encyclopedia of international relations and global politics

The study of international relations has changed rapidly in recent years. One reason is the pace of major political and economic change – the end of the Cold War and the fall of communism; the resurgence of nationalism; terrorism and other forms of fundamentalism; and of course, globalization. Another reason is the development of competing views of how international relations should be defined, conceived and studied. This is reflected in the ongoing debates on the fundamental paradigms most appropriate for understanding contemporary global politics, and the emergence of perspectives such as feminism, postmodernism, constructivism and critical theory.

The *Encyclopedia of International Relations and Global Politics* provides a unique reference source for students and academics, covering all aspects of global international relations and the contemporary discipline across IR's major subject divisions of diplomacy, military affairs, international political economy, and theory. Written by a distinguished group of international scholars, the encyclopedia is largely comprised of substantial entries of more than 1000 words, with 50 major entries of 5000 words on core contemporary topics. Entries are fully cross-referenced, and followed by a listing of complementary entries and a short bibliography for further reading. A comprehensive analytical index guides the user quickly to the required information.

A unique resource, the *Encyclopedia of International Relations and Global Politics* will be an extremely valuable addition to all libraries supporting teaching and research in the social sciences.

Martin Griffiths is an Associate Professor in the School of Political and International Studies at Flinders University, Australia. Amongst his publications are *International Relations: The Key Concepts* (Routledge, 2002) and *Fifty Key Thinkers in International Relations* (Routledge, 1999).

encyclopedia of
international relations
and global politics

edited by
martin griffiths

LONDON AND NEW YORK

First published 2005
by Routledge
2 Park Square, Milton Park, Abingdon, Oxon OX14 4RN

Simultaneously published in the USA and Canada
by Routledge
270 Madison Avenue, New York, NY 10016, USA

Routledge is an imprint of the Taylor and Francis Group

© 2005 Routledge

Typeset in Optima and Univers by Taylor & Francis Books
Printed and bound by TJ International Ltd, Padstow, Cornwall

British Library Cataloguing in Publication Data
A catalogue record for this book is available from the British Library

Library of Congress Cataloging in Publication Data
A catalog record for this title has been requested

ISBN 0-415-31160-8

T&F informa

Taylor & Francis Group is the Academic Division of T&F Informa plc.

contents

consultant editors

contributors

Rita Abrahamsen
University of Wales, Aberystwyth, UK

Amitav Acharya
Nanyang Technological University, Singapore

Sean K. Anderson
Idaho State University, USA

Luke Ashworth
University of Limerick, Ireland

R. William Ayres
University of Indianapolis, USA

William Bain
University of Wales, Aberystwyth, UK

Fran Baum
Flinders University, Australia

Mark Beeson
University of Queensland, Australia

Brett Bowden
University of Queensland, Australia

Jacqueline Braveboy-Wagner
The City College, New York and City University of New York, USA

Bruce Buchan
Griffith University, Australia

Anthony Burke
University of New South Wales, Australia

Peter Burnell
University of Warwick, UK

David Carment
Carleton University, Canada

Philip G. Cerny
Rutgers University, Newark, USA

John Chiddick
La Trobe University, Australia

Theodore Cohn
Simon Fraser University, Canada

David Coleman
University of Sydney, Australia

George Crowder
Flinders University, Australia

Vesna Danilovic
Texas A&M University, USA

Carmel Davis
University of Pennsylvania, USA

Richard Devetak
Monash University, Australia

Tim Dunne
University of Wales, Aberystwyth, UK

Jenny Edkins
University of Wales, Aberystwyth, UK

Colin Elman
Arizona State University, USA

Cynthia Enloe
Clark University, USA

Jonathan Fox
Bar-Ilan University, Israel

Narayanan Ganesan
National University of Singapore,
Singapore

Des Gasper
Institute of Social Studies, The Netherlands

Martin Griffiths
Flinders University, Australia

Rohan Guneratna
Nanyang Technological University,
Singapore

Ted Robert Gurr
University of Maryland, USA

Stefano Guzzini
Danish Institute for International Studies,
Copehagen and, Uppsala University,
Sweden

Peter M. Haas
University of Massachusetts, USA

Emma Haddad
London School of Economics, UK

Marianne Hanson
University of Queensland, Australia

Barbara Harff
Clark University, USA

John M. Hobson
University of Sheffield, UK

Kalevi J. Holsti
University of British Columbia, Canada

Ann Hughes
Keele University, UK

Ian Hurd
Northwestern University, USA

Mir Zohair Husain
University of South Alabama, USA

Robert Jackson
Boston University, USA

Paul James
RMIT University, Australia

Darryl Jarvis
University of Sydney, Australia

Adam Jones
Yale University, USA

Arie M. Kacowicz
Hebrew University of Jerusalem, Israel

Caroline Kennedy-Pipe
University of Sheffield, UK

John Kirton
University of Toronto, Canada

Tonny Brems Knudsen
University of Aarhus, Denmark

Stephen J. Kobrin
University of Pennsylvania, USA

Anthony J. Langlois
Flinders University, Australia

Anna Leander
University of Southern Denmark,
Odense, Denmark

Brett Ashley Leeds
Rice University, USA

Douglas Lemke
Pennsylvania State University, USA

Andrew Linklater
University of Wales, Aberystwyth, UK

Richard Little
University of Bristol, UK

Lorna Lloyd
Keele University, UK

David Lockwood
Flinders University, Australia

Jack Lule
Lehigh University, USA

Rod Lyon
University of Queensland, Australia

Tanya Lyons
Flinders University, Australia

John Macmillan
Brunel University, UK

Samuel M. Makinda
Murdoch University, Australia

David Scott Mathieson
Australian National University, Australia

Philip McMichael
Cornell University, USA

Stephen McNally
La Trobe University, Australia

Oliver Morrissey
University of Nottingham, UK

James D. Morrow
University of Michigan, USA

Layna Mosley
University of North Carolina, Chapel Hill, USA

Grant Niemann
Flinders University, Australia

Kim Richard Nossal
Queen's University, Canada

Terry O'Callaghan
University of South Australia, Australia

Brendon O'Connor
Griffith University, Australia

Rosemary H. T. O'Kane
Keele University, UK

Andrew O'Neil
Flinders University, Australia

Walter C. Opello, Jr.
State University of New York, Oswego, USA

Lionel Orchard
Flinders University, Australia

Ronen Palan
University of Sussex, Australia

Alberto Paloni
University of Glasgow, UK

Matthew Paterson
University of Ottawa, Canada

Andrew Phillips
Cornell University, USA

Elisabeth Porter
INCORE, University of Ulster, UK

Igor Primoratz
University of Melbourne, Australia

Elisabeth Prugl
Florida International University, USA

Heather Rae
Australian National University, Australia

Gregory A. Raymond
Boise State University, USA

Matthew Rendall
University of Nottingham, UK

Robbie Robertson
University of the South Pacific, Fiji

P. Stuart Robinson
University of Tromsø, Norway

Sam Robison
Louisiana State University, USA

Stephen J. Rosow
State University of New York, Oswego, USA

Brad R. Roth
Wayne State University, USA

David L. Rousseau
University of Pennsylvania, USA

Mark Rupert
Syracuse University, USA

Larbi Sadiki
University of Exeter, UK

Mette Eilstrup Sangiovanni
Cambridge University, UK

Mark Schafer
Louisiana State University, USA

Michael Schiavone
Australian National University, Australia

Leonard Seabrooke
Australian National University, Australia

George E. Shambaugh
Georgetown University, USA

Richard Shapcott
University of Queensland, Australia

Timothy J. Sinclair
University of Warwick, UK

Elinor C. Sloan
Carleton University, Canada

Georg Sørensen
University of Aarhus, Denmark

David Sullivan
University of Wales, Bangor, UK

John P. Synott
Queensland University of Technology, Australia

Dirk Willem Te Velde
Overseas Development Institute, UK

Holli Thomas
Deakin University, Australia

Janna Thompson
La Trobe University, Australia

Katharine Vadura
University of South Australia, Australia

Klaas Van Walraven
African Studies Center, Leiden, The Netherlands

Amy Verdun
University of Victoria, Canada

Stephen G. Walker
Arizona State University, USA

John Walsh
University of South Australia, Australia

Craig Warkentin
State University of New York, Oswego, USA

Raechel L. Waters
University of Washington, USA

Patrick Webb
Tufts University, USA

Colin Wight
University of Sheffield, UK

Rorden Wilkinson
University of Manchester, UK

Howard Williams
University of Wales, Aberystwyth, UK

Michael C. Williams
University of Wales, Aberystwyth, UK

Geoffrey Wiseman
University of Southern California, USA

Duncan Wood
Instituto Tecnologico autonomo de, Mexico

Steve Wood
Griffith University, Australia

Vikash Yadav
The American University in Cairo, Egypt

introduction

The study of international relations has changed rapidly over the past decade. In part this is a result of trends and transformations in its subject matter. In part it is a result of changing perceptions among scholars over how that subject matter should be defined, conceived and studied. Among the former one would identify the end of the cold war, the collapse of communism more generally, changing patterns of warfare and collective violence, the disintegration of some existing states and rise of allegedly new kinds of state formation ('failed' states, 'rogue' states), the resurgence of nationalism, terrorism, and various forms of 'fundamentalism' (religious but also economic), regional economic crises in Russia, Latin America and East Asia, and the phenomenon of 'globalization' and its impact on the international system. Among the latter one would include a whole host of academic debates over the nature and limits of the academic field of International Relations (IR). These include ongoing debates over the adequacy of existing approaches or 'isms' such as realism and liberal internationalism; the rise of feminism, constructivism, post-structuralism and critical theory; and the 'return' of normative IR theory in the form of cosmopolitan and communitarian-inspired attempts to generate appropriate moral criteria for assessing the use of force and other issues of global import.

In short, the study of international relations is a site of change, controversy and theoretical plurality. For some observers, this is unfortunate, a sign of impending chaos and indiscipline in the study of global politics. For others, it is a trend to be welcomed as we escape the confines of the cold war era to embrace post-positivist/multi-disciplinary perspectives in a rapidly changing global environment. Either way, the time is appropriate for a reference source that reflects both the enduring stock of concepts we use to comprehend international relations (such as the balance of power, or just war theory), as well as more recent theoretical innovations and agendas (such as constructivism, global governance, and the renewed interest in the nature of sovereignty under the conditions of globalization).

The Routledge *Encyclopedia of International Relations and Global Politics* is a unique reference source for students and academics in the field. Its scope is *empirical*, *normative*, and *conceptual*, with thematic coverage of the main dimensions of the study of international relations – diplomacy, military affairs, international political economy, and international relations theory. Empirically, the encyclopedia includes entries on significant international organizations and the essential phenomena of our subject matter (military, economic, diplomatic, and political). Normatively, it includes entries on contested terms such as 'just war' and 'humanitarian intervention'. Conceptual entries include the key concepts with which we interpret empirical phenomena (such as sovereignty, nationalism, and the nation-state). Finally, the encyclopedia covers the most important theoretical debates/perspectives that have emerged over the past decade. Whilst the title of the encyclopedia mirrors the name of an established sub-field in political science (International Relations), its content discloses the current state of knowledge about global politics, conceived in the widest sense.

In short, the *Encyclopedia of International Relations and Global Politics* is a concise but comprehensive introduction to the study of international relations in the twenty-first century. Its entries range across the field, from diplomatic statecraft and foreign policy analysis, comparative politics, historical sociology, international political economy, international history, strategic studies and military affairs, ethics, and international political theory. The contents of this book reflect both the scope of the study of global politics as well as dramatic developments that have taken place since the end of the cold war.

The *Encyclopedia* contains 250 entries written by 125 contributors from around the world. The entries fall into two broad types. First, lengthy entries provide critical scholarly introductions to key theoretical approaches, concepts, issues and international organizations in international relations. There are 50 such entries, indicated by italics in the list of entries on p. xv. These entries are written by experts in the area under examination, in which the content of the entry often reports on research undertaken by the author in his or her particular area of knowledge and expertise. These entries also provide critical reviews of current research, and thereby represent comprehensive overviews of current scholarship in the area. Second, shorter entries provide succinct overviews of the most important concepts, institutions and issues in contemporary global politics.

Using the volume is simple. All the entries are arranged in strict alphabetical order. Although each entry is self-contained, cross-references to other entries are frequent. Where a term is first used that has its own entry elsewhere in the volume, it is highlighted in a bold typeface. At the end of each entry readers are referred to complementary entries in the text. Finally, each entry is followed by suggestions for further reading in the subject. A comprehensive index has also been provided with references and page numbers to hundreds of words and names referred to in the text. For the reader wanting information on very specific subjects, the index may be the best place to start.

martin griffiths

acknowledgments

I am indebted to Gerard Greenway at Routledge for inviting me to edit the Routledge *Encyclopedia of International Relations and Global Politics*, and for the assistance of Dominic Shryane as the book developed. I would also like to thank the consultant editors for their help and advice in constructing the list of entries, and for their suggestions about appropriate authors. I am particularly grateful to the Faculty of Social Sciences at Flinders University for providing me with a vital period of study leave in 2004, and I owe a considerable debt to the contributors themselves, not least for their patience over the last three years. Final thanks go to my family, especially Kylie and Jade. Your love and support sustained me throughout this project.

list of entries

A
African Union
Agent-structure debate
Alliance
Al-Qaeda
Anarchy
Anti-Americanism
Appeasement
Arab League
Arms control
Arms race
Arms trade
Asia Pacific Economic Cooperation
    Forum
Asian values
Association of Southeast Asian Nations
Asylum
Authority

B
Balance of power
Balance of threat
Ballistic missile defense
Bank for International Settlements
Biodiversity
Biological weapons
Bipolarity
Bretton Woods

C
Capital controls
Capitalism
Casino capitalism
Chemical weapons
Chlorofluorocarbons (CFCs)
Civil war
Clash of civilizations
CNN factor/effect

Cold war
Collective security
Common Agricultural Policy
Common security
Commonwealth
Commonwealth of Independent States
Communism
Communitarianism
Concert of powers
Conditionality
Confidence and security building
    measures
Constructivism
Containment
Corruption
Cosmopolitan democracy
Cosmopolitanism
Crimes against humanity
Crisis
Critical security studies
Critical theory

D
Decolonization
Deconstruction
Debt trap
Democratic deficit
Democratic peace
Democratization
Dependency
Desertification
Deterrence
Development
Diaspora
Diplomacy
Disarmament
Discourse
Disintermediation

African Union

The African Union (AU) was established by a Constitutive Act signed in Lomé, July 2000. The AU replaced, and by and large represents an institutional copy of, the Organization of African Unity (OAU). The OAU was founded in May 1963 and, like the AU, had its headquarters in the Ethiopian capital Addis Ababa. With fifty-three member states, the African Union represents one of the largest international organizations in the world. It includes all states on the African mainland, with the exception of Morocco, which left the OAU in 1984 because of the admission of the Western Sahara. In addition, all independent island states recognized as part of the African region are members of the AU.

The OAU was meant to enhance the reciprocal security of African state elites in the context of their fragile domestic political positions and to augment Africa's collective influence in fora such as the **United Nations**. Its main objectives were to encourage the struggle against colonialism and apartheid, mediate in conflicts between member states, harmonize policies in **diplomacy**, defense and economic **development**; and coordinate Africa's voice in international fora through executive secretariats in New York, Brussels and Geneva.

The organization's struggles against colonial and white minority regimes were waged with varying degrees of success. Generally, the OAU was most effective in upholding the diplomatic isolation of these regimes. Trade **sanctions** were largely ineffective, while assistance to liberation movements was mainly of a token nature. By acquiescing in the informal leadership of the alliance of southern African 'Frontline' states, the pursuit of its anti-colonial mandate was rendered more concrete. If such leadership was lacking or the countries most directly involved were divided, implementation of its anti-colonial ideology proved divisive, as in the crisis over Morocco's occupation of the Western Sahara.

Mediation in member state conflicts represented an important part of the OAU's existence, while economic issues became important after the late 1970s. During its first thirty years, the OAU's record of mediating inter-state conflicts was, contrary to popular perception, moderately successful. As in other areas of activity, however, it was hampered by the absence of effective hegemonic leadership in Africa's inter-state relations (see **hegemony**). Although some countries, like Nigeria, Egypt and South Africa, are important actors in the African state system, their influence has never amounted to undisputed continental leadership. Consequently, the OAU always lacked the clout to execute forceful strategies in conflict mediation or impose the financial discipline necessary to develop strong institutions or launch **peacekeeping** operations. It therefore pursued a minimalist strategy aimed at persuasion, the use of dilatory tactics and **containment** of inter-state hostilities through mediation on a decentralized and *ad hoc* basis.

However, this proved largely ineffective in the management of high intensity conflicts. Usually, such conflicts have been part of intra-state crises (see **crisis**), where the organization's functioning was hindered by a broad interpretation of the non-interference principle. Although this principle was sometimes ignored, the OAU's elitist bias contributed to its institutional disregard for some of Africa's most tragic civil **wars**. African critics of the OAU therefore referred to the organization as a 'trade union' of tyrants. Where the OAU did try to intervene, it usually failed, such as in the various crises that beset Congo (Zaire) during the 1960s and 1970s and, later, in the civil wars in Chad and Somalia.

The end of the **cold war** forced Africa's state elites into action. The OAU formally included the management of intra-state conflicts in its mandate, improved its monitoring of conflicts and introduced a mechanism for conflict prevention, management and resolution. Essentially, this consisted of improved cooperation between the OAU's Secretary-General, whose political prerogatives were upgraded, and the bureau of the Assembly of Heads of State and Government, the organization's highest organ. Its objective was the improvement of reactive capacity *vis-à-vis* conflicts. The OAU's mediatory activity increased, but continued reliance on minimalist tactics geared at the reduction, rather than resolution, of hostilities meant that it was powerless to resolve the worst intra-state wars. The OAU continued to rely on the United Nations

or acquiesce in the growing role played by Africa's sub-regional organizations, as illustrated by Nigeria's intervention in Liberia in the early 1990s under the auspices of the Economic Community of West African States.

Africa's soul-searching during the 1990s also led to renewed emphasis on economic cooperation, which materialized in the establishment of the African Economic Community (1991), which was to consist of the OAU's institutions, buttressed by new organs like a Pan-African Parliament and Court of Justice, and aim at future continental economic **integration**. Many of its objectives were unrealistic and could be interpreted as a psychological rationalization of African elites' despair about the continent's economic predicaments. To some extent, the OAU's transformation into the African Union could be analysed in the same perspective. Nevertheless, during the 1990s the organization's financial regulations became more stringent, with some member states defaulting on their contributions losing out on voting rights. In the absence of a genuine continental leader this did not, however, result in fundamental change. Chronic budget deficits survived into the new millennium and, in spite of an expanding mandate, forced a retrenchment of secretariat staff.

The organization's transformation into the African Union in 2001 was part of the same search for more effective management of Africa's manifold problems, in addition to efforts of some member states, such as Libya, to stake out a more prominent role in continental politics. The AU's structure bears a remarkable resemblance to that of the OAU. Possibly inspired by the example of the **European Union**, the secretariat was renamed 'the Commission', while a protocol for the Pan-African Parliament entered into force in December 2003.

The 'Council of Ministers' was renamed the 'Executive Council' and the Assembly of Heads of State and Government was simply called the 'Assembly', retaining its overall institutional supremacy. The latter's semi-permanent bureau, which became more active in conflict resolution during the 1990s, was renamed 'Peace and Security Council'. Its protocol allows it to mount peace support operations and recommend interventions to the Assembly in member states in case of **war crimes**, **crimes against humanity** and **genocide**.

An explicit commitment to democratic government is one of the Union's novel elements. Hence, it may decide on sanctions against regimes coming to power by unconstitutional means. However, the Union's Constitutive Act also pays lip-service to the principle of non-interference in member states' internal affairs and stipulates that it is the Assembly, made up of heads of state, which decides on possible sanctions. Its record toward unconstitutional developments in member states has so far been ambiguous. The real significance of the OAU's transformation into the African Union, as well as its commitment to peer reviews of democratic behavior seems as yet unclear, depending *inter alia* on the nature of Africa's multi-party regimes. The lack of effective continental leadership in its international relations will continue to affect the Union's record in areas as diverse as the struggle against AIDS, the containment of civil wars and the ending of the continent's social and economic malaise.

Further reading

Amate, C. (1986) *Inside the OAU: Pan-Africanism in Practice*, New York: St Martin's Press.

Maluwa, T. (2001) 'Reimagining African Unity: Some Preliminary Reflections on the Constitutive Act of the African Union', *African Yearbook of International Law* 9: 3–38.

Van Walraven, K. (1999) *Dreams of Power: The Role of the Organization of African Unity in the Politics of Africa 1963–1993*, Aldershot: Ashgate.

See also: decolonization; regionalism; Third World

KLAAS VAN WALRAVEN

Agent-structure debate

The agent-structure debate emerged in international relations (IR) theory in the mid-1980s. The debate is concerned with the theoretical attempt to find a way to integrate both agents and structures into one coherent framework. It is often most closely associated with **constructivism**, although the issues raised in the debate are of much wider significance. During the course of the debate it became clear that contributors were not always addressing the same problem, nor using key conceptual terms in a consistent manner. This is understandable given that the agent-structure problem defies easy definition, let alone resolution. Its essence is captured in Marx's oft-quoted phrase that 'men [sic] make history, but not in circumstances of their own choosing'. Irrespective of how the problem is defined, the debate has demonstrated that all theories of international relations embody an implicit solution to the problem, hence its continued relevance to contemporary theoretical debates.

Historical background

Although the language of agents and structures is a recent development in IR theory the issues underlying the debate have always been fundamental to the discipline. These have generally been discussed under questions concerning the relationship between individuals and society, **levels of analysis**, and issues of micro-macro linkages. The specific terminology of, and interest in, the agent-structure problem, however, was the result of three interrelated factors.

First, during the post-positivist turn in the field there was a tendency for IR theorists to look for inspiration from cognate disciplines (see **Post-positivism**). Social theory was a fertile source of theoretical innovation and the agent-structure problem had been a key feature of contemporary debates among social theorists. Second, arguably the most innovative and important theory in international relations since the late 1970s had been neorealism, a particular variant of **realism**. Neorealism is a structural theory. It attempts to explain international processes and phenomena in terms of the structural properties of the **international system**. Structural theories had dominated the social sciences since the mid-1950s, although they had always come in for consistent criticism. As a structural theory of international relations, and particularly in the context of the turn to social theory, it was inevitable that IR theorists would use critiques of structuralism from cognate disciplines to mount a critique of neorealism.

Critiques of structuralism came from two sources. First, there were methodological individualists keen to place individuals back at the centre of analysis. Second, were those who, whilst dissatisfied with the inherent determinism of structuralism, had no desire to return to methodological individualism. This latter group attempted to develop theoretical frameworks that integrated agents and structures into one account. Roy Bhaskar, Pierre Bourdieu and Anthony Giddens were some of the key social theorists that provided inspiration for the agent-structure debate in IR.

There was, however, a third factor that played a decisive role in shaping the development of the agent-structure debate in IR. The many trenchant critiques of positivism had made their way into IR. One aspect of this set of critiques was the view that positivism was an inappropriate epistemological framework to study social phenomena. Positivism and structuralism were often linked. Neorealism was perceived to be a paradigmatic example of positivism. Hence some critiques of neorealism focused not on its structural aspects but its positivism. These critiques of the epistemological basis of neorealism became conflated with the critique of its underlying social ontology and contributors to the agent-structure debate rarely took the trouble to make clear which aspect they were considering.

Two elements played an important role in the debate as it developed in IR. First there was scientific realism (SR), which was claimed by many of the contributors to be a superior model of science to that of positivism. The appeal of scientific realism lay not only in its very intuitively attractive account of science, but particularly in the way that it permitted reference to unobservables as a legitimate aspects of any science. This meant that unobservables such as social structure could be given a stronger ontological basis. Second, Anthony Giddens' structuration theory was fundamental in the evolution of the debate, as was Roy Bhaskar's Transformational Model of Social Activity (TMSA). Some contributors to the debate have not distinguished between Bhaskar's TMSA and scientific realism. However, whilst Bhaskar is committed to both scientific realism and the TMSA, not all scientific realists are convinced that social ontology necessarily follows from the commitment to SR. Moreover, many contributors to the debate accept the broad contours of Giddens' structuration theory, but reject SR.

The issues at stake

Fundamentally, the agent-structure problem is concerned with the nature of agents, structures and the relationship between them. As such, it is an ontological problem, concerning the constitutive nature of social and political reality. Epistemological and methodological issues concerning appropriate ways to understand that reality are themselves dependent upon how the prior ontological problem is addressed. This account of the problem implies that there may be no 'right' solution. Indeed, understood as competing visions of the social world and its internal dynamics, different resolutions to the agent-structure problem are at the heart of all theoretical and political debate. Traditionally there have been two dominant and opposed answers to this ontological aspect.

The first answer, generally known as methodological individualism, tends to see everything social as a result of individual actions, driven by nothing more than subjective beliefs, desires and wants. A classic expression of this viewpoint is Margaret Thatcher's dictum that 'there is no such thing as society'. Society, it is argued, consists of the actions of individuals. Structures, as the saying goes, 'do not take to the streets'. The alternative approach is structuralism. For structuralists, individuals are mere pawns of society, usually coerced in one way or another into actions over which they have no control. Oft-cited advocates of individualist and structuralist approaches in social theory are Max Weber and Emile Durkheim.

Weber argued that the study of social activity should be concerned with the actions of individuals toward each other

(i.e. social action). Such action can be seen as means employed to achieve particular goals. Moreover, this action must be understood in terms of the meanings that individuals give to it, which Weber called 'subjective understanding'. This stress on subjective understanding should not be taken to imply that Weber denied the existence of societies as entire systems of interconnected institutions and groups. He agreed that societal, or associational, systems formed a distinctive level of phenomena – a 'distinctive configuration' – that was objectively real. He opposed, however, any reification of these as entities; because, in his view, they only existed in the sense that the subjective meanings and motives shared by all members of society sustained them. For Weber, social collectives are solely the result of particular acts of individuals, since individuals alone can be treated as agents.

This can be contrasted with Durkheim's more structuralist account. Durkheim argued that there was more to social life than individuals and their activity. For Durkheim, the most important elements of the social world had an existence over and above individuals. This was a '*l'âme collective*' (or group mind) into which individuals had to be socialized. Whenever a social phenomenon is directly explained by a psychological phenomenon, Durkheim argued, we may be sure that the explanation is false. No theory or analysis that begins from the individual can successfully grasp the specific properties of social phenomena. Society is not the mere sum of individuals. For Durkheim 'social facts' existed as things in their own right and changes in them could only be explained in terms of other social facts. Durkheim argued that social life must be explained, not by the conception held by those who participate in it, but by profound causes that escape individual consciousness.

The agent structure debate in IR theory has been a systematic attempt to think through this issue drawing extensively on a body of literature in social theory and philosophy that has attempted to go beyond the Weberian and Durkheimian poles. The discussion has raised a series of fundamental questions relating to the treatment of key terms such as agency and structure, the relationships between these two key elements and epistemological and methodological questions that derive from differing formulations.

Attempts to unravel the many strands of this problem confront a terminological minefield. These difficulties are compounded by the fact that contributors to the agent-structure debate use differing terms to describe similar ideas, common terminology to refer to different issues, and display a diversity of opinions over which elements of the agent-structure problem should be classified as ontological, epistemological or methodological. As such, it is not always clear that they are talking about the same problem.

In fact, the agent-structure debate in International Relations has tended to conflate four interrelated, but distinct, problems. First, there is the question of the nature of agents and structures and their interrelationship – this is the agent-structure problem in its essence. Second, there is the question of whether the level-of-analysis problem and the agent-structure problem are one and the same. Third, there is the empirical issue of the relative weight of agential versus structural factors in determining specific social outcomes. Finally, there is the question of what are the most appropriate modes of investigation required to study agents and structures. There were a range of subsidiary issues that arose in the debate, but these were not integral to the discussion of the problem.

The first confusion that arose related to the levels of analysis problem and its links to the agent-structure problem. As formulated within the discipline, the level of analysis problem relates to the level at which one wishes to base one's explanation of any particular phenomenon, such as individuals, bureaucracies, states, or the **international system**. It is understandable that this problem should arise in discussions of the agent-structure problem, but it is not the same issue. The level of analysis problem can only emerge as a problem after some resolution, either explicit or implicit, of the agent-structure problem has been achieved. The identification of an individual, or any other level, is dependent upon an a priori understanding of what an individual or level is. Hence the agent-structure problem is neither reducible to the levels of analysis problem, nor analytically dependent upon it. Instead, it sets the conditions of possibility for the level of analysis problem to emerge as a problem.

This can be demonstrated through a consideration of the second issue that became entangled with the agent-structure problem; that of the relative causal weighting attributable to factors in the social field. Was, for example, the end of the **cold war** attributable to Gorbachev, or to structural factors pertaining at the time? Whilst an important issue in its own right, the question itself depends on how the agent-structure problem is resolved at a more abstract level. The question of whether particular social outcomes were the result of agential or structural forces cannot even be raised unless one has first attempted to resolve the agent-structure problem. The issue of relative causal factors is an empirical not a theoretical question, but it is an empirical question that only makes sense within the framework of a resolution to the agent-structure problem. All contributors to the agent-structure debate agree that both agential and structural factors are relevant.

A third confusion arose over the question of differing modes of investigation required to study agents and structures respectively. This has typically become to be known as the 'explaining/understanding' divide within the discipline, although the distinction is derived from hermeneutic and interpretive rejections of the attempt to apply a positivist framework to the study of social phenomena (see **hermeneutics**). The distinction between explaining and understanding is often presented in terms of competing epistemological positions relating to understandings of the scientific method. Underlying this epistemological issue, however, are a set of ontological questions concerning the nature of social objects. For example, even if one begins with an a priori epistemological position such as explanation = X (positivism perhaps), it makes no sense to argue that X (positivism) is inapplicable to the study of Y (the social world) unless one has an account of Y such that it may or may not be susceptible to study by X; that is, an answer to the agent-structure problem. Hence the distinction between explanation and understanding is based firmly on prior considerations about the nature of the entities in the social world. The ontological question of the nature of agents and structures and their interrelationship is prior to the question of the mode of investigation required to study them.

Despite the confusion generated about precise definitions of the agent-structure problem, the debate has identified a series of important issues and pushed research agendas forward in these areas. The first of these was over competing accounts of structure. Although the term structure features regularly in the lexicon of the discipline it is rarely, if ever, clearly defined. The term is often deployed but rarely explained. This changed with the arrival of the agent-structure debate. Contributors to the

debate began raising questions not only about the meaning of structure, but also its status. Was structure an existent, or merely an analytical, construct? If the latter, how could it possess causal power? Initially, contributors to the debate suggested that accounts of structure developed in social theory were largely compatible. For example, both Bhaskar and Giddens had attempted to transcend the agent-structure dichotomy through what Giddens has called the 'duality of structure'. According to him, the structural properties of social systems are both medium and outcome of the practices they recursively organize. Structure should be seen as both enabling *and* constraining. The existence of a social structure in society is a necessary condition for any human activity. The structure provides the means, media, rules and resources for everything we do. Moreover, these structural constraints, it is claimed, do not operate independently of the motives and reasons individual actors have for what they do. Thus, society is considered to be the unmotivated consequence for all our motivated productions, as well as being the outcome of them.

All contributors to the debate endorsed this general articulation of the agent-structure relationship and have used the term 'mutually constitutive' to describe it. However, this term often presents more problems than solutions. For example, it fails to unpack the dynamic nature of the relationship between agents and structures over time and space. Agents and structures may be mutually constitutive but the relationship may not be symmetrical. Moreover, the relationship may change over time or differ in various geographical, cultural, political or economic locales. Certain types of structural configuration may place more limits on human agency than others and the dynamics of this relationship require theoretical specification and empirical investigation. To say that things are mutually constituted does nothing more (or less) than to highlight that there is a necessary relationship that requires investigation.

Agreement on the issue of mutual constitution in the study of international relations has elided serious differences emerging in social theory. For example, the notion of structure developed by Bhaskar was not the same as, or even compatible with, that of Giddens. In an attempt to get around the problems associated with various forms of structuralism, Giddens had moved beyond prevailing definitions within social theory and redefined structure as sets of 'rules and resources'. Bhaskar, on the other hand, specifically theorized structure in terms of social relations. In IR this difference tends to be overlooked with some contributors referring to structure as 'rules and resources' and others employing a more relational account. There were also differences in the ontological status accorded to structure in Giddens' and Bhaskars's accounts that have yet to be fully understood.

The issue of agency received much less attention in the debate than that of structure. In part this is understandable given that the aim was to construct a more robust account of the agent-structure relationship without regressing back to any form of individualism. However, IR theory has no fully developed account of agency, although more recent contributors to the debate have now begun to address this lacuna. In social theory agents were usually associated with individuals. IR has transposed this framework and inserted states in place of individuals. This means that states are often conceptualized as persons having interests, fears and so on. Often this treatment of state agency is implicit rather than explicit, although some contributors

have attempted a sustained defence of state-personhood.

As yet, little attempt has yet been made to consider the implications of alternative solutions to the agent-structure problem for research methodology, which is destined to become a major issue in the evolution of the debate. But it is also clear that these methodological discussions will be shaped and framed by ontological differences. Much the same can be said about epistemology, with accounts of how we might make claims to knowledge about social entities being dependent upon how those social entities are defined. This highlights the fact that no metatheoretical solution to the agent-structure problem can be expected. To label something a problem suggests both the possibility of a solution and the need to elaborate one. In respect of the agent-structure problem, there can be no solution in the sense of solving the conundrum so that we know *the* answer, or the problem no longer appears as a problem. Every theory has its own solution to the problem. We may want to reject some formulations and favour others, but this does not mean that the problem has been solved once and for all.

Further reading

Bhaskar, R. (1979) *The Possibility of Naturalism: A Philosophical Critique of the Contemporary Human Sciences*, Brighton: Harvester.

Carlsnaes, W. (1992) 'The Agent-Structure Problem in Foreign Policy Analysis', *International Studies Quarterly* 36, 3: 245–70.

Dessler, D. (1989) 'What's at Stake in the Agent-Structure Debate?' *International Organization* 43, 3: 441–73.

Doty, R. L. (1997) 'Aporia: A Critical Exploration of the Agent-Structure Problematique in International Relations Theory', *European Journal of International Relations* 3, 3: 365–92.

Friedman, G. and Starr, H. (1997) *Agency, Structure and International Politics: From Ontology to Empirical Inquiry*, London: Routledge.

Giddens, A. (1984) *The Constitution of Society: Outline of the Theory of Structuration*, Cambridge: Polity Press.

Hollis, M. and S. Smith (1990) *Explaining and Understanding International Relations*, Oxford: Clarendon.

Wendt, A. (1999) *Social Theory of International Politics*, Cambridge: Cambridge University Press.

Wight, C. (1999) 'They Shoot Dead Horses Don't They? Locating Agency in the Agent-Structure Problematique', *European Journal of International Relations* 5, 1: 109–42.

See also: constructivism; levels of analysis; Marxism; realism

COLIN WIGHT

Alliance

An alliance is a formal agreement among independent states to cooperate militarily. Alliances are usually codified in treaties, and include promises by states to coordinate their actions in the event of military conflict while retaining their **sovereignty** and identities as independent states. By pooling their efforts, leaders hope to enhance the **security** and **power** of their states by creating a stronger joint fighting force. Most scholars today distinguish between alliances, which are relationships embodied in formal, written agreements between states, and alignments, which are informal expectations about shared interests and cooperative behavior.

There are many different kinds of alliances. Most alliances do not obligate states to cooperate in all military endeavors, but instead specify the conditions under which cooperation is required and the kinds of actions that states are required to take when the obligations are invoked. Some alliances, such as the **North Atlantic Treaty Organization** (NATO), oblige states to come to the assistance of their partners only in the event that an alliance member is a victim of attack on home territory. Others promise active military assistance not only in defense of the sovereignty and territorial integrity of members, but also for offensive goals. Many alliance treaties do not require states to fight together, but instead require that state leaders will consult in the event of **crisis** and pursue a common policy, perhaps involving joint military force. Alliances also vary in their level of institutionalization. While some alliances, like NATO, are highly institutionalized and provide for significant military integration, including joint planning, shared military bases and training, and standardization of equipment and procedures, others have little to no peacetime structure.

One can easily understand why leaders might see the benefit of alliances. Scholars have long argued that in an anarchic system where the use of force is always possible, banding together with other states is the best way to enhance one's power (see **balance of power**). Yet, given that formal agreements are not enforceable under **anarchy**, and thus, relying on the promises of others to enhance one's security may be dangerous, why have formal alliances been a persistent feature in international politics? Modern scholarship suggests two primary functions that alliances serve.

First, states form alliances to take advantage of economies of scale in the provision of defense. Formal alliances serve to regulate behavior among allies. By coordinating training, equipment, and procedures, allies can create a more formidable joint fighting force at lower cost. By cooperating with other states that have different comparative advantages (e.g., land power versus sea power), states can achieve significant gains from exchange. One of the main goals in forming alliances is for member states to reduce their individual defense burdens. By relying on others to help provide security and **deterrence**, states are able to invest less in defense spending. For example, one of the factors that allowed the Japanese to achieve dramatic economic growth during the **cold war** was Japan's ability to rely on the United States for most of its defense needs.

Second, alliances may serve as formal notification to others of a state's intentions should international conflict break out. One of the main motivations for forming alliances is to discourage those with aggressive intentions from initiating military conflict. By warning potential adversaries that any attack will face a multinational force, alliances can deter the initiation of **war**. On the other hand, offensive alliances may serve to encourage potential targets to give up quickly. Knowing in advance that the attacker will receive assistance may encourage immediate capitulation. Thus, state leaders have an interest in making their intent to work together known if doing so may discourage attacks and/or encourage adversaries to give up quickly.

However, outside observers may be skeptical of the message sent by alliances, because state leaders might have an incentive to bluff. Leaders might form alliances whose formal obligations they would not follow in the hope that deterrence will succeed. The costs involved in allying, however, help to impede bluffing. Establishing a credible alliance involves engaging in policy coordination. State leaders give up some of their autonomy in favor of joint decision making, or at least in favor of compatibility in behavior and attitudes on relevant issues. Not only must leaders negotiate the original agreement and

establish any institutional structures, they must also demonstrate common purpose in order to convince others that their alliance is reliable. Finally, the failure to fulfill an alliance commitment if the bluff is called could have negative repercussions. Most leaders are wary of making promises they are unwilling to fulfill because of the negative effect this may have on their future credibility.

Yet, alliances are not perfectly reliable, and states incur some risk in depending on others to maintain their security. Specifically, states must worry that if potential aggressors are not successfully deterred, their alliance partners might abandon them. Alliance members have devised many strategies to limit the risk of abandonment. For instance, during the **cold war**, it was very important to the European allies, and particularly West Germany, that US troops be stationed on the border with East Germany. The fact that any Soviet invasion would cost American lives made it less likely that the US would abandon Europe in a conventional war.

The most direct effect of military alliances is on the probability of violent international conflict. Defensive alliances make war less likely by discouraging likely attackers from attempting a challenge. Offensive alliances, on the other hand, may encourage bellicose behavior. Many scholars believe that when alliance patterns are clear and both sides have a great deal of information about what would happen in the event of conflict, war becomes increasingly unlikely because the parties are more likely to reach an agreement that is acceptable to both sides without war. Alliances may also promote additional cooperation among members. Some, for instance, have noted that allies may trade more with one another and be less likely to find themselves involved in conflicts with one another. Cooperation in the military arena may spill over to other areas, leading, for instance, to the settlement of other disputes and increased economic **interdependence**.

Further reading

Lake, D. A. (1999) *Entangling Relations*, Princeton: Princeton University Press.

Leeds, B. A. (2003) 'Do Alliances Deter Aggression? The Influence of Military Alliances on the Initiation of Militarized Interstate Disputes', *American Journal of Political Science* 47, 3: 427–39.

Morrow, J. D. (2000) 'Alliances: Why Write Them Down?' *American Review of Political Science* 3: 63–83.

Smith, A. (1995) 'Alliance Formation and War', *International Studies Quarterly* 39, 4: 405–25.

Snyder, G. H. (1997) *Alliance Politics*, Ithaca: Cornell University Press.

See also: concert of powers; national interest; North Atlantic Treaty Organization

BRETT ASHLEY LEEDS

Al-Qaeda

Arabic name, meaning 'the base' (alternative spelling, Al Qa'ida; full name, Al Qa'ida al Sulbah, 'the solid base'), for the Islamic fundamentalist organization led by Osama bin Laden, dedicated to fighting regimes and groups regarded as enemies of **Islam**. Its tactics include guerrilla operations, such as against the Soviets in Afghanistan, and **terrorism** directed at civilian and government targets, such as the 11 September 2001 attacks on the World Trade Center and Pentagon. It targets primarily Western nations, such as the United States, perceived to be engaged in **imperialism** or **neocolonialism** against Muslim nations. It also targets pro-US Muslim governments, such as Saudi Arabia or Egypt, as 'apostate regimes'. Finally, it targets rival Muslim groups and secularized Muslim elites. It seeks to restore a pan-Islamic state based on Sunni Muslim precepts. It has developed the first truly multinational terrorist network with a proven global span of operations.

History

Al-Qaeda was formed in 1987–8 by Sheikh Abdullah Azzam, a Palestinian Islamic fundamentalist in Jordan's Muslim Brotherhood. Azzam entered Pakistan in 1979 to aid the Afghan resistance. After Osama bin Laden joined Azzam, they founded the *Maktab al Khidamat* (MAK) or 'Services Office' in 1984, which later became al-Qaeda, to recruit Arabs and other Sunni Muslims to fight the Soviets. After the Soviets withdrew, MAK sought to maintain unity among the veterans who shared an Islamic fundamentalist political program and commitment to violent means to achieve it. Azzam envisioned al-Qaeda becoming a future 'quick reaction force' to aid oppressed Muslims worldwide. His deputy, Osama bin Laden, instead wanted to use al-Qaeda to target the United States, as the principal enemy of Islam, and US aligned Muslim regimes. Azzam opposed these goals, believing that terrorism would be ineffective against the United States or against repressive Muslim regimes, whose retribution would only harm Islamist movements. In addition conservative regimes in Saudi Arabia and the Persian Gulf sheikhdoms had given MAK material and moral aid without which al-Qaeda could not pursue the more limited future mission that Azzam contemplated. This disagreement was due to members of the Jihad Group of Egypt, Ayman al Zawahiri and Muhammad Atef, who joined MAK in 1985 and converted bin Laden to their more radical views. After Azzam was assassinated by a bombing in 1989 bin Laden assumed full control of al-Qaeda.

Although the United States supported various *mujahideen* (holy warrior) groups through the CIA or through Pakistan's Inter-Services Intelligence agency (ISI), there is little evidence the CIA created al-Qaeda or backed Osama bin Laden. During the war against the Soviet Union *mujahideen* groups received support from rival state sponsors: Iran supported the Islamic Party of Gulbiddin Hikmatyar while the Persian Gulf states backed the Islamic Revolutionary Movement of Muhammad Nabi Muhammadi. The United States supported groups led by native Afghans having a nationalistic agenda, whereas Saudi Arabia funded fundamentalist groups such as MAK whose ranks included large numbers of Arab volunteers. Bin Laden denied that he or his group ever received US aid and claims that he has always opposed the United States for supporting Israel. Al-Qaeda commenced operations against US forces following its intervention in Kuwait during the 1991 Gulf War.

Ideology and program

Al-Qaeda is an Islamic fundamentalist group. Such movements hold certain common beliefs. Islam and its laws have comprehensive solutions for all economic, social, diplomatic, criminal and civil problems. Islamic law is perfect, immutable and organic, not requiring reform. The current Muslim world, with its mixture of traditional Muslim and western laws and institutions, and division of the historic *caliphat* (Islamic empire) into several **nation-state**s, deviates from true Islam. Finally, the duty of *jihad* (holy war) permits violence to rid Muslim lands of un-Islamic laws, institutions, rulers and foreign powers. As a *salafist* (purist) group, al-Qaeda rejects reformism or dialogue in favor of revolutionary violence to establish Islamic rule.

Al-Qaeda follows the Wahhabi interpretation of the Hanbali Sunni school of law favoring literal interpretations of the Koran and received traditions but rejecting rationalism, mysticism, and anything not part of primordial Islam. It is close to other Sunni salafist groups such as the Islamic Group of Egypt, the Egyptian Jihad Group and others. Despite Wahhabi scruples rejecting Shi'ite Islam as heresy, al-Qaeda has not shunned contact with Lebanon's Hezbollah or with Iranian operatives. Al-Qaeda seeks not so much to establish Islamic rule within one existing Muslim nation-state but rather to overthrow the **international system** in favor of one caliphat embracing all Muslim nations.

The ideology and program of al-Qaeda are found in several documents, the foremost being the ten volume *Encyclopedia of the Afghan Jihad* (1996), a compendium of military tactics and strategy used in the Afghan war. Other documents include the *Encyclopedia*'s companion volume *Declaration of Jihad against the Country's Tyrants* (Military Series) devoted to terrorist tactics. Originally written in Arabic, they incorporate material culled from US and British military manuals and were secretly circulated among al-Qaeda trainees but not intended for open distribution. In 1999, copies seized by Jordanian police were given to western intelligence agencies which prepared English translations now publicly available under the name *The Al Qaeda Training Manual*. Other public documents include the several *fatwas*, or Islamic religious judicial decrees, issued by al-Qaeda.

On 23 February 1998 one such *fatwa* was faxed to the London Arabic language newspaper, *Al Quds Al Arabi*, signed by bin Laden and three others, declaring it 'the religious duty of every individual Muslim to kill Americans everywhere, whether soldiers or civilians, to free the holy cities of Islam from the presence of foreign, non-Muslim troops'. Such *fatwas* may only be issued by Muslim religious figures of known piety, probity and scholarship in Islamic jurisprudence. Although bin Laden himself is not recognized by reputable Muslim religious leaders as being such a scholar, nonetheless these statements struck a resonant chord among Muslims throughout the world of all social classes who often have blamed the problems of their nations on the United States.

These *fatwas* identify the general objective of countering US power but not the concrete steps to achieve this. Intermediate range goals are found in the *Encyclopedia*: Radicalization of Islamic groups throughout the world; overthrowing of 'apostate' Muslim governments; support for Muslim insurgents in countries around the world; destroying Israel; destroying the United States; and finally, restoration of the Islamic caliphat uniting all Muslim nations. More practical, concrete steps to attain these goals are given in the *Al Qaeda Training Manual*: Surveillance of targets; kidnaping enemy personnel and stealing documents, secrets and arms; assassinating enemy personnel and tourists; freeing imprisoned fellow combatants; spreading provocative propaganda to incite people against the enemy; and also, bombing the enemies' places of socializing and entertainment, embassies, vital economic centres, and key bridges and tunnels in major urban areas. Other documents indicate al-Qaeda's desire to obtain or else develop **weapons of mass destruction**.

Given these goals, how should al-Qaeda be classified along the spectrum of Islamic fundamentalist groups? Specialists on Islamic extremist groups sort them into one of four categories; *revolutionary groups* using violence selectively to target non-Muslims, *ideological groups* using violence as one of several tactics alongside ordinary political activism or providing social services to their Muslim constituencies, *utopian groups* seeking to overthrow the existing political order through unrestrained violence, and *apocalyptic groups* seeking to destroy not only their enemies' political order but also their social, economic and cultural institutions, including civilian as well as political and military targets (Magnus Ranstorp, cited in *Gunaratna* 2002: 92–3). Al-Qaeda is an apocalyptic group and so would be more likely to use **weapons of mass destruction** or mass casualty terrorism to achieve its ultimate objective.

Al-Qaeda has tried to obtain weapons of mass destruction either by buying ready made weapons or by obtaining the materials and technology to assemble them on its own. US troops occupying al-Qaeda camps in Afghanistan found chemical reagents, potassium iodide pills (used to counteract radiation poisoning), numerous notebooks with crude schematics for producing **chemical weapons** and radiation dispersal bombs, and also videotapes of experiments testing poisonous gases on dogs. Concerns over al-Qaeda seeking weapons of mass destruction may be misplaced. After losing its camps in Afghanistan, al-Qaeda has lacked the needed sanctuary and security to develop biological or **chemical weapons**. However it has already developed great expertise in using explosives and creativity in turning western technology into mass casualty weapons, as in seizing the four airliners used as flying bombs in the 11 September attacks. Rather than expecting al-Qaeda to imitate an Aum Shinrikyo poison gas attack it is more likely it will continue using massive bombs, a tactic that has proven effective, easily implemented, and relatively inexpensive.

Leadership

Osama bin Laden is al-Qaeda's *Emir*, or 'commander'. Muhammad Atef headed its military committee and masterminded the 1998 US Embassy bombings but died in US air raids in November 2001. Ayman al Zawahiri, an Egyptian doctor who led the Jihad Group, is bin Laden's personal physician and chief counsel and heads the Islamic study committee. Another al-Qaeda figure, Khalid Sheikh Mohammed, the mastermind of the 11 September 2001 attacks, was captured by Pakistani forces on 1 March 2003 and remanded to US investigators.

Osama bin Laden, born in Riyadh in 1957, was one of fifty-two children of Muhammad bin Laden, a Yemeni contractor who amassed a fortune of about US$5 billion. Osama bin Laden helped run the family business and inherited about US$25 million from his father. When the Soviets invaded Afghanistan on 11 January 1979 bin Laden left his family business to help the *mujahideen*. While in Pakistan in 1979–84 he funded Afghan fighters and built shelters for refugees. In1984–9 inside Afghanistan he built roads and shelters for the *mujahideen* and later participated in actual combat. Together with Abdullah Azzam, he helped organize the MAK, opening offices throughout the world wherever Muslims could be recruited. After the Soviets left Afghanistan in 1989 the *mujahideen* attacked the heavily defended city of Jalalabad. Bin Laden, who led an assault on the airport, was wounded by shrapnel and many of his Arab volunteers were killed. After this he returned to Saudi Arabia and resumed work in the family business.

The deployment of US forces against Iraq in 1990–1, and particularly the stationing of non-Muslim US troops in Saudi Arabia, outraged bin Laden. He viewed the Saudi royal family's permission to station American troops in Arabia as treachery to Islam because the government of Arabia was also the 'Protector of the Two Holy Places', namely the holy cities of Mecca and Medina, which non-Muslims are forbidden to enter but which now in effect were also under US military protection. He moved to Sudan in April 1991, ostensibly so his construction business could help develop a destitute Muslim nation. However by 1994 the governments of Egypt, Algeria and Yemen were accusing him of supporting Islamic fundamentalists seeking to overthrow them. After learning of bin Laden's involvement with domestic opposition groups the Saudi government revoked his passport and Saudi citizenship in 1994 and his family has reportedly disowned him. Al-Qaeda supplied the Stinger missiles used by Somali militias against US helicopters in the autumn of 1993. Although bin Laden initially had good relations with the National Islamic Front ruling Sudan by 1996 he was asked to leave, due to pressure from Egypt, whose President, Hosni Mubarak, survived an al-Qaeda sponsored assassination attempt during his 26 June 1995 visit to Ethiopia.

Bin Laden returned to Afghanistan although his exact movements from 1996 onward remain a mystery. His base outside Jalalabad held about 600 of his followers who were estimated to number around 10,000 or more in over twenty-five countries. He developed close relations with the Taliban leader, Mullah Omar, whose forces seized Kabul in September 1996. Bin Laden contributed over 5,000 trained men to fight alongside Taliban forces which seized all but 10 per cent of Afghanistan by late 1999. On 9 September 2001 two al-Qaeda suicide bombers, posing as Arab journalists, killed Massud Shah, the main leader of the Northern Alliance forces opposing the Taliban. Following the entry of US forces into Afghanistan bin Laden's whereabouts became even more obscure. A videotape dated 9 November 2001, found by US forces in December 2001, placed him in Qandahar, meeting al-Qaeda associates and discussing his role in the 11 September attacks. While he was thought to be hiding in tunnel complexes within the Tora Bora mountains in December 2001, later it was learned that he had ordered a follower to use his satellite phone as a decoy to throw US intelligence off his trail. By late 2003 it was believed that bin Laden and al Zawahiri were hiding in regions bordering Pakistan and Afghanistan ruled by tribes not under Pakistani government control. After December 2001 bin Laden avoided using telephones and other electronic communications that might reveal his location but depended instead on human couriers.

Operations

Al-Qaeda operations included recruitment, logistical support, fund raising, propaganda, and training fighters in special camps in unconventional warfare. Al-Qaeda maintained extensive businesses and charities as front organizations, and traditional financial channels for flows of funds and communications needed to keep its network of allied groups functioning effectively. Some are entities created by al-Qaeda but in many cases it has infiltrated and taken over existing charities, banks, and businesses. Finally al-Qaeda has committed terrorist attacks which won it notoriety.

Al-Qaeda engaged in these operations prior to the 11 September attacks. On 29 December 1992 al-Qaeda bombed a hotel in Aden, Yemen, housing US troops headed to Somalia. In June 1993 Jordanian police discovered an al-Qaeda plot to assassinate Crown Prince Abdullah. On 3 October 1993 al-Qaeda forces crossed into Somalia from Kenya and attacked US forces, killing eighteen Americans and many Somalis. The 26 February 1993 World Trade Center bombing, killing six and wounding over one thousand people, was planned and executed by Ramzi Yousef, an al-Qaeda operative captured in one of bin Laden's safe houses in Pakistan in February 1995. On 24 June 1993 al-Qaeda members were arrested for plotting to bomb the Lincoln and Holland tunnels in New York City. The Egyptian cleric, Omar Abdur-Rahman, whose Islamic Group in Egypt aligned itself with al-Qaeda, was arrested and later convicted for his role in these plots. On 6 January 1995 a police raid on Ramzi Yousef's Manila apartment exposed *Plan Bojinka*, which included plots to assassinate Pope John Paul II during his visit to the Philippines, and also against both US President Bill Clinton and Philippines President Fidel V. Ramos. The plotters planned to bomb eleven US airliners over the Pacific Ocean after they had succeeded in a trial run bombing of a Philippines Airlines flight on 11 December 1994, which killed one Japanese passenger and forced the plane to land at Naha Airport, Okinawa. On 26 June 1995 Egyptian President Hosni Mubarak survived an al-Qaeda assassination attempt during a state visit to Ethiopia.

In Riyadh on 13 November 1995 a Saudi Arabian National Guard office was car-bombed, killing seven foreign employees while wounding forty-two bystanders. On 25 June 1996 US military housing in the Khobar Towers, in Dhahran, Saudi Arabia, was truck-bombed killing nineteen US citizens and wounding some 500 people. On 17 November 1997 the al-Qaeda aligned Islamic Group massacred fifty-eight foreign tourists and four Egyptians at the Temple of Queen Hatsheput outside Luxor, Egypt. On 7 August 1998 two near simultaneous bombings of the US Embassies in Nairobi, Kenya and Dar es Salaam, Tanzania, killed 291 people and wounded about 5,000 in the Nairobi attack and killed ten persons and wounded seventy-seven in the Dar es Salaam attack. On 14 December 1999 US Customs arrested an Algerian, Ahmad Rassam, for smuggling explosives from Canada, which exposed an al-Qaeda plot to bomb Los Angeles International Airport as well as other targets in North America and Europe during upcoming Millennium celebrations. Earlier on 30 November 1999 Jordanian police discovered an al-Qaeda plot to bomb the Radisson Hotel in Amman on New Year's Eve, where a large Millennium celebration was certain to attract many foreigners.

On 3 January 2000 two bombers attempted to sink the USS *The Sullivans* anchored in Aden, Yemen, piloting an explosives laden boat but the operation was botched when the overloaded boat was swamped and sank. A second attempt succeeded on 12 October 2000 when the USS *Cole* was badly damaged by a large bomb deployed by two suicide bombers in a skiff which killed seventeen sailors. Finally al-Qaeda carried out the 11 September 2001 attacks in which suicide bombers hijacked four American domestic flights, crashing one into the World Trade Center north tower and another into the south tower, and another into the east side of the Pentagon. The fourth flight crashed following a struggle between the hijackers and passengers. At least 2,817 persons were killed at the World Trade Center and 125 were killed at the Pentagon. All nineteen hijackers and 238 passengers died in these attacks.

After US forces occupied Afghanistan al-Qaeda has been less able to muster terrorist operations on the scale of those before the 11 September attacks. Yet on 13 October 2002 the al-Qaeda linked Jemaah Islamiyah group bombed several nightclubs in Bali, Indonesia killing 202 persons, including eighty-eight Australian tourists and seven US tourists. In Riyadh, Saudi Arabia on 12 May 2003 al-Qaeda carried out three simultaneous bombings at a housing complex for foreign workers, killing twenty-three people, as well as the twelve suicide bombers. Al-Qaeda is believed to have been behind the 19 August 2003 bombing of UN offices in Baghdad, which killed twenty-three people, including Sergio Vieira de Mello, the top UN envoy to Iraq.

Organization

Al-Qaeda uses novel command structures and tactics to expand vertically by contacting and co-opting other Islamist movements into its network through heady ideological indoctrination, irresistible financial support, and often by sheer force. These organizations include most known violent Islamist militant groups, the major exceptions being the Palestinian groups Hamas and Islamic Jihad, which are wary of al-Qaeda's propensity to absorb its allies. Each co-opted group then transmits al-Qaeda's strategic direction and tactical support horizontally down to its compartmentalized cells and front groups. Up to one-fifth of the bona fide Islamic charities and educational foundations worldwide were also co-opted whose patrons remained unaware until police crackdowns after the 11 September attacks revealed these infiltrations. Many takeovers of Islamist groups have been hostile, involving the murders of leaders or members who did not agree with al-Qaeda's agenda or methods. Oddly enough this group that began by resisting a Marxist–Leninist regime in Afghanistan itself adopted many of the tactics of Leninism in forming its own version of a militant 'Islamist International' complete with its own vanguard leadership.

One must distinguish the central core group of al-Qaeda centered around bin Laden from the loose network of affiliated organizations operating outside Afghanistan and Pakistan. A third layer of 'walk ins' consists of young, committed Islamic fundamentalists attracted to al-Qaeda who volunteer for martyrdom actions with no prior Afghan war experience or training. Acceptance by al-Qaeda requires that one must be a believing Muslim. However acceptance into a leadership position requires proficiency in the Arabic language and some ties of family, friendship or past shared combat experience to vouch for one's integrity to the cause.

Prior to al-Qaeda most terrorist organizations had a central leadership with command and control branches linked to several compartmentalized cells which operated independently but ordinarily could not coordinate attacks due to their mutual isolation. Bin Laden created a system whereby allied groups outside Afghanistan and cells of al-Qaeda operatives in various countries functioned as independent cells but could coordinate their actions through a system of human couriers that eluded the electronic surveillance upon which most western intelligence agencies relied. This system works because the many thousands of members of these different groups and cells share bonds of trust forged in their common experience fighting together in the Afghan war. Most leaders of the allied regional groups formed friendships with bin Laden during the Afghan war as well as with other al-Qaeda leaders.

The al-Qaeda core consists of bin Laden, other leaders, and the roughly 1,000–1,500 men who survived the al-Qaeda training program, passed its rigorous physical and mental tests, and

who have sworn personal fealty, or *bayat,* to bin Laden as their Emir, imposing religious obligations of obedience to him unto death. This core provides the bodyguards, internal security force for preventing infiltration, and also the staff who control the group's personnel records and financial affairs.

The basic organization is headed by the Emir, bin Laden, assisted by his chief counsel, al Zawahiri. Under the Emir is the *shura majlis,* or consultative assembly, of roughly 10–15 men who run the various executive committees. Four permanent committees oversee the work of al-Qaeda: the military affairs committee, in charge of training, planning of operations and logistics; the Islamic study committee, in charge of indoctrination of members into proper understanding of Islamic law; the financial affairs committee, overseeing the holdings of al-Qaeda, the network of financial transfers, and the various fund raising schemes to finance operations; and the Islamic propagation committee, which disseminates al-Qaeda communiques through public mass media and informal channels. Membership in these committees and their structure is not so much governed by rules and written documents but rather by family ties, friendship, and areas of experience and expertise. Al-Qaeda's core members are driven more by their common goals than by formal organizational or procedural precepts.

While twenty-five different radical Islamic groups have been named as forming part of the al-Qaeda network only a few show consistent compliance with the core group. They include, in Subsaharan Africa, the Ittihad al Islamiya; the Jemaah Islamiya group in Malaysia and Indonesia; and the Islamic Group in Egypt. The Lebanese Hezbollah group has provided al-Qaeda with instruction on mass casualty bombing attacks and use of suicide bombers, however their mutual dealings are those of equals rather than al-Qaeda being dominant. In other cases, al-Qaeda has co-opted existing Algerian and Egyptian networks in western Europe. Al-Qaeda has severed links with other groups when their behavior has proved scandalous. In 1998 al-Qaeda ceased supporting the Armed Islamic Group in Algeria after it embarked on massacres of Muslim civilians. It also abandoned the Abu Sayyaf Group in the Philippines for degenerating into a gang interested more in robbery and kidnaping for ransom than in fighting for an Islamic state.

Al-Qaeda planted its own cells throughout North America, Great Britain, and Europe consisting of 'families' of al-Qaeda operatives picked from similar national backgrounds who have trained or fought together in Afghanistan. They are carefully trained in assuming a cover identity and maintaining a plausible occupation, residence and behavior consistent with that cover. Mindful of police surveillance of immigrant Muslim communities they are advised to avoid mixing with local Muslim populations and to avoid attending prayer services in existing Islamic centers or mosques.

Like Ayatollah Khomeini before him, bin Laden believes that the more fundamental conflict between Muslims and their enemies requires them to set aside their own doctrinal differences for the sake of unity. Thus al-Qaeda collaborates with Shi'ite Muslims, such as the Lebanese Hezbollah and official Iranian representatives, in spite of its Wahhabi salafist orientation. Generally al-Qaeda avoids contact with non-Muslims but it has contacted the Liberation Tigers of Tamil Eelam to acquire better suicide bombing expertise and has contacted organized criminal syndicates to raise funds and, in some instances, to attempt to buy nuclear materials. However such contacts with Shi'ites and various non-Muslim groups are short term tactical accommodations rather than part of a long term strategy.

What is the relationship of al-Qaeda to Pakistan and Saudi Arabia, as well as to state sponsors of terrorism, such as Iran, Iraq, and Libya? Although Pakistan's ISI had al-Qaeda contacts and helped create the Taliban, following the 11 September attacks the Pakistani government aligned itself with the US campaign against the Taliban and al-Qaeda and so the issue of Pakistani support for al-Qaeda became moot. After disclosures that the Saudi supported World Muslim League and International Islamic Relief Organization had each financially supported al-Qaeda, members of the US Congress and others have questioned the sincerity of Saudi efforts against al-Qaeda. In the past the ruling elites of Saudi Arabia tolerated fund raising for al-Qaeda and limited activities within their borders on the implicit understanding that in return al-Qaeda would not directly attack them. But with recent al-Qaeda attacks on Saudi targets, including planned attacks within the holy city of Mecca, the question of passive Saudi support for al-Qaeda also became moot.

Ironically Libya was the first nation to issue an arrest warrant for bin Laden in 1998 following the 1994 murder by al-Qaeda of a German couple vacationing in Surt, Libya. The Libyan leader Muammar Qadhafi has always repressed salafist groups in Libya and even aided the Algerian government in its war upon its salafists in the 1990s by interdicting salafists operating along Libya's western border with Algeria and through intelligence cooperation. Following the 11 September attacks questions were raised about Iraqi support for al-Qaeda and in particular about possible Iraqi sponsorship of those attacks. On 16 September 2003 the US Secretary of Defense,

Donald Rumsfeld, stated there was no evidence of Iraqi involvement in the 11 September attacks but that there was evidence of earlier Iraqi aid to al-Qaeda in bomb construction and training in the use of chemical and biological weapons. However with the overthrow of Saddam Hussein by US troops in April 2003 the issue of Iraqi state support for al-Qaeda became moot.

Finally there remains the question of Iranian state support. There is ample evidence of active Iranian aid to al-Qaeda: Hezbollah trainers and Iranian Ministry of Intelligence and Security agents trained al-Qaeda fighters in camps in the Sudan, in Hezbollah camps in Lebanon, and in training bases within Iran. Imad Maghniyah, the Hezbollah mastermind of the 23 October 1983 bombing of the US Marines encampment, is known to have instructed al-Qaeda in his bombing expertise. Recovered records of al-Qaeda's international telephone calls show that over 10 per cent of its calls were routed through Iran. As of October 2003 one of bin Laden's sons, as well as Abu Musab al Zarqawi, the al-Qaeda biochemical weapons expert, and Turki al-Dandani, wanted for the 12 May 2003 Riyadh bombings, were all hiding in Iran. Iranian state support for al-Qaeda has been continuing in spite of Iranian claims to the contrary.

Challenge

Rohan Gunaratna (2002: 223) and other counterterrorism experts concur that the policies of western liberal democracies to counter al-Qaeda should be multilateral, not unilateral (see **multilateralism**). However military actions even by coalitions of nations against al-Qaeda remain half-measures unless conjoined with public **diplomacy** to make their case heard among the developing Muslim nations to which al-Qaeda

directs its appeal. Other counterinsurgency experts note that the true 'center of gravity' of most conflicts is the issue of legitimacy, that of the regime(s) being attacked versus that of its attackers. If so, then disarming al-Qaeda requires exposing its ideology before its intended Muslim constituencies as being an opportunistic distortion of Islamic teaching. This demythologizing is necessary since bin Laden's appeal rests on his image as a pious militant serving Islam. Bin Laden has ingeniously exploited Islamic religious symbolism and Muslim grievances for his self-aggrandizement, promoting himself as a populist folk hero among the Muslims not only of Asia, Africa, and the Middle East but even among the educated and prosperous Muslim diasporas in North America, Europe, and Australia.

Apart from the continuing operations of al-Qaeda and similar groups two other problems of international relations must be addressed to reduce their threats. First is the problem of **failed state**s and of 'gray areas'. After the defeat of the Soviets in Afghanistan in the late 1980s, US foreign policy failed to address the growing political vacuum that the Taliban and al-Qaeda soon filled. Failed states such as Afghanistan and Somalia provide both sanctuaries for groups like al-Qaeda and recruiting grounds for the thousands of young men lacking other ready employment in the midst of devastated economic and political systems. Apart from failed states other sanctuaries are found in remote regions where government authority is lacking, 'gray areas,' such as the frontier bordering Pakistan and Afghanistan, and the region overlapping Brazil, Paraguay, and Argentina, that are also breeding grounds of terrorism. Second is the problem of **rogue state**s, such as Iran and Syria, and formerly, Iraq and Sudan, which use groups like al-Qaeda to pursue their geopolitical aims. Clearly even well financed net-works, such as al-Qaeda, require some state support to obtain identity docu-ments, weapons, explosives, sanctuaries, and other needs. Effective counter-terrorism policies need to correct failed states and gray areas, to isolate and punish rogue states that sponsor terror-ism, and to reward and aid states that withdraw from passive or active spon-sorship of terrorism. Finally the liberal democracies must find ways to ensure that **globalization** brings net material, social and political benefits to develop-ing nations, and in particular to the Muslim nations, to neutralize the grie-vances and resentments that groups such as al-Qaeda exploit.

Further reading

Burke, J. (2003) *Al-Qaeda: Casting A Shadow of Terror*, London: I. B. Tauris.

Bergen, P. I. (2002) *Holy War, Inc.: Inside the Secret World of Osama bin Laden*, New York: Free Press.

Gunaratna, R. (2002) *Inside Al Qaeda: Glo-bal Network of Terror*, New York: Colum-bia University Press.

Ranstorp, M. (1998) 'Interpreting the Broader Context and Meaning of Bin-Laden's Fatwa', *Studies in Conflict and Terrorism* 21, 4: 321–30.

See also: Islam; suicide terrorism; terrorism

SEAN K. ANDERSON

Anarchy

Anarchy is the absence of government. The central role accorded to anarchy is evident in every introductory textbook on international relations, where it is conventional to describe the **interna-tional system** as an anarchy and then to go on to note that this does not imply the presence of disorder or chaos. Rather, anarchy is a formal condition of the international system, a product of the legal independence enjoyed by each **nation-state**. The opposite of anarchy is hier-archy, the condition in which units are organized so that one is entitled to com-mand and others are required to obey.

Any system in which the units are for-mally independent of one another can be characterized as anarchic. That is, there is no overarching center of **author-ity** that has the right to command that the units behave as it wishes. Each actor is legally free to decide its policies as it sees fit, judging for itself the costs, bene-fits, and consequences of each course of action. In this way, anarchy is the logical corollary of **sovereignty**. The fact that the international system is composed of sovereign states necessarily implies a condition of anarchy among them. Sover-eignty describes the qualities of the units in the system (formal, legal autonomy) and anarchy describes the structure of the system in which these units exist.

Any definition of anarchy must make clear what element of government is missing in an anarchic system. Here, controversy abounds. Some, working from a Weberian definition of the state, suggest that the international system is lacking a centralized institution that monopolizes the use of force. This may go too far, since few, if any, states actu-ally succeed in monopolizing the use of force on their territories. Even well-established national governments may be faced with occasional armed internal dissent in the form of (for instance) separatist movements. Milner (1991) provides an excellent discussion of the matter, leading to the conclusion that anarchy is the absence of legitimized authority in the system.

Behavioral consequences of anarchy

The formal autonomy of units entailed by anarchy does not preclude the coercion of the weak by powerful actors. Thus, it is no violation of the idea of anarchy to have strong states pressuring the weak, or to have weak states concerned about retaliation by the strong should they pursue an independent policy. Anarchy does not mean that each gets to do whatever it wants, only that each has no *legal* obligation to obey another. As long as the formal, legal freedoms enshrined in sovereignty continue to exist, so does anarchy. Going a step further, it would be a contradiction of anarchy to have either the strong states eliminating the weak from the system (taking them over) or claiming a legal right to rule over them. The distinction between practical domination and formal hierarchy can be hazy in the real world. Was the British Empire a hierarchical system in which the dominions accepted the British right to rule, or was it simply a system where the weak submitted because of the threat from the strong? The former eliminates anarchy from the system while the latter preserves it.

Anarchy does not imply chaos or disorder in the international system. There may even be a great deal of behavioral regularity among the units in an anarchy. Indeed, the anarchical structure of the international system has been seen by many theorists as a *cause* of the patterned behavior of states. Such theories (known collectively as 'structural theories') include versions of **realism, neoliberalism**, and **constructivism**, and all argue that international anarchy gives states incentives to behave or to see themselves in some ways and not in others. For instance, neorealism begins with the assumption that in an anarchy units must devote some of their energies to ensuring their self-preservation. By dint of there being no super-ordinate agency to protect states from attack by others, each must pursue some version of a 'self-help' strategy, perhaps by **bal-**

ance of power. The structure of anarchy encourages states to behave in this way, and punishes those who do not. Over the long term, this means that the system will come to be populated by states that all look alike in this way. Much like Adam Smith's 'invisible hand', a pattern thus emerges from the uncoordinated and independent behavior of units in the system responding to the exigencies of the anarchic structure.

Wendt, in his famous phrase that 'anarchy is what states make of it' (1992) takes issue with this logic on the grounds that anarchy in itself is insufficient to generate the kind of insecurity presumed by the neorealists. He accepts the description of the system as an anarchy but suggests that this alone cannot make the units feel under threat. Rather, he claims, the incentives presented by an anarchic system depend on the 'culture' that exists among the units: an anarchy of friends is very different than one of enemies. Understanding the culture that exists in the system is crucial for understanding how the units will behave, and Wendt examines the very different kinds of international order that result from three distinct cultures: the Hobbesian, Lockean, and Kantian cultures.

Despite these differences, these 'structural' theories all share the assumption that anarchy is the fundamental reason for certain recurring patterns in international politics. They contrast with the earlier forms of classical realism, liberal internationalism, and idealism precisely on the issue of anarchy. The classical theories identify the causes of patterns in international politics at the level of individual leaders or in the characteristics of particular nation-states. They are therefore not concerned with the structural power of anarchy to shape behavior, even though they still might describe the system as anarchic in form. It is only with the turn to 'structural' theory that anarchy begins to be seen as a cause in itself of outcomes.

The logic of anarchy holds such a central place in International Relations theory that it is hard to image it being displaced. Indeed, it is sometimes suggested that nothing short of the creation of a single world state would qualify as the end of anarchy. However, some trends in contemporary international politics, if extended, might cause us to rethink the centrality of anarchy. Returning to the original definition of the term, international anarchy would end if an international organization came to be seen as having the authority to decide matters on behalf of states. In small ways, this might already be happening: widely shared norms govern what counts as acceptable treatment of citizens by their states; private military companies exist to provide security to states for a price; bond rating companies decide the credit-worthiness of governments (and so affect their borrowing capacity); the **United Nations** Security Council decides when **war**s are legal or illegal. To the extent that the **power** enjoyed by these institutions is seen as legitimate and authoritative, they violate the formal definition of anarchy and would imply that anarchy has been replaced by authority, at least in some parts of the system.

These fragments of authority notwithstanding, the anarchic nature of the system as a whole seems secure, and will last as long as does the sovereign state system itself.

Further reading

Bull, H. (1994) *The Anarchical Society: A Study of Order in World Politics*, New York: Columbia University Press.
Milner, H. (1991) 'The Assumption of Anarchy in International Relations: A Critique',

Review of International Studies 17, 1: 67–85.
Schmidt, B. (1998) *The Political Discourse of Anarchy: A Disciplinary History of International Relations*, Albany: State University of New York Press.
Waltz, K. (1979) *Theory of International Politics.* Reading, MA: Addison-Wesley.
Wendt, A. (1992) 'Anarchy is What States Make of It: The Social Construction of Power Politics', *International Organization* 46, 2:391–425.

See also: global governance; international society; prisoner's dilemma; realism; sovereignty

IAN HURD

Anti-Americanism

Although anti-Americanism is a widely used term, it has no fixed meaning. One of the key problems for precision and clarity is that one person's reasonable criticism of the United States is another person's anti-Americanism. Anti-Americanism needs to be understood as both a descriptive and a pejorative term. It is rightly used to describe hatred of America and often misused to dismiss criticisms of the United States. Thus a key issue is how to distinguish criticism based on anti-Americanism from criticism based on other grounds. Genuine anti-Americanism implies an across-the-board abhorrence of American politics, culture and people. Such a breadth of antipathy is a tall order given the diver3 Zeldin has described anti-Americanism as pathological, arguing that '[t]o hate a whole nation, to love a whole nation, is a clear symptom of hysteria' (Toinet *et al.*, 1990: 35). Similarly Toinet *et al.* suggests that the use of the term anti-Americanism 'is only fully justified if it implies systematic opposition – a sort of allergic reaction – to America as a whole' (Toinet *et al.*, 1990: 219).

Even thought of as an 'ism' rather than a prejudice, the broad range of views that are called anti-Americanism make the concept more incoherent and amorphous than the standard usually expected of ideologies or belief systems. The clearest version of an anti-American ideology has arguably been put forward by Osama bin Laden and **Al-Qaeda**, with the events of 11 September 2001 being quintessential anti-American acts. Al-Qaeda's anti-American belief system principally blames the United States and its client rulers for the world's various injustices. This comes closest to a coherent definition of anti-Americanism, namely a belief that the US is to blame for the ills of the world. In political debates in the west this viewpoint is associated most readily with writers such as Noam Chomsky, John Pilger and Tariq Ali. However, the criticisms of these authors generally focus on American politics, not American culture or the American people. As a result they would all reject the label of anti-Americans, as would most non-fanatics.

At its broadest, it could be argued that someone who is anti-American is simply someone who is not pro-American. This understanding may suffice for bar room conversation or within certain parts of the media but is far too broad. As a result of this obvious problem, writers have tried to break the term down into separate components. The most common approach is to look at what people dislike about the United States and to distinguish between types of anti-Americanism. The principal division is between political and cultural anti-Americanism. Naim (2002), however, goes further and identifies five types: politico-economic, historical, religious, cultural, and psychological. Hollander (1994) examines irrational and rational anti-Americanism at home and abroad. Others have followed a comparative approach, arguing that anti-Americanism is usefully understood in various historical and cultural contexts (Crockatt, 2003).

One way of explaining anti-Americanism is to see it as a function of America's size, influence, and power. If we accept this argument, anti-Americanism would seem little different from anti-English, anti-French or anti-Japanese sentiment. While it needs to be recognized that anti-Americanism is not entirely different from Anglophobia (particularly during the reign of the British Empire), anti-Americanism is different in some important respects. Fairlie (1975) notes the United States' unparalleled impact on other cultures, and the distinct nature of anti-Americanism. Like the French, Americans often see their values as universal; but unlike the French, the language Americans use is the *lingua franca* of our age and American popular culture is consumed by a broader range of peoples than any culture has ever been. These factors make American values, culture, and businesses a major source of inspiration and fashion around the world, but also a great source of anxiety, exploitation, and disruption.

There are other characteristics of the United States that account for the distinctive nature of anti-Americanism. Lipset (1996) has suggested that America is more than a country – it is an ideology. Lipset suggests that liberty, egalitarianism, individualism, populism and *laissez-faire* beliefs are at the core of Americanism. Crockatt (2003) suggests that Americanism is an idealized account of how Americans sees themselves and their role in the world. One potent source of anti-Americanism is the vast gap between the ideals the United States espouses and its actual behavior. It is the hypocrisy of much American activity, particularly in the arena of foreign affairs, which aggravates many so-called anti-Americans. The distinctive character of anti-Americanism inspired by such hypocrisy is that anti-Americans see the United States neither as a source of inspiration nor as a country capable of reform.

In summary, anti-Americanism manifests itself in a wide variety of ways. It is useful to distinguish between at least three levels of analysis. The first level consists of what is often called anti-Americanism but what should be more correctly described as criticism of American politics, values and culture. At level two we move from criticism to stereotype-driven rhetorical attacks on the United States and the American people as a whole. This mindset produces sweeping claims about American people and culture or an inability to see anything admirable about American foreign policy. Finally, there is a form of anti-Americanism which draws on such stereotypes to express not just criticism but hatred. An extreme example of this level of anti-Americanism were the attacks of 11 September 2001, whose targets included symbols of American power as well as civilians who were predominately Americans.

Further reading:

Crockatt, R. (2003) *America Embattled*, London: Routledge.

Fairlie, H. (1975) 'Anti-Americanism at Home and Abroad', *Commentary* 60, 6: 29–39.

Hollander, P. (1995) *Anti-Americanism*, London: Transaction Press.

Lipset, S. M. (1996) *American Exceptionalism*, New York: Norton.

Naim, M. (2002) 'Anti-Americanisms', *Foreign Policy* 128 (January/February): 95–104.

Toinet, M., Lacorne, D., Rupnik, J. and Zeldin, T. (1990) *The Rise and Fall of Anti-Americanism*, London, Macmillan.

See also: empire; hegemonic stability theory; hegemony

BRENDON O'CONNOR

Appeasement

A strategy of conflict resolution in which one state makes unilateral concessions regarding the issues that are the focus of conflict between two or more states. This definition implies that the goal of an appeasement strategy is to settle a conflict between states by avoiding **war** and without dominating the other state. Less obvious is whether the appeasing state can or should submit to the opponent as part of its appeasement strategy. Surrender and appeasement have become confounded as strategies of conflict resolution by the notorious example of Britain's appeasement strategy toward Germany during the 1930s leading up to the outbreak of the Second World War.

In this case the concessions made by Britain's Prime Minister Neville Chamberlain to settle issues with Nazi Germany did not resolve their conflict and thereby did not achieve the goal of peace between the two states. The British failure to prevent the Second World War and the criticism that British strategy may have contributed to the outbreak of war in Europe has given appeasement a bad reputation. However, some defenders of Chamberlain's appeasement strategy have maintained that Britain's submission to Hitler's demands in 1938 was an appropriate way to buy time until Britain could rearm and bargain with Germany from a position of strength in 1939.

During the **cold war**, American presidents from Truman through Reagan invoked the Munich settlement negotiated in 1938 between Chamberlain and Hitler as a classic example of how *not* to resolve conflicts. Instead of pacifying Germany, the Munich agreements to transfer Czech territory to Germany encouraged Hitler to escalate his demands for more territory from Czechoslovakia and Poland, leading to the outbreak of war in 1939. The lesson that American policymakers drew from this example is that appeasement will not work, at least against certain adversaries such as revolutionary regimes and **rogue state**s who will interpret any concessions as signs of weakness. They applied this lesson in dealing with the communist states of Russia, China and North Vietnam during the cold war and have extended it to the post-cold war era in America's relations with Iraq following the latter's invasion of Kuwait in 1990.

A more balanced view of the historical record reveals that appeasement has a mixed record of successes and failures (Rock 2000). Some cases were successes in the short run but failures over the long run, resolving some immediate issues between states while not addressing others that became occasions for war. The pattern of partial success fits the British case, as Chamberlain was successful in resolving the conflict over the Czech Sudetenland but failed to resolve the conflict over Polish territory. Prior to the 1930s, Britain's foreign policy for much of the nineteenth and twentieth century was characterized by a strategy of appeasement with some notable successes as well as the failures of the 1930s (Kennedy 1983). The appeasement strategy's decline in popularity in the twentieth century may be traced to the development of highly nationalistic or revolutionary states with ideologies that made it difficult for their leaders either to grant concessions or to be satisfied with concessions from others. At the same time, the rise of liberal democracies created a zone of democratic peace among other states (see **zone of peace**), characterized by strategies of conflict resolution that have made it very unlikely that any issue will lead to war between democracies (Ray 1995).

The contrast between democracies and dictatorships regarding the cultural norms for the management and resolution of conflict perhaps best explains the appeasement strategy's short-run versus long-run prospects for success. The appeasement strategy is popular among democratic states in dealing with fellow democracies, because they share common cultural traditions and domestic institutions based on negotiation and the art of compromise as norms for conflict resolution. In contrast, authoritarian and revolutionary regimes established in Nazi Germany, the Soviet Union, and some of the new states in the Middle East and elsewhere operate on norms that emphasize coercion and domination by the strong over the weak, or the holy over the infidel. In the absence of shared norms for peaceful conflict resolution, therefore, an appeasement strategy is likely to fail in the long run.

However, all kinds of states have adopted appeasement strategies in the short run to settle a particular conflict for instrumental reasons, e.g., to reduce the number of active conflicts with other states or to buy time to rearm. In August 1939, Nazi Germany signed a nonaggression pact with the Soviet Union in which they mutually agreed to resolve their own differences without the use of force and divide Poland if either state should find itself at war with this third party. This agreement between the revolutionary dictatorships allowed Hitler to focus his attention on the threat from France and Britain in the event that Germany should attack Poland, reducing his number of enemies. Equally, Stalin was able to buy some time to rearm against a possible threat from Germany over the long run while reducing the number of Russian enemies so that he could focus on the threat from Japan in the Far East. In April 1941, Japan negotiated a nonaggression pact with Russia, which reduced Japanese enemies in Asia so that it could focus on the threat from the

United States regarding Japan's expansion into Southeast Asia. These examples of successful appeasement strategies in the short run were directed toward ideological foes by revolutionary regimes. In all of these cases, however, the signatories of such pacts eventually found themselves at war with one another, so they failed to preserve the peace in the long run.

As either a short-run or a long-run strategy to resolve conflicts with other states, the prospects for successful appeasement depend on several conditions. They include the nature and goals of the adversary, the appeasing state's ability to make concessions that address the needs or fears of the adversary, the perception of these concessions by the adversary, and the adversary's incentives to reciprocate with an appeasement strategy. In addition to these features of the situation, the skill with which an appeasement strategy is carried out may influence its degree of success. Depending on the conditions outlined above, concessions that are unconditional or conditional, incremental or radical, gradual or rapid, may have more success (Rock 2000).

Finally, the success of an appeasement strategy must be judged in comparison to the alternatives and their consequences. Depending on the distributions of power and interests between a state and its adversary, an appeasement strategy may be more or less cost-effective compared to strategic engagement, **deterrence** or coercive **diplomacy**. Strategic engagement goes beyond the resolution of conflict between states associated with an appeasement strategy and attempts to foster active cooperation and interdependence between them. Deterrence and compellence are strategies of coercive diplomacy rather than conflict resolution. The goals of these strategies are deadlock and domination, respectively, rather than settlement or submission. They employ the threat or deployment of force rather than concessions to avoid war.

Further reading

Kennedy, P. (1983) 'The Tradition of Appeasement in British Foreign Policy, 1865–1939', in P. Kennedy *Strategy and Diplomacy, 1870–1945*, London: Allen & Unwin, pp. 15–39.

Ray, J. (1995) *Democracy and International Conflict*, New York: Columbia.

Rock, S. (2000) *Appeasement in International Politics*, Lexington: Kentucky.

See also: containment; misperception; pacifism; reciprocity

STEPHEN G. WALKER

Arab League

The League of Arab States, or 'Jami'atu al-Duwal al-'Arabiyyah', was founded in 1945. In the early 1940s, two Arab Prime Ministers were proactive in driving the idea of Arab unity and the creation of the League. However the vision of creating an Arab League was neither clear nor widely popular. The Egyptians originally preferred unification with their Southern Sudanese neighbors within a Nile Valley framework. The Iraqis identified more closely with 'ahl al-Sham', the peoples of the fertile crescent (Iraq, Jordan, Lebanon, Palestine, and Syria). Their plan for unity was geographically modest and perhaps more realistic than uniting the entire Arab World.

Egypt's Mustafa al-Nahas Pasha (1876–1965) had the skill to facilitate the arduous negotiations that resulted in the 1945 Alexandria Protocol, which created the Arab League. More importantly, he placed his country's full political weight behind the project, investing a great deal of effort into mediation and consultation, especially during the two-year talks that culminated in the founding of the League. Al-Nahas continues to be credited with ironing out many of the problems between the small club of founding member states whose original visions for intra-Arab **multilateralism** were narrow in scope and unambitious in objectives. Thus when the League was finally created, Egypt's role was recognized in a number of ways. For example the headquarters of the League have remained in Cairo, except for a ten-year hiatus following Sadat's 1979 Camp David peace treaty with Israel, when the League was moved to Tunis. As the largest Arab state Egypt has also had a monopoly over the General-Secretariat, a post that seems to be reserved for Egyptian former Foreign Ministers. Over a period of 60 years, only one of its six occupants (Chadhli al-Qalibi of Tunisia) has not come from Eqypt.

Iraq's Nuri al-Said 'Pasha' (1888–1958), although known for his pro-British stance, also committed a great deal of energy towards advancing Arab unity. In fact, not only is he the Arab leader credited with inventing the idea of Arab unity, but also the term 'league' (Jami'ah) with its 'Arab' modifier. However in 1943 he concentrated on applying his idea to the countries making up the Fertile Crescent. Nonetheless, Al-Said (who was premier eight times when Iraq was still a monarchy) worked closely with al-Nahas Pasha, inspired by the desire for independence from European colonialism, as well as Arab unity. By virtue of being a key player in the League's creation and supported by petrodollar wealth, Iraq has always seen itself as a natural claimant for the mantle of Arab leadership within the League.

No understanding of the League can be complete without recognizing the different contexts that informed the performance, legitimacy and viability of the institution often referred to as the Arab House, 'al-Bait al-Arabi'. As mentioned, colonialism was important in driving the creation of the League. **Decolonization** widened the League's membership, especially as many new members felt beholden to an institution that pan-Arabists used to promote the cause of liberation in many Arab states, especially in the Arab West, or Maghreb. Arms, money and propaganda were invested to assist in the liberation of Algeria, Morocco and Tunisia. The League, especially during the presidency of Nasser, helped Arabs gain independence. In so doing, it made itself both viable and legitimate. Except in Palestine, colonialism has passed into history.

The Palestinian cause continues to unite an increasingly enfeebled League. The League still renders many services to this cause just as it did in the 1960s when it helped create the Palestinian Liberation Organization (PLO). But the Arab resolve that existed in the 1940s, 1950s, 1960s, and 1970s to commit more than lip service to help the Palestinians, namely, in its commitment to fight wars against Israel, no longer exists. The League remains a source of moral, and to some extent financial, support for the Palestinian cause. But the League has no will of its own outside its member states who are no longer united on how to help the Palestinians, much less how to resolve the whole Arab-Israeli conflict. Two Arab states (Egypt, Jordan) have formal peace treaties with Israel. Other Arab states have overt or covert diplomatic links with Israel. As in the case of Palestine, the League seems to have been enfeebled by its record of failure in resolving intra-Arab conflicts. This failure overshadows its early successes in promoting Arab unity (for example, through the creation of the Arab Development Fund and other pan-Arab institutions in the fields of education, culture, infrastructure and development) and continues to erode its legitimacy. The League did not shield its member states from international **sanctions** (e.g. Iraq, Libya, and Sudan). In fact, Libya has never forgiven its fellow Arab states for observing an embargo that in its view was unjust, and its leader, Mu 'ammar al-Qadhafi, has often threatened to withdraw from the League. The 1950 Arab Mutual Defence and Economic Cooperation Agreement might have served a purpose in the 1973 Yom Kippur war when member states' armies fought alongside Egypt and Syria. But at the turn of the twenty-first century it became outdated. It failed to serve any purpose in preventing the Anglo-American invasions (in 1991 and 2003) of the second most important founding member state of the League, Iraq, or in providing protection for the Palestinian civilians under Israeli occupation.

One could argue that the League itself is blameless even though its member states are not. In the broader context of **modernization**, **globalization** and **democratization**, they have failed to modernize the League, to integrate their economies, to create a borderless Arab region, or to democratize their own regimes and the decision-making processes within the League. They have not created enough of a community of interests worthy of solidarity, commitment or collective defense. The Tunisians do more trade with the French and the Saudis with the Americans than with their Arab neighbors. Egypt, the League's host, remains authoritarian and bureaucratic. The League is almost a replica of how Egypt itself is ruled, with little representation or accountability. Arab regimes have no genuine parliaments with popular representation; nor does the League. Had the Arab World democratized, the Arab League would have an Arab Parliament, with democratic institutions, procedures and laws, modeled on the **European Union**. The League was conceived within a colonial context. But neither its Charter nor procedures have evolved to reflect the spirit of changing contexts from modernization to globalization. The idea of the League remains relevant, but its institutions and procedures demand democratic transformation.

Further reading

Azzam, H. (2002) *The Arab World Facing the Challenge of the New Millennium*, London: I. B. Tauris.
Burdett, A. L. P. (1995) *The Arab League: British Documentary Sources, 1943–63*, Neuchâtel, Switzerland.
Dawisha, A. (2003) *Arab Nationalism in the Twentieth Century*, Princeton, NJ: Princeton University Press.
Hasou, T. (1985) *The Struggle for the Arab World: Egypt's Nasser and the Arab League*, London: KPI Books.
Gomaa, A. (1977) *The Foundation of the League of Arab States: Wartime Diplomacy and Inter-Arab Politics, 1941–1945*, London: Longman.
Hassouna, H. A. (1975) *The League of Arab States and Regional Disputes*, New York: Sijthoff.

See also: regionalism

LARBI SADIKI

Arms control

Arms control is classically defined as a set of cooperative measures undertaken amongst states to improve their joint **security**. Typically, those measures regulate some indicator of military potential or capability. They do so in order to achieve specific objectives, such as reducing the likelihood of **war**, reducing the economic and political costs of preparing for war, and reducing the levels of violence if war actually occurs.

In this sense, arms control is merely the obverse side of the coin of defence policy: it aims at building and enhancing security for its participants. Seeing it as this sort of activity is critical to understanding its scope, its validity and its role. Critics of arms control damn its ability to do too little, its unavailability when most needed and its role in reinforcing adversarial relationships. Many such arguments are well made and well meant, but they sometimes pretend that arms control can be something other than what it is. The limitations of arms control are generic, and people who want to work with arms control are usually intent upon achieving and defending small gains, especially in the context of an adversarial relationship. However, small gains can be valuable.

Critics of arms control can be found on both the ends of the political spectrum. The conservative strategic thinker Colin Gray, for example, in his book *A House of Cards* (1992), mounts an argument the central pillar of which could be endorsed by the more radical commentator Jonathan Schell (2000) – that arms control tempts its practitioners into doing too little. For Gray, arms control during the **cold war** stood in the way of strategic victory, and the overt effort made by American and Soviet arms controllers to reduce the economic burden of the arms competition helped prolong the longevity of the Soviet system. For Schell, arms control during the same period prevented Western policy-makers from pursuing grander visions of disarmament, even when the cold war was over. Both Gray and Schell attack arms control from different directions over what is essentially the same flaw: that it is, at its core, a conservative bargaining activity that constrains its participants and devalues more radical approaches to **security** dilemmas.

Despite its critics, arms control remains an important and valid activity.

Arms control, properly designed, is an instrument that enhances strategic stability, increases predictability, and minimizes arms racing (see **arms race**). It offers to adversaries a tiny window of cooperation, and is most likely to be undertaken when the adversaries see themselves as 'prisoners of insecurity'. But its utility is constrained by one key factor: the adversaries have to want to cooperate in order to reduce the tensions of their adversarial relationship and to manage that relationship better. Where no such desire exists, little can be achieved by forcing the mechanisms of arms control into place. The establishment of a 'hot-line', for example, between strategic rivals, has no meaning without a commitment by the parties to use that mechanism in stabilizing ways.

Is there such a thing as unilateral arms control? Yes. Some countries have voluntarily and unilaterally provided certain pledges, or initiated certain codes of practice that have helped to introduce elements of stability into adversarial relationships, and the value of such initiatives should not be understated. For example, in 1992 President George H. Bush declared that US naval vessels would not routinely carry tactical nuclear weapons during peacetime. Such measures can often be of particular relevance in asymmetrical inter-state contests, such as exists between India and Pakistan. When both countries have only limited resources to devote towards command and control and detecting ballistic missile launches, even a unilateral policy by one of the sides to provide prenotification of ballistic missile test launches could have small but valuable gains for strategic stability on the subcontinent. But unilateral arms control measures are not bound by treaty, nor verified by accepted provisions. They are revocable at the whim of the party that entered into them.

Does arms control require symmetrical competitors? Probably not, although during the cold war some of the most important arms control agreements codified numerical parity between the strategic arsenals of the United States and the Soviet Union. Nor does arms control even demand that states be the initiators of negotiations: the Ottawa convention on land mines, for example, shows that agreements can be initiated by pressure from non-state actors. But at a key point, implementation of arms control agreements does presuppose the existence of strong states, able to exercise governance over their territories, their defense policies and their procurement programs.

Recent commentators note that the field of arms control is undergoing something of a seachange. With the rise of a set of transnational actors onto the global security agenda, the place of arms control is more under question now than it has been for decades. So too, the death of some arms control **regime**s – such as the ABM treaty – has suggested to some of arms control's most dedicated advocates that the activity is more a reflection of the international security environment and less defining of that environment than they would like.

Arms control's key hurdle, however, lies in two inter-related developments within the international security environment. Firstly, in the post-cold war era, it faces a loss of structure and focus in the absence of a symmetrical balance of power. Second, those conflicts that remain within the environment – typically intra-state wars – are much harder to regulate by arms control measures than are traditional inter-state conflicts. It is hard to imagine the sort of arms control agreement to which **Al-Qaeda** might be a party, or even to imagine the negotiation at which its representative had a seat at the table.

The emergence of those two factors at the global level has led some to speculate that the age of arms control is largely over. That conclusion is too sweeping. Indeed, measures to tighten control over existing **weapons of mass destruction** arsenals might be more necessary now than ever, even though the reason for doing so may have changed. Many arms control agreements today have what might be termed useful 'second order' effects: they minimize certain sorts of weapons, and usually improve the regulation and control of such weapons. Since terrorists do not usually manufacture their own weapons, this is a non-trivial gain.

In coming years it will be important for the supporters of arms control to show that new measures are available to address the threats of a changing security environment in productive ways. The mechanisms that proved fruitful in constraining the two **superpower**s in a bipolar world are unlikely to be as useful in a world characterized by a war on terror, the continued proliferation of weapons of mass destruction and enduring regional rivalries. Applying arms control to a globalizing world, and to a range of asymmetrical strategic contests, will be a challenging but necessary enterprise.

Further reading

Gottemoeller, R (2002) 'Arms Control in a New Era', *The Washington Quarterly* 25, 2: 45–58.

Gray, C. (1992) *House of Cards: Why Arms Control Must Fail*, Ithaca, NY: Cornell University Press.

Larsen, J. A. (ed.) (2002) *Arms Control: Cooperative Security in a Changing Environment*, Boulder CO: Lynne Rienner.

Levi, M. and O'Hanlon, M. (2005) *The Future of Arms Control*, Washington, DC: Brookings Institution Press.

Schell, J. (2000) 'The Folly of Arms Control', *Foreign Affairs* 79, 5: 22–46.

Schelling, T. C. and Halperin, M. H. (1985) *Strategy and Arms Control*, Washington, DC: Pergamon-Brassey's (originally published 1961).

See also: arms race; International Atomic Energy Agency; nuclear proliferation

ROD LYON

Arms race

The idea that states are inclined to embark on programs to bolster their armaments in response to perceived enemies and potential adversaries has a strong lineage in strategic theory as well as having been borne out by empirical trends in international politics. Arms race refers to a situation in which two or more states compete actively for strategic advantage by seeking to offset and/or negate relative strengths in their respective military capabilities. The arms race dynamic refers to the action–reaction cycle that drives the arms race process: that is, one state's acquisition of a certain type of weapons system will provoke the acquisition of an equivalent or superior system on the part of its strategic adversary. The global arms race between the Soviet Union and the United States exemplified the logic (some would say the illogic) of the action–reaction cycle. But the phenomenon of arms racing did not end with the passing of the **cold war**. While nowhere near the massive scale of the **superpower** arms race, there exist a number of 'mini' arms races in various regions that contain the potential seeds for **war**.

There are different levels of arms racing internationally. On one level, a distinction can be drawn between quantitative and qualitative arms racing. Quantitative arms racing encompasses attempts to achieve numerical superiority in military personnel and/or a specific type of weapons system. This was

regarded as particularly important by those who subscribed to the strategy of attrition warfare in the early part of the twentieth century and it was a salient feature of the arms race between Britain and Germany that preceded World War One. By contrast, qualitative arms racing involves an attempt to balance or surpass an adversary's possession of a specific weapons system which, by dint of its impact on the balance of military forces, could have a potentially decisive impact in determining the outcome of any conflict. For instance, in the Taiwan Strait, instead of attempting to counter the United States' aircraft carrier force element with a matching acquisition program, China has decided to acquire the Russian-made Sovremenny class destroyer which is equipped with a 'carrier killing' anti-ship missile capability. In most cases, however, arms races incorporate both a quantitative as well as a qualitative dimension.

Central to the arms race dynamic is the existence of the **security dilemma** in international relations. The security dilemma is a situation where state X acquires specific armaments for what decision-makers regard as purely defensive reasons. But given that all military systems can be employed for offensive purposes, state Y sees this acquisition as offensive in intent. State Y reacts by acquiring similar classes of weapons to counter the perceived offensive threat from state X. While both states may genuinely regard their respective acquisitions as being defensive in nature, the logic of the security dilemma suggests that this action–reaction cycle would trigger an arms race and lead to instability and perhaps armed conflict between state X and state Y, even though neither state may want conflict. Given the reality of **anarchy** in international relations, there is no higher **authority** that can compel either side to exercise restraint in the arms acquisition process. Thus arms racing is essentially a symptom of the security dilemma rather than a cause of it. However, instituting a process of **arms control** can help to mitigate the effects of the cycle and pre-empt the potential for further arms racing by formalizing agreed constraints on the procurement of certain types of weapons systems.

The most ambitious and intense arms race in human history was the cold war arms race between the United States and the Soviet Union. Fuelled by a combination of misperception, mistrust and, at times, deliberate provocation, the US–Soviet arms race dominated the strategic landscape for almost half a century. The superpower arms race was evident at two levels: conventional and nuclear force acquisitions. Soviet conventional superiority in Europe in the aftermath of Word War Two was an important stimulant for the acceleration of the US nuclear weapons program after 1945 and provided the rationale for the presence of American tactical nuclear weapons in NATO Europe for most of the cold war period (see **North Atlantic Treaty Alliance**). At the global strategic level, both superpowers invested enormous resources in building up their respective missile and nuclear warhead arsenals, primarily to deter the other side from launching a first strike. Yet both superpowers continually sought to grapple with the perennial question of 'how much is enough in order to maintain deterrence?' The imperative of erring on the side of excess rather than strategic sufficiency led to massive redundancy in the capacity of both superpowers to destroy each other. It is generally agreed that the Soviet Union's diversion of precious economic resources into building up expensive weapons procurement programs that the country could ill-afford was a direct cause of the USSR's eventual collapse in the early 1990s.

Since the end of the cold war, several regional and sub-regional arms races have developed internationally. This is particularly evident in the Asia-Pacific where a number of states have accelerated highly competitive arms acquisition programs. China and Taiwan continue to engage in a qualitative arms race, with Beijing according priority to developing a short-range missile strike force and amphibious warfare capability sufficient to overwhelm Taiwan's ability to defend its maritime approaches across the Taiwan Strait. But the most serious arms race is occurring in South Asia, the only sub-region in the **international system** where two declared nuclear powers remain locked into a relationship of political confrontation. With India and Pakistan fixated on rapidly modernizing their nuclear warhead and missile programs, neither side is devoting adequate attention to developing reliable command and control capabilities. This may have disastrous results in terms of making it harder for both sides to exercise absolute control over their nuclear forces if a **crisis** over Kashmir begins to escalate to the nuclear threshold. Another feature of the Asian region often overlooked is the latent potential for a major nuclear and conventional arms race between deep-seated historical antagonists China and Japan. Should the United States decide to withdraw its strategic presence from the region, it is highly likely that the two strongest indigenous powers in Asia will actively seek to balance each other's military capabilities. This would, in all likelihood, lead to an arms race that neither China nor Japan may necessarily want, but which both sides appreciate could be unavoidable.

Some observers have argued that the decision by the United States in 2001 to accelerate the development and deployment of **ballistic missile defense** has increased the prospect of a new global arms race. Critics maintain that America's deployment of national missile defense assets designed to defend the US homeland against attack will encourage China to acquire greater numbers of long range missiles and nuclear warheads to counter US defensive systems which are regarded by most Chinese strategists as inherently offensive in intent. This, in turn, will spur China's close regional rival India to match the tempo of Chinese acquisitions which will in turn provoke an analogous reaction from Pakistan. This chain of events may have the effect of igniting a new global arms race with unpredictable, though highly destabilizing, consequences.

Further reading

Bracken, P. (1999) *Fire in the East: The Rise of Asian Military Power and the Second Nuclear Age*, New York: HarperCollins.

Bundy, M. (1990) *Danger and Survival: Choices About the Bomb in the First Fifty Years*, New York: Vintage Books.

Buzan, B. (1987) *An Introduction to Strategic Studies: Military Technology and International Relations*, Basingstoke: Macmillan.

Glaser, C. (2004) 'When are Arms Races Dangerous? Rational Versus Suboptimal Arming', *International Security* 28, 4: 44–84.

Mandelbaum, M. (1981) *The Nuclear Revolution*, Cambridge: Cambridge University Press.

Sloss, L. (2001) 'The New Arms Race', *The Washington Quarterly* 24, 4: 135–47.

See also: arms control; ballistic missile defense; cold war; prisoner's dilemma

ANDREW O'NEIL

Arms trade

In monetary terms, the international trade in conventional weapons accounts for roughly less than 1 per cent of total world trade. Yet the attention devoted to the impact of the global arms trade in shaping geo-strategic trends far exceeds its monetary consequence. States, **non-governmental organization**s, and academic think tanks concerned with the issue agree that the international arms trade is a key variable determining the degree of strategic stability in specific regions around the globe. While the volume of global transfers of conventional weapons has declined by between one quarter to one half since the end of the **cold war**, the international market has remained buoyant, with demand being particularly robust in the Asia-Pacific and the Middle East.

Today, the largest global arms suppliers are the United States and Russia which, together, account for more than 60 per cent of all international conventional arms transfers. The five largest suppliers – the United States, Russia, France, Germany and the United Kingdom – provide more than 80 per cent of aggregate arms transfers. In this sense, the composition of key arms exporters has remained largely unchanged since the end of the cold war. However, one salient trend has been that countries such as Israel and North Korea, who were traditionally only recipients of arms transfers, have entered the global market as suppliers of important niche technologies (missile components in North Korea's case and advanced combat software systems in the case of Israel).

As distinct from the acquisition of **weapons of mass destruction** (WMD), the acquisition of conventional weapons by individual states has always been regarded as an entirely justifiable pursuit in safeguarding national **security**. Unlike the situation with respect to WMD, there is no well established norm in international relations that discourages states from acquiring and using conventional forces as an instrument of policy. As a consequence, the trade in conventional weapons – ranging from those at the lower end of the technological spectrum such as light weapons and small arms to those at the higher end including combat aircraft and main battle tanks – continues to enjoy normative legitimacy in international relations. Of course, there are notable exceptions to this general rule, including prohibited weapons exports to states which are subject to **United Nations** sponsored arms embargoes and the transfer of arms to non-state entities such as terrorist groups or criminal syndicates.

During the cold war, conventional weapons were seen as useful tools of superpower **diplomacy** and were supplied by the Soviet Union and the United States to key allies and neutral states alike. Both **superpower**s transferred conventional arms for geo-strategic and ideological reasons and many states (particularly those in the **Third World**) took advantage of this permissive attitude to build up their armouries with the latest equipment. During the Vietnam War, for instance, the Soviet Union provided North Vietnam with crucial air defence assets which included the latest generation MIG fighter aircraft in an effort to support Hanoi against American forces. Similarly, the United States transferred hundreds of 'Stinger' surface-to-air missile (SAM) systems to Pakistan for delivery to Afghan rebels resisting Soviet occupation during the 1980s. While they were fairly liberal in the conventional arms they transferred to client states during the cold war, the superpowers nevertheless retained a tight leash on exports and were generally selective in the way they used conventional arms transfers as a political instrument.

In the wake of the end of the cold war, and the attendant sharp decline in the tempo of conventional arms procurements in North America and Europe (including Russia), arms manufacturers faced significant pressures to compensate by building up alternative markets in Africa, Asia, the Middle East, and South America. The scramble by arms manufacturers (typically with the enthusiastic support of their host governments) to find alternative post-cold war markets has led to important changes in the global arms market overall, which is now characterized by over-capacity. This has had three noticeable effects on the international arms market.

First, a consequence of the increasingly permissive market environment is that existing controls governing weapons sales are being steadily eroded. Government constraints on the approval of specific arms transfers have always been fairly weak when compared with the constraints imposed on the sale of nuclear technology, but they have become even weaker in recent years. In particular, the increasingly competitive market environment has substantially weakened supply-side restraints on Western exporters.

Second, the increasing glut of conventional arms on the international market has provided potential purchasers with greater scope to play off suppliers against one another in an effort to obtain the best deals and the most sophisticated weapons systems. For instance, competition between American, European, and Russian weapons manufacturers for lucrative contracts in Asia has intensified significantly over recent years. This has allowed Malaysia and Singapore, two countries that place a high premium on avoiding single supplier dependence in their respective defence acquisition programmes, to angle for the most competitive price on key platforms and systems by signalling that procurement decisions will be taken strictly on a case-by-case basis, irrespective of the source country.

Third, the glut of cheap weapons on the global market has made it considerably easier for non-state entities (including terrorist groups) to acquire high-tech conventional arms. Although most attention has focused on the possibility of terrorist groups such as **Al-Qaeda** gaining possession of nuclear, **chemical weapons**, or **biological weapons** for use against Western targets, the opportunities for terrorists to acquire major conventional weapons on the international black market has grown appreciably over the last decade. Of particular concern is that a terrorist organization may have already attained SAM systems equipped with optical sight and infra-red sensing mechanisms that are capable of shooting down civilian airliners.

Further reading

Brauer, J. and Dunne, P. (2004) *Arms Trade and Economic Development*, London: Routledge.

Hagelin, B., Wezeman, P. and Chipperfield, N. (2003) 'International Arms Transfers', in *Stockholm International Peace Research Institute, SIPRI Yearbook 2003: Armaments, Disarmament and International Security*, Oxford: Oxford University Press, 439–75.

Klare, M. and Lumpe, L. (1998) 'Fanning the Flames of War: Conventional Arms Transfers in the 1990s', in M. Klare and Y. Chandrani (eds) *World Security: Challenges for a New Century*, 3rd edn, New York: St. Martin's Press, 160–79.

Phythian, M. (2005) *The Business of Arms*, London: Routledge.

See also: arms control; civil war; terrorism

ANDREW O'NEIL

Asia Pacific Economic Cooperation Forum (APEC)

The Asia Pacific Economic Cooperation Forum was founded in 1989 to assist in promoting **free trade** in the broadly conceived Asia-Pacific region. Its successful inauguration suggested that it was an idea whose time had come. APEC's way had been prepared by a number of organizations and epistemic communities that had enthusiastically championed the cause of regional economic cooperation and helped to establish closer ties among regional political and economic elites (see **epistemic community**). However, despite these auspicious beginnings, APEC's subsequent history suggests that its advocates and some of its members may have had unrealistic expectations and/or divergent goals – the result being that APEC has failed to realize many of the hopes of its architects.

Paradoxically, one of APEC's potential strengths ultimately became a source of tension and an important illustration of differential **regionalism**. Despite accounting for more than half of global GDP, from the outset APEC's founding members – Australia, the United States, Canada, Japan, South Korea, China, Hong Kong and Taiwan, plus the original ASEAN (**Association of Southeast Asian Nations**) countries, Brunei, Indonesia, Malaysia, the Philippines, Singapore and Thailand – represented a diverse group with little in common politically, socially or economically. This lack of common identity has been compounded by the subsequent inclusion of Chile, Peru, Vietnam and even Russia – a country with little obvious claim to membership.

The question of inclusion has been a central feature of APEC's development from the outset. Although Japan had long promoted the idea of a free trade area in the Pacific, Japan's inability to provide effective regional leadership – principally a legacy of its wartime role – meant that Australia was able to utilize concern about the emergence of **regional trade blocs** elsewhere to push for something similar in its own region. Significantly, however, Australian Prime Minister Bob Hawke's original proposal did not include the United States, as Australia was primarily concerned about being excluded from any possible East Asian grouping, an area that was home to Australia's major trading partners. Equally significantly, such a grouping was of no interest to prospective Asian members of APEC, as their principal concern was ensuring continuing access to lucrative markets in North America.

The need to accommodate such diverse countries and interests led to the development of a two-speed trade liberalization process and another distinctive APEC phenomenon: 'open regionalism'. The proposed liberalization timetable enunciated in the Bogor Declaration of 1994 envisaged APEC's developed economies achieving trade liberalization by 2010, with the developing economies following by 2020. Significantly, such liberalization measures were not only voluntary and non-binding, but they were applicable to non-members as well. Indeed, APEC was to be distinguished by the concept of open regionalism, in which non-discriminatory trade liberalization was the ultimate goal, and the sort of discriminatory trade blocs associated with the **North American Free Trade Agreement (NAFTA)** and the **European Union** (EU) were deliberately repudiated as a consequence.

The reluctance to adopt mandatory, binding goals and agreements reflects an enduring nervousness, especially amongst APEC's Asian members, about creating a powerful organization that might impinge on an otherwise jealously guarded national **sovereignty**. Consequently, APEC's secretariat is small and lacks both the authority and institutional infrastructure of more powerful organizations like the EU. Although APEC's 'western' members might have preferred a more powerful, legalistic and rules-based mechanism to drive trade liberalization, it is significant that the 'Asian way' of consensus and voluntarism became both APEC's hallmark and a source of some frustration about the pace of, and compliance with, the liberalization timetable. The lack of compulsion in APEC's liberalization process and timetable was captured by another revealing piece of 'APEC-speak': concerted unilateralism.

Potentially, at least, one of APEC's most useful innovations has been the 'Leaders' Meetings', which have occurred annually since 1993. No other forum offered the opportunity for regular meetings between such a disparate group of countries, which significantly includes the leaders of both mainland China and Taiwan. However, the potential effectiveness of such meetings has been largely dependent on the enthusiasm shown by the United States, which has generally not seen APEC as an especially important organization, and which has increasingly eschewed **multilateralism** for unilateralism when pursuing its foreign policy agenda. The lack of leadership within APEC, compounded by the absence of an effective secretariat, has undermined the organization's potential effectiveness.

More fundamentally, perhaps, APEC has been marginalized by other organizations and its own inability to play an effective role at moments of crisis. Not only does the **World Trade Organization**'s possession of dispute resolution mechanisms make it a potentially much more effective agent of trade liberalization, but APEC's near invisibility during the East Asian **crisis** of 1997, led many to question its relevance and utility. Indeed, it is noteworthy that the **International Monetary Fund** played a much more prominent role in crisis management and in pushing through the sort of market-oriented reforms than

APEC did in the aftermath of the East Asian crisis. Perhaps the most telling indication of APEC's limited effectiveness is that many of its members, including the US, Australia, Japan and Singapore, have abandoned the sort of multilateral approach that APEC promotes, in favor of bilateral or more narrowly conceived and discriminatory **preferential trade agreement**s.

Even the more technical trade facilitating initiatives like APEC's economic and technical cooperation strategies, which ought to be a strength and an indicator of the organization's usefulness, have generated few substantive outcomes. The lack of enforcement mechanisms, the need to accommodate such disparate political and economic interests, and major disparities in levels of **development** and state capacities seem to have been major obstacles to cooperation and integration of a sort that has characterized the EU. Indeed it is significant that in the longer term it is likely that APEC will be further marginalized by the development by new inter-governmental organizations that reflect the identity and interests of more narrowly defined regional groupings. The development of 'ASEAN+3', for example, has the potential to reflect and further the interests of its exclusively East Asian members in ways that APEC never could. It is also significant that meetings of the new ASEAN+3 grouping have attracted more media interest than recent APEC meetings, which despite the increased strategic significance of the East Asian region, have passed relatively unnoticed.

The lofty ambitions and hopes that accompanied APEC's inauguration have been downgraded and APEC's significance has steadily diminished as a consequence. Although this is arguably an appropriate recognition of political and economic reality, it may also indicate the end of APEC's potentially most significant contribution: the annual Leaders' Meetings provided a unique forum for the ventilation of regional concerns in ways that might otherwise be unavailable. Given East Asia's enhanced geopolitical importance and the United States' continuing involvement in the region, APEC might yet provide a useful vehicle for regional dialogue if its goals can be expanded beyond the economic and the technocratic (see **geopolitics**).

Further reading

Berger, M. (1999) 'APEC and its Enemies: The Failure of the New Regionalism in the Asia-Pacific', *Third World Quarterly* 20, 5: 1013–30.

Drysdale, P. and Vines, D. (eds) (1998) *Europe, East Asia and APEC: A Shared Global Agenda?*, Cambridge: Cambridge University Press.

Funabashi, Y. (1995) *Asia Pacific Fusion: Japan's Role in APEC*, Washington, Institute for International Economics.

Ravenhill, J. (2001) *APEC and the Construction of Pacific Rim Regionalism*, Cambridge: Cambridge University Press.

Webber, D (2001) 'Two Funerals and a Wedding? The Ups and Downs of Regionalism in East Asia and the Asia-Pacific after the Asian Crisis', *The Pacific Review*, 14, 3: 339–72.

See also: Association of Southeast Asian Nations; regionalism; regional trade blocs

MARK BEESON

Asian values

The end of the **cold war** and the Asian economic 'miracle' provided many Asian states with new opportunities in international politics. A number of them (particularly Malaysia, Singapore, China, Burma, Indonesia and Japan) used this moment to advance their interests through the dissemination and promotion of an ideology called 'Asian Values'. The ideology was promoted at the level of culture, political economy and international relations.

Asian values' proponents argued that Asian societies have a different culture to that of the West. Asian values are defined against the background of the alleged decline and decadence of the West. That decadence and decline is marked by the Enlightenment critique of religion and other traditional values; the rise of individualism; the celebration of personal freedom, autonomy and choice; the *anomie* induced by the economic and social consequences of unregulated **globalization**; and the unchecked and ethically unregulated application of new technology. The response of the 'Asian values' proponents to these challenges is a desperate bid to protect their societies from a similar fate. The paternalism of such a response is an intrinsic aspect of the 'Asian values' cultural agenda.

The claim that Asia constitutes an integrated cultural system which is internally consistent and regionally accepted is, however, false. Rather, cultures are dynamic, overlapping and internally contested. Moreover, culture is not the only basis for the formation of **identity** and community, it can also be a form of ideology, a means for exercising **power**. Claims to promote a specific culture can conceal its internal diversity. Moreover, claims to cultural authenticity are profoundly political claims, partly because cultures are not simply found and experienced, but are constructed, written, developed and represented. Many critics correctly assert that proponents of specific Asian values perpetuate stereotypes of Orientalism/Occidentalism and monolithic constructions of both East and West. After all, Asians freed from 'Asian values' do not automatically become Western liberals.

A particularly insidious aspect of the attempt to promote 'Asian values' has been the defence of enduring **human rights** malpractice and anti-democratic policy formulations in the name of economic necessity. The context here is the old dispute about the priority to be given to, and the relationship between, civil/political rights and social/economic rights. Proponents of 'Asian values' often argue that economic **development** is only sustainable in a climate of law and order, and such a climate requires paternalistic government. Giving freedom to people constrains the state's capacity to promote economic growth and general prosperity. Thus, the West should be supportive of Asian governments' focus on economic conditions and policy, rather than critical of their lack of implementation of civil and political rights. It is argued that the West's one-eyed focus on the latter runs against the doctrine of the indivisibility of rights, which holds that economic rights are as important as, and inseparable from, civil and political rights.

It is at this point however that the arguments of the 'Asian values' proponents start to unravel for, if rights are indeed indivisible, then the argument that a certain level of economic development must be achieved before basic civil and political rights may be granted is mistaken. The indivisibility of rights doctrine logically requires a focus on both economic and political issues, not merely a reversal of priorities from political to economic rights. In short, the argument that there is a necessary link between political repression and economic success is an invalid argument. It is neither borne out by empirical research, nor does it have any firm ethical or philosophical foundation.

One of the fundamental ironies of the Asian values debate is the privileged position that is given to the state by the proponents of Asian values. In a **discourse** that posits a stark divide between what is Western and what is Asian, the principal tool for the implementation of the Asian values ideology is the state. And the state, in its historical provenance and intellectual theorization, is an undeniably Western tool for the organization and administration of human populations.

The coupling of Asian values with the statist principles of **sovereignty** and non-intervention is designed to prevent any form of external critique. The counter argument is that sovereignty and non-intervention are part of a wider package of values, and that the partial and self-interested adoption of some of the principles of the international system of states by Asian governments has the effect of leaving them open to more damning criticisms, rather than vindicating their behaviour on Western terms. After all, **legitimacy** in **international society** is not just a matter of respecting state sovereignty, it also (and increasingly) requires respect for the principles of the rule of law and for human rights.

Since the Asian financial crisis of 1997–8, there has been a decline in the rhetoric of Asian values. Indeed, for some commentators, the crisis was itself in part caused by Asian values. However, a more sober judgement would be that the cultural essentialism which nominated distinctive Asian virtues in explaining economic growth, or which reinterpreted them as vices ('crony capitalism') is misguided. The Asian values and practices which contributed to the financial collapse are local Asian variants of more universal traits: graft, corruption and bad management.

To take this to mean that there are no distinctive Asian values, however, assumes the existence of an underlying universalism in human values, temporarily displaced from view by the rhetoric of political agents. This assumption fails to acknowledge the many Asian voices who dissent both from the claims of their governing elites about peculiarly Asian values, and from the claims of Western liberals about, for example, the universality of specific human rights, or the role of religion in society. Asian Values should be recast as Asians' values – the values held by Asian people. As such, Asian values are varied, diverse, contingent and non-essentialist or foundationalist (see **foundationalism/inti-foundationalism**). They range across the political spectrum, are dependent on religion, tradition, culture and philosophy in complex and sophisticated ways, and defy any attempt at definitive articulation. In this sense, they have much in common with the West and Western values.

Further reading

Bauer, J. and Bell, D. (eds) (1999) *The East Asian Challenge for Human Rights*, Cambridge: Cambridge University Press.

Jacobson. M. and Bruun, O. (eds) (2000) *Human Rights and Asian Values: Contested National Identities and Cultural Representation in Asia*, Surrey: Curzon Press.

Langlois, A. J. (2001) *The Politics of Justice and Human Rights: Southeast Asia and Universalist Theory*, Cambridge: Cambridge University Press.

Sung-Joo, H. (ed.) (1999) *Changing Values in Asia: There Impact on Governance and Development*, Tokyo: Japan Center for International Exchange.

Svensson, M. (2002) *Debating Human Rights in China: A Conceptual and Political History*, Lanham: Rowman and Littlefield.

Van Ness, P. (ed.) (1999) *Debating Human Rights: Critical Essays from the United States and Asia*, London: Routledge.

See also: Association of Southeast Asian Nations; communitarianism; human rights

ANTHONY J. LANGLOIS

Association of Southeast Asian Nations (ASEAN)

The Association of Southeast Asian Nations (ASEAN) was established in 1967. Its founding members were Indonesia, Malaysia, the Philippines, Singapore and Thailand. Its primary objective was to reduce intra-regional tensions between its members. ASEAN's founding document, the Bangkok Declaration, emphasized the importance of fostering economic development, encouraging social stability and protecting the countries of the region from 'external interference'. Nearly four decades later, and despite the fact that a number of the ASEAN countries have, at times, achieved impressive economic growth, the realization of these goals remains uncertain.

When ASEAN was inaugurated, all the original members except Thailand were still coming to terms with the aftermath of the **decolonization** process, which had left a number of unresolved territorial disputes in its wake. Between 1963 and 1966 the undeclared war between Indonesia and the newly independent Federation of Malaysia provided the critical initial motivation for attempting to institutionalize more cooperative relations between the highly diverse countries of Southeast Asia.

The preoccupation with enhancing state **sovereignty** remains one of ASEAN's defining features to the present day. Given Southeast Asia's specific historical experience, especially the impact of colonialism, the challenges of late economic development, and the newly independent Southeast Asian nations' abrupt incorporation into an existent **international system**, the concern with maintaining autonomy is unsurprising. What is more surprising, perhaps, is that non-interference in the domestic affairs of individual member states should have become a guiding doctrine of the nascent organization. Crucially, ASEAN states have been as concerned about maintaining internal stability and order as they have about any possible external threats, a consideration that helps to explain the prominent domestic role of the military in countries such as Indonesia.

As a consequence of this concern with maintaining independence and **order**, the ASEAN grouping has developed a number of distinctive features. One of the most original of these is ASEAN's *modus operandi*, the so-called 'ASEAN way'. The confrontation between Indonesia and Malaysia was instrumental in establishing the principle of non-violent dispute resolution, and helped to establish a pattern of consultative, consensually-determined political outcomes. This evolving regional approach to conflict management allowed ASEAN to defuse another potentially explosive territorial dispute between Malaysia and the Philippines in 1968. Subsequently, the ASEAN way has become synonymous with informality, inclusiveness, and consultation leading to consensus.

Critics have claimed that the ASEAN way has been associated primarily with avoiding difficult issues, rather than resolving them. Certainly in the aftermath of the financial crisis (1997–8) that affected Southeast Asia especially badly, ASEAN appeared unable to act effectively and was dependent on external agencies like the **International Monetary Fund** to organize a bail-out of the region's battered economies. The fact that ASEAN's secretariat, which was not even established until 1976, is small and relatively powerless, meant that there was no effective central mechanism with which to address regional crises. Revealingly, the modest scale of the secretariat reflected a conscious desire not to replicate the powerful administrative apparatus of the **European Union** and the possibility that such an organization might impinge on the sovereignty of individual members.

Nevertheless, the issue of possible interference in the domestic affairs of individual members has become more pressing, not only because of recent crises, but also as a consequence of the expansion of the original organization. Brunei joined ASEAN in 1984, but of greater long term significance has been the incorporation of Burma, Vietnam, Laos and Cambodia in the 1990s. While this expansion helped realize the long-term goal of including all the Southeast Asian nations in one organization, Burma's appalling human rights record has undermined ASEAN's standing and made relations with the rest of the world more problematic as a consequence. ASEAN's hopes that what it described as 'constructive engagement' would have a beneficial impact on Burma have not been realized. This is not to say that ASEAN is without influence, however: the earlier rapprochement with Vietnam was in part testimony to ASEAN's role in achieving a resolution of the Cambodian crisis in which Vietnam was persuaded to peacefully withdraw from Cambodia.

A couple of important caveats about ASEAN's position should be noted, however. First, although the resolution of the Cambodia crisis is generally considered to be ASEAN's finest diplomatic hour, it was made possible because it coincided with the interests of the United States and China. Second, there are enduring disparities of economic development and governmental capacity, especially between the latest additions to ASEAN and its comparatively more established founding members, that make developing and implementing coherent policy positions more difficult than was the case with the smaller organization. Moreover, the issue of 'interference' in member states has become even more pressing, especially as a con-

sequence of trans-boundary problems like environmental management. Consequently, some of ASEAN's more liberal states like Thailand and the Philippines push for greater intervention in domestic affairs, while some of the more conservative states like Burma and Malaysia remain highly resistant to changes to the 'ASEAN way'.

In the aftermath of the **cold war** and the development of a more benign **security** environment, ASEAN pursued a number of important new initiatives. In an effort to increase relatively low levels of intra-regional trade, ASEAN inaugurated the ASEAN Free Trade Area (AFTA) in 1992, which was designed to create an internal **free trade** area within fifteen years. Despite the crisis of 1997 and some formidable domestic obstacles to trade liberalization from politically and economically important industries, there is still a rhetorical commitment to AFTA's goals. However, it remains unclear how successful or necessary AFTA will be in pursuing this goal given the existence of powerful domestic interests that remain opposed to liberalization on the one hand, and competing external agencies like APEC and the WTO, on the other (see **Asia Pacific Economic Cooperation Forum World Trade Organization**).

ASEAN has also been at the center of the ASEAN Regional Forum (ARF) a security organization which, in addition to the ten ASEAN states includes a number of key regional dialogue partners like China, Japan and the United States. A central purpose of the ARF was to institutionalize China's relationship with the region and encourage cooperative behavior over potential regional flashpoints such as the disputed Spratly Islands. It is intended to consolidate ASEAN's improved relationship with China through an expanded free trade area.

China also figures prominently in what may prove to be the most significant spin-off from ASEAN thus far: the 'ASEAN+3' grouping, which comprises the ASEAN countries, China, and the other two East Asian heavyweights, Japan and South Korea. If successfully developed this new grouping would give the region a major international presence. There are a number of intra- and interregional impediments ASEAN+3 must overcome, not the least of which are the competing regional leadership ambitions of China and Japan, and differing attitudes toward the United States' role in the region. For the original ASEAN nations, however, even if such tensions can be overcome, this will be something of a mixed blessing, as the Southeast Asian nations will inevitably be overshadowed by their more powerful neighbors. Despite the longevity of the ASEAN organization, therefore, it has been unable to overcome the enduring asymmetries of **power** and influence that have characterized Southeast Asia's political and economic **development**.

Further reading

Acharya, A. (2001) *Constructing a Security Community in Southeast Asia: ASEAN and the Problem of Regional Order*, London: Routledge.
Haacke, J. (2003) *ASEAN's Diplomatic and Security Culture*, London: Routledge.
Henderson, J. (1999) 'Reassessing ASEAN', *Adelphi Paper 328*, New York: Oxford University Press.
Narine, S. (1999) 'ASEAN into the Twenty-First Century: Problems and Prospects', *Pacific Review* 12, 3: 357–80.
Stubbs, R. (2002) 'ASEAN Plus Three: Emerging East Asian Regionalism?' *Asian Survey* 42, 3: 440–55.

See also: newly industrializing country; regionalism; regional trade bloc; sovereignty

MARK BEESON

Asylum

Political refuge by a host state when the state of origin is unable or unwilling to offer protection as a citizen. Article 14.1 of the Universal Declaration on Human Rights holds that 'every individual has the right to seek asylum'. The right to grant asylum, however, remains a prerogative of the state. Claiming asylum is inherently political: leaving the jurisdiction of one state means entering another and asking for permission to stay on its territory. Moreover, granting asylum means giving the individual **refugee** status or some other form of leave to remain in the host country, such as the United Kingdom's Humanitarian Protection arrangements. This automatically makes a political statement about the country of origin: the home government has been unable or unwilling to protect its citizens and these individuals become a ward of **international society** and must seek an alternative source of protection. Granting asylum therefore recognizes a state failure that could have serious implications for international relations. Accordingly humanitarian considerations have always been influenced by foreign policy and political imperatives, with the result that certain individuals in certain places at certain times are granted asylum while others are not.

The end of the post-war economic boom and the impact of higher oil prices in the 1970s reduced the demand of Western countries for immigrant labor. Meanwhile numbers of refugees in developing countries were increasing rapidly, yet the end of the **cold war** removed the ideological motivations that had been hidden behind refugee assistance programs. Western states started to introduce big reductions in refugee resettlement programs alongside restrictions in accessing the asylum system through physical and bureaucratic barriers. The result was that (political) refugees and (economic) migrants were forced into one single migration route – asylum seeking – and the figure of the 'asylum seeker' emerged. This convergence has caused huge problems in attempts to define and distinguish between 'real' refugees fleeing persecution from others seeking a better quality of life. The difficulty in making the distinction is at the heart of the so-called 'asylum crisis' sweeping Europe.

Being granted asylum means acquiring a specific legal status under **international law**, such as refugee status as contained within the 1951 Convention Relating to the Status of Refugees. However the Convention was drawn up during the onset of the cold war at a time when flows of people were smaller since individuals could not physically leave their country of origin to seek international protection. Politics and borders were frozen, as were movements of persons. As international relations thawed, however, and peoples started moving again, the mass 'problem' of refugees once again came into view. Large-scale displacements had been occurring in developing countries from the 1960s, as a result of **decolonization** and the unrest left behind, yet at the time **Third World** refugees stayed in the Third World and so were physically irrelevant to Europe. But when they started to arrive on Europe's doorstep, a series of myths and exceptions was constructed to make the refugee from the South and the international refugee **regime** seem entirely incompatible, and western states invented a variety of reasons to prevent non-European refugees reaching Europe.

The 'European asylum crisis' is constructed as a new experience, caused by apparently new factors and on an unprecedented scale. This ignores three facts: first, that non-European refugees have been part of the international land-scape for decades; second, that refugees from the South are not fleeing wholly different conditions from their predecessors, indeed today's causal factors have many similarities with pre-1951 flows (related to the formation of new states and associated persecution based on ethnic, national and religious grounds); and third, that numbers of individuals seeking asylum across the globe are not greater than ever before. Flows in the inter-war years were vast and, in comparison with total world population figures, proportionately bigger than today.

Asylum-seekers are often portrayed as threats, upsetting the homogeneous national communities of Western societies that existed in the past. Political hyperbole and media myths seek to justify the exclusion of refugees from Western societies today on the basis of their potential to weaken national traditions and the threat they pose to the very survival of national communities. This can be seen, however, as the reproduction of an invented past that has never existed. Thus the 'asylum crisis' is not new; it is merely a re-writing of the past and the construction of a certain kind of **discourse**.

European states claim they are being flooded with 'bogus' asylum-seekers who bring crime, **terrorism** and drugs into their societies. Of course, since **international law** upholds the right to seek asylum, the concept of an 'illegal asylum-seeker' is a misnomer. Nonetheless, European and other states have become fixated on keeping refugees as far as possible from their territorial borders. Policies aimed at preventing their arrival include the 'safe haven' concept, 'in-country processing', 'safe country' lists, and 'transit processing centers'. Other initiatives, including the denial of welfare provisions, detention, and impediments to accessing the refugee status determination procedure, attempt to impose greater restrictions on individuals if and when they arrive in Europe, in the hope of discouraging refugees from even setting out in the first place.

The contemporary ideal 'durable solution' is therefore posited as (voluntary) repatriation and its cousins, containment and in-country protection. The right to remain is regarded as more important than the right to leave and protection is now sought more and more by the international community on behalf of refugees within the country of origin. This is justified on the grounds that people prefer to stay close to similar national, religious or ethnic groups; that it is no longer always the state that is the source of persecution, and the state may be able to provide sanctuary from a persecuting non-state group in another part of the country; and that it is easier for refugees to go home if they remain near their homelands. Yet the whole underlying concept of being able to seek asylum means the existence of circumstances in the country or region of origin that are seriously threatening the ability of the individual to remain where he or she is for fear of threat to life. Thus justifications for this change in direction of protection can be seen to hide alternative strategies: Western states know it is harder to repatriate refugees across long distances, especially after a significant period of time when a certain degree of integration and adjustment into the host community may have taken place.

Containment and safe area practice effectively limit the opportunities for exit. The confinement of the individual within his or her country of origin close to the source of persecution or danger threatens above all to deny the most basic of rights encompassed within both the refugee protection **regime** and **human rights** law, the right to seek asylum. Asylum has become more a type of entitlement than an act of political humanitarianism and individuals must overcome ever larger obstacles to satisfy the relevant criteria and hence prove their right to the entitlement and the rights and benefits it brings. States have acted to limit the scope of the entitlement by tightening procedural and substantive requirements, yet in so doing they run the risk of denying protection and assistance to individuals in need and thus not fulfilling basic moral and humanitarian obligations.

Further reading

Chimni, B. S. (1998) 'The Geopolitics of Refugee Studies: A View from the South', *Journal of Refugee Studies* 11, 4: 350–74.

Goodwin-Gill, G. (1978) *International Law and the Movement of Persons Between States*, Oxford: Oxford University Press.

Haddad, Emma (2003) 'Refugee Protection: A Clash of Values', *International Journal of Human Rights* 7, 3: 1–26.

Loescher, G. (1993) *Beyond Charity: International Cooperation and the Global Refugee Crisis*, Oxford: Oxford University Press.

Nicholson, F. and Twomey, P. (eds) (1999) *Refugee Rights and Realities: Evolving International Concepts and Regimes*, New York: Cambridge University Press.

See also: cold war; ethnic cleansing; human rights; refugee; solidarism

EMMA HADDAD

Authority

It is scarcely an exaggeration to say that many of the dilemmas of the modern age are intimately bound up with the concept of authority. Since the decline of religious absolutism in Europe and the rise of 'reason', the political authority of leaders has been uncertain. Upon what foundation does political authority stand? By what logic can we justify the duty of citizens to obey? Who has the right to authority, and who has the right to *decide* who has the right to authority?

These are some of the fundamental questions of modern political theory.

Authority is a kind of **power**, but it is fundamentally different from simple coercive force. Joseph Raz (1990, 2) says that political authority is 'a right to make laws and regulations, to judge and to punish for failing to conform to certain standards'. In short, it is a right to command. Authority adds to power the concept of right or **legitimacy** – for those in authority it represents the right to issue binding edicts, and for those who follow it represents an obligation to obey.

What place is there in international relations for such a concept of power? At first glance, there may be none. The dominant paradigms of international thought in the twentieth century ruled out the possibility that authority could exist in international affairs. For **realists** in particular, authority exists only within the **nation-state**. For them, the distinguishing feature of domestic government is that it creates a system of hierarchical authority in which it is generally accepted that some are in positions of command and others in positions of subordination. Even in democratic domestic systems, where the equality of citizens is a well-established principle, a hierarchy of bureaucratic offices exists, leading up like a pyramid to the head of state. No such hierarchy of authority exists in international affairs. Thus Kenneth Waltz takes it to be axiomatic that in an **anarchy** of states no institutions of authority can develop. 'National politics is the realm of authority' he says, while 'international politics is the realm of power, of struggle' (1986: 111).

However, the notion that the **international system** is an 'authority-free zone' has come under fire recently from two directions, opening important empirical and conceptual spaces for new research. The first strand of criticism comes from the fact that the absence of authority from

the international system is, for most IR theorists, a matter of assumption rather than one of proof. There are no studies that set out to examine the evidence and determine whether authority exists or not. Rather, IR scholars have been content to assume that it does not exist and then work out the logical implications of that absence. The realist edifice, for instance, begins with a distinction between international anarchy and domestic authority/hierarchy, and goes on to chart the kinds of order that can exist in anarchy (see **realism**). At no point, however, is that fundamental distinction put to the test.

The second strand of critique comes from more empirically minded scholars who, in the pursuit of interesting real-world problems, have uncovered evidence of international actors that marry power with legitimacy. This casts doubt on the assumed monopoly over authority by nation-states. For instance, the **regimes** that regulate firms in the **international political economy** (IPE) sometimes demonstrate a capacity for rule-making that is at once authoritative and not dependent on state power. For example, certain firms in the financial services industry exercise effective authority in IPE by virtue of the power of the information that they sell. Credit-rating firms such as Moody's and Standard & Poor's collect information on the creditworthiness of their clients and disseminate it to potential investors. This information is important for avoiding potential market failures, but it also plays a more political role when states are the ones using ratings or are being rated. These firms have legitimate power over states by virtue of their place in the market system and the value of the information they sell. This implies that the firms have become institutions of international political *authority*.

Traces of authority might also be found in international governmental organizations such as the **United Nations** (UN). If states or publics come to see the UN as having a *right* to decide issues on behalf of states, then it would qualify as being 'in authority' over them. Hints in this direction were evident in the lead-up to the US–Iraq war in 2003, when several states sympathetic to the US said they would support American action only if it was first approved by the UN Security Council. If this perception comes to be widely shared by states, then it will signal that the Security Council is in a position of authority over nation-states in deciding when international force can rightfully be used.

The empirical suggestions that international authority might already exist, in firms or in international organizations, creates a number of conceptual puzzles and problems. For instance, if some firms now have authority, where did that authority come from? Was it formerly lodged in states and then transferred to firms, or was it created anew? If the latter, then the absolute quantity of authority in the international system must be increasing, but what can that mean?

More fundamentally, if we find strong evidence of political authority in non-state institutions in international affairs, we would have to revise our basic understanding of the system as an international anarchy. A system that is anarchic is one in which there are no institutions of authority. This is a common way of describing world politics, but it is brought into doubt by these new arguments about international non-state actors. Accepting the evidence of authority would mean abandoning Waltz's neat dichotomy between domestic hierarchy and international anarchy. Doing so brings up a very deep question: if the presence of authority means that the international system is not an anarchy, then what is it? To this, we have yet no answer.

Further reading

Cutler, A. C., Haufler, V. and Porter, A. (eds) (1999) *Private Property and International Affairs*, Buffalo, NY: SUNY Press.

Hall, R. and Biersteker, T.J. (eds) (2002) *The Emergence of Private Authority in Global Governance*, Cambridge: Cambridge University Press.

Hurd, I. (1999) 'Legitimacy and Authority in International Politics', *International Organization* 53, 2:379–408.

Raz, J. (1990) *Authority*, New York: New York University Press.

Sinclair, T. (1994) 'Passing Judgment: Credit Rating Processes as Regulatory Mechanisms of Governance in the Emerging World Order', *Review of International Political Economy* 1, 1:133–59.

Waltz, K. (1986) 'Anarchic Orders and Balances of Power', In R. O. Keohane (ed.) *Neorealism and its Critics*, New York: Columbia University Press.

See also: global governance; legitimacy; power

IAN HURD

B

Balance of power

Balance of power may refer to the distribution of **power** between countries, a particular configuration of such a distribution, a foreign policy, or a family of international relations theories. Central to each of these is power. Traditionally, power is assessed in terms of material capabilities. For example, some **realist**s, exemplified by John Mearsheimer (2001), employ only economic and military capabilities as indices of state power while others, exemplified by Hans Morgenthau (1985) include factors such as population and demographic trends; territory, geography, and resources; and political will, morale, and competence.

Different countries have different endowments of the elements of power, and this distribution is one definition of the balance of power. The distribution of power may have a multipolar, bipolar, or unipolar configuration. Multipolarity occurs when there are a number of great powers, exemplified by Europe before 1945, and the balance of power has at times referred to the existence of this particular distribution. Some commentators have identified a 'holder of the balance' and the concept of 'offshore balancing', both exemplified by Britain before 1914. Britain was not committed to any European **alliance** but it was able to join the weaker side and so remedy any imbalance. Bipolarity occurred during the **cold war** as the United States and the Soviet Union were the only two countries plausibly able to counter an attack by the other. The United States has enjoyed a unipolar distribution since the collapse of the Soviet Union in 1991, a situation some have called a unipolar 'moment' which will pass as other countries (such as China) or alliances of states engage in a policy of balancing against it. More loosely, balance of power may refer to the superiority of the power of one country over another.

A country pursuing a balance of power policy assesses the distribution of power and engages in balancing behavior, seeking at a minimum to maintain a distribution that preserves its independence. Countries may do this either externally by forming alliances or internally by generating power. A policy of balancing does not prevent **war**, which might be prevented by strategies of accommodation, **appeasement**, and bandwagoning. The primacy of power over morality in policy has at times made the balance of power a term of opprobrium.

Balance of power theory, a major branch of realism, predicts the continuous formation of balances of power over time. In particular, weaker countries are expected to form alliances to balance against stronger ones to prevent the emergence of a hegemon, or dominant power. A significant outcome is the preservation of the system of states in

anarchy, that is, without a superordinate **authority**. Classical and neorealist variants of realism differ in their attribution of state motivations and whether countries always engage in balancing. Classical realists, exemplified by Morgenthau, focus their analyses at the unit-level of countries, and emphasize deliberate balancing behavior by statesmen. In contrast to the manual balancing of classical realism, neorealist theories focus on the determining role of structure and its production of balances of power over time. The mere existence of actors seeking survival in anarchy causes the recurrent formation of balances of power. Balances tend to form without the intentionality of statesmen. The 'offensive realism' of Mearsheimer argues that countries seek to maximize their power so as to maximize their odds of survival while thwarting others from gaining power at their expense by balancing.

An epistemological critique of balance of power measured in terms of the distribution of power begins with the argument that power is inherently difficult to measure. First, while some individual components can be measured (e.g., economic size), others, such as political competence and morale, are hard to measure, especially in prospect rather than hindsight. Second, having a list of components of power does not tell us much about how to aggregate them. Is a country with a large military and a smaller economy more powerful than one with a smaller military and a large economy? The first might be more powerful inasmuch as it might be able to seize additional increments of economic capability, which was seriously attempted by Germany and Japan in World War Two. The second might be more powerful to the extent that it can convert its economic capability into military capability. The answer to the 'conversion problem' lies in the time available and the efficiency with which a country can translate its stock of economic elements of power into military elements or *vice versa*. Perhaps the optimal situation is to have a large stock of economic elements, which take time to grow, and the time to convert them, which has been the fortunate situation of the United States in two world wars.

A critique of balance of power as a policy and as a family of theories is that it is not clear what actions are sufficient to count as balancing and when those actions must take place. An historical critique of classical realist balance of power theory is that it is debatable how often countries actually engage in balancing behavior. For example many countries have not balanced against the United States after the end of the cold war, contrary to expectations based on realist analysis. Similarly, European diplomatic history in the 1930s is not a story of alliance formation to balance against Germany: Britain did not formally commit to a military alliance with France until early 1939, Belgium, Denmark, Holland, and Norway maintained their neutrality, and the Soviet Union did not form a coalition with Britain until after it was invaded by Germany in 1941. Equally, the diplomatic history of the Napoleonic period features extensive attempts by powers, great and small, to reach an accommodation with France.

Further reading

Mearsheimer, J (2001) *The Tragedy of Great Power Politics*, New York: Norton.

Morgenthau, H. (1985) *Politics Among Nations: The Struggle for Power and Peace*, 6th edn, New York: McGraw-Hill.

Paul, T.V., Wirtz, J. and Fortmann, M. (eds) (2004) *Balance of Power: Theory and Practice in the Twenty-First Century*, Palo Alto, CA: Stanford University Press.

Waltz, K. (1979) *Theory of International Politics*, Reading, MA: Addison-Wesley.

Gulick, E. (1955), *Europe's Classical Balance of Power*, New York: Norton.

Vasquez, J. and Elman, C. (eds) (2003) *Realism and the Balancing of Power: A New Debate*, Upper Saddle River, NJ: Prentice Hall.

See also: balance of threat; bipolarity; polarity; realism

CARMEL DAVIS

Balance of threat

Balance of threat theory argues that countries balance not against **power** but against those countries that appear especially dangerous to them. It attempts to extend **balance of power** theory by considering additional factors. However, threat theory can be hard to test because these factors can be difficult to assess and measure.

Threat theory is closely associated with Stephen Walt, especially his book *The Origins of Alliances* (1987). Walt argues that threat is comprised of aggregate power, geographic proximity, offensive power, and aggressive intentions. Aggregate power is a country's total resources; a country with more resources can pose a greater threat than one with fewer resources. Geographic proximity matters because (other things being equal) countries that are nearby are often more threatening than those that are further away. Offensive power is the ability of one state to threaten the **sovereignty** or territorial integrity of another state at an acceptable cost. Finally, countries that are perceived as aggressive are more likely to elicit balancing behavior from other states. Aggressive intentions specify the propensity of one particular country to compel another to respond, a situation

exemplified by Nazi Germany. Walt emphasizes the significance of aggressive intentions in his theory, rather than material sources of power.

Walt argues that the balance of threat is a far better predictor of **alliance** formation than the balance of power. For example, in explaining the origins of the **cold war**, he argues that the geographic proximity, offensive power, and aggressive intentions of the Soviet Union elicited balancing by regional powers in Europe and Asia in the form of alliances with the United States, and that the Soviet Union subsequently balanced against the United States by generating power internally. Walt has also employed threat theory to analyze alliance formation in Southwest Asia and the relationship between **revolution** and war. The theory explains why, notwithstanding contemporary concerns about American foreign policy after the events of 11 September 2001, it is unlikely that US preponderance will elicit balancing by other countries.

Threat theory is closely related to but distinct from **balance of power** theory, which argues that countries balance against power. However, proponents of threat theory argue that its additional variables allow it to explain cases of balancing that are not readily explained by balance of power theory so that threat theory is a useful extension and refinement of power theory. For example, many countries joined the stronger United States in the cold war rather than the weaker Soviet Union, as a crude version of balance of power theory would predict.

Threat theory is hard to test rigorously because of difficulties in assessing key variables such as 'offensive power' and 'aggressive intentions'. Offensive power is hard to measure because many types of military forces may be used for both defense and offense, and forces with defensive missions may require offensive capability to conduct counteroffensive operations. Equally, aggressive intentions can be difficult to assess. Intentions are rarely bimodal, either 'aggressive' or 'not aggressive'; rather, there is a propensity that may range from high to absent, and that propensity may change over time. Furthermore, aggressive intentions may be informed by implicit cost-benefit analyses: leaderships may be more aggressive if the prospects for success are good and costs appear low so that aggression, and hence threat, may mean mere opportunism in the presence of an imbalance of power.

Aggressive intentions may also be hard to assess because they are the subjective judgments of a group of individuals (perceivers) about the intentions of another group of individuals (the perceived). Individual members of each group may come and go, have variable influence, differ with each other, and change their minds. It may not be clear whose mind, among either group, should be considered and whose should not. In the absence of an official articulation of aggressive intentions or extraordinarily good intelligence, the perceiver may have increasing evidence as the perceived prepares to act but cannot know with certainty the intentions of another until the perceived acts. Hence, the intentions of a leadership can be hard for external (and even internal) observers to know, and it can be impossible to know the intentions of a leadership before it is irrevocably committed to action. The usual situation is that some individuals in one country perceive the leadership of another as aggressive, others disagree, the leadership of the perceived country is divided and is itself making similar judgments about the other country.

Further reading

Kagan, R (1995) *The Origins of War*, New York: Doubleday.

Kaufman, R. (1992) 'To Balance or to Bandwagon? Alignment Decisions in 1930s Europe' *Security Studies*, 1, 3: 417–47.

Schweller, R. (1994) 'Bandwagoning for Profit: Bringing the Revisionist State Back In' *International Security*, 19, 1: 72–107.

Walt, S. (1987) *The Origins of Alliances*, Ithaca: Cornell

Walt, S. (1996) *Revolution and War*, Ithaca: Cornell.

See also: alliance; balance of power; non-offensive defense

CARMEL DAVIS

Ballistic missile defense (BMD)

Ballistic missiles travel quickly: they are propelled upwards by rockets during the initial 'boost-phase' of their flight, and then fall under the influence of gravity back to earth. Their speed has traditionally made them a difficult weapon to counter. But they are relatively inaccurate, certainly in comparison to today's precision-guided weapons. Two means exist for countering that inaccuracy: aiming the missiles at a large target, such as a major city, where inaccuracies of the order of one to five kilometers may not matter very much; and increasing the size of the explosive in the warhead. This second option makes the ballistic missile the natural partner of **weapons of mass destruction**, and it is that partnership which drives concern about ballistic missile proliferation.

As ballistic missiles have proliferated, policymakers have become more attracted to a variety of efforts to halt or slow such proliferation. Ballistic missile defense offers one particular means of diluting the value of ballistic missiles, but only as part of a broader package of anti-proliferation strategies. That broader package typically includes **arms control** measures, such as the Missile Technology Control Regime, and a range of proactive measures (including the Proliferation Security Initiative for the forcible interdiction of sea and air-based cargoes of ballistic missile-related technologies) to slow ballistic missile proliferation.

Pressures toward some sort of ballistic missile defense have been around for decades: they were present in the 1960s before the Anti-Ballistic Missile Treaty (1972) constrained the development of such systems; in the 1980s with President Reagan's Strategic Defense Initiative, which was brought to an end by the fall of the Berlin Wall; and in the 1990s under President Clinton as a means of addressing the particular problems of ballistic missile proliferation by **rogue states**. But serious work on BMD is still a comparatively recent phenomenon. Defensive technologies needed to support an effective anti-ballistic missile system were primitive in the 1960s, and not much more advanced by the 1980s. Some would say they are still maturing only slowly today.

Defending against a ballistic missile threat is technically demanding. For much of the **cold war**, the **superpower**s agreed that no effective defense could be built, and that **mutually assured destruction** (MAD) was a technological fact. Even today, intercepting a ballistic missile in flight is no easy task. Expert opinion is that it might take another three decades before such defenses become reliable. So why do governments persist in throwing large quantities of money at a system that may not work for many years, if ever, and the most immediate effects of which may be to undermine the carefully crafted pattern of strategic stability that was achieved during the cold war?

They do so because ballistic missile defenses are intended to address a continuing concern: that ballistic missile proliferation continues, and that the current tools for containing such proliferation are few in number and uncertain in scope. Furthermore, US policymakers believe that the years of strategic stability are already passé, and that Washington cannot rest content with the slow emergence of MAD relationships with a string of other adversaries. The United States cannot tolerate a MAD relationship between itself and North Korea, for example, because central to the acceptance of such a relationship is a belief that the other party in the relationship is risk averse with a strong commitment to the status quo. Many policymakers believe that North Korea simply does not fit such a description.

So where do strategic problems lie down the path to missile defenses? Many of them concern China's possible reaction to the deployment of such systems. It opposes even defensive systems intended to counter theater range ballistic missiles in Asia, which might be deployed to defend Taiwan. It is true that China's intercontinental ballistic missile capabilities are weak. But China has in place a modernization program to enhance those capabilities and that program will proceed regardless of Washington's enthusiasm for missile defenses.

More broadly, the problems lie where they traditionally have: in technological difficulties and in the abrasive effect that doctrines of missile defense might have in a world where offensive missile technologies will hold the whip hand over defensive counter-measures for the foreseeable future. In such a world, defensive shields, if they show promise at all, will merely spur missile proliferation. And the most logical use of such defenses will be in association with offensive force options, for the simple reason that it will always be easier to defend against a ragged retaliatory strike than against a first strike. But since defenses seem likely to grow in capability only slowly, for many years even a ragged retaliatory strike will be sufficient to penetrate an imperfect shield. So during those years nuclear **deterrence** will continue to provide the backbone of the great power relationships.

Still, we are already approaching a stage where defenses against theater range ballistic missiles are becoming more effective. Since the bulk of missiles in the world fall within that range, the move toward a better offense–defense balance might not be as far away as some critics assume. Few countries now deploy ballistic missiles with an inter-continental range, and those tend to be the great powers anyway, who seem capable of organizing their relationships upon a traditional basis. A key focus of the argument over the wisdom of pro-ceeding down the missile defense path is a debate about the rate at which such specialized capabilities might spread to countries like North Korea, and how much intelligence warning other coun-tries, including the United States, might get about that spread.

After the events of 11 September 2001, it became fashionable to assert that the new war on terror would marginalize ballistic missile defense as a strategic issue. Such judgments were frequently substantiated by the observation that an expensive and perhaps unreliable ballis-tic missile shield could have done noth-ing to avert the tragedies of that day. But so far such judgments have not proven to be correct. Indeed, 11 September appears to have galvanized key sectors of the Western strategic community to press the point that the emergence of a new set of weak actors in the international security environment concentrates, rather than dilutes, the need for Western nations to play to a different set of strategic strengths rather than to continue to rely upon traditional deterrence doctrines. The issue of ballistic missile defense will be with us for the indefinite future.

Further reading

Miller, S. (2001) 'The Flawed Case for Missile Defence', *Survival* 43, 4: 95–109.
Panofsky, W. (2001) 'The Continuing Impact of the Nuclear Revolution', *Arms Control Today* 31, 5: 3–5.
Wilkening, D. (1999) *Ballistic Missile Defence and Strategic Stability*, Adelphi Paper 334. London: International Institute for Strategic Studies.
Wirtz, J. J. and Larsen, J. A. (eds) (2001) *Rockets' Red Glare: Missile Defenses and the Future of World Politics*, Boulder, CO: Westview Press.

See also: arms race; deterrence; mutually assured destruction; non-offensive defense; rogue state

ROD LYON

Bank for International Settlements (BIS)

The Bank for International Settlements (BIS) provides the world's oldest, most developed and rigorous **regime** for supervising and monitoring the interna-tional financial **order**. It provides an institutional space for the sharing of information among central bank gover-nors, the development of international banking regulation, and the collation and dissemination of financial data to international financial institutions and private financial market actors. The BIS is based in Basle, Switzerland, and is governed by a Board of Directors that is chaired by a central bank governor of one of the BIS member states. In addition, the Board of Director includes governors of the central banks of Belgium, France,

Germany, Italy, the UK, and the United States, as well as nine other central bank governors that are elected. New regulatory frameworks are primarily established from discussions within 'Group of Ten' committees (the Finance Ministers of Belgium, Canada, France, Germany, Italy, Japan, the Netherlands, Sweden, the UK, and the US).

The BIS was created under the Young Plan of 1930 to assist with the repayment of German World War One reparations established during the Treaty of Versailles, as well as to act as trustee to loans generated under the Dawes and Young plans. In doing so, the BIS replaced the Agent General for Reparations, based in Berlin, and intended to provide an international organization with fewer political constraints on its behavior. The BIS also provided emergency financing to German and Austrian central banks during the financial **crisis** of 1931–3. Interestingly, the creation of this new regime emerged from cooperation between Belgium, France, Germany, Italy, Japan, Switzerland, the UK, the US, and three US banks during a period of 'interregnum' in the **international political economy**. This defies conventional thinking about the need for **hegemony** to create new international regimes, the central tenet of **hegemonic stability theory**.

Beyond the early period in the BIS's history of attempting to settle reparations issues, its role shifted to focus on coordinating credit networks among member states' central bank governors. Between 1950 and 1958 the BIS supported the European Payments Union that assisted European states' currency convertibility as part of the **Bretton Woods** monetary system. As speculation on the dollar's real value relative to gold (as opposed to its official value of US$35 per ounce), intensified in the 1960s (see **casino capitalism**), the BIS stepped in to assist coordination between central bankers

through the creation of currency swap networks. It did so through the development of a 'Gold Pool'. As the private financial markets were trading on the basis of US$40 per ounce of gold, a network of currency holdings among central bankers was required to prevent the collapse of the international monetary order. During this period the BIS also provided emergency currency support to France, Italy, and the UK.

The BIS's role changed in the 1970s as it responded to new developments in international finance after the collapse of the Bretton Woods system. Following the 1974 collapses of the Franklin National Bank and Bankhaus Herstatt, both as a result of currency speculation, the BIS began to develop new international financial regulation through the development of the Basle Concordat, which would eventually evolve into the Basle Accord of 1988. During the 1970s the BIS noted that the growth of large-scale syndicated lending from Western commercial banks to the **Third World**, particularly to Latin American governments, was endangering the stability of the international financial system. According to the BIS the consequence of such lending practices would be the creation of a **debt trap**, and the Debt Crisis of the early 1980s proved the BIS correct. Particularly important to reversing such international financial instability was for the BIS to encourage international private banks to increase their 'capital adequacy ratios', the amount of capital banks keep aside in case of an emergency. Capital adequacy ratios seriously declined during the late 1970s and their recovery was an immediate goal for the BIS's Basle Accord.

The formation of the Basle Accord can be interpreted in two ways. One interpretation is that the BIS took the initiative in coordinating its member states to share information on their international banks' operations and thereby create a new, more stable, system. This interpretation gives some autonomy to the BIS as an international regime. A second interpretation is that the Basle Accord emerged from great power politics between the United States and Japan, and was then legitimized as an international regime under the auspices of the BIS (see **great powers**). By this account, the US Federal Reserve noted that Japanese international banks were operating with comparatively low capital adequacy ratios, giving them a competitive advantage over US banks due to US domestic regulations that established a 5½ per cent capital adequacy benchmark. Accordingly, the United States and the UK created a new regime on capital adequacy ratios that was presented as a *fait accompli* to the BIS, and to Japan. Support for this version may come from the fiscal windfall the Basle Accord of 1988 generated for the United States. Under the accord Japanese international banks were required to buy up 'safe' capital to raise their capital adequacy to the new global rate of 8 per cent, particularly the **Organization for Economic Cooperation and Development** (OECD) government debt. The Basle Accord is being revised between 2001 and 2006, with a new accord to be released in 2007. The new accord will be based on new risk assessment measurements. Like the first accord, the determination of how risk is assessed is intensely political.

During the 1990s the BIS was called upon as a supplementary financier for **crisis** loans (such as those granted to Mexico in 1995 and to Brazil in 1998) from the **International Monetary Fund** (IMF) due to the sheer magnitude of capital account financial crises. The size and frequency of crises and a rapidly changing international financial environment (see **disintermediation**) has led the BIS to establish forums to generate new international financial regulation. Following the Asian financial and Russian financial crises of 1997–8, the BIS hosts a Financial Stability Forum (FSF), which has become a focal point for new international financial regulation. The FSF is thought to be a more inclusive and consultative body for international financial regulation, providing greater voice to the 'G-20' group of emerging market economies. To what extent this represents genuine inclusion in the formation of new regulations is a matter of great dispute. Criticisms of the BIS center primarily on its incapacity to provide a framework which is more capable of meeting the needs of developing states, and on the supposed ascendant position of large financial institutions in deliberations on new international regulatory frameworks (see **neoliberalism**).

Further reading

Kapstein, E. B. (1994) *Governing the Global Economy: International Finance and the State*, Cambridge, MA: Harvard University Press.

Oatley, T. and Nabors, R. (1998) 'Redistributive Cooperation: Market Failures, Wealth Transfers and the Basle Accord', *International Organization* 52, 1: 35–54.

Seabrooke, L. (2001) *US Power in International Finance: The Victory of Dividends*, Basingstoke: Palgrave.

Simmons, B. A. (1993) 'Why Innovate? Founding the Bank for International Settlements', *World Politics*, 45, 3: 361–401.

Wood, D. (2004) *The Basle Committee and the Governance of the Global Financial System*, Aldershot: Ashgate.

See also: casino capitalism; debt trap; disintermediation; global financial center; International Monetary Fund; international political economy; money laundering.

LEONARD SEABROOKE

Biodiversity

Conserving our planet's biodiversity and the enormous variety of life forms developed over millions of years has come to be recognized as one of the most crucial tasks of our time. Loss of species means depletion of a biological heritage having incalculable moral, practical and scientific value to future generations. There are three general kinds of biodiversity: habitat diversity, genetic diversity, and species diversity. The survival of each is linked to the health of the other two, and together they comprise the health of *ecosystems*.

Habitat diversity refers to the variety of places where life exists, such as coral reefs, old-growth forests in the Pacific Northwest of the United States, tallgrass prairie, coastal wetlands, and many others. Each broad type of habitat is the home for numerous species, most of which depend on that habitat. When it disappears, a vast number of species disappear as well. More often, an entire habitat does not completely disappear but instead is reduced gradually until only small patches remain. This has happened to old growth forest and coastal wetlands in the United States and is now occurring in tropical forests throughout the world. Elimination of all but small patches of habitat is especially damaging because it not only eliminates many local species but also threatens those species that depend on vast acreage for their survival.

To understand *genetic diversity*, it helps to first clarify what biologists mean when they refer to a 'population'. Consider the crows in your garden. They are a population, individuals of a species that live together, in the sense that mates are chosen from within the group. The crows in the population share more of their genes with each other than they do with other individuals from populations of the same species elsewhere, because individuals in one population rarely breed with those in another. Although each population within a species contains some genetic information unique to that population, individuals in all populations share in common the genetic information that defines their species.

In principle, individuals from one population could mate with individuals from another population of the same species. That is a definition of what a species is, a collection of individuals that could, in principle, interbreed. In practice, individuals from different populations within a species rarely interbreed because of geographic isolation.

The genetic diversity within a species is primarily the variety of populations that comprise it. Species reduced to a single population (like the California condor) generally contain less genetic diversity than those consisting of many populations. Song sparrows, found over much of North America, occur in numerous populations and thus maintain considerable genetic diversity within the species. Biologists care about the survival of populations, as well as species, because of the unique genetic information contained within populations. The very survival of a species is dependent on the survival of its populations, for if only a few populations remain, there are few survival tactics that the species can deploy in the face of threats (such as global warming). Each population contains a distinct set of genetic instructions for how the species might adapt to threats.

Finally, there is *species diversity*. This is what most people mean when they talk about biodiversity. There are about one and a half million named species on earth, but we know that many unnamed species exist, and the total number is probably between five and fifteen million. Most of the evidence for numerous unnamed species comes from studies of insects in tropical forests; when the canopy of a tropical tree is fumigated and all the dead insects are collected, large numbers of hitherto unknown insects are frequently collected. Tropical rainforests cover less than 2 per cent of the planet and yet are the only home for at least half and possibly as much as 90 per cent of all species on earth. The higher estimate is based on the assumption that a large share of the yet to be discovered species will be tropical because biological exploration of the tropics is so fragmentary. Other habitats are also poorly explored and undoubtedly contain numerous species unknown to science today.

Each year, during the past several decades, people have been destroying tropical forests whose survival is crucial for maintaining biodiversity. Some of this lost forest, particularly in Central and South America, is burned and then used for cattle grazing or for crops; some, particularly in Asia, is clear cut for its timber; and, particularly in Africa, fuel wood gathering accelerates the pace of deforestation. Over the last century, between one quarter and one half of the rainforests on earth have been destroyed. At the current rate of destruction, there will be only tiny patches of rainforest left by the middle of the twenty-first century.

Because of the tremendous concentration of species in the tropics and their often narrow geographic ranges, biologists estimate that tropical deforestation will result in the loss of half or more of the existing species on earth during the next fifty years. Humanity is now in the process of destroying roughly as many species during the next century as were wiped out every 100 million years by natural causes. This is particularly devastating for birds. On current trends, at least one in ten of the world's remaining bird species will be extinct by the end of the twenty-first century. It

takes only a few decades, as history shows, to drive a once abundant species, like the passenger pigeon, to extinction. The extinction of the passenger pigeon in North America has contributed to the spread of Lyme disease, which can cause neurological damage and flu-like symptoms. The disease is carried by ticks, which thrive on the bodies of deer mice. As passenger pigeons died out, the acorns on which they fed became available to deer mice, supporting much larger populations of the rodents and spreading the disease more rapidly. It is inconceivable that during the coming millennia evolution could replace with new species those lost to deforestation and other human actions.

Although deforestation in the species-rich tropics is currently a focus for outrage, it should not be forgotten that deforestation in North America and Europe has destroyed even larger areas of old growth forest than in the tropics. Virtually all the hardwood forests of the northern United States were cleared prior to the Civil War; the second-growth forests that have sprouted on abandoned farmland during the past century are a poor ecological substitute for what was lost. In recent years, clear cutting in the United States is again destroying some of the most important old growth forest in the world.

The international response to this situation has been slow and inadequate. In 1993, 155 states signed the Convention on Biological Diversity following the historic Rio Conference held a year earlier. The Convention is an attempt to protect biological diversity by establishing some rules for the use of genetic resources and biotechnologies. Parties to the Convention have pledged to develop plans to protect biodiversity, and to submit reports that are to be internationally reviewed. Unfortunately, the rules remain vague and highly qualified.

Further reading

Gaston, K. and Spicer, J. (2004) *Biodiversity: An Introduction*, Oxford: Blackwell.

Heywood, V. (ed.) (1995) *Global Biodiversity: An Assessment*, Cambridge: Cambridge University Press.

Le Pestre, P. G. (2002) *Governing Global Biodiversity*, Aldershot: Ashgate.

Perlman, D. and Addson, G. (1997) *Biodiversity: Exploring Values and Priorities in Conservation*, Oxford: Blackwell Science.

See also: global warming; population growth

MARTIN GRIFFITHS

Biological weapons

These are **weapons of mass destruction** that employ micro-organisms, viruses or toxins to kill or incapacitate humans, destroy livestock, or damage crops. Unlike **chemical weapons** which use man-made chemical compounds to kill, the agents used in biological weapons occur in nature. However, the process of weaponization enhances their lethality considerably. For example, after modification, as little as one millionth of a gram of anthrax is enough to kill an adult human being.

Some experts suggest that, given the right conditions, a biological weapon could kill as many as 300,000 people and injure up to half a million. Others put the figure much lower, arguing that a biological attack on a medium sized city could kill around 100,000 people and injure 125,000. Gaining accurate casualty rates is difficult for two reasons. First, there has never been a large-scale biological weapons attack on a heavily populated area. Consequently, and thankfully, there is no accurate empirical data available. Second, the effectiveness of such an attack depends on such variables as the type and quantity of the agent used, its quality, the delivery system, climatic conditions at the time of its release, and the level of civic preparedness. Regardless, these weapons are quite terrifying and have the potential to wipe out entire cities.

Biological agents are invisible, odourless and colourless. Infected individuals may not develop symptoms for hours or even days after an attack. Moreover, they are relatively easy to produce. A person with a basic science degree and a relatively modest laboratory can produce a crude but effective biological weapon. This makes them a weapon of choice for terrorists, apocalyptic millenarian groups, and criminal organizations.

Almost any biological organism or disease can be turned into a weapon capable of harming humans. The most common organisms used in biological weapons programs since the end of World War Two are anthrax, the plague, smallpox, cholera, tularaemia, brucellosis, and botulinum. Yellow fever, Q fever, dengue fever, lassa fever, dysentery, glanders, influenza, hemorrhagic fever, gas gangrene, ricin, typhoid, paratyphoid, and rinderpest have also figured prominently in these programs. Research into the use of anticrop agents include wheat and rye stem rust, rice blast, potato beetle, and potato blight.

The use of biological agents and disease to kill humans has a long history. The poisoning of wells with human corpses and animal carcasses is a practice almost as old as **war** itself. Since the beginning of the twentieth century, there have been a number of examples where biological weapons have been used. During World War One, the Germans infected French livestock and feed with biological materials. From 1932 to 1945, the Japanese military tested biological weapons on prisoners in Manchuria. In Ping Fan, an estimated 3,000 prisoners died. In 1941, cholera was used in an attack on Chengteh, with an estimated

10,000 casualties. During the **cold war**, the Soviet Union often used ricin, a derivative of the castor bean, to assassinate defectors. In one example, the Bulgarian Secret Service used an umbrella with a spring-loaded tip laced with ricin to assassinate a defector in London. In 1995, Aum Shinrikyo, a Japanese religious cult, released botulinum toxin in Tokyo's subway. The group is also known to have actively sought the ebola virus. More recently, in the days following the 11 September 2001 attacks a number of letters were sent through the US mail containing anthrax spores. Twenty-three people were infected and five died.

The limited number of examples of the use of biological weapons during the twentieth century should not lead to an underestimation of the dangers posed by these weapons. A number of states continue to have active biological weapons programs. They include North Korea, Iran, China, Egypt, Syria, and Taiwan. A number of other states have active research programs, but are not thought to have produced or stockpiled these weapons. It is important to note, however, that despite the fact that extensive biological weapons research and development has been undertaken by a number of states over the last one hundreds years, no two **sovereign states** have engaged in biological warfare against each other, nor have they employed a biological weapon against a domestic enemy. Even Iraq, with its purported biological weapons capability during the 1980s, refrained from using these weapons against the Iranians, the Kurds, or coalition forces in 1991 and 2003.

This is due, in no small measure, to the 1972 Biological Weapons Convention (BWC). This convention has managed quite successfully to control the proliferation of these weapons. The BWC is the first **arms control regime** to outlaw an entire class of weapons. As of late 2003, 166 parties had ratified the treaty. The central pillar of the treaty is that it prohibits the development, production, and stockpiling of organisms that have no therapeutic, protective, or peaceful purpose, as well as the weapons, equipment, and delivery systems designed for use in armed conflict. Since entering into force, much work has been undertaken to strengthen the convention. These include confidence-building measures such as the exchange of relevant data, disclosure of research facilities, publication of biological research results, and declaration of biological research activities since January 1946, verification measures (VEREX), as well as the formation of an Ad Hoc Group charged with responsibility for strengthening and monitoring the convention (see **confidence and security building measures**).

Yet the Convention faces a number of difficulties. The first is compliance. It is difficult to accurately verify that a state is living up to its obligations. Despite being a sponsor of the Convention, for example, Russia admitted in the early 1990s that it continued to operate a biological weapons research program. It is not difficult to hide a laboratory or to disguise it as something else. Second, the Convention has no mechanisms to punish violators, beyond verbal reprimand and censure in the **United Nations**. Third, the dual use problem makes it difficult for monitors to determine what equipment is being purchased for legitimate biomedical and industrial research and what is being used for research into biological weapons. Fourth, states who have not signed the Convention arguably have a significant offensive capability over states that abide by its terms. This situation may, over time, lead to the emergence of a classic **security dilemma** and the subsequent defection of some states from the treaty. In other words, and despite its obvious success in limiting the spread of these weapons, it remains a fragile and conditional agreement.

Since the end of the cold war, the threat of a biological attack by a non-state actor has emerged as a major challenge for the international community. Terrorists, hate groups, cults, and criminal organizations have all sought to acquire biological weapons. In the mid-1990s, for example, one individual in the United States was arrested with enough ricin to kill 30,000 people. There is also evidence to suggest that **al-Qaeda** has actively sought to develop a chemical and biological weapons capability. The 'loose nukes' problem applies equally to biological (and chemical) weapons as it does to nuclear weapons. Moreover, borders have never been more porous and difficult to defend.

It is important not to be alarmist about the dangers posed by biological weapons. The fact that the world managed to avoid a nuclear holocaust during the cold war demonstrates that weapons of mass destruction can be effectively controlled and monitored. The challenge for policymakers and law enforcement officials is to ensure that terrorists groups are unable to acquire the organisms needed to develop such hideous weapons while, at the same time, maintaining the integrity of the BWC.

Further reading

Dando, M. (2001) *The New Biological Weapons: Threat, Proliferation, and Control*, Boulder, CO: Lynne Rienner.

Langford, E. R. (2004) *Introduction to Weapons of Mass Destruction: Radiological, Chemical, and Biological*, New York: Wiley-Interscience.

Falkenrath, R., Newman, R. and Thayer, B. (1998) *America's Achilles Heel: Nuclear, Biological, and Chemical Terrorism and Covert Attack*, Cambridge, MA: MIT Press.

Guillemin, J. (2004) *Biological Weapons: From the Invention of State-Sponsored Programs to Contemporary Bioterrorism*, New York: Columbia University Press.

Hutchinson, R. (2003) *Weapons of Mass Destruction: The No-Nonsense Guide to Nuclear, Chemical and Biological Weapons Today*, New York: Weidenfeld & Nicholson.

Lederberg, J. (1999) *Biological Weapons: Limiting the Threat*, Cambridge, MA: MIT Press.

Zilinskas, R. (1999) *Biological Warfare*, Boulder, CO: Lynne Rienner.

See also: chemical weapons; terrorism; weapons of mass destruction

TERRY O'CALLAGHAN

Bipolarity

A bipolar distribution of **power** within the **international system** refers to a situation where two states of relatively equal strength dominate everyone else. Historical examples include Athens and Sparta on the eve of the Peloponnesian War, the Macedonian kingdoms of the Seleucids and Ptolemies that emerged following the death of Alexander the Great, and the **cold war** confrontation between the United States and the Soviet Union. People often confuse bipolarity with a polarized configuration of military **alliance**s. **Polarity** is defined by the number of dominant states, not the number of blocs of states. Prior to the outbreak of World War One, for example, the European **balance of power** became polarized, consolidating into two rigid blocs: the Triple Alliance and the Triple Entente. Nevertheless, the system was not bipolar because it still contained more than two **great powers**.

Some realist scholars believe that bipolar systems are very stable and experience less **war** than systems containing more than two power centers (see **realism**). To support their claim, they advance the following arguments.

First, the stark rivalry in a bipolar system encourages each leading power to restrain **crisis**-provoking actions by its subordinate allies; hence war is less likely because the dominant states have incentives to prevent conflicts between lesser states from engulfing them in a military maelstrom. Second, unlike a multipolar environment, where any combination of major and minor powers may wage war, within a bipolar system only one pair of **great powers** might face off; hence war is less likely due to fewer possibilities for its onset. Third, the clear, unambiguous nature of bipolarity dampens the chances of underestimating the strength or resolve of one's adversary; hence war is less likely to occur due to miscalculation. Conversely, two general kinds of miscalculation may happen during periods in which resources are evenly divided among three or more dominant great powers. On the one hand, states that believe their **security** is intertwined with the survival of others and perceive that advantages lie with offensive action may chain themselves to reckless allies, only to be pulled toward war if any of their partners stumble into hostilities. On the other hand, states that perceive defensive advantages may not align with others soon enough because of a propensity to pass the buck, trying to ride free on the actions of third parties. Insofar as the dominant states in a bipolar world are not dependent upon their smaller allies for survival, and since their allies cannot confront the opposing superpower alone, miscalculations due to chain-ganging or buck-passing will not occur. Fourth, it is sometimes argued that a system composed of two predominant powers does not breed extreme inequalities between them; hence it will tend to have greater long-run stability. Under conditions of scar-

city, multipolarity engenders serious inequalities in resources among the most advantaged and disadvantaged great powers. Since these inequalities tend to engender contentious efforts to redress perceived imbalances, state systems consisting of three or more poles will experience instability unless some form of compensation is available to avoid conflict. Fifth, the uncomplicated structure of bipolarity makes it easier to establish the rules that facilitate reaching international accords; hence war is less likely because these accords help regularize behavior and institutionalize cooperation. The diffusion of power among multiple, contending states whose alignments ebb and flow makes it more difficult to distinguish ally from adversary. Consequently fears of defection from commitments rise and cooperation declines.

Other theorists assert that bipolarity is more war-prone than other polarity configurations. In particular, they submit that multipolar systems with several roughly equal great powers are more peaceful than bipolar systems. In support of their claim, they make the following arguments.

First, in a multipolar world of shifting alliances, the crusading zeal and intense competition inherent in a bipolar standoff are replaced by a process of political compromise; hence war is less likely because the shifting equilibrium of forces encourages conciliation. Anyone is a potential partner; no one is an implacable enemy. Second, as more states ascend to great power status, the number, range, and diversity of mutually beneficial trade-offs among them rise; hence the prospects for armed conflict decline (see **great powers**). With numerous states interacting on multiple issues, any given pair of states will likely be cooperating in one issue-area or another. Third, as the number of great powers increases, the share of attention that any state devotes to any other state will fall; hence the potential for conflicts to escalate will also drop since states must focus considerable attention on one another in order to become hostile enough to contemplate war. Within a fluid multipolar system, the coupling or decoupling of any two states would be a common occurrence and less threatening to the **security** of others than in a taut, uncompromising world of bipolar antagonism where both great powers are preoccupied with every change in political allegiance. Likewise, weapons accumulation by any single actor in a multipolar rivalry would not necessarily trigger the arms race so characteristic of bipolar rivalry because marginal increases by a combination of like-minded states could easily offset any attempt by a single country to obtain a military advantage. Fourth, it is claimed that the larger the number of major powers, the greater the difficulty of appraising relative capabilities and predicting possible alignments; hence war is less likely within a multipolar system because national leaders are not apt to risk military confrontations so long as they harbor grave doubts about the strength and composition of their opposition. Without a clear way to gauge the probability of success on the battlefield, they will negotiate rather than fight.

The debate between supporters and opponents of bipolarity is inconclusive for two main reasons. First, the distribution of power among states is a variable located at a structural level of analysis (see **levels of analysis**). Its relationship to outcomes such as war has to be assessed in light of the character of particular great powers and their historical relationship. Second, since the origins of the modern state system in the seventeenth century, there are too few cases of different systems across which one can make meaningful comparisons. The balance of power is a dynamic concept which, in practice, has to be understood in context. For example, it is difficult to draw firm conclusions about the alleged stability of the bipolar balance of the cold war when so much of the competition between the **superpower**s revolved around the novel challenges of the nuclear era. Nevertheless, research on the stability of bipolar systems indicates that static distributions of power are not associated with the onset of war. Whether the state system is bipolar or multipolar in structure does not significantly affect the probability of war. The frequency, magnitude, and severity of war is not directly related to the number of great powers within the international system.

Further reading

Kegley, C. W., Jr. and Raymond, G. (1990) *When Trust Breaks Down: Alliance Norms in World Politics*, Columbia, SC: University of South Carolina Press.

Mansfield, E. D. (1994) *Power, Trade, and War*, Princeton, NJ: Princeton University Press.

Mearsheimer, J. (2001) *The Tragedy of Great Power Politics*, New York: Norton.

Vasquez, J. A. (ed.) (2000) *What Do We Know About War?* Landham: Rowman & Littlefield.

See also: alliance; balance of power; cold war; great powers; polarity; superpower

GREGORY A. RAYMOND

Bretton Woods

The town of Bretton Woods, New Hampshire served as the site for a major intergovernmental conference in 1944 to finalize plans for the post-war international economy. The site has since become synonymous with both the liberal international economic **regime** that rose and fell from 1946 to 1973 as well as the two international organizations (i.e., the **International Monetary Fund** and the **World Bank**) that resulted from the conference and have outlived the collapse of the regime (see **liberal internationalism**). The conference planners had also visualized the creation of an International Trade Organization (ITO) but this organization's charter was not ratified by the United States leaving the General Agreement on Tariffs and Trade (GATT) as the primary multilateral convention on global trade from 1947 until the establishment of the **World Trade Organization** (WTO) in 1995 (see **multilateralism**).

The aims of the Bretton Woods conference were not only to rehabilitate the war ravaged countries of Europe, but also to craft an economic 'magna carta' for the **international system** that would eliminate the monetary crises that had been a major source of the enmity between nations (see **crisis**). In essence, the conference represented a constitutional moment; it was an opportunity to organize political space out of **anarchy**. The constitutional task was facilitated by the fact that the international financial crisis of 1929–31 had discredited orthodox *laissez-faire* approaches to international finance. Intellectual space was cleared for more interventionist approaches to economic management. The wartime **alliance** structure initially facilitated the political cooperation necessary to build the new international monetary order, although the USSR chose not to pursue membership after participating in the conference negotiations.

The discussions at Bretton Woods were framed by a plan prepared in advance by the British and American delegations. The Anglo-American Joint Statement was the product of intense and protracted negotiations in which adherence to economic orthodoxy yielded, at least in part, to concerns for national **sovereignty** and social stability.

John Maynard Keynes formulated the original British plan while working at the British Ministry of Information during World War Two. Keynes foresaw a currency system with a continuation of wartime controls on currency convertibility, restricted capital movements, and the creation of a European Rehabilitation Fund. The Fund would supply war ravaged nations with the amount of credit required to purchase food and raw materials from other countries after the war. Limitations on capital mobility (see **capital controls**) would help to preserve the stability and autonomy of sovereign states. A system of bilateral trade arrangements would help the UK make the fullest use of its shrunken resources. In fact, the currency system was particularly suited to eliminate the significant creditor position of the United States after the war. As British imports would be paid only in pounds sterling, US exporters would have to purchase British goods with their sterling denominated payment, thereby reviving the export oriented industry of Great Britain.

In 1941, President Roosevelt prompted his administration to begin negotiations with the Britons on postwar economic policy. The heart of the initial US plan was a multilateral trading system based on the principle of non-discrimination in international trade and current account convertibility. Currency convertibility would permit US exporters to repatriate their profits; non-discrimination permitted protective tariffs but rejected the practice of preferences between imperial and dependent states that would deny competitors equal access to raw materials, markets, and investment. Philosophically, the United States believed that preferential trade arrangements bred aggression, as countries excluded by preferential trade arrangements would seek to obtain by force what they were denied through peaceful trade (see **prefential trade agreement**). Strategically, the Americans wanted to end the British trade system based on imperial preference in order to penetrate those markets.

A series of compromise plans were then developed to reconcile the American and British positions by Keynes and his American counterpart, Harry Dexter White, the Assistant Secretary of the Treasury. The American plans placed greater emphasis on exchange rate stability and less weight on the generous provision of international liquidity than did the British. The Britons believed that the stabilization of currencies was not an end in itself, but only a means to full employment and a rising standard of living. The Britons insisted on the primacy of economic sovereignty and the importance of an expansionary bias in economic policies.

The remaining differences between the US and UK positions were supposed to be hammered out during the negotiations at Bretton Woods. As more work had been completed on the organization and structure of the governing board of the Fund than the Bank prior to the conference, the Fund's Articles of Agreement were used as a model for those of the Bank.

The Bretton Woods **regime** consisted of several major components:

1. a stable but adjustable exchange rate arrangement with the US dollar tied to gold as the key reserve currency;
2. controls on transnational capital flows;
3. a coordinating intergovernmental organization (the **International Monetary Fund**); and
4. a reconstruction and development oriented intergovernmental organization (the **World Bank**).

Although the modest inflation generated by the Bretton Woods system stimulated a long period of global economic growth, the system contained political compromises that generated irresolvable crises.

First, the use of the dollar as an international reserve currency permitted an expansive fiscal policy in the United States, thereby discouraging economic, political, and military restraint during the **cold war**. This problem was only exacerbated by the general failure of other states in the system to fulfill their responsibilities through the process of periodic exchange rate adjustments. The failure of self-discipline and orderly adjustments made the regime rigid and vulnerable to speculative attack. Second, **capital controls** deteriorated once the practice of currency convertibility was restored permitting false invoices to disguise disruptive speculative activity as legitimate international trade financing. Moreover, major states passively encouraged the establishment of **offshore** capital markets that ultimately liberated financial capital from its subordinate status relative to international trade. Third, states ignored their consultative obligations to the IMF when making significant changes to their exchange rates, thereby weakening the authority of the IMF. The Fund also failed to object to a single proposed par value change after 1948, thus passively contributing to the rigidity of the exchange rate system. Fourth, the World Bank's adherence to conservative commercial banking principles initially made it irrelevant relative to other sources of aid such as the US Marshall Plan.

As capital mobility increased after the return of current account convertibility, the threat of capital flight and speculative attacks limited the policy flexibility and financial resources of states seeking to pursue a policy of full employment. Despite the pressure from speculative capital flows, states were unwilling to change national policy priorities because of the growth of organized labor and the extension of the franchise. Politically painful policy prescriptions such as interest rate increases and wage freezes had to be implemented to sustain par values in several countries. As confidence in the priority and ability of states to defend stable exchange rates waned, waves of speculative attacks began against currencies. The system ultimately buckled in 1971 when the United States unilaterally refused to continue bearing the costs in terms of trade from an overvalued dollar and opted for a floating exchange rate system.

Further reading

Eichengreen, B. (1996) *Globalizing Capital: A History of the International Monetary System*, Princeton, NJ: Princeton University Press.

Horsefield, J. (1969) *The International Monetary Fund 1945–1965*, vols 1–3, Washington, DC: International Monetary Fund.

Kapur, D., Toussaint, J. P. and Webb, R. (1997) *The World Bank: Its First Half Century*, vols 1–2, Washington, DC: The Brookings Institution.

See also: capital controls; casino capitalism; International Monetary Fund; World Bank

VIKASH YADAV

C

Capital controls

A broad range of measures that governments undertake to restrict the movement of capital and money across their national borders. In an era of allegedly accelerating **globalization**, and in light of the Asian financial collapse of the late 1990s, international political economists are debating the pros and cons of capital controls. Such controls are not new, although their use has been on the decline since the late 1960s. The debate was sparked by the decision of the Malaysian government to impose capital controls in 1998 to prevent volatile capital flows in and out of its economy, particularly speculative capital. Control on capital flows are usually imposed for two reasons: first, as part of macro-economic management to reinforce or substitute for other monetary and fiscal measures; and second, to attain long term national **development** goals, such as ensuring that residents' savings are locally invested or to reserve certain types of investment activity for residents.

Capital controls may be imposed on capital leaving a country or entering it. The former include controls over outward transactions for direct and equity investments by residents and/or foreigners. For example, restrictions on the repatriation of capital by foreigners can include specifying a period before such repatriation is allowed, and regulations that phase the repatriation according to the availability of foreign exchange. Residents may be restricted as to their holdings of foreign stocks, either directly or through limits on the permissible portfolios of the country's investment funds. Law can also restrict bank deposits abroad by residents. Alternatively, bank accounts and transactions denominated in foreign currencies can be made available to residents, and non-interest bearing capital reserve requirements can be imposed on deposits in foreign currencies, thus reducing or eliminating the interest paid on them and therefore diminishing their attractiveness. The main purpose of controls over capital outflows is to thwart attempts to shift between currencies during financial crises, which can exacerbate currency depreciation.

Controls on capital flowing into a country have been imposed by both rich and poor states, although for different reasons. When freer capital movements were allowed from the 1960s onwards, large capital inflows posed problems for rich states such as West Germany, Holland and Switzerland, boosting the demand for their currency and hence making their exports more expensive for overseas consumers. Consequently they imposed controls such as limits on bank deposits for non-residents.

More recently, some developing countries facing problems due to large speculative capital inflows have also resorted to controls. In 1992 Chile subjected foreign loans entering the country to a reserve requirement of 20 per cent (later raised to 30 per cent). In other words, a certain proportion of each loan had to be deposited in the central bank for a year without being paid any interest. In 1994 Brazil imposed a tax on foreign investment in the stock market, and increased the tax on foreign purchases of domestic fixed interest investments. Similarly, in the same year the Czech Republic taxed banks' foreign exchange transactions, and also imposed limits on short-term borrowing abroad by its banks and other firms. Malaysia imposed capital controls over inflows in 1994 and again in 1998, despite widespread concern in the international finance community.

The debate over the wisdom of imposing capital controls is conducted between those who believe that the state should not interfere with the market, and others who argue that capital controls remain one of the few remaining tools with which governments can attempt to regulate international capital movements that have increased dramatically in recent years. Among economists, the tendency is to argue against them, for five main reasons.

First, they demonstrate an obvious disregard of investors' rights to decide where and how to invest. Second, they drastically reduce the incentive of foreigners and residents to invest when they cannot be sure when they will be able to get their earnings or investments out of a country with capital controls in place. Third, capital controls remove the discipline of the market, which allegedly constantly evaluates and rewards countries that pursue sound, pro-growth policies and penalizes those that do not. Fourth, capital controls tend to grow, because when governments ration foreign exchange they limit not only capital inflows but also consumers' ability to purchase imports. Fifth, controls allegedly isolate emerging economies and, if allowed to linger, cut off the country imposing them from worldwide economic growth. One of the most notable features of the world economy is that labour is plentiful and capital is in short supply. Opponents of capital controls argue that achieving greater capital mobility and moving towards full financial market integration is central to world economic development. This provides the best prospects for transforming the small pool of world savings into the required stock of investment capital.

In contrast, supporters of capital controls believe that the costs have to be weighed against the benefits of reducing extreme volatility in the movement of speculative capital. Remedies for debtor states whose currency is subject to speculative attack all involve pain to the debtor country, and the costs of capital controls may be lower in some circumstances than the standard prescriptions of the **International Monetary Fund**, which usually involve higher domestic interest rates. Emergency restrictions on capital flows might be the best policy if international investors can be assured that they are not imposed as long term solutions to a country's economic problems.

Ultimately, the debate over capital controls is unlikely to be resolved definitely in favour of one side or the other. The increasing **integration** of global capital markets makes it difficult to sustain fixed or managed exchange rates by individual states. Thus for most countries the moves towards more freely floating rates is valuable. But since there are also costs from too free a flow of short-term capital there is a need for capital controls as one tool of macroeconomic policy.

Further reading

Edwards, S. (ed.) (1997) *Capital Controls, Exchange Rates, and Monetary Policy in the World Economy*, Cambridge: Cambridge University Press.

Eichengreen, B. (2003) *Capital Flows and Crises*, Cambridge, MA: MIT Press.

Kahler, M. (ed.) (1998) *Capital Controls and Financial Crises*, Ithaca, NY: Cornell University Press.

Ries, C. and Sweeney, R. (eds) (1997) *Capital Controls in Emerging Economies*, Boulder, CO: Westview.

Schulze, G. (2000) *The Political Economy of Capital Controls*, Cambridge: Cambridge University Press.

See also: Bretton Woods; casino capitalism; development; foreign direct investment; globalization; International Monetary Fund

MARTIN GRIFFITHS

Capitalism

A social and economic system in which social relations are based on the exchange of commodities. Karl Marx (1818–83) distinguished between forces of production (land, labor, capital) and relations of production that are shaped by the forces of production. The main characteristics of the capitalist system are:

1. private ownership and control of the means of production (land, labor, capital);
2. economic production is geared to make profits, which are appropriated by the owners of capital;
3. provision of labor for economic production by workers who are not owners of capital;
4. a market framework regulates the economic activities of production, distribution and consumption;
5. a legal framework ensures and protects property rights and profits.

The general characteristics of the *processes* of capitalism can be described as constant expansion, systematic competition, commodification, and susceptibility to contradictions.

A dominant feature of capitalism is its drive for expansion. The need for the continued accumulation of capital is central to the operation and economic viability of capitalism. The general trend is continuous expansionism although there are alternating 'boom and bust' periods in economic activity. Inherent in capitalism is the imperative for constant growth of investment, trade (commodity exchange), productivity, and profits to ensure that the circulation of capital is not interrupted as this could lead to an economic **crisis**. To ensure the continued accumulation of capital the economy needs to grow. Sustainability for capitalism basically means sustained economic growth. Economic growth refers to the expansion of an economy's capacity to produce goods and services over a prolonged period of time. This increase in production, usually measured as Gross Domestic Product (GDP), is identified with an increase in welfare and hence the major indicator for economic success. Thus economic growth has the highest priority in the economic policies of all countries of the world.

The history of colonialism and **imperialism** is testimony to capitalism's inherent feature of expansion which compels capitalism to find new markets and places for cheap materials and labor for capitalist production. Capitalist expansion and production has a time and space dimension which is not only shown by the history of colonialism and imperialism but also by contemporary global finance capitalism (see **casino capitalism**) in which production and investment move to places which secure the highest economic returns.

A major characteristic of global capitalism is competition. In their quest to maximize their individual economic well-being, there is competition between individuals and groups over, for example, jobs, places in higher education, housing, and limited economic products and services. On the national level, there is competition between firms in their pursuit to maximize profits, over production inputs of capital, labor and land, and over markets for their products and services. On the international level, **nation-state**s are competing against each other to attract and maintain investment, finance, trade and technology transfers in their pursuit of economic growth. **Multinational corporation**s are operating internationally and competing for economic and ecological resources. There is also competition between competing forms of capitalism, such as the Japanese/Asian, European and North American models of capitalism.

Capitalism has an inherent drive towards commodification, which means the transformation of all areas of social life and all social relationships, including our relationship to nature, into economic ones, dominated by economic values and commerce. It is a process of market economization in which society and all its relationships are dominated by the logic of commodity production, circulation and exchange. The increasing subordination of society to the economy and the economic logic of capitalism has intensified under the influence of globalization and neoliberalism over the past two decades, which have accelerated the privatization and deregulation of the global economy .

Historically, capitalism has exhibited and generated important contradictions. At the same time these contradictions are part of the capitalist system. Marx's concern was to identify the inherent contradictions of capitalism and to show that they will ultimately lead to the overthrow of this mode of production. The focus of Marx and his followers was the economic contradictions of capitalism. **Marxism** identifies a fundamental contradiction between the interests of the capitalist class and the proletariat. The cost of labor power needs to be kept down but the purchasing power of the proletariat as buyers of commodities in the market is thus constrained. Market dependence and the increasing commodification of society contributes to the alienation of individuals from each other and from nature, and ultimately leads to social disintegration and conflict.

So far the capitalist world has been able to manage the generation of enormous inequality at the global level. However, the increasing dominance of economics over politics, and of the market over the state, creates problems for democratic control over the economy, both at a national as well as a global level. This means that **global civil society** and the state become subordinate players in the process of **globalization**. Capitalism has shown in its history strong adaptive capabilities to overcome the crises that arise from its internal contradictions. The different historical stages and different locally specific forms of capitalism are the result of its flexibility and adaptation. As a result, and contrary to Marx's expectations, there is no pre-given trajectory to capitalist **development**, and it is impossible to make predictions about the future of capitalism. The internal contradictions are both the strength and weaknesses of capitalism.

Further reading

Gilpin, R. (2002) *The Challenge of Global Capitalism: The World Economy in the 21st Century*, Princeton, NJ: Princeton University Press.

De Soto, H. (2003) *The Mystery of Capital*, New York: Basic Books.

Landes, D. (1999) *The Wealth and Poverty of Nations*, New York: Norton.

Muller, J. (2002) *The Mind and the Market: Capitalism in Modern European Thought*, New York: Knopf.

Schmidt, V. (2002) *The Futures of European Capitalism*, Oxford: Oxford University Press.

See also: casino capitalism; communism; free trade; neoliberalism; socialism

MARTIN GRIFFITHS

Casino capitalism

A term used to describe the dangers of excessive speculation in the international financial **order**. Its most famous proponent was Susan Strange (1923–98), who examined how changes to global financial systems under US **hegemony** transformed the **international political economy** in the post-war period. The argument is that markets within the international financial **order** increasingly operate like a casino, within which financial institutions and investors gamble for wealth and political **power**. **Great powers** permit gamblers to increase the size and risk of their bets, but what is at stake is not simply the gambler's pocketbook but stability within the international political economy. The consequences of instability from financial crises are increasing levels of political, social, and economic inequality; a high price to pay for permitting more speculation in the international financial order (see **crisis**). The argument is dependent on the notion that increased international capital mobility weakens the state. Strange also argued that during the post-war period the United States encouraged financial speculation for short-term benefit but, in doing so, created long-term instability in the international financial order.

The origins of casino capitalism can be traced to the development of the Euromarkets in the 1950s and 1960s, which assisted the doubling of the ratio of private to public capital following the collapse of the **Bretton Woods regime** in the early 1970s.

According to the casino capitalism argument, Bretton Woods collapsed due to the United States' incapacity to maintain the official exchange rate of US$35 per ounce of gold, its support of a massive capital expansion through the Euromarkets (see **disintermediation**), and its export of inflation to the United States' major trading partners. States and financial markets sceptical of the American capacity to maintain the official rate were correct, and Richard Nixon's 'closing of the gold window' (the capacity to exchange dollars for gold at the official rate) on 15 August 1971 signalled the end of the system. Discussions in the early 1970s of what should replace the dollar as a world currency focused on the **International Monetary Fund**'s Special Drawing Rights (SDRs) as the most obvious choice. After all, a currency independent from any one state would not be prone to abuse for domestic political considerations. However, following the quadrupling of oil prices in 1973–4, a rapid expansion of private capital within the international financial order led the United States and the UK to reject the SDR as a viable option. For the casino capitalism argument the American capacity to push the international political economy from a 'gold-dollar' standard to a 'paper-dollar' demonstrates its ongoing **hegemony** despite arguments from some US scholars that Bretton Woods demonstrated the United States' hegemonic decline (see **hegemonic stability theory**).

The 'paper-dollar' standard of flexible exchange rates encouraged financial institutions to increasingly use short term debt trading and 'gambling' on currency positions to guard against risks in rapidly changing currency valuations. The 1974 collapse of two prominent international banks from betting on international currency movements dramatically demonstrated the financial instability of the new order (see **Bank for International Settlements**) and the need for an 'International Lender of the Last Resort' to deal with financial crises. Worse still, the massive expansion of private capital fuelled lending to the **Third World** from international bank syndicates, nearly all of which was US dollar-denominated and with variable rates of interest. Thus when interest rates changed in the United States, Third World states with loans in US dollars found dramatic differences in their short term loan repayments. When the United States raised interest rates in the late 1970s and early 1980s to fight 'stagflation' (a combination of inflation and unemployment) the impact on borrowers led to the debt crisis of the early 1980s that was most pronounced in Latin America and Eastern Europe (see **debt trap**). The crisis transformed the international financial order by encouraging the development of more short term speculative trading so that financial institutions could deal with risks, including the creation of **offshore** financial centres.

Changes in the late 1980s and early 1990s increased speculation within the international financial order. The prevalence of financial 'bubbles' both in the United States and in Japan clearly demonstrated how speculation on future assets (such as real estate) led to expectations of profits far above real prices. Furthermore, US interest rate movements continued to provoke currency problems, with developing states such as Mexico suffering severe financial crises

that have, in turn, strained the IMF's crisis management capacities. In the late 1990s financial crises persisted from financial speculation, culminating in the Asian financial crisis of 1997–8 and the Russian financial crisis of 1998. At the turn of the century ongoing crises in states such as Argentina, again due to changes in international interest rates and short term capital flight, called the stability of the current international financial order into question.

Theoretically, the casino capitalism argument draws upon a number of prominent economists, most notably John Maynard Keynes and Hyman Minksy. According to Keynes, financial market actors are overly concerned with others' perception of how the market behaves, creating a schizophrenic environment that swings wildly between optimism and pessimism. Keynes argued that finance should be the concern of national governments, and not be used by international financial market actors. Building on Keynes, Minsky's 'Financial Instability Hypothesis' (1986) outlines how expectations of future profits on capital assets, and arbitrage in short term securities to manage uncertainty on those profits, leads to financial crises. For Keynes and Minksy, governments should seek economic growth through increasing employment and consumption rather than concentrating excessively on investment.

A number of scholars have put forward proposals to restore states' control over the international financial order. For example, James Tobin (1978) has advocated a tax on international financial transactions to slow speculation. In the 1990s experimentation with **capital controls** in Chile and Malaysia raised interest in national regulation to dampen speculative activity. Ultimately, for casino capitalism arguments, the best source of reform in the international financial order is effective international leadership by the United States. But US leadership is dependent on US domestic politics, which favours **liberal internationalism** in finance, but not coupled with strong state intervention on speculation.

We should take heart, however, that in the twenty-first century the international financial order is under a regulatory and surveillance regime of enormous scope compared with previous periods. Furthermore, scholars have demonstrated that financial market actors have little interest in developed states' domestic policies other than key economic indicators, allowing states some 'room to move'. Third world states are, however, under more scrutiny. This is not to dismiss the basic casino capitalism argument, but to place stronger emphasis on the capacity of national governments to shape their own destinies under the constraints of high international capital mobility.

Further reading

Minsky, H. P. (1986) *Stabilizing an Unstable Economy*, New Haven, CN: Yale University Press.

Mosley, L. (2003) *Global Capital and National Governments*, Cambridge: Cambridge University Press.

Seabrooke, L. (2001) *US Power in International Finance*, London: Palgrave.

Strange, S. (1986) *Casino Capitalism*, Oxford: Blackwell.

Tobin, J. (1978) 'A Proposal for International Monetary Reform', *Far Eastern Economic Journal* 4, 3–4: 153–9.

See also: Bretton Woods; capitalism; embedded liberalism

LEONARD SEABROOKE

Chemical weapons

A class of weapon that relies on the toxic properties of chemicals to incapacitate, injure, or kill human beings. It is important to note that all munitions rely on chemical reactions to kill or injure human beings. The explosive force of TNT and the incendiary capability of napalm is achieved through the interactions of particular chemicals, but their effectiveness as a weapon lies in the energy that is produced and released, not in the toxicity of the chemicals themselves. Sometimes referred to as the poor man's atom bomb, chemical weapons are employed to inflict mass casualties. It is for this reason that they are often referred to as **weapons of mass destruction**.

Chemical weapons have the capacity to kill and injure tens of thousands of people. It is difficult to predict casualty rates from a chemical attack, however. This is because of the number of variables that need to be taken into account. Their lethality depends on such factors as the particular agent used, the number of munitions, the degree of toxic concentration in the weapon, the delivery system, environmental factors such as wind speed and direction, and the population density of the target area. One thing is certain. Chemical weapons are highly toxic to humans and can kill very quickly. One milligram of VX nerve gas, for example, can kill an adult human being in less than fifteen minutes.

Chemical weapons fall into five categories. *Nerve agents*, such as Sarin, Tuban, and VX attack the central nervous system and have the potential to kill individuals very quickly. *Blistering agents*, such as mustard gas, cause severe damage to the surface of the skin, and can also damage the eyes, lungs, and major organs. *Choking agents*, such as phosgene gas and chlorine gas, cause severe damage to the lungs. *Blood agents*, such as hydrogen cyanide, enter the blood stream through the respiratory system and cause lethal damage to the vascular system. Finally, *psychotomimetic agents* affect the mind and the ability of individuals to function normally. This includes impaired decision-making, motor skills, and general incapacitation. While defoliants such as agent orange and riot control chemicals such as mace and tear gas are certainly chemicals, they are not usually classified as chemical weapons.

The effectiveness of chemical weapons depends on a number of factors. Chemical weapons have a number of advantages over other weapons. First, they are relatively cheap to produce and to manufacture. An individual with a basic knowledge of chemistry and some laboratory equipment can build a chemical weapon. Indeed, the CIA has argued that developing a chemical weapon presents no more technical difficulty to a terrorist than the production of chemical narcotics such as heroin. In contrast, the production of a nuclear weapon requires a sophisticated knowledge of nuclear physics and advanced technological capability. Second, as the Sarin gas attacks in Tokyo's subway system in 1995 highlights, chemical weapons are highly portable and easily concealed. Third, from the point of view of the terrorist, a chemical weapon is also likely to create fear and panic in its targets. Chemical weapons do not damage physical infrastructure. This distinguishes them from munitions that employ explosive weapons.

Chemical weapons, like their cousins **biological weapons**, have a long history. The most widespread use of chemical weapons was during World War One, where substances such as phosgene, chlorine, and mustard gas were widely used. There are a number of ways that individuals can protect themselves against a chemical attack. The most obvious defense is protective clothing and the wearing of a gas mask, which provides an effective physical barrier to the entry of toxic chemicals into the body. Researchers have also developed neutralizing agents that deal with the chemicals before they enter the body. Ointments, powders and sprays have been developed for this purpose. In recent years, more elaborate methods of detecting the presence of a chemical attack have been developed. Highly sensitive detection equipment such as gas alarms is available. However, the equipment is expensive, selective in screening for specific chemical weapons, and is only able to give a limited warning of the presence of toxic chemicals in the atmosphere. As yet, there is no foolproof method of defending against a chemical attack. Even a gas mask and protective suit is only useful if it is worn prior to an impending attack.

Further reading

Bothe, M., Ronzitti, N. and Rosas, A. (1998) *The New Chemical Weapons Convention: Implementation And Prospects*, The Hague: Martinus Nijhoff

Hoenig, S. L. (2002) *Handbook of Chemical Warfare and Terrorism*, Westport, CO: Greenwood.

Krutzsch, W. and Trapp, R. (2002) *A Commentary on the Chemical Weapons Convention*, The Hague: Martinus Nijhoff.

Tucker, J. (2000) *Toxic Terror: Assessing Terrorist Use of Chemical and Biological Weapons*, Cambridge, MA: MIT Press.

See also: biological weapons; terrorism; weapons of mass destruction

TERRY O'CALLAGHAN

Chlorofluorocarbons (CFCs)

A group of chemicals created from the combination of fluorine, carbon and chlorine atoms, also known as Freons, which were first manufactured in the late

1800s and later adopted in the 1930s as a safe, non-toxic, non-flammable and non-carcinogenic alternative to dangerous substances like ammonia and sulphur dioxide for purposes of refrigeration, air-conditioning (especially in cars), solvents, foams, and aerosol can propellants. The desirable characteristics of these compounds resulted in an exponential increase in their use and application. Indeed, much of the modern lifestyle of the latter half of the last century was made possible by the use of CFCs. As a consequence, world production, concentrated in the United States and Western Europe, doubled every five years until the 1970s, when the devastating environmental effects of CFCs were first discovered. Subsequently, CFCs have been verified as the primary agents for the accelerated depletion of atmospheric ozone (see **ozone depletion**). In addition, CFCs are a significant greenhouse gas (see **global warming**). They are at least 10,000 times more potent than carbon dioxide and without measures to restrict production it was predicted that they would cause 50 per cent more warming than carbon dioxide. As a consequence of these deleterious environmental effects the production and use of CFCs is now controlled under the auspices of the multilaterally developed Montreal Protocol.

CFCs were first implicated as the main source of **ozone depletion** in 1974. Initial controls over CFC use were established in response to an effective public campaign for a reduction in aerosol can use. This resulted in regulations prohibiting the use of CFCs as aerosol propellants in the United States in 1978, and shortly thereafter in Canada, Sweden and Norway. The European Community also imposed formal reductions. As a result US production of the compounds CFC-11 and CFC-12, the main CFC compounds, fell from 46 per cent of

world production in 1974 to 28 per cent by 1985. However, production increased sharply once more in the early 1980s due to the increased use of CFCs in vehicle air conditioning.

International attempts to establish mechanisms to research the depletion of the ozone layer were initiated by the Vienna Convention for the Protection of the Ozone Layer, signed by twenty-eight countries in 1985. While the Vienna Convention did not contain formal commitments to reduce CFCs, it was an important milestone as it recognized the need for a multilateral approach to a global environmental problem, before the effects, or even the existence of the problem, was scientifically proven. The ratification of the Convention represents the first international adoption of the 'precautionary principle'.

On the basis of the Vienna Convention and in light of growing scientific evidence of dramatic ozone depletion (specifically the discovery, in 1985, of an 'Ozone Hole' over Antarctica), 'the Montreal Protocol on Substances that Deplete the Ozone Layer', negotiated under the aegis of the **United Nations** Environmental Program (UNEP), was ratified in September 1987. The original Protocol was signed by forty-six countries (including the European Economic Community), representing approximately 82 per cent of world consumption of Ozone Depleting Substances (ODS). The Protocol called for the reduction in the use and eventual phase-out of all identified ODS, with stiff penalties for non-compliance and trade restrictions to encourage participation. The requirements of the schedules and the speed at which they were agreed were far greater than was initially expected or hoped for, indicating the shift in the dominance of the 'precautionary principle' from a minor to dominant component of the negotiation process. The Protocol identified phase-out schedules for all identified ODS to come into force in 1989; the most significant of which was the requirement for signatories to make a 50 per cent cut, from 1986 levels, in the production and consumption of the five main CFCs by 1999.

Incorporated in the initial development of the Protocol was the provision that it was constructively flexible: it can be adjusted in response to changes in scientific knowledge or technological developments without having to be completely renegotiated. Consequently, the international response to the growing scientific appreciation of the seriousness of the situation has been rapid. Supplementary agreements were signed in London in 1990 and in Copenhagen in 1992, where the parties of the Montreal Protocol agreed to reduce the time period for CFCs elimination from 1999 to 1995. Further adjustments were made in Vienna (1995), Montreal (1997) and most recently in Beijing (1999) to include newly recognized ODS. The Beijing Amendment (1999) introduced a freezing of HCFC production by 2003. This chemical was introduced as a safe alternative to CFCs but has recently been identified as a highly effective greenhouse gas (see **global warming**). The Protocol now contains phase-out schedules for ninety-six ODS.

Currently, 184 countries have ratified the Montreal Protocol. Approximately two thirds (134) of the signatories are developing countries as described in Article 5 of the Protocol, or countries with 'transition' economies. The inclusion and cooperation of developing countries has been pivotal to the success of the Protocol. In the initial agreement developing countries were granted a ten year grace period before compliance was required, in recognition of the fact that consumption rates were low and to support the basic **development** needs of

these nations. This grace period resulted in a switch of ODS production from developed to developing countries. In 1986, industrialized countries accounted for approximately 82 per cent of the 1.1 million ODP (Ozone Depleting Potential) tons of CFCs consumed globally. However, as developed countries phased out ODS, developing countries continued production. By 1999, the time the Protocol stipulated for developing countries to freeze ODS levels, developing countries accounted for 84 per cent of the 150,000 ODP tons consumed globally. Production in Brazil, China and North Korea accounted for 50 per cent of this amount.

To accelerate reductions in developing countries the London (1990) and Copenhagen (1992) amendments established a Multilateral Fund, which provides funding for technical and financial assistance exclusively to developing countries that would otherwise not have the expertise necessary to phase out ODS. The fund is implemented by the UNEP, the **United Nations Development Program** (UNDP), the United Nations Industrial Development Organization (UNIDO) and the **World Bank**, with contributions to the fund sourced mainly from developed countries. As of 2002, the fund approved nearly US$1.5 billion in funds to phase out consumption of 221,000 ODP tons through projects in 131 countries.

The success of the Montreal Protocol in reducing CFCs and other significant ODS is clear. Between 1986 and 1999, the global consumption of CFCs was reduced from 1.1 million to 150,000 ODP tons. Without the Montreal Protocol global consumption of CFCs would have reached about three million ODP tons by 2010 and eight million in 2060. This rapid achievement was made possible by the ease in finding replacement chemicals or technologies for ODS use. The Protocol has also had the effect of implementing phase-out schedules for significant greenhouse gases, an achievement that has yet to be claimed by the **Kyoto Protocol**. The overall success of the Protocol has hinged on the ability of governments and industry to respond rapidly to changes in scientific knowledge; knowledge that was crucial for constraining policy debates and shaping negotiated agreements. The Montreal Protocol is the greatest success yet achieved in managing human impacts on the global environment and may serve as a role model for current and future multilateral agreements in response to global environmental threats.

Further reading

Liftin, K. (1994) *Ozone Discourses: Science and Politics in Global Environmental Cooperation*, New York: Columbia University Press.

Parson, E. A. (2003) *Protecting the Ozone Layer: Science and Strategy*, New York: Oxford University Press.

Rowlands, I. H. (1995) *The Politics of Global Atmospheric Change*, Manchester: Manchester University Press.

See also: global warming; Kyoto protocol

RAECHEL L. WATERS

Civil war

Civil wars are the most common type of violent conflict in the world, by far outnumbering international **war** since World War Two. The term 'civil war' is open to numerous definitions. Some would limit it to large-scale armed conflict while others would use a very broad definition that encompasses just about any conflict that takes place within a single state. For the purposes of this entry, civil war is defined as any armed conflict within a single state whose object involves some political prize or goal including but not limited to **sovereignty**. This definition has the advantage of including most violent conflict but excludes certain types like government campaigns against criminal elements, unless those criminals are so powerful that they can challenge the sovereignty of a state.

The majority of civil wars take one of two forms: **ethnic conflicts** and revolutionary wars (see **revolution**). Ethnic conflict involves challenges by ethnic groups, usually minorities, against a state apparatus controlled by another ethnic group. Not all ethnic conflicts reach the level of armed conflict, and accordingly are not all civil wars. Those that do generally involve issues of separatism, where the ethnic minority seeks to either form its own state, join with a bordering state, or gain some other form of **self-determination** such as regional autonomy. States have only three options when dealing with these challenges: control, voice and exit. Control is the use of force to repress the ethnic challenge. Voice means to give the ethnic challengers some form of say in the existing government. Exit is to allow the group to fully or partially leave the state. In other worlds, exit means to give in to the separatists' demands. States are sometimes willing to negotiate levels of self-determination that are less than the separatists' original demands. Most states, however, for nationalist reasons, are unwilling to give into separatist demands and choose the control option (see **nationalism**). Examples of well known separatist minorities include the Catholics in Northern Ireland and the Palestinians in Israel.

Revolutionary wars differ from ethnic conflicts in that revolutionaries, rather than wishing to exit the state, want to replace the existing government with another one. Sometimes this involves simply changing rulers rather than the regime type itself. This is more properly called a rebellion. Revolutions generally involve a change in the type of regime. Goldstone *et al.* (1991) identify three factors that are present in all revolutions: state **crisis**, elite alienation, and mass mobilization. A state crisis involves a crisis in the **legitimacy** of a state, especially among elites. This can be caused by economic failures, new political ideologies, or the belief that the state is acting against its people's best interests. Elite alienation involves a sufficient level of alienation that elites feel it is preferable to seek revolutionary alternatives rather than try to fix the existing state apparatus. Mobilization involves mass participation in the opposition movement. Thus, there must be significant and widespread grievances among the population before elites can mobilize them.

There are two other aspects of civil wars that are essential to remember. First, the state is generally a participant. Civil wars are not just conflicts in which the state is a prize. The state apparatus itself, including its bureaucracy, leaders, and military often participate as independent actors. Second, while civil wars occur within states, the international context remains important. The causes of civil wars sometimes include international ones. New ideologies can become important in the **international system**, influencing actors in individual states. The international communist movement influenced civil wars in this way for much of the twentieth century. More recently political **Islam**, another international phenomenon, has been influencing and even causing civil wars in states such as Egypt and Algeria. Civil wars also have an international impact. They can destabilize a region, increasing political tensions in bordering states. They often create international **refugee** flows. Successful revolutions often provide the inspiration for revolutionaries elsewhere

as did the Islamic revolutions in Iran and Afghanistan. Also, successful revolutions are often exported to other states.

From World War Two until the early 1990s, the number of civil wars steadily increased. Over the last decade, however, the number began to drop steadily until 2002, the most recent year for which data is currently available. Ethnic wars, which were the most common and violent type of conflict in the 1990s, dropped to their lowest levels since the 1960s. In fact, the recent trend has been the **containment** and management of such conflicts. While during the 1980s and 1990s civil wars were more or less evenly distributed throughout the world, in the twenty-first century, they are concentrated in south central Asia and sub-Saharan Africa.

Further reading

Ballantine, K. and Sherman, J. (eds) (2003) *The Political Economy of Armed Conflict: Beyond Greed and Grievance*, Boulder, CO: Lynne Rienner.

Goldstone, J. A., Gurr, T. R. and Moshiri, F. (eds) (1991) *Revolutions of the Late Twentieth Century*, Boulder, CO: Westview,.

Horowitz, D. L. (1985) *Ethnic Groups in Conflict*, Berkeley: University of California Press.

Kaldor, M. (1999) *New and Old Wars: Organized Violence in a Global Era*, Cambridge: Polity.

Rule, J. B. (1988) *Theories of Civil Violence*, Berkeley, CA: University of California Press.

See also: failed state; ethnic conflict; war

JONATHAN FOX

Clash of civilizations

Samuel Huntington's 'clash of civilizations' thesis (1996a) has promoted one of the most important debates in international relations in the 1990s. It began with an article in *Foreign Affairs* (1993), which was immediately followed with a number of critiques in the same journal. Huntington responded with several further articles and a book, and his critics have more or less continually faulted the theory since 1993. This debate went beyond a simple discussion of whether a particular theory was correct or incorrect. It was inspired by one key question. What will be the nature of conflict after the **cold war**? Do the old theories still hold true, or are we in a new era? This essay will present Huntington's argument and summarize the arguments of his critics.

Huntington's thesis

Huntington's basic argument is that the **cold war** is being replaced by conflict between civilizations. Huntington (1993: 24) defines a civilization as 'the highest cultural grouping of people and the broadest level of cultural identity people have short of what distinguishes humans from other species. It is defined by common language, history, religion, customs, institutions and by the subjective self-identification of people'. This definition is similar to many definitions of **ethnicity** which are also based on a list of ascriptive traits like language, shared historical experiences or myths, religious beliefs, and region of residence. The basic difference between the two is the breadth of those who are included in the common identity. Ethnic groups are more narrowly defined than are civilizations. Thus, if two groups belong to different civilizations, they most likely are different ethnically as well but the reverse is not necessarily true because the broader definition of civilizations allows for multiple ethnic groups to share in the same civilization. Hunting-

ton is essentially arguing that ethnic identities are amalgamating into a finite number of super-ethnic groups that will become the primary basis for identity, and thus the primary basis for politics and conflict in the post-cold war era.

Huntington identifies several civilizations: Western, Confucian/Sinic, Japanese, Islamic (see **Islam**), Hindu, Slavic-Orthodox, Latin American, and 'possibly' African. Nearly all of these civilizations include some facet of religion in their definition and some of them appear to be wholly defined by religion. The Islamic and Hindu civilizations appear to be defined solely by religion and any group of these religions seem to be automatically included in that civilization, whatever other cultural traits they may possess, The Confucian/Sinic civilization includes Confucianism, and by inference Buddhism, as a major component. However, Huntington seems to be unsure as to whether Buddhism should be part of this civilization or treated as a separate one. In some places in his writings he refers to it as a civilization while in others he clearly states that it is not.

The West is uniformly Christian and is differentiated from other civilizations by religious factors including the influence of the Reformation, its combined Catholic and Protestant cultures, and its adherence to the concept of separation of Church and state. The Slavic-Orthodox civilization is primarily differentiated from the West in that it is based on the Orthodox branch of Christianity which did not experience important religious-related events including the Renaissance, Reformation, and Enlightenment. The Latin American civilization is also distinguished from the West, in part, by religion, in that it is primarily Catholic (Huntington, 1996a: 46). The Japanese civilization has a distinct religious tradition including Shintoism. The African culture is the only civilization which is not religiously homogeneous. The civilization's members belong to various Christian faiths and animist religions. Perhaps it is for this reason that Huntington is unsure whether it should be included in the list of civilizations.

Huntington argues that conflict between these civilizations will become both more common and more violent in the future. He describes three types of conflicts that will occur based on these civilizational identities. The first is core state conflicts. He argues that most civilizations have core states which are the most powerful states in their civilization and, thus, tend to lead them. For instance, the United States is the core state of the Western civilization, Russia for the Slavic-Orthodox civilization, and China for the Sinic-Confucian civilization. He believes that conflicts between these states will become one of the defining elements of international politics.

The second type of conflict is fault-line conflicts between states. That is, where states of different civilizations border each other, there is likely to be increased tension. The third is fault-line conflicts within states. This occurs in states with heterogeneous populations with members belonging to multiple civilizations.

Another important, and perhaps the most well known, argument made by Huntington in this context is his contention that the Islamic civilization has 'bloody borders'. That is, he expects the Islamic civilization to be especially violent and engage in a disproportionate amount of conflict against other civilizations. He also expects the Islamic civilization to challenge the Western civilization and form an alliance with the Sinic-Confucian in order to do so.

Huntington's critics

Since the appearance of Huntington's 1993 article in *Foreign Affairs*, there has been a spirited debate over his argument. One reply, also published in *Foreign Affairs*, was actually written in the form of a poem (Tipson, 1997). Since his later book and articles basically elaborate on the argument made in the original *Foreign Affairs* article, this discussion will evaluate this debate based on the arguments that are made regarding the subject, rather than on a chronological basis. It is important to note that many of the criticisms described below contradict each other and, in fact, some of the individual critics contradict themselves and many of them attack Huntington's theory along several different lines. While it is possible to divide the criticisms of Huntington's theories into several schools of thought, this is avoided here because of the overlapping of critics and criticisms described above. Rather, the debate is presented in terms of the types of arguments that are posed in criticizing Huntington's theory.

First, many argue that conflicts will continue to be fought along traditional lines. Those factors that caused conflict during the cold war will continue to do so. However, there is little agreement over what those traditional lines are. Realists argue that the state, rather than civilizations or any other basis for identity, will remain the basic unit of international relations and the focus of international conflict (see **realism**). Others argue that **nationalism** and ethnicity will be the basis for conflict. The rising trend of ethnic and national groups seeking **self-determination** will continue and, perhaps, increase in importance since the **superpower**s will no longer restrain them. This argument is made in particular with regard to Eastern Europe but is by no means restricted to this geographical region. Whether the basis for conflict will be the state or sub-state groups there seems to be agreement among those who posit that the basis for conflict has not changed with the end of the cold war, that the civilizations Huntington describes are not united and that most conflicts, both international and domestic, will be between members of the same civilization.

Second, many argue that the world is becoming a smaller place and is slowly uniting into a single identity. That is, people will soon consider themselves citizens of the world rather than of civilizations, states, or sub-state entities. This is due to a number of interrelated trends including economic **interdependence**, **globalization**, communications, and the increasing importance of international institutions and organizations. It is expected that a world civilization will slowly emerge from these trends, reducing and perhaps eventually eliminating all violent conflict.

These first two types of argument are the most important to international relations theory and practice. This is because, as does Huntington, they deal with the essential question of what will be the nature of international relations in the future? While there is clearly no agreement on the issue, the debate is an essential one and, whatever one thinks of Huntington's theory, it has clearly helped to mold this debate. Thus, correct or incorrect, the theory has made an invaluable contribution to the study of international relations.

The third type of criticism is that Huntington ignored factors that will impact on conflict, thereby making his theory irrelevant. That is, many argue that some factor other than civilizations will be the basis for world conflict or the lack thereof. These include: that the world is better at managing conflict than it used to be, thus reducing conflict no matter what its basis; that Huntington underestimates the power of modernity and secularism and that people are more interested in economic prosperity than in maintaining their traditions; that Huntington missed the fact that most ethnopolitical conflicts result from protracted discrimination rather than cultural roots; that other civilizations really want to emulate the West; or that some other type of issue will shape global politics in the future.

Fourth, many argue that Huntington has his facts wrong. Many make the argument that Huntington's description of reality is at best incorrect and at worst, manufactured. A number of critics allege that Huntington ignores relevant facts and even bends them to fit his theory. Most of the empirical literature on Huntington's theory fits in this category. That is, nearly every large quantitative study undermines Huntington's arguments. Studies of international conflict using well-known and accepted datasets like the Correlates of War (COW), International Crisis Behavior (ICB), and Militarized Interstate Disputes (MID) have found the predictions of the thesis to be incorrect. They have found intra-civilizational conflicts to be more common than civilizational ones, and that dyads within the same civilization are more likely to go to war than dyads of different civilizations. The end of the cold war did not see a rise in international conflict. There was no increase in conflict between the Western and Islamic civilizations. They also found that cultural factors did not have any consistent influence on international conflict.

Quantitative studies of domestic **ethnic conflict** based on well known and accepted datasets like Minorities at Risk (MAR), and the Uppsala dataset, similarly contradict Huntington's theory. The distribution of civilizational versus noncivilizational conflicts remained nearly identical as did the ratio between the level of violence of civilizational and non-civilizational ethnic conflicts. This includes conflict involving the Islamic civilization.

Studies of general domestic conflict based on well known and accepted datasets like the State Failure and Correlates of War (COW) datasets found similar results. The proportion of domestic conflicts which are civilizational has remained constant since 1965. Moreover, the absolute amount of civilizational conflict has dropped considerably since the end of the cold war. There is no clear evidence that the overall intensity of civilizational state failures is increasing in proportion to non-civilizational state failures. There is no evidence of an increase in conflict by the Islamic civilization as a whole. Rather, its members fight each other more often than groups of other civilizations. Furthermore, political factors are shown to have a greater influence on civil wars than cultural ones.

However, one set of studies which focuses on **terrorism** does find that terrorism is becoming more civilizational in that most new terrorist groups are Islamic and most terrorist incidents in the 1980s and 1990s were by Islamic groups. However, this finding is by no means conclusive proof for Huntington's theory. While Islamic groups seem to prefer the tactic of terrorism, overall world conflict is not particularly civilizational.

The major drawback of all of these studies is that they look at limited time frames. At the time of writing, the most updated look no farther than 2001. Some do not have data past the early 1990s. Thus, it is possible that in the long run, quantitative studies will support Huntington's theory. However, the near unanimity of these studies despite their use of different datasets and methodologies, indicates that such a possibility is unlikely. Thus, the quantitative literature supports the argument that what has caused conflict in the past will continue to do so in the future.

A fifth type of critique of Huntington is to focus on his methodology. As is the case with many of the other critiques, those who make this type of criticism often contradict each other. The critiques of this nature include: that Huntington's theory is an oversimplification; that Huntington's list of civilizations is somehow incorrect or inaccurate; that Huntington often contradicts himself; that Huntington's evidence is anecdotal, leaving room for counter examples; and that Huntington provides no systematic analysis of the link between civilizational controversies and political behavior.

Sixth, many argue that because of his popularity among policymakers, Huntington's theory is a self-fulfilling prophecy. That is, if predictions like those of Huntington combined with the activities of groups like **al-Qaeda** succeed in convincing Western policymakers that Islam is a threat, it will be treated as one. If this occurs, conflicts between the West and Islam would probably be given more attention and provoke a more conflictive response from the West, making escalation more likely and peaceful resolution more difficult.

Seventh, some argue that Huntington's theory is really a surrogate for religion. That is, Huntington develops an elaborate theory to say that religion is important in international relations while overtly avoiding the use of the term religion. Furthermore, civilizations is an inferior substitute for religion as an explanation for international politics and conflict. Thus the debate provides an excellent example of the extent to which international relations scholars have been avoiding the issue of religion. Huntington proposed a theory that while to a great extent is based on religion, systematically avoided making it an overt element of his theory and preferred to couch his theory in terms of civilizations. Despite the intensity of the debate, most of its participants follow Huntington's lead and avoid the overt discussion of religion in international relations. Despite the criticisms, Huntington is not without his supporters, though these seem to be more common in the policy community than in the academy. Even many of Huntington's detractors admit that if he is wrong, he is brilliantly wrong.

The West vs Islam vs the rest

As noted above, the most well known aspect of the 'clash of civilizations theory' is the argument that the Islamic civilization will be particularly violent and will direct this violence at the West. Another aspect of this prediction is that the declining **power** of the West will be a defining factor in world politics which will lead to conflict between the West and 'the rest'.

The Western 'arrogance' which Huntington feels is likely to cause conflict is the belief that Western values like democracy and **capitalism** are universally valid combined with Western willingness to defend its values and interests as the values of the world community. In addition, the West believes that it has led the world into modernity, giving it the right to lead the world. While, democracy and **human rights** tend to be accepted in Christian states, other civilizations are less interested and tend to resist Western influence. On a more micro level, immigrants into Western states are not integrating well into Western society and, accordingly, are increasingly perceived as an internal threat to many Western societies.

According to Huntington, Islam rejects Western culture and prefers to search for the answers to its problems in Islam itself. This response is, to some extent, fueled by the increase in Islamic wealth from oil, but it is more probably due to the failure of governments in Islamic states that were guided by Western ideologies to successfully address pressing domestic social problems. Furthermore, Islam and the West, historically, have mutually feared each other and rejected each other's culture. This is exacerbated by the fact that the Islamic civilization considers itself superior to others and the Islamic religion divides the world into those who follow Islam and those who do not.

Huntington's arguments concerning Islam and the West are, to say the least, controversial. Like the critics of the other aspects of his theory, the critics agree on the fact that Huntington is incorrect but otherwise often contradict each other. Their arguments against this feature of Huntington's theory are as follows.

First, Huntington mistakes economic conflict for cultural conflict. The main grievances of Muslims against the West are economic and if there is any collusion against the West between Muslims and other cultural groupings it is due to common economic interests rather than identity. Second, many argue that the world, including the Islamic world, is secularizing and that religious bases for conflict are disappearing in the modern era. Thus, any clashes between Islam and the West are due to secular causes rather than religious ones. Third, Islamic fundamentalism is more of a threat to authoritarian regimes in Islamic states than it is to the West. The Islamic civilization is internally divided. Conflicts occur more often within it than between it and other civilizations. For instance, **nationalism** is a potent factor within the Islamic civilization. As a result, many Islamic states have better relations with non-Islamic states than with other states that are part of Islam, as illustrated during the 1991 Gulf War.

However, some of Huntington's critics acknowledge some truth in this aspect of his argument. The events of 11 September 2001 and the subsequent US led war on terrorism have reinvigorated the debate over this issue. The phenomenon of civilizational conflict has certainly become more popular in media circles. However, differences between the United States and other Western states, particularly over the invasion of Iraq in 2003, show that the Western civilization is by no means united. Much of the opposition to the United States' agenda came from within the Western civilization from France and Germany.

Conclusions

The 'clash of civilizations' debate instigated in 1993 by Samuel Huntington is one of the most important debates in international relations during the 1990s and beyond. It deals with some of the central questions of contemporary international relations. What will be the basis for international conflict in the future? Has this basis changed from the past or is it immutable? What role, if any, should be given to less tangible factors like culture and identity as opposed to the more concrete elements of material conflict? At the time of writing, there has been no resolution to the debate. Quantitative studies seem to show that Huntington is incorrect but these studies can only look at what has happened up until now and cannot determine whether Huntington will eventually prove to be correct. World events continue to conspire to show both the relevance of Huntington's theory without providing a definitive resolution to the debate. Al-Qaeda seems to epitomize the Islamic challenge to the West, yet many Muslims oppose this terrorist organization. The Bush Administration's prosecution of a war against terror, including the toppling of Saddam Hussein's regime in Iraq, seems to epitomize the Western side of Huntington's predictions. Yet many Islamic states support key aspects of this campaign that are vehemently opposed by a number of states in the West. It is unlikely that the 'clash of civilizations' debate will be resolved soon.

Further reading

Fox, J. (2001) 'Clash of Civilizations or Clash of Religions, Which is a More Important Determinant of Ethnic Conflict?' *Ethnicities* 1(3), 295–320.

Fox, J. (2003) 'State Failure and the Clash of Civilizations: An Examination of the Magnitude and Extent of Domestic Civilizational Conflict from 1950 to 1996' *Australian Journal of Political Science* 38(2), 195–215.

Henderson, Errol A.(1997) 'Culture or Contiguity: Ethnic Conflict, the Similarity of States, and the Onset of War, 1820–1989' *Journal of Conflict Resolution*, 41(5), 649–68.

Hunter, S. T. (1998) *The Future of Islam and the West: Clash of Civilizations or Peaceful Coexistence?*, Westport, CT: Praeger.

Huntington, S. (1993) 'The Clash of Civilizations?' *Foreign Affairs*, 72(3), 22–49.

Huntington, S. (1996a) *The Clash of Civilizations and the Remaking of the World Order*, New York: Simon and Schuster.

Huntington, S. (ed.) (1996b) *The Clash of Civilizations? The Debate*, New York: Norton.

Tipson, F. (1997) 'Culture Clash-ification: A Verse to Huntington's Curse', *Foreign Affairs* 76(2), 166–9.

Walt, S. N. (1997) 'Building Up New Bogeymen', *Foreign Policy* 106, 177–89.

See also: end of history; Islam; standard of civilization; zone of peace

JONATHAN FOX

CNN factor/effect

A term used to describe the possible influence of television news images on foreign policy. The term came into common usage in the early 1990s during crises in northern Iraq, Somalia and other areas (see **crisis**). Continual television news coverage of these crises, particularly by the Cable News Network (CNN), was said to have provoked humanitarian responses by global audiences and government officials. The CNN factor/effect, however, is a subject of debate. The rise of other global television news outlets, such as Fox and Al-Jazeera, has eroded the primacy of CNN. In addition, a direct relationship between foreign policy and television images has proved difficult to isolate. Yet the influence of 24 hour news television on public policy and social life seems impossible to deny.

CNN was founded in 1980 by American entrepreneur Ted Turner. The concept of 24-hour news coverage was then new to television. CNN had aspirations of being a global television network. Bureaux were opened around the world. International news was covered prominently. In 1991, with the onset of the first Persian Gulf War, CNN's experience with round the clock news and its experienced foreign bureaus left it well positioned for continuous **war** coverage. During the war, the network increased in reputation, ratings and influence.

The network followed up its war coverage with reporting on international humanitarian crises. For example, following the Gulf War, much of Iraq's Kurdish population fled to the north for fear of attack from Saddam Hussein's forces. Turkish officials did not allow the Kurds to cross over into Turkey. People were trapped on barren land in northern Iraq with little food, water or medical supplies. CNN reported regularly on the misery of the Kurds. In 1991, US Operation Provide Comfort brought humanitarian supplies to northern Iraq. Commentators questioned whether American officials were moved by televised images of the Kurds.

In 1992, the African state of Somalia was beset by clan violence and famine. Hundreds of thousands of people died or were in danger of death. Again, CNN and other networks brought images of starvation and suffering to television screens around the world. Also in late 1992, a US-led coalition landed in Somalia to bring aid and provide protection for relief workers. Questions again were raised over the relationship between television images and government actions.

In the aftermath of these international interventions, undertaken without traditional national interests at stake, such as military provocations, hostages, or business interests, the concept of the CNN factor/effect gained currency. Officials from the first Bush administration admitted that they were moved to action in Somalia by daily, graphic pictures of starving children.

Discussions of the CNN factor/effect received more urgency the following year when a group of Somalis captured and killed an American soldier, mutilated the body, and dragged it through city streets. Television cameras captured the scenes. Not long after, President Clinton announced that the United States would leave Somalia. Critics charged that America went into Somalia because of horrific television images and left Somalia because of horrific television images.

The CNN factor/effect seemed to place the news media near the center of foreign policy. Around the globe, from Haiti to Bosnia to Rwanda, diplomatic intervention appeared to follow televised pictures of chaos and strife. By broadcasting images of distress and suffering, CNN seemed to galvanize and mobilize public opinion and demand responses from officials. Leading figures from media and government circles publicly worried over the issue and questioned whether the news media should have such **power**.

It appeared that the CNN factor/effect had arrived at a pivotal historical moment. The end of the **cold war** created a vacuum in US foreign policy. Also, technological innovations, from satellites to cell phones to cable, allowed network television unparalleled reporting capacities from around the globe. The foreign policy vacuum and the new reach of media technology offered the possibility that the news media was setting an agenda for public policymakers.

Yet even as the CNN factor/effect entered media and political lexicons, the concept came under question. First, the prominence given to CNN by the term appeared too narrow. CNN alone could not galvanize public opinion or shape policy. The factor seemed really to be television and the totality of images shown by the three traditional networks, Fox, and local news affiliates as well as CNN.

Research began to suggest that the concept itself was a vast simplification of a dynamic, highly complex, symbiotic relationship among officials, the media and the public. Government officials remained very much in charge of foreign policy and critics charged that media coverage actually followed government directives and directions. Rather than the media setting agendas for the government, officials could be understood as using and manipulating the media. For example, in September 1993, one month before the body of the American solider was desecrated in Somalia, the Clinton administration had been discussing plans to withdraw from that country. Perhaps television coverage of the desecration aided administration plans to withdraw.

The CNN factor/effect was also complicated by the advocacy of international relief agencies and **human rights** organizations. These groups have become sophisticated at influencing foreign pol-

icy and manipulating the media. By attracting media attention to particular crises that might generate public and government support for their efforts, humanitarian agencies greatly complicated the concept of the CNN factor/effect.

Despite questions over a direct CNN factor/effect, there can be little doubt that continuous and immediate television news, particularly CNN, has indeed influenced public opinion, government policy and social life. For example, politicians and the news media once worked under a *daily* news cycle. That is, officials needed to provide responses to breaking events before the end of the day, in time for the morning papers and the evening news. With CNN and 24 hour news coverage, the pressure to respond to events is immediate and persistent.

Some researchers have suggested that the CNN factor/effect might be a periodic or occasional force that arises on subjects or countries in which administration officials do not have strongly held views or parochial interests. That is, in the absence of commitments or convictions by government figures, televised images may have more of an impact.

The CNN factor/effect also can be viewed in a wider perspective. Modern society is a '24/7 world' awash in communication and information. CNN can be understood as having laid the foundation for such an era with non-stop programming and the immediate news cycle. The CNN factor/effect thus has proved to be an important if not fully understood concept. Although direct connections between foreign policy and television images have proved difficult to isolate, the influence of 24-hour news television remains a provocative area of study in foreign policy, international communication and journalism.

Further reading

Baum, M. (2003) *Soft News Goes to War: Public Opinion and American Foreign Policy in the New Media Age*, Princeton, NJ: Princeton University Press.

Belknap, M. (2002) 'The CNN Effect: Strategic Enabler or Operational Risk?' *Parameters* 32: 100–14.

Flournoy D. and Stewart, R. (1997) *CNN: Making News in the Global Market*, Bedfordshire, UK: University of Luton Press.

Robinson, P. (2002) *The CNN Effect: The Myth of News, Foreign Policy and Intervention*, London: Routledge.

Volkmer, I. (1999) *News in the Global Sphere: A Study of CNN and Its Impact on Global Communications*, Bedfordshire, UK: University of Luton Press.

See also: cosmopolitanism; diplomacy; globalization

JACK LULE

Cold war

A term used to describe the period 1945–89. During this period the **international system** was defined by a bipolar struggle between a Western **alliance** led by the United States and an Eastern bloc dominated by the Soviet Union (see **bipolarity**). The competition between these two **superpower**s had ideological, economic, military, and nuclear dimensions. However, superpower rivalry never led to direct conflict between the two superpowers. Hence, it was a cold rather than a hot **war**.

The roots of the competition lay in the war years, when after the defeat of Hitler's Germany, both sides struggled for control of Europe. In particular, Stalin sought domination of the countries of East and Central Europe, most notably Poland and the eastern regions of Germany. The Soviet position was strong as after the end of hostilities in Europe in the spring of 1945, Soviet forces continued to occupy parts of East and Central Europe. Soviet policy was governed by the view that the victorious states should define the post-war settlement. In this spirit, in 1944 Stalin had signed a 'percentages agreement' with the British Prime Minister, Winston Churchill. This allowed for a clear division of influence throughout Europe. According to this agreement, Soviet security interests prevailed in countries such as Poland, Bulgaria, and Romania and western interests would dominate in states such as Greece. It is notable that the American President, Franklin Delano Roosevelt, was not a party to these negotiations. The American position was that Central European states should be free to choose their own political futures. Accordingly, at the Yalta Conference in February 1945, the Americans persuaded Stalin to agree to the Declaration on Liberated Europe, which envisaged free elections in East and Central Europe. Western leaders recognized however that this agreement would prove problematic. The continent was already divided by the disposition of military forces and there were few illusions that Stalin would permit democratic elections along western lines.

The ending of the war in the Pacific during the summer of 1945 with the dropping of American atomic bombs on Hiroshima and Nagasaki marked a new period of warfare. The spectacle of nuclear devastation in Japan heralded not just a novel age of military capabilities but also one of East–West confrontation. Stalin resented the fact that Soviet troops were not permitted to take part in the occupation of Japan. He also believed that the use of American atomic weaponry was a vivid warning, directly aimed at Moscow, of future American military superiority. Stalin immediately ordered a massive build up of the Soviet atomic program to achieve some form of nuclear equality with the United States. The nuclear **arms race** was thus born. Until Soviet scientists could achieve a nuclear capability for the Soviet Union, Stalin relied on massive conventional forces, especially in Europe, to counter US nuclear superiority (a preponderance which the Soviet Union was to prove reluctant to abandon). The Soviet search for the raw materials necessary for their nuclear program also necessitated access to uranium resources in both Germany and Czechoslovakia.

It is clear therefore that by the summer of 1945 an age of mutual suspicion had begun. Anxiety on the Soviet side was compounded by the death of Roosevelt in the spring of that year. The Soviet leadership had respected him and his replacement by Harry S. Truman did little to help American–Soviet relations in a difficult phase. The new President made no secret of his suspicion of both Soviet **communism** and the Stalinist agenda for Europe. Western fears of the spread of communism throughout the continent grew steadily from the summer of 1945, and by March 1946, Churchill described in a famous speech at Fulton that an 'iron curtain' now divided Europe. This division ran through the heart of Germany with both Berlin and the entire country subject to occupation between the USSR on the one hand and the western allies, France, Britain and the United States on the other. The subsequent announcement by the US President of the Truman Doctrine in March 1947 heralded a new age of American foreign policy. The Truman Doctrine outlined a strategy of **containment** to counter and halt perceived Soviet territorial and ideological ambitions. The architect of this strategy was George F. Kennan, a State Department official. Kennan believed that the USSR would seek to expand its influence unless the United

States acted decisively. Kennan's views, which were published in the journal *Foreign Affairs* under the pseudonym X, defined American policy for a number of decades.

Central to the success of the Truman doctrine was the US-sponsored program of Marshall Aid. This initiative rested on the American view that the economic recovery of Europe was essential not just for the protection of democracy but to the long term interests of the United States. The Truman Administration believed that America needed its own economic health to invest and trade abroad. This required the reinvigoration of trading partners and the creation of a system of **free trade** based on the ideas of liberal **capitalism**. American-style **liberal internationalism** equated free trade with robust democratic forms of government. Hence, democracy had to be safeguarded as far as possible in Western Europe to provide a new framework for economic integration with the United States.

Historians disagree as to whether economic or political interests defined US policy in Europe. It is perhaps best to see the United States as motivated by both kinds of interest. The US drive for European **integration** did of course contain elements of economic self-interest or even economic **imperialism**, but it should not be forgotten that West European governments were also keen for American economic and political leadership. This was in stark contrast to the growing Soviet control of the East, which involved not free association but political and military repression as a means of ensuring compliance. The British Government in particular was instrumental in setting up the architecture of arrangements and lobbied the Truman Administration intensively on the need for wholesale aid to Europe. These diplomatic initiatives found a sympathetic hearing in Washington. During late 1946 and early 1947, communist parties appeared to be gaining ground politically throughout Western Europe. US officials influenced by the British came to believe that states such as Greece as well as Britain and France were in danger of succumbing to communism. The plan to provide large scale aid to Europe was announced in June 1947. This became known as Marshall Aid after the Secretary of State George Marshall. The subsequent Paris Conference at which the British, the French, and Soviet representatives debated Marshall's proposals proved problematic. Although initially interested in aid and economic coordination, the Soviet Foreign Minister, Molotov, argued that the main American aim was to undermine Soviet control in the east. Specifically, Molotov believed that the Americans were attempting to lure Czechoslovakia into a western bloc. Stalin, after some prevarication, refused to accept the conditions attached to Marshall Aid and instructed the states of East and Central Europe to reject the initiative. This was a relief to US officials, as the Plan was never really designed to include the Soviet Union. The Marshall Plan, at least as far as Western policymakers were concerned, also enabled a satisfactory resolution of the German problem. Western officials feared that the economic plight of Germany was such that Communism would gain ground in the Western zones. The Marshall Plan allowed the western zones of Germany to be integrated economically into the West European economies. Thus, Germany was divided for a generation.

The Soviet response to Marshall Aid was a reinvigoration of confrontation with the United States. The Marshall Plan was hence a catalyst for a further intensification of the cold war. The Soviet response and the refusal to allow countries such as Czechoslovakia to participate meant that the continent was divided not just militarily but also by economic system. In 1949, the Soviet leadership established its own economic framework for the East through the creation of The Council for Mutual Economic Assistance (COMECON). This was designed to coordinate the economies of the east. The Soviet political response was the establishment of the Cominform (Communist Information Bureau) in 1947, which was designed to coordinate the activities and agendas of communist parties outside the Soviet Union. By the end of the 1940s both sides of the cold war preferred separation to cooperation.

To this extent, the hardening of the cold war arose out of a desire on both sides to maintain their own political structures. Therefore, the cold war was an ideological struggle between opposing political and economic systems. For the Soviet leadership, this was to prove problematic. The Soviet leadership in Moscow was never able to impose its politics uniformly throughout the East. Tito's Yugoslavia, for example, broke with Moscow and established a separate pattern of communist politics, a move that prompted a tightening of Soviet control over the remaining Eastern European parties and a wave of repression and show trials. Soviet rule was nevertheless repeatedly subject to resistance and sometimes rebellion, as in Hungary in 1956 and Czechoslovakia in 1968. In contrast, the creation and operation of the American-led bloc was predominantly voluntary. It may be argued that it is in this contrast that we can see why the American led alliance outlasted its communist counterpart.

The coercive nature of communism in the East was not in question and in part explains Western antipathy towards the Kremlin. It is however difficult to evaluate how far American fears of communism were based on a genuine threat of

Soviet expansionism or whether the articulation of such anxieties was a pretext for a vigorous foreign policy aimed at the construction of US **hegemony**. After the trauma of the attack on Pearl Harbor, the United States did fear surprise attacks. Moreover, perhaps it was logical to see the USSR as a threat to its national **security**, especially when the Soviet Union achieved the feat of developing nuclear missiles capable of hitting the American homeland. Nevertheless, this capability was reached only in the 1960s and a decade before there was already a deep seated fear of communism within America. This became apparent in the 1950s when the Truman Administration was itself prey to allegations, made most notably by the Republican Senator Joe McCarthy, that it had failed to adequately deal with domestic communist and 'fellow traveling' activity. The subsequent witch hunts of the 1950s in which a number of individuals were wrongly accused of communist sympathies and liaisons were indicative of the cultural politics of the cold war.

The cold war nearly turned hot in 1948 when the Soviet leadership not only sponsored a coup in Czechoslovakia but also ordered a military blockade of Berlin in a bid to push the Western military presence out of its zone of occupation. A determined Western response with a military airlift of food and supplies ensured that the Western position was maintained in the city but the German capital remained a focus for East–West confrontation. Later, in 1961, the Communist East German authorities ordered the construction of the Berlin Wall to halt people leaving the eastern zones and fleeing to the West.

In 1949, the cold war became somewhat institutionalized with the creation of the **North Atlantic Treaty Organization** (NATO), which heralded a permanent US military presence in Western Europe. The Soviet leadership did not respond with its own military alliance (the Warsaw Treaty Organization) until 1955. In 1949 the USSR finally exploded an atomic device announcing its entry into nuclear competition with the United States. This perception of communist success (the Soviet explosion had not been expected in the West) was further reinforced when the Chinese leader Mao Tse Tung succeeded in bringing mainland China under his control. For many in the West, this signaled a further escalation of competition between communism and capitalism. Although communism was regarded by many in the West as a monolithic entity, Mao and the Soviet leadership became rivals rather than partners with the Sino-Soviet split of the late 1950s.

During the 1950s, the cold war extended from Europe into Asia. At the end of World War Two, Korea was divided at the 38th parallel for occupation purposes between the United States and the USSR. During 1948, South Korea was established and in the summer of 1949, US troops withdrew from Korea. The subsequent Korean War of 1950–3 was waged between the north and the south of Korea. Both the USSR and China backed the North Korean leader, Kim IL Sung, while the United States acting on behalf of the newly formed **United Nations Organization** supported the government in Seoul. A United Nations Command was established under the American General Douglas MacArthur. By 1951, the Chinese had captured Seoul but the United States responded with a massive counter-offensive. The conflict only ended with the death of Stalin in March 1953. The subsequent Geneva Conference of 1953 failed to reach any agreement on Korean unification. The country remains divided. The legacy of the Korean War was crucial to the development of the wider cold war.

Both the USSR and the United States now saw the conflict in global terms and continued to wage wars through intermediaries in the developing world and the Middle East.

It is usual to see the years after Stalin's death and the Korean War as marked by a degree of stabilization in Soviet–American relations. Nikita Khrushchev, the man who emerged as Soviet leader, is generally depicted as seeking a period of peaceful co-existence and a moderation of the worst excesses of the Stalinist system. However, the Soviet launch of the world's first artificial satellite (*sputnik*) and the world's first ICBM (intercontinental ballistic missile) in 1957 fueled American suspicions of a Soviet desire to achieve nuclear superiority. Despite these apparent successes and Khrushchev's propaganda of strength, the Soviet leadership was actually under immense pressure. In reality, at this point in the cold war, the USSR lagged far behind the Americans in the production of nuclear weaponry. The Soviet leadership also faced a series of challenges not least from the Chinese nuclear program and the ambitions of Mao.

Mao made no secret of his disdain for Khrushchev and took great delight in promoting the Chinese model of **development** as more appropriate than the Soviet one. In addition to Chinese independence, Khrushchev was faced with an American strategy of 'roll back'. This was a concerted policy of attempting through organizations such as the CIA (Central Intelligence Agency) to subvert communist rule in Eastern Europe. However, any hopes harbored amongst opponents of communism that the United States might actually intervene to topple authoritarian regimes were misplaced. The Hungarian uprising of 1956 was brutally suppressed and dissent was driven underground. Needless to say, in the wake of such suppression, commu-

nist rule remained deeply problematic. The construction of the Berlin Wall in 1961 should be seen as a measure by the Soviet Union to confront the deepening crisis within the East. The integration of the Federal Republic of Germany into NATO and the successful creation of the European Economic Community particularly troubled Soviet leaders. The Berlin Wall symbolized the fact that the Soviet model of economic and political development was not, contrary to Soviet propaganda, a popular, robust or effective one.

What is again remarkable, perhaps because we now know the extent of the weakness of the Soviet economy and its leadership, is that many believed Soviet propaganda about its nuclear and economic strength. Indeed, during the later 1950s, the idea prevailed in the West that a 'missile gap' had opened to the Soviet advantage. An aging President Eisenhower was accused of having let the Soviet leadership take advantage of the United States and the Democrat John F. Kennedy was elected President, in part at least because his youthful dynamism promised a more effective response to the Soviet threat. The new Kennedy administration was soon tested by one of the most serious confrontations of the cold war, that of the Cuban Missile Crisis.

Fidel Castro, Cuba's revolutionary leader had aligned himself with Moscow and communism. In 1961, the Kennedy Administration launched an attempt to overthrow the Castro regime. The US inspired 'Bay of Pigs' invasion ended in disaster with the defeat of anti-Castro forces attempting a coup. In the autumn of 1962, in part to protect the country against another American-inspired invasion but also to try and break the American strategic advantage, the Soviet leadership attempted to place nuclear weapons in Cuba. This Caribbean **crisis** ended only when President Kennedy, using a naval blockade/quarantine around Cuba, forced the Soviet leadership to back down and remove the weaponry. This is generally thought to be the nearest that the world has come to an actual nuclear exchange. Kennedy was determined that nuclear weapons should not be placed in so a close vicinity to the United States. The Soviet withdrawal from Cuba severely damaged Khrushchev's standing in the Kremlin and within two years he was ousted (albeit bloodlessly) as leader. Kennedy himself remained resolute that the Soviet challenge had to be met militarily and politically, and oversaw the expansion of American military forces (particularly special forces) to deal with the threat of communism in the **Third World**.

The most notable expression of the American effort to confront the threat of communism occurred during the 1960s with the Vietnam War. The United States continued the French campaign in Indochina. Following the signing of the 1954 Geneva Accords, which had divided Vietnam along the 17th Parallel, the communists consolidated **power** in the north, under Ho Chi Minh and looked south to reunite the country. In Saigon, the Americans deposed the French-backed leader. His successor immediately embarked on an anti-communist campaign of the south and those communists who had remained in the south appealed to the north for support. These forces were known as the Vietcong. With the support of China and the Soviet Union, they waged war against Saigon.

Kennedy oversaw a massive increase in the US financial commitment to Vietnam. Kennedy was assassinated in 1963 and his successor Lyndon B. Johnson inherited a complex and difficult legacy in Vietnam. From 1964 onwards Johnson attempted to defeat the Viet Cong through a combination of counter-insurgency tactics and bombing. The first official US ground troops arrived in Vietnam in 1965. Within months, the US troop commitment escalated to 125,000. After years of bloody and controversial conflict, US forces eventually conceded defeat in the early 1970s, finally leaving the country in 1975. The military reputation of the United States was severely damaged in this conflict fought primarily in jungle terrain. Despite vast technological superiority, Northern Vietnamese guerilla forces inflicted a defeat on American counter-insurgency strategy. The loss of 58,000 American troops and the opposition of some parts of the American public led to the so-called 'Vietnam syndrome' in which successive American administrations remained reluctant to place military personnel into war zones.

Indeed, the US defeat in Vietnam and Soviet gains in nuclear technology meant that the second half of the 1970s appeared to see a new mood in international relations emerge. We term this period one of *détente*, meaning a relaxation of tensions. The Strategic Arms Limitations Treaty (SALT) was signed in 1972 amid what appeared to be a new mood of cooperation. Alongside the SALT accords, both sides also signed the ABM (Anti-Ballistic Missile) Treaty, which established a moratorium on the development of defensive nuclear weapons systems. This was an important step as both sides regarded the construction of such systems as deeply disturbing to the prevailing **regime** of nuclear **deterrence** or balance of terror. The doctrine of **Mutual assured destruction** (MAD) meant, at least in theory, that both sides had enough offensive nuclear systems to deter the other side from attacking by threatening massive retaliation against their centers of population.

Part of the US motivation for entering a *détente* with its rivals in Moscow was the military defeat in Vietnam. There were hopes during the early 1970s that Moscow and Beijing could help exert influence on the north to allow some form of settlement short of American military humiliation. On the Soviet side *détente* was fostered primarily by the need for economic cooperation with the United States and a reduction of its crippling arms expenditure. The Soviet economy was still failing to perform and the Soviet leadership under Brezhnev was aware of the need for domestic reform. The Brezhnev leadership was also aware that the United States under President Richard Nixon was seeking an opening to Beijing. In some sense, it may be argued that the cold war at this point became tri-polar.

Détente however failed to bring about a lasting shift in superpower competition. American suspicions of Soviet expansionism were confirmed in 1979 when the Soviet leadership ordered the invasion of Afghanistan in a bid to shore up communist control of this country on the Soviet southern border. The subsequent war became the Soviet leadership's own Vietnam or 'bleeding wound'. Soviet forces, unable to defeat the *Mujahidin*, eventually withdrew from the country in 1988. The war in Afghanistan proved to be damaging for the leadership in the Kremlin. Not only was there widespread international condemnation with the boycott of the 1980s Olympic games in Moscow, but the resulting economic **sanctions** further compounded the situation of weakness in the USSR. The tough stance adopted by the American Republican President Ronald Reagan further isolated the leadership in Moscow. The Kremlin also had to face a rising tide of opposition within Eastern and Central Europe to communist rule. For example in Poland the Solidarity trade union became a serious competitor for political power in 1981.

The period from 1980 until 1985 is known as the second cold war because of increasing tensions between East and West and because a significant escalation of the arms race followed the American announcement that it intended to create a sophisticated and expensive **ballistic missile defense** system, the Strategic Defense Initiative (SDI). By 1985, the economic situation within the USSR was so serious that a new Soviet leader, Mikhail Gorbachev, attempted to introduce major reforms both of the Soviet system and in the relationship with the United States. His domestic agenda envisaged sweeping political and economic changes. *Perestroika* (reconstruction), *glasnost* (openness) and 'New Political Thinking' regarding international relations and the European confrontation became the essential terms of the Gorbachev agenda.

Gorbachev enjoyed a positive relationship with Western leaders, Reagan among them. Not only did both leaders agree to abolish, at least in theory, all nuclear weaponry but also in 1987 the Intermediate Nuclear Forces (INF) Agreement was signed which eradicated a whole (but numerically small) class of nuclear weaponry. Further progress was made in December 1988 when the Soviet leadership, speaking at the **United Nations**, announced sweeping and asymmetric cuts in their conventional forces, thus reducing the historic military threat to Western Europe. The Red Army was to be cut by half a million men. Despite his popularity in the West, though, Gorbachev's stature within the USSR was always precarious. Not only did the Soviet leader have to confront the problems posed by the Chernobyl nuclear disaster of 1987 but also the horror of the Armenian earthquake of 1988. Gorbachev's attempts to reform the relationship between Russian and the non-Russian Republics proved controversial and one by one the Soviet Republics began to agitate for and eventually declare independence from centralized Soviet control. New Political Thinking entailed the weakening of the Soviet hold over Eastern Europe. A 'Sinatra Doctrine' was proclaimed, whereby bloc members would do it their way. This signal of Soviet non-intervention led to a series of leadership crises in bloc countries during 1989, culminating in the breaching of the Berlin Wall by an ecstatic German crowd. This symbolic act is regarded as ending the cold war. The USSR itself broke up within two years without provoking widespread instability. The break-up of the USSR was greeted by the new Bush Administration with a degree of triumph. As Bush declared in May 1989, **containment** had worked and 'freedom' had won the historic post-war struggle. Bush announced that the United States would now work to integrate a democratizing Russia into the community of nations. This was not easy. Although in 1990 Gorbachev won the Nobel Peace Prize, opposition to him mounted at home. In 1991, a coup against him failed but it signaled the end of Gorbachev's time in power.

The new Russian leadership under Boris Yeltsin attempted somewhat uncertainly to forge a path towards democracy but the East and Central European states declared themselves more suited to the politics of Western Europe and particularly the European Union than the politics of the new Russia. The death of the Soviet experiment was lamented by few and left the United States as the lone **superpower**.

Even now, the cold war remains controversial. The origins of the cold war and the responsibility for the division of Europe are still debated by historians. Much controversy centers around the role of Joseph Stalin, with what has been termed the traditionalist view

arguing that while the Soviet dictator was in power the cold war was pre-ordained. The Stalinist desire to control the states of Eastern and Central Europe made it inevitable that the United States had to defend democracy against the tyrannies of communism. Subsequently, Revisionist historians, such as William Appleman Williams (1959) have argued that the United States must bear the responsibility for the conflict. He argued that the United States was determined to find new economic markets in Europe and that it was actually Truman who divided the continent. Revisionists are critical of US foreign policy in general, depicting it as driven by a desire for the creation of an economic and military hegemony. The neo-Revisionist school, writing predominantly in the 1970s and associated with the historian John Lewis Gaddis (1997) attempted to find a middle path between these two interpretations and argued that the cold war, while arising from Stalinist policies, should also be understood as a unique historical period in which both sides but particularly the United States, attempted to get to grips with the new bipolar international system, nuclear weaponry and the disintegration of the European Empires. The cold war was an outcome intended by neither side but provoked by the USSR. In this version of history, the United States was a reluctant superpower.

All of these versions were, because of the nature of the USSR, constructed without access to Soviet or east and central European archives. They were therefore stories based almost wholly on western sources. More recently, with the ending of the communist period and the partial opening of Russian archives, historians and international relations scholars have again been attempting to make sense of the period after 1945. Not surprisingly scholarly opinion is still divided on how and why the cold war began and endured. We do now have access to some of the documents/stories on the communist side. We can begin to make some sense of the experiences of those peoples in east and central Europe who spent a generation under communism. Perhaps the most surprising aspect of the ending of the cold war is that it has been lamented in some quarters. With the passing of the era is the end of the 'long peace', a supposedly golden age of peace and prosperity in which major war was avoided. Maybe, but it might now be time to look at the neglected area of cold war studies, not least the experiences of those in the developing world caught in superpower confrontation. It is perhaps worth remembering that if the cold war structure of a world divided did indeed provide a 'long peace' for some; others paid a high price in terms of their **security** and liberty.

Further reading

Gaddis, J. L. (1997) *We Now Know: Rethinking Cold War History*, Oxford: Clarendon.

Kennedy-Pipe, C. (1988) *Russia and the World*, London: Edward Arnold.

Leffler, M. (1992) *A Preponderance of Power: National Security, the Truman Administration and the Cold War*, Stanford, CA: Stanford University Press.

Westad, O.A. (2000) *Reviewing the Cold War. Approaches, Interpretations, Theory*, London: Frank Cass.

Williams, W. A. (1959) *The Tragedy of American Diplomacy*, New York: Norton.

Young, J.W. and Kent, J. (2004) *International Relations since 1945: A Global History*, Oxford: Oxford University Press.

See also: arms race; bipolarity; communism; North Atlantic Treaty Organization

CAROLINE KENNEDY-PIPE

Collective security

The practice of forming overwhelming coalitions against aggressor states in response to formal, pre-existing obligations. The term is often applied to any **alliance** or **security regime**, but it is best understood as an *alternative* to competing alliances. Collective security schemes have a long history, but the first significant efforts to implement them came in the nineteenth and twentieth centuries, with the most famous being the **League of Nations**. After both the League and its successor, the **United Nations**, failed to block aggression, collective security fell out of fashion until the idea was revived in the 1990s.

Collective security promises an alternative to traditional alliances. Rather than aligning in advance, members of a collective security system are to wait until an aggressor appears, and then form an overwhelming coalition against it. The right to authorize war is generally vested in a collective body: in the nineteenth century, international conferences; in the twentieth, the League and the United Nations. The traditional notion of collective security entailed an international organization with a binding commitment to resist aggression. Some analysts argue, however, that collective security need not be automatic and universal. They consider the early nineteenth century Concert of Europe, which was limited to the **great powers** and entailed no binding commitment to keep the peace, a form of collective security (see **concert of powers**).

Collective security does not presuppose that states ignore the **balance of power**, but rather that they do not form opposing alliances before a conflict arises. Instead, they wait until one of their number poses a threat, and then unite to restrain it. Insofar as collective security promises an alternative to balancing coalitions, one might expect it to be capable of blocking a Napoleon or a Hitler. In fact, however, some of its advocates see it as working best in the *absence* of revisionist great powers. By creating the Security Council veto, the drafters of the United Nations Charter acknowledged that collective security would not be directed against the leading states. This renders it vulnerable to the charge that it works best when not needed. Yet a collective security regime might still play other useful roles: coordinating policy toward minor aggressors and civil wars; and reducing conflict among status quo powers by mitigating the **security dilemma**.

The debate over collective security revolves around two related questions. First, can it replace traditional alliances as a means of preventing aggression? Second, can states overcome their narrow interests and perspectives enough to act in common, particularly in the absence of a unifying threat? Advocates of collective security claim that cooperation is easier in the absence of competing alliances. Collective security confronts an aggressor with overwhelming force. Knowing that others will come to their aid, states have fewer incentives to launch pre-emptive attacks or worry about relative gains (see **relative/absolute gains**). Indeed, they must cooperate to be sure of others' assistance at a later date, and to have a say in the outcome of collective action. Having committed themselves to resist aggression, states are more likely to do so when the crunch comes.

Critics respond that states that are not directly threatened lack sufficient incentives to act. Some states have less of a stake in reversing aggression than do others; other states may pay higher costs in any effort to do so. They will prefer to tolerate aggression or to free ride off the efforts of other states to reverse it. Revi-

sionist states may think they can get away with aggression, while status quo powers can become complacent, and fail to balance promptly against aggressors. Thus the western powers failed to resist Italian and German expansion in the 1930s. The legalistic requirement to resist aggression no matter who commits it might also weaken coalition building against other states that are more threatening.

Critics also note the difficulty posed by states' diverging interests, values and perceptions. Even if they have the will to resist aggression, they may disagree over whom to blame for a **war**, or what to do about it. States may resist action against allies, or other countries for which they feel a particular sympathy or affinity. They will be chary of rescuing or cooperating with traditional enemies. And if collective action involves a rival's intervention in a sensitive region, they may find the cure worse than the disease. States may also disagree about whether an intervention will accomplish its aims. Thus Russia opposed the use of force against the Bosnian Serbs in the 1990s due to longstanding historical ties, the perception that the Serbs were being unfairly singled out for blame for the collapse of Yugoslavia, uneasiness about NATO intervention in Southeastern Europe, and doubts that bombing would work (see **North Atlantic Treaty Organization**).

In practice, collective security's record has been spotty. Proposals to create an international army have invariably fallen on deaf ears. When the great powers have been on good terms and shared common objectives, however, they have sometimes applied collective pressure on belligerents. Faced in the 1830s with the Belgian revolt against the Netherlands, the great powers coordinated their policies through much of the conflict, largely because all had strong reasons for wishing to avoid war among themselves. In the 1990s the United Nations imposed economic sanctions on Libya, Iraq, and the rump Yugoslavia. While states have generally been more willing to agree to economic pressure than the use of military force, in 1950 the Soviet delegate's temporary absence allowed the United Nations Security Council to authorize the use of force against North Korea. In 1991 a dramatic improvement in East–West relations enabled the Council to agree on driving Iraq out of Kuwait, and in 1994 it authorized intervention against Haiti's military leaders.

Even at its most successful, however, collective security has never gone beyond joint *authorization* of intervention. In both Korea and Iraq, a few powers led by the United States did the actual fighting. Often states have refused to agree to collective action. The League of Nations failed to repel Japan's invasion of Manchuria or Italy's attack on Abyssinia in the 1930s, East–West rivalries paralysed the Security Council during the **cold war**, and in 1994 the UN conspicuously failed to prevent **genocide** in Rwanda. Even when the Concert of Europe and NATO after the cold war did undertake multilateral interventions, it was sometimes over the objections of one or more great powers. The Western alliance bombed Yugoslavia in 1999 over both Chinese and Russian protests, and by the time Britain and the United States attacked Iraq in 2003, collective security seemed a quickly receding dream.

Further reading

Bennett, A. and Lepgold, J. (1993) 'Reinventing Collective Security after the Cold War and Gulf Conflict', *Political Science Quarterly* 108, 2: 213–37.

Betts, R. K. (1992) 'Systems for Peace or Causes of War? Collective Security, Arms Control, and the New Europe', *International Security* 17, 1: 5–43.

Claude, I. L., Jr. (1962) *Power and International Relations*, New York: Random House.

Downs, G. W. (ed) (1994) *Collective Security Beyond the Cold War*, Ann Arbor: University of Michigan Press.

Arnold Wolfers (1962) 'Collective Defense versus Collective Security,' in A. Wolfers, *Discord and Collaboration*, Baltimore: Johns Hopkins University Press, 181–204.

See also: common security; concert of powers; humanitarian intervention; League of Nations; peace enforcement; sanctions; United Nations.

MATTHEW RENDALL

Common Agricultural Policy (CAP)

A policy of **European Union** (EU) protection and support of farm production by regulating prices, holding these above market levels by purchasing surpluses, levying imports and subsidizing exports. Formally, the CAP embraces a comprehensive strategy of coordinated agricultural **development** of which price support is logically only one component. In practice the CAP has amounted to little more than price support. The EU has sought to protect farmers' livelihoods and to ensure high levels of agricultural production. This has been costly, in a typical year exhausting about half the total EU budget.

The CAP has not only been an important drain on EU finances. It has also been a central and paradoxical feature of the whole project of European **integration**. The CAP was both an early success of extensive Community policy coordination and a prominent example of its dysfunctional consequences and inability to evolve. The broad policy objectives embodied in the Treaty of Rome gave way to tough negotiations in the 1960s and an arrangement that suited the two most powerful members of the European Economic Community, France, and West Germany. What emerged was a system of producer support with little attention to industrial development or consumer protection. Three decades of reform efforts made little impression on the policy until the 1990s. Over the past decade, the planned eastward expansion of the EU and associated fears of a further escalation of costs, plus outside pressure from the **World Trade Organization** (WTO), have modified the CAP.

The failure of the CAP reflects unique features of agriculture as an industry, including farmers as an interest group, but also the limitations of any general explanation of regional **integration**. The dominant theoretical account in the early years of post-war European integration was known as neo-**functionalism**. Its chief proponent, Ernst B. Haas (1958) suggested that policy coordination in specific issue areas/functional domains tended to generate institutional 'spillover'. This would expand the scope of such policy coordination and generate genuine political integration across national boundaries.

The logic was two-fold. First, domains or sectors are inherently, that is, functionally integrated. An attempt to coordinate policy rationally in one sector leads to similar attempts in others because they will be indispensable to the fulfilment of the initial goal. Creation of a **free trade area**, for example, begins with the removal of direct barriers like import levies but quickly raises the issues of related policy areas that distort trade and create more indirect impediments. The CAP itself seemed to illustrate this logic. By stabilizing food prices the EU removed one crucial pressure on wages and thereby reduced the chances that

relatively low wages, and hence production costs, in one country would provide an effective barrier to imports from the others.

Second, policy coordination tends to create a community of policymakers and relevant interest groups whose roles are likely to be served by a continuation and expansion of the initiative. This, in particular, seems to be where neo-functional logic broke down in the case of the CAP. An alliance of vested interests consolidated the form of policy coordination as it emerged in the 1960s but also produced a powerful block against any further development or expansion of the policy. Consequently, the experience of the CAP seems to have contributed to the widespread rejection of neo-functionalism – not least by Haas himself – and the increasing popularity of models of integration (and potential disintegration) that conceive the process as driven by a combination of inter-state and intra-state bargaining.

Proper understanding of the history of the CAP must take into account the distinctiveness of agriculture not only as an economic activity but also as part of social, cultural and political life. Only then can we fully comprehend how and why agricultural interests shaped key states' policy-positions within the EU and stalled the process of reform. First, agriculture faces unique challenges as an industry. Most importantly, agricultural supply is peculiarly vulnerable to unexpected downturns, primarily because of the dependence of any crop on the vagaries of the weather, while total demand for food is relatively stable. This means that any change in supply resulting from a bounty or poor harvest will instigate large price fluctuations, either to coax reluctant purchasers or to satiate persistent demand. This problem is compounded by the inherent inertia and limited adaptability of agricultural production, which must be planned (in spite of all this uncertainty) sometimes years ahead. Farm incomes are consequently highly unstable. Furthermore, the long term stability of demand for food means that farmers' incomes, relatively speaking, are likely to fall, as general productivity and levels of affluence tend to rise. Absolute incomes are also likely to fall, given continued technological innovation in a context of stable demand. These peculiar economic challenges create huge uncertainty for investors, and generally discourage the choice of farming as a livelihood.

In addition, food production and its rural environment are in most societies considered to be a part of the national heritage, a part of the social and cultural fabric that must be preserved. Furthermore, food production is inherently sensitive politically. The experience of World War Two in particular suggested that lack of self-sufficiency in servicing this most vital of human needs could have the gravest consequences. The war had decimated European agriculture and dramatically increased dependence on imported food. There was therefore a widespread post-war consensus that agricultural production needed a major boost, at least in the short term. It is hardly surprising, then, that this was reflected in the CAP. What is more surprising is that the CAP persisted, essentially unchanged, long after it lost credibility as a rational and affordable policy. This is most directly attributable to the dependence of key political parties (that is, French center-right parties and German Christian Democrats) on small rural constituencies in two of the most powerful members of the Union.

The system of price support works essentially as follows. First, the Council of Ministers sets a target price for each commodity, which EU farmers are encouraged to pursue. If necessary, import levies are applied to prevent non-EU producers from undercutting this price. This suffices to maintain the target price unless the EU produces more than its own market can absorb. Consequently, if prices drop below a predetermined margin of the target level, EU agencies may then buy up produce at this 'intervention price'. With sustained periods of surplus production, this strategy resulted in the creation of huge surpluses held by these agencies, the notorious 'butter mountains' and 'milk lakes' of common market legend. In many cases such surpluses have subsequently been sold off for export at very low prices, bringing charges of 'dumping' from overseas producers.

Although the CAP remains in essence unchanged, some significant progress has been made in the 1990s to begin to separate farm support from production, by linking subsidies to areas of arable land, for example. Negotiations on reform continue under continued pressure from the WTO to reduce subsidies in both the United States and the EU. Ecologically friendly farming practices have also gained in salience among policymakers and, not least, the general public, as a criterion to which subsidies might reasonably be linked. As a whole, the reform process is driven by fears of rising costs in connection with EU expansion, pressure from the WTO to liberalize agricultural trade, and increasing environmental and health concerns regarding an industry and policy community that seems to have placed productivity above all other considerations.

Further reading

Acrill, R. (2000) *The Common Agricultural Policy*, Sheffield: Sheffield Academic Press.

Grant, W. (1997) *The Common Agricultural Policy*, New York: St. Martin's Press.

Haas, E.B. (1958) *The Uniting of Europe: Political, Social and Economical Forces 1950–1957*, London: Stevens.

Moravcsik, A. (1993) 'Preferences and Power in the European Community: A Liberal Intergovernmentalist Approach', *Journal of Common Market Studies* 31: 473–524.

Moyer, W. (2002) *Agricultural Policy Reform*, Aldershot: Ashgate.

See also: European Union; World Trade Organization

P. STUART ROBINSON

Common security

The idea of common **security** owes its popularity to the 1982 report of the Independent Commission on Disarmament and Security Issues, chaired by the late Swedish prime minister Olof Palme. The report set out six principles of common security: all nations have a legitimate right to security; military force is not a legitimate instrument for resolving disputes between nations; restraint is necessary in expressions of national policy; security cannot be attained through military superiority; reductions and qualitative limitations of armaments are necessary for common security; and 'linkages' between arms negotiations and political events should be avoided.

Thus articulated, common security was a fundamental challenge to the prevailing security doctrine in Europe based on nuclear **deterrence**. As the report put it, states cannot achieve security at each other's expense. Viewing security as a zero-sum phenomenon would aggravate the **security dilemma**, in which one state's defensive preparations is construed as being offensive by its rivals. Seeking unilateral security could result in inadvertent war. Hence, argued the report, common security must replace deterrence.

The idea of common security called for replacing deterrence and balancing strategies with reassurance measures including **confidence and security-building measures** (CSBMs), **arms control**, multilateral cooperation (see **multilateralism**) and the enhancement of the collective security functions of the **United Nations**.

The common security concept was institutionalized in Europe through the Conference on Security and Cooperation in Europe (later renamed the **Organization for Security and Cooperation in Europe**, or OSCE). During the 1970s and 1980s, the CSCE started implementing an extensive program of CSBMs that included both transparency and constraining measures and verification procedures. They included, among others, transparency in national defense expenditures, weapons acquisitions and military installations, withdrawal for forces from border areas, and the presence of observers from both sides at large military exercises. The goal of such measures was to reduce tensions between the **North Atlantic Treaty Organization** (NATO) and the former Warsaw Pact and reduce the fear of surprise attack.

Another feature of the CSCE framework was its linkage between domestic political practices and regional/international security. This was achieved through the inclusion of **human rights** issues into the regional confidence-building agenda. Henceforth, the CSCE norms would regulate the internal as well as external political behavior of states. This aspect of the CSCE also distinguished it from other regional groupings which avoided dealing with internal conflicts within their member states.

As the **cold war** came to an end, the success of the CSCE led to the call for similar approaches in other parts of the world, especially the Asia-Pacific region. The ball was set rolling by the then Soviet leader Mikhail Gorbachev who in a speech at Vladivostok in 1987 called for a Pacific Ocean conference alongside the Helsinki (CSCE) conference. The proposal was somewhat ahead of its time, given suspicions of the Soviet Union that still existed in the region. But in 1990, a Canadian proposal offered by External Affairs Minister Joe Clark envisaged a Pacific adaptation of the CSCE. The reference to the CSCE was to be dropped however, following protests from Asian officials and think tank circles who thought differences in political and strategic conditions made the CSCE model inapplicable to Asia. Whereas the CSCE instruments of common security seemed to fit a predominantly continental European strategic landscape, strategic issues in East Asia were primarily maritime in nature. Moreover, critics of the CSCE framework argued that unlike Europe, Asia remained home to a number of unresolved major regional conflicts, which made the task of confidence building so much harder.

As a consequence of these debates, Asia-Pacific security dialogues led to the reframing of common security into 'cooperative security'. The idea of cooperative security rests on three elements. First, security measures should seek to promote reassurance, rather than deterrence or the **balance of power**. Second, security should be pursued multilaterally, emphasizing the principle of inclusiveness. Third, cooperative security envisages a broad agenda of cooperation, encompassing military confidence building as well as political dialogue and other forms of functional cooperation (see **functionalism**). While common security stressed technical measures to reduce military tensions in Europe, cooperative security in the Asia Pacific context is seen as having a more comprehensive and mainly political agenda.

In Asia, the ASEAN Regional Forum (ARF), launched in 1994, represents the closest approximation to the cooperative security idea (see **Association of Southeast Asian Nations**). It has undertaken a program of confidence building measures, albeit on a far more modest scale than the OSCE. The ARF's measures, consisting mainly of voluntary statements on national defense postures and meetings among defense officials, are not intrusive; they do not include as yet constraining measures such as advance notification of military exercises and challenge inspections of national military facilities. Outside Europe and the Asia-Pacific regions, the **African Union** has also created a Conference on Security, Stability, Development and Cooperation in Africa (CSSDCA), which is based loosely on the CSCE model.

Further reading

Clements, K. (1989) 'Common Security in the Asia-Pacific: Problems and Prospects', *Alternatives* 14: 49–76.
Moller, B. (2002) *Common Security and Non-offensive Defence: A Neorealist Perspective*, London: Routledge.
Palme Commission (1982) *The Report of the Independent Commission on Disarmament and Security Issues under the Chairmanship of Olof Palme*, New York: Simon & Schuster.
Wiseman, G. (1992) *Non-Provocative Defence: Ideas and Practices in International Security*, London: Palgrave.

See also: European Common Security and Defense Policy; security; security community

AMITAV ACHARYA

Commonwealth

A voluntary association of independent **sovereign** states consulting and cooperating to promote international understanding, **sustainable development** and international peace. After the **United Nations**, the Commonwealth is the world's largest multilateral organization. It has members from every major region in the world. Its total population exceeds 1,500 million people, more than a quarter of the world's population.

Although the modern Commonwealth is just over 50 years old, the idea took root in the nineteenth century. In 1867, Canada became the first colony to be transformed into a self-governing Dominion, a newly constituted status that implied equality with Britain. The British **empire** was gradually changing. In 1884 a British politician, Lord Rosebury, described it as a 'Commonwealth of Nations'. The Dominion status was extended to Australia (1900), New Zealand (1907), South Africa (1910) and the Irish Free State (1921). They all participated as separate entities in the First World War and were separate signatories to the Treaty of Versailles in 1919. Subsequently, they became members of the **League of Nations**.

After the end of the First World War, the Dominions began seeking a new constitutional definition and a reshaping of their relationship with Britain. The Conferences of Dominions that began in 1887 were resumed and at the Imperial Conference in 1926, the prime ministers of the participating countries adopted the Balfour Report. The report defined the Dominions as autonomous communities within the British Empire, equal in status, in no way subordinate to one another in any aspect of their domestic or external affairs, though united by common allegiance to the Crown, and freely associated as members of the British Commonwealth of Nations. This definition was incorporated into British law in 1931 as the Statute of Westminster. It was adopted immediately in Canada, the Irish Free State, Newfound-

land (which joined Canada in 1949) and South Africa. Australia, and New Zealand soon followed. India, Britain's largest colony at the time, had still not achieved self-government and remained a Dominion under the India Act of 1935 until its independence in 1947. When India gained independence, the new state of Pakistan was simultaneously created, and a wave of **decolonization** followed which saw several colonies become independent and sovereign states.

The London Declaration of 1949 was a milestone on the road to developing the modern Commonwealth. India provided an interesting test case. It wanted to become a republic and to remain a member of the Commonwealth. Would Commonwealth membership only be for countries 'owing an allegiance to the Crown' as the Balfour Report had stated? A conference of Commonwealth Prime Ministers in 1949 decided to revise this criterion and to accept and recognize India's continued membership as a republic, paving the way for other newly independent countries to join the Commonwealth. At the same time, the word 'British' was dropped from the association's title to reflect the Commonwealth's changing character.

The first member to be ruled by an African majority was Ghana which joined in 1957. From 1960 onwards, new members from Africa, the Caribbean, the Mediterranean and the Pacific joined, increasing the diversity and variety that has enhanced the Commonwealth to this day. With its commitment to racial equality and national sovereignty, joining the Commonwealth became a natural choice for many new nations that were emerging out of the decolonization process of the 1950s and 1960s. Since then, the Commonwealth has grown in size and shape, expanding its reach and range of priorities. It is now involved in a wide spectrum of activities, all feeding the greater goals of **good governance**, respect for **human rights**, and international peace.

In 1965, the leaders of the Commonwealth established the Commonwealth Secretariat in London, which became the association's independent civil service, headed by a Secretary-General. A year later, the Commonwealth Foundation was launched to assist the growing number of Commonwealth professional associations and, subsequently, non-governmental Organizations (NGOs).

Two significant events in the history of the Commonwealth occurred in 1971. The first was the Singapore Declaration of Commonwealth Principles which gave the association a formal code of ethics and committed members to improving human rights and seeking racial and economic justice. The second was the creation of the Commonwealth Fund for Technical Cooperation (CFTC), which advanced the idea of technical cooperation among developing countries.

The Commonwealth's structure is based largely on unwritten and traditional procedures and not on a formal charter or constitution. It is guided, however, by a series of agreements on its principles and aims. These are Declarations or Statements that have been issued by Commonwealth Heads of Government at various summits. Together, they constitute a foundation of Commonwealth values and a history of concern in global affairs. The most significant of these are the Singapore Declaration of Commonwealth Principles (1971) and the Harare Commonwealth Declaration (1991), which set out the Commonwealth's commitment to democracy, the rule of law, economic development and good governance.

Further reading

Carter, G. M. (1971) *The British Commonwealth and International Security*, Westport, CO: Greenwood.

Grierson, E. (1972) *The Imperial Dream: The British Commonwealth 1775–1969*, London: Collins.

Lavin, D. (1995) *From Empire to Commonwealth*, Oxford: Oxford University Press.

Somerville, C. (1998) *Our War: How the British Commonwealth Fought the Second World War*, London: Trafalgar Press.

See also: decolonization; empire

MARTIN GRIFFITHS

Commonwealth of Independent States (CIS)

A loose confederation of most of the former constituent republics of the USSR. This ostensibly supra-national body arose from the ruins of the Soviet Union as it collapsed in 1991. By that stage it had become clear that a number of the constituent republics of the USSR were determined to achieve their independence. The abortive coup in August 1991 simply accelerated the process, and added the largest republic, Russia, to those pushing for independence. The formation of the CIS was an attempt to forestall an uncontrollable collapse in the former Soviet republics and the economic ties between them, and to assert that even outside the Soviet Union they had something in common. It has not been successful in either area.

A number of the Soviet constituent republics had long-standing historical aspirations to independence. Among these were Georgia (which had briefly had an independent government after the 1917 **revolution**), Ukraine (likewise) and the Baltic states of Latvia, Lithuania and Estonia (which had been forcibly annexed into the Soviet Union only in

1940). These traditions were encouraged by the limited decentralization of the Soviet economy which was an essential element of the Gorbachev reform program in the late Soviet period. Under Gorbachev, the republics were ceded a certain amount of economic autonomy, contributing to the renewal of **nationalism** in the republics. In addition, the more economically successful regions (mainly the Baltic states, but later Russia itself) began to ask why they should be subsidizing areas that were struggling (the Caucasus and the Central Asian Republics). As with many other aspects of the Gorbachev reforms, decentralization and the rise of nationalism rapidly achieved a momentum of its own, out of the control of the Moscow leadership.

The first mass rally for independence was held in Lithuania in July 1988. Even the Communist Party (CP) in Lithuania endorsed 'economic **sovereignty**' for the republic. The Popular Front, formed to pursue independence, dominated the elections in March 1989 and the following December the Lithuanian legislature voted to remove the CP's monopoly on **power**. In March 1990, Lithuania declared its independence. Moscow's decision to cut off fuel and other supplies forced the Lithuanians to postpone this decision. However, despite further violence in Vilnius and Riga, all three Baltic republics remained committed to independence.

In 1989 the nationalist movement in Georgia had a mass following, especially among the youth. In early April, after several days of pro-independence demonstrations, Soviet troops turned on the demonstrators with a show of force that left nineteen people dead (many from poison gas) and several hundred people injured. This action spurred on the nationalists and helped to secure the election of a nationalist as President of the republic in 1990.

In Russia itself, some two weeks after the election of Boris Yeltsin as President in 1990, the legislature declared that its laws took precedence over those of the Soviet Union. The Baltic states and Georgia had already declared their sovereignty in this way in the first half of the year. Uzbekistan, Moldova, Ukraine, Belarus, Turkmenistan, Tajikistan, and Kazakhstan followed Russia in declarating the supremacy of their laws between June and October.

Gorbachev attempted to forestall the avalanche in two ways. One, he held a referendum in March 1991 asking '[d]o you believe it essential to preserve the USSR as a renewed federation of equal sovereign republics in which the rights and freedoms of a person of any nationality will be fully guaranteed?' The Baltic states, Armenia, Georgia, and Moldova refused to hold the referendum. But in the republics where it was held, it achieved an affirmative vote of at least 70 per cent. Two, he began negotiations (with those republican leaders who would negotiate) for a new Union treaty. It was this treaty, scheduled to be signed on 20 August 1991, that the coup was largely designed to prevent. The coup, and its defeat by the republican leaders (notably Yeltsin), effectively sealed the fate of the new treaty, the Soviet Union and Gorbachev himself.

The Presidents of Russia, Ukraine, and Belarus met near the Belarus capital of Minsk on 8 December 1991 and declared that the Soviet Union no longer existed. The three Presidents formed the Commonwealth of Independent States. They declared that the CIS would have coordinating bodies for foreign affairs, defense and the economy, all of which would be based in Minsk, to prevent any suggestion of Russian domination. There would be, they said, a 'common economic space' and the rouble would function as a common currency. There would be unified control over former Soviet nuclear weapons. And there would be coordinated economic reforms leading to a market economy. The CIS was open to all former Soviet republics (and, it was even suggested, to other nations as well).

At a further meeting in Alma Ata on 21 December 1991, eight more republics joined the new body: Azerbaijan, Armenia, Kazakhstan, Kyrgyzstan, Moldova, Tajikistan, Turkmenistan, and Uzbekistan. This meant that the CIS now consisted of all of the former Soviet republics with the exception of the Baltic states and Georgia (which joined in December 1993). Gorbachev resigned his position as President of the Soviet Union on 25 December 1991. Soviet nuclear codes and the Soviet seat in the **United Nations** were transferred to Russia. A few days later the CIS leaders met again in Minsk. As governing bodies, they set up the Council of Heads of State and the Council of Heads of Government.

As a functioning confederation, the CIS has not been remarkably successful. In the political, economic and military affairs of its constituents it has made little impact. Given the political system from which they emerged, and the tortuous political process that marked their emergence, it was hardly likely that the former Soviet republics would be willing to cede any political power upwards to the CIS. On the contrary, all of them have been fiercely concerned with maintaining their independence and preventing any reassertion of Russian power. The one exception might be Belarus which, under its authoritarian and eccentric President, has sought unification with Russia. This appears to have been motivated partly by Slavic solidarity, partly by nostalgia for the USSR, and largely as a diversion from Belarus' internal problems. Russia, however, mindful of those problems and of Western condemnation of undemocratic practices in Belarus, has thus far kept the Belarussians at arm's length.

Economically, although talk of an economic union within the CIS continues, the results have not been impressive. Initially, the Russian economy dominated the CIS. When Russia liberalized prices (apart from basic food and fuels) in January 1992, many of the other CIS members were forced to follow. The rouble, however, has never taken off as a common currency. With each republic trying to make its own way in the world market – and for practical purposes, this meant attracting as much foreign investment as possible – the space for cooperation between equally poor economies was distinctly limited.

After a rocky start, there has been some military coordination. Despite Yeltsin's initial hope that CIS members would endorse a unified military command under (the Russian) Marshal Shaposhnikov, such a command has never functioned except on paper. The CIS members seem well aware that the fundamental indication of an independent **nation-state** is an independent army. Russia and Ukraine argued over who owned the Black Sea fleet, established by the Soviet Union, stationed in Ukraine. In April 1992 they agreed to divide it. More recently the CIS has dispatched **peace-keeping** forces to the Abkhazia region of Georgia and to Tajikistan. Its members have also signed a number of agreements to prosecute the war on **terrorism**, with the ever present danger of Islamic separatism firmly in their sights.

Further reading

Bremner, I. and Taras, R. (eds) (1993) *Nations and Politics in the Soviet Successor States*, Cambridge: Cambridge University Press.

Brown, A. (1997) *The Gorbachev Factor,* Oxford: Oxford University Press.

Roxburgh, A. (1991) *The Second Russian Revolution,* London: BBC Books.

Suny, R.G. (1993) *The Revenge of the Past: Nationalism, Revolution and the Collapse of the Soviet Union,* Stanford: Stanford University Press.

See also: cold war; integration; regionalism

DAVID LOCKWOOD

Communism

This term refers to two distinct phenomena. As a vision of the future after **capitalism**, it was originally conjured up by utopians, levellers and socialists in the eighteenth century and then taken up and grounded in the realities of capitalist **development** by Karl Marx (1818–83) and Frederick Engels (1820–95). It also was (and is) a term applied to regimes and societies modelling themselves on the Bolshevik revolution of 1917. In both these meanings, confusion often arises over the relationship between communism and **socialism**.

For Marx and Engels, and for most of the pre-1917 classical **Marxists**, communism was a description of the future. Socialism (and more specifically 'scientific' socialism) was the body of political thought adhered to by those who wanted to bring that future society into being. This was not however a rigid distinction. Marx and Engels' most famous tract, *The Manifesto of the Communist Party* (1848) was an exposition of scientific socialist thought rather than a description of the future communist society. Indeed, the classical Marxists were extremely averse to such descriptions since for them (unlike the utopians) communism was not a feat of the imagination, but an inevitable development out of capitalist society. The future would be based not on the capacity for mental creativity but on material reality.

That future was described as communism. As set out in *The Manifesto,* it would be brought about by the elevation of the working class (which, due to the capitalist development of industry would constitute a majority of the population) to the position of a ruling class. In this capacity it would, by degrees, confiscate capital from the bourgeoisie, making inroads on the rights of bourgeois private property. As a result of these measures, it could be expected that class divisions would disappear. Human need would be the basis of society, rather than profit. Democracy would spread from the purely political sphere to the economic and into all other aspects of society. The division of labour would be abolished. The state itself would pass away since its class orientation and its repressive aspects would become unnecessary. Labour would become both universal and universally desired. And since communism was based on the solidarity of labour, the division of the world into competing **nation-state**s would cease.

Importantly, the classical Marxists understood that all of this could come to pass only on the foundations of a mature and advanced capitalist economy. Only such an economy (once cleansed of its inherently exploitative features) could provide the material abundance that was necessary for communism. For this reason, they conceded that a communist society would not burst into full bloom immediately after a successful proletarian **revolution**. Marx identified a first phase of communist society, which would still be marked by the old society from which it had emerged. This phase would operate according to the distributional principle of 'to each according to his work'. But in the higher phase, when all the features noted above were fully operational, distribution of the social product would take place on the basis of the principle 'to each according to his needs'.

The pre-1917 Marxists believed that the first phase would be relatively short (and was certainly not deserving of its own label). This was because they regarded the industrialized economies of Europe as developed enough to supercede capitalism, and they were confident that this was where anti-capitalist revolutions would occur. The Bolshevik revolution of 1917 changed these definitions dramatically. The Bolsheviks insisted that they had successfully carried out a workers' revolution in Russia, and that this revolution could inaugurate a post-capitalist society, provided, they added (but not all the time) that it was followed by revolutions in Europe. Russia in 1917 was not the kind of advanced capitalist economy that the classical Marxists believed to be necessary for communism. In fact, large parts of it (the basic agrarian economy) were hardly capitalist at all. The working class was a social minority and the Bolsheviks, after 1917, were rapidly becoming a minority of that class. Once it was conceded that such a society could push past capitalism – and, in the absence of a European revolution, the Bolsheviks tended to assert this more and more – classical Marxism had to be jettisoned.

The dilemma for the Bolsheviks (now Communists) was that, according to Marx, while a successful workers' revolution was supposed to produce communism the features of communism (abundance, an end to the division of labour, the withering away of the state) refused to appear. The remaining classical Marxists (for example, Karl Kautsky in Germany, the Mensheviks in Russia) pointed out that since Russia had not been ready, in a material sense, to go beyond capitalism, it would continue to reproduce the elements of capitalist society.

The Communists, however, had another solution to the problem. As the period of the new economic policy (NEP – a limited reintroduction of the market into the economy) came to a close in the mid- to late 1920s, they increasingly redefined the phase of social development which the Soviet Union was undergoing. Abandoning the term 'communism' as a description of post-capitalist society, socialism became the first stage of post-capitalism, a stage that preceded communism proper. On the one hand, this enabled the regime to attach the satisfying 'socialist' label to its deeds and institutions (socialist labour, the Union of Soviet Socialist Republics, etc.). On the other hand, it provided a handy explanation as to why the benefits of communism were a long way off.

On occasion however, the old utopianism burst through. Stalin, for example, repeatedly claimed that the Soviet Union had achieved socialism by the mid-1930s, and this claim was duly entered into the new Soviet Constitution of 1936. Stalin however was in a position to throw Marxist logic completely to the wind and simply assert that, despite this achievement, class antagonisms were intensifying and that therefore the state and its security organs had to be continually strengthened. Khrushchev told the twenty-second Party Congress in 1961 that socialism had been firmly established and that the Soviet Union was now engaged in the full-scale construction of communism, which, he remarked on another occasion, should be achieved by 1980. His successors scrapped this optimistic timetable and declared that the construction of communism was not under way; the country was in fact in a new phase called 'developed socialism'. This was assumed to be somewhat better than the socialism they had before, but still left the one-party state and its security apparatus (not to mention the shortages, queues, shoddy goods and alienating jobs) intact.

The Chinese experience was similar. Under Soviet guidance, the regime that followed the Chinese Communist Party (CCP) victory in 1949 regarded itself as neither socialist nor communist, but as a 'new democracy' or a 'people's republic'. Much the same could be said of the regimes in Eastern Europe after 1945, which were classified as 'people's democracies'. But as the Chinese moved out of the Soviet orbit, and as Mao and his supporters became increasingly convinced of the miracles that could be performed by sheer human will, utopian claims of communism emerged. Socialism, said the CCP, had in fact been achieved by 1958 and all that was needed was an economic Great Leap Forward (inaugurated in the same year) to propel China into communism. The Great Leap ended in economic and social disaster. This did not prevent the process from being repeated, this time at the political level (an attempt to get rid of those in authority considered to be obstacles to the Maoist strategy), in the 'Great Proletarian Cultural Revolution' a little under ten years later.

Mao Zedong died in 1976. Talk of communism in China had ceased some years before, but the new leaders (grouped around Deng Xiaoping) wound the developmental cycle back somewhat further in conjunction with the economic reforms that were introduced from 1978. China, they said, was in fact in 'the primary stage of socialism'. This would last until about the year 2050. To many, both inside and outside China, this stage seems increasingly to resemble capitalism. How many more stages would follow was uncertain. But what was clear was that the communism of Marx had been consigned to a distant, and a distinctly uncertain future.

Further reading

Engels, F. (1970) 'Socialism: Utopian and Scientific' in K. Marx and F. Engels, *Selected Works*, Moscow: Progress Publishers, 375–428.

MacKenzie, D. and Curran, M. W. (1997) *Russia and the USSR in the Twentieth Century*, London: Thomson.

Marx, K. and Engels, F. (1970) 'Manifesto of the Communist Party' in K. Marx and F. Engels, *Selected Works*, 31–95, Moscow: Progress Publishers.

Meisner, M. (1999) *Mao's China and After*, New York: Free Press.

Outhwaite, W. and Ray, L. (2004) *Social Theory: Communism and Beyond*, Oxford: Blackwell.

Rozman, G. (1987) *The Chinese Debate about Soviet Socialism, 1978–1985*, Princeton, NJ: Princeton University Press.

See also: capitalism; cold war; Marxism; socialism

DAVID LOCKWOOD

Communitarianism

A political, philosophical and ethical position that stresses the communal origins of moral codes and individual identity. Although communitarianism is often seen as a reaction to liberal individualist accounts of justice especially the work of John Rawls (1921–2004), its origins can be traced back to the German Romantic tradition and the political philosopher G. W. F Hegel (1770–1831). In international relations it has come to denote certain nationalist and anti-cosmopolitan approaches to global distributive justice and international ethics and is often spoken of in terms of a cosmopolitan/ communitarian divide.

Communitarians argue that liberalism misrepresents its own status as an account of political life. Rather than constituting an impartial account of political life, liberalism in fact represented a very particular kind of approach to politics and individuality. Liberalism actually rests on a fairly thick historical culture of shared values such as individuality, autonomy and a public/private distinction. Liberalism also uses a substantive conception of individuality and reason to build its account of justice. Communitarians argue that this conception is more problematic and more culturally specific than many liberals recognize and therefore the liberal theory of justice is not as impartial as it is sometimes claimed. Furthermore liberalism rests on other values that stem from belonging to a particular community, such as nationalism and a sense of the public or civic duty towards members of one's own community. Liberalism therefore is not so much an impartial framework that describes something essentially true and objective about how politics is conducted but is itself a thick cultural artefact. Rather than mediating between different conceptions of the good from a position of right, liberalism contains and is derived from very historically and culturally specific conceptions of the good life.

When these terms are transferred to the field of international relations (IR) they take on a different flavour. The original debates addressed the nature and source of political conceptions of the good and the social construction of individual identity as well as the nature of our knowledge of these values. An essential division existed between those who saw moral knowledge as derived from universal processes of reason and those who argued that all such knowledge stems from languages and meanings generated within specific cultures. Communitarianism is related to **hermeneutics** in this aspect.

In the realm of IR this translated into a concern with the moral significance of national and cultural boundaries. Liberalism is associated with **cosmopolitanism**, and communitarianism with **nationalism** or the idea of a pluralist (see **pluralism**) **international society**. Liberal cosmopolitans argue that there are no morally significant boundaries dividing the human species while communitarians identify the **nation-state** as the primary focus of moral obligation and the primary limit to the expansion of moral community. Beyond the nation-state, authors such as Walzer (1996) claim that we have only minimal moral obligations because we have only a minimal community. There exists a fundamental difference between the 'thick' values and culture available to us as members of a nation and the 'thin' values we may share with those outside. This difference limits our capacity to identify with and work towards more substantive global institutions or values, such as democracy or liberalism. Furthermore, communitarians have identified the lack of a single global moral culture as the major obstacle to the achievement of global justice.

In this context communitarians argue that cosmopolitanism champions universal justice and membership of the human community at the expense of cultural diversity and membership of particular communities. Communitarianism sees any attempt to develop universal moral vocabularies as necessarily destructive of the particular communities in which people actually exist. One example of this can be seen in the so called '**Asian values**' debate. The protagonists in this debate sought to question the universality of Western conceptions of **human rights**.

Overall the communitarian position implies an endorsement of the idea that we have limited moral obligations beyond the boundaries of our national communities. It is not always clear whether this is a result of the practical difficulties arising from incompatible versions of justice or whether it stems from a normative commitment to the preservation of cultural difference.

Communitarianism has also been associated with pluralist accounts of **international society** (see **pluralism**). If all moral values are the product of what Walzer calls 'thick' cultures and the world exhibits a variety of incompatible cultures then it is necessary to come to some agreement about how to coexist in the absence of deeper agreement about common purpose. The rules of international society, including the rules of **just war**, **sovereignty** and non-intervention play this role.

Communitarianism and cosmopolitanism are commonly represented as opposing perspectives. However there is reason to think that the dichotomy has been overstated. In the first instance there are very few cosmopolitans who are in principle hostile to cultural differences, and there are very few communitarians who reject universalism entirely. Therefore these two perspectives can more usefully be viewed as existing at different points along a spectrum. At one end is a global universal morality with a single thin homogeneous culture, at the other end is an relativist world of many thick separate communities, not unlike that depicted by realists (see **realism**). Few contemporary exponents of either cosmopolitanism or communitarianism exist at the far ends of this spectrum.

Certain cosmopolitan or universal elements are present in the argument of many communitarians. For example, Michael Walzer (1996) and Mervyn Frost (1996) acknowledge that human rights provide something of a minimum standard that all states should meet. Moreover, outsiders have a responsibility to intervene to prevent crimes such as **genocide**. Furthermore the defence of cultural difference is itself couched in universal terms; that it is good for all people to belong to a community. It is possible to argue that such a recognition renders the communitarianism position incoherent unless it is able to provide sufficient justification for this normative argument.

Despite their differences, it could be argued that both cosmopolitanism and communitarianism share a fundamental commitment to the value of human equality. What really distinguishes the two perspectives is their interpretation of the meaning of equality, and how it is expressed politically and morally. Cosmopolitans argue that equality can only be achieved in a world **order** based on universal principles which apply to individuals, while communitarians identify the state and the society of states as its appropriate embodiment. If this is the case then the challenge for communitarianism is to identify why the development of a globally 'thick' cosmopolitan community is undesirable, and the challenge for cosmopolitans is to incorporate the recognition of cultural difference into their account of universality.

Further reading

Brown, C. (1992) *International Relations Theory: New Normative Approaches*, New York: Columbia University Press.

Frost, M. (1996) *Ethics and International Relations,* Cambridge: Cambridge University Press.

Mulhall, S. and Swift, A. (1992) *Liberals and Communitarians*, Oxford: Blackwell.

Sandel, M. (1982) *Liberalism and the Limits of Justice*, Cambridge: Cambridge University Press.

Walzer, M. (1996) *Thick and Thin: Moral Argument at Home and Abroad*, Notre Dame: University of Notre Dame Press.

See also: Asian values; cosmopolitanism; foundationalism/anti-foundationalism; pluralism; solidarism

RICHARD SHAPCOTT

Concert of powers

A structured system of cooperation among the **great powers**, in contrast to systems of opposing **alliance**s that have characterized most of modern history. Such concerts generally follow major **war**s that overturn the existing **balance of power**, and during which the leaders of the winning coalition actively coordinate their foreign policies to achieve shared goals. The most famous and durable concert followed the Napoleonic Wars; great power concerts also formed briefly after World War One and World War Two. Some observers believed that a new concert would be formed after the end of the **cold war**, but it failed to materialize.

Great power concerts tend to form at the end of long and devastating wars that draw in all the major powers of the system, and in which one great power suffers a clear defeat. Wartime solidarity within the winning coalition may survive into peacetime, as does the task of dealing with the defeated enemy. Having won the war and dictated the peace, the victors also have a stake in the new status quo. The war's losers, in turn, are either helpless or, once they are rehabilitated as members of good standing in international society, allowed to join the concert. All great powers know the horrors of war firsthand, a further incentive for cooperation and restraint.

Under such circumstances great powers may make a conscious effort to harmonize their policies by establishing rules for cooperation, and through international conferences. For example the victors of World War One cooperated to establish a new system of international relations based on the **League of Nations**. This concert foundered, however, as the United States withdrew into isolationism, and other powers rose that wished to overturn the 1919 Versailles settlement that brought the War to an end. The post-World War Two concert dissolved still more quickly as cooperation between the United States and the USSR was replaced by the cold war.

The Concert of Europe that formed in 1815 proved more durable. Not only did the great powers remain at peace for forty years, but their leaders also met at international congresses to coordinate policy in person. Unfortunately, from the 1830s onward a growing divide opened up between Britain, France, and the conservative eastern courts, culminating in the Crimean War. Nevertheless, balancing alliances did not re-emerge until the second half of the nineteenth century. Moreover, the great powers referred many disputes to international conferences, leading some analysts to argue that the Concert survived all the way to the outbreak of World War One.

In contrast to the brief concerts that followed World Wars One and Two, the Concert of Europe endured because all the major powers were reasonably content with the territorial status quo. Britain lacked territorial ambitions in Europe, while Austria and Prussia had neither the desire nor the power to expand. Russia, potentially the most dangerous aggressor, concluded that it had reached its limits both in Europe and in the Near East. France did not suffer under overly harsh peace terms, and its restored monarchy was conservative and pacific. All the monarchs of Europe also shared a common fear and antipathy to **revolution**.

Did the Concert of Europe merely reflect the great powers' territorial contentment, or did it also *cause* cooperation? Some early twentieth-century scholars saw the Concert as an attempt at international federation. In contrast, Henry Kissinger (1957) attributed the long peace to the moderation of the Vienna settlement, the balance of power that it created, and inspired statecraft rather than international organization or conference **diplomacy**.

In the 1970s and 1980s a new wave of studies appeared on the Concert of Europe, portraying it as a set of norms and rules that actively promoted cooperation. According to Paul Schroeder (1994), the bloody wars of the Revolutionary and Napoleonic eras taught European leaders the need to cooperate. The concert they established prescribed respect for other states' vital interests and mandated joint resolution of key international problems. Drawing on neo-liberal institutionalist theory, Robert Jervis (1985) described the Concert as an early **security regime** based on **reciprocity**. Conference diplomacy, Jervis argued, reduced secrecy and fears of betrayal. European leaders exercised restraint in the expectation that others would show restraint toward them.

Recent analyses, influenced by the rise of **constructivism**, go beyond neo-liberal institutionalism to emphasize the role of **discourse** and changes in collective identity in promoting cooperation. Sceptics have responded, arguing that the great powers' cooperation and restraint during the Vienna era has been greatly exaggerated, and in any case reflected the realities of **power** politics. They note that the great powers repeatedly intervened over the objections of others, formed temporary coalitions, and continued to balance against each other. Increasingly, theories and debates about the Concert of Europe mirror those within international relations as a whole.

With the end of the cold war some observers thought that a new concert would be established. As at the end of other great wars, one side's military and political collapse raised the hope of transcending balance of power politics. The revitalization of the **United Nations**, made possible by Soviet cooperation, and the broad coalition that formed against Iraq's invasion of Kuwait seemed to bear out US President George H. W. Bush's talk of a 'new world order'.

As in the past, however, divisions soon appeared among the great powers. Disagreements over how to handle the **crisis** in Yugoslavia ended in 1995 with the **North Atlantic Treaty Organization** (NATO) bombing the Bosnian Serbs over Russian protests. Four years later, faced with Russian and Chinese opposition, the alliance intervened against Serbia without United Nations authorization. In the spring of 2003 the United States and Britain attacked Iraq despite the objections of the other three permanent members of the Security Council. While the world has not returned to a balance of power system, concerted action by the great powers to sustain international order has yet to be achieved.

Further reading

Jervis, R. (1985) 'From Balance to Concert: A Study of International Security Cooperation', *World Politics* 38, 1: 58–79.

Kagan, K. (1997/98) 'The Myth of the European Concert: The Realist-Institutionalist Debate and Great Power Behavior in the Eastern Question, 1821–41', *Security Studies* 7, 2: 1–57.

Kissinger, H. (1957) *A World Restored*, London: Weidenfeld and Nicolson.

Kupchan, C. A. and Kupchan, C. A. (1991) 'Concerts, Collective Security, and the Future of Europe', *International Security* 16, 1: 114–61.

Rendall, M. (2000) 'Russia, the Concert of Europe, and Greece, 1821–29: A Test of Hypotheses About the Vienna System', *Security Studies* 9, 4: 52–90.

Schroeder, P. W. (1994) *The Transformation of European Politics, 1763–1848*, Oxford: Clarendon.

See also: alliance; collective security; great powers; order; United Nations

MATTHEW RENDALL

Conditionality

The set of conditions and economic policies that the **International Monetary Fund** (IMF) and the **World Bank** (as well as other lenders) expect a borrowing country to implement in order to obtain funding.

As practised by the IMF and the World Bank, conditionality is structured with different levels of obligation. In decreasing order of strength, these are:

1. Preconditions or prior actions. These are reforms, agreed during the loan negotiations, which must be undertaken before the funding is formally approved. Following their implementation, the loan is disbursed, normally in tranches.
2. Legal requirements or benchmark criteria (in World Bank's terminology) or performance criteria (in IMF terminology). Their implementation triggers the disbursement of successive instalments, while failure to achieve the target leads to suspension of the funding until the target is achieved or a new target is agreed.
3. Other commitments, for example structural benchmarks in IMF programmes. If these conditions are not met, tranche releases are not automatically suspended. However, non-implementation could lead to the refusal of further funding or to more extensive and/or tighter conditionality.

The character of conditionality has significantly evolved over time. The issue of intrusiveness of conditionality was not considered at the **Bretton Woods** conference in 1944 where the IMF and the World Bank were founded. The Executive Board of the IMF could decide whether conditions should be attached to its loans. Moreover, while certain goals might be negotiated with the borrowing country, the latter was often free to decide the policy instruments with which to achieve those goals. For example, in the 1960s, the IMF did not insist on the use of devaluation for balance of payments adjustment and accepted the decision made by several countries to rely exclusively on severe demand contraction.

From the beginning, the World Bank has always imposed some conditionality, reflecting the view that project lending would be more effective if upstream and downstream inefficiencies were removed. Its conditions had a macroeconomic focus and were very similar to those of the IMF (covering public sector budget deficits, credit to the private sector, current account deficits), though much less specific, since project lending did not guarantee the Bank enough leverage to negotiate agreements with the highest government authorities and impose detailed conditions.

In 1969, the principle of conditionality was formally included in the IMF's Articles of Agreement. However, up until the mid-1970s, its conditionality remained relatively loose. It became increasingly detailed, specifying the policy instruments to be used to attain the stipulated targets, after the introduction of the Extended Fund Facility in 1974, which represented the formal recognition that countries turning to the IMF would require assistance over an extended period, not just in the short term.

Such expansion of conditionality was criticized by developing country governments, who claimed that conditionality was not tailored to individual countries' circumstances. This prompted an IMF review of its own conditionality in 1979, which recommended greater attention to individual country's priorities and characteristics. At the same time, the IMF introduced a new layer of conditionality, as prior actions were added to performance criteria.

The World Bank initiated structural adjustment lending in 1980, shifting from project-based to policy-based lending and including detailed microeconomic conditionality (see **structural adjustment program**). Moreover, World Bank conditions complemented those of the IMF, since the conclusion of an IMF arrangement was usually a precondition for the Bank's funding. With the debt **crisis**, both the IMF and especially the World Bank attached more conditions to their programs and developing countries had often no option but to accept such conditionality if they were to access new funding.

In 1986, the IMF introduced its Structural Adjustment Facility (SAF) and added a third layer of conditionality, namely, structural benchmarks. These have a definite microeconomic character and reflect the increasing attention paid by the IMF to economic growth. Structural conditionality has increased substantially and by the mid-1990s had been included in almost all programmes supported by the IMF. The introduction of the Poverty Reduction and Growth Facility (PRGF) in 1999 led to a further rise in conditions, which is only partially due to the IMF's widening scope since the number of conditions also increased in traditional areas such as the exchange rate and the fiscal sector. In addition, conditionality has been extended to new areas, such as the environment, gender issues, and the labor market.

World Bank conditionality has also been extended in scope and detail. The area of **good governance** is particularly notable. While the number of structural conditions in World Bank programs is much higher than in IMF programs, the conditionality of the two institutions has converged as a result of their decision to pursue similar aims, namely, economic growth and poverty reduction in their member countries.

Towards the end of the 1990s, the World Bank and the IMF started a process of streamlining of conditionality. In the IMF, this was however restricted to structural conditionality, which also varied greatly from country to country, with no change in the traditional macroeconomic conditionality. In the World Bank, the reduction in the number of conditions occurred in the non-binding conditions. Moreover, the Bank has sometimes taken up some of the structural conditions dropped as a result of IMF streamlining.

The motivation for attaching conditions to lending deems conditionality as a substitute for internationally valuable collateral, which is not available to the countries approaching the IMF or the World Bank. If implemented, such conditions aim to ensure repayment of the loan. The use of conditionality in sovereign lending has a long history, with modern examples being the 'Decree of Mouharrem' in 1881 following the Turkish government's default on its foreign debt or the **League of Nations**' reconstruction schemes of the 1920s.

The use of conditionality may also be advantageous from the borrowing country's viewpoint. First, it is an assurance to the borrowing country that, if previously specified policy measures are implemented, funding will be released. Second, it binds the country to a reform program, since disbursements depend on reform implementation. Third, it lends credibility to the borrowing government's reform plans by signalling its commitment to reform.

By contrast, it has been argued that conditionality has generally failed to bring about policy change because it cannot be made 'incentive-compatible'. In case of a breach of conditions, the threat to suspend funding has low credibility. One reason is that such measure would lead to an inferior outcome, i.e. to default and no improvement in government policy. Another reason is that, once the initial tranche of a loan has been disbursed, the staff of lending institutions have a strong incentive to make the loan 'work'. Knowing that lenders will accept some slippage with conditionality, recipient governments who are not committed to policy reform have incentives to renege on their commitments. Conditionality, therefore, undermines the credibility of the reforms undertaken.

According to this view, conditionality is intrinsically flawed and should be abandoned. Lending and aid should be directed towards countries with 'good' policy environments. However, the application of this recommendation faces a number of problems, among which is that many developing country governments will fall in the category of having neither wholly bad nor wholly good policies.

Further reading

Boughton, J. (2001) *Silent Revolution: The International Monetary Fund, 1979–1989*, Washington, DC: IMF.

Collier, P., Guillaumont, P., Guillaumont, S. and Gunning, J. W. (1997) 'Redesigning Conditionality', *World Development* 25, 9: 1399–407

International Monetary Fund (2001) *Conditionality in Fund-Supported Programmes: Policy Issues*, Washington, DC: IMF.

Killick, T. (1998) *Aid and the Political Economy of Policy Change*, London: Routledge.

See also: debt trap; development; foreign aid; International Monetary Fund; neoliberalism; World Bank

ALBERTO PALONI

Confidence and security building measures

Confidence and Security Building Measures (CSBMs) are usually agreements between two or more states regarding exchanges of information and joint activities regarding the size, composition, movements and use of their respective military forces and armaments. CSBMs aim to reduce tensions by increasing transparency of capabilities and by clarifying intentions about military and political activities. CSBMs provide a way to avoid misunderstandings about ambiguous events and policies, or perceived threats that otherwise might result in confrontation and conflict escalation. A series of CSBMs creates an ongoing set of political exchange relationships and reciprocities that result in graduated reduction in tensions (GRIT) among the rival parties (see **reciprocity**).

By creating points of contact and interaction between parties that require communication of credible information, CSBMs can lead to greater transparency and reduced risks of war caused by miscalculation, misunderstanding of intentions, and miscommunication. CSBMs can modify inaccurate perceptions of motives and thus avoid misjudgements concerning military actions that might provoke violent confrontation. CSBMs are most likely to contribute to normalization in relations where the terms of agreements are clear and accepted by both sides, and where the international community is supportive of the initiatives.

CSBMs require technologies for maintaining direct, regular and quick communication and monitoring among governments and militaries. These measures may make use of a third party state or organization to help monitor the exchange of information and to provide institutions and regimes for the exchange of information. For example, in 1963, during the talks between the United States and the USSR following the Cuban Missile Crisis, open lines of communication contributed to the agreement on the Partial Nuclear Test Ban Treaty and the eventual emergence of detente. During the period between 1969 and 1972, when the US and Soviet governments were negotiating the first Strategic Arms Limitation Treaty and the Anti-Ballistic Missile Treaty, a series of cultural and other exchange agreements helped to improve public perceptions of the other.

Though traditionally associated with inter-state relations, CSBMs also apply in situations of complex, identity-based, intra-state conflict. Strengthening conflict prevention and the transition to cooperative positive-sum relationships are strongly dependent on the development of CSBMs.

In an environment of protracted conflict between ethnic groups, fundamental shifts towards normalized peaceful relations are unlikely in the short term. The development of state structures within multi-ethnic states can lead to a sense of exclusion and failure in the social and political world, which amounts to the systematic denial of the aspirations of particular ethnic minorities. **Ethnic conflict** arises from this sense of exclusion. CSBMs are difficult to apply in these situations. There are two reasons for this. First, unlike states, ethnic groups have neither diplomats nor armies and therefore gradually escalate their conflicts through violence. Second, armed struggle is the result of an ethnic group's quest for **identity**, positive group distinctiveness and in-group cohesion. It is a means of challenging the existing order. For rebellious ethnic communities, proactive violence, which aims to appropriate new entitlements, is a likely instrument for mobilization.

An important consideration is whether ethnic diversity impedes or enhances the prospects for non-violent solutions and the application of CSBMs. Consider the size and number of groups as a potential impediment. It is not unrealistic for as many as five or more 'multiple sovereignties' to be engaged in a confrontation at any given time in an **civil war**. In some instances these groups may be insurgent movements, representatives of legitimate political parties, factions within ethnic groups or clans, allied on some issues and divided on others. The essential problem is an emerging **anarchy** where groups that lack many of the attributes of statehood must pay attention to the primary problem of their **security**. The **security dilemma** applies to situations where the pursuit of security by one group serves only to antagonize the other. A general lack of trust in the other's intentions compels belligerents to pursue conflict through gradual escalation. The behavior of each of the belligerents inhibits them from making conciliatory concessions, since each expects the other to exploit any conciliatory gesture.

In instances of extreme hostility between warring groups and in the absence of a mutually recognized process for discussion, a neutral third party is indispensable for introducing CSBMs. Ethnic groups with a history of hostility and violence between them cannot resolve or manage the conflict without some form of mutual understanding and communication that is usually brought about by the active participation of a third party. A political foundation for reciprocal risk-taking must be established before any party will agree to make concessions, and relinquish assets (tangible, such as land, or intangible, such as recognition of **legitimacy**) in the hope that this will lead to a *quid pro quo* from the other parties. In such a framework, the mutual benefits of cooperation can be made evident by the third party.

Through their involvement at the earliest stages, third parties help mitigate open hostility and smooth the way towards direct negotiations and formal agreements between warring factions. Techniques include efforts to define the sources of conflict in a non-zero sum fashion and to identify mutual interests and values. Third party-initiated dialogue focuses on mechanisms and processes of dialogue and on the design and scope of specific measures to de-escalate violence such as cease-fires, peace agreements and troop withdrawals. At this stage, key features of the process include sustained support from the international community and commitment by both sides to implementing any settlement process.

When a commitment to CSBMs has been made, third parties are there to help the belligerents make difficult concessions involving significant risks, setting aside non-negotiable issues and focusing on those areas where there is mutual interest. On occasion, intensive multi-party negotiations can succeed through sustained pressure by the third party on positive unilateral concessions and processes. The concessions by one side can be replaced by mutual CSBMs over time.

CSBMs can also take the form of technical cooperation where violence is not immanent and relations between parties are stable. These include joint economic and environment initiatives where spillover is anticipated and mutual gains can be expected. CSBMs might also take the form of cooperation between parties to face a common threat such as planning for joint responses to natural disasters, such as earthquakes and drought. These forms of confidence building measures create the basis for long term **integration** and cooperation and deeper recognition of common interests. For example, CSBMs played a role in the transition that took place in Europe between 1974 and 1990 through the Conference on Security and Cooperation (CSCE).

Further reading

Axelrod, R. (1987) *The Evolution of Cooperation*, New York: Basic Books.

Ben-Dor, G. and Dewitt D. B. (eds) (1994) *Confidence-Building Measures in the Middle East*, Boulder, CO: Westview.

Hampson, F. O. (1999) *Multilateral Negotiations – Lessons from Arms Control, Trade, and the Environment*, Baltimore, NJ: Johns Hopkins University Press.

Mahiga, A. P. and Nji, F. M. (1987) *Confidence Building Measures in Africa*, New York: United Nations.

Platt, A. (ed.) (1992) *Arms Control and Confidence Building in the Middle East*, Washington, DC: US Institute of Peace.

See also: peace-building; peace studies

DAVID CARMENT

Constructivism

An approach to the study of international relations that emphasizes the primacy of non-material variables – specifically norms, culture, identities and ideas – in accounting for agents' behavior. Emerging from the 'third debate' between rationalists and critical theorists that dominated international relations scholarship during the 1980s (see **critical theory**, constructivism emphasizes the socially constructed character of agents' identities and interests within global politics. Whereas rationalist approaches to international relations bracket processes of identity and interest formation, focusing instead on the strategic interactions of self-interested actors dwelling in **anarchy**, constructivists study the processes by which the identities and interests of agents are produced, reproduced and occasionally transformed in the course of continuous social interaction with other actors. While critical international relations theorists laid the intellectual foundations of constructivism in their meta-theoretical critiques of the discipline during the 1980s, constructivism as a distinctive approach to international relations emerged only in the more fluid disciplinary context that followed the end of the **cold war**. From the early 1990s, constructivists have demonstrated the value of incorporating ideational factors into the study of global politics in the course of addressing empirical puzzles in the areas of **security** and **international political economy**, and have also contributed disproportionately to the study of 'new agenda' issues such as **feminism**, the environment and the global diffusion of **human rights** norms. Nevertheless, disagreements persist regarding the appropriate relationship (competitive or complementary) that should obtain between constructivist and rationalist approaches to global politics. Constructivists also remain divided over the extent to which the normative concerns and political commitments that animated critical international relations theory in the 1980s should continue to inform constructivist scholarship.

Antecedents and origins

Constructivism's origins can be traced to two trends apparent in the social sciences from the late 1970s onwards. The first of these trends was the growing intellectual influence exerted by a range of Continental thinkers – most prominently Foucault, Habermas, Bourdieu and Derrida – within Anglophone academic circles. In their respective fields, these authors had sought to demonstrate the ways in which relations of **power** and domination were continually produced and reproduced through a range of non-material practices left largely unexamined and uncriticized by conventional social scientists. These theorists shared a commitment to exposing the ways in which ostensibly value-neutral structures of knowledge and meaning were themselves implicated in – and indeed inseparable from – broader relations of domination within society.

The growing influence of Continental critical theories in the Anglophone academy overlapped with and reinforced a second major trend, namely the advent of the 'cultural turn' within the social sciences. While cultural factors had been periodically privileged in social scientists' analyses previously, the early 1980s saw a renewed emphasis on culture as a determinant of political and social phenomena. Within political science, this tendency was initially slow in manifesting itself, alternately complementing and competing with historical sociologists' concerns to 'bring the state back in' to the study of comparative politics and international relations. But by the mid-1980s, the influence of both Continental critical theory and the 'cultural turn' within the social sciences was sufficiently pronounced as to lay the foundations for critical international theory, the direct intellectual antecedent to constructivism.

The introduction of critical theory into international relations in the 1980s saw a diverse range of critical international theorists attack what they perceived to be the inherently conservative and uncritical stance assumed by mainstream international relations scholarship in its engagement with world affairs. These authors dismissed as analytically naïve and politically irresponsible the view that international relations scholars should devote themselves to providing policy relevant insights about the world 'as it really is'. To the extent that existing scholarship naturalized and thereby fortified existing power structures, taking concepts such as the **sovereign state** and the condition of anarchy to be objective and immutable features of global politics, it was to be opposed as but a further expression of relations of domination extant within **international society**. Critical international theorists proposed alternatively that the real task of international relations scholars should be to critique existing power structures with a view towards opening up the possibility of imagining more emancipatory alternatives.

Given their commitment to positivistic conceptions of the nature and purposes of intellectual inquiry, many mainstream international relations scholars initially struggled to appreciate the relevance of the meta-theoretical critiques of the discipline that were being advanced by critical theorists. Some rationalists insisted that critical theorists demonstrate the practical relevance of their claims by applying their insights to the empirical study of problems of immediate concern to social scientists. Conversely, critical theorists protested that the ontological, epistemological, methodological, and normative assumptions of mainstream and critical approaches were each so divergent as to preclude a fruitful synthesis of perspectives. Crucially, this condition of mutual intellectual estrangement was destabilized before it could ossify, with the **cold war**'s peaceful and abrupt conclusion exercising profound and contradictory effects on the discipline of international relations. On the one hand, rationalists' failure to anticipate or account for the cold war's peaceful end seemed to confirm critical theorists' claims that rationalists were incapable of adequately imagining or explaining large-scale changes within international politics. Conversely, the very fact that rationalists had been so obviously wrong-footed by history also suggested that critical theorists had overstated the significance of international relations scholarship in naturalizing and sustaining global structures of domination. These observations aside, the cold war's end did serve as an intellectual circuit breaker, exposing the limitations of existing approaches and thus providing an opening for the development of a more diverse range of explanations for contemporary international phenomena. It was in this more fluid disciplinary context that constructivism emerged as a distinctive approach to the study of international relations.

Foundational assumptions of constructivism

Constructivism is distinguishable from other approaches to international relations in that it is not explicitly anchored within a broader political philosophy. Unlike **realism**, **liberal internationalism**, and Marxist approaches to international relations (see **Marxism**), there are no distinctive prescriptive claims that are constitutive of constructivism. While constructivism finds its origins in critical international theory, constructivism as an analytical approach remains potentially compatible with a range of political perspectives. Consequently, constructivism is best characterized as an analytical approach analogous to rational choice, rather than as a substantive theory of international politics equivalent to realism or liberalism. This observation aside, constructivists are nevertheless distinguishable from rationalist international relations scholars through their subscription to a common set of ontological, epistemological, and methodological claims.

Ontologically, constructivists and rationalists differ on three points. First, constructivists are idealists rather than materialists, in that they argue that material structures acquire social significance only via the intersubjectively shared meaning structures through which they are mediated. Constructivists do not deny the phenomenal reality of material processes such as **nuclear proliferation**, but they do argue that one can only understand actors' behavioral responses to said phenomena by reference to the shared meaning structures through which these processes are perceived and understood. Whether nuclear proliferation will be perceived as threatening international stability, enhancing it, or even exercising a neutral effect will depend on actors' interests and identities, interests and identities that are socially constructed rather than being logically inferable from one's structural position within the **international system**.

Second, constructivists posit a mutually constitutive relationship between agents and structures. Drawing from the insights of sociology, constructivists argue that the question of 'who am I?' is both logically and ontologically prior to the question of 'what do I want?' and that agents' identities are in turn governed by the normative and ideological structures that they inhabit. These structures themselves are not ontological primitives, but are rather sustained patterns of social practice that are continuously produced and reproduced through the actions of these agents. Constructivists see the international system as being a constitutive rather than merely a strategic domain. States' conceptions of who they are and what interests they possess as a corollary of these identities are held to derive from intersubjectively shared meaning structures rather than forming autogenously prior to social interaction. This position contrasts with rationalists' beliefs that agents are analytically separable from the environments they inhabit, and that the study of international politics consists of the study of agents' instrumentally rational pursuit of pre-social interests that remain constant over the course of social interaction.

Third, rationalists and constructivists diverge in their conceptions of the dominant logic governing agents' actions. Behavior through constructivist eyes is seen as essentially norm-driven, with states seeking to ensure a correspondence between their own conduct and the internalized prescriptions for legitimate behavior that states have derived from their identities. Far from being of purely ornamental value, norms are seen as exercising a profound influence on state behavior both by helping to constitute states' identities and interests in the first instance, and by further conditioning and constraining the strategies and actions undertaken by states in the furtherance of these interests. This position contrasts with rationalists' belief that agents' behavior is governed not by a logic of appropriateness but merely by a logic of consequences. States through this optic are conceived as rational egoists pursuing interests formed exogenously to social interaction in a rationally instrumental manner, with cooperation or conflict being determined not by the presence or absence of norms, but rather by a combination of resource constraints (owing to states' finite capabilities) and the congruity, or lack thereof, that states perceive between their own interests and those of other states.

The ontological disagreements between rationalists and constructivists are mirrored in epistemological and methodological differences. Constructivists endorse a post-positivistic approach to the social sciences, arguing that the socially constructed character of agents' interests and identities, and the attendant diversity of possible meaning structures through which these interests and identities might be constituted, preclude the possibility of developing all but the most elementary trans-historically (or trans-culturally) valid claims about international politics (see **post-positivism**). This contrasts with rationalists' conviction that there exists sufficient commonality in state behaviors across different cultural and historical contexts as to warrant the development of law-like generalizations about international politics, and their concomitant belief in the possibility of developing robust predictive claims about global politics on the basis of these generalizations. From the mid-1990s onwards, many modern constructivists have moderated their hostility towards positivism by pursuing contingent rather than universal generalizations about international phenomena in the course of their empirical research. Nevertheless, the aversion to both prediction and the development of nomothetic covering laws about global politics remain distinctive features of constructivist scholarship.

Methodologically, rationalists' commitment to a positivistic epistemology has manifested itself in recourse to quantitative methods such as statistical regression analysis and **game theory**, in addition to more traditional methods such as the use of analytic narratives. Conversely, in light of their emphasis on the centrality of shared structures of meaning in constituting agents' identities, interests, and actions, constructivists draw from a highly eclectic range of methodologies, including discourse analysis, comparative historical case studies, ethnographic research, and qualitative and quantitative content analysis, in order to excavate these meaning structures and thus better enable them to apprehend the underlying power dynamics of the international system.

Divisions within constructivism

While the foregoing comments illuminate the main differences separating rationalist and constructivist approaches, constructivism's internal diversity must also be noted. Two key points of division within constructivism are the distinctions between systemic, unit-level, and holistic constructivism, and between modern and postmodern constructivism. With regards to the first of these distinctions, constructivists disagree on the extent to which state interests, identities, and actions are constituted by either system-wide ideational structures, domestic ideational structures, or ideational structures that bridge the domestic-international divide (Reus-Smit 1996: 220–1). Systemic constructivists acknowledge that states may possess certain very elementary pre-social interests (e.g. the interest in continued survival), but nevertheless emphasize the primacy of system wide normative structures in constituting the social identities and interests of state actors, and in accounting for the varying levels of competitive and cooperative behavior manifest in different international systems. Conversely, unit-level constructivists note variations in state responses to systemic pressures (e.g. global economic shocks or the growth of **terrorism**), and place greater emphasis on differences in the domestic sources of state identities and interests in order to account for this variation. Holistic constructivists differ once again from their systemic and unit level counterparts in emphasizing the co-constituted character of political order at a domestic and an international level. These theorists accord analytical priority to ideational structures that bridge the domestic-international divide, and focus primarily on explaining the dynamics of large scale change both within international systems (e.g. the end of the cold war) and between international systems (e.g. the shift from feudalism to the Westphalian state system (see **Westphalia**).

While systemic, unit-level and holistic constructivists differ in terms of the types of questions they ask and the analytical priority they place on different types of ideational structures, a more fundamental division within constructivism centers on the cleavage between modern and postmodern constructivists. While both variants of constructivism derive their ontological, epistemological, and methodological bearings from critical international theory, postmodern constructivists remain more self-consciously committed to advancing critical theorists' normative agenda of critiquing structures of power, hierarchy, and domination as they inhere both within global structures (e.g. the sovereign state system, the global capitalist economy), and within the intellectual discipline of international relations. Postmodern constructivists are deeply concerned with the presumed nexus between power and knowledge, and are principally committed to excavating the sociolinguistic practices through which particular truth regimes in international politics are constructed and alternative **discourse**s rendered unimaginable.

Conversely, since their emergence in the early 1990s, modern constructivists have largely abjured meta-theoretical critique and instead sought to answer more empirically based questions than those asked by their postmodern counterparts. Ranging across fields of inquiry formerly dominated by rationalists, modern constructivists have attempted to provide competing (and occasionally even complementary) solutions to empirical puzzles that have long preoccupied rationalist scholars. This effort to engage with rationalists has seen modern constructivists pursue the development of contingent rather than all-embracing generalizations based on their research, and has also triggered recourse to a more eclectic range of methods beyond the sociolinguistic approaches favored by critical theorists and postmodern constructivists. Unsurprisingly, neither of these developments has been welcomed by postmodern constructivists, who maintain that there is a fundamental incompatibility between the task of critiquing power and the attempt to intellectually engage with rationalists, whose very commitment to positivism and the search for objective truths is seen to implicate them in the reproduction of global structures of power, hierarchy, and domination.

Applications of constructivism

From the early 1990s, constructivists have enhanced the discipline's understanding of key questions across a wide range of issue areas. In the area of international security, constructivists have contested realist claims that the self-help practices of security seeking states are a logical consequence of the anarchic structure of the international system, arguing instead that 'anarchy is what states make of it', and that a wide range of 'cultures of anarchy' may exist that diverge widely from the Hobbesian form that has preoccupied realist scholarship (Wendt 1994). This insight has been further developed in the growing literature on security communities, where constructivists have sought to trace the processes through which definitions of the self have been expanded in ways that have facilitated the evolution of enduring cultures of security cooperation between states. Finally, constructivists have also explored the evolution of norms governing the conduct of war, employing a range of interpretive and genealogical techniques to reveal the processes through which particular norms (e.g. the anti-nuclear taboo, prohibitions on the use of chemical weapons and landmines) have become established within international society.

In the field of political economy, constructivists have contested the claim that processes of economic **globalization** are compelling societies' inevitable convergence towards a single most efficient form of economic and social organization. Evidence of the continuing diversity of varieties of **capitalism** within the global economy has been adduced by a range of scholars, who have pointed to the enduring significance of institutionalized domestic ideas about the appropriate relationship between states and markets to account for the variety of state responses to putatively homogenizing global economic trends. Conversely, other scholars have applied interpretive techniques to explain the systemic shift from the **embedded liberalism** of the **Bretton Woods** era to the neo-liberal 'Washington Consensus' that has prevailed internationally from the 1980s onwards.

Given constructivists' recognition of the socially constructed character of even the most fundamental social institutions, constructivist scholars have also pioneered research into the origins, evolution, and potential transformation of the Westphalian sovereign state system. Constructivists have drawn from the insights of **historical sociology** to explain phenomena such as the genesis of sovereign territoriality within early modern Europe, the diversity of cooperative institutional forms that have prevailed across different systems of states, and the post-World War Two extension of **sovereignty** to encompass the colonial non-European world. Concern with the ideational sources of change within global politics has also pervaded constructivist contributions to 'new agenda' issues such as feminism and the global diffusion of human rights norms, topics that had previously received less sustained attention within international relations scholarship.

Criticisms

Given the strong points of disagreement between constructivists and rationalists, the application of constructivist approaches to questions formerly monopolized by rationalists has inevitably yielded controversy. One of the earliest charges lodged against constructivism related to its perceived utopianism. Realists in particular decried what they perceived as a fundamental naïveté on the part of those who questioned the inevitability of armed inter-state conflict while the structural condition of anarchy continued to prevail. The notion that self help behaviors were contingent rather than inevitable by-products of anarchy met with sustained criticism, as did the claim that institutions such as the **North Atlantic Treaty Organization** (NATO) alliance could constitute anything more than fragile and ephemeral expedients designed to balance against common threats. Ironically, realists' charges of naïveté found echoes in criticisms from postmodern constructivists, who remained convinced in the inevitability of forms of alienation, hierarchy, and domination continuing to suffuse social relations, and who were consequently sceptical of modern constructivists' belief in the capacity of human agents to work together to construct more emancipatory alternatives to the status quo.

Criticisms of utopianism carry special resonance within a discipline that was initially forged in the inter-war debate between realists and so-called 'idealists', and in which the concern with securing a modicum of **order** within an anarchic world has historically trumped questions concerning the advancement of international justice. Moreover, the plausibility of this critique was inadvertently fueled by the early research agenda of constructivists, in which questions concerning the genesis and evolution of 'good' norms (e.g. human rights norms, the anti-apartheid norm) were disproportionately emphasized over the 'bad' norms that are often more immediately implicated in the perpetuation of relations of violence and domination within the international system.

Its rhetorical power notwithstanding, the persuasiveness of the utopian critique is nevertheless blunted by the existence of constructivist studies on topics such as the militarization of **gender** roles in armed conflicts, the production of cultures of insecurity, and the resort of states to pathological practices of population management including ethnic cleansing and **genocide**. The initial bias in the constructivist research program towards the study of progressive norms and morally inclusive conceptions of political community should not be misconstrued as evidence of limitations that are inherent to constructivism as an analytical approach. Neither adherence to a particular political philosophy nor scholarly inclinations towards either optimism or pessimism should be automatically inferred from the analytical concern with the socially constructed character of norms, cultures, identities, and ideas that has distinguished con-

structivism from other approaches to international relations.

Despite their theoretical commitment to an ontology emphasizing the mutual constitution of agents and structures, constructivists have also been charged with leaving too little room for agency in their empirical work, given their emphasis on the determining role played by domestic and global normative structures in governing agents' actions. In emphasizing the agreement between an existing norm or identity and a state's subsequent actions, constructivists have been accused of failing to seriously engage with questions of intentionality and active decision-making on the part of social agents. Critics have further pointed out the multiplicity of norms and identities to which agents are routinely subject, and the attendant dilemmas that are raised when actors are forced to reconcile the incompatible logics of appropriateness that might be mandated by these disparate norms and identities. In such instances, agents would appear to be compelled to make conscious and calculated decisions about the most appropriate course of action, suggesting a degree of self-consciousness and selectivity in norm compliance that is not always adequately accommodated within constructivist accounts.

These observations notwithstanding, criticisms of constructivism's alleged structuralist bias are often overstated. With regards to the genesis of normative structures, constructivists have long sought to capture the crucial role played by actors such as epistemic communities (see **epistemic community**) and Transnational Advocacy Networks in generating and diffusing international norms. From the late 1990s onwards, constructivists have also attempted to more explicitly parse out the micro-foundations underpinning broader processes of norm genesis, diffusion, and transformation.

Increasing attention has been paid to identifying the respective roles played by communicative action (argument, deliberation, and persuasion) and various social influence mechanisms (e.g. back-slapping and shaming) in securing actor compliance with norms (e.g. Johnston 2001). The variability of actor compliance with norms has also been acknowledged, with scholars increasingly seeking to trace out the different sources of norms extant at an organizational, unit, and systemic level in order to better establish which norms matter and when in accounting for states' actions. Finally, as constructivists do not bracket processes of identity and interest formation but rather see them as forming endogenously to social interaction, constructivist approaches are arguably more open to studying agents' direct involvement in processes of identity contestation than are rational choice approaches.

In addition to their alleged neglect of agency, constructivists have also been accused of analytical imprecision in their attempts to operationalize ideational phenomena such as norms and identity. The very multiplicity of diverse norms and identities in social life has prompted critics to observe that it is possible for constructivists to provide *post hoc* explanations for virtually any outcome by reference to a corresponding norm or identity, thereby threatening to render constructivist arguments non-falsifiable. Rationalists have further pointed to the difficulties associated with quantifying ideational variables, arguing that these difficulties seriously complicate efforts to measure the relative importance of ideational variables vis-à-vis other factors in influencing agents' conceptions of interest and the attendant strategies and actions undertaken in pursuit of these interests.

Admittedly, many constructivists would recoil from attempts to conceive of norms and identities as discrete variables that are separable from actors' interests and actions, claiming that they seek to advance constitutive rather than causal explanations for social phenomena, and that rationalists' criticisms merely reflect the incommensurability of the respective ontological and epistemological positions assumed by the two approaches. Nevertheless, some scholars from both sides of the divide have tried to eschew positions of epistemological absolutism in favor of a more eclectic analytical approach. The post-cold war resurgence of ethno-nationalist violence and the continued growth of religious fundamentalism have captured the attention of rationalists as well as constructivists, prompting more concerted efforts to render intangible concepts such as social identity more amenable to empirical analysis. Scholars working on both sides of the rationalist-constructivist divide have employed a range of methodologies, ranging from quantitative and qualitative content analysis through discourse analysis and cognitive mapping techniques, in order to capture the precise pathways of influence through which different ideas, norms, and identities condition actors' conceptions of self and interest, their decision-making procedures and causal beliefs, and their resulting strategies and actions.

The turn towards analytical eclecticism has prompted speculation on the degree of possible complementarity between constructivist and rationalist approaches, a tendency that has been encouraged by the overlapping research interests of many scholars working on both sides of the analytical divide. Nevertheless, the discipline of international relations has long distinguished itself from other sub-fields within political science in relying upon paradigmatic struggle as the organizing framework for debate and the primary catalyst for disciplinary progress. Consequently, dis-agreement persists regarding the extent to which constructivism should con-stitute a complement or an alternative to existing approaches. Some postmodern constructivists have deplored attempts to close the distance between con-structivism and mainstream international relations scholarship, perceiving any attempt at *rapprochement* as endanger-ing the scholar's overriding commitment to critiquing existing configurations of power/knowledge. These scholars argue that constructivism should neither be read as a complement nor as a com-mensurable competitor to existing para-digms, given the fundamental differences in intellectual purpose (rationalist expla-nation versus constructivist under-standing and critique) informing the two approaches.

Purists on the rationalist side of the debate have similarly downplayed the significance of the constructivist chal-lenge, arguing that constructivists' con-cerns with the role played by ideational factors in conditioning social action can be easily accommodated within ration-alist approaches. Exponents of this view arguably favor a strategy of hegemonic assimilation, whereby norms, culture, and identities may be invoked as the need arises to mop up any residual var-iance in outcomes that cannot be accounted for by recourse to the expla-natory variables traditionally favored by rationalists. Scholars occupying the epistemological center have advanced a more charitable alternative in proposing an intellectual division of labor between constructivists and rationalists, whereby the former are left to explain the forma-tion of identities and interests, while the latter focus upon the strategies and actions adopted by agents in accordance with these identities and interests. Nevertheless, some constructivists have challenged even this position, arguing

that 'stage complementarity' is not with-out its problems given that strategic and institutional **rationality** may share with identities and interests the condition of being constituted by culturally and his-torically specific inter-subjective values and meanings.

The future of constructivism

The turbulence that has characterized the post-cold war period has been mir-rored in the discipline of international relations. The unanticipated end of the cold war, the recrudescence of ethno-nationalist violence and religious funda-mentalism, and the continuing extension and intensification of globalizing forces have conspired to create an intellectual environment that is more conducive to the study of large-change in interna-tional politics and the role played idea-tional factors in shaping this change. This observation notwithstanding, several factors militate against constructivism's emergence as a coherent paradigmatic alternative to existing approaches. First, even though the United States academy served as the initial cradle of constructivism, the commitment to a positivistic conception of the social sciences remains particularly strong within the North American academy. Consequently, while constructivists have demonstrated the value of interpreta-tion, critique, and the search for contingent rather than universal general-izations as legitimate purposes of intel-lectual inquiry, these purposes remain overshadowed by positivistic commit-ments to explanation and prediction as the primary drivers of empirical interna-tional relations research.

Second, the development of a dis-tinctive constructivist macro-theory about international politics is stymied by the fact that constructivism is not anchored within a broader political philosophy.

Constructivists' claims regarding the socially constructed nature of reality and the primacy of ideational factors in world politics are accessible to a multitude of traditions, thereby limiting the scope for the development of a distinctive constructivist theory of global politics. While realist, liberal, and Marxist approaches to international politics are themselves marked by a high degree of internal diversity, they are each nevertheless distinguishable from rival traditions in their subscription to a common set of putatively universal analytic assumptions and prescriptive claims about human nature and the essential purposes and character of political life. Conversely, constructivism lacks a distinctive theory of politics and consequently remains more analogous to rational choice as an analytical approach that is open to scholars favoring a multitude of different political positions.

Finally, disagreements between constructivists as to whether their arguments are intended to subsume, complement, or even bypass rationalist explanations for international phenomena serve as a further impediment to the ascendancy of a constructivist paradigmatic alternative. Nevertheless, the absence of a coherent constructivist alternative to existing theories of international politics should not be construed as evidence of a broader intellectual failure. The search for universal generalizations about politics that are applicable regardless of cultural or historical context, and that are the essence of substantive theories of international politics, runs counter to the constructivist way of thinking. In any case, international relations scholarship is progressively shifting away from a preoccupation with the paradigm wars that dominated the 1980s and 1990s, with scholars increasingly appreciating the virtues of assuming an analytically eclectic stance to the study of empirical

puzzles within international politics. From its inception, constructivism has forced international relations scholars to become more theoretically self-conscious about their ontological, epistemological, and methodological positions. The constructivist emphasis on the role of norms, culture, identity, and ideas as determinants of international phenomena has strengthened the discipline as a whole, enriching the work of not only scholars working within the constructivist tradition but also rationalist scholars as well. And while constructivists and rationalists will remain divided by ultimately unresolvable disagreements on matters of high theory, scholars on both sides of the divide will continue to benefit from ongoing debates concerning the best ways of addressing the empirical puzzles within international politics to which they are commonly drawn.

Further reading

Finnemore, M. and Sikkink, K. (2001) 'Taking Stock: The Constructivist Research Program in International Relations and Comparative Politics', *Annual Review of Political Science* 4: 391–416.

Hopf, T. (1998) 'The Promise of Constructivism in International Relations Theory', *International Security* 23, 1: 171–200.

Johnston, A. (2001) 'Treating International Institutions as Social Environments', *International Studies Quarterly*, 45:3, 487–515.

Katzenstein, P. (ed.) (1996) *The Culture of National Security: Norms and Identity in World Politics*, New York: Columbia University Press.

Price, R. and Reus-Smit, C. (1998) 'Dangerous Liaisons? Critical International Theory and Constructivism', *European Journal of International Relations* 4, 3: 259–94.

Reus-Smit, C. (1996) 'Constructivism', in S. Burchill, A. Linklater *et al.*, *Theories of International Relations*, 2nd edn, Basingstoke: Palgrave, 209–30.

Wendt, A. (1994) 'Anarchy is What States Make of It: The Social Construction of Power Politics', *International Organization* 46:2, 391–425.

Wendt, A. (1999) *Social Theory of International Politics*, New York: Cambridge University Press.

See also: agent-structure debate; critical theory; deconstruction; English School; identity/difference; levels of analysis; post-positivism; poststructuralism

ANDREW PHILLIPS

Containment

In the West, and certainly in most Anglo-American studies, the **cold war** years are described in terms of containment. Historians have argued that in the early years of the cold war, from 1946–8, Western policy was designed to contain Soviet **power** and prevent a **communist** take-over of the European continent. The clearest expression of this strategy was the Truman Doctrine, announced by President Harry S. Truman in early 1947. The doctrine was inspired by the belief that Stalinist foreign policy was inherently uncooperative, ideologically expansionist and politically aggressive. Specifically, Western policymakers pointed to a pattern of Soviet behavior designed to subvert Western influence. It was claimed that Stalin had, in 1946, despite wartime treaties, sought to take control of Iran (and its oilfields) and had meddled in the Greek Civil War, which had broken out in the winter of 1946. Moscow, through Yugoslav intermediaries, was seeking to mobilize resistance to undermine British influence in Greece. Indeed, it was around the fate of Greece and Turkey that the strategy of containment was born. In February 1946, the American State Department was informed that the situation in Greece was increasingly serious and that the British-backed Greek Government might collapse, thus paving the way for a communist triumph. While Greece was not in itself strategically critical to Washington, the Truman Administration came to see the Greek civil war as part of a larger Soviet plan to dominate Europe. George Kennan, the US diplomat, and the original architect of the strategy of containment, noted that a communist victory in Greece would be followed by a similar fate for Turkey and Italy. Once Italy had fallen, he predicted little could prevent France, Britain, and the western occupied zones of Germany succumbing. This was an early version of what would become the domino theory.

Even before World War Two had ended, Kennan argued that the West should accept a divided Europe, based on a spheres of influence agreement, and act robustly to stop communist interference beyond the Soviet sphere. He believed that the Soviet Union was not capable of genuine cooperation and was ideologically committed to an expansionist strategy and competition with the West. Kennan was aware that the creation of a Soviet Empire would prove problematic and indeed, he predicted that the nature of the Soviet political system contained within it the seeds of its own destruction. Not least, he foresaw that those subjugated by the USSR would eventually rebel. In a document, which became known as 'the Long Telegram' sent from Moscow in February 1946, he outlined his views on Soviet foreign policy. These beliefs were later articulated in an article (published under the pseudonym X) in the American journal *Foreign Affairs*. The problem for Kennan was that, even if in the longer term the Soviet Empire would collapse, in the short term, the European powers lacked the political, economic and institutional energy to confront communism.

War weary and beset by economic woes, West European states, Kennan warned, lack the resources to resist the appeal of communism. Kennan, while thus condemning the authoritarian nature of communism, feared its potency.

Kennan was not the only statesman worried by Soviet behavior and its effects on the European powers. Frank Roberts, working from the British Embassy in Moscow warned that the Russians were becoming interested in areas outside of Europe, and any Soviet gains certainly in for example the Middle East would fatally undermine British and thus American interests in the Arab world. Roberts, like Kennan, advocated containing Soviet power. There was thus a strong British influence on the developing view of the USSR as a threat.

The winter of 1946–7 proved particularly troublesome to those who feared communist influence. A poor harvest in 1946 was followed by a severe winter. It was clear that the American loans already made to individual states would not actually meet the needs for economic recovery. The prospects for the economic collapse of several states appeared strong. In February 1947, the British Cabinet warned the Americans that Britain was heading for a financial crisis and that funds for British commitment abroad, especially in Greece, would have to be reduced. In May, the French coalition government fell. Western officials believed that Soviet intransigence at meetings to discuss the future of Germany was inspired by a belief that Western Europe would indeed succumb to communism. The situation was regarded as particularly acute in Germany. By early 1947 such was the poverty of the Western zones that even basic foodstuffs were been imported. This placed a huge burden on the occupying powers of France and Britain and had contributed to the British inability to continue to support Greece and Turkey. The economic revival of the western zones was deemed necessary for the revival of the rest of Europe. Containment therefore was initially designed to provide quick military and economic aid to Greece and Turkey but also to prevent Germany degenerating into disarray.

The Truman Doctrine announced in March 1947 made further financial aid available to both Greece and Turkey. More importantly, the Truman Doctrine articulated a new American worldview. It proclaimed that the United States was engaged in a global battle between two opposing political systems. One was characterized by free institutions and representative government. The other was based upon coercion, terror, and the suppression of liberty. The United States, therefore, had according to Truman, little choice but to support freedom. The implications of the Truman Doctrine were vast. The United States appeared to be assuming the responsibility for resisting all challenges to democracy. This meant that the United States, at least in theory, saw any struggle involving the forces of communism as one that necessitated US engagement. In the longer term, the Truman Doctrine paved the way for the subsequent American involvement in a number of **civil war**s and ultimately in the tragedy of the Vietnam War. As such the Truman Doctrine marked a decisive shift in US foreign policy. Isolationism was rejected in favor of struggle with the Soviet Union. Rather surprisingly, Truman's speech drew a muted reaction from the Kremlin. Perhaps the Soviet leadership assumed (wrongly) that this was yet more capitalist rhetoric. The second part of the strategy of containment, that of Marshall Aid, did however bring about shifts in Soviet foreign policy.

The Secretary of State, George Marshall, announced Marshall Aid on 5 June

1947. The purpose was to strengthen the structures, economies, and institutions of West European states to withstand the threat from communism. The theoretical basis of this initiative was ideological: democratic structures based firmly on liberal ideals, combined with robust market economics, could not be subverted by communism.

Some historians have argued that the fears of European collapse in 1946 and 1947 were exaggerated. The West Europeans were not as demoralized as the Americans liked to claim. Indeed, revisionist historians argued that in order to understand containment and the program of Marshall Aid it is necessary to acknowledge the severe problems with the American economy. The American system was heavily dependent on its wartime markets in Europe and would be deeply affected by the inability of the Europeans to purchase American goods and foodstuffs. Hence, the system of Marshall Aid did indeed benefit the West European states but it was also a means through which the United States created a hegemonic economic system (see **hegemony**). The American Empire post-1945 therefore had self-interested as well as ideological roots.

In this version of history not only is there a claim that the **crisis** in Europe in 1946 was exaggerated by US statesmen but that there was a deliberate inflation of the threat posed both by the USSR and by communism. Stalin, it is argued, did not seek to move beyond the areas already under Soviet control. Soviet forces simply stayed in their areas of occupation. Critics of containment and the Marshall Plan also argue that it is difficult to find concrete evidence that Stalin inspired those communist forces at work in Greece, Italy or France. In short, according to some scholars, Soviet policy was defensive and focused upon control of the East. Those instances in which the

Soviet leadership appeared to have moved beyond their areas of wartime influence, as the venture into Northern Iran in 1946, were in fact short lived.

Soviet motives and American reactions remains an area of controversy. There were great hopes that with the opening of some of the Russian archives after 1989, we would know what caused Soviet behavior in 1946–7. However, historians dispute the meaning of much of the new evidence. Stalin does seem to have been motivated predominantly by insecurity and caution. His main aim was to control Eastern Europe. Yet there were elements of further ambition, as the foray into Northern Iran and the pressure exerted on Turkey demonstrated. Soviet foreign policy was a mixture of insecurity, ambition, and need.

Nevertheless. Soviet adventures in Iran and the militancy of communist parties in Europe not surprisingly fueled western suspicions of Soviet ambitions. Indeed, the lesson drawn from Iran in 1946 was that the United States in conjunction with the British had to act decisively to repel Soviet ambition. It should also be noted that containment inevitably meant that the peoples of Central and Eastern Europe were, initially at least, consigned to Soviet rule. In 1946–7, western policymakers accepted division, despite Truman's rhetoric of freedom. The price of economic and political freedoms in the West was the enslavement of the peoples of the eastern part of the continent.

As William Taubman (1982) has argued it might well be that the West gave up on the possibility of cooperation with Stalin before the Soviet dictator gave up on cooperation with the West. It is clear that Stalin wanted continued economic cooperation. Hence the initial Soviet interest in participation in Marshall Aid. Could the West have exerted greater influence over Stalin through the extension of Marshall Aid to the East?

We can only speculate. Nevertheless, it remains the case that Stalin, given his paranoia over the West, would only have accepted cooperation on his own terms. It was hardly likely that Western policymakers were going to subsidize Stalin and the Stalinist system in the East. Marshall Aid, whilst reconstructing the Western regions of Europe, ensured the prosperity of half a continent. Soviet reactions were severe. Stalin responded with the closing down of avenues of cooperation, the Czech coup of 1948 and the blockade of Berlin.

This is not the full story of containment. US policymakers were not prepared to accept the existence of Soviet rule. Kennan himself had not envisaged coexistence with the USSR over the longer term. From 1947 onwards, containment in its original sense was abandoned. US policy aimed not so much at rebuffing the spread of communism westwards but developed into a strategy designed to weaken fatally Soviet control in Eastern Europe and communism in a global context. Containment in its original context implied that the United States would accept the status quo, after 1948 this was not the case. Neither was the status quo of the late 1940s accepted on the Soviet side. The cold war accordingly developed with resolute efforts on both sides to increase their influence throughout Europe, Asia, Africa, and the Middle East. Winning the cold war thus became more important than containing it.

Further reading

Gaddis, J. L. (1997) *We Now Know, Rethinking Cold War History*, Oxford: Clarendon.

Gaddis, J. L. (1987) *The Long Peace. Inquiries into the History of the Cold War*, Oxford: Oxford University Press.

Lundestad, G. (1998) *Empire by Integration The United States and European Integra-*tion, *1945–1997*, Oxford: Oxford University Press.

Mayers, D. (1988) *George Kennan and the Dilemmas of US Foreign Policy*, Oxford: Oxford University Press.

Taubman, W. (1982) *Stalin's American Policy. From Entente to Détente to Cold War*, London: Norton.

See also: appeasement; cold war

CAROLINE KENNEDY-PIPE

Corruption

Corruption has long occupied a prominent place in Western political thought. Like many of the most important concepts, however, its meaning has remained elusive. Corruption has been variously defined in the West as an abuse of **power** for private gain, the pursuit of private gain by those entrusted with public office, the violation of rules governing the allocation of resources, or as the **World Bank** defines it, the misuse of public office for private gain. While some definitions focus on corruption as an individual failure, others emphasize its collective characteristics when undertaken to enrich a particular group. The broad range of activities associated with corruption then, tends to focus on the activities of public officials, such as bribery, kickbacks, or other illicit payments for information or favours, embezzlement, extortion, sale of office and patronage. Sometimes, corruption may characterize entire regimes, where rulers regard the country as a source of private revenue. Corruption however, need not involve direct monetary payment, but may take place through 'payments in kind' (such as free media exposure for political parties) or the concealment of conflicts of interest. Other corrupt activities may have more to do with the private sector, such as insider trading or collusion on pricing.

This ambiguity over the precise meaning of the term is matched by vigorous debates in non-Western countries where, for example 'corrupsi' has become a major concern in Indonesian politics, or the Koranic term 'rasuah' to refer to anti-corruption activities in Malaysia. The global focus on corruption in the early twenty-first century has two main sources. First, the flows of investment capital associated with **globalization** have facilitated corrupt activities while also increasing the chances of their exposure. The international ramifications of corruption are increasingly apparent in the number and scope of international agencies committed to anti-corruption. The **United Nations**, **African Union**, and the **Organization for Economic Coop-eration and Development** (OECD) have each released declarations against corruption and bribery. The Asian Development Bank has its own anti-corruption policy, and the World Bank and **International Monetary Fund** have already moved to make loans and assistance provisional on recipient countries committing to anti-corruption campaigns. **Non-governmental organization**s such as Transparency International, have also contributed to the growing awareness of corruption world wide, and actively work to ensure that international agreements and declarations are enforced. In this way, corruption has become a problem of neoliberal (see **neoliberalism**) **global governance** requiring the involvement of **global civil society**.

A second source of the global focus on corruption, partly related to the first, lies in the increasing challenges to sovereign states from **transnational crime** and terrorist groups (see **terrorism**). The fact that such clandestine organizations do not respect the **sovereignty** of states or their borders means that the corrupt activities in which they engage (such as **money laundering** or buying influence) has become entwined with the problem of **failed state**s. The prospect of state failure intensifies the problem. Widespread corruption imposes a range of economic costs on citizens who face increased costs to obtain services. High levels of corruption may also deter foreign investment. In both cases, the perception that a government is corrupt fuels the loss of public trust in public institutions, thereby increasing the likelihood of state failure. To the extent that other governments and international organizations commit themselves to combating state failure, anti-corruption measures are crucial.

Although a growing body of literature is addressed to the empirical study of corruption, conceptual research is characterized by considerable ambiguity on how best to define corruption. By focusing exclusively on the western **discourse** of corruption, some salient features of the concept do stand out. First, social scientists have tended to define corruption as a breach of (usually public) office for the sake of (usually pecuniary) gain. Second, political theorists have tended to emphasize that corruption denotes a strong moral condemnation, a charge of ethical turpitude, negligence, or abject failure to uphold moral standards. In both cases the literature on corruption indicates a blurring of the distinction between public responsibilities and private interest. A tension can be identified therefore between corruption as a technical breach of public office, and corruption as a moral failure. Both of these connotations of corruption have a long history in western political thought.

In recent literature on corruption there has been a tendency to speak of modern definitions of corruption as much narrower than older understandings of the term. These older understandings tended to represent corruption as a decay of or falling away from public virtue. In recent governance literature however, corruption has been construed as one of the structural impediments to **good governance**, an activity that threatens to subvert the separation of government and economy, and impose wasteful costs.

One criticism that has been made of this approach is that it obscures the fact that corruption is a normative concept, its identification depending on some conception of what has been corrupted, and hence of a particular vision of the boundaries supposed to have kept it secure. The identification of political corruption then, assumes an ideal image of uncorrupted politics. This language of corruption has traditionally played a crucial role in Western political thought by tracing the health of the community to its moral qualities, and especially to the emulation of virtue among its members.

The emergence in the seventeenth and eighteenth centuries of a language of civilization conceived the polity as an artifact of governmental activity premised on the separation of public and private interests. Importantly, this meant that the political health of the polity was not held to depend, as it had in medieval political thought, on virtue, but on the governmental management of separate but interdependent political, social and economic realms. In tracing the shift between these **discourse**s, corruption emerges as an important indicator of the elasticity and the development of Western political thought. It also illustrates the way in which current debates over the definition of corruption, and the application of the term in contemporary governance strategies emerged from a long history of debate about virtue, vice and the responsibilities of public office.

Corruption – origins of Western definitions

According to Aristotle's (384–322 BC) physics, all earthly bodies are in a constant process of change, either in 'coming to be' (generation) or 'passing away' (corruption). As a form of change, passing away or corruption denoted the physical decay, degeneration, or other aberration from the optimal condition of that body. Aristotle likened moral degeneracy to physical decay by contrasting it with the optimal condition of the human body, which he identified as a moral and physical mean. In moral terms then, virtue denoted a carefully judged mean between excess and deficiency. Thus corruption might refer to the process by which a virtue, such as liberality, gives way to vices such as prodigality (wastefulness) or illiberality (stinginess). In his political writings Aristotle endorsed a different kind of mean in which the polity is conceptualized as combining elements of democracy, monarchy and aristocracy, and in which neither alone prevails. While such a community could be described as imperfect, it has the greatest chance of preservation and longevity, and therefore of staving off the horrors of political dissolution. For Aristotle then, the political problem of corruption was not defined by private misuse of public funds, though he recognized this as a problem, but the larger problem of how to prevent the corruption (understood as the degeneration or dissolution) of the polity itself.

Classical Roman sources can be said to have amplified this concern over corruption as a cause of political dissolution. Cicero (106–43 BC) in particular, drew attention to the necessary connection between political stability and citizen virtue. Citizens, he argued, must be dedicated, honourable, and above all, frugal. If holding public office, they must avoid the temptations of decadence and luxury and remain committed to the pursuit of the common good. Significantly, Cicero helped to establish himself as a leading orator in his prosecution of Verres, the corrupt governor of Sicily in 68 BC. His famous, but mostly undelivered 'Verrine Orations' implored the Senators to act in the name of honour and Roman virtue by punishing Verres' corruption. The problem of the Roman **empire**, Cicero argued, was that it imposed high standards of moral responsibility, but facilitated enormous temptation to those given the responsibility to govern it. Polybius (c. 203–122 BC) magnified this problem into a theory of the cyclical dynamics of all empires. The Romans, he argued, had won their empire through virtue because they were committed to martial values and not to decadence and luxury. Empire however, would eventually lead to corruption, as the temptations of wealth and indolence weakened the commitment to virtue. Corruption, Polybius warned, was the fate of all empires, and it signalled not only the decay of virtue, but the collapse of order as the shared commitment to the common good gave way to faction and self-interest.

Corruption – body politic

The combination of Aristotelian thought with Christian theology during the Medieval period overlaid Aristotle's doctrine of the moral mean with measures of moral praise or condemnation in reference to the tenets of divine teaching. Significantly, the very basis of Medieval Biblical interpretation placed human beings and their earthly polities entirely within the sphere of corruption (of the flesh), and that only in resurrection could the truly faithful triumph over death. For St Augustine (354–430 AD) this led to abiding pessimism about the very possibility of any escape from corruption on this earth. Ordinary human polities (the City of Man) might aspire to high ideals, but the sinful nature of human beings meant that vice and lust would prevail. Only in the heavenly polity under God (the City of God) could a truly just political order be achieved.

Corruption here denoted the physical and moral decay of human beings and their polities. Corruption was fuelled by the pursuit of vices that carried with them the taint of sin. In this sense, particular forms of activity such as venality or simony might not be described as corrupt as such, but were identified with the sin of avarice. Avarice constituted a grave moral failing in Medieval thought, and consisted in the immoderate love of money supplanting the love that human beings should have for God or for each other. The solution to the problem of avarice was framed in distinctly Aristotelian terms, requiring the restoration of the right order of things by the exercise of virtues such as liberality. Consequently, the key to the public, political well being of the community lay in the exercise of the appropriate virtues by its members.

Medieval thinkers often represented the political community as an organic unity, regularly speaking of it through the analogue of the body politic. As John of Salisbury (1115–80) described it, the political community could be thought of as consisting in several connected members, just like a human body. The Church, responsible for the spiritual well being of the community, was the soul in the body of the republic; the prince occupies the head and rules subject only to being ruled by the soul; while judges and provincial governors are like the political body's sensory organs. Significantly, John's image of the body politic made special mention of the treasury as resembling 'the stomach and intestines' which 'engender innumerable and incurable diseases' in the body politic if unregulated.

In Medieval thought then, corruption could denote the process by which a body decays, its members falling away or disintegrating like the rotting flesh of the human corpse. For Medieval Christians, this kind of corruption was the fate of all human beings. The physical decay of the body was the necessary step to the resurrection of the soul. Importantly, death and corruption was a fate that levelled all human beings, even once mighty kings.

Corruption – towards separate realms

The problem of sin or vice in politics however, was that if it took hold in one segment of the body politic it may cause the disease to spread. If all members of the body politic were connected, the corruption of disease in one might not be prevented from infecting the others. Some Medieval writers however, were beginning to develop more a modern conceptualization of the community consisting of discrete realms. Marsilio of Padua (1275–1342) for example marshalled an Aristotelian scheme of good and bad polities to show that the latter were those in which secular, public authority was under the sway of those who were not motivated by or able to protect the common good. Marsilio's approach suggested that there were distinct and identifiable boundaries between spheres of responsibility. In particular, the boundaries between secular and religious authorities were especially important. One of Marsilio's chief concerns was that Church authorities were especially prone to avarice and decadence. Marsilio's references to corruption implied that there were different and distinct spheres of authority

within the state, and that the transgression of the boundaries represented a kind of corruption. They also implied that corruption consisted in a particular kind of transgression, namely, the control of public authority by those with dubious financial interests.

Niccolo Machiavelli's (1469–1529) use of the term corruption suggested two dimensions of his understanding, first a loss of discipline or virtue, and second, a preponderance of private interests over the public interest. For Machiavelli, the health of a republic depended on the constant struggle and contest between popular and oligarchic or aristocratic forces. Successful rulers had to seek a mastery of uncertain fortune through decisive leadership and/or by wisely designed and vigorously maintained institutions that enabled individual rulers and the citizens as a whole to emulate necessary virtues. Virtue consisted in those behaviours (such as decisiveness, courage, discipline, fortitude, sacrifice) opposed to those that tended towards corruption (indolence, decadence, cowardice). Most importantly, he identified a citizen's militia as the vital mechanism by which individual citizens could receive training in the virtues of **war** (discipline, courage, fortitude), and the virtues of political stability (loyalty, obedience, and love of homeland).

Machiavelli thus tended to refer to corruption in the context of describing the falling-away of regimes from a former glory, attributable to indulgence in excess, luxury, or a loss of discipline among the citizens. Crucially, the danger of corruption was explicitly associated not only with those who hold public office, but with the entire populace and the institutions of the republic. For Machiavelli then, one dimension of corruption centred on the loss of virtue. The other dimension connected the loss of virtue to a more modern conception of a separation of public and private interests. Above all other dangers to the republic, Machiavelli warned of the corruption caused by 'gentlemen'. Gentlemen were the chief promoters of all corruption because they lived in splendor, idleness, and indulgence, and were especially dangerous when they maintained castles and armed followers. For Machiavelli, the autonomy of politics consisted in the contest between political actors for glory or supremacy within the city. The second dimension of corruption in particular threatened the collapse of this autonomy when the public interest was supplanted by the private interests of gentlemen or a tyrant.

The sting in the tail of Machiavelli's analysis however, was that the pursuit of virtue, if successful, would lead republics to a policy of conquest and empire. The glory of empire however, would lead inevitably to the temptation of power and wealth, and hence to corruption. A corrupted polity is one in which faction and private interest prevails over the common interest, and thereby the republic becomes weak, enervated and prone to conquest by more vigorous polities. For Machiavelli, the problem of corruption was not simply a personal moral failing, but a political problem with systemic implications. As the analysis of corruption and empire suggests, Machiavelli was aware that temptations of power and wealth undermined the pursuit of virtue, and hence threatened the dynamics of healthy political contest. Significantly, a range of thinkers influenced by Machiavelli came to identify other sources of corruption in the rise of new forms of financial and commercial wealth that challenged the Renaissance image of the virtuous ownership of land. In this new environment, private pecuniary corruption came to be seen as a chief danger to virtue and to stable politics.

Corruption – public and private

While commerce was thought to expand the possibilities for corruption, the gradually narrowing definition of corruption also suggests a series of other conceptual shifts in western political thought. The changing contours of corruption can be correlated, for example, with the decline of the metaphor of the body politic, and the identification of new dynamics of political development focused on ensuring the financial viability and military security of sovereign states, and a political balance between newly emerging social classes.

Nonetheless, it does not necessarily follow that corruption was uniformly identified simply with the undue influence of private interests in public life. Throughout the Renaissance, patronage remained a central feature of political life at royal courts across Europe. The practitioners and beneficiaries of the often subtle game of seeking and receiving patronage may have been just as keen to protect it *from* corruption, as its critics were to construe it *as* corruption. This resulted in the concept of corruption becoming a crucial ideological weapon in political contests between King and Parliament in seventeenth-century England. In the context of this struggle, corruption was used as a rhetorical charge to attack particular forms of royal revenue raising and patronage. In the language of the body politic there were few options for re-thinking the place of the sovereign in relation the other members of the 'body'. Re-casting that relationship required a language able to separate the monarch's private person from their persona as embodiment of the 'body politic', and a narrower conception of corruption was an important tool in that quest.

Throughout the Renaissance, the outline of new dynamics of political, social and economic well-being were being developed, though often associated with the older discourse of virtue and vice. In particular, the problems of inflation and a money economy were seen to require a new dynamic art of good government. This art consisted in the regulation of exchange and coinage as a means of mediating between the interrelated but independent sectors of society engaged in separate economic pursuits. In this context, corruption gradually came to be more closely associated with financial misdemeanours in public office (as it did in the impeachment of Sir Francis Bacon in 1621 for instance).

In the contest between King Charles I (1600–49) and Parliament in the 1640s Parliament complained of the 'corrupt and ill-affected party' advising the King who had managed to 'corrupt' the bishops. Here corruption denoted both the doctrinal deviations or perversions of the bishops, and the greedy and grasping financial measures of the Crown. The King responded by buttressing his own claim to a divine sanction to rule by rejecting Parliament's charge. Some eight years later, as he was about to pay for defeat in the Civil War (1642–9) with his life, Charles reflected that divine sanction or no, only in resurrection could any human, even a king, triumph over corruption. As he stood upon the scaffold in Whitehall his final comment to Dr Juxon echoed the older biblical connotation of corruption. 'I go' he said 'from a corruptible, to an incorruptible Crown; where no disturbance can be, no disturbance in the World.' The very image of the 'body politic' itself was transformed by the trauma of the decapitation of the King as 'head' of the English 'body politic', and the rulership of the infamous 'Rump' Parliament.

As the new political settlement in England was forged in the latter half of the seventeenth century, corruption appeared in the efforts that political writers were making to define the role of commerce and its relationship to the distribution of power. By conceptualizing political **legitimacy** in terms of a contractual bargain between self-interested individuals seeking protection of life and property, Thomas Hobbes' (1588–1679) thought played a pivotal role in the post-Medieval rejection of the Aristotelian foundations of Western political thought. Nonetheless, Hobbes' 'modernity' was still coloured by a striking use of the analogy of the body politic in his analysis of the various 'infirmities' and 'diseases' to which a commonwealth may be exposed. His use of the term corruption however, was much closer to modern usage in speaking of the use of bribes to 'buy' judicial opinion. For Hobbes then, corruption denoted undue private interest in the application of the law. This could only be interpreted as a vicious subversion of law as the expression of sovereign power, and reinforced a slowly sharpening distinction between 'public' office and 'private' interest.

The charge of corruption then, was slowly detached from claims of moral decay and increasingly associated with specific kinds of misdemeanour in the exercise of public office. Though few went as far as Bernard Mandeville (1670–1733) in endorsing the beneficial effects of the 'slipp'rey... Perquisite' in public office, he did express a more popular trend in dismissing the 'body politic' metaphor. As even his strongest critic, Daniel Defoe (1660–1731) recognized, the market was transforming the nature of government, and this required new boundaries to insulate trade and commerce from undue government interference, but also to prevent unscrupulous traders from attempting to 'corrupt and procure' political power.

What writers like Defoe and Mandeville were grasping towards, in very different ways, were new theories of social and political stability and progress pre-mised on the extension of commerce and trade. The eighteenth century emer-gence of such theories in France and Scotland helped to recast western poli-tical thought in significant ways. One important change lay in the develop-ment of new ways of speaking of the 'health' of the state in terms of its civili-zation, that is, in terms of its conformity to presumed standards of modernity, civility, and **good governance**. Though this new language did not necessarily replace older metaphors of the body politic, it made their application seem increasingly anachronistic. By the terms of the new language of political thought, the political community came to be seen as an artefact of governmental activity decoupled from citizen virtue. As a con-sequence, the 'health' of the political community came to be defined in terms of the requirements for a flourishing market and solvent state. This was an image of a political community freed from the moral physics of decay, and in which the contours of corruption began to coincide with the boundaries that separated private interests from public responsibilities.

Corruption – from empire to good governance

The nexus between empire and corrup-tion has been a significant trope in Wes-tern thought, and its echoes have shaped the contemporary discourse on corrup-tion and **global governance**. Edmund Burke's (1729–97) celebrated impeach-ment of the former British East India Company Governor-General of Bengal, Warren Hastings, hinged on the issue of corruption. In the many speeches he made on the impeachment, Burke self-consciously echoed Cicero as he sought to use Hastings as a warning to the Brit-ish people and its government of the

hazards and the responsibility of imper-ial rule. The need to preserve British lib-erties at home was matched, he argued, by the imperative to rule other peoples for their benefit, not just Britain's, and certainly not the Company's. Hastings and the Company he maintained were little more than a band of extortionists and peculators who ruthlessly exploited the people of India for their own private gain. In doing so, not only did they dis-play their own corruption, they corrupted the entire frame of empire, undermining its only possible justification.

While Burke's rhetoric harked back to the old language of moral failure, his references to corruption were over-whelmingly modern, referring most often to Hastings' engagement in unauthorized financial measures, bribery or pecula-tion. Significantly, Burke had been an early convert to the new political econ-omy of Adam Smith and his con-temporaries. What is now referred to as the Scottish Enlightenment produced the most systematic of early modern theories of society premised on the existence of an economy with its own dynamics of **development**. This significantly con-tributed to the emergence of a modern art of good government premised on the identification of the autonomy and inter-nal dynamics but mutual inter-dependence of society and 'economy'. Most importantly, once identified, it was the responsibility of government to allow those dynamics to operate freely and efficiently. To interfere was to corrupt those processes and to endanger the partly unintended benefits of their unhindered operation, the generation of wealth, the augmentation of sovereign power, and the extension of personal liberty.

It is this framework of ideas that informs the contemporary discourse of corruption. The so-called 'Washington consensus' between the US government and international agencies such as the **World Bank** and **International Monetary Fund** (IMF) on the requirements for successful development have reinforced a distinctly western vision of good governance (including fiscal discipline, privatization, and trade liberalization). Among other things, these requirements are supposed to ensure that developing states conform to western standards of accountability. In this environment, Transparency International (TI) has linked the prevalence of corruption with the absence of good governance. According to TI, corruption consists in the misuse of public power entrusted to officials, which not only imposes wasteful economic costs on society, but undermines national integrity and the quality of life it is supposed to ensure. TI's approach is premised on a National Integrity System in which the goods of 'quality of life' and 'rule of law' are held to depend on relations of internal and international surveillance and accountability; hence the focus on transparency. Above all, this vision of accountability suggests that 'transparency' means that the polities involved must comply with western standards of good governance. Because transparency is associated with a western model of good governance, non-western polities are thereby characterized as most likely to be 'corrupt'.

Historically, the concept of corruption has had wide contours of meaning, but its meaning in twentieth century western social science has been more restricted, and tends to denote breaches of rules governing the role of private (usually pecuniary) interests in public office. The concept has been largely shorn of explicit reference to older notions of a loss of virtue, or political decay. Nonetheless, the charge of corruption still carries with it a strong implication of moral condemnation. The search of a rigorous and consistent definition of corruption

among social scientists today is not likely to be successful. Perhaps then, the virtue of the term is that its wide contours of · meaning incorporate both the suggestion of a breach of office, and connotations of grave moral failure.

Further reading

Harris, R. (2003) *Political Corruption*, London: Routledge.

Heidenheimer, A. J. and Johnston, M. (eds) (2002) *Political Corruption: Concepts and Contexts*, 3rd edn, New York: Transaction Publishers.

Kidd, J. B. and Richter, F-J. (eds) (2003) *Corruption and Governance in Asia*, Basingstoke: Palgrave.

Lindsey, T. and Dick, H. (eds) (2002), *Corruption in Asia: Rethinking the Governance Paradigm*, Sydney: Federation Press.

Pocock, J. G. A. (1975) *The Machiavellian Moment: Florentine Political Thought and the Atlantic Republican Tradition*, Princeton: Princeton University Press.

Rose Ackerman, S. (1999) *Corruption and Government: Causes, Consequences, and Reform*, Cambridge: Cambridge University Press.

Transparency International (2004) *Global Corruption Report 2004*, London: Pluto Press.

See also: failed state; good governance

BRUCE BUCHAN

Cosmopolitan democracy

Cosmopolitan democracy is a radical model for rethinking democracy and governance at the global, regional and national level. It does not seek to do away with states, however their structure and **power** is to be considerably altered through the construction of new forms of political institutions and substantial changes to existing political structures. Cosmopolitan democracy refers to democratic governance on a multiplicity of levels, from the local to the global.

The institutional arrangements of cosmopolitan democracy start from the recognition that given the number of issues that cross the boundaries of states and the extent of interconnections between peoples and states, the state alone is incapable of providing for the most basic needs of individuals. **Globalization** generates the need for the extension of democracy beyond the confines of the **nation-state**. Thus the political project of cosmopolitan democracy can be understood as 'the attempt to reconcile the phenomenon of globalization with the success of democracy' (Archibugi 2002: 28). Advocates of cosmopolitan democracy therefore question and reconstruct some of the key concepts of the Westphalian state system (see **Westphalia**), particularly the assumed congruency between **sovereignty**, territoriality and political community. They argue that there exists a fundamental disjuncture between the formal political authority that states claim and the dynamics of the global economy, international organizations, **international law**, global environmental issues and global communications. While liberal democracy was developed within the nation-state and constructed upon territorial foundations, democracy today is faced with a boundary problem. Overlapping communities of fate have arisen as issues and actors across state borders.

While cosmopolitan democracy retains states and recognizes their important role, the concept of state sovereignty is considerably altered as the locus of power and authority is dispersed above and below the state. Cosmopolitan democracy requires that new institutions of governance are created at the local, regional and global level. These political institutions would coexist with the existing system of states but would result in states no longer being regarded as the sole centres of **legitimate power** within their own borders. While governance already exists to some extent at the local, regional and global level, international institutions are usually accountable to sovereign states rather than to individuals or transnational actors.

Cosmopolitan democracy requires the development of multiple levels of **global governance**, such as the establishment of institutions with a legitimate right to govern over specific issues at the local, state, regional, and global level. The guiding principle in determining the structures of cosmopolitan democracy is that local issues should be determined directly at the local level, issues of regional significance at the regional level and global issues with global consequences at the global level. The basic principle is that individuals affected by decisions should have their interests represented in the decision making process. This, it is argued, will promote a more participatory democracy, as individuals become active members of more than one political community and thus have access to several avenues for participation. Individuals would hold multiple citizenships at these various levels, including global citizenship. The ultimate objective of the project is to create symmetry and congruency between those involved in the decision making process and those affected by its outcome.

Besides advocating multiple levels of governance, the model of cosmopolitan democracy entails a number of key institutional changes to the contemporary **international system**. It requires the reformation, extension and strengthening of existing global institutions such as the **United Nations** (UN) and also the creation of new institutions and governing mechanisms. In the short term the aim is to enshrine cosmopolitan democratic law within state constitutions and international assemblies such as the UN. This would involve reforming the Security Council, the General Assembly and other UN governing institutions as well as enforcing key elements of the **human rights** legislation that are part of UN conventions, thereby strengthening existing cosmopolitan laws. In addition, global institutions such as the **World Bank**, **International Monetary Fund** and **World Trade Organization** would be open to public examination and their procedures made more accountable and democratic. In the long term the cosmopolitan model would seek the creation of transnational legislative and executive bodies at both the regional and global levels. This would require the creation of regional parliaments and the holding of referenda which would cut across territorial boundaries to consult individuals and groups on regional issues. Ultimately, the UN would become a global parliament rather than an instrument of sovereign states. Important to the protection and enforcement of these rights is the development of regional and international courts which individuals could appeal to and thereby hold states and international bodies to account. Cosmopolitan democracy also requires that new enforcement mechanisms are developed to ensure the implementation of international law and especially cosmopolitan law (that body of international law that applies to individuals rather than states).

These proposals together provide for a fundamentally changed world order, and many critics have dismissed cosmopolitan democracy as a vague utopian project. Its defenders counter this charge by arguing that **democratization** confined within territorial boundaries is incapable of providing citizens with the means to shape the forces of globalization.

Further reading

Archibugi, D. (2002) 'Demos and Cosmopolis', *New Left Review* 13: 24–38.

Archibugi, D. and Held, D. (eds) (1995) *Cosmopolitan Democracy: An Agenda For a New World Order*, Cambridge: Polity Press.

Archibugi, D., Held, D. and Kohler, M. (eds) (1998) *Reimagining Political Community: Studies in Cosmopolitan Democracy*, Cambridge: Polity Press.

Held, D. (1991) 'Democracy, the Nation-State and the Global System', *Economy and Society Economy and Society*, 20(2): 138–72.

Held, D. (1992) 'Democracy: From City States to a Cosmopolitan Order?', *Political Studies*, 40: 10–39.

Held, D. (1995) *Democracy and the Global Order: From Modern States to Cosmopolitan Governance* Cambridge: Polity Press.

See also: cosmopolitanism; democratic deficit; global civil society; global governance; globalization; sovereignty

HOLLI THOMAS

Cosmopolitanism

The term is derived from the Greek word *kosmopolities*. One of the first expressions of cosmopolitanism is attributed to Diogenes the Cynic who proclaimed himself to be a 'citizen of the world'. All cosmopolitans believe that we should view ourselves as deeply linked to humanity as a whole, although what this should mean at a more concrete level is a hotly debated issue in the study of international relations. However, over the past decade cosmopolitan expressions such as 'global citizen' and 'global community' have come into common usage, partly in response to the intensification of **globalization** and a growing **global civil society**. Cosmopolitanism has also emerged as an important philosophical approach in contemporary debates concerning the scope of justice, the extent to which we owe duties to our fellow compatriots as opposed to those who live outside our national communities, and the character of **global governance**.

Although cosmopolitanism has been conceived in a variety of forms, it is generally agreed that there are two core elements shared by all of them. These are the principles of individualism and universality (Pogge 1994: 89). The first principle, individualism, takes human beings to be the ultimate unit of moral concern. Individuals are seen as belonging to a single moral realm, where each person is of equal moral worth and should be treated accordingly. Regardless of where individuals are born or brought up, cosmopolitanism asserts the irreducible moral status of each and every person. From a cosmopolitan point of view it is individuals, not states, or nations, or communities that are the primary object of concern. States only have value to the extent that they protect and provide for the individuals within them. Hence, cosmopolitanism questions the moral significance of the state and views the state in an instrumental manner.

The second element of generality emphasizes that persons are the ultimate unit of concern for *everyone*, not simply for fellow compatriots or those who share the same religion. From a cosmopolitan perspective, the understanding that we are individuals with equal moral worth and who share a common humanity, requires that the scope of justice should be global.

It is helpful to distinguish between *moral* and *institutional* cosmopolitanism. Moral cosmopolitanism is concerned with the basis upon which cosmopolitan principles and institutions can be justified. Thus moral cosmopolitanism claims that there are universal standards of moral judgement and universal princi-

ples of right, and seeks to justify this claim. While moral cosmopolitanism does not specify or demand any particular set of institutional arrangements, value or ethical significance is only attached to institutional arrangements that promote human worth.

Institutional cosmopolitanism is concerned with what political institutions should be established to ensure that cosmopolitan principles are protected and promoted. There is no particular institutional arrangement that is supported by all cosmopolitans despite the common misconception that cosmopolitanism means support for a world state. In fact, few cosmopolitans have ever supported the idea of a world state and most of them remain sceptical that individual liberty and freedom could be protected or provided for through one universal government. Many cosmopolitans argue that it is both necessary and desirable to maintain some form of state structure. For example, David Held has advocated a model of global democratic governance based upon a system of **cosmopolitan democracy**. Within such a model, although the existing state structure is retained, it exists alongside a network of overlapping institutions at the local, state, regional and global level. **Power** and **authority** would be dispersed to both supranational institutions and local levels of governance. From a cosmopolitan perspective state sovereignty should be conditional, not absolute. Sovereignty has value only insofar as the sovereign state protects the freedom and well-being of its citizens, and is part of an **international system** that promotes these values globally. However, states are not equal and some states are in a better position than others to provide for their citizens' well being. Accordingly, cosmopolitans advocate a global vision of distributive justice. They share the view that the contemporary state system itself is inadequate to support moral cosmopolitanism.

Thus cosmopolitanism is both a philosophical perspective as well as a political project. It is the articulation of a set of moral principles and a commitment to the establishment of political institutions to support those principles. As a philosophical concept, cosmopolitanism has been expressed in a variety of ways across many ethical traditions over history. Cosmopolitanism has also been the target of fierce critique from many quarters in the discipline of International Relations. Its critics include realists, communitarians and poststructuralists (see **realism**, **communitarianism**, **poststructuralism**).

Further reading

Beitz, C. (1999) 'Social and Cosmopolitan Liberalism', *International Affairs* 75(3), 515–29.

Caney, S. (2001) 'International Distributive Justice', *Political Studies* 49, 974–97.

Held, D. (2004) *Global Covenant*, Cambridge: Polity.

Jones, C. (1999) *Global Justice: Defending Cosmopolitanism* Oxford: Oxford University Press.

Lu, C. (2000) 'The One and Many Faces of Cosmopolitanism', *Journal of Political Philosophy* 8(2), 244–67.

Pogge, T. (1994) 'Cosmopolitanism and Sovereignty', in C. Brown (ed.), *Political Restructuring in Europe: Ethical Perspectives*, London: Routledge, 89–122.

Vertovac, S. and Cohen, R. (eds) (2002) *Conceiving Cosmopolitanism: Theory, Context and Practice*, Oxford: Oxford University Press.

See also: communitarianism; cosmopolitan democracy; democratic peace; global civil society; global governance; human capabilities; human rights

HOLLI THOMAS

Crimes against humanity

In international criminal law, a crime against humanity is an international crime and is distinguished from a domestic crime on the basis that its breach is of concern to the whole of humanity. The victims are not only those persons directly affected by the commission of the offence but all of humanity. Such crimes include murder, extermination, enslavement, deportation, imprisonment, torture, rape, and persecution on political, racial or religious grounds.

Crimes against humanity are distinct from **war crimes** because they are not restricted to periods of armed conflict. It was not until the end of World War Two that vague references were formally categorized as a new species of international crime. The Charter of the International Military Tribunal for Nuremberg (1950) expressly created the category of Crimes Against Humanity, and provided sanctions for their breach. The crimes were to attract individual criminal liability for the perpetrator.

The drafters of the Nuremberg Charter had to grapple with the non-intervention principle which provided that **international law** had no application to events that occurred within the borders of a country. In other words international law only applied to events that had occurred during the course of an international event such as an armed conflict. This meant that the crimes committed by the Nazis against their own people prior to the outbreak of the war could not be punished by an international tribunal. The Nuremberg Charter broke new ground in creating a category of international crime that was punishable under international law.

For a crime to be classified as a crime against humanity it must be directed at a civilian population. There is also a need for the crime to exhibit the characteristics of system or organization and be of a certain scale and gravity. The crime cannot be the work of an isolated individual acting alone. It must be shown to be part of a wider plan or policy, but there is no requirement that the crime be carried out pursuant to the policy of a state. In other words, the perpetrator of a crime against humanity must know that his/her act is part of a widespread or systematic attack against civilians, even if a perpetrator is motivated by personal reasons for committing the crime.

The widespread or systematic nature of such crimes must be distinguished from random acts of violence unconnected to any system or organization. The term 'widespread' refers to frequent, large-scale action carried out collectively with considerable seriousness and directed against a multiplicity of victims. The term 'systematic' refers to activities that are thoroughly organized and which follow a regular pattern of abuse.

Is **terrorism** a crime against humanity? This is a fiercely debated question since the events of 11 September 2001. Certainly, crimes against humanity can include acts of terrorism. A single act can be a crime against humanity if the act is carried out pursuant to an organized policy. Thus the attack on the Twin Towers in New York September 2001 was directed against a civilian population and formed part of an organized and systematic plan.

Unfortunately, whilst individual acts of terrorism may be defined as crimes against humanity, there does not exist a universally recognized definition of terrorism in international law. The inability of the international community to reach a consensus on the meaning of terrorism means that terrorism is not automatically a crime against humanity. One of the fundamental principles of international humanitarian law is that there be certainty in international crimes before persons

are tried for their breach. In the absence of a definition of terrorism in international law, it cannot be prohibited.

It has not been for want of trying that an acceptable definition of terrorism has not been found. Numerous conventions have been drafted under the auspices of the **United Nations** to solve the problem. Nor have individual states been slow in drafting their own definitions of what they consider to be acts of terrorism. The problem is that there is no real consistency between the various definitions.

Consequently, not all terrorist acts amount to crimes against humanity. If terrorism means the use of politically motivated violence in order to create public fear, then a terrorist act may or may not be a crime against humanity. For example a political activist may commit a terrorist act by detonating a small explosive device in a crowded cinema. The explosion may not kill or even seriously injure anyone. Thus it would not be a crime against humanity despite being an act of terrorism. However, if the bomb had killed a large number of people then the terrorist act may constitute a crime against humanity. Accordingly the magnitude of the crime is a very relevant consideration. When the size of the attack against the civilian population becomes very large and when it is motivated by a desire to destroy an identified group of human beings, the offence becomes the most serious of all international crimes, namely **genocide**.

International criminal law is still in the developmental stage. In some cases, crimes such as torture and slavery (which are the subject of specific legal conventions) are interpreted as crimes against humanity. The expansion of the category has been particularly notable with respect to sexual assaults including rape. For example, sexual slavery during armed conflict has been recognized in international criminal law as both sexual slavery and torture. As customary international law develops alongside or in addition to statute or treaty law it is likely that other crimes will be added to the list.

Further reading

Cryer, R. (2005) *Prosecuting International Crimes,* Cambridge: Cambridge University Press.

May, L. and Postema, G. (eds) (2004) *Crimes Against Humanity: A Normative Account,* Cambridge: Cambridge University Press.

Ratner, S. and Abrams, J. (2001) *Accountability for Human Rights Atrocities in International Law: Beyond the Nuremberg Legacy,* Oxford: Oxford University Press, 2nd edn.

Robertson, G. (2000) *Crimes Against Humanity,* Harmondsworth: Penguin.

See also: gendercide; genocide; war crime

GRANT NIEMANN

Crisis

The most general definition of a crisis refers to a diplomatic, economic, or military turning point in which the relations between the states in question are in flux, or in the case of a military crisis, in transition from peace to **war**. However, it is also customary to employ the concept to refer to a disruption in normal economic or diplomatic relations between states (see **diplomacy**). Examples of each kind include a crisis between states in a conflict occasioned by the threat or deployment of force (military), a crisis between rich and poor states precipitated by the possibility of the latter defaulting on their loans (economic), a crisis between signatories to a treaty when a state announces it will violate the provisions of the treaty (diplomatic). In each of these examples,

there are also some common characteristics that define them as crises. They include a threat to the core values of at least one state, the presence of increased uncertainty in the future pattern of relations between the states involved, and a sense of urgency reflecting that the disruption in relations is volatile and needs to be stabilized.

There is also the possibility that a crisis may be transformed from a diplomatic or economic crisis into a military crisis if efforts to resolve it include the introduction of military force. Therefore, the study of international crises has tended to gravitate toward the most severe disruptions of international relations involving the threat or deployment of military force and a corresponding increase in the diplomatic efforts of states to resolve the conflict and alleviate the threat posed to them. Diplomatic historians and political scientists have focused on these military confrontations between states in an effort to explain why some crises end in war while others produce a diplomatic settlement or fade away to lower levels of conflict. The introduction of nuclear weapons into the arsenals of several states after World War Two accelerated these efforts in response to the increased costs of war as a crisis outcome. The results of these efforts include a vast inventory of crisis characteristics collected by scholars, a greater understanding of the external and internal origins of crises, and the identification of strategies favoring the escalation or de-escalation of crises toward war or peace.

The most exhaustive inventory of crises is the collection of crisis data by Brecher and Wilkenfeld (1989), who catalog over eighty characteristics of several hundred international and foreign policy crises in the twentieth century. Scholars have mined this source for connections between antecedent conditions and crisis outcomes. Other scholars have focused their attention on particular cases that appear to be particularly important, such as the 1914 crisis among the European **great powers** leading to World War One or the 1962 Cuban Missile crisis between the United States and the Soviet Union ending in a diplomatic settlement. These two cases illustrate the link between **arms race**s and crises posited by those international relations theorists who argue that the **balance of power** between states has an important impact on the development and the outcome of conflicts between them.

The **security dilemma** posed by a state's need to arm in self-defense at the risk of provoking a similar move by other states fosters increased tension and an arms race among states with a greater likelihood that a triggering event may create a military crisis. In June 1914, the assassination of the Austrian Archduke Franz Ferdinand by Serbian nationalists triggered a military crisis between Austria and Serbia. This confrontation brought Russia, France, and Britain into the conflict on the side of Serbia with Germany backing Austria. None of these **great powers** wanted war over this issue, but the history of arms races and the rivalries between the parties along with a bipolar **alliance** pattern resulted in war rather than a peaceful resolution of the crisis. Similar background conditions were present at the onset of the Cuban Missile crisis in 1962. The arms race between the **superpower**s was accompanied by mounting tension between the United States and the Soviet Union as leaders of rival **alliance**s. However, their leaders coped with the triggering event of America's discovery of Russian missiles in Cuba and the Soviet resistance to removing them by first escalating and then de-escalating the crisis short of war.

Given the different outcomes following from similar external conditions, cri-sis analysts examined the internal characteristics of the states to explain the difference. The decision-making processes of the participants in each crisis were marked by sharp contrasts. **Misperception** of the hostility expressed by each side toward the other fueled a conflict spiral in 1914 ending in war. In 1962 the leaders of the United States and the Soviet Union perceived each other's actions and intentions more accurately and were able to recognize and respond to overtures to settle the crisis. Differences among the protagonists in their emphasis on offensive versus defensive military strategies also affected the outcomes of the two crises. The 1914 crisis spiraled into war fueled with an emphasis by the great powers on the advantage of striking first; the 1962 crisis was a successful test of the strategy pursued by both superpowers of **deterrence** to prevent a first strike. The lessons learned from these cases included the need for establishing and maintaining clear communication during a crisis and the importance of coupling an assessment of the balance of power between states with the strategic doctrines governing the use of force by each side.

Subsequent research on international crises has charted the comparative anatomy of international crises and refined our knowledge of crisis management strategies and decision-making processes. Although crises may have territorial, ethnic, cultural, or economic origins, territorial crises between adjacent states are most likely to escalate into war. While almost all crises have a recognizable triggering event, the tempo of subsequent developments and their resolution in war or peace varies according to the distribution of capabilities between the states engaged in the conflict and their crisis bargaining strategies.

Crisis bargaining strategies influence the outcome of crises independently of power relationships between states. The most effective strategy even against a stronger opponent is a strategy of **reciprocity** in which a state establishes its resolve not to be bullied by responding to coercive moves in kind while taking cooperative initiatives when the opportunity occurs. Strategies of bullying and **appeasement** are less likely to avoid the undesirable outcomes of war or submission while reciprocity is more likely to achieve a mutual settlement and reassure the opponent by eschewing domination as an outcome. States also demonstrate a capacity for learning and adaptation in repeated crises with the same opponent. States that achieve a successful outcome of domination in one crisis are likely to repeat this strategy in subsequent confrontations with the same opponent. States that suffer military or diplomatic defeat are likely to escalate their coercive strategies in subsequent confrontations with the victor.

Further reading

Allison, G. and Zelikow, P. (1999) *Essence of Decision*, Boston: Little, Brown.

Brecher, M. and Wilkenfeld, J. (1989) *Crisis, Conflict, and Instability*, New York: Pergamon.

Hermann, C. (1972) *International Crises.* New York: Free Press.

Holsti, O. (1972) *Crisis, Escalation, War,* Montreal: Queen's University Press.

Lebow, R. (1981) *Between Peace and War,* Baltimore: Johns Hopkins University Press.

Leng, R. (2000) *Learning in Recurring Crises,* Ann Arbor, MI: University of Michigan Press.

Wilkenfeld, J., Young, K., Quinn, D. and Asal, V. (2005) *Mediating International Crises*, London: Routledge.

See also: misperception; preventive diplomacy; rationality

STEPHEN G. WALKER

Critical security studies

An approach that challenges the state-centric and primarily military orientations that have dominated the study of **security**. Developed since the 1980s as part of the broader post-positivist movement (see **post-positivism**), Critical Security Studies (CSS) argues that traditional approaches to security are often analytically, politically, and ethically inadequate as foundations for understanding or addressing contemporary security challenges and dynamics. The basic claim of CSS is that security is not an objective condition, assessing threats to security is not simply a matter of correctly perceiving a constellation of material forces, and the object of security is not stable. Instead, questions of how the object to be secured (nation, state, or other group) is constituted, and how particular issues (economic well-being, the risk of violence, environmental degradation) come to be portrayed and accepted as threats (or not) is placed at the center of analysis. Security, and especially its dominant forms constituted under the rubric of 'national security', is understood as a particular set of historical **discourse**s and practices that rest upon institutionalized shared understandings.

Theoretically, this reconsideration involves deconstructive and reconstructive elements (see **deconstruction**). Deconstructively, CSS critically examines the assumptions and knowledge claims of traditional strategic studies, and seeks to demonstrate that they rest upon a series of contestable methodological and political assumptions rather than directly reflecting reality, as many realists claim (see **realism**). Reconstructively, it argues for the need to incorporate a concern with the social construction of social order and action, and with the relationship between identities and interests, in order to accurately understand both conflictual and cooperative security relations, as well as processes of transformation. A central task of critical security analysis thus becomes to determine how security issues and threat thresholds are constructed and defined, and how they change as a result of different policies and political practices.

CSS argues that it is necessary to both *broaden* and *deepen* the agenda of security studies. Broadening refers to the need to consider a range of threats and challenges beyond military relations between territorial states. Economic or environmental dynamics, for example, are frequently cited as presenting direct and pressing threats to security that escape a more traditional view. Deepening involves challenging the dominance of the state as the major or sole object of security, and incorporating a concern with security at levels both above and below the state. At the highest level, all human life depends upon a healthy biosphere, a factor which is beyond the control of any single state and requires that the global environment itself be seen as something to be secured. At the other end of the scale, focusing upon the security of the individual (sometimes linked to the idea of human security) can reveal how for many people the state is not the agent of their security, but one of the most pressing threats to it, or (as feminists have argued) how **gender** relations are central in understanding the security situations of women, and the role of gendered identities in security relations. Finally, this allows a focus on sub- or non-state groups, which have been at the center of **ethnic conflict**s in the past decade, as well as allowing an incorporation of new security issues such as, for example, migration, where a key issue is the perception of threats to collective identity arising from migration flows.

Two broad directions of analysis can be discerned within CSS, sometimes terms 'small c' and 'large c' views of the term 'critical'. 'Small c' CSS is part of a wider movement in security studies that includes constructivists and poststructuralist analyses (see **constrictivism poststructuralism**), and focuses upon issues such as the social construction of threats, the relationship between state identities and policies, and the role of media information technologies in security politics. Research within this trajectory has often addressed core subjects of traditional security studies, examining the way in which appropriate *responses* to the threats are constructed in security policymaking. These analyses have stressed the ways in which **security dilemma**s are not inevitable or inescapable, examining the development of cooperative security policies and transformations such as those involved with the evolution of the **North Atlantic Treaty Organization** and the **Organization for Security and Cooperation in Europe** at the end of the **cold war**. Similarly, constructivist and poststructuralist analyses have sought to demonstrate how the construction of security policies involves not the straightforward securing of a stable political entity from external threats, but is actually implicated in the production and reproduction of state and national identities through their contrast to Others and, in extreme cases, in the casting of these others as enemies.

'Large C' thinking is linked to **critical theory** associated with the Frankfurt School in social theory, and sometimes linked to Gramscian approaches in IR. It places the idea of *emancipation* at the center of security. Emancipation is both a universal definition of security – to be free from constraints is to be secure; and a means to security, since conflict is a consequence of these constraints. 'Security' is in this view powerful both as an analytic concept and a politically mobilizing rhetoric through which change can be effected. Finally, the emancipatory side of CSS argues that an explicit concern with ethics is essential if an expanded security agenda that takes into account, for example, perceptions of migration as a security issue are to make ethical and political judgements about such concerns.

Two major criticisms have been levelled at CSS. The first, generally coming from a traditional security studies perspective, stresses that because it lacks an objective understanding of what security is and what threats are, CSS risks reducing security to little more than a synonym for whatever the analyst finds objectionable or distressing, resulting in a loss of analytic focus. The second criticism takes the opposite position, asserting that-particularly in those positions stressing emancipation – CSS treats security as a real condition to be achieved, a yardstick against which political structures can be judged. This, in the eyes of some critics, marks a return to an essentialized view of security that stands in tension (if not contradiction) with the constructed and contingent focus of CSS. A variation on this critique, often suggested by post-structurally influenced analysts, is that CSS risks placing too high a premium on security. Security is seen as something good, and the more security the better. This, the critics argue, risks overlooking how security is in practice connected to claims of threat that risk undermining emancipation rather than promoting it. Despite such criticisms, it is widely recognized that CSS has played a key role in energizing security studies in the post-cold war era, and that it continues to play an important and challenging role within ongoing debates over contemporary security challenges.

Further reading

Booth, K. (1991) 'Security and Emancipation', *Review of International Studies* 17, 4: 313–26.

Buzan, B., Waever, O. and De Witt, J. (1997) *Security: A New Framework for Analysis*, Boulder, CO: Lynne Rienner.

Dalby, S. (2003) *Environmental Security*, Minneapolis, MN: University of Minnesota Press.

Krause, K. and Williams, M. (1997) *Critical Security Studies: Concepts and Cases*, Minneapolis, MN: University of Minnesota Press.

Wyn Jones, R. (1999) *Security, Strategy, and Critical Theory*, Boulder, CO: Lynne Rienner Press.

See also: critical theory; security; post-positivism

MICHAEL C. WILLIAMS

Critical theory

The establishment of the *Institute for Social Research* in Frankfurt, Germany on 22 June 1922 marks the beginning of Frankfurt School critical theory. The principal members of the School have been the founders of the Institute, Max Horkheimer (1895–1971) and Theodor Adorno (1903–69); Herbert Marcuse (1898–1979), the major 'New Left' theorist of the 1960s; and Jurgen Habermas (b. 1929), the foremost critical theorist of recent times.

Their writings develop an approach to society which is faithful to the spirit but not to the letter of **Marxism**. Classical Marxism or historical materialism used the 'paradigm of production' to analyse particular social systems and to comprehend human history. This paradigm maintains that the forces of production (technology) and the relations of production (class relations) provide the key to understanding political systems and historical change. In particular, class conflict has been the greatest influence on how societies have developed.

Karl Marx (1818–83) and Friedrich Engels (1820–95) argued that the struggle between the bourgeoisie (the class that own the means of production) and the proletariat (the class that has to sell its labour-power in order to survive) is the central dynamic in capitalist societies. They believed that class conflict would destroy **capitalism** and lead to a socialist system in which the forces of production would be used to benefit the whole of society rather than to maximize bourgeois profit (see **socialism**). They also had a vision of global political progress in which the whole of humanity is eventually linked in a socialist world order. Crucially, Marx and Engels thought that the purpose of social inquiry was to promote the emancipation of exploited members of the proletariat. Marx maintained that 'philosophers have only interpreted the world: the point is to change it'. This, in a nutshell, is the commitment to emancipatory social science that is defended by the Frankfurt School.

Its members sought to preserve this conception of social inquiry while breaking with what they saw as the fatal limitations of the paradigm of production. It was plain to Horkheimer and Adorno in the 1930s that the stress on the centrality of production and class conflict could not explain violent **nationalism** in the fascist societies, the rise of totalitarian state power and the outbreak of total **war**. Their writings displayed increasing pessimism about the possibility of emancipation. Nowhere is this more striking than in Adorno's claim that human history has led from the slingshot to the A-bomb. To them, the promise of emancipation which had united the members of the Enlightenment (such as Kant) with their successors (such as Marx and Engels) seemed impossible

to fulfil in the modern era. This was to agree with Max Weber's bleak vision in which society is increasingly dominated by pressures to administer society more efficiently and economically.

Later members of the Frankfurt School sought to recover the emancipatory project without relapsing into classical Marxism and without neglecting the dangerous side of modernity. Herbert Marcuse (1898–1979) analysed how capitalism created 'one dimensional man' caught up in the satisfaction of manufactured material needs; but he believed that the student movement of the 1960s and the struggles for national liberation and socialism in the **Third World** represented a major political effort to create the free society. Habermas has focused on how efforts to administer capitalist societies have led to what he calls the 'colonisation of the life world' – that is to the encroachment of administrative rationality on everyday life – but he sees in the social movements which promote human **security**, equality for women and environmental restoration the promise of a new kind of society which replaces the quest to control nature and administer society with the struggle to enlarge human freedom.

Habermas also regards the **European Union** as an important new experiment in developing 'post-national communities'. These are political communities in which the state is no longer primarily linked with a single nation and dedicated to promoting its selfish interests. States in the European region are not alone in coming under pressure to create political arrangements which respect the multicultural nature of society (see **multiculturalism**). The greater mobility of peoples in recent decades has encouraged this 'post-national' development, as have economic **globalization** and the growing realization that democracy must be established on a world scale if it is to survive at all. In Habermas's view, cosmopolitan democracy can link peoples and cultures which do not have a common language (see **cosmopolitanism**), common symbols and the shared history which have underpinned the **nation-state** for the past two centuries.

The influence of Kant's ideal of perpetual peace and Marx's internationalism is evident in Habermas's vision of postnational communities. Indeed he has been more concerned than earlier members of the Frankfurt School with reflecting on international relations. Marx largely neglected this dimension of human affairs; Engels recognized the importance of war and military strategy without considering the difficulties they raised for the paradigm of production; Horkheimer and Adorno were well aware that **nationalism**, totalitarianism and war had shattered the vision of a socialist utopia but they did not theorize these phenomena. Although Habermas has not set out to develop a critical theory of world politics, he has addressed global issues such as the 1991 Gulf War, the **North Atlantic Treaty Organization**'s intervention over Kosovo in 1999 and the recent Iraq war in various interviews and journalistic essays. His main theoretical ambition has been to equip critical theory with ethical foundations and with universal moral commitments which were either absent from earlier Frankfurt School inquiry or inadequately theorized by its leading proponents. By developing critical theory in this way, Habermas (1990) looks back to Kant's moral philosophy which he reworks in the 'discourse theory of morality' (see later). This is a controversial standpoint, and Habermas's critics have argued that the search for ethical universals always contains the danger of privileging one cultural standpoint and imposing its ethnocentric values on others. The question of ethical universalism has been the central controversy surrounding Frankfurt School critical theory in recent times, and the importance of this controversy for the study of international relations has been immense. It is necessary to analyse Horkheimer's distinction between 'traditional' and 'critical' theory before considering these issues in more detail.

Traditional and critical theory

In the 1930s Horkheimer defended critical theory from the rising tide of positivism (traditional theory). In broad terms, positivism is an approach to society which strives to emulate the natural sciences; it uses scientific methods and quantitative means to uncover social laws and to predict human behaviour. The adequacy of positivism remains one of the central controversies in the philosophy of the social sciences. Horkheimer's main objection was that positivism produces knowledge that makes the more efficient administration of society possible. With the results of social scientific inquiry at their disposal, those that administer the social world can have greater confidence in their ability to steer society. Now this may seem a curious objection given that nineteenth century positivists such as the French sociologist, Auguste Comte (1798–1857) believed the application of science to the study of society would improve human circumstances. With an unprecedented ability to predict how their actions would affect society, they hoped to realize the Enlightenment ambition of increasing human freedom. Horkheimer's argument was that positivism cannot keep faith with Enlightenment ideals.

The main problem, as he saw it, was that positivists believed that objective knowledge of society was possible whereas visions of moral preferences were subjective or arbitrary preferences. Positivism can explain the most rational means of achieving chosen ends, but it denies that human beings can have objective knowledge about what they should do. Weber made this point in *Science as a Vocation* (1919) when quoting Tolstoy's observation that science cannot tell us what we should do and how we should live.

Horkheimer drew the conclusion that positivism left human beings at the mercy of those with the **power** to use knowledge to administer society and to maximize economy and efficiency. It offered no challenge to what Weber saw as the 'iron cage' in which the members of modern society seemed destined to be trapped (whether their society was capitalist or socialist was immaterial in his view) because of the dominance of administrative rationality. Positivism left human beings in the grip of a form of rationality ('instrumental reason') which was concerned with the economy and efficiency of means. In *Dialectic of Enlightenment* (1947), Horkheimer and Adorno argued that the triumph of instrumental reason was the main achievement of the Enlightenment; increased success in mastering the physical world had the effect of extending the political control of society and of diminishing human freedom in the process. Individuals had become more bureaucratized and disciplined in the course of developing greater power over nature.

The Frankfurt School had aimed to develop a vision of social inquiry that had the Enlightenment ideal of universal emancipation at its centre. As Bottomore (1976, p. 49) has argued, it hoped to recover 'subjectivity against the idea of an objective, law-governed process of history'. But Horkheimer and Adorno came to believe that the Enlightenment project was lost in the 1930s, and not least because of the demise of the revolutionary proletariat that Marx and Engels regarded as the historical subject

that would realize universal emancipation. As noted earlier, the main legacy of the Enlightenment for Horkheimer and Adorno was the triumph of instrumental reason and the rise of the 'totally administered society'. Adorno believed all that remained was a 'negative dialectics' in which the theorist could highlight the inadequacy of social arrangements (especially by showing how art exposed the absurdity of the world of instrumental reason and represented human suffering) while conceding there was no evidence that the good society would be realized.

The importance of Marx's thought for the Frankfurt School cannot be over-estimated although its relationship with Marxism has been one of ambivalence. As noted earlier, Horkheimer believed it was essential to follow the spirit but not the letter of Marxism. In particular, this meant accepting Marx's claim that human beings make their own history but not under conditions of their own choosing. The fundamental political question for Marx and for the Frankfurt School subsequently is how human beings can make history more freely. In terms used in more recent debates in International Relations, it is how they can exercise greater 'agency' in the face of constraining 'structures'.

The Frankfurt School did not view Marxism uncritically. Indeed, a central complaint about Marxism in the twentieth century, and specifically about Soviet Marxism, was that it had become transformed into a positivist social science. It was thought that the antecedents of that positivism could be found in Marx's discussion of how the iron laws of capitalist development would lead to political crisis and the transition to socialism. Whether this is a sound summary of Marx's approach has been contested by those who stress his belief that revolutionary class consciousness was necessary for the achievement of socialism. It is certainly true that Soviet Marxism became crudely positivist in its approach to the transition from capitalism to socialism. Horkheimer's claim that positivism left human beings at the mercy of those that wield political power seemed to be confirmed by the Soviet Union where the idea that the revolutionary elite could use advanced technology to promote freedom descended into totalitarian domination. Writers such as Marcuse were highly critical of the theoretical shortcomings and destructive political consequences of Soviet Marxism. Consequently, for later theorists such as Habermas, the question was how to preserve the emancipatory ideals of critical theory from the challenges of positivism and Soviet Marxism.

How then do critical theorists defend themselves from the positivist criticism that it is impossible to have knowledge of the ends that human beings should promote? How do they ground their claims about freedom, and how do they ensure that political efforts to promote human freedom do not degenerate into some form of domination? How should the commitment to human freedom inform social and political inquiry, and what can it contribute to the study of international relations?

Habermas is the main critical theorist to deal with these questions (and although he has not been concerned with the theory of international relations, his writings have influenced efforts to apply critical theory to world politics). To understand his approach it is useful to consider how Marx developed standards for assessing social and political arrangements, and how Habermas has tried to overcome the limitations of his approach and to move beyond Horkheimer and Adorno's pessimism about the dominance of instrumental reason.

Marx was mainly concerned with the critique of ideology (*ideologiekritique*).

The approach is evident in his analysis of capitalist ideology, the doctrine that maintains that private property, the division of labour and the free market were natural phenomena rather than socially constructed and changeable features of human life. Crucially, for Marx, capitalist society referred to the freedom and equality of all of its members to justify these practices. In so doing it provided the suffering victims of capitalism with a language with which to criticize labour exploitation and with which to envisage a world in which human beings could enjoy the freedom and equality that capitalism claimed to realize. For Marx one of the central tasks of critical theory was to engage in the critique of ideology; it was to show how the terms in which societies legitimated their arrangements were in tension with actual social conditions; it was to analyse the ways in which revolutionary social forces emerged from the tension between ideology and practice; and it was to understand and support their efforts to create a society in which the ideology of freedom and equality would no longer be contradicted by forms of exploitation and subordination.

The critique of ideology is linked with immanent critique, the notion that it is necessary to judge societies by the terms they use to defend themselves. The main alternative is to criticize society by appealing to moral standards that are said to be inherent in human nature or human reason. Marx and Engels rejected the belief (which is defended by Kant who in turn is a major influence on Habermas) that universal ethical standards can be used to criticize social arrangements. Their approach, taken up by the first generation of the Frankfurt School, aimed to subvert society from within by showing that moral standards which are said to be true for all (as in the case of freedom and equality in capitalist society) serve sectional interests and stand in the way of a genuinely free and equal society. In this approach one can see how critical theory as defended by the Frankfurt School differs from traditional theory or positivism. Critical theory focuses on political struggles that reveal in broad outline how an alternative society is already immanent within the current social order, whereas positivism aims to explain social laws and, on this basis, to predict future behaviour. For the Frankfurt School, the decision to concentrate on the recurrent and repetitive features of social life can have the dangerous effect of perpetuating unjustifiable constraints on human beings and reinforcing existing inequalities. Traditional theory is inadequate because it lacks the emancipatory intent that informs the critical standpoint.

The critical approach as outlined above does not explain why it is right to judge society by the ideals that it sets for itself. Why should these ideals be privileged? There is an implicit assumption in the Frankfurt School that freedom and equality are the highest moral ends, but they are not valued everywhere and they are understood in different ways in those parts of the world in which they have most support. Habermas's reworking of critical social theory endeavours to overcome this lacuna in Frankfurt School thinking.

To understand Habermas's position it is necessary to analyse one of the main themes in his 'reconstruction of historical materialism', namely that Marx and classical Marxism were too concerned with 'labour' or the activity of working on nature to satisfy material needs. They thought the conquest of nature held the key to human emancipation although the rise of totalitarianism in the inter-war years revealed the error of their thinking (and this explained, as we have seen, Horkheimer and Adorno's pessimism). What classical Marxism had ignored was

'interaction' – the sphere in which human beings negotiate the organizing principles of society. This for Habermas is the domain in which the main hope for progress towards greater freedom resides. A comprehensive study of society and history which reconstructs historical materialism must recognize that human beings do not only labour to satisfy basic needs; they also use language to discuss how society should be organized and how they should live. Habermas's argument that labour and interaction should be granted equal place in a theory of history and politics stresses that the classical Marxist commitment to the 'paradigm of production' must be complemented by the 'paradigm of communication' which recognizes the importance of language or 'communicative action' in the social world. This paradigm saves critical theory from the pessimism of Horkheimer and Adorno by focusing on forms of communication that cannot be reduced to instrumental reason according to Habermas.

In a striking formulation, Habermas argues that the unification of the human race was promised by the first use of language or first 'speech act'. What Habermas means by this statement is that all language users are committed to the same presuppositions: that what they say is intelligible; that it is true; that it is said sincerely; and that they have the right to communicate it. Efforts to deceive others can only succeed because others are committed to these basic principles. Of course, the extent to which societies are committed to public dialogue varies considerably and most societies in human history have certainly not been liberal democracies. But Habermas believes that moral standards can be derived from everyday language and used to judge social conditions and to envisage more free social relations.

Habermas has used the term 'ideal speech' and 'undistorted communication' to describe future possibilities for radical or deliberative democracy which are already immanent in everyday language. He does not suppose, it must be stressed, that ideal speech is ever likely to govern the whole of society. The main point is that the notion of ideal speech provides a critical yardstick with which to point to deficiencies in social life, especially where coercion and domination prevail over dialogue and consent. A central addendum is that human beings do not only learn in the sphere of labour, for example by creating more sophisticated ways of exploiting the physical environment; they also learn in the sphere of interaction, for example by developing more sophisticated tests of the legitimacy of institutions, policies and decisions. A key element of what Habermas calls 'moral-practical learning' is the modern idea that the **legitimacy** of social arrangements depends on the extent to which they are answerable to everyone who is affected by them. The constituency of those with rights to be involved in making such decisions can often be limited to the members of the **nation-state** or to some smaller association. But since people everywhere are affected by decisions about the global environment or the world economy it is increasingly necessary that this constituency should include the whole human race. This is the basis for Habermas's defence of **cosmopolitan democracy** (Habermas 1997).

It is important to note that Habermas builds on Kant's moral philosophy to create new ethical foundations for critical social theory and to defend the idea of the evolution of normative codes. He breaks with Kant's belief that each moral agent must reflect separately on whether the principles informing action can apply to all human beings in similar circumstances. For Habermas, decisions about such matters can only be found through forms of dialogue in which moral agents search for the best possible argument using 'public reason'. Despite this break with Kant's perspective, Habermas shares Kant's belief that the proper task of moral philosophy is to search for universal principles – principles which are true for all and capable of bringing the human race closer to the ideal of perpetual peace. The approach stays true to the method of immanent critique because Habermas appeals to principles that are present in existing societies. But they are not only found in modern liberal democratic societies: they are central to social interaction at all times and places, and that very fact holds out the promise of a global order in which all human beings and all human cultures can confront each other as equals in forms of public dialogue in which 'no one knows who will learn from whom'.

Habermas argues that the goal of joining all other human beings in 'a universal communication community' has even greater importance in the contemporary age because radically different moral perspectives come into daily contact and because there is no obvious reason why any culture should yield to another's vision of how everyone should live. But given their common commitments as language users, all human beings can agree on basic procedures with which to communicate their respective positions and, where possible, reconcile competing claims. They may never be able to agree on a moral code that establishes how all human beings should be organized. Habermas's central point is that they can agree on the nature of a free dialogue which does justice to their different points of view. Realizing this vision of 'undistorted communication' is the central task not only for politics within but for politics between states. In this vision, Habermas creates a conception of human progress that replaces the pessimism of earlier years.

Critical theory and international relations

Critical theory has been a central element in the challenge to the realist claim (see **realism**) that **anarchy** forces all states to behave in much the same way, so perpetuating a world in which competition, distrust and violent conflict prevail. Echoes of Horkheimer's distinction between traditional and critical theory are evident in the critique of realism. In particular, neo-realism has been associated with the positivist interest in understanding patterns and regularities in social life and with predicting human behaviour. In his criticism of neo-realism, Ashley (1982) argued that it is predicated on a 'technical interest' in controlling the social world as much as possible; what is sacrificed in the process is an approach based on an 'emancipatory interest' in removing constraints on human beings which appear natural and immutable but which can be broken down by the exercise of human agency or subjectivity.

This stress on human interests that shape approaches to understanding the social world has a definite purpose which is to show that explanations of the social world are not objective but grounded in specific aspirations. Habermas made this claim in his account of 'knowledge constitutive interests' that Ashley (1982) was the first to apply to the study of international relations.

Robert Cox (1981, 1983) also applied the critical method to international relations in his celebrated discussion of the opposition between 'problem-solving' and 'critical theory'. The main influences on Cox are the twentieth century Italian Marxist, Antonio Gramsci (1891–1937)

and the early eighteenth century Italian philosopher of history, Giambattista Vico (1668–1744) rather than the Frankfurt School. There are parallels nonetheless between Horkheimer's distinction between traditional and critical theory and Cox's identification of two main approaches to international relations. Cox argues that problem-solving approaches take the world for granted and ask how it can be made to function as smoothly as possible. This method informs realism which maintains that international anarchy is unalterable and asks how **order** can be maintained in the face of geopolitical competition (see **geopolitics**). For realists, order depends ultimately on the **balance of power**.

In contrast, critical theory asks how current global arrangements came into being and whether they are changing through political struggle. In particular, it aims to identify 'counter-hegemonic movements' which challenge dominant structures and principles and develop visions of alternative ways of organizing the world. The most promising political actors for Cox when he developed this analysis in the early 1980s were states (especially in the **Third World**) and social movements which challenged the global capitalist economy and the forms of labour exploitation and social inequality which are intrinsic to it. In common with the long tradition of critical theory, Cox is concerned with alternative principles of world political organization that are immanent within existing structures. The emphasis it should be noted is not on the political actors which have the greatest impact on the world as it is (these remain the **great powers**) but on political movements which are in the vanguard of efforts to imagine and create global political structures which deal with the plight of the most vulnerable members of humanity.

Cox's critical approach shifts attention from the anarchic political system to the organization of the world political economy and to the forms of dominance and **hegemony** it generates. Whereas realists argue that political actors have no choice but to resign to the constraints inherent in international anarchy, Cox argues that many political actors are already involved in collective efforts to change the principles of world political organization. In Marx's language, the latter are actively involved in trying to make more of their history under conditions of their own choosing. This leads Cox (and Ashley in his early writings) to advance a central claim which has its origins in Marx's thought, that theories of the social world can assist the perpetuation of arrangements which disadvantage sections of humanity. Cox argues that realism has the ideological effect of inviting human beings to resign to an allegedly unchangeable international anarchy. This criticism is reminiscent of Marx's argument that bourgeois theories of political economy contributed to the perpetuation of social inequalities by arguing that private property, the division of labour and market competition are natural phenomena. As noted earlier, the point is that theories of the social world are not neutral and objective accounts of an external reality. In Cox's much-quoted phrase, theories are 'always for someone and for some purpose': they tend to work for some interests and against others. A central task of critical theory is to uncover the political implications of claims to analyse the world in the spirit of neutrality: it is to show that theories of the social world do not stand outside politics but have consequences for the distribution of political power, material resources and meaningful opportunities in domestic and global society.

Cox sets out a broadly materialist interpretation of the nature of world politics but he does not defend a reduc-

tionist version of 'the paradigm of production'. His starting point is labour and production although he does not regard them as more influential than state power and the structure of world order in shaping society and politics. Each level (production, the state and world order) influences the others and shapes the environment in which the struggle between hegemonic and counter-hegemonic movements takes place. Although Cox has privileged labour over interaction – in Habermas's use of these terms – he turned in his later writings to the role that different civilizational perspectives play in world politics (Cox 1996). Other approaches to applying critical theory to international relations have been more concerned with the sphere of interaction and specifically with the idea of dialogue that is central to Habermas's version of critical theory.

This alternative, but complementary, approach to Cox's perspective starts with the Habermasian notion of learning in the moral and cultural sphere. The emphasis shifts to the evolution of more cosmopolitan tests of the legitimacy of political institutions, policies and decisions (see **cosmopolitanism**). To return to an earlier point, the argument is that every human being has a right to be represented in dialogue where the likelihood is that decisions will affect them. The emphasis here is on 'the triple transformation of political community' at the national and global levels so that communities are more cosmopolitan for the reasons just mentioned, sensitive to cultural and other differences and committed to reducing material inequalities. New forms of political community are required in the 'post-Westphalian era' to ensure that vulnerable groups everywhere have a greater opportunity to influence decisions which harm their vital interests and endanger their **security** (Linklater 1998).

Several critics of the Habermasian approach doubt that this cosmopolitan commitment can avoid creating new forms of power and domination. Postmodern or poststructuralist approaches (see **poststructuralism**), and feminist (see **feminism**) critiques of the **discourse** theory of morality, have argued that the project of including all human beings in the 'universal communication community' may lead to different forms of social exclusion, such as those who do not accept Habermas's essentially Western liberal belief that decisions should be reached through a process of dialogue in which all persons are treated equally and where no persuasion is ruled out as illegitimate in advance. But many critics agree with the idea that political life should be determined by dialogue even though they are not convinced by the Habermasian vision of unconstrained communication. Some of the most important debates between Habermas and his critics are concerned with whether there any firm foundations for ethics, and with the extent to which all forms of knowledge, including knowledge orientated towards emancipation, may achieve nothing more than reorganizing social and political power (see Devetak 2001). All are especially concerned with what Adorno once called the danger of annexing 'the alien in a kind of philosophical imperialism'.

Despite many differences with Frankfurt School critical theory, feminist and poststructuralist approaches to international relations are equally opposed to realism. They are broadly committed to showing how claims about the immutable nature of international politics can help to reproduce this very condition, and how such claims can obscure the existence and possibility of political efforts to remove unnecessary social constraints and end needless suffering.

Members of the Frankfurt School have been especially prominent in ensuring that what Adorno called the desire 'to lend a voice to suffering' remains important for the analysis of contemporary political life.

Further reading

Ashley, R. K. (1982) 'Political Realism and Human Interests' *International Studies Quarterly* 25(2), 204–36.

Bottomore, T. (1984) *The Frankfurt School*, Chichester: Ellis Horwood.

Cox, R.W. (1981) 'Social Forces, States and World Orders: Beyond International Relations Theory', *Millennium* 10(2), 126–55.

Cox, R. W. (1983) 'Gramsci, Hegemony and International Relations', *Millennium* 12, 2: 162–75.

Cox, R. W. (with Sinclair, T.) (1996) *Approaches to World Order*, Cambridge: Cambridge University Press.

Devetak, R. (2001) 'Critical Theory' in S. Burchill *et al.* (eds) *Theories of International Relations*, 2nd edn, Basingstoke: Palgrave

Habermas, J. (1979) *Communication and the Evolution of Society*, London, Heinemann.

Habermas, J. (1990) *Moral Consciousness and Communicative Action*, Cambridge: Polity Press.

Habermas, J. (1997) 'Kant's Idea of Perpetual Peace, with the Benefit of Two Hundred Years' Hindsight', in J. Bohman and M. Lutz-Bachmann (eds), *Perpetual Peace: Essays on Kant's Cosmopolitan Ideal*, London: MIT Press.

Horkheimer, M. and Adorno, T. (1977) *Dialectic of Enlightenment*, New York: Herder and Herder.

Linklater, A. (1988) *The Transformation of Political Community*, Cambridge: Polity Press.

Rasmussen, D. (ed.) (1999) *The Handbook of Critical Theory*, Oxford: Blackwell.

See also: cosmopolitanism; global civil society; Marxism; order

ANDREW LINKLATER

D

Debt trap

A situation in which a state has to spend much of its earnings from trade on servicing its external debts rather than on economic and social **development**. The debt trap is one of the most crippling problems for **Third World** countries (or more accurately, the vast majority of their citizens). The origins of the debt trap for poor states lie in the formation of the **Organization of Petroleum Exporting Countries** (OPEC) in 1973 and the dramatic rise in oil prices that year. The OPEC states deposited their new oil wealth in western banks. Since idle money loses against inflation (which was rising rapidly at the time), the banks needed to find countries to take loans. Many states in Eastern Europe and the Third World borrowed huge sums of money in the expectation that interest rates would remain stable.

The expectation was shattered by two trends in the global economy over the next twenty years. First, the fixed exchange rate system that had been established after World War Two collapsed, and states began to use interest rates to stabilize their exchange rates. Second, interest rates rose in the 1980s in response to trade and budget deficits in the United States. This triggered a recession in many industrialized states, thereby reducing export markets for poor states. As their export earnings fell, debt repayment obligations rose, leaving much of Africa and Latin America in a state of financial bankruptcy. In the recession the price of raw materials, on which many poorer states depend for earning foreign exchange, collapsed. Debts incurred were so large that they needed new loans to finance them.

Between 1982 and 1990 US$927 billion was advanced to poor states but US$1,345 billion was remitted in debt service alone. The debtor states began the 1990s 60 per cent more in debt than they were in 1982. Sub-Saharan Africa's debt more than doubled in this period. When the issue of debt remission or debt forgiveness was raised, western banks argued that it would create what economists call 'moral hazard' – failing to honor debts would simply encourage poor states to continue borrowing in the expectation that they would never have to repay their debts. In contrast, some commentators argue that moral hazard should cut both ways. Overborrowing is overlending, and creditors should pay their share of the costs of mistakes made in the 1970s.

By 1997 Third World debt totaled over US$2.2 trillion. The same year US$250 billion was repaid in interest and loan principal. By 2004 the debt burden surpassed US$3 trillion. The debt trap represents a continuing humanitarian disaster for over one billion of the world's poorest people. During the last decade the world's most heavily indebted continent, Africa, has experienced falling life expectancies, falling incomes, falling investment levels and rising infant and maternal mortality rates.

In October 1996 the first real attempt was made to deal with the problem when the **World Bank** and the **International Monetary Fund** (IMF) won agreement from their Boards of Governors for the establishment of the Highly Indebted Poor Country (HIPC) Initiative. At its launch, the policy offered the promise of poor countries achieving a 'robust exit' from the burden of unsustainable debts. Campaigning groups and non-governmental organizations (NGOs) welcomed this policy as the first comprehensive approach to debt write-offs with an enormous potential for poverty reduction.

The Initiative was only open to the poorest countries, those that:

1. were eligible for highly concessional assistance from the World Bank's International Development Association (IDA) and the IMF's Poverty Reduction and Growth Facility (formerly called the Enhanced Structural Adjustment Facility);
2. faced an unsustainable debt situation even after the full application of traditional debt relief mechanisms; and
3. had a proven track record in implementing strategies focused on reducing poverty and building the foundation for sustainable economic growth.

Despite its limitations, the Highly Indebted Poor Countries (HIPC) Debt initiative is the first debt reduction mechanism that promises to deal with the ongoing debt trap in a comprehensive and concerted way. It is designed to tackle not only commercial debt and debt owed by HIPCs to bilateral creditors, but also debt owed to multilateral creditors: the World Bank, the IMF, and regional development banks. The central aim of the HIPC initiative is to enable the most highly indebted poor countries to achieve a sustainable debt level within a period of six years. During this period, a country must implement a World Bank/IMF-supported **structural adjustment program**. At the 'decision point', which marks the end of the first three years, creditors re-examine the country's debt problem and determine whether it can exit the HIPC scheme or, if it cannot, how much debt relief it will need to reach a sustainable level of debt at its 'completion point', three years down the line.

What is a sustainable level of debt? This has been defined by the World Bank/IMF as a level at which a country is able to meet its current and future debt repayment obligations in full without compromising economic growth and without resorting to rescheduling or building up arrears in the future. In the HIPC scheme, a country undergoes a Debt Sustainability Analysis (DSA), on the basis of which it is decided exactly how much debt relief is needed for the country to fulfill the sustainability targets of the initiative: a debt burden within the range of 200–250 per cent of the country's annual exports and a debt service of 20–25 per cent of annual exports.

As of September 2004, twenty-seven countries were receiving debt relief under the Initiative. Fourteen of these countries had reached the completion point and were receiving debt relief. Thirteen countries are between decision point and completion point. The remaining countries that are potentially eligible for the Initiative have been beset by persistent social difficulties such as continual internal civil strife, cross-border armed conflict, governance challenges, and substantial arrears problems. A few of them, however, have made progress towards establishing a track record of macroeconomic performance which is a requirement for qualifying for debt relief. At present, the HIPC Initiative framework has provided debt relief amounting to more than US$50 billion.

Further reading

Dent, M. and Peters, B. (1999) *The Crisis of Poverty and Debt in the Third World*, Aldershot, Ashgate.
George, S. (1991) *The Debt Boomerang*, London, Pluto.
Lehman, H. P. (1993) *Indebted Development*, Basingstoke, Palgrave.
Payer, C. (1991) *Lent and Lost: Foreign Credit and the Third World*, London, Zed Books.
Roodman, D. and Peterson, J. (2001) *Still Waiting for the Jubilee: Pragmatic Solutions for the Third World Debt Crisis*, Washington, Worldwatch Institute.

See also: conditionality; dependency; development; International Monetary Fund; structural adjustment program; World Bank

MARTIN GRIFFITHS

Decolonization

Decolonization refers to the end of formal European colonial **empires**, the transfer of **authority** (but not necessarily **power**) from the colonizer to the colonized, and the creation of a **sovereign state** from a former colony. In 1945 approximately one third of the world's population (750 million people) lived in non-self-governing territories, geographically located primarily in Africa and Asia. The process of decolonization began in earnest after World War Two. European colonial powers committed themselves to the new **United Nations** Charter that stipulated the right to **self-determination** for all colonies.

What accounts for this remarkable historical process? Some argue that **nationalism** was primarily responsible for the dismantling of the colonial empires. Others contend that decolonization was a product of imperial policy and planning. The two approaches tell the story of decolonization in the context of colonial–imperial relations, singling out either demands in the colonies or deliberations in the imperial capitals. A third approach places decolonization in the context of changes in the international system. The Great Depression of the late 1920s and early 1930s was particularly critical. It wreaked havoc on the world economy ruining the lives of millions of people and in the process stoking the fires of nationalism. Among the **great powers** it led to growing protectionism and imperial rivalry. As might be expected given their underdeveloped and dependent status (see **dependency**), colonial economies were hit hardest. People in the colonies blamed their falling commodity prices and wages and deepening material hardships on colonialism, which lost any **legitimacy** it may have acquired. The World War Two brought death and destruction on a scale never before experienced in world history. Millions of colonial subjects were conscripted to fight on behalf of their respective masters, and many millions more were commandeered to produce 'strategic raw materials' for the war effort. Colonial political economies were profoundly shaken and transformed by the war. Besides the hardships, the war changed attitudes and expectations on both sides of the colonial divide.

Decolonization was undoubtedly a product of many factors. It involved a complex interplay of the prevailing international situation, the policies of the colonial powers, the nature and strength of the nationalist movements, and the ideologies and visions of the postcolonial world promoted by the **superpowers**. There were clearly variations in the patterns of decolonization among regions and colonies, conditioned by the way in which these factors coalesced and manifested themselves. Decolonization was also affected by the relative presence and **power** of European settlers and each colony's perceived strategic importance.

Political power was usually handed over to westernized or at least western-educated elites who would be able to maintain many of the colonial structures and networks. Such 'conservative transitions' resulted in minimal changes to the political economies of these former colonies. While formal political independence was achieved, the former colonizers often maintained substantial links to their former colonies in relation to trade and foreign policy issues. In other cases however, decolonization was rapid, leaving little if any infrastructure and human resources to ensure the developmental success of the former colonies (see **development**).

East Timor, located in the Indonesian archipelago north of Australia, is the most recent country to achieve national independence from its former colonizers. East Timor was initially colonized by the Portuguese who withdrew from the region in the mid-1970s. In the power vacuum that resulted, Indonesia invaded East Timor and remained an occupying force until 1999 when a referendum was held. The people of East Timor who had been fighting a liberation struggle since Portugal departed voted unanimously for national independence and self-determination from Indonesia, thus becoming the newest state in the **international system**.

More than 80 new states have been created as a result of decolonization. However, today over 2 million people still live under colonial or foreign rule, with 16 non-self governing territories remaining in the international system. While decolonization has achieved political independence for many peoples, the process has had significant effects on the postcolonial states, in particular their economic and political development trajectories (see **postcolonialism**). Many of them have been labeled as **Third World** countries, with low socio-economic status, high levels of poverty and corruption, and marginal positions in the global economy.

Further reading

Betts, R. F. (1998) *Decolonization*, New York: Routledge.

Le Sueur, J. (ed.) (2003) *The Decolonization Reader*, London: Routledge

Freund, B. (1998) *The Making of Contemporary Africa: The Development of African Society Since 1800*, 2nd Edition, Lynne Rienner.

Waites, B. (1999) *Europe and the Third World: From Colonisation to Decolonisation c.1500-1998*, New York, St. Martin's Press.

See also: dependency; League of Nations; neocolonialism; Third World

TANYA LYONS

Deconstruction

A specific, technical term much in evidence in approaches in international relations labelled poststructuralist (see **poststructuralism**). It is occasionally used very loosely by scholars to mean the opposite of 'construction', or in other words, to mean something like 'taking apart', but this is not what it means in the work of its chief exponent, Jacques Derrida (1930–2004). It is also misleading to equate 'deconstruction' with 'destruction'.

It is ironic that an entry purporting to define 'deconstruction' should even appear in an encyclopedia. Derrida's work, and his discussion of deconstruction in particular, is a critique of the very possibility of definition, and an analysis of the outcomes of attempts to delineate concepts and specify methods and programs. He claims that such attempts to produce certainty are totalizing moves that close off the possibility of what he calls the 'ethico-political'. To understand what this means it is necessary to examine the basics of Derrida's critique of western metaphysics, or 'logocentrism'.

Logocentrism, a way of reasoning that is fundamental to contemporary thought, specifically that derived from the European world, operates through the production of dichotomies such as inside/outside, man/woman, memory/forgetting, presence/absence. Every dichotomy of this sort is more than just an opposition between two terms. Each sets up a hierarchy in which the first term of the pair is seen as primary and is valued more highly than the second. However, as Derrida points out, the prioritized term cannot operate without its shadow. It only has meaning in relation to the spectral second term, which is sometimes called 'the constitutive outside'. In other words the second term has to be excluded to bring the first term into being. For example, 'memory' only has meaning if we also have in mind the concept 'forgetting'. In that sense memory is *haunted* by forgetting. Derrida's work suggests that rather than thinking of *ontology*, or what exists, we should be looking at *hauntology* (Derrida 1994: 10).

Most importantly, Derrida uses this analysis to critique the centrality of the notion of presence in western thinking. He suggests that 'presence' is something that is brought into being by a particular way of thinking, and that the drive for presence has certain political implications. Through endless debates and discussions of what *exists* or how things

should be *defined* (questions like: 'What *is* the state?' or 'What *is* terrorism?') structures of authority are put in place. These structures of authority have no foundation other than the violence of the hierarchies or the dichotomies and exclusions on which they are based. In the end though, since dichotomies and the structures they authorize are reliant on concepts that cannot by definition be pure but rather are always haunted by their opposites, they have an in-built tendency to collapse, or to *deconstruct*. Deconstruction takes place of its own accord, as the structures set up by logocentric thinking falter and collapse.

What about deconstruction as a method of analysis, or as a way of demonstrating the fallibility of logocentrism? It is necessary to be careful here, because although deconstruction is regarded by some as a *method* that can be used in international political analysis, and indeed it can – though perhaps not as a method so much as an *intervention* in international politics – Derrida himself prefers to emphasize that *deconstruction is the case*.

But if we choose to intervene through a deconstructive move, how does this work? How do we go about 'deconstruction'? Such an investigation can take place either through the examination of specific concepts – 'justice' or 'writing', for example – or it can work by scrutinizing texts. Often in Derrida's work the first part of a piece will examine a concept and the second a specific text.

In both these instances, after noting the dichotomies or exclusions around which the concept or text is structured, a deconstructive move goes through two related phases or steps: a stage of *inversion* or overturning and a stage of *displacement* (Derrida 1987: 41). Inversion involves the reversal of the hierarchy; displacement entails the attempt to remove the hierarchy altogether. In challenging a hierarchical dichotomy the first stage, that of inversion, is no good on its own. If a dichotomy is just inverted, the structure remains in place. For example, if the dominance of 'man' is challenged, and 'man' is replaced by 'woman', nothing much has changed: the system of domination and authority remains in place. The only difference is that we have exchanged a matriarchal system for a patriarchal one. However, the first stage is absolutely necessary for strategic reasons, otherwise it may not be possible to retain a purchase on the opposition that it is to be challenged. Too quick a move of neutralizing the dichotomy would not be effective politically. To move immediately beyond the opposition man/woman to a terminology of 'persons' that forgets the violence of the hierarchy involved will not make any practical difference. However, the move to displacement is the one that disorganizes the previous hierarchy, and makes new ways of thinking possible.

An example of this that has arisen above is hauntology. In *Specters of Marx* (1994), Derrida discusses the dichotomy between 'to be' (presence) and 'not to be' (absence) in Shakespeare's *Hamlet*. The hierarchy is first overturned, and death or absence reemphasized, but the immediate next move replaces *ontology*, the study of being or presence, with *hauntology*, a concern with spectrality and ghosts. The second stage of deconstruction involves the introduction of what Derrida calls 'undecidables' (Derrida 1987: 43), terms that inhabit a dichotomy but do not constitute a third term in a Hegelian sense. These are terms such as *pharmakon* and *supplement*. The pharmakon, for example, is neither remedy nor poison, and a 'pharmacotic war' can either harm the body politic or strengthen it (George 2002). In another example, the supplement to a book is something that challenges the integrity of the book. It is neither necessary for the book, since it is supplementary, nor superfluous to it.

A deconstructive approach can also examine what is set to one side in a piece of writing in order for the analysis to continue. What has to be excluded is instructive, and bringing this 'back in' can reveal the contingent nature of the analytical frame that has been set up. It demonstrates how the argument relies on the very thing that it excludes. In his analysis of speech act theory, Derrida demonstrates that a successful speech act relies on the very thing that is ruled out, that is, the possibility of failure, or a speech act that does not do what it purports to do (Derrida 1988).

As we have seen, deconstruction in a sense is not an option or a choice: it is inevitable. Importantly, this means that those adopting this approach to analysis are not destroying something. It is not *destruction*. Deconstruction as a method involves no more than gently nudging or helping along a process that is inevitable at some point in any case. It involves drawing the attention of logocentric thinking to the way in which its foundations are unstable or indeed untenable, and demanding instead a properly political approach. Logocentric thinking proceeds on the assumption that knowledge and 'truth' are attainable, and can be arrived at through various forms of logic, reason and analysis. A deconstructive approach points out that this way of thinking can be problematic and calls instead for a recognition of the need for ethico-political decisions and an acknowledgement of the impossibility of full knowledge or ontological presence (Campbell 1994).

A philosophical or metaphysical analysis based on abstractions or general rules gives an illusion of certainty and closure that can be politically very dangerous. Derrida calls for an acceptance of openness, and a recognition of the importance of the ethico-political process of 'decisioning'. Specific decisions must be taken in a particular case, even though 'knowledge' will not be sufficient to guarantee them. Derrida is emphatically not calling for indecisiveness or relativism but demanding the recognition of the impossibility of specifying in the abstract what action should be taken.

Further reading

Campbell, D. (1994) 'The Deterritorialization of Responsibility: Levinas, Derrida, and Ethics after the End of Philosophy' *Alternatives* 19, 455–84.

Caputo, J. D. (ed.) (1997) *Deconstruction in a Nutshell: A Conversation with Jacques Derrida*, New York: Fordham University Press.

Derrida, J. (1987) *Positions*, London: Athlone Press.

Derrida, J. (1988) *Limited Inc*, Evanston, IL: Northwestern University Press.

Derrida, J. (1994) *Specters of Marx: the State of the Debt, the Work of Mourning, and the New International*, New York: Routledge.

George, L. N. (2002) 'The Pharmacotic War on Terrorism: Cure or Poison for the US Body Politic?' *Theory Culture and Society*, 19, 161–86.

Patton, P. and Smith, T. (eds) (2001) *Jacques Derrida: Deconstruction engaged: The Sydney Seminars*, Sydney: Power Publications.

See also: discourse; genealogy; hermeneutics; post-positivism; poststructuralism

JENNY EDKINS

Democratic deficit

The term 'democratic deficit' has appeared most in the context of ongoing debates about the **European Union** (EU) since in the 1990s, although it has also been applied more generally. Despite the absence of a single definition, the term has been used to signal the lack of recognizable democratic characteristics of EU governance. Its usage emerged due to the increase in power of EU institutions that increasingly resembled those of national government systems, yet were different in a few key aspects. Thus the EU lacks the traditional checks and balances that characterize national systems of governance.

What is the democratic deficit? One can differentiate between four ways in which the term is used. The first description of the democratic deficit is a *lack of democracy*. A democracy can be defined as a political system with a *demos* (a people). The EU lacks such a demos. The EU consists of multiple peoples (*demoi*) that are governed by national governments that are still sovereign (see **sovereignty**). In the EU the most important *representative government* is at the national level, thus EU institutions do not represent 'the people'.

A second description of the democratic deficit is that the EU *lacks democratic and representative institutions*. As was mentioned before, most of the traditional checks and balances of EU governance run through the national systems and few EU institutions resemble national ones. Yet, an estimated two thirds of all laws originate in EU laws in one way or another. For example, the EU executive (the European Commission) consists of a group of appointed individuals who have each been put forward by their respective 'home' **nation-state** and subsequently approved by the European Parliament (EP). These Commissioners swear an oath to protect the interests of the EU rather than the member states. Because there are no elections for the Commission, the Commissioners do not run on a public platform, and once in office they normally do not make explicit the political choices they face (i.e. they act more as technocrats than as traditional politicians). The single institution that is elected by the EU citizens, the EP, has only limited (albeit expanding) powers in the decision making process. Regarding the Commission, the EP cannot dismiss an individual Commissioner, but can only dismiss the entire body of Commissioners. The role of the Commission is that of guardian of the treaties and the Commission has the right of initiative to propose laws. Finally, decision making is influenced importantly by the 'Council of Ministers' (who have to pass laws that are initiated by the Commission, often after consulting the EP). However, because the Council consists of national ministers, each of whom represents his/her national member state, that body as a whole can also not be dismissed. Any disciplining of the Council would have to be done by national parliaments in relation to their 'own' minister.

Third, the term democratic deficit has been used to describe the *lack of transparency and accountability of the EU*. Because the EU has its own set of rules and regulations, its own particular way in which laws are made, adopted, implemented and enforced, it has often been felt that the EU is insufficiently transparent. The sense that the EU is also insufficiently accountable follows from the EU decision making process. Because the institutions all have some role to play in the policymaking process but none of them holds full responsibility for the outcome, it is difficult to hold anyone accountable. The European Court of Justice (ECJ) may be asked to consider any negative side effects (or failure to act) on the part of one of the institutions, but turning to the ECJ is not a real option for most citizens. The ECJ is a very powerful institution as EU law is superior to national law. But again, this characteristic makes EU governance daunting to citizens who no longer

understand why the national government is no longer fully sovereign in the policymaking process.

The fourth description of the democratic deficit refers to the *lack of public debate and poor state–society relations in the EU*. There are plenty of democratic channels in national systems (debates in the media, such as newspapers, television, opinion pieces and so on), but these types of societal reflections are lacking with regard to EU policies and EU laws. There are very few 'European' newspapers, or 'European' television programmes. Thus there are no public debates of the issues on the agenda in the EU outside the national context. This lack of debate on EU issues becomes even more clear on the eve of EP elections. The political parties that do run on a political platform before the EP elections often 'make the mistake' to run on national issues, even though the prospective Member of the EP (MEP) will not have much to do with national politics but rather with EU issues. State–society relations suffer if public debates are lacking.

As can be seen, although there are many dimensions of the democratic deficit they are all interconnected. The basic problem underlying the democratic deficit of the EU is that its institutional design resembles partly an international organization and partly a fully fledged federal state. Over the past decade the EU has responded to the democratic deficit in a number of ways. For example, it has facilitated greater freedom of information regarding its practices, and has created the position of an ombudsperson. The powers of the EP have also grown over this period of time. In 2000 a Convention was established to create a base document for the EU that would function as a Constitution, and to find ways to simplify EU governance. Some elements of 'direct democracy' were also adopted in the new EU Constitution (such as a pan-European Citizens' Initiative Right, giving one million EU citizens the same power of initiative as a majority in the EP). The Constitution has yet to be ratified by all 25 EU member states before it enters into force, but suffice to say that the democratic deficit debate will have had a major impact on the discussions on the future of Europe.

Further reading

Born, H. and Hänggi, H. (eds) (2004) *The Double Democratic Deficit*, Aldershot: Ashgate.

Chryssochoou, D. N. (2003) 'EU Democracy and the Democratic Deficit' in Cini, M. (ed.) *European Union Politics* Oxford: Oxford University Press, pp. 365–82.

Crombez, C. (2003) 'The Democratic Deficit in the European Union: Much Ado about Nothing?' *European Union Politics* 4(10), 101–20

Eriksen, E. and Fossum, J. (eds) (2000) *Democracy in the European Union*, London: Routledge.

Lord, C. (1998) *Democracy in the European Union*, Sheffield: Sheffield Academic Press.

See also: cosmopolitan democracy; democratic peace; democratization; European Union

AMY VERDUN

Democratic peace

Democracies do not (or virtually never) go to **war** with each other. Since the end of the **cold war** the idea of a democratic peace has been the subject of much debate, which tends to focus on three issues. First, is there a direct causal relationship between democracy and peace? Second, if there is, what best explains the relationship? Finally, what are the implications of the relationship for world order?

In the twenty-first century, democracy refers to a system of government characterized by: regular elections for the most powerful government positions; competitive political parties; near universal franchise for elections of key office-holders; secret balloting; widespread respect for civil liberties and political rights (or basic **human rights**). Prior to the twenty-first century, scholars relaxed this definition in light of the marked absence of secret balloting, competitive political parties and the limited nature of the franchise.

If a democracy refers merely to a state with periodic, competitive elections that also acknowledges a body of citizens with equal rights, it is clear that democracies rarely, if at all, go to war with each other. If one defines an international war as a military engagement in which 1,000 people or more are killed, then 353 pairs of states engaged in such wars between 1816 and 1991. None were between two democracies, 155 pairs involved a democracy and a nondemocratic country, and 198 pairs involved two nondemocratic states fighting each other.

The significance of these empirical facts is unclear. Do they expose a deep and persistent feature of democracy or are they a mere statistical curiosity, like the fact that no two countries with McDonald's franchises have gone to war prior to 1999? This precarious relationship between the presence of McDonald's and the absence of war collapsed when NATO attacked Serbia in March 1999 (see **North Atlantic Treaty Alliance**). Unlike this relationship, however, the lack of war between democracies has been tested in different ways for other periods, other definitions of democracy, and other ways of defining war. In each case it has been significant.

It remains unclear, however, whether democratic states do not fight each other *because* they are democratic. Some scholars argue that the relative peace between democracies can be explained on the basis of other factors. For example, it could be argued that the lack of war between democracies during the cold war was really due to the overwhelming threat from the Soviet Union. On the other hand, even if this alleged threat accounted for the particular lack of war between democracies since 1945, what about other periods?

If one accepts that there is a causal link between democracy and peace, a variety of factors have been suggested to explain it. First, it could be argued that democratic leaders are restrained by the resistance of their people to bearing the costs and deaths of war. However, if this were true, democracies would be peaceful with all kinds of states, since wars against non-democracies are just as unpleasant as wars against democracies. But democratic states fight as often as other states do; their peaceful tendencies are only alleged to extend to one another. The putative law that democracies do not fight one another stands out because the evidence is conclusive that democratic states have been involved, proportionately, in as many wars as non-democratic states.

Second, the diversity of institutions and relations within and between democracies creates checks and balances and cross-pressures inhibiting belligerence among them. Whilst this may well be a contributing factor to the democratic peace, it also has a dark side. Democracies are not monolithic; they are divided into many agencies, some of which operate in secrecy and are really authoritarian subsystems connected only at the top to democratic processes. Examples include the military, especially in wartime, and secret services such as the Central Intelligence Agency (CIA).

The most plausible explanation is cultural. The presence of a democratic culture of negotiation and conciliation means that in their interaction with other democracies, democratic leaders are basically dovish. They share the same values, and thus are more willing to negotiate than fight. Disagreements among the citizens of a democracy are resolved through compromise and negotiation rather than conflict and coercion. When confronted with international disputes, democracies seek to resolve them in the same ways. Democracies reciprocate attempts at compromise and enjoy peaceful relations with one another. Because undemocratic states do not follow norms of compromise, however, democracies distrust them and treat them with hostility.

The final issue in the debate revolves around the implications of the relationship for world **order**. Optimists believe that democracy will spread around the world, which in turn will therefore become more peaceful. Pessimists note that democratic states are generally hostile towards nondemocratic states. Unless today's democracies actively encourage the process of **democratization**, there will not be a peaceful world order; at best, democracies will enjoy peace among themselves but the rest of the world will remain plagued by war.

It will take a large investment of resources by democracies to help other states democratize. Such aid will be more forthcoming only if there is a wider understanding among the democracies that by providing it they are not only promoting the freedom and prosperity of other countries but also contributing to international peace.

Further reading

Barkawi, T. and Laffey, M. (eds) (2001) *Democracy, Liberalism and War:*

Rethinking the Democratic Peace Debate, Boulder, CO: Lynne Rienner.

Brown, M., Lynn-Jones, S. and Miller, S. (eds) (1996) *Debating the Democratic Peace,* Cambridge, MA: MIT Press.

Lipson, C. (2003) *Reliable Partners: How Democracies Have Made a Separate Peace,* Princeton, NJ: Princeton University Press.

Weart, S. (1998) *Never at War: Why Democracies Will Not Fight Each Other,* New Haven, CT: Yale University Press.

See also: democratic deficit; democratization; liberal internationalism; war

MARTIN GRIFFITHS

Democratization

A process whereby countries move towards a more democratic political system. Since the mid-1970s, and particularly since the end of the **cold war**, this has been one of the most striking political trends in the **Third World** and in the post-communist world. Globally this period has seen a significant decline in the number of authoritarian regimes, and today the majority of countries in the world hold some form of multi-party elections, leading to characterizations of our time as the 'age of democracy'. The initial optimism that accompanied the transitions has however faded somewhat, as democracy has not improved the living conditions for the majority of people in poor countries. Some countries have also experienced a reversal of the democratization process.

The current 'wave' of democratization started in the mid-1970s, when the military dictatorships of Spain, Portugal, and Greece gave way to democratic rule. In Latin America, the process began in the 1980s, when Argentina, Brazil, Bolivia, and Chile amongst others held competitive multi-party elections. In the early 1990s, following the fall of **communism**,

democratization took place in numerous countries in Eastern Europe, in Asia, as well as in most of sub-Saharan Africa. By the mid-1990s, democratically elected governments had become the norm in most regions of the world, and only the Middle East remains largely unaffected by this global trend towards liberal democracy.

Explanations and interpretations of the trend towards democratization vary. Early explanations regarded it as part of a **modernization** process. Democracy was expected to occur as countries achieved a higher stage of social and economic **development**. The fact that democracy is more commonly found in rich, or more developed countries, is frequently cited in support of this theory. Following the recent 'wave' of democratization in poor countries, explanations have tended to focus more on political choice and agency and democracy is said to require no preconditions such as a high level of economic development. Instead democracy is seen as the result of political bargains and negotiations between political elites. The voluntaristic character of this explanation differ significantly from a third, more structural approach, which explains democratization primarily with reference to long term structural changes in relations of **power**, focusing on the relationship between classes, state power and transnational power structures.

While the different theoretical approaches assign different weight to various explanatory factors, depending on country and time period, most agree that the end of the cold war is of central importance to an understanding of recent transitions. The fall of **communism** is seen to have deprived authoritarian systems and one-party states of ideological **legitimacy**, making liberal democracy the only legitimate form of rule. At this point, most Western aid donors and international institutions like the **World Bank** made

foreign aid conditional on political reforms towards democracy, and such aid conditionality is an important explanatory factor in economically dependent countries, particularly in sub-Saharan Africa. The large scale popular protests against authoritarian rule in Eastern Europe is also said to have inspired similar protests in distant parts of the globe, and it is in this sense that democratization is said to be 'contagious' and facilitated by **globalization** and the existence of global communication and civil society networks.

While few would dispute that the world is now more democratic than ever before, in the sense that the majority of countries hold regular, competitive elections, critics argue that this is a highly limited form of democracy, allied to the global expansion of **capitalism**. This form of democracy, often referred to as liberal democracy, restricts the influence of citizens to periodic elections and does not facilitate or advocate the extension of democratic accountability to other spheres such as the economy, the workplace or the local community. Critics argue that in poor countries, liberal democracy makes little difference to the majority of people, who despite their right to vote every fourth or fifth year continue to suffer social and economic deprivation. Summarized in the phrase 'you cannot eat votes', this view maintains that unless accompanied by social and economic rights, the political and civil rights associated with liberal democracy remain of limited relevance to poor people. The contemporary global dominance of **neoliberalism**, however, has ensured that democratization has often gone hand in hand with an intensification of economic liberalization and **structural adjustment program**s.

It is also important to note that democratization is not an irreversible process and that a transition to democracy does not guarantee that democracy will survive. It is for this reason that consolidation is frequently treated as a separate phase of democratization. While difficult to define, a consolidated democracy can be described as one that is able to survive considerable social, economic and political turmoil. Many new democracies cannot yet be described as consolidated, and in some of them, the process has suffered significant reversals or been aborted by military coups. In some new democracies, political and civil rights have been gradually eroded since the initial transition in the early 1990s, and although there are regular elections in which all adults are allowed to vote, these are often marked by significant irregularities and restrictions on the activities of opposition parties. Such countries can be described as partial electoral democracies, although it must be noted that democracy is difficult (if not impossible) to measure and that even the most consolidated democracies such as the United States are not immune to electoral irregularities.

While domestic politics has been democratized in recent years, no similar process has taken place on the international level. This significantly restricts the impact of democratization, as globalization has meant that sites of power are frequently located outside the territorial boundaries of national democracies. For example, international institutions and organizations like the **World Bank**, the **International Monetary Fund** (IMF) and the **World Trade Organization** (WTO) have profound effects on the welfare and security of millions of people, but are not subject to democratic control or procedures of accountability. In other words, as a result of globalization both the democratic autonomy of states as well as the influence of citizens as voters is severely compromised, and this has led to calls to democratize **global governance** and to reform international institutions like the **United Nations** and the World Bank.

Further reading

Hippler, J. (ed.) (1995) *The Democratisation of Disempowerment: The Problem of Democracy in the Third World*, London: Pluto Press.

Huntington, S. (1991) *The Third Wave: Democratization in the Late Twentieth Century*, Norman: University of Oklahoma Press.

O'Donnell, G., Schmitter, P. C. and Whitehead, L. (eds) (1986) *Transitions from Authoritarian Rule*, (4 volumes), Baltimore: Johns Hopkins University Press

Potter, D., Goldblatt, D., Kiloh, M. and Lewis, P. (eds) (1997) *Democratization*, Cambridge: Polity.

Schraeder, P. (ed.) (2002) *Exporting Democracy: Rhetoric Versus Reality*, Boulder, CO: Lynne Rienner.

See also: cosmopolitan democracy; state formation; end of history

RITA ABRAHAMSEN

Dependency

Theories of dependency challenged the dominance of **modernization** strategies in the mid- to late twentieth century. Modernization strategies mapped pathways to modernity for **Third World** states based on the use of external agents for change. Dependency analysts declared such agents exploitative. Without autonomous economic growth, Third World societies could expect no change in their economic fortunes. The result, so dependency theorists argued, could never be modernization or **development**, only underdevelopment.

Dependency's language of neocolonial denial proved extremely influential during the 1960s and 1970s and contributed to international efforts to transform unequal trading relationships (see **neocolonialism**). But not all dependency theorists regarded exchange as the cause of underdevelopment. Others stressed exploitative internal relations of production instead. The debate robbed dependency of its theoretical unanimity. By the 1980s, the rise of newly industrializing countries in the Third World appeared to rob it also of its universality (see **newly industrializing country**). Dependency and modernization, critics declared, were simply two sides of the same coin. Both focused on national solutions and both were ill equipped to counter the growing influence of new **globalization** strategies at the end of the twentieth century.

Certainly dependency theories derived from the same postwar global landscape that bred theories of modernization. In industrial societies state-based Keynesian initiatives, which provided citizens access to education, housing, health services and work, replaced the divisive bitterness and destruction of prewar strategies. Within the space of a single generation, industrial societies were transformed and the consumerism of empowered citizens became the means to achieve sustainable growth.

But in the Third World no similar domestic focus existed. Colonialism had denied people both the opportunity and capacity for self-governance. Above all it had denied them the empowerment that invariably flowed from domestically focused wealth generation, and left them dependent on external demand to generate growth. It never permitted them the opportunity to achieve the same degree of economic autonomy enjoyed by the first world.

Although aspirations for self-reliance had been inherently dangerous for prewar industrial states, they remained central to most Third World national agendas. However, aspirations alone could not transform dependency. Most Third World states remained producers of cheap labor and raw materials dependent on the health of distant markets. They never reinvented their economies drawing on the strength of their own domestic needs. These realities informed the central theses of early dependency theorists. Continued dependency and unequal exchange, they argued, produced **neocolonialism** not liberation, underdevelopment not development.

This simple argument made the notion of dependency extremely attractive as a way of accounting for the inability of many former colonies to transform themselves into democratic consumption-based societies, the goal of modernization. Not only had colonialism systematically underdeveloped their capabilities, it also left their internal economic sectors bereft of overall coherence. Each sector existed separately to meet external demand.

Some dependency theorists argued that this vast developmental gap between internal sectors bestowed on states a centrality no longer possessed in the first world. In newly independent Africa, local elites quickly seized control of these states to maintain their privileges. Linkages with foreign owned enterprises similarly strengthened their status. Since most elites depended also on fragile political and economic bases to maintain their access to state resources, they quickly learned to exploit regional, ethnic, religious or tribal differences to their advantage. Unfortunately these strategies did little for national development. Nations fragmented, capitalist classes failed to flourish, poverty and dependency worsened.

South America's solution to foreign dependency lay with import substitution. But its leaders also benefited from the status quo. They were reluctant to introduce the necessary packages for land reform, income redistribution and political change that successful industrialization required. Consequently import substitution never generated sufficient internal market growth to remove industry's dependence on foreign markets. Nor did it prevent the penetration of transnational capital keen to take advantage of protected markets or to exploit for export purposes the internal colonial relationships that industry relied upon to remain competitive.

Supporters of modernization blamed this situation on internal obstacles to development, not foreign domination. Tradition and the lack of entrepreneurial spirit determined the backwardness of rural sectors and prevented their integration with modern urban sectors, which had no choice but to turn to foreign markets in order to grow. Dependency theorists disagreed. When the industrialized world created colonial economies, they conserved only those pre-capitalist social formations functional to **capitalism**. This created an impression of duality, of contradictory modern and traditional sectors. In reality traditional sectors were integral to the survival of the modern economy. They were not separate from it, although the nature of their integration differed from rural sectors in the first world. In that difference lay disadvantage and underdevelopment, not empowerment and autonomy.

Many consequences flowed from this lack of internal coherence. It created internal colonial relationships that differentiated town and country. It enabled modern urban sectors to remain globally relevant only by exploiting rural sectors as a cheap resource. Such unequal internal relationships kept wages low, reduced political pressures for reform and made development difficult. At the same time they sharpened uneven development and social conflict.

However, the dependency idea that the experience of colonialism most explained differences between first and Third Worlds, provided elites with a convenient scapegoat. The Third World's numerical dominance of most international fora by the 1970s also provided post-colonial leaders with an opportunity to create a powerful new Third World bloc to address these historical legacies and lobby for global reform (see **post-colonialism**). A Non-aligned Movement (1955) attempted to create Third World solidarity. A **United Nations** Conference on Trade and Development in 1964 sought a Third World alternative to the first world's think tank, the **Organization for Economic Cooperation and Development** (OECD). Both organizations demanded a New International Economic Order (1975) and a redistribution of first world surpluses to the Third World.

No new order materialized. The only surpluses redistributed were petrodollars that arrived as cheap loans of dubious value. By the 1980s the cost of servicing debt negated any gains made during preceding decades. Although the European Community and the United States did improve terms of trade, their actions affected only small groupings of Third World countries and only a narrow range of commodities. Moreover these efforts to address unequal exchange promoted foreign rather than domestic markets as the basis for economic growth. They reinforced arguments that dependency and modernization theories were simply two sides of the same coin. Indeed, as globalization intensified towards the end of the twentieth century, debates concerning dependency withered. Civil society organizations developed alternative localized programs for community capacity building instead. In East Asia, states successfully transformed export-led strategies into domestic growth. Colonial pasts were not always the absolute constraint that dependency analysts had suggested. Thus the political

significance of dependency also abated over time.

Further reading

Blomstrom, M. and Hettne, B. (1984) *Development Theory in Transition: the Dependency Debate and Beyond*, Third World Responses, London: Zed Books.

Seers, D. (ed.) (1981) *Dependency Theory: A Critical Reassessment*, London: Frances Pinter.

Seligson, M. A. and Passé-Smith, J. T. (eds) (1993) *Development & Underdevelopment: The Political Economy of Inequality*, Boulder, CO: Lynne Rienner.

Wolfe, M. (1996) *Elusive Development*, London: Zed Books.

See also: development; interdependence; modernization; neocolonialism

ROBBIE ROBERTSON

Desertification

Degradation of formerly productive land in arid, semi-arid and dry sub-humid areas due to climatic variation (e.g. prolonged drought or flooding) and/or unsustainable human activity, associated primarily with food production. While the standard view of desertification conjures up images of advancing desert sand dunes, the reality is complex and sporadic. Consequently, desertification is not confined to desert fringe areas such as the Sahel region of Africa and western Rajasthan in India. To date, significant land degradation has also occurred in the United States (30 per cent of land), Latin America and the Caribbean (one quarter is now desert or dry land), China (loss of 700,000 hectares of arable land) and Europe (e.g. one fifth of land in Spain is under threat). Current estimates suggest that this problem affects approximately one third of the earth's land surface (four billion hectares), impacting on the lives of approximately 250 million people, resulting in an estimated loss in annual income of US$42 billion.

Desertification can occur naturally due to fluctuations in climate conditions. For example, the vegetation of the south of the Sahara may be able to move by up to 200 kilometres when a wet year is followed by a dry one and vice versa. The ecosystems of the Sahara, and other regions susceptible to desertification are, however, highly adapted to these fluctuations. Problems occur when additional pressures are imposed on these fragile ecosystems by unsustainable human activity. Examples of activities that may accelerate land degradation, and subsequent desertification, include: overgrazing, deforestation, poor irrigation, extended monoculture (single crop farming: a common practice in the production of cash crops) and the overuse of pesticides or herbicides. These practices result in the loss of vegetation, subsequent erosion of precious fertile topsoil and potential soil salinization (increased salt content), together with the potential for decreased productivity due to reduced nutrient levels or increased soil toxicity. Environmental outcomes in the wider region or community may include silting of river or lake systems, contamination of water supplies and the increased occurrence of dust storms, resulting in increased air pollution with consequences for public health and potential damage to machinery, buildings and livestock.

Overexploitation of land and subsequent degradation is particularly prevalent in poverty-stricken areas where limited food supply necessitates overexploitation of productive land or cultivation of marginal land. Increased land use in these areas may be further compounded by increases in local populations due to changes in cultural practice from nomadic to settled communities or

dislocation of communities due to conflict and natural disasters. Unsustainable farming practices may also be adopted in countries where food is not in shortage and is instead being grown in pursuit of profit, often in conjunction with highly mechanized or technologically advanced approaches. Here the issue is poor education and an ignorance of the importance of local environmental conditions.

One such example is the infamous American Dust Bowl of the 1930s when, during drought conditions, farmers used ploughing practices more suited to the temperate conditions of Western Europe, resulting in the loss of productive top soil over an area of approximately 100 million acres. In these two scenarios, poor and affluent, the environmental outcomes may be similar, however effective control or reduction of desertification will require different types of political, economic and educational intervention.

The need for a global response to the issue of desertification was first formally addressed in 1977 at the **United Nations** Conference on Desertification (UNCOD), which was attended by officials from ninety-five countries, fifty United Nations offices and a host of **non-govermental organizations** (NGOs). The outcome of UNCOD was the Plan of Action to Combat Desertification (PACD) which was implemented centrally by the Desertification Control Program Activity Centre (DAPAC), launched in 1985 by the then head of the United Nations Environment Program (UNEP). The success of this program was limited, due to a lack of a formal implementation framework. The issue was therefore raised again in 1992 at the United Nations Conference on Environment and Development (UNCED) or the so-called Earth Summit. Here negotiations resulted in the recommendation for the United Nations Convention to Combat Desertification (UNCCD), which was adopted in June 1994, ratified in 1995 and entered into force, as a legally binding agreement, in December 1996. To date the Convention has been ratified by 190 countries.

The primary aim of the convention is to foster international cooperation to combat desertification. This is achieved through member parties engaging in the collection, analysis and exchange of information, research, technology transfer, capacity building and awareness building, together with assistance in ensuring that adequate financial support is available to combat desertification and mitigate the effects of drought. Current estimates suggest an effective global effort will cost US$10–20 billion a year. Programmes to combat desertification are funded by the contributions from the developed Convention members, multilateral bank loans, foreign private investment, the **World Bank**, the International Fund for Agricultural Development (IFAD), NGOs and the affected countries themselves.

The Convention is implemented through national action programs (NAPs), which target the causes of desertification in affected member states and identify measures for preventing and reversing deleterious outcomes. In recognition of the fact that regional circumstances differ, NAPs are developed under five regional implementation annexes for Africa, Asia, Latin America and the Caribbean, the northern Mediterranean and Central and Eastern Europe.

Two key components central to the success of the NAPs are education and technology, which need to be modified to local circumstances. Examples of technologies that can help combat desertification include modern communication, satellite imagery (for improved weather forecasting) and genetic engineering (e.g. drought resistant and salt-resistance plants).

In recognition of the need for a local approach to the problem of desertification the Convention uses a 'bottom-up' approach, which is a radical departure from usual 'top–down' approach of previous UN programs. This approach decentralizes decision-making, and works at a local level, in direct consultation with local communities, stakeholders, NGOs and community based organizations (CBOs), women's and youth organizations. This participatory process is time consuming and labor intensive but ensures the local relevance of the proposed activity and more importantly, the sustainability of the program once foreign experts have left.

This approach of the Convention provides a framework to consider the many facets of the issue of desertification as a whole, thereby recognizing that this environmental issue is one of **sustainable development**. Potential solutions must therefore consider environmental management with reference to issues of poverty, social and political stability, migration, food availability, improved civil society, and local or regional governance. In addition, responses to desertification must be considered with reference to strategies that address **biodiversity** and that combat **global warming**. The interplay between desertification, food supply and global warming is predicted to be of particular significance.

Further reading

Middleton, N. and Thomas, D. (eds) (1997) *World Atlas of Desertification*, 2nd edition. London: Arnold.

Secretariat of the United Nations Convention to Combat Desertification (UNCCD) (1996) *Down to Earth: A Simplified Guide to the Convention to Combat Desertification*, Bonn: UNCCD.

Thomas, D. S. G. and Middleton N. J. (1994) *Desertification: Exploding the Myth*, Chichester: John Wiley & Sons.

See also: global warming; population growth

RAECHEL L. WATERS

Deterrence

Since both compellence and deterrence may be simultaneously pursued by states in their foreign policies, it is important to make a distinction between these two principal forms of strategic bargaining. Compellence is where one side attempts to force another into taking a desirable course of action. In contrast, the goal of deterrence is to prevent the other side from taking an unacceptable action in the first place. In other words, deterrence refers to a strategy of *dissuasion*, intended to prevent a specific action, and as such it is distinct from a policy of *coercion*. Both the challenger's unacceptable action and the deterrer's threatened retaliation may be undertaken through the use of military, economic, diplomatic, or other means. Thus deterrence can be manifested in a number of issue areas, but the most common focus of deterrence research has been in **security** studies.

The scholarly analysis of deterrence was particularly prompted by the advent of nuclear weapons, which marked a new era of military doctrine in which weapons primarily served deterrent purposes. Resulting from the apocalyptic consequences of the use of nuclear weapons, the first wave of deterrence scholarship was concerned with the intricacies of nuclear deterrence in the context of the **cold war**. Yet conventional deterrence, a strategy of dissuasion by threats of retaliation with conventional weapons, has been practiced throughout history. Acknowledging

this ubiquity of deterrence regardless of the type of weapons, the deterrence literature since the 1980s has been less concerned to focus on the alleged uniqueness of the nuclear age.

It is common to understand deterrence in terms of cost-benefit calculations, that is, threats are assumed to convince one's opponent that the costs and risks of a given course of action would outweigh their potential benefits. In addition to threats, deterrence may also operate through the promise of positive inducements through rewards, but this is not the central focus of most deterrence studies.

Additionally, the distinction is often made between basic or direct deterrence, in which a threat is issued to prevent an attack on one's own territory, and extended deterrence, when a deterrer attempts to prevent an attack on a third party. Another common distinction is made between general and immediate deterrence, depending on whether the deterrent policy is pursued to *prevent* challenges to the status quo that can trigger imminent militarized crises (general deterrence) (see **crisis**) or whether it is pursued *in response* to such imminent threats of attack (immediate deterrence). This is an important distinction because, as some authors claim, the conditions related to the failure of general deterrence may be different from those related to the failure of immediate deterrence.

Some typical problems in empirical studies of deterrence concern case selection and outcome identification. While case studies often suffer from selection bias by examining only cases of deterrence failure such as **war**, quantitative studies may have the same selection bias problem, and also may tend to oversimplify the notion of deterrence outcomes. Specifically, deterrence success is often identified with all cases that did not result in the use of force, thus attributing peaceful outcomes to deterrent threats. Yet, peaceful resolutions of disputes may result from many conditions, not all of which need be related to a deterrent threat. A potential challenger might refrain from upsetting the status quo for a number of reasons, including its satisfaction with the status quo. Recent studies attempt to rectify this problem by differentiating among types of peaceful outcomes, revealing that not all of them necessarily represent deterrence success (Danilovic 2002).

The central question for deterrence theory concerns the conditions under which deterrence is expected to work. Traditionally, strategic thinkers assume two basic requirements for successful deterrence: a deterrer must have sufficient capability to retaliate if deterrence fails and its threat must be perceived as credible. Simply put, for deterrence to work, the challenger must be convinced that the deterrer can and will execute his threats if the attack occurs. Based on these two commonly accepted factors, capability and credibility, for understanding the dynamics of deterrence, different schools of thought have emerged over the last five decades concerning each requirement.

Regarding the military balance as a deterring factor, the literature emerging immediately after World War Two, mainly focused on nuclear weapons as a potential deterrent. In this respect two schools of thought developed over the following two decades, one advocating the stability of the balance of terror resulting from **mutually assured destruction** (MAD), and another questioning the credibility of such massive retaliatory threats. In this second approach, the strategy allowing for the possibility of limited nuclear war became not only a thinkable option, but also one that presumably resolved the credibility problem of suicidal wars as exemplified in the MAD scenario. Quantitative empirical studies, however, seemed to indicate that nuclear weapons did not have unique deterrent properties and thus nuclear deterrence was not substantially distinguishable from conventional deterrence. The focus consequently switched to the traditional issue of conventional military balances that had a deterring effect, especially in the context of immediate deterrence, when military attack is an immanent possibility. Empirical findings tend to indicate that, in this respect, the deterrer's advantage in the short-term balance of forces and those that can be immediately employed if an attack occurs, have a stronger deterring potential than threats utilizing long-term forces as a weapon for retaliation (Huth 1988).

With respect to the issue of threat credibility, two main approaches can be discerned. As a principal representative of the 'second wave' deterrence theorists, Schelling (1966) developed a 'signaling theory' of a deterrer's resolve. He maintained that the nuclear credibility problem could be solved through manipulative strategies signaling a deterrer's strong resolve, including the possibility of irrational behavior if the threat fails. At the heart of Schelling's theory is his understanding of deterrence as a 'competition in risk-taking' which 'involves setting afoot an activity that may get out of hand, initiating a process that carries some risk of unintended disaster' (Schelling 1966, 91). By increasing the risk of military conflict and consequent high costs for backing down, costly signals are thus intended to reveal information about the deterrer's irrevocable commitment to act upon its threat.

In the late 1960s and 1970s, the third wave of deterrence scholars offered an alternative view of threat credibility as a function of 'intrinsic interests' in the issue at stake (e.g., George and Smoke 1974), which can significantly limit the relevance of manipulative tactics advocated in the signaling theory. The primary criticism of signaling theory is directed at its apolitical and technical approach to policy problems, whereas '[t]he fact of the matter is that the task of achieving credibility is secondary to *and dependent upon* the more fundamental question regarding the nature and valuation of interests' (George and Smoke 1974, 559). Over the last two decades, this approach in deterrence theory has been examined in the context of the issues at stake in a series of innovative quantitative studies (e.g., Huth 1988) and a formal-theoretic analysis of the related notion of 'inherent credibility' (Zagare and Kilgour 2000). This alternative approach to credibility as a requirement for deterrence was further elaborated as a function of national interests prioritized through the regional stakes of major powers in their mutual deterrence (Danilovic 2002). However, since Schelling's signaling theory also continues to find advocates in current literature (e.g., Fearon 1994), the debate concerning the requirements for successful deterrence is far from being resolved, explaining the continued research interest in this area.

Further reading

Danilovic, V. (2002) *When the Stakes Are High: Deterrence and Conflict among Major Powers*, Ann Arbor: University of Michigan Press.

Fearon, J. D. (1994) 'Signaling versus the Balance of Power and Interests: An Empirical Test of a Crisis Bargaining Model', *Journal of Conflict Resolution* 38(2), 236–69.

George, A. L., and Smoke, R. (1974) *Deterrence in American Foreign Policy: Theory and Practice*, New York: Columbia University Press.

Huth, P. (1988) *Extended Deterrence and the Prevention of War*, New Haven, CT: Yale University Press.

Schelling, T. C. (1966) *Arms and Influence*, New Haven, CT: Yale University Press.

Zagare, F. C., and Kilgour, D. M. (2000) *Perfect Deterrence*, Cambridge: Cambridge University Press.

See also: ballistic missile defense; confidence and security building measures; mutually assured destruction; nuclear utilization theory; pre-emptive use of force; security dilemma

VESNA DANILOVIC

Development

Development is a universal ideal, and, as such, it is virtually irreproachable. It is positively associated with material and psychological improvement as humans learn to manipulate the natural world. It is often associated with democratic outcomes. However, one of the key problems of development is that it is often realized through inequality, and so has not always enlarged human freedom. Indeed, sometimes it restricts the scope of democratic decision-making. For example the **United Nations** *Human Development Report* (1990), which represented a broadening of official understandings of development beyond its primary concern with economic growth, arose at a time when economic and social gains across the **Third World** were being reversed via **structural adjustment programs** that were implemented during the so-called 'lost decade' of the 1980s.

Another dilemma is that while improving material benefits may be the promise of development, there are high costs to be paid. Technological progress does not come as an unmitigated good; it involves continual (if not accelerating)

change in social and environmental relations. If development is evaluated in terms of outcomes and gains (e.g., incomes, goods and services, convenience), the evaluation misses some of the conditions of these outcomes, such as what people lose, give up, and even resist, in the process of development.

A further dilemma lies with the assumption that development involves directional change. Social scientists routinely characterize change as occurring in the governing beliefs of societies (from religious to secular rule), in their spatial patterns (from rural to urban living), or in their material means (from animal to machine power) – all leading to rising prosperity and a reduction of the burdens of agrarian existence. The dilemma arises where prosperity does not reach the majority of the world's population, whose development choices are narrowed by the shrinking of public capacity and the privatization of public services. Further, a significant portion of the global minority experiencing prosperity also experience complications, as 'developed societies' experience declining living standards when jobs move offshore, rising diseases of affluence, and the alienation and stress of post-modern lifestyles.

Finally, there is the conventional understanding of development as realization of the western lifestyle, and as a path pursued by each national society, following tracks laid by the 'developed countries'. The dilemma here is that while development is represented as a universal achievement, its realization at the national level is evidently quite variable. Is development a natural process to be realized in all countries, or is its claim to universality a projection of the European experience as the destiny of human kind? The sub-text here concerns whether and to what extent development is really a global, rather than a national (path-dependent) process.

The legacy of colonialism is instructive. Colonialism was an extractive **power** relationship through which the developed world gained a head start on the so-called development path. At the same time, the colonies were forced to specialize in primary goods production for export to the imperial centers in Europe. The dialectic of development/underdevelopment has been coined to describe this essentially global process, which generated the experience of development as a national outcome in the imperial centers. While development was identified as a European achievement, it was also a profoundly global process realized through inequality, dramatically represented in the colonial relationship. The twentieth century episode of **decolonization** itself was in part fueled by the power of the development ideal, as a lodestar to which postcolonial states could aspire (see **postcolonialism**). It was in this juncture that 'development' assumed its most powerful role as an organizing principle for independent nations, most systematically in the series of mid- to late twentieth century development decades. In so doing, it (mis)-represented a world historical process as a national goal and outcome.

Representations of development often contradict its historical relations insofar as it is represented as a desirable outcome. Historically, development is a political, economic and social process, with profoundly unequal consequences. Bringing colonized subjects into the mainstream of western civilization has been characterized variously as 'human destiny', 'the white man's burden', psychological 'enslavement', or even a 'holocaust'.

More recently, development has been presented with some unsettling counter-trends: religious fundamentalist challenges to westernization (if not modernity); environmental challenges to the sustainability of resource dependent consumer lifestyles; the natural world's challenge (for example, in the form of **global warming**) to human depletion of its ability to replenish its renewable (and non-renewable) resources; the rising tide of informal activities as marginal habitats expand on the fringes of urban areas and commercial agricultures; growing structural instability of employment, and declining public services, in 'developed economies'; and proliferating resistance to development culminating in the World Social Forum movement, as the counterpart to the World Economic Forum of the 'developed economies'. Contemporary resistance formulate and experiment with alternative conceptions of development, often linked to the relatively recent conception of **sustainable development**, and more generally linked to finding ways to address the inequalities and power relations through which development operates. Situating this growing tendency to problematize development requires a retracing of its historical steps.

In the nineteenth century, 'development' was understood philosophically as the improvement of humankind. However, in practice, development was understood by political elites as the social engineering of emerging national societies. It meant formulating government policy to manage the social transformations wrought by the rise of **capitalism** and industrial technologies. Development was identified simultaneously with industrial and market expansion, and the regulation of its disruptive social effects. These effects began with the displacement of rural populations by land enclosures for cash cropping, creating undesirables such as menacing paupers, restless proletarians and unpleasant, unhealthy factory towns. Development meant balancing the apparent inevitability of technological change with social intervention, under-

stood idealistically as assisting human society, and perhaps more realistically as managing citizen-subjects experiencing wrenching social transformations.

Unsurprisingly, this social engineering framed European colonization of the non-European world. Not only did colonial resource extraction underwrite European industrialization, but also colonial administrators assumed the task of developing, or controlling, their subject populations. Here, development served a legitimating function, where, compared to Europeans, native peoples appeared backward. The proverbial 'white man's burden' was an interpretation of this apparently natural relation of superiority and an invitation to intervene, in the name of development.

Development became, then, an extension of modern social engineering to the colonies, as they were incorporated into the European orbit. Subject populations were exposed to a variety of new disciplines, including forced labor schemes, schooling, and segregation in native quarters. Forms of colonial subordination differed across time and space, the overriding object being either to adapt or marginalize colonial subjects to the European presence. A minority of colonial subjects was socialized into civil service functions as a requirement of colonial rule over the laboring majority. Punctuality, task specialization, and regularity were the hallmarks of the new discipline of adaptation, breaking down social customs and producing individual subjects who confronted a new, rational order, which they reproduced and/or resisted. Civil servants learned the new disciplines required of developing societies and were busy displacing peasant culture with plantations, and managing armies of migrant labor, building an infrastructure of roads, canals, railways, telegraphs and ports. Across the colonial divide, industrialism was transforming metropolitan and colonial societies alike, producing new forms of social discipline among laboring populations and middle class citizen-subjects. While industrialism produced new class inequalities within each society, colonial development, everywhere, produced a form of international inequality steeped in racial distinctions.

Non-European cultures were irrevocably changed through colonialism and the subsequent movement to wrest independence from the colonizers. The colonial division of labor developed European capitalist civilization (with food and raw materials extracted from the colonies) at the same time as it disrupted non-European cultures. As European industrial society matured, the exploding urban populations demanded ever increasing imports of sugar, coffee, tea, cocoa, tobacco, and vegetable oils from the colonies, and the expanding factory system demanded ever increasing inputs of raw materials such as cotton, timber, rubber, and jute. The colonists, deploying an intermediary class of civil and military servants, forced more and more colonial subjects to work in cash cropping, employing a variety of methods such as enslavement, taxation, land grabbing, and recruitment for indentured labor contracts.

Western secular and religious crusades in the forms of administration, education, and missionary efforts accompanied colonial rule to stimulate progress along the European path. But the ruling Europeans misunderstood and denied the integrity of non-European cultures. Bringing progress to colonized peoples denied their **sovereignty**, a paradox experienced daily by colonial subjects, who enlisted in anti-colonial movements seeking independence from Western occupation. They appropriated the European **discourse** of the rights of man, turning it against their colonial masters as a mobilizing tool for independence.

National independence nevertheless expressed the unequal legacy of colonialism and international development. Despite the modern ideal of sovereign **nation-state**s, some were more equal than others, and these were defined as 'undeveloped' in a hierarchy of economic development informed by a western standard. The leaders of newly independent states had little choice but to operate in an international framework that was not of their making, but through which they acquired political legitimacy by pursuing development. While this goal was irreproachable from the perspective of redressing the impoverishing legacies of colonialism, it carried the questionable assumption of whether development, that is, replicating the European path, was possible given the dependency of that path under the colonial relationship.

This relationship represented the key puzzle of development. The juxtaposition of European industrialization with non-European agricultural specialization, in national terms, suggested that Europe had paved the way for the backward, non-European states to follow. This representation of development as a national process ignored the historic **interdependence** forged through colonialism. But by viewing this international specialization as relational (interdependent) rather than sequential (a matter of catch-up), the conventional understanding of development as a direction comes into question. Further, if European industrialization depended on colonial monocultures, then development (as experienced in Europe) was more than a national process. It was in fact an international, albeit unequal, relationship, represented as a national process. Such a representation served the interests of the dominant states, insofar as their power relations with the non-European world were obscured by aid relations premised on the formula of 'catch-up' development.

In the post-1945 period, which was marked by the collapse of the European empires as decolonization took hold, development was elaborated as an international initiative. It sprung from two related sources, the aspiration for independence on the part of post-colonial peoples, and second, the determination by the European states (including the United States) to retain access to ex-colonial markets and resources. At this time, the capitalist first world had 65 per cent of world income with only 20 per cent of the world's population, whereas the colonial and post-colonial third world accounted for 67 per cent of world population but only 18 per cent of its income. This economic disparity generated a vision of development that would energize political and business elites in each world to overcome the division of humanity between developed and undeveloped regions. This division of the world projected a singular destiny for all states.

Development, or modernity, became the standard by which other societies were judged. It was a new and specific ideal of **order** (including a bureaucratic state, industrial production, rational law, specialization, technical innovation, professionalism, price-based value) that, given the concentration of wealth and power in the first world, came to seem like order itself. Development assumed the status of a master concept. It was a way of looking at the world, a new paradigm. It presumed that with the end of the division of the world between the colonizers and the colonized, modernity was there for the taking by the underdeveloped world.

The development paradigm offered a strategy for improving the material con-dition of the Third World. It was also a strategy for reimposing order in the world, inscribing first world power and privilege in the new institutional structure of the postwar international economy. Development was simultaneously the restoration of a capitalist world market to sustain first world wealth, through global access to strategic natural resources, and the opportunity for Third World countries to emulate first world civilization and living standards.

The power of the new paradigm arose in part from its ability to present itself as a universal, as autonomous, and therefore uncontroversial, indeed natural. In these terms, development discourse expressed western international hegemony, naturalizing development by ignoring the double role of colonialism. In a postcolonial era, Third World states could not repeat the European experience of developing by exploiting the resources and labor of other societies. Moreover, development's aura of inevitability devalued non-European cultures and discounted what the West could learn from the non-European world.

Development was the enabling principle for the national and international goal of equality, as proclaimed by the United Nations Declaration of Human Rights (1948). The responsibility of realizing these rights by individual Third World countries constituted the social contract that underlined the development project. Deploying the **Bretton Woods** institutions (the **World Bank** and the **International Monetary Fund**), as well as bilateral programs of economic and military assistance, first world states constructed an aid **regime** linking development with the **containment** of communism during the **cold war**. Within this framework, Third World elites legitimized their rule by complementing foreign aid (which often reproduced the colonial division of labor) with programs of economic **nationalism** to reverse the colonial legacy. Such initiatives sometimes strengthened patronage systems at the expense of **democratization**.

During this period, US strategic interests were framed in terms of 'free worldism' and 'freedom of enterprise' in establishing an **empire** of containment. This empire was founded on military alliances, disbursements of the dollar (as the international reserve currency) and export credits. It was not dissimilar to the structure of power in the post-September 11, 2001 world, the difference being that twentieth century development, included a domestic protocol of state intervention inspired by a discourse promoting public goods and equality. The United Nations Charter (1945) proclaimed a rising standard of living as the precondition for the social contract, measured by the commercial output of goods and services within a country and *per capita* gross national product (GNP), or the national average of *per capita* income. While *per capita* income was not the sole measure of rising living standards (health, literacy, etc. were allied measures), the key criterion was measurable progress towards the goal of the good society, characterized by high mass consumption.

In the minds of many Western economists, development required a kind of jump-start in the Third World. Cultural practices of sharing wealth within communities were perceived as traditional obstacles to the transition. The solution was to introduce a market system based on private property and wealth accumulation. It required a range of modern practices and institutions designed to sustain economic growth, such as banking and accounting systems, education, stock markets and legal systems, and public infrastructure. Within this framework, national accounting methods standardized wealth in price terms across states, reducing the value of productive activity to monetized transactions, thereby devaluing subsistence activity. Thus farming and indigenous cultures, women's work, and environmental relations were all either discounted or marginalized. The consequences, including the systematic disregard for equity, ecology and diversity, have recently precipitated reformulations of development that include cultural rights, sustainability, social justice and inclusion.

In the meantime, across the last half of the twentieth century, the development trajectory was shaped by some key moments that express ideas as much as changing power relations. The viability of the development state depended originally on the principle of economic nationalism, popularized by the executive secretary of the Economic Commission for Latin America, Raul Prebisch, in the 1950s. This principle was based on the concept of 'import-substitution industrialization', designed to reverse the effects of the colonial division of labor. It inspired two decades of building domestic industrial and complexes, including agro-industrial complexes (known as the 'green revolution'), in strategic states in the Third World (often subsidized with World Bank loans, which in turn enabled the import of western technology). Indeed, a disproportionate amount of aid and investment was concentrated in a relatively small number of key states in Asia (South Korea, Taiwan, Hong Kong and Singapore) and in Latin America (Brazil and Mexico). These states became known as the Newly Industrializing Countries (NICs), and were presented as showcases to the remaining Third World countries to legitimize the development paradigm (see **newly industrializing country**). Each of these states held strategic **geopolitical** positions in the international order, as consequential states in their regions, with all but Hong Kong distinguished by one party or military rule during their period of maximum economic growth. Industrial measures of development notwithstanding, these states held a special relation to the security and ideological requirements of the West in context of the cold war.

The cold war over determined the development trajectory. Third world patterns of authoritarian or military rule served strategic international interests at the same time as they were often associated with the principle of economic nationalism. However, when Third World states extended this principle to the nationalization of foreign-owned resources, the West intervened to stem the nationalist tide. Notable examples include the CIA-sponsored coup in 1953 against Guatemalan President Arbenz's land reforms, which threatened United Fruit holdings, the bloody overthrow of ultra-nationalist Indonesian President Sukarno in 1965, with Britain and the United States as co-conspirators, and the assassination of Chilean President Allende, spurred by his nationalization of US copper holdings.

The economic nationalist phase culminated in a lending and borrowing binge of the 1970s, as a global money market emerged, fueled by offshore dollars and recycled oil rents (when the **Organization of Petroleum Exporting Countries** formed a cartel to inflate prices). Development states borrowed easily and heavily to finance industrial and infrastructural projects, with some regimes flaunting their wealth (and corruption) through unnecessarily grandiose projects. Such financial overreach laid the groundwork for the 1980s debt crisis. A debt regime, instituted through the World Bank and the IMF as debt collection agencies, reversed the course of development and the illusion of Third World upward mobility (represented by

the NIC phenomenon). A new technology of financial discipline arose, with a discourse of **good governance** to justify and enable privatization and economic liberalization, effectively challenging the social contract of the original development project.

In this context, economic nationalism experienced its final *denouement* in a relocation of sovereignty from the state to the market, with the World Bank redefining development as successful participation in the world market. Protectionism was replaced by export orientation, as global economic integration proceeded apace, driven by transnational corporate use of 'global sourcing' of labor and other inputs into the manufacturing process. Rather than replication of a national model of development, specialization in the world economy became the development elixir in the post-cold war, or 'post-socialist', world of the 1990s. It was premised on the doctrine of comparative advantage, whereby states would pursue their relative efficiencies in a new trade regime. To facilitate this transition, the first world founders of the GATT Uruguay Round (1986–94) promised, disingenuously, to lower barriers against Third World exports in return for Third World adherence to the rules of the emerging project of **globalization** (liberalization of agriculture and its trade, of investment and services, and their privatization, and the institutionalization of intellectual property rights). This initiative culminated in the formation of the **World Trade Organization** (WTO) in 1995.

Under the WTO regime, development has been redefined further as market rule, meaning that the function of states is to facilitate private forms of development through trade, two-thirds of which is managed by, or internal to, **multinational** corporations. Development became a reward for joining the global market. The WTO institutionalized, through its protocols, the original axiom of the World Bank, that development now involved strategic positioning in the global economy. The difference is that whereas once development was managed by states, it is now being actively privatized. That is, decisions about the allocation of resources are increasingly governed by the market, which is dominated by the ubiquitous transnational corporation.

The shift in emphasis, from national/ public to global/private development, informed the WTO Agreement on Agriculture (1995), which codified a dramatic liberalization of farm sectors and agricultural trade across the global South. Reversing a long-standing commitment by governments to national food self-sufficiency (whether realistic or not, given varying ecological endowments and public capacities), the privatization of food security subjects food production and distribution decisions to agribusiness and consumer choice. Since not all consumers are equal, such decisions tend to be driven by the superior purchasing power of affluent consumers. The classic example is the global substitution of food grains by feed grains to supply an animal protein revolution (lot-fed beef, pork, and poultry, and shrimp and fish aquacultures) driven by rising incomes among the upper segments of the world's population. The proportions of this substitution are underlined by the fact that the quantity of feed grains fed to US livestock equals the combined food grains consumed by the populations of India and China (in a world where 1.2 billion people are undernourished). In this scenario, then, a basic human right to adequate food, which might be understood as a foundation for development, is institutionally relocated from the public to the private sphere.

The turn to development as a private, global initiative fundamentally alters the socio-political, or civic, content of development. When public services are privatized, the meaning of citizenship switches from membership of the public household with rights to social protections, to membership of the market with rights to produce, exchange and consume. Access to goods and services is determined less by need and more by income. Privatization policies accentuate the individual (as opposed to the civic) content of citizenship, subordinating social rights to economic rights in the marketplace. In the global South, where more than half the population is engaged in informal activity, economic rights in the marketplace are scarce.

The WTO's General Agreement advances privatization globally on Trade and Services (GATS). GATS protocols opened markets for trade in services by establishing the rights to corporate presence in member countries for the delivery of a service in the areas of finance, telecommunications and transport. The new 'GATS 2000' protocol is intended to be more far-reaching in compelling governments to provide unlimited market access to foreign service providers, without regard for social and environmental impacts of the service activities. All services are targeted, including health, education, water, social security, prisons, libraries, postal, and a variety of municipal services. Represented as a trade agreement in the WTO, GATS 2000 expects cross-border provision of services as a condition for opening Northern markets in garments, textiles and agricultural products. The nature of this asymmetrical trade-off is to privilege foreign ownership of the social infrastructure of economies in the global South in exchange for tropical, and out-sourced, commodities. As before, development is realized through an unequal, international relationship, increasingly interpreted as corporate globalization.

In this sense, the WTO tends to regulate states as much as trade, and has the effect of replacing the inclusive social contract between state and citizen with an exclusive private contract between corporation and consumer. To facilitate this, the multilateral agencies, in addressing the social impact of structural adjustment and the **debt trap**, have refined **global governance** mechanisms by linking new loan criteria to 'state effectiveness,' and deepening liberalization, with the explicit goal of stimulating private global economic activity, and perhaps the implicit goal of securing Northern access to Southern resources given the international relations of development.

How this trajectory of global **neoliberalism** will play out is an open question, as shifts in the geopolitical balance are bound to occur. For example, a new bloc of Southern states, led by Brazil, India, and China, challenged Northern protectionism at the 2003 WTO Ministerial in Cancun, Mexico, suggesting that a Southern alliance led by states with large populations and industrial complexes and a growing stake in the world trading system might alter the terms of global development. Brazil, Russia, India, and China (the so-called 'BRICS') may become more consequential in the global economy over the next fifty years. At present they are included in the world's ten largest economies, but they are certainly not the richest (measured by income *per capita*). How that will further redefine the conditions of development, officially, is a question that will depend on prevailing power relations.

The tradition of representing development as a universal ideal is viewed by some as a confidence trick, or an illusion, because the metropolitan centers of the world economy have always depended on an exploited periphery. Others, such as Susan George and Fabrizio Sabelli (1994), view development as a success because they believe it was never intended to be an egalitarian process. Whatever the case, it is clear that development has been a process wherein states *attempted* to manage national economic integration, but the integration was often incomplete. States have different points of departure, and different resources with which to work, but capitalist development is an unequal and uneven process. In addition, the industrial fixation marginalized rural communities and their redundant populations, who found their way into the shantytowns bordering cities. By 2006, the global South's share of world urban population will exceed 50 per cent. States almost routinely exploit weaker communities in their hinterlands (such as forest dwellers or peasant villages), in order to build dams, to expand mines, plantations and commercial farms for export revenues, or to relocate other displaced peasants, justifying this action in the name of national development.

In short, large social segments of the Third World have remained on the margins or experienced displacement through development. Only about one-fifth of the world's six billion people participate in the cash or consumer credit economy. In many ways development has been quite limited, and often undemocratic, however inclusive its (western) ideals. The emerging corporate form of global development is decidedly less stable and certainly not homogeneous in its effects. Although it is certainly true that more people across the world in the twenty-first century consume standardized goods, it is also true that the conditions under which many of these goods are produced are quite diverse, and uncertain. China is emerging as the world's manufacturing powerhouse with a seemingly unlimited supply of cheap labor, which exerts a powerful destabilizing and disorganizing impact on Northern labor forces and the welfare state.

The modern European welfare state rested on a common organizing drive by the labor forces in Europe, demanding adequate wages, job and employment protection, the right to organize into unions, and a voice in national politics. This trend, representing the social gains of development, has subsided as industrial restructuring, **offshore** investment, public works downsizing, labor demobilization, and the steady relocation of blue, and increasingly white, collar jobs to the global South have swept across the global North. On the other side of this process new, mobile labor forces across the world are incorporated into commodity chains of global production. Peasant contractors, *maquila* workers, child labor, casual female and male labor, sweatshop work, plantation labor, homework, and even slave labor constitute a quite heterogeneous mix of labor in the global economy. With jobs concentrating in the South and consumers concentrated in the North, development is manifestly global, but profoundly destabilizing as governments lose their tax base, employment becomes more tenuous, and national payment imbalances grow.

The record for the era of 'globalization,' coinciding with the WTO era, has been decidedly mixed. Despite positive indices of global economic growth, the World Bank estimated that 200 million more people were living in abject poverty at the end of the 1990s than at the beginning of the decade. In 1997, the United Nations reported that while the income of the wealthiest 20 per cent of the world's population was 30 times that of the poorest 20 per cent, by 1997 the difference was 74 times; and a UN report in 2002 claimed that for the poorest 49 countries, living standards were lower than 30 years previously.

Perhaps just as telling as these statistics is the mushrooming of alternative movements and forms of development across the world. These alternatives often reject the dominant paradigm, maintaining that its definitions of poverty and wealth are culturally biased, discounting the wealth of non-market cultures and the poverty of market cultures. The movements are known variously as global justice movements, anti-globalization movements, or alternative sovereignty movements. Many of them question the commercial and mono-cultural principles of official development practices, under the slogan of 'our world is not for sale'. In this regard, the emphasis is on finding alternative, sustainable development paradigms that revalue cultural diversity, community, biodiversity, and the self-organizing principle central to enlightenment philosophy. These initiatives occur in the form of community and producer cooperatives, movements of the landless, regional/ethnic autonomy movements, fair trade schemes implementing ecological and social accounting, seed saving schemes to preserve biodiversity and farmer autonomy, agricultural multi-functionality and community-supported agriculture, commons recovery schemes, and alternative currency movements.

The essential point is that these movements work against the grain of a global development project that seeks to impose a singular logic and pattern on a culturally, ecologically, and politically diverse world. They offer alternative visions and practices, some of which the global developers actively appropriate to their ends. In this dialectic, compounded by increasing ecological turbulence, and the possibility of a new, but unstable, world empire based on US military expansionism to secure strategic resources and counter stateless **terrorism**, lies the future trajectory of development.

Further reading

Aronowitz, S. and Gautney, H. (eds) (2003) *Implicating Empire. Globalization & Resistance in the 21st Century World Order*, New York: Basic Books.

Brecher, J., Costello, T. and Smith, B. (2000) *Globalization From Below. The Power of Solidarity*, Boston: South End Press.

Cowan, M. P. and Shenton, R. W. (1996) *Doctrines of Development*, New York: Routledge.

Davis, M. (2000) *Late-Victorian Holocausts. The Making of the Third World*, London: Verso.

Escobar, A. (1996) *Encountering Development. The Making and the Unmaking of the Third World*, Princeton, NJ: Princeton University Press.

George, S. and Sabelli, F. (1994) *Faith and Credit: The World Bank's Secular Empire*, Boulder, CO: Westview Press.

Hoogvelt, A. (1997) *Globalisation and the Postcolonial World: the New Political Economy of Development*, London: Macmillan.

Houtart, F., and Polet, F. (2001) *The Other Davos. The Globalization of Resistance to the World Economic System*, London: Zed Books.

McMichael, P. (2004) *Development and Social Change. A Global Perspective*, Thousand Oaks: Pine Forge Press.

Rist, G. (1997) *The History of Development: From Western Origins to Global Faith*, London: Zed Books.

See also: dependency; modernization; sustainable development; United Nations development program; world-system theory

PHILIP McMICHAEL

Diaspora

The study of global diasporas is a growing academic field that is not confined to any one discipline in the social sciences. Once considered the preserve of Jewish studies and the US immigrant story, the study of the physical movements of groups around the world now includes Chinese, Korean, Latino, Indian, and countless cultural groups residing outside their original homelands. A hallmark of diaspora studies is the examination of cultural continuities and adaptations characteristic of such movements. Scholars are primarily concerned with how well diasporic groups retain their home cultures and how much is lost in the process of absorption into another culture. In an era of **nationalism**, **globalization** and increased flows of immigrants and **refugee**s, one can expect diasporas to attract greater scholarly attention in the study of international relations than has been the case thus far.

The term 'diaspora' was originally coined to describe the circumstance of Jews who lived outside of Palestine after the Babylonian exile. Since then, its scope has been enlarged to include any group that has been scattered far from its original homeland, with most attention paid to the descendants of Africans who were forcibly removed from Africa and brought to the New World as slaves in the seventeenth century.

In light of the diversity of the diasporic experience, it would be futile to insist on an exclusive definition of what is and what is not a diaspora. Instead, it is more useful to note that there are different types of diaspora, and it is important to distinguish between them. There are three main types. First, one can identify *victim* diasporas, such as Jews, Armenians, and Africans. These are groups whose history is one of systematic oppression in which they have either fled or been forcibly removed from their homeland. Second, there are *labor and imperial* diasporas, such as the Indians and British, respectively. Many groups have moved from their place of origin and established communities overseas as a consequence of the history of imperialism. In the case of British diaspora, these are often descendants of British colonial administrators who have remained in former colonies rather than returning home. Finally, there are *trade* diasporas such as the overseas Chinese or Lebanese, groups whose entrepreneurial skills have enabled them to flourish outside their country of origin.

Given this diversity of experience, is it possible to make any useful generalizations about diasporas? Not really. What can be said is that diasporas share a common problem of cultural identity that they respond to in vastly different ways. Diasporic identity points in two directions, the place of origin and the location of domicile. Members of diasporas have often never been to their homeland, whilst the experience of assimilation to their new home can exacerbate rather than alleviate the sense of marginality for which it was supposed to be the cure. The condition of the diaspora is thus an interesting state of suspension. Their nationality is rarely fixed or definitive. Instead, they represent forms of sociocultural organization that transcend and even predate the state, itself a relatively new form of political organization born about four hundred years ago.

Further reading

Brah, A. (1997) *Cartographies of Diaspora: Contesting Identities*, London: Routledge.

Braziel, J. E. and Mannur, A. (2003) *Theorizing Diaspora: A Reader*, Oxford: Blackwell.

Cohen, R. (1997) *Global Diaporas: An Introduction*, Seattle, WA: University of Washington Press.

Friedman, J. and Randeria, S. (eds) (2003) *Worlds On The Move*, London: I. B. Tauris.

Okpewho, I, Davis, C. and Mazrui, A. (eds) (1999) *The African Diaspora*, Bloomington, IN: Indiana University Press.

See also: globalization; nation-state; refugee

MARTIN GRIFFITHS

Diplomacy

The conduct of relations between sovereign states by their accredited representatives. Normally, such diplomats are professionals, in the sense that they are career foreign service officers. But they are often supplemented by the secondment to conference delegations and resident missions of experts from other government departments , those dealing, for example, with defense, finance, or trade. Such individuals are temporary diplomats. Additionally, the holders of political office will from time to time (increasingly so in recent decades) play *ad hoc* diplomatic roles at summit meetings and at international conferences and organizations.

The *significance* of diplomacy is that it enables states to engage in peaceful relations with each other. States are commonly spoken of as if they are persons, but they are so only in a notional sense. Accordingly, their views or wishes have to be transmitted via representative human persons (as is the case with all notional entities). Diplomacy is the means whereby this is done, and without some such scheme it is hard to see how states could engage in any external relations other than the bald use of force. Thus diplomacy provides the essential communications system that states need in order to engage in international relations.

The necessity of such arrangements where distinct groups wish to have peaceful dealings with each other is historically clear. The first decipherable written records of international relations, dating from the early third millennium BC, provide evidence of diplomacy, as do the mid-fourteenth century BC Amarna letters that record the conduct of relations between Egypt and the other states of the ancient Near East (the first **international system** known to us). By 500 BC the Greek city-states had developed a recognizable diplomatic system that greatly influenced later thinking about diplomacy.

Modern diplomacy emerged among the Italian city-states in the late fifteenth century. The resident diplomatic missions then established are the forerunners of those found today, which have by no means been overshadowed by the concurrent despatch of permanent missions to international organizations such as the **United Nations**. It is now virtually unknown for the heads of such resident missions not to be of the highest diplomatic class. Thus they are either ambassadors; or, for **Commonwealth** missions, high commissioners; or, in the case of missions despatched by the Holy See, *nuncios*.

The functions of a resident mission, as set out in the 1961 Vienna Convention on Diplomatic Relations, include representation; protecting nationals; negotiating; reporting home about conditions and developments in the receiving state; developing economic, cultural and scientific relations; and promoting friendly relations. That last assertion, however, reflects diplomatic correctitude rather than analytical accuracy. A diplomat's duty is to advance the interests of her or his state, which may involve actions that by no means advance friendship. As one aphorism puts it, 'a diplomat's job is to do and say the nastiest thing in the nicest way'.

During the twentieth century some important alterations occurred in the ways in which diplomats go about their business. Some commentators regard these developments as major challenges to the very institution of diplomacy. That goes too far, confusing the manner in which tasks are executed and the content of the diplomatic agenda with the basic nature of the activity. But these changes do deserve note.

First, the openness of diplomacy has increased markedly. This dates from World War One, when those who blamed the 'old', 'secret' diplomacy for precipitating the War called for a 'new', 'open', and more democratic system. They were powerfully reinforced when, in 1918, the US President Woodrow Wilson famously called in the first of his 'fourteen points' (in which he outlined a peace program) for 'open covenants openly arrived at'. What Wilson meant has often been misunderstood. He did not mean that all negotiations, however sensitive and delicate, should be conducted in the full glare of publicity. He did mean that the outcome of negotiations should be made public, a principle that has since been generally accepted. The idea of open diplomacy was also reflected in the practice of the **League of Nations**, in that almost all its meetings were held in public. Indeed, the League Assembly (which contained representatives of every member state, each having one vote) came to be seen as a kind of world parliament, hence the emergence of the phrase 'parliamentary diplomacy'. Today it is vividly exemplified in the formal meetings of the United Nations.

Second, the huge growth in the ease and speed of communication and travel since 1945 has affected the way diplomats work. Heads of mission can more easily be given detailed instructions or edged aside by a visiting politician; but they can also be brought closely into discussions occurring at home and be swiftly transported there for urgent consultations. Consequently, and contrary to what some allege, their influence has not greatly declined. Moreover, they remain well placed to gather and interpret information. They do valuable preparatory work in preparing for summits and high level conferences, provide guidance during them, and do follow-up work. Most of them are culturally aware communicators who can deliver messages personally to the appropriate official and in the most telling way.

Third, during the same period the phrase 'new diplomacy' has been used to describe certain specific changes in its scope and conduct. These include the extension of diplomatic missions' traditional remit beyond strictly political matters to encompass promoting their states' commercial and economic interests, and the occasional direct involvement in external relations of domestically-focused government ministries. And fourth, in the last thirty-odd years **terrorism** has made diplomacy a more dangerous and much more security-conscious profession.

It remains the case, therefore, that diplomacy is central to the conduct of relations between states, and that in its absence states would hardly be in a position to engage in any such relations. It is, however, important to be aware that the term is also used internationally in ways other than that which has so far been described. On the one hand, it is sometimes employed more narrowly. Often, for example, it refers solely to negotiation, and as regards some types of negotiation new phrases have been coined. Thus 'track one diplomacy' describes the efforts of a state or inter-governmental organization to resolve an inter-state or even an intra-state conflict;

and 'track two diplomacy' refers to the same process when undertaken by non-state agencies, such as **non-governmental organizations**. 'Two-track diplomacy', however, describes separate but coordinated negotiations of either a 'track one' or a 'track two' type, or both. Then, too, the term diplomacy is commonly used to refer to the skill with which a particular diplomatic task has been undertaken, as when some inter-state matter has been conducted with notable tact or skill ('very diplomatically').

On the other hand, the term is often used more broadly than in this entry. In the United States, especially, 'diplomacy' is frequently treated as synonymous with foreign policy. Used in this way, diplomacy refers, either generally or in part, to a state's external relations (as in 'French diplomacy at the United Nations' or 'American diplomacy under President Clinton'). Similarly, it may be used to refer to the fora in which states pursue their foreign policy goals (as in 'diplomacy at the United Nations'). This terminology tends to obscure the very important distinction between the substance and the execution of foreign policy. Diplomacy, most usefully conceived, has to do with the latter. But diplomacy is not simply one of a number of optional tools which may be employed in carrying out policy. Rather, it provides the essential framework for states to engage in any kind of non-forceful inter-state activity. Without it, they would be either hermits or have nothing at their external disposal except **war**.

Further reading

Berridge, G. R. (2002) *Diplomacy: Theory and Practice*, 2nd edn, Basingstoke: Palgrave.

Berridge, G. R. and James, A. (2003) *A Dictionary of Diplomacy*, 2nd edn, Basingstoke: Palgrave.

Hamilton, K. and Langhorne, R. (1995) *The Practice of Diplomacy*, London: Routledge.
James, A. (1980) 'Diplomacy and International Society', *International Relations* 6(6), 931–48.

See also: CNN factor/effect; international society; preventive diplomacy; recognition

LORNA LLOYD

Disarmament

The attempt to eliminate or radically reduce armaments. It can be distinguished from the concept of **arms control**, which entails restraint but not necessarily reduction in the number and kinds of weapons available to states. Most disarmament proposals are based on the assumption that weapons are an important source of conflict in themselves. Historically, disarmament has taken place in two contrasting ways. First, after a **war**, disarmament has often been *imposed* on the defeated state by the victor. For example, in 1919 the Treaty of Versailles limited the German army to 100,000 troops, thereby effectively eliminating an army that could be capable of offensive activity, and a similar restriction was placed on Germany and Japan after World War Two. Historically, the victors have been unable to remain united and unwilling to act together to enforce these prohibitions. Nazi Germany established training areas and munitions factories in the Soviet Union after World War One without suffering any penalties, and as the **cold war** intensified after 1945, a primary concern of US foreign policy became rebuilding the military might of Japan and West Germany.

The second type of disarmament is *voluntary* disarmament, in which states seek to negotiate a mutually acceptable framework within which all parties will reduce the size of their military establishments. While the ultimate logic of disarmament points to the total elimination of all weapons, three main types of disarmament plans can be identified. The first is typified by attempts to reduce the size of the German armed forces to the bare minimum. A second type of disarmament is General and Complete Disarmament (GCD), which seeks the total elimination of all weapons. If this ever happened, the fundamental nature of international relations would be radically transformed. Unfortunately, GCD is usually associated with extreme idealism although there are historical examples of such proposals. During the Reykjavik Summit in 1986, General Secretary of the former Soviet Union Mikhail Gorbachev proposed – and President Reagan of the United States accepted – a plan for the elimination of all nuclear armed ballistic missiles by 1996. Although the plan was never implemented, it did increase public support for Gorbachev at a time when many people feared that the nuclear arms race was reaching dangerous levels of intensity.

A third form of disarmament is *regional* disarmament. It seeks to reduce or to eliminate weapons from a particular geographic area. Over the last five decades regional disarmament plans have frequently taken the form of proposals for nuclear-free zones. A major barrier to the successful negotiation of such agreements is that, once a state in a region has acquired nuclear weapons, it is difficult to prevent others from doing likewise. This was the main problem that ultimately prevented the implementation of the (often proposed) South Asian Nuclear Free Zone. Today, both India and Pakistan possess nuclear weapons, and the proposal looks very unlikely to be implemented in the foreseeable future. However, the history of regional disarmament is not all hopeless. Four main regional agreements remain in effect. In 1967, the Treaty for the Prohibition of Nuclear Weapons in Latin America, also known as the Treaty of Tlatelolco, was signed. This treaty prohibits the testing, possession, and deployment of nuclear weapons in the region. Similarly, the 1959 Antarctic Treaty bans the use of Antarctica for military purposes, including nuclear testing. In 1971 a treaty was signed banning states from placing nuclear weapons on the seabed, and in 1967 a similar treaty prohibits states from placing nuclear weapons in earth orbit or stationing them in outer space.

While the existence of such treaties may provide supporters of disarmament with some hope that they can be extended, it should be pointed out that treaties such as those just mentioned are not strictly about disarmament. Rather, they represent agreements by states not to develop weapons that they are not planning to build in the first place, and not to deploy weapons in areas that are of peripheral strategic value. Were these conditions ever to change, it is unlikely that the mere existence of such treaties would deter states from breaking them.

There are two main problems with the concept of disarmament. First, it is not clear that the underlying assumption (arms cause war) is correct. In the 1980s, many supporters of the Campaign for Nuclear Disarmament (CND) and European Nuclear Disarmament (END) claimed that the nuclear arms race was out of the control of politicians. They advocated unilateral nuclear disarmament in order to break the cycle of the arms race. However, the end of the cold war has been followed by radical arms reductions by the **great powers**, suggesting that **arms race**s are caused by underlying political conflicts. Disarmament proposals that treat only the symptoms of a problem rather than its causes are unlikely to work. A second problem

with the concept is the difficulty of verifying disarmament agreements. In the absence of reliable verification, disarmament can make the world a more dangerous place. Having said that, disarmament is most likely to proceed when there is a consensus among states that the possession of particular weapons can no longer be justified and when there exists reliable systems of verifying agreements.

Further reading

Berdal, M. (1996) *Disarmament and Demobilization After Civil Wars*, Oxford: Oxford University Press.

Karp, R. (ed.) (1992) *Security Without Nuclear Weapons*, Oxford: Oxford University Press.

Wittner, L. (1995) *The Struggle Against the Bomb*, Stanford, CA: Stanford University Press.

See also: arms control; arms race; pacifism; security dilemma

ANDREW O'NEIL

Discourse

The word derives from both the French *discours* and Latin *discursus*. Gee (1996) usefully distinguishes between 'small d' and 'big D' discourse. Small 'd' discourse refers to any meaningful stretch of language. It is a general term for talk or conversation, extending also to a sermon or a treatise. In linguistics, it refers to a unit or piece of connected speech or writing that is longer than a sentence. It can also be used to mean extended samples of spoken dialogue as opposed to written text. Beyond this the term also covers different types of language used in different social contexts, for example classroom discourse as different from doctor–patient discourse. In linguistics, discourse analysis analyses speech and writing and their relationship to the contexts in which they are used. The discourse analyst focuses on the more 'micro' linguistic features such as the patterns of lexis and grammar at the level of the clause. An example in international relations is the analysis of the choice of lexical term used to describe the combatants in armed conflicts, variously 'freedom fighters' or 'terrorists'. How does a reader interpret the choice of either in a piece of discourse, and what is the significance of choosing one over the other in producing a text as a product of discourse?

At the grammatical level the same discourse analyst may examine the choice of agency, that is, the 'doer' of an action. Note the difference in the phrase 'coalition forces bombed Baghdad' from the phrase 'bombs fell on Baghdad'. In the first example it is the coalition forces that are the agents of the action. In the second example the agent is deleted, so there is no named 'doer' of the action, which implies that the bombs acted independently without human volition. Further, compare the phrase 'coalition forces bombed Baghdad' with the phrase 'F-117 radar-evading jets dropped bombs on Baghdad'. In the second example the responsibility for the action now sits with technology rather than humans. Discourse analysts from a linguistic background work from the assumption that these different lexical and grammatical choices create different readings of reality. A stronger position suggests that there are in fact different realities created via the texts produced within discourses.

What Gee calls 'big D Discourse' refers to the larger, more pervasive sets of values, beliefs and ideas through which humans are positioned in social settings. In this view, derived from continental philosophical traditions, people are limited in the thoughts they can hold and express through language. Their ideas are restricted by the boundaries of Discourse, the structure within which humans operate. In this usage of the term, Discourse moves away from being something only to do with language and closer to the idea of discipline. It encompasses gesture, dress, and bodily disposition. Discourse refers to ways of behaving, interacting, valuing, thinking, believing, speaking, reading and writing which are accepted as instantiations of particular roles by specific groups of people. Thus the ways in which different cultural or ethnic groups perceive each other can be viewed as the products of Discourses (see **ethnicity**). For example the Irish could be construed as 'stupid' in one English Discourse, as are 'Poles' in a parallel American Discourse.

Discourse analysis from this angle places more weight on the more 'macro' considerations inherent in the social, cultural or political context. Discourses are defined by 'what can be said' and exclude those ideas which fall outside their boundaries. Such exclusion contains the ability to shape thought and also to shape truth via a pressure or a power of constraint on other Discourses. For some scholars working from a post-structural perspective, truth is itself a construction of Discourse (see **post-structuralism**). In particular, Foucault's work can be seen as an attempt to uncover the **genealogy** of Discourses in which ideas that at one time were considered the truth are abandoned at another time via processes of discursive progression. Discourse shapes reality rather than reality shaping Discourse, a **power** which is masked by the nature of Discourse itself. The Discourse is viewed as benign and participants believe they are capable of holding any idea or expressing any thought, limited only by their individual creativity. It is very difficult to recognize that the society and social practices with which we engage on a daily basis are in fact 'preconstructed'. They are not a 'natural' result of our interactions with others and our world. Rather, each Discourse incorporates a tacit theory of what counts as a normal person and the appropriate ways to think, feel, and behave. Discourses resist internal criticism and self-scrutiny. To offer a point of view which seriously questions or undermines them would define a person as standing outside the Discourse. To question our Discourses is tantamount to challenging what we know and who we are. This extends from the individual through to the level of the state. The Discourse itself defines what can be offered as criticism, excluding other ideas from the created reality. Those who do proffer ideas outside the discursive boundaries are rejected using the criterion of reason.

A number of scholars have attempted to synthesize both types of discourse in proposing a dialectical relationship between the micro and the macro, between discourse and Discourse. For example, Fairclough (2003) defines discourse not only as a 'mode of representation', that is the traditional linguistic use of the term, but also as a 'mode of action' through which people act on the world and also on each other. This dual definition discloses a dialectical relation between discourse and social structure. The products of discourse, or texts, are produced, distributed and consumed differently across different social groups. He proposes a three-dimensional model such that any instance of discourse is at the same time a piece of text, an instance of discursive practice and also an instance of social practice, allowing the analyst to attend to the different levels of analysis, the text itself, the types of discourses drawn on, and the institutional and organizational context. Kress (1985)

argues that ideology is the politics of Discourse, wherein ideology marshals the variety of Discourses into a congruent structure. Through ideology, Discourses are aligned in the cause of larger political aims. Texts are the products, the realization of Discourses, and an individual instantiates Discourses every time s/he acts, speaks or writes. To refer to the earlier example of whether one should refer to 'terrorists' or 'freedom fighters', the decision is inextricably linked to the 'big D Discourse' in which one is located.

Further reading

Fairclough N. (2003) *Analysing Discourse: Textual Analysis for Social Research*, London: Routledge.

Gee J. P. (1996) *Social Linguistics and Literacies: Ideology in Discourses*, London: Taylor & Francis.

Kress, G. (1985) *Linguistic Processes in Sociocultural Practice*, Oxford: Oxford University Press.

McHoul A. and Grace, W. (1995) *A Foucault Primer: Discourse, Power and the Subject*, Melbourne: Melbourne University Press.

See also: deconstruction; genealogy; post-structuralism

JOHN WALSH

Disintermediation

Disintermediation refers to a fundamental change in how financial markets operate, from traditional forms of mediation, like bank lending, to the trading of short-term debt securities. The term is misleading in that disintermediation is a process that has not displaced banks from domestic and international financial markets. On the contrary, banks have been forerunners in furthering disintermediation, as it allows them greater leverage in managing their assets and partially averting the burdens imposed by international financial regulatory **regime**s. Disintermediation encourages banks to act less as we traditionally think of them, as depositories of capital for lending, and more like brokerage houses, especially in trading debt securities for short term financing. Accordingly, banks' clientele begin to act more like investors than depositors, encouraging the development of financial innovations that afford competitive advantages. Disintermediation also encourages the development of anonymous and untaxed investment vehicles, such as those typically found in **offshore** financial centers (see **global financial center** and **money laundering**). The disintermediation process is commonly associated with technological advances that allow the consumer to bypass the traditional financial institutions and invest directly in securities through the Internet.

Disintermediation is not, however, a mere consequence of recent technological innovations. It is a consequence of state policies, particularly those of the United States and Britain, which emerged in the post-war period to provide states and private financial institutions greater flexibility to protect their interests. The process can be traced to the emergence of the Euromarkets in the late 1950s and 1960s; a market for the trading of debt securities and currencies that was legally offshore and unregulated by any national government.

There are various views on how the Euromarkets emerged, such as those suggesting that both China and the former Soviet Union did not want to have their overseas investments captured if invested under the jurisdiction of specific western states. The Bank of England informally encouraged British banks to trade in this offshore market to retain a British share of the international financial marketplace in the face of US competition. British banks could attract deposits in US dollars, invest in the Euromarkets, and provide large profits to the investor. Because the Euromarkets were untaxed, anonymous, and not regulated by any national authority (and therefore had no ceilings on interest rates, stipulations on reserve requirements, or deposit insurance) they could offer returns on investment up to 4 per cent higher than most forms of nationally based investment. The United States also encouraged its international banks to trade in the Euromarkets through a series of domestic regulations that restricted domestic credit extension but permitted it to expand overseas, fueling the criticism that the United States was able to export inflation in the late 1960s. The number of US banks' foreign subsidiaries grew at a rate of 70 per cent per annum in the late 1960s while international banking grew at 25 per cent per annum well into the 1970s (compared to only 8 per cent per annum, for domestic financial systems). The trading volume of the Eurocurrency market grew almost thirty-fold between 1960 and 1970, while the Eurobond market grew nearly seven-fold during the same period. The consequent expansion of credit led to speculation that the US dollar-gold exchange rate of US$35 per ounce of gold established under the **Bretton Woods** agreement was unrealistic. This speculation, and growing US domestic economic worries, led to the collapse of the Bretton Woods international monetary regime in 1971.

The massive expansion of credit under the Euromarkets and the 'petrodollars' that emerged from the 1973–4 oil embargo imposed by the **Organization of Petroleum Exporting Countries** (OPEC), trumped any real chance of imposing **capital controls** and fixed exchange rates on the new international financial and monetary system. To cope with the doubling of the amount of private capital compared to public capital within the international financial system, international banks increasingly turned to more disintermediated forms of investment (such as short term trading of debt securities), often with disastrous results. Massive private flows of capital also contributed to the **debt trap** and the debt crisis of the early 1980s, which furthered disintermediation as US banks made a clear shift from syndicated bank lending to greater investment in debt securities. As a consequence, bank lending as a proportion of all long term international capital flows dropped from a third to a tenth within a decade.

These events had a dramatic impact on the international financial order, as well as the US domestic financial system, the only state with fully developed disintermediation. Within the United States there was a joint government/private push on socializing disintermediation, more generally through the encouragement of greater household investment in debt and equity securities and, particularly, through the emergence of 'securitization' that could benefit both mortgage holders and banks. Securitization allowed banks to funnel the outstanding debt on a mortgage and all interest repayments into a pooled investment purchased by a third party. This pool of capital would then be resold as a debt security based on a dependable flow of capital (the servicing of the mortgage debt). US banks welcomed this financial innovation because it allowed them to move assets from their balance sheets and avoid the scrutiny of the capital adequacy ratios requirements imposed by the Basle Accord of 1988 (see **Bank for International Settlements**). By the mid-1990s over 90 per cent of asset-backed securities in the US were provided by banks. As banks were increasingly willing to provide mortgages in the United States the growth of securitization permitted homeownership to reach record highs, although this trend also raised concerns about the massive indebtedness of US households. Disintermediation has, therefore, generated a 'social source' of international financial power for the United States, providing a deep and broad domestic pool of capital from which to draw on for global financial operations.

The United States' major financial competitors, particularly Japan, have been slow in socializing their financial systems to accommodate disintermediation, but the process has had a substantial international impact. Most notable is the impact of disintermediation on capital account crises created by the flight of short term debt securities (such as in Mexico in 1994 and Asia in 1997). The efflorescence of **regime**s to control on data dissemination and improve financial surveillance is a direct consequence of a more fragmented international financial order based on the trading of short term debt. The power of private financial regulators, such as credit rating agencies, is also noteworthy and provides much fodder for those who argue that the international financial system is impinging on state **sovereignty** and destabilizing national governments' capacity to govern their own economies (see **casino capitalism**). The contrary view is that disintermediation permits the use of short term debt instruments to manage risks and encourages stability and transparency within the international financial order.

Further reading

Germain, R. D. (1997) *The International Organization of Credit*, Cambridge: Cambridge University Press.

Helleiner, E. (1994) *States and the Reemergence of Global Finance*, Ithaca, NY: Cornell University Press.

Hester, D. (1969) 'Financial Disintermediation and Policy', *Journal of Money, Credit,
and Banking* 1(3), 600–17.

Seabrooke, L. (2001) *US Power in International Finance*, Basingstoke: Palgrave.

Sinclair, T. J. (1994), 'Passing judgement:
credit rating processes as regulatory
mechanisms of governance in the emerging world order', *Review of International
Political Economy*, 1(1), 133–59.

See also: Bank for International Settlements;
casino capitalism; debt trap; global financial
center; globalization; International Monetary
Fund; international political economy

LEONARD SEABROOKE

E

Embedded liberalism

A term used to describe the combination of international economic openness (hence 'liberalism') with domestic social protection, particularly for those individuals and groups likely to suffer trade-based dislocations (hence 'embedded'). In theory, it represents a political compromise between advocates of efficiency-producing trade openness and proponents of equity-enhancing employment and income protections. National policies based on embedded liberalism were exemplified by post-war West European countries. Over the past twenty years, many argue that the acceleration of trade and financial openness known as **globalization** threatens embedded liberalism by making it more difficult, in fiscal as well as in competitive terms, for governments to provide generous domestic social policies.

Historical background

Karl Polanyi usually is cited as the modern progenitor of the notion that economic openness should be combined with social protection. In *The Great Transformation* (1944), he argues that the self-regulating market, and the free market system more generally, is a utopian ideal. A market system subsumes society, rather than the reverse, ultimately leading to the collapse of market-based systems.

Such a collapse is exemplified by the Great Depression during the 1930s. According to Polanyi, the turmoil of the interwar years stemmed not from a breakdown in the world economy, but from the flawed separation of the economic and the social: 'the origins of the cataclysm lay in the utopian endeavor of economic liberalism to set up a self-regulating market system' (Polanyi 1944, 29). Although economic **integration** was not, in and of itself, detrimental to the functioning of democratic societies, economic integration without an accompanying system of social protection was doomed to failure. The gold standard **regime**, to which many European states subscribed, and to which several peripheral countries pegged their currencies, set broad parameters for government behavior, requiring them to privilege external adjustment over internal policy autonomy, and to allow for the unfettered movement of capital (Eichengreen 1992). Polanyi argues that policymakers did not frequently even *consider* deviating from the economic orthodoxy implicit in the exchange rate system.

The gold standard facilitated the growth of trade and capital flows, and it allowed governments to borrow at low rates of interest; but, ultimately, it proved politically unsustainable. The classical gold standard system, in place from the 1880s until World War One, rested on the political domination by the wealthy of less prosperous groups. As long as governments could force large segments of domestic society to accept the costs of domestic economic adjustment, they were able to maintain their commitments to gold. It was only during the interwar period, when governments faced increased demands from expanded domestic constituencies, that governments were faced with the choice between their exchange rate commitments and their commitments to domestic interest groups (Simmons 1994). Or, in Polanyi's terminology, they encountered the fundamental tension between social protection and the market economy (Polanyi 1944, 129). European publics ultimately rejected the notion that currency values were the penultimate policy achievement. Many governments, then, chose to focus on internal demands, rather than on external pressures. More broadly, after World War Two, and as a result of broader suffrage, popular mobilizations, and changes in electoral institutions, European governments embraced the role of social protection. In Polanyi's terms, governments acknowledged that free market practices were only politically sustainable when embedded in a system of social policies and social protections.

Polanyi's account, of course, is rich with normative underpinnings, as well as with political choices. In Polanyi's view, it is not only that free market economies often *are* coupled with systems of social protection, but that they certainly *ought* to be. More generally, the choice of economic and social policies reflects the political dominance of certain interest groups and ideologies: if fully free market economies are utopian ideals, how do they still manage to come into place? The answer lies in political interests:

monarchs promote trade within countries, and towns serve as loci for protecting nascent commercial interests. In the nineteenth century, the *raison d'être* of the state became the creation and the preservation of the self-regulating market (Ruggie 1982, p. 386). During the interwar years, however, another 'great transformation' occurred: various domestic groups demanded the restoration of a social dimension to economic policies. In light of these demands, the restoration of trade and financial openness, and of the gold standard exchange rate system, was doomed to failure. By implication, after World War Two, political interests in economic openness – as a means of increased efficiency, as well as a means of rebuilding a war-torn Europe – remain. But ideas (normative and positive) about how best to facilitate economic openness shift.

Drawing on Polanyi's distinction between embedded and disembedded economic systems, John Ruggie (1982) deployed the term 'embedded liberalism' to describe the international economic regime that prevailed after World War Two. This system was similar, in some features, to the systems that precede and follow it, but different in fundamental ways. The character of the embedded liberalism regime was, in Ruggie's account, determined not only by state power, but by the 'fusion of power with legitimate social purpose' (Ruggie 1982, 382). More specifically, the framers of the post-war economic order held beliefs about the need for social protection, and the need for (international) market regulation, that were similar to Polanyi's. While the final post-war economic system did not reflect all of John Maynard Keynes' and Harry Dexter White's early ideas about the need for regulation, it did reflect a fundamental shift in the extent to which market regulation was embraced. This shift may have been normatively desirable, but it also was politically expedient. 'Polanyi, White and Keynes were also correct in their premise that, somehow, the post-war international economic order would have to reflect this change in state–society relations if the calamities of the interwar period were not to recur' (Ruggie 1982, 388).

For Ruggie, too, normative forces play a major role in the shift from *laissez-faire* economics to embedded liberalism. British economic and political power undoubtedly facilitated the late nineteenth century economic order (as **hegemonic stability theory** emphasizes). But ideas about the appropriate balance between states and markets, and the extent to which external economic commitments should be privileged over domestic social conditions, also played a key role. Most importantly, individuals, interest groups and governments from across the ideological spectrum rejected pure economic liberalism. Instead, they coalesced around a compromise of embedded liberalism: 'unlike the economic nationalism of the thirties, it would be multilateral in character; unlike the liberalism of the gold standard and free trade, its multilateralism would be predicated on domestic interventionism' (Ruggie 1982, 393). Citizens promised to accept a return to economic openness (particularly trade openness), and governments were committed to protecting citizens from trade-induced volatility, via a variety of social protections.

The specific manifestations of this compromise were efforts toward trade liberalization (first, via the failed International Trade Organization, and then via the General Agreement on Tariffs and Trade); the multilateral management of fixed exchange rates, with prohibitions on competitive devaluation (via the **International Monetary Fund**), but with relatively closed capital markets; and the development of national welfare states, with provisions for unemployment insurance, education and training, and income redistribution. International commitments to non-discrimination and **reciprocity** in trade policy not only were coupled with domestic intervention, but also were limited in scope; the GATT, for instance, allowed for a variety of exemptions and safeguards, particularly during times of national economic distress. Along these lines, deviations from GATT and IMF rules during the 1950s and 1960s could be seen not as evidence of non-compliance with international commitments, but as an indication that the embedded liberalism compromise, and the framers of the postwar economic order, did not always privilege external over internal obligations (Ruggie 1982, 398–99).

Embedded liberalism and government policies

The emergence of embedded liberalism as an organizing principle affected the character of international economic institutions as well as the development of national welfare state policies in the advanced industrial democracies. At the international level, institutions facilitated the reduction of some trade barriers, and a resulting rapid growth of trade flows. At the domestic level, efforts at embeddedness were exemplified by a variety of state-led efforts to minimize unemployment (Blyth 2002). The focus on Keynesian full employment, and the resulting policies of compensation and income redistribution, reflected a general approval of public intervention in private markets. Broad acceptance of intervention notwithstanding, public policies for social protection varied somewhat between states, as the result of different domestic constellations of ideas, interests, and institutions. The US model, based on less interventionism and a smaller public sector, stands in marked contrast to the Scandinavian social democratic model, exemplified by Sweden.

Despite these divergent types of welfare capitalism, a consistent link between economic liberalization and public intervention emerged in postwar societies. Since the late 1970s, scholars of comparative politics have found a strong positive correlation between a country's degree of openness to international trade and the size of its public sector. Cameron (1978), for instance, finds that in the postwar era, the states with the greatest openness to international trade (measured in terms of trade flows as a percentage of gross domestic product) also have the most generous welfare states. The causal claim, then, is that the most economically exposed states are most in need of embeddedness, or social protection.

Likewise, Peter Katzenstein's *Small States in World Markets* (1985) described patterns of democratic corporatism in western Europe. Given their relatively small size, states such as Austria, Belgium, and the Netherlands had little choice, economically, but to open themselves to world markets. Engaging the global and regional trading systems allowed for a much more efficient allocation of goods and services, and for lower consumer prices. At the same time, however, this openness created a need for domestic compensation. In Katzenstein's account, this combination of liberal external policies and compensatory domestic measures had its roots in the interwar years. Openness without compensation simply was not a viable political strategy. Of course, Katzenstein does not suggest that the external economy is the only factor determining patterns of domestic compensation. Rather, he identifies two configurations of small states – liberal corporatism, character-

ized by weak, decentralized labor unions and strong, centralized business associations (Belgium, the Netherlands, and Switzerland); and social corporatism, with strong labor unions and weak business associations (Austria, Norway, and Denmark; Sweden is an intermediate case).

More recent accounts also identify a strong correlation, based on cross-sectional time series analyses, between trade openness and domestic compensation, specifically, the size of the public sector. In their analyses of trade openness and the size of government, both Geoffrey Garrett (1998) and Dani Rodrik (1997) discover a positive relationship. The effects of exposure to trade on public sector size are, according to Garrett, mediated by domestic institutional structures, particularly the interaction of government ideology and labor organization. Where 'left-labor power' is greater, trade openness has stronger effects on the size of the public sector. Again, these results are consistent with the notion that government spending helps to reduce risk and income volatility in states with high external exposure, and that this pattern persists after Europe's 'Golden Age' of **capitalism** (the 1950s and 1960s).

Interestingly, evidence for an embedded liberalism compromise can also be found, to some extent, in the developing world. Rodrik (1998) investigates the extent to which the trade–government size relationship holds within in a broader set of countries (he examines over one hundred). Again, the positive statistical association between trade and the size of government holds for both low and high income sets of states, and for most aggregate measures of government spending (including public consumption and public investment). This relationship also is robust after the inclusion of a wide range of control variables, such as country size, public debt, and the rate of inflation. Additionally, Rodrik provides evidence for a causal, not merely a correlative, relationship between trade exposure and public compensation. The extent of trade openness in 1960 is a significant predictor of the growth of government consumption over the next three decades. Furthermore, Rodrik demonstrates that external risk (operationalized as terms of trade volatility, and the product concentration of exports) is significantly associated with income volatility, and that the effects of trade openness on public sector consumption are greatest in states with the highest external risk. The political pathway, then, is consistent with an embedded account: trade exposes certain groups in society to risk; these groups demand protection from and compensation for increased risks to their incomes; and governments respond by providing more generous social policies.

While Rodrik's account of the causal steps behind the trade–government spending relationship is an advance beyond simply demonstrating correlations, it fails to examine the trade–compensation relationship at the micro-level, and it assumes rather than demonstrates a model of political activity that produces domestic compensation under conditions of high external risk. Adserá and Boix (2001) partly address these shortcomings by considering the joint importance of democracy and trade openness in generating public spending. While recognizing the compensation logic inherent in the notion of embedded liberalism, Adserá and Boix also point out that democracy has an additional impact on levels of government spending. In authoritarian political systems, the losers from external openness are unable to express their political preferences, so governments have little need to compensate or insulate them. In

democratic systems, though, governments have political incentives to compensate, particularly under conditions of high openness. Empirically, they demonstrate that such a pattern exists: public spending is greatest where trade openness is high and regimes are democratic; spending is lowest with limited trade openness and an authoritarian political regime. Based on this analysis, Adserá and Boix suggest that states with competitive export sectors may be able to sustain a policy of high compensation, even in the contemporary global economy; this is particularly true if public spending is used to supply goods that help to improve economic competitiveness. Their model provides a political logic to accompany past empirical findings, and the logic is consistent not only with developing country experiences in the 1980s and 1990s, but with the experiences of European states in the pre-World War One and interwar years. Without mass enfranchisement, openness without compensation was a viable political strategy; with democratization, such a strategy was much less successful.

At the same time, though, research in comparative and **international political economy** has yet to provide systematic evidence of the political mechanisms underlying compensation. That is, the politics that are part of the embedded liberalism compromise often are identified mostly at the macro-level (e.g. a linkage between openness and compensation, or among democracy, openness and public spending). Rodrik's (1997) analysis of the possibilities for a backlash against globalization, for instance, provides evidence that trade openness generally increases the risk and volatility of incomes in advanced industrial democracies. The data do not, however, reveal exactly how external risk and income volatility are distributed within countries. We might assume that, in the developed world, sectors in labor-intensive sectors or firms are most affected by external risk, or that low-skilled workers are most affected by income volatility.

Once we identify the factors of production, firms or sectors that are most affected by external risk, we must ask about their capacity to mobilize politically, and about the forms this mobilization takes. First, to what extent do individuals and interest groups attribute increased income risks to the global economy? In reality, some of the increase in risk is due to increased economic integration; but another part of the increase in risk stems from technological change. Technological advances render some types of unskilled labor redundant, and the skill sets necessary for individual economic success change over time. The *perceived* sources of risk, though, are more important for politics: it matters less what the true sources of risk are and more what individuals and interest groups believe the sources of risk to be. Here, economic globalization often surfaces as the enemy of those hurt by a combination of technological change and competition from foreign producers. The challenge for scholars interested in the domestic effects of globalization is to collect data on individuals' opinions regarding income risk, trade openness and domestic compensation, in order to gain a systematic understanding of how public opinions regarding economic globalization are formed, as well as how individuals who perceive themselves as harmed by trade openness mobilize politically. While some research has sought to analyze existing data on public opinion and globalization, or to generate new data for this purpose, there remains a tremendous need for better information on this subject (see, for instance, Scheve and Slaughter 2001).

Second, how does public opinion regarding economic globalization combine with domestic interest groups and institutional structures to produce demands for, and ultimately the supply of, public policies? The domestic politics of trade policy could occur at the sectoral or at the factoral (capital versus labor) level, or at some combination of the two (see Hiscox 2002). Additionally, where labor is better organized, or where certain industries have more direct access to policymakers, some interest groups will be more effective in their demands for compensation or protection. And, where political institutions allow for the representation of more narrow interests (e.g. where majoritarian electoral systems combine with geographically-concentrated sectors to produce some staunchly protectionist legislators), anti-trade advocates are more likely to achieve their policy demands. Even where individuals and industries face similar threats from the global economy, patterns of political demands – and the supply of public policies – likely will differ.

Finally, when groups that face external risk demand government policies, for what do they ask? Most broadly, those hurt by trade could ask for protection, or they could ask for compensation, or for some combination of the two. Embedded liberalism entails policies of compensation, rather than of closure (although, in its post-World War Two form, embedded liberalism did not include full trade openness, so some space for protectionist policies remained). If governments provide protectionist policies, though, the embedded liberalism pattern – relatively open trade, but with compensation – will not attain. More specifically, if compensatory policies are offered in response to externally-generated risks, what sorts of policies are they? Compensatory policies could be general (that is, available to all members of society), or specific (targeted toward certain categories of voters); this, coupled with voters' own economic positions, will affect public support for social protection (see, for instance, Moene and Wallerstein 2001).

Challenges to the compromise of embedded liberalism

Beyond the need, in academic research, for better research on the contemporary domestic politics behind the compromise of embedded liberalism, the compromise itself also faces challenges. Ruggie's (1982) seminal article on embedded liberalism concludes with an inventory of challenges to the compromise, taken in the late 1970s and early 1980s, including the position of developing states, the growth of private capital flows, and the pervasiveness of inflation. While inflation has receded from the political agenda in recent years, particularly in the developed world, the other two challenges – the extent to which the compromise will hold in the developing world, and the ways in which financial globalization further restricts governments' ability to provide social protection – remain highly salient. Moreover, the reduction of inflation in the 1980s reflects an ideological change (the rise of monetarism and the decline of Keynesianism) that also has implications for the survival of embedded liberalism.

Beginning in the late 1960s and early 1970s, dominant ideas about the role of government intervention in the economy began to change. These changes were brought on by a variety of events and their interpretation at the time, including the rise of monetarism, public choice, and rational expectations in economics; stagflation in the late 1970s; and the buildup of debt in the developing world (see Blyth 2002, Helleiner 2003, for a discussion of ideological change on the

specific subject of embedded liberalism). This ideational change was based on the notions that inflation was more of a threat than unemployment, and that governments were more likely to do harm, rather than good, through intervention. Whereas the early proponents of embedded liberalism worried about private market failures, the advocates of deregulation and supply-side economics worried about government failures.

This shift in ideas went hand in hand with shifts in government policies, including the domestic policy shifts of Ronald Reagan and Margaret Thatcher; the reduction of barriers to capital flows; the trend toward politically independent central banks; and the promulgation of a 'Washington consensus' view of structural adjustment for developing countries. The renewed ascendancy of economic liberalism also helped promote the restructuring of centrally planned economies, in the late 1980s and early 1990s, into democratic capitalist systems with *laissez-faire* underpinnings. Of course, these ideational shifts did not occur independently of political interests, but, rather, operated in tandem with the interests of certain domestic and international actors.

The ideational shift toward disembeddedness, and the policy shifts that were generated by and helped to reinforce the shift, challenged the domestic compensation model in a variety of ways. One very important change was the growth of economic globalization, in terms of trade as well as finance and production. During the last decade, scholars have devoted substantial attention to specifying the impact of economic globalization on national policy choices (see Mosley 2003 for a review). This theme has attracted interest not only in the academic realm, but also within media and policymaking circles. Much of the popular literature on the subject offers grim prognoses for government policymaking autonomy, as well as for the compromise of embedded liberalism.

The academic literature falls into two broad groups predicting greater convergence and divergence. Predictions of cross-national policy convergence rely on the imperatives of international competition and economic efficiency; the type of convergence predicted tends to be downward, rather than a common trend toward an intermediate position. As 'races to the bottom' ensue, governments lose the ability to provide goods and services to their citizens. Predictions of divergence, meanwhile, are based upon the continued diversity of national institutions and on persistent domestic demands for compensation.

In the realm of capital markets, the capacity for exit, and the political voice it confers on investors, is central to convergence-oriented accounts. While capital market openness provides governments with greater access to capital (and, therefore, to funding), it also subjects them to external discipline. Governments must sell their policies not only to domestic voters, but also to international investors. Because investors can respond swiftly and severely to actual or expected policy outcomes, governments must consider financial market participants' preferences when selecting policies. More generally, financial globalization represents a transfer of author from the public to the private sector.

The alternative perspective, which predicts continued diversity in economic policies and institutions, relies on two arguments. First, national specialization is possible within globalization. Firms and consumers have different preferences over taxation, services and regulation; governments offer different combinations of these goods; and consumers and firms locate in the jurisdiction that best matches their preferences. Second, economic globalization serves to heighten, rather than to reduce, pressures for government intervention. This implies expanded or sustained domestic demands for government intervention. Governments continue to have domestic political incentives to insulate individuals from externally generated insecurity and volatility; governments might pay an external economic price (in higher interest rates, for instance) for maintaining welfare state policies, but this price is offset by the internal political benefits of compensation.

Recent empirical work assessing the validity of the convergence and divergence hypotheses, particularly in the advanced capitalist democracies, reveals a mixed pattern. Substantial cross-national diversity remains in areas such as government consumption spending, government transfer payments, public employment, and the public taxation, but growing cross-national similarity characterizes aggregate monetary and fiscal policies. The latter often is associated positively with economic internationalization, while the former reveals the continued influence of domestic politics and institutions. Moreover, the impact of international capital markets on policy outcomes is contingent on earlier choices over exchange rate policies, just as it was during the gold standard era.

How, specifically, does capital mobility affect the positive relationship between trade openness and the size of the public sector – identified by Cameron (1978), Rodrik (1998) and others? Garrett (1998, 2001) suggests that when assessing the impact of the international economy on national government policies, it is important to look at both trade and financial openness. Earlier studies focused only on trade openness. In a study of a wide range of countries, Garrett finds no evidence of a relationship between the level of capital market openness and the level of government spending; the trade openness-size of government relationship remains. At the same time, though, Garrett (2001) finds that changes in (rather than levels of) trade and capital market openness matter for the size of the public sector. States in which trade openness grew more quickly after 1985 tended to have public economies that grew less quickly, as a 'disembedding' trend might suggest. This pattern was exacerbated in countries where capital mobility also increased quickly. Embedded liberalism, then, may be most under threat, or least likely to take root, in those countries that experience dramatic growth in both trade and capital market openness. Again, then, the prospects for compensatory social protection are least in the developing world.

Studies of international capital markets also suggest that capital mobility renders more difficult the provision of social protection, particularly in the developing world. It is this difficulty that lies at the heart of Rodrik's 'backlash' argument: the demands for insulation from externally-generated risk persist in the developed world, particularly among unskilled workers, but, given capital market pressures on government policymaking, governments are less able to respond effectively to these demands. Along similar lines, Mosley (2003) provides evidence that the consideration of government policies by financial market actors varies markedly across groups of countries. This pattern is driven by variation in investors' certainty regarding governments' creditworthiness, as well as the relative costs and benefits of employing information. In the advanced capitalist democracies, market participants consider key macroeconomic indicators, but not supply-side or micro-level policies. Market participants can charge high prices for certain government policies, but the range of policies used to set these prices is limited. In OECD countries (see **Organization for Economic Cooperation and Development**), governments are pressured strongly to satisfy financial market preferences in terms of overall inflation and government budget deficit levels, but they retain domestic policymaking latitude in other areas. The result is a strong but narrow financial market constraint in the developed world; these governments remain able, assuming there is domestic political support to do so, to provide generous welfare state policies. For developing nations, however, the scope of the financial market influence extends to cover both macro- and micro-policy areas. Market participants, concerned with default risk, consider many dimensions of government policy when making asset allocation decisions. Domestic policymaking in these states is more likely to conform to the convergence view, as the financial market constraint is both strong and broad; it is here that the challenges to embedded liberalism are greatest.

Another important change during the last two decades is the integration and, sometimes, the reintegration of developing countries into the global economy. In many cases, integration has been painful at the domestic level, occurring as part of broader **structural adjustment programs**, and sometimes associated with increases in poverty levels and income inequality, at least in the short to medium run. Developing states, on average, have greater difficulty attracting international investment, and they often must compete on the basis of low labor and production costs, rather than on the basis of skilled labor or product innovations. Furthermore, developing country governments generally have a smaller revenue base. These features do not augur well for a coupling of trade openness with social protection. Rather, they suggest that developing countries might find themselves in a position similar to interwar European governments – attempting to maintain liberal economic policies as well as to democratize, but with little capacity for compensating those hurt by liberalization. Recent empirical studies suggest that the picture is mixed in the developing world. Economic globalization creates stronger pressures on governments, but some room for diversity in policy remains (e.g. Brooks 2002, Garrett 2001, Rudra 2002). Possibilities for redistributive and social protection policies depend, as in the developed world, on political institutions, government ideology, and on the strength of labor market institutions.

Recent events, then, suggest that there has been some, albeit not complete, disembedding during the last two decades. The extent of this trend varies across countries, so that some cross-national diversity persists. With a general movement toward economic liberalism, the interwar era might hold lessons for contemporary policymakers and scholars. If the gold standard's rules – coupled with the evolving domestic political ambitions of governments – sowed the seeds of its demise, can the same be said for contemporary economic globalization (James 2002)? Given the development and growth of the modern welfare state, today's governments have a greater variety of domestic demands placed on them, in terms of providing not only infrastructure and national defense, but also in terms of providing education, health care, and social security. At the same time, however, the global economy also offers a variety of opportunities to individuals and firms; governments may be more able to maintain public support for economic openness, even if domestic compensation declines.

Further reading

Adserá, A. and Boix, C. (2001) 'Trade, Democracy and the Size of the Public Sector: The Political Underpinnings of Openness', *International Organization* 56(2), 229–62.

Blyth, M. (2002) *Great Transformations: Economic Ideas and Institutional Change in the Twentieth Century*, Cambridge: Cambridge University Press.

Brooks, S. M. (2002) 'Social Protection and Economic Integration: The Politics of Pension Reform in an Era of Capital Mobility', *Comparative Political Studies* 35(5), 491–525.

Cameron, D. (1978) 'The Expansion of the Public Economy: A Comparative Analysis', *American Political Science Review* 72(4), 1243–61.

Eichengreen, B. (1992) *Golden Fetters: The Gold Standard and the Great Depression 1919–1939*, New York: Oxford University Press.

Garrett, G. (1998) *Partisan Politics in the Global Economy*, Cambridge: Cambridge University Press.

Garrett, G. (2001) 'Globalization and Government Spending Around the World', *Studies in Comparative International Development* 35(4), 3–29.

Helleiner, E. (2003) 'Economic Liberalism and Its Critics: The Past as Prologue?' *Review of International Political Economy* 10, 4: 685–96.

Hiscox, M. J. (2002) *International Trade and Political Conflict: Commerce, Coalitions, and Mobility*, Princeton, NJ: Princeton University Press.

James, H. (2002) *The End of Globalization: Lessons from the Great Depression*, Cambridge, MA: Harvard University Press.

Katzenstein, P. (1985) *Small States in World Markets*, Ithaca, NY: Cornell University Press.

Moene, K. O. and Wallerstein, M. (2001) 'Inequality, Social Insurance and Redistribution', *American Political Science Review* 95(4), 859–74.

Mosley, L. (2003) *Global Capital and National Governments*, Cambridge: Cambridge University Press.

Polanyi, K. (1944) *The Great Transformation*, Boston: Beacon Press.

Rodrik, D. (1997) *Has Globalization Gone Too Far?* Washington, DC: Institute for International Economics.

Rodrik, D. (1998) 'Why Do More Open Economies Have Bigger Governments?' *Journal of Political Economy* 106(5), 997–1032.

Rudra, N. (2002) 'Globalization and the Decline of the Welfare State in Less Developed Countries', *International Organization* 56(2), 411–45.

Ruggie, J. (1982) 'International Regimes, Transactions and Change: Embedded Liberalism in the Postwar Economic Order', *International Organization* 36(2), 379–415.

Scheve, K. and Slaughter, M. (2001) *Globalization and the Perceptions of American Workers*, Washington, DC: Institute for International Economics.

Simmons, B. A. (1994) *Who Adjusts? Domestic Sources of Foreign Economic Policy During the Interwar Years*, Princeton, NJ: Princeton University Press.

See also: Bretton Woods; casino capitalism; end of history; globalization; liberal internationalism; managed trade

LAYNA MOSLEY

Empire

Empire has returned as both a serious subject of scholarly interest and, arguably, a serious object of international **diplomacy**. Derived from the Latin *imperium*, the term 'empire' and its place within Western thought derives from the classical Greek and Roman efforts to project geopolitical supremacy over other peoples (see **geopolitics**). For the ancient Romans *imperium* referred simply to the civil and military powers of Roman magistrates. At a very general level, empire may be characterized as the formal administration of different peoples by a central (or metropolitan) power. Considerable elaboration on this basic definition is required in order to see that the 'return' of empire is as much a product of the end of the **cold war** as it is part of a complex of political and moral problems deeply embedded in Western thought.

Empire: promise and problem

For the Ancient Greeks, empire was conceived as both a means of extending Greek civilization, and a structure of geopolitical order. Herodotus (c. 480–c. 430 BC), for example, drew a firm line between the Greeks and non-Greeks or 'barbarians' who lived a fitful and uncertain life beyond the bounds of the Greek polis. Many Greeks clearly derived a strong sense of their superiority over other peoples by virtue of their civilization, including their art, knowledge, society, trade, and form of politics. Plutarch (c. 45–125 AD) claimed that Aristotle advised his pupil Alexander the Great to treat the barbarians as brute beasts and conquer them. Although Plutarch also reported that Alexander was wise to ignore this advice, his account of Alexander's life portrays him as the world's first great 'civilizer', introducing the barbarians to agriculture, cities, and Greek learning by means of empire.

If this constituted the promise of empire, the Greeks were also aware of its problems. Thucydides (c. 460–395 BC) for instance, recalled of Pericles' policy in the Peloponnesian War, that the 'imperial dignity' of Athens depended on its mastery of the oceans. This would bring the benefit of greater reach, mobility and flexibility for Athenian military forces. Furthermore, Pericles argued that empire required conquest and this involved both harsh sacrifice at home and incurring hatred and envy abroad. Empire, he argued, was akin to tyranny and it raised insoluble questions about the justice of conquest. More importantly however, having won it, the Athenians could not let it go, for to do so would invite disorder and ruin.

Throughout its subsequent history, empire denoted both the pretension to subdue and to rule over others, and a structure through which an international **order** and peace could be created and maintained. The accomplishments of Augustus listed outside his mausoleum recounted the common themes of empire; foreign conquest, benevolent rule, colonization, the extension of boundaries, the pacification of hostile peoples, and the submission of client states and supplicant rulers. For St Augustine (354–430 AD), the Roman Empire and the moral qualities displayed in its conquest were admirable, but he also argued that the worth of empire hinged on its justice, by which he meant its obedience to the will of God. Conquest for the sake of grandeur or dominion was wicked, but it was 'stern necessity' that petty rulers be kept in order even under the empire of an unjust ruler. For Niccolo Machiavelli (1469–1527), empire was a **power** that could only be won by virtue. Importantly, republics could conquer empire only through the virtue of citizen soldiers. While empires may be maintained by active conquest and policies of colonization, he warned that the inevitable fate of all empires was moral decadence and corruption. Significantly then, the western tradition of conceptualizing empire represented it as both a promise of order and peace, but one that also raised the problem of decline, collapse, and ensuing chaos.

Defining empire

Throughout the history of European empires between the sixteenth and twentieth centuries, the concept continued to denote a range of characteristics rather than a clear definition. The salient features implied by the term drew from both classical sources and contemporary imperial practice, and may be summarized in general terms. First, an empire is a political entity that is said to be distinguished by its artificiality. Empire has thus been separated from other forms of polity on the grounds that it involves the spatially extended government of culturally diverse peoples within an overarching framework of laws and administrative structures. Empire has been distinguished thereby from the nation understood as a culturally homogeneous people, and from the state as a political institution defined by its claim to enjoy a legitimate monopoly of force within a delimited territory (see **nation-state**). On this view, empire is distinguished by its territorial extension and its administration of diverse peoples, or by the absorption within it of distinct states. While this characteristic is helpful, it must also be remembered that the distinction rests on an oversimplification. Nations and states are themselves artificial creations, and while a state may have clearly delimited borders, so too may an empire. Indeed the modern state of Great Britain was first conceived in the sixteenth and seventeenth century as an empire built on the absorption of formerly independent crowns, and nations that remained distinct. Exactly where one is supposed to draw the conceptual line between nation, state and empire is unclear.

Perhaps for this reason writers have turned to a second feature of empires, that they are characterized by the conquest of peoples and territories by the forces of a central power. Perhaps the most often cited feature of empire, conquest is also said to separate the classical empires of the ancient world from the mercantilist empires of Britain and Holland in the seventeenth and eighteenth centuries (see **mercantilism**) and the global **power** of the United States today. While it is certainly true to say that most empires have rested on the conquest of other peoples and territories, equally, few if any have rested on that alone. The Athenian empire, Thucydides claimed, rested as much on the control of the oceans as it did on the conquest of cities. Furthermore, while the mercantilist empires of Britain and Holland were achieved, at least in part, by the activities of private companies such as the Dutch and English East India Companies, both organizations boasted substantial naval and military establishments that were capable of, and actively engaged in conquest in the name of metropolitan monarchs or pretensions to rule. Nor would it be correct to suggest that the European empires of the eighteenth and nineteenth centuries forbore conquest.

A third feature of empire then, is that it is usually associated with the pursuit of economic gain, whether that takes the form of the exaction of tribute (as in ancient Athens), widespread plunder (as in the Mongol empire), a system of land rents (such as that of the Mughal empire), extraction of resources (as in the Spanish and Portuguese empires), the monopolization of trade (as in the European mercantile empires), or securing foreign markets and conditions for investment (such as the European and US involvement in China in the early twentieth century).

Empires have thus approached the challenges of revenue from a variety of angles. The mercantile European empires in the 'New World' of the sixteenth and seventeenth centuries aimed at accruing wealth as a chief objective, but the methods adopted varied considerably. The Spanish empire originated in the effort to monopolize the spice trade, but became synonymous with the extraction of mineral wealth. The British

and French empires were forged in the effort to mimic Spanish success, but became more closely associated with the monopolization of the lucrative fur trade (France), or the establishment of colonies based on agricultural exploitation (Britain). The Dutch empire began as a series of trading centers or factories, which grew over time into colonies.

Although Machiavelli had recommended it as a means of holding conquered territory, colonization has not always been a common feature of empire. Undertaken to a considerable extent by the Romans but largely eschewed by the Mongols, in modern times the most systematic colonizers were the British, who adopted it as an alternative to more lucrative endeavors. Even for the British however, colonization and the mercantile economics on which it rested remained controversial. In the wake of Adam Smith's critique of the economics of the British Empire, there has been a strong tendency among liberal political economists to oppose the dynamics of **free trade** to the stifling effects of empire. Empire did not result, on this view, in the control of trade as much as in its channeling, leading to the impoverishment of the peripheries of empire, the enrichment of a select few among the metropolitan elite, and to the general distortion of the flows of wealth that free trade would create.

Nonetheless, liberal imperialists in Britain and elsewhere retained the image of a global reach of free trade within the empire. For Marxist political economists however (see **Marxism**), there was a direct association between European **imperialism** and the development of **capitalism**. Empire in effect signaled the last phase of capitalist development, and was interpreted as a drastic response by metropolitan capitalists to manage the tensions within the economy by creating new markets, exporting excess working class population and exploiting new resources. In the late twentieth century, debate was generated on the question of whether the influence of global financial institutions constituted a new kind of empire. While this claim is deserving of consideration, it would appear to be the case that few empires considered the control of trade or material enrichment on its own a sufficient purpose of empire. Empires such as those of Britain or France could deploy force informally to secure the conditions for investment (in China for example) without annexing territory. But such interventions were effective only because they represented the force of the formal empires behind them. While the pronouncements of the **World Bank** or the **International Monetary Fund** (IMF) today carry considerable coercive clout, they appear to be of a markedly different kind to the instructions of the British Colonial Office in the nineteenth century.

The attempt to define empire has thus usually involved turning to a fourth feature, namely, territorial expansion. The expansion of the territory of the imperial power is the paradigmatic instance of empire. Territorial expansion is not simply about the extension of borders, but should be seen as hosting a range of other phenomena. In particular, territorial expansion suggests a fifth feature of empire, the extension of particular kinds of rule, government or administration of the imperial power over subject peoples. At its height in the late nineteenth century, the British Empire consisted in a variety of centrally administered colonies, dependencies whose rulers were obliged to accept British advice, or largely self-governing dominions. This empire had its origins in the sixteenth century claim of the English crown to the 'empire' of Wales, Scotland, and Ireland. Within this empire, the formerly independent monarchies were thought of as

having been absorbed into a new composite polity in which the English crown reigned supreme. All empires confront the problem of how to develop and sustain some kind of administrative apparatus for governing peoples subject to it. The effort to construct this mechanism provided solutions that varied from the uniform extension of metropolitan law, to highly variegated structures involving the employment of nominally autonomous rulers of dependencies, self-governing colonies, to local laws and forms of rule.

Related to this, then, is a sixth characteristic of empire, the construction and imposition of an ordered set of geopolitical or international relations (see **geopolitics**). Polybius noted this as a defining characteristic of Roman imperial history, the integration of formerly independent and unconnected peoples into a new set of international relations. Rome's empire was conceived as a kind of **globalization**, a force that brought political, economic, legal and cultural coherence to a formerly chaotic and disjointed world. In the eighteenth century, a similar process of global **integration** would be hailed by the luminaries of the European Enlightenment as leading toward the culmination of the universal history of humankind. Significantly, these thinkers identified the emergence of powerful **sovereign state**s in Europe controlling extensive empires abroad, as the building blocks of a new international **order**. This order was conceptualized as a **balance of power** between states sustained by delicate **alliance**s and based on 'rational', calculations of the **national interest**. We may conclude then, that the modern study of international relations was born of empire. While not all of the Enlightenment thinkers celebrated empire, they saw in it a new international order that, albeit by less than just means, could forge a universal human community based on the fruits of European civilization. While there has been a tendency to speak of the order of empire as a 'Pax Romanum' or a 'Pax Brittanica', the subjects brought within its orbit may not have been as convinced of the peacefulness of empire.

Civilization raises a seventh feature of empire, the ideological justification of the imperial claim to conquer, colonize, control or rule over the periphery by virtue of metropolitan superiority variously conceived, as it was for the Greeks, on visions of cultural pre-eminence, or for the Europeans of the nineteenth century on spurious theories of racial supremacy. A consistent feature of the western history of empires is the claim that by means of empire the metropolitan power is able to bring the benefits of its superiority to other inferior peoples, in effect to civilize them. Derived from Latin origins, civilization denoted the benefits of an urban life under settled laws, regular government, and economic abundance.

When Europeans spoke of their superior civilization and of their right to civilize others, it was to the example of ancient imperial Rome that they looked. Edmund Burke (1729–97) helped to shape the modern vision of the British Empire as a benevolent institution ruling other peoples in trust in the 1790s during his famous impeachment of Warren Hastings, the former British East India Company Governor-General of Bengal. His model was Cicero's prosecution of Verres, the corrupt Roman governor of Sicily in 68 BC. Both men defined the burden of empire as a trust, to exercise power over others by upholding Natural Law and *jus gentium*. The quest to justify imperial rule implies that the ideology of empire was two-sided. Imperial ideologies sought both to convince the populace of the ruling power of their right to empire, and to persuade its actual or potential subjects that they should sub-

mit to it. Ideologies however, are notoriously porous and always contestable. As Edward Said suggested, the claims of imperial ideology (or colonialism) are especially prone to subversion, or as Franz Fanon demonstrated, to radical inversion. The quest to convince or to persuade may not always have been successful, but once made, the effort tied the fate of empire to the struggle not only for mastery of its geopolitical terrain, but of its ideological terrain as well.

Empires then, may be said to consist in several interrelated features, each of which may take a variety of forms. An empire is thus an extended political entity conceived as a framework of administration encompassing a variety of peoples and territories. Empires are constituted by a central or metropolitan power conquering, controlling, or ruling over subordinate or dependent peripheral powers and peoples. Empires usually involve territorial expansion, but may also be focused on the control of trade and commerce, and the imposition of an ordered set of relations between the central power and formerly independent powers. The rank inequality of these relations is articulated within complex ideological theories of superiority and inferiority, which give form to the claim that the ruling power has a right to govern the peoples subject to its rule. A large part of the allure of empire has been the promise that it may allow the creation of an international or global order, the formation of a supra-national entity capable of binding and holding potentially mutually hostile petty powers within an overarching structure of dependence to the metropolitan power.

In the wake of the collapse of the Soviet empire in the early 1990s, the prospect of 'Balkanization' loomed as a consequence. While few lamented its passing, some commentators at least suggested that for all its ills, the Soviet empire had been able to impose a structure of rule and enforcement capable of preventing the horrors of **nationalism**. Nonetheless, it is also important not to overstate the orderliness of empires. Concentration on the effort to impose order has often masked the complex interrelations between center and periphery. The very structure of empire facilitates a complex interplay of political and cultural influences between center and periphery, helping to shape the identities and outlook of the inhabitants of both. It is in the wake of the collapse of empire however, as both Pericles and Polybius warned, that the dangers of international disorder reveal themselves most forcefully. This ancient warning has echoed throughout the history of the twentieth century, and continues to reverberate in the twenty-first century.

Empire and global politics

In large part, the experience of empire over the last four hundred years has decisively shaped the nature and structure of contemporary global politics. While no systematic study can be undertaken here, some key features do stand out. First, empires have reconstructed the religious, ethnic and cultural distribution of humanity. Many empires have used the forced or voluntary movement of peoples as a technique of rulership. In the early-modern and modern period, however, empires moved vast numbers of people across entire oceans and continents. Slavery and mass migration eventually gave rise to multiethnic and multicultural societies in which the effort to project a unified national identity free from the injustices of their imperial past continues to excite controversy (see **multiculturalism**).

Second, the rise and decline of European empires have aided the spread of that other European creation, states. The European empires formed in the sixteenth century fueled the formation of sovereign states in Europe. The structure of empire facilitated the spread of states worldwide. Many European empires expanded into regions in which there were political entities more extensive than those in Europe, such as the empires of the Aztecs of present day Mexico, or the Incas of present day Peru and Chile. Other regions lacked institutional structures comparable to the sovereign states that were emerging in parts of Western Europe in the seventeenth and eighteenth centuries. In the wake of the collapse of those empires in the twentieth century however, states were the successor institutions.

Beginning in North America in 1776, Haiti in 1804, and the wars of independence in South America in the 1820s, the struggle to break free of empire has created a host of states and an enduring aspiration for national **self-determination**. In the twentieth century, this aspiration fueled wars of national liberation across Africa and Asia, but also spawned a series of bitter internal conflicts as the states that broke free of empire during **decolonization** (such as India in 1947) found that their new borders contained a host of tensions. The borders that were drawn – sometimes hastily, often arbitrarily – by the retreating imperialists reflected the exigencies of hasty retreat, and echoed the boundaries created by imperial rule between racial, national or ethnic subject populations. Little thought had been given to the viability of those states, and to the enormous challenges they would face in a world where the economic power of Europe, the United States and the international institutions created after World War Two were said to constitute a new kind of empire.

Empire has also framed many of the key issues of contemporary **international law**. The Romans had conceived their empire as giving substance to laws they considered to have universal application. The pretension to the universal reach and application of law remained a foundational aspiration of European empires in the early modern and modern period. The Spanish Thomists Bartolomeo de Las Casas and Francisco de Vitoria attempted to apply the principles of Natural Law to the problem of how the Spanish were to regulate their affairs with Indigenous Americans. The justification of empire was tied thereby to the development of *jus gentium*. Hugo Grotius' explication of the laws of **war** and peace and to the use of the sea emerged from the growing rivalry between his native Holland and its imperial rivals, and aimed in part to justify Dutch imperial designs. Samuel Pufendorf (1632–94), John Locke (1632–1704) and Christian Wolff (1679–1754) each contributed to the development of international law by articulating norms governing the acquisition of new territory and the rights (or lack of them) of the indigenous inhabitants. Despite the rhetoric of Natural Rights and reason, their theories usually remained firmly Eurocentric. In the nineteenth and early twentieth century, doctrines of international law could be used to justify the system of capitulations by which European powers took effective control of formerly independent powers, and principles of fiduciary duty by which European powers were to govern other peoples in trust. In more recent times however, international law has been used by indigenous peoples to claim their **human rights**, especially to the return of lands denied to them by the colonial states that empire left behind.

Finally, the experience of empire in the twentieth century has underlined the ancient problem of the collapse of order. Polybius had defined the problem of empire in terms of its inevitable corruption and decay. Machiavelli followed him, and suggested that the disorder following the decline of empire could be creative of a new order only by those with the cunning and the power to aspire to a new empire. In the early twenty-first century, that dream of empire seems to have faded and the world created by the collapse of empire seems to defy the control of any one state. Nonetheless, the ideal of order associated with empire continues to exert influence. In the cold war period, two **superpowers** (the United States and the Soviet Union) vied for global supremacy. **Deterrence**, **Mutually Assured Destruction** and détente were the mechanisms of a bipolar **balance of power** (see **bipolarity**). Some considered this a contest between two empires, but in the wake of the collapse of the Soviet Union, the evils of **ethnic cleansing** and the prospect of **failed state**s, the question of empire has taken on new relevance.

The United States: a new empire?

The Berlin Wall came down in 1989, and with it collapsed, if not Ronald Reagan's 'Evil Empire', then certainly a paradoxical empire whose origins lay in dynastic expansion, but whose later form was buttressed by the anti-imperial ideology of Marxism–Leninism. While the lineaments of the 'new world order' declared by President Bush (Snr) in the wake of the First Gulf War (1991) remained unclear, Francis Fukuyama (1992) suggested that humanity stood on the verge of the **end of history**. Widely interpreted as a triumphalist account of the victory of Western liberal democracy and **capitalism** over its ideological foes, there was an element of lament in his pronouncement that the end of ideologically motivated conflict signaled the end of a central axis of global order. In this post-ideological world, the biggest struggle would revolve around the global extension of liberalism and the **democratic peace** in the face of reversions to atavistic **nationalism** and the insular 'politics of identity'.

The apparent triumph of liberal democracy signaled not only an end to ideological conflict, but also, it was hoped, to the imperial dream of conquest and subjection of other peoples. The commitment to the pacific values of liberal democracy became a mantra among many western political thinkers and international relations theorists. If the peaceful illusion was not shattered, it was at least disturbed by those scholars who seemed to want to revive older terms of political discourse such as civilization and empire. Samuel Huntington (1996) proposed that the world was on the verge of a new era of conflict motivated not by ideology, but by a form of 'identity politics' based on the values of different civilizations. Civilization, a term long associated with the western drive to empire, would become in Huntington's view, a potent source of division, and nowhere more obviously than in the **clash of civilizations** between the West and Islam.

Huntington was far from endorsing a return to empire. Nor did he seek to revive the association of civilization with the claim to rule other peoples in their best interests. Nonetheless, he maintained that the United States had particular responsibilities to shoulder the burden of maintaining (along with Europe) the values of western civilization. For others however, the language of civilization was ill-equipped to convey the complexities of globalization and the place of the United States within it. For Hardt and Negri (2000), empire was the term that best conveyed the extraordinary dynamic of globalization linking the world in an ever changing,

extending and transforming fabric of relations. The power that drove this process was not conceived as imperialist conquest, but as a shifting and renewing 'network power' that brought more of the world's people and its resources into processes of production and exchange. The constant extension and transformation of this network power, however, can only be experienced as 'omnipresent crisis', breakdown or **corruption**.

Whatever the merits of these theories, none saw what was coming in the form of the attacks of 11 September 2001. The 'war on terror' these traumatic events precipitated revived calls once again for the West, and the United States in particular, to assume the mantle of empire. In contrast to the federative structure of the **European Union**, the United States appears to be a more likely candidate for empire, but exactly what kind of empire it is supposed by some to be, or is supposed by others to become, remains unclear. For those attempting to define it, the United States has been variously described as an 'incoherent', 'liberal', 'virtual', or 'consensual empire', an 'empire of invitation', and even a 'protection racket'. One school of thought maintains that the United States is and always has been an empire that has used its overwhelming military force and political influence not to annex territory, but to uphold the global terms of trade that allows US domination of foreign markets. For Chalmers Johnson (2004), the American empire is a creation of the post-cold war environment, disguised by the global **discourse** of **free trade**. Nominally independent global financial institutions such as the **International Monetary Fund** (IMF) are merely surrogates of the US government, but US influence is distributed and directly felt through the network of military bases it maintains worldwide.

Alternatively, it has been suggested that if the United States is an empire, it is not like the empires we have known in the past, and indeed is in a paradoxical situation. The United States undoubtedly possesses overwhelming conventional military might, considerable political clout and enormous economic influence. Nonetheless, it does not seek (like the Ottomans of the sixteenth century or the British in the nineteenth century) to annex new territory or to colonize other peoples. Nonetheless, like those empires, it is responsible for the enforcement of **order**, this time on a truly global scale. The ability of the United States to mobilize and deploy its military might exceeds that of any previous empire, but it must also devote considerable time and energy to the persuasion of other, independent states to acquiesce in its designs. The current 'war on terror' reveals the paradox of the United States' position most clearly: the unrivalled, pre-eminent global power is struggling to subdue an elusive enemy capable of attacking it in its own metropolitan heartland.

Some observers chide the United States with not being enough of an empire. On this view, the US Empire is the best hope of sustaining a peaceful global order – a 'Pax Americana'. It must learn the lessons of the British Empire and commit itself to the extension of liberal values and free trade, but it must also be prepared to step in to avert state failure. Other critics would prefer to see a 'new imperialism' or 'empire lite' among Western powers and **non-governmental organizations** (NGOs) without subscribing to a US Empire as such. For these critics, **terrorism**, **ethnic cleansing** and state failure requires **humanitarian intervention** in the name of universal or humanitarian values, but armed and capable of buttressing states and maintaining order. Others suggest that the very idea of a US empire, whether it actually exists or is merely a 'temptation', is not sustainable, and speak instead of US **hegemony** or 'hyperpower'. It is doubtful that the question of whether the United States is an empire can ever be satisfactorily resolved. Indeed, uncertainty lies at the heart of empire. At once a dream of global order and a pretension to superiority, we can detect in the rhetoric and the policies of the US government more than a distant echo of the promise and problem of empire.

Further reading

Barber, B. (2003) *Fear's Empire: War, Terrorism and Democracy in an Age of Interdependence*, New York: W.W. Norton.

Ferguson, N. (2004) *Colossus: The Rise and Fall of America's Empire*, London: Allen Lane.

Fukuyama, F. (1992) *The End of History and the Last Man*, London: Penguin.

Hardt, M. and Negri, A. (2000) *Empire*, Cambridge, MA: Harvard University Press.

Huntington, S. (1996) *The Clash of Civilizations and the Remaking of World Order*, New York: Simon and Schuster.

Ignatieff, M. (2003) *Empire Lite: Nation-Building in Bosnia, Kosovo and Afghanistan*, London: Vintage.

Johnson, C. (2004) *The Sorrows of Empire: Militarism, Secrecy, and the End of the Republic*, New York: Metropolitan.

Louis, W. R. (ed.) (1998–9) *Oxford History of the British Empire*, New York: Oxford University Press.

Machiavelli, N. (1996) *Discourses on Livy*, Translators: H. C. Mansfield and N. Tarcov, Chicago: University of Chicago Press.

Mann, M. (2003) *Incoherent Empire*, London: Verso.

Pagden, A. (2002) *Peoples and Empires: Europeans and the Rest of the World, From Antiquity to the Present*, London: Phoenix.

See also: imperialism; order; sovereignty

BRUCE BUCHAN

End of history

Since the publication of his article 'The End of History?' in the Fall 1989 edition of *The National Interest*, Francis Fukuyama's claim that we are at the end of history has been the subject of intense discussion. Many critics at the time dismissed the idea as one that would pass quickly from view, arguing that it received a wholly unforeseen, and largely unmerited, boost through the accident of its publication coinciding with the fall of the Berlin Wall. But both the concept and the writer have proved far more resilient. To some extent the attempt to dismiss the idea rather than subject it to a proper critical analysis was due to misunderstandings of what precisely Fukuyama meant by the phrase 'the end of history'. The very 'catchiness' of the phrase, and the way in which its meaning appears to be straightforward, partly explains why many people criticized the article, and especially Fukuyama's subsequent book *The End of History and the Last Man* (1992), without paying close attention to the details of his argument. A close reading of the texts shows that Fukuyama was aware that his ideas were part of a much longer tradition of thought, and that he owed a particular debt to aspects of Hegel's philosophy.

Fukuyama's definition of 'the end of history'

So what does Fukuyama mean by 'the end of history'? The answer is complex precisely because of Fukuyama's conscious dialogue with the earlier writers in the tradition of speculation on the subject. Fukuyama is influenced very strongly by Hegel's view that ideas are the driving force of history, rather than material forces such as economic relationships or war. The end of history is fundamentally an intellectual process. It

is marked by the recognition (a key word for Fukuyama) by governments of the inherent rights and dignity of the citizens they represent, which has only become fully possible by the development of liberal democracy. At the heart of Fukuyama's definition is the claim that the *ideal* of liberal democracy cannot be improved upon. The end of history is concerned with the culmination of political events and the triumph of democracy, but not in a literal and straightforward way.

The end of history is a process, not an event, which has been going on since the second half of the eighteenth century marked especially by the American Revolution and, more ambiguously, by the French Revolution. It is marked by the growth of representative government, the rule of law and, in time, democratic elections. But no single event or set of events marks the end of history precisely because it is fundamentally an intellectual process which is expressed imperfectly through institutions and forms of government, although these should draw closer to the ideals as time passes.

Marx, communism and the end of prehistory

The end of history thesis of the early 1990s was explicitly anti-Marxist, and anti-communist (see **Marxism, communism**), and gained much of its immediate resonance from that opposition, but this should not obscure the fact that a very important focus of the argument was the theory of history implicit in communism, which was institutionally coming to an end in Eastern Europe and Russia. Marx and Marxism had complex theories of history, dividing it into several stages in a manner similar to Hegel. Indeed in his historical view of human consciousness and human society, Marx was very much the pupil of Hegel. Hegelian ideas were already implicit in the phenomenon of the collapse of communism with which Fukuyama was trying to deal.

Marx's theory of history was laid out in its most accessible form in the *Communist Manifesto* (1985) where he and Engels argued that the motor of historical **development** is class struggle. Marx identifies the following historical stages: slave society (Greek); patrician and plebeian (Rome); lord and serf; guild-master and journeyman (feudal society) and bourgeois and proletarian (the modern epoch). Implicitly there was an upward development towards higher forms of society culminating in modern capitalist society. Marx's novel thesis was that this was not the final social form. There was yet one more stage to be gone through. **Capitalism** itself would be superceded by **socialism**.

This argument was closely connected to the view that 'the history of all hitherto existing society is the history of class struggle' (Marx 1985, 79). What led to strife amongst social classes, according to Marx and Engels, was the control that one class exercised at the expense of óthers over society's means of production. Domination over the means of production, or the main economic forces of the society, was used to extract a surplus of wealth for the controlling class. Although class relations had taken a number of varying forms throughout history; surplus extraction was a persistent feature. The surplus and the manner it was extracted was self-evident in a slave society but less so in later societies. In feudal society the surplus was removed through dominant class ownership of the land. Under capitalism the class struggle is between employers and workers, or the bourgeoisie and the proletariat.

Marx's argument is that social transformations from one form of production or one type of economic order to another occur not as a result of violent intervention from an external agency but as a result of the inner dynamic of the economic order itself. 'At a certain stage of development, the material productive forces of society come into conflict with the existing relations of production or – this merely expresses the same thing in legal terms – with the property relations within the framework of which they have operated hitherto. From forms of development of the productive forces these relations turn into their fetters. Then begins an era of social revolution' (Marx 1971, 21). Marx devoted his scholarly life to seeking to demonstrate that such an inner dynamic governed modern capitalist society. Economic forces within capitalist society would drive the bourgeoisie into ever more intense clashes with the working class. For its own defense the proletariat would organize itself as a class, socially, economically and politically to overthrow the rule of the bourgeoisie. The success of the proletarian revolution would inaugurate an entirely new society where classes would cease to exist. It was the apparent failure of this prognostication in the late 1980s with the internal dissolution of Soviet and Eastern European society, ostensibly driven by Marx's ideas, that motivated Fukuyama's remarkable counter thesis.

For Marx, the transformation of capitalism to socialism would herald the end of the pre-history of the human race. Marx's engaging thesis about a future classless society without exploitation convinced millions of people. The impact of Fukuyama's argument relied upon turning this idea upon its head. Fukuyama argued that the end of history had already occurred. The collapse of communism simply confirmed this. As Fukuyama's argument is a direct reaction to the teleological view of history implicit within communism, and which draws heavily on the work of G. W. F. Hegel (1770–1831) and to a lesser extent

Immanuel Kant (1724–1804), it is important to clarify the key features of these earlier accounts of historical transformation as well.

Kant and the hopes for perpetual peace

Kant was a vital influence on the development of the philosophy of history. Stimulated by Jean-Jacques Rousseau (1712–78) and Johann Gottfried Herder (1744–1803), Kant put together his considerations on historical development in several essays published in the 1780s and 1790s. Like Marx, Kant puts the emphasis on looking at history from the standpoint of the forward **development** of the human race. Although Kant thinks it is impossible to prove with certainty that mankind is improving 'we may hope that what strikes us in the actions of individuals as confused and fortuitous may be recognized, in the history of the entire species, as a steadily advancing but slow development of man's original capacities' (Kant 1991, 41). For Kant there is an inner dynamic in human relations that may drive us in this direction. He refers to this as our asocial-sociability: our need both to have the company of others of our kind but our need also to be different from them and our need from time to time not to be with them. This asocial-sociability leads to rivalries both within states and among them.

Political progress lies in the development of civil society and the establishment of a republican form of government. This progress is charted in one of Kant's most famous publications *Perpetual Peace* (1795). The book is set out in the form of an imaginary peace treaty which is intended to form the basis for a flourishing world society. The imaginary treaty has three definitive articles which outline the key steps the human race has to take to ensure lasting harmony. These definitive articles are supported by six preliminary articles that spell out the obstacles that have first to be removed (such as standing armies, and the finance of **war** through the extension of national debt) if the three larger milestones are to be achieved. The key step will be taken when states adopt for themselves republican constitutions. This is stipulated in the first definitive article. Peoples who live under republican constitutions are inclined towards peace because it is they, through their representatives, who have to decide on war and it is they who have to fund and fight in them. The second definitive article outlines the next decisive step. This is the formation on a voluntary basis of a federation of free states that has peace as its aim. This federation will provide the foundation for a functioning **international law** since its members will commit themselves to regulating their relations as though they have a common sovereign. The third definitive article calls for the recognition of a cosmopolitan right for visitors throughout the globe to be treated without hostility (see **cosmopolitanism**). Kant does not believe that these articles will inevitably be brought into force by the process of world history, but he does think that from a moral perspective they should be deemed indispensable by the human species.

Kant has a clear path of improvement mapped out for the human race. He also thinks that history can lend a helping hand. In the essay he includes a supplement called 'On the Guarantee of Perpetual Peace'. Paradoxically Kant sees war as placing upon us the greatest pressure to improve our condition. Although war represents the greatest evil where it occurs it nonetheless forces upon us the need for reform. On pain of death the human race is obliged to invent and improve its skills, consequently to increase its knowledge and regulate its activities effectively. War is not the path to follow but when we descend into it the processes of history can work in our favor.

Hegel: history as spirit

Hegel's account of history represents a considerably altered emphasis from that of Kant and prepares the way for Marx's dramatic and dialectical view of the outcome of history. Hegel gives history an unequivocal direction and impetus by invoking the concept of *Spirit* (Geist). Spirit or Mind might broadly be regarded as a modification of the Christian idea of God. For Hegel Spirit is the moving force behind history. As he puts it, 'world history is the necessary development, from the concept of the freedom of spirit alone, of the moments of reason and hence of spirit's self-consciousness and freedom' (Hegel 1991, 372). Kant neither expresses this certainty about there being an author of the historical process nor does he have the same firm belief in history's upward direction. For Kant the *hypothesis* of future progress acts as a spur to the moral actions of contemporary individuals. He sees the idea of a final goal of history or the highest political good as something that the human species has the potential but not necessarily the moral capacity to achieve. The project of progress may always miscarry at any time because of our own frailties. Hegel's monistic account of history brushes aside any misgivings of this kind. Progress will inevitably occur and has indeed already occurred. The embodiment of this progress is the modern state: 'the present has cast off its barbarism and unjust arbitrariness, and truth has cast off its otherworldliness and contingent force, so that the true reconciliation, which reveals the state as the image and actu-

ality of reason, has become objective' (Hegel 1991, 380).

Hegel divides world history into four broad stages or epochs. He describes these stages as the oriental world; the Greek world; the Roman world; and the modern world of the 'Germanic' or Protestant spirit. For Hegel the progress of world history follows the path of the sun, traveling from east to west. The path forward from east to west is equivalent to the development of different stages of freedom. In the oriental world only the despotic ruler is free. In the Greek world a few only are free, namely, the slave holding citizens of the city-states. In the Roman world the many, those who are land owning farmers, are free. The great glory of the modern Germanic period is that all are free. Whereas the hallmark of Kant's account of history is the hope that humankind may grasp the opportunities offered by its own strife torn development, the chief characteristic of Hegel's account is the optimism that this has already happened and may be discerned to be continually occurring under the aegis of spirit.

Recognition and thymos

Hegel is a major influence on Fukuyama's development of the idea of the end of history, although it is Hegel mediated through the work of Alexandre Kojève (1902–68), Hegel's most famous interpreter in the twentieth century. Kojève's reading of Hegel sometimes has peculiar implications and Fukuyama's understanding of Hegel is perhaps too much affected by Kojève at times. Nonetheless, the influence of Hegel is most apparent in Fukuyama's use of the concept of *recognition*, and Fukuyama goes to considerable lengths to acknowledge this in both the article and the book. Fukuyama begins his account of recognition with a discussion of one of

Hegel's most celebrated passages, his account of the primitive 'first man' at the dawn of history and the struggle to the death for recognition in the *Phenomenology of Spirit*. This first man shares with the animals certain basic natural desires such as the desire for food, sleep, shelter and, above all, for the preservation of his own life. But the first man is radically different from the animals in that he is also a social being who needs to be recognized by other people. His own sense of worth and identity is intimately connected with the value that other people place upon him, upon their willingness to acknowledge his value as a human being. The most fundamental way in which a man can assert his own value, and be recognized as a man by others, is through risking his life. Thus his encounter with other men leads to a violent struggle in which each seeks to make the other recognize him by risking his own life. Fukuyama does not claim that this violent battle ought to be recreated in modern society, any more than Hegel does. What he does claim is that the desire to be recognized as a human being with dignity, worth and value, is one of the major forces at work in modern society. It provides, so he argues, a powerful insight into the success of modern liberal democratic society, which provides this recognition in a fuller way than any other possible society.

Fukuyama claims that Hegel's concept of recognition is echoed in the works of many other writers, which in itself shows the great importance of the concept. Of these, the one which Fukuyama singles out for most discussion is Plato's concept of *thymos*. According to Plato, a person leads a just or good life when the three parts of the soul, reason, *thymos* and desire, are kept in balance. Usually this means that reason controls *thymos* and desire and ensures that they are kept in their proper place. But sometimes *thymos* needs to prompt reason to act according to a proper sense of honor or justice rather than simply follow the precepts of logic. 'If human beings were nothing but reason and desire, they would be perfectly content to live in a South Korea under military dictatorship, or under the enlightened technocratic administration of a Francoist Spain, or in a Guomindang-led Taiwan, hell-bent on rapid economic growth. And yet, citizens of these countries are something more than desire and reason: they have a thymotic pride and belief in their own dignity, and want that dignity to be recognized above all by the government of the country they live in' (Fukuyama 1992, 206). For Fukuyama, liberal democracy provides the best political context in which all men and women can find true recognition. This is why the triumph of the idea of liberal democracy marks the end of history.

American democracy

Fukuyama has often been accused of being an uncritical supporter of American democracy, almost at times as being the 'in house' philosopher for the first President Bush's New World Order. In fact he is surprisingly sharp in his criticism of aspects of American democracy and of American society as a whole. Democracy, he argues, takes different forms and will evolve over time, and there is much in American democracy that can be improved upon.

In particular, 'Anglo-Saxon democracy', as he calls it is flawed because it gives too much emphasis to the idea of individualism. This has led to the increasing isolation of individuals and to the breakdown of a proper sense of community. Fukuyama stresses the importance of the community and of civic associations in the growth and maturity of democracy, referring frequently to the work of Alexis de Tocqueville. In contrast to Anglo-Saxon individualism the newly emerging democracies of South East Asia have a much stronger and more robust sense of community from which Americans can learn. This is connected to the idea of recognition, because in order to gain a true sense of self-worth a person must be recognized as equal by other members of his or her own community. A fiercely competitive society where every individual is consumed with his or her own importance is not a place to encourage the mutual respect that is the basis for a truly human community.

Global politics at the end of history

Where do the ideal and the practice of democracy fit into the international sphere? It has often appeared in the past that democratic states are at a distinctive disadvantage in their relationship with illiberal states because those states do not have to worry about the potentially divisive effects of public opinion. This is not so, according to Fukuyama, because governments depend for their long term existence on having a legitimate right to rule and non-democratic states are inherently vulnerable in this respect. Fukuyama describes this as 'the weakness of strong states' and both the phrase and the accompanying argument seemed particularly compelling when applied to the Soviet Union and its vassal states.

At the heart of Fukuyama's argument is his claim that **legitimacy**, rather than force, ought to be recognized as being the central category of political analysis, even in the study of international relations. This places him at odds with realists who, he argues, have too simplistic a view of the states that make up the international system (see **realism**). 'States do not simply pursue power; they pursue a variety of ends that are dictated by concepts of legitimacy. Such concepts

act as powerful constraints on the pursuit of power for its own sake.' Moreover, realism 'does not take account of history', but 'portrays international relations as isolated in a timeless vacuum, immune from the evolutionary processes taking place around it' (Fukuyama 1992, 258). The most significant element in this evolutionary process is the intellectual triumph of liberal democracy and the rapidly growing number of liberal democratic societies in the world. Embracing the idea of **democratic peace**, Fukuyama argues that democracies do not fight each other, and so we should see a gradual decrease in interstate **war** and non-peaceful international conflict generally as democracy spreads. But why should we assume that democracy will keep on spreading? Because, says Fukuyama, democracy is infectious and as the peoples in non-democratic regimes see the enormous benefits of living in democratic societies they will seek to change their systems to reap the same benefits.

In arguing this way Fukuyama is heavily influenced by Kant's arguments in *Perpetual Peace*. Like Kant, he claims that a pacific union of liberal democratic states provides a just and equitable way of confronting world issues. The purpose of the pacific union is not imperialistic but idealistic, to extend justice, in the form of human rights and universal recognition, to all societies.

Fukuyama divides non-democratic states into three categories. First are the states of the undeveloped world, particularly in Africa. Warfare at both the interstate and intrastate levels may continue here for a long time but they pose no threat to the advanced democracies which are technologically far in advance of them. The way out of this conflict is for them to embrace the ideals of liberal democracy and establish legitimate governments committed to justice and fairness.

A second group are the capitalist states of East Asia such as Singapore, Taiwan and Indonesia which, when *The End of History and the Last Man* was published in 1992 had not embraced democracy. Perhaps in part because of his own Japanese ancestry Fukuyama is both more acutely aware of the differences between these societies and those of the West and more inclined to overstate the significance of those differences. In a tantalizing passage which he never fully develops, he writes that 'despite the apparent absence of systematic alternatives to liberal democracy at present, some new authoritarian alternatives, perhaps never before seen in history, may assert themselves in the future' (Fukuyama 1992, 235).

The third group are the states of the Islamic world. Whereas Fukuyama takes the threat to liberal democracy from South East Asia seriously, he is dismissive of the long term threat to democracy from Islamic states, believing that they present no plausible alternative ideology. He has dismissed the **terrorism** of **al-Qaeda** and the anti-western rhetoric of many Islamic governments as examples of 'Islamo-fascism'. In other words, bin Laden and the governments of states such as Saudi Arabia are in practice wedded to an ideology which reflects the values of an outmoded world view, not a bright new hope for the future. Fukuyama is careful to distinguish between the ideals and activities of radical Islamists and more moderate Muslims, but underlying his thinking in this area is a general belief that religion is at best a marginal issue in the modern world. This in turn is linked to his belief in the importance of science.

Science

In *The End of History and the Last Man*, science is presented as one of the driving forces that propels history forward and which promotes democracy. There are several reasons for this. One is that science brings wealth and **power**. Cheap medicine and greater material well being offer the prospects of life that is much longer and of much higher quality than the vast majority of people have known in the past. A second, related reason is that science produces new weapons that make scientifically advanced societies much less vulnerable to threats from potential enemies. Neither of these factors in themselves is inherently supportive of democratic values, but the third reason very decidedly is. Science grows through open debate and criticism and in science there are no sacred texts or absolute authorities. Hence science produces a culture in which criticism and the rejection of authority are crucial components. Such a culture is inherently favorable to democracy, and indeed requires democracy for its long term stability and development.

This in turn raises the question of whether it is possible to accept modernity in the form of science and technology while rejecting the western civilization from which they arose. Samuel Huntington (1996) argues that it is possible, pointing to the way in which non-western civilizations use modern technology to further their religious beliefs – videos, audio tapes, the internet, etc. – while decrying western decadence. But it may be that as they continue using these technologies they will have to come to accept some underlying western ideas, or simply remain reliant on the West to produce new technologies. This is a point which Fukuyama makes strongly, as he argues that one of the driving forces toward the end of history is the growth not only of modern technology but also the science which underlies it and which is inevitably secular and rational in nature.

After the end of history

Fukuyama was in his early forties when *The End of History and the Last Man* was published and while it is not quite a young man's book it is the work of someone who was just beginning a remarkably fruitful engagement with a whole host of central social and political issues. He has continued this engagement in a number of important books and a large number of articles as well as serving on important government committees, expressing particular interest and concern in recent years over the ethical and political impact of biotechnology. Because this engagement is continuing, and one would expect many more years of innovative and illuminating contributions from him, it would be premature to attempt a definitive assessment of his thinking and of the significance of his contribution to the concept of the end of history.

There is, though, one particularly serious challenge to the end of history thesis, one which Fukuyama himself has recognized and written about in his more recent book, *Our Posthuman Future* (2002). This is the claim that science, which Fukuyama sees to be one of the key driving forces in history, has not come to an end. Quite the opposite, it seems to be about to make a giant, and very dangerous, leap forward in the area of biotechnology. In 1992, Fukuyama made much of the supposed Hegelian roots of his central argument, but he lacked anything approaching a metaphysical account of history along the lines of Hegel's own concept of Spirit. Indeed, Fukuyama offered a strikingly secular (and very un-Hegelian) account of Spirit in terms of human consciousness. In practice, Fukuyama's fundamental philosophical orientation never was as Hegelian as it appeared to be. The concept of recognition was – and

remains in his later work – enormously important, but it is treated quite independently of Hegel's metaphysics. Perhaps the most important way in which Fukuyama differs from Hegel is in his view that human nature is unchanging. His view is that there are certain elements in human nature that remain constant and the ability to express these is the key to a happy and healthy life, both for the individual and for society. This is also central to the notion that the end of history has arrived because liberal democracy is the only form of government that can fully allow for the free expression of human nature. Only democracy allows for true human flourishing. The view of human nature is far more Aristotelian than Hegelian, and in *Our Posthuman Future*, Fukuyama refers to Aristotle explicitly in this connection. Hegel makes no appearance in the book.

A posthuman future would not be the end of history because it would involve a derailment of our present historical development and the setting off on a new track altogether. All those values that make the end of history so attractive – values such as individual liberty, a sense of honor and integrity, the recognition of our worth by others – depend upon a stable, enduring human nature. Until now there was no possibility of that nature being changed, but biotechnology threatens to alter this. And if human nature is changed, there is no telling what will happen as a consequence. It is hard to emphasize this point too strongly. If we succeed in changing human nature we may cease to be the kind of beings that we have hitherto been. Fukuyama places human dignity as one of the central elements in human nature. In this he is echoing one of the central themes of *The End of History and the Last Man*, and he explicitly links it again with the idea of recognition.

In his later work Fukuyama reiterates the end of history thesis with the important addition that it is now firmly grounded in a concept of a universal human nature and an Aristotelian view of the world. But the acknowledgment of the importance of human nature also brings us back to modern science. Liberal democracy represents the end of history because it is superior to all alternative ideologies. But its superiority rests upon its meeting the most basic requirements of human nature. If that human nature changes through biotechnological innovation whose scope we can only imagine today, then democracy may no longer fulfill the role it now does. In which case history may start again.

Further reading

Fukuyama, F. (1992) *The End of History and the Last Man*, London: Penguin.

Fukuyama, F. (2002) *Our Posthuman Future*, London: Profile Books.

Hegel, G. W. F. (1991) *Elements of the Philosophy of Right*, Cambridge: Cambridge University Press.

Huntington, S. (1996) *The Clash of Civilizations and the Remaking of World Order*, New York: Simon and Schuster.

Kant, I. (1991) *Kant's Political Writings*, Cambridge: Cambridge University Press.

Marx, K. and Engels, F. (1985) *The Communist Manifesto*, Harmondsworth: Penguin.

Marx, K. (1971) *Contribution to the Critique of Political Economy*, London: Lawrence & Wishart.

Williams, H., Sullivan, D. and Matthews, E. G. (1996) *Francis Fukuyama and the End of History*, Cardiff: University of Wales Press.

See also: clash of civilizations; democratic peace; democratization; liberal internationalism

DAVID SULLIVAN and
HOWARD WILLIAMS

English School

The English School (also called the **international society** approach) is a particular theoretical perspective in the study of international relations. It holds that states and other actors do not merely operate in an anarchical **international system** (see **anarchy**). They have also established common rules and institutions for the conduct of their relations, i.e. an international society informed by common values and interests and providing for international **order** and elements of justice. In accordance with its focus on the shared understandings inherent in international norms, rules, institutions and practices, the English School is generally in favor of a classical interpretive methodology inspired not only by traditional quarters of International Relations and political science, but also by related fields like history, sociology, political theory, philosophy, **international law**, international ethics and diplomatic studies (see **diplomacy**).

The intellectual roots of the English School and its central idea of international society can be traced back to the naturalist and positivist streams of the European tradition of international law (i.e. Suarez, Grotius, Pufendorf, Vattel and the nineteenth century legal positivists) and to the European tradition of political theory (i.e. Locke and Burke). More contemporary sources of inspiration include the opposed early and mid-twentieth century liberal internationalist (see **liberal internationalism**) and classical realist streams of thought, although the first generation of English School scholars had quarrels with both. As a distinctive and original theoretical perspective on international relations the English School took shape during the 1950s, 1960s and 1970s (although it was not so named until 1981). Its institutional bases were the International Relations

Department of the London School of Economics and the British Committee on the Theory of International Politics (1959–84).

By stressing the habitual, orderly and social nature of international politics, the English School was from the beginning at odds with both the realist preoccupation with **anarchy** and **power** politics and the idealist quest for radical international transformation. Both of these competing traditions of thought have long been recognized and in some respects incorporated in the work of the English School, but its basic conception of international relations derives from what Martin Wight identified as a rationalist tradition associated with the early seventeenth century thinker Hugo Grotius (1583–1645). Following Martin Wight's original work on the three main traditions of thought, this conception can be contrasted with both **realism** and what he called 'revolutionism'. As opposed to realism, the Grotian position holds that international society is characterized and constituted by societal features such as common values, rules and institutions and thus by a substantial element of international **order**. Consequently, what is sometimes referred to as the 'domestic analogy' (which describes international relations as a Hobbesian state of nature given the absence of a central government at the international level) must be rejected. As opposed to idealism, the Grotian tradition holds that the primary, but not exclusive, agents or members of international society are states rather than individual human beings, although the rights and duties of the latter are recognized especially by the solidarist writers in the rationalist tradition (see **solidarism**). According to English School theorists, the imperatives of reason, morality and law do not demand the dissolution of international society in favor of a world government or a universal society of humankind. Rather, they require the maintenance of orderly, peaceful and meaningful coexistence, i.e. the continuation and improvement of modern international society.

Drawing on the Grotian tradition of thought, the main theoretical ambition of the English School is to develop analytical concepts and categories by which the nature, dynamics and central normative questions of international society can be grasped. According to Hedley Bull (1977), an international society exists when a group of states are conscious of certain common interests and common values, conceive themselves to be bound by a common set of norms and rules in their relations with another, and share in the working of common institutions. In modern international society, the most basic common goals include the maintenance of international society itself, mutual recognition of **sovereignty**, peace as the normal condition of interstate relations, constraints on violence, and the keeping of promises between states. To the extent that common goals give rise to common rules and corresponding practices there will be a degree of international order: patterns of activity that sustains the primary goals of international society as a whole. The point is not that every single norm or pattern of behavior expresses this instrumental and universal rationality, but that the historical development of some rules and practices reflects the basic goals that most states have shared at most times, for instance to order and place some limits on international violence. Relatively stable norms and practices may also reflect a shared meaning originating from common values and morality. It is possible, then, that norms, rules, and practices reflecting shared values and justice can be incorporated into, or added to, a system of norms, rules and practices that also allows for the establishment and maintenance of international order. This facilitates a dynamic analysis, for instance in light of the attempt by the West to promote values like democracy, **human rights**, freedom, and the rule of law after the end of the **cold war**. In this sense, world society – as something that goes beyond interstate order and provides for systems of **global governance**, a mature system of rights and duties for the individual in relation to international society, an advanced international legal order, global communication not only in the political system, and a multitude of social relations across borders and involving many different types of actors and sectors – is not unthinkable, indeed, it may even be said to be a fact of contemporary international life.

To the English school the link between common interests and patterns of activity is established by international rules such as domestic sovereign jurisdiction, equality and therefore non-intervention, as well as institutions which provide guidance and opportunities of common governance. According to members of the English School an institution does not necessarily imply an organization or administrative machinery, but rather a set of habits and practices shaped towards the realization of common goal. These include practices that are fundamental in the sense of being universal in scope and of constitutive significance for international society and its elements of order and cooperation. Thus the mutual **recognition** of sovereignty, the **balance of power**, great power management (see **great powers**), diplomacy, international law and even **war** (understood as a set of shared expectations and practices governing the use of force) can be seen as institutions. Overall, the impact of this element of international society on state behavior is both enabling and constraining. On the one hand, rules and institutions make meaningful interaction

possible. On the other hand, they guide this interaction in certain directions.

It follows that modern international society is a mental, discursive, an institutional and a physical reality. As an idea, it exists inside the minds of state leaders, diplomats, representatives of **non-governmental organization**s, journalists and ordinary citizens throughout the world. As a shared idea it is often appealed to in national and international dialogue. At a more concrete level, the idea of international society has a normative and institutional existence in shared rules, codes of conduct and fundamental institutions such as the mutual recognition of sovereignty, **diplomacy**, international law and great power governance, and a physical expression in, for instance, embassies, documents of international law, governmental and non-governmental international organizations and internationally sponsored programs of **peace-building** and the reconstruction of war-torn societies. Finally, it exists as a shared language of social, orderly and just interaction referring to common rules, social norms, moral standards and political practices.

An international society is thus much more than an **international system**, since the latter can be conceived of simply as a group of interacting states, meaning a state of affairs in which two or more states have sufficient contact with each other to cause them to behave as parts of a whole. However, while the focus of the English School is on shared understandings leading to many of the qualities that we find also in domestic society such as order, peace, and justice, it is important to stress that the international practices that spring from such understandings may be about, or may lead to, conflict, war, and injustice as well. Consequently, this perspective on international relations may seem unduly pluralistic and eclectic in so far as it borrows from and incorporates some of the insights and themes of realism, liberalism, **regime** theory and **constructivism**. The English School has developed a number of more specific lines of enquiry, analysis and discussion. Two, in particular, are worth noting.

The first is the emerging debate within the school between pluralist and solidarist conceptions of international society. According to the pluralist conception, states can only be expected to be able to agree on the minimum requirements of international order, such as mutual respect of sovereignty, non-intervention, the codes of diplomacy and conventional international **peace-keeping**. Consequently, order, justice and the rule of law in international society depend primarily on the ability of states to provide for these qualities in their own national societies, and in accordance with their own values. On this view, there can be many different versions of the good life and the good society in the world at a given point in time, and the main function of the rules and institutions of international society is simply to prevent war and conflict between them. This is the essence of the term pluralism which points to a decentralized international order based on the principle of toleration and the acceptance of wide diversity in the domestic arrangements of states.

In contrast, the solidarist conception of international society is based on the assumption of solidarity or potential solidarity among states with respect to the conduct of international relations and the enforcement of common rules and principles. As a matter of international practice and legal principle, international cooperation is not confined to relationships between states. Individuals too have rights and duties under international law, and under some circumstances the enforcement of these rights and duties may be a legitimate concern for international society as a whole, either on behalf of the individual or on behalf of groups of individuals, for instance an ethnic minority looking for protection.

General or specific changes in international society can thus be discussed and evaluated in terms of pluralist and solidarist values and conceptions. Traditionally, scholars of the English School have been inclined to regard solidarist developments in international society with suspicion and caution due to a fundamental concern for international order. More specifically, state leaders have a responsibility for their own citizens and countries (*raison d'etat*), the maintenance of international order, peace and security (*raison dé système*), and to uphold the minimum standards of humanity, the prerequisite for world order. State leaders are inclined to rank these concerns in the just stated order, but hard choices must be expected

A second focus of the English School is more historical and comparative. In this line of inquiry the English School has discussed questions of culture, historical and contemporary criteria of membership in international society, the mechanisms separating insiders from outsiders, standards of civilization and the historically known as well as imaginable alternatives to the Westphalian international order (see **Westphalia**).

Critics argue that members of the English School have been too preoccupied with states and interstate society at the expense of other actors and overly concerned with continuity at the expense of change. Moreover it is sometimes argued that the meta-theoretical foundations of the English School are unclear and confused, and that the School has shown little interest in the international political economy of international society, past and present. Despite these criticisms, since the end of the **cold war** there has been a renewed interest in the English School. Under the leadership of Barry Buzan, the School has reconvened with a new generation of scholars less concerned with the debates of their predecessors and more interested in renewing the relevance of their insights for the challenges of the twenty-first century.

Further reading

Bull, H. (1977) *The Anarchical Society*, Basingstoke: Macmillan.

Bull, H. and Watson, A. (eds) (1984) *The Expansion of International Society*, Oxford: Oxford University Press.

Butterfield, H. and Wight, M. (eds) (1966) *Diplomatic Investigations: Essays in the Theory of International Politics*, London: Allen and Unwin.

Buzan, B. (2004) *From International to World Society? English School Theory and the Social Structure of Globalisation*, Cambridge: Cambridge University Press.

Dunne, T. (1998) *Inventing International Society: A History of the English School*, Basingstoke: Palgrave.

Wight, M. (1991) *International Theory: The Three Traditions*, Leicester: Leicester University Press.

See also: constructivism; international society; pluralism; solidarism

TONNY BREMS KNUDSEN

Epistemic community

The term 'epistemic community' is often invoked by constructivist scholars of international relations to focus analytic attention on the process by which states formulate interests and reconcile differences of interest (see **constructivism**). Epistemic communities are a principal channel through which consensual knowledge about causal understandings is applied to international policy coordi-nation, and by which states may learn through processes of international cooperation.

Epistemic communities are networks of knowledge-based communities with an authoritative claim to policy relevant knowledge within their domain of expertise. Their members share knowledge about the causation of social or physical phenomena in an area for which they have a reputation for competence, and a common set of normative beliefs about what actions will benefit human welfare in such a domain. In particular, they are a group of professionals, often from a number of different disciplines, who share the following characteristics. First, a set of shared con-summatory values or principled beliefs. Such beliefs provide a value-based rationale for social action of the members of the community. Second, a set of shared causal beliefs or professional judgment. These beliefs provide analytic reasons and explanations of behavior, offering causal explanations for the multiple linkages between possible policy actions and desired outcomes. Third, they share common notions of validity, or intersubjective, internally defined criteria for validating knowledge. Finally, they comprise a common policy enterprise: a set of practices associated with a central set of problems which have to be tackled, presumably out of a conviction that human welfare will be enhanced as a consequence.

If contemporary international relations is characterized as a setting of complexity and uncertainty, as argued by constructivist scholars, particularly under contemporary circumstances of complex **interdependence**, increasing **globalization**, and the emergence of new technical issues on the international agenda with which traditional decision makers are habitually unfamiliar, then state interests are often unknown, or incompletely specified. In this context, policymaking is a matter of applying embedded and institutionalized beliefs about the nature of problems and the appropriate means of collective response, rather than the process of resolving rationally formulated state preferences. Changes in information processing are likely to follow well-publicized shocks or crises (see **crisis**). Only at such times are decision makers likely to recognize major anomalies and to pursue new policy patterns. During subsequent, less revolutionary periods these new doctrines or orthodoxies assume the status of taken for granted assumptions or dogma, which persist until called into question again by external stimuli.

Because of the disjointed equilibrium nature of policy change, an evolutionary focus on institutional learning and path dependence may provide an appropriate model by which to understand the international recognition of and response to global change. Such a research program may provide a better understanding of factors which influence the introduction of new policy frames, collective understandings or doctrines as well as illuminating mechanisms to identify those factors which may influence the degree of irreversibility of national and collective actions.

Epistemic communities are among the principal actors responsible for aggregating and articulating knowledge in terms of state interests for decision makers, and disseminating those beliefs internationally. In a broader political context, epistemic communities provide one of the major channels by which overarching **regime** principles, norms and rules are articulated for the international community, and disseminated internationally. The extent to which such regimes become more deeply diffused and embedded internationally has to do with the political influence of epistemic community members; their ability to persuade others, their ability to consolidate bureaucratic influence in important institutional venues, and their ability to retain influence over time.

Epistemic communities are likely to be found in substantive issue areas where scientific disciplines have been applied to policy oriented work, and in countries with well established institutional capacities for administration. Only governments with such capacities are likely to see the need for the technical skills which epistemic community members command, and such professionals would only be attracted to governmental service when they believe that their policy enterprise can be advanced. Crises or widely publicized shocks are probably necessary precipitants of environmental regime creation, but crises alone are insufficient to be able to explain how or which collective responses to a perceived joint problem are likely to develop. Epistemic communities can help to identify cause and effect relationships, elucidate links between problems, help to define the consulting state's or organization's interests, and help to formulate policy. Their aggregate effect depends upon the extent to which their ideas become embedded in influential multilateral institutions more generally (see **multilaterism**). Overall, learning will occur in the **international system** as new policy relevant knowledge is identified and applied to a common problem.

Empirical work has found that in environmental issues, many of these experts have been members of an ecological epistemic community. Members of the epistemic community that have dominated technical discussions in environmental regimes have subscribed to holistic ecological beliefs about the need for policy coordination subject to ecosystemic laws. Thus, they promote international environmental regimes which are grounded in policies which offer coherent plans for the management of entire ecosystems, sensitive to interactions between environmental media (such as air and water), sources of pollution, and contending uses of the common property resource, rather than being limited to more traditional policies for managing discrete activities or physical resources within fairly short term time horizons.

When it was first elaborated in the early 1990s, the concept of an epistemic community was initially favorably received in the study of international relations because it provided a means for focusing on the ideational component of politics as well as allowing for the role of agency in theorizing about **global governance** and policymaking. Studies of the **European Union** (EU) in particular have analyzed the role of various epistemic communities in shaping EU directives as well as in building a broader sense of European identity. The ideational focus was absorbed into the broader constructivist research program developed in international relations and comparative politics. Among other things, constructivists examined the role of beliefs and ideas in shaping state interests and practices, with epistemic communities serving as one of the mechanisms by which new ideas are developed and circulated.

However, questions have also been raised about the role of such epistemic communities, and whether they constitute a neutral agent or a politically biased group of experts. Their defenders argue that, normatively, epistemic communities ultimately provide more impartial advice than other modes of policy advice. More importantly, they are worth studying because they represent a causal pathway by which ideas come to inform political practices.

Further reading

Haas, P. and Kanie, N. (eds) (2004) *Emerging Forces in Environmental Governance*, Tokyo: UNU Press.

Hall, P. (1993) 'Policy Paradigms, Social Learning and the State', *Comparative Politics* 23, 275–96.

Hasenclever, A., Mayer, P. and Rittberger, V. (1997) *Theories of International Regimes*, Cambridge: Cambridge University Press.

Jacobsen, J. K. (1995) 'Much Ado About Ideas', *World Politics* 47, 283–310.

Zito, A. (2001) 'Epistemic Communities, Collective Entrepreneurship and European Integration', *Journal of European Public Policy* 8(4), 585–603.

See also: communitarianism; regime

PETER M. HAAS

Ethnic cleansing

When ethnic populations are minorities in territories controlled by rival ethnic groups, they may be driven from the land or (in rare cases) systematically exterminated. By driving out the minority ethnic group, a majority group can assemble a more unified, more contiguous, and larger territory for its **nation-state**. The term 'ethnic cleansing' was coined in the context of the dissolution of Yugoslavia in the 1990s. It is a literal translation of the expression *etnicko ciscenje* in Serbo-Croatian/Croato-Serbian. The precise origin of this term is difficult to establish. Mass media reports discussed the establishment of 'ethnically clean territories' in Kosovo after 1981. At the time, the concept related to administrative and non-violent matters and referred mostly to the behavior of Kosovo Albanians (Kosovars) towards the Serbian minority in the province.

The term derived its current meaning during the war in Bosnia and Herzegovina (1992–5). As military officers of the former Yugoslav People's Army had a preponderant role in all these events, the conclusion could be drawn that the concept has its origin in military vocabulary. The expression 'to clean the territory' is directed against enemies, and it is used mostly in the final phase of combat in order to take total control of the conquered territory.

Analysis of ethnic cleansing should not be limited to the specific case of former Yugoslavia. This policy can occur and have terrible consequences in all territories with mixed populations, especially in attempts to redefine frontiers and rights over given territories. There is a new logic of conflict that relies on violent actions against the enemy's civilian population on a large scale, rather than on **war** in the traditional sense, i.e. between armed forces.

It is important to underline that the policy of ethnic cleansing fundamentally represents a violation of **human rights** and international humanitarian law. Only when the means and methods of ethnic cleansing policies can be identified with genocidal acts (see **genocide**), and when a combination of different elements implies the existence of an intent to destroy a group as such, can such actions represent genocide. Ethnic cleansing lacks the precise legal definition that genocide has, although it has been widely used in **United Nations** General Assembly and Security Council Resolutions, documents of special *rapporteurs*, and the pamphlets of **nongovernmental organization**s.

Some suggest that ethnic cleansing is merely a euphemism for genocide. There would seem, however, to be a significant difference between them. The former seeks to 'cleanse' or 'purify' a territory of one ethnic group by use of terror, rape, and murder in order to convince the inhabitants to leave. The latter seeks to destroy the group, closing the borders to

ensure that none escape. This observation should not be taken to imply that ethnic cleansing is not a barbaric international crime. It is most certainly punishable as a crime against humanity (see **crimes against humanity**).

Further reading

Carmichael, C. (2002) *Ethnic Cleansing in the Balkans: Nationalism and the Destruction of Tradition*, London: Routledge.

Mann, M. (2004) *The Dark Side of Democracy: Explaining Ethnic Cleansing*, Cambridge: Cambridge University Press.

Naimark, N. (2002) *Fires of Hatred: Ethnic Cleansing in Twentieth Century Europe*, Boston, MA: Harvard University Press.

See also: civil war; ethnic conflict; ethnicity

MARTIN GRIFFITHS

Ethnic conflict

Conflict is 'ethnic' when one or more of the parties to the conflict claims to represent the interests of an ethnic or communal group. Ethnic and communal groups are non-state entities whose active members share a distinctive and enduring collective identity based on common descent, shared experiences, and cultural traits. This broad concept includes ethno-nationalist groups such as Basques and Kurds, indigenous peoples such as Navajos and Miskitos, communal contenders such as Yoruba in Nigeria and Maronite Christians in Lebanon, and ethno-classes such as people of African descent in the Americas and overseas Chinese in Southeast Asia. It also includes religious minorities who share common descent such as Shi'is in Sunni-dominated Islamic states and Catholics in Northern Ireland.

When ethnic groups mobilize to pursue political objectives against the state or rival groups they are described as 'ethno-political'. Their aims may be to win political autonomy or independence from existing states, to gain greater rights and privileges within states in which they reside, or to establish dominance over rival groups. Which objectives ethno-political groups pursue, the means they use, and the strategies with which regimes and international actors respond have important consequences for world politics. The consequences are especially serious when ethnic disputes become violent. In the last fifty years more than seventy ethno-national groups fought armed conflicts for **self-determination**, including some of the most deadly wars fought since the end of World War Two (see Marshall and Gurr 2003). During the same period as many as forty communal groups were targets of state policies of **genocide** or political mass murder because government elites saw them as threats to state **security**.

This essay begins by examining some international consequences of deadly ethnic conflicts, and then summarizes expert views and evidence about their causes. It concludes by outlining doctrines and practices that are being used in the early twenty-first century in international efforts to contain and resolve ethno-political disputes.

International dimensions of ethno-political conflict

If a global atlas of politically active ethnic groups could be compiled, it would highlight the fact that most such groups transcend the boundaries of existing states. While most ethnic conflicts occur within particular states, ethnic groups usually are linked by similar interests and social networks with kindred groups elsewhere. The Kurds live in five contiguous Middle Eastern states. Tutsis and Hutus inhabit not only Rwanda and Bur-

undi but also are politically significant minorities in neighboring Congo and Uganda. Immigrant Muslims and Roma (gypsies) are interconnected peoples who live in most European states. A transcontinental political network links indigenous activists in the Americas, Asia, Scandinavia, and parts of Africa. Therefore any campaign of ethnic mobilization, any armed conflict, any government policy aimed at suppressing or accommodating an ethnic group impacts on the hopes and actions of similar groups elsewhere, and also influences the policy decisions of other governments facing similar challenges.

Ethno-political conflicts, especially violent ones, also have immediate and tangible international consequences. Numbers of major ethnic **war**s being fought world-wide increased steadily from four in the 1950s to a high of thirty-two in the early 1990s before declining to eleven in 2002. Many lesser armed conflicts have been fought by ethno-political groups using **terrorism** and sporadic armed attacks. Such conflicts have potentially serious international ramifications, four of which are discussed below (see Ganguly and Taras 1998; Lake and Rothchild 1998). External actors often support ethnic contenders in pursuit of their own interests; 'spillover effects' decrease **security** in neighboring states; humanitarian and security crises (see **crisis**) are increasingly likely to prompt remedial action, including intervention, by international actors; and **diaspora**s may be formed and activated in ways that reshape future conflicts, both within and among states.

Foreign support for ethnic contenders

During the **cold war** the United States helped arm and finance ethno-political warriors in Angola, Afghanistan,

Nicaragua, Laos, and Vietnam to counter Soviet, Chinese, or Cuban-supported regimes in those countries. Regional rivals have repeatedly supported rebellious minorities in one another's countries with the aim of weakening their opponent. For example, during and after the Iran–Iraq war of the 1980s each country provided operating bases and material support for one another's Kurdish rebels. Pakistan provides safe havens and support for Muslim rebels fighting for an independent Kashmir while India allegedly provides clandestine assistance to internal opponents of the Pakistani regime.

The Yugoslav government's sponsorship of rebellions by Serbs in Croatia and Bosnia in the early 1990s illustrates the motives and means of international support for irredentist rebellions (see **irredentism**). The aim is to enable kindred groups in neighboring states to gain autonomy and align more closely with their homeland country, if not formally to be incorporated in it. The Republic of Armenia's support for Armenian rebels in Azerbaijan's Nagorno-Karabakh province is another instance, the result of which is that Nagorno-Karabakh has *de facto* become part of Armenia. Irredentist wars are less common than surrogate wars; most recent instances occurred as a consequence of the break-up of the USSR and the Yugoslav Federation (see Saideman 2001 for a general analysis and detailed examples).

Spillovers from ethnopolitical wars

Ethnic conflicts within states can no longer be regarded as localized problems; it is widely recognized that they are nested problems that substantially affect, and are affected by, their regional political environment. Ethno-political rebels seek external support, from friendly governments or **diaspora** communities. If they control scarce resources they can purchase arms, sometimes on a large scale. Under military pressure rebels often seek base areas in neighboring states, whose rugged terrain may place them outside the reach of any government authority. The more severe the conflict, the greater are **refugee** flows into neighboring countries, which bring their own share of problems. Refugees require assistance, compete with host communities for land and resources, and may harbor armed rebels. The root cause of **civil war**s that have ravaged eastern Congo since the mid-1990s was the flight of Hutu refugees from Rwanda in the aftermath of the 1994 **genocide**. The genocide ended when Uganda-based Tutsi rebels seized control of the government, but warfare continued because Hutu militants among the refugees fought a cross-border war. This in turn prompted Rwanda's new leaders to support a series of wars in eastern Congo, aimed at eliminating the external Hutu threat.

The fact and fear of spillover effects such as these creates insecurity among leaders of neighboring countries. They often respond by increasing their military and security forces and cracking down on their own minorities, especially those who are kindred to cross-border rebels. These policies, along with the demonstration effects of ethnic rebellion elsewhere, in many instances motivate new ethnic wars and justify preemptive regime campaigns of repression. 'Protracted conflict regions' is Marshall's (1999) term for the areas afflicted in these ways by spillovers from major civil conflicts. His and others' comparative evidence shows that ethnic and revolutionary warfare is a consistent predictor of future ethnic and political instability in neighboring countries (see **revolution**).

International responses to regional crises

Ethno-political wars and their spillover effects create a number of problems for international and regional organizations. Usually the most immediate issue is helping refugees fleeing the fighting. In 2002 about two thirds of the world's 15 million international refugees had fled from ethno-political conflicts and repression and at least twice as many others were internally displaced by force or famine.

When fighting spreads into neighboring countries, and when it threatens the security interests of major powers, it is increasingly likely to lead to intervention authorized by the **United Nations** Security Council. During the **cold war** the UN rarely agreed on intervention because of great power rivalry (see **great powers**). Since 1991, however, the Security Council has become increasingly likely to use its authority to impose arms embargoes, sanction repressive governments (see **sanctions**), and authorize **peacekeeping** missions. Most of the fifteen UN peacekeeping operations in place in 2002 aimed at containing conflicts within states, mainly ethnic wars.

Some regional organizations also are playing a more vigorous role in responding to ethno-political conflicts. Diplomatic and political efforts to head off emerging ethnic violence have been widely and effectively employed by the **European Union** and by the High Commissioner for Minorities of the **Organization for Security and Cooperation in Europe** (OSCE). The **North Atlantic Treaty Organization** (NATO) was the instrument the United States and Europeans used in 1999 to check by force the Serbian campaign to ethnically cleanse Albanians from Kosovo province. In Africa the **African Union** is increasingly likely to use its limited political and diplomatic resources to encourage peaceful solutions to new and ongoing communal conflicts. The AU has few resources for peacekeeping, however, and the most substantial military efforts to check ethnic wars in Africa have been mounted either by the UN (for example in the eastern Congo in 2002–3) or by Nigeria at the head of a regional coalition (in Sierra Leone and Liberia). Regional organizations representing the Islamic and Asian states have played little political and no military role in containing communal conflicts in those regions.

Diasporas

The role of diasporas in ethnic conflict processes is complex and has only recently received close analytic attention. Diasporas come into existence as a result of economic and political migration, including peoples fleeing from ethnic conflicts who settle permanently in their country of refuge. Long-settled diaspora peoples in democratic countries are ever more likely to use political means to pressure their governments to act in support of their kindred. Campaigns of support for Israel by Jewish communities in Western Europe and North America are widely emulated by other diaspora groups, such as Armenian-Americans who have promoted US federal legislation to aid the government of Armenia in its conflict with Azerbaijan, Irish-Americans who back US government efforts in support of a negotiated end to the Northern Ireland conflict, and Arab-Americans who give financial and political support to the Palestinian cause.

The darker side of diaspora politics is the flow of funds to warring kindred groups. Sikh activists in Canada in the 1980s supported militant Sikh opposition to the government of India, including planting a bomb that destroyed an Air India plane in flight. Canada is also home to a large population of Sri Lankan Tamils who from 1975 to the early 2000s were the major external source of support for the Tamil Tigers' war for independence. The 1984–2001 war between Turkish Kurds and their government was funded in part by Kurdish immigrants and refugees in Europe, and was echoed in clashes and terrorism between Kurdish and Turkish activists in Germany.

The etiology of ethno-political conflict

Efforts by scholars to postulate a single general explanation for ethno-political conflict have foundered on the sheer diversity of groups, issues, circumstances, and forms of conflict. Below three approaches are summarized to explaining ethno-political conflict, a general framework that can be used to organize the analysis of causes is outlined, and some specific theories are commented on.

Approaches to explaining ethno-political conflict

Most explanations, whether general or specific, are shaped by their assumptions about the nature of ethnic identities and action. The *primordial* approach assumes that ethnic identities are more essential and transcendent than others. Thus groups with deep social, historical, and genetic foundations are more enduring than others, and threats to ethnic solidarity are a recurring source of conflict with states and other groups. This assumption underlies arguments that ethnic diversity inevitably leads to open conflict.

The *instrumental* view is that ethnicity is one of many alternative bases of identity. It becomes significant, and a basis for political action, when ethnic symbols are invoked and manipulated by political entrepreneurs in response to threats and opportunities. This assumption leads to theories that attribute ethnic conflict to group leaders and how they take advantage of changing political circumstances.

The *constructivist* approach begins with the premise that ethnic identities are social constructions that emerge and change over time (see **constructivism**). An identity such as 'the Kurdish nation' or 'African-American' is a social construction that may have been imposed by outsiders, shaped by intellectuals, and reinforced by conflict with other groups. However identities originate, they are passed on by families and teachers, reinforced and reshaped by leaders, and used by political movements. They also shape who is and who is not judged to be a group member. This does not mean that ethnic identities are totally malleable, as some contend. Rather they are enduring social constructions. Their content and significance may change, but usually slowly and in response to changes in the group's social and political environment. The constructivist approach calls attention to the ways that conflict among groups shapes and intensifies ethnic identities.

Another implication of the constructivist approach is that ethnic conflict is itself a construction. For example civil war in Afghanistan during the cold war was widely seen as a revolutionary (or counterrevolutionary) conflict between mujahadeen rebels and the Soviet-backed regime in Kabul. During the 'war on terrorism', declared after the 9/11 attacks on the United States, the Afghan conflict was redefined as one between Islamic extremism, exemplified by the Taliban, and their northern opponents. Underlying all civil conflicts in Afghanistan during the last century is the enduring rivalry between the Pushtun majority, who were principal supporters of the communist regime (see **communism**) and the Taliban, and their regionally based Uzbek, Tajik, and Hazari challengers. Thus Afghanistan's civil wars can be interpreted through the lenses of revolutionary, fundamentalist, or ethnic conflict.

A theoretical framework for analyzing causes of ethnopolitical conflicts

The first general question asked by most theories of ethnic conflict is this: When and why do ethnic groups mobilize to defend and promote their collective interests? The second is: What factors determine the strategies they choose, i.e. conventional politics, protest, terrorism, or warfare? Here a four-variable framework is outlined that can be used to answer those questions. It assumes that the origins of ethno-political conflict are mainly internal to groups themselves and their relations with societies in which they reside. International factors, when they are relevant, act mainly to exacerbate or moderate the effects of group and societal causes.

Four general factors or variables are specified in the framework: the *salience of ethnic identity*, the group's *incentives for political action*, its *capacities for action*, and the *opportunities* provided by the group's political environment.

The greater the *salience* of ethnic identities for a group, the more likely members are to define their interests in ethnic terms and the easier it is for leaders to mobilize them. This proposition problematizes the primordial assumption: one cannot assume ethnic identity is fundamentally important, instead it is necessary to determine how important it is for members of a notional group and why. The most general proposition is that the salience of ethnic identity depends on how much difference it makes in people's lives. Three specific factors help determine salience. One is the extent to which a group differs culturally from other groups with whom they interact: cultural differences provide the basis for differential perceptions and treatment. The second is the extent to which group members are advantaged or disadvantaged relative to other groups. The third is the intensity of their past and ongoing conflicts with rival groups and the state: discriminatory treatment and a history of repression leave bitter residues in collective memories. Victimization helps create and sharpen group identities.

International factors also contribute to the salience of group identities. Most important is the diffusion of information about mobilization and collective action by similar groups elsewhere. **Decolonization** in Asia and Africa during the 1950s and 1960s helped define and sharpen the sense of ethno-national identity among groups elsewhere, even in Europe (Bretons in France, Scots in the UK) and North America (the Quebecois). The civil rights movement by African-Americans had a strong effect on how minorities elsewhere interpreted their status and rights.

The second question is how much group members think they have to gain by collective action: their *incentives*. Three general kinds of incentives can motivate ethno-political action: the desire to redress grievances about losses suffered in the past, a fear of future losses, and hopes for gains relative to other groups. In objective terms this directs attention to the extent to which an ethnic group is disadvantaged relative to other groups: most ethnic protestors and rebels seek economic gains and greater access to political power. Also relevant is a group's historical memory of lost autonomy. Virtually all ethno-nationalists, national minorities, and indigenous peoples were once independent of external control or were part of states other than the states that now govern them. The aim of regaining autonomy or independence is one of the most powerful incentives underlying wars of self-determination. Repressive control of an ethnic group is the third source of incentives for ethno-political action. The use of force against minorities and conquered people initially inspires fear and caution but at the same time creates resentment and enduring incentives to resist and retaliate.

Empowering doctrines about self-determination and collective rights play a special role in motivating ethno-political action because they connect group identities and incentives to a program of action. The process is called framing (Tarrow 1994). The doctrines most widely used to frame contemporary ethno-political movements are national self-determination, indigenous rights, and minority rights. These doctrines travel easily across borders, encouraging new and rising aspirations among ethnic and communal groups elsewhere.

The third analytic question concerns a group's *capacity for collective action*. The greater a group's cohesion and mobilization, the more frequent and sustained its political action, and the more likely it is to gain concessions and greater access to power (see Tilly 1978). Cohesive groups are those held together by dense networks of communication and interaction. Mobilization is the process by which members of ethno-political organizations are recruited and motivated. Empirical studies have consistently shown that territorially concentrated minorities are more likely to rebel (see Fearon and Laitin 2003), presumably because groups with a regional base have greater cohesion and are easier to mobilize. Leadership skills are crucial in building a group's capacity for action. Effective leaders must be able to articulate a program of organization and

action that is consistent with the beliefs and experiences of group members, forge coalitions within the group, overcome the recurring tendency toward factionalism, and build alliances with external actors.

The ways in which identity, incentives, and capacity are translated into ethno-political action depend on the *opportunities* in a group's domestic and international environment. Most protest campaigns and ethnic rebellions are shaped by the strategic assessments and tactical decisions of leaders and activists which in turn are based on their assessments of opportunities. Some general principles about opportunities are well-established. Established democracies are relatively open to ethnic political activism and thus ethno-political leaders usually chose protest rather than rebellion. In autocracies ethnic rebellions are more common because limited forms of political action are usually suppressed; rebellion is the only alternative to passivity. State **power** is also a significant factor: ethnic activists have more to gain from powerful states, and also more to lose if their actions trigger repressive responses.

In new and weak states, including those in transition to democracy, the opportunities for ethno-political action are greatest. State institutions command few resources or legitimacy, their leaders need all the allies they can get, and their capacity to repress opponents is limited. This is a major reason why the dissolution of the USSR and the Yugoslavian Federation was accompanied by an upsurge in ethno-political protest and rebellion in the successor states. It is also why new states in Asia in the 1950s and Africa in the 1960s experienced so much ethno-political rebellion. And the continuing weakness of most African states provides ever-present opportunities for new and renewed ethno-political action by communal contenders and separatists.

Important sources of group capacity and opportunities come from the international arena. Some are mentioned above, including support from kindred groups and friendly foreign governments. The availability of light arms, readily obtained from foreign backers and the illicit international trade in arms, contributes substantially to ethno-political groups' capacity and opportunities for action, especially in weak states (see Sislin and Pearson 2001). At the most general level, any substantial change in the structure of the international system, including the breakup of **empire**s, shifting **alliance** patterns, and international warfare can provide ethno-political groups with new resources and opportunities to act.

Some specific theories of ethno-political conflict

The framework sketched above is broad enough to incorporate most of the more specific theories advanced to explain ethno-political conflict. These are some examples.

Enduring ethnic rivalries and hatreds

A commonly held theory is that ethnic diversity in a society is a more or less inevitable source of ethnic rivalry, hostility, and recurring conflict. This theory has been used to explain the eruption of ethno-national wars in Yugoslavia, to argue that minorities in the United States and France must be assimilated, and to justify the suppression of nationalist aspirations by peoples like the Kurds in Turkey. In fact empirical studies show no strong connection between ethnic heterogeneity in modern societies and their extent of ethnic conflict, for reasons that are easily interpreted in larger theoretical

terms. Not all ethnic groups have a strong sense of group identity, and many of those that do pursue their group interests by conventional political means. Ethnic mobilization and open conflict are most likely when group identities and interests are threatened, and when the balance of political opportunities favors rebellion.

Inequalities

A competing theory is that poverty and disenfranchisement are the root causes of ethno-political mobilization and rebellion. The theory gains plausibility from the fact that most politically active minorities are poorer and politically marginalized by comparison with other groups, and that their leaders put these issues high on their agenda of grievances. What this theory does not explain is why some of the poorest groups do not rebel, while some advantaged groups do. The indigenous peoples of the Americas are among the most disadvantaged peoples anywhere in the world, but rather than rebelling they are either quiescent or use the nonviolent political strategies of the indigenous rights movement. In contrast, some economically advantaged groups, like the Basques in Spain, have fought persistent rebellions.

Inequalities are an important source of group incentives for action but not necessarily the most important. Some ethnic groups are more concerned about protecting their culture and securing recognition of their status than with overcoming inequalities. Others, like communal contenders in Lebanon and Afghanistan, and Hutus and Tutsis in Central Africa, want state power in order to subordinate rival groups and promote their own interests. These are the goals of the ambitious and contentious, not of the poor. And whatever the mix of economic, political, and cultural incentives for ethno-political mobilization, group capacities and opportunities for action vary widely.

Predation

Recent work by researchers at the **World Bank** emphasizes the importance of predation, or greed, as a motivating factor for civil conflict in poor countries. They find that lack of **development** and dependence on natural resource exports are closely associated with ethnic and political warfare (Collier 2003). Lack of development in countries such as Sierra Leone, Liberia, Angola, and the Democratic Republic of Congo intensifies conflict among groups for control of scarce resources and state power. Economic decline in low-income countries also accelerates the risk of civil war. In poor and economically stagnant countries natural resources like diamond fields and timber are prizes that, in the hands of rebels, can be used to buy loyalty and arms. Wars fought by well-armed and well-financed rebels in weak states are very persistent and difficult to control, and often end only when the rebels are guaranteed a share of state power or regional autonomy, both of which help preserve their resource and human support base.

This argument and evidence help explain the rise and persistence of ethno-political rebellions and communal warfare in poor countries, but does not account for pervasive ethno-political protest, nor for the ethnic rebellions that sometimes erupt in more developed countries. It needs to be extended by analyzing how less tangible resources such as cultural identities, ideologies of empowerment, and external encouragement affect the onset and persistence of ethno-political conflict.

Ethnic entrepreneurs

A fourth approach indicts extremist ethno-politicians for encouraging and organizing ethnic warfare. The rise of Serbian and Croat **nationalism** and subsequent wars in Bosnia and Croatia often are attributed to manipulative rivalries and hate-mongering of politicians such as Yugoslavia's Slobodan Milosevic, the Bosnian Serb Radovan Karadzic, and the Croat leader Franjo Tudjman. As suggested above, leaders of ethno-political groups usually play a crucial role in framing, mobilization, and capacity building. They also make strategic choices about issues such as whether to use exclusionary appeals to outbid rival leaders, where to seek allies and external support, and whether to fight or seek agreements with existing governments. But they make these choices within limits set by the expectations and experiences of their ethnic kindred, the means at their disposal for mobilizing and rewarding followers, and the political threats and opportunities facing them. In other words the success of ethno-political leaders depends on their followers and their circumstances. Most Serbs and Croats, confounded by political uncertainties, chose to support extremist leaders. And by so doing they contributed to what Posen (1993) calls a **security dilemma** in which the group's survival seemed to depend on striking at rivals before they had a chance to act. In brief, understanding why ethno-political leaders do what they do, and with what results, depends on analysis of the other factors in the general framework.

Containing ethno-political conflict in heterogeneous societies

The increase in ethno-political conflict at the end of the cold war was a strong stimulus to international problem solving that aimed at ending ongoing ethnic wars and heading off future ones. By 2003 five widely accepted general principles had been established about how best to do so.

States and civil society should recognize and promote the rights of minorities

The **human rights** regime that emerged in Western societies in the 1970s has led to major gains in legal and institutional protections for minorities in democratic societies. The European Union has urged new democracies in East Central Europe to implement such policies as the price of membership in the EU. Latin American constitutions have been amended to recognize indigenous rights. Some autocratic regimes also have sought to improve their images by reducing discriminatory treatment of minorities. These shifts are not merely symbolic. They give ethno-political groups greater incentives and opportunities to pursue electoral and interest group politics. They also expose regimes that do not protect minority rights to international scrutiny and criticism. Most of the Islamic world is resistant to Western human rights doctrines but even here a few religious and other minorities (including the Copts in Egypt and some regional groups in quasi-democratic Indonesia) have made some gains.

Democratic institutions and power-sharing are preferred means for protecting group rights

The worldwide shift from autocracy toward democracy in recent decades provides the context in which deadly ethno-political conflict has declined. In the mid-1970s autocracies outnumbered democracies by more than two to one whereas by 2002 there were eighty-three fully democratic countries and nearly fifty transitional regimes with a few democratic traits, but fewer than thirty autocracies. The democratic principle is that all peoples in ethnically diverse societies have equal civil and political rights. Democratic governance also implies acceptance of peaceful means for resolving civil conflicts. From the viewpoint of ethno-political leaders, democratic institutions give them incentives to pursue moderate political goals by nonviolent means.

Some democratic institutions are better than others for promoting group rights. Decentralized or federal democracies give politically organized minorities a greater voice in state or provincial politics. Proportional representative electoral systems mean that minority parties gain representation in proportion to their votes and thus are more likely to participate as a collectivity in coalition governments.

Conflicts over self-determination are best settled by negotiations for autonomy within existing states

Armed separatist conflicts, including those using low level terrorism, increased from five in the 1950s to a global maximum of forty-one in 1991, before falling even more abruptly to a low of twenty-two in early 2003. Several general factors contribute to this decline. One is the recognition by many governments and ethno-political leaders that autonomy within existing states, such as that gained by Tatars and Bashkirs in Russia, Nagas and Mizos in India, and Miskitos in Nicaragua, is preferable to wars for total independence. A second is the democratic shift cited above: it is easier to negotiate solutions for separatist disputes in democratic and federal political systems. This permissive environment has encouraged many groups to claim the right to self-determination; nearly 100 such groups were active in 2003. But only twenty-two are currently using violent means while seventy-six rely on nonviolent political strategies. Most of these disputes will be channeled into conventional politics and result in modest concessions; few are likely to escalate into rebellion.

International actors should protect minority rights and promote settlement of ethno-political wars

Since the end of the cold war the UN, regional organizations, the major powers, and a great many NGOs have actively promoted minority rights and the settlement of civil wars. The reasons are compelling: to check humanitarian crises, contain spillover effects of internal crises, and avert further fragmentation of the international state system. The means are diverse. They include media campaigns to call international attention to emerging ethno-political conflicts; observer missions and diplomacy to encourage contenders to seek accommodation; international mediation and arbitration; and incentives to all parties to adopt reforms. The ethno-political war begun in 2001 by the Albanian minority in Macedonia, led by rebels from neighboring Kosovo, prompted this kind of response. Hard line Macedonian and Albanian nationalists wanted a war but moderate politicians on both sides recognized that this risked breaking up the Macedonian state. Heavy European pressure on all parties led to an internationally brokered agreement backed up by a short-term European peacekeeping mission that supervised disarmament of the rebels. The agreement recognized Albanians as a national people within Macedonia, guaranteed their cultural rights, and committed the government to expanding Albania's partici-

pation in security forces and civil administration. International actors continue to monitor and press for implementation of the agreement.

The Israeli–Palestinian conflict has thus far defined settlement by such means. It exemplifies ethno-political conflicts that have persisted so long, and created such entrenched hostilities, that they are thought to be intractable. But allegedly intractable conflict over *apartheid* in South Africa was settled peacefully and protracted ethno-political wars in Sudan and Sri Lanka shifted in 2002 from fighting to negotiations. It is premature to write off any ethno-political conflict – in Tibet, Kashmir, Chechyna, the West Bank, and Gaza – as intractable.

International actors may use coercive means to stop civil wars and mass killing of civilians

When preventive means and peacekeeping fail to contain deadly conflicts that threaten regional stability, it is increasingly accepted that international actors have the right and responsibility to respond with sanctions and **peace enforcement** operations. This has been called the doctrine of coercive prevention, which means the use of credible threats of military action and preventive deployment of troops to deter fighting and gross human rights violations, as well as to compel an end to them once underway. This doctrine is not consistently applied, in part because the major powers do not necessarily agree that it is desirable and feasible in specific situations, and in part because conflicts in the realms of international powers such as Russia, China, and India are off limits to any international action other than low-key diplomacy.

A further step in the evolution of the international doctrine of engagement is the principle that, when **authority** and security have collapsed, multilateral force can be used to maintain international protectorates while civil governance is reestablished. This strategy has been employed in Cambodia in 1991, in Bosnia after 1996, in Kosovo and Timor after 1999, and the Bush administration is moving toward acceptance of international responsibility for Iraq. It also is generally recognized that coercive international intervention creates long-term responsibilities. As a practical matter, early withdrawal risks losing any gains achieved by intervention.

Conclusion

In conclusion, the five principles for managing ethno-political and other conflicts have taken firm hold in international norms and practice since 1990, but they also have their critics. Some liberal political theorists contend that individual rights but not group rights deserve international protection. Leaders of new states fear that autonomy arrangements for communal groups will weaken national identity and contribute to political fragmentation. Many in the global South reject the right of international actors to judge and intervene in their domestic affairs. Nonetheless the principles are widely asserted and acted upon. And application of the principles has contributed to a substantial improvement in the status of minorities in most world regions and a steady diminution of deadly ethno-political conflict.

Further reading

Berdal, M. and Malone, D. M. (eds) (2000) *Greed and Grievance: Economic Agendas in Civil Wars*, Boulder, CO: Lynne Rienner.

Collier, P. (2003) *Breaking the Conflict Trap: Civil War and Development Policy*, Washington, DC: World Bank and Oxford University Press.

Fearon, J. D. and Laitin, D. D. (2003) 'Ethnicity, Insurgency, and Civil War,' *American Political Science Review* 97(2) 75–90.

Ganguly, R. and Taras, R. C. (1998) *Understanding Ethnic Conflict: The International Dimension*, New York: Longman.

Gurr, T. R. (2000) *Peoples Versus States: Minorities at Risk in the New Century*, Washington, DC: US Institute of Peace Press.

Hampson, F. O. and Malone, D. M. (eds) (2002) *From Reaction to Conflict Prevention: Opportunities for the UN System*, Boulder, Colorado: Lynne Rienner.

Harff, B. and Gurr, T. R. (2004) *Ethnic Conflict in World Politics*, 2nd edn, Boulder, CO: Westview Press.

Jentleson, B. W. (2000) *Coercive Prevention: Normative, Political, and Policy Dilemmas*, Peaceworks No. 35, Washington, DC: US Institute of Peace.

Lake, D. A. and Rothchild, D. (eds) (1998) *The International Spread of Ethnic Conflict*, Princeton, NJ: Princeton University Press.

Marshall, M. G. (1999) *Third World War: System, Process, and Conflict Dynamics*, Lanham, Maryland: Rowman and Littlefield.

Marshall, M. G. and Gurr, T. R. (2003) *Peace and Conflict 2003: A Global Survey of Armed Conflicts, Self-Determination Movements, and Democracy*, College Park, Maryland: Center for International Development and Conflict Management.

Posen, B. R. (1993) 'The Security Dilemma and Ethnic Conflict,' *Survival* 35(1), 27–47.

Saideman, S. M. (2001) *The Ties that Divide: Ethnic Politics, Foreign Policy, and International Conflict*, New York: Columbia University Press.

Sislin, J. and Pearson, F. S. (2001) *Arms and Ethnic Conflict*, Lanham, Maryland: Rowman & Littlefield.

Tarrow, S. (1994) *Power in Movement: Social Movements, Collective Action, and Politics*, New York: Cambridge University Press.

Tilly, C. (1978) *From Mobilization to Revolution*, Reading, MA: Addison-Wesley.

See also: civil war; ethnic cleansing; ethnicity; war

TED ROBERT GURR

Ethnicity

Terms such as 'ethnic groups' and '**ethnic conflict**' have become common, although their meaning is ambiguous and vague. Most of the major armed conflicts in the world are internal conflicts, and most of them could plausibly be described as ethnic conflicts. In addition to violent ethnic movements, there are also many important non-violent ethnic movements, such as the Quebecois independence movement in Canada. Political turbulence in Europe has also moved issues of ethnic and national identities to the forefront of political life. At one extreme, the former Soviet Union has split into over a dozen ethnically based states, and issues of nationhood and minority problems are emerging with unprecedented force. At the other extreme, the situation seems to be the opposite, as the **nation-state**s of Western Europe are moving towards a closer economic, political and possibly cultural **integration**. But here, too, national and ethnic identities have remained important. Many people fear the loss of their national or ethnic identity as a result of European integration, whereas others welcome the possibilities for a pan-European identity to replace ethnic and national ones.

The word ethnicity is derived from the Greek *ethnos* (which in turn derived from the word *ethnikos*), meaning heathen or pagan. It was used in this sense in English from the mid-fourteenth century until the mid-nineteenth century, when it gradually began to refer to racial characteristics. In the United States, 'ethnics' came to be used as a polite term referring to Jews, Italians, Irish, and other people considered inferior to the dominant group of British descent. In everyday language, the word ethnicity still has a ring of 'minority issues' and 'race relations'. In international relations, it refers to aspects of relationships between groups that consider themselves, and are regarded by others, as being culturally distinctive.

A few words must be said about the relationship between ethnicity and race. Whereas it used to be common to divide humanity into different races, modern genetics tends not to speak of races, for two main reasons. First, there has always been so much interbreeding between human populations that it would be meaningless to talk of fixed boundaries between races. Second, the distribution of hereditary physical traits does not follow clear boundaries. In other words, there is often greater variation within a racial group than there is systematic variation between two groups.

Ethnicity can assume many forms, and since ethnic ideologies tend to stress common descent among their members, the distinction between race and ethnicity is problematic. Ideas of race may or may not form part of ethnic ideologies and their presence or absence does not seem a decisive factor in inter-ethnic relations.

The relationship between the terms ethnicity and nationality is nearly as complex as that between ethnicity and race. Like the words 'ethnic' and 'race', the word 'nation' has a long history, and has been used in a variety of different meanings in English. Like ethnic ideologies, **nationalism** stresses the cultural similarity of its adherents, and by implication, it draws boundaries against others, who thereby become outsiders. The distinguishing mark of nationalism is by definition its relationship to the state. A nationalist holds that political boundaries should be coterminous with cultural boundaries, whereas many ethnic groups do not demand command over a state. Although nationalism tends to be ethnic in character, this is not necessarily the case.

It should be noted that ethnic organization and identity, rather than being primordial phenomena radically opposed to modernity and the modern state, are frequently reactions to processes of modernization. When we talk of ethnicity, we indicate that groups and identities have developed in mutual contact rather than in isolation. But what is the nature of such groups?

The words 'ethnic group' have come to mean something like 'a people'. But what is a people? Does the population of Britain constitute a people, does it comprise several peoples, or does it form part of a Germanic, or an English-speaking, or a European people? Does this imply that ethnic groups do not necessarily have a distinctive culture? Can two groups be culturally identical and yet constitute two different ethnic groups? These are complicated questions. Contrary to a widespread commonsense view, cultural difference between two groups is not the decisive feature of ethnicity. Two distinctive groups may well have widely different languages, religious beliefs and even technologies, but that does not entail that there is an ethnic relationship between them. For ethnicity to come about, the groups must entertain ideas of each other as being culturally different from themselves. Ethnicity is essentially an aspect of a relationship, not a property of an isolated group. Conversely, some groups may seem culturally similar, yet there can be a socially highly relevant (and even volatile) interethnic relationship between them. This would be the case of the relationship between Serbs and Croats following the break-up of Yugoslavia. There may also be considerable cultural variation within a group without ethnicity. Only in so far as cultural differences are perceived as being important, and are made politically relevant, do social relationships have an ethnic element.

Ethnicity is therefore an aspect of a relationship between agents who consider themselves as being culturally distinctive from members of other groups. It can thus also be defined as a social identity (based on a contrast vis-à-vis others) characterized by metaphoric or fictive kinship.

There are four main types of ethnic groups. First, *urban ethnic minorities*. This category would include, among others, non-European immigrants in European cities and Hispanics in the United States, as well as migrants to industrial towns in Africa and elsewhere. Research on immigrants has focused on problems of adaptation, on ethnic discrimination from the host society, racism, and issues relating to identity management and cultural change. Although they have political interests, these ethnic groups rarely demand political independence or statehood, and they are usually integrated into a capitalist system of production and consumption.

The second type of ethnic group is *indigenous peoples*. This word is a blanket term for aboriginal inhabitants of a territory, who are politically relatively powerless and who are only partially integrated into the dominant nation-state. Indigenous peoples are associated with a non-industrial mode of production and a stateless political system.

Third, there are *proto-nations* or *ethno-nationalist movements*. These groups, the most famous of ethnic groups in the news media, include Kurds, Sikhs, Palestinians, and Sri Lankan Tamils, and their number is growing. By definition, these groups have political leaders who claim that they are entitled to their own nation-state and should not be ruled by others. These groups, short of having a nation-state, may be said to have more substantial characteristics in common with nations than with either urban minorities or indigenous peoples. They are always territorially based; they are differentiated according to class and educational achievement, and they are large groups. In accordance with common terminology, these groups may be described as nations without a state.

Finally, there are *ethnic groups in plural societies*. The term 'plural society' usually designates colonially created states with culturally heterogeneous populations. Typical plural societies would be Kenya, Indonesia, and Jamaica. The groups that make up the plural society, although they are compelled to participate in uniform political and economic systems, are regarded as (and regard themselves as) highly distinctive in other matters. In plural societies, secession is usually not an option, and ethnicity tends to be articulated as group competition. Most contemporary states could plausibly be considered plural ones.

Further reading

Cornell, S. and Hartmann, D. (1998) *Ethnicity and Race*, Thousand Oaks, CA: Pine Forge.

Glazer, N. and Moynihan, D. (1976) *Ethnicity: Theory and Experience*, Boston, MA: Harvard University Press

Hutchinson, J. and Smith, A. (eds) (1996) *Ethnicity*, Oxford: Oxford University Press.

See also: ethnic cleansing; ethnic conflict; multiculturalism; nationalism

MARTIN GRIFFITHS

Euro

The **European Union** (EU) introduced a single currency, the euro, in 1999. It was first introduced in financial markets and in national accounting, but euro banknotes and coins were introduced on 1 January 2002. The creation of the euro was the final step of the process of economic and monetary unification or 'Economic and Monetary Union' (EMU). It was created to strengthen the European **integration** process and was considered to be more beneficial than having fixed exchange rates. In EMU monetary policy is pursued by the European Central Bank (ECB) located in Frankfurt that sets interest rates for the entire 'euro area' that contains 320 million inhabitants. The twelve countries that together form the euro area at the time of writing are Austria, Belgium, Germany, Greece, Finland, France, Ireland, Italy, Luxembourg, the Netherlands, Portugal, and Spain. The exchange rate vis-à-vis other countries remains the responsibility of the Ministers of Economic and Financial affairs of the twelve Member States euro area. However, the day-to-day management of the exchange rate **regime** is conducted by the ECB. The value of the euro depreciated considerably in the first three years of its existence (the period 1999–2002) but returned to its introduction value in summer 2003 and has since remained more or less stable at that level. The introduction of the euro can be seen to be a success: the euro is the second most traded currency after the US dollar and before the Japanese yen.

EMU was created in the EU to enhance economic and political integration and to provide the EU with an important symbol of integration. Following the process of European integration since the 1950s, the EU and EMU were officially introduced in the 'Treaty on European Union' or 'Maastricht Treaty', signed in 1992, that entered into force in November 1993. The treaty envisaged a three-stage process to completing EMU with those countries that were ready to join the single currency. The euro would then become legal tender, replacing the national currency of those EU Member States that would have met the so-called 'convergence criteria'. These criteria referred to performance in the following areas: inflation rate, sustainability of public debt and budgetary deficits, stable exchange rates, and stable long term interest rates. Besides these criteria aspiring Member States needed to have an independent central bank.

All these provisions were put in place to secure price stability in the EU and to ensure that EMU would continue the regime that had been in place during the 1980s. This was the European Monetary System (EMS) with its exchange rate mechanism (ERM) that enabled stable exchange rates in the EU, and that was dominated by the German central bank, the *bundesbank*, which focused in particular on price stability. It has been pointed out that the **hegemony** of Germany (in particular the *bundesbank*) was replaced by an institutional structure that was closely modeled on the German institutions and monetary policy. Furthermore, back in the 1970s the founding fathers of EMU, envisaged further economic and monetary integration to go hand-in-hand with political integration. One interpretation of that aspiration would be to create an economic government to flank the newly to be created ECB. However, in the 1990s there was a fear that a new supranational economic government for the EU would restrict the independence of the ECB, and moreover, that responsibility should remain with the Council of Ministers of Economic and Financial Affairs.

Thus EMU became an asymmetrical one: it has an independent supranational monetary **authority** in the form of the ECB, whereas economic governance stays in the hands of national ministers of Finance and Economics. Rules are used to coordinate macroeconomic policies (in particular the level of budgetary deficits and public debts). Further details have been developed in the Stability and Growth Pact that envisages that Member States keep their budgetary deficits below 3 per cent of Gross Domestic Product (GDP). The SGP became controversial in 2003 when Germany and France persuaded others in the Council of Ministers of Economics and Financial affairs to suspend the rules for them.

The introduction of the euro banknotes and coins in 2002 proceeded without any major difficulty and the new currency circulated in as many as twelve Member States, many more than originally expected. Furthermore, some **microstates** (Monaco, Vatican City, and San Marino) have officially adopted the euro, whereas others have de facto accepted the euro as their currency (e.g. Andorra, Kosovo, and Montenegro).

Not all EU Member States were keen to join EMU. Denmark and the United Kingdom were skeptical from the outset and both managed to keep an official 'opt-out' from EMU since the early 1990s. Sweden joined the EU in 1995 and has also stayed outside EMU. The majority of the population in these countries prefer to keep the national currency. The UK is planning to hold a referendum in the near future, but to date polls have indicated that a majority would currently oppose joining EMU. The Member States that have recently joined the EU (May 2004) are in general positive about the prospect of joining EMU. The eight former communist (see **communism**) countries (Czech Republic, Estonia, Hungary, Latvia, Lithuania, Poland, Slovakia, and Slovenia) and the two Mediterranean states (Cyprus and

Malta), will need to meet the convergence criteria in order to qualify to join. However it seems that on the whole these countries are looking forward to the prospect of adopting the single currency. They see the euro as a token that symbolizes importantly their full membership of the EU.

Many economists and political scientists are puzzled that such an important instrument and symbol of national **sovereignty** was abandoned seemingly without difficulty. Various theoretical schools of thought have offered explanations, ranging from **realism** (the strongest and largest countries wanted it, thus it happened), to institutionalism (EMU was effectively the institutionalization of an exchange rate **regime**), to **constructivism** (EMU institutionalized a certain neoliberal paradigm (see **neoliberalism**) with principles such as sound money and stable finances, brought to the fore by an **epistemic community**, whilst simultaneously offering an important symbol of European unity) to **functionalism** (arguing that policies would be more effective if pursued centrally and by technocrats rather than politicians). Others have stressed the importance of the general environment of **globalization** and **global governance** that envisages that national Member States no longer have the ambition to have all policies be pursued all the time at the national level, when they effectively can be pursued at the supranational level without giving up too much de facto sovereignty (already lost by accepting to be in the ERM of the EMS and being part of the EU). Despite the many convincing individual analyses of the EMU process, there is no one convincing theory that is best able to explain the outcome.

The euro is an important symbol and success story of European integration. It is also an interesting international relations phenomenon. Why did so many governments of developed **nation-state**s give up monetary sovereignty in one part of the world (Europe) whereas in other parts of the world this sovereignty is eagerly preserved? Why are some EU Member States not eager to join EMU whilst the majority of them are enthusiastic? These are questions that will be addressed by the researchers of the future.

Further reading

Baldwin, R., Bertola, G. and Seabright, P. (eds) (2003) *EMU: Assessing the Impact of the Euro*, Oxford: Blackwell.

Dyson, K. and Featherstone, K. (1999) *The Road to Maastricht: Negotiating Economic and Monetary Union*, Oxford: Oxford University Press.

Gros, D. and Thygesen, N. (1999) *European Monetary Integration: From the European Monetary System to Economic and Monetary Union*, 2nd edition, New York: Longman.

Jones, E. (2002) *The Politics of Economic and Monetary Union: Integration and Idiosyncrasy*, Lanham: Rowman and Littlefield.

Verdun, A. (ed.) (2002) *The Euro: European Integration Theory and Economic and Monetary Union*, Lanham: Rowman and Littlefield.

See also: European Union; integration

AMY VERDUN

European Common Security and Defense Policy (CESDP)

The European Common Security and Defense Policy (CESDP) refers to a series of initiatives taken since 1998 to give the **European Union** (EU) a capacity for autonomous military action. Since 1998, EU Member States have undertaken to strengthen the Union's Common Foreign and Security Policy (CFSP) by developing a common policy on **security** and defense within the overall framework of CFSP. The emphasis on developing a military profile for the Union signifies a fundamental shift away from the civilian nature of the EU and from its institutional relationship with the **North Atlantic Treaty Alliance** (NATO). However, persistent shortfalls in capabilities and disagreement over fundamental policy objectives leaves doubt as to whether the EU will be able to marshal the military capacity and political will to deliver a security and defense policy that is independent from NATO in the foreseeable future.

The Member States of the EU committed themselves to a common foreign, security and defense policy in the wake of the **cold war**. In the early post-cold war years, several pressures combined to promote the idea of a stronger security role for the EU. First, there was increasing uncertainty about US military involvement in Europe. With the cold war over, Europe became less strategically relevant to the United States. A European security dimension would serve as 'insurance' in case America was to disengage. Another motivation was to strengthen the European pillar of NATO. During the 1990s, Washington began to question why, in a post-cold war world, American taxpayers should continue to underwrite European security. At the same time, growing gaps between US and European military capabilities made allied defense cooperation and interoperability increasingly difficult. These problems came into sharp focus during the 1999 Kosovo air campaign, which revealed stark disparities in force capabilities between America and its European allies.

Due to these pressures, a gradual consensus emerged among European governments that they must assume greater responsibility in military affairs. The first step was taken with the 1992 Maastricht Treaty, which substituted CFSP for the system of 'European Political Cooperation' (EPC) which had served since 1970 to coordinate the actions of European foreign ministries. CFSP replaced the informal and strictly intergovernmental EPC with a new system that involved the EU's central institutions – including the Commission, the European Council and the Council of Ministers – in the elaboration and implementation of foreign policy. As defined at Maastricht, CFSP would eventually cover all questions related to the security of the Union, including the framing of a common defense policy. Since then, there has been a growing focus on mustering military capabilities for the Union. The initial decision to launch CESDP was taken in December 1998 during a summit meeting in St. Malo, where French President Jacques Chirac and British Prime Minister Tony Blair agreed to provide the EU with a capacity for autonomous action, backed up by credible military forces in order to respond to international crises. The objective of 'autonomous forces' took concrete form in December 1999 with the formulation of a military 'Headline Goal', which stated that, by 2003, the Union should be able to deploy 60,000 soldiers within 60 days and to sustain them for one year as part of a European Rapid Reaction Force (RRF). To give political and strategic guidance to the RRF, a new decision making apparatus was created within the European Council, consisting of a Political and Security Committee, a Military Committee and a Military Staff. Together with the prior creation of the post of 'High Representative' of CFSP, this gave an institutional presence to EU security policy.

Since 1999, the process of force generation has progressed steadily. A Capabilities Commitment Conference in

November 2000 allowed EU Member States to commit forces to the RRF. Based on these forces, the RRF was declared operational in December 2001, and in January 2003 the EU took over the UN police mission in Bosnia-Herzegovina as its first mission under CESDP (see **United Nations**). This was followed by the dispatch of a stabilization force to Macedonia in March 2003 and by a peacekeeping mission to the Congo in June 2003.

Despite these successes, however, the EU faces some major hurdles before it can emerge as a credible actor in the security and defense field. First, critics charge that CESDP lacks clear political objectives and a strategic concept that assigns priority to different policy goals. The basic objectives of CESDP are defined by the so-called Petersberg Declaration. Adopted by the EU in 1998 it defines the range of operations that the EU could undertake in support of the UN or the **Organization for Security and Cooperation in Europe** (OSCE), specifically humanitarian and rescue missions, **peacekeeping** and peacemaking operations. To these objectives has been added the goal of countering terrorist threats. But beyond these open-ended aims, questions of military scale and ambition, geographical reach and the priority conferred on different policy areas remain poorly defined. This lack of strategic direction is compounded by an institutional framework that is ill suited to the kind of rapid and resolute decision making favored by most military organizations. In particular, the EU's tradition for consensus in decision making poses an obstacle to decisive action.

CESDP also lacks resources. When the RRF was declared operational in 2001, significant capability shortfalls remained in areas such as air-to-air refueling, attack helicopters, early warning systems, special operations forces, strategic airlift and surveillance. Some of these gaps have been filled but many remain. Gaps in capabilities not only testify to a lack of political will but also reflect budgetary constraints. In the 1990s, European defense budgets have come under pressure due to demands for a 'peace dividend'. Faced with uncertain economic growth prospects and the fiscal constraints imposed by Economic and Monetary Union, defense budgets are likely to come under increasing strain in the future. In such circumstances it is uncertain whether EU members will be prepared to make the requisite investments to sustain an autonomous military capacity.

However, the greatest obstacle to a potent European security and defense policy remains the enduring conflict over the basic purpose of CESDP, in particular its relationship to NATO. The quest for autonomous capabilities has triggered a vigorous debate over the future of the transatlantic relationship. Does European security cooperation present an alternative to the Atlantic Alliance or is CESDP mainly a vehicle for strengthening the European pillar of NATO and securing fair burden sharing? So far, EU members appear split on this question. One group, led by Britain, has argued that CESDP must reinforce the European pillar of NATO and has opposed operational independence for the EU, while another group, led by France, has fought to eliminate the EU's dependence on NATO in crisis management operations. Until these contrasting views are reconciled, the EU may find it difficult to achieve the political unity necessary to become a credible security actor.

CESDP is today a reality. With the dispatch of policing and peacekeeping missions in Bosnia, Macedonia and the Congo, the EU has taken on an explicit security role. However, continued disagreement over finance and decision-making, and persistent ambiguities over the relationship to NATO means that the EU's operational capabilities are likely to remain limited in the medium future. A further obstacle looms once eastern enlargement brings the number of EU Member States to twenty-five, thereby adding to the complexity of decision-making. Given these hurdles, the success of CESDP remains uncertain.

Further reading

Andréani, G., Bertram, C. and Grant, C. (2001) *Europe's Military Revolution*, London: Centre for European Reform.

Hill, C. and Smith, K. (2000) *European Foreign Policy: Key Documents,* London: Routledge.

Hoffmann, S. (2000) 'Towards a Common European Foreign and Security Policy' *Journal of Common Market Studies* 38(2), 189–98.

Nuttall, S. J. (2000) *European Foreign Policy*, Oxford: Oxford University Press.

See also: common security; European Union; North Atlantic Treaty Organization; security community

METTE EILSTRUP SANGIOVANNI

European Union (EU)

A unique assemblage of **nation-state**s and institutions that, though its origins as an idea date back further, had its substantive beginnings in the European Coal and Steel Community (ECSC), founded in 1951, and the European Economic Community (EEC) and European Atomic Community (Euratom), established by the Rome Treaties of 1957. A gradual extension of policy and legal competences, and a steady growth in membership, marked an evolution of the combined communities and states into the European Union (EU), which became an official designation in 1993. On 1 May 2004, ten states, most of them from Central and Eastern Europe (CEE), acceded to the EU and increased the membership to twenty-five. This was the biggest of several enlargements since the original six (France, West Germany, Belgium, the Netherlands, Luxembourg, and Italy) initiated the project.

In historical perspective half a century of very successful existence has been accompanied by extensive discussion about the character and limits of **integration**, how far the membership might extend, and even what the EU actually is. Some observers view it as primarily a legal jurisdiction, others consider it a political arrangement, a genuine economic and social union, or a **free trade** zone.

Most scholars of the EU interpret its inception as a response to recurring conflict among European states, and most especially between France and Germany. Jean Monnet, a French economic planner, and Robert Schuman, French foreign minister, believed that the harmonization of national policies and resources for long term collective benefit would present a clear and justifiable alternative to economic rivalry and **war**. The Schuman Plan was designed to merge French and German coal and steel making capacities as the initial step to this end and instigated the ECSC. Along with Konrad Adenauer, the first chancellor of the Federal Republic of Germany (FRG), and the Belgian and Italian statesmen, Paul-Henri Spaak and Alcide de Gasperi, Monnet and Schuman were leading lights in the 'hagiography' of European integration. These pioneers considered that the promotion of strong institutions would lead to a 'supranational' form of governance, and, they hoped, lead to a European federation, as Schuman declared on 9 May 1950 (later 'Europe Day'). Neo-functionalist theorists saw integration as an incremental and bureaucratic process – the '*méthode Monnet*' – through which **national interests** would be enmeshed and potential conflict diluted. This approach generated the concept of 'spillover', which referred to the acquirement of ever increasing levels and areas of authority by institutions and a corresponding diminution in the **sovereign power** and influence of states. Others argued that integration was undertaken by states with the deliberate intention of revitalizing their own economies and international status. 'Europe' was a means by which to 'rescue' the nation-state. Another view subordinated intra-West European affairs to encompassing international circumstances. It impressed the role of American military protection and political, technical and economic assistance. Through Marshall Plan aid, a dominating presence in the **North Atlantic Treaty Organization** (NATO), and its espousal of democracy, the United States chaperoned European integration. Others, often associated with the constructivist school (see **constructivism**), stress a 'specific institutional environment', and correlated norms, which qualitatively differentiates the EU from other forms of international interaction. This, they argue, countermands realist theories emphasizing state power, independent national interests, and **security** concerns in global politics.

Evolution

Incremental progress in integration has been punctuated by significant forward steps and by major setbacks. The launching of the ECSC was followed by the failure of the European Defence Community in 1954. The entire undertaking was again shaken by the so-called 'empty chair' **crisis** in 1965. The 'Luxembourg Compromise' that resolved the crisis impressed the rule of unanimity in

voting for another two decades. Both episodes were characterized by French resistance, most decisively that of President Charles de Gaulle, to any supranational authority. Despite intermittent attempts at revitalization, like the Colombo Plan of 1981, a period of 'Eurosclerosis' in the 1970s and early 1980s then threatened another indefinite stagnation.

Following a u-turn in economic policy by the government of François Mitterrand in 1983, negotiations led by France, the FRG, and the United Kingdom (UK), resulted in the Single European Act (SEA), signed in 1986. Although she often opposed their preferences, the British Prime Minister, Margaret Thatcher, was, along with Mitterrand and German Chancellor Helmut Kohl, a central figure in the negotiations leading to the signing of the SEA. It focused on extensive economic liberalization, culminating in the single internal market introduced on 1 January 1993. The SEA also introduced Qualified Majority Voting (QMV) and other political features that went unnoticed or underestimated by Mrs Thatcher. QMV meant that the principle of unanimity that had been reinforced by the Luxembourg Compromise, was, in certain areas and instances, now superseded. A member state, or several, could potentially be overruled by agreement among a majority of others.

The relationship between institutions, including that of the Council of Ministers and the European Parliament (EP), which gained rights of co-decision, also changed. Soon after the SEA came into force, preparations for Economic and Monetary Union (EMU) were formally initiated. Its chief architect was the then president of the European Commission, Jacques Delors, one of the most influential figures in the history of European integration. The 1988 Delors plan aimed at the creation of a common currency, which would replace those of participating states, and the merger of national monetary policies under the control of a European Central Bank (ECB).

In 1989–90 the sudden collapse of communist regimes in CEE (see **communism**) and the emergence of German reunification as imminent activated a sweeping revision of world politics. These upheavals upset the style and conventional summitry of the insulated West European system. Contrasting with the 'Europhoria' that accompanied the fall of the Berlin Wall and the end of the **cold war**, there were alarmist reactions in some capitals, above all in Paris, London and Warsaw. Prominent figures, including Thatcher and Mitterrand, were apprehensive about a sovereign united Germany of 80 million people. Their concerns were outweighed by the accord between George Bush Snr, Mikhail Gorbachev and Kohl. Mitterrand eventually perceived that the only viable option was to contain the enlarged Germany within a strengthened European framework. In April 1990 he and Kohl presented a letter to the then Irish presidency of the European Council, proposing an intergovernmental conference (IGC) on political union to complement that already projected for EMU. The Mitterrand–Kohl partnership, and Europe itself, were recast and moved into a new phase.

Although integration was initially concentrated on economic matters, other fields came to command more attention. European Political Cooperation (EPC) was introduced in 1970 to develop positions in non-economic external affairs. As diverse foreign, defense and **security** issues emerged in the 1990s, the reluctance or incapacity of some member states to cooperate effectively contributed to several intra-European crises, most starkly over Yugoslavia. New imperatives were rushed onto an already packed agenda as the Soviet Union (despite attempts to preserve it) began to disintegrate. Almost simultaneous to the Maastricht summit of December 1991, when the text for a Treaty on European Union (TEU) was first approved, the Soviet Union expired.

As the nascent EU had to contend with a chaotic, humbled Russia and several volatile ex-Soviet republics, the prospect, or necessity, of a major geographic extension to include CEE, sooner rather than later, appeared. In February 1992 the TEU was signed. The treaty's three-pillar structure enabled an innovative division of authority. The first pillar was one of community (supranational) competence, consisting of regulatory policy areas with decision making by QMV. The second pillar transformed EPC into the Common Foreign and Security Policy (CFSP). Both the CFSP and the third pillar, Justice and Home Affairs (JHA), were intergovernmental, requiring unanimity among member states. The policy areas assigned to pillars two and three were now incorporated in a treaty-based framework.

The TEU did not come into effect until November 1993. The long ratification period coincided with turbulence and recession in several major European economies. As the pound sterling came under pressure from speculators in 1992, the UK left the European Exchange-Rate Mechanism (ERM) that was intended to maintain equilibrium among national currencies. The French Franc was also attacked on currency markets, which had the effect of severely straining Franco-German relations. The German government's room for manoeuvre was restricted as powers bestowed upon the constitutionally independent *Bundesbank* gave it control over German monetary policy (and, de facto, everybody else's). Exchange-rate volatility, economic downturn, high unemployment, and vocal Euroskepticism meant that the TEU was barely passed in the French referendum of September 1992. In Denmark, the treaty was rejected in the country's first referendum. After changes tailored to the Danish context were introduced it was accepted in a second referendum the following year.

Meanwhile, before any admissions of Central and Eastern European countries (CEECs) to the EU could occur, the region had to be stabilized and an enormous reform program implemented. 'Europe Agreements', comprising special assistance packages, were instigated, first with Poland and Hungary. At the Copenhagen summit in 1993 a set of pre-requisites for any state wishing to join the EU (they also pertained to those presently in it) were proclaimed. The 'Copenhagen Criteria' included: a democratic political order, the rule of law, a functioning market economy, the capacity to withstand competition, and the upholding of **human rights** and protection of minorities. Aspirants also had to comply with the *acquis communautaire*, the legal basis of the union, divided into 31 chapters corresponding to various policy areas and other requirements.

Opening the possibility of EU membership for CEECs added the long-term task of 'widening' to the existing goal of 'deepening' integration in the west. The two objectives were not always compatible and it would be a protracted and difficult process. Although Sweden, Finland, and Austria joined the EU without disruption in 1995, the realization that a large scale expansion to include most of CEE was inevitable precipitated a need for extensive reform of institutions, procedures, policies and budgets. In 1996, with some member states especially conscious of the internal situations in CEE associates, of potential geopolitical developments, and of migration pressures, another IGC was launched to tackle the present and approaching challenges.

A rapid expansion of new demands and threats within the responsibility spheres of the CFSP or JHA pillars, or even straddling both, further increased the pressure for effective coordination and response. Many argued that this necessitated the transfer of more authority to supranational decision making structures. At the Amsterdam summit of June 1997, some tasks formerly covered by intergovernmental cooperation, prominently immigration and asylum policy, and visa administration, were shifted to the 'community pillar'. Europol, the agency for cooperation among police forces was strengthened, though ultimate authority remained with the states. *Ipso facto*, a central feature of a united Europe is the dissolution, or at least irrelevance, of internal borders. Already in 1985 the Schengen Agreement had, on paper, introduced the first phase of a plan to make them redundant. The UK and Ireland were not parties to this arrangement and maintained controls on their national borders, though they later joined the Schengen Information System (SIS). For the rest of the EU (and Norway and Iceland, which were not members) Schengen was incorporated into the *acquis*, and the abolition of passport controls was completed by 2001.

Improving performance and capability in foreign, security and defense policy was also targeted, motivated by disasters experienced in the EU's backyard, the Balkans. The Amsterdam Treaty, in force from May 1999, prised ajar the door to areas over which the states had hitherto asserted their undivided **sovereignty**. While the adoption of broad 'Common Strategies' for the CFSP required unanimity, the implementation of more specific measures – 'Common Positions' or 'Joint Actions' – under the auspices of such a strategy could, theoretically, occur against the wishes and vote of one or more member states. Given the sensitivity of all states about foreign policy interests, and to the possibility of being outvoted, the likelihood of such a decision was minimal. As an insurance, the right of veto (in practice a continuance of the Luxembourg Compromise) remained. To strengthen the EU's profile in this field, the Amsterdam Treaty also created the post of a 'High Representative for Foreign and Security Policy', to be ensconced in the (intergovernmental) Council as its Secretary-General. In 1999 the former NATO Secretary General, Javier Solana, was appointed (see **North Atlantic Treaty Alliance**).

In 1998 the EU opened entry negotiations with Cyprus, the Czech Republic Estonia, Hungary, Poland, and Slovenia. These were referred to as the 'Luxembourg Group'. In 2000 negotiations began with the 'Helsinki Group' of Bulgaria, Latvia, Lithuania, Malta, Rumania, and the Slovak Republic. Turkey acquired candidate status. In March 1999, after intense and sometimes acrimonious bargaining, the European Council meeting in Berlin approved the Commission's 'Agenda 2000' program. It was chiefly concerned with reforming the **Common Agricultural Policy** (CAP), regional policy (structural and cohesion funds), financing, and voting procedures. Much of this was motivated by the desire of net payers to the EU budget, led by Germany and including the Netherlands and the UK, to restrict their net payments in light of the forthcoming enlargement. This came into sharp conflict with the demands of entrants-in-waiting, notably Poland, for the same eligibility in agricultural or structural disbursements as current members, and several of the latter, prominently Spain, who were net receivers from the budget. Gruelling distributional battles were to become a feature of the enlargement process.

Another IGC began in February 2000 and concluded with the Nice summit of December that year. Although it also proclaimed a EU 'Charter of Fundamental Rights', the IGC's primary intention was to deal with the so-called 'leftovers' of Amsterdam: the composition and size of the Commission; voting arrangements in the Council; and possibilities for the extension of QMV. In the first instance the Commission was limited to one representative per state from 2005 until the EU increases to 27 members. Thereafter the total complement of commissioners will be reduced and a rotation system introduced. While this streamlines the Commission, it also affirms its weakening position *vis-à-vis* the states. In the second case, voting was made more, not less, complicated. Now 71 per cent of Council votes, with the approval of over half the member states, and 62 per cent of the total EU population, were required for a decision under QMV terms.

As a result the potential permutations of blocking minorities increased. Some smaller and medium-sized states considered that a mere 'double majority' – over 50 per cent of states and 60 per cent of the total EU population – would shift the power balance too far in favor of the larger ones. Voting weight was bound with the third area of focus, the extension of QMV. While a number of provisions were placed in this category, and the CFSP opened to 'enhanced cooperation' (whereby a quorum of eight states could pursue an agreed initiative), taxation, and control over structural funds, were subject to unanimity, as was any form of military cooperation. Social policy remained largely a national domain. For those urging the practical application of measures that would enable the EU to deal with burgeoning challenges, Nice provided a partial solution at best. Reform that would enable cohesive decision-making in a Union of twenty-seven or more states was insufficient. As many critical observers perceived it, outcomes were determined by short-term compromises, rather than a shared and demonstrable strategic vision. This (again) raised perennial questions of the communal **identity**, if there was one, that underpinned the Union, and where, if anywhere, it was headed. Thus while some movement in the direction of an integrated polity and expanded legal and political space could be noted, so too could a renationalizing in several policy fields, in financial matters, and the determination of member states to retain control over what they still regarded as 'vital national interests'. By most accounts the rancorous debates at Nice both confirmed and encouraged these attitudes.

Concurrent to the Amsterdam and Nice IGCs, and the enlargement preparations, progress was made in EMU. Replacing the European Currency Unit (ECU), which had served as an antecedent accounting device based on a 'basket' of European currencies, the **euro** was introduced in non-cash form in 1999. Under strong German pressure the EMU convergence criteria were oriented to maintaining a hard currency and guaranteeing price stability. Each participating national currency had a fixed value relative to the Euro. €1 was now equivalent to 1.955 Deutsche Marks, 6.559 French Francs and 1,936 Italian Lire. On 1 January 2002, despite the protests and other obstacles, the Euro was introduced as cash. National banknotes and coins remained in use for some months before being phased out of circulation. After a difficult start, when it diminished appreciably in value against the $US and some other major currencies, the Euro recovered and later strengthened to well over parity with the dollar. The UK, Denmark, and Sweden, where a 2003 referendum on joining

returned a negative vote, remained out of the Eurozone. All things considered, the Euro's induction and early years, at least, were a success. However, if the monetary component of EMU could be evaluated as positive, the economic part began to waver as debt and deficit levels increased over the levels specified in the criteria. Its main promoters, Germany and France, transgressed the 'stability pact' of 1997 that was intended to reinforce adherence. Other states did likewise. Some, such as Italy and Belgium, had experienced debt-to-GDP ratios of over 100 per cent since EMU was introduced and, if the criteria had been strictly applied, could not have joined.

The 'motor' – and the rest

From its beginnings, France and Germany provided the main impetus to European integration. The rest, de Gaulle reportedly said, 'don't matter'. Advancement involved a bilateral initiative or ongoing mutual interest of these two, interrupted by occasional cool spells. A common interpretation of the 'French position' is that Europe was employed as a means for France to acquire and maintain international influence and prestige; to bind Germany institutionally; counter US supremacy; and extract national benefit from 'community' policies.

The 'German position' is usually explained as a need for international rehabilitation after 1945; the representation of national interests in European form; of security against its own waywardness or isolation; and privileged access to markets for German goods. This dyad inspired many 'odd couple' analogies. Tensions set in from November 1989, and, despite their accomplishments, were sustained into the next century. The catalyst for a revival of the partnership was the mounting international crisis over Iraq in 2002.

A more or less shared Franco-German standpoint on the future of European integration is often contrasted with 'the British position', one of being an 'awkward partner'. The UK is regarded as favoring open markets and investment, and suspected, in some quarters, as desiring little more than a European free trade zone. It has also been viewed as a Trojan horse of the Americans, or as playing continental states off against each other as it traditionally has done. Nonetheless the EU needs the UK for, among other reasons, its expertise in foreign affairs, its military capability, the role of the City of London as a financial center, and its special global connections. At certain junctures, or in particular policy fields, the UK has drawn closer to one or other engine of the Franco-German 'motor', and, rather than a permanent dichotomy of these two versus the skeptical British, a triangular politics of the 'big three' could be construed.

The Anglo-French defense initiative at St Malo in 1998 was one instance, appealing, as it may have, to French aspirations for developing an independent 'military power Europe'. French aversions to a diminution of the nation-state and a corresponding ascendancy in supranational controls are in alignment with prevalent British attitudes. Conversely, the UK is more disposed to the FRG's greater support for free markets.

Of the other states, Ireland has proved one of the EU's outstanding successes, benefiting enormously from membership. In less than a generation it moved from near the lower end of the then EEC's per capita income scale to be among the richer member states. Three former dictatorships, Greece, Spain, and Portugal, which all joined in the 1980s, transformed their political systems, societies and economies. They were greatly assisted by the **Common Agricultural Policy** (CAP) and structural funding. For the CEECs, their accession (with Romania and Bulgaria due in 2007, which will raise the total EU population to almost 500 million) was the institutional confirmation of a 'return to Europe' and overcame the artificial division of the cold war. Only then could the continent become a 'space of freedom, security and justice'. During the pre-accession phase Poland, especially, vigorously pursued its preferences and indicated that as a member state it would continue to do so. For Poland and the Czech Republic, in particular, EU accession was contemporaneous to bilateral reconciliation with reunified Germany. Like much else that had been subordinated to the macro-exigencies of the cold war, eastern enlargement opened several Pandora's boxes; some containing unresolved issues dating back to the World War Two.

Institutions

The principal institutions of the EU are the European Council, which is the regular congress (around every three months) of the Heads of State and Government. The European Council is not a declared 'organ of the EU', though the TEU specifies its purpose as providing 'the Union with the necessary impetus for its development' and defining 'the general political guidelines'. In practice it is the premier forum for states to present positions, assert their interests, and debate differences. Although legally distinct, in day-to-day business this role is adopted by the Council of Ministers, which became the Council of the European Union in 1993. In it national officials represent the states in different policy areas, for example, through regular meetings of the finance, transport, fisheries, or agriculture ministers. The Council has a rotating presidency, with a different member state taking over the role every six months. Changes were proposed that would extend the term to two and a half years.

Intergovernmental theorists maintain that the Council is the most significant of the EU institutions. The European Commission is a quasi-executive that has the sole right of initiative to present draft legislation in community policy fields. If the Council accepts a Commission proposal, it (the Commission) then undertakes tasks of practical implementation. The Commission is the most supranational of EU institutions. Despite its formal prerogatives and designated duties, since its halcyon days under Delors the Commission has lost power to the states. In 1999, following the publication of a report that found it had engaged in 'fraud, mismanagement and nepotism', the entire Jacques Santer-led Commission, resigned. Correspondingly, the EP, which had threatened the Commission's dismissal, has grown in stature. First directly elected in 1979, it has moved beyond rights of consultation or co-decision, to accruing various powers of assent. It has also enlarged numerically, reaching 732 members with the accession of the 2004 entrants. Another institution that has increased in importance commensurate to the expanding body of community law is the European Court of Justice (ECJ). The ECJ is responsible for ensuring the observance of community law in the member states. In contexts established by the treaties it is superordinate to national courts. One judge from each member state is appointed to the ECJ. The Court of Auditors scrutinizes the EU's financial administration, including all aspects of revenue and expenditure. One official per member state is appointed. There is also a Committee of Permanent Representatives,

whose main tasks are to prepare regular summits of the European Council, as well as IGC's and any extraordinary meetings. The Committee of the Regions is an 'organ of the EU', introduced by the TEU in 1993. It monitors the 'subsidiarity' principle of having control reside at local or regional levels where possible. An Economic and Social Committee consults with the Commission and representing views from employee, employer, consumer, and other interest groups.

Quo vadis?

The EU is more than an international organization and not (yet) a state. It is officially represented in over 120 countries by delegations with functions similar to those of national embassies, and in major international organizations such as the **United Nations** (UN) and **World Trade Organization** (WTO). Reciprocally, the EU receives ambassadors. In the course of its evolution the EU has demonstrated that it has a magnetic attraction for poorer European states. The larger it grows, the more it is shown to be a concordance and compromise system under ever increasing strain. Persisting differences in preferences and broader conceptions of what the EU is or should be have caused it to falter.

This is related to another recurring theme: that of the EU's end state. Few have definitively explained what the terminus shall be or how it will be achieved. One notable exception is the German Foreign Minister, Joschka Fischer. Fifty years after Schuman, Fischer has advocated the formation of a European federation, now with extensive powers conferred on the EP. Fischer has many opponents, however. Skeptical commentators have disparaged the EU as a process without a goal, bureaucratic and wasteful, illusionary and incapable of dealing with major challenges and threats. For its supporters, the EU is the premier example of 'multi-level governance' or complex **multilateralism**: a 'civilian power' that impresses the primacy of the rule of law, upholds **human rights**, is the world's largest **foreign aid** donor, and has been crucial in the generation of prosperity for Europe's citizens. Its bureaucracy is small, they note, compared to those of its member states. Moreover, states alone are incapable of coping with many contemporary developments. Psychological aspects, it seems, are very important to the EU's internal solidarity and dynamics, as the continent is often swayed to either optimism or pessimism regarding its collective future.

Another difficulty facing the EU is its alleged **democratic deficit**, manifested chiefly in the unelected Commission, and the indirectly (via national elections) elected Council, which often meets and reaches decisions in secret. The directly elected EP is, despite an expansion in its rights and responsibilities, less powerful than the Council. It also has low turnout figures for its elections with potential voters perceiving it as unimportant. Seeking to prevent centralization and lack of transparency, some politicians have called for a clear division of competences between the European, national, and sub-national levels, and the fortification of subsidiarity. At the Laeken summit in December 2001 another venture got underway with a declaration to inaugurate a 'Convention on the Future of Europe'. It was chaired by former French President, Valéry Giscard d'Estaing, and charged with preparing a proposal for a Treaty Establishing a Constitution for Europe. This was presented in June 2003 and incorporated variations on the voting procedures that had been rejected at Nice. The member states failed to reach agreement on the draft constitution in

December 2003. The voting issue again ended in impasse and resulted in many commentators depicting the summit as a 'debacle'.

In the foreign and security policy sphere, the Kosovo conflict of 1999 again demonstrated a dependence of the EU on the United States, even if it was also the locus for significant developments, like Germany's first post-1945 military participation in a 'hot war' – and without a UN mandate. Worsening relations between some EU states and the United States, intensifying over Iraq but present in other fields before and after this conflict, is a major concern. In contrast to some other member states, the CEECs saw their interests as contingent on a strong American interest in European affairs, and EU enlargement closely paralleled that of NATO. In the early twenty-first century, global insecurity is a problem that neither the EU, nor individual states, can evade. An unwillingness or inability on the part of the collective EU to sufficiently provide for its own security and defense invokes a dilemma: pacifist societies (see **pacifism**) and political cultures averse to military expenditure and involvements could mean that threats are inadequately addressed. The menace of **terrorism** may impel more integrated counter-measures. Shortly after the Madrid train bombing in 2004, the establishment of an EU office for domestic security, charged with coordinating the relevant agencies of member states, was one response to the demand for concerted action.

Turkey presents another huge challenge for the EU, which has officially opened negotiations on Turkish membership. Turkey's accession would intensify pressure on already stretched budgets. Besides economic factors, some arguments focusing on political (democratic) credentials and cultural suitability were made against Turkey's entry. If

Turkey was admitted, or negotiations on its entry began, it would strengthen the *prima facie* case of states such as Ukraine, Moldova and Russia to join on the grounds that any European state may apply to join the EU. Bearing the concept of 'common values' in mind, the question 'are the Balkans European?' might also be tested.

European integration has been impelled by a history of conflict and seismic geopolitical changes. It was also central to the creation and sustaining of prosperity, albeit under the conditions of **bipolarity**. Although it has become a global economic power, foremost in trade matters, there are some examples in the economic domain where the EU is less than united; among them taxation, social welfare payments, and adoption of the Euro. One of the most contentious issues, internal and external to the EU, is the CAP. In the 1970s over 70 per cent of the community budget was expended on agricultural subsidies and related measures. It took almost thirty years to reduce the figure to around 50 per cent. Structural and cohesion funds are another focus of intense political controversy. Both policy areas were again tested by the 2004/2007 enlargement. More broadly, global economic forces imperil the 'European social model' and what was largely a west European invention, the welfare state. Europe is also ageing. In Italy and the FRG about 18 per cent of people are 65 or older, in France 16.5 per cent. The emergence of a young entrepreneurial class in the new member states could provide an impetus to enliven the EU, yet the overall rise in pension claimants relative to workers is a huge predicament.

Partly to encourage reflection on more than financial questions, there have been many appeals to the common spiritual, religious, and intellectual ancestry of Europe. This, it was hoped, would encourage feelings of identification and belonging that the EU has struggled to inspire. Yet the effect of these shared origins has been diluted by immigration, new economic and technological developments, lifestyle changes, and the continued potency of diverse national identities. It might be asked what overwhelming influence a Greco-Roman and Christian past exerts on the EU's present and future. The EU has been the world's most successful experiment in regional integration, though the project is not complete. Notwithstanding its exceptional achievements, the challenges ahead may be as immense as any in the past.

Further reading

Van den Boer, P., Bugge P. and Wæver, O. (1995) *The History of the Idea of Europe*, London: Routledge.

Judt, T. (1996) *A Grand Illusion*, London: Penguin.

Mayhew, A. (1998) *Recreating Europe: The European Union's Policy Towards Central and Eastern Europe*, Cambridge: Cambridge University Press.

McCormick, J. (2002) *Understanding the European Union*, Basingstoke: Palgrave.

Milward, A. (2000) *The European Rescue of the Nation State*, 2nd edn, London: Routledge.

Moravcsik, A. (1998) *The Choice for Europe*, Ithaca, NY: Cornell University Press.

Schimmelfennig, F. (2003) *The EU, NATO and the Integration of Europe: Rules and Rhetoric*, Cambridge: Cambridge University Press.

See also: Common Agricultural Policy; cold war; Euro; European Common Security and Defense Policy; integration; North Atlantic Treaty Organization; Organization for Security and Cooperation in Europe; regionalism; sovereignty

STEVE WOOD

Extraterritoriality

In **international law**, extraterritoriality refers to instances in which the jurisdiction and laws of one sovereign state extend over the territory of another, usually under a treaty granting such rights. In general, extraterritorial jurisdiction is most frequently exercised by consuls and diplomats in specific countries who, in addition to their ordinary consular duties, are vested with judicial powers. The term is also sometimes defined as the immunity from the laws of a state enjoyed by diplomatic representatives of other states. Such immunity has often been extended to armies in permitted transit and to warships. Extraterritorial rights may be surrendered by treaty, abolished by the annexation of the country granting extraterritorial rights to a country not granting such rights, or abolished by voluntary renunciation on the part of the state enjoying such rights.

Extraterritoriality is rooted in the concept of sovereignty, if only because it is traditionally considered a violation of it. In **international law**, sovereignty refers to a state's claim of exclusive jurisdiction over individuals or activities within its borders. Extraterritoriality therefore can be defined as a state's claim of jurisdiction over individuals or activities beyond its borders.

Extraterritorial claims can be differentiated into four types. They can be *regional* (applying to individuals or activities within a specific area outside the territory of the state), *global* (applying to individuals or activities regardless of their location outside the territory of the state), *exclusive* (no other actor has jurisdiction over the individual or activity) or *shared* (other actors may have some jurisdiction as well).

Beginning in the late eighteenth century and continuing well into the twentieth century, western states claimed at least partial extraterritorial jurisdiction over their citizens in countries in Africa, Asia, the Middle East, and the Pacific. They believed that 'uncivilized' countries were not subject to the Christian law of nations and therefore were not sovereign. Christian states had a right and an obligation to protect their citizens in non-sovereign, non-Christian states. The development of the principle of **self-determination** made this conception of sovereignty increasingly untenable. Self-determination held that sovereignty was not a privilege of civilized states but a right of all states. In some cases, extraterritorial claims were renounced when countries became 'civilized'. In other cases, the West gave up its claims based purely on the right of self-determination. Today, regional extraterritoriality is dead. Legal reform in the affected countries and the rise of the principle of self-determination killed it. Shortly after the end of World War Two, the principle of sovereignty based on exclusive territorial jurisdiction was extended to all countries, Christian and non-Christian.

It should be noted that the arrogance of many Europeans in equating civilization with the particular civilization of Europe was no less than that of the Chinese. Nor was the European belief that their religion was the one true faith any less dogmatic than that of the Muslim peoples with whom they came into contact. The standard of civilization on which the Europeans insisted did indeed lead to unjust treatment. However, the demand of Asian and African peoples for equality of rights in international law was one that they did not put forward until they had first absorbed ideas of the equal rights of states to sovereignty and of peoples to self-determination, which before their contact with Europe played little part in their experience.

Further reading

Gong, G. (1984) *The Standard of Civilization in International Society*, Oxford: Clarendon Press.

Lang, D. and Born, G. (eds) (1987) *The Extraterritorial Application of National Laws*, Deventer: Kluwer.

Neale, A. and Stephens, M. (1988) *International Business and National Jurisdiction*, Oxford: Clarendon Press.

See also: international law; international society; self-determination; standard of civilization

MARTIN GRIFFITHS

F

Failed state

State failure means that a state breaks down in decisive respects. Instead of protection of the citizens there is domestic chaos and often **civil war**. Laws are not made, **order** is not preserved; central political **authority** is absent or highly deficient. In many cases the economic system has failed as well, being unable to provide even the most basic elements of welfare for the population. Somalia, Liberia, Sierra Leone, Congo (former Zaire), Angola, Rwanda, Afghanistan, and Sudan are recent examples of state failure in various degrees and forms.

State failure most often takes place in states that are already fragile and weak. Compared to fragile states, failure is a matter of degree: the problems related to fragile statehood magnify. That means that the distinction between fragile state and failed state is blurred: failure is when fragility intensifies. So in order to appreciate state failure it is necessary to understand the fragile, weak state from which failure emerges. The basic characteristics of such states can be outlined in ideal typical terms.

Fragile states are deficient in several respects. One major problem is economic; there is a lack of a coherent national economy, capable of sustaining basic level of welfare for the population. The poorest, least developed countries are in

Africa south of Sahara, but there are also considerable pockets of poverty in Central America and Asia (Burma, Nepal, Bhutan). It should be added that a relatively large part of the world's poor are in India, a country of enormous internal economic variation. Other large countries in the **Third World** (China, Brazil, Indonesia) also have many poor people.

The second problem in fragile states is political, concerning the institutions of the states and their **legitimacy** in the population. States that function well sustain a number of activities which are more or less taken for granted by their citizens: **security** against external and internal threat; order and justice in the sense of a functioning rule of law; and personal freedom including basic civil and political rights. Fragile states sustain such functions only to a limited extent or not at all. On the one hand, the institutions of the state are weak, lacking capacity, competence, and resources. On the other hand, **power** is frequently concentrated in the hands of elites who exploit their positions for personal gain.

The system is known in sub-Saharan Africa as 'personal rule' or rule of the 'strongman'. The most important positions in the state apparatus, whether in the bureaucracy, military, police or in the polity, are filled with the loyal supporters of the strongman. Loyalty is strengthened through the, albeit unequal, sharing of the spoils of office.

The strongman thus controls a complex network of patron–client relationships. The state does not exist to provide public or collective goods except in a very limited sense. Rather, the state apparatus is a source of income for those fortunate or clever enough to control it. Such a state is by no means a source of security, order, and justice for its citizens. It is a threat, an apparatus against which the population must seek protection.

For obvious reasons fragile states lack legitimacy. Vertical legimacy is low because large parts of the population have no reason to support the government; and the government has no authority in the sense that people support or follow its rules and regulations. Horizontal legitimacy – i.e. people's sense of belonging together in a nation – is also low because the state is captured by specific groups; it is not a state for the whole people. Fragile states comprehensively lack the ability to create a sense of moral community.

There is a partial overlap between lack of economic substance and lack of political and institutional substance. Not all economically wanting states are weak in political-institutional terms; Uruguay, Chile, or Costa Rica are Less Developed Countries (LDCs) economically, but they are not weak states in political terms, although they may contain some elements of weak political statehood. The reverse also holds; not all states that are weak in political and institutional terms are LDCs. Yugoslavia earlier and Bosnia today, as well as Russia, are in many respects weak without being LDCs. Yet in most cases there will be an overlap, so that states which are weak are also LDCs. It is in this category that we find the vast majority of states that are in danger of becoming failed states.

The concept of fragile state is an ideal type. In the real world states approximate that type in varying degrees. Most of the fragile states are in sub-Saharan Africa. But the least developed Central American states and the Central Asian states which have emerged from the former Soviet Union, together with other Asian states and even some states in Europe (e.g. Albania) share many of the characteristics of fragile states outlined here.

How did fragile states emerge?

There are three major approaches to answering that question. The first relies on the realist (see **realism**) tradition in international relations (IR) and focuses on the role of the leading states, the **great powers**. The second stems from the liberal tradition in IR and concentrates on the role of social forces in society. The third is connected with theories of **international political economy** (IPE) and focuses on the global capitalist system (see **capitalism**). I look at each approach in turn.

Before World War Two, the possession of colonies was considered legitimate and even necessary, given the backward condition of the colonized areas. After the **war**, colonialism came to be considered fundamentally wrong, even 'a crime' according to a UN General Assembly Resolution (see **United Nations**). That normative change led to decolonization which in turn helped produce a peculiar type of weak player in the **international system**, the fragile state. Decolonization took place in a new international order, dominated by the United States and the Soviet Union. Both countries pushed for an end to colonial empires. The old colonial powers, Britain and France, were much more hesitant but they now held second rank in the international system.

The leading states in the post-war international system pressed for decolonization, meaning the independence of existing colonial territories, no matter how weak they were in terms of political, economic, or any other substance. The **United Nations** General Assembly Declaration (Resolution 1514) stated that 'all peoples have the right to **self-determination**'. The formulation did not mean that individuals and groups were to decide about which communities they wanted to belong to. The 'nations' that were entitled to self-determination were not nations in any community sense. They were the people living within given colonial borders. In effect, the right of 'peoples' meant the right of existing colonies to independence.

Furthermore, it did not matter that the colonies were weak states politically, economically, and in terms of national cohesion. Declaration 1514 explicitly declared that 'inadequacy of political, economic, social or educational preparedness should never serve as a pretext for delaying independence'.

The new norms of decolonization combined with **superpower** competition in the context of the **cold war** virtually guaranteed that there would be no old-fashioned, imperial take-overs of fragile states, even though the mere differentials in **power** would seem to point in that direction. The newly sovereign, fragile entities could survive as independent states because they were not subjected to the classical **security dilemma**: they did not face external threats that could amount to a matter of life and death for the state. Both states and regimes were protected from the outside threat by strong international norms, backed by the **great powers**.

During the cold war, intervention by the superpowers did take place in some cases where the Soviet Union (and Cuba) came to the aid of so-called 'progressive' forces and the United States supported anti-communist rulers. Yet the East–West confrontation helped strengthen the new norms of the right of fragile states to sovereign statehood. That confrontation created a situation where fragile states could, to some extent, play on the fact that the global competitors were looking for partners elsewhere in the world; at the least, the leading powers were anxious to avoid that too many countries lined up on the side of the opponent.

Unfortunately, the lack of external threat did not create domestic security for the peoples of the newly sovereign, fragile states. Rather to the contrary; it created a situation where state elites could be self-seeking predators to the extent that domestic chaos and violent conflict could go to any extreme without paying the ultimate price: termination of the state.

In sum, the first approach focuses on the role of the great powers in creating new international norms after World War Two. These norms allowed the existence of formally sovereign, yet very fragile entities in the **international system**. Even fragile states that are not former colonies are protected by the same set of norms which guarantee the formal persistence of such weak entities.

The liberal approach to fragile statehood is different and much more optimistic. It starts by pointing out that **development** experiences in the world show great variation. For example, not all states with a colonial background have become weak and underdeveloped; some have done better than others. In general, developing countries can be expected to follow the same path of development as taken earlier by the now advanced countries in the West: a progressive transition from a traditional, pre-industrial, agrarian society, towards a modern, industrial, liberal society. Development means overcoming the barriers of agrarian production, backward institutions, and parochial value systems which impede the process of growth and **modernization**. But in some countries, the traditional forces in society, that is, big landowners, money-lenders, religious elites, farmers, and so on, remain strong. In alliance with political elites they can halt the process of modernization and economic progress. The liberal explanation, then, stresses the role of groups in society that resist modernization.

Radical **dependency** theorists in the study of **international political economy** argue that underdevelopment and fragile statehood is caused by factors external to the poor countries. It is due to domination by foreign economic interests originating in the developed West. These exploitative economic forces cripple and distort societal structures inside fragile states. Fragile statehood is therefore based on economic dependency and processes of underdevelopment in a context of uneven global capitalist development. The radical dependency explanation thus emphasizes the negative role of foreign economic interests as the primary factor in creating fragile statehood.

All three explanations appear to contain relevant insights. The role of leading states is undeniable. They were the major players, both as holders of colonial **empire** and, in a later phase, as leaders in the process of decolonization. The fragile states would hardly be able to exist if the **international society** had not set up a framework within which they can disintegrate in the extreme (for example Somalia, Sierra Leone, Liberia), but still retain formal membership of the international society of states and be officially recognized as independent, sovereign entities.

Yet liberals are perfectly right in underlining the fact that the experiences of developing countries vary. A colonial past and a process of decolonization do not inevitably lead to underdevelopment and misery. Some countries with a colonial past have done very well, such as Taiwan or South Korea. It takes the active effort of social forces in society in alliance with state elites to create development and prosperity. But it takes an equally active effort of those forces to create underdevelopment and misery, as liberals point out.

Radical dependency theorists have a point when they call attention to the possibly negative effects of foreign economic interests. But these theorists tend to overly downplay the fact that foreign economic interests do not create underdevelopment – or development – on their own. The effects of their presence are always connected to the environment in which they function, especially to the economic and political capacities of host countries. It is true that fragile states are poorly equipped to benefit from foreign investment. But foreign investment does not always and everywhere produce underdevelopment.

In sum, we need insights from all three approaches in order to fully explain the emergence of fragile states. I have implied that my own ordering of the approaches in terms of relative explanatory value corresponds to the order in which they have been presented above.

From fragile to failed state

Several factors help explain why fragile states are in permanent risk of entering a process of further breakdown and failure. The lack of legitimacy of state elites basing themselves on patron–client relationships creates the need for coerced compliance; governments without legitimacy must depend heavily on force. The need for coercion leads to authoritarian forms of rule. In sub-Saharan Africa, for example, military, quasi-military, or one-party regimes thoroughly dominated the political scene by the early 1980s. Rulers in such systems do not give up power easily. On the African continent, there is not a single case, before 1990, of an opposition party actually coming to power after having defeated the incumbent regime in an election.

The lack of public services, poor administration and corruption creates an unfavourable climate for economic growth. It is difficult to attract foreign investment; many fragile states depend on the export of a few primary products or raw materials. That leaves the economy very vulnerable to price fluctuations in the world market. From the late 1970s, increasing energy prices and decreasing prices for the major export items created fiscal crises in many fragile states. That in turn increased the pressure on farmers when governments attempted to create additional revenue by squeezing producer prices to artificially low levels.

By the 1980s the **International Monetary Fund** (IMF) and the **World Bank** began to demand the adoption of **Structural Adjustment Program**s (SAPs) in fragile states. The idea was to reduce the role of the state and to create more open, liberalized market-economies. State elites responded by trying to secure more economic aid without seriously implementing reforms that might be a threat to their power. By the early 1990s, focus shifted towards reform of the state itself; that led to new demands for **democratization** and **good governance**.

It is extremely difficult to install democracy in fragile states, especially in the short term. There is ample evidence on this from the African scene. With the introduction of multi-party systems, swarms of political parties have been formed. They are most often separated along ethnic lines and led by individuals with no clear ideological visions but with ambitions of becoming strongmen in their own right, controlling their own political patron–client networks. Undeniably, there has been some democratic progress in fragile states; but in a sig-

nificant number of cases, incumbents have managed to remain in power through a combination of divide and rule tactics, which have often involved repression and the use of violence against political opponents.

Instead of producing political goods for the population in terms of economic welfare and political freedoms, the economic and political reforms recorded here have often led to more instead of less violent conflict. Such conflict is nothing new in fragile states; but armed opposition movements against the state have been a marked feature of both the 1980s and 1990s. Especially since the end of the cold war state decay has, in a number of cases, led to state failure involving immense human and social cost.

Some of the major general factors leading to state failure have been recorded above. But a concrete analysis of cases must also include the triggers: the specific events unleashing the crisis. In Rwanda, for example, there was a long history of ethnic and economic tensions between the Hutu majority and the Tutsi minority. The conflict escalated during the early 1990s. The killing of President Habyarimana through the shooting down of his airplane on 6 April 1994 started the **genocide** that cost the lives of more than 800,000 people.

In Sierra Leone, a small Revolutionary United Front (RUF) force came in from Liberia in March 1991 and attacked a village in eastern Sierra Leone. Soldiers from Sierra Leone's army aided by a Liberian group managed to contain the incursion. But junior officers from the army noted that there was little support forthcoming from the corrupt government in Freetown. They ousted President Momoh in April 1992. Yet the new military regime under Captain Strasser only exacerbated the war. Strasser recruited a private military company from South Africa, Executive Outcomes, in return for access to diamond operations. RUF was on the defensive and entered peace negotiations, but violent conflict soon again escalated. Each of the state failures has its own specific trajectory.

During the 1989–2000 period there were between fifty-two (1992) and thirty (2000) intra-state armed conflicts. During the period, intra-state conflict involving more that 1,000 casualties per year has taken place in: Colombia, El Salvador, Guatemala, Peru, Algeria, Angola, Burundi, Chad, Congo, Ethiopia, Guinea Bissau, Liberia, Mozambique, Rwanda, Sierra Leone, Somalia, South Africa, Sudan, Uganda, Afghanistan, Cambodia, India, Indonesia, Myanmar, the Philippines, Sri Lanka, Tajikistan, Iraq, Lebanon, Turkey, Yemen, Azerbaijan, Bosnia and Herzegovina, Russia, and Yugoslavia. The relationship between fragile statehood and intra-state conflict ought to be clear.

Humanitarian intervention

State failure has attracted the attention of international society in a more dramatic way than was the case with fragile states. That is partly connected with the level of casualties; four conflicts alone have cost the lives of 500,000 to one million people; they were in Sudan, Ethiopia, Mozambique, and Rwanda. It is also connected to the fact that possibilities for response by the international society of states have been improved with the end of the cold war. UN Security Council decisions are no longer completely blocked by an East/West confrontation. Together with an increased awareness of **human rights** as a universal value, **humanitarian intervention** has taken place in a number of cases of state failure, including Rwanda, Haiti, Somalia, Liberia, Bosnia, and Serbia/Kosovo.

Humanitarian intervention means that the international society attempts to alleviate the crises in failed states by intervening in the conflict. From a humanitarian viewpoint, this would appear to be the right thing to do, but there are also major problems connected with such intervention. First, humanitarian intervention always takes place after the fact. It follows upon a situation where the population, or substantial parts of it, has already been exposed to violent threat. Even when 'early warning' systems are successful in terms of relaying information to the international society about impending humanitarian disasters, the international society, and especially the great power members of it, is slow to react (see **great powers**). That is because intervention involves cost for those undertaking it, material cost as well as potential human cost in that intervention forces are themselves exposed to violent threat. Therefore, the humanitarian crisis in question must have developed to a certain stage, which includes that of having caught the attention of Western public opinion, before humanitarian intervention becomes a realistic possibility. In other words, significant human cost is a necessary precondition for intervention.

Second, any humanitarian intervention always involves considerations that are not humanitarian; power and interest are the most important additional factors. Power is reflected in the rules of the game of international society; the great powers play a special role in that game, evidenced by their special position in the Security Council. Consequently, humanitarian intervention cannot be conducted against the great powers themselves even if there may be good humanitarian reasons for doing so in places such as Chechnya or Tibet. It also means that given the level of necessary resources to conduct humanitarian interventions, such undertakings rely on the willingness of the great powers to shoulder most of the burden. That willingness, in turn, is connected not only to the humanitarian issue, but also to consideration concerning perceived **national interest**. In other words, behind the innocent label of humanitarian intervention is a much more mixed palette of motives. Furthermore, after the terrorist attacks of 11 September 2001, American decision makers are worried that fragile/failed states may be a breeding ground for terrorists. Recent US operations in Afghanistan and Iraq are connected to such fears.

A third consideration concerns the operational problems involved in humanitarian intervention. Even with the purest of motives, concrete operations can come upon practical difficulties that run counter to the achievement of humanitarian aims. The first UN intervention in Somalia, for example, had no clear long term aims and lacked knowledge of local conditions; it was difficult to find out which clans were the perpetrators and which were the victims. The intervention thus provided some short term relief but was not able to help construct a political framework for sustaining order. The second intervention became entangled in military confrontations with the clans, especially the clan led by Aideed. Partly as a consequence of this, the UN force was no longer seen as a neutral player and it never succeeded in the planned disarmament of the clans. In Liberia, the intervention force was too small to undertake a disarming of the contending groups; and the original plan, according to which the intervention force should only take up arms in self-defence, quickly had to be abandoned. In sum, humanitarian interventions have certainly helped save lives, but there is no reason to expect that humanitarian intervention can provide effective long-term solutions to the problems of failed statehood. This has led to speculations about more durable answers.

Problems of effective state building

The most radical proposals to the problems of fragile/failed states suggest to increase the pressure on incumbent state elites in order to promote the formation of viable states with domestic order and legitimacy. One recommendation is that the international society should accept the creation of new states in a much more radical manner than has been the case so far. This also means accepting warfare as a means of creating capable states. The reasoning is straightforward: if peaceful means do not strengthen the state why not give war a chance?

The creation of such a Darwinian scenario would require that the international society should disregard the human cost involved; that is the very logic of 'giving war a chance'. It would also require a willingness to abandon the former practice of recognizing existing jurisdictions and begin a fundamental redrawing of borders. Both of these requirements are highly unlikely to be accepted by the international society because they run directly counter to current procedures. But if for a moment we set such 'practical' considerations aside, what would be the consequence of this reinvention of war?

There is no reason to expect that established great powers from the North would begin recolonizing fragile/failed states. The latter would be left to struggle among themselves. In view of the weakness of these states, large and small, any productive Darwinian payoff in terms of effective state building should surely not be expected in the short and medium run. A certain outcome, by contrast, would be a much larger number of collapsed states. Given the substantial number of casualties in current state failures, such a development would definitely involve extremely high human cost.

If the war option is neither realistic nor desirable, are there better ways of promoting rapid and effective state building? Different proposals connected with a more flexible approach to **sovereignty** have been put forward. They include changing the rules of **secession**, making the formal formation of new states easier; and the decertification of states by the international community. In the latter case, highly ineffective states should have their sovereignty put on hold; this could be combined with giving international aid to regions instead of states. In the African context that would establish a connection to pre-colonial African conceptions of overlapping jurisdictions not based on control of terrritory, but on power over people.

In order to simplify, let us focus on secession. The suggestion is that better possibilities for secession would lead to a larger number of viable states better capable of protecting and providing other political goods for their populations. Who should be allowed to secede? At present, for example, there are evolving secession conflicts in the following weak states in sub-Saharan Africa: Somalia, Ethiopia, Senegal, Cameroun, Angola, Sudan, and Congo. Which of these cases should benefit from a policy change?

Sceptics argue that secession most often will create more problems than it solves. Both in the former Soviet Union and in the former Yugoslavia, secession has been accompanied by massive acts of so-called **ethnic cleansing**. In sub-Saharan Africa, the human cost would probably be even higher. The question is also where to stop; which groups should be allowed to create new states following which specific criteria? A major problem in this respect is that many fragile states hold a very large number of different ethnic groups. If some groups are allowed to secede why would others not make similar demands? And if they

do, how many new states is it relevant to accept? Surely the number would have to be much lower than the total number of ethnic groups in Africa (some 5,000).

It appears to be a genuine dilemma: the old borders are holding together groups that fight against each other because they cannot agree on forming a political community. The result is insecurity and underdevelopment. Splitting them up appears to create more problems than it solves; they cannot stay together and they cannot split up. The very different views on the possible benefits of secession are tied to different calculations concerning short term as well as long terms benefits of the undertaking. Proponents are rather optimistic, opponents very pessimistic. One way of addressing the dilemma would be to favour secession in cases where the benefits are clearly deemed to outweigh the cost, and to reject secession in other cases. That would appear to speak more in favour of independence for Somaliland than for the other cases mentioned above. At the same time, even such moderate changes would increase the incentives for potentially seceding groups to seek control of their own state because of the potential benefits of such control; that, in turn, will spur violent domestic conflict perhaps to the extent of requiring a new basis for the calculation of costs and benefits of secession.

The considerations in this section demonstrate how difficult it is to increase external pressure on post-colonial state elites (see **postcolonialism**) in a way that will both avoid excessive human cost and lead to the creation of effective states with capacities for delivering security and other political goods to their citizens. State building and development in fragile states is not impossible. Some countries, such as Botswana and Mauritius, have made good progress. But progress cannot be taken for granted; it requires certain domestic and international preconditions that are frequently absent and hard to generate. Ours continues to be a world of sovereign states that first and foremost look after their own populations. We must expect that popular insecurity, often combined with perennial threat of violent domestic conflict, will continue to characterize a large number of fragile states. The local populations cannot solve the problem; and the measures taken by the international society are bound to be constrained in such a way that they are not capable of effectively addressing it.

Further reading

Clapham, C. (1996) *Africa and the International System*, Cambridge: Cambridge University Press.

Fukuyama, F. (2004) *State – Building*, Ithaca, NY: Cornell University Press.

Herbst, J. (2000) *States and Power in Africa*, Princeton: Princeton University Press.

Holsti, K. (1996) *The State, War, and the State of War*, Cambridge: Cambridge University Press.

Jackson, R. (1993) *Quasi-states: sovereignty, international relations and the Third World*, Cambridge: Cambridge University Press.

Job, B. L. (ed.) (1992) *The Insecurity Dilemma. National Security of Third World States*, Boulder, CO: Lynne Rienner.

Milliken, J. (ed.) (2003) *State Failure, Collapse and Reconstruction*, Oxford: Blackwell.

Prunier, G. (1995) *The Rwanda Crisis. History of a Genocide*, London: Hurst & Company.

Reno, W. (1999) *Warlord Politics and African States*, Boulder, CO: Lynne Rienner.

Rotberg, R. (ed.) (2004) *When States Fail*, Princeton, NJ: Princeton University Press.

Zartman, W. I. (ed.) (1995) *Collapsed States. The Disintegration and Restoration of Legitimate Authority.*

See also: civil war; corruption; good governance; humanitarian intervention; state formation

GEORG SØRENSEN

Famine

A situation characterized by food deprivation among large numbers of individuals, often leading to elevated mortality rates. Constrained access to food is central to the famine experience and starvation is a widely used synonym for famine, but an absence of food is not always the most significant aspect of this phenomenon, nor is starvation typically the immediate cause of death (since cholera, typhus, and even measles carry direct responsibility). Famine is not simply the result of a decline in food availability linked, say, to poor harvests or the devastation of **war**; it is a set of mutually reinforcing failures in political, social and economic policy that together cause geographically concentrated shortfalls in food consumption, social turmoil, market disruption, and a collapse of public services (health system, law and order) all leading to unnecessary deaths if left unchecked.

Famine was once a common feature of human society. Historical records are full of the misery associated with population-wide food deprivation. Whether in medieval Europe, colonial India or present day Ethiopia the manifestations of famine are similar: massive increases in the price of food, a breakdown of social norms (neighbors fighting over handfuls of grain, the abandonment of the elderly or infirm, the sale of a daughter for food), consumption of unusual foods (rats, cats, saw-dust, tree bark), the sale or mortgage of valued assets (the roof of a dwelling, a plow, the last cow, a sewing machine, farm-land), distress migration of adults or entire families looking for work and food, skeletal children, and the daily apparition of fresh rows of graves.

These outcomes describe an accelerated destitution of people who were already among the most vulnerable and marginalized of society. Thus, while the symptoms of famine may be universal, the outcomes of famine are not. Some groups of people (the wealthy and powerful) often gain from the distress of others, buying up cheap land and assets, claiming local power where a vacuum has been created, securing a monopolistic edge in disrupted markets for food, or strengthening a claim to national leadership by undemocratic means.

Some governments have been toppled when food riots became the touchstone of mass discontent (the French Revolution, the fall of Haile Sellasie's government in Ethiopia in 1974). Yet, famine has also been used as a tool to leverage government policies regardless of the human cost. For example, famine in the Ukraine from 1932 to 1934 killed as many as eight million people, but it served to cement Stalin's control of the Soviet political apparatus. The great famine in China from 1958 to 1962 resulted in as many as 33 million excess deaths, possibly the largest single event of mass mortality linked to food deprivation in history. The central government was unperturbed by the disrupted patterns of production, marketing and consumption which led to famine since these changes were seen as a necessary consequence of the Great Leap Forward. More recently the famine in North Korea (1995–9) claimed more than three million lives, but the government remained in **power** insisting all the while that it needed to spend scarce resources not on enhancing food **security** but on developing its nuclear program.

The total death toll from famines in the twentieth century has been estimated at more than 70 million. These people died in the context of some thirty major multi-year events. In each case droughts, floods or epidemics were proximate triggers for unusual conditions but it was pre-existing government policy and/or government inaction in the face of distress that determined the nature and severity of outcomes.

A nation's commitment to protecting its weakest citizens during times of vulnerability requires adequate institutional and financial investments not only in famine warning and response systems, but also in functioning safety nets that prevent citizens from destitution during non-crisis years. It was not until the second half of the nineteenth century that most European governments acknowledged an innate responsibility for the wellbeing of all citizens, not just for the wealthy few with a political voice. Prior to that time large numbers of Europeans died in famines. 1816/17 saw the last pan-European famine with distress across the entire continent, from Scotland to Sicily. There were still crises in individual nations in subsequent years, such as in Ireland in 1848–50, when natural events evolved into humanitarian disasters because of a lack of prior investment in smallholder agriculture, combined with political inaction in the face of widespread destitution.

Today most developed and developing country governments have accepted the political duty to support the public and private sector systems required to protect vulnerable citizens. Additionally, much progress was made during the 1990s in professionalizing humanitarian responses to emergencies, resulting in fewer famines (thanks to better early warning, higher levels of public recognition in affected countries, and more timely responses), and far fewer deaths in the contexts of famine. For instance, armed conflicts in East Timor and Bosnia produced famine-friendly conditions in the mid-1990s, but famine itself was averted (even if other human and political catastrophes were not). Similarly, the serious droughts in southern Africa in 1991/92, and again in 2001/2, caused massive shortfalls in food supply but no famine deaths ensued thanks to rapid, coordinated, multi-sectoral interventions.

Unfortunately, while a crisis of 'Biblical proportions' was averted in Africa in 2002 there is a lingering feeling across the continent that underlying problems have not disappeared. Indeed, the southern Africa crisis focused attention on a new contributor to famine – HIV/AIDS. Africa is burdened with the highest prevalence of HIV/AIDS in the world. The drain on household and national resources caused by daily funerals and lost productivity contributes to increased hunger, falling life expectancy, and increased vulnerability to even small shocks like drought or price increase. HIV contributes to the progressive destitution of already chronically poor and malnourished people, opening the door to future vulnerability.

Of course not all of Africa is equally affected, not are all people in famine prone regions. Countries with more vibrant economic and political systems, such as Botswana and Senegal, are relatively less prone to succumb to conditions whereby large numbers of citizens will want for food. By the same token, such countries tend to invest in appropriate warning and response systems that mitigate climatic or economic shocks. An enduring international challenge is to find ways to assist poor and/or economically and politically closed societies to tackle the conditions that make them vulnerable to food-mediated crises, and to enhance their domestic capacity to mitigate their worst effects. In either case, appropriate long-term development policy, not just effective famine relief, is the key to success. An important part of sound **development policy** is active recognition of **human rights**, even for people in remote famine prone regions, and the responsibility of political cadres to promote and protect those rights. A future rights based agenda in **international law** is likely to insist that contributors to famine (by way of policies enacted or by way of allowing public inaction), should face prosecution for **crimes against humanity**.

Further reading

Sen, A. (1981) *Poverty and Famines*, Oxford: Clarendon Press.

Von Braun, J., Teklu, T. and Webb, P. (1999) *Famine in Africa: Causes, Responses and Prevention*, Baltimore, MD: Johns Hopkins University Press.

Webb, P. (2002) 'Emergency Relief during Europe's Famine of 1817: Anticipated Crisis Response Mechanisms of Today', *Journal of Nutrition* 132(7), 2092–5.

See also: desertification; foreign aid; humanitarian intervention; pandemic; refugee

PATRICK WEBB

Feminism

A complex set of understandings about how **power** (both private and public) is dependent both on controlling both the thoughts and bodies of women and on controlling notions of femininity and masculinity. Feminism prompts a lively interest, therefore, in **gender**, what any social group thinks being male or being female means. Feminism is a distinct form of gender studies in that it raises explicit questions about power – about how, when and for whose benefit power is employed to create, sustain and (sometimes) alter the meanings of femininity and masculinity.

Feminists have learned over the years that an investigator has to move between micro and macro arenas; if one is seeking to understand politics, it is not sufficient to stay just at the level of governments. For instance, if one wants to understand the workings of power inside homes, then one will need to be curious about the gendering of power inside workplaces and governments. Likewise, if one is trying to make sense of the workings of power inside a government or an international agency, one will need to chart the causes of femininity's and masculinity's relationships inside families. This necessity makes a feminist approach to political exploration self-consciously interdisciplinary; feminist students of politics know they need to draw up the work of feminist anthropologists, geographers, economists and, always, historians.

By the early 2000s, many teachers, researchers and writers using feminist questions and methodologies to shed light on the obvious and the hidden workings of national and international power have come to refer to feminism in the plural: feminisms. What they mean is that they now see feminist theorizing, feminist empirical research and feminist policy interventions as taking several forms. They have developed a collective wariness about speaking in universal terms. They avoid referring to a single homogeneous feminism because they have watched women's advocates in so many countries working to build alliances across the politically constructed chasms of class, race, religion, **ethnicity**, nationality, generation and sexuality. Today there is a realization among feminist political observers that there exist simultaneously proponents of: *liberal feminism* (with its focus on individual rights and equality for women), *socialist feminism* (see **socialism**) (with its focus on the genderings of economic class, as

shaped by the dynamics of local and international **capitalism**), *radical feminism* (highlighting the causes and consequences of patriarchy and misogyny), *postmodern feminism* (paying close attention to identities, images and culture), and *post-colonial feminism* (prioritizing the subtle workings of gendered racialized hierarchies that sustained colonialism and have persisted even long after formal colonial rule has been dismantled). Feminist international relations thinkers today tend to accept that users of these different feminist political and analytical foci exist simultaneously and seek to enrich the entire feminist intellectual enterprise by ensuring that they engage with one another – in their academic course readings, in their conference sessions, in their journal publications, in their activist organizing.

What is political?

There are, nonetheless, several significant common conclusions that are shared by most feminist international relations teachers and scholars. First, in order to make sense of international relations and the global political economy, feminists believe that one must pay serious attention to women, to women's complex lives, to women's ideas, conditions, actions; paying attention to women in all their diversity sheds analytical light on how and why states act the way they do, as well as on how states rise, persist and sometimes crumble. Closely related to this conclusion has been the shared feminist understanding that women are not homogeneous; thus one must be alert to how any woman's life is shaped by the dynamics of gender ideology, the class system, notions of race, generational memories and ethnic identity formation. Furthermore, feminists have found that there may indeed be some remarkable consistencies in women's conditions across time, place and social system (e.g., subordination in marriage, lower pay than men, exclusion from the centers of power), but those consistencies across women's diverse locations need to be discovered, never simply presumed.

Moreover, most scholars employing a feminist curiosity to shed light on the realities of local and international politics have come to realize that men have to be investigated *as men*. Any study that assumes that the particular constructions of masculinity of generals or prime ministers or clerics or bankers or labor union organizers or militia fighters are irrelevant, will produce a political analysis that is not reliable. That is, such analyses will not explain enough. Thus among feminist scholars studying politics there is agreement that there is a lot more power being wielded (to keep some women in 'their place' or to alter the existing relations between femininity, masculinity and the state, or to bolster certain relations between governments or between culture and capital) than previously has been assumed. Non-feminist analyses of national and international politics, that is, seem to have seriously underestimated the amount and the types of power at work in local and international political affairs.

Consequently, what is deemed to be political, feminist investigators are now convinced, is far more wide-ranging than many international commentators have imagined. Beauty turns out to be political; so are marriage and motherhood; factory work is political; prostitution and sex trafficking are political; cultural standards of manliness and feminine respectability are political; so too is paid and unpaid housework. For example, some of the most interesting research exposing the political workings of the global economy today is being conducted by feminists taking seriously

the experiences, ideas and organizing efforts of women who have migrated from the Philippines, Sri Lanka, and Mexico to earn money cleaning the kitchens and bathrooms of affluent women living in Hong Kong, Kuwait, Italy, and the United States. Scrubbing a tub can become political. Feminists agree: what is worth investigating in order for us to make reliable sense of yesterday's or tomorrow's global politics starts close to home and stretches far towards the distant horizon.

Feminist curiosity about states and nations

A principal shortcoming in the conventional, non-feminist approach to international politics, according to feminist students of international relations, is its practitioners' tendency to assume that states are the natural actors – coupled with a risky presumption that states speak for the nations they claim to rule. In fact, a feminist analysis questions not only the 'naturalness' of states, but of nations too. Feminist informed investigations of societies as different as Ireland, Yugoslavia, Canada, and Sudan have revealed that both the state and the nation have been constructed out of particular ideas about femininity and masculinity. Most often the building blocks are those ideas about femininity that have been wielded in ways to marginalize women in state affairs, as well as in nation-building movements. Where women have become prominent in the decision-making circles of a state or a nationalist movement it has usually been because some women have organized to force open those spaces in the masculinized leadership. Thus feminist political analysis takes seriously the ways that ideas about motherhood, sexual purity, the good wife, and family stability shape policymaking within nationalist movements, political parties and state institutions.

Most states, feminists have discovered, have sought in the past and still today to entrench – in popular culture and in formal law – those particular ideas about women's 'natural' belonging to the private sphere to legitimize men's allegedly 'natural' place in the public sphere. This feminist finding has helped to explain why officials of states as diverse as that governing sixteenth century Japan and that governing the contemporary United States each have become so anxious around challenges to contemporary marriage practices. Virtually every state has taken an intense interest in marriage – to keep working women's wages low, to collect taxes, to enlist young males into armies, to take the census, to promote its own notions of morality, and to distinguish itself from rival states.

Since the rise of liberal democratic states in the late eighteenth century, the very idea of the 'citizen' as the elemental and legitimizing member of what became known as the **nation-state**, has been imbued with ideas about manliness. This discovery has prompted feminist scholars to assign importance to movements for women's suffrage. Those suffrage movements – in l890s New Zealand, 1900s Australia, Canada, Britain, and the US, 1920s Philippines, Egypt, Brazil, and Mexico, and 1990s Kuwait – were, in the eyes of feminist political analysts, not merely about efforts to gain a single right; suffrage activists are better understood as having launched basic challenges to the very concept of the masculinized state as a powerful web of institutions run by allegedly naturally public men for the sake of protecting allegedly maternally privatized, domesticated women. Any woman (suffragists Huda Sha'rawi in Egypt, Alice Paul in the United States, or Emmeline Pankhurst in Britain) or any man (nineteenth century reformer John Stuart Mill) who tries to topple this pillar propping up the state can be labeled not merely a 'radical', but a threat to state security, or what is mistakenly called 'national security'.

Feminist researchers take seriously local and international debates among policymakers about population control. Some state officials today see **population growth** as the key to their state's international economic and diplomatic stature. Thus French, Russian, and Japanese politicians currently express anxiety about their own countries' falling birthrates: if their 'own' women refuse to have larger families, how will they staff their factories, generate tax revenues for workers about to join the pension rolls? By contrast, other policymakers, acting on behalf of international **development** agencies and governments in Vietnam, China, and Nigeria, express alarm at the alleged pressures that population growth impose on their scarce resources. As dissimilar as these two groups of officials are in their attitudes toward current population trends, what they share is the belief, feminist researchers find, that women's reproductive capacity is a matter of state and international political concern. Controlling women's bodies, thereby, is transformed by them into a matter of state **security** and global stability: the state that fails to ensure that women give birth to, and nurture into healthy maturity, more children, like the state that fails to ensure that women give birth to fewer children, is a state in trouble both in its internal affairs and in its relationships to its neighbors, allies, trading partners and international bankers. Investigating how so many state officials and international agencies come to these positions and act upon them to intervene in women's lives and how women themselves react to those interventions thus has become a serious topic for feminist students of international politics.

Women's rights, patriarchy and femocrats

Out of women's international organizing during the **United Nations'** 1975–85 Decade of Women and the later follow up to the Decade, the 1995 UN sponsored international meeting held in Beijing, came a widespread official and popular **discourse** on women's rights. Women's rights, women's activists declared, could not be simply subsumed under the gender neutral concept of **human rights** because the latter were too mired in patriarchal presumptions that the feminized private sphere was separate from the masculinized public sphere, and human rights referred only to those accorded in the public sphere. At international conferences convened throughout the 1990s (held in Vienna, Cairo, and Beijing), women's advocates asserted that a woman had the right to be free from violence, whether on the street, in the workplace, in someone else's kitchen or in her bedroom. Second, they asserted at these international meetings that women had the right to control their own bodies, including their reproductive capacities, Third, they argued that no ideological claim that these were private (not political) matters and no diplomatic (see **diplomacy**) claim that these were realms for which the sovereign state alone was responsible were sufficient to keep women from demanding that these rights be actively protected by **international law** and practice.

The outspoken (and even more subtle) resistances mounted by state officials and party politicians to these women activists' rights claims confirmed what many feminist theorists of the state had long suspected: not only were state building and state maintenance policies rooted in gendered strategies meant to privilege masculinity, but the very principle of state **sovereignty** – the holy grail of so much international relations thinking – was gendered. That is, the sovereign state is gendered in a way intended to keep most women, regardless of their class or race privilege, politically marginalized.

Patriarchy is a societal system of structures and beliefs that sustains the privileging of masculinity. Feminists approach every state – and the state as a global phenomenon – as problematic. That means that feminists understand that the state is neither natural nor inevitable. Rather the state is a particular sort of social structure held together (often tentatively) by questionable relationships between women and men and by artificial, historically concocted notions about femininity and masculinity. Feminists ask who inside the state's apparatus and who among those subject to that state's laws and practices do these gendered relationships and gendered ideas privilege: all men? Most men? Some women? Feminists do not a priori assume that every state at every stage of its evolution is partriarchal. But feminists always ask: is this state – the post-revolution French state, the World War Two American state, the 1950s Soviet state, the 1990s Chinese state, the 2005 Iraq state – patriarchal? The answer their investigations have generated have been so often 'yes' that many feminists have come to suspect that the very model of the state may be itself inherently (inescapably) patriarchal.

This suspicion leaves feminists everywhere coping with an obvious quandary: should any person dedicated to improving the lives of women by reducing masculinity's political privilege even try to pursue those goals by working through or in a given state? Feminists in many countries have debated this important question, for it has profound implications. Should an Israeli battered women's shelter take funds from the Israeli state with its statist strings attached? Should Indian feminists pour their energy and scarce resources into running for parliamentary seats? The risk of cooptation may appear too high. Australian feminists decided in the 1980s, when a liberal political party was in power, to take this risk with their eyes wide open and their monitoring skills at the ready. They coined the term 'femocrats'. Femocrats are women intent upon pursuing feminist goals working as civil servants and as administrative policy-makers inside the state, despite knowing that taking this step is fraught with risk. Today there are feminists working to de-privilege masculinity working inside the **European Union**, the **International Labor Organization**, the **World Bank**, the newly established **International Criminal Court**, and many agencies of the UN. One might think of them as global femocrats. A femocrat, though, does not just work on gender questions; a femocrat is a feminist and thus examines how and why ideas about and practices of gender shape the dynamics of power.

A short history of feminism in the study of international relations

Feminist theories of and analytical approaches to international relations (which academics often call 'IR') have not come out of the ether. Individual scholars' own innovative, often daring, thinking, teaching and writing have been crucial. But those alone would not have created what by the early 2000s has become widely known (if not always embraced) as 'feminist IR' or 'gender and IR'. This intellectual transformation had been generated by an energizing network of women scholars (and some men)

working together to reform university curricula and tenure criteria, to change publishers' political science lists, to reimagine professional associations' annual programs and to launch new scholarly journals. This network was created self-consciously across boundaries, not just across the more obvious state boundaries, but also across the more daunting boundaries of race and culture, professional rank, and scholarly specialty.

The year 1988 marked a beginning. At that time the second wave of women's movement activism was at its height in many countries: raising individual consciousnesses of women; transforming state policies concerning conditions of paid and unpaid work; shining bright lights on the power dynamics inside marriages, parties, legislatures, courts and peace movements; converting acts of male violence against women from a private problem into a public issue. The UN-sponsored Decade of Women, 1975–85, had helped to make these mobilizations more genuinely international. Many women studying for their doctorates and some lucky enough to have academic posts took part in conferences that brought together feminist activists and researchers. By the late 1980s, too, Women's Studies courses were being launched in many universities in Australia, the Philippines, India, Canada, Britain, Germany, Ireland, Scandinavia, and the United States, their teachers often overcoming skepticism and direct opposition from their own faculty colleagues, who had cast aspersions on the alleged 'lack of intellectual rigor' of such a new upstart field of inquiry.

By the late 1980s, new Women's Studies journals such as *Signs, Women's Studies International Forum, The Women's Review of Books* and *Feminist Review* also had been created and were attracting manuscripts from scholars working in history, literature, sociology, art history, and anthropology. While some courses in 'Women and Politics' had been created by individual academics as early as the mid-1970s, and while there had been moves by feminist-informed political scientists to organize women's caucuses inside professional groups such as The American Political Science Association, little was being done in the late 1980s to bring feminist ideas into the field (and the 'world') of academic International Relations. IR appeared to be a fortress of intellectual and professional resistance when confronted with feminist insights into the workings of power. It was in this heady atmosphere, however, that the British International Studies Association (BISA) convened its annual gathering at the London School of Economics that spring of 1988. It was there that a small number of women making careers inside academia began collectively to find their voices to insist that women's movement concepts (e.g., the feminization of unpaid labor; the patriarchal state; marginalization of women) and the wealth of Women's Studies research were indeed relevant for understanding international politics.

BISA, along with the US based International Studies Association (ISA), had become the institutional arena for determining what would be taken seriously in the scholarly study of international politics. Thus in the formal panel sessions where professors were presenting papers on their own research on international politics' myriad questions, but also in the conference's crowded hallways and over beer in the pub after sessions, academics explicitly and implicitly confirmed what was to be 'counted' as 'real IR'. The overwhelming majority of these 1988 program organizers, paper presenters and pub patrons were male, and most of them were white men from Britain,

Canada, and the United States, although this profile was seemingly so naturalized that very few participants either noticed that demographic profile or thought it worthy of political analysis. That is, until a handful of women, including Rebecca Grant, Kathleen Newland, and Spike Peterson began to raise questions, began to express a public curiosity about how this distinctive profile of the BISA conference and the larger trans-Atlantic IR academic discipline might be both professionally and intellectually distorted by the unquestioned prevalence of unacknowledged masculinist assumptions and practices.

At about this same time, a small group of American scholars led by Ann Tickner persuaded the Ford Foundation to sponsor a modest, but intellectually innovative, conference on women, gender and the study of international politics. It was held at Wellesley College in Massachusetts. Though a college long renowned for its dedication to women's education, its own political scientists, just like those in scores of political science departments across the country, taught IR to their undergraduates and graduate students in a fashion that insured not only that women's lives were invisible, but that men were deemed analytically irrelevant as well. The lively conversations begun at BISA and at Wellesley set off intellectual sparks. By the early 1990s, several feminist editors inside British and US academic publishing houses began to accept manuscripts that put these emergent feminist ideas about international politics into print so that they could be more widely debated, applied, and assigned to students; among those early books were *Bananas, Beaches and Bases: Making Feminist Sense of International Politics* (Enloe 1990), *Gender and International Relations* (Grant and Newland, editors 1991) and *Gender in International Relations* (Tickner 1992).

The next step in creating 'feminist IR' was to open up a professional space in which these questions and hunches could be explored by more than a handful of interested scholars. A group of academics including Spike Peterson, Ann Tickner, Jan Pettman, Sandra Whitworth, Christine Sylvester, and Anne Sisson Runyan already were active in the International Studies Association. They decided to make it their arena for an ongoing exchange of feminist ideas about IR. That meant persuading the association's officers to open up new panel sessions, to acknowledge that these fresh questions could be 'counted' as IR. Fifteen years later, due to their and new colleagues' steady work with the association, with publishers, with graduate students, with colleagues, when thousands of academics were preparing for the ISA's 2004 annual conference in Montreal, Quebec, several significant things had been accomplished.

First, there was a Women's Caucus now operating inside the ISA, to monitor and challenge all the sorts of sexism which so often thread their ways through any academic association. Second, the Feminist Theory and Gender Section (FTGS) of the ISA had been institutionalized, helping to mentor younger scholars, to encourage participation by feminist scholars in the running of the ISA, to sponsor papers and panels at meetings, to broaden the cultural and geographic profile of feminist IR specialists beyond its early largely white female base. Third, in the run up to the 2004 ISA conference, eighteen full panels were proposed for FTGS sponsorship, while an additional eighty-one individual papers were proposed on gender, feminism and IR. These numbers suggested the sheer volume of feminist research being conducted in the expanded discipline of international relations.

Fourth, and equally important, by the time the three thousand ISA members descended on Montreal in March, 2004, not only were courses on 'Gender and IR', 'IR Feminist Theory', 'Women and Human Rights', 'Gender and International Development', 'Gender and Globalization', and 'Gender and War and Peace' all becoming more commonly offered in universities around the globe, but the professors teaching those courses were more likely to be seen as tenurable by senior faculty at their institutions. In addition, while many members of the IR profession still remained dismissive of feminist theorizing and feminist empirical research (for instance, they rarely incorporated those insights and findings into their own research on trade, security or international organization) there were increasing numbers of non-feminist IR faculty who, when they came to design their own 'Introduction to International Relations' undergraduate courses or their graduate seminars on 'IR Theory', now thought it was necessary to devote at least a week or two to feminist approaches and feminist theories. A week in a full term's worth of thinking was rather tokenist, but it did represent an intellectual toe-hold. It also signaled to more and more young scholars interested in the genderings of power and the patriarchal dynamics of globalized political economy that they did not have to migrate to History or Anthropology; they could pursue their research interests within the academic arena of IR.

Members of the FTGS members also had launched a new journal, *The International Feminist Journal of Politics* in 1999. Five years later, IFJP's number and international range of writers, editors, readers and subscribers continued to grow. In the late 1990s, when the journal's founders talked together about why they thought the time was ripe for creating such a new journal and what values and practices they wanted to inform such a journal, they collectively drew on their direct experiences as women, as feminists, and as professionals in academia and in the field of IR to craft the new publication. They brought to bear their feminist insights into not only scholarship but also contemporary world affairs. These feminist teachers and scholars furthermore agreed that 'feminist' should be put in the journal's title. They knew that it might be professionally 'safer' to use the blander term 'gender'. Still, they jointly decided that by inserting 'feminist' in the title, they would be declaring what their own research efforts had revealed: that is, to encourage a scholarly conversation about the workings of constructed femininities and masculinities in local and international affairs. This new journal was to serve as a place where the diverse interactions of gender and power would be explored. Furthermore, during the initial discussions about the journal's practices, the founders agreed that not just the content should reflect a feminist investigatory stance, so too should its editorial practices. To these scholars that meant that 'professional' should be disentangled from an institutional culture that was competitive, hierarchical, secretive and exclusivist. They sought to encourage younger scholars to submit articles, to urge external reviewers to conduct their evaluations of manuscripts in a spirit of mentoring, and to make transparant the internal processes of the journal.

The feminist IR scholars who founded the IFJP made sure from the start that their discussions were multinational. Canadian, Australian, US, and British scholars took part from the outset. Yet they also explicitly made a commitment to move the journal beyond this narrow geographic range, first by ensuring that the Editorial Advisory Board was more truly international, and, second, by

inviting feminist scholars in the Global South to submit papers and serve as manuscript reviewers. They encouraged men as well as women to submit manuscripts and asked several male scholars to serve on the journal's advisory board. In addition, the journal's founders decided that there should be a three-person senior editorial team, not just a single editor; each of the three core editors would be based in a different geographic region, so as to structurally push the IFJP to adopt a genuinely global approach to the creation and distribution of new knowledge. Toward this same end, the founders decided that the operational headquarters of the journal would not be placed in the United States. While one of the three principal editors at any time might be a scholar based in the United States, the journal's main editorial office would be placed at the home university of one of the other two non-US editors. Their reasoning was derived from their own scholarly understanding of the disproportionate influence of the United States in international affairs and of the role that the cultural production of knowledge played in producing that radical lopsidedness. Thus, at its launch, the IFJP was headquartered at the Australian National University's Women's Studies Center, the academic home of Jan Pettman, who, along with Gillian Youngs of Britain and Kathy Jones of the United States, were selected by the founding group to serve as the first three-member editorial team. By 2004, the journal's operational base had moved to the Department of Politics, at Britain's University of Leicester, the home base of Gillian Youngs, and the three member team now was comprised of Youngs, Jones and Rekha Pande, a feminist scholar at the University of Hyderbad, India.

Feminist research and teaching in the newly expanded field of international relations remains a work in progress. In its content, as well as its explanations and practices, feminist international relations explorations seek to keep the intellectual conversation open and fresh. In 1988, few people understood how paying serious attention to Filipinas scrubbing other people's bath tubs in Hong Kong and Kuwait would make us smarter about the deeply gendered workings of local and international politics. What will surprise us when we look back at the early 2000s?

Further reading

Carver, T. (2004) *Men in Political Theory*, Manchester: Manchester University Press.

Grant, R. and Newland, K. (1991) *Gender and International Relations*, London: Open University Press.

Enloe, C. (2000) *Bananas, Beaches and Bases: Making Feminist Sense of International Politics*, Berkeley, CA: University of California Press.

Enloe, C. (2004) *The Curious Feminist: Searching for Women in a New Age of Empire*, Berkeley, CA: University of California Press.

Marchand, M. H. and Runyan, A. S. (eds) (2000) *Gender and Global Restructuring*, London: Routledge.

Peterson, V. S. (2003) *A Critical Rewriting of Global Political Economy*, London: Routledge.

Pettman, J. (1996) *Worlding Women: A Feminist International Politics*, Sydney: Allen and Unwin.

Tickner, J. A. (2001) *Gendering World Politics*, New York: Columbia University Press.

Whitworth, S. (2004) *Men, Militarism and UN Peacekeeping: A Gendered Analysis*, Boulder, CO: Lynne Rienner.

Youngs, G. (2004) 'Feminist International Relations', *International Affairs* 80(1), 75–88.

See also: gender; gendercide; identity/difference; women and development

CYNTHIA ENLOE

Foreign aid

Although foreign aid funding is reviving following years of decline, continuing tension between different objectives and policy drivers is no less problematic than during the **cold war** when flows were close to their peak. The core of foreign aid is official **development** assistance, defined by the Development Assistance Committee (DAC) of the **Organization for Economic Cooperation and Development** (OECD) as resources transferred on a concessional basis for the promotion of the economic development and welfare of developing countries. Since the early 1990s assistance has fluctuated around US$50 billion. The United States and Japan are the largest donors, but the **European Union** together with its member states' own aid budgets now provides over half the total. Around two-thirds of development assistance is transferred bilaterally and around one-third is channeled through multilateral organizations (see **multilateralism**). The **Bretton Woods** institutions and **United Nations** bodies are pre-eminent. Official aid, earmarked for certain post-communist transition economies (see **communism**) and substantial US aid to Israel, and aid from **non-governmental organization**s make up the rest. Alongside all these flows there is a long history of military assistance and other **security** related transfers. Over the years soft loans have given way to grants; program and budget support and technical assistance now often prevail over aid for projects. Precise definitions of aid can be rather specious, and measuring its volume is a contingent exercise. The intended purposes and the objects that transfers actually support can vary considerably; the effects can diverge from donor and recipient intentions.

The language of development cooperation and partnership is more fashionable than aid. This is in keeping with perceptions that if development assistance is to make a sustained impact there must be recipient ownership of the projects or programs and the related conditionalities (see **conditionality**). Partnership is a vague, contested idea. In reality the relationship tends to be one where **power** and accountability are both asymmetrical. A further idea is that the donors' partners must be the authors of the development solutions; they should not simply accept ownership of solutions the donors propose.

Since the early 1980s donors have increased the layers of aid conditionality, beginning in the 1980s with economic policy and institutions (reflecting the 'Washington consensus'). In the 1990s political and governance conditionalities (ranging from democracy and **human rights** to anti-**corruption** measures) were added. Since 1999 the trend has been to insist on strategies for poverty reduction too (policy process conditionality). The **World Bank**, a major influence on development aid thinking, believes that assistance can significantly reduce poverty in the right policy and institutional environment. The effectiveness of conditionalities, however, is increasingly questioned. There is currently a move to elevate allocative 'selectivity' over conditionality, thereby concentrating assistance more on countries already committed to a supportive environment. However arguments persist that aid can still deliver worthwhile benefits elsewhere. Disaster relief is one example.

The demand for aid is expressed in the form of a wide range of disparate but also inter-locking economic, financial, social, environmental and political needs. The scope for **humanitarian intervention** in complex emergencies and post-conflict reconstruction has grown, following the increase in sub-state violence in the post-**cold war** disorder. Yet the 1990s witnessed declining flows of development assistance aid, reaching a low of 0.22 per cent of the Gross National Income of the DAC donors in 2000. Explanations must account for the supply side: donor interests rather than recipient needs. Most donors have traditionally emphasized national **security**, economic and commercial motivations, especially in their bilateral aid.

Aid's seemingly terminal decline in the 1990s was occasioned by two main developments. First was the end of the cold war and the collapse of the Soviet Union, which removed a strategic rationale that had been a powerful driver in the United States. Second, donor confidence in aid's developmental effectiveness was eroded by an accumulation of critiques highlighting aid's misuse by corrupt, incompetent governments and the risk of aid **dependency**. The superior merits of trade and commercial investment flows were stressed as agents of world development. At most aid's role came to be likened to a catalyst.

The mood changed in 2002, with the US government's unexpected announcement of increased funding around the time of the international conference in Monterrey, on 'Financing for Development'. The European Union committed its members to significantly increasing their aid. So, aid's drivers now can be summed up by reference to two agendas: the discontents of **globalization**, and the post-11 September 2001 war on international **terrorism** and other perceived threats to international security. The critical issue for aid's developmental objectives is whether and how far these different agendas can combine: will the second serve the purposes of the first, or will the first be captured, distorted, or drained by the second?

On the one side, there is growing recognition of the importance of **international public goods**. Addressing the challenge of world poverty is illustrative. Even globalization's enthusiasts recognize the persistence of absolute poverty and increased relative poverty or inequality, notwithstanding notable improvements in certain human development indicators around the world. Globalization and the rich countries' protectionism that makes for uneven global liberalization creates losers as well as winners. And there are marginalized peoples who simply get left behind. Some analysts argue that our understanding of how aid can tackle these problems and the chances of it doing so are better now than ever before. Others claim that economic malaise giving rise to poverty and grievance over the great and increasing inequalities also account for many of the new threats to international security, partly through fomenting internal conflict and instability. Security here refers not simply to threats to territorial **sovereignty** but other dangers posed to human well being, for instance the global transmission of 'diseases of poverty', international crime including drug trafficking, environmental degradation, and the large scale movement of illegal migrants. Directing aid at development for the poor could address these issues at their source. Moreover aid that generates economic growth expands international markets for the donor countries' exports. All these rationales have different implications for an optimal geographical and sectoral allocation of aid, but together they make a strong case for increasing the flows. 2003 for instance saw high level political support in some rich countries for tackling Acquired Immune Deficiency Syndrome (AIDS) in Africa in particular.

However, although concern about international terrorism and other security risks can constitute a case for aid where unresolved development problems and poverty are believed to be root causes, an alternative reading sees the causes lying more in political structures. One view holds that political authoritarianism and religious extremism fuel the appeal of anti-Western terrorism in the Middle East for instance. There, regime change and democracy assistance can seem more important than tackling poverty. Yet political change can also create political instability, which in turn can have negative economic social consequences, thereby increasing the requirements for humanitarian and development aid. Iraq is illustrative. A conflicting view urges financial support to strategically placed governments that cooperate in the war on terror, even if their democratic credentials and commitment to pro-poor development are both questionable. Pakistan is an example. Either way, poor, needy states that pose no serious and imminent threat would appear to present a much weaker case for aid.

Foreign aid is set to increase after years of decline, but fundamental tensions between aid policy objectives and the driving forces persist, alongside intellectual confusion over the true nature of relationships among key social, economic and political variables. Competing perspectives on aid's developmental purpose continue to complicate assessment of its developmental effectiveness. The future could yet see a repetition of the past, when aid's developmental performance was severely constrained by competing political interests and other disagreements bearing down on all sides.

Further reading

Burnell, P. and Morrissey, O. (eds) (2004), *Foreign Aid in the New Global Economy*, Cheltenham: Edward Elgar.

Sogge, D. *Give And Take: What's the Matter with Foreign Aid?* London: Zed.

See also: conditionality; development; foreign direct investment; good governance

PETER BURNELL

Foreign direct investment (FDI)

Foreign Direct Investment (FDI) has become a key phrase in the vocabulary of economists and politicians. Attracting FDI has become a policy priority for many governments. Significant FDI inflows are considered to be a sign of a healthy and competitive economy. Yet, not all countries are able to attract significant FDI inflows, nor have all countries developed on the basis of FDI. There are also voices, including from Northern NGOs, arguing that FDI and the activities of subsidiaries of **multinational corporations** are associated with sweatshops, environmental degradation and a lowering of labor and environmental standards. The importance of FDI in national **development** strategies remains a hotly debated issue.

Despite the growing importance of FDI, there is confusion about how FDI is normally defined. According to the **Organization for Economic Cooperation and Development** (OECD) and the **International Monetary Fund** (IMF), FDI reflects the objective of obtaining a lasting interest by a resident entity in one economy in an entity resident in an economy other than that of the investor. The lasting interest implies the existence of a long term relationship between the direct investor and the enterprise and a significant degree of influence on the management of the enterprise, usually at least 10 per cent of the shares. FDI flows are recorded in the balance of payments and include equity capital, reinvested earnings, and other capital flows associated with various inter-company transactions between affiliated enterprises.

FDI should not be confused with other measures of multinational activity such as the share of employees or value added under long term control of foreign firms. Nor should FDI be mistaken for fixed capital investment, which enters the national account as investment. FDI can involve building up the capital stock, but also simple financial transfers of assets as in mergers and acquisitions. In developed countries, most FDI has taken this form.

While countries have been interconnected through FDI before, particularly at the beginning of the twentieth century, FDI has become a significant form of international economic activity only in the past few decades. Over this period, the value of FDI has been growing faster in most developing and developed countries than the value of other types of economic activity such as trade and national incomes. Most of the rise of FDI has occurred amongst developed countries (in the **European Union**, the United States, and Japan), but developing countries have traditionally been able to attract more FDI when accounting for market size. FDI flows to developing countries have become concentrated in a handful of emerging markets such as China, Mexico, Brazil, and Southeast Asia. FDI used to be most prominent in natural resource industries, such as mining, and oil and gas, and this is still so in sub-Saharan Africa, but globally the services sector has overtaken manufacturing, and manufacturing has overtaken natural resources in importance. The rapid rise in FDI and the boom in mergers and acquisitions over the 1990s have given way to years of decline more recently, reflecting in part the global slowdown.

There are various debates about the motivation of FDI and why FDI has increased so rapidly. Traditional trade theory suggests that FDI is a response to differences in production factors rewards. For instance, due to labor scarcity at home the same type of labor may be cheaper abroad. Such differences in factor rewards will be exploited by the movement of capital (when trade and movement in people are restricted) until factor reward convergence has been achieved. However, it has been argued that this theory fails to explain observed North–South investment in capital-intensive industries. Recent theories suggest that FDI occurs because of the existence of firm-specific assets that cannot be exploited in other ways such as through exports, predicting that FDI occurs in knowledge and capital-intensive industries.

Another significant force behind the increase in FDI is policy liberalization at both national and international levels. Across the world, countries have begun to liberalize their national FDI regime. Some Asian NICs (see **newly industrializing country**), such as Singapore, which actively pursued FDI, and Hong-Kong with its more *laissez-faire* approach, opened up to foreign capital in the 1960s. Other Asian countries soon followed. Even South Korea, which had restricted FDI in many sectors, had opened up by the late 1990s. Latin American countries began to liberalize in the 1980s and 1990s when the failure of the import-substitution model had become apparent and when the financial crises of the 1980s had starved their economies of external capital. African countries opened up many sectors to foreign firms in the 1990s. It has become clear that without such widespread liberalization of FDI policies, some FDI could not have taken place. Moreover, a passive, open door policy is by no means a guarantee for further FDI inflows.

International policy towards FDI has also moved into the direction of providing more rights and market access to investors. There are now more than 2,200 bilateral investment treaties spelling out the rights of foreign investors. Regional arrangements increasingly include investor rules (with the **North American Free Trade Agreement (NAFTA)** as a prime example), reflecting a shift from restrictive approaches such as those adopted in the 1970s. At a multilateral level (see **multilateralism**), the **World Trade Organization** (WTO) Agreement on Trade Related Investment Measures contains rules that protect the rights of investors in manufacturing while WTO members can voluntarily sign up service sectors to be opened up for FDI under the General Agreement on Trade in Services.

While the debate on motivations for investment has coincided with the increase in FDI, the debate on the effects of FDI has come to the forefront only slowly with interest picking up from the mid-1990s. In the 1970s, FDI was associated with uncompetitive behavior and the exploitation of developing countries through profit repatriation. Since the 1980s and 1990s, it has become associated with more positive forces. Not only was FDI seen to be a relatively stable source of external finance, surpassing official aid flows to developing countries, but increasingly FDI is being considered a key driver of economic growth and productivity by providing access to new technology, management techniques and worker skills.

There is now a majority view that FDI and economic growth are associated, although it is less clear whether FDI causes growth, or whether FDI follows growth, or both. The economic effects of FDI have been found to depend on many factors including MNC strategies, the nature of specific sectors, and conditions and policies in host countries, suggesting that it is unlikely that FDI has the same (or even a positive) effect everywhere. There have also been attempts to assess the environmental and social impacts of FDI, which also vary and depend on many factors. While there are positive and negative cases, the spotlight of environmental campaigners has been directed onto individual FDI projects involving environmental damage. Regarding the social effects, large corporations are sometimes associated with poor working conditions in individual cases in export processing zones. At a more general level FDI does not seem to provide poorer working conditions than do local investors. However, FDI does tend to benefit the already well off, and hence is more likely to perpetuate inequalities rather than narrow them.

Policymakers in most countries appreciate the positive economic effects of FDI and have made attracting FDI a policy priority. The **Bretton Woods** institutions include FDI attraction as important policy prescriptions. Some national governments bend over backwards to lure investors into their country (or state) and compete on the basis of incentives, efficient regulatory frameworks and basic economic conditions, while other governments are more passive. There seems to be relatively less attention on actively pursuing policies that are effective and efficient in capturing the benefits of FDI on behalf of everyone.

Further reading

Dunning, J. H. (1993) *Multinational Enterprises and the Global Economy*, Reading, MA: Addison-Wesley.

Markusen, J. R. (1995) 'The Boundaries of Multinational Enterprises and the Theory of International Trade', *Journal of Economic Perspectives* 9, 169–89.

Moran, T. H. (1998) *Foreign Direct Investment and Development*, Washington, DC: Institute for International Economics.

Mundell R. A. (1957) 'International Trade and Factor Mobility', *American Economic Review* 47, 321–35.

See also: international political economy; multinational corporation; neoliberalism; political risk analysis

DIRK WILLEM TE VELDE

Foundationalism/anti-foundationalism

Foundationalism means an adherence to the belief that systems of knowledge must be secured on fixed, permanent foundations. Foundations are posited to offer reassurance, **authority**, and certainty in the realm of knowledge. Modern philosophical and political thought has displayed a strong desire for, and faith in, foundations. Anti-foundationalism is skeptical about the possibility of, or requirement for, fixed or permanent foundations. At stake is the question of whether and how knowledge claims can be justified.

It was against the backdrop of considerable intellectual and political upheaval in the sixteenth and seventeenth centuries that the clash between foundationalism and anti-foundationalism came into sharp relief. This period not only saw transnational religious violence reconfigure the political landscape, but also brought to the surface profoundly unsettling questions about the sources and legitimation of knowledge. This was in no small part due to the Renaissance revival of Pyrrhonian skepticism associated with the thought of Michel de Montaigne (1533–92). The words he had inscribed on a beam in his house nicely capture the gist of his skepticism: 'All that is certain is that nothing is certain'.

Tremendous intellectual and social change transformed Europe during this time. Feudal social relations slowly gave way to modern ones based on **sovereignty** and territoriality, and closed medieval cosmologies like the 'great chain of being' gradually gave way to post-Copernican worldviews of an infinite universe. The Scientific Revolution and heliocentric astronomy together with baroque aesthetics and absolutist political ideologies radically altered the order of things by emphasizing **order**, coherence, harmony among the parts, and a governing center. It was believed that in the absence of foundations, moral, theological and political disagreement would fuel disorder and destructive violence. The quest for political stability thus ran parallel to the quest for certitude.

It was in this intellectual and social atmosphere that René Descartes (1596–1650) inaugurated the modern quest for certainty. In response to skepticism, Descartes sought to establish firm foundations for knowledge. Driven by this epistemological imperative, Descartes' aim was to reach certainty by casting aside loose sand and arriving at solid bedrock. This ground clearing exercise to establish unshakable grounds had to be the first move of the modern philosopher. It required demolishing extant philosophical edifices and beginning anew on solid ground.

For Descartes this meant revisiting the foundational assumptions or 'first principles' of philosophy which were commonly based on errors and falsehoods. To remedy the situation Descartes would withhold his assent from all but the most indubitable beliefs. Doing so momentarily throws the modern thinker into a chaotic vortex. The anxiety of being

without foundations is, however, only a fleeting feeling, for the rational thinker quickly realizes that there is one thing that survives radical philosophical doubt: the thinking self. The quest for certitude ends when we discover the indubitable foundation of the philosophical subject, the 'I' who thinks and doubts: *cogito ergo sum,* 'I am thinking therefore I am'. This arrests the anxiety generated by doubt and the temporary absence of foundations, returning the philosopher's feet to philosophical bedrock, and providing grounds of justification.

Geological and architectural metaphors were common to seventeenth century attempts to establish firm foundations. Both Thomas Hobbes (1588–1679) and Gottfried Leibniz (1646–1716) joined this Cartesian quest. They wrote, respectively, of the dangers of building states or knowledge on sandy ground, emphasizing the necessity of solid ground. Common to Descartes, Hobbes and Leibniz was the imperative to use reason to question shaky foundations and replace them with surer ones. What they do not do, however, is question the grounds of reason.

By questioning the grounds of reason, thinkers such as Friedrich Nietzsche (1844–1900), Max Weber (1864–1920), Michel Foucault (1926–84) and Jacques Derrida (1930–2004) challenge the trust placed in foundations by questioning reason's reasonableness. In famously declaring 'God is dead!' Nietzsche cast doubt over the possibility of offering any reassurances about the authority or objective rationality of knowledge claims. Weber similarly questioned the possibility of rationally grounding moral, legal and political norms because reason itself is divided. This returns us to the threat of cognitive and normative chaos.

Because Nietzsche's original declaration that 'God is dead!' comes from the mouth of a madman, it is often assumed that to question foundations or the need for them is to side with irrationality against **rationality**, or relativism against objectivism. It seems to imply that all knowledge claims are equal, and that 'anything goes'. In short, it seems to lead to a fatalistic, nihilistic anti-foundationalism. When framed in this way, the opposition between foundationalism and anti-foundationalism is simply another form of the time honored political dualisms between reason and unreason, order and disorder, sovereignty and **anarchy**, male and female that feminists (see **feminism**) and poststructuralists (see **poststructuralism**) have convincingly deconstructed (see **deconstruction**).

In the post-positivist study of international relations (see **post-positivism**), anti-foundationalism is almost always associated with poststructuralism. Poststructuralist theorists of international relations have drawn attention to parallel crises in the realms of knowledge and politics by casting doubt over the faith in sovereign certitude. What is at stake, Ashley and Walker (1990) argue, is the very question of sovereignty. Sovereignty here needs to be understood simultaneously as a predicate of the state and as a symbol of authoritative foundation. Under conditions of **globalization** the conceptual and political supremacy of sovereignty has been considerably challenged. New social, political and economic dynamics have generated empirical and normative challenges to the sovereign state as the foundation of the political realm and the guarantor of **authority** and certainty.

Critics have argued that poststructuralism, taken to its logical conclusion, leads to a hazardous epistemological and political anarchy. If we are deprived of foundations, they enquire, how are knowledge claims to be justified? To retreat from the poststructuralist abyss, some international relations theorists have proposed a 'minimal foundationalism'. While sharing the skepticism towards absolute, permanent foundations, the more interpretive or hermeneutic (see **hermeneutics**) theorists are equally skeptical of anti-foundationalist assertions. They and critical theorists such as Jürgen Habermas (see **critical theory**) have expressed concern about the apparent normative incoherence or relativism in poststructuralism's alleged anti-foundationalism. They seek to move beyond the antithesis of objectivism and relativism.

While it appears that we must choose between foundationalism and anti-foundationalism as if it were a choice between reason and madness, or objectivism and relativism, critical theorists and poststructuralists both suggest that the antithesis is overdrawn, or even false. Indeed, poststructuralists are perhaps better described as *non*-foundationalists than *anti*-foundationalists. They question and critically analyze all foundations, while positing none of their own. They urge us to expose what foundations mean, and how they function to authorize certain forms of rationality and exclude particular types of knowledge. The key point for both poststructuralism and critical theory, however, is that there are no foundations that cannot be questioned and contested. There may well be foundations, but the most important thing is to continue questioning them and their status. The certitude afforded by faith in absolute foundations, like that invested in absolute monarchs, has been subjected to an ongoing critical questioning, one consistent with a democratic ethos.

Further reading

Ashley, R. K. and Walker, R. B. J. (1990) 'Reading Dissidence/Writing the Discipline: Crisis and the Question of Sovereignty in

International Studies', *International Studies Quarterly* 34(3), 367–416.

Bernstein, R. (1983) *Beyond Objectivism and Relativism: Science, Hermeneutics, and Praxis*, Oxford: Blackwell.

Brown, C. (1994) 'Turtles All the Way Down: Anti-Foundationalism, Critical Theory and International Relations', *Millennium* 23(2), 213–38.

Cottingham, J., Stoothoff, R. and Murdoch D. (1985) *The Philosophical Writings of Descartes*, Volumes I and II, trans. J. Cottingham, R. Stoothoff and D. Murdoch, Cambridge: Cambridge University Press.

Derrida, J. (1978) 'Structure, Sign, and Play in the Discourse of the Human Sciences', *Writing and Difference*, trans. A. Bass, London: Routledge and Kegan Paul.

Habermas, J. (1987) *The Philosophical Discourse of Modernity: Twelve Lectures*, Cambridge: Polity.

See also: critical theory; deconstruction; feminism; hermeneutics; poststructuralism; post-positivism; reflexivity

RICHARD DEVETAK

Fourth world

The indigenous societies of the 'new world', as imagined in medieval cartography, identified the new world as an undiscovered zone of mystery, riches and conquest after the 'First World' of Europe, the 'Second World' of Asia, and the 'Third World' of Africa (Shapiro 1997: 22). More recently, the term has been folded into the Eurocentric **development** schema that constructs a hierarchy of 'worlds' based on assumed levels of wealth, scientific sophistication, and political organization. In both cases, the term devalues the centrality and significance of indigenous peoples to world politics, while preserving a useful trace of how they were only made visible to the Western gaze through enlightenment cartography. In short, the indigenous societies and struggles of the 'fourth world' are the hidden, marginalized and devalued *Other* of international relations – lost in both realist state based accounts of high politics (see **realism**), and idealized liberal accounts of global economic **integration** or the universal norms of **international society** and law.

Yet the fourth world is also International Relations *enabling* Other: the peoples dispossessed in the colonization and growth of Canada, the United States, South America, and Australasia, and whose lands there and in the Asia-Pacific are now exploited for oil, timber and minerals to fuel the world economy; the African societies robbed of their people to fuel the slave economies that underpinned Europe and America's industrial development, and who now struggle to reconcile tribal forms of social organization with the **nation-state** and the destructive legacies of colonialism; the Pacific and Australian societies whose lands were poisoned by nuclear testing, and who (like the Mirrar of Kakadu) continue to resist the cultural, environmental and military impacts of uranium mining; and most profoundly, the peoples whose forms of politics, society and culture resist and contrast with the fundamental unit of the **international system**, the modern **sovereign state**.

In short, indigenous peoples struggle for survival, autonomy and **self-determination** from within sovereign states either imposed by colonizers or created through the first wave of **decolonization**. In many **Third World** states they struggle against elites who see their forms of life as 'backward' and refuse to acknowledge the integrity of their cultural systems, their rights over land, or their custodianship over the environment. However indigenous peoples continue to struggle for justice and recognition. Such struggles can involve a rejection of state control, modern religion and capitalist economics (see **capitalism**), or complex combinations of appropriation, accommodation and resistance.

Even though there are over 150 million tribal people in sixty countries, literature on indigenous politics in the study of international relations is 'a rather slim file', a poor contrast to that in law, politics, social theory, and global cultural studies (Shaw, 2002: 65). Yet even a cursory survey reveals native peoples deeply involved in key international processes. One of the last nomadic tribal peoples in Brazil, the Awa, has been struggling to preserve its society against violence and encroachment by ranchers and industry. With the support of international and local **non-governmental organization**s (NGOs), in 2002 they won a significant court case securing large areas of their land against further encroachment. A similar victory was also secured by the Yora of Peru in 2002 – a ban on logging inside a reserve of 80,000 ha – after earlier forcing Exxon-Mobil to cease oil exploration on their land. In 1993, Shell's oil operations in the Niger delta made global headlines when Ken Saro-Wiwa and eight other Ogoni activists were executed by the military regime of Sani Abacha. The Movement for the Survival of Ogoni People (Mosop) had in December 1992 demanded 4,000 million dollars from Shell in reparation for their destroyed environment and another 6,000 million dollars in unpaid rents and royalties.

In West Papua, Melanesian people formed the backbone of the secessionist movement *Organisasi Papua Merdeka* (OPM), which has broad support across the territory for its campaign for independence from Indonesia. Indonesian security forces have fought the OPM since the mid-1960s, killing tens of thousands of people and routinely committing **human rights** abuses. This war saw a massive **refugee** crisis in the

1980s, rising tensions between Indonesia, Papua New Guinea (PNG) and Australia, and the involvement of the **United Nations** High Commissioner for Refugees. Along with wealth in oil and timber, the territory contains the world's largest gold and copper mine, Freeport, which has been a locus of conflict between security forces, the OPM and local Amungme landowners.

Conflict between indigenous people, **multinational corporation**s and governments is inevitable while national laws fail to acknowledge indigenous ownership of land and resources, and while unequal patterns of trade and **development** force Third World states to rely heavily upon resource income. In PNG, resources corporation BHP was successfully sued by landowners over the environmental damage caused by its Ok Tedi mine, and the worst conflict broke out in 1989 when landowners at the Panguna mine on Bougainville began a war of **secession** which was brutally repressed by the PNG military. The war and blockade killed 10,000 people until a negotiated solution was reached in 2001 with the assistance of New Zealand, Australia and other Pacific countries.

The task then, for the study of international relations, is to recognize how the peoples and history of the fourth world raise profound questions about modern sovereignty and international law. It means recognizing that the exclusion of indigenous peoples is not incidental but constitutive of international relations and that while **international society** continues to defend states, it has failed to acknowledge the **legitimacy** of unresolved indigenous claims against the state. For example, the United Nations has yet to adopt the Draft Declaration on the Rights of Indigenous Peoples, which enshrines rights to self-determination, to ownership of land, resources and water, and prohibitions against physical and cultural **genocide**. The Declaration has languished since 1993, stalled by the United States, Britain, Australia and Canada.

Further reading

Coates, K. (2004) *A Global History of Indigenous Peoples*, Basingstoke: Palgrave.

Keal, P. (2003) *European Conquest and the Rights of Indigenous Peoples: The Moral Backwardness of International Society*, Cambridge: Cambridge University Press.

Shapiro, M. (1997) *Violent Cartographies: Mapping Cultures of War*, Minneapolis: University of Minnesota Press.

Shaw, K. (2002) 'Indigeneity and the International', *Millennium* 31(1), 55–81.

Wilmer, F. (1993) *The Indigenous Voice in World Politics*, Newbury Park: Sage.

See also: imperialism; microstates; Third World

ANTHONY BURKE

Free trade

In theory, free trade implies the absence of barriers to the movement of goods and services across borders. According to its defenders, commerce should be allowed to flow freely across geographical spaces and to respond to the twin factors of supply and demand. Thus state regulation of trade in the form of border controls, tariffs, licensing requirements, quality controls, subsidies of domestic producers, and (in some cases) health and safety standards is seen as an impediment to the effective functioning of free trade. In this sense free trade supposes a reduced responsibility for the state in the economy, as governments should have a minimal role in organizing commercial relations.

The theoretical origins of free trade can be found in the thought of the physiocrats, an ideological movement that began in France in the eighteenth century. They argued for a reduction in state control of the economy and that the free movement of goods coincided with the tenets of natural law. Although it had little effect in France, the ideology of the French physiocrats deeply influenced the early liberal economic thought of British political economists such as Adam Smith (1723–90) and David Ricardo (1772–1823). Smith postulated that human beings have a natural propensity to 'truck and barter' and saw free trade playing a central role in increasing the wealth of states. Smith attacked **mercantilism** by arguing that national wealth depended not on the accumulation of precious metals but rather of goods. Free trade, he argued, maximized the amount of productive goods a nation could accumulate and proposed that states concentrate on the production of goods in which they held an absolute advantage, claiming that in each nation nature had provided the conditions for the efficient production of a particular set of goods.

In the early nineteenth century, Ricardo supported the idea of free trade but modified Smith's ideas to introduce the concept of comparative advantage. He noted that although a state might not be the most efficient producer of any goods in particular, it should concentrate on those goods it can produce comparatively efficiently. By focusing on the production of these goods, and exporting them to other countries, the country can then import the goods that it has difficulty in producing. This principle, Ricardo claimed, would lead to the expansion of wealth not only in individual countries but in the **international system** as a whole and his argument continues to provide the theoretical basis for free trade.

In theory, then, free trade is connected to the liberal idea of the harmony of interests. It is also linked to peace and as such is a key element in **liberal internationalism**. Liberals have long argued that the spread of trade will bring states closer together; as states increase their levels of trade they will become more and more dependent on each other. As such **interdependence** and the benefits from trade grow, states will be less likely to risk what they have gained from trade by going to **war**.

It is important to note that free trade was a revolutionary concept when introduced by Smith. Traditionally commerce had been strictly regulated by the state as a source of **power**, control and wealth. Liberal ideas of free trade thus challenged the dominant notion of mercantilism and suggested that the goal of trade should be the creation of wealth, not power. As such, free trade was not readily adopted by national governments, and it was not until the nineteenth century that it became established as a widely used international commercial strategy.

The first country to look to free trade as an international commercial strategy was Great Britain. As the first state to go through the industrial revolution, Britain led the world in productivity in the first half of the century and looked to free trade as a way to expand its international markets. It also looked to the free flow of imports to lower its production costs, particularly the cost of food. In the 1840s a national debate raged between farmers and manufacturers over the liberalization of the trade in agricultural goods. British farmers feared the influx of cheap grain imports from overseas, whilst manufacturers sought cheaper food for their workers to enable them to reduce labour costs.

Ultimately the industrialists won the day and legislation that had been in place since the end of the Napoleonic Wars to protect British agriculture (the Corn Laws) was repealed in 1846. After the repeal of the Corn Laws, Britain rapidly liberalized its international trade, removing barriers unilaterally in the expectation that others would follow its example. In many cases this occurred, although British persuasion and sometimes coercion was necessary to bring some countries to open up their domestic markets. Throughout the nineteenth century Britain remained the leading trading nation, both with friends and enemies alike. Even at the height of a naval arms race with Germany, Britain saw its bilateral trade with that country grow rapidly.

In the twentieth century free trade played an important role in the theory and practice of international relations. After World War One free trade was seen by the **League of Nations** as essential to securing peaceful international relations; indeed a third of US President Woodrow Wilson's Fourteen Points for the attainment of peace spoke of removing all economic barriers to trade. Later, the breakdown of trading relations between the great powers in the 1930s was seen by many as a significant factor in the tensions leading to the outbreak of World War Two. As a consequence the **Bretton Woods regime** that was created in 1944 was built around the idea that trade must be allowed to prosper between states. Although efforts to create an International Trade Organization (ITO) through the Havana Charter failed, the General Agreement on Tariffs and Trade (GATT) was created in 1947 and functioned as the world's trade liberalization regime until 1995, when it was superseded by the **World Trade Organization** (WTO).

Throughout the post-war period the **international system** experienced an impressive expansion in international trade, with overall trade levels increasing ten fold from 1965–85. This was achieved in part by the progressive reduction of tariffs between advanced industrialized states. But, despite the impressive expansion of overall levels of international commerce, trade at the global level is hardly free. Although **regional trade blocs** have spread throughout the world, a large number of protectionist measures still exist in most countries, in the form of both tariffs and **non-tariff barriers** (NTBs). Since the 1970s **managed trade** has become an enduring element in international economic relations.

Free trade has always been controversial and has created conflict between those who support and those who oppose it. Producers who are competitive will be able to take advantage of the opportunities presented by free trade, while those who are not will have to adjust to increased competition. Consumers will benefit from wider choice in the goods available to them, but workers may lose their jobs as uncompetitive domestic producers cut costs or fail. The debates over free trade have become one of the most significant elements in the ongoing controversy concerning **globalization**.

Further reading

Bhagwati, J. N. (2002) *Free Trade Today*, Princeton, NJ: Princeton University Press.

Irwin, D. (2003) *Free Trade Under Fire*, Princeton, NJ: Princeton University Press.

Russell R. (1994) *The Choice: A Fable of Free Trade and Protectionism*, Upper Saddle River, Prentice Hall.

Smith, A. (1994) *An Enquiry into the Nature and Causes of the Wealth of States*, New York, Modern Library.

See also: globalization; managed trade; mercantilism; regional trade bloc; World Trade Organization

DUNCAN WOOD

Functionalism

Any attempt to define functionalism in the study of international relations is hampered by two problems. First, the term means something very different in sociology and comparative politics. Second, the man who is credited with the theoretical elaboration of functionalism, David Mitrany (1888–1975), never used the term, and actually rejected it as an unnecessary, even dangerous, step towards dogmatic thinking. Mitrany preferred the term functional 'approach', which he upgraded to 'functional theory' in his last work published in 1975, the year of his death. Despite this, the term functionalism has continued to this day as the preferred title for the set of ideas developed by Mitrany.

Mitrany's functional approach grew out of a rich liberal tradition, often referred to as the new liberalism, which emerged at the end of the nineteenth century. Until World War One new liberalism did not have much to say about International Relations and was more concerned with the problems of domestic politics. Indeed, the first use of the terms function and functionalism in their Mitranian sense, are found in L. T. Hobhouse's influential *Liberalism* (1911), and later on in the writings of the Guild Socialists R. H. Tawney and G. D. H. Cole. The earliest attempts to convert this functionalism into an international theory can be found in the writings of Mary Parker Follett and Harold Laski. Mitrany's contribution to the development of functionalism was to construct a coherent and exclusively international functionalism that toned down its strongly socialist associations (thus making it more acceptable to non-socialist practitioners and scholars) (see **socialism**).

Functionalism is based on two key premises. The first is that individuals are not, as classical liberals had claimed, self-contained beings forced by necessity to live in a society. Rather, individuals are defined (and also define themselves) by their social functions. People identify themselves by what they do in society (their role in the family, occupation, recreational activities, or political allegiance), and hence the individual is a node in a cobweb of social functions that link each individual with every other individual. The second premise is that society should be based around the provision of need. Mitrany often contrasted the political ethos of the nineteenth century state, which privileged the development of the rule of law and the nightwatchman state, with the new politics of the twentieth century welfare state, where the provision of need was now central to political activity. The nineteenth century had solved the problem of the rule of law, he claimed, and the twentieth century was doing the same for needs. This privileging of need as the central organizing factor of the new liberal politics was seen as a logical progression from the nightwatchman state.

David Mitrany's main contribution to functionalism was to popularize its application to the international sphere. Although by no means the only writer to do this, his influence on the development of international functionalism is unsurpassed. In a series of books, pamphlets and articles – of which the best known are *The Progress of International Government* (1933), *A Working Peace System* (1943) and *The Road to Security* (1944) – Mitrany laid out his view of a global functional order.

The main goal of a functional order was **security**. In an earlier unpublished paper from 1933–4, Mitrany defined the security problem as a misfit between the social life of a society (the self-contained mass of functions that reproduce the society) and the security system that protects it. While the social life grows gradually, expanding beyond the boundaries of the security system, the political structures of the security system are more rigid. Social life eventually bursts the boundaries of its security system, and when this happens the security system goes from protecting the social life to being a parasitic political institution.

Thus, for Mitrany, the feudal order at the end of the Middle Ages was no longer capable of containing the new social life led by Europeans, and once it no longer served its security role it began to work against what it was supposed to protect. Its replacement by the territorial state was the swapping of an obsolete security system for a larger one that contained and protected new social realities. Thus, the development of security systems was marked by long periods of inactivity, followed by the rapid replacement of one system by another.

It was Mitrany's contention that the territorial state was no longer capable of protecting the social life, which since the nineteenth century had now become truly global. The problem for Mitrany, therefore, was fundamentally one of security rather than an issue of **integration**. The world is already socially integrated, it is our political/security organizations that need to be updated.

Mitrany's contention that the future security system should be based around function-specific global organizations emerged from his disillusionment with the arguments for international federalism. While he was sympathetic with the goals of federalism, he regarded it as naïve. First, international federalism tries to unite people by what divides them. The use of the United States as a template was misleading, since the United States federated at a time when government functions were limited to, perhaps, four key areas. The Australian federation a hundred years later took almost twenty years, despite their shared values and legal systems. How would it be possible to unite such a culturally and politically diverse world a hundred years on? The second problem with federalism is that it tends to create regional federations, which then merely behave like large states. The replacement of lots of smaller states by larger federations does not deal with the problem of state competition in a globalized world.

The functionalist answer is this problem is to bring people together by what unites them. The new global security system should be constructed function by function, starting with uncontentious areas such as transport and communications infrastructure. This process, which Mitrany saw as an emerging reality through the development of specialized organizations, **non-governmental organization**s and even multinational firms, would not directly challenge the state and the emotive symbols that went along with it. The pull of the new functional order would be the fulfilment of need. Since the functional organizations would be the most efficient providers of need they would gradually begin to supplant the loyalty to older organizations like the state without directly confronting the state order. Since the organizations would be fit around specific functions, their size and reach would be dependent on the size and reach of the function, and the state would continue to be the main provider of any function that still made sense when organized on a state, rather than continental or global, level.

Although Mitranian functionalism is largely about the development of an alternative political security system, because it looks beyond the state for the development of new systems of government, the myth developed that Mitrany's approach was largely an economic one. This myth spurred the development of neo-functionalism, an approach that gave more prominence to state involvement and the role of interest groups. Neo-functionalism's major difference with Mitrany's functionalism, however, is in its goal. Neo-functionalists saw the creation of an integrated regional super-state as their goal, rather than a new globalized functional **order**.

Further reading

Ashworth, L. and Long, D. (eds) (1999) *New Studies in International Functionalism*, Basingstoke: Macmillan.

Groom, A. J. R. and Taylor, P. (1975) *Functionalism: Theory and Practice in International Relations*, London: University of London Press.

Mitrany, D. (1943) *A Working Peace System*, London: Royal Institute for International Affairs/Oxford University Press.

See also: European Union; interdependence; relative gains/absolute gains; sovereignty

LUKE ASHWORTH

G

Game theory

A formal theory of strategic interaction used by some scholars to explicate theories of international relations. It provides a tool for the mathematical analysis of situations where all actors can influence the outcome, and so all must consider others' actions when deciding what to do. As strategic interaction has been considered central to many questions in international relations, game theory can be a useful tool to examine the logic of arguments about such interactions. Some topics that have been studied using game theory are: **balance of power**, **democratic peace**, **deterrence**, **ethnic conflict**, **hegemonic stability theory**, **power transition theory**, and **reciprocity**.

Game theory falls into two branches, cooperative and non-cooperative. Cooperative game theory addresses how players agree to divide their possible gains. There are two main questions here; what group of players will coordinate their actions and how will they divide the gains of that coordinated action? A variety of solution concepts strive to capture bargaining dynamics in cooperative game theory. Typically, the precise way the players coordinate their actions is not analyzed in cooperative game theory.

Non-cooperative game theory analyzes actors' incentives to take certain actions within the context of their interaction. A non-cooperative game specifies who the actors are, what their choices are, the order of those choices, how the choices lead to outcomes, what the actors know when they must choose, and their values for the outcomes. Non-cooperative game theory has been used to analyze general questions such as; when actors honor their agreements, and how an actor can communicate information that only he or she knows. Such games are solved by finding their equilibria. An equilibrium is a set of actions in the game where no actor can make itself better off by changing its action, assuming that all actors correctly anticipate what one another will do. Behavior in equilibrium is stable in the sense that all believe they are doing what is in their own interest, and no actor holds anticipations of the future actions of others that are consistently incorrect.

Games fall into the classes of zero sum and non zero sum. The latter are of greater interest as models of international politics because they do not require that the gains of one player be matched by the losses of another. **Prisoner's dilemma**, the best-known game, is non zero sum.

Games are abstractions of social situations. Such abstractions may be useful in stripping away the complexity of a situation so that its basic principles can be analyzed. For example, prisoner's dilemma illustrates how individual incentives can lead to a situation where all are worse off. Game theory then is not a theory of international politics; it is a tool for the explication of theories of international relations.

For example, bargaining is commonly modeled using game theory. Real cases of bargaining are very complex. The parties have idiosyncratic political and economic motivations, the subject of negotiations may have unusual characteristics that make striking a bargain difficult, and the parties may have a history that influences how they bargain with each other. Most bargaining games strip away all this complexity in favor of focusing on a few strategic issues. These models typically have two parties bargain over a fixed cake with a given sequence of offers and responses. The roles of impatience for a settlement, values attached to the share of the cake received, the effect of the possibility of breaking off bargaining in favor of another option, and knowledge of the other side's value for the cake can all be analyzed in these games. These bargaining games highlight strategic dynamics that may be obscured in the complexity of an actual negotiation. General principles deduced from such models can then be applied to understand actual cases.

Game theory allows us to test the logic of a theory by examining the strategic interactions that are central to that theory. In many cases, our intuition is correct; in others, simple models show that strategic interaction either produces unexpected effects or is more complicated than thought. Further, the need to specify a particular game for analysis requires the theorist to be explicit about the strategic situation in the theory. This formalism can both reveal unstated assumptions or inconsistencies in the argument and aid communication of the argument among analysts knowledge-

able in game theory. At their best, such models can also help the analyst discover novel conclusions about international politics. Of course, the value of such models depends on the value of the theory being explicated; bad theory does not give rise to good models.

Specific conclusions developed from game theoretic models include: the central role of costly signals in the credible communication of deterrent threats (see **deterrence**), how a greater concern for the future makes agreements easier to enforce but more difficult to negotiate, how the combination of distributional and informational issues lead to the failure of bargaining, and when the difficulty of making binding commitments contributes to **ethnic conflict**. Arguments that game theoretic models have suggested are more complicated than generally thought include: when states join together against a common threat, the effects of long term shifts of power on the likelihood of **war**, and the role of international institutions in the communication of information in bargaining and enforcement.

The application of game theory to international relations has been criticized. Some claim that it cannot model theories of social structure because it is based on methodological individualism, that is, it analyzes the choices of individuals apart from their social context. However, a game does specify the social setting under which those individual choices are made. Of course, this description of the social setting may not incorporate all of the elements that some think of as social structure. Others argue that game theory cannot model theories that draw on **constructivism** such as structuration because they claim that games assume the interests and identities of the players – a central question in such theories. Those who use game theory respond that there are games where interests and identities are not fixed by the rules of the game. Much of the problem here lies in the lack of clear identification between the primitive concepts of game theory and concepts from constructivism like identities and interests. Further research will have to answer these questions, with the prospect of improving our understanding of both game theory models and those theories of social interactions.

In short, game theory as a tool has produced some important results for international relations theory. It is not, however, a central methodology in the field, and its use is largely limited to political scientists at US universities, and to economists.

Further reading

Gibbons, R. (1992) *Game Theory for Applied Economists*, Princeton, NJ: Princeton University Press.

Morrow, J. D. (1994) *Game Theory for Political Scientists*, Princeton, NJ: Princeton University Press.

Morrow, J. D. (1999) 'The Strategic Setting of Choices: Signaling, Commitment, and Negotiation in International Politics', in D. A. Lake and R. Powell (eds) *Strategic Choice and International Relations*, Princeton NJ: Princeton University Press, 77–114.

Powell, R. (2002) 'Game Theory, International Relations Theory, and the Hobbesian Stylization', in I. Katznelson and H. V. Milner (eds) *Political Science: State of the Discipline*, 3rd edn, New York: Norton, 755–83.

See also: prisoner's dilemma; rationality

JAMES D. MORROW

Gender

A system of **power** relations governing the interaction of males and females which usually privileges the former over the latter. Gender analyses have primarily criticized the absence of or under-representation of women both from international political decision making, and from traditional narratives in the study of international relations (IR).

Gender analysis in IR is an extension of the broader feminist critique (see **feminism**) and global activist project that has taken shape since the early 1960s. What binds together diverse feminist approaches to IR is a focus on women as political and historical actors; a foundation in the realm of women's and girls' lived experiences; and a normative contention 'that women and the feminine constitute historically underprivileged, under-represented, and under-recognized social groups and 'standpoints', and that this should change in the direction of greater equality' (Jones 1996: 406).

One cannot pinpoint a foundational text in feminist IR, but there is perhaps a foundational question: Where are the women? It was first posed in the most enduringly popular work of the subfield, Cynthia Enloe's *Bananas, Beaches and Bases* (2000), originally published in 1989. Various features of the feminist IR literature in the 1990s were anticipated in Enloe's book: the critique of classical theories of IR that shunted women and other subaltern actors to the sidelines; its global scope, asserting that gender was universally operative in international politics; and its diligent and imaginative location of women as agents in IR. Many of its core themes also received deeper exploration, including by Enloe in subsequent works: women and militarism; women in the international political economy; and gender and **nationalism**.

At the heart of the feminist IR literature is a critique of the classical (basically realist) tradition (see **realism**), although feminists have also leveled a critical gaze upon liberal internationalist (see **liberal internationalism**) and socialist (see **socialism**) formulations. Both from a distinctive slant and together with other exponents of **critical theory**, feminist IR scholars have assailed a wide range of basic tenets in the field: the universalization of man/men as the essential 'rational actors'; the idea of a unitary, 'black-boxed' state that obscures divisions of class, race, and not least gender; and modernist/masculinist epistemologies that underpin the classical tradition and bolster hierarchies of knowledge, **power**, and material privilege. Among the most fervent critics have been poststructuralists (see **poststructuralism**), who have sought to undermine dominant epistemologies, notions of stable identity, and all generalizing terminologies. The apogee of this trend was perhaps reached with the publication of Christine Sylvester's *Feminist Theory and International Relations in a Postmodern Era* (1994).

As noted, the study of gender and IR has been deeply affected by global trends in feminist theory and activism. In the activist sphere, women's mobilizations for equality have scored striking successes over the past four decades. National and international initiatives have addressed the plight of women, and entrenched women's issues at all institutional levels, though women still remain woefully under-represented in leadership positions nearly everywhere. The process was mirrored in academia, where feminist critiques came to constitute both a discipline in their own right and a standard component of introductory courses across the humanities and social sciences. In IR, the feminist subfield was by the mid-1990s one of the most flourishing in the discipline.

As feminism has become global, so has it been globalized (see **globalization**). The internationalization of feminist activism, once a Western monopoly, was symbolized by the **United Nations** Decade for Women and the UN-sponsored World Conferences on Women, the fourth and most recent of which was held in Beijing in 1995. Encounters between first world and **Third World** feminists at these and other gatherings led to a dramatic reappraisal of 'women' as a unitary global category. It prompted greater attention to divisions of culture and class among women; the role of women in female oppression (for example, as employers of female domestic servants and adherents of xenophobic nationalist movements); the relationship of feminism to other emancipatory critiques (such as anti-imperialism); and the possibility of men and women working towards common goals, a strategy that Third World women emphasized more than their developed world counterparts.

Mention should be made of a related trend prominent from the early 1970s: the growth of a **women and development** (WID) critique within **development** studies and international organization. The critique focused on women's situation in developing countries, quantifying many of the relevant issues for the first time, and arguing that women (and children) should be integrated into national development initiatives and international development work. In the 1990s, WID was increasingly replaced by a gender and development (GAD) critique that called for gender relations (rather than women) to be adopted as the primary analytical tenet.

Increasingly in the 1990s, as part of a broader revisioning of **security** studies, explorations of gender have revolved around conflict and conceptions of security. Rejecting traditional state-centric formulations, feminist scholarship has pointed to the gendered insecurity that afflicts women (for example, through domestic and sexual violence), even within superficially secure **nation-states**. Increasing attention has been paid to women's and girls' gender specific vulnerabilities in wartime. A central theme here is the **war rape** of females in wars and **genocide**s from Bangladesh to Bosnia. As well, the collapse of **communism** in Eastern Europe has prompted skeptical, feminist informed appraisals of the impact of **democratization** processes on gender relations.

Early feminist contributions were sometimes marked by gender essentialism: the notion that women and men held beliefs and attitudes that reflected their differing physiologies. Thus, a greater nurturing orientation for women could result from their capacity to bear children. Such essentialism was decisively supplanted, however, by a stricter demarcation between biological sex (male versus female) and socially constructed gender (masculinity versus femininity), with the overwhelming explanatory weight assigned to the latter. Hence, women were not necessarily predisposed to peace, nor men to violence. Rather, cultural formations shaped embodied men and women to behave according to limited and stereotypical visions of masculinity and femininity.

Is gender thus to be defined as exclusively a cultural formation? Increasingly, gender theorists have come to view sex and gender as mutually constitutive. Among feminists, the shift has perhaps been prompted by the feminist emphasis on damage done to the female body under conditions of male dominance, through violence and labor exploitation. The corporeality of gender seemed not only evident, but integral to feminist normative prescriptions.

What of the subject of men and masculinities in the study of gender and IR? It is fair to say that the attitude of most IR gender theorists has tended to be skeptical or hostile. Males have figured primarily as leaders, powerbrokers, and gender oppressors. Attention to diverse, especially subaltern masculinities has until recently been extremely limited.

Further reading

Cleaver, F. (ed.) (2003) *Masculinities Matter! Men, Gender and Development*, London: Zed Books.

Connell, R. W. (2002) *Gender*, Cambridge: Polity.

Enloe, C. (2000) *Bananas, Beaches and Bases: Making Feminist Sense of International Politics*, 2nd edn Berkeley, CA: University of California Press.

Jones, A. (1996) 'Does Gender Make the World Go Round? Feminist Critiques of International Relations', *Review of International Studies*, 22(4), 405–29.

Pettman, J. (1996) *Worlding Women*, London: Routledge.

Sylvester, C. (1994) *Feminist Theory and International Relations in a Postmodern Era*, Cambridge: Cambridge University Press.

Tickner, J. A. (2001) *Gendering World Politics*, New York: Columbia University Press.

See also: feminism; gendercide; women and development

ADAM JONES

Gendercide

Gender-selective mass killing. Whether directed against females or males, the practice is as old as history. In the politico-military context, sources from the Old Testament to Thucydides record instances of mass killing of 'battle-age' males, usually accompanied by the enslavement and forced concubinage of women and girls. In a sociological context, gendercidal institutions such as female infanticide, witch-hunts, forced labor, and military conscription are among the more venerable and destructive human institutions.

The term 'gendercide' derives etymologically from the term **genocide**, referring to the destruction of human groups. Under the 1948 Genocide Convention, genocide was limited to national, ethnic, racial, and religious groups. Groups structured according to political identity or socio-economic class were excluded. So, too, were gender groups. It is notable, however, that the most far reaching internal reappraisal of the Genocide Convention, the **United Nations** Whitaker Report of 1985, *did* recommend incorporating 'sexual groups' as targets of genocide. These included both biological men and women, and minorities (such as homosexuals) defined by actual or imputed sexual identity (Charny 1999).

Even a cursory glance at the numerous genocides of the twentieth century, along with other campaigns of mass killing, attests to gender's prominence as a variable. The most common trend has been the gendercidal targeting of battle age but non-combatant males, between roughly 15 and 55 years old. Such gendercidal massacres constitute an end in themselves and/or a means of weakening and undermining the broader target community.

Quite commonly, as in Bangladesh in 1971 and Bosnia-Herzegovina in the 1990s, the selective killing of adult men and adolescent boys has been seen as both a necessary and a *sufficient* genocidal strategy, at least as far as mass killing is concerned. Accompanied by other measures that are usually not fatal, such as mass expulsion and widespread **war rape** of women, the gendercidal killings of males serves to terrify a target population and reduce its will and capacity to resist. Gendercide of community males alone is genocidal, though it falls short of full-scale genocide. As Daniel Goldhagen argues in his study of the Jewish holocaust, '[t]he killing of the adult males of a community is nothing less

than the destruction of that community' (Goldhagen 1997: 153).

For contemporary observers, the paradigmatic case of gendercidal killing was the July 1995 slaughter at Srebrenica in Bosnia. In the worst massacre in Europe since World War Two, over 7,000 Muslim men and boys were separated from the community and executed *en masse*, or hunted down by Serbian regular and irregular forces in the surrounding hills (Honig and Both 1996). Children and women, along with some elderly men, were allowed to flee to safety in Muslim controlled territory.

In many other cases, including (by definition) the most extreme genocidal campaigns in history, gendercide against 'battle age' men has served as a tripwire or precursor of genocide against all members of the target population. The three classic genocides of the twentieth century (against Turkish Armenians in 1915–16, European Jews from 1939 to 1945, and Rwandan Tutsis in 1994) all share this feature. Armenian men, including eventually the very old and the youngest boys, were mercilessly eliminated from the population prior to, or at the start of, the death marches to the Syrian Desert for which the genocide is notorious. These forced expulsions eventually killed hundreds of thousands of Armenian children and women. Hitler's campaign against the Jews began with roundups and selective killings of Jewish men, such as after the *Kristallnacht* (Night of Broken Glass) in 1938. It was overwhelmingly gendercidal in the earliest stages of mass killing by *Einsatzgruppen* death squads in occupied Poland and Russia during summer 1941, at a time when millions of male Soviet prisoners of war were also being corralled for subsequent extermination. But the killing of Jews rapidly expanded beyond traditional gender parameters, and was extended to children and women. As many scholars have noted, this caused considerable psychological stress to the Nazi killers, and led to the development of distancing technologies such as gas vans and eventually gas chambers to implement the extermination orders. As for Rwanda, although mass slaughters of Tutsis took place almost from the start of the 1994 genocide, they were accompanied by an especially merciless targeting of Tutsi males, who appear overall to have constituted a substantial majority of those killed. Tutsi women were exposed to systematic **war rape** and sexual slavery that can itself be considered both genocidal and gendercidal.

Gendercide may be old, and a regular feature of contemporary conflicts worldwide. But the term itself is a product of modern feminist social inquiry (see **feminism**). It was coined by the American scholar Mary Anne Warren in her book *Gendercide: The Implications of Sex Selection* (1985). Warren drew an analogy between extermination on racial grounds (genocide) and gendercide, the deliberate extermination of persons of a particular sex (or gender). A particular advantage, in her view, was the gender inclusive character of gendercide, compared with female specific terms like gynocide and femicide.

Jones (2000) built on Warren's gender inclusive framing by applying it beyond the female-focused cases stressed by Warren, in particular by focusing on the vulnerabilities of non-combatant males during politico-military genocides. An institutional critique was also offered. As Warren had cited female infanticide and the European witch hunts as examples of gendercide against women, Jones coined the term 'gendercidal institutions' to describe both such enduring female-targeted phenomena, and institutions such as forced labor and military conscription that have generally or exclu-sively targeted males. The recent academic debate over gendercide is encapsulated in *Gendercide and Genocide* (Jones 2004), in which an interdisciplinary group of scholars examines, extends, or rejects Jones's formulations.

It is important to note that whereas the term 'genocide' in international legal parlance describes an extraordinary broad range of actions against human groups, from outright killing to transportation of children and impedance of births within the group, the debate over gendercide has focused almost exclusively on the dimension of mass killing and/or large scale mortality. In this sense, the term perhaps resonates more with popular conceptions of genocide (implying killing and physical extermination) than with the broader framing of the legal one. Any study of gendercidal institutions must extend the issue of agency far beyond direct state killing, as in the case of female infanticide, which is institutionalized through decentralized, family-level killings of girl infants. But it remains to be seen how useful the framework is in exploring more insidious forms of structural discrimination – for example, the educational and nutritional deficit of girls in most countries, or self-destructive lifestyles among younger men leading to high rates of injury and mortality.

If gendercide is such a regular feature of genocide, then the framework should hold some predictive value, enabling more effective forms of **humanitarian intervention**. For example, if gender selective crackdowns, roundups, and/or widespread executions of 'battle age' men are a reliable indicator of the prelude and onset phases of genocide, then such massacres should set alarm bells ringing in the halls of international governmental and **non-governmental organizations**. If younger men are the most vulnerable and consistently targeted population group, through time and around the world today, then governments as well as intergovernmental and non-governmental organizations should direct appropriate attention and resources to members of this group, by, for example, assigning them priority in evacuations from besieged communities.

Gendercidal killings of men also inflict immense trauma and deprivation upon surviving group members – disproportionately women, the elderly, and children. Interventionist strategies that protect civilian males therefore have important and positive repercussions for the rest of the community. Greater attention to gendercidal institutions that target women and girls – such as female infanticide and maternal mortality – could help to address underlying patterns of discrimination and neglect that afflict females in most countries of the world. Supplementing the study of discrete genocides with an institutional analysis of this type can also help to ameliorate gendercidal institutions that disproportionately harm men and boys.

Further reading

Charny, I. W. (1999) 'The Whitaker Report' In I. W. Charny (ed.) *Encyclopedia of Genocide*, Santa Barbara, CA: ABC-CLIO, 581–7.

Gendercide Watch. Web-based activist project with over 20 detailed case studies of gendercide and a compendium of media coverage.

Goldhagen, D. J. (1997) *Hitler's Willing Executioners: Ordinary Germans and the Holocaust*, New York: Vintage.

Honig, J. W. and Both, N. (1996) *Srebrenica: Record of a War Crime*, London: Penguin.

Jones, A. (2000) 'Gendercide and Genocide', *Journal of Genocide Research* 2(2), 185–211.

Jones, A. (ed.) (2004) *Gendercide and Genocide*, Nashville, TN: Vanderbilt University Press.

Warren, M. A. (1985) *Gendercide: The Implications of Sex Selection*, Totowa, NJ: Rowman and Littlefield.

See also: crimes against humanity; feminism; gender

ADAM JONES

Genealogy

When approaches to international relations labelled poststructuralist (see **poststructuralism**) mention the term 'genealogy', they are generally referring to the work of Michel Foucault (1926–84), who himself borrowed the notion from Friedrich Nietzsche (Foucault 1998). Unfortunately the term 'genealogy' is often used more broadly, and inaccurately, to refer to any history of a concept or a social practice.

Foucault draws attention to the problematic nature of any attempted history of ideas. For him history is always 'a history of the present'. It is inevitably composed from the perspective of the time in which it is written, and it views the past from the worldview of the present. What is more, the purpose for which it is compiled is located in the present. Foucault opposes any attempt to search for origins, or to trace the 'history' of an idea or concept through the ages, as if that concept somehow retains an identity through several periods, each with distinct ways of thinking. His work demonstrates that outlooks in different epochs (or *epistemes*, as he calls them) are radically incompatible with each other. It is not just that distinct concepts are recognized in each historical period but that in a sense what counts as rational thought, or as a suitable topic of study, changes. Ways of thinking, explaining and understanding change, as do ways of ordering. For example, although at present the human being – 'man' – is considered an appropriate subject of study, this was not always the case, and, according to Foucault, will not always continue to be so: Man may well 'be erased, like a face drawn in sand at the edge of the sea' (Foucault 1970: 387). A genealogy attempts to trace these differences and discontinuities.

What is accepted as rationality and what is necessary for something to be considered 'true' is dependent on the prevailing *regime of truth.* This term emphasizes the way in which the mechanisms and conventions for validating knowledge are tied up with systems of **power**. For Foucault power and knowledge are so closely related that he speaks of *power/knowledge.* He argues that there is no way in which truth can be seen as separate from power: on the contrary, systems of power are needed to produce truth, and, in turn, truth induces effects of power (Foucault 2000a: 132). What counts as true in any particular historical period depends on the social structures and mechanisms that are in place to validate particular methods or certain people or institutions as capable of producing truth. In the contemporary world, 'Truth is centred on the form of scientific **discourse** and the institutions that produce it' (Foucault 2000a: 131). It is science as a practice and as a method which these days is credited with the ability to produce 'truth'.

Because of the way in which genealogy attempts to uncover ways of thinking entirely distinct from each other and unfamiliar to current thought, it requires extensive and detailed historical research. Often, it means examining thinkers, writings and practices not generally considered important from the perspective of the present day. It also includes the uncovering of ways of thinking that, while taking place in the present, do not accord with generally accepted positions. In addition, and most importantly, it entails establishing the functionality of social practices in terms of power relations and the production of subjectivities.

It is this type of work that brings to light the possibility of intervening in contemporary regimes of truth. Exacting, meticulous historical scholarship leads to the rediscovery of the history of struggle and conflict that the systematizing thinking that goes along with the search for cause and effect disguises. But it does not work on its own; it also involves the resurrection of local, marginal or 'subjugated knowledges', disqualified or regarded as insignificant by the current regime of truth, repressed memories of struggles, and so on. As Foucault puts it, it is 'the coupling together of scholarly erudition and local memories, which allows us to constitute a historical knowledge of struggles and to make use of that knowledge in contemporary tactics' (Foucault 2003: 8). This is what he calls 'genealogy', which can be effective in fighting 'the power effects characteristic of any discourse that is regarded as scientific' (Foucault 2003: 9). Genealogies are antisciences.

This is not an unproblematic enterprise, since it is a struggle against the forms of power that go along with certain forms of (scientific) knowledge. And often, as soon as genealogical fragments are excavated, they will be re-colonized by the unitary, scientific discourses that previously rejected them. They then become part of the power/knowledge effects of the dominant discourse into which they are incorporated. A related danger is the risk of building the fragments of subjugated knowledges themselves into an alternative unitary system, with equally repressive consequences.

Further reading

Foucault, M. (1970) *The Order of Things: An Archaeology of the Human Sciences*, London: Routledge.

Foucault, M. (1998) 'Nietzsche, Genealogy, History', in P. Rabinow, (ed.) *Essential Works of Foucault 1954–1984*, Vol. 2, New York: The New Press, 369–91.

Foucault, M. (2000a) 'Truth and Power', in P. Rabinow, (ed.) *Essential Works of Foucault 1954–1984*, Vol. 3, New York: The New Press, 111–33.

Foucault, M. (2000b) 'The Subject and Power' in P. Rabinow, (ed.) *Essential Works of Foucault 1954–1984*, Vol. 3, New York: The New Press, 326–48.

Foucault, M. (2003) *Society must be Defended: Lectures at the College de France, 1975–76*, London: Allen Lane.

Sheridan, A. (1980) *Michel Foucault: The Will to Truth*, London: Routledge.

See also: deconstruction; discourse; identity/difference; poststructuralism

JENNY EDKINS

Genocide

Genocide, according to Article 2 of the **United Nations** Genocide Convention, refers to 'acts committed with the intent to destroy, in whole or part, a national, ethnical, racial, or religious group, as such: (a) killing members of the group; (b) causing serious bodily or mental harm to members of the group; (c) deliberately inflicting on the group conditions of life calculated to bring about its physical destruction whole or part; (d)imposing measures intended to prevent births within the group; (e) forcibly transferring children of the group to another group'.

The definition is fraught with ambiguities and as such has given rise to innumerable claims of victimization. The question is whether or not the UN definition fits episodes in Bosnia, Rwanda, Burundi and some 40 similar cases since 1945. The answer is probably yes. Let us examine the usability of the definition by looking at a real case, that of Cambodia between the years 1975–9. This well documented case exemplifies the horrors of genocide. The quasi-Marxist regime was known as the Khmer Rouge – Khmer refers to the largest ethnic group in Cambodia – and Rouge (red) refers to the Marxist origin of the political ruling elite at the time. This regime was responsible for the death of approximately 1.2 million people out of a total population of 7 million. Its agents killed, starved and transferred whole populations from the cities to the countryside. They removed children from their families and trained them to become cadres that also would kill and maim. They would prevent families from living together and would not allow husbands to live with their wives, therefore preventing procreation.

Given the facts on the ground it appears that events in Cambodia had all of the trimmings of a classic genocide, yet legally this was not the case. Throughout the years in question representatives of the Khmer Rouge occupied the official seat of Cambodia in the UN, and with the active help of their supporters were able to block attempts by the UN to act. As of today Khmer Rouge atrocities are sometimes referred to as mass slaughters, auto-genocide, or politicide. Why? The majority of the victims as well as the perpetrators were of the same ethnic group whereas the assumption implied in the language of the Convention was that victims had to be members of another group. The other real stumbling block was that there had to be intent to kill in whole or in part. After the Holocaust, who would have anticipated that an ethnic would turn against its own people?

The failure to recognize this episode as genocide can be traced back to the Convention's lack of inclusion of political victims. During the late 1940s **international law** experts had to pacify the former Soviet Union by excluding political victims from the language of the Convention, otherwise Stalin's representatives would have been instructed to halt its creation. Why? The answer is that Stalin would have been then identified as one of the great mass murderers of the twentieth century, having been responsible for the death of millions of men, women and children, who died in the name of an ideology that targeted real or perceived enemies of **communism**, similar to the goals of the Khmer Rouge, who wanted to eliminate all traces of previous regimes and of modern civilization.

What can be learned from this tragic failure to identify some cases of mass murder as genocides? At least in theory cases labeled as genocide should produce a flurry of preventive activities in the UN and other international bodies. Potential victims would enjoy the legal protection of the Convention and perpetrators could be held responsible and brought to trial. At the very least, we need to include political victims in the language of the Convention. Many scholars now include cases in which the primary victims are members of political groups; here these cases are reffered to as politicides.

The Khmer Rouge case highlights another problem, that of how many people need to be killed before an episode can be called a genocide. Although most victims were Khmer (political victims), some belonged to ethnically and religiously identifiable groups, such as Chinese, Vietnamese, and Buddhist monks, who were Cambodian citizens. Numerical criteria do not make sense, because it is not the body count that makes a genocide but rather the intent of the perpetrators, their sustained efforts and the group traits of the victims. Thus, isolated massacres or pogroms that are spontaneous and directed at peoples irrespective of their ethnic origin typically are not considered genocides. Nonetheless the threshold between massacres and genocide is somewhat fluid.

What are the key problems in recognizing a genocide before large numbers of peoples are killed, and what are the essential differences between killings in **war** and killings due to state repression, **civil war**, and genocide? One way of approaching this question is to look at what makes genocide unique. Looking back at the original definition, we find the words intent, deliberate, calculated, identity of victims, and physical destruction. If we compare these concepts to cases of civil or international war, we find that the identity of victims is key because during war all members of a society are potential victims. State repression typically refers to cases in which state authorities target members of political opposition groups by incarcerating or selectively killing some, but typically do not attack family members. If they were to do so, this could be construed as a case of politicide.

This is a brief description of what has been learned about what causes genocide and how to prevent it. The prevention of mass atrocities gets further attention in the entry on **humanitarian intervention**.

Individual and comparative case studies have shed some light on general conditions that contribute to the outbreak of genocide. A handful of more systematic and quantitative studies have tested some of these theories. The results of a recent empirical study (Harff 2003) support some assumptions and cast doubt on others. First, all genocides of the last half century were preceded by political upheaval, defined to include ethnic and revolutionary war (see **revolution**), regime collapse, and involvement in international war. Only 35 of 126 such upheavals between 1955 and 2000 led to genocides, however. Analysis showed that countries with high magnitudes of upheaval were twice as likely to have genocides as those with low magnitudes. Genocides were three times more likely in countries with political upheavals that had committed prior genocide. Autocratic regimes were three and a half times more likely to commit genocides than democratic regimes. States adhering to an exclusionary ideology were two and a half times more likely to experience genocide following political upheaval. The term 'exclusionary ideology' includes strict **Marxism/Leninism**; governance by *sharia'h* law, as in Saudi Arabia, that forbids the expression of other religions; rigid anticommunist doctrines found in some military dominated Latin American countries during the 1960s and 1970s; doctrines of ethnic and ethnonationalist superiority and exclusivity as practiced in South Africa during the era of apartheid; and narrowly secular nationalist doctrines that exclude the political participation of religious movements. Genocides were two and a half times more likely in unstable countries in which the political elite was based entirely or mainly on an ethnic minority. Iraq is an example in which Saddam Hussein's Tikriti (his home town) Sunni clan dominated a Shi'i majority.

Further contributing factors such as international political and economic **interdependence** were tested, on the theoretical assumption that if a country is connected to the international community it is more likely to be scrutinized in its internal behavior. The effect of economic connectedness was tested using as an indicator trade openness (indexed by exports plus imports as a percentage of GDP). Political interdependence was tested by using a country's membership in international organizations. Such membership would sensitize regimes to rules of laws and fair practices and/or provide more resources to avert internal conflict. Trade openness proved to be highly significant because states in upheaval with low degrees of trade openness were two and a half times more likely to experience genocide. These factors alone made it possible to distinguish between upheavals that led to genocide and those that did not with 74 per cent accuracy. These are exceptional results given the limitations of social science data and they provide a basic framework for explaining why genocides occur.

Despite convergence of expert's views about what constitutes genocide and politicide, and solid comparative evidence about the factors contributing to its occurrence, we are a fair distance from preventing future genocides. Why? Two arguments are frequently made. First, we do not know exactly when a genocide is being planned. Second, political leaders have little political will to engage in situations that are costly and dangerous. At present the United States government routinely does risk assessments based on the model described above. Thus, we know that a country is at risk, but not when exactly a genocide will occur. However, early warning models are being tested on high-risk cases that would narrow the time frame in which we can forecast when a genocide is likely to begin. This implies that policymakers can no longer say that they did not know. The lack of political will is an enduring issue but, with warning capabilities at hand, preventive action would be far less costly in political and material terms than inaction. The cases of Cambodia, Bosnia, and Rwanda make it clear that inaction, and belated reaction, have serious international consequences. They contribute to massive **refugee** flows, regional instability, and demands for reconstructive assistance, in addition to the human and moral costs of inaction.

What is key now is to develop better means to help potential victims and states to avoid genocide. In other words, policymakers and activists need to know what works, in which situations and at what time, to prevent genocides and political mass murders.

Further reading

Chalk, F. R. and Jonassohn, K. (1990) *The History and Sociology of Genocide: Analyses and Case Studies*, New Haven: Yale University Press.

Fein, H. (1993) *Genocide: A Sociological Perspective*, London and Newbury Park, CA: Sage.

Harff, B. (2003) 'No Lessons Learned from the Holocaust? Assessing Risks of Genocide and Political Mass Murder since 1955', *American Political Science Review* 97(1), 57–73.

Power, S. (2002) *A Problem from Hell: America and the Age of Genocide*, New York: Basic Books.

Weitz, E. (2003) *A Century of Genocide*, Princeton, NJ: Princeton University Press.

See also: crimes against humanity; humanitarian intervention; war crime

BARBARA HARFF

Geopolitics

Geography has always played an important role in human affairs. It has shaped the identity, character and history of **nation-state**s, helped and hindered their social, political and economic **development**, and played an important role in their international relations. Geopolitics is the study of the influence of geographical factors on state behavior – how location, climate, natural resources, population, and physical terrain determine a state's foreign policy options and its position in the hierarchy of states.

The term 'geopolitics' was first coined by Rudolf Kjellen, a Swedish political scientist, in 1899. However, it did not come into widespread use until the 1930s when it was championed by a group of German political geographers and in particular the retired Major General Dr Karl Haushofer in the Department of Geography at the University of Munich. Haushofer's association through Rudolf Hess with Adolf Hitler brought the concept to the attention of the world when Hitler consolidated **power** for himself and the Nazi party in Germany during 1933. Numerous scholars in the West and in Russia, China and Japan developed an interest in geopolitics as a science of statecraft, a method of thinking through the supposed significance of geographical factors in international relations.

As a field of study, geopolitics was inspired by the work of two major nineteenth century scholars, Alfred Thayer Mahan (1840–1914) and Sir Halford John Mackinder (1861–1947), although one might also note the influence of the German pioneer of geopolitics, Friedrich Ratzel (1844–1904) and the French geographer Pierre Vidal de la Blache (1845–1918). Writing in the late nineteenth century, Mahan argued that naval power was the key to national power. A state that controlled the high seas (as Britain did at the time) could dominate international relations. The ability to achieve such control, however, was dependent on a large well-armed navy, long coastlines, and adequate port facilities. In 1919, Sir Halford Mackinder advanced a territorial counterpart to Mahan's thesis (which he repudiated in 1943). Referred to as the 'Heartland theory', Mackinder argued that the state that controlled the territory between Germany and Siberia could control the world. As Mackinder expressed it in a memorable phrase; 'who rules Eastern Europe commands the Heartland, who rules the Heartland commands the World Island, who rules the World Island commands the World'.

Despite its unfortunate association with Nazi Germany's foreign policy in the 1930s and 1940s (Hitler was obsessed with expanding Germany's 'living area' or *lebensraum*), geopolitics is a serious field of inquiry. The various dimensions of geopolitics coalesce around the significance of the location of states on the world map. A state that is landlocked between two other states is likely to have very different foreign policy objectives than one that is surrounded by sea or other natural barriers. It has often been suggested, for example, that the isolationist tendencies in US foreign policy are directly related to its distance from Europe and that (prior to the invention of nuclear weapons) the Atlantic and the Pacific oceans provided it with a natural defense. This also accounts for the particular emphasis that the United States has placed on naval power over the last hundred years or so. In contrast, the location of Russia on the fringes of the West and its lack of secure borders helps to explain its historically difficult relationship with the West.

For geopolitical analysts, there is also an important connection between location, wealth and power. States that are located in areas with a temperate climate tend to be economically and militarily more powerful than other states. A wider variety of agricultural products can be grown, facilitating the extraction of natural resources. By the same token, those located around the equator or in the frigid areas of the planet tend to be economically underdeveloped and continually at the mercy of the environment.

Climate also impacts on the ability of a state to prosecute a **war**. The large number of French and German soldiers who froze to death whilst trying to conquer Russia in the nineteenth and twentieth centuries is an excellent example. In addition, climate affects terrain and this has an impact on warfare. Deserts, jungles, and mountain ranges require special training and equipment, and can either benefit an army or be the cause of spectacular military defeats. Thus, location can have important strategic implications. Consider, for example, the obvious advantage a state that controls the headwaters of a large river system has over a downstream neighbor. Not only would the foreign policy objectives of each state vary according to their position along the river system, but it would also lead to very different strategic responses in the event of a military crisis.

At the heart of geopolitical analysis is a belief that states' economic and military capability, their position in the hierarchy of states, and how they relate to their neighbors is a consequence of geographical factors. In international relations, geography is destiny. But it is important not to fall into the trap of reducing a complex area of inquiry like international relations to a single factor. There are many ways of interpreting state behavior and geopolitics is only one of them. Some scholars even argue that in the twenty-first century geopolitics is obsolete, superceded by 'chronopolitics'. Arguably, the strategic value of the 'non-place' of speed has supplanted that of place as electronic communications and accelerated modes of transport have compressed time and space.

Further reading

Agnew, J. (2003) *Geopolitics*, London: Routledge.

Braden, K. and Shelley, F. (2002) *Engaging Geopolitics*, New York: Longman.

Kupchan, C. (2002) *The End of the American Era: US Foreign Policy and the Geopolitics of the Twenty-first Century*, New York: Knopf.

Snow, D. (2003) *National Security for a New Era: Globalization and Geopolitics*, New York: Longman.

See also: globalization; realism; war

TERRY O'CALLAGHAN

Global cities

Global cities can be defined as large population centers (usually of more than three million people) with significant connections to other clusters of international populations. These connections are most often in the form of trade and economic ties, communications, transportation and ethnic diversity. In addition such cities act as social, political and economic centers for surrounding regions. Increasingly, these cities act as hubs in a growing global information network.

The world has entered the urban millennium. In 1950, only 30 per cent of humanity lived in towns and cities, rising to 45 per cent in 1995. Today a majority (over 50 per cent) of the world's people are now city dwellers and there are continuing trends towards rapid urbanization. There are uneven patterns to this scenario. For example, in the world's two most populated countries (China and India) some 30 per cent of the population live in urban areas while, by contrast, 80 per cent of Australians, Americans, East Asians (Japan and South Korea), and South Americans live in urban areas. However in India and China the situation is changing rapidly under capitalist economic systems (see **capitalism**) that attract people from rural to urban areas. The fastest rate of urbanization is in developing states in Africa, with current growth accelerating a trend that has been underway since the 1970s. Currently, the world's urban population is growing 2.5 times faster than the rural population. By 2015, the ten largest cities in the world will be in Asia, Latin America, and Africa. Nine of them will be in developing countries: Bombay, India (27.4 million); Lagos, Nigeria (24.4 million); Shanghai, China (23.4 million); Jakarta, Indonesia (21.2 million); Sao Paulo, Brazil (20.8 million); Karachi, Pakistan (20.6 million); Beijing, China (19.4 million); Dhaka, Bangladesh (19 million); and Mexico City, Mexico (18.8 million). The only city in a developed country that will be in the top ten is Tokyo, Japan (28.7 million).

The world's cities are growing by one million people each week. Projections for the year 2025 show that more than two-thirds of the Earth's population of 8 billion people will be city dwellers and with an anticipated doubling of the world's population by 2050, 90 per cent of that growth will occur in the South, mostly in the cities. Most of this growth will take place in small and medium sized towns and cities.

The role of global cities can be understood by considering the way they meet emerging population and social needs. Trends towards increased urbanization contribute to lower mortality rates through improved nutrition and health care, while urbanization also contributes to a decline in birth rates with increased education in family planning and changes in the status of women. Thus cities are factors in overall **population growth**, and also stimulate rises in the overall standards of living. The future of humanity lies in cities. Of all human habitats cities are best able to meet the rapidly growing demands for food, water, housing and other basic needs.

Around the world the population trends of young people are important for the future and these will be most strongly experienced in cities. Currently Asia has 1.6 billion children and Africa 333 million. By 2020 the regional proportion of children under the age of 15 years will be: Asia – 57 per cent; Africa – 24 per cent; developed countries (incl. Australia) – 11 per cent; Latin America – 9 per cent; Oceania – 1 per cent. The engagement of this young population with key issues in globalization is one of the most important factors that will determine the human future in the following ways:

- in terms of access to and use of technology;
- in impacts on and attitudes to the natural environment;
- in consumption of resources such as water;
- in access to education at all levels;
- in intergroup and intercultural relations;
- in gender relations;
- in opportunities for work and/or other meaningful activities;
- in engagement with political systems.

Certainly, many of the future impacts and relationships of this globally young population will take place in growing cities and urban complexes. The trend in globalization is thus towards a continued growth in the size and importance of cities around the world.

The growth of global cities

While the oldest cities are acknowledged to be in the Indus valley as early as 4000 BC other early cities flourished in such places as China, Korea, Africa and Central America through the first millennium. However urban growth was slow,

such that by 1800 less than 3 per cent of the world's population was urban. In pre-modern kingdoms cities were the domain of royalty and ruling classes, while the majority population of agricultural workers lived outside cities. The late middle ages brought the growth of cities such as Budapest and Prague along the great river trading routes of central Europe. The historical growth of cities can be identified with emerging capitalist economic activities, particularly in the growth of industrialism and modern international trade stemming from colonialism. Port cities such as London and New York grew on the basis of trade, partly to each other. In the eighteenth century the English city of Liverpool thrived on the international slave trade, building ships on which people were transported. Melbourne grew as a major city on the back of the gold rushes in Victoria, as did San Francisco from the gold industry in California. In industrialized nations around the world, from Manchester to Osaka to Baltimore, cities thrived through the nineteenth century as centers of manufacturing and industrial resources, to which large number of workers shifted from the rural regions.

However, features that enabled cities of the industrial revolution to grow have not necessarily maintained their comparative advantage in the period of globalization. In fact many of the previous industrial centers have declined in recent decades, sometimes becoming industrial wastelands. This is so particularly in the industrial cities of the former Soviet Union. Also former industrial centers in the United States and England like Baltimore and Manchester have had to revitalize at tremendous cost as their manufacturing industries declined.

They are being replaced by new cities offering advantages in areas like finance, high technology, or consumption. For instance, the center of the new industry information technology is Silicon Valley, near San Jose, a concentrated urban area in California. Cultural industries like media are also concentrated in urban areas. The world's largest media corporations like CNN, Time-Warner and News Ltd have their headquarters close to each other in downtown Manhattan, New York.

Globalization is accelerating the trend towards intensifying urbanization. A group of global cities have emerged as the networked center of global information flows, finance and services. These include New York, London, Paris, Frankfurt, Hong Kong, Tokyo, and Sydney.

Third world cities

The **Third World** has been characterized by the continuing growth of cities since the **development** period of the 1960s. The prospects for jobs, health, housing and education have been much better in cities around the developing world rather than in rural areas. Cities account for 50 to 80 per cent of most developing countries' gross national product and the urban poor are three to ten times better off economically than the rural poor.

The change from subsistence and local market economies towards national systems, export industries and corporate production structures is at the basis of this population trend. Cities have better services such as electricity and sewage. The spreading values of **modernization**, the desire for products like motor cars and televisions, and fashion clothes like denim jeans have stimulated the trend towards urban centers. Around the developing world the dream for a better life and wealth other than rural poverty calls many young adults and families towards cities.

The scale of the migration to cities and the failure of the cities to meet these expectations has resulted in the con-

tinuous growth of slums on the fringes of cities, where, at a global level, hundreds of millions of people struggle to survive in makeshift dwellings with very few basic services. In terms of living standards it is a fine line between **refugee** camps and fringe slum cities, many of which are technically illegal and occasionally get bulldozed by governments. They are made from old sheet iron, pieces of plywood, plastic and cardboard. Cities with major slum cities around them include Mumbai (Bombay), Rio de Janeiro, Brasilia, Johannesburg, Lagos, Kingston (Jamaica), Bangkok, Kuala Lumpur, Manila, Jakarta, and many others. Sometimes built around and under freeway systems, shelters are tiny. The only space for washing, cooking, sitting and playing may be the fringe of the road outside, crammed constantly with loud, polluting trucks and buses. Or else these shelters may be located along an alleyway passing between rows of lamp lit, tumbling shacks intersected by open drain ways of polluted waste, or perhaps a railway line. Other fringe cities grow up around airports.

It is a tribute to human spirit and resilience that families manage to cope, cook and keep their children clean in such urban squalor. However, in all fringe cities ill-health effects tend to be widespread. Many of the fringe cities merge into equally difficult older sections of the major cities where overpopulated ghettoes and irregular services like electricity force stringent conditions on the communities.

The rural areas vacated in this great migration to cities in developing countries are increasingly inhabited by old people and sons without prospects of wives, or wives and children left behind by husbands who have left for the cities. The burden of crop production weighs heavily on women and the young, especially with falling commodity prices.

Rural productivity declines and communities deteriorate. The concentration of services in cities further deprives rural areas of services like health, employment, and finance. This increased separation between cities and rural communities is one of the key aspects of globalization. In China, for instance, rapid growth is occurring in cities like Shanghai, yet in distant Yunan province, home to one-third of China's ethnic minorities, most communities do not have electricity or bridges across rivers. As China powers ahead in the development race, they fall further behind.

Some cities in developing countries have taken advantage of the opportunities in globalization for wealth creation and have developed high technology industries, becoming virtual islands of global urbanization, surrounded by rural, poverty level regions. The best-known example of this phenomenon is Bangalore, India, which since 1989 has established a wide range of information-technology based industries, building on an existing presence of education and aviation industries. Bangalore has established one of the world's largest software industries, producing over 30 per cent of India's software exports. It has also established such industries as data entry and telephone call centers that are used by companies around the world.

Cities as networks

The New Economy, with its emphasis on services, knowledge and communications technology has resulted in a new configuration of cities. The 'global village' to a large extent is the global marketplace of connected globally-oriented cities, each with their own internal social and economic structures (that look increasingly similar). Within these local contexts the elite classes are engaged in economic and cultural transactions with similar elites in other major cities. Patterns of networks between cities tend to reflect the patterns of airline services between them. The most recognized world cities like New York and London are networked centers of finance, information, legal and transport services. So are Seoul, Istanbul, and Buenos Aires. They are also regional centers of knowledge-based industries in education, media and the arts. Global cities are not only multi-functional but also the boundaries between different activities, such as industry and education, are flexible and open.

The concentrations of wealth, **power**, technology and services mean that cities are also centers of employment. While the capacities of information technology allow in a sense for networked regional development, and for increasing scope for work to be done from home, cities remain magnets for young people from rural areas in the West, as in the developing world. With work and the fulfillment of ambitions, the attractions of city life in such areas as entertainment, galleries and libraries, sport, urban and historic architecture allow lifestyles of relative ease, fun and diversity, if you can afford it. Cities have an allure of individuality and freedom. Important services like medical help and education are concentrated in cities, providing extra drawing power. Cities also have their distinctive histories and social distinctions, crimes and organized corruption. They are strengthening their role as centers of political power as rural regions decline.

Cities: sources and sites of investment

The freer flows of capital, electronic commerce and knowledge in globalization, and the market based criteria that determine the direction of those flows, have opened up new opportunities for cities as hubs of regional investment and services. The financial centers, particularly those with major stock exchanges such as London, New York, Frankfurt, Hong Kong, Sydney and Tokyo represent a networked group of cities where huge financial transactions take place at electronic speeds. These cities are also the most expensive in terms of property and living costs.

In order to achieve growth, cities are in fierce competition against each other to improve their attractiveness to holders of investment capital. In this global competition for economic growth, cities in the West have been the most successful, which is to be expected given their baseline advantages. However cities in NIC (see **newly industrializing country**) economies like Seoul, Bangkok, and Singapore are also globally oriented competitors for **foreign direct investment**. In the case of Singapore, this is built on a long history of strategic location along the world's transport routes and deliberate planning to remain a nexus of finance and communications.

The competition for investment means that cities must deliver the facilities and services demanded by big business as a precursor to investment. Using the South Korean case as an example, the Inchon International airport, which opened prior to the World Cup soccer tournament in 2002, was conceived and designed to be a regional 'hub', attracting trade and commerce in a globally linked air transport system. Vast amounts of money were spent on the facilities, services and overall quality of Inchon International Airport, hoping that it would attract recognition, prestige and business. This is a development model being implemented around the globe. However, this competitive drive sometimes means that city governments ignore the needs of local residents as they invest in projects to attract outside investors.

In their efforts to compete, cities in the Third World borrow excessive amounts of money from international sources to develop infrastructure projects that will attract foreign investors, such as 'Western' apartment blocks for employees or freeways to international airports, or indeed airports themselves. However, if they are not successful, these projects may become unfinished, under-utilized urban wastelands, for which the local population carries extra burdens of national debt. On the other hand, when they are successful, projects like airports and apartments are themselves capital assets that add to a city's value as well as providing infrastructure services for foreign investors.

The huge expenditure made on cities to make them attractive to foreign investors means that the population that lives in such cities experiences the costs and benefits of government decisions. Even in Western cities this focus on attracting investment has intensified existing socio-economic gaps in cities. While one area of a city may receive lavish resources to improve its investment potential, this is often done by reducing resources and services to other areas. Perhaps these are residential areas that were located around industries such as manufacturing that have now declined as a result of globalization. Consequently the globalizing of cities produces this differential effect whereby some areas become wealthy, networked and provided with a world of services, where the information-rich pursue money and careers, while other areas have chronic poverty, unemployment and a deteriorating urban landscape – or slumscape.

In major cities around the world the trend is towards denser centers where business, services, residences and entertainment converge, so that the traditional

CBDs (Central Business Districts) become CLDs (Central Lifestyle Districts). The rapid and continuing growth of apartment complexes in inner cities is an indicator of this trend.

Social and ethnic divisions

The socioeconomic division in cities, which is more gradual in Western cities than in the Third World, produces chronic inequalities between rich and poor people. Across the world, there are many examples of large populations living in city slums and on garbage dumps under freeways and below billboards with spectacular advertisements for global consumer products like Coca Cola, Ray-ban sunglasses, or Nokia cell phones. Extreme wealth inequalities are typical of cities like Lagos, Manila, and Mexico City, but also are the case in US or European cities that show increasing crime, drug use and further social breakdown.

One further feature of cities in the era of globalization is the way elite groups have responded to the problems of inequality and increasing violence by protecting their residences behind walls in so called 'gated communities', protected by private **security** guards and expensive security systems. In response to the inability of public police forces to protect them, the elite classes invest increasing amounts of money in their personal security. Not surprisingly security industries have grown rapidly in recent years. These well-resourced walled communities of professionals and successful capitalists are just one aspect of the growing ghettoization of cities.

Social patterns in global cities show the formation of increasingly more complex community clusters based on identity markers, such as ethnicity, age, gender and work. Language enclaves become established across these communities (and their sub-cultures). Ethnic community groups, which have been long present in world cities like London or San Francisco, will commonly use ethnic languages rather than that of the standard language used by government, civil officials and mainstream media. While English may be the unofficial main language in a city, many non-English speaking members of the city will go through their lives without knowing the English language. Their family and ethnic community contacts render it less essential to speak English, or any other dominant language. Moreover, as English is fast becoming the global language of business and information technology, many foreigners live and work in non-English speaking cities with no need to learn the local language because their English is sufficient for professional work and social life.

Increasing cultural diversity is a key characteristic of the globalization process and cities represent a challenge for multicultural (see **multiculturalism**) communities of different value orientations and priorities of interests to work and live peacefully together in the same space. One area of concerns expressed in debates over the future of cities relates to problems of conflict and violence between different communities within cities as they struggle for dominance over each other, or compete for access to resources of wealth and political power. Cities divided into war zones based on **ethnicity** are not entirely new. Jerusalem is the prominent example of this and there are many historical examples. The boundaries between ethnic communities are flexible and at times may be quite open, while at other times completely closed. The process of building cooperative multicultural communities requires much community building and education. Where cities have been divided on hostile grounds, such as racism, issues of justice and reconciliation have to be successfully resolved.

Consequently, one of the factors considered important for external investors relates to security and order issues. Multinational companies (see **multinational corporation**) are reluctant to establish operations in cities where political wars are being fought violently or law and order is breaking down. This explained the exodus of firms from Jakarta, Indonesia, when social order collapsed briefly after the Asian Economic crisis in the late 1990s. While firms increasingly operate **offshore** from their home countries they quickly move on if the conditions for doing business deteriorate. This was one of the main concerns in Manila, following a failed army coup in July 2003. The actual insurrection was hardly likely to succeed, but it created an air of political instability that threatened the globally oriented economic policies of the city and the country as a whole.

Cities as information hubs

The impacts of the **information revolution** on cities are many and varied. In South Korea, Singapore, and Hong Kong, for instance, the concentrations of high rise apartments make for easier, cheaper networking to the broad band communication system which gives faster, flexible access to the Internet and other information networks than conventional telephone lines. Another impact of the information revolution is the multi-node development of cities, physically, functionally and socially. In many places cities focused around a single CBD are being replaced by spreading metropoles of several centers. Contributing to this is a trend for sprawling outer areas of cities to merge into each other, and the city becomes one urban megapolis. Manila, Sydney, Tokyo,

Beijing, and Los Angeles are all examples of this trend.

Managing global urban challenges

The management of global cities has become one of the key issues in globalization. While in developing countries the key issues are provision of basic infrastructure such as water and sewage, in the West the increasing complexity of cities produces crises in areas like transport, environmental degradation, pollution, and provision of services in health and welfare. Increasingly, the efficient functioning of cities is dependent on networked information technology. Computer synchronized traffic lights to coordinate the flow of traffic are a prominent example. Trains, roads, buses and monorail services operate on detailed and complex information systems.

New laws have been introduced in Singapore, regarded as a model city for the human future, to ensure that the city functions as an integrated system. This placed certain restrictions on civil liberties in the demand for urban efficiency. Critics argue that such social engineering is dehumanizing to the population, who become cogs in some huge urban machine whose sole goal is efficiency for financial growth. It is often argued that the emphasis on functionality and efficiency undermines a sense of community. Modern Singapore has been described often as a 'soulless' city.

The trends of globalization towards increasing power and influence for large corporations becomes very evident in cities, through advertising displays, ownership of buildings, including former public spaces like sport stadiums and parks, and sponsorship of a wide range of events. Much urban space is available for rent to advertisers. The electronic advertising in Times Square, New York, has become a major tourist attraction in itself. People increasingly wear corporate logos on their clothes and shoes, and motor vehicles are prominently badged. In this dense cityscape there is no recognizable boundary between the personal and the commercial other than the 'choice' of the consumer, people exercising their freedom to choose from the range of products and brands on offer. This concentrated city environment is increasingly replicated across the globe as the products, food and brands become globally distributed. In this sense there is a growing sameness to world cities, or large segments of them. The proliferation of transnational corporate activities is a major factor in this process, with shopping malls, supermarket chains, and other icons of cities having similar features, products and ownership.

The visible urban presence of these corporations makes them vulnerable to protest, and sometimes acts of violence. Cities are also centers of terrorist activities (see **terrorism**). The terrorist bombing of the luxury Marriot Hotel in Jakarta in early August 2003, where over 100 people were killed or injured, is an example of this exposure of MNCs in cities to hostilities. The Marriot chain is based in the United States with operations in sixty-three countries. The strike was made because of the recognition of Marriot as part of a global chain and the protest was against the hegemonic (see **hegemony**) commercial and political forces that the Marriot represents as much as the particular hotel company.

Cities are also centers of political and civil activity and globalization presents challenges and opportunities in these respects. Cities offer social spaces that bring together people in civil activities. **Non-governmental organization**s (NGOs), political parties and social movements tend to be based in cities. Cities, then, become sites for political action by civil groups. In the age of globalization cities can be seen to play an important role in the spread and expression of a growing **global civil society**.

The 'learning city'

Over recent years the concept has emerged of 'learning cities' being forged that build on the benefits of globalization and the concentration of knowledge economies. Such cities work to achieve a better integration of structures, technology and global values to produce people with appropriate expertise and knowledge systems that will give the city a comparative advantage in the knowledge based society of the twenty-first century. Technology infrastructure such as broadband and other rapid communications are essential in learning cities. Networking and partnerships between firms, universities, civic organizations and other learning organizations are promoted to deal with a continuous exchange and flow of information about products, processes and innovation.

Thus a city for the knowledge economy places a focus on learning institutions and activities, knowledge production (research and culture) and the dissemination of information. This web of activities creates a shared identity for the city and diverse social capital. The goal of the learning city concept is to create globally competitive, knowledge intensive industries and services. Modern economies thrive on trade and the learning city is outward and export oriented, seeking to market and sell its skills and knowledge resources into the global market. The social capital of a city extends well beyond its technology industries however and learning cities also become centers of the arts, intellectual activities and even sport.

Global village – sustainable cities

In 1986 the **World Health Organization** introduced the Healthy Cities Program for the Twenty-First Century with a goal to improve public health in urban areas. A healthy city is one that improves its environment and expands resources to improve the opportunities for people to reach their potential. The Healthy Cities Program established the following areas of focus for urban development: development planning; community participation; health impact assessment of projects; **sustainable development**; health aspects of transport; urban governance and planning to promote healthy cities. These areas of focus provide a set of references and valuable criteria for urban development. Indeed, sustainable urbanization will ease the pressures caused by encroachment on fragile natural habitats. The Global Report on Human Settlements released in March 1996 by the **United Nations** Center for Human Settlements (Habitat) established the key goals and strategies for achieving sustainable urban futures.

While some cities are well positioned to reap the benefits of globalization, the impoverished living conditions in large parts of Third World cities are likely to become global crises and **human rights** issues. Despite growing investment, more than one third of the urban population live in substandard housing. Forty per cent of urban dwellers do not have access to safe drinking water or adequate sanitation. The high rate of urban population growth in most regions has led to common problems: congestion, lack of funds to provide basic services, a shortage of adequate housing and declining infrastructure, to name a few. Nevertheless cities will remain the engines of social, economic and environmental development in the next century and provide the greatest opportunity for the poor to improve their living conditions. Transnational corporations will increasingly control the economies and employment of cities, as well as their information systems, ownership of transport systems and utilities like gas and water, yet governments will remain responsible for the provision of services, law and order and other infrastructure. Sustainable cities will be the outcome of partnerships between governments, corporations and civil society.

Further reading

Bishop, R., Phillips, J. and Yeo, W. (eds) (2003) *Southeast Asian Cities and Global Processes*, London: Routledge.

Clark, D. (2003) *Urban World/Global City*, London: Routledge.

Graham, S. (ed.) (2004) *The Cybercities Reader*, London: Routledge.

Miles, M. and Hall, T. with Borden, I. (eds) *The City Cultures Reader*, London; Routledge.

Savitch, H. V. and Kantor, P. (2002) *Cities in the International Marketplace*, Princeton, NJ: Princeton University Press.

Short, J. R. (2004) *Global Metropolitan: Globalizing Cities in a Capitalist World*, London: Routledge.

Thorns, D. C. (2002) *The Transformation of Cities: Urban Theory and Urban Life*, Basingstoke: Palgrave.

See also: global financial center; globalization; information revolution

JOHN P. SYNOTT

Global civil society

In the domestic setting civil society refers to a social and political space distinct from the state in which individuals and collectives freely pursue and engage in social and political activities. Civil society exists between the private or family sphere and the public sphere of the state, and either incorporates or partially overlaps with the marketplace. Global civil society is conceived of in two ways: as the spread of domestic civil society across the globe to states without a strong tradition of civil society; and the **globalization** of civil society above and beyond the domestic arena such that it compliments and/or represents an alternative to intergovernmental organizations in **global governance**.

Civil society is said to be made up of a wide range of **non-governmental organizations** (NGOs) that both work with and provide a counterbalance to the pervasive **power** of the state. It is of interest to social and political commentators from across the political spectrum as it is thought to encompass a judicious mix of both individualist and collectivist sentiments, and of rights and responsibilities. It is the space in which social capital or social trust is generated and maintained. A strong and stable civil society is important because it goes hand in hand with the principles of democratic government, playing a crucial role in keeping at bay the potential for state authoritarianism. Similarly, global civil society incorporates a diversity of NGOs, many of them international in scope in that they are either physically located or conduct operations in multiple countries. To the activist, as in the domestic sphere, global civil society both works with and provides a countervailing force to the power of states, intergovernmental organizations, and the agents of global **capitalism**. In this sense global civil society is seen by some as globalization from below or the **democratization** of globalization 'from above'.

Global civil society is a contested concept used to describe an amorphous entity that means different things to different people, some even doubt whether it exists. Given the rapid increase in the number of international NGOs since the 1960s, and in the 1990s in particular it is difficult to deny the existence of at least an incipient global civil society. Many commentators on global civil society argue that it was conceived in the 1950s and the 1960s when many of the well-known NGOs were established. Others claim that its foundations are more long standing and point to the eighteenth and nineteenth century origins of organizations like the Anti-Slavery League, or the longevity of the Socialist International. A good case in point is the international feminist movement (see **feminism**) which traces its institutional origins to the International Congress of Women, established in 1888, the International Women's Suffrage Alliance (1904), and the Socialist Women's International (1907).

Discussions of global civil society generally include NGOs, **transnational social movement**s, and advocacy networks. Social movements or networks work on the knowledge or the belief that the agents of a movement in one country are reciprocally supported by similar groupings of potential political agents in other states. This motivational factor is important because even if the ideal of internationalism does not exist in actuality via formal organizational links, there remains a general awareness of shared experiences across the globe. One of the reasons why there has been an increase in the presence and effectiveness of these organizations and networks is their ability to utilize relatively cheap and sophisticated communications and information technology to organize and mobilize.

Common to most elements of global civil society is a focus on issues and areas of concern that transcend territorial boundaries. These can be single issue concerns such as **human rights**, health (e.g. the spread of HIV/AIDS), and environmental degradation (e.g. **global warming**), or broader areas of concern such as **sustainable development**, the detrimental aspects of global **capitalism**, and global distributive justice. The capacity of global civil society actors to mobilize and protest their concerns over such issues has been highly visible at meetings of the **World Bank**, the **World Trade Organization**, the **International Monetary Fund**, and the World Economic Forum. It is in this respect that some see global civil society (or more accurately, coalitions of actors within it) as having the potential to combat the perceived injustices of global capitalism. A particular target of this opposition is the allegedly exploitative tendencies of **multinational corporation**s.

In this regard global civil society is viewed as having a significant and essential role in global governance. To varying degrees it is embraced with the potential to make globalization more democratic, equitable, and ecologically sustainable. At its best, it is thought to be a superior alternative to the **international society** of states and intergovernmental organizations for the resolution of issues of international significance, and is thus viewed as a legitimate challenger to state **sovereignty**. At the very least, actors within global civil society endeavor to act as a countervailing force that can influence and compete with states in key aspects of global governance.

Discussions of global civil society are not all positive and they give rise to a number of difficult issues. For instance, there is contention over whether non-state actors such as terrorist organizations fit into the global civil society schema, as their organizational infrastructure resembles that of many NGOs or transnational civil society networks. Some critics see the emergence of a global civil society as a symptom of the withering of the state that marks the internationalization of social welfare, which is itself evidence of the globaliza-

tion of economic **neoliberalism**. To other critics global civil society is complicit in the spread of global capitalism and as such perpetuates the **hegemony** of neo-liberal orthodoxy.

As with most debates, reality lies somewhere in between these extremes. Claims that the invigoration of global civil society ushers in the decline of the state and the principle of state sovereignty are greatly exaggerated. For instance, NGOs are not completely autonomous organizations as they are restricted to a certain degree by the laws, policies, and conditions imposed upon them by the state(s) in which they are based. Equally, the claim that global civil society represents an unqualified good, or some kind of panacea with the potential to overcome all humanity's ills is an embellishment. This view is naïve and relies too heavily on the assumption that global civil society is a unified and coherent body that speaks with one voice, when in fact it is made up of a diversity of actors with different and not necessarily compatible motives and agendas.

Further reading

Anheier, H., Glasius, M. and Kaldor, M. (eds) (2002) *Global Civil Society Yearbook 2002*, Oxford: Oxford University Press.
Colas, A. (2002) *International Civil Society: Social Movements in World Politics*, Cambridge: Polity Press.
Keane, J. (2003) *Global Civil Society?* Cambridge: Cambridge University Press.
Keck, M. and Sikkink, K. (1998) *Activists Beyond Borders: Advocacy Networks in International Politics*, Ithaca, NY: Cornell University Press.

See also: cosmopolitanism; critical theory; global governance; human rights; multinational corporation; non-governmental organization; transnational social movement

BRETT BOWDEN

Global Compact

The **United Nations** Global Compact is a voluntary initiative designed to promote good corporate citizenship. Participating organizations undertake to apply the Global Compact's Nine Principles to the entirety of their operations. The Nine Principles cover the areas of **human rights**, labor standards and the environment.

First announced at the World Economic Forum in January 1999, the Global Compact is a direct initiative of the UN Secretary-General, Kofi Annan. It builds upon a range of United Nations Declarations, the most pertinent of which are the Universal Declaration of Human Rights, the Rio Declaration on Environment and Development, and the International Labour Organization's Declaration on Fundamental Principles and Rights at Work. By basing the Global Compact on these existing Declarations, Annan was able to coopt indirectly the support of member countries, without needing to have the initiative directly approved by the UN General Assembly.

Although the Global Compact sees a role for **non-governmental organizations**, business associations and organized labor, its primary focus is the private sector, and in particular **multinational corporation**s. Voluntarily participating corporations are expected to publish in their annual reports the ways in which they are supporting the Global Compact's Nine Principles.

Principles one and two of the Global Compact relate to human rights: businesses should support and respect the protection of internationally proclaimed human rights, and assure that they are not complicit in human rights abuses.

Principles three to six focus on labor standards: businesses should uphold the freedom of association and the effective recognition of the right to collective bar-gaining; businesses should eliminate all forms of forced or compulsory labor; should abolish child labor, and should eliminate discrimination in respect of employment.

Principles seven to nine deal with environmental practices: businesses should support a precautionary approach to environmental challenges; should undertake initiatives to promote greater environmental responsibility, and should encourage the development and diffusion of environmentally friendly technologies.

At the Global Compact Leaders Summit in June 2004, participating organizations agreed to add a Tenth Principle: business should work against **corruption** in all its forms, including extortion and bribery.

In a June 1999 speech to the United States Chamber of Commerce, Annan made clear that a primary objective of the Global Compact is to give the global market more of a 'human face'. The statement showed prescience, as six months later the Seattle meetings of the **World Trade Organization** were rocked by anti-**globalization** protests.

To 'humanize' the globalization of socio-economic activity, participating entities are encouraged to pursue their enlightened self-interest in developing (and then sharing) best practice activities. The hope is that quasi-collective activity at the corporate level will simultaneously arrest the 'race to the bottom' in environmental and labor standards, and broaden the social and economic benefits that may flow from trade. To advance its objectives, and to include NGOs, labor organizations and government in the initiative, the Global Compact Secretariat has developed 'engagement mechanisms' such as Policy Dialogues, Learning Fora, Local Networks, and Partnership Projects. The Global Compact is managed through a network of five UN agencies. These are the Office of the High Commissioner for Human Rights, the United Nations Environment Program, the **International Labor Organization**, the **United Nations Development Program**, and the United Nations Industrial Development Organization.

The UN Secretariat is at pains to point out that the Global Compact is not a code of conduct, nor does it seek to replace or compete with existing regulation. However, a case could be made that the Global Compact finds its historical origins in UN sponsored code making that began in the 1970s. Between 1975 and 1994, the UN Commission on Transnational Corporations sought to develop a code of conduct that would regulate the operations of transnational/multinational corporations. However, the proposed code of conduct was never finalized, and therefore was never brought to vote in the UN General Assembly. This had much to do with the politicized nature of the UN in this period, with entrenched **cold war** positions, ongoing post-colonial divisions (see **postcolonialism**), and a simmering conflict over the would-be New International Economic Order (NIEO). The proposed code of conduct on transnational corporations became bogged in international negotiations, and its failure to progress beyond a draft form was symptomatic of these geopolitical realities.

In contrast, the 1999 Global Compact avoided opposing **national interest**s by dealing directly with the private sector and other non-state stakeholders. It won swift support, and the International Chamber of Commerce was an early champion. In 2000, thirty-eight entities signed up, and by the early 2000s, the Global Compact had in excess of 1,700 participants. Just over half of these were based in an OECD country (see **Organization for Economic Cooperation and Development**). Other countries with large numbers of participating organizations included the Philippines, Brazil, India, China, Sri Lanka and Cameroon.

There has been some government backlash against the Global Compact. In the 2001 session of the General Assembly, for example, many country representatives resisted the push for 'global partnership', especially where these moves were seen to de-emphasize the primacy of states in international governance. Given thirty years of debate over the appropriate UN based mechanism for the global regulation of private industry, Annan may have found it preferable to at least achieve universal voluntary guidelines than to have no progress on a state-endorsed code of conduct.

Critics of the initiative argue that the Global Compact's voluntary and self-reporting nature render it effectively meaningless, and allow corporations to 'blue-wash' their operations with the UN's reputation. Supporters counter that the Global Compact builds upon existing regulations and codes of conduct, and that its main purpose is to bring greater transparency, responsibility and innovation to the activities of global business.

At its core, the Global Compact represents an attempt to standardize existing UN Declarations regarding environmental rights, human rights and labor rights, each of which are unevenly adhered to by signatory countries. The logic is that the growing importance of corporate citizenship may encourage greater social and environmental responsibility in corporate activities, with policy timelines longer than the electoral cycle. With the key proviso that participation in the Global Compact is seen to be in the corporate interest, it is possible that the narrow profit agenda of international business may be guided towards more sustainable social and environmental targets than has been the case thus far.

Further reading

Coleman, D. (2003) 'The United Nations and Transnational Corporations', *Global Society* 17(4), 339–57.

Feld, W. J. (1980) *Multinational Corporations and UN Politics: The Quest for Codes of Conduct*, Frankfurt: Pergamon Press.

Tesner, S. (2000) *The United Nations and Business: A Partnership Recovered*, Basingstoke: Palgrave.

See also: global governance; multinational corporation; United Nations

DAVID COLEMAN

Global financial center

A global financial center is a territorially demarcated area in which financial intermediaries are concentrated and within which a high volume of financial transactions takes place. Normally we think of New York, London, and Tokyo when considering global financial centers. Accordingly, many studies within **international political economy** have traced the development of the international financial order according to **power** shifts between principal financial centers. From this view London, Paris, and Amsterdam shared power in the eighteenth-century global economy. In the nineteenth century London was the dominant center, followed by New York in the 1920s. Today, some believe that the dominant financial centers of the world are to be found in London, New York, Paris, Frankfurt, and Tokyo.

There is strong evidence to suggest that London, in particular, developed the **offshore** and unregulated Euromarkets in the 1960s with the approval of the British state, and to take advantage of US domestic financial regulations that were pushing capital offshore (see **casino capitalism**). As a consequence the number of foreign banks within the London financial center ballooned during the 1960s and help explain its contemporary prominence. From 1980 the United States explicitly did the same in New York with the development of International Banking Facilities, a regulatory shift that explicitly recognized the growing prominence of offshore financial markets and the US need to guarantee its own market share within this new international financial environment (see **disintermediation**).

If we combine trading volume with the number of foreign financial intermediaries within its territory, then the leading global financial center is clearly London. Indeed, London has nearly twice the number of foreign banks that are present in New York, more than twice that of Frankfurt, and more than five times that of Tokyo. Similar comparisons can be made using measures such as foreign exchange turnover. However, to focus on London, or New York, or Tokyo, is not sufficient in understanding how global financial centers shape the international political economy. To restrict our understanding of global financial centers to these localities obscures the place of offshore financial centers or tax havens, which are an important part of the general debate on whether financial **globalization** is a threat to state autonomy and **sovereignty**. Three broad types of global financial centers can be identified based on the degree to which they empower or diminish sovereignty and state autonomy.

First are 'principal financial centers' that engage in high volume financial transactions and provide highly diversified financial services, including traditional centers such as London, New York, Paris, and Frankfurt, as well as

Toronto, Singapore, Hong Kong, Sydney, and others. These principal financial centers strengthen a state's autonomy by permitting the state's positive engagement with the international political economy and increasing its potential to invest and attract capital. Although London and New York provide the cases with the strongest international effects, all of the above principal financial centers operate with state support rather than discord. For example, 'Big Bang' financial regulations demonstrate their state's active role to make the financial centers more internationally competitive. Any diminution of sovereignty is the choice of the state itself and is reversible. Principal financial centers strengthen both sovereignty and state autonomy, although there is some dispute on the extent to which a financial center heightens income inequality within the state itself.

The second and third type of global financial center are commonly grouped together as offshore financial centers or 'tax havens', but they should be differentiated into two types. The second type can be thought of as global financial centers that act as 'capital service providers' with rigorous, if not deep, state-like institutional structures and broad social support for their presence. Many of these can be found on the European continent, such as Switzerland, Luxembourg, Liechtenstein, and Monaco. Financial centers within this group provide not only a means to place capital but typically also provide financial services and tax benefits to investors. By providing financial services and taxation exemptions to investors, states in this group use global financial centers to boost their autonomy by strategically using their sovereignty. In doing so, they are dependent upon the protections afforded by investor rights under international financial **regime**s. Their power in these

regimes is strong. For example, both Luxembourg and Switzerland sit on the **Bank for International Settlements'** Basle Committee. Typically, investors within states that host principal financial centers use these capital service providers to boost their comparative advantages on taxation and investment returns. Arguably, this makes such investors 'free riders' on the services provided by the 'genuine' tax revenue of their own states.

The third type may be described as 'capital shells' (more commonly known as 'brass plates') in which investment is strategically 'placed' for short periods of time. Such capital shells provide dubious social benefits to their host states. These financial centers are located in peripheral areas, both in geography, socioeconomic status, and political **power**. Unlike the second type, the benefits for state autonomy are questionable, as is their position within the international political economy as they come under much greater scrutiny from changes in international financial regulation. States that host 'capital shells' vary in their size, but include well known locations such as The Bahamas and the Cayman Islands in the Caribbean through to lesser known locations such as Vanuatu in the South Pacific. Following the 11 September 2001 terrorist attacks, these capital shells have come under even greater scrutiny as possible sites for terrorist financing. Under the hegemonic leadership (see **hegemony**) provided by the United States, the 'Financial Action Task Force' on **money laundering** through the auspices of the **Organization for Economic Cooperation and Development** has threatened the use of capital shells for **sustainable development**. States may use their legal sovereignty to act as geographical sites for 'capital shells', but it may cost them their autonomy. Critics argue that the existence of capital shells reflects the systematic underdevelopment of global financial regulation under the pressures of neoliberal (see **neoliberalism**) **globalization**.

All three types of global financial centers encourage the process of **disintermediation** and are thought to encourage excessive international financial speculation and tax evasion. The key question for the future will be whether the international re-regulation of global financial centers strengthens or diminishes stability within the broader international political economy.

Further reading

Agnew, J. and S. Corbridge (1995) *Mastering Space: Hegemony, Territory and International Political Economy*, London: Routledge.

Hudson, A. C. (1998) 'Placing Trust, Trusting Place', *Political Geography* 17(8), 915–37.

Langley, P. (2002) *World Financial Orders: An Historical International Political Economy*, London: Routledge.

Palan, R. (2003) *The Offshore World: Sovereign Markets, Virtual Spaces and Nomad Millionaires*, Ithaca: Cornell University Press.

Thrift, N. (1994) 'A Phantom State?' *Political Geography* 13(4), 299–327.

See also: Bank for International Settlements; casino capitalism; debt trap; disintermediation; global cities; globalization; International Monetary Fund; international political economy; money laundering; offshore

LEONARD SEABROOKE

Global governance

Like **globalization**, global governance is understood in widely differing ways by scholars and policymakers. Although for many global governance is no more than a synonym for technocratic management or just a new name for the study of international institutions, in the hands of others global governance offers a fresh perspective on newly emerging phenomena in international relations.

The idea of global governance is in part a response to the exhaustion of earlier ideas about world **order**. Two ideas about international relations competed at the end of World War Two. On the one hand, for many in the academic community and amongst the political establishment, **war** seemed to show the folly of the idealism of the 1920s. Idealists had suggested that cooperation between states was possible, and that misunderstanding and **misperception** were the reasons why cooperation failed. Against this idealism, a new **realism**, as it came to be known, pervaded thought on international relations after 1945. In the realist view, states were always driven to pursue their advantage at the cost of other states. The world was a zero-sum game and relative gains were the focus (see **relative/absolute gains**), to be acquired through tough negotiation. 'Human nature' did not allow for another way of behaving. Realists thought the liberal internationalist (see **liberal internationalism**) views championed by President Woodrow Wilson and the **League of Nations** had proven wrong and may have even encouraged the onset of conflict in the 1930s.

This view, despite half a decade of war and many years of severe economic difficulties, did not stop the victorious Allies from establishing the body we know as the **United Nations** (UN) in October 1945. Unlike the League, the UN was conceived as an active peacemaker. Indeed, the Allied Powers had used the term 'United Nations' from early 1942 to designate their **alliance** against German and Japanese military **power**. After World War Two, UN forces again undertook a peacemaking role, fighting in the Korean peninsula.

The UN enjoyed prestige in the 1940s and 1950s. This was a time of high tension between the East and West, and the United Nations was a place in which elements of this tension were managed, where the high politics of peace and **security** could be addressed in practical ways. During this period, the idea of international organization came firmly into focus in academic and policy-making circles. International organization, although never clearly articulated, was nevertheless an ambitious concept that suggested most problems between states were not about survival, and therefore could be dealt with through the application of science, expertise and resources.

International organization, unlike the idealism of the interwar years, was promulgated in a period of strong hegemonic leadership (see **hegemony**) by the United States. This meant that international organization, despite the ambition to solve problems, was always a limited concept that reflected the core interests of the richest and most powerful states. Not surprisingly, these core states were largely satisfied with the way international relations was organized and major problems were addressed. They were interested in refining and developing systems and institutions, not in remaking the world order into a fairer, less exploitative place. In this sense, international organization was what Robert Cox (1996), following the Frankfurt School of social theory, has called a problem-solving concept. International organization was plainly not a critical concept that could form the intellectual basis for a fundamental rethinking of how the world was governed.

The idea of international organization fell into disfavor in the 1960s and 1970s. In Africa and Asia, many new states emerged from colonial control in the late 1950s and 1960s. The end of colonialism had a major impact on the institutions of international organization. Discussion took on a decidedly more radical flavor. New agendas came to the fore in the UN and its specialist agencies, including importantly, the idea of a New International Economic Order (NIEO) between North and South. This called for a major redistribution of resources between rich and poor. The non-aligned bloc appeared, and General Assembly votes increasingly reflected the views of the world's poor.

The late 1960s and 1970s were also an era in which American **hegemony** was perceived to suffer relative decline. This was hardly a surprise given that the United States was responsible for half of world GDP in 1945 after the most deadly conflict in history, but relative decline was significant for the direction of US foreign policy. Some scholars have suggested that this period sees the onset of a more unilateral self-interested policy by the United States. This stance generated overt hostility to the United States even among rich countries. An example of this tendency was the US policy of printing dollars to finance both the Vietnam War and the Great Society programs of the second half of the 1960s. This flood of dollars stimulated the rise of inflation and a decade or more of economic policy problems for industrial countries.

The new assertiveness of the post-colonial societies eager to redress past wrongs came at the same time as the industrial countries experienced these tensions with US leadership. Conflicts over economic resources, rules for trade and finance, and the operation of the UN and its agencies became endemic. These were fundamentally political conflicts. The United States, or at least parts of the US Government, became increasingly uncomfortable with the UN and the views championed within it. During the

1980s, the United States grew tardy about funding the organization, and debates within the US Congress sought to link US financial contributions to UN reform, including the abandonment of some of its goals, such as the idea of a UN standing army.

From the late 1960s and into the 1970s, the idea of international organization itself fell into disuse. *International Organization*, the major journal that carried its name, increasingly drew back from matters of international policy and instead became a vehicle for the development of rigorous academic theory. It seemed that the idea of international organization as a policy goal was no longer feasible. The concept belonged to an earlier, more optimistic, more hegemonic age. The realities of the world of the 1970s were not ones in which the concept could thrive.

The abandonment of the idea of international organization signaled the end of faith in the post-war dream of a controlled world in which states could plan their way out of conflict and toward peaceful prosperity. International organization had proven to be a notion born of the confidence of victory that could not address new unanticipated conflicts. Despite the failure of international organization as a concept and a reality, the debate about managing international affairs did not end. Several new challenges came together in the 1970s and 1980s to rekindle the ambition that had underpinned the idea of international organization.

The **Bretton Woods** system of fixed exchange rates had come to an end in 1971, a consequence of the imbalance between US gold stocks and increasing US dollar holdings created to finance war and domestic social programs without a commensurate increase in taxes. The Bretton Woods system had been created at the end of 1944. Its purpose was to facilitate the balancing of liabilities between countries without the need for states to deflate their economies, putting people out of work. This sort of contraction in economic activity had been the normal way in which countries adjusted to each other prior to World War One. The architects of Bretton Woods saw this adjustment process as impossible after World War Two given the heightened expectations of returning soldiers and their families for a good life. The planners were also keen to avoid the return of destabilizing capital flows between societies, which they blamed for the development of trade frictions in the 1930s.

The end of Bretton Woods, and the re-emergence of global finance in the 1970s and 1980s (characterized by increasingly mobile capital movements) did create problems. Volatility, especially in exchange rates, was a great concern. Europeans in particular were worried about the negative implications of floating currencies. For them, the attractions of a more ordered world were very strong. This anxiety produced the Basle capital accord of 1986, which regulated the reserves that banks had to hold as a consequence of their lending. The 1980s was also a time in which cooperation between rich country central banks and finance ministers became increasingly formalized.

Another key challenge that emerged in the 1970s and 1980s was the environment. While anti-pollution measures were not new – England had put in place clean air laws in the 1950s to beat the London smogs – an awareness of the transborder nature of environmental problems was novel. This was illustrated by the case of 'acid rain' created by 'dirty' coal burning power stations in the United States. Although created in the United States, the acid rain actually fell on lakes in Canada, poisoning fish and plant life and killing the ecosystem of many waterways. One key product of this challenge was the United Nations Conference on Environment and Development (UNCED), in Rio de Janeiro, June 1992.

The Less Developed Country (LDC) debt crisis of the 1980s was another crucial moment in the development of new ideas about global management. The crisis had its origins in the desire of these states to avoid borrowing from the **International Monetary Fund** (IMF) and the **World Bank**. Official lending came with conditions that sought to limit what the LDCs could do with the money they had borrowed. Private sector money did not have the same conditionality attached and was plentiful in the mid-1970s because of the massive rise in the price of oil. These 'petrodollars' were deposited in Western banks that needed to find a way to earn income on these funds. As a result, credit standards fell and many loans were made that would not have been made had there not been such a flood of money. Because inflation was high during this period, the money was borrowed by the LDCs in the form of floating rate loans. When interest rates rose, so would the rates on these loans. The rise in rates, when it came in 1979, has come to be known as the 'Volker shift' after chairman of the US Federal Reserve Paul Volker. This effort to tackle inflation helped to create a severe recession in the early 1980s and a collapse in commodity prices. By the early 1980s, the LDCs were paying much more for their loans, but their exports had collapsed in volume and value because of weak demand in the recession-hit rich countries. The debt crisis developed rapidly, not just creating severe problems for these countries, but destroying the balance sheets of many rich country banks, threatening the functioning of the global financial system. Ironically, this effort on the part of LDCs to get around the restrictions of the international financial institutions had the opposite effect and helped to substantially alter the receptiveness of these states to market-based solutions to their problems. By undermining the potential for domestic strategies of economic growth, the LDC debt crisis created the conditions for an even more invasive program of scrutiny than these countries had experienced previously.

These problems, and many others such as **human rights**, land mine clearance and migration, made policy analysts and academics alike think again about the management of global problems. International organization had been overly optimistic, and closely linked to the prevailing pattern of American hegemony in the context of an ongoing **cold war**. What was needed in the new conditions was a more pragmatic idea, one that was not dependent on the support of one key state, and that focused on outcomes rather than just institutional processes.

The first widely circulated statement that used the concept of global governance is the report of the Commission on Global Governance, published as *Our Global Neighborhood* in 1995. Stimulated by the end of the cold war and what the Commission called a 'heightened sense' of an 'endangered future', the report asserted that governance 'is the sum of the many ways individuals and institutions, public and private, manage their common affairs' (1995: 2). This is a managerial vision of global governance, one concerned with dealing with feasible, tractable problems, and definitely not with broad issues of blame for poverty and exploitation, or adjustment of the prevailing world order. As many of the explicitly political dimensions of the relations between rich and poor states as possible were avoided by deploying this implicitly managerial concept of global governance.

A central feature of global governance as articulated by the Commission was the role of private, non-state institutions in the creation and enforcement of governance. Economic **integration**, especially the growth of capital markets, has created a multitude of new actors. In some cases, the Commission suggested, governance will rely on markets and market institutions. The incorporation of private sources of governance such as **non-governmental organization**s (NGOs), citizens' movements and multinational corporations (MNCs) was necessary today in order to acknowledge the broader scope of governance after the cold war. Previously, governance had primarily been understood as a consequence of intergovernmental relations. Accepting the role of private institutions in governance would, suggested the Commission, increase their effectiveness. But emphasis on these newly relevant private sources of governance fitted neatly into a more managerial vision of how to deal with global problems. The management focus of the global governance concept could be reinforced by the priority given to private agents, because private agents are not – in the common-sense understanding of the term – political. They are by nature technical. Even if they are lobby groups like NGOs, their main focus is on practical projects, not political change.

During the 1990s, the concept of global governance became part of the lexicon of the **development** policy community, including the international financial institutions, NGOs, think tanks, government agencies and academics. It has become the term of choice because it avoids the unequivocally political connotations of 'government', and the even worse implications of other labels such as **power** and **authority**. It provides a non-emotive language in which major issues of societal rule can be deliberated by experts and officials without making explicit what is implicit in the idea of global governance. Global governance seems safe, balanced and neutral.

Although global governance is a new concept within international relations scholarship it is already possible to distinguish some main strands to research. Full discussions of these tendencies can be found in Murphy (2000) and Hewson and Sinclair (1999). The first strand of scholarly global governance thinking is associated with Rosenau's (1995) discussions of the relocation of authority. Rosenau suggested that rising skill levels made the traditional organization of authority problematic, and placed emphasis on a secular shift from 'government' to 'governance'. Global governance in this account seems less like a traditional international relations notion and more like an entire perspective on global life. A second strand is concerned with the global expansion of democracy via civil society, and is particularly associated with the work of David Held (1995). In his view, *humane* global governance as an end incorporates democratic and cosmopolitan values can usefully be promoted by **global civil society**. This concern has recently been the focus of feminist authors who see global governance as a gendered realm.

A third approach is concerned with the role of globalizing elites, or what Cox calls the Transnational Managerial Class in furthering the development and implementation of neoliberal models of economic and social policy (see **neoliberalism**). Miller and Rose (1990) argue that 'technologies of thought' such as writing, numbering, compiling and computing render a realm knowable, calculable and thus governable. These 'procedures of inscription' make objects such as the economy and the firm amenable to intervention and regulation. Such 'humble and mundane mechanisms', combined with interventionist policy goals (what Miller and Rose call 'programs of government') have over time dissolved the distinction between state and civil society. What has been most vital, they contend, are the ways in which these indirect mechanisms of rule have enabled 'government at a distance'. This form of domination involves 'intellectual mastery' by those at the center over persons and events distant from them, based on the possession of critical information. The objective of rule at a distance is to create a framework in which social entities will become self-regulating within the norms of the system. This view, which is clearly less optimistic about the humane potential of global governance, could be thought of as the start of a critical political economy perspective on global governance.

Global governance is also associated with **regime** theory and the study of international organization. In this context, however, global governance is perhaps little more than a new label for research agendas that have their origins in traditional international relations concerns. There is little sign of a distinct global governance literature here.

The future for global governance is clearly a contested one. Global governance is an attractive idea for policy elites and they are likely to continue to deploy it in their work. It is an appealing notion for those interested in reforming the international policy process too, as it suggests some minimal mutuality to policy that reformers can seize upon to hold policymakers to account. For many scholars, however, global governance is likely to be used as no more than a synonym for the traditional study of international institutions.

Further reading

Commission on Global Governance (1995) *Our Global Neighborhood: The Report of the Commission on Global Governance*, Oxford: Oxford University Press.

Cox, R. W. with Sinclair, T. J. (1996) *Approaches to World Order*, Cambridge: Cambridge University Press.

Held, D. (1995) *Democracy and the Global Order: From the Modern State to Cosmopolitan Governance*, Cambridge: Polity Press.

Hewson, M. and Sinclair, T. J. (eds) (1999) *Approaches to Global Governance Theory*, Albany, NY: State University of New York Press.

Miller, P. and Rose, N. (1990) 'Governing Economic Life', *Economy and Society* 19(1), 1–29.

Murphy, C. N. (2000) 'Global Governance: Poorly Done and Poorly Understood', *International Affairs* 76(4), 789–803.

Rai, S. M. (2004) 'Gendering Global Governance', *International Feminist Journal of Politics* 6(4), 578–601.

Rosenau, J. N. (1995) 'Governance in the Twenty-First Century', *Global Governance* 1(1), 13–43.

Scholte, J. A. (2002) 'Civil Society and Democracy in Global Governance'. *Global Governance* 8(3), 281–304.

Wilkinson, R. and Hughes, S. (eds) (2002) *Global Governance: Critical Perspectives*, London: Routledge.

See also: conditionality; cosmopolitan democracy; regime; United Nations

TIMOTHY J. SINCLAIR

Globalization

The concept of globalization has in an extraordinarily short time become the dominant motif of the contemporary social sciences. Initially, the most common images of contemporary globalization were those beamed back from the Apollo missions. Planet earth floated in a dark void and swirled with clouds and oceans. This was the time of David Attenborough's television series *Life on Earth* (1979), watched world-wide by an estimated 500 million people. For all its colourful complexity, it was a *National Geographic* world, a planet without visible inhabitation. Partly qualifying the *terra nullius* naivety, political commentators strained their eyes to see 'man-made' signs such as the Great Wall of China, and environmental writers used the image to signify a fragile earth. The four horsemen of the apocalypse (war, famine, pestilence, and plague) rode this world, but they were shrouded by aspirational ideologies proclaiming that high-technology communications would happily bring us together in what earlier had been called a 'global village' (McLuhan 1960). This concept became the precursor to a series of other concepts including the graceless term 'glocalization', signifying the merger of the local and the global.

From its first academic use in the early 1980s, by the early 1990s globalization had taken on the kind of compelling urgency that we now take for granted and, like its French equivalent *mondialism*, the term had become politically loaded. Explaining the exponential rise of the term is difficult. It is not sufficient to point to the dramatic markers of the shift across that period, including the fall of the Berlin Wall (1989), the end of the **cold war**, the collapse of **communism** in the Soviet Union and the subsequent dissolution of the Soviet **empire** itself. Concepts such as 'Coca-colonization' had already been coined, but the two major political shifts of the twenty-first century were yet to have any effect on global politics: the uneven emergence of an anti-corporate globalization sensibility and the explosion of a global paranoia foisted on the world in the shape of a 'war on terror'. It was if we were setting up the conceptual apparatus for a phenomenon that we had just discovered and the naming made it real. Like the discovery of the New World in the sixteenth century, we could not at this time admit to the significance of its deeper (pre)history. Only later, as I will describe, did historians and sociologists come to talk about the different periods of globalization, and therefore its different social modes.

Despite, or more precisely because of the novelty of the realization, fields of study such as international relations and sociology faced 'winds of change' buffeting through the assumptions of their dominant approaches. In international relations the realist (see **realism**) emphasis on **nation-state**s as black boxes came under considerable pressure, as did the emphases of its critical counterparts, including even **Marxism** that had long recognized the global reach of material processes and ideas. Earlier, **world-system theory** and theoretical analyses of **dependency** had signalled a shift away from classical **imperialism** studies as the major scholarly vehicles driving the study of globalizing relations and the dynamics of global **capitalism**. However, it took a sociologist of religion and later a couple of anthropologists – Roland Robertson (1992), Jonathan Friedman (1994) and Arjun Appadurai (1996) respectively – to write the first major books on globalization as such. International relations as a discipline had profound problems in dealing with globalization, but across the 1990s and into the new century we started to get books from writers crossing the boundaries of the discipline, including the international critical theorist Jan Aart Scholte (2000) and the international political economists Robert O'Brien (1992) and Mark Rupert (2000).

Defining globalization

Too many definitions of globalization are reductive, with a tendency to include sweeping generalizations about the obsolescence of territoriality, to exaggerate the economic basis of global relations or to focus on the **information revolution** as the defining characteristic of the phenomenon. For example, Malcolm Waters (2001: 5) defines globalization as '[a] social process in which the constraints of geography on economic, political, social and cultural arrangements recede, in which people become increasingly aware that they are receding and in which people act accordingly'. This definition is either a complete overgeneralization and/or it relies on a subjectivist qualification which implies that globalization does not exist until people recognize it. One of the most quoted and broadest definitions identifies globalization as 'a process (or set of processes) which embodies a transformation in the spatial organization of social relations and transactions, assessed in terms of their extensity, intensity, velocity and impact – generating transcontinental or inter-regional flows and networks of activity, interaction and the exercise of **power**' (Held *et al.* 1999: 16). According to this definition, globalization is a process, not a state of being. As a process it involves organized social connections across transcontinental or regional space. The definition is useful but vague. We might well ask, what *degree* of extensity, intensity, velocity and impact is sufficient for globalization to come into being? Why is the inter-regional or even transcontinental reorganization of space sufficient to call it 'globalization'? Why have changes in the mode of organization become the defining basis of globalization?

I suggest that globalization is best defined not in terms of inter-regional reorganization. Nor is it, as some other definitions have suggested, the annihilation of space, the overcoming of distance, or a terminus that we will reach when the local is finally subsumed by the global. Globalization may become more totallizing than it is now, but it can never be complete, at least while we remain human and therefore bound to some extent by our bodies and immediate relations. Rather, globalization is no more than the extension of matrices of social practice and meaning across *world-space*, where the notion of 'world-space' is itself defined in the historically variable terms in which it has been practised and understood phenomenally through changing *world-time*. Globalization is thus a layered and uneven process, changing in form over time. Globalization is not a specific condition. Globalization is the extension across world-space of ongoing practices, ideas and sensibilities, patterned as *modes* of social practice in production, exchange, enquiry, organization and communication. In addition, these modes of social practice manifest themselves through analytically distinct *forms* of globalization, as described below.

At this point we need to take seriously the critical analysis of Justin Rosenberg (2000). He argues that changes in the nature of time and space have been elevated by some writers into a grand architecture of explanation that has the potential to dehistoricize the processes of global extension. As he points out, if globalization involves spatial extension it cannot be explained by invoking the claim that space is now global. The explanation and the 'thing being explained', he rightly says, cannot be part of a self-confirming circle. 'Globalization as an outcome cannot be explained by invoking globalization as a process tending towards that outcome' (Rosenberg 2000: 2). Notwithstanding this crucial methodological injunction against the reification of globalization, it is still legitimate to treat globalization as a *descriptive* category referring to processes of extension across a historically constituted world-space. With a few refinements, that is all that I am attempting to elaborate in this entry. An explanation as to *why* the dominant modes of practice contribute to the genie of globalization is not tautologously contained inside the definition provided above, even if a method for beginning such an enquiry is inferred. I will develop this methodological argument later. First, we have to be clear that approaches to globalization also have to take into account ideas about the global from notions of heliocentrism in the fifth century BCE to the emphasis on freedom and **free trade** in the present day.

This leads us to the associated concept of 'globalism', which needs to be distinguished from globalization. Globalism refers to the ideologies and/or subjectivities associated with different historically dominant formations of global extension. It is therefore much more than the ideology associated with the *contemporary* dominant variant known as **neoliberalism**. The definition implies that there were pre-modern or *traditional* forms of globalism and globalization long before the driving force of capitalism sought to colonize every corner of the globe. We might, for example, go back to the Roman Empire in the second century BCE, or perhaps to the Greeks of the fifth century BCE. Interestingly, international relations scholars such as Chris Reus-Smit (1999) draw on classical Greek examples to begin their constructivist (see **constructivism**) analyses of the changing nature of the state. In relation to globalism, Greek scholars conceived of world-extension as a contested field mostly confined to a mode of enquiry with little impact on other

modes of practice. Later, the Roman Empire drew lines of organizational connection across vast expanses of the known world. Although they were very restricted in comparison to what might be called *modern* globalization, the Roman Empire still had pretensions to colonize a world-space. Claudius Ptolemaeus (*c.* 90–*c.* 150) revived the Hellenic belief in the Pythagorean theory of a spherical globe. He wrote systematically about a world-space stretching from Caledonia and Anglia to what became known as Java Minor. Alongside the secular empire, the Roman Catholic Church (as its name suggests; *katholikos* means universal, *kata* in respect of, *holos* the whole) had globalizing pretensions. This does not mean that during these times that globalism was the dominant or even a generalized understanding of the world. Sacred universalism, for example, was and is not the same as globalization.

Periodizing globalization

The definition of globalization provided above is sensitive to Roland Robertson's (1992) argument that globalization is a deep historical and variable process. By suggesting that the Roman Empire possessed globalizing sensibilities (globalism) and globalizing practices (globalization), the definition extends Robertson's chronicle of the 'germinal stage' back long before the beginning of (*modern*) forms of globalism in the fifteenth century which saw the *revival* of a spherical view of the world.

Consequently, we must be sceptical of claims linking globalization to modernity. For example, Anthony Giddens (1990) suggests that globalization is a consequence of modernity, whilst Martin Albrow (1996), in a fit of theoretical exuberance, claims that globalization is in the process of replacing modernity. However, processes of globalization developed long before modernity (understood in epochal terms only as a dominant social formation), and they will probably continue long after its heyday. We can distinguish between traditional, modern and even postmodern forms of globalization, but it is important not to think of such forms as unique properties of specific periods of time. For example, Robertson (1992) distinguishes between five 'phases' of globalization that he labels the 'Germinal Phase' (from the early fifteenth century to the mid-eighteenth century), the 'Incipient Phase' (from the mid-eighteenth century to the late nineteenth century), the 'Take-off Phase' (from the late nineteenth century to the mid-1920s), the 'Struggle for Hegemony Phase' (from the 1920s to the late 1960s) and finally, the 'Uncertainty Phase' (from the late 1960s onwards). Despite Robertson's concern with globalization, his typology of such phases rests on a specific focus on developments in Europe. Moreover, the typology implies a mysterious teleology of development with such loaded terms as 'take-off'. I am not suggesting that we should avoid identifying contingently dominant patterns of historical practice and putting dates around them, but there is a tendency in much of the literature towards a kind of 'epochalism' that reduces a period to a certain form of practice, and vice versa.

Theorizing globalization

Just as in the area of defining and periodizing globalization, when it comes to theorizing globalization there is a tendency to focus on changes in either the market or the area of information exchange. There are notable exceptions across the fields of international relations, international political economy, sociology and social theory, but quite often we find the implicit suggestion that

if the steam engine brought us the industrial revolution then information communication technologies (ICTs) have brought us globalization. It is not that these developments are not crucial, but we should recognize that the contemporary form of globalization is driven by a matrix of modes of practice, including changes in modes of production, exchange, enquiry, organization and communication.

Susan Strange (1996) provides an interesting perspective that avoids the tendency in the literature to exaggerate the role of communication. She uses the categories of security, credit, knowledge, and production as the basis for analysing changes to systems of **power** in globalization. Strange's categories are adequate for what she wants to understand (namely, who gets what in the context of **casino capitalism**) but her categories leave out too much for a broader understanding of globalization. After all, even if it is not the single determinative basis of globalization, changes in the mode of communication have to be recognized in the matrix of explanation at some point.

Perhaps by working across modes of production, exchange, communication, organization and enquiry we would be in a better position to engage with a fuller range of questions across the spectrum of concerns about globalization and localization. In the contemporary period, the dominant *mode of production* is computer-mediated and less dependent on 'labor-in-place' or 'single-site integration'. *Exchange* is increasingly dominated by the manifold processes of commodity marketing and abstract capital trading. *Enquiry* is techno-scientific and rationally decontextualizing of locality. *Organization* is abstract and governed by rational-bureaucratic modes of decision making; and *communication* is dominated by electronic interchange, including mass broadcasting whose content is sourced across the globe, but which is largely controlled from corporate headquarters in the United States. Changes in each of these modes contribute to the extensions of globalization.

Even if they are not *the* keys to understanding globalization, the modes of communication and exchange provide good illustrations of epochal change over the past century. After all, it was only at the end of the nineteenth century that, for the first time in human history, cabling and telegraph systems lifted communication out of the restraints of messages being physically carried by people. Long-distance communication tended to depend upon embodied agents of institutions such as the state. By the beginning of the twenty-first century, relations of communication had changed dramatically. In April 2003 Rupert Murdoch closed a $US6.6 billion contract to buy US pay-television group DirecTV, thus giving the News Corporation–Fox Entertainment nexus the first global pay television satellite network, including Star Asia, Star Plus (India) and British Sky.

This is an empirically powerful illustration of globalization in action, but it does not tell us much about the political nature of the process, or about the relationship between the local and the global. For example, Fox News succeeded in winning the largest cable-audience share in the United States during 'Operation Freedom for Iraq' (2003), presenting the **war** through a matrix of gung-ho **nationalism**. The stars and stripes fluttered in the top left-hand corner of the screen while presenters such as Bill O'Reilly spoke a language of 'us' and 'them', 'good' and 'evil'. *The O'Reilly Factor* had a daily US audience of 5.4 million viewers in the first week of April 2003. Thus despite the global reach of Fox News, this is evidence that might be equally taken as substantiating claims about counter-globalization tendencies, suggesting a return to the boundaries of the nation-state and the reciprocal feedback between the social form of globalization (in this case, the mode of communication) and the re-emergence of bellicose nationalism.

However, despite its variable content (local, national, regional or global) the media is globalizing in its interconnections, points of reference and technological sourcing. Whether it is Fox News, CNN, or even Al-Jazeera, the dominant telecommunications systems are satellite-based, cross-referential, and watched by more than their local or national audiences. For example Fox News, like all of the major news groups, has a globally accessible website. Neilsen/NetRatings reported that in the week ending 23 March 2003, more than two million people accessed Fox News on the Web, over eight million accessed MSNBC and over ten million people logged on to CNN.COM. In March 2003, Nielsen estimated the 'active internet universe' at 247.5 million users, a massive expansion even from March 1994 when the US Vice-President Al Gore presented 'his' project for a network of networks – the so-called Global Information Infrastructure.

The worldwide internet population is now variously estimated at between 580 and 655 million people. Starting with the letter 'A', there are 10.5 million internet users in Australia, 3.7 million in Austria, 2.0 million in Argentina, 24,000 in Aruba and no information on Afghanistan. This is an indicative list showing how the take-up of such technologies is related to the economic and political standing of the populations concerned. Nevertheless, we can say that the immediate reach of those media of communications is global. A person can now stand anywhere in the world from Aruba to Afghanistan to Australia and, through satellite-linked communications systems including the Global Positioning System (GPS), be technologically and globally 'networked' in some way or other. 'Welcome to your new office', proclaimed an advertisement in 1998 for iridium.com, introducing the world's first hand-held global satellite phone, 'it measures 510,228,030 square kilometres'.

Turning from communication to exchange, we can quickly see how the various modes of practice are bound up with each other. Concomitant with the development of electronic, computerized, and mediated codification as a new dominant means of communication, the overlaying of coinage and paper money by electronic exchange systems has been fast, confusing and increasing integrated with the modes of production and organization. Despite his understanding of money as a material abstraction, Karl Marx could not have envisaged the pace of change in this area of globalization.

Although many of the developments had slow antecedents, the changes have multiplied quickly. For example, the first globally linked credit cards such as American Express, MasterCard, and Visa expanded across the 1960s; cheque-clearing systems were developed in the 1970s; electronic funds transfer systems (EFTPOS) and automatic teller machines (ATNs) consolidated in the 1980s. In 1985 the Netherlands communications corporation Phillips and the British bank Lloyds announced a joint global funds transfer system called Sopho-net WAN, spanning countries from Peru to Papua New Guinea. Electronic banking through global browsers such as Netscape and Internet Explorer took hold in the 1990s, as did new schemes for electronic marketing, merchandizing, and computer-assisted share trading. IBM made a corporate comeback in the late 1990s popularizing the new concept of 'e-business' under its slogan 'solutions for a small planetTM'. Incidentally, IBM advertisements juxtaposed the old and the new: one newspaper e-business advertisement in 1998 showed a contemporary businessman pondering over a laptop and sitting next to a giant Egyptian Tutankhamen figure, itself appearing to hold an ancient ledger book.

Working at this level of what might be called *conjunctural analysis* is useful for examining modes of globalization in the present and making comparisons with the past, but by shifting to a more abstract level of analysis, there are possibilities for taking the analysis much deeper. For just as we can distinguish between different dominant *modes* of globalization (in production, exchange, communication, organization and enquiry), we can also distinguish between different dominant *forms* of global integration.

Forms of globalization

The concept of 'dominant forms' used here is crucial, for across human history we have seen the uneven intersection of at least four different forms of integration from the local to the global. First, there is 'face-to-face' or embodied integration where persons are readily present to each other in a physical sense. Second, there is a form of 'object-extended' integration where objects from gifts to commodities carry a relationship between individuals beyond the immediacy of embodied integration. Third, there is form of 'institutionally-extended' integration where agents of different institutions and corporations extend the possibilities of social relationships. This is the level of integration focused on by conventional international relations scholars who participate in a **discourse** of inter-state relations. Fourth, there is a form of 'disembodied' integration where social relations are abstracted from any agencies of mediation. These forms of integration, it should be pointed out, are quite independent of globalization and pertain to the constitution of *all* forms of sociality. However, they are useful as a way of giving analytical precision to processes of global extension that are uneven, transhistorical and changing.

Embodied globalization refers to the way that movements of people extend across the globe in a way that binds world-space. In a trivial sense it could be argued that this is the oldest form of globalization and was the unintended outcome of long processes of human movement conducted long before any self-conscious subjectivity of globalism was possible. It could simply be used as the name for human beings spreading out to settle the globe. However, to the extent that we want to treat the process as integrative, embodied globalization needs to be understood as extending lines of lived interconnection. It is relevant today as the patterned movements of **refugee**s, emigrants, travellers and tourists act to integrate the globe through transnational **diaspora**s of known others drawing lines of embodied connection sustained by stories, memories, and visits. The second form, *object-extended globalization*, involves the movements of objects, in particular traded commodities, as well as those ubiquitous objects of exchange and communication: coins, notes, stamps, and postcards. Traded global commodities today range from the objects under the gaze of the **World Trade Organization** to the relics and treasures of antiquity such as Cleopatra's Needle and the Ram in the Thicket from Ur, reported as stolen from the Iraq National Museum during the collapse of Saddam Hussein's regime in 2003. The third form, *institutionally-extended globalization*, depends upon the movement of the agents of institutions such as **multinational corporation**s and states,

beginning with the legions of expansionist Roman Empire and the proselytizing agents of Christendom, and today including McDonald's, Coca-Cola, Greenpeace and the **United Nations** as they administer their respective projects across the known world. Finally, *disembodied globalization* is characterized by the interchange of immaterial things and processes including images, electronic texts and encoded capital. This is the only really new form of globalization, at least in its systematized reach and intensity, but it has taken on an unprecedented generality with the intersection of electronic communications, computerized exchange, techno-science and casino capitalism.

Conclusion

Despite the volume of literature on globalization, one could argue that scholarship in this area is still in a formative stage. It is still searching for adequate definitions, for ways of periodizing history that do not reduce the diversity of phenomena to crudely demarcated epochs, and for a theoretical approach that can make sense of the complexity of globalization without giving it a strange life of its own. We need to recognize that the modes of globalization have been, and continue to be in flux. Moreover, globalization can take fundamentally different dominant forms across world history, or even within one historical moment, but without that form coming to characterize the period in and of itself. In any particular period, globalization ranges from embodied extensions of the social, such as through the movements of people, to disembodied extensions, such as through communications on the wings of textual or digital encoding. Across human history, and into the present era, the dominant forms of globalization range from *traditional* forms (primarily carried by the embodied movement of peoples and the projections of traditional intellectuals) to *modern* and even *postmodern* forms (primarily carried by disembodied practices of abstracted extension). Studying globalization in a systematic fashion therefore requires a new interdisciplinary thrust that will see international relations scholars working more closely with disciplines such as anthropology, sociology and history.

Further reading

Albrow, M. (1996) *The Global Age*, Cambridge: Polity Press.

Appadurai, A. (1996) *Modernity at Large: Cultural Dimensions of Globalization*, Minneapolis, MN: University of Minnesota Press.

Friedman, J. (1994) *Cultural Identity and Global Process*, London: Sage.

Giddens, A. (1990) *The Consequences of Modernity*, Cambridge: Polity Press.

Held, D., McGrew, A., Goldblatt, D. and Perraton, J. (1999) *Global Transformations*, Cambridge: Polity Press.

McLuhan, M. (1960) *Explorations in Communication*, Boston, MA: Beacon Press.

O'Brien, R. (1992) *Global Financial Integration: The End of Geography*, London: Pinter.

Reus-Smit, C. (1999) *The Moral Purpose of the State*, Princeton, NJ: Princeton University Press.

Robertson, R. (1992) *Globalization: Social Theory and Global Culture*, London: Sage.

Rosenberg, J. (2000) *The Follies of Globalization Theory*, London: Verso.

Rupert, M. (2000) *Ideologies of Globalization: Contending Visions of a New World Order*, London: Routledge.

Scholte, J. A. (2000) *Globalization: A Critical Introduction*, Basingstoke: Palgrave.

Strange, S. (1996) *The Retreat of the State: The Diffusion of Power in the World Economy*, Cambridge: Cambridge University Press.

Waters, M. (2001) *Globalization*, 2nd edn, London: Routledge.

See also: cosmopolitanism; embedded liberalism; casino capitalism; global cities; information revolution; regionalism

PAUL JAMES

Global warming

The terms global warming, climate change and greenhouse effect are all used in public **discourse**. While there are nuances in the meaning of each of these terms, for present purposes they will be treated as synonymous. Global warming was propelled on to the international political agenda in 1988. It rapidly became one of the major, arguably the principal, environmental issues on the international agenda and a centrepiece of the rising importance of environmental problems in international relations during the 1990s. Global warming refers to the (projected) rises in global temperatures caused by emissions of a range of gases from human activities. Such temperature rises are widely regarded to entail serious (and mostly negative) consequences, including sea level rise, substantial changes in weather patterns, migration of agricultural zones, and increases in extreme weather events. Several things have ensured that the political stakes in global warming are high, and that proposals to mitigate it are highly controversial. These include the human consequences of such ecological changes, mostly in terms of the generation of significant numbers of **refugee**s, their impacts on agriculture, as well as the possible economic and political consequences of mitigating global warming involving radical changes in energy use.

This entry is divided into six parts. The first lays out a history of international climate politics. The second describes the basic science of global warming, and the political controversy over the scientific claims regarding it. The third outlines the human activities involved in producing greenhouse gases. The fourth describes the main international agreements on global warming, such as the **United Nations** (UN) Framework Convention on Climate Change (FCCC), and the **Kyoto Protocol**, while the fifth introduces the main controversies involved in debates leading up to these agreements and in the elements that make them up. The final part examines three analytical perspectives that might be used to explain international climate politics.

History of international climate politics

Global warming was propelled on to the political agenda in 1988 by a combination of the US drought that summer, the realization that the six hottest years on record were all in the 1980s, and the sharpening consensus amongst scientists that carbon dioxide emissions were likely to cause global warming. This culminated in two events: the testimony of James Hansen, a well known climatologist from NASA, to the US Congress, where he stated that 'it is time to stop waffling so much and say that the greenhouse effect is here'; and the Conference in Toronto on 'The Changing Atmosphere: Implications for Global Security', which was highly publicized around the world, and where the proposal that industrialized countries should reduce their emissions by 20 per cent by 2005 was first articulated.

The principal outcome of these events was the establishment of the Intergovernmental Panel on Climate Change (IPCC) in late 1988 by the World Meteorological Organization and the United Nations Environment Program (UNEP). The IPCC was charged with reporting on the state of knowledge concerning the basic science of climate change as well as about possible impacts of and policy responses to climate change. The IPCC reported in 1990. Its report stated that should greenhouse gas emissions continue to rise, global temperatures would also rise, and would have broadly negative social and economic implications. Shortly afterwards, the United Nations General Assembly established the Intergovernmental Negotiating Committee for a Framework Convention on Climate Change (INC), charged with negotiating a treaty in time for adoption at the United Nations Conference on Environment and Development (UNCED) at Rio in June 1992. Also during 1990–1, governments from most industrialized states developed unilateral targets to limit or reduce their greenhouse gas emissions. Most of these coalesced around commitments to stabilize their CO_2 emissions at 1990 levels by 2000, but notably the United States government did not adopt such a target.

The negotiations leading up to Rio started in February 1991, and the UNFCCC was agreed in May 1992 and adopted formally at Rio (see below for its main provisions). Following Rio, there were a series of negotiations to develop the FCCC. Quickly, many parties argued that the provisions of the FCCC were inadequate to the task of responding adequately to climate change. This debate led to what became known as the 'Berlin Mandate', so called because it was adopted at the first Conference of the Parties (COP1) in Berlin in 1995. It contained a declaration that the parties should agree a 'protocol or other legal instrument' which would involve reductions in greenhouse gas emissions, in time for COP3 in 1997. The negotiations which followed produced what became known as the Kyoto Protocol, agreed in Kyoto in December 1997.

Kyoto's provisions were quickly controversial, as US legislators made it clear that they would not ratify it, given that it did not contain commitments for developing countries also to limit their emissions. At the same time, many of its provisions, particularly the new flexibility mechanisms were complex and much of their detail was unresolved. Over the next two years (at COPs in Bonn, Buenos Aires and The Hague), strenuous efforts were made both to develop the detail of these commitments, and to elicit US ratification. These efforts significantly relaxed the rules for emissions trading, Joint Implementation (JI) and the operations of the Clean Development Mechanism (CDM) to make it possible for parties to meet almost all of their commitments by buying up emissions permits from other parties or through investments in developing countries through the CDM, over the opposition of some parties and many **non-governmental organizations** (NGOs). However, the international process was then further affected by the election of George W. Bush as President of the United States. In March 2001 Bush stated that he would not submit Kyoto to the Congress for ratification and he was himself opposed to its provisions. Although Kyoto has now entered into force after Russia ratified it in 2004, many states have begun to explore other avenues for developing an international response.

Climate change science and its politics

The basics of global warming science are not disputed, even by climate change sceptics. There are three principal elements. First, certain gases in the atmosphere act as 'greenhouse gases'. They allow incoming radiation from the sun to pass through, but when it is re-emitted from the earth's surface, at different wavelengths, they absorb the energy. Thus the earth's average surface temperature is approximately $33°C$ higher than it would be without the presence of these gases. The principal naturally occurring greenhouse gases are water vapour and carbon dioxide (CO_2), with some methane also.

Second is the rise in concentrations of greenhouse gases in the atmosphere. The concentrations of CO_2 and methane have risen substantially since the industrial revolution. CO_2 and methane have been joined by a set of other greenhouse gases, notably nitrous oxide, **chlorofluorocarbons (CFCs)**, hydrofluorocarbons, perfluorocarbons and sulphur hexafluoride which are not naturally occurring. All of the rise in concentrations of these gases is due to human activities.

Third, there has been a rise in the global average surface temperature of around $0.6°C$ during the twentieth century. Much is also often made of the observation that the hottest years on human record have all occurred from the mid-1980s onwards.

Beyond this however, there is some disagreement. Strictly speaking, the controversy is about whether there is any disagreement or not. For supporters of the IPCC, the controversy is really about the ability of a very small number of sceptical scientists to gain media attention to denounce the IPCC consensus as a false, politically constructed one. There is in fact, for these IPCC supporters, no real disagreement about the main elements of the three main IPCC reports that have been produced, in 1990, 1995, and 2001.

For most participants, then, the IPCC reports constitute a statement regarding the current state of knowledge about climate change science. This has a number of main elements. First, from 1995 onwards (in its Second Assessment Report, or SAR), the IPCC was prepared to claim that the best explanation for the observed rise in temperatures is the rise in atmospheric greenhouse gas concentrations and that the balance of evidence suggests a discernible human influence on global climate.

Second, the IPCC has made a range of projections concerning rises in temperatures and in the sea level. Sea-level rise due to global warming is principally a response to the thermal expansion of the oceans, not the melting of ice-caps. There is some contribution from melting of glaciers and other land based ice, but melting of sea ice has no effect on sea level. These projections have emerged from the running of large computer simulations of climate known as General Circulation Models (GCMs). The IPCC's Third Assessment Report (TAR) projected increases of 1.4–5.8°C between 1990 and 2100, and the sea level to rise by between 0.09 and 0.88 m during the same period.

Third, while there may regionally be some positive impacts of climate change, in general the impacts will be largely negative. These negative impacts will primarily be associated with sea level rises, agricultural/ecological migrations, the health effects of temperature extremes, possible increases in extreme weather events, economic costs to agriculture, insurance, banking, tourism, and other industries.

For critics of the IPCC, however, there is still a significant controversy about whether their basic claims can be sustained. The main elements of criticism of the IPCC's conclusions are that: remaining uncertainties (in particular concerning feedback mechanisms) are too great to act as a guide to action; the nature of GCM models means the methodology

for making projections about temperature rises is inadequate; the IPCC has excluded people from many scientific disciplines with relevant knowledge; they underestimate the possible benefits of a warmed world; and that there has been too much focus on CO_2 to the exclusion of other greenhouse gases.

More strongly, many critics of the IPCC allege that the organization and its senior leaders have been driven by a political agenda to increase their own levels of research funding and personal prestige, and by a government agenda serving the interests principally of European states, most of which have few fossil fuel resources or opportunities for carbon sequestration (reforestation). Conversely, of course, critics of the sceptics, apart from pointing out their small number as compared to those involved in IPCC activities, focus on the funding they receive from companies whose interests are threatened by proposals to limit greenhouse gases (in particular CO_2) emissions.

Causes of climate change

The three gases responsible for the bulk of anthropogenic global warming, CO_2, methane, and nitrous oxide, are responsible, according to the IPCC, for approximately 60 per cent, 20 per cent and 6 per cent of the global warming currently being caused. The bulk of the CO_2 produced comes from the burning of fossil fuels (oil, coal, natural gas), with smaller amounts coming from deforestation and cement manufacture. Methane is produced principally by certain forms of rice agriculture, ruminant animals, and leakage from natural gas production and distribution. Nitrous oxide comes primarily from agricultural fertilizer use, with some contribution from transport and energy use. The principal area therefore which requires policy attention is energy use (including transport), with forestry and agriculture also important. Regarding CO_2, the IPCC suggests emissions need to be reduced by over 60 per cent in order to stabilize atmospheric concentrations. And given the ubiquity of energy use, in transport, industrial production, to heat and cool homes and workplaces, for food storage and cooking, the challenges in mitigating climate change are clear.

The two main international climate change agreements

The main provisions of the FCCC are contained in its objective (article 2), commitments to limit emissions (article 4.2), and the establishment of a range of procedural institutions and mechanisms. The stated objective of the Convention is to achieve 'stabilization of greenhouse gas concentrations in the atmosphere at a level that would prevent dangerous anthropogenic interference with the climate system' (article 2). Article 4.2 then contains the principal commitments of the Convention. This states that 'developed country Parties shall adopt national policies ? with the aim of returning individually or jointly to their 1990 levels of these anthropogenic emissions of carbon dioxide and other greenhouse gases not controlled by the Montreal Protocol' (article 4.2 [a] and [b]). The language is in fact more complex and confusing than this summary, weakening the force of this injunction to stabilize emissions.

The Convention also contains a range of measures to facilitate financial and technology transfers to developing countries to enable them to carry out inventories of their emissions and sinks, and to limit their emissions growth (articles 4.3, 4.5, 11). It also establishes a range of mechanisms to enable parties to develop the climate regime, including a Conference of the Parties (article 7), a

Subsidiary Body for Implementation (article 9), a Subsidiary Body for Scientific and Technological Advice (article 10) and a Financial Mechanism (article 11).

The Kyoto Protocol contains two principal elements. The first is a set of quantified commitments by industrialized countries to reduce their emissions of a basket of six greenhouse gases by 'at least five per cent' as compared to 1990 levels by some point in the period 2008–12 (article 3). This meets the principal requirement of the Berlin Mandate.

The second element is what have become collectively known as the 'Kyoto mechanisms', or 'flexibility mechanisms'. These are means of providing for countries to be able to meet their emissions obligations without necessarily reducing their actual national emissions. The three elements are emissions trading, JI, and the CDM, as alluded to above. Emissions trading (article 17) is a system whereby countries may trade their emissions permits with other countries. Thus countries that find it relatively easy to reduce their emissions could reduce by more than their required amount, and then sell surplus permits to countries for whom reductions are more expensive to pursue. Joint Implementation (article 6) builds on the 'individually or jointly' provision in article 4.2 of the FCCC by developing a system for crediting of investments amongst industrialized countries ('Annex 1' countries in the FCCC, 'Annex B' countries in the Kyoto Protocol) against their emissions obligations. Thus, for example, the UK might invest in an energy efficiency project in the Ukraine, and claim the reduced emissions from the project as part of its efforts to reduce UK emissions under the Kyoto Protocol. The CDM (article 12) is a rough equivalent to JI but between industrialized countries and developing countries, which have no commitments to reduce their own emissions. It allows for industrialized countries to invest in projects in developing countries that would reduce greenhouse gas emissions and count those against their emissions reductions obligations.

Controversies in climate politics

These elements in the Kyoto Protocol have proved to be highly controversial since they were first proposed. In part this is due to their operational complexities; much of the international effort since Kyoto has been directed to the details of how these mechanisms can be put into practice, concerning for example the rules by which emissions reductions from JI or CDM projects should be both calculated and distributed between participating parties. At the same time they have been highly political, principally in terms of how 'flexible' the flexibility mechanisms should be. The principal question here has been how much of a countries' commitment to limit its emissions could be met through these mechanisms. Parties (especially the UK) wanting to make it easier for the United States to sign have been keen to have relatively relaxed rules, while others (and most environmental **non-governmental organizations**) have wanted to insist on strict limits for the use of such mechanisms, so that parties would have to meet most of their obligations through action to reduce emissions within their own country. Another aspect of this has been the problem of 'hot air'. As 1990 was used as a baseline against emissions would be judged, this meant in particular that there is a possibility that the Kyoto targets would not in fact lead to significant emissions reductions. This is because emissions from the former Soviet bloc countries had already declined significantly after 1990 because of their economic collapse, and thus in practice many countries could avoid emissions reductions by buying up the substantial surplus of emissions allowances from Russia or the Ukraine.

These particular controversies reflect more general conflicts endemic to climate politics. Principal amongst these have been those over the usefulness of targets (and how stringent they should be), conflicts between North and South, and the particular position taken by the United States. From early on in the negotiations, there was a sharp contrast between the United States and other industrialized states over the question of targets. Most states proposed a stabilization target as a binding commitment in the Framework Convention. The United States was strongly opposed to this. It argued that targets would be inflexible and economically inefficient, but opponents claimed that they simply did not want to be committed to meaningful action. The dynamics of this debate has persisted since then. This deadlock was to an extent broken by the proposal for emissions trading, made initially by the United States in 1996, which retains the clarity of quantified targets but introduces the flexibility sought by the United States. But it persists in terms of conflicts over the stringency of commitments, with 'leader' and 'laggard' states present.

A second principal controversy has been between Northern and Southern countries that mirror more general North–South conflicts. The global distribution of greenhouse gas emissions is highly skewed. Industrialized countries produce approximately 75 per cent of greenhouse gas emissions with only 25 per cent of the world's population, with the proportions for developing countries correspondingly reversed. Thus developing countries have tended to claim that they are not causally responsible for global warming, and thus have no responsibility for mitigating it. This is overlaid with an economic argument about the different resources available to rich and poor countries. Meanwhile, some industrialized countries, especially the United States, have often argued that while industrialized countries' emissions are relatively stable, those in developing countries are growing rapidly, and thus for industrialized countries to reduce emissions alone would be worthless. This underlying dynamic has produced a series of specific conflicts in negotiations over in particular: the concept of 'common but differentiated responsibilities' (FCCC, article 3); whether the Financial Mechanism of the Convention should be administered through the **World Bank**'s Global Environmental Facility; Joint Implementation; and whether and when developing countries should take on emissions limitations commitments.

Finally, the position of the United States has been a consistent problem for other players. Although it only has 4 per cent of the world's population, it accounts for 25 per cent of global greenhouse gas emissions, and thus any global strategy to deal with climate change has to attempt to affect the pattern of United States' emissions. But the United States has been the holdout or laggard state throughout the period of negotiations on climate change. Given its political, economic and military dominance, it is able to resist pressure from other states relatively easily. This position of the United States intensified after George W. Bush announced he was withdrawing from the Kyoto Protocol in March 2001, which for many spelled the death of the Protocol. The negotiations have often contained a tension between those who wished to appease the United States to get its signature and those who preferred that countries in favour of action agree between themselves and wait until the United States was willing to join them.

International relations theories and global warming

For scholars and students of international relations, a number of theoretical and analytical questions arise regarding global warming. This section deals with three theoretical perspectives. For the dominant traditions of **realism** and **liberal internationalism**, the most obvious framework with which to analyse climate politics is as a collective action problem. Global warming is thus seen as a problem where there is a basic contradiction between its nature as a global problem, not respecting international borders, and the organization of world politics into separate sovereign states (see **sovereignty**). Resolving global warming requires action by all states, but there is no authority capable of imposing such action, and the **international system** contains a number of features that make such collective action difficult to achieve.

Realists and liberals share this starting point but then differ in their prognosis regarding how difficult cooperative action may be to pursue. For realists, the possibility of cooperation is very strictly limited by the way that international **anarchy** means that states are jealous about their sovereignty and thus reluctant to cooperate even where they have common interests with other states, but also because given that they are preoccupied with their physical, territorial security, they act as relative gains maximizers when engaging in potential cooperative ventures (see **relative/absolute gains**). The persistent conflicts between Northern and Southern countries, the failure of other states to persuade the United States to stay with the Kyoto regime, the weakness of the IPCC as and institution of international scientific cooperation to generate sufficient cognitive authority to overcome entrenched economic and political interests, could all be highlighted by realists as evidence in favour of their approach.

For liberals, by contrast, while international anarchy remains the central problem, the prospects for international cooperation and **regime** building are significantly more optimistic. First, for liberals states usually have wide margins of survival and therefore act as absolute gains maximizers. In this situation there is much more latitude for pursuing cooperation as states all need to gain but not necessarily equally. Second, the realist image of cooperation is based on assumptions within **game theory** about one shot games. By contrast, international cooperation involves repeated games over time, and thus states can build strategies to elicit cooperation from others, to deter free riding, and so on. As a consequence, international institutions and organizations can play a greater role in enabling states to find cooperative solutions. They can act to facilitate information transfer, build trust (to overcome free rider problems), and to reduce transaction costs, in particular.

In contrast to realists, therefore liberals would emphasize that against the background of these entrenched differences in state interests, what is remarkable is the extent of cooperation that has been achieved. Given all of the problems realists would highlight as above, one would perhaps be surprised to learn that states had agreed to collate and communicate to each other extensive details of their greenhouse gas strategies, for industrialized countries to commit themselves first to aiming to stabilize their emissions (in the FCCC), and then to reducing them by an average of 5 per cent (in Kyoto), as well as to develop elaborate and highly innovative institutional mechanisms (the Kyoto flexibility mechanisms, as well as more general mechanisms for reporting, scientific advice, financial transfers, and so on).

Liberals would also argue that international institutions had in fact shaped the pattern of cooperation, for example by making it increasingly difficult to argue that there was too much scientific uncertainty to justify action to reduce emissions.

From a political economy perspective, two rather different sorts of arguments emerge. First, both realist and liberal perspectives fail to explain the systemic nature and depth of the North–South conflict over global warming. From a political economy point of view, this is rooted in the structural inequalities operating within the global economy. The second is a focus on the power of business within contemporary polities, to explain the patterns of policy development both within and between states. From this perspective, the central analytical starting point is the relationship between states and social forces in capitalist society (see **capitalism**), in which business is structurally dominant, rather than relations between states.

Three broad business interests can be discerned in climate politics. The first has been a coalition of mostly US firms from the oil, automobile, electricity, steel, and coal industries in particular, to try to undermine action to reduce emissions. They have been organized mostly through the Global Climate Coalition (GCC), which was set up in the early 1990s and has: attempted to undermine the credibility of the IPCC; emphasized remaining scientific uncertainties; lobbied politicians both in the United States and internationally; and engaged in advertising campaigns (especially in the run-up to Kyoto) emphasizing the economic costs to the United States and to individuals of emissions reductions and the alleged unfairness that developing countries have no emissions obligations under Kyoto. Members of the GCC had very close ties to the incoming Bush administration, which has taken a position very close to that of the GCC regarding climate change.

Second are those businesses with interests in mitigating greenhouse gas emissions. These 'sunrise' industries of renewable energy (solar, hydro-electricity, wind, in particular) alongside energy efficiency and conservation industries, have provided countervailing pressure and evidence regarding the economic costs of action. They have been joined by some oil companies (especially Shell and BP) whose joint holdings in gas and oil mean they have interests in reductions to promote their gas business, and who have also become significant players in renewable energy development. These 'progressive' business voices have found outlets in organizations like the Business Council for a Sustainable Energy Future, and the Pew Center on Global Climate Change.

Third, some industries are likely to be significantly affected by the impacts of climate change itself. The most prominent of these is the insurance industry, parts of which have been making noises about the potential impact of the increases in the frequency and severity of extreme weather events since the early 1990s, which at their extreme could cause major disruption to financial institutions and thus the global economy. Insurers have been courted initially by Greenpeace and then from around 1994 onwards by UNEP, in attempts to build support for action to mitigate climate change.

The power of business in climate politics is therefore complex. But at its heart is an account of global warming politics which focuses on the structural power of business in capitalist society. Capitalist society in this view is fundamentally dependent on growth. And in a growth dependent system, those who organize the investment that generates growth are structurally powerful. Throughout climate politics, debates about whether to reduce emissions or not, and by how much, are dominated by considerations of impacts on GDP growth. But while for most of the twentieth century the widespread assumption was that this required growth in (fossil) energy consumption, since the oil crisis of 1973–4, this assumption has been increasingly challenged. The splits in business interests over global warming outlined above reflect this challenge, and we can now discern two distinct blocs of interests, with distinct growth strategies underpinning their positions.

The first is a bloc comprising the GCC, the Bush Administration in the United States, and OPEC (see **Organization of Petroleum Exporting Countries**), arguing for a continuation of cheap fossil fuel energy as a basis for economic growth. The second is a bloc comprising most European governments, renewable energy (and in some cases nuclear) and energy efficiency firms, and supported ideologically by environmental NGOs (see **non-governmental organizations**), operating with what can be called a discourse of ecological modernization – that growth can and should be pursued while aggressively pursuing emissions reductions, and indeed that emissions reductions are an opportunity to improve economic efficiency and dynamism through fostering rapid technological **development**. Climate politics is thus from a political economy perspective not so much a question of how to explain collective action problems and promote cooperation between states, but how to articulate (transnationally) coalitions to support growth strategies that reduce emissions, and reduce global inequalities in emissions.

Further reading

Athanasiou, T. and Baer, P. (2002) *Dead Heat: Global Justice and Global Warming*, New York: Seven Stories Press.

Boehmer-Christiansen, S. and Kellow, A. (2002) *International Environmental Policy: Interests and the Failure of the Kyoto Process*, Cheltenham: Edward Elgar.

Leggett, J. (1999) *The Carbon War*, London: Penguin.

Newell, P. (2000) *Climate for Change; Non-State actors and the Global Politics of the Greenhouse*, Cambridge: Cambridge University Press.

Paterson, M. (1996) *Global Warming and Global Politics*, London: Routledge.

Sprinz, D. and Luterbacher, U. (eds) (2001) *International Relations and Global Climate Change*, Cambridge MA: MIT Press.

See also: biodiversity; chlorofluorocarbons; desertification; Kyoto protocol

MATTHEW PATERSON

Good governance

While by no means a new topic in the area of economic **development**, the issue of good governance has been given new impetus by five important factors. First, the issue is a response to the development failures in the 1980s, in particular, the difficult experience with and mixed record of **structural adjustment programs**. Second, it is a recognition of the failure of command economies and the emergence of a consensus within the **World Bank** and the **International Monetary Fund** (IMF) on the relative efficacy of neoliberal development strategies. Third, the rise of pro-democracy movements in Africa and other parts of the developing world has been accompanied with the demand for good governance and more responsive forms of government as a rallying point. Fourth, there has been growing concern that widespread **corruption** is siphoning away both domestic and external resources of developing states. And fifth, the phenomenal increase in **globalization** has generated strong imperatives for sound domestic policy environments and economic management.

Governance means the act or manner of governing, of exercising control or **authority** over the actions of subjects through a system of regulations. In essence, therefore, governance may be taken as denoting how people are ruled, and how the affairs of a state are administered and regulated. In international relations, governance is usually linked to the exercise of state **sovereignty**. However, in an increasingly globalized world, states are bound together by a web of multilateral and bilateral agreements that create mutual binding obligations and place governments under greater scrutiny.

The trend towards globalization deserves special attention. It is manifest in the growth of **regional trade bloc**s that cooperate in such areas as trade and the elaboration of common legal frameworks. It is also observed in the **power** of intergovernmental institutions and in the spread of **multinational corporation**s. Globalization is altering the world's economic landscape in fundamental ways. It is driven by a widespread push towards the liberalization of trade and capital markets, increasing internationalization of corporate production and distribution strategies, and technological change that is rapidly dismantling barriers to the international tradability of goods and services and the mobility of capital. Globalization has profound implications for governance, including the erosion of state sovereignty as transnational bodies increasingly mediate national concerns and press for universal laws. Another dimension is the increased globalization of political, social, economic and environmental problems.

Thus good governance cannot be considered a closed system. The role of the state is to find a balance between taking advantage of globalization and providing a secure and stable social and economic domestic environment. Against this background, governance can more appropriately be defined as the manner in which power is exercised in the management of the affairs of a nation, and its relations with other nations. It follows therefore, that solutions to some governance problems, such as corruption and excessive military expenditure, can be facilitated by actions at the global level.

There is a consensus that good governance should build on effective states, mobilized civil societies, and efficient private sectors, three factors necessary for sustained development. Effective states create an enabling political and legal environment for equitable economic growth. Active and vibrant civil societies mobilize individuals, groups and communities, facilitate political and social interaction, help to generate social capital, and foster societal cohesion and stability. Productive private sectors generate jobs and income. There is also a wide consensus that the key elements of good governance include accountability, transparency, combating **corruption**, participatory governance and an enabling legal/judicial framework.

Accountability is defined as holding responsible elected or appointed individuals and organizations charged with a public mandate to account for specific actions, activities or decisions to the public from which they derive their **authority**. In a narrow sense, accountability focuses on the ability to account for the allocation, use, and control of public spending and resources in accordance with legally accepted standards, i.e. budgeting, accounting, and auditing. In a broader sense, it is also concerned

with the establishment and enforcement of rules of corporate governance.

Transparency is broadly defined as public access to knowledge of the policies and strategies of government. Among other things, it involves making public accounts verifiable, providing for public participation in government policy-making and implementation, and allowing contestation over decisions impacting on the lives of citizens. It also includes making available for public scrutiny accurate and timely information on economic, financial and market conditions.

A general definition of *corruption* is the misappropriation of public assets or public office/trust for private gains. This definition sufficiently covers most forms of corruption in both the private and public sectors. Combating corruption is considered to be a key indicator of a commitment to good governance.

Stakeholder participation refers to a process whereby stakeholders exercise influence over public policy decisions, and share control over resources and institutions that affect their lives, thereby providing a check on the actions of government. In the context of governance, participation is focused on the empowerment of citizens, and the interplay between a broad range of civil societies, actors, and actions. It concerns the creation of an enabling regulatory framework and economic environment in which citizens (including women) and private institutions can participate in their own governance, generate legitimate demands and monitor government policies and actions.

The term 'good governance' also covers the *legal and judicial framework* for economic development, referring to a legal and judicial system in which the laws are clear and are uniformly applied through an objective and independent judiciary. Good governance promotes the rule of law and respect for **human rights**, and private capital flows.

The elements of good governance highlight the complex nature of the concept. Good governance covers two distinct but closely related dimensions: one is political, and relates to the degree of genuine commitment to the achievement of good governance; the other is technical, and relates to issues of efficiency and public management. Both must be addressed to create an enabling environment where private operations can flourish and poverty can be reduced.

Poor governance manifests itself through the following: failure to make a clear separation between public and private resources; failure to establish a predictable framework of law and government behavior conducive to development; excessive rules and regulations, which impede the functioning of markets and encourage rent-seeking; priorities inconsistent with development, resulting in a misallocation of resources; and narrowly based or non-transparent decision-making. The absence of good governance has proved to be particularly damaging to the 'corrective intervention' role of government. Programs for poverty alleviation, for example, have been undermined by corruption, lack of public accountability and participation of the beneficiaries. Pervasive corruption is damaging to development. It weakens the ability of governments to carry out their functions efficiently, including by diluting equity from the provision of government services. Other causes of poor development management are the high degree of concentration of decision-making power. The trend toward the disengagement of the state from productive activities, while re-emphasizing the government's crucial responsibilities for the provision of public social and infrastructural services and for the creation of an enabling environment, has a major

impact on governance. Distinct, though related, is the parallel trend toward decentralization and the empowerment of local communities. Popular participation, more specifically that of women and disadvantaged groups, fosters more efficient delivery of services, equitable distribution of resources, and is, therefore, germane to poverty reduction. Empowerment, decentralization, greater accountability, participation, creation of an enabling environment will not assure better governance unless agencies at central, intermediate and community levels are made more competent. This brings to the fore issues of technical management and of skills acquisition. It also highlights the need for institutional and capacity building.

Further reading

Adedeji, A. (1999) *Comprehending and Mastering African Conflicts: The Search for Sustainable Peace and Good Governance*, London: Zed Books.

Hoen, H. W. (2001) *Good Governance in Central and Eastern Europe: The Puzzle of Capitalism by Design*, Cheltenham: Edward Elgar.

Munshi, S. and Abraham, B. P. (eds) (2004) *Good Governance, Democratic Societies and Globalization*, London: Sage.

Poluha, E. and Rosendahl, M. (eds) (2002) *Contesting Good Governance: Cross-cultural Perspectives on Representation, Accountability and Public Space*, London: Curzon.

See also: conditionality; corruption; foreign aid; political risk analysis

MARTIN GRIFFITHS

Great powers

Great powers are the most powerful states in the **international system**. They are of interest to international relations scholars studying international conflict and **war**, **international political economy**, and international organizations because their massive reserves of resources allow them to be disproportionately active in diverse fields of international behavior. They are not only the most powerful, but also are the most active of international actors.

Students of international conflict and war are interested in the great powers because they are the most likely to wage war, intervene in ongoing conflicts, be involved in military **alliance**s, supply arms to belligerents, and participate in post-war settlements. One explanation for this increased propensity of great powers to be active militarily is that they alone have the ability to project power over vast distances. Minor powers might have intentions just as belligerent as the great powers, but be unable to act on them because they lack the capacity to transport their forces to distant crises (see **crisis**) and wars. At the same time, great powers, because of their vast capabilities, are more likely to provoke **security dilemma**s. As a result, they are more likely to be the targets of other states' aggression. They have more reason to suspect other states of acting against them, and thus more incentive to enter conflicts on their own terms in order to preempt the possibility of being subsequently targeted by the belligerents. It is hardly surprising that many theories about international conflict (see **realism**, **power transition theory**) self-consciously focus their attention on the great powers.

Students of international political economy are also keenly interested in the great powers. One of the components of great power status, directly or indirectly, is the possession of a large domestic economy. Great powers are thus invariably among the richest states in the international system. They are disproportionately involved in international trade and are the primary source of **foreign direct investment**. Most **foreign aid** originates from great powers, thereby providing another great power source of foreign capital. One great power in particular, the United States, has instituted more than half of the trade **sanctions** observed in the post-World War Two international system. All of this great power activity is of no surprise to scholars of international political economy. Gravity models are the most successful econometric predictive tools for those interested in anticipating how much trade a state will engage in. These models identify the size of a state's economy, its population size, and its wealth (measured as gross national product per capita), as the three most powerful predictors of trade levels. Great powers lead most other states in all three regards, having the biggest economies, largest populations, and generally the highest levels of wealth. It is their disproportionate presence in international exchange that provides them with the leverage to make their sanctioning more likely to succeed than would-be sanctions issued by poorer states. Thus, the qualities that make a state a great power enhance its international market presence, and mutually reinforce a wide range of other international economic behavior.

International organization scholars also focus considerable attention on the great powers. This is because the great powers are the leading actors in the establishment and maintenance of most of the world's international organizations. The **League of Nations** emerged from great power negotiations at the Paris peace talks that concluded World War One. The **United Nations** was negotiated among allied great powers as World War Two drew to a close. The UN's Security Council wields tremendous influence over UN membership, **peace-keeping** activity, and decisions to authorize the use of force by member states. Thus it is clearly revealing of great power influence over the UN that the five permanent members of the Security Council (China, France, Great Britain, Russia, and the United States) are all widely recognized as great powers. These permanent members have the ability to veto any resolution presented to the Security Council, and thus can prevent the UN from acting.

The existence and behavior of great powers help international organization scholars solve theoretical problems. Specifically, the construction of international organizations, as well as their continued maintenance, are seen as **international public goods** for members of the international system. The problem with collective goods is that everyone who stands to benefit from their provision will do so whether they contribute to the construction of the collective good or not. Consequently everyone has an incentive to free ride and let others pay the costs associated with creating international organizations. One theoretical school of thought, **hegemonic stability theory**, suggests that some great powers might behave as privileged actors, actors whose tremendous resources allow them to pay the costs of providing the collective good for everyone. Thus hegemonic stability theorists recognize great power activity in constructing international organizations as examples of privileged actors overcoming international collective action problems.

Various scholars have generated lists of states they identify as great powers. Singer and Small's Correlates of War (COW) project identifies great powers (or major powers as they call them) by consensus among political scientists, historians, and military scholars. Their list identifies the great powers as: the

Austrian empire (and then Austria–Hungary, 1816–1918), the People's Republic of China (1950 on), France (1816–1940, 1945 on), Germany (previously Prussia, 1816–1918, 1925–45 and 1990 on), Great Britain (1816 on), Italy (1860–1943), Japan (1895–1945 and 1990 on), Russia and then the USSR and again Russia (1816–1917 and 1922 on), and the United States (1898 on). Mearsheimer (2001) identifies the great powers based on his perception of their ability to wage sustained war against the strongest state in the system. His list includes: the Austrian empire (and then Austria–Hungary, 1792–1918), the People's Republic of China (1991–2000), France (1792–1940), Germany (previously Prussia, 1792–1945), Great Britain (1792–1945), Italy (1861–1943), Japan (1895–1945), Russia and then the USSR and again Russia (1792–2000), and the United States (1898–2000). While this list is similar to the COW compilation in many regards, there are big differences between the two specifically in the post-World War Two great power sub-system.

Some scholars offer cautions against the pervasive attention international relations researchers devote to the great powers. For example, Neuman (1998) argues that the emphasis of great power activity in international relations research results in theories with little or no relevance for the developing world. Great power bias amounts to Eurocentrism, with attendant problems such as the inability to understand the international behavior of non-great powers and of states in the **Third World**, then over-emphasis on international conflict to the detriment of analyses of internal conflict, and the inability to understand why some developing states fail to develop. Critics of great power bias do not contend that all great power-inspired research is suspect, rather they ask scholars who focus primarily on the great powers to think about the relevance of great power-inspired theories and research for other types of states.

Regardless of disagreements among scholars about which states qualify as great powers, and in spite of criticisms of pervasive great power bias in international relations research, the great powers remain among the international system's most active participants, and thus will always be of special interest to international relations research.

Further reading

Mearsheimer, J. (2001) *The Tragedy of Great Power Politics*, New York: Norton.

Neuman, S. G. (1998) *International Relations Theory and the Third World*, New York: St. Martin's Press.

Singer, J. D. and Small, M. (1972) *The Wages of War*, New York: John Wiley & Sons.

See also: concert of powers; group of eight; middle power; superpower

DOUGLAS LEMKE

Group of Eight (G8)

The Group of Eight (G8) is an informal intergovernmental institution of the world's major market democracies, formed in 1975 to preserve and promote open democracy, individual liberty, and social advancement. The G8 is currently composed of France, the United States, Britain, Germany, Japan, Italy, Canada, Russia, and the **European Union** (EU). It deals with the major political and economic issues facing members' domestic societies and the international community as a whole.

The G8 was established to deal with several crises arising in the early 1970s that the existing **United Nations** and Atlantic institutions failed effectively to address. These crises included the collapse of the **Bretton Woods** system of fixed exchange rates in 1971, the still-born launch of the Tokyo Round of multilateral trade negotiations in 1973 (see **multilateralism**), the Middle East war and OPEC oil embargo in 1973 (see **Organization of Petroleum Exporting Countries**), the Indian nuclear explosion of 1974, the defeat of the United States in Vietnam in 1975, and the spread of 'Eurocommunism' across southern Europe. In response, following meetings of G5 finance ministers in the Library of the White House since 1973, and a meeting of the four major western leaders on the margins of a Summit of the Conference on Security and Cooperation in Europe in July 1975, the first G8 Summit was held in Rambouillet, France, in November 1975. Its visible founders were Valery Giscard D'Estaing of France and Helmut Schmidt of Germany. But its primary architect and creater was US Secretary of State Henry Kissinger, who drew inspiration from his scholarly work on the nineteenth century Concert of Europe, and who saw a modern democratic concert as a form of governance able to respond to the crises of the times.

The G8 system centers on an annual two or three day Summit of the leaders, held in late spring or summer. Additional special Summits, sometimes with a more limited membership, have taken place in 1985, 1996, and 2003. The hosting and the Chair of the Summit rotate annually among the member countries in a seven year cycle, starting with France and continuing in turn with the United States, Britain, Germany, Japan, Italy, and Canada. Russia will host for the first time in 2006. Linked to the Summit, in some cases very loosely, are several standalone institutions of G8 ministers. These include those for trade starting in 1982, foreign affairs in 1984, finance in 1986, the environment in 1992, employment and labor in 1994, information in 1995, **terrorism** in 1995, crime in 1997, energy in 1998, health in 2001, and **development** cooperation in 2002. This wider G8 system is supported by a host of official bodies that deal with specific subjects, often operate for a limited time and at times reach out to involve other countries, intergovernmental organizations and **non-governmental organization**s (NGOs) and private sector firms. Throughout the year, the leaders' personal representatives, known as 'sherpas', 'sous-sherpas', finance deputies and political directors, meet regularly to create the Summit agenda, prepare the Summit discussions, monitor progress with Summit commitments, and deal with breaking and related issues.

The first Summit at Rambouillet included France, the United States, Britain, Germany, Japan, and Italy. Canada came in 1976 and the EU in 1977. The Soviet Union and then Russia have participated ever more fully since 1991, with a now democratic Russia becoming a permanent member in 1998. The leaders of selected other countries and intergovernmental organizations have been involved on the margins of the Summit since 1989 and met with G8 leaders collectively in 1996 and from 2001 to 2003. Outsiders also participate, as functionally appropriate, in the G8-centered ministerial and official bodies.

Since its start the G8 has dealt consistently with a broad range of economic issues such as exchange rates, macroeconomic management, international trade, and relations with developing countries, transnational and global issues such as energy, and the environment and political-security issues such as east–west relations and terrorism. The G8's flexible agenda has steadily expanded to embrace micro-economic issues such as employment and information technology, global issues such as nuclear safety,

organized crime and drugs, and issues such as arms control, regional security, and **human rights**. At times Summits concentrate their agenda on specific themes, such as terrorism, **weapons of mass destruction** and Africa at the Kananaskis Summit of 2002.

Their annual G8 Summit allows busy leaders to discuss directly, on a sustained, face-to-face basis, in a private club of peers, the most complex and challenging international issues and the domestic constraints they face in dealing with them. These discussions enable leaders to develop the personal relations that help them take difficult decisions at home and to respond collectively, quickly and effectively to sudden crises or shocks. The Summit also gives direction to the global community by setting priorities, defining new issues and issue areas, and affirming or introducing principles and norms to guide global **order**. The G8 Summits often produce collective, public decisions or commitments that are precise, concrete, forward-looking, and ambitious, and that contain instructions for members and outside governments, and for intergovernmental organizations to follow.

There has been a generally steady expansion of the range of issues discussed, the novelty of the principles and norms created, and the number of commitments produced at the annual G8 Summit. Compliance with these commitments by the member countries has generally been positive. As the post-**cold war**, rapidly globalizing **international system** has taken hold, compliance has risen, with the United States and France now complying at the substantial levels that the other members, led by Britain and Canada, long have. The G8 Summits have generated many major achievements. These include fostering the largely peaceful transformation of the Soviet Union into a democratic, market oriented Russia that is now a full G8 partner, launching the **war** to prevent **genocide** in Kosovo in 1999, brokering the global environmental conventions on climate change and **biodiversity** announced at Rio in 1992, ending the second oil shock of 1979, launching and completing rounds of multilateral trade liberalization, containing the global financial crises that erupted in the second half of the 1990s, and combating 'skyjacking' and other forms of terrorism, especially in the wake of the 11 September 2001 attacks in the United States. The Summit has also created and strengthened international **regime**s to deal with new international issues, revitalized and reformed existing international institutions, and provided a center of **global governance** to deal with new challenges.

The success of the G8 Summit has led to a phethora of institutionalized, plurilateral Summit level institutions in the 1990s. Yet the G8 Summit remains the only place where the leaders of all of the world's major democratic powers regularly meet to provide global governance, based on democratic principles, as a whole.

As an increasingly effective center of global governance, the G8 has become a focal point for the global political process. The annual Summit now attracts demands from many outside countries and organizations seeking to influence, particpate in, or become members of the Group. Thousands of journalists attend, and up to hundreds of thousands of non-governmental and civil society organizations and citizens come to lobby or demonstrate. The G8's emerging centrality is raising questions about whether the membership needs to be broadened, whether and how the G8 might involve **global civil society** on a more institutionalized basis, and whether the G8 needs a permanent Secretariat of its own.

Further reading

Bayne, N. (2000) *Hanging In There: The G7 and G8 Summit in Maturity and Renewal*, Aldershot Ashgate.

Fratiani, M. and Kirton, J. (eds) (2003) *Sustaining Global Growth and Development: G7 and IMF Challenges and Contributions*, Aldershot: Ashgate.

Hodges, M., Kirton, J. and Daniels, J. (eds) (1999) *The G8's Role in the New Millennium*, Aldershot: Ashgate.

See also: great powers; group of 77; Organization for Economic Cooperation and Development

JOHN KIRTON

Group of 77 (G77)

The late 1950s and early 1960s saw the emergence to independence of most of the African and Asian nations. A common characteristic of these new nations was economic vulnerability stemming from dependence on primary production. Economies were generally undiversified and dependent on the markets of former colonial metropoles. Thus once the euphoria of anti-colonial success faded, these developing (or **Third World**) countries moved on to address problems arising from what they called 'neo-colonialism,' that is continued dependence on the industrial nations. They saw the need to restructure their economies and to correct imbalances in the international economic and financial systems. In the 1970s, African and Asian countries were joined by Latin American nations which, having gained their independence in the nineteenth century, had not felt the urge to associate with the anti-colonial Afro-Asians until then. Under **United Nations** auspices, and supported by **development** economists such as Argentine economist Raúl Prebisch, the Third World sought relief from their unfavorable and declining terms of trade (ratio of export to import prices), from aid **dependence** and **conditionality**, and from investment patterns that they saw as harmful.

Although Western industrial nations initially opposed efforts to change the system (in particular, the rules governing **free trade**), the developing countries soon gained the support of the Soviet Union. Subsequent easing of Northern opposition led to the holding of the first United Nations Conference on Trade and Development (UNCTAD) in Geneva in 1964. Seventy-seven developing countries were represented at this conference. This 'Group of 77' (G77) became a permanent caucusing group for the developing nations when UNCTAD became institutionalized as a UN organ under the General Assembly. The G77, with a membership today of 133, has gone on to become the chief interlocutor of the South at all relevant UN forums. China often formally joins in to endorse the group's positions. Although based at UN headquarters in New York where it meets in ministerial session before the General Assembly begins every year, the G77 has established offices led by separate chairmen in Geneva, Washington, Rome, Vienna, Paris, and Nairobi. The G77's activities are funded by member contributions, with specific South–South collaborative activities funded by a trust fund (the Perez-Guerrero Trust Fund) established in 1986.

Although the global context or environment has changed since the 1960s, the G77 countries have never changed their essential goals. Beyond their specific pleas for reform of the international economic and financial systems has been a concern for development, defined in the first development decade (1960s) primarily in terms of GNP growth but moving more strongly to incorporate social (or human) development in the nationalist 1970s and in the 1980s and 1990s when liberalization policies engendered deep concerns about poverty alleviation. In addition, by the 1990s, developing countries, though initially wary, came to embrace the concept of **sustainable development**, not only in its meaning of proper environmental management but also as integrated social and economic growth, or 'comprehensive development' embracing political (governance), human, and ecological and economic adjustments.

As far as specific strategies are concerned, the G77 has focused efforts on trade stabilization, seeking to eliminate trade (and financial) volatility by means of commodity agreements, preferential access arrangements, regional **integration** and broader South–South collective self-reliance. Like industrial countries, the G77 countries agree that trade is the engine of growth. However, developing countries have found it difficult to secure stable markets and prices for their agricultural products and raw materials, and their manufactured products have been less competitive than those of the early industrialized countries. In the 1970s the G77 were mildly successful in getting UNCTAD to sponsor difficult commodity negotiations in a number of products, but their main success came with the adoption of the Generalized System of Preferences (GSP), whereby industrial countries agreed to eliminate import duties on most products from the developing world. Although developing countries had sought a comprehensive nondiscriminatory system, they agreed to a system whereby each developed country could make product and country exclusions. Developed countries have established criteria for excluding politically unfriendly countries and for graduating countries as their economies improve. Nevertheless, the GSP, established in

1968 and implemented in all developed countries by 1975, has become a mainstay of the global trading system, accepted as an exception under the rules of free trade.

Efforts to improve access to developed country markets have been accompanied by a G77 thrust to integrate developing markets themselves. UNCTAD was an early champion of regional and subregional integration. Moreover, in the 1970s the developing countries, buoyed by the success of the **Organization of Petroleum Exporting Countries**, managed to obtain reluctant support from the developed countries for the negotiation of a New International Economic Order (NIEO) that, among other things, endorsed collective self-reliance in trade and technical assistance. This thrust came to be known familiarly as 'ECDC/TCDC' or 'economic cooperation/technical cooperation among developing countries'. In trade this led to a push by the G77 in the 1980s for a global system of preferences or trade concessions among developing countries (GSTP). By the early 2000s, a GSTP agreement was in force among forty-four developing countries. Meanwhile, after a period of eager experimentation with regional integration in the 1960s, developing countries lost some of their enthusiasm for this strategy when confronted by the unequal distribution of integration benefits, the limitations of even expanded regional market size, and difficulties in overcoming political and philosophical differences. However, in the 1990s, with the renewed global emphasis on liberalization and the formation of blocs in the developed world, G77 countries moved to revive moribund integration movements and initiate new ones.

Recent changes in the global system toward increased emphasis on global free trade have had both a negative and positive influence on the G77 as a group. On the negative side, the G77's protectionist agenda and its **power** as a single bargaining unit were diluted by the adoption of the once-disliked liberal agenda, as well as by the breakdown of Third World cohesion in the rush to bilateral and regional arrangements. On the positive side, the industrial countries' forceful push for global liberalization also brought G77 countries together to counter developed country efforts to hasten the removal of trade and financial barriers. Thus today the G77 trade agenda has moved from the broader UNCTAD arena to the **World Trade Organization** (WTO). Developing countries were never enthusiastic supporters of the WTO's predecessor, the General Agreement of Trade and Tariffs (GATT) whose rules of reciprocity and antiprotectionism they saw as heightening their disadvantaged position in international trade. But today, most developing countries have joined or are seeking to join the WTO, even though their influence in that forum has generally been weak. That weakness shows signs of changing, however, as North–South antagonisms have sharpened on issues such as trade in services, intellectual property (including pharmaceutical issues), removal of agricultural subsidies, and investment rules. The G77 has again found a united voice, pushing the developing country agenda based on special and differential treatment for developing countries. When the perceived intransigence of the industrial countries on the issue of reduced farm subsidies led to a walk-out by an informal group of developing countries leading the negotiations with the WTO (the Group of 21 led by China, India, Brazil, and South Africa), the G77 as the umbrella unit also gained greater influence.

In the companion area of financing for development, the G77 has always stressed, among other things, the need for compensatory financing to help developing countries meet balance of payments shortfalls, increased transfers of concessional aid and technical assistance from developed to the developing countries, transfer of technology and skills to the developing countries, and structural changes in international institutions to foster greater participation of developing countries in their decision making processes. A focus on controls on **foreign direct investment** in the nationalistic 1970s gave way by the 1980s to a general welcoming of investment as long as it involved 'good corporate citizenship'. In fact, the G77 itself institutionalized cooperation with business stakeholders through the establishment of a Chamber of Commerce and Industry of Developing Countries (G77CCI), a network of such organizations interested in South–South cooperation. The 1980s were also a decade when many developing countries floundered amid high debt burdens, giving the G77 another focus: external debt relief.

In March 2002, the G77 achieved one of its major aims: the holding of a global conference on Financing for Development (Monterrey, Mexico). Conference participants agreed in principle to a number of actions intended to mobilize both domestic and external financial resources for development, including – at the domestic level – greater transparency, sound macroeconomic policy planning, investment in social services, strengthening the domestic financial sector, and encouraging microfinance initiatives, and – at the external level – encouraging foreign investment flows and the transfer of technology, promoting initiatives by regional and international institutions, strengthening financial support for export diversification and other trade related initiatives, a substantial increase in foreign aid (given

the alarming decline over the years) and better management of such aid, external debt relief, and effective participation of developing countries as well as economies in transition in international institutional processes. The target for foreign aid transfer had already been renegotiated at a conference on least developed countries in 2001: that conference endorsed a transfer target of 0.7 per cent of GNP to developing countries and 0.15 to 0.20 per cent of GNP to the least developed countries.

As in trade, so in aid the G77 also strongly endorses and funds efforts at South–South cooperation. In this respect, a High level Committee on TCDC has worked to strengthen technical exchanges from the more developed to less developed developing countries in areas such as energy, information, and science and technology.

In evaluating the performance of the G77, one must take into account the difficulties faced by any large group in seeking to incorporate the concerns of diverse constituencies. The G77 has had to advocate for newly industrializing countries as much as for primary producers, for landlocked countries, for Small Island Developing States (SIDS), small states in general, Highly Indebted Poor Countries (HIPCs), marginalized African states, and least developed states (LDCs). Since these countries have different goals, it has sometimes been difficult to ensure solidarity and develop common negotiating strategies. The G77 has also had to be careful to avoid politicization of its agenda: although an economic caucus, the group's members naturally have distinct political positions and perceptions and the group itself often cooperates with the Non-Aligned Movement. In fact, formal interventions on behalf of the group are made on a range of socio-economic, ecological, and **global governance** issues.

On balance, the G77 has been effective in bringing the concerns of the South to global attention, though the record is mixed with respect to its ability to actually negotiate solutions. In the 1980s the group lost ground by continuing for too long to espouse rhetorical positions that were out of step with the changing global climate and the move of many members to adopt more liberal policies. However, as **globalization** has heightened the economic and social vulnerabilities of the developing countries, the G77 seems to be regaining some lost bargaining power.

Further reading

Spero, J. and Hart, J. A. (1997) *The Politics of International Economic Relations*, New York: St. Martin's Press.
Williams, M. (1991). *Third World Cooperation: The Group of 77 in UNCTAD*, New York: St. Martin's Press.

See also: Group of eight; Third World

JACQUELINE BRAVEBOY-WAGNER

Groupthink

A term made famous by Irving Janis's 1972 book of the same name. It refers generally to faulty decision making in a group that is caused by in-group norms, poor structure of the group, poor information processing, and a desire to avoid disagreements and conflict within the group. The most common fault associated with groupthink is premature consensus by the group that results in misunderstanding the problem and missing possible alternatives that might be effective in the problem area.

While the most famous applications of groupthink have been in the field of foreign policy, scholarly work on the subject is common in many other fields as well including business and management, psychology, sociology, public policy, and anywhere else where small groups play a role in decision making.

In international relations the term is associated with the foreign policy decision making school, which investigates intragovernmental factors associated with the process of decision making including psychology, group structures, and advisor systems. The most prominent critics of this approach are realists (see **realism**) and adherents of the rational-actor model of foreign policy behavior. These schools generally argue that micro-level phenomena (such as psychology and group processes) play at best a small role in affecting international relations, and that instead much of international relations can be explained by factors at higher **levels of analysis** such as **power**, interests, and rationality. Other critics have said that groupthink is either too broad (being used as a synonym for all kinds of group based decision flaws) or it is too specific and limited, referring only to premature consensus – and that scholars need to move beyond thinking about groupthink to understand other group decision making problems. In spite of these critics, the concept remains very important in understanding foreign policy decision processes and has received much attention in the literature in terms of both theory and empirical investigations.

While groupthink is generally thought of as the final stage of decision making, it has been argued theoretically and supported empirically that faulty decision making has its origins much earlier in the process. Janis laid out a causal chain that begins with situational constraints on decision making, such as limited time, high level of stress, a recent failure by the group, or a **crisis** situation. Additionally, groupthink can be affected by the traditional structures and roles of members of the group prior to an occasion for decision; these include a biased leader, poor tradition of methodical procedures, group homogeneity, and the illusion of invulnerability in the group.

Due to these antecedent conditions, decision making becomes ripe for a series of possible information processing errors by the group, including poor information search, failing to survey objectives and alternatives, and stereotyping the situation or the out-group. When these symptoms of groupthink take place, the result is often dangerous in-group norms, collective rationalizations, and self-censorship. Groupthink occurs when the group engages in these psychologically supportive, pathological group decision making processes.

Janis argued that decisions marked by groupthink were likely to produce optimal outcomes and to result in escalations in international conflict. His initial work reviewed a handful of case studies that looked for groupthink factors in terms of faulty group structures and poor information processing. Two of his cases come from John F. Kennedy's administration: the Bay of Pigs and the Cuban Missile Crisis. The Bay of Pigs decision making is called the perfect fiasco and demonstrates the extent to which an otherwise highly intelligent group developed very poor in-group norms that left many assumptions unchallenged and alternatives not discussed. Only a short while later the Kennedy administration had undergone structural change within its decision making apparatus and handled the Cuban Missile Crisis with patience, careful deliberation, and due consideration of alternatives.

Three additional terms are helpful in understanding some of the practices associated with groupthink: self-censorship, mindguards, and gatekeeping. Self-censorship happens when an individual fails to raise concerns, objections, or questions regarding a course of action so as not to be seen as deviating from the group's consensus or interrupting the group's norms. A mindguard is someone who directly tries to stifle adverse information as a way to keep the group cohesive and minimize dissent. Robert McNamara is purported to have played such a role in the Bay of Pigs decision making when he essentially told Arthur Schlesinger, who had significant reservations, that the decision might be good or bad but the time for questioning was over and the President needed everyone to be on board with the invasion plan.

A gatekeeper is someone who has some control over the flow of information and individuals, and uses that control to keep dissenting viewpoints from moving forward. White House officials played this role during the Reagan administration, not in terms of keeping information from the President, but from other key players on the foreign policy team. Secretary of State George Schultz and Secretary of Defense Caspar Weinberger were kept completely 'out of the loop' during the decision making process for Reagan's Strategic Defense Initiative in the 1980s; the Secretaries were not even told that the White House was working on the proposal until a couple of days before Reagan was scheduled to make the stunning announcement.

While many have argued that Janis's purposive sample could hardly be considered scientific, other researchers have conducted more thorough investigations using large numbers of cases and creative, replicable methodologies, and have found strong empirical support for much of Janis's theory. The one exception coming out of the empirical research is that evidence does not support Janis's assertion that situation variables, such as crisis situations or short time constraints, contribute to faulty group decision making.

The most important empirical findings from the groupthink research program are that the structures and processes in decision making groups significantly affect the quality of decisions and outcome in a case. Poor structures are likely to lead to poor information processing, and together they are likely to result in harm to **national interest**s and a rise in international conflict.

The gist of these empirical findings is fairly good news for decision making groups: the situation factors, which cannot generally be controlled, do not have an adverse effect on decision quality, but structural factors and information processing do have an effect, and the latter are matters that leaders and groups can improve. Indeed, the groupthink research program is one that has direct prescriptive implications for decision making groups: set up good structures, develop rational and thorough information processing procedures, reduce biases and stereotypes, implement a 'devil's advocate' system to check assumptions, and the decision process is much more likely to be optimal. These prescriptions are fairly simple, low cost, and easy to implement, and have been shown to be very effective. Preventing groupthink is largely a matter of establishing good structures and practices in decision making.

Further reading

George, A. (1980) *Presidential Decisionmaking in Foreign Policy: The Effective Use of Information and Advice*, Boulder, CO: Westview Press.

Janis, I. (1972) *Victims of Groupthink*, Boston: Houghton Miffin.

Hart, P. and Eric K. S. (eds) (1997) *Beyond Groupthink: Political Group Dynamics and Foreign Policy Making*, Ann Arbor, MI: University of Michigan Press.

Schafer, M. and Crichlow, S. (2002) 'The Process-Outcome Connection in Foreign Policy Decision Making: A Quantitative Study Building on Groupthink.' *International Studies Quarterly* 42, 433–60.

See also: crisis; misperception; rationality

MARK SCHAFER and SAM ROBISON

Hegemonic stability theory

Hegemonic stability theory posits that a hegemonic state is required to provide stability to the international political and economic system through the establishment of **international public goods**, such as international finance and trade **regime**s. In doing so, however, the hegemon allows other states to 'free ride' on the provision of such goods, thereby raising their costs, threatening hegemonic decline and increasing the probability of international political and economic disorder. Hegemonic stability theory (hereafter HST) proposes that while the hegemon may encourage other states to participate in enjoying international public goods, it also needs allies to support this provision by taking on some costs to themselves.

The notion that the **international political economy** is underpinned by a combination of political and economic muscle was first expressed in Charles Kindleberger's (1973) study of the sources of the Great Depression, but is also attributed to a development of Mancur Olson's (1971) theory of collective action. Kindleberger asserted that the Great Depression was caused by the failure of the **great powers** of the time to provide leadership – that Britain was politically willing but economically incapable, and that the United States was economically capable but politi-

cally unwilling. For Kindleberger a political and economic leader is required to provide a stable market for distressed goods, a stable exchange rate system, stable long term lending, a system for macroeconomic coordination among states, and a lender of the last resort function. The failure to provide these functions allowed the deepening of the Great Depression and clearly signalled the need for a political and economic leader in the post-war period.

Within the sub-field of international political economy, HST was popularized by a debate on US political and economic decline following its post-war '**hegemony**'. Proponents of HST, particularly 'neorealist' scholars such as Robert Gilpin (1987), argued that the United States, as the hegemon, provided international regimes through the **International Monetary Fund** and the **World Bank** (which together comprise the **Bretton Woods** regime), and the General Agreement on Tariffs and Trade (now the **World Trade Organization**) to govern and encourage an open, multilateral international political economy. It also provided a new **security structure**, particularly through the **North Atlantic Treaty Organization** (NATO). US hegemony, so the argument goes, permitted the relative economic rise of its allies, particularly Japan and West Germany, during the post-war 'long boom'.

In doing so, the United States declined as the burden of carrying these international public goods outweighed its political and economic capacity. The shrugging of this burden was signified by the closing of the 'dollar-gold window' in 1971 when Richard Nixon's administration was plagued by persistent (and correct) speculation that the United States could not maintain the Bretton Woods fixed exchange rate of $35 per ounce of gold. This 'collapse of Bretton Woods' brought the international political economy to a temporary halt and also represented a shift in US foreign economic policy from 'benign' to 'malign' hegemony. Following this collapse a debate emerged (most furiously during the 1980s) within which scholars debated whether the consequences of hegemonic decline would be widespread international political and economic instability, a shared international political and economic leadership between the United States and Japan, or perhaps the maintenance of international regimes even after hegemony.

This last 'after hegemony' argument provided the greatest challenge to the notion that a hegemon was required to initiate, or maintain stability, within an international regime. The 'liberal institutionalist' school of thought (which is distinct from **neoliberalism**), led by Robert O. Keohane (1984), argued that states realizing their self-interest would bind themselves into continuing support for international regimes to reduce information asymmetries between their members, lower transaction costs (an argument based on fears of market failure), and generate positive-sum outcomes rather than the zero-sum view of the international political economy purported by realist scholars. Other studies have since pointed out how some international institutions were created without the presence of a hegemon,

including the **Bank for International Settlements**.

Another problem with the HST is that scholars seeking to validate it are accused of distorting history in the process. The largest problem here is the oft-made comparison between British and US hegemonies, where Britain's supposed hegemonic power is established in order to demonstrate that HST does indeed have relevance. This is especially the case for the years when Britain is alleged to be at its hegemonic zenith, the mid-nineteenth century. While it is sometimes alleged that Britain provided stability to the international political and economic system by encouraging free trade, carrying a great military burden, and encouraging states to adhere to a stable fixed exchange rate system known as the Gold Standard, there is no academic consensus that Britain actually carried out any of these tasks. Various studies have pointed out that Britain was unwilling or incapable of performing these functions. Accordingly, the five requirements of political and economic leadership, established above, may therefore be seen as a wish list rather than as an historical fact, no matter how one may try and present Britain's role as a hegemonic leader.

Plagued by empirical problems, HST remains a theory based on one case, the United States in the immediate period after World War Two. And even on this ground HST has been persistently attacked, both for exaggerating the extent of US **power** at the time or its subsequent decline. HST has also been criticized for providing a far too simple view of power, seeing power as simple military or economic capacity based on resources, rather than the US capacity to use 'structural power' or 'soft power' to set new agendas and influence actors' preferences. In addition, the US economic resurgence of the 1990s, for example, undermined many analyses of US decline that were popular a decade earlier.

Further reading

Gilpin, R. (1987) *The Political Economy of International Relations*, Princeton, NJ: Princeton University Press.

Hobson, J. M. (2002) 'Two Hegemonies or One? A Historical-Sociological Critique of Hegemonic Stability Theory', in P. K. O'Brien and A. Cleese (eds), *Two Hegemonies*, London: Ashgate, 305–25.

Keohane, R. O. (1984) *After Hegemony: Cooperation and Discord in the World Political Economy*, Princeton, NJ: Princeton University Press.

Kindleberger, C. P. (1973) *The World in Depression, 1929–1939*, Berkeley, CA: University of California Press.

Olson, M. (1971) *The Logic of Collective Action*, 2nd edn, Boston, MA: Harvard University Press.

Webb, M. C. and Krasner, S. D. (1989) 'Hegemonic stability theory: an empirical assessment', *Review of International Studies* 15(2), 183–98.

See also: great powers; hegemony; historical sociology; international public goods; neoliberalism; power

LEONARD SEABROOKE

Hegemony

A term used to explain the relative stability of political **authority** and control in and between capitalist democracies, such as the United States and many West European countries, despite economic crises (see **crisis**) and World Wars. The original theorist in this vein is Antonio Gramsci (1891–1937), an Italian who wrote his major work as a political prisoner in the 1920s and 1930s. Gramsci (1971) began with the insight that, most of the time, **power** in liberal democracies is exercised not overt coercion

(such as imprisoning political dissenters), but through a dominant worldview, or ideology. This common set of ideas and symbols legitimates existing rulers, helping them to win the citizens' consent, or at least acquiescence. Thus, in a medieval feudal economy, where serfs (agricultural laborers in bondage to the lords who owned the land they worked) were ruled over by an aristocracy, and the aristocracy by a monarch, a whole set of political structures and ideas had to be invented to legitimate and perpetuate the aristocracy's and monarch's exclusive control of property. The notion that kings had a divine right to rule, given to them by God, is a good example of an idea that seems archaic to us today, but which served to support centuries of rulers.

Although Gramsci's main inspiration was Karl Marx (1818–83), his theory is quite different from traditional **Marxism**. Classical Marxists often viewed society as a kind of building where the economy was the base, upon which sat a 'superstructure' of political, civil and cultural institutions and beliefs. For them, the economy was the foundation of society, and it determined people's behavior and thinking in the political and cultural spheres. To use the above example, a feudal economy caused people to dream up the idea that kings had a divine right to rule. In contrast to traditional Marxists, Gramsci suggested that the ideas and symbols of the ruling ideology could be as powerful and determining as the economy. The relationship of base and superstructure is dialectical. Each affects and changes the other. We can still speak of the economy (or culture) as determining, but only if determination means setting limits to how we act or think, rather than causing us to act or think this way in some mechanical manner. So the theory of hegemony knocks the economic foundation out from under classical Marxism, arguing that ideas and cultural institutions can shape us as powerfully as how we make a living.

Gramsci also saw the ruling forces of society in a more complex manner than did Marx. Marx tended to portray society's rulers as those who owned the means of production: factories, land, industrial infrastructure, whatever was used to produce goods. For Marx, governments and other institutions of capitalist societies (see **capitalism**) had little independence from the owners of capital. The state was simply the committee for managing the common affairs of the whole bourgeoisie. Gramsci, on the other hand, did not reduce the ruling forces of a society solely to the capitalist class, but saw society as governed at any given time by an 'historical bloc'. Historical blocs are shifting coalitions of interests that share some political solidarity at a point in time. These blocs may be bound as much by ideological ties as by shared economic interests, and they are subject to change. They are not necessarily from one economic class, but may represent fractions of several classes.

Gramsci defined hegemony as the process by which the dominant classes or class fractions, through their privileged access to social institutions (such as the media), propagate values that reinforce their control over politics and the economy. These values form a dominant ideology. The dominant ideology in any society is a set of common sense assumptions that legitimates the existing distribution of power. Ideology makes this structure of power seem inevitable, and therefore beyond challenge.

Through ideology, ruling groups attempt to universalize their own interests as the interests of all. An example might be the notion that cutting taxes on the rich encourages them to invest this money and create jobs for the rest of us.

How do we know that they will create jobs? How do we know that these will be decent paying jobs? Most importantly, why should we give the wealthy the power to decide whether to make jobs for us, rather than using the money for other purposes? Gramsci argues that it is by these ideational means, rather than through the coercive force of the state, that ruling groups maintain their power. And power is most effectively exercised not through overt inculcation and censorship, but also and especially by the ability to define the parameters of legitimate discussion and debate over alternative beliefs, values and world views.

A note on the common usage of ideology is in order here. Often the word is used negatively, as an epithet. Gramsci argued that we all have some kind of ideology, in the sense that we have a framework of ideas that allows us to locate our identities (as Americans, or Californians, or working class or middle class), and our interests (in higher wages, or control over our work, or the prevention of abortion). Ideology, in this version, is both constraining and enabling. Moreover, ideologies are not simply concocted and spread by small conspiracies of rulers. Instead, for theorists of hegemony, the creation and spread of ideology is a very complex process. Cultural institutions play a key role in perpetuating aspects of the dominant worldview. These include the family, religious organizations, and the mass media, among others. Some argue that hegemonic ideology acts primarily as a kind of social glue that holds together diverse peoples of contemporary democracies. Ideology takes on a particularly important role in welding together a ruling bloc, and in ensuring others' consent to be ruled.

For example, US ideology after World War Two portrayed the globe as a battleground between the 'Free World' and a dangerous, expansionist communist bloc, led by the former Soviet Union (see **communism**). This worldview helped legitimate the terms of the peace after 1945. At this time, the United States moved to bring as many countries as possible into a global capitalist system dominated politically and economically by the United States. **Cold war** thinking ensured consent among Americans for US leadership abroad, and the sacrifices it required, from higher taxes to pay for increased defense spending to risking American soldiers' lives in Korea, Vietnam, and elsewhere. The picture of an imminent and pervasive communist threat (often inflated beyond reality) also justified an increasingly secretive foreign policy to protect national security, concealing from Americans much of what the military and intelligence agencies did in the name of protecting them.

Gramsci was greatly preoccupied with the character of state and civil society relations prevailing in relatively modern societies, especially capitalist democracies. He challenged the reductionist conception of the state as exclusively a class state, a mere instrument of ruling class coercion and domination. He insisted on the educative role of the state, its significance in constructing alliances that could win support from different social strata, and the state's role in providing cultural and moral leadership. Although the economic structure may be, in the last instance, determinative, Gramsci gave much greater autonomy to the effects of the actual conduct of the struggle for leadership, across a wide front and on a variety of sites and institutions. He argued that the role of the communist party was to engage and lead in a broad, multi-faceted struggle for hegemony with the capitalist state. A shift in socialist political strategy (see **socialism**) was necessary, away from an outright frontal assault on the state to the winning of strategic positions on a number of fronts. Socialist struggle was conceived as a 'war of position' in the first instance against the forces of capitalist hegemony in civil society and culture.

Understood in this way, hegemony at a global level is not necessarily to be equated with material or military dominance (as in some forms of **realism**, particularly in the way that realists elaborate **hegemonic stability theory**), nor is it necessarily to be regarded as a desirable international public good (see **international public goods**) (as in some forms of **liberal internationalism**).

Further reading

Gramsci, A. (1971) *Selections from the Prison Notebooks*, New York: International Publishers.
Mann, M. (1970) 'The Social Cohesion of Liberal Democracy', *American Sociological Review* 35, 423–39.

See also: authority; critical theory; hegemonic stability theory; international public goods; legitimacy; Marxism; power

MARTIN GRIFFITHS

Hermeneutics

The study of the relationship between meaning, interpretation and understanding. The term is derived from the name of the Greek messenger god *Hermes* and it signifies the act of the transfer of meaning. While originally referring only to the interpretation of Biblical texts hermeneutics now also refers to the interpretation and study of meaning in general. In the field of international relations hermeneutics is associated with emergence of post-positivist and anti foundationalist approaches (see **post-positivism**; **foundationalism**). **Critical theory, constructivism, post-structuralism** and some varieties of

feminism all employ or incorporate hermeneutic insights.

Prior to the nineteenth century hermeneutics referred to the interpretation and understanding of texts. In the nineteenth century Wilhem Dilthey (1833–1911) developed hermeneutics as a methodology for the study of the humanities or human sciences. Dilthey introduced a distinction between explanation and understanding that is still used by many today. Explanation is concerned with establishing the causal connections between facts (the 'how' of natural phenomena). Understanding refers to the interpretation of meanings (the 'why' of social action). Dilthey argued that it was possible to be objective and scientific in one's interpretations of human beliefs and social products such as texts, art, and artefacts and therefore to equal the achievements of the natural sciences.

In German the hermeneutic tradition is also commonly known as the *verstehen* methodology and is associated with the work of the famous sociologist Max Weber (1864–1920). This form of hermeneutics characterizes contemporary constructivist (see **constructivism**) approaches to the study of international relations, according to which understanding the meanings and values which actors bring to the international realm are as, if not more, important than explaining their material capabilities.

In the twentieth century hermeneutics was characterized by a distinction between the modes of 'recovery' and 'suspicion'. The first refers to idea of understanding from 'the native's point of view'. The aim is to place oneself in the culture or period of another and attempt to understand it, as best as is possible, on its own terms and thereby 'recover' its meaning. The hermeneutic circle is an essential concept in this approach. It refers to the idea that understanding an individual or a work of art or an idea can only be successful by understanding the larger context in which they exist and by recognizing that understanding the larger context can only occur through understanding its particular and individual elements. Thus interpretation finishes where its starts (hence a circle).

The hermeneutics of suspicion sees the hermeneutic circle as a vicious cycle. It refers to the task of investigating the hidden or systematically distorted meanings that may come about through the deployment of **power** or **misperception**. In that sense it is suspicious of received beliefs. It is most often associated with the idea of the critique of ideology and the Frankfurt school critical theoretical project of emancipation (see **critical theory**). It can also be seen in the work of poststructuralists (see **poststructuralism**).

In the hands of Hans-Georg Gadamer (1900–2002) hermeneutics became not just a methodology for the human sciences but a description of the human condition. Gadamer used the work of Martin Heidegger (1889–1976) to deepen the project begun by Dilthey and to develop what he called 'philosophical hermeneutics' (PH). Gadamer argued that our primary mode of relating to each other and to the world was through language. This means that we are always in an interpretive enterprise or environment. All understanding is interpretation. Furthermore, Gadamer argued that the best way to think about interpretation was to understand it as a dialogue between the reader and a text, or between two people. A genuine dialogue is a search for truth and this, he believed, is what interpretation ought to be about.

In addressing the topic in this way Gadamer was able to suggest an answer to one of the enduring issues of hermeneutic practice: how to judge between interpretations. Gadamer argued that judgement was possible and indeed inescapable but that it was not possible to settle on the final or objective meaning of acts, texts or interpretations and that good judgement could only come about as a result of a good dialogue. Gadamer argues that our judgements are based on a mixture of our historical and linguistic context, personal experience, and reflective reasoning. Aristotle's account of practical wisdom provides the appropriate model of judgement in the humanities and social sciences. This development places hermeneutics on the side of those who see the interpretation of meaning as closer to an art than a science.

Gadamer also argued that language carries the past within it and therefore we are always informed or affected by the past more than we may care to acknowledge. Thus one of the outcomes of a hermeneutic understanding was consciousness of the effects of history, which ironically also means that we may recognize that the past has effects without knowing exactly what those effects are. This in turn means that we can never be entirely certain whether our knowledge or beliefs are free from the unseen effects of previous contexts, languages, or viewpoints. So for example when the Bolsheviks took **power** in 1917 it became clear that not everything from the past had been rejected. They inherited not just Tsarist palaces but also the Tsarist mode of government despite their efforts to make something new in the Soviet Union.

Gadamer applied this insight to the enlightenment goal of universal reason. He argued that not only can we never entirely free ourselves from tradition and prejudice but also that the language we inherit from our forebears enables us to understand and make sense of the world. Therefore we should not be 'prejudiced' against tradition. This was arguably the most controversial of Gadamer's claims.

Some critical theorists have argued that Gadamer's account was too sceptical about the liberating power of reason. He was uncritical towards tradition and was conservative rather than emancipatory. However others believe that this reading of Gadamer is overstated. More importantly it became clear that PH was not a rejection of reason in favour of tradition but rather a contextualization of the conditions and epistemological status of reason. In this way hermeneutics is compatible with elements of **communitarianism**.

Roger Epp (1998) has pointed to the similarities between hermeneutics and the **English School**. The common thread here is an emphasis on history and the idea of a dialogue with the past. More importantly they share an understanding of the limits on, and conditions in which, political and moral reasoning takes place which places them closer to the classical study of the art of politics than the modern technocratic scientism which dominates the contemporary discipline of international relations. The approach starts from a recognition that while the future is open the past still continues to shape and constrain the possibilities for taking action in the present.

Further reading

Epp, R. (1998) 'The English School on the Frontiers of International Society: A Hermeneutic Reflection', *Review of International Studies* 24(4), 47–53.

Gadamer, H. G. (1989) *Truth and Method*, 2nd Edition (Trans, J. Weinsheimer, and D. Marshall), London: Sheed & Ward.

Rabinow, P. and Sullivan, W. M. (1979) *Interpretive Social Science: A Reader*, Berkeley, CA: University of California Press.

See also: constructivism; critical theory; deconstruction; English School; foundationalism/anti-foundationalism; genealogy; post-structuralism; post-positivism; reflexivity

RICHARD SHAPCOTT

Historical sociology

A body of theoretical and empirical scholarship that emerged in the 1980s as a critique of mainstream ahistorical and asociological international relations (IR) theory, and which developed much further after the end of the **cold war** as the need to understand international/global change became pressing within the discipline. However, the major *rationale* of historical sociology (HS) has been not merely to understand the process of international change as a counterweight to the emphasis on continuity promoted by **realism** in the study of international relations. Above all, its mandate is to reveal differences in **international systems** through time thereby forcing us to rethink the origins, unique properties and changing dynamics of the present international or global system. Put differently, its purpose is not simply to tell us more about the past but to shed light on the trajectory of the contemporary global system as well. In this context historical sociologists view the ahistoricism and asociologism of mainstream IR theory as a fundamental obstacle to a more adequate analysis of the present system.

Mainstream IR theory suffers from what has been called *tempocentric* ahistoricism. Tempocentrism is a mode of ahistoricism that takes a snapshot of the present system and then extrapolates this picture back through time, thereby smoothing over and obscuring discontinuities or ruptures between historical international systems. In the process the international realm appears to be marked throughout history by a regular tempo that beats according to the rhythm of the present. Tempocentrism is in fact an inverted form of path dependency. Tempocentrism reconstructs all international systems in the past to conform to that of the present, so that all systems are imagined as homologous or isomorphic, governed by the same structure and displaying the same properties. Accordingly, the study of IR can be conducted through *transhistorical* analysis. That is, the familiar concepts of the modern system – **anarchy**, the **balance of power**, states as 'like-units', and great power politics (see **great powers**) such as **imperialism** or **superpower** rivalry – can be applied unproblematically to all times and places.

This transhistorical methodology effectively converts history into an intellectual laboratory wherein mainstream theories of the present can be tested and confirmed. Thus, for some realists, the superpower contest between the United States and the USSR after 1947 can be explained in exactly the same way as that of the rivalry between ancient Athens and Sparta. Similarly, Athenian imperialism is conflated with British imperialism. Or the United States as a great power finds its analogy with nineteenth century Britain, or seventeenth century Holland, or sixteenth century Spain. By explicitly dismissing the specificities of the socio-historical context within which these processes are embedded and informed, so realists can present the timeless presence of anarchy as the central property of the international system.

For example, **hegemonic stability theory** (HST) demonstrates its tempocentric properties by arguing that great power politics is governed by a universal 'hegemonic cycle'. And by taking American **hegemony** as a given, theorists extrapolate this conception back in time to characterize nineteenth-century Britain. But a number of historical sociologists have claimed that Britain was not a hegemon. The upshot of this claim is not merely that it tells us new things about nineteenth century Britain but that it renders problematic our understanding of *modern* US hegemony.

In sum, the main problem with tempocentrism is that in 'flattening out' international history and tarnishing it with the same 'presentist' brush, mainstream IR theory not only misguides our conceptions of the past but also misinforms our understanding of the constitutive properties of the present system. In order to best understand the emergence of HS in the 1980s/1990s it is necessary to revisit the genealogical development of the discipline.

Historical sociology and the study of international relations

It is generally assumed that HS first emerged in the discipline in the 1980s. But it would be more appropriate to assert that ahistorical/asociological mainstream IR theory emerged in the 1980s as a counter to traditional historical and sociological enquiry that had been a core component of the discipline in the eighteenth, nineteenth and first half of the twentieth, centuries. Put differently, historical and sociological analysis has been the norm for most of the discipline's long history.

Between roughly the eighteenth century to the late 1940s, IR scholarship eschewed analysis of the world according to strict disciplinary divides. Instead, scholars combined **international law**, history, sociology, and political theory. What we commonly think of IR as a discipline today is in fact an aberration in terms of its own history. The discipline is conventionally traced back, at least in its formal guise, to 1919 with the establishment of the first Department of International Politics at the University of Wales, Aberystwyth. Of course, while this occasion marked the formal institutional inception of the discipline, it obscures the long tradition of work that stems back at least to the eighteenth century, if not much earlier. IR scholars characterize the 1919–*c*.1948 period as that of the 'First Debate', conducted between liberals and classical realists. Moreover, the emergence in the First Debate of the so-called 'realist quest' for an abstract science of international politics is usually thought to be the vital moment in the birth of an exclusive IR discipline, itself abstracted from other disciplines such as history and sociology.

But as a growing number of scholars are now appreciating, some of the founders of this abstract science themselves worked within the traditional framework of historical and sociological thinking. So while Hans Morgenthau's classic text, *Politics Among Nations* (1948) is remembered chiefly for the ahistorical and 'scientific' six principles of political realism outlined in the first chapter, the fact is that the ensuing thirty-one chapters are an implicit rejection of the possibility of an ahistorical understanding of international relations. Martin Griffiths (1992) perceptively labelled Morgenthau a 'nostalgic idealist' – nostalgic because of his admiration for the nineteenth century Concert of Europe, and idealist because Morgenthau saw this era as one in which states entered into a cooperative European international society, whose moral boundaries were defined not by sovereign borders (see **sovereignty**) but by the relatively peaceful norms of aristocratic international society. Such norms preached cooperation and a fundamental commitment to the balance of power as a means to ensure the collective reproduction of the society of states, rather than as a product of the unintended politics of individual state survival. Morgenthau posited a fundamental break in international history, which he located in the nineteenth century. This was caused by the rise of democracy and therefore the development of new sovereign states that were morally beholden not to the international collectivity of states but to their own individual populations. The upshot of this change was the contraction of an inclusive (albeit aristocratic) international moral boundary into exclusively competitive national sovereign states, thereby leading to a shift from cooperative international relations to a world dominated by power politics. In short, while Morgenthau is traditionally imagined to be one of the most important scientific realists in the field, he was in fact truer to the historical–sociological methodology that had characterized the 'discipline' prior to 1919.

Similarly, E.H. Carr's *The Twenty Years' Crisis* (1939), which is often viewed as the exemplar of modern realism in the study of international relations, also rejected the notion of the international as a realm of continuity. Moreover, in his book *Nationalism and After* (1945) he provided an historical-sociological interpretation which essentially reproduces the framework of Morgenthau's vision of the sources of historical change. Carr developed a critical analysis which posited that **liberal internationalism** was not a genuine moral project but was merely a protective front that maintained the dominance of the great powers at that time.

In contrast to the historical and sociological analyses of Morgenthau and Carr, the narrowing of the discipline's boundaries is a trend that emerged during the second half of the twentieth century. Notable here was the behavioural revolution (prevalent in the United States), which effectively swept aside historical and sociological analysis in favour of an empiricist approach. Even so, historical–

sociological methodology never completely dominated the study of international relations, particularly since, on the other side of the Atlantic, the members of the **English School** fought something of a rearguard battle against the trend.

Arguably, it was only as late as 1979 with the publication of Kenneth Waltz's *Theory of International Politics* that the discipline's boundaries suddenly narrowed or regressed sharply into a highly exclusive intellectual domain that rejected the utility, or inclusion, of historical and sociological analysis. Waltz was explicitly concerned to deny the use of HS when constructing a 'theory of international politics', and sought instead to define a theory as legitimate only in terms of its ability to explain 'continuity'. By continuity, he meant that international politics has always comprised conflict between political units, whether these units were **empire**s, city-states or nation-states. To explain this alleged *uniformity* of international outcomes, Waltz made four major claims, all of which sought to banish historical–sociological enquiry from the mainstream IR research agenda. They are worth revisiting if only because their rejection informed the basis of the subsequent historical–sociological challenge.

First, international anarchy ensures that states have no choice but to adapt or conform to the structural logic of competition. Accordingly, the politics of 'agency' drops out (and was effectively consigned or banished to the discipline of Comparative Politics). Second, Waltz posits a strict dividing line between the autonomous or self-constituting international realm and the residual national/domestic realm, in order to retain the primacy of international anarchy (again banishing the analysis of domestic politics to Comparative Politics/Economics). Third, he insists on the omission of social processes and the politics of identity formation – again so as to preserve the centrality of the structural/materialist logic of anarchy. Finally, he dismisses the study of international change by arguing that the international realm is and always has been marked by a dismaying persistence of recurring events. Indeed, Waltz's theory contains only a reproductive rather than a transformational logic because by conforming to the competitive logic of anarchy, states unintentionally reproduce the structure of anarchy. Since states are required to emulate the leading powers and to engage in balance of power politics to ensure their individual survival, so it becomes impossible for any one state to take over the system and transform the anarchic multi-state system into an imperial hierarchy.

The return of historical sociology

The debate between Waltz and his critics dominated the mainstream IR theory research agenda since the early 1980s up to the end of the **cold war**. From the outset his worldview was contested by a number of prominent scholars who viewed history and sociology as important aspects of the discipline. Perhaps the most influential book of the 1980s was Keohane's edited volume, *Neorealism and its Critics* (1986). John Ruggie's chapter in that book is particularly important, for it contains the key 'anti-tempocentric' insight which is that by failing to appreciate fundamental differences between the medieval and the modern international system, Waltz has no way of understanding the unique spatial relationship between *modern* states. In the same volume, Richard Ashley points out that Waltzian neorealism is a 'historicism of stasis' which freezes the political institutions of the current world order thereby ruling out the possibility of future change beyond the pre-

sent system. The critical theorist Robert Cox took this point furthest by differentiating conservative *problem-solving* theory from **critical theory**. Unlike problem-solving theory, critical theory refuses to take the present system for granted and rejects the search for ways of making the present system work more efficiently. Instead critical theory is fundamentally concerned to unravel the socio-historical origins of the present system, discover the dynamic processes that underpin its development as well as to uncover the possible social processes which might lead to its transformation. Building on these criticisms, international relations scholars have turned increasingly to historical sociology in order to counter mainstream tempocentrism.

Problematizing the general assumptions of mainstream IR theory

It is hardly controversial to assert that the most common disciplinary assumption is that the international realm has always comprised an anarchic system of political units which can be understood as 'like-units' whose inner characteristics are irrelevant to the conduct of interstate behaviour. This seemingly anodyne and unproblematic assumption is however, fundamentally challenged by historical sociologists. First, they reveal as problematic the claim that 'like-units' have predominated, asserting that for *unlike-units* have been the norm in world history. For example, in the European medieval system, feudal polities coexisted with city-states (as in Italy), city-leagues (such as the German Hansa) as well as various imperial formations at different times. Fittingly John Ruggie (1986) uses the term 'heteronomous' to describe the pre-modern European system. Thus the alleged existence of sovereign 'like-units' found today is in fact unique to the present system and are not a timeless, universal property of world politics. This in turn means that we need to rethink the origins of the uniquely modern 'like-unit', the sovereign state. Moreover, we need to realize that anarchy (which also existed albeit to varying degrees before the present system) could not in itself have been the cause of either unlike-units before 1648 or like-units thereafter.

Second, the assumption that sovereign states are spatially demarcated by hard and fixed sovereign borders seems incontrovertible. But to explain their emergence *is* controversial. Historical sociologists reveal that medieval European polities functionally overlapped. Borders did not exist in a rigidly defined way but were loose or fluid. Thus for example, the King of England owned territories in France (a contributory factor in the Hundred Years' War from 1337–1453). Thus inter-spatial relations between polities have varied through historical time. The significance of this claim lies in the point that without a conception of inter-spatial relations as a variable rather than as a constant, mainstream IR theorists are unable to explain the emergence of rigidly defined sovereign borders in the modern period. Clearly this lacuna robs mainstream IR theorists of the capacity to explain one of the most important constitutive features of the present system.

Third, historical sociologists reveal that anarchy is not monolithic but *differentiated*. Realists tend to see anarchy and hierarchy as two parts of a dichotomy. But historical sociologists reveal that sub-system hierarchies and heteronomies have always coexisted alongside anarchy. Thus sub-systemic heteronomies coexisted within multi-polity systems in medieval Europe. Indeed feudal polities overlapped with numerous hierarchies including the Mongol

Empire, Merovingian and Carolingian Empires, as well as the Habsburg Empire and Holy Roman Empire. And upon these multiple political formations was superimposed the Catholic Church; hence the designation of Europe as Christendom (or the *Respublica Christiana*). Mainstream IR theorists might respond by arguing that even if this was the case, the modern system is clearly anarchic. But historical sociologists reveal that sub-system hierarchies/heteronomies have been a prominent feature of the modern world (e.g. British and French empires, the Warsaw Pact and the European Union). Hendrik Spruyt argues that mainstream IR theorists have mistaken the Westphalian 'moment' for the ontology of the international system (Spruyt 1998: 19). But HS reveals that even the Westphalian moment itself has been reified and hijacked, and therefore needs to be reconsidered anew through historical-sociological enquiry.

By the late 1980s/early 1990s a small number of scholars sought to draw explicitly upon historical–sociological insight in order to counter the direction that the discipline was now taking. Various scholars saw Weberian historical sociology (WHS) as providing a useful first-cut into developing an alternative direction.

First and foremost, WHS insists that domestic social processes (alongside international pressures) are important in shaping state behaviour. Paradoxically, one expression of this lies with the renewed emphasis on the autonomy of the state. In the Weberian context, the most well-known conceptualization is Michael Mann's (1986) distinction between infrastructural and despotic state power. The former refers to the ability of rulers or governments to logistically reach into society and to make policy in collaboration with important social groupings. By contrast, despotic power refers to the ability of rulers to undertake a range of actions that do not require routine negotiation with civil society groups. Second, WHS offers a means to transcend *systemic* structuralism by revealing the co-constitutive relationship between the national and international realms. Most significant here is Mann's claim that societies, and by implication international systems, 'are constituted by multiple overlapping and intersecting socio-spatial networks of power' (Mann 1986: 1). Third, WHS offers a means to counter the excessive materialism of mainstream IR theory. Anthony Giddens' (1984) structurationist approach, which explains the process of change by giving equal weight to agents and structures, was seminal. And Mann's emphasis on the importance of what he calls the *immanent* power of ideology preempted the later claims made by constructivists (Mann 1986). Fourth, such writers emphasize the importance of international change *and* discontinuity in contrast to Waltz's thesis of continuity. These four major insights amount to the *promise* of WHS for IR.

More generally it became a common perception that the greatest insight of WHS lies in its ability to uncover the historical origins of states and to view states as governed by historically contingent processes. This, of course, would counter the tendency to view the existence of fully-formed Westphalian sovereign states, analogous to Hobbes' individuals, as if they appeared by magic in 1648. Thus WHS offered a means to problematize the state itself. Ironically, however, historical sociologists have been criticized for reproducing realist premises in treating the international realm as one of geopolitical competition between states and, above all, for understanding **nationalism** within the alleged context of the geopolitics of international anarchy. In this way, the first wave of historical sociology has arguably failed to live up to its early promise.

Nonetheless, the ultimate point of undertaking historical–sociological analysis has been to reveal not just the different forms that IR has taken in the past but to highlight the point that the modern system is unique and cannot be treated simply as an ontological given that characterizes IR through world-historical time. And all historical sociologists are unanimous in asserting that rethinking the constitutive properties and dynamics of the modern system can be successfully achieved only by applying a more sensitive 'non-tempocentric' historical-sociological lens.

Further reading

Biersteker, T. J. and Weber, C. (eds) (1996) *State Sovereignty as Social Construct*, Cambridge: Cambridge University Press.

Buzan, B. and Little, R. (2000) *International Systems in World History*, Oxford: Oxford University Press.

Carr, E. H. (1939) *The Twenty Years' Crisis*, London: Macmillan.

Carr, E. H. (1945) *Nationalism and After*, London: Macmillan.

Giddens, A. (1985) *The Nation-State and Violence*, Cambridge: Polity.

Griffiths, M. (1992) *Realism, Idealism and International Politics*, London: Routledge.

Hobden, S. (1998) *International Relations and Historical Sociology*, London: Routledge.

Hobden, S. and Hobson, J. M. (eds) (2002) *Historical Sociology of International Relations*, Cambridge: Cambridge University Press.

Jarvis, A. P. (1989) 'Societies, States and Geopolitics: Challenges from Historical Sociology', *Review of International Studies* 15(3), 281–93.

Keohane, R. O. (ed.) (1986) *Neorealism and its Critics*, New York: Columbia University Press.

Mann, M. (1986) *The Sources of Social Power*, Cambridge: Cambridge University Press.

Morgenthau, H. (1948) *Politics Among Nations*, New York: Knopf.

Rosenberg, J. (1994) *The Empire of Civil Society*, London: Verso.

Ruggie, J. (1986) 'Continuity and Transformation in the World Polity', in R. Keohane (ed.) *Neorealism and its Critics*, New York: Columbia University Press.

Skocpol, T. (1979) *States and Social Revolutions*, Cambridge: Cambridge University Press.

Spruyt, H. (1998) 'Historical Sociology and Systems Theory in International Relations', *Review of International Political Economy* 5(2), 340–53.

Tilly, C. (1990) *Coercion, Capital and European States AD 990–1990*, Oxford: Blackwell.

Waltz, K. N. (1979) *Theory of International Politics*, New York: McGraw Hill.

See also: agent-structure debate; constructivism; critical theory; English School; international society; Marxism; post-positivism; realism; reflexivity; revolution

JOHN M. HOBSON

Human capabilities

A term closely associated with the work of Martha Nussbaum (1947–), in which she has elaborated and extended the Aristotelian concept of human capabilities – which refer to what a person can be and do; and what, normatively, a human person should specifically be able to do. Nussbaum's 'capabilities approach' offers a reconstruction of ethical and normative political theory. She argues that the approach provides a grounding for **human rights** and for national constitutional frameworks.

Nussbaum identifies a series of concepts associated with the term: basic capability, internal capability, combined capability, and central human capability. First, a 'basic capability' is an inborn potential. In most cases basic capabilities need to be fostered to fulfil that potential; for example, the capability to speak is lost after a few years of life if it has not been appropriately fostered.

Second, an 'internal capability' is a skill or **power**, that typically results from the appropriate fostering of a basic capability; such as the ability to speak. It is internal to the person, and whether it can be used will depend on the person's environment.

Third, a 'combined capability' is a real ability to do or to be something; for example, a capability to speak in public, given both the internal capability and the absence of external threat, prohibition or lack of opportunity. This is the main sense of 'capability' as used by Nussbaum, and matches what her associate, the Indian economist Amartya Sen (1933–), calls 'functionings'. Sen introduced the term 'functionings' for the various things that a person does or is; for example, how long she lives, her pattern of health and sickness, and her form of participation in political life. (Combined) capability refers to the functionings which are attainable for a person.

Fourth, a 'central human capability' is a combined capability which is deemed a high priority, necessarily present in a decent human life or a life with dignity. Sometimes Nussbaum uses the term 'basic (human) capability' here too. She asks the classical Greek question: what are the features without which a life cannot be deemed human, or (her more demanding criterion) humanly decent? For example, a life in which one cannot exercise one's faculties in a reasoned manner and to mix with other people in various rewarding ways will not meet the minimum standards for a decent human life. Whether a person chooses to use such capabilities is a different matter. Once people have the capability to attain the basis for leading a good life, then Nussbaum adopts a Rawlsian 'political liberalism' which tolerates different ethical perspectives, each of which provides substantive content for the good life of an individual.

The capabilities approach attempts to construct a humanist and in some respects a cosmopolitan (see **cosmopolitanism**), internationalist ethic. It builds selectively and critically on ideas from Aristotle, Kant, Marx, Rawls, Sen, and from the human rights tradition. From Aristotle come concerns with what is distinctively human; with what persons can do in their lives, not only with what they possess; and with many distinct aspects of life, each deserving attention and protection. However, Nussbaum rejects Aristotle's restricted focus in terms of persons, particularly his exclusion of women. From Kant comes her insistence on treating each person as of moral importance and equal importance. She rejects, however, Kant's social contract stance in considering global relations; it is, she argues, insufficient when considering relations between the strong and the weak. From Marx she draws strengthened Aristotelian ideas of the diversity of a person's needs and capacities, and the significance of living in a way guided by reason and in association with others. From the human rights tradition she takes a willingness to propose universal priority requirements, but seeks a sharpened formulation and theoretical basis for human rights. Human rights are seen as rights for specified combined capabilities, based on the criterion of human dignity. From Rawls comes ideas of a staged construction of ethical theory and the search for a reflective equilibrium. However, Nussbaum criticizes Rawls' social contract approach, includ-

ing its partial extension to the international arena.

From Sen, Nussbaum elaborates the content of ideals such as capabilities and functionings, and an orientation to issues in or affecting low-income countries, not only high-income ones. The world's affairs are run to a large degree on the basis of monetary calculations that exclude many human concerns as well as those who have little or no purchasing power. The monetized sphere dominates attention, and tends to expand and annex other spheres of life as economic power buys political and judicial influence and influences the production and distribution of ideas. A preoccupation with production and consumption that are only recorded in monetary terms reflects or implies certain assumptions: that the amounts that people pay or are willing to pay for goods adequately measure the goods' normative importance, either because they measure the satisfaction that people acquire from the goods, which can supposedly be treated as a good measure of their associated well-being; or because they reflect people's free choice and/or preferences. Sen has led the way in demonstrating the impoverishment of public policy based on these assumptions. He argues for functionings and capability, especially capability, as primary evaluative categories in public policy discussions. To some extent, his ideas have been adopted in the Human Development approach of the **United Nations Development Program** – notably in its annual *Human Development Reports* and set of indices of human development.

Nussbaum's approach differs from Sen's in several ways. She promotes a central focus on human dignity rather than on human freedom, and paints a richer picture of personhood, including the emotions and their role in shaping our identity. Nussbaum's list of essential human capabilities is controversial. Over the years it has evolved through discussion, and she considers it permanently corrigible and provisional, as well as open to 'plural specification' and 'local specification' in light of the culture(s) and conditions in specific contexts. In addition, it must be acknowledged that any list is inevitably partly fuzzy, not a sharply delimited set of necessary and sufficient features for a decent life. Nussbaum's capabilities approach has evolved and deepened, and should be read in its recent rather than early formulations.

Further reading

Nussbaum, M. (2000) *Women and Human Development*, Cambridge: Cambridge University Press.
Sen, A. (1999) *Development as Freedom*, New York: Oxford University Press.

See also: cosmopolitanism; development; foundationalism/anti-foundationalism; human rights

DES GASPER

Humanitarian intervention

Humanitarian intervention has been defined as 'reliance upon force for the justifiable purpose of protecting the inhabitants of another state from treatment which is so arbitrary and persistently abusive as to exceed the limits of that authority within which the sovereign is presumed to act within reason and justice' (Stowell 1921: 53). The principle of humanitarian intervention is a widely accepted but still controversial international legal principle that has a long history in the guise of the **just war** doctrine. A brief historical overview makes the connection between just war and humanitarian intervention clearer.

Intervention in legal discourse means essentially reliance upon force, thus **war**, fought to redress a wrong (*ergo* a defensive action). The Roman thinker Cicero (106 BC–43 BC) argued that wars undertaken without reason are unjust wars. Just wars could only be fought for the purpose of avenging or repulsing an enemy. Early Christian **pacifism** changed in the fourth century to endorse wars fought to defend principles consistent with Christian doctrine. Philosophers such as St. Augustine (354–430) and Thomas Aquinas (1225–1274) hoped that through just war a just order would emerge, true to the Gospel and infused by the divine will. Essential requirements were added later. These are that:

(a) just war must have a just cause,
(b) 'intervenors' must have just intentions,
(c) an authoritative sovereign must declare war, and
(d) good has to result from war.

The debate over whether or not it is possible to fight a 'just war' has continued throughout the ages. It was revived during the later part of the nineteenth century, but shifted from the philosophical realm to the legal (jurisprudential) realm. The philosophical debate over whether war and justice are compatible continues today. Scholars such as Michael Walzer (1977, 1995) have changed their position from categorical denial to a reasoned endorsement of humanitarian intervention in cases of **genocide** or other massive violations of **human rights**. This is not to say that they would endorse in principle unilateral interventions as a matter of right or acceptable practice. The **international law** community remains divided between those who think of humanitarian intervention as legal and those who deny its legality. Among many writers some classics are especially important. Historically, supporters include Rougier (1910), Stowell (1921), and Lauterpacht (1975), all of whom argue that humanitarian intervention is an established legal principle. Numerous others disagree, among them Hall (1895) and Franck and Rodley (1973), who contended that humanitarian intervention is essentially a moral imperative not a legal doctrine. Today the debate is more diffuse, varying between qualified support and rejection (see Weiss and Collins 2000).

Enduring legal issues

With the emergence of international law in the seventeenth century the territorial integrity and inviolability of national boundaries of the sovereign state became the cornerstone of international relations (see **sovereignty**). In legal discourse no state had the right to intervene in the internal affairs of another state. But with the post-1945 emergence of doctrines and conventions (such as the Human Rights Conventions and Genocide Convention) that seek to protect individuals and groups from abuse by their governments, the balance between rights and obligations of governments versus those of individuals has changed. International law is no longer the domain of the all powerful state. Instead groups and individuals are also subjects of international law who are endowed with rights and obligations to the state and the international community. But major obstacles remain. On the one side it is unclear whether or not the right to intervene is part and parcel of what is called intervention by right, and if so what are the specific criteria that would allow states and international bodies to invoke the language of law. Equally troublesome are provisions found in the **United Nations** Charter which includes language that says nonintervention is the general rule (article 2, paragraph 7) but allows for self-defense and collective action (chapter VIII and article 51). Article 35 empowers the Security Council to investigate disputes that endanger peace and article 46 authorizes member states to take action when needed. The question has to be whether or not the abusive treatment of individuals by their states constitutes a threat to peace and **security**.

The underlying issue is whether the rights of individuals are equal to the rights of states. If states' rights reign supreme then it follows that they can conduct their internal affairs as they wish, which at worst means committing genocide. If individual and group rights and liberties are protected by international law, it follows that states can be held responsible for wrongs committed. Recent history provides examples of states held responsible for delicts such as fighting aggressive wars, and to a lesser degree for committing **crimes against humanity**. Current practices are even less ambiguous in bolstering individuals' claims against abusing states, as shown by judgments emanating from the European Court of Human Rights and the genocide trials against perpetrators of atrocities committed in Rwanda and Bosnia. It is quite clear that individuals and groups are subjects of international law and enjoy rights and obligations similar to those of municipal law vis-à-vis their states. It is also clear that individuals can be held responsible for crimes against humanity, but it is uncertain whether or not states can be held criminally liable in cases of massive **human rights** violations.

Here we enter the realm of essential barriers to humanitarian intervention. If other states intervene on behalf of threatened minorities, the action is directed against a collectivity, the state, which would in theory amount to collective punishment against all subjects minus the victims. However, if we were to think of the potential intervener as the representative of the international community of peoples fighting for the rights of peoples, and punishing certain regimes made up of abusive peoples, the grounds on which humanitarian intervention could become an accepted legal principle are less problematic.

But other difficulties remain. Intervention is often only thought of as punishment for wrongs committed (a sanction against a delict). Yet, international law in practice does not prescribe specific punishments nor does it automatically attach sanctions, but instead challenges states to accept responsibility and to change unacceptable practices. Also, collective action against criminal offenders is possible but not required. One may doubt the utility of a law that has no enforcement mechanism in place or that relies on good will to endorse norms of behavior. But recall that we are dealing with a global community of actors numbering less than 200 in which self-reliance and rational self-interest are the norm and altruistic behavior the exception. Today, most states routinely abide by the rules of international law, out of some combination of necessity, fear, and a multitude of other reasons. But some states commit criminal offenses, such as abusing their citizens, committing genocide, or engaging in aggressive warfare. Often these behaviors are based on rational calculations by leaders who think they can get away with crimes because:

(a) the international community will do little or;
(b) oppression of specific groups is tacitly approved by outside powers which regard the target groups as potentially more dangerous than their oppressors.

Classic examples were international inaction in the face of death squad killings in Guatemala and El Salvador during the **cold war**, and Idi Amin's genocide in Uganda in the 1970s. A current example is Algeria, where government forces routinely persecute Islamists who are held responsible for mass killings. Given the complexity of these issues we need to think of humanitarian intervention not as punishment but instead as part of the preventive machinery that could stop massive human rights violations before they escalate to genocide.

The late twentieth century should serve as an example for what can happen if humanitarian intervention is not legally available or consistently used to stop atrocities. The Holocaust surely shattered the **security** of the world and led to new rules that sought to protect ethnic, racial and religious groups from annihilation, yet little was done to put teeth into these new rules. We have yet to invent means to stop potential genocides in their track. And new problems are potentially equally deadly. With the emergence of newly independent states, ethnonational groups claiming the right to secede, and individuals insisting on new and expanded rights vis-à-vis their states, the old rules neither fit, nor are all conflicts likely to be solved in a peaceful fashion.

New thinking is required. First, consider that the state is just one actor among many, important to be sure, but not all powerful against groups or individuals. Thus, when states sign agreements and Conventions they are legally bound to abide by the rules – arguably they are bound even if they did not sign, provided a majority of states were signatories. It follows that they can be held legally responsible just as any person under international law. Thus, logically the state is a person similar to other individuals or groups, and can be held responsible for criminal offenses. But, think of the above argument re collective punishment. We know that a state is an abstraction, made up of an amalgam of peoples with different degrees of **power** depending on the type of regime. We also know that the state is governed by a few people who can easily be identified as those formally representing their state. It is that group, referred to as a regime or government, which can be held responsible for state actions directed against its' citizens. Second, some contend that intervention by right cannot be extended to include humanitarian intervention because **sovereignty** reigns supreme. Third, supporters of the doctrine's legality are unsure whether or not an intervention has to be a collective action, thus making unilateral intervention illegal. Fourth, others insist that since crimes against humanity are part and parcel of international law, there is no need to sanction punishment in the guise of humanitarian intervention, since punishment should be meted out against perpetrators after crimes are committed.

This is the crux of the problem. Humanitarian intervention should not be thought of as punishment alone but also as a means to prevent massive human rights violations. If sanctioned as a legal instrument and widely recognized as a preventive means and policy option, combined with assurances that intervenors have the support of the international community, humanitarian intervention could become a powerful tool in the hand of righteous states for upholding international standards and preventing atrocities.

Solving the legal dilemmas

Recall that nonintervention was to be the general rule in international law as exemplified in article 2, paragraph 7 of the UN Charter, which forbids outside intervention because it threatens the legally guaranteed territorial integrity and political independence of states. But exceptions to the rule of nonintervention do exist, known as intervention by right. For example, intervention is allowed when the lawful government of a state asks for outside help, or when the rights of neutrals are violated during a conflict, or if the citizens of one state are maltreated by another state. Typically, however, plaintiffs are asked to settle claims peacefully. In other words they should exhaust all remedies including diplomatic protests, mediation, and arbitration, and should accept decisions rendered by the International Court of Justice before resorting to force.

The problem with seeking redress or invoking the intervention by right clause is that:

(a) human rights abuses are not issues between two states but rather they pit the community of states that try to uphold international standards of behavior (norms) against offenders, and

(b) by the time disputes might be dissolved by these means many victims may be dead, thus defeating the purpose of the original claim.

Imagine a domestic situation in which assault victims have to live in the house of the offender, knowing quite well that at any time they could be killed. This pretty much sums up the situation today. Genocide tribunals have been convened after the end of atrocities in Bosnia and Rwanda to punish offenders. Such *ad hoc* tribunals are ill equipped to handle the complex issues of state sponsored murder, in part because of limited funds and, in Rwanda, a lack of legal personnel or political expediency have made them little more than showcases. Such tribunals do little to deter future offenders, whereas the larger goals of criminal justice systems include prevention and **deterrence** as well as punishment. With the establishment of a permanent court (the **International Criminal Court**, which was established in 2002) this may change, but only time can tell, and in the absence of support from the world's most powerful country, the United States, the Court's chances of success are dim.

To summarize, from a legal perspective it would be highly desirable to include humanitarian intervention in the arsenal of preventive means at the disposal of the international community of states to uphold minimal standards of justice, such as freedom from genocide or torture. This could be done in two ways, by elevating its status to intervention by right and by including it among legally accepted conflict resolution measures such as arbitration. Humanitarian intervention, as mentioned earlier, should be a preventive tool, one that should be invoked when other means, such as mediation, have failed, but before many people are dead. Some scholars invoke the principle of using force only as a last resort in cases such as pre-genocide Rwanda. The problem with the 'last resort clause' is that we know that mediation, good office and persuasion rarely work in situations that are at risk for genocide. Conversely too little effort may have been made to dissuade likely perpetrators from escalating violence. Using force to prevent genocide is the lesser of two evils. Savings lives can be costly since it may take the sacrifice of some to save many. But according to General Dallaire, UNAMIR commander in Rwanda at the onset of the genocide, a few hundred trained combatants and a different mandate could have saved the lives of hundreds of thousands.

Assuming that the legal status of humanitarian intervention remains ambiguous, as seems to be the case now, what can be done? Of course international actors can ignore international law and intervene, thus presenting the world with a *fait accomplis*, as in Iraq in 2003. Assume for a moment that the US and British intervention was primarily a humanitarian mission. Although the United States and Britain, supported by a few other states, claimed that this was a defensive action justified by the threat of weapons of mass destruction, few other states agreed that the threat was imminent, or left no choice of means or time to respond in a less aggressive fashion (which are requirements for defensive action under international law). Surprisingly, it would have been more reasonable for the intervenors to justify their actions by invoking the Baathist regime's human rights violations. The problem however is that of claiming imminent danger. Was Saddam Hussein a greater threat to his people in 2003 than in the past? Was he planning to attack others outside his territory or supporting international terrorism? Unfortunately these are real issues facing potential intervenors, all of whom must provide proof that intervention was/is justified. Given these formidable obstacles, it is no wonder that states are reluctant to take action to save lives in cases that do not threaten the immediate survival of their own peoples, regimes, or vital interests.

How to activate legal mechanisms

Much can be done to circumvent the *impasse* posed by legal authorities who react but seldom proact, which is essentially part of legal tradition. Consider that international law supposedly reflects the mores of **international society**. In its role as a representative of global society the United Nations needs to agree to change the rules, for it is after all the legislative arm of the international community.

Because international law is case law, which relies on precedent (*stare decisis*) in order to evolve, lawmakers could instead refer to a few 'successful' humanitarian interventions to help guide them in drafting new principles. Furthermore given the existence of Conventions, signed by most states, that spell out obligations, right and duties, it is long overdue for the UN to spell out the rules by which violators can be punished or, preferably, deterred from violating international standards of behavior. Elevating the status of humanitarian intervention to intervention by right would mean three things:

(a) it could be used for prevention in cases in which abusive regimes are poised to attack their citizens,
(b) it may serve as a deterrent to future genociders, and
(c) it is a punitive act against offenders.

What remains is the formulation of rules that clearly spell out what needs to be done and when. From here it gets difficult. Unfortunately there are only few precedents of successful humanitarian interventions from which legal experts can learn. And, in a handful of cases intervenors have been accused of intervening for less than altruistic reasons. Despite these less than perfect models the alternative of leaving things the way they are, i.e. doing nothing, encourages apathy and inaction despite Rwanda, Bosnia, Sierra Leone and Congo-Kinshasa to name just a few cases where early intervention could have saved many lives. Unfortunately, in some cases intervenors were accused of aggression and lawlessness, thus would-be helpers may be dissuaded from future preventive action. Today's international policymakers are ever more cautious in advocating intervention because the political costs and material costs of going it alone are prohibitive given the risks, lack of support and international criticism.

The current situation

The advent of the European Court of Human Rights, fully functioning as a single court since 31 October 1999, the projected permanent International Criminal Court adjudicating crimes against humanity, and the existence of *ad hoc* tribunals dealing with specific cases of genocide, all are supposed to deter future perpetrators, establish precedents and allow for representation of survivors and punishment of offenders. Much can be learned from the proceedings. For one thing we can discover how events unfolded and help future generations detect signals that may lead to future episodes. We may find out what motivated perpetrators and how they mobilized others, used institutional resources and gathered support to commit crimes. From this information we may be able to devise tools to interrupt at each stage a process that leads to disaster. Ideally, using force should enter the equation at later stages but may be needed early depending on how fast a situation deteriorates. A classic example is Rwanda in which massive killings were planned and carried out in a relatively short time in the early 1990s.

As observed above, we need clear rules on how to intervene and when. This presupposes an understanding of what factors contribute to the situation in question and knowledge of what is the best time at which the use of force is warranted and effective to halt escalation. Below I briefly describe the state of early warning in cases of massive human rights violations.

At present we simply do not know how best to proceed in halting humanitarian disasters. But given the arguments above, the least we can do is authorize intervention by outside powers to halt massive abuses of human rights, e.g. to stop genocide. These points have been made. First, humanitarian intervention should be elevated in law to intervention by right and should be part and parcel of conflict resolution tools. Second, the use of force, i.e. humanitarian intervention, should be restricted to cases in which we have clear signals that massive human rights violations are imminent or already underway. Use or threat of force should be accompanied by incentives to allow would-be violators to change course. Force should be sparingly used and only as long as necessary to establish a situation that is deemed safe for potential victims. No material benefits should accrue to the intervener, but legal, moral and material support should be forthcoming from other actors whether they are directly involved or not.

Political obstacles

During the cold war distrust of great power politics (see **great powers**) led critical scholars to argue that using force could and should not be justified, even for a good cause. The typical argument was that so-called humanitarian intervention was a prelude to greater oppression or, at best, troublesome meddling by superpowers pursuing their own global agendas. With the end of the cold war, the emergence of increased **ethnic conflict**, and the danger of genocide, some have abandoned their pacifist tradition or simply changed their minds by endorsing the use of force to end atrocities, mindful of the fact that events similar to the Holocaust could and did recur. Thus **peace-building** entered into international strategic and legal language, essentially affirming the right to use force to protect the global citizenry.

However, it is also understood that a peaceful world should best be achieved through peaceful means. Humanitarian intervention (using force) should be a last resort to redress wrongs and it should be a collective action. The intervener must prove necessity and use proportional means to achieve stated goals.

Where does this leave us? It is difficult to know what 'last resort' means in the absence of effective tools that would prevent genocides or similar situations. Furthermore collective actions, although desirable, seldom come about in time to prevent tragedies. Thus, there should be a place in legal language that would allow for unilateral intervention on behalf of the international community in cases deemed necessary. This recommendation is of course highly controversial. But there is such a legal means. Under chapter VIII of the United Nations Charter the UN can delegate action to individual states, a clause rarely invoked given the often acrimonious and competitive relations among states. Unfortunately, one always finds supporters even of the most abusive regimes, for many reasons. At least a few are worth mentioning. One, other similarly abusive regimes would of course be threatened by potential international action. Two, because of a greater sense of community, Western or Asian or Islamic states may in principle support unsavory regimes in their midst. Or, conversely, powerful states can support abusers for material benefits or political expediency.

Despite the dismal picture painted above, there are also states that would take action if supported by the international community. The Northern European states, such as Sweden, Norway, and Denmark have a long tradition of committing resources, political will and support for humanitarian missions. Canada and the United States are at times willing and able to commit to cases that are outside their immediate **national interest**s defined narrowly by changing administrations. There are many states of lesser status such as Jordan in the Middle East, South Africa, Australia, Japan, Bulgaria, and others that would take part in efforts to prevent future human tragedies.

Early warning of humanitarian crises: a prerequisite for effective intervention

Who could forget the Holocaust, when forceful early intervention by the allied powers could have saved the lives of millions? Did the international community know what was happening and ignored the evidence, or was the evidence sketchy and not believable? Experts believe that both factors were at work, in addition to a lack of moral fortitude and political will.

The academic and policy communities have evolved to recognize international law's shortcomings in protecting individuals and groups from the omnipotent state. But much work needs to be done. We need to do better in a variety of ways. Changing the law is one thing, making sure that we have adequate means to prevent or halt humanitarian disasters. But providing early warnings based on information that is reliable and persuasive, not based on intuition or opinion, is difficult. In order to do reliable risk assessment and provide early warning, evidence is needed on a number of similar events, which would lead to systematic comparison and the testing of hypotheses on why these events took place. We now have enough empirical knowledge to do global **political risk analysis**. The data and model are readily available and thus at the disposal of anyone interested in future risk assessment. This kind of procedure enables us

to scan the world for trouble spots and estimate the chances that a humanitarian disaster or similar scenario may develop in any given country within the next few years. The next step is to develop early warning capacity, to allow policymakers to narrow the time frame in which such events are likely to begin from years to months. Models developed for this purpose are being tested but the data used are not publicly available. Given such progress, more attention can be given to prevention. But few scholars have identified tools that deflect or deter genocide. We know that standard forms and means of conflict resolution such as mediation, sanctions, and arbitration did not prevent genocide in Rwanda in 1994. But it is unknown whether or not such means could have worked better if applied earlier. And there is lack of political will to use and assess effects of preventive actions.

What is certain is that human suffering has not abated to a significant degree since World War Two, though there are signs that ethnic warfare is on the wane and the danger of genocide has somewhat receded since the end of the cold war. It is also true that many states monitor the global human rights situation and many **non-governmental organization**s (NGOs) have emerged that provide early warning and seek to alleviate human suffering. Increased communications are creating a global village, in which it becomes ever less likely that states will get away with murdering their citizens without scrutiny and repercussion. As argued earlier, international law needs to be clear and unambiguous about what constitutes legal intervention, who can intervene, under which circumstances, and using which means. Early warning mechanisms need to be perfected in order to detect years and months in advance when gross human rights violations are likely. This would allow policymakers to choose preventive options that are less expensive in personnel and material. We also need to know much more about which incentives and **sanctions** work at which point in time to de-escalate conflict. Finally, we must have better ways of mobilizing the global citizenry and international policy to act in the face of imminent threats.

Learning from the past

Of the handful of successful humanitarian interventions such as India in Bangladesh, Tanzania in Uganda, and Vietnam in Cambodia, the latter is clearly the most controversial. Vietnam intervened in December 1978 and freed the country from the murderous Khmer Rouge regime led by Pol Pot. The killings stopped, but Vietnamese occupation began. Eventually the Vietnamese leadership decided to leave (occupation was costly in men, material and international opinion) and a Cambodian-led coalition emerged (including former Khmer Rouge members) that became the ruling regime of Cambodia until the present. Cambodia became the orphan child of the United Nations, probably the most costly project in recent history. The UN regime tasked to rebuild Cambodia was ill equipped to do so, fraud and waste was rampant, but despite these failures the political will was laudable. Cambodia is symptomatic of the problems that do occur when nothing is done to prevent a situation from evolving into genocide. Vietnam as the intervenor was hailed by some in the human rights community as a savior, but the majority of scholars and international public opinion condemned Vietnam for its aggressive intervention into Cambodia.

The collective intervention in early 1999 in Kosovo to halt Serbian aggression against Albanian (Muslim) Kosovars had its critics. Some considered it a situation that was not approaching genocide, therefore bombing the potential perpetrator into submission was in itself a criminal act. Others saw it as siding with a people themselves responsible for a guerrilla war against Serbian authorities.

What lessons can be drawn from these two episodes? First, no humanitarian mission (intervention) will ever satisfy all critics. Second, intervention prior to escalation to genocide, although desirable, will be problematic because we will never know if we have stopped a genocide or some lesser disaster. Third, unilateral intervention, although in some cases desirable, is fraught with obstacles, not the least of being accused of selfish motives and imperialist goals (see **imperialism**). Despite the shortcomings of these two interventions, what counts for the human rights community is that greater disasters have been prevented and the killings stopped.

Further reading

Franck, T. and Rodley, N. (1973) 'After Bangladesh: The Law of Humanitarian Intervention by Military Force', *American Journal of International Law* 67(2), 275–305.

Gurr, T. R. and Marshall, M. G. (2003) *Peace and Conflict 2003: A Global Survey of Armed Conflicts, Self-Determination Movements, and Democracy*, College Park, MD: Center for International Development and Conflict Management.

Hall, W. E. (1895) *A Treatise on International Law*, 4th edn, Oxford: Clarendon.

Harff, B. (1984) *Genocide and Human Rights: International Legal and Political Issues*, Denver: Monograph Series in World Affairs, University of Denver.

Harff, B. (1995) 'Rescuing Endangered Peoples: Missed Opportunities,' *Social Research* 62 (spring), 23–40.

Harff, B. (2003) 'No Lessons Learned from the Holocaust? Assessing Risks of Genocide and Political Mass Murder since 1955,' *American Political Science Review* 97(1), 57–73.

Harff, B. and Gurr, T. R. (1998) 'Systematic Early Warning of Humanitarian Emergencies,' *Journal of Peace Research* 35: 551–79.

Johnson, J. T. (1981) *Just War Tradition and the Restraining of War: A Moral and Historical Inquiry*, Princeton, NJ: Princeton University Press.

Lauterpacht, E. (ed.) (1975) *International Law. Collected Papers of Hersch Lauterpacht*, vol. 1, Cambridge: Cambridge University Press.

Rougier, A. (1910) 'L'intervention d'humanite,' *Revue Generale de Droit International Public*, 17: 468–526.

Stowell, E. C. (1921) *Intervention in International Law*, Washington, DC: John Byrne.

Walzer, M. (1977) *Just and Unjust Wars: A Moral Argument with Historical Illustrations*, New York: Basic Books.

Walzer, M. (1995) 'The Politics of Rescue', *Social Research* 62: 53–66.

Weiss, T. and Collins, C. (2000) *Humanitarian Challenges and Intervention*, Boulder, CO: Westview Press.

See also: failed state; genocide; just war; peace enforcement; peacekeeping; sovereignty

BARBARA HARFF

Human rights

Human rights have become one of the central political ideologies of our day. This is a considerable achievement, given that prior to World War Two the idea of human rights had little if any standing either in international relations or within the broader intellectual and political milieu of the day. The central organizing doctrine of international relations prior to World War Two held that the state was the basic unit and that each state was autonomous and sovereign (see **sovereignty**). The corollary of this doctrine was the norm of non-intervention: that each state had final jurisdiction over its own territory and was not to be subject to interventions from other states. The provision of political autonomy, economic sustenance, social infrastructure, religious freedom and physical security was the responsibility of the state alone. Consequently, **international society** was largely unconcerned with the manner and extent to which states fulfilled these expectations, providing they did not impact upon the stability of the **international system**.

The human tragedy of World War Two displayed the inadequacy of this approach to international relations. The atrocities committed by Nazi Germany during the holocaust were rightly judged a crime against humanity (see **crimes against humanity**), precipitating questions about the **legitimacy** of an international system which valued 'peace' above the life of innocent individuals and their communities. This was the setting for the new language of human rights, which served to facilitate a defense of the sanctity (inviolability) of each human person. Its emergence represented a harsh critique of an international society that had been complacent in the face of atrocity against individuals and their communities.

The idea of human rights was written into the **United Nations** Charter, promulgated in 1945. Human rights were seen as a key part of the new international policy mix required to forestall the sort of aggression manifest by Germany, Japan and Italy in World War Two. They were also a central component of the Nuremberg and Tokyo trials of those who had committed what were now called crimes against humanity. Both of these developments furthered the recognition that each individual had basic human rights which could not be legitimately violated in any circumstance.

The incorporation of the human rights idea into our contemporary international human rights **regime** was initiated with the adoption, in 1948, of the Universal Declaration of Human Rights. This declaration was not binding in **international law**, nor was it endorsed by all states (including the USSR, South Africa, and Saudi Arabia). While the negotiation process for the drafting of this document was broad, it nonetheless privileged the **liberal internationalism** of the allied West. It was not until 1966 that the process of translating the aspirational claims of the Universal Declaration of Human Rights into formal treaties bore significant fruit. These treaties are the **International Covenant on Civil and Political Rights** (ICCPR) and the **International Covenant on Economic, Social and Cultural Rights** (ICESCR). A further decade was to pass before the stipulated number of signatories required in order for the Covenants to come into force for full members was attained.

It has become customary to refer to these and subsequent instrumentalities as successive 'generations' of human rights, first through to third, with the numerical ascription representing their temporal recognition within human rights **discourse**. The First Generation of rights refers to the civil and political rights of the ICCPR. These rights are the traditional rights of Western political thought, such as freedom of speech, association and religion, which emerged to protect the negative liberty of the individual against the encroachment of sovereigns (be they monarchs or states). The Second Generation of rights are designed to not merely constrain the behavior of sovereigns, but to require them to provide the basic economic and social environment needed for the flourishing of human persons and communities. These rights are to such things as subsistence levels of income, appropriate work conditions and basic education. Instrumentalities subsequent to the two International Covenants comprise a Third Generation of Rights, which attend more to the communal or social nature of being human, including the preservation of culture and the protection of group identity. A Fourth Generation of rights has been mooted in response to criticisms of the feminist movement (see **feminism**) that rights discourse in its origin and practice catered only for male, middle class property owners. Even when extended to women, it is argued, these rights have little application to the situations in which most women find themselves. This requires that further rights be developed – or at the very least, that our rights systems be altered, so as to be inclusive and more **gender** sensitive. Developments on this front, however, can be best descried as embryonic. The Second and subsequent generations of rights have all caused considerable political and philosophical controversy because of the manner in which they extend the original ambit of liberal rights. These controversies mark one of the points at which the claims about the universalism of human rights come under scrutiny.

By 2005, 140 states (out of a total of 191) had signed on to the International Covenants. At a broader level, all states have signed on to at least one human rights law instrumentality. Compliance with these treaties is far from complete. Nonetheless, that even those who practice a politics that denies the value of human rights engage with the discourse demonstrates the distance that the international community has come in its recognition of the value of human rights in global politics.

Intellectual history

The atrocities of World War Two served to provoke the international community to search for an idiom through which its members could express their outrage and their conviction that such events should not be allowed to happen again. The idiom grasped was that of the natural law and of natural rights, the rights of 'man'. This idiom has a long intellectual and political history within Western traditions of political thought; indeed, it serves as the foundation for many of the political ideas we take for granted today. Why, then, was it that this language of rights had to be disinterred from the intellectual museum? Why was it that these natural rights were not invoked to prevent the atrocities of total **war** in the twentieth century?

The answer lies partly in our attempts to articulate the exact nature of human rights. In all the periods of its historical development, the idea of human rights is tied up with a particular worldview or intellectual framework. The origin of human rights, the content of human rights, the moral justification for human rights – these all depend upon the broader worldview of the day. The rise and eventual decline of the idea of human rights prior to its twentieth century revival is intractably linked with the rise and decline of the various intellectual milieu with which the idea of rights was associated.

Thus, the idiom of natural rights is, in its historical gestation, intimately bound up with the idea of a natural law. While this idea has pre-Christian antecedents in ancient Greece and Rome, it is within the intellectual tradition of Christendom that it comes to full flower. The identification of the idea of natural rights and natural law with Christian theism was such that as the latter became passé for the intellectual elite of the day, natural rights and law were part of the collateral damage. Their justification was dependent upon the Christian traditions in which they were nested.

Of course, the decline of Christian theism did not stop the use of rights language. Indeed, the Enlightenment period is famous for its declarations of rights: in 1776 there was the 'unanimous declaration of the thirteen united States of America'; fifteen years later we have the French Declaration on the Rights of Man and Citizens. At the same time, however, many Enlightenment philosophers were challenging the intellectual foundations of these politically efficacious claims. New intellectual tools – sociology, epistemology, empiricism, historical criticism – were used to elevate humanity itself as the highest tribunal for judgements of any kind. Nonetheless, because of its political effect, the language of natural law and essential rights that pointed beyond human will or reason was appealed to in the ongoing project of political and social reform.

The most vivid example of critique came from the utilitarian Jeremy Bentham, who dismissed the language of natural rights as 'rhetorical nonsense – nonsense upon stilts'. Such rights were 'unreal metaphysical phenomena'. They did not exist because the law that they claimed to be based upon, the natural law, itself did not exist. Natural law did not exist because there was no divine lawgiver. Thus, the apparent demise of the Christian theological traditions led to the demise of all associated political doctrines (such as, for example, the divine right of kings) as well as the doctrines of natural law and natural rights.

There were many other critiques of the natural rights doctrine. Edmund Burke provided a conservative critique; Karl Marx a radical critique. The point that this serves to illustrate is that the political ascendancy of natural rights in the eighteenth century came too late to receive intellectual respectability; it was too closely linked to philosophical and theological traditions that were being eclipsed by intellectual and sociological changes. As these changes took hold and became established, the idiom of rights became the preserve of legal regimes – positive laws – within individual states.

The historical revitalization of human rights served as a way of articulating absolute moral judgments about the atrocities associated with World War Two. It is not clear, however, that simply revitalizing the term provides answers to the many questions and critiques that saw it fade from view prior to the twentieth century. Many contemporary political and intellectual controversies about human rights are caused by these unresolved issues.

The nature of human rights

Some have argued that these theoretical debates are a diversion from the real game: the protection of rights under our contemporary internationally recognized human rights regime. The most recent development of this regime is the now permanent **International Criminal Court** which has the **power** to try people for crimes against humanity. This is the argument from legal positivism, and it is reminiscent of Bentham's position: the rights we have are those enshrined in positive law.

To ask about the nature of human rights in this context is to expect an answer denominated in treaties, conventions, declarations and international law. The difficulty is soon apparent. Human rights are not *protected* by the legal structures of a state, an international community or international laws, but are *reduced* to such legal structures. Human rights become merely the constraints or obligations imposed by positive law and policed by the state. Human rights, on this account, come into existence with the creation of a legal regime or several working in concert; they change when the regime changes and they go out of existence when the regime ceases to be enforced. Beyond this, there are no human rights.

At first glance this may appear to provide relief from the theoretical difficulties which have previously dogged human rights. However, the problem with a positivistic ontology for human rights is that it removes from human rights that with which it has traditionally been identified: the capacity to act as a form of moral criticism against state power – a form of moral criticism that is effective and persuasive because it appeals to something above and beyond the self-claimed prerogatives of the state, prerogatives to which human rights are assimilated under the positivist approach. The belief that in some sense human rights exist beyond positive law has been an essential mainstay and motivation for the critique of inadequate positive law protections of freedoms and privileges considered due to the human person.

A positivistic account of human rights can only serve the traditional function of the human rights doctrine for as long as states are ruled by benign governments. And if the ontology of human rights does not go any further than codifying state behavior then those who believe that the state is not a law unto itself and should not be allowed to act with impunity will have to appeal not to human rights but to one of the more traditional grounds of moral critique such as natural law, religious tradition, classical philosophical anthropology, or metaphysics, with all their ambiguities. In short, the positivistic account of human rights robs human rights of any claim to moral universalism, which in turn enables states to justify their intransigent moral irresponsibility and maintain their impunity.

Universalism

The universality of human rights has been, and continues to be a source of philosophical and political controversy. It is the universalism of human rights which is seen to give them their moral force – the idea that everyone everywhere is accountable to certain basic moral norms which brook no exception. Once it is asserted that particular groups of people, for reasons of their culture or religion or philosophical creed, are exempt from the observation of human rights, then much of what the idea is thought to stand for is compromised. This, indeed, is the force of the word 'human' in the term 'human rights', the idea that these rights accrue to all people simply by virtue of their being human. They do not need to belong to a particular class or religion, their sex or race has no impact, their wealth or status is neither here nor there. Under a human rights regime, it is their humanity which serves as the basis for their recognition, and the basis for the universalism of the human rights doctrine.

There is much that is attractive here. And there is very little need to elaborate the way in which the events of World War Two gave great impetus to this vision. In the Holocaust, specific groups of people were defined *out* of the category of humanity on the basis of their ethnicity, religious affiliation, and in some cases their utility to society (for example, the old and the infirm, though not necessarily Jewish, who met their death in the concentration camps). The revived vision of human rights, it was hoped, would prevent such occurrences from happening again by the simple expedient of proclaiming rights which could under no circumstances be legitimately taken from any human person.

Universal moral ideas, however, always come in the garb of particularist moral accounts of what it means to be human – and this is as much the case for human rights as it is for any other moral idea. The translation of the general idea that human beings are inviolable and of equal worth into a political program which can be implemented the world over is a political process. This process requires the identification and codification of a whole range of values which are sufficiently concrete that specific political, legal and social action may be taken in their name.

Liberalism

The particular moral account of what it is to be human that is expressed through the doctrine of human rights is that of Western political liberalism. Far from being a universal account of what it means to be human, human rights articulates in declaratory form that particular way of organizing society that emerged in the West during the late Medieval and Enlightenment periods. These periods saw the West move from political and social organization based on the vestiges of feudalism and Christendom, to new, liberal, forms of organization. These were premised on Enlightenment ideals which rejected the place of received authority, traditional moralities, transcendental religious faiths and local or customary **identity**. In place of these, the new critical rationality of the Enlightenment was to erect a universal civilization, secular and humanist. The ideas of natural rights based upon a natural law given by God were transformed by this approach, in which the idea of a self-creating, self-ruling 'man' is placed at the apex of the cosmos. As a consequence, the doctrine of natural rights became an individual, rational, universal, secular, democratic, and radical doctrine.

The particular philosophical anthropology assumed by liberalism provides the *rationale* for later elaborations of human rights as rights which inhere in the person, which are inalienable, inviolable, and universal; rights which we cannot choose to adopt nor from which we can be voluntarily quitted. These are rights that we have, not because of positive law, communal practice, social or religious tradition. These are rights we have because they explicate the essence of what it means to be human.

This vision of the human is one where the individual self is preeminent and basic. The self is conceptualized at the most foundational level as a willing self. Our capacity to will, to act, to choose, is our most important human capability (see **human capabilities**). For social arrangements this means that the freedom to will, to act, to choose, becomes the overriding value, to the point where our freedom restricts that of others. We can see the application of this conception of the self quite clearly in the history and development of the human rights discourse. It has only been in recent decades that the focus of rights discourse has moved away from clearing a space in which the individual may will, choose and act, unhindered by state (and later, societal) pressures. Even with recent communitarian developments (see **communitarianism**) which acknowledge the constitution of the individual by society and that rights are primarily a social relation not an individual ambit claim, rights discourse is still largely about enabling the individual (albeit now an individual formed within the community) to will, choose and act – now more explicitly protected against not just state and society but against particular structural (group oriented) aspects of society.

Despite these communitarian amendments it nonetheless remains the case that the liberal narrative posits an essential human subject to which rights adhere. This subject is the transcendental self, or the essential self. It is the self which is the core of all human persons, despite the accretion of culture, religion, society, politics, and philosophy through the self's existence. And this is critical to the applicability of human rights to all human persons despite these accretions, when these lead to claims for social behavior which are not mirrored by human rights.

Pragmatic diversity, normative pluralism

It is at this point that the political nature of human rights, elided by the claim of universality, most commonly comes to the fore. Moving from the general idea that there are certain forms of behavior which are so heinous that they must be absolutely proscribed, to concrete lists and bills of rights which not only proscribe such behaviors but also articulate basic ground rules for acceptable behavior – this transition is one which is fraught with difficulty and controversy. The articulation of lists of human rights, basic standards of behavior below which no human should sink (in either the giving or receiving of such rights) is a positive rather than a negative endeavor. The UDHR and the other human rights instrumentalities which have been developed by the UN do not merely proscribe behavior. Rather, the strategy for the prevention of undesirable behavior is the imposition of a basic list of behaviors to which adherence from all signatories is required.

Once we move from the general to the specific, from the abstract to the particular, the issue of which behaviors should be nominated as human rights and accepted as such becomes critical as well as controversial. Ever since the UDHR was promulgated, it has been mired in political controversy for this reason. The earliest international political controversy about human rights began with the commencement of the **cold war**, and indeed human rights became one of the many pawns in the cold war era. The controversy centered around the relative priority which should be given to political and civil rights in relation to economic, social and cultural rights. The United States and other liberal Western democracies held the view that the fundamental human rights were civil and political. The riposte from the USSR was an argument to the effect that there was not much point in having the right to vote if you did not have food to eat and a roof over your head.

More recently there has been the so-called **Asian values** debate. In this debate the political elites of states such as Malaysia, Indonesia, Singapore, China, Japan, and Burma have asserted that to a significant degree the UDHR and the broader ideology of human rights is an artifact of neo-imperialism. The human rights discourse originated in the West, was structured by Western religious and philosophical views, was molded by historical and sociological developments within Western history, and – after a **war** which was caused by the follies of Western politics – was foisted upon the rest of the world. It is yet another instance of the rich and powerful Western elite using moral categories to camouflage the structures by which it pursues its own political and material interests.

By contrast, so the argument goes, the non-Western regions of the world (in this case Asia, but a similar debate has taken place in Africa) are comprised of societies which have very different cultural, religious, and philosophical back-

grounds to those of the West. They are not, for example, necessarily democratic, they are not secular, and they do not privilege ontological individualism in their understanding of the human condition. Thus Islam, Buddhism, Hinduism, Confucianism, and indigenous cultural practices are not always compatible with (Western liberal) human rights. Moreover, it is argued, there is no *prima facie* reason why such an incompatibility should always mean subservience to liberalism (except when the pre-eminence of Western thought has already been accepted or assumed). The world is a plural world; human rights are a good idea, but even when accepted in their liberal form they must be mediated through the plural cultural traditions of the world, and at times this will mean different societies have different accounts of the nature and content of human rights. Consequently, a range of different religious and political organizations from across the spectrum have promulgated alternative human rights declarations, which owe their specific content, for example, to **Islam** or Hinduism or African cultural values.

According to this argument, while the idea of human rights may continue to be seen as an important development for justice both within and between societies and states, it is mistaken to assert that human rights (either concretely as international laws, or normatively as a moral code) are unproblematically universal. Hard core relativists will argue against any yardstick which may be used to judge one code against another. Pluralists, communitarians and multiculturalists (see **pluralism**; **communitarianism**; **multiculturalism**) can all be arrayed on a spectrum between hardcore relativism and the exclusive universalism of perfectionist liberalism. The points on the spectrum represent different strategies which have been employed to mediate between the normative claims and institutional aspirations of a universal human rights culture, and the range of challenges which are thrown up against this project by the plurality of different ways of being and understanding what it means to be human.

The politics of human rights

The central difficulty for the idea of human rights may be put in these terms. The declaratory nature of human rights rhetoric posits human rights as universal, absolute, self-evident, natural, inviolable, inalienable, and non-derogable. As such they are givens, which are above both political dispute and philosophical questioning. As we have seen, however, the idea of human rights itself is derived from a philosophical tradition which is not above question; and the practical realization of human rights in international relations is the consequence of a managed political campaign.

Far from being an incontrovertible statement of fact about the human condition, universal human rights are a deeply political and philosophically controversial vision of what can be made of the human condition. Rather than being a statement about human nature, it is a vision of human possibility. Like all such visions, however, it is deeply partisan, owes its provenance to a specific historical and cultural tradition of thinking about humanity, has changed and developed in fundamental ways over its active history, and is not transcendental. In other words, however much some of its protagonists may insist that it represents a moral order which exists beyond our humanity, human rights as an expression of that order is always mediated through particular human persons and groups of persons; is dependent for its explication on philosophical traditions maintained and developed by humans; and becomes practical through institutions created by human persons. Manifestly, neither the idea nor the practice of human rights is 'above the fray' in the sense that may be derived from its rhetoric.

This, however, should not deter human rights partisans from arguing their case and defending the vision of an international regime of rights (which some would say largely exists) and an international, even global, culture of rights (which most would recognize as a more tenuous description of present affairs). The recognition that human rights is not above the fray should not signal the end of the vision for human kind as articulated by the likes of Eleanor Roosevelt when the UDHR was inaugurated. It would be more desirable for it to signal the transition to a more sophisticated intellectual defense of the idea of human rights.

Most people affected by human rights abusing states (or other agents) are neither philosophers nor theorists. Nonetheless they are people of a diverse range of political, religious, traditional, philosophical and communal belief systems. Given this, a politics of human rights which proceeds on the basis of respect for these differences, rather than proceeding on the assumption that these differences only represent superficial or incidental differences from the liberalism which informs human rights, will be most effective in making the human rights vision of the human condition one which people desire to endorse and implement.

Further reading

Dunne, T. and Wheeler, N. (eds) (1999) *Human Rights in Global Politics*, Cambridge: Cambridge University Press.

Forsythe, D. (2000) *Human Rights in International Relations*, Cambridge: Cambridge University Press.

Frost, M. (2002) *Constituting Human Rights: Global Civil Society and the Society of Democratic States*, London: Routledge.

Ignatieff, M. (2001) *Human Rights as Politics and Idolatry*, Princeton, NJ: Princeton University Press.

Langlois, A. (2001) *The Politics of Justice and Human Rights: Southeast Asia and Universalist Theory*, Cambridge: Cambridge University Press.

Perry, M. (1998) *The Idea of Human Rights: Four Inquiries*, Oxford: Oxford University Press.

Shute, S. and Hurley S. (eds) (1993) *On Human Rights: The Oxford Amnesty Lectures 1993*, London: Basic Books.

See also: Asian values; communitarianism; cosmopolitianism; crimes against humanity; foundationalism/anti-foundationalism; human capabilities; International Covenant on Civil and Political Rights; International Covenant on Economic, Social and Cultural Rights; multiculturalism; war crime

ANTHONY J. LANGLOIS

Identity/difference

There is no identity without difference, and no world politics without identity, no people, no states, no **international system**. The question for International Relations is the *relationship* between them: how representations of identity and difference, sameness and otherness, take on meaning and manifest themselves in world politics and social life. This theme has seen a profusion of scholarship in International Relations, and sub-fields such as **critical security** studies, inspired by sources in **critical theory**, **feminism**, **post-colonialism** and **poststructuralism**. This scholarship takes an anti-foundationalist stance (see **foundationalism/anti-foundationalism** to argue that identity, whether that of individuals, nations, regions or civilizations, is not a political or ontological given, but is socially constructed through language and thus becomes manifest in social relations and structures of **power**. It has broken down the key distinction in International Relations between the domestic and international, showing how domestic struggles over identity are played out in international policy, making both realms part of a single political and cultural dynamic, and showing how representations of self and other are implicated in everything from the distribution of **foreign aid** to **genocide**.

The identity/difference question in International Relations has been manifested in two related ways. One is as an interrogation of the discipline itself as a critique of the way its intellectual givens are structured by a dichotomous strategy that privileges facts over values, **order** over **anarchy**, masculinity over femininity, truth over opinion, reason over passion, self over other, and the state over the world, while simultaneously disavowing their intimate interconnection (George 1994). The second is through a potentially limitless array of practical analyses which examine and question how linguistic constructions of identity and difference have worked to constitute world politics, how they frame and limit policy, generate and drive events, shape political and bureaucratic truths, and enter into conflicts.

Most fundamentally, the identity/difference question has resulted in a challenge to International Relations' bedrock images of **sovereignty** and the **nation-state**, to its assumption that the state is the fundamental space of political community and the privileged locus of allegiance, **security** and identity, creating closed and exclusive moral communities and limiting obligations to outsiders. International Relations, by beginning its narrative and structure with the peace of **Westphalia**, naturalizes the nation-state and its model of identity, and stifles questioning about how that identity is formed and reformed, both prior to and through the operations of global politics.

The dominant image of the sovereign state internalized by International Relations is that of the 'body-politic' of Hobbes, Locke and Rousseau: the state as a 'general will', 'a multitude united in One Person'. Such accounts deny the violence inherent in the founding of sovereignty: how sovereignty invents the 'people' who ground and authorize it, and how it is secured through a violent relationship to challenges from within and without. This modern political subject is constructed as radically estranged from the *Other*: of the criminal, the socialist, the aboriginal or the ethnic minority, entrenching a powerful image of sovereign identity as perpetually under threat and providing realist images of domestic security and international anarchy with a hidden ontological depth. Feminists in turn have shown how existing images of the nation-state are *gendered* by a dichotomy between masculine identity and feminine difference, constructing the state as a self-reliant patriarchal protector of its citizens using the instruments of strength and force rather than dialogue and cooperation (Tickner 1992).

In the philosophy of G. W. F. Hegel (1770–1831), the primal antagonism between identity and its others took on a progressive, 'dialectical' cast: the absorption of difference into a higher synthesis was a new motor of historical progress, of which Hegel saw the United States as a beacon. Such a 'philosophy of history' justified the destruction of indigenous cultures and societies, the imperial control of the Middle-East, Africa and Asia, and was revived in 1989 by Francis Fukuyama, who saw the twin 'triumphs' of liberal democracy and free markets as harbingers of the **end of history**. This illuminates how the sovereignty of the United States was historically constructed through war and dispossession of native Americans, an antagonism externalized during the **cold war**, which was often portrayed as an existential struggle between wholly irreconcilable value systems.

Such rhetoric has since been revived by the Administration of George W. Bush in its images of a post-9/11 war between civilization and **terrorism**. Conversely, the Soviet Union systematically repressed ethnic minorities and dissidents while militarily confronting the capitalist West, creating (an all too common) form of identity constructed against enemies without and within.

Mainstream and critical security scholars have also identified rigid identity constructs as central to conflicts such as those between China and Taiwan, the two Koreas, India and Pakistan, and Israel and the Palestinians, in combination with economic interests and military **security dilemma**s. In Rwanda and the Balkans, conflicts based on identity constructs which sought the absolute annihilation of the *Other* became genocidal. Conflict and identity create destructive feedback cycles, hardening structures of identity into political forms that are extremely difficult to shift, as has occurred in Israel since 2000, when a torrent of suicide bombings and Israeli opposition to Palestinian statehood combined to strengthen hardliners' views that coexistence and dialogue between 'Arabs' and 'Jews' was futile.

While the dissolution of barriers to trade, capital and information characteristic of **globalization** has undermined claims about the absolute autonomy and centrality of the state, it has been matched by (the seemingly atavistic) resurgence of violent and xenophobic discourses of sovereignty and identity. The erection of ever higher barriers to **refugee**s and **asylum** seekers in Europe and Australia, and the intensification of counterinsurgency wars in Chechnya and Aceh, are examples of a perverse perseverance of sovereignty that reminds us of the ongoing need to critique and rethink the identity constructs under-pinning the nation-state and ultimately the international system.

To this end, a diverse body of feminist and critical scholarship has sought to explore how identities can be refash-ioned to enable more ethical, empa-thetic, cooperative and dialogical relations with Others, in the hope of reducing conflict, demilitarizing secur-ity, achieving reconciliation, and mov-ing towards a new definition and practice of global justice. In this there are potentially fruitful convergences with (and innovations of) existing efforts to promote **preventive diplomacy** and con-flict resolution, and political affinities with liberal International Relations dis-courses of **cosmopolitanism** and **inter-national society**. A new synthesis, a new absorption of intellectual difference into disciplinary identity, is not needed, but we might hope that eventually Interna-tional Relations can create a global space in which its myriad identities and differences will meet in a spirit of com-mon concern, political exchange and ethical possibility.

Further reading

Burke, A. (2001) *In Fear of Security: Aus-tralia's Invasion Anxiety*, Sydney: Pluto.
Campbell, D. (1992) *Writing Security: US Foreign Policy and the Politics of Identity*, Manchester: Manchester University Press.
Connolly, W. E. (1995) *The Ethos of Plur-alisation*, Minneapolis, MN: Minnesota University Press.
George, J. (1994) *Discourses of Global Poli-tics*, Boulder, CO: Lynne Rienner.
Inayatullah, N. and Blaney, D. (2004) *Inter-national Relations and the Problem of Difference*, London: Routledge.
Tickner, J. A. (1992) *Gender in International Relations*, New York: Columbia University Press.

See also: genealogy; feminism; post-structuralism

ANTHONY BURKE

Imagined community

This concept is the brainchild of one of the most original students of nationalism, Benedict Anderson. In his well-known book *Imagined Communities: Reflec-tions on the Origin and Spread of Nationalism* (1991), Anderson is parti-cularly interested in how people come to believe that, as individuals, they are members of a particular nation that is entitled to **sovereignty** over a piece of territory and can feel so loyal to their nation that they are prepared to die in its defense.

Anderson focuses on the historical process of collective imagination that he believes to be constitutive of nation-hood. The nation is imagined as both limited and **sovereign**. It is imagined because the members of the nation never know most of their fellow members. It is imagined as limited because no nation sees itself as coterminous with humanity. Anderson examines three paradoxes of nationalism in some depth; first, the objective modernity of nations in the eyes of historians versus their subjective antiquity in the eyes of nationalists; sec-ond, the formal universality of nation-ality as a sociocultural concept versus the particularity of its manifestation; third, the political **power** of nationalism versus its philosophical poverty.

Anderson argues that nationalism has to be understood not in relation to self-consciously held political ideologies, but the large cultural systems that preceded it. Nationalism arose at a time when three other cultural conceptions of identity were decreasing in importance.

First, there were changes in religion. Nationalism represented a secular transformation of fatality into continuity, magical contingency into worldly meaning. The unselfconscious coherence of religion declined after the Middle Ages because of the explorations of the non-European world and the gradual demotion of the sacred language itself. Older communities lost confidence in the unique sacredness of their language (the idea that a particular script offered privileged access to sacred ontological truth). Second, there were changes in the dynastic realm. In feudal forms of imagination, states were defined by 'high centers', borders were porous and indistinct. With the decline of the **legitimacy** of the sacral monarchy in the seventeenth century, however, people began to doubt the belief that society was naturally organized around 'high centers' such as Rome. Third, and here Anderson is most original, he argues that we must take into account the feudal conception of time, in which cosmology and history were indistinguishable. It was changes in the conception of time that made it possible to 'think' the nation. The pre-modern era is characterized by a conception of *simultaneity-along-time* in which time is marked by 'pre-figuring and fulfilment'. This is gradually replaced by the conception of *simultaneity-across-time* in which time is measured by clocks and calendars. The idea of a sociological entity moving calendrically through time is a precise analogue of the idea of the nation, which also is conceived as a solid community moving steadily through history.

The decline of old ideas set the stage for a new form of collective cultural consciousness. The reason it took the form of nationalism is due to the fortuitous interaction between **capitalism**, a new technology of communication (print) and the fatality of linguistic diversity. Capitalism was important because the expansion of the book market contributed to the revolutionary vernacularization of languages. This was given further impetus by the mass production of bibles during the Reformation and the spread of particular vernaculars as instruments of administrative centralization. In turn, printed languages laid the foundation for national consciousness by creating unified fields of exchange and communication. In combination, print capitalism created the possibility for nationalism by providing a medium for the new representations of time and space.

In short, by treating nationalism as a response to epochal change, and by examining the material and cultural conditions for the possibility of the nation as an imagined community, Benedict Anderson's work is essential reading for students of nationalism. Thinking of the nation in this way raises interesting questions about whether new forms of communication in the twenty-first century are shaping the imagination of alternatives to the nation. Anderson himself is somewhat skeptical. He points to the emergence of long distance nationalism by members of ethnic minorities in the West who can take advantage of new technology (such as email) to intensify their sense of belonging to imaginary homelands far away from the state in which they live. It remains to be seen whether contemporary spatiotemporal accelerations enhance or retard nationalism in the future. Either way, Anderson's contribution to the study of international relations remains his examination of the impact of such accelerations three hundred years ago.

Further reading

Anderson, B. (1991) *Imagined Communities: Reflections on the Origin and Spread of Nationalism*, 2nd edn, London: Verso.

Anderson, B. (1998) *The Spectre of Comparison*, London: Verso.

Chatterjee, P. (1994) *Nationalist Thought and the Colonial World*, London: Zed Books.

Ullock, C. (1996) 'Imagined Community: A Metaphysics of Being or Becoming?' *Millennium: Journal of International Studies* 25, 425–41.

See also: nation-state; nationalism

MARTIN GRIFFITHS

Imperialism

A policy undertaken by a state to directly control foreign economic, physical, and cultural resources. The concept of imperialism has a long history within international relations. Imperialism has been traditionally thought of as distinct from **hegemony** because it radiates from a political center rather than through more diffuse forms of **power**. While much of the recent work on imperialism makes a distinction between formal and informal types of imperialism, to cope with diffuse forms of power, imperialism is still, at root, the extension of sovereign forms of control over foreign resources. Identifying either formal or informal imperialism therefore requires drawing a causal relationship between the imperial state and the foreign resource to be expropriated.

There is a large and complex literature on theories of imperialism from the far left to the far right of the political spectrum. Theories of imperialism can be differentiated by the extent to which they view economic goals as primary or by the extent to which they emphasize cultural identity formation as important. More importantly, theories of imperial-

ism can be differentiated by whether imperialism is viewed as inextricably linked to the evolution of **capitalism** or associated with certain types of capitalist activity in conjunction with a **great power**'s foreign policy choices. This distinction is the crucial difference between Marxist (see **Marxism**) and liberal internationalist (see **liberal internationalism**) views of imperialism. With this in mind we can immediately distinguish between the 'classical' theories of imperialism by John A. Hobson (1858–1940) and V. I. Lenin (1870–1924), which are often (wrongly) conflated as the 'Hobson–Lenin' thesis.

On the liberal internationalist side, Hobson argued that imperialism arose from 'underconsumption' in the domestic economy, which sent capitalists to irrationally look abroad for secure economic profits under the false claim that 'trade follows the flag'. His cure for imperialism was for the state to encourage capitalists to boost domestic consumption and thereby their own profitability. Such a 'social liberal' union of state action and capitalist activity would not only enhance welfare for all within the state, but also encourage the state to support peaceful **multilateralism**. Such a change would also involve dismantling the racist **standard of civilization** that underpinned the imperial mentality. Similarly, Joseph A. Schumpeter (1883–1950) argued that imperialism was a social and psychological warrior-like hangover from the absolutist autocratic period, and that capitalism would develop large corporations, which would then lead to a strong labor movement that would encourage their states to coexist peacefully with **free trade** and social welfare.

By contrast, Lenin argued that imperialism was not a hangover from absolutism but a product of late capitalism in which, also due to a domestic declining rate of profit, capitalist ruling classes used states to divide up the world's economic resources to secure monopoly profits. The squabbling over these monopolies would inevitably lead imperial **great powers** into a world **war**. On the other hand, he believed that imperialism would spread capitalism, which would then provide the environment for socialist **revolution**.

Both Hobson and Lenin view imperialism as supported by a capitalist ruling class who favor economic monopolies and 'unproductive' finance capital. However, Hobson argues that states can reverse imperialism without abandoning capitalism by eliminating parasitic capitalists. For Lenin, however, imperialism was inextricably linked to capitalism and the state has little autonomy from the capitalist ruling class. From this view warfare between classes, particularly the bourgeoisie and the proletariat, is inevitable.

Following the delegitimation of imperialism as a viable state strategy after World War Two, imperialism was long viewed as an ideological term employed not by conventional international relations scholars, but primarily by 'radical' scholars. From this radical viewpoint post-war **embedded liberalism** had not removed imperialism but instead generated macrostructures that permitted the developed North to systematically exploit economic and labor resources from an underdeveloped South. Though not always clearly specified, radical scholars argued that the North exploited the South through unequal exchange via **multinational corporations** (MNCs) that exacerbated adverse terms of trade. They also believed that liberal internationalism was a cloak for imperialism, as were its key institutions such as the **International Monetary Fund** and the **World Bank**. Indeed, through liberal internationalism,

imperialist activity changed from costly formal means, such as the direct administration of territories, to more informal means, such as Western MNCs locating themselves in **Third World** states for cheap labor and tax breaks.

In the same radical tradition, much work on cultural **identity** formation has been a significant variation on older theories of imperialism to cope with more informal forms of imperialist activity. Particularly important here is the concept that imperialism is, historically and contemporaneously, the 'white man's burden' to civilize the irrational barbarians that inhabit non-European lands. As discussed by a number of scholars, most notably Edward Said (1978), the construction of an inferior 'Other' by Western imperial powers intends to produce a culture of inferiority among non-imperial peoples, and superiority among imperial peoples, that assists access to economic and physical resources.

This view also associates **globalization** with cultural imperialism, as a form of 'Americanization' that is of benefit to US state and corporate interests. Also of significance here is the argument that neoliberal (see **neoliberalism**) discourses underpin **global governance** and have constructed a modern standard of civilization that can promote imperialist interests through popular causes such as **humanitarian intervention** and **democratization**. A key point for these arguments is that imperialism does not have to radiate from a central point but is intertwined within diffuse forms of power, such as cultural identity construction. A key question here, then, is how does one meaningfully distinguish imperialism from **hegemony**?

Unfortunately, there is no clear answer to this question. Many international relations scholars previously concerned with hegemony argue that the United States is now better understood as an imperial power precisely because power is seen to radiate once more from a central point. A stronger form of this argument puts forward the view that the United States, as the world's leading economic and military power, is failing to meet its 'imperial responsibility' to impose its values across the globe through direct action. For other scholars all imperial activity is dead because it is inherently tied to state actions that have come under attack from globalization. From this view imperialism has been replaced by a market civilization that still serves US interests, but does not radiate from a central point.

Again, the most important distinction is whether imperialism is inextricably tied to capitalism, or whether it is linked to a great power's foreign policy choice. Clearly a great power's formal choice between unilateralism and multilateralism is helpful in separating imperialism from hegemony, although we should also be aware that cultural and informal forms of power help to structure the world economy to reflect great powers' interests.

Further reading

Brewer, A. (1980) *Marxist Theories of Imperialism*, London: Routledge.

Ferguson, N. (2004) *Colossus: The Price of America's Empire*, New York: Penguin.

Fieldhouse, D. K. (1967) *The Theory of Capitalist Imperialism*, London: Longman.

Hardt, M. and Negri, A. (2000) *Empire*, Cambridge, MA: Harvard University Press.

Harvey, D. (2005) *The New Imperialism*, Oxford: Oxford University Press.

Said, E. W. (1978) *Orientialism*, New York: Routledge.

See also: empire; neocolonialism; postcolonialism

LEONARD SEABROOKE

Information revolution

A term assigned to the digital-based and electronically delivered technology systems that emerged in the late twentieth century. These systems have radically altered financial, production, governmental, communication, and transport systems across the world and, more recently, have impacted significantly on consumer, personal, and domestic activities. The information revolution refers to the technology employed, such as computers and automated industrial production, their operating systems, and their applications, such as the Internet. The information revolution is characterized by rapid time and space dissemination, such that transactions can take place in real time through an apparent compression of time and space. The information revolution thus has made the world smaller and faster and as such is one of the defining features of **globalization**. The information revolution has emerged out of the contexts of rapid changes and developments in technology that have been evolving over the past two centuries.

Historical emergence

The information revolution is the third of the modern technological revolutions. The First Industrial Revolution emerged in mid-eighteenth century England and transformed Britain from an agrarian to an industrial economy. Changes in the mode of production led to new forms of industrial employment, a disruptive shift of population from rural areas to the cities and the formation of new social classes. The profound economic and social impacts ensured that science was forever after the handmaiden of technology, and applied science became the driving force of new scientific knowledge.

The First Industrial Revolution contributed to the historical emergence of globalization. For instance the development of industrialization throughout Europe was a major factor in the colonial 'scramble for Africa' during the nineteenth century in the drive to access resources. In another respect, the First Industrial Revolution transformed the world trading system. The First Industrial Revolution also introduced world society to some of the miseries with which it continues to struggle: environmental pollution and degradation as a consequence of the industrial process, exploitation of workers including children, the social and psychological effects of rapid urbanization. The First Industrial Revolution, bringing about new forms of social relations, spawned the emergence of new fields of inquiry, particularly sociology and psychology.

The Second Industrial Revolution occurred in the United States at the end of the nineteenth century, with a wave of technological and scientific innovations that further reshaped the nature of work and the way societies, institutions and individuals operated. Some of the innovations of this period set the trends for aspects of our modern lifestyles, particularly the mass production of automobiles and telephones (invented in Boston in 1876 by Alexander Graham Bell).

The Second Industrial Revolution saw the further integration of science and technology. Electricity grids were established that serviced whole regions for the first time. In the telegraph and telephone arenas, this period brought the introduction and diffusion of new communication technologies that were to radically change the speed and extent of communications – that is, the speed and volume of information delivery and exchange.

The social impacts of the revolution in telecommunications and automobiles were significant. The changes in the spheres of work and personal lifestyles as a result of the mass production of automobiles after 1913 were immense. Increased efficiency in industrial production and transportation produced wealth along with a culture of consumerism as commodities became cheaper. The social group of white collar middle-class workers expanded and, increasingly, complex administrative systems developed in government and commerce sectors.

For example, many African-Americans moved out of southern states to take up work in the new industrial centers of the north. This work was low skilled, repetitive and involved humans working at a pace to keep up with the machines. Cities like Cleveland, Ohio, grew rapidly around the burgeoning automobile industries and most of the workers were poorly educated, lowly paid and comprised largely of African-Americans, or the recent immigrant arrivals from Europe. Thus, the class structures that emerged out of the Second Industrial Revolution in the United States consolidated social divisions on the basis of race and ethnicity.

The period brought a demand for increased standards of education and health care. Those able to take advantage of new technologies received higher wages, while there were more luxury goods available for consumption. Advertising proliferated from this period on and contributed to the growth of mass media and entertainment with national newspaper corporations and Hollywood cinema industries emerging as new industries and cultural icons.

The Second Industrial Revolution signaled the emergence of the United States as a great power (see **great powers**). The automobile industry became a dominant international industry while the inventions in telecommunications, such as the telephone, not only were major exports for the United States but also established a totally new model of 'real-time' international communications that was valuable in politics and business. In addition, the technological innovations established an intellectual dominance in many fields of science and technology. Important developments in the social sciences also showed the growing influence of US values on other nations, such as the rapid growth of the disciplines of psychology, sociology and anthropology. Thus the Second Industrial Revolution shifted the balance of wealth, intellectual and military power from Europe to the United States.

Information: the third revolution

The third of the modern technology revolutions is that which we are living through today, generally called the information revolution, but sometimes called the 'digital revolution' or the 'electronics revolution'. It is characterized by a group of modern technologies and their applications in areas such as computers, cell phones, and the Internet that are driving worldwide and rapid changes in patterns of human interaction and behavior. This revolution is closely associated with concepts such as the knowledge economy. The section below will briefly review the historical emergence of some of the phenomena of this revolution, then discuss some of their main social and global impacts.

Military origins

Since ancient times **war** has inspired technological development. The use of iron-clad 'turtle-boats' to defend Korea against Japan's invasion in 1592 remains one of the great military technological innovations, as was the Manhattan Project in the 1940s that produced the atomic bomb. Through history the drive for ever more powerful weaponry has driven research and innovation, culminating in the so-called 'smart' weapons of contemporary warfare.

For military purposes major breakthroughs in electronics were made during and after World War Two. The first programmable computer was introduced in the early 1940s. Transistors, the beginning of microelectronics, were invented in 1947 at Bell Laboratories, New Jersey. The production of semiconductors, or 'chips', soon followed and by 1954 these were produced for the first time from crystals of silicon that were able to hold increased volumes of information.

During World War One research to improve the effectiveness of **chemical weapons** used by both Britain and Germany was the basis for contemporary **weapons of mass destruction**. The **cold war** between the United States and the Soviet Union was sustained through a massive build-up of nuclear weapons and a range of delivery systems. The **arms race** of the cold war was matched by a political competition in space research and application, which culminated in the first moon landing by American astronauts in 1969.

Some of the science and technology innovations of this period also found their way into commercial application. Particularly in Japan, the electronics industries developed consumer products like televisions, sound systems, and cameras from the technical knowledge of the space and weapons laboratories, to which they added their own innovations. The Japanese car manufacturers also applied the new technologies to the motor car production process particularly enhanced automation of the assembly line.

While the application of the technologies brought rewards to Japan, the fundamental research that produced new technologies was based in the United States. A major development came about in the United States with the invention of integrated circuits. The new systems resulted in a technological explosion whereby prices fell by 85 per cent and production increased by 20 times, again mainly for military purposes. This trend was enhanced by the invention of the microprocessor (a computer on a chip) by Ted Hoff, in Silicon Valley California, which had been the center of electronics research in the United States since the 1950s. The advent of microprocessors began another cycle of innovation and miniaturization, the scale of which can be recognized by the fact that, whereas in 1971 2,300 transistors could be fitted on one chip, by 1993 that number had risen to 35 million, representing a vast increase in the volumes of information that could be stored and rapidly transmitted. While the applications of these powerful micro-technologies had many possibilities, their biggest commercial impact was on the new industry in computers. The information revolution had arrived.

Computers

The construction of large-scale machines for storing, processing and calculating data was conceived during World War Two and the first general purpose computer was produced in 1946 at the University of Pennsylvania. It weighed 30 tons and occupied the area of a gymnasium. Similar models followed with government, research and commercial applications. International Business Machines (IBM) dominated the market with Intel actively engaged in the development of computer technology throughout the 1960s.

The new technology of the computer presented a mode of storing and manip-ulating information when it is expressed in binary codes, which is still the basis of contemporary computers. The new technologies work by coding information in numbers – expressed in series of 1s and 0s – and designers are able to move information around by moving these numbers. Computers and communication systems combine to form computer networks. Computer networks are the basis of information infrastructures.

From the early 1970s, the advent of microprocessors began a race to design a small-scale computer. One of the early groups to stimulate new ideas was the 'Homebrew Computer Club', which met at a garage in Menlo Park, California. Research was also conducted in Canada, Japan, Europe and Russia. In 1976 Steve Wozniac and Steve Jobs demonstrated their new computer (called Apple I) to the Homebrew Computer Club. Earlier, Wozniac had approached Hewlett-Packard with the Apple I but they weren't interested, saying it had no future. Wozniac and Jobs established the Apple Computer Company on April Fools Day, 1976. The subsequent outstanding commercial success of the Apple computer was due to its rapid diffusion into a myriad of venues not possible previously, such as businesses of all scales, educational facilities, transport and finance industries. For some time, however, the large companies like Altari and Hewlett-Packard were not interested in producing personal computers.

The industry giant IBM introduced its version of a microcomputer in 1981, with the tag PC (Personal Computer, a term coined by Ed Roberts in 1975 and which had been used in the industry for some years), and the basic design was rapidly remodeled by a number of other electronics companies and diffused around the world, signaling the era of the home computer.

In 1984 Apple introduced its Macintosh model, with a focus on user-friendly computing through such features as icons and symbols, and thus started the trend toward drop-down windows that are now standard in all personal computers. The trend in the development of the technology was toward personal and domestic consumer use. The increased miniaturization and flexibility of the machines were accompanied by decrease in prices, such that computers were available to ever-expanding numbers of users.

The next breakthrough was in the software or systems of codes and electronic languages that functioned in the computers. Early computers functioned on complex languages of which Cobol and Fortran were the most widely used, and these were followed by a range of DOS languages, that were implemented in most non-Apple machines (while Apple had their own software). The most significant of these was BASIC, designed by Bill Gates and Steve Allen. The changing uses of computers and the quest for more sophisticated, faster, more flexible languages produced dynamic competition to design ('write') universal and user-friendly computer languages. Two leaders in this quest were Bill Gates and Steve Allen who founded a company called Microsoft in the 1970s. Initially Microsoft products were operating systems but these expanded to become a range of software for a variety of applications in the micro-computing market as a whole. Microsoft Corporation has become the world's dominant computer software company, so much so that in 2000 it was charged and convicted in the courts for operating as a monopoly.

Since the 1980s computers have expanded rapidly in scope and capacity. Networking has multiplied these capacities through computers in different locations sharing their information. The shift from centralized computer data storage to networked systems has produced a decrease in costs as well as increased capacities. Key to their functionality is their rapidly growing miniaturization and adaptation into more areas of society. Computers have become intrinsic to all modern industries, from aviation to banking to small-scale businesses. They are vital to education, government, and basic urban services such as traffic lights and gas stations. We can barely think of contemporary activities where computers are not used in some role.

Like the new technologies of the First Industrial Revolution, computers both have created and have shed jobs done by people. They have radically impacted on many areas of institutional, work and personal lives such that they are at the center of the information revolution.

Telecommunications

In telecommunications, the increased capacity of cable systems through the use of optic fibers and advanced switching techniques provided the basics of Internet technology. At the same time advances in using the radio spectrum for such activities as satellite broadcasting and microwaves have led to the proliferation of communications systems.

The invention of the cell phone in the United States in the 1970s paved the way for the mobile phone revolution that continues unabated. Like early computers, the original cell phones were heavy and cumbersome. Initially, they were designed for car phone systems. Engineer Ted Cooper realized that the potential of the new technology lay with personal mobile phone systems and he established Motorola, still one of the major cell phone companies. However the cell phone phenomena has spread rapidly around the globe to become one of the iconic products and cultural symbols of globalization, both fashion symbol and tool for global people. Increasingly, cell phones are merging with personal computers, such that palm-size items merge the capabilities of both systems, being used as phones, computers, cameras and able to convey images as well as words to other users.

Internet

The origins of the Internet reside in the **cold war** technological competition between the United States and the USSR. In 1957 the Soviet Union launched the world's first satellite, called Sputnik. This motivated the US government to establish the Advanced Research Projects Agency (ARPA), who developed the first successful US satellite within eighteen months. The same cold war fears encouraged ARPA to design a networked communications system that would be invulnerable to Soviet attack. It planned for a system that could operate independently of command centers, and by which messages could be sent and collected together at any point in the system. Thus, theoretically, the system as a whole could not be disabled by enemy attack.

Dr. J. C. R. Licklider, who sought to make computers more interactive and who involved the inputs of university researchers, led the project. The first computer network, ARPANET, went online on 1 September 1969, connecting research centers in four US universities (University of California Los Angeles and Santa Barbara, Stanford University, and State University of Utah). The first word sent across this system was 'login', well, not exactly, for the system crashed after the first three letters! Although the network was supposed to be exclusively for military use, the scientists used it for their own purposes and the number of users grew rapidly. The ever-popular

email was initiated by US academic Ronald Tomlinson in 1971.

Through the 1980s new networks were created and the ARPANET was closed down when the National Science Foundation took over the system under its new name of INTERNET. In 1989 the concept of the World Wide Web was developed at the European Centre for Particle Research by a Swiss physicist looking for a new way to organize online data. In 1993 a hypertext system called MOSAIC was introduced to link documents from different media (text, images, sound) to each other, with this system evolving into Netscape.

While these expansions and improvements were taking place the Internet remained under the control of the National Science Foundation and its uses were primarily for government and research. However, it was clear that this system had massive commercial applications and there was immense pressure on the government to open the system up for both commercial and non-commercial interests. Subsequently ARPANET closed in April 1995, and the Internet became available for private use with no central, regulating authority in the United States or anywhere else in the world. The Internet remains resistant to regulation and is widely regarded as being a free, open and anarchic technological innovation.

One of the main innovations since the Internet has been that of the search engines, or directories, that act as electronic librarians, bringing information to users on request. The first of these was Yahoo! followed soon after by Google, both from young computer teams in Silicon Valley, California. The search engines provided important pathways into the vast fields of data and made the Internet into a contemporary encyclopedic tool for every knowledge inquiry, including selling and shopping, banking, conducting research or just meeting people from all over the planet in cyber-space.

Social Impacts of the information revolution

As with previous technology revolutions, the Information revolution has brought profound consequences to societies around the globe. Information has become a key commodity in global social and economic processes. Another phrase used to describe the current phenomena is that of the 'knowledge society' or in Castells' (2000) phrase the 'network society' whereby the flow and quality of specific types of information determine the social construction of fundamental economic, political and social transactions. As the early analyst of the impacts of new technologies Marshall McLuhan (1967) observed, 'we shape our tools and thereafter our tools shape us'. Since the knowledge society is in its infancy we can expect these impacts to increase over coming decades.

Many of the technical skills learned by the older generation have had to be radically altered and new ones learned during their lifetimes. The most fearsome challenges have been posed in the workplace as workers have had to learn the skills for computerized tasks, or else lose their jobs. Research indicates that many individuals experience severe anxiety when confronted by having to use new technology. Technophobia – reaction and aversion against using the new technologies – was first charted by Alvin Toffler in his groundbreaking book *Future Shock* (1971). In contrast, there is also widespread technomania – a passion for new technology at personal, business and institutional levels. As daily life, work and household activities become more technology-based new technology skills become an economic and social advantage. The relationship

between consumer demands and innovations of products is a constant feedback loop that drives continuous change of both products and tastes.

While these psychological characteristics are experienced at an individual level, other aspects such as the implications of the so-called 'digital divide', the growing differential gap between societies in the global North and South in access to technology, have profound meaning for regions and nations and the patterns of globalization. The Digital Divide represents a new form of global social categorization, identifying those who are and are not able to participate in the information revolution.

Technology is at the heart of the global process. It enables centralized control of dispersed production and distribution systems and produces the vital information-based tools for global financial transactions. Importantly it facilitates the process of deregulation of societies and cross-border relationships, paving the way for **free trade** and open societies. This deregulation, with technology as its facilitator, produces an increasing pace of production, distribution, exchange and consumption. The deregulation, whereby technology has increased the pace of production faster than human capacity, enslaves humans and passes regulation to the machines. In various ways humans are motivated to give more time and effort to protect jobs, to achieve more, to earn more, to survive and to consume, but their efforts are not valued relative to the productive output of machines, and they have decreasing time, more stress, and more health breakdowns. In other words their own regulatory systems of sleep, rest and meaningful healthy activities become deregulated. Social effects include increasing debt and family separations. Recent concerns over new developments in gene technology and biomedical research have added another dimension to the debates over the relationship between humans and technology.

Information revolution in business and finance

The capacities of the information revolution are at the heart of the globalization of business and finance and the many social effects flowing from those phenomena. The speed and interactivity of computers has changed the dynamics of international investment and currency exchange. Financial entrepreneurs and speculators are able to shift vast amounts of money from one state, stock market or currency market to more profitable ones with the click of a computer mouse. With the value of global foreign exchange transactions amounting to something like US$1.3 billion per day, the constant shifts and flows of money produce an international money maze in the international capital market. All of this activity is conducted electronically. Similarly, the flow of investments on global stock markets is generated through the constant streams of electronic information that can be accessed – and responded to – by people using computers.

Networked

The information revolution has allowed corporations to develop decentralized networked operations around the world. The speed of communications and information-sharing permits real time communication between distanced locations, so that decisions, data, finances and other information vital to business activities can be readily transmitted. However, networking also has dissolved the boundaries between home and office and other social spaces so that for many people their social worlds are increas-

ingly characterized by a seamless flow of transactions, information and relations related to their participation in computer-enabled networks. The disadvantages of this networked society include a dissolution of our privacy, so that records regarding our finances, for instance, can be accessed easily, so that our 'personal computers' become the delivery point for unwanted advertising or criminal scams. Or perhaps the files on our computers – our records, books, files – could be wiped out as part of a networked cyber war.

A global labor market

One of the effects of the networked information based production systems has been to relocate jobs from the North to the South. In this sense, the dissolution of space/time boundaries by modern technologies has created a worldwide pool of labor for some industries, particularly service industries dealing in information and finance. For example, credit card and telephone companies have relocated their call centers to India where labor costs are much cheaper than in the North. The **International Labor Organization** (ILO) has emphasized in its reports that the majority of technology-based jobs shifted to the South from the North are provided to women who work for lower wages than men, and who work longer hours yet still carry the burden of domestic work. This feminization of poverty is recognized in such documents as the **United Nations** Millennium report. Analyses such as these emphasize that the effects of this technology driven transfer of labor are to increase profits to corporations rather than benefit the poor, and they call for greater regulations and equity principles, rather than increased deregulation.

Automation and its impact on work

One other major impact of the Information revolution has been in respect to the computerization of the production process. Robots and other digitalized machines have replaced human workers in key industries, particularly automotive and electronics industries. This practice continues the trends of the first and second industrial revolutions of replacing human labor with mechanization of work. Factory jobs relocated to the **Third World** are being automated quickly. For example, new technology in China is predicted to produce 300 million unemployed people within a decade.

In any local economy rising unemployment brings an increase in social problems. **Modernization** values break down older network supports such as extended families, and individual families rely more on employment for maintaining standards of living. Welfare is not a choice. Thus workers dislocated from traditional work face major challenges. As the technology-based production system becomes globally distributed the impact of automation in the shedding of people's jobs is likely to increase social tensions.

The digital divide can be regarded then as a much broader concept than just differential access to computers, it relates to the control and ownership of the automated means of production. This includes areas like agriculture, medical technology, services like communications, education or finance, and manufacturing.

Information revolution and militarism

The concept of 'network-centric-warfare' refers to the capacity to use advanced technologies for surveillance and battlefield strategies and simultaneously conduct campaigns on a number of different fronts. The delivery systems of computerized missiles and bombs have been shown to be extremely accurate, so that individual buildings can be clearly targeted by computers from great distances using satellites and laser-guided technology. Sophisticated 'night vision' technologies permit military assaults to be conducted twenty-four hours each day in an unrelenting onslaught on the enemy. Apart from these capacities, the war-making capacities of the most advanced aircraft such as B-2 stealth bombers, that cannot be detected by radar, have demonstrated clearly that the decades of research into information technologies for military purposes have produced deadly results.

In another dimension, recent wars are notable for the way in which they are broadcast to the world by the military system and global media corporations using advanced technologies for live broadcasts, digital cameras and other devices of the information revolution. It is difficult to separate the notions of entertainment and information in this process.

Information revolution and social life

The information revolution has greatly changed social life. Whether in regards to maintaining contacts, shopping, and entertainment or in household management and maintenance, new technologies have been embraced around the world by those who can access and afford them. This is an unfinished revolution and there is no end in sight. New technologies are being introduced continuously, and frontiers being extended as innovations impact on social life. There is an ongoing social debate over the assumption that most social (including medical) problems can be solved through technological means, irrespective of the moral and human implications. Issues of human unemployment caused by new technology, impacts of new weapons, environmental impacts of new technologies, personal issues of privacy rights are some of the current debates. The important debate over the primacy given to technology (and the science that produces it) goes to the heart of the human condition and is at the center of debates over global policy.

There is an increasing spillover effect between technologies. Phones become cameras and fridges have a computer function. One of the new frontiers is in gene technology and biomedicine. The boundaries between organic and inorganic are being dissolved, with the promise of solutions to some of humanity's intractable health problems such as cancer. New ethical issues are generated from these developments as to what is good and appropriate for humans and what, if any, limits should there be to scientific research and application. Practices such as euthanasia and social engineering through cloning that interfere in the natural processes of life and death challenge values across all cultures.

The central issues over the social impact of technologies revolve around political and ethical debates rather than technical ones. Thus social debates arising from the continuing information and technology revolution consider the goals or ends towards which this revolution should directed.

A further social phenomenon associated with new technology is the formation of global virtual communities. Certain events like sporting events have drawn global television audiences of two billion people. Such events fulfill increasingly important roles in promoting a consciousness of participating in a world community. The sense of being a member of that global society is encouraged by the advertising that inevitably accompanies such events, along with the global reach of the media corporations that present them.

The information revolution has generated contradictory social impacts. On the one hand it provides greater accuracy and regulation. For instance due to computers, international aircraft not only fly more efficiently but they usually arrive on schedule. Computerized terminals process people and goods efficiently. Computerized traffic lights control the flow of people and vehicles around cities with what is ideally a robot-like efficiency. The demands of computer-based banking, teaching and learning, even shopping impose new types of order and control on social activities. Yet most workers struggle to match the speed and efficiency of the computers with which they work in some form. If the computers are down it is almost impossible to work, to conduct transactions, to communicate. The virtual realities are anarchic and can lead anywhere; people can get as lost (and bewildered) mentally doing a computer search as trying to find their way out of an unfamiliar shopping mall. The technology-based society is geared toward consumer choice and freedom to select from a vast array of items available. However, the social skills required for balancing these contradictions, negotiating impacts and making appropriate ethical choices require some insight both into the nature of the information revolution and to the opportunities and pitfalls that it presents to global human society.

Further reading

Castells, M. (2000) *The Rise of the Network Society*, 2nd edn, Cambridge, MA: Blackwell.

Hajnal, P (ed.) (2002) *Civil Society in the Information Age*, Aldershot: Ashgate.

Logan, R. K. (1995) *The Fifth Language*, Toronto: Stoddart.

McLuhan, M. (1967) *The Medium is the Message*, Harmondsworth: Penguin Books.

Servon, L. (2002) *Bridging the Digital Divide: Technology, Community and Public Policy*, Oxford: Blackwell.

Schiller, D. (1999) *Digital Capitalism: Networking the Global Market System*, Cambridge, MA: MIT Press.

Toffler, A. (1967) *Future Shock*, London: Pan Books.

See also: global cities; globalization; revolution in military affairs

JOHN P. SYNOTT

Integration

The concept of integration is closely related to that of **interdependence**, and suffers from similar problems of ambiguity. Integration is both an explanation of certain processes in international relations and a prescription for solving global and regional conflicts. The main exemplar of successful integration at the regional level is the **European Union**, which still remains the benchmark for other weaker **free trade** areas and customs unions. The emphasis in the integration literature has been on integration as a voluntary process, although coercive integration has a long history, and is still widely practiced.

Integration can be divided into three main types, each defined by its goal. The first is integration of previously separate territories into a single state. The emphasis here is the creation of a single national identity and loyalty where there were previously two or more. In many of these cases there has often been a blurring of the voluntary and coercive aspects. While this form of integration was responsible for creating a number of modern **nation-state**s, such as the United Kingdom, the United States, Greater Romania, Indonesia, and Malaysia, the tendency in the last four decades has been for the disintegration, rather than integration, of existing national entities. Previously integrated states, such as Czechoslovakia and Yugoslavia, have disintegrated, while experiments such as the West Indies Union and Central African Confederation were still-born.

The second type is regional integration, where the goal is greater cooperation between states in the region. The emphasis here is on pooled **sovereignty**, and the efficiency that results from cooperation on issues such as **security**, economic policy or **development**. For some observers, regional integration will result in the creation of a regional superstate, and therefore resembles the first type of integration. For others, the goal is the creation of a separate political entity that is neither a state nor merely a conglomeration of states. While the most visible example of regional integration is the European Union, there have been a series of examples with a more limited scope, such As the **Association of Southeast Asian Nations** (ASEAN), ECOWAS in West Africa, and even the **North Atlantic Treaty Alliance** (NATO) within the narrow confines of the **security** realm. Perhaps, though, what is often ignored by the integration literature is the success of smaller bilateral or trilateral arrangements. The customs union between the United Kingdom and the Republic of Ireland remains one of the deepest and most stable integrations between neighboring states, only rivaled by similar arrangements such as the trilateral BENELUX customs union between Belgium, the Netherlands, and Luxembourg. In both of these cases close ties succeed despite historical animosities between the main protagonists. To a certain extent the trilateral **North American Free Trade Agreement** (NAFTA) has more in common with these customs unions than with the more deeply integrated EU or ASEAN.

The final type refers to integration into the dominant social, economic, cultural and political norms of the world, and overlaps with many of the concepts associated with **globalization**. This form of integration is also frequently referred to as Westernization, since integration into **international society** invariably means the acceptance of a Western-sponsored trade regime, a Western organization of government, and Western **human rights** legislation. While this form of integration does not necessarily require or presuppose a formal organizational structure, aspects of this third type of integration are actively promoted by organizations such as the **World Trade Organization** (WTO), the **World Bank** or the **International Monetary Fund** (IMF). On top of this are the disparate processes of cultural integration.

To a large extent the concept of integration cannot be discussed without reference to its opposite phenomenon, that of disintegration. There are at least two reasons for this. First disintegration defines the ultimate goal of, and hence the ideological drive for, integration. It was the fear of the economic and political disintegration of the 1930s that gave the initial impetus to European integration, while the disastrous role played by protectionism during the same period remains the major ideological prop to the establishment and maintenance of the WTO trade **regime**. Similarly, memories of **civil war** in the 1960s lay behind Indonesia's often coercive integration policies, while Ireland's customs union with Britain is a child of the ruinous economic **war** that preceded it.

Second, integration can also be an agent of disintegration. This danger is keenly felt by those who oppose regional federalism, which can bring together states in a single region to the detriment of ties with entities outside of the region. Thus, Britain's closer ties with the rest of Europe caused problems for its close economic ties with New Zealand, NAFTA caused problems for North American firms that imported many of their component parts from outside of North America, while the unification and integration of the United States broke many of the trading, cultural and even family links that had previously existed between New England and Nova Scotia. Integration can, therefore, be a particularly destructive force that undermines other forms of integration. It was for this reason that early advocates of **functionalism** stressed the development of transnational links and welfare provision, rather than integration, as the benchmark of success for their alternative functional form of government.

Further reading

Held, D. and McGrew, A. (2002) *Governing Globalization: Power, Authority and Global Governance*, Cambridge: Polity.

Murray, P. and Rich, P. (eds) (1996) *Visions of European Unity Boulder*, CO: Westview.

Pentland, C. (1973) *International Theory and European Integration*, London: Faber and Faber.

See also: European Union; functionalism; regionalism

LUKE ASHWORTH

Interdependence

A concept that gained prominence in International Relations (IR) in the 1970s, most famously with the publication of Robert Keohane and Joseph Nye's *Power and Interdependence* (1977). By 1979 former US ambassador to the European Communities J. Robert Schaetzel could describe interdependence as one of the few words that 'capture the essence of our time' (Schaetzel 1979: ix). Although Keohane and Nye's definition of interdependence included **alliance**s, and was not necessarily incompatible with a realist (see **realism**) view of international relations as **power** politics, the word rapidly became associated with a liberal alternative to the realist paradigm. In the 1980s liberal interdependence was seen as forming one of three paradigms in the **inter-paradigm debate**. While realism stressed conflict between states according to a 'billiard ball' model, and structuralists stressed the ubiquity of **dependence** in a global class structure, theorists of interdependence sat between the two, playing up the connections between peoples and states in what became seen as a 'cobweb' model of world **order**.

Although the word is relatively new, the idea of an integrated or integrating world is not, and many scholars have traced the origins of ideas of interdependence to the nineteenth century and beyond. Here it is important to distinguish between a broad and a narrow definition of interdependence. In its narrow sense it refers primarily to economic and social links, particularly economic ones, between states. In its broader sense interdependence can refer to a host of interconnections between peoples and states, and hence can be interpreted as a natural condition of all human societies. In this broader sense, ideas associated with interdependence predate both liberalism and the academic discipline of IR.

Perhaps the oldest and most basic conception of interdependence in the Western canon is the old stoic idea of the natural unity of humanity. Our shared biology makes us citizens of one imagined world city, or *Cosmopolis*. This idea remains a central pillar of many modern religions, such as the Muslim idea of the *Dar al Islam* or the Bahá'í 'Oneness of Mankind'. This stoic conception found a home in eighteenth century Enlightenment political thought, where the political and economic divisions of humanity were contrasted with its natural moral unity. This common humanity, manifest most prominently in our common reason, was a central plank in Kant's moral **cosmopolitanism**. Interdependence in this sense is not based on material need, but rather on the moral need to function together in a rational way. For Kant this moral interdependence was an attribute of all communities, and even a society of devils would need rational moral laws in order to function. The same would also, at a rather thin level, apply to **international society**.

An alternative material conception of interdependence developed in the second half of the nineteenth century, especially in Britain where liberal and industrial interests latched on to economic interdependence as an alternative to Tory foreign policy. Yet, much of the agitation for peace and **free trade** in the middle of the century assumed that economic interdependence was a choice, rather than a reality. It was only in the last decades of the century that pacifists and free traders began arguing that the interdependent nature of the world was a reality, and that consequently foreign policies based on power politics were suicidal. These late Victorian ideas of interdependence were summarized and developed by Norman Angell in his 1911 classic, *The Great Illusion*. Angell anticipated much of the interdependence literature of the late twentieth century. He argued that the world economy was now so inter-linked, and so reliant on intangible forms of wealth such as credit, that **war** no longer served any material purpose. Wars would continue to occur as long as people still believed the mantra of a previous less sophisticated age according to which war brought material benefits to the victor. For Angell, the only justification for war would be as a policing action to help prevent violence that would otherwise upset the sensitive system of interconnections that made our global prosperity possible.

At a policy level, ideas of interdependence found form in the establishment of the Public International Unions, such as the Universal Postal Union and the International Telegraph Union in the late nineteenth century. These organizations were seen by their founders as evidence that the links between states were now too strong to allow the economies of the world to be regulated at a state level alone. In the intervening years, before the use of the term interdependence in the 1970s, ideas about the interconnectedness of the global economy took both a descriptive and prescriptive form. Sometimes these were combined together. For example, David Mitrany's functional approach was simultaneously a description of the social interdependence of the modern world, and a normative theory that saw this interdependence as the basis upon which to build a more peaceful world. The idea that encouraging interdependence would reduce the risk of armed conflict found institutional form in organizations such as the European Coal and Steel Community and the General Agreement on Tariffs and Trade. Both often used the rhetoric of interdependence to justify their existence.

Keohane and Nye (1977) combine both the descriptive and prescriptive elements associated with interdependence. Their central prescriptive element was the development of complex interdependence, which was designed as an alternative to the realist model of international relations. Complex interdependence challenged the idea of the state as a unitary actor, cast doubt on the effectiveness of the use of force, and recognized that social and economic relations were no longer subservient to **security** and political concerns in global politics. While Keohane and Nye championed a broader definition of interdependence, taking in issues such as interdependence in **alliance**s, the term increasingly became associated with economic **integration**. This fed into two literatures. First, there were the studies of European integration, which tended to highlight how growing economic interdependence spilt over into other areas of cooperation. Second, there were the studies of the global political economy, which stressed the extent to which interdependence was usually asymmetrical, with many smaller and poorer states being heavily dependent on larger and richer states.

Although many of the writers who have used the term interdependence are well aware that an interdependent relationship need not be symmetrical, fair or inherently peaceful, it is often associated with these qualities. The idea that interdependence might lead to a more peaceful world has found critics on both the left and the right. For the left, it can be a mask for inherently dependent relations, while for the right it is not always clear that people dependent on each other will not resort to violence. Indeed many realists argued that growing interdependence would lead to wider possibilities for conflict.

Further reading

Angell, N. (1911) *The Great Illusion*, Toronto: McCelland and Goodchild.

Keohane, R. and Nye, J. (1977) *Power and Interdependence*, Boston: Little Brown.

Schaetzel, J. R. (1979) *The Unhinged Alliance: America and the European Community*, New York: Harper & Row.

See also: dependency; functionalism; liberal internationalism; integration; international political economy

LUKE ASHWORTH

International Atomic Energy Agency (IAEA)

The International Atomic Energy Agency (IAEA) is a specialized agency within the **United Nations** system. Established in 1957 as an independent, intergovernmental science and technology-based organization, it is the focal point of the international community's attempts to regulate the use of nuclear technology. Its principal tasks are to facilitate cooperation in the peaceful uses of nuclear technology, and to establish and to implement nuclear safeguards and inspection measures, both for civilian nuclear programs and to verify that states comply with their obligations under the nuclear Non-Proliferation Treaty. Its fundamental aim is to ensure that nuclear material is not diverted from civilian to military uses. The IAEA has come into prominence in international politics largely as a result of the discovery of the extent of **weapons of mass destruction** capabilities in Iraq after the 1991 Gulf War and growing concerns about nuclear proliferation in a range of states in the early part of the twenty-first century.

The IAEA emerged from the 'Atoms for Peace' proposal suggested by US President Eisenhower in 1953, eight years after the United States used nuclear weapons against Japan and four years after the Soviet Union acquired a nuclear weapons capability. The proposal called for nuclear materials to be stored within a new organization as an **arms control** measure. Although Eisenhower's full plan was never implemented, the idea of establishing an international agency to promote the peaceful use of nuclear energy and to ensure that nuclear technology would not be used for military purposes, did come to fruition. The IAEA was never, however, seen as an organization for restraining the military ambitions of the existing nuclear weapon states.

A key element of the IAEA is its provision of safeguards, a process involving declarations by individual states and verification through multilateral inspections and evaluations. The IAEA's Statute had indicated the need for nuclear safeguards, but a proper safeguards system, as opposed to simple bilateral measures, was not established until 1961, with the adoption of a model safeguards agreement. Even so, compulsory safeguards did not come about until the early 1970s, within the context of the nuclear Non-Proliferation Treaty (NPT) signed in 1968. These 'fullscope safeguards' represented an important component in a new international effort to prevent the spread of nuclear weapons, with the NPT requiring a system that would bring nuclear materials and facilities within member states under close surveillance and monitoring controls.

Fullscope safeguards were followed by a program of 'strengthened safeguards' in the 1990s. The fact that the IAEA had not detected the extent of Iraq's nuclear weapons program until after that state's defeat in the Gulf War in 1991 was a wake-up call to the international community. Strengthened safeguards would henceforth rely not only on declared inventories and flows of nuclear material, but would seek to make an evaluation of the state as a whole, provide credible assurances of the absence of undeclared nuclear materials and activities, and diversify the methods of detection used by the IAEA. The aim was to provide a more robust system of monitoring and verification and to strengthen the international community's confidence in the abilities of the IAEA.

The strengthened safeguards system can be implemented partly through a more rigorous application of existing agreements between member states and the IAEA. Full implementation however requires an additional legal instrument allowing the IAEA to proceed with more intrusive measures. This instrument, drafted by the IAEA Board of Governors in 1997, and known as the Additional Protocol is not, however, compulsory for member states. The organization's 'Program 93 + 2' was further evidence of the wish to move towards a more rigorous system. The IAEA's history of a slowly strengthening system of safeguards and inspections has been heeded by others, most notably by those who drafted the 1993 Chemical Weapons Convention with its attendant intrusive inspection measures.

Importantly, the IAEA has no enforcement mechanisms of its own. It is required to report any findings of non-compliance to the **United Nations** Security Council and General Assembly; the Security Council can subsequently authorize political, economic or military actions against a non-complying state. There have been two such clear episodes. The first was the report in 1991 that Iraq had breached its NPT obligations; the result was a series of **sanctions** and UN/IAEA inspections ordered by the Security Council. These continued until 1998, were resumed under Security Council pressure in late 2002, but did not satisfy the United States which eventually launched military action against Iraq in March 2003 on the basis of Iraq's alleged **weapons of mass destruction** program.

The second clear case of the IAEA reporting on non-compliance occurred in April 1993 when it notified the UN that North Korea was in breach of its safeguards agreements. In this case, the United States was able to conclude, with the assistance of other states, an Agreed Framework by which light-water reactors and oil would be supplied to North Korea in exchange for that state abandoning its nuclear weapon ambitions. While this appeared to resolve the issue, rising political tensions between the United States and North Korea in 2002 and early 2003 resulted in North Korea withdrawing from the NPT and the IAEA system of inspections.

A further case concerns Iran. In May 2003, the United States, suspecting a substantial Iranian nuclear weapons program, requested that the IAEA find Iran in material breach of its NPT obligations. No clear ruling has been delivered by the IAEA as at May 2005, although it has requested that Iran conclude an Additional Protocol, thereby allowing for fuller inspections of its nuclear program, a proposal rejected by Iran.

This latter case points to a moderate but nonetheless significant level of discord between the IAEA and the United States, a factor exemplified to an even greater extent in the US–UN relationship which suffered a serious blow over the March 2003 US decision to launch military action against Iraq without a UN mandate. In terms of Iraq too, the United States and other Security Council members had expressed dissatisfaction at the slow progress being made by the IAEA and UN weapons inspectors. These problems were further complicated by accusations from Iraq and other sources that weapons inspectors were acting in the interests of the United States.

Limitations on its ability to inspect nuclear programs and to detect breaches quickly may continue to hamper the IAEA in its efforts to ensure that nuclear materials and technology are used for peaceful purposes. Even its strengthened safeguards system is arguably insufficiently rigorous, although history suggests that progress can be made in this area. The IAEA is also hampered by an inability to push for nuclear disarmament in the recognized nuclear weapon states, something it was not designed to do but which is increasingly being called for by non-nuclear weapon states as a logical extension of its program.

Notwithstanding these limitations, the main significance of the IAEA has been its contribution to developing a norm of compliance and accountability. Analysts have noted that it is the organization that pioneered the idea and practice of multilateral on-site inspections, a practice that was barely developed in the 1950s. By fostering a climate of restraint and compliance, it has done much to reinforce the nuclear taboo among states and to strengthen the nuclear non-proliferation **regime**.

The IAEA's policymaking organs are the 35 member Board of Governors, its executive body, and the General Conference, consisting of representatives of all member states (numbering 137 as of September 2003). The IAEA is located in Vienna.

Further reading

Fischer, D. (1997) *History of the IAEA: the First Forty Years*, Vienna: IAEA.

See also: arms control; arms race; nuclear proliferation

MARIANNE HANSON

International Covenant on Civil and Political Rights (ICCPR)

The International Covenant on Civil and Political Rights (ICCPR) is, together with the **United Nations'** Universal Declaration on Human Rights (UDHR) and the **International Covenant on Economic, Social and Cultural Rights** (ICESCR), one of the key constituents of the International Bill of Rights. Unlike the UDHR, the two Covenants were each designed as legally binding treaties. The need for treaties, and indeed for treaties which enumerated two very different categories of rights, stemmed from the ideological cleavage which divided states after World War Two and which was associated with the **cold war**. The UDHR had the handicap of listing rights which were privileged by the 'free world', or those on the capitalist side of the ideological cleavage (see **capitalism**), along with rights which were privileged by those on the socialist and communist side of the ideological cleavage (see **socialism**; **communism**). The antagonism between these sides was such that those on the right did not consider economic, social and cultural rights to be rights as such, while those on the left felt that civil and political rights meant nothing if the subject of these rights had neither food nor shelter. The political way forward was the creation of two covenants, each a UN Treaty. They were drafted by the Human Rights Commission of the UN's Economic and Social Council.

The distinctive contribution of the ICCPR in the protection of human rights may be found in articles 6 to 27. The earlier articles and preamble share with the ICESCR a commitment to a broad program in which the protection of human rights are made central to the purpose and conduct of states. Then the ICCPR goes on to delineate its specific rights agenda. Commencing with the right to life, the covenant requires that no one be subject to torture; cruel, inhuman or degrading treatment or punishment; slavery or compulsory labor, arbitrary arrest or detention. Those deprived of their liberty must be treated humanely, and people must not be imprisoned just because they cannot fulfill a contractual obligation. Further, there are provisions for freedom of movement, the lawful presence of aliens, equality of persons before courts and the law, and guarantees in criminal and civil proceedings. There are prohibitions on retroactive criminal law, and on arbitrary or unlawful interference in an individual's affairs, reputation and standing. The Covenant protects the rights to freedom of thought, conscience and religion, and the freedom to have and express opinions. Propaganda for war is prohibited, as is the advocacy of hatred (national, racial, or religious) that would constitute incitement to discrimination, hostility or violence. It protects the rights to peaceful assembly, freedom of association, marriage, and the founding of a family (including the equality of rights and responsibilities within and in the event of the dissolution of marriage). Children's rights also are affirmed. Citizens are recognized to have the right to partake in public affairs, to vote, be elected, and have equal access to public service. All are equal before the law and are entitled to equal protection from the law. Ethnic, religious, and linguistic minorities are to be protected. The final article of the Covenant provides for a Human Rights Committee to be established in order to supervise the implementation of these rights.

Certain limitations and exceptions were granted in the provision of these rights. In emergency situations that threatened the life of the nation rights might be suspended, but only as strictly necessary and in accordance with the nature of the emergency. Such suspensions may not involve discrimination on the basis of race, color, sex, language, religion or social origin. Suspensions must be reported to the UN. Some rights

may never be abrogated; these are the rights to life and to equal recognition before the law; the freedoms of thought, conscience and religion; and freedoms from torture, slavery, imprisonment for debt and retroactive penal laws.

There were, in addition, two optional protocols. These protocols were optional in the sense they were in addition to the basic Covenant, and were to be subscribed to independently. The first optional Protocol is symbolic of the radical changes to be wrought in international politics by the **human rights** movement. Through this Protocol, individuals are given legal standing in international relations – in contrast to the prevailing doctrine that only states had legal personality. Under the Protocol, states which are signatories recognize that the Human Rights Committee established by the Covenant has the competence to receive communications from individuals who claim to be victims of rights violations, and who have exhausted all domestic means available to them for redress. The Committee, if it determines the communication to be admissible, brings the communication to the attention of the state party, which must then offer an explanation within a certain time frame, indicating what steps if any have been taken to ameliorate the complaint.

The second Optional Protocol to the ICCPR aimed at the abolition of the death penalty. No individual within the jurisdiction of state parties to the protocol may be executed; states must offer information about the steps they have taken to ensure that this is the case; and individuals may use the procedures of the first protocol in relation to the subject of the second (unless the state in question withdrew this option at the time of ratification or accession).

It took the Human Rights Commission from 1948 until 1966 to develop the two

Covenants, in large measure because of the ideological divide expressed in international affairs as the cold war, noted above. The express wish of the General Assembly of the UN was that the two Covenants, once tabled, would be ratified and come into effect without delay. Another decade was to transpire, however, before this was to be fulfilled. The delay was caused by the requirement that thirty-five states become parties to the Covenant before it could enter into force. Once the target number was eventually reached, the Covenant continued to be dogged by lack of support from the **superpowers** and many other key states.

The implementation of the ICCPR is facilitated by the Human Rights Committee (HRC). The Committee has two roles. The first is the operation of the state reporting mechanism. The Covenant requires that state parties place periodic reports about their compliance to the terms of the treaty. The Committee reviews these reports, returns comments to the reporting states and produces its own report. This report notes any relevant problems with state behavior and reiterates the terms of the treaty. Second, the Committee accepts and acts on communications delivered via the Optional protocols, as discussed above.

The expectation is that state parties, in response to these reports, will make changes to their domestic legal systems and political practices in order to conform to the requirements of the treaty. The HRC often holds states to be in violation of their treaty requirements; how efficacious the committee's reports are in changing the conduct of offending states is another matter. Even in cases of significant positive change in state behavior, other causal factors (such as domestic politics) apply. Further, the Covenant has no influence over states who are not parties to the treaty, or to the protocols. By 2003, the ICPCR had 149 member states, but fewer than 100 of these signatories had ratified the optional protocols.

Further reading

Alston, P. (ed.) (1992) *The United Nations and Human Rights: A Critical Appraisal*, Oxford: Clarendon.

Conte, A., Davidson, S. and Burchill, R. (2004) *Defining Civil and Political Rights*, Aldershot: Ashgate.

Forsythe, D. (2000) *Human Rights in International Relations*, Cambridge: Cambridge University.

McGoldrick, D. (1991) *The Human Rights Committee*, Oxford: Clarendon Press.

Steiner, H. and Alston, P. (eds) (1996) *International Human Rights in Context: Law, Politics, Morals*, Oxford: Clarendon.

See also: human capabilities; human rights; International Covenant on Economic, Social and Cultural Rights; United Nations

ANTHONY J. LANGLOIS

International Covenant on Economic, Social and Cultural Rights (ICESCR)

The International Covenant on Economic, Social and Cultural Rights (ICESCR) is one of two binding international treaties, developed under the auspices of the **United Nations** (UN), which, together with the UN Universal Declaration on Human Rights (UDHR) comprise the International Bill of Rights. The **International Covenant on Civil and Political Rights** (ICCPR) is the second treaty. The development of the International Bill of Rights by the UN after World War Two represented a significant departure from the established ideologies and practices of international relations.

In particular, both at the theoretical and the institutional level, individuals take on an importance and standing which had been absent from **international society** until this point. Only states were deemed to have legal personality in international affairs, with the inevitable result that the rights and well being of individuals or groups of individuals within the state were superseded by the **national interest**. With the development of an international **human rights** culture, and the treaties and institutional mechanisms put in place through the UN and the two Covenants, the door was opened to the development of an international order whose institutional design fundamentally included as paramount the rights of individuals. The human rights covered by the ICESCR go beyond the political and civil rights at the core of the liberal political tradition, to encompass a concern with the overall well being of the human person. This extension of the ambit of human rights has not been without controversy.

The opening articles of the ICESCR cover the same ground as those of the ICCPR: both Covenants build their list of rights out of an initial right to **self-determination** due to all individuals. 'By virtue of that right they freely determine their political status and freely pursue their economic, social and cultural development.' Both Covenants affirm that all human persons have the right to enjoy all human rights, and enjoin states to pursue this end. Further, both Covenants set out protections against the destruction, limitation or misinterpretation of rights such that the rights outlined in the Covenants cannot be used to curtail the enjoyment of any other rights; they also guard against the possibility that stronger affirmations of rights and more extensive lists of rights than those in the Covenants, already enjoyed by citizens of states, should not be eroded or diminished by what may be a less fulsome exposition in the Covenants.

The specific rights that the ICESCR then lists are the following: the right to work, and in so doing to enjoy just and favorable conditions of work; to form and join trade unions; to social security and social insurance; the right to the provision of the most extensive protection of the family, noting especially mothers, children and young persons; the right to a standard of living deemed adequate; and to standards of physical and mental health which are the highest attainable; the right to education; and to participation in cultural life.

That these rights are of a different class to those in the ICCPR has been recognized by the various ways in which they are described, which in turn are linked to the different institutional approaches that need to be developed in order to provide these rights. The rights of the ICESCR are usually categorized as Second Generation rights, which describes their chronological place in the development of rights theory and practice within the liberal tradition. The rights of the ICESCR are often referred to as positive rights, in contrast to the negative rights elaborated through the ICCPR. Negative rights, it is argued, require only that governments restrain themselves from interfering with the lives of their citizens. By contrast, positive rights, or so it is argued (not without controversy), require constant provision and maintenance on the part of a government. Positive rights insist that the government act and not cease acting for as long as it is necessary to sustain the economic, social and cultural rights in question.

It is not surprising, then, that the rights of the ICESCR are termed promotional or aspirational rights. Within the Covenant itself, the difference is obvious. The approach taken is one of progressive implementation. The hard line supporters of negative rights argue that the rights of the ICESCR represent goals towards which societies should aim; but that they were not rights *as such*, which must be implemented immediately and absolutely in order to be implemented at all. Many states simply lack the economic capacity to provide these rights, which is recognized in part by the developmental language of the Covenant. It is also recognized by the provision for acceptable limitations on rights. Rights may be limited by law, but such limitations must not go against the nature of the rights in the ICESCR, and are only acceptable when intended to promote the general welfare within a democratic framework.

As with the ICCPR, the ICESCR was not tabled in the UN General Assembly until 1966, and did not come into force until 1976. The development of effective institutions for monitoring and compliance however were further delayed. An initial committee was formed in 1978 within the UN Economic and Social Council; this committee, however, proved to be incompetent and was replaced in 1986 with an independent committee of experts, which operates along similar lines to those of the Human Rights Committee in relation to the ICCPR. The new committee has demonstrated commitment and enthusiasm in its work, in which its principle agenda has been the pursuit of a minimum base line for state policy with regard to the rights in the Covenant. Unfortunately, there is little support for its mandate in the international community. States routinely fail to submit reports – a common problem within the UN system, but especially so with this Covenant. There has been a lack of resources and information; an unwillingness on the part of governments and **non-governmental organization**s to pursue the committee's agenda as an agenda for rights rather than for **development**; and, not least, difficulties with the interpretation of the Covenant.

Further reading

Alston, P. (ed.) (1992) *The United Nations and Human Rights: A critical Appraisal*, Oxford: Clarendon.
Forsythe, D. (2000) *Human Rights in International Relations*, Cambridge: Cambridge University Press.
Steiner, H. and Alston, P. (eds) (1996) *International Human Rights in Context: Law, Politics, Morals*, Oxford: Clarendon.

See also: International Covenant on Civil and Political Rights; human rights; United Nations

ANTHONY J. LANGLOIS

International Criminal Court (ICC)

A court of law established by the international community to try persons accused of committing international crimes. The court sits in the The Hague, the Netherlands. It officially began to operate in July 2002. The Court is made up of judges, prosecutors and other court officials appointed from the international community.

The coming into existence of the International Criminal Court (ICC) represented a historic step in the development of international criminal law because for the first time a court existed that was specifically established to address breaches of international criminal law. Notwithstanding the criticisms of its detractors, the ICC is no threat to democratic states that uphold the rule of law. The Court's work is directed to those atrocious **human rights** abuses which have become all too familiar, where the international community has hitherto stood by and watched human beings being killed, raped, and tortured with impunity.

With the ending of the **cold war** and the success of the International Criminal

Tribunal for the former Yugoslavia (ICTY) the idea of an ICC gained much more acceptance than had previously been the case (see **International Criminal Court**). In 1994 the **United Nations** General Assembly requested the International Law Commission (ILC) to produce a draft statute for the Court. Following the completion of the draft, a Conference of all States was then organized. On 17 July 1998 the representatives of 120 states met in Rome and one month later they voted to adopt the Statute for the ICC. Only 21 states abstained and seven were opposed. Unfortunately the opposition states constituted most of the population of the world. They included the United States, China, Indonesia, and India.

The Court is established by Treaty and has jurisdiction over **genocide**, **crimes against humanity**, **war crime**s and the crime of aggression. Genocide does not include conspiracy to commit genocide as in the ICTY Statute nor does it include rape as a crime of genocide. War crimes and crimes against humanity are specified in considerable detail under the Statute.

By 11 April 2002, the sixty ratifications required for the Rome ICC Treaty to enter into force had been reached. The Court began work almost immediately. The structure of the Court is similar to that created for the ICTY. It has four main organs, including the Presidency (responsible for the functioning of the Court), the Judiciary (comprising pretrial, trial and appeal chambers), the Prosecutor (responsible for the investigation and prosecution of crimes specified under the Statute), and the Registry (responsible for the administration of the ICC). The Judges and staff of the Court including the Prosecutor and the Registry staff are employed on a full time basis.

The jurisdiction of the Court is based on the principle of 'complimentarity'. The Court may exercise jurisdiction if

(1) a state party refers a matter to the Court;
(2) the Security Council of the United Nations refers a matter to the Court under Chapter VII of the UN Charter;
(3) the Prosecutor initiates an investigation of a State party which the Court then approves.

The Security Council can stop the Prosecutor from proceeding with the investigation initially for a period of one year.

The Court has a great deal of control over the Prosecutor. The Court will not permit a case to be investigated or prosecuted where the accused has already been investigated by a State investigator or tried by a State court, unless the investigation or trial was a sham. But more specifically the Court will not allow a matter to proceed unless the Prosecutor has a 'reasonable basis' to proceed.

Under the Statute, the Prosecutor is given the authority to take a 'unique investigative opportunity statement'. The purpose of this statement is to preserve evidence in those cases where a witness may not be subsequently available to testify.

Individual criminal responsibility is firmly entrenched as a principle of liability under the Statute. A person can be criminally liable if they commit the crime as an individual or jointly with another, irrespective of whether the other person is found liable or not. Criminal liability may attach if the accused 'solicits, induces, aids abets or otherwise assists' in the commission of the crime.

Under the Statute there is a higher level of culpability for a military commander than a civilian superior. The military commander is liable if he/she 'knew or should have known' of a crime, whereas the non-military superior is liable if he/she 'knew or consciously disregarded information' about a crime.

The defense of 'superior orders' is available under the ICC Statute, if an accused can show that he/she was under a legal obligation to obey the order, that he/she did not know it was unlawful and that it was not manifestly unlawful. The important exception to this is that if the crimes charged are genocide or **crimes against humanity** the defense is not available. Other defenses provided under the Statute include insanity and self-defense. Intoxication is a defense where the person cannot appreciate the unlawfulness of their conduct.

The Prosecutor is required to investigate in such a way as to establish the 'truth', by being required to investigate 'incriminating and exonerating' circumstances equally. The rights of a person during investigation as provided for under the Statute include the right not to be subjected to coercion, duress or threat, or arbitrary detention. If questioned an accused must be allowed an interpreter, the assistance of counsel, and the person must also be informed of the purpose of the investigation and be advised that he/she has the right to remain silent.

The ICC Statute creates an Assembly of States Parties, which acts in the capacity of rule maker, budget approver, and overseer of ICC operations. Decisions of the Assembly must have the support of two-thirds of members in the Assembly. The Court is also funded by the States Parties although the General Assembly of the United Nations may provide funds to the Court, especially with respect to those investigations referred to the ICC by the Security Council under the Statute.

The existence of the Court will act as a deterrent to those persons who might otherwise commit international crimes. The Court is founded on the basis of a legal treaty. Accordingly, its decisions are likely to be accepted by the international community as legitimate legal precedents rather than mere decisions of national courts.

Further reading

Broomhall, B. (2003) *International Justice and the International Criminal Court – Between Sovereignty and the Rule of Law*, Oxford: Oxford University Press.

Kittichaisaree, K. (2001) *International Criminal Law*, Oxford: Oxford University Press

Politi, M. and Nesi, G. (eds) (2004) *The International Criminal Court and the Crime of Aggression*, Aldershot: Ashgate.

Schabas, W. (2004) *An Introduction to the International Criminal Court*, 2nd edn, Cambridge: Cambridge University Press.

See also: crimes against humanity; human rights; sovereignty; war crime

GRANT NIEMANN

International Labor Organization (ILO)

One of the specialized agencies of the **United Nations** (UN) charged with promoting labor rights and social justice in the world of work. The ILO was created, together with the **League of Nations**, through the 1919 Versailles Treaty. Unlike the League it survived World War Two and became the first specialized agency associated with the newly formed United Nations Organization in 1946. At its conference in Philadelphia in 1944, the ILO affirmed a set of core commitments that have become its hallmark:

(a) the understanding that labor is not a commodity;
(b) **human rights**, in particular freedom of expression and association;
(c) combating poverty;
(d) tripartism, i.e. the collaboration of governments, workers and employers in efforts to fight poverty and promote social justice.

In 1969, the ILO won the Nobel Peace Prize for its work. In the early twenty-first century, it has emerged as an international force in efforts to rein in the negative social consequences of economic **globalization**.

The ILO emerged from humanitarian commitments paired with political considerations. Since the late nineteenth century, the goal of establishing uniform labor standards in order to improve working conditions in industry and prevent unfair competition had brought together governments and non-governmental experts in various international meetings and led to the creation of the International Association for Labor Legislation in Basel in 1901. The 1917 Russian revolution and the specter of **communism** gave these efforts new impetus. The contracting parties at Versailles understood social justice to be a prerequisite for the peace they were negotiating and created the ILO as a means to accomplish this goal.

In its early years, the organization's work focused on formulating a set of legal instruments (binding conventions and non-binding recommendations) to improve working conditions (working hours, occupational health and safety, rest periods and holidays) and workers' welfare (social insurance). It also sought to regulated specific categories of workers, in particular seafarers, workers in agriculture, and women. For the latter, protective conventions called on states to provide maternity leave, but also to limit women's work at night and under ground. At the same time conventions affirmed the principles of equal treatment and condemned forced labor. Between 1919 and 1939, the ILO passed sixty-seven conventions and sixty-six recommendations, comprising almost a third of today's International Labor Code. The rapid rate of international rule making became a target of critique as governments had difficulty adopting ILO conventions at the national level and the number of ratifications remained low.

The ILO's tripartite structure is unique among international organizations. In the International Labor Conference (the ILO's assembly comprised of all member states), and in the ILO's Governing Body (the ILO's executive council comprised of ten states of chief industrial importance plus four elected states), states are represented by two government members, one employer and one worker member. After the Soviet Union (together with a number of socialist states) joined the organization in 1954, the independence of employer and worker representatives became a bone of contention and the ILO's commitment to furthering human rights became entwined in **cold war** politics. The alleged erosion of tripartism, combined with the accusation that the ILO was politically biased in its application of human rights standards led the United States to withdraw from the organization from November 1977 to February 1980. Among other things, US complaints referred to the fact that the 1974 International Labor Conference had condemned the Israeli occupation of Arab territories while its Committee of Experts refused to adopt a report condemning forced labor in the Soviet Union.

With decolonization and the rapid formation of new states in Africa and Asia ILO membership increased from fifty-two at the end of World War Two to 121 in 1970, and the organization became increasingly involved in providing technical assistance to newly independent states. In the 1950s, the bulk of such activity focused on human resources **development** and vocational training. In the 1960s, in the context of the UN Development Decade, job creation moved to the foreground of ILO technical assistance activities. In 1969, it launched the

World Employment Program (WEP) and reoriented its technical assistance efforts towards combating unemployment while seeking to make employment a primary consideration in international development efforts. The program sponsored a series of employment missions to provide analytic assessments of labor markets in various countries. WEP research led to the identification of the informal sector as a primary source of jobs and as a target for development in Africa, Asia, and Latin America. The task of improving working conditions and social security in the informal sector has become a matter of debate and programmatic intervention in the ILO.

In the 1980s and 1990s, the rise to prominence of neoliberal economic orthodoxy increasingly complicated the ILO's standard-setting activities. Efforts to regulate flexible work arrangements encountered considerable opposition from employers and governments that viewed such regulation as an obstacle to job creation. In the late 1990s, the organization found a new voice in debates about economic **globalization** and increasingly has helped insert a concern for social justice into international trade negotiations. In 1998, it adopted the Declaration on Fundamental Principles and Rights at Work, which defines five core labor rights: freedom of association and collective bargaining, the elimination of all forms of forced or compulsive labor, the abolition of child labor and the elimination of discrimination in employment and occupation. The declaration obligates all states to respect these fundamental principles, regardless of whether they have ratified the relevant ILO conventions, providing a clear social benchmark for government learning and for negotiating the rules of global economic governance.

The International Labor Office is the permanent secretariat of the ILO based in Geneva. A Director-General with strong executive powers heads the office and provides leadership in setting the organization's agenda. The two longest-serving Directors-General were Albert Thomas (from 1919 to 1932), a French socialist who established the ILO as an energetic organization with an ambitious agenda, and David Morse of the United States (from 1948 to 1970) who oversaw the expansion of the ILO in the 1950s and 1960s and spearheaded the focus on technical assistance to **Third World** countries. Juan Somavia of Chile became the first Director-General from the South in 1999, leading an organization with 243 member states in 2003. He forcefully has inserted the ILO into debates around globalization by making the notion of 'decent work' a benchmark for judging the effects of globalization. To realize the decent work agenda, the ILO is focusing its efforts on promoting core labor standards, job creation, enhancing social protection, and strengthening tripartism. Achieving **gender** equality and development have become central crosscutting issues.

Further reading

Cox, R. W. (1977) 'Labor and Hegemony', *International Organization* 31(3), 385–424.

Imber, M. F. (1989) *The USA, ILO, UNESCO and IAEA: Politicization and Withdrawal in the Specialized Agencies*, New York: St. Martin's Press.

Riegelman Lubin, C. and Winslow, A. (1990) *Social Justice for Women: The International Labor Organization and Women*, Durham, NC: Duke University Press.

Weisband, E. (2000) 'Discursive Multilateralism: Global Benchmarks, Shame, and Learning in the ILO Labor Standards Monitoring Regime', *International Studies Quarterly* 44(4), 643–67.

See also: global governance; International Covenant on Economic, Social and Cultural Rights; labor internationalism

ELISABETH PRUGL

International law

A body of norms, emanating primarily from the interaction of **sovereign state**s, that international actors recognize as imposing legal obligations. Contemporary international law reflects a wide range of standard-setting endeavors, from traditional efforts to regulate navigation, commerce, and the exchange of diplomats, to more recent and controversial efforts to constrain the use of force, to implement fundamental **human rights**, and to impose criminal justice on individuals acting under state **authority**. Notwithstanding significant earlier developments, modern international law is frequently said to date from the 1648 Peace of **Westphalia** that ended the Thirty Years War in Continental Europe. The twentieth century saw major qualitative and quantitative advances, with first the **League of Nations** and then the **United Nations** introducing far greater institutional complexity to the international order, and facilitating the development of a much more elaborate body of substantive law.

Whereas domestic systems characteristically possess a legislature, a judiciary, and an executive, the **international system** is marked by highly decentralized modes of lawmaking, adjudication, and enforcement. The system is often described as 'horizontal' rather than 'vertical', as states formally relate to one another on the basis of sovereign equality. The United Nations General Assembly, albeit a deliberative body that often works to develop binding legal standards, lacks any authority to bind a dissenting minority of states to the terms of a majority vote. The International Court of Justice (ICJ), although its decisions are binding on the parties to the dispute before it, has adjudicatory authority only where – and only to the extent that – the states in question have consented to its jurisdiction; moreover, no international court, including the ICJ, has the formal power to render 'precedents' that control future decisions and thereby constitute interstitial lawmaking. The United Nations Security Council, albeit having the authority to bring coercive (political, economic, and military) measures to bear on states, may do so only in response to perceived threats to international peace, not mere violations of international law; moreover, where the Security Council makes coercive demands on states, these demands reflect policy judgments rather than international legal standards. Thus, lawmaking, adjudication, and enforcement in the international system remain largely uninstitutionalized; these functions are nonetheless frequently, if inconsistently and incompletely, fulfilled through *ad hoc* arrangements and an array of issue specific international structures.

International law often furnishes rules of decision for standing international courts or quasi-judicial bodies, for *ad hoc* international tribunals, or for domestic (municipal) courts. Much of the time, however, formal adjudication is unavailable, and the application of international law rests with the political organs of governments and international organizations. Even where invoked outside of legal institutions, legal obligations can be distinguished from purely political ones: they are deemed to be binding on states irrespective of intervening changes in government, and their violation, unlike breaches of purely political pledges or expectations, can license aggrieved states to engage, within strict limits, in otherwise unlawful 'countermeasures' to prevail upon the violating state to resume compliance. International law can also be distinguished from the moral views of the international community; while often overlapping with moral concerns shared across state boundaries, international law frequently concerns matters of coordination rather than high principle, can be created and changed from time to time through mere exercises of the will of relevant actors, and can be accessed through technical arguments rather than appeals to conscience.

Methodology

The study of international law is neither a strictly empirical inquiry, seeking to describe the salient features or to ascertain the causes of a particular social phenomenon, nor an exercise in normative political theory, applying abstract principles of justice to the international arena. Rather, the inquiry seeks to find, interpret, and apply standards of conduct that are immanent in international practices. International law derives from the application of accepted methods for identifying international norms of a legal character. Exactly what those methods are – and upon exactly whose 'acceptance' their validity rests – remain topics of fierce debate within the discipline.

The traditional approach to international law is positivist, in that it seeks, by the value-neutral application of formal criteria, to deduce from observed social behavior a body of rules accepted as law within the pertinent community. One deduces the existence of a rule specifying obligatory conduct by evaluating empirical data according to the criteria of the community's 'secondary' rules – the standards that a community is observed to have adopted as its bases:

(a) for acknowledging primary rules as authoritative ('rules of recognition');
(b) for applying them in practice ('rules of adjudication'); and
(c) for changing them from time to time ('rules of legislation').

In this approach, the international system's rules of recognition identify three primary sources of law. They are custom, treaties, and 'general principles of law'. Each source of law entails a separate method for establishing the existence of a legal obligation. Each, however, remains subject to substantial controversy, centering less on the means by which a given empirical proposition can be reliably established (method as understood by social scientists) than on which empirical propositions are legally probative. To establish the existence of a legal norm is ordinarily to overcome the a priori presumption that states remain juridically free to act as they choose. Disputes that purport to turn on the strength of the adduced evidence are most frequently, in reality, disputes about the nature and strength of the presumption. Thus, even within legal positivism, the primary methodological problem is not one of 'research design', but of foundational principle.

The most prominent alternative methodology in the international law field is that of the 'New Haven School'. This policy oriented approach regards law not as a body of rules, but as a purposive process. Although it shares with positivism an appreciation for established expectations and authorized procedures, this approach also draws on considerations typically associated with legal realism (policies of the powerful) and natural law (principles inherent in any legal project, properly so called). On the one hand, policy oriented jurisprudence asserts that lawmaking authority depends, not on pre-established and general secondary rules, but on the dynamic empirical capacities of international actors to exert effective authority in particular contexts; the weight of particular states in norm-creating processes may thus be differential and variable, and the exertions of efficacious non-state actors may also figure in norm creation. On the other hand, in contrast to positivism's insistence on value neutrality, policy oriented jurisprudence posits a set of underlying values, said to be broadly shared in the international community, that orient legal interpretation; legal processes are ascribed a *telos*, in keeping with these supposed shared values, of founding and maintaining 'minimum public order' and advancing toward an 'optimum public order'.

Although the New Haven approach is appealing at a high level of abstraction – since legal positivism, legal realism, and natural law each seem to disclose part, but only part, of the essence of legality – it is often unclear how the pieces fit together to produce determinate conclusions about concrete problems. A central concern of critics is that, absent a formally structured account of their supposed juridical authority, the assertions of various international actors can be invoked or ignored, as convenience dictates, by those who have the **power** to create facts in disregard of the long term accommodations that positive norms represent. Concessions to legal realism, in overcoming the inflexibility of established sources of law, may tend to render short run efficacy both the necessary and the sufficient condition of normativity, thereby undermining any role for law as a restraint on power.

Meanwhile, concessions to natural law may tend to neglect the extent to which the inherent purposes of legal order are contested; any community, let alone the global community, is beset by disagreement about underlying values –

if not about their validity, at least about their order of priority. Appeals to authoritative goals such as minimum public order, employed to attribute to arid formalism the failure of established sources of law to support the proposed outcome, tend to obscure the real limits of consensus and the corresponding need for accommodation. Critics of the policy oriented approach fear that it does not adequately distinguish law, in principle, from 'justice as interpreted by the strong', and therefore, in practice, from the purposes of a hegemonic power (see **hegemony**).

Foundational assumptions

The primary bearer of international legal personality is the state. It is states to which international legal norms are presumptively addressed, although some norms go further to establish rights and obligations for non-state entities and individual persons. Furthermore, whatever the role of non-state actors in spurring the adoption of international norms, states – acting severally or jointly through intergovernmental organizations (IGOs) – are traditionally considered the sole bearers of norm creating **authority** in the international system. Under the principle of sovereign equality, states are deemed to be juridically equal and bound only to obligations that can be attributed (albeit, perhaps, 'constructively') to exercises of their own will.

Although the literature most frequently defines a state in terms of empirical attributes, the state is best understood as an abstract entity, a political community to which the international system has attributed sovereign right. An existing state is not automatically extinguished by a loss of its classic empirical attributes (a population and territory under the effective control of an independent government), nor does the presence of such empirical attributes automatically bring a state into existence. In the late 1970s, for example, Lebanon was a state, while Rhodesia was not.

The concrete representation of the state in the international system is the government, a ruling apparatus that acts on behalf of the state in international affairs, performing such legal functions as asserting rights, incurring obligations, and conferring immunities. The relationship of government to state is that of agent to principal. It is the state, not the government, which is sovereign. Traditionally, however, the ruling apparatus that exercises effective control of a recognized state through 'internal processes' (i.e., not through unlawful foreign intervention) is acknowledged to have authority to act on that state's behalf for the purposes of international law. Obligations undertaken by a government continue to be binding upon states even should the government be overthrown.

One of the puzzles of the international system is that states bound by international norms appear to retain residual sovereign prerogatives that can serve to obstruct implementation. The system's strict prohibitions on coercive interference in states' internal affairs appear to remain applicable even where the interference is ostensibly undertaken to secure compliance with an international obligation. Although discord between powerful and weak states has so far precluded any authoritative delimitation of the scope of permissible 'countermeasures', there can be little doubt of the international system's resistance to any transborder use of force to coerce compliance, and serious questions have been raised about the admissibility of certain non-forcible remedial exertions directed toward effecting a change in the norm-violating government, such as secondary boycotts and covert funding of internal opposition movements.

In addition, notwithstanding an ever-expanding set of international legal obligations that pertain to internal governance, the precise relationship of international to domestic legal authority remains a controversial issue. Unquestionably, domestic legal norms and governmental decisions that are incompatible with international obligations constitute international wrongs, to be duly redressed through international processes. Nonetheless, a state's acceptance of international obligations does not ordinarily amount to a renunciation of its ultimate authority over public order within its territory, and only the rare domestic legal system accords international law supremacy over all local sources of authority.

Consequently, while incompatible domestic law cannot be pleaded in the international system as a defense of the violation of an international norm, it does not necessarily follow that international law regards an incompatible domestic norm or decision as *ultra vires* (i.e., beyond the scope of prescribed authority) and thus a legal nullity, as if it was a product of rogue officials operating under mere 'color' of state authority. Rather, in attributing the breaching act to the state, international law may shelter officials and other individuals from personal liability for their participation in the breach, and may treat the breaching act as creating a legal fact (as where a state's internationally wrongful expropriation of real property is deemed to have nonetheless effectively transferred title to that property). The extent of this phenomenon is variable and highly debatable, especially where the breaching act constitutes a serious violation of internationally-recognized human rights.

Sources of international law

Mainstream doctrine recognizes three primary sources of international law:

(a) custom,
(b) treaty, and
(c) 'general principles of law accepted by the community of nations'.

Court decisions and scholarly writings are invoked as 'subsidiary' sources, insofar as they adduce evidence for the presence or absence of the factors required to establish the existence of a customary, treaty-based, or 'general' norm.

Customary international law

The existence of a customary norm is traditionally said to turn on the presence of two components:

(1) a consistent pattern of state practice that conforms to the putative norm; and
(2) a manifest sense of legal obligation (known as *opinio juris*) on the part of state actors to conform to the putative norm.

Behavior conforming to a particular pattern does not alone establish that pattern as law, as that behavior may stem from courtesy or convenience or even inadvertence; there may have been no intent to yield the right to act differently on the next occasion. By the same token, pious pronouncements about how states ought to behave, without a supporting pattern of conforming practice, can be dismissed as diplomatic posturing, especially where the pronouncements pertain exclusively to the behavior of *other*, dissimilarly situated states.

There is little agreement, however, about how much of either component is needed to establish the existence of a legal norm. Traditionalists emphasizing the need for enduring patterns of practice clash with the champions of 'instant custom', who see in certain unanimous IGO resolutions (or even near-unanimous resolutions, where support cuts across established interest groups and ideological factions in the international community) the requisite expression of collective commitment to determinate standards. While the hortatory rhetoric and programmatic proposals characteristically contained in IGO resolutions clearly do not rise to the level of expressions of *opinio juris*, other language in such resolutions can be read as a shared interpretation of pre-existing customary or treaty law, as the 'crystallization' of a theretofore emerging norm, or as an articulation of a standard that will eventually ripen, through invocations in the subsequent course of state practice, into customary law. Contemporary interpretations of customary international law rely increasingly on such language, especially in fields such as human rights, where states' actual performance tends to fall far short of the standards that those same states acknowledge, expressly or tacitly (often through concealment of violations), to be applicable.

State practice and *opinio juris* are invoked not only for the making, but also for the un-making of legal norms. Where disregard of a previously established customary or treaty norm becomes not only commonplace, but generally accepted in the community of states, the one-time norm is nullified by 'desuetude'. Lawbreaking conduct can thus overturn old norms and create new ones; the legal effect of a pattern of violations turns on whether other states respond by reaffirming the wrongfulness of the acts, or by manifesting an acceptance of the conduct. Since law's mission is precisely to constrain behavior, fierce jurisprudential controversy rages over the precise conditions under which lawbreaking conduct can be said to succeed in changing international norms.

Although customary law is rationalized as the product of consent, or consensus among, free and equal states, the attribution of a norm to the will of the bound state is often a legal fiction. Not only may consent be inferred from mere acquiescence, but customary norms, once 'crystallized', are deemed to be binding on newly emerging states or on states newly participating in the activity governed by the norms; these states are deemed, by virtue of joining the community of states or of entering a pre-existing field of interaction, to have consented to the established pattern of conduct. Once norms have crystallized, a mere disavowal of consent does not free a state from its customary obligations. On the other hand, if a state persistently objects to the emergence of a customary pattern of interaction that nonetheless crystallizes among the other participants, theory suggests that the objecting state remains unbound by the new customary norm. There is, however, considerable dispute, both over the validity of this 'persistent objector rule' and over the existence of 'peremptory norms' (*jus cogens*) to which the rule does not apply.

Peremptory norms are norms so strongly insisted upon by almost all states and international institutions – presumably because so inherent in the project of international legal order – that states cannot be heard to repudiate them. Most frequently referenced in this category are the norms against aggression and **genocide**, although no state can be said to have sought an exemption from these. A more instructive illustration may be the transformation of an indeterminate principle of **self-determination** of peoples, contained in the United Nations Charter and unanimous IGO declarations, into a concrete legal demand for the relinquishment of colonial territories and an end to *apartheid*, over the persistent objections of Portugal and South Africa. It is unclear, though, how many further *jus cogens* norms have achieved general acceptance in the international community, and to what extent assertions of peremptory norms are grounded in natural law doctrines rather than in positivistic inquiries.

Treaties

Treaty-based norms operate against the background of customary law governing the operation of treaties (now largely codified in the Vienna Convention on the Law of Treaties), much as contracts in domestic systems operate against the background of contract law. Notwithstanding the apparent similarity of some multilateral treaties to legislation (see **multilateralism**), multilateral treaties are best conceptualized as a web of bilateral treaty relationships. Although some multilateral treaties seek to codify customary norms that the parties regard as independently binding on all states, treaties, as such, typically do not bind non-party states.

Moreover, the operation of multilateral treaties is frequently subject to 'reservations', appended by individual parties to their instrument of ratification, which change the terms of treaty obligations for particular parties. A reservation operates in roughly the same manner as a counteroffer in the context of bilateral treaty negotiations; except where the treaty language forbids reservations (or all reservations of a particular type), each other state party has the choice to respond to the reserving state by:

(a) accepting the bilateral treaty relationship as amended by the reservation;

(b) accepting a bilateral treaty relationship that omits all mutual obligations concerning the subject matter of the reservation; or

(c) repudiating the treaty relationship altogether.

Thus, two states may be parties to the same treaty, and yet owe each other no obligations under it, or may owe each other a different set of obligations than other parties owe one another. This phenomenon may have limits, to the extent that adjudicatory bodies acquire the authority to invalidate certain reservations as incompatible with the treaty's 'object and purpose', irrespective of the positions taken by the other treaty parties. Such authority has rarely been clearly established, however, and the effect of its exercise would most logically be to expel the reserving party from the treaty regime, rather than to 'sever' the reservation, thereby holding the state to the very obligations to which it had refused consent (a heterodox solution that some jurists have proposed).

The favored approach to treaty interpretation emphasizes the 'objective' meaning of the instrument, rather than seeking to ascertain the substance of a subjective meeting of the minds. Thus, under Articles 31 and 32 of the Vienna Convention, one is to interpret treaty terms based on their 'ordinary meaning' in the context of the instrument as a whole (and any appended documents), in light of both the treaty's manifest 'object and purpose' and other applicable norms of international law. Only where this objective analysis yields an ambiguous or unreasonable outcome should the interpreter have recourse to extrinsic evidence, such as the records of negotiation (*travaux préparatoires*) or the overall circumstances of the treaty's conclusion. The treaty terms may further be interpreted according to meanings established by subsequent agreement of the parties, as indicated expressly or by subsequent practice in the treaty's application. These interpretive standards often raise more questions than they answer, especially in regard to varied and dynamic understandings of morality-based concepts invoked in the language of certain multilateral treaties, such as those pertaining to human rights.

On the one hand, the contemporary law of treaties sharply limits the traditional notion, often abused to subvert the duty to observe treaty commitments (*pacta sunt servanda*), that treaties contain an implied clause voiding obligations in case of a fundamental change of circumstances (*clausula rebus sic stantibus*). On the other hand, the present-day approach, unlike previous ones, invalidates treaty provisions that are extracted by unlawful uses or threats of force against a state's territorial integrity or political independence, or that violate peremptory norms of the international system (*jus cogens*).

General principles of law

The final source of law, 'general principles,' has traditionally been limited to the background norms that facilitate the operation of all major legal systems. Such norms include elemental principles of interpretation (e.g., specific provisions control over general ones; subsequent documents control over prior ones), adjudication (e.g., previously adjudicated claims are presumptively precluded from reconsideration), and equity (e.g., parties should not benefit from their own wrongs; parties should be protected in their reasonable expectation that a well established course of conduct will continue). More recent jurisprudence has asserted, often controversially, that the category extends further to substantive norms – most importantly, elements of crimes –

common to all major legal systems. It is not clear, however, which such norms can properly be transposed from domestic systems to the international system, absent manifestations of *opinio juris* specifically establishing these common internal practices as having implications for external affairs (and thus, as having the status of customary law). Moreover, invocations of general principles may tend to trade on common 'concepts' while neglecting conflicting 'conceptions'; an illusory commonality is sometimes invoked to circumvent the very international discord that precludes the emergence of desired customary and treaty-based norms. Nonetheless, where the international legal order must address circumstances of utter lawlessness, general principles of law may be indispensable to filling the void.

The international law of peace and security

The international system's most ambitious project of legal regulation has been the twentieth century effort to construct a peace and security **order**. Although standards governing the conduct of warfare (*jus in bello*) were the subject of a series of treaties concluded from the mid-nineteenth century to the early twentieth century (culminating in the 1907 Hague Regulations), there existed in this period neither treaties nor customary law purporting to regulate the decision to resort to hostilities (*jus ad bellum*). Rather, it was generally accepted that states retained the sovereign prerogative to undertake warfare in the service of their **national interest**s, and to acquire territory by the use or threat of force.

After World War One, the League of Nations was established to facilitate orderly settlement of international disputes, and its Covenant imposed legal conditions on the use of force. Shortly thereafter, in the 1928 Kellogg-Briand Pact of Paris, most of the international community (with the lone major exception of the Soviet Union) officially renounced and condemned recourse to **war** as an instrument of national policy. A corollary, announced by the United States, was the Stimson Doctrine, which called on the international community to deny recognition to the fruits of unlawful uses of force.

Such developments, however, lacked both the institutional mechanisms and the political will to render them efficacious in the face of the events of the 1930s: the Japanese invasion of Northern China, the Italian conquest of Abyssinia (Ethiopia), and the German annexation of Austria and extortion of territorial concessions in Czechoslovakia. Moreover, opinion in some quarters perceived the new legal norms as attempts by the entrenched **great powers** to safeguard an arbitrary territorial status quo, itself a product of force, from the advance of emergent powers. Although one might question whether any legal strictures on the use of force meaningfully remained in place by 1939, the pan-continental aggressions of Germany and Japan in World War Two came almost universally to be viewed as criminal acts, inspiring both punishment by Allied military tribunals and the creation of a new, more elaborate post-War peace and **security** order.

Article 2(4) of the United Nations Charter of 1945 bars 'the threat or use of force against the territorial integrity and political independence of any state' (including, according to subsequent authoritative interpretations, the arming of insurgents), subject only to two overt qualifications: Article 51, licensing 'individual or collective self-defense' in the event of an 'armed attack'; and the prerogative of the Security Council under Chapter VII to order or license the use of force – by a vote of nine of its fifteen members, absent a veto by any of its five permanent members – in response to a perceived 'threat to the peace, breach of the peace, or act of aggression'. Legal scholars frequently debate whether certain other non-Security Council-authorized uses of force remain implicitly licensed: anticipatory self-defense against an evidently imminent armed attack; proportionate forcible countermeasures against violations of Article 2(4) that do not rise to the level of armed attack (e.g., counterattacks against insurgents' forward bases located within the territory of a harboring state); armed intervention by invitation of a state's legitimate government; material assistance to certified 'liberation movements' fighting against 'colonial domination, foreign occupation, or racist regimes'; and perhaps most controversially, armed intervention to forestall imminent humanitarian catastrophe. Although the Charter era has seen a substantial number of violations of use-of-force norms, almost all states have consistently affirmed their commitment to those norms, even while quibbling about their application or distorting the factual record to feign compliance.

Whereas the geopolitical divisions of the **cold war** era greatly impeded the role of the Security Council in maintaining peace and security, a post-cold war revitalization of that institution seemed evident in its authorization of a forcible response to the flagrantly unlawful 1990 Iraqi invasion of Kuwait. In 2003, however, the decision by the United States and its allies to initiate a 'preventive war' against Iraq (without even an allegation that an armed attack by Iraq was imminent) – after having tried and failed to obtain Security Council authorization to use force in response to Iraqi 'material breaches' of previous disarmament resolutions – raised renewed questions

about the efficacy (and, among some critics, the desirability) of the legal regime governing the use of force.

The status of individuals in international law

Whereas international law traditionally provided individuals residing or traveling in foreign territory with certain protections (derivative of the reciprocal respect that the territorial state owed to the state of which they were nationals), only in the twentieth century did it begin to regulate sovereign states' treatment of their own nationals. The League of Nations era saw two major efforts in this regard: treaties sponsored by the newly established International Labor Organization (ILO) to set minimum labor standards, and treaties designed, in the wake of post-World War One territorial solutions, to protect minority ethnic groups in the new states of Eastern and Central Europe. It was not until the United Nations era that international law sought more generally to protect human rights. The atrocities that Nazi Germany and its allies committed against their own civilian nationals occasioned both new categories of international crime (**crimes against humanity**, as prosecuted at Nuremberg, and **genocide**, as defined in a 1948 convention) and new international legal obligations of states to respect the basic rights of individuals.

According to its Charter, the United Nations counts among its animating purposes the promotion of respect for human rights (Art. 1(3)). To that end, the General Assembly issued a Universal Declaration of Human Rights (UDHR) in 1948. The contents came subsequently to be embodied, with some modifications, in two sweeping human rights treaties – the **International Covenant on Civil and Political Rights** (ICCPR) and the **International Covenant on Economic,**

Social and Cultural Rights (ICESCR) –
and an array of other treaties focusing on
such specific ills as **gender** discrimination, racial discrimination, and torture.
Most states, representing all regions and
all major cultures, are today parties to
treaties that establish not only negative
duties to refrain from violations of the
physical integrity of the person and from
impositions on fundamental human
freedoms, but also affirmative duties to
provide for individuals, so far as is
materially feasible, the basic conditions
of human flourishing. The most basic of
these duties are also widely deemed to
have the status of customary international law. On the other hand, while
regional human rights systems in Europe
and Latin America have succeeded in
establishing effective mechanisms for the
international adjudication of human
rights claims, such success at the global
level has thus far been elusive, largely
relegating responsibility for human rights
implementation to the political organs of
IGOs and to the foreign policy apparatuses of influential states.

At the frontier of international law lies
the emerging phenomenon of international prosecution of state officials for
serious human rights violations committed under supposed 'sovereign'
authority. In the 1990s, the Security
Council authorized the creation of special tribunals for the prosecution of
crimes against humanity and acts of
genocide, as well as more traditional war
crimes, that took place in the former
Yugoslavia and Rwanda. The International Criminal Tribunal for the former
Yugoslavia (ICTY) and the International
Criminal Tribunal for Rwanda (ICTR)
have generated a substantial jurisprudence of human rights-related
crimes, and have provided a model for a
new **International Criminal Court** (ICC),
a treaty-based institution established in
2002 to address similar crimes committed subsequently by the nationals of,
or on the territories of, its states parties.
Meanwhile, atrocities committed previously in Sierra Leone and Cambodia
have given rise to plans for mixed tribunals, staffed by both local and international prosecutors and judges, to try
criminal cases of such magnitude. And
finally, court systems in a few states have
begun to assert extraterritorial jurisdiction over human-rights-related crimes,
even where the prosecuting state has had
no connection to the alleged perpetrator,
the victim, or the territory on which the
crime was committed (on the theory of
'universal' jurisdiction).

Emerging trends in perspective

As human rights have become a more
prominent component of international
law, often at the expense of legal inviol-
abilities once accorded to sovereign
states, controversies have arisen that
reflect a clash of underlying perspectives
on the fundamental aims of the international legal order. On one side lies an
interpretation of that order's animating
principles, drawn largely from the history of United Nations efforts to bridge
East–West and North–South divisions,
that emphasizes the need for respectful
accommodation among radically differing systems of domestic public order;
international order thus remains largely a
matter of assuring reciprocal respect for
sovereign prerogative. A contrasting
interpretation of the international legal
order emphasizes universal principles of
justice that transcend the boundaries of
territorial communities; sovereign prerogative thus appears largely as a resi-
duum of lawlessness that incrementally
diminishes as international law advances. The future of international law will
largely be determined by the outcome of
this clash of perspectives.

Further reading

Brownlie, I. (2003) *Principles of Public International Law*, 6th edn, Oxford: Oxford University Press.

Ku, C. and Diehl, P. F. (eds) (2003) *International Law: Classic and Contemporary Readings*, 2nd edn, Boulder, CO: Lynne Rienner.

Malanczuk, P. (2004) *Akehurst's Modern Introduction to International Law*, 8th edn, London: Routledge.

Reus-Smit, C. (ed.) (2004) *The Politics of International Law*, Cambridge: Cambridge University Press.

Scott, S. (2004) *International Law in World Politics*, Boulder, CO: Lynne Rienner.

Shaw, M. (2003) *International Law*, 5th edn, Cambridge: Cambridge University Press.

See also: international society; law of the sea; reciprocity; sovereignty; uti possidetis; Westphalia

BRAD R. ROTH

International Monetary Fund (IMF)

The International Monetary Fund was established in 1945 as a specialized agency of the **United Nations** system and the institutional centerpiece of the **Bretton Woods regime** to rebuild and stabilize the international monetary order after World War Two. The IMF provides loans, technical assistance, and economic surveillance for its 184 member states. The US$300 billion in financial resources of the Fund are based on the pooled contributions of member countries and supplemented by large gold reserves and standing agreements with creditor members to borrow in case of a systemic crisis. Contributions are organized through a quota subscription system based on a member's relative economic strength in the world economy. Members may borrow from the pool of subscriptions contingent on accepting certain conditions. In recent decades, the Fund has become increasingly involved in controversial **structural adjustment program**s and financial **crisis** management efforts.

The organization is composed of a Board of Governors, an Executive Board, an International and Monetary Financial Committee (IMFC), a Development Committee, a Managing Director, three Deputy Directors, and a staff of 3,000 technocrats based at the headquarters in Washington, DC. The Board of Governors is the highest decision making body within the organization. The Board is composed of the Finance Ministers and Central Bank Governors of the respective member countries and meets once per year. The daily operations of the Fund are delegated by the Board of Governors to a group of 24 Executive Directors. The directors represent either single member constituencies (i.e., the United States, Japan, Germany, France, Britain, Saudi Arabia, and Russia) or combined member constituencies. The IMFC, which is composed of 24 Governors, meets biannually to advise the Board of Governors on the management and functioning of the international monetary system and the proposals of the Executive Board. A parallel committee to the IMFC, the Development Committee, reports to the joint Board of Governors of the IMF and World Bank on broad questions of economic assistance to the developing countries. The Managing Director is selected by the Executive Board and serves as the chair of the Executive Board and chief of the organization's staff. The Fund is divided into geographically contiguous *area departments* (e.g., African, Central Asian, Western Hemisphere, etc.); *functional departments* (Legal Department, Research Department, Statistics Department, etc.) which support and review area work;

and *support services* departments. The diverse national composition of the Fund's staff roughly reflects the relative quota size of each member country. Most staff members hold an advanced degree in economics. In July 2001, an Independent Evaluation Office (IEO) was established by the Executive Board to provide objective and independent evaluation of the Fund's policies, advice to members, and completed country operations.

The distribution of **power** at the Fund is a product of the political and economic agreements embodied in the quota regime. The quota regime is the basis for determining:

1. a member's required contribution to the organization, and thus the overall size of the Fund;
2. the level and character of access to Fund resources for each member country; and
3. the distribution of voting rights within the organization, including the right to a permanent or single member constituency seat on the Executive Board.

The quota regime accords the greatest voice to the largest contributors. While it is true that consensus rather than actual voting characterizes most decisions by the Fund's Executive Board, it is also the case that member countries will usually not submit issues which are likely to be defeated by the majority of member votes. In essence, the distribution of voting power implicitly influences the character and scope of issues on the Fund's agenda.

The quota regime is subject to review every five years and upon the request of individual member countries. The quota formula specifications and the weight of variables involved in calculating a member's quota have become matters of political compromise that are intended

to distribute **power** in a way that will command wide support from member countries. In addition, the quota regime effectively permits the largest creditor member, the United States with 17.49 per cent of the total votes, to retain veto power over decisions that require a supermajority of 85 per cent (e.g., concerning the adjustment of quotas, balance of payments financing, expulsion of members, and any amendment to the Articles of Agreement). There have been several attempts to rationalize and reform the quota system, with no results that were acceptable to the broad range of members.

The role of the IMF in the global economic and financial system has gradually changed in response to the demands of member countries, major economic and financial crises, global political and economic trends, intra-organizational debates, and criticism by academics and **non-governmental organizations**.

The IMF was originally designed as an intergovernmental organization to stabilize the post-war international exchange rate agreement and to coordinate controls on transnational capital movements. The organization was empowered to monitor national economic policies and to extend balance of payments financing to member countries experiencing temporary difficulties. However, the financing role of the institution was initially overshadowed by the US Marshall Plan in 1947. The Fund's balance of payments financing aimed to preserve the liberal economic order by providing members an opportunity to correct maladjustments in the balance of payments without resorting to restrictions on the use of foreign currency or increased tariff barriers on imports to protect their currency reserves.

The IMF also sought to prevent policies of competitive exchange rate depreciation by promoting a stable exchange rate and an orderly adjustment process. Adjustments within the exchange rate regime up to 10 per cent to correct a 'fundamental disequilibrium' were to be carried out by member countries in consultation with the IMF. Exchange rate adjustments larger than 10 per cent would require approval of three-quarters of the Fund's voting power. The consultation requirement was a constitutional device designed to guarantee official accountability and hence deter competitive devaluation strategies without imposing undue rigidity.

The governing board of the IMF was empowered to sanction governments responsible for policies such as chronic trade surpluses that destabilized the international system through its 'scarce currency clause' (see **sanctions**). The scarce currency clause permitted states to impose controls on imports from countries that ran persistent surpluses and whose currency became scarce within the Fund. Nevertheless, the actual authority of the Fund was rather restricted. The Fund was not authorized to propose a change in the par value of any member country. The Fund could not compel a sovereign member to change its par value even if the currency was in fundamental disequilibrium.

In effect, the consultative mechanisms of the regime only became relevant after significant problems had already developed. Moreover, the IMF was not given the authority or resources to compel an exchange rate adjustment to resolve the problem. The limitations on the authority of the Fund were the product of the compromises between the American and British visions of the postwar monetary order that shaped the Bretton Woods regime. Due to the precarious financial position of the UK, the Britons had insisted on maintaining the sovereign authority to act unilaterally to change the exchange rate if necessary.

The resources of the Fund remained inadequate because of American reluctance to provide generous support to weak-currency countries.

The authority of the IMF *vis-à-vis* major states failed to mature during the lifespan of the Bretton Woods regime. Major adjustments to the exchange rate arrangement were rarely carried out in consultation with the IMF. For example, when Britain devalued its currency in 1949, it informed the IMF only twenty-four hours in advance instead of the requisite seventy-two hours. In 1967, when the British government devalued its currency by 17 per cent, the IMF received only one hour's notice. The Nixon administration did not consult with the IMF when it made a unilateral decision to take the dollar off of the gold standard in 1971 – thereby effectively terminating a core component of the Bretton Woods system. The IMF never invoked the scarce currency clause to sanction government policies that threatened the **international system**. The uncritical behavior of the Fund helped to increase the rigidity of the exchange rate arrangement because reluctant politicians easily deferred necessary changes in par values.

The underlying problem of the Bretton Woods regime was the stable exchange rate agreement. The use of the dollar as an international reserve currency had increased US official foreign liabilities on a limited supply of gold. By 1960 the value of gold on the private markets was US$40 per ounce. The increased value of gold implied that traders believed there was a possibility of a dollar devaluation. The United States was not forced to devalue its currency immediately, because the international liquidity shortage made the dollar desirable as a reserve currency to supplement gold. However, there was a limit to the willingness of foreign governments to absorb dollars because of the risk of importing inflation by accepting devalued dollars. In 1964, frustrated and provoked by American unwillingness to establish an alternative reserve currency, Charles de Gaulle proposed a return to the gold standard as the only way to restore symmetry to the international system. The Bank of France accelerated its conversion of dollars into gold.

In response the United States reversed its position and negotiations began to amend the Fund's Articles of Agreement to allow for the creation of an alternative international reserve asset (i.e., Special Drawing Rights, SDRs) within the IMF to take pressure off the US dollar. As a provision of the amendment the United States was required to eliminate its balance of payments deficit on an official reserve basis (i.e., the supply of dollars relative to the US supply of gold) before the new reserve asset could be distributed. The US would have to adhere to a strict monetary policy if it hoped to meet the requirements of the amendment.

By the time the new reserve assets were finally distributed in 1971, the problem was no longer one of inadequate liquidity. In 1971, for the first time since 1893, the US current account balance fell into deficit as it imported more goods and services than it exported. The tacit assumption of a permanent surplus in its balance of trade, on which the United States had negotiated the Bretton Woods agreement, was no longer tenable. Speculators believed that a devaluation of the dollar was inevitable.

Massive capital flight from the dollar and speculative attacks against the increasingly rigid exchange rate arrangement began in 1971. On 15 August 1971, the Nixon administration decided that it would no longer allow the conversion of foreign official dollar holdings into gold. Nixon not only took the United States off the gold standard, he also terminated all other measures for supporting the dollar in direct violation of the obligation under IMF rules to keep one's currency stable. Even after two devaluations of the dollar, the United States would not commit to defending the dollar and actively continued to talk down the value of the dollar in order to transfer the burden of adjustment to other countries. By March 1973, it became evident to major states that the only way to stem the recurrent waves of capital flight and speculative attacks was to allow their currencies to fluctuate freely for a temporary period. As states could not agree on a new exchange rate arrangement, a permanent floating exchange system emerged as the only feasible solution. In the following years, the major monetary components of the Bretton Woods system were gradually dismantled or reconfigured. In 1978, the Articles of Agreement for the IMF were amended to allow floating exchange rates and to eliminate the special status of gold.

Even though the United States terminated the Bretton Woods exchange rate agreement, it did not push for the elimination of the IMF. US policymakers, confronted with a chronic trade deficit, may have viewed the IMF as a useful forum for pressuring change in the economic policies of rival countries. However, the end of the Bretton Woods exchange rate agreement coupled with the dramatic growth of **offshore** capital markets as a source for balance of payments financing substantially reduced the importance of the IMF amongst advanced industrialized countries. Consequently, since the 1970s the financial services and technical resources of the Fund have focused almost exclusively on those developing countries without sufficient access to international capital markets. The IMF came to serve as a **crisis** manager since the developing country debt crisis began to emerge in the late

1970s. With the end of the **cold war**, the Fund also acquired an important facilitating role in coordinating the economic transition of the former Soviet bloc countries.

Ideologically, by the mid-1980s the IMF moved away from the normative belief in mutual burden sharing and policies geared toward short-term economic stabilization in favor of an asymmetric conception of conditional lending and long-term structural adjustment that places the burden of reform on the developing countries. The change in the ideological position of the IMF corresponded with changes amongst elite academics and policymakers in many parts of the developing world. It is reductive and historically inaccurate to view the IMF as merely an enforcer of a policy consensus derived in Washington, DC. The turn toward neo-classical economic ideas by the mid- to late 1980s in the developing world reflected frustration with failed strategies to enhance national autonomy and reduce economic vulnerability, as well as political concerns regarding the centralization of economic power in predatory bureaucracies. The collapse of the Soviet Union served to further undermine strategies based on economic centralization, widespread price controls, and long-term planning.

Although the IMF had been involved in renegotiating and rescheduling the debt of member states since the 1950s, the IMF became the central multilateral actor in debt renegotiations for developing countries after the late 1970s. In exchange for securing additional lending, developing countries agreed to submit to an IMF monitored program of short-term economic stabilization and later, as short-term solutions failed to restore creditworthiness and economic growth, longer term **structural adjustment programs** (SAPs). As this process of

'conditional lending' became routinized, practices of 'cross-conditionality' emerged whereby an IMF administered program became a precondition for the rescheduling or refinancing of official and private debt.

It is difficult to evaluate the overall impact of conditional lending policies as their design and implementation reflected political bargaining and compromises at multiple levels of governance. Moreover, as countries requesting assistance were often experiencing a severe economic crisis, it is difficult to gauge how the country would have fared without IMF financial assistance. Of course, a number of low income countries did become prolonged users of Fund resources throughout the 1980s for a variety of complex, often case-specific reasons.

The Fund sought to address this problem through a joint program with the **World Bank**, known as the Heavily Indebted Poor Country (HIPC) Initiative launched in 1996, to reduce the external debt burden of low-income member countries. In 1999, the HIPC initiative was enhanced through the transformation of the Enhanced Structural Adjustment Facility (ESAF) and the Enhanced Structural Adjustment Facility Trust (ESAF Trust) into the more broadly designed Poverty Reduction Growth Facility (PRGF) and the Poverty Reduction Growth Facility Trust (PRGF Trust). When these programs are fully implemented, approximately $50 billion in debt service relief will be granted by the IMF and World Bank to 37 eligible countries, with an additional $7 billion in concessional loans from the IMF to 77 eligible countries. Furthermore, these facilities have placed greater emphasis on including civil society groups in program design, strengthening governance of borrowing countries, accommodating flexibility in fiscal budget targets, reducing conditional criteria, and reorienting government spending toward social programs that demonstrably benefit the poor.

A dramatic challenge to the technical competence and institutional capacity of the Fund to manage crises occurred with the East Asian financial crisis of 1997–8. Critics charged that the push for fiscal austerity and increased interest rates by the IMF in the midst of a financial panic exacerbated the depth of economic crisis. As the crisis spread from East Asia to Russia and finally Latin America, the resources of the Fund appeared limited to cope with the scope of the problem.

The failure to manage the financial crisis competently coupled with global economic trends have mobilized **non-governmental organizations**, students, and workers around the world to protest the perceived inequities in the operation of the global economic system, and specifically the policies of global institutions like the IMF. Organizations in **global civil society** have denounced the **democratic deficit** as well as the lack of transparency and public accountability within intergovernmental financial institutions.

The democratic deficit in the IMF results from a decline in the weight of the 'one state one vote' principle relative to the 'one dollar one vote' principle in the Fund's voting system. This has tilted **power** excessively toward creditor countries and reduced the voice of smaller countries within the IMF. The democratic deficit also stems from biases in the calculation of economic strength that have caused the IMF to neglect the strength of emerging market economies. Although developing countries as a group have achieved the fastest expansion of trade and now account for one-third of world trade (up from one quarter in the early 1970s) a great disparity still exists between the economic strength and voting power of the emerging market economies and smaller European countries on the IMF's Executive Board.

For example, in 2001 India had 41,832 votes at the IMF compared to 51,874 for the Netherlands despite the fact that India's GDP was almost US$100 billion greater than the Netherlands at market exchange rates and US$1,820 billion greater when valued in terms of purchasing power parity. Notably, India's population exceeds one billion inhabitants while the Netherlands has only 16 million inhabitants.

In response to its critics, the IMF has increased the transparency of its policy-making process by making many documents available on-line and declassifying many archival records. The Fund has also created an Independent Evaluation Office to assess the effectiveness of its policies and programs. The IMF has commissioned groups of experts to give advice on reforming the voting structure within the organization. Finally, the IMF is attempting to enhance the scope of its economic surveillance and to harmonize rules related to member countries' banking and financial systems to strengthen the international financial architecture. Nevertheless, the democratic deficit in the IMF will persist until there is a comprehensive reform of the quota regime.

Further reading

Blustein, P. (2003) *The Chastening: Inside the Crisis that Rocked the Global Financial System and Humbled the IMF*, New York, NY: Public Affairs.

Boughton, J. (2001) *Silent Revolution: The International Monetary Fund 1979–1989*, Washington, DC: International Monetary Fund.

See also: Bank for International Settlements; Bretton Woods; conditionality; international political economy; structural adjustment program; World Trade Organization

VIKASH YADAV

International political economy (IPE)

An interdisciplinary field of study that has close ties with International Relations (IR), and draws on contributions from political scientists, economists, sociologists, anthropologists, historians, and geographers. IPE theorists often argue that the political, economic, and social aspects of IR are closely intertwined. Thus, they criticize some economists for *economism*, or for focusing only on economics and largely ignoring political factors. They also criticize some political scientists for *politicism*, or for disregarding economic structures and processes.

IPE is concerned with the interaction between the *state* and the *market*. The state is a sovereign territorial political unit with a government and population, and the market is a coordinating mechanism where sellers and buyers exchange goods and services at prices and output levels determined by supply and demand. The state is often associated with the pursuit of **power**, and the market with the pursuit of wealth. However, the state also has concerns related to the accumulation of wealth, and the market is not totally removed from power considerations. The interaction between the state and the market sometimes contributes to tension and conflict. Whereas the state is concerned with preserving national **sovereignty** and unity, the market is associated with economic openness and the breaking down of state barriers. For example, the 1988 Canada–United States (US) Free Trade Agreement (CUSFTA) contributed to an open market between the two countries, which some Canadians considered a threat to their national sovereignty in energy, foreign investment, and cultural industries. When CUSFTA was extended to form the **North American Free Trade Agreement (NAFTA)** in 1994, Mexicans were concerned that NAFTA threatened their national sovereignty in energy and agriculture. Despite the dominant US position in North America, many Americans feared that NAFTA would lead to a loss of national control over employment and the environment.

Although there is inherent tension between the state and the market, they also have a complementary relationship. Domestically, states establish rules to protect private property rights and provide infrastructure such as transportation and communications required for the adequate functioning of markets. Internationally, states form agreements and organizations to promote economic openness and stability that are necessary for market transactions. Furthermore, there is often a close relationship between a state's wealth and market size on the one hand, and its military and political power on the other. As **interdependence** has increased, states have been drawn into the competitive forces of the world economy. Thus, states today are involved with restructuring of industry, supporting research and development in high technology sectors, and deregulating financial markets. The impressive economic growth rates of some states seem to be closely related to their success in establishing a symbiotic relationship with the competitive marketplace. For example, the East Asian newly industrializing economies (NIEs) – Hong Kong, Singapore, South Korea, and Taiwan – successfully fostered state-market relationships in the 1960s to the 1980s.

In addition to state-market interactions, IPE also involves relations of states with **multinational corporations** (MNCs), the main non-state actors in the global economy. The 600 largest MNCs each benefit from worldwide sales of over US$1 billion, and together they produce more than 25 per cent of world gross domestic product. Although an MNC has foreign branch plants in 'host' countries, its financial, and research and development activities are most often closely linked with the headquarters in the 'home' country. Directors and shareholders in the home country have primary responsibility for managing the MNC's foreign operations, and the home state provides the legal structure within which the MNC functions. However, a second type of MNC is referred to as 'stateless,' because it has internationalized its ownership, board of directors, and overall policies to increase its freedom of operation. In a third type of MNC, the host state has a greater role in determining the policies and strategies of the branch plant operations, and the directors of the branch plant are often drawn from the host state. Although home state-based MNCs continue to be the most common type, all three types of MNC-state relations are evident in different corporations. Which type of relationship is prevalent depends on various factors, such as the nature of goods and services produced, and the nature of the home and host states.

In addition to MNCs, IPE scholars are also devoting increased attention to other non-state actors today, including labor groups, **non-governmental organizations** (NGOs), and social movements representing various interests including the environment, women, **human rights**, and the disadvantaged. Considerable attention is also being given to the role of capital. Thus, IPE has become a far more complex area of study, focusing not only on state-market relations, but also on relationships involving MNCs, capital, labor, NGOs, and **transnational social movements**.

The complexity of IPE is obviously magnified when we consider that it is interdisciplinary and focuses on political economy at the international level. How does one develop an IPE theory that examines international influences and also accounts for the multitude of social, cultural, economic, political, and developmental variations across **nation-state**s? Furthermore, IPE scholars find it more essential than **security** specialists to focus on international-domestic linkages. Domestic groups and individuals are normally willing to leave decision-making on security and defense issues to the government experts. In contrast, domestic groups often see a close relationship between their own economic welfare and international economic issues such as trade and foreign investment, and they demand a greater role in government decision-making on these issues. IPE scholars therefore have the daunting tasks of focusing on domestic as well as international interactions and of crossing the boundaries between a number of social science disciplines.

The discussion that follows has three parts. The first part examines why IPE is a relatively new area of academic study; the second most detailed part examines the main IPE theoretical perspectives; and the third part discusses the main substantive problems and issue areas in the study of IPE.

Why is IPE a relatively new area of academic study?

The relative novelty of IPE as an academic area is ironic, because awareness of political-economic linkages extends back to ancient times. Several factors led to the tendency to view politics and economics as distinct areas of study. First, liberal economists such as Adam Smith (1723–90) believed that economic activity operated under naturally harmonious laws, and that the economy would therefore function best with minimal government interference. Smith's association with '*laissez-faire*' **capitalism** contributed to the views that economics and politics were fully separable, and that political economy was not a useful area of study. Like Smith, IR scholars after World War Two viewed politics and economics as largely separable. However, whereas Smith prioritized economic issues over political issues, postwar IR scholars reversed these priorities and devoted their attention to political-security issues. During the **cold war** postwar scholars generally viewed political-security issues as 'high politics' of the utmost urgency, and economic issues as 'low politics' which were far less worthy of study. It was not until the 1970s that events such as US President Richard Nixon's decision to suspend the convertibility of the US dollar into gold, the **Organization of Petroleum Exporting Countries'** (OPEC's) dramatic oil price increases, and the foreign debt **crisis** demonstrated the political importance of economic issues and resulted in the focus on IPE in universities. Third, the inflexibility of many universities, with reward systems based on membership in traditional disciplines, slowed the process of introducing IPE as an interdisciplinary area of study.

Theoretical perspectives

The study of IPE is most often divided into three main theoretical perspectives: **realism**, liberalism, and what may be termed historical structuralism. Several general points should be made about these perspectives. First, the three main perspectives do not adequately address some newer IPE issues and approaches such as environmentalism, **feminism**, **constructivism**, and **poststructuralism**. However, they continue to be the most widely accepted perspectives in the study of IPE. Second, each perspective contains a wide diversity of writers, who are grouped together because they generally agree on a core set of assumptions. Third, the perspectives are not mutually exclusive ideologies. The margins between the perspectives are sometimes blurred, and they interact and influence one another over time. Thus, each of the three main perspectives has evolved in response to criticisms from both within and outside of the perspective.

Realism

Realism is the oldest theoretical perspective in IR, and the most influential school affecting US foreign policy leaders after World War Two. Despite its prominence in IR, realism has been less important in IPE because realists place greater emphasis on power and political-security issues than on wealth and economic issues. Unlike most domestic societies, there is no central authority in the **international system** and each state must look after its own interests. Thus, realists consider the state to be the principal actor in IR, and they emphasize the importance of national survival, national security, and the acquisition of power to defend state interests. Realists also generally assume that the state is a rational, unitary actor that seeks to maximize the benefits and minimize the costs involved in achieving national objectives. Furthermore, realists argue that states are most concerned about *relative gains* (see **relative/absolute gains**), with each state trying to improve its position relative to other states. This position contrasts with the liberal view that states are more concerned about *absolute gains,* in which each state seeks to maximize its own gains and is less concerned with the gains or losses of others.

Despite the realist attention to the distribution of power, realists are mainly concerned with relationships among the **great powers** within the capitalist system and they share the liberals' commitment to capitalism. Historical structuralists, by contrast, focus on the poor and disadvantaged and believe that a more equitable distribution of power and wealth is not possible under **capitalism**. Since realists give priority to politics over economics, they assume that the state has considerable capacity to structure economic relations at the international level. **Globalization** (to the extent that it is occurring) increases only because states permit it to increase. Thus, the most powerful states have the capability of either opening or closing world markets, and they can use the globalization process to improve their power positions *vis-à-vis* weaker states.

Although realist writing on IR and IPE can be traced back at least to the time of Thucydides (*c.* 471–400 BC), it was the classical mercantilists of the sixteenth to nineteenth centuries who first engaged in *systematic* theorizing on IPE from a realist perspective. After the demise of feudalism, mercantilism played an important role in state building and territorial unification through its emphasis on national power. Mercantilists believed that a state's power depended on the amount of gold and silver it could accumulate in the public treasury. With these precious metals, the state could build up its armed forces, hire mercenaries, and influence its allies as well as its enemies. Mercantilist states therefore took all necessary measures to increase their exports and decrease their imports as a means of accumulating gold. It is impossible for all states to have a balance of trade surplus, so mercantilists believed that conflict was central to international economic relations and that relative gains were more important than absolute gains. Thus, the mercantilists stood firmly within the realist school of thought.

In the eighteenth century, liberal economists such as Adam Smith (1723–

90) launched a vigorous attack on mercantilism, arguing that it encouraged states to take advantage of their neighbors and caused trade and commerce to become a source of conflict. The liberal criticisms of mercantilism were highly effective, and liberal views of free trade became dominant in England – the major power of the time – for much of the nineteenth century. Although the liberal critics of mercantilism were highly successful, some realist practices continued. Mercantilism was basically a preindustrial doctrine, and the advent of the Industrial Revolution gave a new impetus to realist thought. Foremost among the realist thinkers at this time were the first US Secretary of the Treasury, Alexander Hamilton (1755–1804); and a German civil servant, professor, and politician, Friedrich List (1789–1846). Hamilton and List both placed considerable emphasis on the development of manufacturing industries for a country's economic **development**. Although states can benefit from freer trade in the long term, List argued, the economic development of Germany and the US would be constrained in an open competitive economy as long as they lagged behind Britain. It was therefore necessary for the United States and Germany to impose some protective trade policies as a means of building up their productive potential.

Although many early realists such as the mercantilists, Hamilton, and List were highly attuned to economic issues, US realist scholars after World War Two focused almost exclusively on security issues. With the rapid development of the **cold war**, security matters were a major preoccupation, and international economic issues by contrast seemed to have little political importance. However, major economic changes occurred in the 1970s and 1980s, including the relative decline of US economic **hegemony** or leadership, the dramatic increase in OPEC prices, and the emergence of a foreign debt crisis. The new sources of instability forced realists to confront the fact that international economic issues were of central importance and could no longer be relegated to the category of 'low politics'.

With their emphasis on the state and power, the newer realists argued that the distribution of power among states is the most important factor determining whether international economic relations will flourish. A major issue to consider is whether there is a global hegemonic state with predominant power. Thus, many realists became strong advocates of **hegemonic stability theory** (HST), which draws linkages between the existence of a hegemonic state and the nature of global economic relationships. Although some liberals are also hegemonic stability theorists (and a liberal economist Charles Kindleberger is credited with introducing the theory), HST is central to realist thought because of its emphasis on power relations. HST asserts that a relatively open and stable international economic system is most likely when a hegemonic state is willing and able to provide leadership in creating and maintaining a liberal economic order, and when other major actors believe that the hegemon's policies are beneficial. If a global hegemon is absent or declining in power, economic openness and stability are more difficult – but not impossible – to maintain. It is generally agreed that hegemonic conditions have occurred at least twice – under Britain in the nineteenth century, and under the leadership of the United States after World War Two. HST has spawned a vast array of literature as well as lively discussion and debate in the field of IPE. Scholars have critiqued virtually all aspects of the theory, some simply calling for revisions, and others questioning its basic assumptions.

Although realists are very concerned about relative gains, their preoccupation with power and influence usually leads them to examine distributional issues only among the most powerful states, that is, among the advanced industrial states of the North. Realists in IPE have written more studies on North–South relations in recent years, but this is primarily because some Southern countries have posed a challenge to the power position of the North. In the 1970s, for example, realists became interested in OPEC when it wrested control over oil prices and production levels from the international oil companies. When OPEC supported the South's demands in the **United Nations** for a New International Economic Order (NIEO) to alter the North–South power imbalance, realists also wrote a number of studies on the NIEO's possible impact. In the 1980s, realists turned their attention to the East Asian newly industrializing economies, which seemed to pose a new economic challenge to the North's power position. Even when realists study North–South relations, they generally do not have a sustained interest in the poor and marginalized in developing countries as a legitimate area of inquiry.

Liberalism

Liberalism is the most influential perspective in IPE. It gives primacy of place in society to the individual consumer, firm, or entrepreneur, and assumes that individuals have inalienable rights that must be protected from collectivities such as labor unions, churches, and the state. Liberals believe that international economic interactions can be mutually beneficial if they are permitted to operate freely. All states and individuals are likely to gain from open economic relationships, even if they do not gain equally. Liberals also believe that the international economic system will function most efficiently if it ultimately depends on the price mechanism and the market. According to liberals, the purpose of international economic activity is to achieve the optimum or most efficient use of the world's scarce resources and the maximization of economic growth and efficiency.

Despite these common characteristics, there are many variants of liberalism. Three variants are especially relevant to the study of IPE. *Orthodox* liberals are mainly concerned with promoting 'negative freedom', or freedom of the private sector and the market to function with minimal interference from the state. *Interventionist* liberals believe that the market will not always be progressive and produce widespread benefits, and they therefore see benefits from some government involvement to promote more equality, fairness, and justice in a free market economy. *Institutional* liberals also believe that some outside involvement is necessary to supplement the market, and they favor the development of strong international economic institutions.

The earliest economic liberals such as Adam Smith (1723–90) and David Ricardo (1772–1823) adhered to orthodox liberalism. They were strong supporters of trade liberalization, based on the theories of absolute and comparative advantage. John Maynard Keynes (1883–1946) was an interventionist liberal, who believed that orthodox liberals provided little guidance for dealing with the high unemployment levels in the 1930s Great Depression. In contrast to the orthodox liberal view that markets tend toward a socially beneficial equilibrium, Keynes argued that market-generated equilibrium between production and consumption might occur at a point where there are high levels of unemployment and capital is underutilized. Thus, Keynes emphasized the need for governments to implement fiscal policies (and to a lesser extent monetary policies) to increase demand, and he supported government investment in public projects. Keynes's emphasis on full employment caused him to place less priority than orthodox liberals on specialization and international trade. He argued that it was sometimes justifiable to limit imports in order to bolster domestic employment, even if the goods could be produced more cheaply abroad. Keynes favored government intervention, not for the purpose of replacing **capitalism**, but to rescue and revitalize it.

Post-World War Two liberal economic theories developed in efforts to avoid the economic problems of the interwar years, including trade wars, financial crises, and the Great Depression. Influenced by the ideas of Keynes and Karl Polanyi (1886–1964), the postwar planners designed the international economic order on the basis of an interventionist or embedded liberal compromise. The 'embedded' term refers to the fact that postwar efforts to maintain an open liberal international economy were embedded in societal efforts to provide domestic economic stability. Thus, movement toward greater openness in the international economy included measures to cushion domestic economies and societies from external disruptions, and policies to provide domestic stability in turn were designed to minimize interference with global economic expansion. In addition to interventionist liberalism, institutional liberalism also was important after World War Two. Thus, three major international economic organizations were established in the 1940s: the **International Monetary Fund** (IMF), the International Bank for Reconstruction and Development (IBRD) or **World**

Bank, and the General Agreement on Tariffs and Trade (GATT). These institutions upheld liberal economic principles, and at the same time helped cushion their member states from the disruptive effects of growing economic **interdependence**.

Interventionist liberalism maintained its centrality during the expansive years of the 1950s–60s. However, the 1973 OPEC oil price shock and the prolonged global recession after 1974 made it more costly for governments to continue supporting welfare and full employment policies. Writings of orthodox liberal economists therefore began to exert more influence over government policies. Foremost among political leaders pushing for a revival of orthodox liberalism, or **neoliberalism**, were British Prime Minister Margaret Thatcher and US President Ronald Reagan. In the view of many critics, the Thatcher–Reagan policies concentrated on revitalizing business confidence, largely rejecting the attempt to ease the effects of liberalism on vulnerable groups. As these changes spread to other countries, there were growing pressures on governments to adopt orthodox or neoliberal policies in the 1980s and 1990s, with an emphasis on privatization, deregulation, and the promotion of **free trade** and foreign investment. International institutions such as the IMF, World Bank, and **World Trade Organization** or WTO (which replaced the GATT in 1995) also more assertively promoted these neoliberal policies.

While hegemonic stability theory has been central to realist IPE, interdependence theory and **regime** theory have been central to liberal IPE. Interdependence theorists explicitly question the realist assumptions that states are unitary, rational actors and that states are the only important actors in IR. States not only interact at the official governmental level, according to interdependence theorists. They are also involved in *transnational relations* in which at least one actor is non-governmental (such as an MNC), and in *transgovernmental relations* among subunits of national governments (such as Departments of Environment). These many points of contact create webs of interdependence that increase the vulnerability of states A and B to each other, making it more costly for them to alter or disrupt their relationship. Since the use of military force can be highly disruptive, force becomes less useful in promoting a state's **national interest** in highly interdependent relationships. Thus, interdependence theorists question the realist argument that military security issues are more important than socio-economic issues in IR. Since force is normally not used among highly interdependent states, interdependent relationships increase the opportunities for bargaining and permit smaller states to achieve their objectives in disputes with larger states more often than one might anticipate.

Although interdependence theorists criticize the realist tendency to give priority to military and security issues, they are acutely aware of the importance of power in IR. Interdependence is often asymmetrical, and this asymmetry is a source of power for the larger, less dependent state. For example, states A and B may be highly interdependent in trade, but if B depends on A for 80 per cent of its exports, and A depends on B for only 20 per cent of its exports, the disruption of their trade will be far more injurious to B. This provides a source of power to A, since B is more likely to make concessions to preserve the trade relationship. It is also important to note that interdependence theorists view their model as supplementing rather than replacing realism. Indeed, they acknowledge that realism is still the best model for understanding many security situations, in which power and force are of prime importance. They maintain, however, that interdependence theory is more applicable than realism in explaining international socio-economic relations.

In addition to interdependence, liberals also place considerable emphasis on international institutions as a means of promoting cooperation among states. In the liberal view, 'cheating' by states can inhibit cooperation, but a global hegemon and international institutions can limit cheating and facilitate movement toward cooperation. International institutions prevent cheating simply by bringing states together on a regular basis. A state that interacts regularly with other states in international organizations is less likely to cheat because the other states will have many opportunities to retaliate. International institutions also enforce principles and rules to ensure that cheaters will be punished, and they collect information on each member state's policies, increasing transparency or confidence that cheaters will be discovered. Furthermore, international organizations contribute to a mutual learning process in which states become aware of the mutual gains that can result from cooperation. Because realists place so much emphasis on states' concerns with relative gains, they are far more skeptical than liberals about the role of international institutions. International institutions can play a significant role in promoting cooperation, according to realists, only if the institutions can ensure member states that their gains will be balanced and equitable. However, gains are rarely equal, so this will be an extremely difficult objective for international institutions to achieve.

In view of the importance liberals attach to institutions, they have been major proponents of international regime theory. Most commonly, regimes refer to the convergence of actors around certain principles, norms, rules, and decision-making procedures in a given area of IR. For example, nondiscrimination, trade liberalization, reciprocity, and safeguards are important principles of the global trade regime. To promote the trade liberalization principle, the World Trade Organization provides rules that outlaw import quotas and export subsidies (with some exceptions), and decision-making procedures such as multilateral trade negotiations to decrease tariff and **non-tariff barrier**s to trade. In the liberal view, regimes can provide countries with reliable information, decrease the likelihood of misunderstandings, and increase the possibilities for cooperation. Regimes can also induce national governments to follow consistent policies, become less responsive to special interest groups, and limit actions that adversely affect other states. To say that regimes can influence international behavior does not indicate that their effect is always as positive as liberals imply. As realists point out, the principles, norms, and rules of a regime may sometimes reflect or further the interests of the most powerful states, and it is the least powerful states that are expected to abide by them.

Historical structuralism

Critical perspectives question the status quo in IPE, and the mainstream theoretical perspectives of realism and liberalism. Prevailing power arrangements that critical perspectives oppose may be associated with capitalism, **gender**, race, or **ethnicity**, and they call for replacing the prevailing power hierarchy with more just and equitable structures and relationships. Critical perspectives are more explicitly normative than the realist and liberal perspectives, because of their commitment to altering the status quo.

Instead of accepting existing political, economic and social relationships as objective facts to be explained, critical theorists view these 'facts' as emerging from historical and social arrangements that privilege some actors and marginalize others.

This section focuses on the most prominent critical perspective in the study of IPE, which can be termed historical structuralism. The term historical structuralism encompasses a wide range of theoretical approaches, including **Marxism**, **dependency theory**, **world-system theory**, Gramscian analysis, and regulation theory. All of these approaches have some roots in Marxism, but some have diverged quite substantially from mainstream Marxist ideas. The term 'structuralist' reflects this perspective's focus on structural means of exploitation, in which one class dominates another or rich Northern states in the core of the global economy dominate poorer Southern states in the periphery. However, some realists are also structuralists, since they explain state behavior on the basis of the structure of the international system; for example, states behave quite differently according to realists in unipolar, bipolar, and multipolar international systems. To differentiate the third perspective from structural realism, the word 'historical' is added because many theorists in this perspective engage in historical analysis and believe that history is marked by exploitation.

Historical structuralists consider economic relations to be basically conflictual, with exploitation taking the form of a struggle between classes, or between developed countries in the North and developing countries in the South. The views of historical structuralists evolved partly in efforts to explain why some of their predictions proved to be inaccurate. For example, Karl Marx (1818–83) and Friedrich Engels (1820–95) initially predicted that contradictions within capitalism would contribute to poverty of the working class, surplus production, economic downturns, and collapse of the capitalist system. When the capitalist system persisted, Vladimir Lenin (1870–1924) maintained that **imperialism** delayed the downfall of capitalism because colonies provided the metropole states with a cheap source of agricultural and raw materials, and a market for the metropoles' surplus capital and manufactures. When **decolonization** marked an end to the age of imperialism, capitalism continued to demonstrate resilience, and historical structuralists turned their attention from colonialism to *neocolonialism* as the explanation. Although the imperial powers had ceded direct political control, they continued to exert economic control over their former colonies.

Others who have sought to explain the persistence of capitalism and Southern underdevelopment include dependency theorists and world-system theorists. Dependency theorists argue that the world is hierarchically organized, with the leading capitalist states in the core of the global economy exploiting poorer states in the periphery. Only the core states can make autonomous policy choices, and market mechanisms simply reinforce socioeconomic and political inequalities. Some (but not all) early dependency theorists asserted that the core states 'underdeveloped' the peripheral states. However, success stories in the periphery such as the emergence of the newly industrializing economies caused later theorists to acknowledge that development is possible in some Southern states. These theorists argue that economic growth in the South takes the form of 'dependent development', which involves a close association between elites in the core and the periphery. World-system theorists also have attempted to address the fact that some Southern states are in fact developing by establishing a new category of states – the semiperiphery – between the periphery and the core. States in the *semiperiphery* include the newly-industrializing economies, and some OPEC countries.

Gramscian theorists have revised the third perspective to address criticisms that Marxism is overly economistic. The domination of capitalism, Gramscians argue, depends only partly on economic factors such as the private ownership of the means of production. To understand capitalist domination, we must also be familiar with the political, ideological, and cultural aspects of class struggle. Thus, Gramscians place more emphasis than Marxists on the role of culture, ideas, and institutions in explaining societal organization and change. Unlike realists, who identify hegemony solely with the predominant power of a state or group of states, Gramscians also view hegemony in terms of class relationships. A dominant class has hegemony when it legitimates its power through institutions, and makes concessions to encourage subordinate groups to support the existing social structure. Thus, the hegemonic rule of a particular class is based not only on coercion, but even more importantly on social and moral leadership. The ruling class gains the active consent of the subordinate class on the basis of shared values, ideas, and material interests.

Substantive issue areas in IPE

Much detailed analysis of IPE of course focuses on specific substantive issue areas. It is impossible in this short space to examine the range of IPE issue areas in any detail. Instead, this section briefly discusses which issue areas tend to receive the most attention. IPE specialists in different countries of course emphasize different issue areas, but the discus-

sion here addresses the subject in more general terms.

There is a tension between two major tendencies in the study of IPE: those who focus on more traditional subjects, and those who focus on a more comprehensive range of subjects including a number of newer issues. The most common traditional subjects include international trade, MNCs and foreign investment, and foreign debt and international development. Interest in these subjects in IPE has stemmed from the fact that they are highly political as well as economic in nature. For many years, international monetary relations were studied primarily by economists (and only a small number of political scientists). In contrast to trade and foreign investment, monetary relations was considered to be highly technical, and of little concern to interest groups and the general public. In more recent years, however, monetary and financial relations has become one of the most researched topics in IPE with the collapse of the **Bretton Woods** system of fixed exchange rates in the early 1970s; the foreign debt crisis in the 1980s; the financial crises in East Asia, Russia and Latin America in the 1990s; and the creation of the **Euro** as a potential competitor to the US dollar as the key international currency.

Those who take a more comprehensive approach to the study of IPE examine the traditional areas, but in addition also examine newer areas such as the environment; gender; migration; **human rights**; health issues stemming from globalization such as AIDS, SARS, and West Nile virus; illegal activity such as **money laundering**, drug trafficking, and the financing of **terrorism**; and military-economic interconnections. Those focusing on the traditional areas believe it is impossible to adequately examine a wider range of issues. Those taking a more comprehensive approach argue that newer areas such as the environment, gender, and migration deal with issues and groups that are often disregarded in society and do not receive sufficient attention.

In sum, IPE is a complex field that focuses on a diverse range of theoretical perspectives and substantive issue areas, and examines the linkages between domestic and international relations. As an interdisciplinary area of study, IPE presents a fundamental challenge to those who wish to adhere to traditional disciplinary boundaries. The message of many IPE specialists is that we should be concerned primarily with focusing on important issue areas, and with adopting relevant theoretical perspectives. The growing number and range of challenges confronting us in the global political economy should be of major concern to us, even if it means questioning our traditional disciplinary boundaries.

Further reading

Biersteker, T. (1993) 'Evolving Perspectives on International Political Economy: Twentieth Century Contexts and Discontinuities', *International Political Science Review* 14(1), 7–33.

Cohn, T. (2003) *Global Political Economy: Theory and Practice*, 2nd edn, New York: Addison-Wesley Longman.

Cox, R. (1987) *Production, Power, and World Order: Social Forces in the Making of History*, New York: Columbia University Press.

Gilpin, R. (2001) *Global Political Economy: Understanding the International Economic Order*, Princeton, NJ: Princeton University Press.

Keohane, R. (1984) *After Hegemony: Cooperation and Discord in the World Political Economy*, Princeton, NJ: Princeton University Press.

O'Brien, R. and Williams, M. (2004) *Global Political Economy*, Boulder, CO: Lynne Rienner.

Palan, R. (ed.) (2000) *Global Political Economy: Contemporary Theories*, London: Routledge.

Strange, S. (1996) *The Retreat of the State: The Diffusion of Power in the World Economy*, Cambridge: Cambridge University Press.

See also: foreign direct investment; free trade; global financial center; interdependence; International Monetary Fund; World Bank

THEODORE COHN

International public goods

Awareness that all countries are interrelated to a greater degree than in the past has given new impetus to discussions of global or international public goods – actions or activities that affect the well being of people throughout the world. The best examples are global efforts to address contagious diseases, especially HIV/AIDS, preserve the environment or promote global **security**. The **United Nations Development Program** (UNDP), in a publication in 1999, promoted the concept of global public goods as a way of thinking about how to address global problems. Since then, much has been written on the topic, concentrating on how to finance the provision of global (or international) public goods. While there are debates about what actually constitutes an international public good, there is widespread agreement that there are global problems that require concerted and coordinated global action. The **discourse** on international public goods is concerned with global action on global problems, but the discussion here concentrates on the underlying concept.

Precise definitions are difficult, but the essential requirement is that the activity (providing the public good) generates a benefit that is available to the public.

This benefit could be the activity itself, or could be actions to address a problem. Whether or not this is global or international depends on the 'spill over' range. For example, reducing **global warming** potentially benefits people everywhere, so actions to reduce global warming provide an international public good. A similar argument could be made for actions to reduce international **terrorism**. In contrast, policing to reduce crime in a town or city provides a public benefit to residents, but does not spill over internationally.

The concept originated in economics, where a distinction is made between private (or market-provided) goods and public goods, which would not be adequately provided by the market. A pure public good must exhibit two characteristics. First, the good is non-excludable: once it has been provided, no agents can be excluded from enjoying its benefits. As long as it is difficult or costly to exclude, private providers will not find the market attractive. They cannot exclude non-payers from deriving benefit and therefore cannot recover the costs of production. Consequently, there is a role for the public sector in providing the good (as the public sector can use non-price mechanisms to finance provision). Second, the good must be non-rival in consumption: when it is consumed by one person this does not diminish the amount available to others, therefore the market would under-supply the good (relative to the amount that is best for society).

In practice, goods are 'impurely public' as they exhibit neither characteristic completely. Eradication of a contagious disease is an example. The benefit of eradication is both non-rival and non-excludable. However, the method of providing the public good may be both rival and excludable (e.g. vaccinations). The knowledge of how to make the vaccine is non-rival in that many firms could use the technology without displacing others from using it, but is excludable insofar as not all are *able* (or enabled) to use the technology. The discussion about public goods is thus one about degree of excludability and rivalness, whereas the issue of whether they are international depends on the spill over range of the benefits.

A closely related concept in economics is that of externalities – when the activities of one agent have non-market effects on others not engaged in that activity. An example of an external benefit is when children are vaccinated against contagious diseases; not only do those children benefit, but the chances of others catching the disease are reduced also. Such external benefits mean that there are public good elements in providing health care. An example of an external cost would be pollution by a factory, as others suffer from the pollution. Actions to reduce pollution this provide a public good in the form of a cleaner environment from which all can benefit. The concept of international public goods encompasses all actions that provide widespread public benefits, or reduce public costs.

The fundamental point about public goods is that they will be under-supplied if provision is left to the market (i.e. market failure). This arises for two reasons. First, to an agent, the investment cost of provision may exceed the returns. This follows from the inability to exclude potential beneficiaries, which implies that some or all of the beneficiaries will not pay for the benefits, that is, they will free-ride. Second, even if charging for the benefits (exclusion) is possible, it may not be desirable from society's point of view if the social benefit exceeds the private benefit. This will be the case if benefits are non-rival, or there are significant external benefits.

Traditional discussions of public goods were at the national or community level – the government would provide **security** within its borders, or a local community could provide its own street lighting or policing. However, the spillover or spatial range over which benefits (or costs) are meaningful can extend from the local to the truly global level. The term international public good signifies that the benefits extend well beyond national boundaries, whether regional or truly global.

Broadly speaking, three types of benefits can give rise to public goods: directly providing utility, reducing risk or disutility, and enhancing capacity (to increase welfare). A public good may provide all three types of benefits. In a sense, all public goods provide utility, they provide something that is potentially of benefit. In many cases the benefit (utility) lies simply in knowing that the public good is provided – preserving **biodiversity** or conserving rainforests are examples. Note that the benefit is provided for all (within the spillover range), even to individuals who do not actually derive utility (e.g. some people are not concerned about preserving biodiversity).

Many public goods do more than provide utility, in particular they may provide a benefit that takes the form of reducing or eliminating a risk, where the risk is a disutility. For example, reducing global warming reduces the associated risks of damage to property or crops from extreme weather for everybody. However, reducing the risk (e.g. of illness) associated with the pollution of a common property resource, such as a lake, provides a public good with a more limited spatial range (regional or national). Eliminating a disease like malaria would reduce the risk (of catching it) globally, although the benefit is greater to those in countries most afflicted with the disease.

Public goods can also confer a benefit by enhancing the capacity to produce goods, where the enhanced capacity is a benefit available to all. It is the enhanced capacity that constitutes the public good, not necessarily the goods that may be produced as a result. Knowledge is an example: in principle, it is available to all but some may be constrained in their ability to access or use the knowledge, implying the need for complementary public goods. Knowledge itself is nevertheless an international public good. Education enhances national capacity, including the capacity to use global knowledge, and has positive externalities, so can be considered an international public good. Education also enhances the capacity to produce global knowledge, and is therefore an activity complementary to providing the international public good.

As a concept, therefore, an international public good encompasses activities that reduce risks or enhance capacity for the public at an international level, or that simply provides something that people consider beneficial in itself (such as peace or a cleaner environment). In practice, providing international public goods amounts to the same thing as addressing global problems. The public goods concept is useful because it provides a link to a literature on how to finance and coordinate action to address these problems.

Further reading

Ferroni, M. and Mody, A. (eds) (2002) *International Public Goods: Incentives, Measurement and Financing*, Boston and London: Kluwer Academic Publishers for The World Bank.

Kaul, I., Grunberg, I. and Stern, M. A. (eds) (1999) *Global Public Goods: International*

Cooperation in the 21st Century, New York: Oxford University Press for UNDP.

Kaul, I., Conceicao, P. Le Goulven, K. and Mendoza, R. (eds) (2003) *Providing Global Public Goods: Managing Globalization,* New York: Oxford University Press for UNDP.

See also: hegemonic stability theory; hegemony; regime

OLIVER MORRISSEY

International society

The concept of a society in social theory has generally presupposed notions of cultural cohesion and social **integration** associated with national societies. Consequently, the idea that relations among states may take place within the context of an international society appears somewhat strange. Nonetheless, a number of scholars associated with what has become known as the **English School** have developed a rich body of scholarship based on this idea.

The concept refers to a group of states that share certain common interests or values, and who participate in the maintenance of international institutions. In the past it was possible to point to a shared civilization among states that facilitated communication and cooperation among them. For example, one could argue that Western Christendom in the sixteenth and seventeenth centuries, or perhaps European political culture in the eighteenth and nineteenth centuries, restrained states from pursuing their self-interests in a totally anarchical environment. Most scholars trace the origins of contemporary international society to Europe, and in particular the 1648 Peace of **Westphalia** that generated the constitutive rules of interstate co-existence. Today's international society encompasses the globe, raising the question of whether the religious and cultural diversity of contemporary international relations renders the concept redundant as a tool of analysis. Members of the English School suggest that this is not the case, since the rules of contemporary international society continue to play an important role in sustaining international **order**. **International law** continues to affirm and reinforce the primacy of the states system, it specifies the minimum conditions of co-existence among states, and regulates the terms of cooperation among them in a variety of different issue areas.

The term 'international society' is important in drawing our attention to two fundamental aspects of international relations. First, it suggests that attempts to construct a rigid dichotomy between domestic politics (the site of hierarchy, order, and perhaps justice) and international relations (**anarchy**, absence of order, the site of **power** politics) are doomed to fail. Insofar as international relations are rule governed in the sense that rules are not mere expressions of power but also help to restrain that power, the realist approach is fundamentally flawed. Second, it suggests that the sources of state conduct cannot be deduced solely on the basis of observable and measurable factors. The term 'international society' implies that relations among states are infused with normative significance. States relate to each other in the context of claims about rights and obligations rather than mere struggles for power.

Both these aspects of international relations raise a number of interesting questions. If international relations cannot be understood adequately simply as a manifestation of power politics (realism), is it therefore unnecessary to radically transform the international order to achieve global peace and justice – as some critical theorists and cosmopolitans claim (see **critical theory; cosmopolitanism**)? Whose interests are served by the rules of co-existence among states? Are those rules capable of adaptation in the interests of individuals, or are they designed to protect states alone? Is international society a concept that is applicable across the globe, or is its scope confined to particular states and regions?

Although it is impossible to answer these questions in any definitive manner, the range of answers continues to be at the heart of contemporary debates in the field. For some scholars, the concept of international society adds little to our understanding of international relations. The rules of co-existence may be expressed neatly in constitutional charters, international institutions may flourish, but in the end international relations remains a realm in which a 'logic of consequences' prevails over a 'logic of appropriateness'.

International society is not a static concept. Its strength varies over time and space. During the height of the **cold war**, when international relations appeared to be the site of a dangerous ideological struggle over the terms of international order, evidence of a society of states was weak. In the months following the end of the cold war, it re-emerged as a powerful element in facilitating collective action to reverse Iraq's invasion of Kuwait.

Finally, some scholars suggest that the concept is analytically obsolete. In an era of **globalization**, we need to explore the possibility of international relations taking place within a broader global society in which states are but one of a number of important actors shaping the world. Moreover, even if the element of international society can be said to contribute to international order, it is hostile to ideas of cosmopolitan justice. If the latter is to be achieved at all, it is not enough that states tolerate each other. They need to participate in a broader

common project that begins to tackle common problems, such as those presented through environmental degradation and human inequality.

Further reading

Bellamy, A. (ed.) (2004) *International Society and its Critics*, Oxford: Oxford University Press.

Buzan, B. (2004) *From International Society to World Society?* Cambridge: Cambridge University Press.

Fawn, R. and Larkins, J. (1996) *International Society After the Cold War*, Basingstoke: Palgrave.

See also: anarchy; constructivism; English School; global governance; pluralism; solidarism

MARTIN GRIFFITHS

International system

The modern international system is a system of states. It was neither inevitable, nor essential. Whether the world **order** will continue to take the form of a states system is not at all clear. Current challenges are profound, from computerization and new communications technology, to population movements straining national identities, to the advent of non-state forms of collective violence, to environmental dangers and to increasing **transnational social movement**s for social and political justice.

The modern international system describes a transformation of political space in Europe from approximately the Renaissance to the twentieth century. While recent international relations theory tends to refer to the system as beginning with the Peace of **Westphalia** (1648), Martin Wight (1977) is undoubtedly correct in arguing that it develops slowly from the middle of the fifteenth through to the eighteenth centuries. Through colonialism the European states system becomes global by the end of the nineteenth century. During the twentieth century the system is further transformed by the dissolution of European **empire**s, the development of international organizations, and the emergence of post-colonial states. In the early twenty-first century, the technologies and accelerations associated with globalization seem to be realigning space and time in ways that render the international system an ambiguous ordering of international relations.

While international systems have existed at other places and times, the European states system has distinctive properties that have been crucial in defining modernity. Most notable is the **sovereignty** of the territorial state and the mutual **recognition** of that sovereignty by other states. These states communicate through regular institutions of law and **diplomacy** and sometimes engage in **balance of power** politics.

The international system is territorial. Political community is defined first and foremost within territorial borders. International political relations are constituted as relations between states with fixed borders and mutually recognized rights to make policy, provide justice, and enforce order within those borders. A complex balance of **power** operates, involving military power, diplomacy, economic resources and propaganda. The tradition of 'Reason of State' provided the first rationale for the balance of power. Drawing on Enlightenment ideas of space and time, the Peace of Utrecht (1713) embodied the idea of the international system as a self-regulating system. The Congress of Vienna (1815) established the idea that the balance of power could be managed by concerts of the **great powers**. In the twentieth century attempts were made to create multi-lateral institutions to manage **collective security** in the system, such as the **United Nations** Security Council.

The contemporary international system is a cultural and political ordering of space and time. Space is seen as abstract and empty, no principles of order preexist its division into states. This modern cartography requires, among other things, accurate descriptions of borders and boundaries, which might then be the basis for the determination of state borders and thereby the differentiation of political communities.

Temporally, the international system links the fate of all peoples within it to a single trajectory, a single future, in spite of the different histories of the states and peoples within it. The presumption of order in the system often obscures the differences between peoples and the complex, multiple histories that constitute them. In this respect, the very concept of the international system is totalizing, creating the appearance of unity and order while obscuring the contingency and historicity of political community. Moreover, in the contemporary international system, political authority, to be recognized as legitimate, must be organized with a sovereign center that can 'see' from the singular perspective of the state.

As such, the system shares an ontological assumption with the institution of modern private property, the presumption of unitary ownership of land and resources. Just as the principle of private property limits the legitimate habitation on the land to its use by an owner for individual gain and the accumulation of wealth, the principle of territoriality confines legitimate politics within national borders and undermines alternative forms of political organization which do not assume a unitary perspective and authority, such as empires, or the more nomadic political associations of the native North Americans. Through such a common ontological assumption, the institution of private property and territoriality in the system could work together to enable the expansion of European states and the transformation of the system into a global order.

During the **cold war**, a mechanistic account of the balance of power came to define the field of **security** studies as well as international relations more generally, drawing on neoclassical economic accounts of the state as a rational actor. According to this account, order in the international system could be understood primarily in terms of a system-level analysis of the interaction of states, conceived abstractly as interest maximizing units. With the advent of détente and the growth of economic **interdependence** in the 1970s, this account has been modified but remains a central feature of **realism** in the study of international relations.

The current international system is global. Time and space have been, and continue to be, compressed. In military and economic affairs speed seems to be overtaking space and reducing the significance of the territorial state. Demographic shifts are routinely challenging fixed national identities. Transnational corporations have grown so large and complex that they limit the power of most states to regulate them. The 'global commons' asserts itself over and through the borders of **nation-state**s. Sovereignty seems to be both being transcended by alternative transnational orderings and devolving to more local and parochial formations based on ethnic, religious or national imaginaries.

Yet, the dominant political imagination remains moored to the nation-state with its supposedly secure and sacrosanct territorial borders. What all this will mean for international ordering is yet unclear. Some propose an increase in **multilateralism**. Others highlight the contributions of **non-governmental organization**s and social movements to a **global civil society** based on alternative ordering principles to the current international system. Still others are returning to a neo-Kantian vision of a global cosmopolitan democracy (see **cosmopolitanism**) in which the state declines in favor of international juridical institutions and procedures. Clearly, the international system remains a modern states system, yet its edges and liminal spaces – with all the uncertainty and contingency these imply – are pressing into the center with ever greater speed and insistence.

Further reading

Bartelson, J. (1995) *A Genealogy of Sovereignty*, Cambridge: Cambridge University Press.

Opello, W. C., and Rosow, S. J. (1999) *The Nation-State and Global Order*, Boulder, CO: Lynne Rienner.

Ruggie, J. (1993) 'Territoriality and Beyond: Problematizing Modernity in International Relations', *International Organization* 47, 139–74.

Wendt, A. (1999) *Social Theory of International Politics*, Cambridge: Cambridge University Press.

Wight, M. (1977) *Systems of States*, Leicester: Leicester University Press.

See also: anarchy; English School; international society; levels of analysis

STEPHEN J. ROSOW

Inter-paradigm debate

A particular way of describing the state of international relations theory in the 1970s and 1980s, and still used even today as a heuristic device to organize competing schools of thought in the field. It is sometimes referred to as the third debate in the study of international relations, following the alleged 'realist–idealist' debate in the 1930s and 1940s and the second so-called 'great debate' between historians and positivist social scientists in the 1950s and 1960s.

The term 'paradigm' came to prominence in the philosophy of science in the 1960s, mainly through the work of Thomas Kuhn (1970). Briefly, he argued that a paradigm consists of a set of fundamental assumptions about the subject matter of science. A paradigm is both enabling and constraining. On the one hand, it helps to define what is important to study and so a paradigm is indispensable in simplifying reality by isolating certain factors and forces from a multitude of innumerable possibilities. On the other hand, a paradigm is constraining since it limits our perceptual field (what we 'see' as the most important actors and relationships in a particular field of study). In examining the history of science Kuhn argued that what he called *normal* science proceeded on the basis of particular paradigms, the truth of whose assumptions were taken for granted. A paradigm is therefore a mode of thinking within a field of inquiry that regulates scientific activity and sets the standards for research. A paradigm generates consensus, coherence and unity among scholars. However, periods of normal science are punctuated by periods of *revolutionary* science as scientists confront problems (or *anomalies*) that cannot be solved within the terms of the dominant paradigm. A new period of normal science can only resume on the basis of a 'paradigm shift' and the establishment of a new set of assumptions to account for anomalies that could not be accommodated within the assumptions of the old paradigm.

Although Kuhn had little to say about the social sciences, many scholars in the latter domain quickly seized upon his arguments in order to strengthen and clarify the historical, organizational and sociological foundations of their own disciplines. Students of international relations were no different in this regard.

Arend Lijphart (1974) was among the first to import the Kuhnian notion of a paradigm into International Relations. Writing in the mid-1970s, he argued that the general pattern of development in international relations theory paralleled Kuhn's version of theoretical progress in the natural sciences. He described the traditional paradigm in terms of state **sovereignty** and international **anarchy**. For Lijphart, **realism** had such a ubiquitous presence in the field that it qualified as a paradigm. It set out the key questions, determined the core concepts, methods, and issues, and shaped the direction of research. In the mid-1970s, however, realism came under sustained attack from both liberals and radicals. Thus the inter-paradigm debate refers to an alleged debate between realists, liberals and radicals concerning the adequacy of the dominant realist paradigm, although it should be noted that scholars use different terms to refer to the various 'paradigms' within the debate.

For realists, relations among states take place in the absence of a world government. The **international system** is anarchical, and international relations are best understood by focusing on the distribution of **power** among states. Despite their formal legal equality, the uneven distribution of power means that the arena of international relations is a form of 'power politics'. Power is hard to measure; its distribution among states changes over time and there is no consensus among states about how it should be distributed. Nonetheless, international relations is a realm of necessity (states must seek power to survive in a competitive environment) and continuity over time. When realists contemplate change in the international system, they focus primarily on changes in the **balance of power** among states, and tend to discount the possibility of fundamental change in the dynamics of the system itself.

In contrast to realists, liberals see international relations as a potential realm of progress and purposive change. They value individual freedom above all else, and they believe that the state ought to be constrained from acting in ways that undermine that freedom. Domestically, the power of the liberal constitutional state is limited by its democratic accountability to its citizens, the need to respect the demands of the economic marketplace and the rule of law. Liberals believe that despite the difficulties of replicating these constraints at the international level, they must be established to promote stability among, as well as within, sovereign states.

Finally, radicals are primarily concerned with the sources of structural inequality allegedly inherent in the international system, as well as the ways in which it might be overcome. Often inspired by, but not limited to, the Marxist tradition of thought (see **Marxism**), they examine how international relations among states makes possible (and tends to conceal) the inequities of a global capitalist system (see **capitalism**). In contrast to liberals, radicals are not content with international reforms that are limited to regulating relations among states, particularly if they rely on the capacity and the will of the **great powers**. Radicals believe that both realism and liberalism serve to maintain the basic distribution of power and wealth. They think that students need to reflect far more critically on the historical conditions underlying inequality between global *classes*, the material and ideological forces that sustain it, and the potential for revolutionary change towards a just world order.

There is no need to go into a detailed analysis of each of these so-called paradigms in the study of international relations. However, three points are worth making about the inter-paradigm debate as a 'self-image' of the discipline.

First, the inter-paradigm debate was a rather odd 'debate'. Some scholars have suggested that there was never any real debate, if by this is meant open and meaningful dialogue. After all, Marxism has never had the kind of impact on the discipline that realists and liberals have enjoyed, and there is little evidence to suggest that realists ever seriously engaged with the radicals at all. Although there has been a sustained debate between realists and liberals, it would be hard to argue that their differences were ever so serious as to constitute an inter-paradigm debate in the Kuhnian sense.

Second, despite its heuristic appeal in organizing opposing views for pedagogical purposes, the character and boundaries of each of the three 'isms' is far more complex than their interpretation as coherent paradigms, raising important questions about the wholesale transplant of Kuhn's arguments from the history of science to the study of international relations. There are, for example, important philosophical differences among realists that are glossed over when one employs the language of paradigms.

Third, the metaphor of the inter-paradigm debate is now dated. Not only was it somewhat simplistic as a way of summarizing the main fault lines in the discipline when it became popular in the 1970s, but today it is wholly inadequate because there are important 'schools of thought' (for example, **feminism**, **constructivism** and **poststructuralism**, to name but three) that escape the typology altogether.

Further reading

Elman, C. and Elman, M. (eds) (2003) *Progress in International Relations Theory*, Cambridge, MA: MIT Press.

Kuhn, T. (1970) *The Structure of Scientific Revolutions*, 2nd edn, Chicago, IL: University of Chicago Press.

Lijphart, A. (1974) 'The Structure of the Theoretical Revolution in International Relations', *International Studies Quarterly* 18, 41–74.

Waever, O. (1996) 'The Rise and Fall of the Inter-Paradigm Debate', in S. Smith, K. Booth and M. Zalewski (eds) *International Theory: Positivism and Beyond*, Cambridge: Cambridge University Press, 149–85.

See also: discourse; interdependence; realism; reflexivity; Marxism

TERRY O'CALLAGHAN

Irredentism

A political movement to unite the territory and people of an ethnic group with other territories held by members of that same group across international boundaries. There are two subtypes of irredentism, depending on the circumstances of the group in question: 'motherland irredentism', which consists of an attempt by an established **nation-state** already dominated by an ethnic group to incorporate its ethnic kin and their territory from a nearby nation-state; and 'Kurdish-style irredentism', which involves several segments of an ethnic group, none dominant in any nation-state and divided by international boundaries, uniting across those boundaries to form a single, new independent nation-state.

The first type was a cause of conflict in the Balkans in the 1990s, where an irredentist Serbian government attempted to incorporate groups of Serbs living in neighboring countries (Bosnia and Croa-tia) into a 'greater Serbia'. Irredentist conflicts have also been fought in East Africa between Ethiopia and Somalia, and in the Caucasus between Armenia and Azerbaijan. The long-running dispute between India and Pakistan over Kashmir is considered to be an irredentist conflict, as the Muslim Kashmir region could seek to join with Pakistan if it gained its independence from India. The second type of irredentism has been confined mostly to discussions of the Kurds in the Middle East, spread out across Iraq, Iran, Turkey and Syria, who might desire to unite into a larger, independent Kurdistan.

Because irredentism necessarily involves breaking away from the **authority** of an existing state, it is closely associated with **secession**. Scholars have pointed out that the conditions for both secession and irredentism exist throughout the world. Most societies are ethnically diverse, and many ethnic groups live in relatively compact geographical areas. Moreover, many ethnic groups are divided by international boundaries, with segments of those groups living in different countries (as is the case with the Kurds, but also Ossetians in Georgia and Russia, Tamils in Sri Lanka and India, Chinese throughout Southeast Asia, Hutus and Tutsis in Rwanda, Burundi, and eastern Congo, and Serbs in Serbia, Croatia, Bosnia, and Montenegro.

Yet despite these conditions, which create the possibility for both secession and irredentism, there have been relatively few irredentist movements in the last fifty years, although there have been many more secession attempts. Scholars have pointed out that irredentism, because it involves states expanding at the expense of other states, is less likely to receive political support internationally, where the inviolability of international boundaries has been a key principle in **international society** since the end of World War Two. Moreover, segments of ethnic groups that live far from the 'center' or 'motherland' may not be seen as being 'true members' of the group; their loyalty may be questioned, or they may be accused of becoming too much like the other groups they live among. Irredentism is thus closely related to **nationalism**, as common identity and group loyalty are necessary to motivate a reunification movement.

Finally, irredentism involves secession as a necessary first step; but secessionist movements often are led by local political leaders who may not want to give up their authority and **power** to the government of a larger neighboring state, however much they may be ethnically related. This also helps explain the extreme rarity of 'Kurdish-style' irredentism, which would necessitate several successful secessions, followed by a pooling of the newly independent areas into a single entity – an extraordinarily unlikely convergence of events. Thus, while secession and irredentism are usually seen as alternatives which ethnic groups can choose between, the former remains more attractive than the latter as a political strategy.

Irredentism and secession are generally treated differently on the international level as well. In the wake of World War Two, the international community adopted new norms and expectations about how nation-states should treat each other. Many of these expectations are embodied in the **United Nations** Charter and related principles of **international law**. Chief among these are provisions discouraging **war** between states, and prohibiting aggression by one state against another – the latter a clear response to Nazi Germany's aggression in Europe, which began as a series of irredentist claims against neighboring states (Austria, Czechoslovakia) which

had German-speaking populations. There is thus a strong international bias against states making irredentism claims on their neighbors, for fear that these will lead to war. While this was not sufficient to deter Serbia's irredentism attempts in the 1990s, the Serbian case – ultimately resolved without the changing of international boundaries, and with no successful irredentism – serves to reinforce the general fear of irredentism and its potential consequences. Some vulnerable parts of the world – Africa in particular, where nearly all states serve as host to ethnic groups that cross boundaries – have largely refrained from irredentism out of fear that if any one movement were successful, it would call into question the entire arrangement of states and borders, generating an expanding number of international and **civil war**s.

On the other hand, movements of 'national liberation' to free an 'oppressed' people, have been granted much more international legitimacy, going back to the **self-determination** principle articulated by US President Woodrow Wilson at the end of World War One. Thus, states that wish to pursue irredentism will often not do so openly, but will encourage secessionism among their ethnic kin in a neighboring state. For example, both Pakistan and Serbia denied having any designs on their ethnic kin in nearby states (Kashmir and Bosnia, respectively), but both have actively engaged in promoting and assisting secessionist movements on those territories, while claiming that those movements are both independent and legitimate under international norms of self-determination. These efforts become problematic under international norms primarily when they involve the **ethnic cleansing** of the region by driving out other, rival ethnic groups. Modern irredentism is therefore most likely to take the form of assistance to ethnic secessionist movements, which can be withdrawn or denied if necessary in the face of international pressure.

While it will likely remain relatively rare, therefore, irredentism will continue to be a concern well into the next century. Upheaval in nearly any region of the world – Africa, Asia, and the Middle East in particular – can create conditions which might encourage ethnic groups to try to reunite with their kin nearby, or for ethnically-dominated states to expand at the expense of their neighbors.

Further reading

Carment, D. and James, P. (1997) 'Secession and Irredenta in World Politics: The Neglected Interstate Dimension', in Carment, D. and James, P. (eds) *Wars in the Midst of Peace: The International Politics of Ethnic Conflict*, Pittsburgh, PA: University of Pittsburgh Press, 194–231.

Chazan, N. (ed.) (1991) *Irredentism and International Politics*, Boulder, CO: Lynne Rienner.

Gurr, T. (2000) *Peoples Versus States: Ethnopolitical Conflict and Accommodation at the End of the Twentieth Century*, Washington, DC: United States Institute of Peace.

Saideman, S. (1998) 'Inconsistent Irredentism? Political Competition, Ethnic Ties, and the Foreign Policies of Somalia and Serbia' *Security Studies* 7(3), 51–93.

Saideman, S. and Ayres, R. (2000) 'Determining the Causes of Irredentism', *Journal of Politics* 62(4), 1126–44.

See also: ethnic cleansing; ethnic conflict; nation-state; secession; self-determination; sovereignty

R. WILLIAM AYRES

Islam

Islam is one of the fastest growing and most influential religions with over 1.3 billion Muslims (comprising one-fifth of the world's population). Islam is the second largest religion after Christianity, which has 2.3 billion followers. Muslims comprise a majority of the population in fifty-five countries and a minority in many others. Muslim countries possess innumerable raw materials, producing over half the petroleum consumed in the West, and controlling as much as two-thirds of the world's known petroleum reserves. The Muslim world possesses a substantial pool of inexpensive labor and provides a lucrative market for goods and services from the West. Islam is one of the most misunderstood religions. It is, therefore, imperative for students and scholars to attain a deeper and more meaningful understanding of Islam.

Islam, Muslim, and Muhammadanism

The word Islam, as well as the word Muslim, stem from the Arabic root *slm* or *aslama*, which literally means to submit or to surrender. Therefore, the religion of Islam has come to mean submission, surrender, resignation, and obedience to the Will of God and His guidance. Muslims believe only by totally submitting to God's Will, as embodied in the Qur'an, can one achieve happiness in this world and in the hereafter.

Muslims believe that the Qur'an, God's last message to humankind, was revealed to Prophet Muhammad ibn Abdullah (570–632 CE) over a period of twenty-two years (610–632 CE). The Qur'an emphasizes *tawhid* (the absolute oneness, unity, and uniqueness of Allah/ God). *Salaam* or peace, is one of the ninety-nine attributes of or names for God. Muslims often say *salaam alaykum* (peace be upon you) when they greet another Muslim, and are given the response of *wa' alaykum as-salaam* (peace be upon you, too). The term

'Muhammadanism' has often been incorrectly used synonymously with Islam. Prophet Muhammad did not create Islam, the Qur'an does not consider him divine, and Muslims do not worship him. The worship of Prophet Muhammad would be regarded as *shirk* (associating someone with God), which violates the central Islamic belief in *tawhid,* the defining doctrine of Islam. Moreover, Muslims acknowledge *all* the Old Testament prophets and revere Muhammad as Khatam al-Nabieen (the seal of the Prophets) or the last in a long line of God's prophets sent to guide humankind on 'the straight path'. The Qur'an describes Islam as the totality of the messages God revealed to all His messengers, from Adam to Muhammad. While Muslims view Prophet Muhammad as *insan-i-kamil* (perfect human being), they believe God established Islam and created everything in the universe.

Muhammad: Islam's last prophet

The name Muhammad comes from the Arabic verb *hamada*, to praise, to laud, and to glorify. Thus, Muhammad means the praised one or the one who is glorified. Muhammad was born in the oasis town of Makkah in the Arabian Peninsula (present day Saudi Arabia) in 570 CE. His father, Abdullah, died before his birth and his mother, Aminah bint Wahab, died when he was six years old. His grandfather, Abd al-Muttalib, died when he was eight and Muhammad's upbringing was assumed by his uncle, Abu Talib, his guardian for the next forty years.

Muhammad was deeply disturbed by the ignorance, polytheism, and primitive customs prevalent in Arabia. The practice of female infanticide was common; slavery, alcoholism, and gambling were widespread; wealthy and influential men kept large harems; widows and orphans suffered poverty and terrible indignities; and tribal wars were frequent. Although Muhammad quietly sought spiritual answers to these social ills, he earned his living as a merchant. By his mid-twenties, Muhammad had acquired a reputation in Makkah for honesty and integrity, earning the titles *Al-Sadiq* (honest and truthful) and *Al-Amin* (the trustworthy). Khadijah bint Khuwaylid, a wealthy and influential woman in Makkah, employed Muhammad. Muhammad's exceptional character, personality, and work habits were so impressive that Khadijah proposed marriage based on love and respect, as opposed to the more common arranged marriages of the day.

In his thirties, Muhammad meditated regularly in the Makkan cave of Hira. Muslims believe Muhammad was visited in the cave by the Archangel Gabriel in 610 CE, who told him he should announce his prophethood and preach the message of Islam. His wife, Khadijah, and a few relatives converted immediately to Islam.

The first Muslims suffered extremely brutal persecution by corrupt pagan leaders of Makkah. Responding to this persecution in 622 CE, Muhammad led his followers to the nearby town of Yathrib, renamed Madinat un-Nabi (the Prophet's city) or Madinah, where a small band of converts had invited him. This migration from Makkah to Madinah, called the *Hijrah,* marks the beginning of the Islamic lunar calendar. The year 622 CE is thus designated as the First *Hijri* and all subsequent years are referred to as 'After *Hijrah*' (or AH). The establishment of the first Islamic state in Madinah illustrates the centrality of the *ummah* (community of believers/Muslims) and the fusion of religion and politics in Islam.

Once in Madinah, Muhammad established and governed the Islamic state. However, the Makkans gave the Prophet no peace, and a series of wars between the Makkans and the Muslims ensued for nine years. When Muhammad conquered Makkah, most of his former enemies converted to Islam. Muhammad died in 632 CE, at the age of 62, leaving behind a young and dynamic faith.

The Qur'an

According to Muslims, Prophet Muhammad's greatest miracle was the *Qur'an*, which literally means *recitation* in Arabic. The Qur'an is a collection of God's revelations, which Muslims believe the Archangel Gabriel conveyed to Prophet Muhammad. Most often, these revelations were communicated to Muhammad in classical and eloquent Arabic prose. Muhammad, in turn, recited these revelations to his companions, who wrote them down, memorized them, and recited them to others. The name Qur'an was later given to the sacred book containing these revelations and provides guidance for almost every aspect of a believer's life.

Muslims consider the Qur'an the last sacred book containing the authoritative Word of God. The Qur'an comprises 114 *surahs* (chapters), each one further divided into *ayats* (verses). The majority of Muslims around the world learn to recite the Qur'an in Arabic, regardless of their native language. They believe it is God's final guidance to humankind until Judgment Day.

Iman

Iman literally means faith, belief, or spiritual convictions. It comprises five fundamental articles of faith. First, the belief in Allah (God) is the most important tenet of Islam. The Islamic term, Allah, represents one omnipotent, omnipresent, omniscient, just, and merciful God or Supreme Being. The second article of faith is a belief in God's angels.

Archangel Gabriel is believed to have brought God's messages to all His prophets. Third, Muslims profess a belief in God's prophets who came to earth as guides for humankind. Muslims believe in a long line of prophets starting with Adam and including Noah, Abraham, Ishmael, Isaac, Jacob, Joseph, Job, Moses, Aaron, David, Solomon, Elias, Jonah, John the Baptist, Jesus, and Muhammad. Fourth, Muslims believe in God's Holy Books. Muslims believe that God revealed the *Suhuf* (Scrolls) to Abraham, the *Zabur* (Psalms) to David, the *Tawrah* (Torah) to Moses, the *Injil* (Gospels) to Jesus, and the *Qur'an* to Muhammad. Each of these Holy Books, when they were revealed, showed their respective people 'the straight path' God wanted humankind to follow. However, Muslims also believe that the Qur'an contains God's final, complete, and authentic message to humankind. Finally, Muslims believe in *Yaum al-Akhira* (the Day of Judgment). The Qur'an informs Muslims the world will come to an end and the dead from the time of creation will be resurrected, to be judged by God. Righteous human beings, who have done good deeds in this world, will be rewarded with an eternal happiness in Heaven/Paradise, while those who have refused to follow God's guidance will be sent to Hell and suffer.

Faraidh

Muslims believe that neglecting the five *faraidh* (compulsory duties or obligations), also known as the five 'pillars of the faith', will be punished in the hereafter, while their fulfillment will be rewarded. The five pillars of the faith include the professing or declaring of one's faith, the ritual of daily prayers to worship God, charity (Muslims are encouraged to donate at least 2.5 per cent of their net worth, not just their annual income, to the welfare of the poor and needy), observing the fast from dawn to dusk during the ninth Islamic calendar month of Ramadan (the month Prophet Muhammad started receiving God's revelations), and to make a pilgrimage to the sacred shrine of *Ka'abah* in Makkah at least once in their lifetime.

Shariah

Shariah is the comprehensive, eternal, immutable, and divine law of Islam, which governs all aspects of the public and private, social and economic, religious and political life of every Muslim. The shariah's provisions were compiled by the *ulama* (Islamic scholars) during the middle ages using the discipline of Islamic jurisprudence, Prophet Muhammad's ethos of consultation and consensus, and the method of *qiyas* (deduction by analogy). Shi'ahs, representing the minority sect of Islam, substitute independent reasoning and judgment by *mujtahids* (revered ulama) instead of deduction by analogy, and confined the scope of consensus to their Imams and/or their Grand Ayatollahs (supreme *ulama*). A Muslim country must impose the shariah as the law of the land for recognition as an Islamic state. This explains in large part why all Islamists want to impose the shariah in Muslim societies.

Reign of the first four caliphs

The influential Muslim leaders of Makkah nominated the sixty-year old Abu Bakr, a close companion of Prophet Muhammad, as his successor and as the first *khalifah* (caliph). During his brief reign (632–4 CE), rebellious bedouins were suppressed, Islamic rule consolidated over the Arabian Peninsula, and Muslim armies were sent to conquer Iraq and Syria. Abu Bakr nominated

Umar ibn al-Khattab to be the second caliph. During Umar's reign (634–44 CE), his armies conquered Mesopotamia, Egypt, Syria, Palestine, the greater part of Persia, Azerbaijan, Armenia, and even some parts of Turkey. He was the first Muslim leader to assume the title of 'supreme commander of the faithful'. As a competent public administrator, Umar created a police department to maintain law and order, a welfare service to assist the needy, an education department, and established a consultative body to deliberate on public policy and guide him in its implementation. After Umar's assassination, Muslim tribal leaders chose Uthman ibn Affan to be Islam's third caliph. A wealthy merchant, he married Prophet Muhammad's step-daughter Ruqayyah and, after her death, her sister Umm Kulthum. During Uthman's reign (644–56 CE), his armies conquered much of Persia and North Africa. Although Caliph Abu Bakr started the process of collating the Qur'an, a process that continued under Caliph Umar, it was during Uthman's reign that Islamic experts completed the project. Just before Uthman's death, a standard edition of the Qur'an was published and distributed, introducing the first organized news service in Islamic history. Ali ibn Abi Talib (656–61 CE) was the last of the *Khulafah-i-Rashidun* (first four rightly-guided caliphs). He was the cousin and son-in-law of Prophet Muhammad and the first convert to Islam after Khadijah, Muhammad's wife. He was raised by the Prophet and married the Prophet's daughter Fatimah.

Islamic sects

The Muslim world is divided into two major sects, the Sunnis and the Shi'ahs. Sunnis, the majority Islamic sect, comprise 80–85 per cent of the Muslim world. The Arabic term, *sunni*, means those who follow the *sunnah*. There are four main Sunni subsects, the Hanafi, Maliki, Shafi'i, and the Hanbali, named after the Islamic scholars instrumental in developing these four major schools of Islamic jurisprudence

Hanifis, follow the Islamic jurisprudence of the Iraqi-born Imam Abu Hanifah al-Nu'man ibn-Thabit (699–769 CE). The Hanafi sect was actively promoted by a number of Abbasid and Ottoman rulers and is widely prevalent in Turkey, Afghanistan, Egypt, Central Asia, China, and South Asia.

Malikis follow the Islamic jurisprudence of Imam Abu Abd Allah Malik ibn Anas (716–95 CE). Imam Malik codified Islamic common law in a treatise entitled *The Book of the Trodden Path*. In his research, Imam Malik strayed little from the *sunnah*. The Maliki sect spread in Muslim Spain and Africa.

Shafi'is follow the instruction of Imam Muhammad ibn Idris ash-Shafi'i (767–820 CE). He traveled throughout the Muslim Middle East, teaching in Baghdad, Egypt, and Makkah; Shafi'i promoted a moderate and eclectic brand of Islam, which embodied the continuity of tradition and change through independent reasoning. The Shafi'i sect spread in southwestern Asia and northern Egypt. The Shafi'i decline began when the Ottomans, comprising members mostly of the Hanafi sect, propagated their beliefs throughout the Ottoman Empire.

Hanbalis belong to the most revolutionary, puritanical, and iconoclastic of the four Sunni schools of Islamic jurisprudence. The founder of the Hanbali sect was the Iraqi-born theologian and jurist Imam Ahmad ibn Hanbal (780–855 CE), who condemned innovations in defense of the purity of Islamic beliefs and practices. However, the Hanbali sect's puritanism, the Ottomans promotion of the Hanafi sect, and the suppression of Wahhabism (a subsect within the Hanbali sect), resulted in the Hanbalis

being the smallest of the four Sunni sects. In the last quarter century, Saudi Arabia, dominated by the Hanbali sect, has made a significant effort to promote the ideology of Wahhabism to the four corners of the world.

The term Shi'ah literally means party, partisan, follower, or split. Shi'ahs are the second major Islamic sect, comprising 15 to 20 per cent of the ummah. They believe Prophet Muhammad nominated Ali as the first *Imam* (leader) or caliph because he was best qualified for the job. The first major schism in the House of Islam owes its origins to this succession. The Arabic term Shi'ah is an abbreviation for *shi'at-i-Ali* (Ali's faction). Within the Shi'ah sect, there are a number of subsects, namely, the Ithna Asharis (Twelver), Bohris, Ismaelis, and Alawites. The Ithna Ashari Shi'ahs are the majority sect in Iran, Iraq, Bahrain, and Lebanon. Additionally, they comprise 15 to 20 per cent of the Muslim population in India and Pakistan.

Major differences between Sunnis and Shi'ahs

In addition to the *shahadah*: 'There is no God but God, and Muhammad is His Messenger', Shi'ahs often add the phrase, 'Ali is the beloved of God'. While Sunnis revere the first four caliphs, many orthodox Shi'ahs reject the legitimacy of Ali ibn Abi Talib's three predecessors and all his successors. Sunnis insist that Prophet Muhammad was a fallible human being through whom God revealed His message, whereas Shi'ahs contend that the Prophet was close to infallible with some divine attributes because of the 'Divine Light' shared by all of God's prophets. Moreover, Shi'ahs assert, elements of the 'Divine Light' were bestowed upon Muhammad's daughter Fatimah, her husband, Imam Ali, and their descendants through their male progeny. While Sunnis respect Ali and his descendants, they do not revere them to the extent that Shi'ahs do. Indeed, the Sunnis reject the Shi'ah contention that Muhammad selected Ali to be the first *Imam* of the Islamic state and thus repudiate the Shi'ah institution of the Imamate, the divine right of Ali and his male descendants to govern the *ummah.*

Additionally, while Sunnis recognize four schools of Islamic jurisprudence, Shi'ahs only follow the Islamic jurisprudence that Jafar-I-Sadiq (who died in 765 CE), the sixth Shi'ah Imam, compiled and codified. Furthermore, differences exist between Sunnis and Shi'ahs in the laws of marriage, divorce, and inheritance. Some Shi'ahs, for example, permit temporary marriage. Sunnis disavow and consider sinful any marriage contract which sets a limit to the duration of marriage. Shi'ahs, by contrast, place greater restrictions than do Sunnis on the husband's right to divorce his wife. Relatively speaking, the inheritance received by female heiresses is far more generous in Shi'ah law than under the four schools of Sunni beliefs. Also, Shi'ahs differ from Sunnis in their exclusively Shi'ah practice of 'concealment', which permits an individual to conceal his or her true religious, ideological, or political beliefs to avoid persecution or death at the hands of enemies. This practice evolved as a response to 1,500 years of Shi'ah persecution throughout the Muslim world.

The practice of daily liturgical prayers differs between Shi'ahs and Sunnis. Shi'ahs are permitted to perform their five daily prayers three times a day between dawn and sunrise, between midday and sunset, and between sunset and midnight. The Sunnis, however, perform their prayers five times daily: before sunrise, around midday, in the late afternoon, at dusk, and before midnight. Sunnis and Shi'ahs also differ in how they pray; Shi'ahs stand with their arms hanging straight down, while most Sunnis fold their arms in front of themselves.

Although Shi'ahs and Sunnis have their differences, as do adherents of the four Sunni sects, Muslims of all sects and subsects agree that they have much in common. Thus, Muslims of all sects are sharing in the Islamic revival sweeping through the Islamic world.

Status of women in Islam

Many non-Muslims believe Muslim women are unfairly treated in Islam. This misperception is based on the improper practice of Islam by some Muslims. The negative perception of Muslim women as uneducated, subjugated, and abused, with no rights and no opportunities, is a stereotype born of ignorance or malevolence.

For example, in the Qur'anic account of Creation, woman was not created from the rib of man. Rather, the first person (indefinite gender) was created, followed by the creation of the person's mate (4:1). Moreover, Eve was not considered the temptress and the cause of original sin; both Adam and Eve were equally responsible for the mistake (not sin) in the Garden of Eden. The Qur'an prohibits the pagan Arab practice of female infanticide prevalent in pre-Islamic Arabia. In the Arabian Peninsula, during the sixth century CE, women were sold into marriage by their fathers, kidnapped, raped, and purchased both as concubines and as members of large harems. Some tribal chieftains had as many as fifty wives. Prophet Muhammad abhorred the practice of forced marriages made by a woman's guardian and instead converted marriage into a legal agreement or civil contract between two consenting individuals.

Based on a Qur'anic revelation, Muhammad also limited the number of women any one man could marry to four. As there were several tribal wars, resulting in numerous male fatalities and consequently an overabundance of widows and orphans, Muhammad believed through marriage the warring tribes could be brought closer while providing care for widows and orphans. The Qur'an later added that it was impossible for a man to do justice to more than one wife.

Islam gave women inheritance rights in the sixth century. Although women were given only half the amount assigned to corresponding males, it was a substantial reform in the patriarchal society of Arabia. This is in sharp contrast to many Western cultures, which until only a couple of centuries ago denied daughters inheritance if there were sons in the family. In addition, a woman could earn her own living as an independent individual, without any obligation to contribute her income or wealth to her husband or her family. Prophet Muhammad's open-minded and progressive attitude toward women can best be illustrated in his first marriage to Khadijah. She was a confident, mature, enterprising, business woman. Khadijah owned a successful trading company and earned her living outside the home in a patriarchal, chauvinistic society. She was the first person with whom Muhammad shared Archangel Gabriel's visit in the cave. Khadijah was able to reassure her husband God anointed him as His prophet. Besides her conversion to Islam, Khadijah contributed her entire fortune, time, and support to the spread of Islam despite Makkan persecution.

Four additional points can be made to demonstrate that Islam does not discriminate against Muslim women. First, a Muslim woman can retain her name; she does not have to adopt her husband's surname. Although in Islam women are encouraged to dress mod-estly in public, non-Muslims rarely mention that Islam instructs men to dress modestly as well. Second, women have assumed leadership positions in several Muslim countries. Mrs Bhutto was sworn in as Pakistan's prime minister in 1988. Although she lost power in 1990, she was popularly reelected by millions of Pakistanis in 1993. Bangladesh has had two female prime ministers since 1991. In 1993, Turkey elected Tansu Ciller as prime minister. Although she lost her position as prime minister in 1996, she was appointed as foreign minister. Ciller was to serve as prime minister again in 1997, but her coalition government lost its majority later that year. Finally, in 2001, Megawati Sukarnoputri became president of Indonesia, the most populous Muslim country in the world, with over 220 million people.

The success of these women provides role models to other Muslim women that Islam supports their societal contributions as well as the role they play in the home. The male chauvinism and patriarchal cultural traditions often found in Muslim countries should not be confused with Islam *per se*.

Islam and terrorism

Islam emphatically condemns and prohibits terrorism or the intentional and indiscriminate killing of innocent human beings. It considers terrorism to be a sin because human life is considered sacrosanct and only God has the right to bestow it and take it away. In fact, Islam opposes all types of violent extremism which results in the death of innocent civilians.

The Organization of the Islamic Conference (OIC), which represents fifty-seven Muslim countries, wasted no time strongly condemning the terrorist attacks in the United States on 11 September 2001. The OIC response was soon joined by political leaders and Islamic clerics from many Muslim countries, which viewed the tragic events as an affront to Islam and a distortion of *jihad*. In the non-Muslim world, *jihad* is often erroneously defined as 'holy war'. In fact, the Arabic term for 'holy war' is *harb un-muqaddastu*, which is not found in the Qur'an. In Arabic, *jihad* literally means to strive and to struggle. In Islam, *jihad-i-akbar* (the greatest *jihad*) is the nonviolent spiritual struggle to control and vanquish one's baser instincts and impulses; and *jihad-i-asghar* (the lesser *jihad*) is to actively defend oneself against tyrants, aggressors, and colonizers.

Islamism

Islamism is a comprehensive ideology in which Islamic symbols, ideas, and ideals are cultivated for political purposes. Islamism promotes the spread of Islam from homes, mosques, and *madrassahs* (Islamic schools) into the mainstream of not only the sociocultural life of Muslim societies, but also the legal, economic, and political spheres of Muslim states. Coming at a time of great disparity of wealth and in most Muslim societies, Islamism's emphasis on socioeconomic equity and justice has considerable populist appeal.

The individuals, groups, and movements which fuel Islamism fall into three ideal-typical categories: *Revolutionary* Islamists tend to be radical and puritanical in their religious and political orientation. They reject Western ideas and ideologies and work to establish an Islamic state governed by Revolutionary Islamists and based on the comprehensive and rigorous application of the *shariah*. *Traditionalist* Islamists are often Islamic scholars who want to conserve Islamic laws, customs, and traditions practiced in the classical and medieval periods of Islamic history. Finally, *pro-*

gressive Islamists (also called modernists, pragmatists, adaptationists, apologists, syncretists, and even revisionists) are religiously devout but advocate the reconciliation of traditional Islamic ideas with secular scientific rationalism. They also advocate adopting beneficial ideas from anywhere in the world and adapting them to Muslim societies.

Further reading

Esposito, J. (ed.) (1999) *The Oxford History of Islam*, Oxford: Oxford University Press.

Fuller, G. (2003) *The Future of Political Islam*, Basingstoke: Palgrave.

Glasse, C. (1989) *The Concise Encyclopedia of Islam*. New York: Harper and Row.

Halliday, F. (2003) *Islam and the Myth of Confrontation*, London: I. B. Tauris.

Hashmi, S. (2002) *Islamic Political Ethics*, Princeton, NJ: Princeton University Press.

Husain, M. Z. (2003) *Global Islamic Politics*, 2nd edn, New York: Longman.

Lewis, B. (2003) *The Crisis of Islam: Holy War and Unholy Terror*, New York: Random House.

Saikal, A. (2003) *Islam and the West: Conflict or Cooperation?* Basingstoke: Palgrave.

Schulze, R. (2002) *A Modern History of the Islamic World*, London: I. B. Tauris.

See also: al-Qaeda; clash of civilizations

MIR ZOHAIR HUSAIN

Isolationism

In the most general sense the term 'isolationism' implies a degree of disengagement from international affairs. Perhaps the most radical instance of isolationism was the Japanese **empire**'s attempt to exclude external cultural influences until forcible foreign intervention in the nineteenth century made such an endeavour forlorn. Such examples are historically rare, however, and in practice isolationism is best seen as one side of a continuum, with internationalism or interventionism on the other side. In the modern world countries have expressed isolationist tendencies rather than being totally removed from international affairs. Thus, for example, the North Korean regime has sought to safeguard its position by minimizing international contact available to its citizens, while maintaining economic and military relations with other states. Switzerland has eschewed membership of such bodies as the **North Atlantic Treaty Organization** (NATO) and the **European Union**, while being open to international engagement of a less formal kind.

The concept of isolationism is most frequently discussed in the context of American foreign policy, where it is identified with aversion to foreign wars and alliances, especially those originating in the European 'Old World'. Care should be taken to distinguish American isolationism from other positions with which it may be linked, such as **pacifism** (the principled opposition to all military action).

While the word itself does not predate the twentieth century, the ideas informing isolationism may be traced back to the early years of the American republic. A classic statement was that of George Washington, whose farewell address in 1796 advocated the 'great rule of conduct' that in extending commercial relations with foreign nations, America should have as little political connection as possible with them, and should avoid permanent **alliance**s, although temporary ones to meet specific emergencies were acceptable. Washington linked his views to America's geographical location, noting that 'our detached and distant situation' facilitated and rendered advisable a different course from that typical of European **great powers**. This message was reinforced by Washington's

presidential successors, notably Thomas Jefferson, who famously warned against 'entangling alliances', and James Monroe. Another isolationist theme that emerged in the nineteenth century was the fear that American liberties would be imperilled by prolonged foreign military commitments. The subsequent history of isolationism may be understood as the attempt to preserve as much as possible of these tenets in the face of America's expanding economic interests, and the emergence of potential imperial challengers.

In contrast to Britain, whose imperial interests led it into the Crimean War with Russia in the 1850s, the United States was able in the nineteenth century to expand its territorial control without going to war with a European rival. A more ambiguous case was the Spanish–American War of 1898, as a result of which Cuba and the Philippines became American dependencies. While this did not involve sending American forces to Europe, they were sent outside the American continent. Furthermore, the arguments advanced for the war often had a 'moral imperialist' character, urging Americans to lead the world's less fortunate peoples to more enlightened conditions. This episode prompted Rudyard Kipling to appeal to the United States to 'take up the White Man's Burden', but also provoked the foundation at home of the Anti-Imperialist League, which urged the United States to lead the world by example rather than by the use of force.

The war with Spain was at least partly driven by the need to protect US trading interests, a task rendered more urgent by the 1890s economic depression. Another expression of the same concern was the Open Door policy, adopted in 1899, whereby the United States insisted on its right to equal access with other great powers to the putatively vast Chinese market. American economic expansion may be adduced as a ground for questioning the usefulness of the term 'isolationist' as a description of its policies even in this period. Another criticism is that, in the light of the comparison with British policy mentioned above, the term has a Eurocentric flavor.

America's initial neutrality in the First World War served to allay isolationist misgivings. Even the Wilson Administration's decision to enter the war in 1917 did not break unequivocally with tradition, for it was provoked by the threat to American merchant shipping posed by German submarine activity, and by an apparent pledge by Germany to assist Mexico in the recovery of territory lost to the United States. These direct challenges to American interests led normally isolationist members of Congress to vote for war against Germany. Wilson's post-war attempt to secure American membership of the newly founded **League of Nations** proved less acceptable, since it threatened to commit America to precisely the kind of permanent engagement against which Washington and others had warned. The Senate voted not to join after attempts to reach a compromise failed.

In the 1920s the United States did not face any major international **crisis** such as would revive debate about foreign policy fundamentals. That came in the 1930s and early 1940s, in the face of the challenges posed by German and Japanese expansionism, and the outbreak of the Second World War in Europe. In the 1930s traditional isolationism had been reinforced by the pacifist reaction against the carnage of the 1914–18 War, and Congress had passed a series of Neutrality Acts. When war broke out in 1939, President Roosevelt moved by gradual steps to a strategy of assisting Britain by means short of **war**. This aroused opposition from a new isola-tionist formation, the America First Committee, but their case was undermined by Hitler's conquest of Western Europe in 1940 and the subsequent bombing of Britain, and collapsed altogether with the Japanese attack on Pearl Harbor in December 1941.

After the Second World War the Truman Administration adopted the policy of **containment**, designed to counter Soviet power in the emerging **cold war**. Traditional isolationists objected to aspects of this policy, including the NATO **alliance**, which committed America to the defence of European powers. In July 1949 the Senate ratified membership of NATO by 82 votes to 13, a decision that is often regarded as the end of an era in American history. There have nonetheless been a number of occasions since when 'neo-isolationist' trends have been detected in US foreign policy debate, such as the demand voiced during the Korean War for a reduction in the military commitment to Europe, and the support of many Democratic Party activists for Senator McGovern's 'Come Home, America' call in the early 1970s.

More recently, since the collapse of the Soviet Union, anti-interventionist arguments of a more traditional kind have been advanced by the conservative Pat Buchanan, who supported the containment of **communism**, but maintains that more recent American wars, such as those against Iraq, serve no American interest. Some commentators even dubbed the early attitudes of President George W. Bush 'isolationist', but this was surely a misdescription. He did at one stage suggest a more 'humble' foreign policy, and showed himself sceptical about or opposed to various international treaties, but this is a long way from isolationism. The term 'unilateralism' may be more appropriate, implying readiness to act without the endorsement of allies or international bodies, rather than the relative disengagement implied by 'isolationism'.

Further reading

Adler, S. (1966) *The Isolationist Impulse,* New York: The Free Press.

Cole, W. S. (1983) *Roosevelt and the Isolationists, 1932–45,* Lincoln: University of Nebraska Press.

Jonas, M. (1990) *Isolationism in America 1935–1941,* Chicago: Imprint Publications.

Radosh, R. (1978) *Prophets on the Right: Profiles of Conservative Critics of American Globalism,* New York: Free Life.

See also: containment; liberal internationalism; multilateralism

JOHN CHIDDICK and
BRENDON O'CONNOR

J

Just war

The term is used in two senses. In one, more general sense, it means 'morally justified **war**', a subject admitting of a wide range of views. In the second, narrow sense, it refers to one particular view on the morality of war, just war theory. This entry discusses just war in each of these senses in turn.

Main views on the morality of war

War gives rise to two moral questions: What are the conditions of a morally justified recourse to war? What is morally legitimate to do in the course of fighting a war? Just war theory provides the heading *jus ad bellum* (justice of war) for the former and *jus in bello* (justice in war) for the latter. These headings are thought to be useful even by those who do not subscribe to the theory, and have long been in general use. Any theory of the morality of war needs to give an account of both *jus ad bellum* and *jus in bello*.

There is, however, an approach to the morality of war that stands outside of any classification of positions within the ethics of war. That is **realism**, the view that there is no such thing as the ethics of war, since war is not subject to moral judgment and regulation. This view may be held as part of a more comprehensive conception of international relations as but a **balance of power**, beyond moral evaluation and restraint. Alternatively, the claim may be that while morality may have a role in international relations in peacetime, war is an exception. It is an extreme condition where the most basic **national interest**s and often the very survival of states are at stake. It is also the realm of extreme violence that, once unleashed, cannot be restrained until it runs its course.

Still, the distinction between *jus ad bellum* and *jus in bello* makes it possible to distinguish two varieties of the realist approach to war. The comprehensive variety puts both the ways and means of waging war and the decision to go to war beyond moral judgment. The restricted variety is captured in the phrase 'war is hell'. It allows for moral considerations with regard to recourse to war, but rejects the notion that, once started, war must be fought in accordance with rules enjoined by morality. Attempts at restricting warfare by means of such rules are considered misguided and counterproductive, as they get in the way of bringing the war to as quick and satisfactory a conclusion as possible.

Realist authors tend to be long on assertion but short on argument. It is difficult to make a good case for a position that flies in the face of human experience throughout history. Wars have always been criticized and defended in unmistakably moral terms. Those responsible for making war have tried to show that they had a just cause, while their critics have tried to rebut those claims. And both warriors and others have judged acts of war, as well as tactics and strategies, in terms of some conception of the warrior's honor or the civilized, morally defensible way of fighting. Some of this **discourse** may be hypocritical; but even the need for hypocrisy shows the importance of moral judgment of war.

Other views consider war a proper subject of moral judgment, but differ on what that judgment is. For **pacifism**, moral judgment of war is clearly and emphatically negative: war is extremely wrong and must not be waged. 'Pacifism' covers a range of views differing both in regard to what is being rejected and in regard to the argument leading to the rejection. The most sweeping type of pacifism finds all violence morally unacceptable. A less sweeping version objects only to state violence, while allowing that violence in individual self-defense, for example, may be morally legitimate. Yet another, even more narrowly focused variety of pacifism rejects war, while leaving room for other types of state violence, for instance in law enforcement. The nature of the opposition to violence or war differs too.

Absolute pacifism rejects one or the other in principle, under any circumstances. Some of the arguments in support of this rejection point at what violence or war does: at the killing, maiming, and destruction it involves. Other arguments focus on long-term effects of violence or war upon individuals and society. Contingent pacifism allows that war may be justified under certain circumstances, but argues that while such circumstances may have obtained in the past, they no longer do in our time. The indiscriminate character of modern military technology in general and of **weapons of mass destruction** in particular, as well as the tendency of modern war to evolve into 'total war' that resists any moral or legal regulation, make it virtually impossible to wage war in accordance with the rules laid down in *jus in bello*. Just war belongs to the past.

Opponents of pacifism find it a noble, but unrealistic position. Some argue that absolute pacifism is plagued by a contradiction: it is an opposition to violence so simplistic and sweeping that it rules out violence necessary to oppose and defeat unprovoked, aggressive, and unrelenting violence, and therefore in effect, if not in intent, gives passive support to such violence. This argument does not withstand critical scrutiny. Absolute pacifism rules out violent response to violence, or the waging of war of defense against aggression, but at the same time enjoins non-violent resistance to it. But a weaker version of this objection has considerable force. Advocates of absolute pacifism bring up cases such as Gandhi's non-violent campaign against British rule in India as proof that non-violence can succeed. Their critics need not deny that; they point out that the prospects of non-violent resistance depend on just what is being resisted. A non-violent strategy that succeeded against the British in India would not have been very effective in the face of Nazi aggression or Greater Serbian **'ethnic cleansing'**.

Another criticism of pacifism aims at both its absolute and contingent varieties: absolute pacifism is oblivious to the moral difference between killing human beings and killing *innocent* human beings (noncombatants, civilians), while contingent pacifism is too quick to despair of the possibility of observing this distinction in contemporary warfare. That makes both types of pacifists, in effect if not in intent, complicit in the rampant skepticism concerning moral constraints on warfare. The military, in particular, are not at all tempted to embrace pacifism. But they are often ready to accept the suggestion that the distinction between killing *simpliciter* and killing innocent people need not or no longer can be observed, and to proceed to kill as many of the latter as they feel they need to in pursuit of victory.

Pacifism is a position on the morality of war, but does not really offer much in the way of an ethics of war. The ethics of war is based on the view that some wars, and some acts of war, tactics, and strategies, are morally justified and others are not, and offers a criterion or criteria for distinguishing between the two. It reflects the basic division in ethics into *consequentialism* and *nonconsequentialism*, and is readily divided into consequentialist ethics of war and just war theory.

Consequentialism is an ethical theory that grounds moral judgment of actions, policies, and practices exclusively on the balance of their good and bad consequences. Consequentialist ethics of war is but an application of this general approach to moral issues to do with war. It settles both the question of recourse to war and the question of ways and means of fighting in war by looking into the good and bad consequences of various options and choosing the one that can be expected to have the best, or least bad, consequences for all those concerned.

Consequentialism is exposed to two standard objections: it is overly permissive, and often misses what everyone but the consequentialist sees as the crux of the matter. It denies that actions, policies, and practices are right or wrong in themselves, and ascribes the moral force of moral rules to the good consequences of their adoption. When its consequentialist justification does not apply, a moral rule – say, that of promise-keeping –

no longer binds; we are permitted, and indeed enjoined, to break it, when that is the option with the best consequences. And by focusing on consequences and advising us to break a promise because that is the option with the best consequences, consequentialism ignores the intrinsic significance of what is surely the central moral consideration in the case at hand, namely the simple fact that we made that promise.

The same problems arise in consequentialist ethics of war. It is too permissive with regard to the rules of warfare, and it often ignores what everyone but the consequentialist holds to be the central moral consideration. The prohibition of deliberately targeting noncombatants, for instance, is seen as a useful rule since its adoption reduces the killing, maiming, and destruction in war. But in cases where observing the rule will not have the best consequences, and where, on the contrary, attacking enemy noncombatants will have better consequences than either attacking enemy combatants or doing nothing, we are permitted and indeed advised to attack them. Thus noncombatants are made hostage to the vagaries of war, rather than protected by an extremely strong moral prohibition. And with regard to their immunity, too, the consequentialist misses what anyone else, and in particular a noncombatant in wartime, considers the central, decisive point. Faced with the prospect of being killed or maimed by enemy fire, a noncombatant will surely not make her case in terms of disutility of killing and maiming noncombatants in general, or of killing or maiming her then and there. She will rather point out that she is a civilian, not a soldier; a bystander, not a participant; an innocent, not a guilty party. She will protest that she has done nothing to deserve such a fate. Such arguments, couched in personal terms and relating to the past and present, seem to be much more to the point than the impersonal calculations of future consequences, by means of which the consequentialist proposes to settle the matter.

Consequentialist ethics of war does not lack adherents; but the other main position in the ethics of war, just war theory, has been much more influential both in philosophy and political and legal theory, and in the shaping of laws and customs of war. It offers a more complex account of what it takes for recourse to war to be morally legitimate, and what it is to wage war in a morally defensible way. The remainder of this entry deals with this theory.

Just war theory

The central tenet of any non-consequentialist is the rejection of consequentialism. That, of course, is not tantamount to denying that consequences of our actions, policies, and practices matter to their moral evaluation. What is denied is the consequentialist's claim that *only* consequences matter. Nonconsequentialist ethics takes into account good and bad consequences of action; but it also takes into account justice and rights as considerations different from, and irreducible to, the good and bad consequences of acting justly or unjustly, or of respecting or violating rights. Consequentialism is a monistic ethical theory; nonconsequentialism is pluralistic.

Just war theory provides an alternative to consequentialist ethics of war. While the latter seeks to couch, and settle, all moral questions concerning war – those of *jus ad bellum* and those of *jus in bello* – in terms of consequences of one's options, just war theory takes into account those consequences, as well as an array of considerations of a different order: the justice or injustice of various courses of action, individual and group rights that will be respected or violated, and the way in which certain harms will be brought about: with or without intent.

There is also an important structural difference between the two approaches. In consequentialist ethics of war, issues of *jus ad bellum* and those of *jus in bello* are of a piece; the division is one of convenience. In just war theory the two prongs are related, but logically independent, each with its own set of moral requirements. A nation at war may live up to both, or only one of them, or neither. Its recourse to war may be justified and it may fight 'clean', in accordance with the rules of war. It may lack justification for resorting to war, and compound the wrong of going to war for no good moral reason by fighting 'dirty', in disregard of the rules of war. It may be justified in going to war, but compromises its cause by fighting 'dirty'. Or it may go to war without justification for doing so, but at least fights 'clean'. It is only in the first of these cases that a nation's war will be fully morally justified. Historically, however, wars that were justified in terms of both *jus ad bellum* and *jus in bello* have been quite rare.

The historical sources of just war theory include Christian philosophers St. Augustine (354–430) and St Thomas Aquinas (1225–74), and political and legal thinkers such as Francisco de Vitoria (1480–1546), Francisco Suarez (1548–1617), Hugo Grotius (1583–1645), and Emmerich Vattel (1714–67). Over its long history, some of its central notions have undergone significant change, while others have remained much the same. Some of the tenets of the theory have been accepted as part of international laws and customs of war in legal documents such as the Hague Conventions (1899, 1907), the Geneva Conventions (1929, 1949), and the Geneva Protocols (1977).

Just war theory: *jus ad bellum*

The first prong of the theory sets down six requirements. Resort to war is justified:

1. if the cause is just and
2. the intention right;
3. if the decision is made and declared by a legitimate authority and
4. as a last resort;
5. if there is reasonable hope of success, and
6. if the harm caused by war will be proportionate to the benefits achieved (the proportionality clause of *jus ad bellum*).

The first and most important requirement is that of just cause. It has undergone considerable change over time, but this change has taken place under a single heading. For any version of just war theory, to have a just cause for going to war means to be responding in some appropriate way to a grave injustice.

In medieval and early modern statements of the theory, the idea of war as punishment for grave wrongdoing figures prominently, although not as the only just cause. St Augustine took the two causes acknowledged by Roman law, defense against aggression and retrieval of property unjustly taken, and added a third: punishment for wrongdoing. St Thomas combined the distinctively Augustinian notion of war as punishment for wrongdoing with the idea of self-defense of the community. So did Vitoria and Suarez. Subsequently, however, this understanding of war as, at least in part, punishment for wrongdoing, came to be discarded. By the times of Grotius and Vattel, it was replaced by defense against aggression as the central, and eventually sole just cause for going to war. The injustice that provides the just cause for war is that of aggression; the appropriate response to it is defense. In the aftermath of World War Two, this view was codified in the Charter of the **United Nations**: the Charter expressly restricts legitimate resort to war to national defense against aggression. The unduly narrow focus on already existing states was later corrected by acknowledging the right of peoples under foreign rule to liberation through armed struggle. Such struggle, too, can be seen as communal self-defense.

The understanding of just cause as defense raises an array of questions. One has to do with the moral foundations of this principle. A state has a just cause for war when it falls victim of grave injustice. This happens when its **sovereignty** or territorial integrity – paramount prerogatives of an independent state – come under attack. Such attack is unjust because a nation has a right to **self-determination**, and that normally amounts to a right to statehood, state sovereignty, and territorial integrity. Are these rights to be understood as collective rights of states, and thus the starting point of just war theory, as some **communitarian** thinkers hold? Or are they to be grounded in the rights of individuals who comprise the state, of citizens of the polity – most likely in the rights of individuals to life and liberty, which generate their rights to *common* life and liberty, and to a patch of land where their common life can take root and common liberty can be exercised – as liberals tend to argue?

Another issue is whether virtually any state is to be accorded such rights and accordingly has just cause for war when subject to aggression, or only states that live up to certain moral standards qualify. Proponents of just war theory who tend to rely on the existing world **order**, such as Michael Walzer (2000), advance the former view. Others, who hark back to earlier statements of the theory and put more emphasis on its critical potential, like A. J. Coates (1997), take the latter approach.

If only aggression provides just cause for war, must a state wait to be attacked before it can legitimately use military force? Just war theory does not countenance preventive war, but some of its advocates permit **pre-emptive use of force**. While the former seeks to anticipate and frustrate a threat of aggression expected at some, possibly distant, point in the future, the latter aims at defeating aggression that has not yet begun, but is clearly imminent.

Finally, defense against aggression is normally self-defense, but it can also be defense of others – of another state, or population, that is victim of aggression and unable to defend itself. Just war theory allows for **humanitarian intervention** beyond the state's borders.

The first, paramount condition for a recourse to war to be justified is that of a just cause. But it is not enough that such a cause should obtain; it must also be the reason for going to war. Only then will the war be declared and waged with the right intention. If a state as a matter of fact has a just cause but that cause is only a pretext, while it goes to war in order to expand its borders or to gain some economic advantage, its war will not be justified, for the right intention will be lacking. Some authors hold that this rules out any intention beyond that of vindicating the just cause; others argue for a less restrictive interpretation.

If resorting to war is to be morally legitimate, the decision to do so must be made and declared in an appropriate way. Not anyone – any individual or group – can do that. Only the highest authorities of a state, authorized to decide in matters of war and peace, can do so. This, at least, used to be the standard understanding of the requirement of legitimate **authority** from the early state-

ments of just war theory in the Middle Ages to (roughly) the mid-twentieth century. It was assumed that war is always a conflict of states. But, as civil wars and wars of liberation from foreign rule show, that need not be the case. Nor will it do to relegate all such wars beyond the realm of moral and legal regulation; that would indicate an overly statist approach. More recent interpretations accordingly allow sub-state parties to claim the status of morally legitimate belligerents. If, say, a liberation movement is representative of the population on whose behalf it sets out to fight, if it is organized in a way that provides for a chain of command and responsibility and enables it to make good on its commitments – things taken for granted with regard to states – then it may have a good case to be recognized as a belligerent party, and its leadership may qualify as legitimate authority so far as resort to war is concerned.

The first three requirements of *jus ad bellum* relate to the justice of a decision to go to war; the next three relate to consequences of such a decision. Even if it would be just to go to war because the cause is just, the intention right, and the decision made by a legitimate authority, if the consequences of going to war will be worse than those of not doing so, the decision to go to war will not be morally justified. There is more to the morality of war than its justice. If war is not the last resort since the aims sought could also be attained by peaceful means, such as diplomacy or political or economic pressure; or if the war stands no reasonable chance of success; or if, even if the war is won, the price of victory will be too high, then going to war is neither rational nor morally justified.

While the last resort clause will often not be very hard to satisfy, the application of the other two clauses concerning the consequences of war will frequently prove difficult. For both 'success' and 'balance of good and bad consequences' of a war may be interpreted in various ways. As soon as these notions include not only military and civilian casualties and economic gains and losses, but also imponderables such as a state's sovereignty or territorial integrity, the aggregation and balancing of consequences becomes an extremely complex task. How many human lives, for instance, is a reasonable and morally acceptable price to pay for defending national independence? These difficulties are compounded by the need to consider not only gains and losses to one's own state, but also those to the enemy, as well as to any third parties that may be involved. For just war theory is not about the wisdom of going to war, but about the morality of doing so; and the moral point of view is not that of one's own nation, but of humanity.

Just war theory: *jus in bello*

The second prong of just war theory, too, addresses both issues of justice and rights and those of good and bad consequences. It lays down two requirements, two rules of war. An act of war, a tactic, or a strategy is morally justified:

1. if it respects noncombatant immunity (the principle of discrimination); and
2. if the harm it causes will be proportionate to the military aim achieved (the proportionality clause of *jus in bello*).

The latter clause is relatively straightforward, at least in theory, if not in practice. Proportionality figures in both prongs of just war theory. Whereas *jus ad bellum* enjoins that the harm caused by war be proportionate to the benefit achieved by it, the proportionality requirement in *jus in bello* relates to the harm inflicted and military advantage gained by particular acts of war, tactics, and strategies. It rules out gratuitous or excessive employment of military force. This requirement, too, refers not only to loss and advantage to one's own forces, but also to the harm inflicted on enemy forces, enemy noncombatants, and enemy economy and society; for this, too, is a mandate of morality, rather than counsel of sheer prudence.

Noncombatant immunity is a more complex matter. This is a central tenet in any ethics of war and in the laws and customs of war. Both seek to limit the killing and destruction inherent to war, and accord immunity from harm to those who are not involved in the waging of war and therefore do not constitute a legitimate target of deadly violence: noncombatants, civilians, the innocent. In just war theory one finds differing views on the best wording, on the scope of the class of those protected, and even, albeit to a lesser degree, on the ground of the immunity.

The terms 'noncombatants' and 'civilians' overlap to a large extent, but not completely: the former, but not the latter, applies to medical personnel in the armed forces and military chaplains, and therefore seems preferable. But any wording will generate problematic cases: are soldiers on leave, or civilians working in arms production, to be granted immunity? A deeper disagreement concerns the basis of this immunity. Some reference to 'innocence' might be thought inevitable, but this term can be taken in two senses. Its etymological meaning is *innocentes*, Latin for 'not harming', i.e. not engaged in fighting or in supplying those who fight with the means of fighting. This has nothing to do with individual responsibility for taking part in fighting or for the war being fought; 'innocence' lacks its ordinary, moral content, and serves as a technical term. According to the mainstream view in just war theory, this understanding of 'innocence' provides just the right scope of noncombatant immunity: only soldiers and workers in arms and ammunition production are legitimate targets in war, while everyone else has a right not to be attacked. This conception is also enshrined in the **international law** of war.

If 'innocence' were taken in a moral sense, implying lack of responsibility for the fighting, that might restrict the class of those who can claim immunity in at least two ways. Some noncombatants in a country waging a war of aggression might be considered responsible bystanders who can, and therefore ought to, help prevent or put an end to the aggression. If they fail to do so, they become complicit in it, perhaps to a degree that makes them, too, legitimate targets of military attack. That might especially be the case in democracies, whose citizens have ways and means of influencing government policies. Moreover, democracy is based on popular sovereignty; the military and the government do not act on their own, but on behalf of the people, as its agents. That in itself might be thought to implicate democratic citizens in their country's unjust war, possibly to a degree that makes them legitimate targets of military attack. To be sure, both lines of argument suggest that attacking noncombatants of the relevant type might be legitimate only on the further condition that doing so serves a sufficiently important military purpose. Modern just war theory, unlike its medieval and early modern versions, does not understand war as punishment of the guilty, but as defense against aggression. Even so, most of its adherents today would resist

these arguments, and keep to the former, technical conception of 'innocence'.

Except when fought at sea or in a desert, modern war always harms noncombatants. If noncombatant immunity were taken to refer to any harm, however caused, that would rule out virtually all war. Just war theory draws on the doctrine of double effect, developed in Catholic ethics, and takes noncombatant immunity to refer to harm inflicted with intent. Harm to noncombatants is permissible when it is a foreseen, but not intended effect of an act of war and when it is proportionate to the importance of the military objective. Michael Walzer (2000) adds the proviso that soldiers must do their utmost to reduce this harm to a minimum, and must be willing to take risks to life and limb in doing so.

Prospects

Just war theory is the most important theoretical account of the moral import of, and constraints upon, war. It has informed international laws of war and made an invaluable contribution to attempts at containing the killing, mayhem, and destruction involved in war. But there are doubts concerning its present and future relevance. Military technology is becoming ever more destructive. Social and political developments making for 'total war' – war of total mobilization of society and total attack on enemy society – seem very difficult to resist. **Terrorism** has become an international, indeed global menace. Ethnic wars of the 1990s and some of the rhetoric of the 'war against terror' seem to indicate a revival of the punitive understanding of war coupled with crude, premodern notions of collective responsibility. In view of these developments, some argue that just war theory no longer has much application.

Its insistence on proportionality, discrimination, or legitimate authority can no longer be heeded.

Many would contest these claims. Yet even if they are granted, there are two very different conclusions that might be drawn. One is that just war *theory* has failed and is now a thing of the past, and that we must reconcile ourselves to a world in which war, when it breaks out, takes us beyond all moral restraint and concern. The other is that just war theory still offers the correct account of the morality of war. If the nature of war and society have indeed changed so much that its prescriptions and prohibitions can no longer be observed in a sustained and effective way, that means that just and morally justified *war* is a thing of the past and that we must wage war no longer. In this way, just war theory can turn out to be a roundabout way of reaching the conclusion enjoined by contingent pacifism.

Further reading

Coates, A. J. (1997) *The Ethics of War*, Manchester: Manchester University Press.

Coppieters, B. and Fotion, N. (eds) (2002) *Moral Constraints on War: Principles and Cases*, Lanham: Lexington Books.

Gilbert, M. (2003) *New Terror, New Wars*, Edinburgh: Edinburgh University Press.

Holmes, R. L. (1989) *On War and Morality*, Princeton, NJ: Princeton University Press.

McKeogh, C. (2002) *Innocent Civilians: The Morality of Killing in War*, Basingstoke: Palgrave.

Norman, R. (1995) *Ethics, Killing and War*, Cambridge: Cambridge University Press.

Primoratz, I. (2005) 'Civilian Immunity in War', *The Philosophical Forum* 36(1), 41–58.

Walzer, M. (2000) *Just and Unjust Wars: A Moral Argument with Historical Illustrations*, 3rd edn, New York, Basic Books.

See also: humanitarian intervention; pacifism; pre-emptive use of force; realism; war; Westphalia

IGOR PRIMORATZ

K

Kyoto Protocol

An agreement signed by 160 countries in 1997 committing industralized states to reduce emissions of greenhouse gases, principally carbon dioxide, by around 5.2 per cent below 1990 levels over a five-year period (2008–12). The initiation and consequent amendments of the Protocol have resulted from significant international negotiation and debate, fuelled primarily by the scientific uncertainty surrounding the links between greenhouse gas emissions and **global warming**. Questions concerning the cost effectiveness of implementing the Protocol remain unanswered which is the principle issue for non-ratification by some of the larger greenhouse gas emitters, specifically the United States, the Russian Federation, and Australia. Non-participation by these states places the success of the current policy framework in jeopardy, requiring new approaches to address this problem, which is unquestionably the greatest environmental challenge to face international policymakers to date.

International discussion around the topic of global warming began in earnest in 1992, at the **United Nations** Earth Summit in Rio de Janeiro, in response to the scientific evidence of the potential enhancement of global warming due to anthropogenic greenhouse gas emissions presented by the Intergovernmental Panel on Climate Change (IPCC). The outcome of the Earth Summit was the United Nations Framework Convention on Climate Change (UNFCCC): a landmark, but non-binding agreement that aimed to stabilize greenhouse gas emissions by industrialized countries (listed in annex I to the Convention) at 1990 levels by the year 2000.

To achieve this target the agreement required signatories to 'adopt national policies and take corresponding measures on the mitigation of climate change'. The framework agreement was signed by 186 countries, including the United States, and was adopted in 1992. As an instrument to mitigate climate change the UNFCCC failed. Few policies were implemented and in the period to 2000 greenhouse gas emissions rose rather than decreased. The UNFCCC did however establish the mechanism for the negotiation of climate change policy to continue, termed the 'Conference of the Parties' (COP) meetings.

At the first Conference of the Parties (COP1) held in Berlin in 1995 it was recognized that commitments identified in the UNFCCC were insufficient for the Convention to succeed. The resulting 'Berlin Mandate' established a process of review to 'set quantified emission limitation and reduction objectives' (QELROs) for annex I parties. In addition, the decision was made that negotiations should not introduce any new commitments for non-annex I countries, in recognition of the fact that developing countries had made a minimal contribution to atmospheric concentrations of greenhouse gases and that imposed emissions restrictions would negatively impact on social and **development** needs. COP2, held in Geneva in 1996, identified the additional need to identify specific time frames for emissions reduction targets.

COP3 was held in Kyoto in December in 1997. The outcome of this meeting, after 72 hours of negotiations, was the Kyoto Protocol: a binding treaty with explicit reduction targets and associated time frames for the thirty-nine countries listed in annex I. On average, reduction targets equated to 5.2 per cent below levels in 1990. Individual parties negotiated country specific targets in order to address varying national circumstances. For example, the United States committed to a 7 per cent reduction while Japan's target was 6 per cent to reflect decreases in emissions prior to 1990 due to the adoption of energy efficient technology. Australia set its cap at an 8 per cent increase based on the argument that its high dependency on coal power would make reductions difficult. The agreed non-uniform targets had to be accomplished within the 'commitment period' of 2008–12. The Protocol covered emissions of four gases: carbon dioxide (CO_2), methane (CH_4), nitrous oxide (N_2O), sulphur hexafluoride (SF_6) and two halocarbons: hydrofluorocarbons (HFCs) and perfluorocarbons (PHCs). Targets could be met by a mix of carbon-equivalent reductions in these scheduled compounds.

The initial design of the Protocol was intentionally flexible in terms of potential compliance mechanisms. Nationally, reduction strategies were completely at the discretion of individual countries and included the provision for emissions to be offset by the development of domestic 'sinks' which reduced atmospheric carbon dioxide concentration through positive land-use change and forestry (LUCF) activities. Internationally three innovative mechanisms were developed. The first two are market-based (emissions trading and project-based credit trading) and allow annex I countries to buy, sell or trade greenhouse gas reductions and emission allowances. The third strategy is the Clean Development Mechanism (CDM) which allows annex I parties to offset domestic emissions with carbon credits earned from emissions-reduction projects in non-annex I (developing) countries. The aim of CDM is to assist developing countries to achieve **sustainable development** by promoting technological knowledge transfer and environmental friendly investment from the governments and private sectors of industrialized countries. These mechanisms may be the key to the success of the Protocol, however there are concerns regarding the transfer of domestic responsibilities to the international market place and the potential exploitation of developing states involved in CDM projects.

Subsequent COP meetings have focused on the need to identify the operational details of the Protocol that were not discussed in the 1997 Protocol negotiations. Specifically, these refer to issues surrounding standardizing emissions-measurement techniques, monitoring compliance, penalties for non-compliance, and the role of developing countries in CDM projects. The negotiation process was severely slowed in March 2001 when President George W. Bush announced that the United States would withdraw from the Protocol on the grounds that compliance would damage the US domestic economy. After some hesitation negotiations continued and the 'Kyoto rulebook' was finally agreed upon at COP7 in Marrakech in

November 2001. The effectiveness of these measures has yet to be tested.

The loss of the United States has put the future of the Protocol in significant jeopardy. The United States, after all, is responsible for 36 per cent of global greenhouse gas emissions. The reasons for non-ratification by the United States are purely economic. The United States is particularly concerned about the potential economic advantage that would be enjoyed by annex II countries such as China. In addition, the uncertainly surrounding the science of global warming means that human benefits of compliance cannot be measured, in contrast to the costs of compliance. The implementation of climate changes policies therefore requires investment in future contingencies rather than present realities, which represents a challenging policy decision for any head of state.

Although the shortcomings of the Protocol are easy to identify, it is important to recognize that even without ratification, the ongoing negotiations surrounding the Kyoto Protocol have successfully placed climate change policy in the domain of the global agenda. This has resulted in increased individual, NGO (see **non-governmental organization**) and private sector participation in emissions reduction activities. The solution to the apparent current deadlock may therefore be to explore mechanistic alternatives that incorporate private sector and NGO involvement in CDM and innovative technology activities. In addition, the initial 'precautionary principle' adopted by the UNFCCC in 1997, which required a focus on halting climate change rather than adapting to changing conditions, may no longer be realistic.

Further reading

Boehmer-Christiansen, S. and Kellow, A. (2002) *International Environmental Policy: Interests and the Failure of the Kyoto Process.* Cheltenham: Edward Elgar.

Grubb, M., Vrolijk, C. and Brack D. (eds) (1999) *The Kyoto Protocol: A Guide and Assessment,* London: Earthscan.

McKibbin, W. J. and Wilcoxen, P. J. (2002) Climate change policy after Kyoto, Washington, DC: Brookings.

Victor, D. G. (2001) *The Collapse of the Kyoto Protocol and the Struggle to Slow Global Warming,* Princeton, NJ: Princeton University Press.

See also: chlorofluorocarbons; global warming; ozone depletion

RAECHEL L. WATERS

L

Labor internationalism

The forging of ties across national borders between unions and/or rank-and-file workers to achieve a range of goals, varying from good collective bargaining agreements to social change. Labor internationalism has a long history, whether through such organizations as the International Working Men's Association (First International) or between specific unions. For example, in 1899 Australian unions sent £30,000 to support striking British dockworkers.

The recent history of unionism in the developed world, particularly in the United States, is a history of business unionism. Business unionism is concerned with narrowly defined 'bread and butter' issues, such as union members' wages and working conditions. Business unionism is primarily concerned with the welfare of local unionized workers to the detriment of workers worldwide. The **nationalism** of the US union movement was especially rampant during the **cold war** as the American Federation of Labor-Congress of Industrial Organizations (AFL-CIO) was an ally of the US government in its fight against **communism**.

However, business unionism could not deal with the attack on the 'social contract' by employers and the government beginning in the United States in the late 1970s following the ascendancy of **neoliberalism**. Over the past couple of decades, there has been a significant decline in US workers' wages and conditions in real terms. For example, between 1980 and 1996, the total share of income of the bottom 60 per cent of Americans fell from 34.2 per cent to 30 per cent. In addition to declining workers' wages, there has been a dramatic decline in union membership. Unions only represent 12.9 per cent of the US workforce compared to 26 per cent in 1973. While not as pronounced, union membership declined significantly in many other countries.

In recent years a number of scholars have argued that if unions engage in labor internationalism they may be able to renew their lost influence. It is important to note, however, that while some union leaders now argue that unions should adopt an international strategy, many activists have been arguing this case for a number of years.

The AFL-CIO's current international strategy demonstrates the shift in policy of unions and labor federations since the end of the cold war. During the cold war, the AFL-CIO was an ally of the US government in its fight against communism. This led the AFL-CIO to attempt to destabilize leftist overseas unions in countries such as Brazil, Chile and El Salvador. Moreover, in Chile as well as Brazil, the AFL-CIO helped to organize fascist coups against existing governments.

However, since the late 1980s, with the collapse of communism and the growth of **globalization**, the AFL-CIO is starting to develop an international focus. For example, the AFL-CIO has sent delegations to South Africa to meet union officials who, in the past, they would have accused as being communists. Likewise, since the election of John Sweeney as President in 1995, the AFL-CIO has begun to support independent trade unions in Mexico, something that would have been unthinkable under the previous administration.

Labor internationalism, in addition to forging solidarity between workers worldwide, has led to unions attaining better collective bargaining agreements than might otherwise have been achieved. For example, as part of its campaign against the United Parcel Service (UPS) in 1997, the International Brotherhood of Teamsters sought to build international alliances. This was partly because UPS was planning to expand its overseas operations. International support came from Belgium, Germany, Italy, and Spain and helped the Teamsters achieve a remarkable victory.

Furthermore, workers worldwide, particularly in Mexico, have benefited because of the increasing international activities of unions. The United Electrical, Radio and Machine Workers of America (UE) is arguably at the forefront of labor internationalism in the United States. Since 1992, the UE has maintained a strategic alliance with the Mexican labor federation *Frente Autenico del Trabajo* (Authentic Labor Front (FAT)). The alliance was formed in response to **multinational corporation**s (MNCs) moving their production plants from the United States to Mexico. While of course there is self-interest involved in the UE's commitment to the principle of international solidarity, this is not its only concern in sustaining such alliances. The UE

argues that corporate globalization will lead to a global 'race to the bottom', with no concerns for labor and the environment. The UE provided FAT with financial support, research capability, and rank-and-file action in the United States in support of Mexican organizing drives. In return, FAT has helped the UE in its campaigns in the United States.

Nevertheless, it remains the case that most unions that engage in labor internationalism do so on the basis of self-interest. For example, despite the positive changes within the AFL-CIO, it still primarily focuses on American workers. Nonetheless, as part of its internationalist strategy, the AFL-CIO has begun to address the role of international economic institutions. For example, the AFL-CIO argues that the **World Trade Organization** (WTO) should enforce workers' rights by the use of 'side agreements' in all **free trade** negotiations. On the other hand, John Sweeney has endorsed the US government's goals for ongoing WTO talks, which include the opening up of overseas markets. In other words, Sweeney hopes that greater overseas market access for US corporations will ultimately benefit US workers. This expression of business unionism demonstrates that the AFL-CIO has not entirely broken away from its past.

Likewise, in its opposition to the **North American Free Trade Agreement** (NAFTA), the AFL-CIO argued that the Agreement would result in US job losses to Mexico. It is examples like these that have led some overseas unions to question the AFL-CIO's internationalist stance. Moreover, the AFL-CIO still undermines overseas unions and governments. For example, in Russia during 1999 the AFL-CIO's Free Trade Institute collaborated with the US coal industry to weaken Russian trade unions in an effort to broker a new coal policy that would benefit US corporations. More recently, since

2003 the AFL-CIO through its 'Solidarity Center' has been attempting to destabilize the Venezuelan government.

These examples demonstrate that it would be a mistake for rank-and-file workers to totally rely on unions and official international labor bodies (such as the International Trade Secretariats, which are federations of national unions, or the International Council of Free Trade Unions) to promote more effective labor internationalism. Most existing Western unions are bureaucratic in nature, and are essentially business unions. Likewise, while the European Work Councils (the **European Union** requires businesses in more than one EU country to form Work Councils) can help facilitate an increase in cross-border contact between workers, they rely on the European Union for funding. It is doubtful whether the European Union would continue to fund Work Councils were they to engage in protracted campaigns against European MNCs.

In their book *Unions and Free Trade: Solidarity vs. Competition* (1992), Kim Moody and Mary McGinn outline six proposals to promote more effective forms of labor internationalism. They argue that a first step is for local unions to form an international solidarity committee. The committee would educate its members on the benefits of international solidarity, and form alliances with overseas unions and workers. Second, there is a need for a national grassroots network on free trade that would coordinate campaigns and help facilitate international contacts. Third, international union conferences could improve relations between unions in different countries. Fourth, unions should engage in industry-wide networks as many industries have production facilities in different countries. These networks could exchange information on issues such as wages and working conditions,

while developing common agendas for change. Fifth, unions that operate within MNCs should engage in internationally coordinated bargaining. The final step for an effective international solidarity is for rank-and-file workers to join unions that are effectively controlled by their members.

If unions and rank-and-file workers embrace this type of labor internationalism, they may yet regain some of the strength that has been lost through decades of business unionism.

Further reading

Breitenfellner, A. (1997) 'Global Unionism: A Potential Player', *International Labour Review* 136(4), 531–55.

Moody, K. (1997) *Workers in a Lean World*, Verso, London.

Moody, K. and McGinn, M. (1992) *Unions and Free Trade: Solidarity vs. Competition*, Detroit, MI: Labor Notes.

O'Brien, R. (2000) 'Workers and world order: the tentative transformation of the international union movement', *Review of International Studies* 26, 533–55.

Waterman, P. (1998) *Globalisation, Social Movements and the New Internationalisms*, London: Mansell.

See also: International Labor Organization; liberal internationalism; Marxism; transnational social movement

MICHAEL SCHIAVONE

Law of Peoples

In *The Law of Peoples* (1999), John Rawls (1921–2004), the pre-eminent liberal political philosopher of the twentieth century, argues for a set of basic normative principles to guide international relations. The distant ancestors of Rawls's law of peoples include the classical notion of *jus gentium* and the Christian concept of natural law, but

Rawls's focus is narrower than these. His central question is as follows: what principles would be acceptable to liberal democratic and non-liberal but 'decent' societies in their dealings with one another and with other societies? The rules he arrives at, and the method by which he justifies those rules, have provided a major focus of debate in recent international relations theory. In particular, critics have questioned Rawls's view that liberal states should refrain from challenging the values espoused by some non-liberal states, his refusal to extend to the international sphere the redistributive principles that he defends domestically, and his assumption that international norms should primarily address the well-being of societies rather than that of individual persons.

Rawls's argument

The starting point for Rawls is his famous account of domestic distributive justice in *A Theory of Justice* (1971). There he seeks principles of justice in the sharing out of a society's 'primary social goods' – its rights, liberties, income, wealth, and self-respect – that would inform the society's basic institutions and be acceptable to all of its citizens. His justificatory model is the social contract: the just principles would be those principles that free and rational people would choose under fair conditions. The fair conditions are represented by Rawls's classic device of the 'Original Position'. Here the parties know enough to choose rationally, but they are prevented by a 'veil of ignorance' from knowing certain things about their own situation – for example, their natural talents, income bracket and ideas about 'the good life' – that would tempt them to bias the choice of principles in their own favor. The Original Position thus ingeniously combines self-interested (or

mutually disinterested) motivation with impartiality. From this starting point, Rawls argues, the parties to his contract will choose two principles of justice, the first distributing rights and liberties equally among citizens, the second allowing social and economic inequality but only on condition:

1. that people be given 'fair equality of opportunity' to compete for the unequal rewards, and
2. that any such inequality work to the advantage of the least advantaged members of the society.

These two qualifications to inequality, in particular condition (2), the 'difference principle', suggest that the practical implementation of Rawls's domestic theory of justice will involve a very considerable degree of wealth transfer from the rich to the poor. Rawlsian domestic justice will be strongly, perhaps even radically, redistributive.

Rawls subjected his theory to a major revision in *Political Liberalism* (1993b). While the content and effect of the principles remained the same, he tried to amend their justification to meet complaints that his Original Position was not the impartial starting point he had claimed it to be. The critics alleged that Rawls's staring point concealed a bias in favor of liberal or individualist ways of life, implicit for example in the requirement that the parties to the contract put aside their cultural or religious beliefs when making their choice. In *Political Liberalism* Rawls replied that his theory was not intended to be universal but rather a theory of justice for a particular kind of political culture, namely that of constitutional democracies like those of the West. Within such a political culture, however, the acceptability of the Original Position did not depend on any particular 'comprehensive moral doctrine', such as liberalism. Rather, it could be understood as a point of 'overlapping consensus', that is, supported on the basis of many different streams within the larger culture. Rawls's position was thus restated as 'political' in two senses: it was local rather than universal, and it did not depend on any single comprehensive moral or religious doctrine. Its claims were therefore both more modest than they had seemed before, and more ecumenical.

Rawls first considered the international implications of his position in *A Theory of Justice*. There he argued that his contract methodology could be applied at the international level, but he also refrained from internationalizing his domestic principles of redistribution. Principles of international justice could be chosen from an original position in which the parties were 'representatives of nations' (1971: 378). These representatives would be subject to a veil of ignorance in which they were deprived of knowledge of the 'particular circumstances of their own society', modeling the same commitment to impartiality as in the domestic case. Unlike the domestic case, however, the international contract, Rawls believed, would yield a 'familiar' set of principles. The most central of these was the fundamental equality of 'independent peoples', who consequently possessed rights of **self-determination** and obligations of non-intervention in the affairs of other peoples, and duties of treaty keeping and **just war**. Conspicuous by their absence were any principles requiring justice in economic distribution. Rawls's assumption appeared to be that questions of distributive justice arose only within a 'scheme of social cooperation' in which people were engaged for mutual benefit, generating rights and duties in relation to the benefits available. While a domestic society counted as a cooperative enter-

prise, giving rise to claims of justice, there was no **international society** in quite the same terms. Distributive justice was appropriate to the internal affairs of independent peoples, but not to their international relations.

The view of international law sketched in *A Theory of Justice* was elaborated and developed by Rawls, first in his Oxford Amnesty Lecture (1993a) and later in *The Law of Peoples*. The latter contains his mature statement. The argument commences with a distinction between five types of society:

1. liberal peoples;
2. non-liberal but 'decent' peoples;
3. outlaw states;
4. burdened societies;
5. benevolent despotisms.

Rawls says little about the last of these. His concern is to show that a Law of Peoples can be formulated which is acceptable to both liberal and decent peoples, who together constitute the category of 'well-ordered' peoples, and who can thus join with one another in a law governed 'society of peoples'. Under current 'nonideal' conditions, however, not all societies are liberal or decent. Falling outside this group are outlaw states, which refuse to comply with the law of peoples, and burdened societies, which cannot comply because of their 'unfavorable conditions', in particular poverty. The law of peoples does not yet govern these societies in fact, but it is morally binding on them, and it prescribes the proper conduct of well-ordered peoples towards them.

As in *A Theory of Justice*, Rawls justifies his law of peoples by extending his contract method from the domestic to the international sphere. As before, he imagines an international original position in which the parties are representatives of 'peoples'. A 'people' is a society governed by just or decent institutions, united by a common culture, and willing to exercise reasonable restraint in its dealing with its own members and other societies. These parties will choose principles of international justice in the knowledge that all peoples have certain fundamental interests, including independence, culture, **security**, material well being and self-respect. But once again a veil of ignorance will prevent the parties from bias in favor of their own people. Rawls argues that they will agree, as before, to 'certain familiar principles of equality among peoples', including:

1. the freedom and independence of peoples;
2. treaty keeping;
3. equal moral and legal status of peoples;
4. non-intervention;
5. right of self defense;
6. honoring of human rights;
7. just war;
8. a duty of assistance for burdened societies (1999: 37).

To begin with, Rawls imagines that the parties to the international original position are representatives of liberal peoples. He then extends the contract to non-liberal but decent peoples, arguing that they too can accept the terms of the original position and, given that starting point, will choose the same principles as those acceptable to liberal peoples. 'Decent' societies are defined as less than fully just in liberal terms, but nevertheless meeting standards of minimal legitimacy. In particular, Rawls speaks of 'decent hierarchical societies' (1999: 64–7). Although not liberal, they are not aggressive or expansionist, they respect minimal standards of human rights, and they operate under a 'common good conception of justice' which

aims to take into account the interests of all the society's citizens. Although not wholly democratic, such societies typically involve a 'decent consultation hierarchy', under which the grievances of different groups are given a hearing. As suggested by Rawls's imaginary example of 'Kazanistan', he evidently has in mind moderate Islamic states among others. Clearly, he regards it as important that the law of peoples be acceptable to societies of this non-liberal kind as well as to liberal societies. This echoes the central concern of *Political Liberalism* that just institutions should, as far as possible, be justifiable on 'political' grounds rather than tied to a comprehensively liberal outlook that many people of good will do not share.

At this point Rawls has established the terms of a law of peoples to which well-ordered societies, whether liberal or decent, can be party. What about those societies that are not well-ordered, in particular outlaw and burdened societies? Such societies cannot be party to the law of peoples, but they are still bound by it. Further, Rawls is especially concerned to spell out the implications of the law for the way in which these societies should be treated by the well-ordered societies. The most general goal is to bring about a world in which all societies are well-ordered. How exactly this goal should be pursued, and with what qualifications, depends on the kind of non-well-ordered society one is dealing with.

First, Rawls considers outlaw states, those which refuse to comply with the law of peoples. The immediate concern of well-ordered societies in this case is self-defense, and so the law of peoples prescribes a right to **war** in self-defense for both liberal and decent peoples. Self-defense is the only justification for war; moreover, the conduct of war is subject to certain ethical restrictions, in particular relating to the proper treatment of civilian populations. Beyond self-defense, well-ordered societies can legitimately work to bring outlaw states into compliance with the law of peoples, for example by creating international institutions to expose and criticize violations of the law. The intransigently non-compliant may be subjected to deliberate pressure, in the form of rewards or penalties. This contrasts with Rawls's insistence that where non-liberal societies count as decent, liberal societies ought not to promote their liberalization as a matter of policy, even through the use of incentives. Finally, well-ordered societies may, in some cases, impose **sanctions** on outlaw states in order to prevent violations of **human rights**, and even, for the same reason, intervene in an outlaw state's territory.

Second, Rawls discusses burdened societies. In this case the society is unable to comply with the law of peoples because of 'unfavorable conditions' such as extreme poverty. 'Well-ordered peoples', Rawls argues, 'have a duty to assist burdened societies' (1999: 106). This goes further in the direction of redistribution than *A Theory of Justice*, which required no assistance at all, but Rawls is explicit that the duty to assist falls short of a principle of distributive justice. While international distributive justice would involve a principle permanently regulating the relative wealth of different societies, Rawls's 'duty to assist' aims only to ensure that each society has the capacity to be well-ordered. As soon as that target is reached, the duty to assist is discharged. In this connection, Rawls emphasizes his view that a society's economic and social health is determined more by its political culture than by its material resources. Some resource-rich societies fail to be well-ordered, while some well-ordered societies are resource poor. What matters crucially,

according to Rawls, are cultural values, for example attitudes to women. Material assistance, therefore, is not the most important factor in overcoming unfavorable conditions. Rawls also sees degrees of affinity among peoples as a 'legitimate concern' in motivating assistance, suggesting that societies cannot be expected automatically to help those with whom they have little in common. But he also notes that 'relations of affinity are not a fixed thing', but can be expanded (1999: 112).

In summary, Rawls presents a picture of the possibilities of international cooperation based on a liberal starting point, acceptable also to non-liberal but decent societies, and ultimately transmissible to currently outlaw and burdened societies. The overall vision is of a world of political societies, each internally well-ordered – although not necessarily liberal – and engaged in peaceful and just relations with others, although this does not necessarily involve economic equality. Rawls sums up his picture as a 'realistic utopia': utopian in the sense that it does not yet exist, but realistic in that it could do so given existing widely shared beliefs and motivations.

Critical responses

The most sophisticated critical responses to *The Law of Peoples* have come from Rawls's fellow liberals. Their comments fall into two broad schools. Some see Rawls's theory as a sensibly moderate approach to international relations, one that avoids demonizing all non-liberal regimes and is realistically wary of the justice and prospects of **foreign aid**. Others regard Rawls's global position as a betrayal of the fundamental values of liberalism and of his own earlier case for egalitarian justice in economic distribution. These accusations of betrayal have focused on two main aspects of the theory: his treatment of human rights, and his reluctance to globalize distributive justice.

Human rights

One basic complaint against Rawls is that the list of human rights protected by his law of peoples is too thin. Rawls is clear that the law of peoples does not recognize all those rights that would be defended by liberals, but only 'a special class of urgent rights, such as freedom from slavery and serfdom, liberty (but not equal liberty) of conscience, and security of ethnic groups from mass murder and **genocide**' (1999: 79). While liberals would applaud the list so far, they would also draw attention to what it leaves out: freedom of speech or expression, full and equal freedom of conscience (e.g. on religious questions), rights of democratic political participation, and equal treatment of the sexes. For many, if not most, liberals these goods are essential to the well being of all human individuals, and no adequate political theory can fail to stand up for them, not only domestically but also internationally.

The reason why Rawls's list of internationally recognized rights is so conservative is that he wants the law of peoples to be acceptable not only to liberals but also to non-liberal but decent peoples, in particular 'decent hierarchical societies'. Such societies do not accept the full list of liberal rights, and so could not be expected to agree to a law of peoples that insisted on the full list. Yet these societies 'do have certain institutional features that deserve respect', including recognition of the urgent rights mentioned, a common good conception of justice, and a decent consultation hierarchy (1999: 84). Rawls is not saying that such societies are the moral equals of liberal societies; on the contrary, he makes it clear that by liberal standards they are not fully just. But the 'decent' features that he emphasizes, taken together, bring these regimes closer to liberal societies than to outlaw states or burdened societies.

Still, many liberal critics maintain that Rawls is too generous to decent hierarchical societies, and that an adequately liberal view would not be so tolerant of them. First, it remains true, the critics would say, that Rawls's toleration of hierarchical societies licenses the oppression of the individual members of these societies. The full list of liberal human rights is in fact essential to a good life for any human being, and anything less is a serious limitation on the prospects for a person's well being. Women, in particular, are rendered vulnerable by hierarchical systems, their lack of legal, political and economic equality giving men the power to reduce their lives to subhuman levels (Nussbaum 2002: 283–5).

'Oppression' or 'subhuman' by what standards, however? Rawls would reply that we cannot simply assume the validity of specifically liberal standards, especially at the global level. While there may be some moral agreement among cultures, or 'comprehensive moral doctrines', moral disagreement is also widespread. Moreover, much of that disagreement comes down to the rival claims of general conceptions of the good life. At that level moral conflict is ineradicable because 'reasonable'. Even if one or more parties to a dispute in the field of morality is mistaken, it may still not be possible to demonstrate that mistake in terms that all the parties can accept. Reasonable disagreement of this deep kind is likely to be permanent in the absence of overwhelming force, and a humane politics will try to accommodate rather than overcome it. All this is true of moral conflict within liberal democratic societies, Rawls argues in *Political Liberalism*. The same reasonable disagreement over the good will be even more in evidence, he suggests, when it comes to global morality. Therefore, just as domestic political liberalism accommodates reasonable non-liberal moral doctrines, so too should the law of peoples accommodate moderate non-liberal societies.

However, a second objection to Rawls's toleration of decent non-liberal societies is that his international and domestic positions are not consistent after all. In the domestic case, in *Political Liberalism*, non-liberal practices are tolerated only in the private realm and only so far as they do not conflict with full liberal rights, which are guaranteed to all citizens. Under the law of peoples, however, the citizen of the decent hierarchical society is protected only by the thin list of 'urgent' rights. In addition, the decent consultation hierarchy will give a voice to dissenters, but not to the extent that dissent challenges the limited terms of the consultation process itself (Beitz 2000; Miller 2000). As Nussbaum points out, the effect of Rawls's view is that the same individuals will be treated very differently depending on whether they happen to be members of a subgroup within a state or citizens of an independent state (2002: 290–4). Why this difference? It results from Rawls's analogy between tolerating reasonable non-liberal moral doctrines in the domestic case and tolerating decent non-liberal societies in the international case. If liberals ought to tolerate non-liberal minorities within the liberal state, then they ought to tolerate similarly non-liberal societies outside the state. In the law of peoples the same principle of toleration that had been justified in political liberalism is simply extended from the domestic to the international case. Consequently, even if the effects are different, the basic principle remains the same.

Several commentators have argued that this domestic-international analogy is 'deeply flawed' (Tan 2000: 28). First, as already pointed out, the toleration of non-liberal views is much more qualified at the domestic level, in which the full range of liberal rights is overarching, than in the international case where only the most 'urgent' rights are recognized. Second, in the domestic case the position of the individual member of the non-liberal group is strengthened by the real possibility of exit from the group into the surrounding liberal society. Such a right of exit is very much more problematic in the international case, where movement can only be from one society to another. In this connection Kok-Chor Tan notes that most liberal theorists, including Rawls, are happy to endorse a right on the part of the individual to emigrate but reluctant to admit a corresponding duty on any society to authorize a given individual's immigration (Tan 2002: 42). More generally, when Rawls moves from the domestic to the international sphere he has been accused of shifting between two quite different senses of 'toleration'. In political liberalism toleration is 'person-centered', concerned with respecting individuals by accommodating their comprehensive moral doctrines; in the law of peoples it is the group or culture that is the real focus of toleration, 'and that actually shows deficient respect for persons' (Nussbaum 2002: 293). Similarly, Tan sees the law of peoples as highlighting a serious tension between the toleration of non-liberal groups and the liberty of their members that is deep seated in Rawls's political liberalism as a whole (Tan 2000: 38).

Rawls might reply as follows. There is indeed a tension in the law of peoples (and political liberalism) between group toleration and individual liberty. That situation is far from ideal, but unavoidable given other important considerations. What alternative is there to toleration of decent hierarchical societies? Many liberals would say that liberal states should be prepared to criticize any regimes that fall short of liberal standards, and to work actively to liberalize those regimes. But there are dangers in this kind of activist policy. The most obvious is the possibility of international conflict. But Rawls also emphasizes the likelihood that liberal criticism will wound the self-respect of decent societies, creating resentment and bitterness and undermining the mutual respect that is one of the foundations of a Society of Peoples. Again, Rawls does not deny the superiority of liberal principles or the desirability of a world of fully liberal states. But he counsels patience in the means by which those goals are pursued, arguing that too vigorous a policy of liberalization may be counterproductive. Rather, 'a decent society, when offered respect by liberal peoples, may be more likely, over time, to recognize the advantages of liberal institutions and takes steps toward becoming more liberal on its own' (1999: 62). Whether Rawls is being too cautious or his critics too precipitate remains the issue.

Distributive justice

The second major target of the critics has been Rawls's reluctance to extend his domestic principles of justice in distribution to the global stage. Once again, the most frequent complaint is that Rawls's position is too conservative. *The Law of Peoples* is more demanding in this respect than *A Theory of Justice*, where Rawls mentioned no foreign aid requirements at all. Moreover, the duty he now lays on well-ordered states to assist burdened societies marks, from an egalitarian point of view, an advance on the current international status quo (Beitz 2000). However, many commentators believe that the duty of assistance is too limited. There is no duty to assist well-ordered societies at all; the purpose of the duty is to enable burdened societies to become well-ordered, not to make them prosperous or more equal with other societies; and no challenge is issued to the existing basic structure of international political economy, for example the principle of **free trade** or the tendency to regard one's own fellow-nationals as having superior claims to assistance to those of other people. In general, *The Law of Peoples* has confirmed in many readers the view that Rawls shows insufficient concern for the vast inequalities of global economic distribution, especially in the light of his intense desire to rectify the less extreme inequalities found within liberal democracies.

The most celebrated critique of this aspect of Rawls is that of Charles Beitz in *Political Theory and International Relations* (1999). Beitz is a prominent representative of the 'cosmopolitan' school that argues, contrary to Rawls and others, that international relations theory should be primarily concerned with the well being of individual persons rather than 'peoples' or states. Concerning Rawls's view of international distributive justice, Beitz's basic argument is that the logic of Rawls's own theory points to more radical conclusions than those he allows. First, Rawls's domestic original position ought to be globalized directly: instead of imagining a second original position in which the parties are peoples, we should simply admit all human beings as parties to the first original position. Since the parties' nationality is morally arbitrary, that will be screened off by the veil of ignorance, and they will choose principles of justice in the knowledge that some countries are wealthy and some poor, but without knowing in which of these they will end up. As a result, Beitz argues, they will choose a global version of the difference principle, under which wealth will be redistributed to the least well-off human beings, whoever and wherever they may be. The problem with this argument is that it assumes a global context of cooperation for mutual advantage on a level with that of a domestic society, and that such a global scheme of cooperation does not exist. Beitz (1983) has conceded the merit of this criticism, although he maintains his conclusion in favor of redistribution, basing this now on a Kantian commitment to universal respect for persons. Alternatively, Beitz argues, if we assume a contract among societies rather than individuals, we can still mount a case for redistribution if we emphasize the arbitrariness of the distribution of natural resources. With natural resources behind the veil of ignorance, rational representatives of peoples will opt for principles that will compensate them should they turn out to be resource-poor. A similar argument has been taken up by Pogge (1994), who proposes that heavy users of resources should pay a Global Resource Dividend, which will then be available for redistribution.

Rawls considers but rejects these egalitarian theories. First, he argues that we cannot assume that liberal egalitarianism will be acceptable to the decent non-liberal societies he is anxious to accommodate. This concern takes us back to the issues discussed in the previous section. It may also be asked whether non-liberal societies, even if they reject liberal egalitarianism domestically, would necessarily reject it as an international principle – since in most cases greater international equality would be to their economic advantage (Tan 2000: 168–71). Second, Rawls supposes that the duty of assistance is sufficient to ensure the goal that all societies become well-ordered. This supposition has been challenged on the ground that an important element of being well-ordered is self-respect, and that self-respect can be undermined by large scale social and economic inequalities. In other words, substantial redistribution may be justifiable even given Rawls's limited goal. Third, Rawls argues that more substantial redistribution may be unjust. He imagines a case in which Society A makes choices that lead to a high degree of prosperity, much of which is then redistributed to Society B, whose poverty is largely the result of its own poor choices. The question this raises is whether and to what extent poorer societies can be held responsible for their predicament. Arguably, the typical causes of a country's poverty are factors beyond its control, such as global patterns of production, finance and trade. And even when economic failure can be attributed to the decisions of the country's government, it is a further question whether the individual citizens should be held responsible, especially since most of these governments will be non-democratic.

In these debates over Rawls's resistance to global redistribution, two underlying issues are especially important. The first is the causes of poverty. A striking feature of Rawls's position, to which he returns several times, is his insistence that the social and economic well-being of a country is determined less by its possession of material resources than by its political culture. If this is true, then there is much to be said for Rawls's general view that substantial transfers of money from richer to poorer societies will not necessarily help matters for many members of the latter. But is this true? This large empirical question appears to be very much open (Beitz 2000: 690).

The second issue is fundamental not only to the question of redistribution but to Rawls's international theory as a whole. This is the conceptual debate between two broad approaches to international political thought: one accepting the existence of separate societies and states as having moral weight, and the other denying this. The former position is favored by Rawls (although he is far from a supporter of unlimited state **sovereignty**), the latter by his cosmopolitan critics (see **cosmopolitanism**). Here, too, it may fairly be said that the jury is still out. For the cosmopolitans, the boundaries between states and peoples are historically arbitrary and morally irrelevant. Rawls replies that the arbitrariness of boundaries does not detract from their moral significance: in the absence of a world state, politically organized peoples are necessary to take responsibility for the care of particular territories. Against Rawls it has been argued that his assumption of a world of separate societies has been falsified by **globalization**, and that consequently his law of peoples amounts to a set of 'Rules for a Vanished **Westphalia**n World' (Buchanan 2000). But this misses the point that Rawls's notion of a people is not merely descriptive but in part an ethical ideal (Brown 2002: 178). Rawls's law of peoples is disappointing from a cosmopolitan perspective, but his sensitivity to national identity and diversity amounts to a challenge that cosmopolitan thinkers should take seriously.

Further reading

Beitz, C. (1983) 'Cosmopolitan Ideas and National Sentiment', *Journal of Philosophy* 80, 591–600.

Beitz, C. (1999) *Political Theory and International Relations*, 2nd edn, Princeton, NJ: Princeton University Press.

Beitz, C. (2000) 'Rawls's Law of Peoples', *Ethics* 110, 669–96.

Brown, C. (2002) *Sovereignty, Rights and Justice: International Political Theory Today*, Cambridge: Polity.

Buchanan, A. (2000) 'Rawls's Law of Peoples: Rules for a Vanished Westphalian World', *Ethics* 110, 697–721.

Caney, S. (2001) 'International Distributive Justice', *Political Studies* 49, 974–97.

Miller, D. (2000) *Citizenship and National Identity*, Cambridge: Polity Press.

Nussbaum, M. (2002) 'Women and the Law of Peoples', *Politics, Philosophy and Economics* 1(3) 283–306.

Pogge, T. (1994) 'An Egalitarian Law of Peoples', *Philosophy and Public Affairs* 23(3), 195–224.

Pogge, T. (2002) *World Poverty and Human Rights*, Cambridge: Polity.

Rawls, J. (1971) *A Theory of Justice*, Oxford: Oxford University Press.

Rawls, J. (1993a) 'The Law of Peoples', in S. Shute, and S. Hurley (eds) *On Human Rights: the Oxford Amnesty Lectures 1993*, New York: Basic Books.

Rawls, J. (1993b) *Political Liberalism*, New York: Columbia University Press.

Rawls, J. (1999) *A Law of Peoples*, Cambridge, MA: Harvard University Press.

Tan, K-C. (2000) *Toleration, Diversity, and Global Justice*, University Park, PA: Pennsylvania State University Press.

See also: cosmopolitanism; order; pluralism; solidarism

GEORGE CROWDER

Law of the sea

Historically, rules concerning use of the oceans were established by customary **international law**, a term used to describe practices considered legally required by most states from time to time. The uncertainties inherent in such an approach led, in 1958, to the adoption of four international Conventions on oceans governance. The Conventions were promptly ratified by the United States and many other countries, but soon came to be seen as insufficient. In particular, during the 1960s, the United States became increasingly concerned about the growing number of coastal states asserting control over vast reaches of the oceans. New issues, including marine pollution, gained greater prominence. In 1973, negotiations were launched for a comprehensive Convention on the Law of the Sea.

The Convention was finally adopted in 1982. The Convention on the Law of the Sea is sometimes called a constitution for the oceans. Its provisions include recognition of navigational and overflight freedoms, limits on coastal state jurisdiction to a 12 mile territorial sea, the establishment of 200 mile exclusive economic zones, and rights to the ocean floor to the edge of the continental shelf. Negotiations over the Convention's deep seabed mining provisions were launched in 1990. These talks concluded in 1994 with an agreement on deep seabed mining. At present, there are no commercial deep seabed mining projects, largely because costs are much higher than for land-based mining. Cost is expected to remain a significant barrier to mining in the deep ocean for years to come.

Historically, the lack of clear property rights was also a barrier to development. The high seas and ocean floor beneath them have long been considered part of the global commons, beyond the reach of national jurisdiction. As such, it was unclear how states or companies might establish legal title to minerals retrieved from the ocean floor. Investors were not expected to commit the substantial funds needed for commercial development in the absence of assurance that property rights would be widely recognized.

In 1994, more than 100 states adopted a set of rules governing deep seabed mining. The 1994 agreement applies free market principles to deep seabed mining, establishing a mechanism for vesting title in minerals in the entity that recovers them from the ocean floor. The agreement establishes an International Seabed Authority (ISA) with responsibility for supervising this process. The ISA is an independent international organization, not a part of the **United Nations**. It is governed by a Council (with principal executive authority) and an Assembly (which gives final approval to regulations and budgets). Technology transfer requirements (a principal objection in 1982) were deleted from the agreement. The 1994 agreement is a legally binding modification of Part XI of the Law of the Sea Convention. The 1994 agreement also recognized the longstanding view that the deep ocean floor is part of the global commons and beyond the reach of national jurisdiction. Also in 1994, the Convention entered into force after the sixtieth state joined. On 25 February 2004, the Senate Foreign Relations Committee unanimously recommended that the United States join the Convention.

Today, more than 140 countries are parties to the Law of the Sea Convention. In November 2004, the treaty was open for amendment for the first time. Under the Convention, no amendment may be adopted unless the parties agree by consensus (or, if every effort to reach consensus failed, more than two-thirds of the parties present agree both on certain procedural matters and on the proposed amendment).

The Convention is a major achievement in establishing a legal framework for international cooperation both to exploit and to preserve the world's oceans. First, the navigational freedoms recognized under the Convention provide a stable environment for global commerce. Clear rules with widespread acceptance facilitate international trade and reduce risks to the many industries that depend upon marine transport.

Second, the Convention offers a ready set of procedures for delineating the limit of each country's continental shelf. These procedures help provide the certainty needed for major capital investment in offshore oil and gas facilities. The Convention also contains a set of provisions concerning revenue sharing of proceeds from the outer continental shelf. Under the Convention, no payments are owed for the first five years of production (which are typically the most productive). Beginning in year six, payments equal to 1 per cent of the value of production at the site, increasing 1 per cent each year to a maximum of 7 per cent, are owed to the International Seabed Authority.

The Law of the Sea Convention provides a comprehensive framework for international cooperation to protect the marine environment. The ocean environment is under enormous stress. Many fisheries are depleted or collapsing. Pollution plagues highly populated coastal regions. Non-native species threaten ocean ecosystems around the globe. The Law of the Sea imposes minimum requirements to protect and preserve the marine environment. Under the Convention, states are required to take measures to address pollution from vessels and land-based sources, to prevent the introduction of alien or invasive species, and to conserve and manage coastal fisheries.

The Convention also requires states to work together to protect the oceans. States are required to cooperate in the management of high seas fish stocks, as well as stocks that migrate between the high seas and exclusive economic zones, setting the stage for regional agreements essential to managing ocean fisheries. States are also required to work together to protect marine mammals, which are given special protections under the Convention.

Further reading

Churchill, R. and Lower, A. (1999) *The Law of the Sea*, New York: Juris.

Klein, N. (2005) *Dispute Settlement in the UN Convention on the Law of the Sea*, Cambridge: Cambridge University Press.

Nordquist, M. and Moore, J. (2001) *Current Marine Environment Issues and the International Tribunal for the Law of the Sea*, Amsterdam: Martinus Nijhoff.

Sohn, L. and Noyes, J. (2004) *Cases and Materials on the Law of the Sea*, New York: Transnational.

See also: international law; international public goods; sovereignty

MARTIN GRIFFITHS

League of Nations (LON)

The League of Nations was the world's first general international organization. It sought to limit the likelihood of **war** by preserving peace, promoting disarmament, the peaceful settlement of disputes and the rule of law, prescribing 'open, just and honourable' inter-state relations, and generally organizing international cooperation to further the moral and material welfare of humanity.

The League came into existence in January 1920 when the Treaty of Versailles (the major peace treaty following the First World War, of which the Covenant formed a part) entered into force. The detailed ideas embodied in the Covenant came almost wholly from Britain, but it was thanks to the determination of the US President, Woodrow Wilson, that the Covenant was drafted at the 1919 Paris Peace Conference.

Wilson had, however, failed to take sufficient account of American hostility to foreign entanglements and the obligations of League membership, and in particular to Article X of the Covenant which guaranteed the territorial integrity of member states. Thus the Senate refused to ratify the Treaty of Versailles, and in consequence the United States could not become a founder member of the League. Nor did it ever apply to join.

America's abandonment of the League severely weakened it as a **collective security** organization, and left Britain and France as largely unenthusiastic leaders of an organization that was different from what they had wanted and expected. France lacked faith in the League's ability to protect it against Germany, and Britain worried about having to bear the burden of keeping the peace. In fact, the Covenant did not provide for mandatory military sanctions against aggressors. What it said was that in certain circumstances the League Council had a duty to 'recommend' military action to the members (Article XVI). The Covenant legally obliged members to impose far reaching economic sanctions on any state that made war in defiance of the Covenant's stringent requirements regarding the pacific settlement of disputes. But it was left to each member to decide whether events had precipitated that obligation and, if so, to determine the exact method of its execution. This reflected the fact that the League was based on the idea of cooperation rather than direction. It could not order states to do anything, as was implicit in the fact that all substantive decisions of the League's organs had to be unanimous.

The League began with forty-two members; twenty states were later admitted; seventeen withdrew; and one – the Soviet Union – was in effect expelled after it invaded Finland in 1939. The League's headquarters were at Geneva, Switzerland, where it was serviced by a multinational secretariat headed by a Secretary-General, the first instance of an impartial international civil service.

The secretariat served two principal organs: the Assembly and the Council. All member states (each having one vote) were represented in the Assembly, which met once a year for about a month. The Assembly gave small member states a voice in international relations, and they eagerly made the most of it. In the process, they turned the Assembly into a dynamic body whose resolutions were often deemed to be important indicators of world opinion. However, there was a fair amount of 'hot air' and self-interest in many members' speeches. It cost the small states nothing to proclaim their devotion to League ideals; as consumers of collective security they had everything to gain from trying to strengthen the League.

The League's other principal organ was the Council, which held three or four meetings each year, and special meetings as required. It represented the institutionalization on a global scale of the nineteenth century Concert of Europe. Permanent seats on the Council were occupied (during the period of their membership) by the **great powers**: Britain, France, Italy (until 1936), Japan (until 1933), Germany (1926–33) and the Soviet Union (1934–9). There were also some non-permanent Council members, elected by the Assembly for three years on a rotating basis.

Like the Assembly, the Council was envisaged as a purely deliberative body. It had some specific tasks, such as formulating plans for disarmament, and keeping an eye on the administration of mandated territories and the well being of national minorities in certain states. More generally, it could discuss any matter within the League's competence 'or affecting the peace of the world'

(Article IV). The Covenant had been drafted on the premise that a public rebuke from the Council would usually be all that was needed to deter a wrong-doer. This assumed the existence of a sense of community and common interest that in fact proved to be lacking (and is probably always lacking in a world of sovereign states). However, the League was right in recognizing that it could only act effectively when states were in agreement.

The experience of the League reflected its circumstances. During the 1920s, when the international climate was favourable, the League was fairly successful. But in the 1930s its weakness was revealed. When Japan invaded the Chinese province of Manchuria in 1931, the League simply sent a commission of inquiry, condemned Japan, and refused to recognize the puppet state of Manchukuo that Japan had set up in China. America's absence from the League was an important barrier to effective League action, but the circumstances were anyway unpropitious. China was a long way off; there was initial confusion about what was going on; many members had some sympathy for Japan; there was a general unwillingness to risk war; and no-one favoured applying economic **sanctions** at a time when the world was in recession.

The League's failure in Manchuria weakened it as a collective security organization. The Abyssinian (Ethiopian) **crisis** effectively killed it. Italy's invasion of that East African member state in 1935 was a clear case of aggression and League members swiftly applied some economic sanctions. However, because Britain and France feared driving Mussolini into Hitler's arms, these sanctions were half-hearted and ineffective, and they were lifted shortly after the fall of Addis Ababa (the capital) in March 1936. Having been discredited as a collective security organization, the League had only a shadowy existence, and was virtually closed during the Second World War. In April 1946 its final Assembly transferred the League's powers, functions, buildings and archives to the new **United Nations**.

The circumstances of its decline resulted in the League generally being judged a failure. However, it was by no means a continuous or complete failure, and it had a number of important achievements. These were mostly, but not exclusively, in non-political areas such as the promotion of **international law** and of functional cooperation in the regulation of health and nutrition. Moreover, the Covenant represented certain important milestones in the development of ideas about how international relations should be conducted, notably, its condemnation of aggression and its assertion that any war or threat of war was a matter of general concern. Perhaps most significantly of all, the League established the idea that the world needed such a body. Unsurprisingly, its imprint on the shape of its successor was far reaching. As one of the drafters of the Covenant put it, the League was 'a great experiment'.

Further reading

Knock, T. (1995) *To End All Wars: Woodrow Wilson and the Quest for a New World Order*, Princeton, NJ: Princeton University Press.

Northedge, F. S. (1986) *The League of Nations, Its Life and Times*, Leicester: Leicester University Press.

Walters, F. P. (1960) *A History of the League of Nations*, Oxford: Oxford University Press.

See also: decolonization; sanctions; United Nations; war

LORNA LLOYD

Legimacy

Legimacy is a crucial concept in social science, standing as it does between **authority** and **power**, but it is one that has not been well incorporated in the field of International Relations. From Max Weber (1864–1920), we know that legimacy is a mode of social control that is distinct from either self-interest or coercion, and that legimacy causes an actor to believe that a rule or an institution ought to be obeyed. This generates an internal motivation in the actor to follow the rules, and leads to social **order** without the need for overt enforcement of the rules or offers of material incentives.

The power of legimacy comes in two ways. At the individual level, the internalization of an external rule shapes the actor's perceptions of its own interests, and so changes the orientation of the individual toward the rule. This can cause actors to behave differently than they would in the absence of the legitimated rule or institution. But the effects are potentially more widespread since these changes then also change the strategic environment faced by all actors, including those not affected by the internalization. When enough actors are affected by internalization, it creates new incentives and patterns in the system more generally. In this way, legimacy affects both individual level and structural features of a social system or, put differently, it affects both believers and non-believers in the normative content of the rule.

For International Relations, it is common to hear that international organizations and rules are stronger to the extent that they are seen as legitimate, but the meaning and operationalization of this claim are far from clear. Recent scholarship has identified several ways in which these two aspects of legimacy's power affect world politics. Each defines the key terms somewhat differently and is directed at a different kind of empirical problem.

First, legimacy may be at the heart of international norms. Since norms (by definition) cannot rely on coercive enforcement, part of their behavioral effect comes from states perceiving them as being legitimate rules of state conduct. In a recent study of how norms are created, Christopher Gelpi (2003) has found that international **crisis** negotiations can legitimize norms of peaceful settlement, and these norms make subsequent crises less likely to turn violent, even among committed adversaries. This displays the power of legitimized ideas to affect the policies that states choose.

Second, and more deeply, notions of legimacy may shape the entire **international system**, either by defining what counts as a legitimate actor or by defining legitimate relations among them. On this theme, Mlada Bukovansky (2002) argues that there is an 'international political culture' that contains legitimated ideas about acceptable forms of statehood, and that this changes over time. New forms of domestic governance and new intellectual currents redefine legitimate units. The American and French revolutions, she argues, are examples of shifts in the international system from one dominant form of legitimation to another. Theorists of **globalization** might suggest that we are in the midst of another change today, toward the legitimation of firms or other non-state actors as acceptable international actors.

Finally, legitimation may occur around international organizations themselves. States may be socialized to accept some international organizations as legitimate, and this changes how states approach decisions about compliance and noncompliance. For instance, to the extent that states accept the institution of

sovereignty as legitimate, we can expect them to challenge existing international boundaries less often. Formal international organizations rely heavily on perceptions of their legitimacy for their power, and so have an incentive to succeed in their legitimation. It is common to see both critics and defenders of the **World Trade Organization**, the **European Union**, and the **United Nations** Security Council discuss how the power of those bodies might be increased by increasing their legitimacy.

Legitimacy presents several interesting problems, both for students of International Relations and for practitioners. For students, the methodological problems associated with as big and vague a concept as legitimacy are daunting. It is very hard to distinguish empirically between legitimacy and other explanations for rule following. For instance, with international norms, the counter-argument to the legitimacy explanation is that states follow norms that accord with their self-interest, abiding by or ignoring norms depending on how they suit their interests. The behavioral result of legitimacy and self-interest is the same; the difference comes from the different *motivations* behind the two, and this is very hard to distinguish. For that matter, it is difficult even to show that legitimacy is having an effect at all, making it easy for skeptics to deny that it matters in the first place.

For practitioners, legitimation creates challenges both for strong states and weak states in world politics. The strong have an interest in legitimizing their dominance because it makes that dominance 'cheaper' but this means giving up some control. The strong must behave in ways that maintain the belief in their legitimacy, and this may mean forgoing some of the policies (such as exercises of brute force) that appeal to those who see themselves as in charge. Hypocrisy by the **hegemon** is a sure path

to delegitimation. The weak gain some leverage over the strong out of this relationship, since it is their approval that the strong must seek, but they too are constrained by its logic.

A final problem affects both scholars and practitioners, and concerns the constant tension between legitimation and delegitimation. Legitimation is never complete, and it is always subject to critique by critics who succeed in propagating alternative interpretations. This instability in legitimacy is inherent in its subjective nature. As a result, legitimacy is very difficult to study empirically in International Relations, and it is a very slippery foundation on which to build a 'real world' foreign policy for states.

Further reading

Bukovansky, M. (2002) *Legitimacy and Power Politics: The American and French Revolutions in International Political Culture*, Princeton, NJ: Princeton University Press.

Coicaud, J.-M. (2002) *Legitimacy and Politics: A Contribution to the Study of Political Right and Political Responsibility*, Cambridge: Cambridge University Press.

Gelpi, C. (2003) *The Power of Legitimacy: Assessing the Role of Norms in Crisis Bargaining*, Princeton, NJ: Princeton University Press.

Hurd, I. (1999) 'Legitimacy and Authority in International Politics', *International Organization*, 53(2), 379–408.

Hurd, I. (2002) 'Legitimacy, Power, and the Symbolic Life of the UN Security Council', *Global Governance* 8(1), 35–51.

See also: anarchy; authority; reciprocity; recognition; power

IAN HURD

Levels of analysis

Vantage-points of relative breadth or aggregation – most commonly the individual, state or **international system** – around which to organize inquiry, usually in terms of identifying important causes behind some aspect of international behavior. The notion that there are major alternative levels at which to study international politics retains considerable academic currency. Such levels feature in most introductory texts as important organizing devices for students. While the global level is of comparatively recent vintage, the 'old favorites' can be traced at least as far back as 1959 and the publication of Kenneth Waltz's *Man, the State and War*. Although Waltz actually spoke of alternative 'images' of international relations, these could clearly be conceived as levels of abstraction, aggregation or breadth, as J. David Singer (1961) argued. Singer invited fellow scholars to think through the alternative levels as a central theoretical and methodological issue.

The characterization of the 'problem' was shaped by a major upheaval in the field of international relations, the so-called 'behavioral revolution'. Behavioralists sought to emulate the rigorous standards of validity routinely enjoyed by the natural sciences, advocating the elimination of statements of norms or values from empirical study and emphasizing methodological rigor and cumulative knowledge building. Above all, it was important to generate more reliable generalizations and even laws of human behavior, to be achieved by conceptually isolating variables that could then be examined for evidence of their statistically significant correlations. This 'quantitative turn' was inspired by a positivist view of social inquiry (that is, value neutral and empiricist) traceable to David Hume (1711–76), and was widely thought to lead eventually, through incremental steps, to more reliable aggregative theory.

Behavioralists advocated systematic theory that was *analytical* in the sense of breaking observations down into discrete components, that is, simple propositions or hypotheses that might feasibly be 'operationalized' and tested. The results can be seen in a comparison of two of the most influential theoretical texts of the time: the complex, nuanced but disparate theoretical observations of Hans Morgenthau's *Politics Among Nations* (1948), and the systematic but simplifying rigor of Waltz's own *Theory of International Politics* (1979) published thirty years later.

If the central goal of social science was to generate universal laws of human behavior it seemed natural to situate international relations more self-consciously within a broader range of academic disciplines and categories of social inquiry. Hence international relations and political science in the 1960s and 1970s were heavily influenced by systems theory emanating from the field of sociology. A system was understood as a simplified model of some set of relatively autonomous processes. This might reveal the operation of a relatively closed structure of causal mechanisms. Hence the study of the state became, in the United States at least, the study of the political system while the study of **diplomacy** and **war** became the study of the **international system**. The discussion of levels of analysis began, then, as a consideration of the general problems and pitfalls of compartmentalizing the field of international relations in the form of simplifying models and hypotheses. Most salient of all, in this regard, was that emerging literature attempting to compartmentalize the most abstract dimension, to theorise the broad 'nature' of the international system.

Used coherently, levels of analysis constitute levels of abstraction. The state might be considered in terms of its component parts and processes or as a 'system' in itself. On the other hand, it might be taken as a relatively straightforward, largely undifferentiated 'given' to form the essential unit collectively populating a broader system. Such an approach allows the construction of more parsimonious theory.

Waltz, for example, sought to establish those factors at a highly aggregated level that shape, in the manner of permissive causes, states' broad patterns of interaction. The system's decentralized political order of **anarchy** leads to the competitive behavior of states, which, as rational actors, are first and foremost preoccupied with **security**. It is this common preoccupation that leads states to behave so alike and justifies their treatment as relatively undifferentiated units (comparable to firms in a market). The relative instability (or bellicosity) of such competition broadly reflects the distribution of military capabilities. Relatively concentrated capabilities in the hands of two **superpowers** tend to be more stable. The simple cleavage of such a **bipolar** order is more transparent and predictable than, for example, the fluid and often secretive **alliance** formations between the five **great powers** who eventually participated in World War One.

The level of analysis is a useful device for illustrating logical pitfalls in the study of international relations, illuminating the benefits as well as the limitations of certain kinds of analytical focus. Take, for example, a fairly typical state-level argument that the general tendency of liberal democracies to emphasize the 'the rule of law' produces a corresponding tendency in foreign policy to adhere to the rules of diplomatic procedure and international organization. How much effect this will have on interactions more generally arguably depends on constraints of **power** and conflict arising

from the general patterns or relationships of the international system. In other words, the state level of analysis can indicate a force in a certain direction in foreign policy that may or may not translate into observable patterns at the system level because of intervening variables or 'externalities'.

The biggest pitfall is reductionism: to reduce characteristics of complex relationships to those of their constituent units. It is important to recognize that a psychological theory of human aggression, for example, cannot explain war in any sense beyond the identification of a *potential* contributory factor. For aggressive feelings in individuals, although they might trigger or prolong wars in certain specific circumstances, can be regarded as neither a necessary nor sufficient condition of wars *per se*.

The limitations of lower levels of abstraction should not blind us to the dangers of isolating particular levels of analysis. The chief danger is to exaggerate the autonomy of the domain or abstraction upon which one chooses to focus. Use of an abstraction like the international system logically depends on making claims at lower levels. The units of the system, for example, must be assumed to have simple, relatively undifferentiated characteristics. Although simplifications are appropriate and necessary to the construction of broad theoretical claims, they run the risk of failing to do justice to the phenomena they signify. Waltz's characterization of the structure of the international system, for example, paradoxically risks the charge of reductionism. Its governing logic requires the assumption that states respond to structural constraints in the manner of coherent and rationally instrumental human beings, reducing the complex institution of the state to a simple human writ large.

Further reading

Morgenthau, H. J. (1948) *Politics Among Nations*, New York: Knopf.

Singer, J. D. (1961) 'The Level-of-Analysis Problem in International Relations', *World Politics* 14(1), 77–92.

Rosenau, J. N. (1980) *The Scientific Study of Foreign Policy*, London: Frances Pinter.

Waltz, K. (1959) *Man, the State and War*, New York: Columbia University Press.

Waltz, K. (1979) *Theory of International Politics*, Reading, MA: Addison-Wesley.

See also: agent-structure debate; constructivism; realism

P. STUART ROBINSON

Liberal internationalism

The application of liberal thought and political principles to the international and trans-societal levels. Underlying liberal internationalism is the assumption that one can apply reason to extend the possibilities for individual and collective self-rule, or freedom. Liberal internationalism emerged as a coherent if variegated doctrine in the Enlightenment and reached its apogee as a systematic statement of international reform with Woodrow Wilson's Fourteen Points, intended to form the basis of the post-First World War peace. Liberals tended to believe that the outbreak of the First World War had vindicated their critique of the prevailing system of international relations and sought to establish a liberal peace marked by open **diplomacy**, the right of **self-determination**, **free trade**, disarmament, the peaceful settlement of disputes, and the establishment of an international **security** organization in the form of the **League of Nations**. The role of the League would be to resolve differences between states, guarantee their political independence and territorial integrity, and address a range of other contemporary international questions such as the position of labor and minorities. However, hopes for a reformed world, already badly damaged by the punitive Versailles Peace Treaty (1919), were shattered with the militarization and expansionism of Italy, Germany and Japan in the 1930s, culminating in the Second World War. These events and the rapid onset of the **cold war** after 1945 generated a number of influential realist critiques (see **realism**) that were widely (if not necessarily fairly) perceived as devastating to liberal internationalism, both as an intellectual construct and as a guide to the practical conduct of international relations. Since the 1980s, however, liberal internationalism has attracted renewed interest both on empirical and normative grounds and it may be that the academic subject of International Relations is moving towards a position in which it can provide a more satisfactory account of liberal internationalism's legacy, potentialities, and limitations.

Liberal assumptions and historical overview

Liberal Internationalism reflects the broader liberal philosophy of which it is part in that it comprises several political/philosophical traditions, has emerged in a number of diverse national and historical contexts, has evolved over time in response to changing domestic and international conditions, and rests upon a body of elastic concepts that invite the exercise of judgement and interpretation in order to draw out their political and policy conclusions. When considered in these terms, liberalism is better understood not as providing a blueprint for thinking about international relations or foreign policy, but rather a cluster or matrix of underlying values, principles and purposes that provide a guide and framework through which one can think flexibly about international relations, albeit with the benefit of a series of moral and historical reference points.

Despite this apparent indeterminacy, however, it is nevertheless possible to identify both a conceptual core within the tradition and the main strands of international thought. Historically the tradition's central normative and critical concerns have been to expand the capacity for collective self-rule and address the perennial problems of the abuse of **power** and illegitimate violence. Conceptually, one finds at the centre of liberalism an insistence upon the moral primacy of the individual and a tradition of political and philosophical interest in the conditions of individual freedom, or autonomy. When taken in conjunction with liberalism's egalitarian assumption of the moral equality of individuals one can appreciate why liberals have advocated republics, constitutional monarchies, or what in contemporary terms are often referred to as 'liberal democratic' political systems. These are regarded as offering a rational means of facilitating the greatest collective domain of freedom for equal individuals through being bound by the principles of the accountability of power, independence of the legislature and the rule of law. When the universalist liberal assumption that the human species possesses a certain moral unity is also taken into account one has the bases of the cosmopolitan (see **cosmopolitanism**) sentiments that pervade liberalism. Two areas in which this universalism plays out politically are in the tension between liberalism and the **Westphalia**n notion of state **sovereignty**, and in underpinning the cosmopolitan doctrine of **human rights**.

Within liberalism persons are not only the subject of moral inquiry, but are also regarded as key agents of historical and political change. But what concep-

tion of the individual do liberals hold? Whilst accounts vary, Kant's qualified endorsement of the human character (marked by self-interest and a desire for self-preservation yet also possessing the capacity for moral thought, reason and human sympathy) avoids the extremes of either naivety or cynicism. This conceptualization is consistent with the traditional liberal emphasis upon education, individual and collective responsibility for action, and the notion of enlightened self-interest as some of the best hopes for individual and collective progress.

In nineteenth-century Europe, whilst the absence of systemic challenges after the Napoleonic Wars enabled liberals to concentrate primarily upon the achievement and consolidation of domestic political gains, they also applied themselves to the international realm. At this time, the international requirements of the development of liberal politics at home and the legitimacy of intervention to assist liberal movements abroad were the key issues for liberal internationalism. One finds in this period a largely uncritical faith in the universal benefits of **free trade**, self-determination (at least for Europeans), and the peaceful arbitration of disputes. The notion that a market-based realm of unhindered transsocietal relations would be beneficial for civilization was implicit in Richard Cobden's (1804–65) famous dictum 'as little intercourse as possible between Governments, as much connection as possible between the nations of the world'. However, this belief in the operation of providence or some other form of pre-ordained or natural moral progression of human history could not survive the turmoil of the twentieth century. Whilst many liberals attributed the First World War as much if not more to a systemic failure than to wilful design, the expansionism and raw brutality of the 1930s and the collapse of free trade presented a clear and unambiguous rebuttal to the optimistic assumptions of nineteenth century liberalism.

It was also in this period that E. H. Carr published his influential critique of liberalism, *The Twenty Years Crisis* (1939). Whilst several of Carr's specific points present virtual caricatures of the liberal tradition one of its key arguments, that liberalism's claim to present universal values and identify universal goods were the unwitting reflection of particular national and class interests, remains pertinent. It is ironic, however, that Carr's work, often thought of as an astute commentary upon the character of political life, itself misjudged the requirements of **security** policy, for Carr himself advocated the **appeasement** of Hitler whereas, with hindsight, the early application of some form of collective resistance might have averted the Nazi leader's expansionism.

As the cold war superseded the Second World War mainstream liberalism became increasingly absorbed with the question of the Soviet threat and rallied round the policy of **containment** as a way to prevent the spread of state socialist or **communist** regimes. A combination of military, political, economic and ideological measures were employed, but with the expectation that ultimately state socialism would fail due to internal inefficiencies and domestic unpopularity. The containment doctrine came under criticism, however, from liberals on both the Left and the Right. On the Left containment was criticized for the pervasive militarization of foreign policy and support of authoritarian regimes with appalling human rights records, so long as they were anti-communist. On the Right, despite the initial retreat from 'rollback' in the 1950s, containment was often regarded as too moderate a doctrine and, particularly in the Reagan years, greater efforts were made to provide military aid for movements resisting communism in the Middle East, Central Asia, Central America and elsewhere.

In the late 1980s, however, the implosion of the Soviet system was widely hailed by mainstream liberals as a vindication of containment, whilst the Right claimed that it vindicated Reagan's military build-up. The contingent nature of this latter claim has become more apparent since the end of the cold war as disaffected and repressed social forces within authoritarian states allied with or formerly supported by the United States have emerged as hostile to the cold war victors. Whilst the problem is not new – witness the Iranian Islamic Revolution of 1979 against the US supported regime of the Shah – the rise of anti-American Islamic militancy in Saudi Arabia (see **anti-Americanism**) and the protracted issue of Iraq have created major new security problems for the United States. All three of these cases raise the question of the long term wisdom of supporting authoritarian regimes and failing to conduct one's foreign policy in accordance with liberal principles and values, even when there may seem to be short term or instrumental reasons for doing so.

This question of liberal foreign policy is but one aspect of the major debate with **realism** over the nature of international relations and the possibilities for their reform. The liberal emphasis upon the determining power of factors at the state level – such as the spread of liberal democratic regimes – and the ability of states to refashion their **national interest**s through the development of commerce has received fresh interest in recent years following the end of the cold war as well as empirical support from the **democratic peace** research program.

Before discussing liberalism's contribution to international affairs in more detail it is sobering to consider the scale of the task a reformist ideology such as liberalism faces as it is required to operate effectively across four distinct but properly inter-related dimensions: the critical, the normative, the political and the administrative or managerial.

Liberalism's critical spirit was first directed to the bastions of privilege and tradition under the *ancien regime* but for those at the progressive edge of the tradition the responsibility to continue to scrutinize political institutions and practices and the underlying terms and horizons of politics remains incumbent. Once liberalism fails to address itself to contemporary claims of justice and abuses of power it is prone to become the doctrine of the already privileged and increasingly conservative or elitist in character. Liberalism's normative dimension has been manifest in the presentation of appealing normative claims such as self-determination, human and minority rights, economic justice, and more recently notions of cosmopolitan democracy (see **cosmopolitanism**). But, if liberalism fails to generate inspiring normative and political visions or fails to abide by those it does present, then it becomes open to charges of complacency, double standards or hypocrisy and may generate disillusionment and cynicism, thereby squandering this valuable political resource.

As a practical as well as a theoretical project a further dimension of the liberal project has been to develop a politics through which to achieve its goals. Central to this dimension is a significant liberal societal base composed of political parties and/or civil society organizations that are in positions of power or influence. Without this strong societal base liberalism faces political marginalization or irrelevance.

Finally, the maintenance of liberal gains and achievements requires managerial and administrative competence to avoid liberal institutions and programs becoming inefficient and wasteful. To consistently achieve any of these requirements individually, let alone strike an effective balance between them, is a major challenge for liberal internationalists, particularly at the international level in which **anarchy** has often been thought to produce disincentives to cooperation and to the realization of normative goals.

The historical emergence and development of liberal internationalism

Whilst the philosophical roots of liberalism are often located in the Judaeo-Christian traditions, it is in the eighteenth century European Enlightenment that one first finds a systematic statement of liberal internationalism. Liberals tended to regard international relations as a function of domestic politics and from this premise they identified a range of international practices, most centrally **war** itself, as the external buttresses of the *ancien regime's* hierarchical domestic political order. The French *philosophes* in particular developed the fundamentals of what was to become the classic liberal and Radical critique of the **Westphalia**n international system. Politics, they argued, should concentrate primarily on developing and perfecting the domestic realm rather than satisfying the pursuit of glory overseas. Under the *ancien regime* **diplomacy** was conducted secretively in order to serve the personal intrigues and ambitions of rulers rather than the interests of the people at large; treaties were regarded as temporary armistices; the **balance of power** an inherently unstable system prone to shocks and conflicts.

The promise of contemporary liberal internationalists was to supersede this 'war system' through responsible government, commerce and ultimately the rule of law, with the rising European bourgeoisie and its intellectuals as the harbingers of the new age of reason. The most forceful popular manifesto of liberal (or republican) internationalism can be found in Thomas Paine's *The Rights of Man* (1791); its most brilliant political-philosophical statement in Immanuel Kant's *Perpetual Peace* (1795); and the foundations of liberalism's economic or commercial internationalism in Adam Smith's *Wealth of Nations* (1776).

Whilst most liberals did come to regard war and the use of force as legitimate in certain circumstances, it was generally regarded as a failure of reason and an impediment to the liberal vision of political life. When it did occur it was typically regarded as a product of the bellicosity of despots or monarchical rulers, the consequence of faulty or unjust domestic political arrangements, or else the result of poor communication or of misunderstanding between parties. It is, however, the link between war and injustice that provides the most enduring and theoretically interesting insight into the analysis of war and violence. The importance liberals have attached to the problem of war is apparent when one considers the central place it has occupied across a range of key areas liberals have sought to reform in accordance with their normative and political concerns. These include civil-military relations, **international political economy**, and self-determination, as well as the emphasis liberals have put upon such themes as the international rule of law, arbitration and disarmament. Underpinning this major theme in liberal thought has been the view that war and preparation for war corrodes liberal domestic political structures and impedes the pursuit of liberty. This restraining influence sits in tension, however, with the argument that force

might sometimes be legitimate for liberal political reasons, such as for purposes of **collective security** or the protection of human rights as well as the traditional right of self-defence.

Civil-military relations

A fundamental issue for emerging constitutionalist and liberal movements has been the need to provide for defence against foreign threats whilst at the same time avoiding the creation of a military force that threatens civilian rule and liberal politics domestically. Among the methods historically devised in Europe and North America have been legislative control of the military and its funding and reliance upon civilian militias alongside or instead of a professional military.

However, increased military specialization, industrialization, the experience of total war, and most of all the onset of the cold war and the development of nuclear weaponry so radically transformed the conduct of warfare that military **authority** became increasingly removed from society and concentrated in the hands of military professionals and the executive branch of government. The rise of the 'imperial presidency' and proliferation of executive agencies in the United States is the clearest example of this trend, with the emergence of a military–industrial complex during the cold war indicative of the broader militarization of society in this period.

Following the end of the cold war, whilst there was an initial decrease in military expenditure in the United States and the reassertion of Congressional influence, the trend towards a populist cultural militarism apparent in the glamour of hi-tech and smart weaponry and encouraged by state agencies and the entertainment industry, receives remarkably little critical attention in mainstream liberal thought. Most recently the emergence of the 'War on Terror' since 2001 has raised afresh questions regarding the motives and accountability of executive agencies, the role of the intelligence services in the democratic foreign policy process, and the tensions that exist between war, security and human rights.

Political economy

Liberal political economy emerged as a critique of **mercantilism** which was a doctrine that sought to harness economic activity to the pursuit of state power. Mercantilism assumed the level of wealth in the world to be fixed and encouraged the 'beggar-thy-neighbour' policies of maximizing exports and minimizing imports. By contrast, liberal thinkers such as Adam Smith, reflecting the views of earlier writers such as the French *physiocrats* and the Scot, David Hume (1711–76), argued that the purpose of economic activity should be to increase overall levels of wealth and that increased division of labour and specialization could achieve this end. The market, Smith argued, was guided by an invisible hand that made it self-regulating. Accordingly, state intervention would lead to distortions and inefficiencies. In this *laissez faire* vision, the state's role was to be confined to the protection of society from external threats and the provision of certain public goods. Externally, free trade would increase the absolute wealth of all parties, as further articulated by Ricardo's theory of comparative advantage (1817), and foster bonds of interdependence and peace between peoples. Indeed, this perceived progressive cosmopolitan role has been one of the principle reasons why free trade became for many liberals a fundamental article of faith.

However, the equity of free trade as an international doctrine was challenged by some in later industrializing nations such as imperial Germany and the United States who argued that it favoured the most advanced national economies and that some measure of state protection was required in order to allow their economies to catch up. Similarly, the success of the East Asian economies in the 1980s required strong and efficient state apparatuses, which were (in varying degrees) able to negotiate the terms of engagement with neoliberal economic forces.

The doctrine of *laissez faire* was also to become increasingly challenged as left-liberals in the late nineteenth century increasingly advocated greater public regulation of the economy in order to balance the claims of economic liberty with those of equality and social justice. 'New Liberals' identified growing tensions between democracy and **capitalism** and argued that the state should play a more active role in the development of 'positive freedom', understood as developing the social and economic conditions whereby persons were able to properly exercise and enjoy the formal rights and freedoms liberalism offered. This break with classical liberalism laid the foundations for the Keynesian economic doctrines that were to form the economic bases of the social democratic programmes that became the orthodoxy in many liberal states from 1945 until the late 1970s. Indeed, this split between 'classical' and 'welfare' or 'social' liberals constitutes one of the most fundamental dividing lines within the liberal tradition and carries with it important international implications. Social liberals saw that growing levels of domestic inequality were generating their own injustices, and argued that this was becoming expressed internationally in terms of trends towards autarky, greater militarism, imperialism and conflict.

Keynes himself, in *The Economic Consequences of the Peace* (1919) warned that, given pre-war levels of **interdependence**, the recovery of the German economy was a necessary prerequisite of a broader European recovery and of continental stability. One finds in Keynes' critique of the Versailles settlement a vindication of Norman Angell's argument in *The Great Illusion* (1913) that the extent of the international division of labour and the credit-dependent structure of modern wealth meant that conquest was no longer rational as a means through which states could expand their wealth. Keynes also published in the inter-war years a powerful critique of *laissez-faire* and, for a brief period during the Depression, even argued for greater economic **nationalism** in order that political communities might pursue their respective political ends (such as full employment) without facing a 'flight of capital' from the national economy. Liberal thinkers, then, have been willing to re-evaluate liberalism's doctrinal elements in light of changing political circumstances and considerations of justice.

The inter-war collapse of the European economies and the rise of political extremism brought a greater recognition among political leaders of the need for public regulation of the international economy and of the need to pursue a benign rather than a punitive peace after the Second World War. Under US leadership the **Bretton Woods** institutions and General Agreement on Tariffs and Trade established a relatively open and non-discriminatory international trading and financial **order**. Politically, probably the greatest success of this period was to have successfully managed the peaceful **integration** of the defeated powers into the reconstructed international order. West Germany and Japan were led to accept the desirability of a democratic domestic political system, which for the liberal victors was a condition of their future peacefulness, and encouraged to participate in an open international economy that they were able to recognize as an avenue that would allow their dynamic economies to grow and prosper through non-military means.

This aspect of liberal political economy pertaining to the management of relations between advanced economies has received considerable academic attention through the literature on interdependence, regimes, and institutions and is generally regarded as the mainstream liberal research agenda in the academic study of International Relations. Central to this agenda is an engagement with realism in order to demonstrate that even under conditions of anarchy it is rational for self-interested state actors to develop patterns of cooperation. This research agenda has been criticized, however, for its proximity to the key concerns of United States foreign policy, particularly the possibilities of maintaining a favourable trading and financial order following the decline of US **hegemony** in the 1970s and 1980s. The problem, however, is less the nature of the research programme (as argued above the 'managerial' is a legitimate and important aspect of the liberal project, particularly given contemporary trends towards unilateralism and protectionism in the United States) but rather that the managerial dimension has become the predominant strand of academic inquiry at the same time that it has tended to disconnect from the other dimensions, notably the critical and the normative.

Scholars such as James Richardson (2001) criticize the neoliberal insistence upon the virtue and necessity of the unregulated market that has emerged since the late 1970s and which has been promoted by the **World Bank** and the

International Monetary Fund (IMF) and governments of states such as the United States and the United Kingdom. A liberal alternative to this is a **development-centered** approach along the lines advocated by the **United Nations Development Program**. The changing political climate is reflected in the neglect among key policymakers of the work of scholars such as Charles Beitz (1979) who has argued that under conditions of interdependence there are moral obligations upon the North to pursue redistributive policies towards the South, and Henry Shue (1980) who has insisted upon the North's obligation to provide the basic right to subsistence towards those in need.

(National) self-determination

Implicit in the liberal pursuit of individual and collective freedom or autonomy is the right to self-government. During the French Revolution this principle was combined with nationalism to generate the principle of national self-determination, which legitimated the right of a people or nation to their own self-governing sovereign state. It is, however, important to disentangle this combination in order to appreciate the evolution of liberal thought on the topic. In the nineteenth century liberals were generally sympathetic to the independence struggles of the Greeks, Hungarians, Poles, and Italians. However, following the unification of Germany under Bismarck between 1860 and 1871 by 'blood and iron', it became increasingly apparent that nationalism could develop in non-liberal forms suited more to the development of states and **empires** as centralized power units rather than as republics engaged in the pursuit of liberal freedom. There developed, then, tensions between nationalism as the claim to maintain an exclusive territorial, political and moral domain, and the liberal ideal of self-determination, concerned with the right and ability of a people to establish political control over the forces and decision making processes that determine their social and political fates, compatible with the right and ability of others to do the same.

Following the First World War the problematic aspects of national self-determination became further apparent when applied to the multicultural regions of Central and Eastern Europe. Increasingly, liberal notions of self-determination came to require modifications or limitations upon the principle and practice of **sovereignty**. This has led liberal internationalism in the direction of support for minority rights, federalism, and the establishment of the partially post-sovereign institutions of the **European Union**: the European Coal and Steel Community and the European Economic Community. One current effort to re-imagine the question of self-government under conditions of **globalization** is the project of cosmopolitan democracy (see **cosmopolitanism**). The challenge this project faces is to devise ways in which centres of power and decision making can be influenced by and answerable to those groups they affect, despite the disjuncture between the (global) territorial scale of economic/political relations and the juridical/political division of the world into states.

Residual dilemmas of intervention and imperialism

The questions of whether to intervene to assist movements for national independence or to relieve violations of human rights or human suffering have generated legitimate differences of opinion within the liberal tradition. Most liberals have tended to fall somewhere between absolute non-interventionism and pro-interventionism. Immanuel Kant (1724–

1804), for example, was a strong non-interventionist but did sanction the right of forced constitutional change against regimes that were persistent and serious violators of **international law**. John Stuart Mill (1806–73), following the suppression of the liberal revolutions in 1848, came to sanction a right of counter-intervention in cases where a foreign power had intervened to suppress liberal forces.

More recently, the diverse responses to crises in the 1990s in areas such as Somalia, Bosnia, Rwanda, Sierra Leone, and Kosovo indicate both the lack of settled norms on the **legitimacy** of intervention and the enduring importance of certain classic questions pertaining to the question of intervention. These include the question of the authority to intervene, the interests and motives of the intervening parties, and the likely balance of good and harm that intervention will bring. Most recently, liberals have struggled to offer either analyses of, or alternative policies to, the 'new security agenda', as defined by Washington under the Bush administration, characterized by a willingness to use 'preventive force' and to pursue regime change in the 'War on Terror'. Two areas in which liberalism has shaped the recent international agenda, however, are the development of international law and the promotion of the idea of **good governance**.

The development of the international as a law governed realm has long been an aspiration for liberals and, accordingly, the rediscovery of the legal responsibility of individuals for **war crime**s and **crimes against humanity** as developed at Nuremberg after the Second World War is at face value a positive development. However, whilst the *ad hoc* tribunals for former Yugoslavia and Rwanda have come into operation the more ambitious Permanent International Criminal Court has yet to function, due in large part to the absence of an increasingly unilateralist United States. Further, the lack of legal rights afforded to detainees at Camp Delta at Guantanamo Bay by the United States discredits the wider turn to law in the **international system** through demonstrating the selectivity of the attachment to due process.

The conventional liberal attention to the internal character of states has become manifest recently in the requirement for good governance by states in transition or in the underdeveloped regions of the world and is often a condition of aid and loan transfers by Western donors and financial institutions. Good governance has been popular on both the right and left of the tradition, not least for the way in which it bundles together a number of political goods – human rights, development, the rule of law, participatory political structures, and peace – as interdependent and mutually reinforcing. Differences in how these concepts are understood and over what their political implications are reflect the differences noted above between right-liberals who stress the importance of a hospitable environment for foreign capital and left-liberals who are primarily concerned with the development of civil society and participatory politics. The intrusive nature of this agenda does, however, raise the question of whether and to what extent 'governance' represents a new form of **imperialism**.

Historically, whilst many liberals such as Adam Smith, Kant, Cobden and Bright were critics of colonialism, others such as John Stuart Mill went as far as to sanction despotism as a legitimate mode of government for 'uncivilized' non-Europeans. Whilst imperialism came increasingly to be perceived as illegitimate as the colonized claimed for themselves the 'universal' right of self-determination that the Europeans enjoyed, the broader issue of the widespread liberal presumption of moral superiority remains. Accordingly, it is one of the residual liberal dilemmas whether to retreat from international engagement or to seek to better pursue some form of global justice that acknowledges liberalism's tendency to treat non-liberals less than equally but which seeks to overcome this long-standing tension. For social welfare liberals the issue of poverty and under-development would be an obvious place to start, as would greater emphasis upon what duties liberals themselves might have towards international peace, development, the ecological balance of the planet, and non-liberal others.

Conclusion

Liberal internationalism's reformist nature has been at the forefront of efforts to modify the international system of states and its political and moral character and evolution. National self-determination, free-trade, international organizations, the promulgation of universal rights and responsibilities all feature as part of the liberal problematic of seeking the pursuit of individual and collective freedom in a diverse and anarchical international system. Liberalism's most significant achievements lie in the efforts to develop politics in accordance with the perceived requirements of justice and to develop ways through which states can move beyond the realist representation of international relations as a war bound realm with strictly limited potential for cooperation. Among its weaknesses, however, are a problematic association with capitalism, a presumption of moral superiority and inclination towards imperialism, and an inconsistent level of engagement with international affairs and issues.

Liberal internationalism's future remains uncertain, as does the ability of liberalism to generate success in any of its critical, normative, political or administrative dimensions, let alone achieve a sustainable working balance between them. Theoretically, however, the most profitable route for those who wish to maintain liberal internationalism as a critical and normative project is to avoid an insular stance and embrace the concerns and insights of a number of other perspectives and methodologies that have contributed to the academic study of International Relations in the past two decades or so. **Historical sociology**, for example, is valuable through complementing liberalism's own philosophical and normative concern with greater awareness of the operation of structural power in international relations. **Feminism** and post-colonial studies are particularly strong in drawing attention to the position of the 'other' in contemporary theory and contemporary politics, which has been one of liberalism's most significant shortcomings. At the same time, liberalism's central concern with individual and collective freedom and its historical contribution to reshaping the conceptual categories and normative horizons of international relations, as well as its own political experience of pursuing reformist projects, ought to ensure that in one form or another it continues to be at the forefront of efforts to develop more humane and democratic global politics.

Further reading

Carr, E. H. (1939) *The Twenty Years Crisis*, London: Macmillan.

Franceschet, A. (2002) *Kant and Liberal Internationalism*, Basingstoke: Palgrave.

Howard, M. (1981) *War and the Liberal Conscience*, Oxford: Oxford University Press.

Keohane, R. and Nye, J. (1989) *Power and Interdependence*, Glenview, IL: Scott and Foreman & Co, 1989.

Long, D. and Wilson, P. (eds) (1995) *Thinkers of the Twenty Years Crisis: Inter-War Idealism Reassessed*, Oxford: Clarendon Press.

MacMillan, J. (1998) *On Liberal Peace*, London: I. B. Tauris

Richardson, J.L. (2001) *Contending Liberalisms in World Politics*, Boulder, CO: Lynne Rienner.

See also: democratic peace; embedded liberalism; end of history; order; realism; zone of peace

JOHN MACMILLAN

M

Managed trade

Managed trade involves efforts by states to direct trade by regulating imports and exports through the negotiation of trade outcomes rather than allowing the market to determine the results from trade. The practice trade hearkens back to the days of **mercantilism** when governments controlled international trading relationships in order to increase their national **power** but in the modern world it most often reflects the influence of protectionist elements in the domestic economy. In recent years managed trade has become an increasingly popular method for the stronger economies to seek greater benefits from their trading relationships with weaker states. Managed trade thus stands as an example of the exercise of power in the **international** political economy.

One common manifestation of managed trade is Voluntary Export Restraints (VERs). Under a typical VER agreement (sometimes known as a Voluntary Restraint Agreements or VRA) negotiations between two states lead to the setting of an upper level to which exports from one country to another may rise before higher tariffs come into use. Though officially termed 'voluntary' the negotiation of a VER usually involves the threat of punitive tariffs by the importing state if agreement cannot be reached. VERs have been a relatively common

tool of international trade statecraft since the 1930s but became increasingly popular in the post-war international trading system as tariff levels were reduced under the General Agreement on Tariffs and Trade (GATT), exposing producers in the developed states to higher levels of international competition. Managed trade became a central element of the 'New Protectionism', as the industrialized countries imposed a series of **non-tariff barriers** (NTBs) on international trade.

The highest profile VERs have been seen in the relationships between developed states. The commercial relationship between the United States and Japan in particular has been marked by the use of VERs since the 1950s, with a dramatic rise in their use in the 1980s and 1990s. In the early 1980s, as soaring gasoline prices pushed consumers to buy smaller, more fuel-efficient vehicles, the American automobile sector lost a large portion of its domestic sales to Japanese competitors and faced shrinking profits and high levels of unemployment. In response to calls for protection from US automobile producers, the US government pushed the Japanese to accept a VER on auto exports in 1981, an agreement that was regularly renewed over the next decade. Other states, such as Britain, negotiated similar agreements with the Japanese, using the threat of market closure to gain Japanese compliance.

Another form of managing trade that has become more common in recent years is the Voluntary Import Expansion (VIE). In contrast to a VER, it relies on the importing state to guarantee a minimum level of imports to the exporting state, thus guaranteeing market share. In 1986, the US government negotiated a bilateral agreement to limit Japanese semiconductor exports to the United States and at the same time to guarantee a 20 per cent market share to foreign producers in the Japanese market. The use of this kind of forced market opening increased in the following years, first with the Bush (senior) administration using the Structural Impediments Initiative (SII) talks to force Japan to open up to US exports, then with the Clinton administration opting for a more aggressive, 'results oriented' trade policy and the setting of numerical targets in bilateral trade.

Strategic Trade Policy (STP) is the official term used to describe such methods of managing trade. The goal of an STP is to protect key sectors in the economy and to improve overall national economic growth. A defensive STP protects the domestic market from competition, whilst an aggressive STP forces open foreign markets for national industries. In some cases a state may use these same policies to govern trade in sensitive areas, such as defense-related materials. This is usually justified in national **security** terms since states are unwilling to lose control of key technologies in this sector.

It can sometimes be confusing to distinguish between managed trade and **free trade**. For whilst some international agreements are promoted by governments as trade liberalization moves, they in fact micro-manage the process of liberalization to protect domestic producers

and workers from the negative effects of naked competition, at least in the short term. The **North American Free Trade Agreement (NAFTA)**, for example, excluded some important sectors in all three member countries (the United States, Canada, and Mexico), and provided transition periods for other sectors, to allow producers to adjust to competition from firms in the other NAFTA member states.

There are many debates over the economic pros and cons of managed trade, with free traders arguing that it compromises not only the economies of the targeted states, but also of the state employing such trade policies. It has been claimed, for example, that the 1981 VER on automobiles raised the average price of cars in the United States by US$2,000, and that each job saved by the agreement actually cost the US consumer US$180,000. Thus even without considering the effects on Japan's economy or on long-term US economic efficiency, managed trade can be a highly costly option.

Managed trade has also been a feature of the economic relations between rich and poor states. In the 1950s, as developing countries became more competitive in the production of low technology goods such as textiles, producers in the developed states called for protection against low cost imports. Initially, industrialized states negotiated bilateral agreements with the leading exporting states, but in the 1970s the major exporters came together with the major importers to negotiate a multilateral agreement on textiles called the Multi-Fibre Agreement (MFA), that set an upper limit on the market share that each of the major exporters could expect in the major importing states. This quota-based system continued until 1994 when the Uruguay Round of GATT negotiations renamed the MFA the Agreement on Clothing and Textiles (ATC) and phased out the quotas over a ten-year period. Another sensitive sector for developing states is agriculture, still one of the most protected economic areas. Many developing states argue that agricultural protectionism by the developed states has eliminated a potentially lucrative source of export revenue for them.

Thus a key issue relating to managed trade is its impact on economic **development**. Developing states have long argued that the protection of key sectors of the advanced industrialized economies damages their long-term development prospects. On the other hand developing countries called for multilaterally negotiated agreements to manage the trade in commodities during the abortive attempt to establish a New International Economic Order (NIEO) in the 1970s to stabilize their export revenues. The powerful states refused to negotiate such agreements and the international trade in commodities (with the notable exception of oil) continues to be defined by market principles.

Further reading

Cohn, T. H. (2003) *Governing Global Trade: International Institutions in Conflict and Convergence*, Aldershot: Ashgate.

Flamm, K. (1996) *Mismanaged Trade? Strategic Trade Policy and the Semiconductor Industry*, Washington, DC: Brookings.

Roberts, R. (1994) *The Choice: A Fable of Free Trade and Protectionism*, Upper Saddle River, NJ: Prentice Hall.

Tyson, L. and Bergsten, C. F. (1996) *Who's Bashing Whom: Trade Conflict in High Technology Industries*, Washington, DC: Brookings.

See also: embedded liberalism; free trade; most-favored nation; non-tariff barrier

DUNCAN WOOD

Marxism

Deeply enmeshed in intellectual and political projects spanning well over a century and across much of the world, Marxism – the tradition of 'practical critical activity' founded by Karl Marx (1818–83) – defies reduction to any simple doctrine or single political position. Nevertheless, it is possible to understand this constellation of intellectual and political positions as constituting variants of historical materialism (the core of the Marxist theoretical tradition) insofar as they are animated by a critique of **capitalism**, understood as a particular historical form of organization of human social life rather than a natural or necessary expression of some innate and invariant human nature. Without pretending to speak for the whole of Marxism, this entry will present a particular synthetic interpretation of historical materialism and its relevance for global politics.

Contrary to the caricatures which retain in some quarters a measure of academic currency, historical materialism has focused its attention upon capitalism as a material way of life, an ensemble of social relations which has never been coterminous with 'the economy' as we know it in the modern world, nor with the so-called 'domestic' sphere putatively contained within the boundaries of the sovereign state. Marxism has much to say about historically evolving structures and practices which have crossed national boundaries and linked the domestic and the international, the economic and the political – much to say, in short, about the social production of global politics. Historical materialism suggests that states and systems of interstate and transnational **power** relations are embedded in and (to a significant degree) produced through systems of relations which encompass (among other things) the social organization of production. This latter is itself structured according to relations of class (and, many contemporary Marxists acknowledge, by race and **gender** as well as other relations of domination), and is an object of contestation among social classes, state managers, and other historically situated political agents. Thus politics is not confined to the formally public sphere of the modern state, but permeates the economic sphere as well: just as the state and interstate politics can profoundly shape economic and social life, so the politics of the economy can have enormous implications – not generally recognized within the terms of liberal worldviews – for the historical form taken by particular states and world **orders** constructed among states. The point here, it must be emphasized, is not to reconstruct global politics on the basis of an economistic reductionism in which all causality is seen as emanating from an already constituted, foundational economic sphere (a sort of universal independent variable), but rather to argue something very nearly the opposite – that politics and political struggle are essential aspects of the processes by which all social structures are (re)produced, and hence that the analytical separation of political from economic life – as well as domestic and international aspects of these – represents a false dichotomy which obscures much of potential political importance.

Historical materialism

Historical materialism begins from the premise that humans become what they are in large part because of the social forms through which they organize their material reproduction, a process that is at once both natural and social. Human social beings continually (re-)produce the conditions of their existence through socially organized productive activity which, because we are human and not animals, necessarily involves thinking, speaking, planning and organizing together. Through this process, the material world, social relations and ideas, and human beings themselves are continuously reproduced or transformed. Thus, to paraphrase Marx, people make their own history and in the process determine what it means to be human in a particular socio-historical context; but they cannot just make themselves anew, *de novo*, in any way they please. Rather, historically situated social agents – whose actions are enabled and constrained by the social relations and self-understandings which constitute their identities – inherit particular social forms from preceding generations and proceed to (re-)produce, alter, or transform the social world in which they find themselves situated. No longer need we understand the world as a collection of apparently objective facts mutely confronting and constraining us, nor is the only alternative to imagine our world and ourselves as the creation of some mystical superhuman subject; rather the material and social world as it exists for us may be understood as a human social product, and since we are ourselves integral to that world, we are (potentially) capable of social **self-determination** in and through our socially organized productive activity. Under historical circumstances of capitalism, our inability collectively to determine the social organization of our productive activity, the kind of society we will live in and the kinds of people we will become, is for Marx an index of our unfreedom.

The critique of capitalist social life

Capitalism as Marx represents it is not a seamless web of oppression, but rather a contradictory life of 'dual freedom'. On such a dialectical Marxian view, capitalism entails liberation from the relations of direct political and economic dependence characteristic of feudalism and other pre-capitalist forms, and hence presents possibilities for social individuation and 'political emancipation' within the parameters of republican forms of state. But capitalism simultaneously limits the historically real emancipatory possibilities it brings into being by (re-)subjecting individuals to social domination through the compulsions of market dependence and the disabling effects of fetishism and its reification of social **power** relations. These dialectics of freedom and unfreedom, the powers they generate and resistances they engender, have produced families of capitalist historical structures that are fraught with tension and possibilities for change. Whether any such possibilities are realized, and in what particular ways, depend upon open-ended political struggles in which the power relations of capitalism will necessarily be implicated.

One of the enduring insights of Marxian theory is that the seemingly apolitical economic spaces generated by capitalism – within and across juridical states – are permeated by structured relations of social power deeply consequential for political life and, indeed, for the (re)production of social life as a whole. These powers may be ideologically depoliticized (and thus rendered democratically unaccountable) in liberal representations separating a naturalized and privatized economy from the formally political sphere of the state. The operation of this economy (and the implicit social powers residing within it) may then be represented as something approaching a universal social good, the engine of economic growth and a generalized prosperity. However another of these enduring Marxian insights is

that social power relations are also *processes* – dynamic, contradictory and contestable.

The critical leverage of a Marxian critique of capitalism is generated by its explicit focus on the social power relations that inhere in, and yet are obscured by, the structures and practices of capitalist production and exchange. Under historical conditions of capitalism, social relations are mediated by things – commodities. Although the social division of labor under capitalism has brought together and collectively empowered human producers as never before, capitalism simultaneously divides and disables them by representing their social relations as naturalized relations of exchange between commodities (the famous 'fetishism of commodities'). To the extent that social relations are subsumed into a world of putatively independent objects – 'things' – communities of human producers are correspondingly disempowered. 'The social world of capitalism appears as something we inhabit ... rather than some of the ways we are, and it is this estrangement of the real content of social life that grounds the abstractions which come to stand in for it: modernity's representations ... of both society and self' (Sayer, 1991: 88). Inhabitants of the capitalist market, the subjects of capitalist modernity, are represented to themselves as abstract (i.e., atomistic) individuals who, as such, are largely unable to discern – much less communally to govern – the social division of labor in which they are embedded. The social division of labor takes on the appearance of objectivity, an uncontrollable force of nature, the mystical market whose price signals and compulsions individuals neglect at our peril. Concomitantly, capitalism's fetishism and reification serve to mystify social power relations by making power appear as a property of things that may be possessed (or not) by abstract individuals.

The implications for democracy are deeply ironic. For even as capitalism realizes 'political emancipation' through the development of the liberal republic in which citizens are formally equal, it effectively reifies, privatizes and de-politicizes class based social powers (by associating them with ownership of 'private property') and thereby evacuates from the purview of political democracy much of the substance of social life, vitiating democracy's promise of social self-determination.

Capitalism and class power

Behind these mystifications, capitalist social relations generate the possibility of asymmetrical social powers distributed according to class. Socially necessary means of production are constituted as private property, exclusively owned by one class of people. The other class, whose exclusion from ownership of social means of production is integral to the latter's constitution as private property, are then compelled to sell that which they do own – labor power, their capacity for productive activity – in order to gain access to those means of production and hence through wages) their own means of survival. As the consumer of labor power, the capitalist may control the actual activity of labor – the labor process – and appropriate its product, which is then subsumed into capital itself as part of the process of accumulation. As a consequence of their position within the social organization of production, then, capitalists may exercise two kinds of social power.

As *employers*, capitalists and their managerial agents attempt to assert control over the transformation of labor power – the abstract, commodified capacity for labor – into actual labor.

Driven by the imperatives of competitive accumulation, they seek to maximize the output of workers in relation to wages paid for labor power, and may lengthen the workday or transform the labor process itself in order to do so. This latter tendency was instantiated in struggles surrounding Fordist workplace regimes. Displacing predominantly craft-based production in which skilled laborers exercised substantial control over their conditions of work, Fordist production entailed an intensified industrial division of labor; increased mechanization and coordination of large scale manufacturing processes (e.g., sequential machining operations and converging assembly lines) to achieve a steady flow of production; a shift toward the use of less skilled labor performing, *ad infinitum*, tasks minutely specified by management; and the potential for heightened capitalist control over the pace and intensity of work. At the core of the Fordist reorganization of production, then, was the construction of new relations of power in the workplace; to the extent that these relations of power could become established parameters of the work process, capital would reap the gains of manifold increases in output per hour of waged labor. The promise of massive increases in productivity led to the widespread imitation and adaptation of Ford's basic model of production through the industrial core of the US economy, and in other industrial capitalist countries.

The social institutions of Fordist mass production began to emerge in the United States early in the twentieth century and – bitterly, if episodically, resisted by workers – were at the center of a decades-long process of social struggle which extended into the immediate post-World War Two era. **Cold war** ideology played a crucial role in the political stabilization of Fordist institutions in the United States, providing the common ground on which de-radicalized industrial labor unions could be incorporated as junior partners in a coalition of globally oriented social forces which worked together to rebuild the 'free world' along liberal capitalist lines, and to resist the encroachment of a presumed communist (see **communism**) menace globally and at home. Institutionalized Fordism, in turn, enabled the United States to contribute almost half of world industrial production in the immediate postwar years, and thus provided the economic dynamism necessary to spark reconstruction of the major capitalist countries after World War Two, and to support the emergence of both the consumer society and the military-industrial complex in the postwar United States (Rupert, 1995).

The second social identity through which capitalists are socially empowered is as *investors*. Deciding when, where, and how to invest is a prerogative attendant on ownership of private property in the means of production. As owner-investors, capitalists routinely make decisions which directly determine the social allocation of labor and resources (the pace of aggregate economic activity and the shape of the social division of labor) and indirectly limit the scope of public policy through the constraint of 'business confidence' and the implicit threat of 'capital strike' and/or transnational capital flight. These social powers have been amplified in recent decades. In increasingly globalized financial markets, astonishing volumes of foreign exchange trading and speculative international investment now dwarf the currency reserves of governments and can readily swamp, or leave high and dry, the financial markets of particular states. Responding to short term differences in perceived conditions of profitability and variations in business confidence between one place and another, as well as speculative guesses

about future market fluctuations, these enormous flows are highly volatile. Massive amounts can be shifted from one currency (or assets denominated in one currency) to another literally at the speed of light via the computer modems and fiber optic cables that link together the world's financial markets and enable 'round the clock' trading. These changes have been consequential, for the new historical structures embody an enhancement of the social powers of capital, and especially finance capital, which can effectively pre-empt expansionary macro-policies aimed at increasing employment or wage levels. This disciplinary power has the effect of prioritizing the interests of investors, who are as a class effectively able to hold entire states/societies hostage.

Insofar as the social powers of capital are effectively privatized – associated with private ownership and exchange of property among juridically equal individuals in an apparently de-politicized economic sphere – they are ideologically mystified and democratically unaccountable. Anti-democratic and disabling as they might be, however, these class-based powers are neither uncontestable in principle nor uncontested in fact. Like all relations of social power, capitalist power relations are reciprocal, constituting a 'dialectic of power' subject to ongoing contestation, renegotiation, and restructuring. The reproduction of these powers is always problematic, and must be politically secured on an ongoing basis in particular contexts. Successful reproduction of class power is hardly assured.

However, the process of challenging these powers may be significantly more complex than more fundamentalist versions of Marxism have been prepared to contemplate. For class powers must be actualized in various concrete sites of social production where class is articulated with other socially meaningful identities resident and effective in those historical circumstances. Capitalist power over waged labor has been historically articulated with gendered and raced forms of power: separation of workplace from residence and the construction of ideologies of feminized domesticity rationalizing unpaid labor; ideologies of white supremacy rationalizing racial segregation and inequality; gendered and raced divisions of labor; and so forth. Indeed, these relations of race and gender have had important effects on class formation. This implies that in concrete contexts class cannot be effectively determining without itself being determined. However this is not to say, in some pluralist sense, that class is only one of a number of possible social identities all of which are equally contingent. Insofar as productive interaction with the natural world remains a necessary condition of all human social life (as Marx maintained), I would suggest that understandings of social power relations that abstract from the social organization of production must be radically incomplete. To the extent that capitalism and its putatively private relations of power organize crucial parts of social life on a transnational scale, the struggles surrounding these relations and their various articulations in sites around the world merit serious study as part of the question of global power and resistance.

Gramsci: capitalism, ideology, hegemony

If Marx left us with incisive theorizations of capitalism, its core structures and constitutive tensions, it was the Italian political theorist and communist leader Antonio Gramsci (1891–1937) who contributed to the historical materialist tradition a conceptual vocabulary with which to enable processes of transfor-

mative politics. Marx suggested that socialist transformation might emerge out of the confluence of capitalism's endemic crisis tendencies, the polarization of its class structure and the intensified exploitation of the proletariat and, most importantly, the emergence of the latter as a collective agent through the realization of its socially productive power, heretofore developed in distorted and self limiting form under the conditions of concentrated capitalist production.

Gramsci accepted in broad outline Marx's analysis of the structure and dynamics of capitalism, but was unwilling to embrace the more mechanical and economistic interpretations of Marx circulating in the international socialist movement. Contrary to vulgar Marxist dogma, progressive social change would not automatically follow in train behind economic developments, but must instead be produced by historically situated social agents whose actions are enabled and constrained by their social self-understandings. Thus, for Gramsci, popular 'common sense' becomes a critical terrain of political struggle. His theorization of a social politics of ideological struggle – which he called a 'war of position' to distinguish it from a Bolshevik strategy of frontal assault on the state – contributed to the historical materialist project of de-reifying capitalist social relations (including narrowly state-based conceptions of politics) and constructing an alternative – more enabling, participatory, intrinsically democratic – social order out of the historical conditions of capitalism.

Popular common sense could become a ground of struggle because it is an amalgam of historically effective ideologies, scientific doctrines and social mythologies. Gramsci understood popular common sense not to be monolithic or univocal, nor was **hegemony** an unproblematically dominant ideology that simply shut out all alternative visions or political projects. Rather, common sense was understood to be a syncretic historical residue, fragmentary and contradictory, open to multiple interpretations and potentially supportive of very different kinds of social visions and political projects. And hegemony was understood as the unstable product of a continuous process of struggle, 'war of position,' or 'reciprocal siege'. Gramsci's political project thus entailed addressing the popular common sense operative in particular times and places, making explicit the tensions and contradictions within it as well as the socio-political implications of these, in order to enable critical social analysis and transformative political practice.

Beginning with the seminal work of Robert Cox (1981), Gramscian concepts have been deployed by scholars of world politics (not all of whom would be at home with the label 'Marxist') seeking to counter the predominant intellectual climate of state-centric atomism and its deeply conservative implications. Drawing on the relational and process-oriented conceptual underpinnings of historical materialism, Cox stressed the historical construction of various forms of state in the nexus between social forces (classes, social movements, and other collective social agents) on the one hand, and world orders on the other. He stressed that this relational nexus necessarily involves economic, political and cultural aspects, all of which are bound up with systems of power which are not coterminous with sovereign states. Drawing on Gramsci's conceptualization of hegemony, Cox suggested that these systems of power could be meaningfully distinguished depending upon the relative balance of coercive and consensual forms of power. The re-thinking of world politics produced by Cox and other neo-

Gramscian scholars has provided a critical alternative to conventional understandings that take sovereign states (understood as territorially based wielders of coercive power) to be axiomatic.

The state and the interstate system

More orthodox Marxian scholars of world politics have in recent years made important contributions to understanding the historical production of the state and interstate system as modern social forms historically linked (if not genetically twinned) with capitalism. In his incisive critique of orthodox realist (see **realism**) International Relations theory, Justin Rosenberg (1994) argues that 'geopolitical systems' are not independent of, and cannot be understood in abstraction from, the social organization of material life and its processes of reproduction. Rosenberg challenges realism's reification of the state as a transhistorical essence, and its typical reduction of political agency to state policy. Abstracting the modern state from those social relations in which it is embedded, such that the state may be determining without itself being determined, realism understands the politics of economic relations in terms of the instrumental machinations of states extracting resources for deployment in international geopolitical competition. This reveals a crucial theoretical weakness at the heart of orthodox international relations theory, a blindness to the political relations intrinsic to the capitalist world economy which are not reducible to the interests or actions of sovereign states.

Following the logic of historical materialist critique, Rosenberg situates the sovereign state and its geopolitics – as well as the seemingly separate sphere of the capitalist economy – in the historically specific social relations of capitalist modernity: 'the separation of the political and the economic indicates precisely the central institutional linkage between the capitalist economy and the **nation-state**: that is, the legal structure of property rights which removes market relationships from directly political control or contestation and allows the flow of investment capital across national boundaries' (Rosenberg 1994: 14). It is through these latter processes of transnational economic activity that the privatized powers of capital have been projected on an increasingly global scale.

While acknowledging Rosenberg's insight that capitalist geopolitics are qualitatively different from absolutist or feudal geopolitics, Hannes Lacher (2002) offers a powerful theoretical and historical argument against the thesis that the modern state – and, by extension, the system of states – had its genesis in the very historical processes which gave rise to capitalism. He argues instead that the emergence of a system of states (a process driven by the historically distinct politico-economic imperatives of absolutist rule) preceded the emergence of capitalist production relations and cannot adequately be understood as their product. On this view, the modern state emerged from irreducibly geopolitical processes rooted in the pre-capitalist milieu of absolutist states.

Subsequently, with the emergence of capitalist agriculture and primitive accumulation in Britain, the pressures of interstate political competition contributed to the articulation of this geopolitical state system with capitalism, integrating and transforming both and generating thereby the primary structural forms of modern social life. Following the emergence of capitalist production relations in England, the dynamics of absolutist geopolitics were transformed by the competitive dynamics characteristic of capitalism, and the system of territorial states was internalized within, and became integral to, a distinctly capitalist system of social relations. In this historical system, political authority was organized through territorially defined states even as economic transactions and capitalist competition overflowed state boundaries. Geopolitical competition among states thus became bound up with transnational processes of competitive capitalist production.

Imperialism: then and now

Among the most familiar and long-standing contributions of Marxist theory to the understanding of world politics are its theorizations of **imperialism**, initially developed in the early twentieth century. By the dawn of the twenty-first century, the concept of imperialism appeared to have lost much of its currency, displaced by a focus upon the less directly coercive mechanisms of capitalist **globalization**. Recent episodes of military adventurism by major capitalist powers, however, serve as a reminder that this branch of Marxian theory, even if no longer novel, remains significant for contemporary world politics.

Since capitalism entails a structural separation between the economic and political aspects of social life (the depoliticization and privatization of the economy which makes possible capitalist property and wage labor), the state in a capitalist context is generally dependent upon the economic activities of capitalists in order to generate resources which it can tax, and to create enough economic growth and prosperity within its territory to minimally legitimate the government and the social order as a whole. The state has, therefore, a compelling interest in the overall success of accumulation by capitalists whose operations are based within its territory. But since capitalist economic activity routinely overflows those boundaries, and encounters in the world market capitalist competitors based in other states which may well be geopolitical rivals of the home state, the imperatives of capitalist and geopolitical competition may converge to generate imperialism, the deployment of military power in the service of capital accumulation. This has entailed forcibly integrating new areas into the world market, destroying non-capitalist ways of life and commodifying social relations to create an exploitable proletarianized labor force, or enforcing the dominance of private property and capitalist access to important resources.

Capitalist imperialism – as distinct from pre-capitalist tribute-extracting or commerce-controlling empires – involves the use of coercive power in order to create and maintain conditions necessary for capitalist production, exchange, and investment (in short, for capital accumulation) to occur on a transnational scale (Wood, 2003). This is not to say that all modern instances of imperialism have had a purely capitalist character. As a consequence of the globally uneven development of capitalist social relations we may identify historically hybrid instances such as the British Raj with its militarily enforced **mercantilism** and tributary taxation, or King Leopold's Belgian Congo where partial commodification was attended by outright extortion and the massive and ruthless exercise of coercive force to compel hyper-exploited labor. Viewed from a world historical perspective, however, the spatial expansion of capitalist social relations and processes has prepared the way for the recession of explicitly political coercive force into the background of global capitalism, never entirely absent but not as a rule directly present or transparent.

Globalization

When conditions of transnational accumulation have been more or less secured, capitalism can function without regular recourse to directly coercive exploitation: rather than the sharp point of a bayonet, it relies on what Marx called 'the dull compulsion of the economic', the relentless pressure in a commodified society to earn enough to secure the material necessities of life. William Robinson (2004) argues forcefully that by the late twentieth century, much of the globe had been successfully integrated into the capitalist world market, such that the commodification of labor and of the conditions of material life was very nearly complete.

On this view, globalization represents an 'epochal shift' in which the displacement of pre-capitalist relations is completed and capitalist commodification is universalized, national circuits of accumulation are subsumed within global circuits (through the globalization of commercial, productive, and financial capital), a transnational capitalist class emerges and the nation-state is transformed, superceded by and incorporated within a multi-layered 'transnational state' as the political aspect of capitalist social organization. Patterns of nation-state based political accommodation between capitalist and popular classes (such as the Fordist accommodation), and the constraints on accumulation that these have represented, have been increasingly vitiated by the transnational re-organization of capitalist power, displaced by the hegemonic project of the neoliberal *Washington Consensus*. Despite the perhaps overly confident tone of his extrapolations regarding the emergence of a qualitatively new transnational capitalism and transnational state, Robinson explicitly acknowledges the continuing presence and significance of nationally-based phenomena, and ongoing contradictions between national and globalizing aspects of capitalism. Increasingly global, capitalism is nonetheless a deeply contradictory system and faces recurrent accumulation crises and political tensions among factions of the global capitalist bloc as well as between that bloc and the great bulk of the world's people who are politically and economically marginalized by this system of power.

Ellen Wood (2003), another important contemporary Marxist theorist, is resistant to Robinson's strong 'transnational state' thesis, and suggests that under capitalist conditions market-mediated economic relations readily outdistance the social organization of political rule, so that globalizing capitalism is increasingly reliant on nation-states for the political mediation of unevenly developed and variously regulated local spaces. On this view, contemporary capitalism is likely to generate an intensification of the contradiction between economic expansionism and the territorially defined forms of political authority upon which capitalism depends for social stability and political reproduction. Wood sees the US quest for unquestioned military supremacy as a response to this contradiction, an attempt to exert control over the system of states in order to maintain conditions of profitability for US based firms operating in a world economy.

Marxism in the twenty-first century?

Although not without its tensions and limitations, Marxian theory provides critical leverage for understanding the structures and dynamics of capitalism, its integral if complex relationship to the modern form of state, the class based powers it enables and the resistances these entail; and Gramsci's rich legacy suggests a conceptual vocabulary for a transformative politics in which a variety of anti-capitalist movements might coalesce in order to produce any number of future possible worlds whose very possibility is occluded by capitalism.

In the present context of globalizing capitalism and neo-imperialism, such resistance has taken the form of a transnational confluence of movements for global justice and peace. It contains elements that are explicitly class-identified, but also encompasses a rich variety of social forces opposed to the depredations of globalizing neoliberal capitalism and the arrogant US power which enforces it. Insofar as the multifarious movements for global justice and peace inhabit common ground, it is a world where massively unequal wealth and divergent life chances are underpinned by historical concentrations of both economic and military power; an implicitly undemocratic world that, while historically real, is neither natural nor necessary. In their diverse but convergent challenges to this concentrated power they embody a rejection of capitalism's abstract individuals in favor of more relational and process oriented visions of social reality, and an affirmation of the historical situatedness of political knowledge and practice. To the extent that they are forging a transnational culture of solidarity across meaningful social differences, and together effect resistance to the power relations which variously and commonly oppress them, they may represent the germ of a transformative political process which need not be contained by capitalism's reified separations of economics/politics, state/society, domestic/international.

Further reading

Brewer, A. (1991) *Marxist Theories of Imperialism: A Critical Survey*, London: Routledge.

Cox, R. (1981) 'Social Forces, States, and World Orders', *Millennium* 10, 126–55.

Lacher, H. (2002) 'Making sense of the international system: the promises and pitfalls of the newest Marxist theories of international relations' in M. Rupert and H. Smith (eds) *Historical Materialism and Globalization*, London: Routledge.

Robinson, W. (2004) *A Theory of Global Capitalism*, Baltimore: Johns Hopkins University Press.

Rosenberg, J. (1994) *Empire of Civil Society*, London: Verso.

Rupert, M. (1995) *Producing Hegemony*, Cambridge: Cambridge University Press

Sayer, D. (1991) *Capitalism and Modernity*, London: Routledge.

Wood, E. (2003) *Empire of Capital*, London: Verso.

See also: agent-structure debate; communism; critical theory; revolution; socialism

MARK RUPERT

Mercantilism

Mercantilism is often seen as one of three approaches to the theory and practice of **international political economy**. The first is *laissez faire* liberalism, which advocates **free trade** and minimal state intervention in both the domestic and the international economy. The second perspective seeks to understand the workings of the global capitalist system (see **capitalism**) in order to demonstrate its inherently exploitative nature. There are different versions of this general approach, but all share a Marxist heritage (see **Marxism**). The most-well known of these is **world-system theory**. The third perspective is mercantilism. Sometimes referred to as economic **nationalism**, it is the oldest of the three perspectives. It was the dominant economic philosophy of European states from the fifteenth century to the late seventeenth century. Since that time, it has gone through a number of manifestations and continues to be an important economic alternative to both liberalism and Marxism.

Essentially, mercantilism is an economic philosophy that believes that the economic management should be part of the state's pursuit of its **national interest**s defined in terms of wealth, **power** and prestige. Francis Bacon (1561–1626), an early defender of this philosophy, wrote that there was a direct line 'from shipping to Indies, from Indies to treasure, and from treasure to greatness'. Consequently, mercantilists are not interested in improving the quality of life of humanity or of fostering mutual cooperation among states in the **international system**. Their primary goal is the maximization of power and they see economic activity as a vehicle for achieving this end.

In order to achieve 'greatness' through 'treasure', mercantilist states typically do two things. First, they orient their domestic economy so as to produce a favorable balance of trade. Their goal is to produce goods for export while at the same time keeping imports low. Second, they will gear their industries to producing value-added products from cheap imported raw material. Thus, mercantilist states tend to discourage agricultural production in favor of manufacturing, to impose high import duties on foreign made products, and offer subsidies to domestic industries. Mercantilist states, then, are highly interventionist.

One should distinguish between *benign* or *defensive* mercantilism and *malevolent* and *aggressive* mercantilism. The former is designed to protect a state's core values and safeguard its autonomy in the face of the internationalization of production. The other variant (popular in the 1930s) wages economic warfare against other states in order to triumph over them.

In theory if not in practice, mercantilism fell into disrepute toward the end of the eighteenth century. One reason for this was the publication of Adam Smith's *Wealth of Nations* (1776). This rightly famous liberal text set out explicitly to demonstrate that mercantilism was flawed. Among other criticisms of mercantilism, Smith suggested that it was inefficient for a state to produce a product that could be produced more cheaply elsewhere. Later this would become the basis for the theory of comparative advantage and the basis for free trade. It would be a mistake to think that mercantilism is dead and buried, however. Protectionist and neo-mercantilist policies continue to be a part of the economic thinking of some states.

Further reading

Ekelund, R. and Tollison, R. (1997) *Politicized Economies: Monarchy, Monopoly, and Mercantilism*, Houston, TX: Texas A&M University Press.

Heckscher, E. and Magnusson, L. (1994) *Mercantilism*, London: Routledge.

Ormrod, D. *et al.* (eds) (2003) *The Rise of Commercial Empires : England and the Netherlands in the Age of Mercantilism, 1650–1770*, Cambridge: Cambridge University Press.

See also: free trade; managed trade; world-system theory

TERRY O'CALLAGHAN

Mercenary

Mercenaries fight for profit in a conflict or country which is not their own. Mercenaries have been a regular feature of organized warfare for centuries, serving lords, kings, and states in place of 'people's armies'. Professional formations of soldiers were employed by states to wage **war**s on their behalf, or were utilized for their skill in certain military tactics such as archery, cavalry and artillery. These privateers fought throughout Europe and its colonies. Many famous military formations began as mercenary operations, and technically still are, such as the French Foreign Legion, and the Nepalese Ghurka regiments which serve Britain and India. In some cases they were raised and controlled by **multinational corporation**s such as the British East India Company.

Having done much to generate the rise of **nation-state**s, mercenaries soon became antithetical to its principles. The consolidation of the sovereign state and its monopoly over the use of legitimate violence ended the routine use of mercenaries as professional people's armies began to ensure states interests. New national armies were seen as more reliable, professional, and legitimate than profit motivated militias, they could be controlled by government and they served to support the **legitimacy** of the state.

Modern mercenaries came to prominence in the 1960s when they were widely used in wars of **decolonization** and post-colonial state building in the **Third World**. Many states in Africa used individual mercenaries or units to support their rule. Mercenaries were also employed by anti-government or revolutionary forces to take control of the state, in some cases mounting coups against established governments. Their unaccountable actions and brutal reputation evinced the label 'dogs of war', and led most states to ban the use of mercenaries in modern conflicts.

Mercenaries are outlawed by **international law**, contained in Article 47 of the

Geneva Convention (1977 Additional Protocol), which stipulates that foreign mercenaries are those that take direct part in conflicts that they or their country are not party to, for the sole purpose of private gain, being usually paid in excess of the local combatants. In 1989, the **United Nations** (UN) created the International Convention against the Recruitment, Use, Financing and Training of Mercenaries, but this was met with little international support and attracted few signatories. The UN Special Rapporteur on Mercenaries releases regular reports on mercenary activities in civil conflicts.

Change in the international **security** environment after the **cold war** has witnessed a dramatic rise in the use of mercenaries. The many ethnic **civil war**s that broke out after 1989, particularly in Africa, the former Yugoslavia, and Central Asia, the increased criminalization of many civil wars, and the growth in **transnational crime** have seen renewed employment of mercenaries to bolster war fighting capability. Their clients now include states, multinational corporations, insurgent groups, transnational criminal organizations and narcotics producing syndicates. The breakdown in the state's monopoly of violence has seen multiple **power** holders emerge within and across the sovereign boundaries of the nation-state. These non-state actors have taken advantage of the surge in privatization in the global economy, seeking alternatives in the expanded network of privatized security services.

There are two main types of mercenaries. The first are individuals who hire out their skills to states, insurgent groups and criminal organizations for specific duties attached to combat or support units. Many of these mercenaries prefer to be called 'contract soldiers'. Second, there are private military companies (PMCs), corporate entities that maintain large contracts with clients that are usually states. PMCs employ hundreds of professionals and maintain a roster of personnel that they can draw upon for specific duties. They often work to bolster weak but legitimate regimes, protect state assets from criminal insurgents, and offer a range of force augmentation training and tactics. These larger firms are often involved in complex corporate structures that connect the provision of security with the extraction of natural resources such as oil, diamonds, and other large-scale multinational projects.

The privatization of security has increased in tandem with the global economy and the drive to privatization. The end of the cold war necessitated the downsizing of many militaries. The market was subsequently flooded with professionals from a host of European and Western armies. Some elite units were demobilized and then reestablished as profit oriented PMCs. Weapons and equipment from old Soviet arsenals also became available, providing many firms with sophisticated equipment to conduct operations.

The size of the private security industry has been estimated at US$200 billion annually. There are now hundreds of firms that operate in many of the world's civil conflicts. PMCs offer a wide array of services. These can include technical support, transport, logistics, training, and aerial reconnaissance, as well as the more traditional task of conducting military campaigns on behalf of clients. Their operations range from multi-million dollar contracts awarded to the US firm Military Professional Resources Incorporated (MPRI) to retrain and re-equip national armies such as those of Croatia and Bosnia-Herzogovina, to specific military operations to reestablish state control over vital national assets, such as those engaged in by the South African firm Executive Outcomes (EO) in Sierra Leone and Angola in the 1990s. In one case, a Russian firm provided a small air fleet of fighter planes and helicopters, including pilots and support staff, to the government of Ethiopia to provide air cover for its 1998 war against neighboring Eritrea. A notorious case involved a British based firm, Sandline International, commissioned by the government of Papua New Guinea to train its defense forces in order to end a secessionist movement that had wrested control of a lucrative mine. The contract was ended when domestic and international pressure toppled the PNG government and the contract with Sandline was terminated.

Larger PMCs are also employed by states to provide support services, such as transport, housing, guarding sensitive installations and detention facilities that have been privatized by governments. These are often in developed states that have privatized support services. Training of foreign troops in security, tactics, weaponry, and computer software has also increased. These activities now account for the largest share of modern mercenary contracts.

While many of the larger PMCs rely on close contacts with Western governments to maintain their access to markets, smaller firms can be more unscrupulous in their choice of contracts, working with insurgent groups known for their **human rights** abuses, or for narcotics producing syndicates seeking professional advice and training in how to avoid government interdiction. The resurgence of mercenary firms reflects the changing security environment in the developing world. Their use also demonstrates trends towards privatization and the use of the private sector in the absence of state services.

The legality of many PMCs is questionable. Efforts to outlaw their activities are thwarted by a maze of parent-subsidiary companies, the extensive use of outsourcing, and their ties to large multinational corporations and states. PMCs are not expressly prohibited by **international law**. In many cases, established PMCs have been granted approval by governments to pursue contracts as an adjunct to state policy. Some commentators argue that PMCs could even replace multilateral **peacekeeping** operations due to their reduced costs, rapid deployment capability, and corporate accountability, freeing states from having to contribute their own forces to dangerous and difficult interventions. A 2002 report by the British Government recommended regulation of the industry to serve such a purpose. Arguments such as these have been condemned by the United Nations and human rights groups, who see no role for mercenaries in conflict resolution.

Further reading

Adams, T.K. (1999) 'The New Mercenaries and the Privatization of Conflict' *Parameters* 29(2), 103–16.

Arnold, G. (1999) *Mercenaries. The Scourge of the Third World*, Basingstoke: Palgrave.

Mandel, R. (2002) *Armies Without States: The Privatization of Security*, Boulder, CO: Lynne Rienner.

Singer, P.W. (2003) *Corporate Warriors. The Rise of the Privatized Military Industry*, Ithaca, NY: Cornell University Press.

Shearer, D. (1998) 'Outsourcing war', *Foreign Policy* 112, 68–72.

See also: civil war; decolonization; failed state; peacekeeping; war

DAVID SCOTT MATHIESON

Microstates

When the **United Nations** was launched in 1945, small size proved no obstacle to the membership of wealthy Luxembourg and later, Iceland, both with populations below 500,000, but like the **League of Nations**, the organization drew the line on admission of the very small European states of Monaco, Liechtenstein, and San Marino. These states were viewed as too small to be able to carry out the responsibilities of membership in a global political body. Instead, the European microstates, which also include Andorra and the Vatican, were relegated to observer status. Today, except for the (non-territorial) Vatican, these countries are full members of the United Nations, even though their populations range from only 28,000 (San Marino) to 69,000 (Andorra).

The change in attitude toward very small states (*microstates*) on the part of the global community owes much to the wave of **decolonization** beginning in the 1960s and the attendant embrace of anti-colonialism on the part of the United Nations. By the end of 1968, the UN had admitted the following countries having less than a million inhabitants: The People's Republic of the Congo, Cyprus, Gabon, Zanzibar (later merged with Tanganyika), Gambia, Barbados, Botswana, Guyana, Lesotho, Equatorial Guinea, Mauritius, Swaziland, and the smallest, Maldives, with only about 100,000 inhabitants. In turn an enlarged UN in which **Third World** countries of all sizes came to predominate fully endorsed the notion that all independent (sovereign) states should be members regardless of size. The movement to universality in UN membership was completed after the **cold war** when the small Baltic republics joined the organization, and the once-rejected tiny European principalities applied and were finally accepted as full members in the early 1990s.

In the late 1960s and the early 1970s the UN, concerned about the growing numbers of very small member states, tried to address the issue of whether these states could realistically carry out their international obligations. Prior to this period, 'small' referred primarily to European states such as Belgium, Austria, and Switzerland. At the UN and elsewhere, the subcategory of ministate or 'microstate' was therefore coined to denote states that had very small populations: somewhere between 100,000 and one million people. Interestingly, the focus of the global community was not only on whether these states were economically and financially viable and therefore internationally responsible, but also on the relationship between size and influence in international organizations, particular with regard to voting equity. There was some sentiment among the larger states and some analysts that microstates should have less than full membership; they should confine their interests to selected issues and be given only limited decision making involvement in global forums. Although the norms of one state, one vote democracy and full participation eventually prevailed, it is clear that microstates have over the decades had to overcome unique obstacles in order to survive and be noticed, both in the institutional sphere and in the world at large.

The definition of a microstate remains problematic today inasmuch as any population limit one sets must of necessity remain shifting and relative. The organization which has perhaps done the most policy work on small states is the **Commonwealth**, which has thirty-two small states among its fifty-four members. The Commonwealth's latest definition of what it prefers to call simply 'small' (1997) refers to states with fewer than 1.5 million inhabitants, but it is telling that the organization had to include Jamaica, Lesotho, and Papua New Guinea with populations well above 1.5 million, on the basis that they share certain common characteristics with the smaller group. Along with these three microstates, the Commonwealth group included Belize, Guyana, and the English-speaking Caribbean island states; the African states Botswana, The Gambia, Mauritius, Namibia, Seychelles, and Swaziland; Brunei and Maldives in Asia; the South Pacific islands; and Cyprus and Malta in the Mediterranean.

For purposes that go beyond the Commonwealth focus, Papua New Guinea with nearly 5 million people (2001) would not normally be included as a microstate, whereas the following would certainly be added: Suriname in South America; Comoros, Djibouti, Cape Verde, Equatorial Guinea, Gabon, Guinea-Bissau, and Sao Tome e Principe in Africa; Bhutan in Asia; Bahrain and Qatar in the Middle East; and Estonia in Eastern Europe. All of these had populations below 1.5 million in the early 2000s. Some analysts might even use a slightly higher population cut off, allowing for the inclusion of Kuwait and Oman, with populations somewhat below 2 million, and Slovenia, Macedonia, Latvia, and Mongolia which have populations below Jamaica's 2.6 million. To all these must be added the traditional microstates of Europe.

There is great variation in economic and social **development** among the microstates. Not unexpectedly, the older European microstates are generally wealthier and more socially developed, with Luxembourg in particular ranking as one of the wealthiest countries in the world, and one that is also highly advanced in human development. However, even among developing states, there is a fair amount of variation. In income per capita, the Middle Eastern small states rank as highly developed; the East European and Caribbean microstates tend to be high or upper middle income with a few in the lower middle income category; the Pacific states are generally lower middle income; and the African group contains a number low income members along with middle income Botswana, Gabon, and Mauritius.

Social or human development ranks tend to be less unevenly distributed: small states are well represented in the high human development category of the UN's Human Development Index, and those that are not generally score in the medium group. In fact in 2003 Barbados ranked first among all developing countries (save Hong Kong) and number 27 of all countries in the world. The fact that these small states score relatively well on these indices may lead observers to discount their very real vulnerabilities. For although to some extent very small states are easier to administer well, their progress is also just as easily disrupted by market and environmental uncertainties. Apart from the Middle Eastern countries, Gabon, and Trinidad and Tobago, which are fortunate in possessing abundant oil resources, and a few others with mineral endowments, these microstates are generally dependent on vulnerable and variable economic sectors, namely agriculture, tourism, and various financial services.

The unique qualities shared by most of these states, in particular the developing microstates, are: open economies, usually dependent on external markets and grounded in a narrow resource base and a small range of products or activities; related difficulties in achieving economies of scale; high infrastructural costs and transportation problems; limited access to external financing; and vulnerability to natural disasters. These countries tend to be reactive to and often buffeted by events in the **international system**, and they are vulnerable to external intervention by, and pressure from, larger powers, international financial institutions, and elements of **international society** in general. They also share common environmental problems, many related to or affecting the tourist industry that is a mainstay of so many economies. In the case of the islands in particular, these problems include susceptibility to beach erosion, marine pollution and, in the longer term, a rise in sea levels. Finally, as **globalization** has intensified, these countries have also proven to be highly vulnerable to transnational threats, including financial crime and narcotics trafficking.

In view of these vulnerabilities, non-European microstates have had to work hard to convince the global community of the need for special and differential treatment. They have benefited from preferential trading arrangements with North America and Europe, and are today seeking slower timetables for global liberalization to allow them time to adjust their economies and societies to compete against the larger countries. In the diplomatic sphere, all microstates – European as well as Third World – recognize that it is in their interest to maintain friendly and cooperative relations with as many states as possible, but especially with their larger neighbors on which they tend to rely for economic assistance, transportation links, and in some cases, foreign policy decision making and defense.

One of the common strategies used by these very small states to overcome the limitations of size is regional cooperation. Economic **integration** and cooperation have been the goals of the Caribbean Community (Caricom) since the late 1960s and the South Pacific Forum (SPF) since the 1970s. In Europe Luxembourg was a founding member of the European Community, and the small Eastern European states are negotiating their entry to that union. Similarly, the Middle Eastern states are members of the Gulf Cooperation Council; Bhutan and Maldives of the South Asian Regional

Association for Regional Cooperation (SARC); African states belong to the Economic Community of West Africa (ECOWAS), Economic Community of Central African States (CEEAC), or South African Development Community (SADC). In addition to these and their economic and political memberships in groups ranging from the Non-Aligned Movement and the **Group of 77** to the **Arab League**, **African Union**, and Organization of American States, many of the microstates belong to two important cross-regional organizations: the African-Caribbean-Pacific (ACP) group which lobbies the **European Union** for special treatment, and the Alliance of Small Island States (AOSIS) formed to draw global attention to their unique environmental problems.

Overall, the early skepticism of the global community with regard to the ability of microstates to conduct themselves responsibly in international relations now seems outmoded. These small states have, in fact, shown themselves capable of influencing the international agenda through their alliances and coalitions. However, for every one of them that has compensated for limited size by displaying skilled **diplomacy** and active participation in certain international forums, there are others that continue to lack the financial or human resources necessary to pay much attention to matters beyond their immediate domestic and regional environments. In this regard, globalization brings with it the danger of increased microstate marginalization.

Further reading

Commonwealth Advisory Group (1997) *A Future for Small States: Overcoming Vulnerability*, London: Commonwealth Secretariat.

Hey, Jeanne A. K. (ed.) (2003) *Small States in World Politics: Explaining Foreign Policy Behavior*, Boulder, CO: Lynne Rienner.

Jazbec, M. (2001) *The Diplomacy of New Small States: The Case of Slovenia with Some Comparison from the Baltics,* Aldershot: Ashgate.

Sutton, P. and Payne, A. (eds) (1993) *Size and Survival: The Politics of Security in the Caribbean and the Pacific,* London: Frank Cass.

See also: globalization; state formation; United Nations

JACQUELINE BRAVEBOY-WAGNER

Middle power

This term is commonly used in the foreign policy **discourse** of a number of countries in contemporary global politics. It is, however, a slippery and ambiguous concept. There are two main ways of defining middle powers.

The first is *positional.* In this view, middle powers are those states in international politics whose size and power put them in the 'middle' between the **great powers** on the one hand, and smaller states on the other. Indeed, Carsten Holbraad (1984) demonstrates that the idea of ranking powers hierarchically from 'large' to 'small', with 'medium' powers located in the middle, has been a persistent feature of descriptions of international relations for centuries: German authors in particular were interested in the idea of *Mittelmacht,* those middle-sized powers located *physically* in between the great powers. There is, however, little agreement on the precise measures to be used for this ranking exercise. For some, determining the 'middle' is little more than an intuitive assessment. For others, by contrast, 'power ranking' can be determined by such measures as geographic size, size of population, size and nature of the economy, level of industrial and technological **development**, degree of economic dependence, and the size and sophistication of military capabilities.

The other definition of middle powers is *behavioral.* In this view, a state is a middle power not because of what it is, but rather because of what it does. In other words, middle powers pursued a particular kind of **diplomacy** in international affairs, a style of politics that a former Canadian diplomat, John W. Holmes, termed 'middlepowermanship' (a tongue-in-cheek reference to the tendency of American officials to describe US **diplomacy** toward China and the Soviet Union in the 1950s and 1960s as 'brinkmanship').

But what is 'middle power diplomacy'? There are three essential features that can be identified. First, middle power diplomacy seeks multilateral solutions to global problems and issues. While governments of middle powers may on occasion embrace unilateral positions, unilateralism is seen as a distinctly second-best solution.

Second, middle power diplomacy tends to favor compromise in global politics. Middle powers – in large part precisely because they are not great powers – recognize that conflict is an unavoidable condition of global politics. While conflicts of interest can be resolved by a 'winner take all' approach, middle power diplomacy is animated by the idea that the conditions of peace in global politics are not forged by attempts at zero sum wins. Rather, compromise, in which parties to a dispute are able to get some part of their interests, is seen as a more effective and durable means of conflict resolution. Thus, middle power diplomacy has always been concerned with bringing two sides together, putting an emphasis on negotiating peaceful resolution to the differences that will be an inevitable feature of global politics.

Finally, middle power diplomacy is marked by what Australia's minister of foreign affairs from 1988 to 1996, Gareth Evans, called 'acts of good international citizenship'. Evans was referring to the tendency of some states in international affairs to involve themselves in global politics in ways that might not be expected if a very narrow definition of self-interest were being used. Thus, for example, involvement in most of the international **peacekeeping** operations during the **cold war** was rarely in the narrow self-interest of most of the governments which contributed to these operations. But the middle powers that contributed to peacekeeping operations had a somewhat wider definition of self-interest at work, one that was usually more indirect. In other words, contributing to peacekeeping operations in a distant region might bring stability and **order** to that region, and thus contribute to the creation and maintenance of a broader global peace. But acts of good international citizenship were also animated by morality, and the idea of doing the 'right thing'.

But even if one is armed with such a behavioral definition of middle power, it is nonetheless difficult to identify middle powers clearly or unambiguously. For example, since during the cold war middle powers were the prime contributors to peacekeeping operations, peacekeeping became a defining characteristic of middle power diplomacy. But with the advent of 'second generation' peacekeeping after the cold war, it is no longer possible to determine from peacekeeping operations who the middle powers are, since numerous countries, including great powers and much smaller states, increasingly contribute to these operations.

Perhaps because of these definitional difficulties, the term middle power has increasingly slipped into disuse, particularly in policy circles. Thus, for example, while Canada was often considered the quintessential middle power – in large measure because this is how the Canadian government described its global role during the immediate post-1945 period – Canadian politicians no longer use the term, even though governments in Ottawa continue to pursue what in essence is a middle power foreign policy.

Further reading

Chapnick, A. (1999) 'The Middle Power', *Canadian Foreign Policy* 7(2), 73–82.

Clarkson, S. and Cohen, M. (eds) (2004) *Governing under Stress: Middle Powers and the Challenge of Globalization*, London: Zed Books.

Cooper, A. F., Higgott, R. A. and Nossal, K. (1993). *Relocating Middle Powers: Australia and Canada in a Changing World Order*, Vancouver: UBC Press.

Glazebrook, G. P. (1947) 'The Middle Powers in the United Nations System', *International Organization* 1(2), 82–103.

Holbraad, C. (1984) *Middle Powers in International Politics*, London: Macmillan.

Holmes, J. W. (1966) 'Is There a Future for Middlepowermanship?' in J. King Gordon (ed.), *Canada's Role as a Middle Power*, Toronto: Canadian Institute of International Affairs: 13–28.

See also: great power; multilateralism; power; superpower

KIM RICHARD NOSSAL

Misperception

Misperception happens when an actor draws incorrect inferences in an interaction situation with one or more other actors. The most commonly known type of misperception is when an actor interprets the intentions or actions of another differently from the way the other actor intends them. But misperception can also include mistakenly understanding the level of capabilities of the other actor or the level of one's own capabilities.

Perception is one's sensory awareness of the world. Thus, some have argued that the term misperception is actually a misnomer. Perception is specific to the actor and, therefore, technically cannot be wrong; perception simply is what the actor senses. Nonetheless, the term misperception is used extensively in international relations to refer to those times when an actor's perceptions are not in line with some objective reality. This, of course, raises classic poststructuralist and constructivist questions about the nature of reality (see **poststructuralism; constructivism**).

The term misperception is further complicated because it is often applied when an actor's probabilistic guess about another actor's move turns out to be wrong. For instance, misperception has been ascribed frequently by analysts to Argentina's belief that the United Kingdom would not act militarily to retake the Malvinas (Falkland) Islands in 1982. But case study materials show that their perception was quite accurate regarding views of UK Cabinet members with one exception: Margaret Thatcher. One can easily see how that case might have turned out very differently. Since leaders are always required to make decisions based upon less than perfect information, it should not be considered a case of misperception every time those probabilistic estimates turn out to be wrong.

Nonetheless, it is the case that some human information processing errors result in less than optimal assessments – that is, leaders sometimes misperceive situations that seem to be reasonably clear to others. An example is the United States' misreading of China's intentions prior to its entry into the Korean War (1950–3). As the United States moved north on the Korean peninsula and came closer to the border, China began signaling that it would not tolerate further US advances. China mobilized vast numbers of troops on the border and gave formal diplomatic warnings through several channels; in addition, China has a legacy of taking strong defensive actions in response to threats along its borders. It is difficult to imagine much more that the Chinese could have said or done to make the message clearer to the United States. And yet, the United States ignored these messages and marched on toward the Chinese border, thus resulting in some of the greatest military defeats in US history.

Why is it the case that humans sometimes perceive inaccurately? As perceivers, it is impossible for humans to be perfect or to approach complete information processing. It is simply impossible for a human actor or group of actors to take in every detail, nuance, and dimension of an object. Cognitive psychologists are quick to point out that most of the time we do not need to be perfect with information processing to function. Take the concept of a chair for instance. We know what a chair is, how to use one, where to go when someone gestures and says take a seat. But that other person could take forever to perfectly describe the chair he was referring to: size, shape, color, fabric, amount of padding, type of wood, type of construction, history, nicks and scratches, and so on. Even if he or she were to get to the level of the molecule, he would not be complete and perfect. Of course, such perfect description is not necessary or even helpful in functionally telling someone where to sit.

As humans, we instinctively know that we cannot and indeed need not know every detail. Cognitive psychologists refer to humans as cognitive misers: concerned with our cognitive limitations, we continuously engage in filtering, taking in what we think we need given the limits we have, and leaving the rest unknown or unprocessed. While being a cognitive miser is necessary and functional, it sometimes results in major errors in judgment and perception. Sometimes the cognitive filters and shortcuts that humans use become dysfunctional, and in international politics, that can be dangerous.

One of the common cognitive shortcuts that actors use is called the image. An image is a belief or theory about another actor. For instance, President Ronald Reagan's famous image of the Soviet Union being the 'evil empire' was an obvious oversimplification of reality, but it served a function for Reagan and demonstrated the prism through which he viewed the Soviets.

Another cognitive shortcut that humans use is the analogy. When actors see situations in international relations that provide a challenge, they often turn to lessons in history to find guidance. Of course, history never perfectly repeats itself, and while learning from history seems reasonable, sometimes the extent to which the new situation does not fit history is more important than the ways it does. All too frequently leaders have invoked the Munich/**appeasement** analogy as a lesson in the post-World War Two world when often appeasement or cooperation may lead to a better outcome than the alternative.

Sometimes actors misperceive a situation because it simply does not fit with their existing beliefs, resulting in cognitive dissonance. Individuals do not usually like dissonant information and so actively take steps to reduce the dissonance. This can mean changing perceptions, but more often it means dismissing the dissonant information, seeking out alternative supportive information, reinterpreting the information so it fits the original beliefs, or even discrediting the messenger.

Finally, sometimes our unconscious psychological traits predispose us to interpret information in a certain direction, one that is often the wrong direction. For instance, an individual who harbors high levels of anger is much more inclined to see anger in the actions of others even when it is not present. A person with a high need for **power** may perceive others as more controlling than they are. Or a person who is clinically depressed might fatalistically see only negative alternatives in a situation and take actions that then become a self-fulfilling prophecy. This might be one of the reasons why Russia and Germany escalated leading to Word War One, the **war** that no one wanted and everyone believed was being started by the other side.

Misperception, by itself, is non-directional, meaning that one could misperceive the other as being more hostile than they are, thus leading to a preemptive escalatory move, or one could misperceive the other as being more friendly than they are, thus leading to a preemptive cooperative move. However, most of the literature on misperception focuses on how it can lead to escalation, war, and disaster: Chamberlain misperceived Hitler's broader intentions in the 1930s; the United States misperceived North Vietnam's will and determination in the 1960s; Saddam Hussein misperceived US reaction to the invasion of Kuwait in 1990.

The literature on misperception calls into question rational actor models of foreign policy analysis, and indeed research on misperception comes out of the decision making school, which is quite critical of rational assumptions. We know that actors make information-processing errors; we know they are subject to human limitations and biases;

and we have seen the effect of some of those errors time and time again in history. In the end this means that, at least some of the time, misperception produces results that are far from rational.

Further reading

Holsti, O. R. (1962) 'The Belief System and National Images', *Journal of Conflict Resolution* 6, 244–52.

Jervis, R. (1976) *Perceptions and Misperception in International Politics*, Princeton, NJ: Princeton University Press.

Levy, J. (1983) 'Misperception and the Causes of War', *World Politics* 36(1), 76–99.

Stoessinger, J.G. (2001) *Why Nations Go To War*, New York: St. Martin's Press.

See also: appeasement; crisis; deterrence; rationality

MARK SCHAFER and SAM ROBISON

Modernization

Modernization defined a new experience for human societies. During the late nineteenth and early twentieth centuries, imperial rivalries, bolstered by nationalist and civilizing ideologies, shaped industrial relationships and produced colonialism, protectionism, depression and world **war**s. The post-war years were very different, however. Although the **cold war** existed as a reminder that the past had not been entirely left behind, the decades that followed the Second World War ushered in **decolonization**, reduced barriers to trade, economic prosperity, and an end to military rivalry between many competing industrial nations.

The **democratization** of industrial societies provided the basis for this remarkable transformation in relations between the world's main industrial states. Democratization empowered citizens as consumers and fuelled growth in employment, health services and education. The process of change became known as modernization, and its fame spread rapidly in a world now more interconnected than at any time in the past and expecting much from the **development** strategies promised with decolonization.

The architects of modernization certainly believed their postwar miracle possessed universal application. Not only did it define the goals of the new American-dominated world **order**, it also differentiated that order from its predecessors. However, the language and ideas it employed weakened its case for universality and differentiation. They enabled critics to dismiss it as Westernization or Americanization.

First, the very name chosen to describe their ideology derived from the idea that humankind had experienced a fundamental shift in its trajectory beginning with the Renaissance in the trading cities of Italy, the second millennium rebirth that signalled Europe's recovery from post-Roman collapse, and which ultimately produced the Scientific Revolution and Enlightenment; in short, modernity.

In fact modernity derived from humanity's growing interconnectedness, and in particular from the global changes wrought by the late fifteenth-century European discovery of the silver-laden Americas. Although change quickened further with subsequent industrialization, we should not imagine that Europeans either planned or successfully managed the transformation. Nonetheless, as the initial beneficiaries of modernity, they regarded themselves and not the interconnections exploited as the actual motor for human change. Non-Europeans sometimes concurred; since the shock of modernity arrived in the form of Western colonialism, they confused modernity with Westernization. The ideology of modernization continued this tradition.

Second, the champions of modernization presented the former industrial rivals as a homogeneous first world whose **development** had followed a common trajectory. No historical basis existed for this assertion. Once Britain industrialized at the start of the nineteenth century, the circumstances under which all countries subsequently industrialized changed. Indeed, those differences fuelled competition and **imperialism**, and ultimately contributed to global instability. Circumstances differed again for the postwar world. Cold war, decolonization and reconstruction fostered a sense of Western unity and homogeneity that was unprecedented.

Third, the supporters of modernization implied that the engine for growth in developing countries had to be external. Again no historical precedent existed for this argument, but it was justified on the grounds that unchanging tradition differentiated the **Third World** from the technologically modern first world, and held it back; hence the need for external agents of change.

Colonialists had made similar claims, that the most advanced and civilized societies presented inferior societies with an image of their future. Development, then, was not a process that colonized people might own and shape, but something they had of necessity to copy. When applied to the postwar era, it dangerously ignored the crucial role deepening democracy and social transformation played in stabilizing all societies, no matter what their state of development.

The idea that societies should be judged according to the extent they mirrored dominant industrial societies spawned a sense of failure whenever differences produced divergent results. Dichotomies were not new as explanatory tools for

policymaking. Colonialism had thrived on them, denying equality to colonial subjects on the grounds that they were backward. Now modernization strategists similarly dismissed non-modern sectors in Third World countries as traditional, static, and beyond redemption.

Many late industrializers had also dismissed their rural sectors as backward, and with similar consequences. Industries denied the crucial domestic base for growth had no choice but to reach outside of their own borders for alternatives, thereby fuelling international competition and contributing to **war**. Domestically, uneven development also generated social and political instability. The supporters of modernization neglected this historical lesson; like colonialists before them, they focused instead on dynamism from external sources.

In many respects the idea of a tradition–modernity dichotomy derived from appearances. In reality dichotomies were impossible. Just as no society could insulate itself from the changed postwar global environment, so no one sector of a society could remain isolated from changes affecting other sectors. Modern and traditional sectors interacted. The latter ensured a plentiful supply of cheap labour, kept costs low, and reduced political pressures for change. In other words, far from being the static obstacle to change that the critics alleged, so-called traditional sectors were functional to the operation of modern sectors, and to the welfare of national elites who demonstrated few qualms about treating their members like colonial subjects. Nonetheless, the subservient manner of their incorporation impacted on all society, and reinforced the modernization drive to seek growth from external sources.

This was the greatest weakness of modernization, as it was sold to the world. Its focus on external linkages for growth suited the new postwar global emphasis on reducing selected trade barriers. It also suited the economic strategies pursued by major industrial powers and an increasing number of transnational businesses. But it did little for capacity building within developing countries and fostered perceptions of a tradition–modernity dichotomy that all too easily blended with and fed post-colonial angsts and cold war tensions. In the long term its greatest legacy in the Third World was a **democratic deficit** that encouraged ethnic tensions, funda-mentalism, environmental disasters, economic collapse, and military coups. By the mid-1960s many supporters of modernization had abandoned **demo-cratization** as their goal. It was just as modern to produce guns as to educate people, and dictatorships could more rapidly produce the kind of short-term stability required for externally focused economic growth.

By the 1970s modernization had run its course. Internationally, theorists attacked modernization theory for the **dependency** it induced in Third World countries. Within the first world itself, the confidence that had driven moder-nization strategies foundered in the inflation of the 1970s. International finance and transnational corporations chaffed at the constraints imposed by a theory that prioritized national entities and attacked its neo-Keynesian roots and central planning features. During the 1980s monetarist economic strategies completed the rout. By the time the cold war ended, modernization was all but dead. Within a short while a new ideol-ogy of globalization held centre stage.

Further reading

Huntington, S. (1968) *Political Order in Changing Societies*, New Haven, CT: Yale University Press.

Meier, G. M. and Seers, D. (1984) *Pioneers in Development*, Washington, DC: World Bank.
McClelland, D. (1962) *The Achieving Society*, Princeton, NJ: Van Nostrand.
Rist, G. (1997) *The History of Development: From Western Origins to Global Faith*, London, Zed Books.
Robertson, R. (2003) *The Three Waves of Globalization: A History of a Developing Global Consciousness*, London: Zed Books.
Rostow, W. W. (1961) *The Stages of Economic Growth*, Cambridge: Cambridge University Press.

See also: cold war; decolonization; demo-cratization; dependency; development; Third World

ROBBI ROBERTSON

Money laundering

The process by which illegally generated profits are processed into the mainstream economy to evade official detection. Money laundering is the transformation of money from illegal to legal status for the purpose of concealing unlawful profits. The process involves moving funds through banks, financial institu-tions, currency conversions, and invest-ment in property or business, in order to create a paper trail, or 'history', which conceals its illicit origin from investiga-tors. Money laundering has increased in volume as the international economy and financial system has become more technologically sophisticated. The majority of money laundering is pursued by transnational criminal networks and terrorist organizations (see **terrorism**), and has grown in line with the interna-tional trade in narcotics, weapons, human trafficking, and other illicit trade. The term can also encompass tax evasion and illegal flight capital or the falsifica-tion of records by legitimate business.

Money laundering distorts markets, erodes the tax base of states, creates greater volatility in international capital flows, affects exchange rates, and reduces the public trust in banking institutions. For the developing world, money laundering inhibits efforts at **development** and deters international investment, breeds **corruption**, weakens state institutions, and erodes the tax base. Money laundering reduces the tax base of the developing world by at least US$50 billion per year.

While impossible to accurately gauge the extent of money laundering, in 1998 the **International Monetary Fund** (IMF) estimated that global money laundering accounted for between 2 and 5 per cent of global gross domestic product (GDP), amounting to some US$800 million to US$2 trillion. The difficulty with money laundering is proving which money is illegal, as each step through the system moves it further from its origin.

A money laundering cycle operates through three stages. The first is the initial, or placement, stage, where large sums of illegally generated funds are broken into smaller amounts and enter the financial system through a variety of means, including small bank deposits or are converted to money orders and cheques that are deposited in financial institutions. This usually occurs in the country where the funds are generated. As effective as this process can be for small depositors, the volume of much money laundering operations mitigate against using such a tactic, and most successful operations utilize corrupt associates in banking institutions.

The second stage, layering, disperses these deposits to other, predominantly international, financial institutions. Layering entails multiple steps of financial transactions that seek to distance the funds from their illicit origin, through bank accounts, wire transfers, loans, payments, and invoices. Multiple wire transfers are conducted in a matter of hours through several accounts, making detection difficult.

Another method involves being purposefully overcharged for imported merchandise or services, with the overcharged balance being deposited in a bank in another country. Layering often involves the use of 'shell companies' or brass plate operations, financial entities that have no staff or physical presence, but are registered in a jurisdiction to facilitate the transfer of laundered money or create service receipts to legitimize funds. These are often **offshore** financial centers (OFCs), predominantly located in small states with weak financial regulation and law enforcement. Caribbean and Pacific microstates are often implicated in this process, although it can also include Western states with strict customer privacy laws that inhibit investigators. Before better regulation in the late 1990s, the Cayman Islands, with a population of 35,000, had 570 banks, 2,240 mutual funds, 500 captive insurance firms, and 45,000 offshore businesses, with total banking assets estimated at US$670 billion.

The final stage, integration, is when the laundered proceeds are established in the legal economy and can be utilized legally in any business or venture. This often involves repatriating funds to US banks and European banks where the funds can be used for investment in legitimate business, property, and savings. Drug traffickers choose existing trades to conceal their laundered profits. For example Colombian and Mexican drug producers use the black market peso exchange system to layer drug profits, while Burmese drug producers invest in the legal gem trade and construction. Integration permits the originators of criminal finance to use these funds legitimately.

Financial **globalization** has assisted the spread of money laundering. Higher volumes of currency in international markets make identifying and tracking illegal transfers exceedingly difficult. A further problem is that money laundering often involves a combination of legal and illegal channels. This intersection of networks makes detection a complex undertaking. The dilemma is how to strike the right balance between privacy laws, a major component of banking systems, and the right of authorities to investigate the origin and legality of financial transfers. Changes to technology, particularly the Internet, have facilitated the ease of transferring money. Many banks now have online services that make the speed and volume of transfers difficult to detect if they are orchestrated by a skilled money laundering operation.

Attempts to curtail the trade have been a recent addition to international regulation. The United States was the first state to expressly outlaw the activity in 1986. International action to stem money laundering emerged from multilateral cooperation to fight drug trafficking, exemplified by the **United Nations** 1988 Vienna Convention that increased cooperation amongst states against the international drug trade. The Basel Accords on international banking regulation also provided a model for this type of international regime. In 1989, the G-7 group of major industrialized states created the Financial Action Task Force (FATF), which now operates under the purview of the **Organization for Economic Cooperation and Development** (OECD). The FATF acts as a standard setting and monitoring body for international trends in money laundering. It created forty recommendations for states to counteract money laundering and institute legal measures in their domestic jurisdictions and in cooperation with other states and international regulatory bodies. These recommendations are not binding, but they provide a framework for states to adopt in the global cooperation against money laundering. Failure to adopt these guidelines results in the public listing of recalcitrant states. In 2003 the FATF listed nine Non-Cooperative Countries and Territories (NCCTs) that have failed to enact comprehensive anti-money laundering legislation and pursue effective action against the trade.

There are also unilateral measures that states enact in their jurisdiction. Many governments insist on financial institutions filing suspicious transaction reports, in which financial transfers that are questionable or overly large must be reported to regulatory authorities. Deposits over a certain amount, in the United States it is US$10,000, must be adequately accounted for. More stringent 'know your customer' laws, which establish the legal credentials of depositors, also assist in identifying agents of money laundering. Another method is for financial transfer services, such as CHIPS and Fedwire, to compel their customers to declare their identity and the origin of funds, creating a closed circuit system of legal international transfers and blocking obvious money laundering transactions.

The fight against money laundering is inhibited by three key factors. The uneven regulation between developed and developing states leads some poorer states to permit laundering activities in their economy to accrue rents for corrupt officials or central government revenue. Second, the difficulty of detecting the movement of illicit money as it traverses both legal and illegal channels in the financial system. Finally, there is a limit to regulation that states can impose on their own financial system without disrupting the flow of funds by lawful business. This tension between **free trade** and crime sustains money laundering.

Further reading

Baker, R. (1999) 'The Biggest Loophole in the Free-Market System', *The Washington Quarterly* 22(4), 29–46.

Fabre, G (2003) *Criminal Prosperity: Drug Trafficking, Money Laundering and Financial Crisis after the Cold War* London: Routledge Curzon.

Masciandaro, D. (ed.) (2004) *Global Financial Crime: Terrorism, Money Laundering and Offshore Centres,* Aldershot: Ashgate.

Morris-Cotterill, N. (2001) 'Money laundering', *Foreign Policy* 124, 14–22.

Wechsler, W.F. (2001) 'Follow the Money' *Foreign Affairs* 80(4), 40–56.

See also: arms trade; globalization; transnational crime; terrorism

DAVID SCOTT MATHIESON

Most-Favored-Nation (MFN)

The principle around which much contemporary international trade is organized. In its pure form, MFN requires that all trading partners be treated as if they were the 'most favoured nation'. As such, any preferential treatment extended to one country must be extended to all third parties without exception or qualification. In practice this means any that tariff concessions negotiated between, say, Britain and Japan must be extended to all other countries without compensation.

MFN occupies a hallowed place in liberal political and economic thought. In liberal political thought, the adoption of MFN, and thus a non-discriminatory commercial policy, is perceived as a means of mitigating the possibility for conflict to develop among states (assuming that the deployment of discriminatory behavior can act as a catalyst for tension). For liberal economists, MFN, if applied in the spirit of **free trade**, is perceived as a means of generating efficiency through the nurturing of specialization and the realization of comparative advantage.

The prominence of MFN in trade agreements has grown steadily throughout the development of the modern state system. An MFN clause was included in the 1417 *Treaty for Mercantile Intercourse* between England and Flanders; and by the mid-nineteenth century the principle had become a staple of international commercial agreements (the 1860 Cobden-Chevalier Treaty between Britain and France is a landmark in this regard). MFN's popularity lasted until the outbreak of the First World War. Thereafter, the principle fell into disrepute. President Woodrow Wilson unsuccessfully attempted to have a commitment to MFN included in the legal framework of the **League of Nations** (though Article 23 did pledge member states to 'equitable treatment' in international commerce). And the principle came under increasing attack from the isolationist and protectionist sentiments that followed the onset of depression in the interwar years.

Wartime discussions on the shape of the post-war order saw the allied planners, and in particular the United States and the UK, begin the process of reinstating MFN as a norm of international commerce. This was first articulated in the 1941 Atlantic Charter and subsequently in the 1942 Lend-Lease Agreement. MFN was to form the cornerstone of the international commercial **order** overseen by the ill-fated International Trade Organization (ITO). The principle nevertheless played a key role in the General Agreement on Tariffs and Trade (GATT) – the ITO's more limited, provisional, but ultimately much more successful, sibling. Moreover, the centrality of MFN to international commerce was extended with the establishment in 1995 of the **World Trade Organization** (WTO).

It is important to note, however, that throughout its history MFN has not been applied in its unconditional form (nor is it applied in such a way under current GATT/WTO rules). Until 1923 the United States operated a conditional form of MFN. Rather than conveying, without condition, any negotiated preferential treatment to third parties, the United States saw fit only to extend such treatment if third parties granted the United States concessions judged to be of equivalent value in return. It was only after 1923 that the United States adopted the practice of automatically extending negotiated concessions to third parties. Even then, however, the policy was accompanied by a tariff increase and was followed a few years later by the infamous Smoot-Hawley tariff (which significantly increased the US tariff on imported agricultural produce).

The primary reason for adopting a conditional approach to MFN is to curtail the degree to which third countries can 'free ride' by receiving concessions extended to them without making an equivalent offer in return. The United States was itself the recipient of third party concessions without reciprocation prior to its adoption of the unconditional form of MFN. During this time the United States operated a high, non-negotiable tariff enabling it to benefit from the concessions of third parties without reciprocation.

The tariff increase that accompanied the United States' adoption of unconditional MFN illustrates a limitation of the principle. Unconditional MFN is not itself an engine for free trade. It is merely a mechanism for ensuring equality in tariff and other barriers to trade. It is just as conceivable to envisage the extension of unconditional MFN to result in higher overall tariff levels as it is in lower schedules.

To counter the potential impact of free riding as well as to ensure that the principle was applied in 'good faith', the institutionalization of MFN in the GATT came with a number of qualifications. First, signatories to the GATT agreed to extend MFN only to other contracting parties (and, thus, to withhold preferential treatment from non-signatories). Second, signing the GATT brought with it an obligation to engage in negotiations (periodic trade 'rounds') designed to lower the general incidence of tariffs and other barriers to trade. Trade rounds would only reach conclusion once the satisfaction of all was assured. And this satisfaction would inevitably only result once every participant had contributed in an equivalent manner. And third, the GATT operated a system of 'binding' tariffs at their negotiated levels thereby shielding against any re-inflation.

The application of MFN within the GATT was also qualified in other ways. Largely as a result of American and British pressure, the 1950s saw the exemption of agricultural produce and textiles and clothing from GATT rules. At a time when **decolonization** was fueling an increase in the number of contracting parties to the GATT, the removal of these areas from the trade liberalization process was a significant disappointment to developing states (given their reliance on the production of these goods for their economic wellbeing). The qualification of MFN was also deemed appropriate in instances wherein customs unions and free trade areas had been established; with regard to quantitative restrictions; balance of payments difficulties; general and **security** exceptions; nullification and impairment; anti-dumping; the settlement of disputes; and the establishment of infant industries. However, perhaps rivaling the removal of agriculture and textiles and clothing for its contention was the inclusion of a provision (Article XXXV) enabling existing contracting parties to the GATT to withhold their procurement of MFN to new signatories should they see fit to do so. The clause was included largely at the insistence of India, which did not want to convey preferential treatment to apartheid South Africa. Yet, it was Japan that suffered most under this provision. Upon joining the GATT 40 per cent of the then contracting parties invoked Article XXXV enabling them to withhold MFN.

The creation of the WTO augmented, rather than eroded the number of instances wherein MFN could be qualified. This is in spite of the reinsertion of agriculture and textiles and clothing into the trade agenda. That said, the WTO's burgeoning legal framework and its centrality to international trade has firmly enshrined a qualified form of MFN as a cornerstone of the global commerce. The future expansion of the WTO's remit and the preference for MFN as a centerpiece for new agreements is likely to secure the principle's future further.

Further reading

Curzon, G. (1965) *Multilateral Commercial Diplomacy: The General Agreement on Tariffs and Trade and its Impact on National Commercial Policies and Techniques*, London: Michael Joseph.
Patterson, G. (1966) *Discrimination in International Trade: The Policy Issues 1945–1965*, Princeton, NJ: Princeton University Press.
UNCTAD (1999) *Most Favoured Nation Treatment*, New York: UNCTAD.

See also: managed trade; multilateralism; preferential trade agreement; World Trade Organization

RORDEN WILKINSON

Multiculturalism

Many societies have been 'multicultural' in the sense that they have in fact contained multiple cultures, or ways of life. The Roman and Ottoman empires, for example, showed considerable toleration for religious and ethnic minorities in their midst. Multiculturalism, however, is the relatively recent idea that cultural diversity within a single political society is not only a tolerable reality for most states, but also positively desirable. Further, multiculturalists typically argue that the ideal of cultural diversity should be recognized as a matter of public policy. Such recognition may take various forms, and its supporters offer a range of justifications for these. Much multicultural policy has become widely accepted, at least in liberal democratic societies, although some of its more radical forms and arguments remain highly controversial even there. In its global dimension, multiculturalism is sometimes in tension with **human rights** and **globalization**.

The origins of multiculturalism lie in a combination of factors characteristic of the modern age, in particular of the past century. First, the spread of liberal democratic ideas has encouraged minority social groups to reject inferior social and political status, and to demand rights of equal treatment and participation in their societies' central institutions. Second, moral and political dogmatism and evangelism have been undermined by an increased moral skepticism and pressure to toleration, owed in part to modern experience of the human costs of slavery, colonialism and world **war**. Third, accelerating processes of economic and technological globalization have made it increasingly difficult to maintain cultures as separate entities. Fourth, the end of the **cold war** has led to the upsurge of 'identity politics', often based on ethnic or nationalist affiliations that had been suppressed during the global contest between **capitalism** and **communism**.

As a result of these pressures, liberal democratic states have become increasingly accommodating of their minorities. The beginnings of this tendency can be traced as far back as the seventeenth-century movement for religious toleration, championed by thinkers like John Locke (1632–1704) and Pierre Bayle (1647–1706) in the wake of the European wars of religion. In the twentieth century the rights of minorities were strengthened by legislation designed to protect them from unfair discrimination in politics, education and employment.

Multiculturalism proper, however, goes further still. Beyond toleration and non-discrimination, contemporary multiculturalists argue for the public recognition and promotion of minority cultures. This may take several forms. At its weakest, multiculturalism may be simply rhetorical, involving public statements to the effect that a society values diversity and respects its cultural minorities. A stronger form of multiculturalism would concede its minorities 'special' or 'group' rights, claimable only by members of those particular groups rather than by all citizens. Such special rights may extend certain legal exemptions to the group: for example, permitting Sikh motorcyclists to wear turbans rather than helmets. Special rights might also grant educational or other welfare opportunities to members of a group, as in the case of newly arrived immigrants who seek help with integrating into their host society. Alternatively, the goal may not be integration but the maintenance of a distinctive culture. In this connection many indigenous peoples claim special entitlements to use land and other natural resources for traditional purposes. In their strongest form, again typically invoked in the case of indigenous groups, multicultural policies may promote a group's **self-determination**, perhaps even involving the institution of a parallel legal system.

Such policies are sometimes highly controversial. By according some citizens entitlements that others do not have, special rights may seem to depart from standard liberal democratic notions of equality. Moreover, some minority groups subscribe to values and practices that violate widely held notions of human rights: for example, restrictions on religious and other freedoms, female genital mutilation and even 'honor killings'. Can such conduct be accommodated by even the most open-minded modern societies?

One way of justifying multiculturalist policies might be to appeal to cultural relativism: the view that there are no universal moral standards, only the particular moral codes of particular cultures. Any moral judgment is necessarily made from within some such code, and there is consequently no neutral ground from which to judge that one code is superior to another. Consequently, all cultures are morally equal, and all deserve equal respect. This may sound like a humane and tolerant view, but it is in fact a very shaky basis for tolerance and multiculturalism. If moral justification depends entirely on cultural perspective, then those cultures that reject toleration or respect for other cultures cannot be criticized.

More reliable defenses of multiculturalism have been mounted by liberal thinkers committed to universal notions of human rights and personal liberty. The leading name in this respect is that of Will Kymlicka, who supports special rights for cultural minorities, but subject to the prior value of individual autonomy (Kymlicka 1995). For Kymlicka, membership of a flourishing culture provides the necessary context within which people can make sense of their life choices; consequently, liberal states have good reason to protect cultures in the name of individual liberty. Special rights should be seen as compensating members of minority groups for the disadvantage inherent in their situation rather than as unequal privileges. However, there is a limit to the extent to which cultures should be protected, since there can be no protection for those practices that undermine individual autonomy, the value on which the whole argument is based. Indeed, Kymlicka sees his argument as justifying the liberalization of non-liberal cultures, although he argues that this need not be coercive or intrusive because there is room for prudence and restraint in the means by which such a policy is pursued.

Kymlicka's view has been extremely influential, but it has also drawn a good deal of criticism. Some critics argue that his view does not do enough to accommodate non-liberal minorities. According to one account, such groups need not be liberalized as long as they allow their members to exit from the group when they choose (Kukathas 2003). Another response is that a genuinely multicultural society must be strongly democratic, not merely granting special rights but ensuring that cultural minorities have an active voice in making the rules that govern them (Parekh 2000). On the other hand, some commentators argue that Kymlicka concedes too much to cultural traditions, which are often oppressive, inegalitarian and patriarchal. The strongest criticism along these lines comes from Brian Barry, who sees much of the literature of multiculturalism as a damaging distraction from more important dimensions of social injustice (Barry 2001).

At the global level, multiculturalism raises two problems in particular. The first is the possible conflict with human rights already mentioned. In this connection much attention has been devoted to the debate over **Asian values**, in which some people have argued that the idea of human rights itself is distinctively Western and that a genuinely universal morality would have to assimilate 'Asian' norms emphasizing **order** rather than liberty (Bell 2001). Second, there is considerable disagreement over whether cultural diversity is increased or decreased by globalization. Some writers understand cultural globalization as essentially homogenizing, leading to the worldwide dominance of Western culture, while others see it as inevitably producing a backlash in which 'McWorld' is confronted by its 'Jihad' opposite (Barber 1995). Still others emphasize the tendency of globalization to produce 'hybrid' personalities and societies that may add to diversity (Scholte 2000).

Further reading

Barber, B. (1995) *Jihad vs McWorld*, New York: Ballantine.

Barry, B. (2001) *Culture and Equality*, Cambridge: Polity.

Bell, D. A. (2001) *East Meets West: Human Rights and Democracy in East Asia*, Princeton, NJ: Princeton University Press.

Kukathas, C. (2003) *The Liberal Archipelago: a Theory of Diversity and Freedom*, Oxford: Oxford University Press.

Kymlicka, W. (1995) *Multicultural Citizenship*, Oxford: Oxford University Press.

Parekh, B. (2000) *Rethinking Multiculturalism: Cultural Diversity and Political Theory*, Cambridge, MA: Harvard University Press.

Scholte, J. (2000) *Globalization: a Critical Introduction*, Basingstoke: Palgrave.

See also: ethnicity; nationalism; nation-state

GEORGE CROWDER

Multilateralism

Multilateralism is a term much used in international relations but seldom precisely defined. At its simplest, it is taken to mean action by or among a group of three or more states. In this way, multilateralism is distinct from unilateralism – independent action by a single state – and bilateralism – action by or between two states. Multilateralism does not, however, always refer solely to formal organizations, as is often assumed. It refers to all arrangements wherein three or more states act in concert. Like its counterparts, unilateralism and bilateralism, the term multilateralism also conveys a sense of the kind of relationship or form of action under observation. Unilateral behavior is generally associated with independent, often self-serving, potentially 'against the grain' action; bilateral arrangements are commonly deemed to be discriminatory, in that they preclude third parties, as well as open to abuses of **power** within the relationship (particularly if one party is significantly more powerful than the other). Multilateralism is generally deemed to be qualitatively different. Acting multilaterally is perceived to have value. This value is derived from the appearance of an inclusive, collective, even consensual approach to international action.

These qualitative distinctions are best demonstrated by way of example. In international trade, unilateral efforts by the United States designed to open up Japanese markets outside of the confines of the General Agreement on Tariffs and Trade (GATT) in the late 1980s and early 1990s were much criticized for being aggressive and at variance with the spirit of multilateral trade liberalization. Similarly, the bilateral exchange of trading concessions is deemed discriminatory, in that such concessions are withheld from third parties in a way that a more inclu-

sion collective orientated, multilateral approach is not. A strong preference for multilateralism is also exuded in debates on the procurement of international aid wherein multilateral arrangements are generally deemed to be more transparent and, as a result, less open to the imposition of inappropriate **conditionality**. Likewise, in the field of **humanitarian intervention**, multilateral action is deemed to be more legitimate and less open to the pursuit of self-interest than unilateral or bilateral actions.

There are of course problems with simply associating multilateralism with international arrangements perceived to be valuable. Though appearing otherwise, multilateral arrangements can and do obscure relationships of inequality. The ability of the permanent members of the **United Nations** Security Council to set the Organization's agenda and veto any actions that are contrary to their individual interests (most harrowingly demonstrated by the inaction of the UN during the Rwandan genocide of 1994) but which are often in contravention to those of the wider membership, and the systems of weighted voting operated by the **International Monetary Fund** (IMF) and **World Bank** wherein Western states predominate, provide apposite examples.

The lack of a precise definition of multilateralism, and the problems arising therefrom, spurred scholars to investigate its underlying meanings. Ruggie's work (1993) is perhaps the most familiar. By exploring a series of commonly agreed upon instances of multilateralism Ruggie concluded that common to multilateral arrangements are a set of rules which organize relations among a group of three or more states in accordance with certain general principles of conduct. These principles specify the behavioral patterns necessary to achieve a particular goal; but crucially the rules crafted to operationalize these principles are applicable to all participating states (as opposed to discriminating among them). Such a claim leads Ruggie to make two important assertions. First, in multilateral arrangements states behave as if the goal pursued is achievable only through their collective action. In this sense the goal is 'indivisible'. Second, in pursuit of that goal, multilateral arrangements tend to operate on the basis of 'diffuse reciprocity'. This means that the benefits derived from the pursuit of the goal are not derived immediately, but are rather accumulated in the aggregate and over time from the active participation of all involved.

Ruggie's claims are best illustrated by way of two examples. Under GATT – and now **World Trade Organization** (WTO) – rules governing commercial relations among the participating states are organized in accordance with the principle of **most-favored-nation**. With a few exceptions, this principle requires that each participant is treated in a manner consistent with the most-favored trading partner. Here, the perceived economic gain associated with **free trade** is deemed to be indivisible; and the benefits of pursuing such a goal are derived in aggregate and over time as each state benefits from the trading concessions conveyed by others. In the realm of international security, the **North Atlantic Treaty Organization** (NATO) provides an equivalent example. NATO is based upon the principle – known as **collective security** – that an attack on one of the participating states constitutes an attack against them all. **Security** (and thus the ensuing peace) is treated as indivisible. Each state benefits from the security NATO provides, which is provided by the pooling of military resources among the collective.

Ruggie's final comment, and one worth repeating here, is that while we can deduce a common core to multilateralism, its contemporary manifestations have tended to be constructed in such a way that they preserve the **national interest** of that state most associated with their creation: the United States. To put it slightly differently, those multilateral institutions created in the post-World War Two era have been fashioned in such a way that they have tended to assist in the preservation of the United States' pre-eminent role rather than contributed to its dilution. We need think no further than the examples of the UN Security Council and the weighted voting systems of the IMF and World Bank cited above to underline this point. It is precisely because of this imbalance, as well as a lack of broad-based representation within multilateral institutions, that a more recent body of literature has emerged. The principle concern of this literature has been with the promotion of grassroots inclusion and broad based representation in multilateral forums thereby overcoming the **democratic deficit** endemic to much contemporary multilateralism. It is something of a paradox, then, that this preferred form of international organization has so far eschewed an extension in its parameters to facilitate greater representation.

Further reading

Cox, R.W. (1992) 'Multilateralism and World Order', *Review of International Studies* 18(2), 161–80.

Cox, R.W. (ed.) (1997) *The New Realism: Perspectives on Multilateralism and World Order*, Basingstoke: Palgrave.

Gill, S. (ed.) (1997) *Globalization, Democratization and Multilateralism*, Basingstoke: Palgrave.

Ruggie, J. (ed.) (1993) *Multilateralism Matters*, New York: Columbia University Press.

Ruggie, J. (1994) 'Third Try at World Order: America and Multilateralism after the Cold

War', *Political Science Quarterly* 109(4), 553–70.

Schechter, M. (ed.) (1999) *Future Multi-lateralism*, Basingstoke: Palgrave.

Schechter, M. (ed.) (1999) *Innovation in Multilateralism*, Basingstoke: Palgrave.

Wilkinson, R. (2000) *Multilateralism and the World Trade Organisation*, London: Routledge.

See also: embedded liberalism; global governance; most-favored nation; World Trade Organization

RORDEN WILKINSON

Multinational corporation (MNC)

The Multinational Corporation (MNC) is now visible in everyday life across the globe. Prominent examples of MNCs include fast food chains, energy and construction companies and IT firms. The emergence of MNCs over the past decades has resulted in several, often polarized, debates. On the one hand, researchers have pointed to the benefits that MNCs provide, including technology, skills, capital and other spillover effects. This has led many governments to try to attract such firms. On the other hand, anti-**globalization** protesters have pointed to the increasing dominance of MNCs associated with poor working conditions, environmental degradation, **human rights** abuses and **corruption** scandals.

The MNC is a company that controls and manages production plants located in at least two countries, and hence constituting a special case of a multi-plant firm. Neoclassical economics cannot explain the existence of MNCs. Instead, international business researchers have examined the emergence of multinationals extensively for at least five decades, at which time the first studies considered the operation of American multinationals in Europe. One prominent international business researcher, John Dunning, developed an eclectic model to explain the existence of multinationals: the Ownership Location Internalization (OLI) framework. It was emphasized that MNCs needed to have some 'firm specific' asset that differentiated them from domestic firms to compensate for the extra costs, for example in terms of local knowledge, that a foreign firm must incur to operate in foreign markets. The firm specific asset is called an ownership (O) advantage and this was recognized early on by international business researchers. Later it was acknowledged that MNCs should also have an internalization (I) advantage to internalize business contacts, because otherwise they could engage in other business contacts such as outsourcing (which frequently occurs in the global value chains of supermarkets and clothing retailers). Finally, the reason why a multinational invests in one country but not in another depends on the host country's locational advantage (L).

Various categorizations of MNCs have arisen in the literature. One often cited categorization is by motivation of investment. Natural resource seeking MNCs aim to exploit natural resources, such as oil and gas, available in host countries. Market seeking MNCs invest abroad to serve markets through their affiliates. Efficiency seeking MNCs invest abroad because this supports the efficiency of their operations, for example the use of low labor costs in assembly operations. Finally, strategic asset seeking MNCs invest because it helps their competitiveness and productivity. This may be the case when investors want to 'plug into' a cluster of innovation associated with superior technological and human capabilities.

Market seeking MNCs have traditionally involved building replicas of the same plant (horizontally integrated) in other countries in order to overcome high tariffs which cause trade to be expensive or impossible. But a significant part of the recent increase in the spread of multinational activity is due to vertical specialization or fragmentation of production processes. Global firms have relocated parts of the production process in their search for cheaper production costs, which has been made technically possible by the development of support services and technological activities. Firms may maintain design, R&D or marketing functions in the headquarters in developed countries, while relocating and communicating with labor and less skill intensive production processes such as assembly operations to low cost developing countries. Globalization of production occurs through the fragmentation of production processes and often manifests itself in **foreign direct investment** (FDI) by efficiency seeking and vertically integrated MNCs.

There are various ways in which MNC activity can be measured including capital assets, sales, exports, value added, and employment. Each measure will provide a different picture of the globalization of MNCs. The measures can also be used to assess the relative importance of MNCs in a national economy. According to the sales and exports measure, MNCs can dominate whole sectors of an economy. According to the value added measure this is less so, because MNCs are often involved in processing, and value added is measured net of raw materials purchased. Nevertheless, value added by affiliates of foreign owned MNCs is more than half the total of manufacturing value added in countries such as Hungary, Ireland and Singapore.

MNCs and non-MNCs differ in performance. This is most often shown empirically by comparing performance measures of foreign owned firms (MNCs) and local firms (mostly comprising non-MNCs). Econometric and case studies show that foreign owned firms in general are larger, more productive, more export intensive, more skill intensive and use more up to date and complex technologies. They also tend to pay more to their workers than local firms even after accounting for other factors associated with higher wages such as size, location and sector. In particular, skilled workers are able to gain a wage premium when working in foreign owned firms.

The spillover effects of MNCs on the wider economy are subject to intense debate. In the OLI framework the effects of MNCs depend on the type (market seeking, efficiency seeking, resources seeking or strategic asset seeking) and distinctiveness of the MNC, the characteristics of the home and host countries, including policies, and the ability of local firms to assimilate and deploy MNC assets and to maintain competitiveness. Productivity spillover effects on local firms are based on various channels including demonstration effects of using new technology, the spread of workers trained in MNCs and the effects of the presence of MNCs on competitive behavior. A significant body of evidence finds that while MNCs are more productive, the effects of MNCs on productivity levels and growth in domestic firms are mixed. Domestic firms could be better off as (foreign) competition forces them to upgrade technologies (as found in Indonesia); they could be worse off when foreign firms take the market of existing local firms (Venezuela); or they could learn little due to a large productivity gap (Mexico). In Morocco, Venezuela and the Czech Republic, the presence of foreign firms lowered productivity growth in domestic firms.

While superior economic characteristics are usually recognized, the image of MNCs has become tarnished through much publicized negative cases. MNCs have been implicated in corruption scandals, poor working conditions and human rights abuses. They have also been portrayed as having significant **power** over sovereign states and using this to extract significant rents from their operations. The annual profits of individual companies can surpass the level of income of several developing countries. As a response to this poor image MNCs have begun to develop voluntary codes of conduct showing how MNCs perform in the area of corporate social responsibility (CSR). CSR is now considered to go beyond philanthropic giving and extends into more general areas such as identifying the business 'imprint' on the wider society. Voluntary codes of conduct have long been enshrined in the Multinational Guidelines for MNCs of the Organization for **Economic Cooperation and Development** (OECD) and the **International Labor Organization** (ILO). New initiatives include the Extractive Industries Transparency Initiative and the Publish As You Pay campaign aiming to persuade MNCs and host country governments to be more transparent and to publish full financial flows between governments and MNCs.

Further reading

Caves, R. E (1996) *Multinational Enterprise and Economic Analysis,* 2nd edn, Cambridge: Cambridge University Press.

Dunning, J. H. (1993) *Multinational Enterprises and the Global Economy,* Reading, MA: Addison-Wesley.

See also: foreign direct investment; offshore; globalization; political risk analysis

DIRK WILLEM TE VELDE

Mutually assured destruction (MAD)

A policy and theory of nuclear force deployment designed, not for direct protection, but to deter any nuclear attack by credibly threatening the reciprocal annihilation of lives and property on a catastrophic scale. Often reduced to the simple acronym MAD, this quasi-military strategy routinely risked the charge of being precisely that, mad. It is perhaps the most important among many remarkable developments in **cold war** nuclear **deterrence** that spurred one critic to describe its policy architects as 'the wizards of Armageddon'.

All satire aside, the theory and practice of MAD was and is deadly serious. Many of its weapons systems remain. Throughout the cold war, **security** specialists theorized and American policymakers implemented a 'strategy' of deterrence, which entailed the accumulation of weapons of unprecedented destructive power. Since its very political impact was meant to preclude the wartime use of the weapons in question, however, this was a novel form of strategy – traditionally a **war** plan tailoring the direct use of force to policy objectives. The novel usage reflected the perceived novelty of the weapons, as virtually unusable. The new strategy was thus designed to conceive a comprehensible political role for such weapons where their direct military use seemed inconceivable. Their unprecedented destructive power and range (aided by ballistic missile technology) suggested that defense must now hinge on a deterrent threat of reprisal rather than the direct use of force to prevent or impede attack.

The demonstrative effects of the World War Two bombing of Hiroshima and Nagasaki seemed to suggest the American atomic monopoly could be enough to protect American security. The main impetus behind the rapid growth of an unprecedented civilian industry of Western 'strategists' lay in the way the Korean War (1950–3) directly challenged this assumption. Against all expectations, the American-led **United Nations** (UN) efforts to unify Korea by force met a response in kind from China, undeterred by the (presumably remote) possibility of nuclear retaliation. The Korean experience may well explain the emphasis strategists subsequently placed on the importance to effective deterrence not only of capabilities but also *credibility*, achieved by convincing the potential challenger of one's resolve to use those capabilities. At any rate, the war seemed to underscore the need for a nuclear strategy. The first step was Secretary of State John Foster Dulles's announcement in 1954 of a policy of 'massive retaliation', explicitly threatening a full-blown nuclear reprisal against any challenge anywhere that the United States deemed an 'act of aggression'. Massive retaliation formed the central pillar of MAD as it evolved in the early 1960s, in direct response to the increasing salience and approaching rough parity of Soviet nuclear forces. Broadly speaking, American strategy came to reflect the enhanced collective destructive power of the world's nuclear arsenals.

The strategy required that the composition and state of readiness of American bombers and missiles convey the message that any nuclear attack (or even a conventional attack on Western Europe) could and would be met with massive retaliation. A large scale Soviet attack would thus 'at best' result in 'mutually assured destruction', that is, catastrophic, socially decimating losses on both sides. Conveying such a message convincingly required that American forces could mount such a reprisal, even in the event of a full-scale nuclear attack.

The key would be forces that had what strategists called 'second strike capability', meaning that they were not vulnerable to a disabling initial counter force strike. This was achieved, in the face of improving satellite surveillance technology and missile precision, by putting bomber aircraft on a high state of alert, developing smaller and more mobile missiles and/or hardening their silos and, most effective of all, deploying a substantial fleet of armed submarines. The latter were mobile, hard to detect and, increasingly, able to deliver relatively accurate missile payloads over huge distances.

Perhaps the biggest challenge was to threaten credibly that such capabilities would or at least might be used. Here deterrence built on the much debated paradox of eliciting rational restraint from attack *via* a threat to respond *irrationally* (and immorally) should deterrence fail. For once deterrence of a nuclear attack had failed, what could really be gained by 'evening out' the catastrophic loss of innocent human life, by what, at this point, would be little more than an act of misdirected vengeance? Thus the effectiveness of deterrence rested implicitly on the assumption of a kernel of human instrumental **rationality** as well as its practical and emotional limitations. One obvious solution was to dehumanize the response by instituting an automated 'launch on warning' system, but the unwillingness to do this reflects another dilemma of mutual deterrence. Improvements of deterrence *credibility* readily detract from deterrence *stability*, increasing the danger that some sequence of errors, accidents and incremental acts of escalation might precipitate the apocalypse. Also, any increase in the apparent propensity to use nuclear weapons raises the fear of a pre-emptive first strike and hence even the apparent utility of resorting to such a first strike oneself. The interest in stabilizing deterrence was reflected in **arms control** initiatives (undermined by the American Strategic Defense Initiative or 'star wars' program in the 1980s) to impede deployment of **ballistic missile defense**, which might, by promising to 'mop up' any reprisal, itself encourage a pre-emptive attack.

Here deterrence builds most clearly on the paradoxical logic of the **balance of power**, especially as expounded by realists (see **realism**). If the balance of power is to maintain **order** then strength and resolve must be tempered with forbearance and moderation. This is the challenge of prudent statesmanship, perhaps never more acute than in the era of nuclear weapons, to achieve the delicate task of defending without provoking.

The subsequent debate about strategy and arms control was rooted in the central tensions of deterrence exemplified by MAD. Efforts to improve credibility threatened to undermine stability and vice versa. The doctrine of 'flexible response', for example, was meant to embody a credible threat to retaliate at an equivalent escalatory level or, if needed to ensure 'escalation dominance', an incremental step up the 'escalation ladder', depending on the nature and scale of the attack. This meant, for example, a continued policy of 'first use', albeit of the newer, smaller tactical or battlefield nuclear weapons, in response to a Soviet conventional attack on Western Europe. Flexible response constituted a subtle and paradoxical modification, not a substitution, of the logic of MAD. The deterrent effect rested on the expected likely escalation to a full-scale nuclear exchange once the nuclear 'firebreak' had been broken. The credibility of the threat, however, rested on communicating a willingness to believe such escalation could nevertheless be controlled.

On this condition, the use of tactical nuclear weapons might seem comprehensible, even rational, and more minor security threats than nuclear attack could be deterred.

The much criticized warfighting or **nuclear utilization theory** (NUT), popular in policy circles if not targeting policies in the early 1980s, contained a similar logic. This replicated the apparent Soviet practice of simply adopting a traditional war plan that included the more or less extensive use of nuclear weapons. As deterrence this still rested on conveying a belief in the possible utility of using nuclear weapons, and thereby deterring their use by an opponent because of the probability, nonetheless, of escalation to MAD. The problem is that increased credibility comes at the cost of stability. Unlike MAD, a warfighting strategy favors counterforce over countervalue targeting (of cities and human populations), raising the perceived danger on both sides of a willingness and incentive to mount a disabling first strike.

Nuclear deterrence strategies emerged from the renewed Soviet–American enmity after World War Two and, in particular, the American policy of **containment**. Policymakers perceived both communist ideology (see **communism**) and Soviet power to be inherently expansionist. MAD was thus part of a full spectrum effort to field possible incursions or attacks in any context, at any level, from cultural infiltration to nuclear attack. With the end of the cold war the apparent danger of a nuclear exchange receded. The thinking behind deterrence persists, however, drawing considerable credibility from its roots in realist theory and the concept of the balance of power. Its salience promises to re-emerge with continued **nuclear proliferation** and the emergence of new conflicts where nuclear weapons – if only implicitly – are likely to play a role.

Further reading

Bundy, M. (1990) *Danger and Survival*, New York: Vintage Books.

Freedman, L. (1989) *The Evolution of Nuclear Strategy*, 2nd edn, New York: St. Martin's Press.

Kaplan, F. M. (1983) *The Wizards of Armageddon*, New York: Simon and Schuster.

Paret, P. (1986) *Makers of Modern Strategy*, Oxford: Clarendon.

See also: arms control; ballistic missile defense; deterrence; nuclear proliferation; nuclear utilization theory; security dilemma

P. STUART ROBINSON

N

National interest

Despite its centrality to foreign policy **discourse**, national interest is probably one of the most elusive and controversial concepts in the study of international politics, not yet finding its way into the standard dictionaries, including the latest updated third edition of the *Oxford English Dictionary* (2000). In the most general sense, implicit in the notion of national interest is an idea of preferences for the policy that is best for a nation or state as a whole. Yet this notion has been conceptualized in three different ways:

1. as an analytic construct to describe and explain the sources of state preferences in foreign policy;
2. as a criterion for evaluating particular strategies or courses of action; and
3. as a justification for foreign policy decisions taken by policymakers.

While the third usage of national interest (i.e., as a means for justifying particular courses of action) is practiced by policymakers to mobilize domestic support, political scientists are mainly concerned with national interest in terms of the first two usages.

In terms of the first (analytic) usage, we can distinguish between 'objectivist' and 'subjectivist' approaches (Frankel 1970). The former assumes that national inter-ests can be objectified into clearly discernable sources of state preferences, whereas the latter conceives it as a changing set of subjective preferences. As for those who define national interest in terms of subjective preferences, we may further distinguish between domestic (decision making) and international (social constructivist) versions.

The 'objectivist' approach is best exemplified by the influential realist school of Hans Morgenthau (1948) and other followers. In his classic principles of the realist theory of international relations, Morgenthau identifies **power** maximization (later to be expanded into **security** maximization by neorealists such as Kenneth Waltz) as the omnipresent national interest of any state. In his oft-quoted statement, Morgenthau postulates that realism assumes that 'statesmen think and act in terms of interest defined as power,' which is understood to be an objective category that is universally applicable (1948, 5). Accordingly, international relations are not seen through the lenses of intersubjective reality, shaped by individual idiosyncrasies or the bureaucratic preferences of decision makers, but rather as an arena of contestation between states, treated as unitary actors, each driven by the national interest of power and security maximization.

In another important realist analysis of national interest, Krasner (1978) initially departs from the assumption of states as unitary actors, by contending that national interests indicate the preferences of central decision makers. Yet his view is also objectivist as he stipulates that 'such a set of objectives must be related to general societal goals, persist over time, and have a consistent ranking of importance in order to justify the term national interest' (Krasner 1978, 13). Applying this notion in the context of US policy in international raw materials, he argues that several basic aims can be discerned in this issue area (such as insuring security of supply), which have persisted over time and intended to advance the welfare of the US society as a whole.

In contrast, a domestic version of the 'subjectivist' approach maintains that there is no single national interest, and that it is defined by the subnational interests of those who have the capacity to translate their preferences into policy (e.g., Trubowitz 1998, 4). In the 1960s and 1970s, the rise of decision making approaches to foreign policy analysis particularly challenged the 'objectivist' realist approach and instead adopted a procedural conceptualization according to which the national interest is shaped by the bureaucratic or idiosyncratic interests of individuals and groups who participate in the decision making process. In other words, the national interest is subjectively defined by the participants in the policy process and does not reflect the interest of an entire nation. Instead, it is reflective of various societal or bureaucratic interests that manage to prevail in the policy formulation process.

More recently, the emergence of a constructivist approach to international relations gave rise to a different 'subjectivist' conceptualization of the national interest. Instead of focusing on the agent (state) in the agent-structure dichotomy (see **agent-structure debate**), constructivists emphasize the impact of international structures (often normatively understood in terms of shared values, transnational collective identities or norms of behavior) on state preferences. That is, international norms, often assumed to be socially constructed through international institutions, structure the ways in which states endogenize these norms as their foreign policy preferences. Finnemore (1996), for example, provides historical case studies to show how international institutions were able to reshape state interests, examining, for example, the role of the **World Bank** in redefining the ways that states approached **development** problems by institutionalizing new antipoverty norms.

Apart from its usage as an analytic construct that describes and explains the sources of state preferences that qualify as national interests, the term national interest is also often used as a value laden concept, serving as a criterion for evaluating particular foreign policies. As a normative, rather than descriptive or explanatory, construct, the national interest has divided scholars in terms of the content they believe should constitute the national interest. In the early stages of the modern study of international relations, this division was reflected in a well known debate between 'idealists' and 'realists'. The former argued that moral aspirations (such as justice) best serve the public interest, even in the area of foreign policy. Realists, on the other hand, considered a 'rational' foreign policy, based on the pursuit of power and security as the ultimate national interest, to be good foreign policy from a prescriptive point of view as well.

More recently, the end of the **cold war** revived interest in this issue, as the United States found itself searching for a new role in world politics and thus undergoing a redefinition of its national interests due to changed global circumstances. The debate is centered on the question of the content and priorities of national interests, specifically concerning the issue of what distinguishes vital from peripheral interests. This issue was largely ignored during the cold war due to the 'unrestricted' global nature of the **containment** policy. In this respect, different schools of thought emerge, somewhat mimicking the earlier idealist–realist debate of whether moral aspirations should be considered national interests.

The advocates of 'universalism' (or, some would call it, renewed Wilsonianism) clash with geopolitical schools. The former include **human rights** as an important element of vital national interests for a democratic state such as the United States, thus justifying **humanitarian intervention**s on moral grounds, considered to represent a national interest priority. The latter advocate different policies, ranging from globalism to selective engagement, depending on the tangible elements (such as economic wealth or military power) that are prioritized in the national interest. However, in the absence of a theory with generalizable criteria for distinguishing between those issues that belong to vital as opposed to secondary national interests, it is likely that the debate about the national interests of powers such as the United States will continue to be based on value laden (normative) rather than theory driven arguments. That is, while this question might be resolved in the policy arena, it is unlikely to be resolved in the realm of political science any time soon.

Further reading

Finnemore, M. (1996) *National Interests in International Society*, Ithaca, NY: Cornell University Press.

Frankel, J. (1970) *National Interest*, New York: Praeger.
Krasner, S. D. (1978) *Defending the National Interests: Raw Materials Investments and US Foreign Policy*, Princeton, NJ: Princeton University Press.
Morgenthau, H. J. (1948) *Politics Among Nations: The Struggle for Power and Peace*, New York: Alfred A. Knopf.
Trubowitz, P. (1998) *Defining the National Interest: Conflict and Change in American Foreign Policy*, Chicago, IL: University of Chicago Press.

See also: agent-structure debate; constructivism; humanitarian intervention; power; realism; security

VESNA DANILOVIC

Nationalism

A sense of national consciousness that exalts one nation above all others. Nationalism is a very broad term that has been interpreted in many different ways, and in general terms it has both a cultural and political dimension. The study of nationalism has come to the fore since the beginning of the twentieth century, and has been a focus for scholars trying to understand the development of the **nation-state**, the concept of a nation and the character of contemporary **ethnic conflict**. There are a number of different schools of thought in relation to the origins of nationalism ranging from the historical (or primordial) to the modern. Modernists believe that nationalism has its origins in modern times, that is, since the development of the nation-state, whilst other scholars argue that its origins lie in pre-modern social formations, particularly those associated with discrete ethnic groups. Similarly, there is a range of views concerning the trajectory of nationalism in the twenty-first century. Finally, the study of nationalism has become increasingly interdisciplinary in recent years, resulting in a range of perspectives and interpretations. Originally the study of nationalism was confined to historians, but has since developed to include perspectives from anthropology, sociology, psychology, philosophy, law, economics, linguistics, and political science.

The nation

Despite the importance of nationalism, there is a lack of consensus about why it has maintained a firm hold over much of the world's population. Any examination of nationalism must be preceded by an analysis of what constitutes a nation. This analysis is complicated by the manner in which people often use the terms 'nation', 'state', and 'country' interchangeably. The last two terms refer to political entities. The first is a term used to describe a group of people who may or may not live in the same state or country. The difference is conveyed in German by the words *Staatsangehorigheit* (citizenship) and *Nationalitat* (nationality). A person can be of German *Nationalitat* without being a German citizen.

Definitions of nation or nationality rely either upon objective or subjective criteria, or on some combination of the two. Most objective definitions of nationality rely on the commonality of some particular trait among members of a group. Shared language, religion, ethnicity (common descent) and culture have all been used as criteria for defining nations. A casual examination of the history of national differentiation indicates that these factors often reinforce each other in the determination of a nationality. Certain nationalities, such as the Croats, are now defined as distinct from Serbs almost exclusively on the basis of religious differences. Likewise, Urdu-speaking Pakistanis are distinguished from Hindi-speaking Indians largely

because of religion. In other cases, however, a shared religion seems a less accurate method for drawing the boundaries of a nationality. The German nation, for example, is divided mainly among Protestants and Catholics. Conversely, the inhabitants of France and Italy, though both overwhelmingly Catholic, belong to two different nationalities.

One of the most often used of all the objective marks of nationality is a common language. Indeed a shared language has been a very powerful factor in national unification. Yet this definition, too, is fraught with difficulties. For one thing, what we today call national languages are, to one degree or another, artificial constructs. This is certainly true in the case of many of the languages of east-central Europe and of the non-European world. Other national languages have been created for imperial purposes. The various languages of central Asia, e.g. Uzbek, Kyrgyz, and Khazak did not exist until they were conjured out of local dialects by Soviet linguists during the 1920s. The languages were then used as evidence to support Soviet claims of the existence of several nations in Central Asia, which was then divided into separate Soviet Socialist Republics as part of a 'divide and rule' strategy

Even in cases where a popular vernacular becomes a national language this transformation typically happens after the foundation of a nation-state. For example, French became a national language only after the creation of a French nation-state. In 1789, only about half of the population in the Kingdom of France spoke French. To the nationalist Revolutionaries, making French the common language of the nation was of the utmost importance. The same could be said of German, Italian, Hungarian, and other modern European languages. A common vernacular language of administration, state education, and military command was an important tool in the extension of the modern state's bureaucratic control. Thus, national languages are largely the creation of modern nation-states, not the other way around.

It seems, therefore, that pre-existing common linguistic or religious attributes may not be absolute indicators of a nation. **Ethnicity** and common descent are other possible criteria for national boundary drawing. These were especially popular during the late nineteenth and early twentieth centuries and blended with that era's fascination with racial pseudo science. To the modern student, however, ethnicity seems a much less compelling criterion. The people of the various Mediterranean nations, for example, are plainly the product of centuries of inter-ethnic marriages. Likewise, the American, Mexican, or British nations are made up of people of many different ethnic backgrounds.

Hence, while objective traits can be useful as very rough criteria for defining the existence of a nation, they are not enough. Indeed, a nation may be a very subjective entity. Many students of nationalism are eventually led to the (almost tautological) conclusion that people belong to a certain nation if they feel that they belong to it.

As a political ideology, nationalism is the claim that people belonging to a particular group called a nation should inhabit a particular area and control a state of their own. Defined in this manner, nationalism is not the same thing as **patriotism**, which refers to a sense of loyalty to an existing nation-state. Such a definition points to nationalism as a method of drawing boundaries among people.

Whether nationalism is viewed as an ideology or a state of mind, one can still ask why did so many people abandon earlier, universalist ideologies (e.g. Christianity) and non-national self-iden-

tifications (for example, by occupation or social status)? Some trace the roots of nationalism to the Reformation. The Reformation itself was important in the development of proto-nationalist feeling, especially when considered in light of the revolution in printing and the subsequent surge in publications in various vernaculars (as opposed to the universalist Latin), which weakened the church hierarchy as interpreters of the Bible and laid the groundwork for the establishment of the nation. While the print revolution may have sown the seeds of national self-consciousness, most people continued to identify themselves by their religious affiliation rather than their nationality.

Most students of nationalism draw a causal link between the changes underway in Europe during the end of the eighteenth century and the development of nationalism during that same period. As people left their villages and farms for the growing cities, they also left behind many of their previous attachments and were receptive to new ones. The great social and economic changes underway during the late eighteenth century were accompanied by change in political thought as liberalism began to compete effectively against the ideas of divine right of kings and absolutism. The American War of Independence, for example, was both a manifestation of the idea of national **self-determination** and an assertion of radical liberal principles. The American nationality was defined by the belief in a set of liberal propositions which, the Americans believed, applied not only to themselves but also to all humankind. Similarly, English nationalism as it developed during the eighteenth and nineteenth centuries maintained its roots in the idea of individual liberty.

The growth of the centralized state as well as the fascination with vernacular languages fostered the growth of nationalism. The modern state needed to promote a common language among its subjects. Public (i.e. state-run) schools emerged at precisely the time when nationalism was growing. The state used its schools to teach a common national (i.e. enforced) language, partly to reinforce a sense of loyalty to the state, but also to facilitate state functions, such as tax collection and military conscription. The extraction of revenues from the population and the formation of vast military organizations for territorial aggrandizement drove the evolution of the modern state system in Europe. The subsequent emergence of nationalist ideology is closely connected to this process. As direct rule expanded throughout Europe, the welfare, culture, and daily routines of ordinary Europeans came to depend on which state they happened to reside in. Internally, states undertook to impose national languages, national educational systems, national military service, and much more. Externally, they began to control movement across frontiers, to use tariffs and customs as instruments of economic policy, and to treat foreigners as distinctive kinds of people deserving limited rights and close surveillance. As a result, two mutually reinforcing forms of nationalism emerged: one refers to the mobilization of populations that do not have their own state around a claim to political independence, the other to the mobilization of the population of an existing state around a strong identification with that state. Besides these aspects of the growth of the modern state it is no accident that the participation of the masses in politics coincided with the age of nationalism. As politics became more democratic and monarchs lost the last vestiges of their previous **legitimacy**, rulers needed something new upon which to base their **power**.

Both liberalism and nationalism shared a healthy loathing of dynastic absolutism

and of the censorship and oppression that it brought, linking their fates closely together through the eighteenth and early nineteenth centuries. The Revolutionary and Napoleonic Wars, however, succeeded in destroying many aspects of individualism and liberalism that had existed in nationalism. Beginning in the middle of the nineteenth century, the history of nationalism on the continent of Europe would be dominated by increasingly anti-liberal, or anti-individualistic, themes. The emerging nations of Europe became acquainted with nationalism not as a vehicle of individual liberty but as an adoration of collective power.

In much of Western Europe the geographic boundaries of the nation-state had preceded the building of the nation itself. For example, there was a Kingdom of France before there was a French nation. In central and Eastern Europe the situation was completely reversed. In these areas nations were born before nation-states. Much of east-central Europe was controlled by four great multinational **empires**, namely the German, Russian, Habsburg, and Ottoman. Many of the people who inhabited these empires had no historical state with which they might identify. For the peoples living in central and Eastern Europe, the liberal aspirations of nationalism were submerged while the goal of building a nation-state became paramount. The development of nationalism in Asia, and later in Africa, was greatly influenced by the growing role of European powers in those areas. It is, in fact, in Asia and Africa where nationalism developed last and where many of its worst manifestations are today in evidence.

The role of nationalism in international relations is ambiguous. On the one hand, nationalism provides a justification for dividing humanity on the basis of territory. On the other hand, since many territorial boundaries were determined prior to the rise of nationalism (particularly in Asia, the Middle East and Africa), the principle of national self-determination is deeply subversive of contemporary **international law** based on state **sovereignty**. There are no signs that this paradox is about to come to an end in the foreseeable future.

Nations and states

Nations and states may seem identical, but they are not. States govern people in a territory with boundaries. They have laws, taxes, officials, currencies, postal services, police, and (usually) armies. They wage war, negotiate treaties, put people in prison, and regulate life in thousands of ways. They claim sovereignty within their territory. By contrast, nations are groups of people claiming common bonds like language, culture, and historical identity. Some groups claiming to be nations have a state of their own, like the French, Dutch, Egyptians, and Japanese. Others want a state but do not have one, including the Tibetans, Chechnyans, and Palestinians. Others do not want statehood but claim and enjoy some autonomy. The Karen claim to be a nation trapped within the state of Burma/Myanmar. The Sioux are a nation within the boundaries of the United States, and the Scots within Britain. Each of these nations has its own special territory, rights, laws, and culture, but not statehood. Some imagined nations are larger than states or cross state boundaries. The Arab nation embraces more than a dozen states, while the nation of the Kurds takes in large areas of four states.

Some people assume that states are fixed and permanently established across most of the globe. But in fact states are in flux. State boundaries are often changed – by **war**, negotiation, arbitra-tion and even by the sale of territory for money (Russia sold Alaska to the United States, for example). A few states have endured, but others may be here today and gone tomorrow. Over the past decade a number of states have disappeared – Czechoslovakia, East Germany, North and South Yemen, and of course the Union of Soviet Socialist Republics.

Diplomatic **recognition** confers legitimacy on a new state (or on the government of a state) but sometimes there is dissensus within the international community. For example, the Palestinian people are largely under the jurisdiction of other states, although they are seen by the majority of the international community as having strong claims to independent statehood. Other nations claiming the right to independent statehood fail to win backing and are dismissed as frivolous or illegitimate (such as Kosovo). When the United Nations was founded, it was composed of just fifty-one member states. Today there are more than 190 member states. The great majority of today's members were then either colonies (as in most of Africa) or parts of other states (such as those that emerged after the collapse of the Soviet Union).

The classical nation-states in Northern and Western Europe evolved within the boundaries of existing territorial states. They were part of the European state system that took on a recognizable shape with the Peace of **Westphalia** in 1648. By contrast, the 'belated' nations – beginning with Italy and Germany – followed a different course, one that was also typical for the formation of nation-states in Central and Eastern Europe; here the formation of the state followed the trail blazed by an anticipatory national consciousness. The difference between these two paths (from state to nation *versus* from nation to state) is reflected in the backgrounds of the actors who formed the vanguard of nation and state builders. In the former case, they were lawyers, diplomats, and military officers who belonged to the king's administrative staff and together constructed a state bureaucracy. In the latter case, it was writers, historians, scholars, and intellectuals who laid the groundwork for the subsequent diplomatic and military unification of the state. After the Second World War, a third generation of very different nation-states emerged from the process of **decolonization**, primarily in Africa and Asia. Often these states, which were founded within the frontiers established by the former colonial regimes, acquired sovereignty before the imported forms of state organization could take root in a national identity that transcended tribal differences. In these cases, artificial states had to be first filled by a process of nation-building. Finally, with the collapse of the Soviet Empire, the trend toward the formation of independent nation-states in Eastern and Southern Europe has followed the path of more or less violent **secessions**; in the socially and economically precarious situation in which these countries found themselves, the old ethnonational slogans had the power to mobilize distraught populations for independence.

The nation-state at one time represented a response to the historical challenge of finding a functional equivalent for the early modern form of social integration that was in the process of disintegrating. Today we are confronting an analogous challenge. The **globalization** of commerce and communication, of economic production and finance, of the spread of technology and weapons, and above all of ecological and military risks, poses problems that can no longer be solved within the framework of nation-states or by the traditional method of agreements between sovereign states. If

current trends continue, the progressive undermining of national sovereignty may necessitate the founding and expansion of political institutions on the supranational level.

Some observers believe that the role of the nation-state has been reduced to that of a municipality within the global capitalist system, responsible for providing the necessary infrastructure and services to attract capital investment. However, this is much too simplistic. Societies also demand identity, and the nation-state has sometimes been successful in providing this where other identities have been weak. It can therefore play an important part in expressing to the outside world a unique identity associated with a particular locality. The nation-state is less successful in those situations where the population is fragmented between several large groups who do not wish to surrender portions of their different identities in order to produce a national identity. Malaysia, Indonesia, and Yugoslavia are just a few particularly good contemporary examples. In these cases, the national ideology for various reasons fails to assimilate large sections of the population, causing an on-going crisis of belief within the society, that is generally responded to with the use of (sometimes violent) coercion by the apparatus of the state and by the dominant group.

The cultural effects of accelerating globalization have brought with them disintegrating factors that tend toward the atomization of societies, and toward the breakdown of older social, political, and cultural units, including that of the nuclear family unit. This tendency is most pronounced in the economically advanced nation-states of the West, and has tended to reduce the authority, importance and relevance of the nation-state as an institution.

Alongside this atomization within societies, especially Western societies, has come a seemingly contradictory tendency toward **regionalism**. The surrender of many of the economic functions of nation-states to regional entities has been a feature of this latest round of globalization. Perhaps more significant has been the growth of **global cities** and their increasing independence from the nation-state to which they ostensibly belong. New York, London, and Tokyo have been identified as being global cities of the first order, whilst cities such as Los Angeles, Frankfurt, Zurich, Paris, Sydney, Singapore, among a dozen or so others, can be considered second-order global cities. The relationship of these global cities to national governments is changing, especially in critical areas such as monetary policy, interest rates, commercial treaties, and immigration.

The development of global cities has been accompanied by the growth of territory that has become peripheral from the major social and economic processes, and which cuts across the boundaries of rich and poor countries. Whilst including much of what was known as the **Third World** and the countries of the former communist bloc, this peripheral economic wilderness now includes large regions within the developed countries themselves.

However, it should be remembered that controlling population movements has become a key function of the modern nation-state, and keeping the poor immobile has become a principal concern, especially for those wealthy regions of the world that do not want their cities 'flooded' with people – usually unskilled – for whom their economy has no useful purpose.

In the next century we may witness the further decay of the nation-state as the all-powerful and sole center of power, and with that we will see the further growth of non-state organizations, and the concentration of actual power within the global cities. Some of these organizations stand above the state – for example, the **European Union**. Others are of a completely different kind, such as international bodies and **multinational corporations**. What they all have in common is that they either assume some of the functions of the nation-state or manage to escape its control. Being either much larger than states or without geographical borders, they are better positioned to take advantage of recent developments in transportation and communications. The result is that their power seems to be growing while that of the nation-state declines.

Is it possible to view nationalism in the abstract as either 'beneficial' or 'threatening'? In one sense nationalism could be perceived to be beneficial in that it can assist in promoting democracy, encouraging **self-determination**, discouraging **imperialism**, and allowing for economic **development**, and the pursuit of freedom. Alternatively, it could be interpreted as threatening in that it encourages hatred between groups, rise of xenophobia or racism, internal oppression of minority rights, and external aggression.

Further reading

Anderson, B. (1991) *Imagined Communities*, 2nd edn, London: Verso

Brubaker, R. (1997) *Nationalism Reframed: Nationhood and the National Question in the New Europe*, Cambridge: Cambridge University Press

Gellner, E. (1983) *Nations and Nationalism*, Oxford: Blackwell.

Hutchinson, J. and Smith, A. (eds) (1994) *Nationalism*, Oxford: Oxford University Press

Puri, Y (2004) *Encountering Nationalism*, Oxford: Blackwell Publishers

Smith, A. (1998) *Nationalism and Modernism*, London: Routledge

Vincent, A. (2002) *Nationalism and Particularity*, Cambridge: Cambridge University Press.

See also: communitarianism; nation-state; patriotism; self-determination; state formation

MARTIN GRIFFITHS and
KATHARINE VADURA

Nation-state

The nation-state is a basic component of global society. Every square mile of the globe, except the open oceans and Antarctica, falls within the exclusive domain of one nation-state or another. The nation-state as a form of governance is so ubiquitous that its existence is taken for granted, rarely noticed, even by scholars of international relations. The nation-state, or something like it, is often assumed to have always existed and to be a universal, immanent part of human nature. What is not recognized is that the present dominance and exclusiveness of the nation-state as a form of governance is a recent historical development and was produced by the peculiar political and military conditions prevailing on the continent of Europe in the first centuries following the collapse of the Roman Empire. After its emergence in Europe, Europeans exported the idea of the state to the rest of the globe to the detriment of all other forms of governance.

The nation-state has the following characteristics which set it apart from other forms of human governance: first, the state has a distinctive geographically defined *territory* over which it exercises jurisdiction; second, it has *sovereignty* which means that its jurisdiction is exclusive of outside interference by other states or entities; third it has a *government* that directly controls and administers the territory and population subject to the state's jurisdiction; fourth, the state has *fixed boundaries* recognized by other states and marked on the ground by entry and exit points and, in some case, by fences and border guards; fifth, the government of the state has a *monopoly on the legitimate use of physical coercion* over its territory and population; sixth, the state has, to a greater or lesser degree, a sense of *national identity* among its inhabitants based on an invented and imagined shared history, culture, language, religion, and customs; and seventh, it can rely on, to a greater or lesser degree, the *obedience* and *loyalty* of its inhabitants. These characteristics make the state fundamentally different from the other forms of human governance that have existed historically on the globe such as city states, empires, tribes, and theocracies.

Formation of the state

The dominance and exclusiveness of the nation-state as a form of governance can be seen by tracing its formation from medieval Europe to the present. The Western Roman Empire was followed by a collection of Germanic kingdoms. Over time, the Roman conception of centralized, direct, public, governance was erased and replaced by the Germanic conception of politico-military power being a private possession of the ruler that could be bought and sold, divided among heirs, mortgaged, and given in marriage. In other words, public politico-military **power** as it had existed during the Roman Empire became thoroughly 'privatized'. While these semi-autonomous units existed in what eventually came to be known as 'Christendom', there was no clearly defined hierarchy of **authority** downward as had existed during the Roman period. Not even the Pope, the religious leader of

Christendom who claimed authority over all Christians, nor the Holy Roman Emperor, the Germanic heir to the Roman emperors who claimed secular authority over Europe, could control the religious and political life within their respective domains in ways that are now routine for the fully formed nation-state. Territory was not determinative of identity and political loyalty. Rights, obligations, and loyalty were determined by one's location in a complex matrix of personal connections called 'vassalage'.

Gradually, this situation of politico-military heteronomy began to reverse itself. From about the year 1200 CE the competing units began to consolidate around the idea of bounded, mutually exclusive territory and politico-military power began to centralize and de-privatize. Governance gradually became more direct and bureaucratic. The lineaments of the current global **order** of territorially defined, mutually exclusive sovereign states within which there exists a centralized continuous, institutionalized politico-military authority possessing the legitimate use of physical coercion, and expecting obedience and loyalty from its inhabitants came into view.

The force behind this reversal was **war**, which gradually transformed the heteronomy of the medieval period into the homonymy of the current global order. Military activity and the formation of the nation-state were inextricably linked. Changes in the way war was fought and innovations in the technology of warfare drove the formation of the nation-state.

War making was gradually transformed from episodic, limited combat about property to combat with a strategic purpose, such as the conquest of the territory of the enemy, by a major shift in the way that war was made and organized. This shift in the manner of war making was brought about by a series of innovations in the technology of warfare. The most important of these innovations was gunpowder and the development of weapons that used it to propel projectiles with great force: the handheld firearm and the canon. Projectiles fired from even primitive firearms and cannons could penetrate the plate armor worn by knights and could bring down the high stonewalls of medieval strongholds in a few hours. Eventually, groups of foot soldiers carrying firearms replaced mounted knights as the main military formation and high stone-walled castles were replaced by low profile earthen fortifications designed to absorb sustained pounding from heavy cannons.

The emergence of the infantry based army, backed up by artillery, ensconced in massive low-walled fortifications, changed armies from small retinues of mounted aristocratic warriors to large and complex organizations composed of infantry, artillery, and light cavalry units. Training and discipline were introduced. Logistics systems to support large armies in the field were developed. Military training schools, which taught young unruly aristocrats parade ground drill, discipline, tactics, and scientific gunnery, were founded. The infantry regiments became the basic unit of military organization. Regiments became permanent institutions with a fixed headquarters in a particular city where it recruited its soldiers, and, from the surrounding countryside, its officers who were drawn from the local aristocratic families. Soldiers began to wear standardized clothes (uniforms) and displays of individual fighting prowess, which had been central to medieval combat, were discouraged.

Recruiting, training, paying, and supplying such large armies required unprecedented amounts of money. War being a private affair, the king or prince who had sufficient personal money to recruit, train, equip, and supply a large well disciplined army and build large low-walled fortifications could prevail over others, within or without his realm. In order to pay for such armies, especially during times of war when costs skyrocketed, kings borrowed money, debased the coinage, sold crown lands, and at times, pawned the crown jewels when they ran short of money from their personal treasuries. Such methods of raising the revenue necessary to pay for large infantry based armies were inefficient and monarchs began to find ways to extract the money, as well as the men and *materiel* from all the lands in their realms and from the entire subject population. In order to do so, monarchs had to receive the approval of the great council of the realm composed of upper members of the nobility, the higher clergy, and important members of the commoners, usually 'well to do' individuals from the most important towns in the realm. Because the king needed the consent of the great council to levy a tax to fight wars, a struggle ensued between the crown on the one hand, and the great council, on the other, over the control of taxation. Eventually, medieval monarchs began to levy taxes directly on their subjects. At first the concessions granted to the king were only for the purpose for which they had been requested. The idea of a regular tax to pay for war came about slowly.

The granting to the monarchs the power to tax to pay for increasingly expensive war gradually created a new apparatus of rule that was increasingly separate from the person of the monarch. The members of the king's household staff, who collected his revenues from his private estates and administered his justice, were slowly transformed into public officials who provided these functions for the entire realm on a regular basis. The development of financial and judicial institutions staffed with a small but growing body of professional administrators loyal to the king meant that monarchs were able to collect revenue directly and control their realms without the help of intermediaries. Over time, medieval monarchs gathered to themselves the instruments of uniform, territorial rule. The imperatives of raising money to support enormously expensive infantry armies impelled monarchs to construct the administrative apparatus that made centralized, territory-wide rule possible. These embryonic state structures gradually became public and penetrated into every nook and cranny of the realm. Politico-military power was steadily centralized and concentrated into the hands of the king.

As politico-military power became more and more lodged in the institutions of the centralizing monarchy; such power was increasingly distinguished from the person of the king and viewed as an attribute of the state itself. Politico-military power came to be less identified with the decisions of the monarch as a private person and more as a manifestation of the action of an ongoing set of offices, institutions, and processes, which were under the supervision of the monarch. Gradually, the logic of loyalty to the person of the monarch was replaced with loyalty to the institutions and processes of politico-military power. The monarch ceased to be the embodiment of sovereignty and became the minister of sovereignty. Governing became less about land and property and more about managing the institutions of the state to ensure its own survival. The monarch came to more view his subjects and his realm as objects to be administered and protected. The result of these changes was the emergence of territorialized political space. Now, only the state could provide the administrative, technical, and financial resources required to make war.

Types of states

After **Westphalia**, monarchial sovereignty became the only legitimate form of the state in Europe. Increasingly, other forms of rule, such as the imperial state of the Habsburg Empire, the successor to the Holy Roman Empire, became illegitimate. Also, increasingly, the ecclesiastical unity of Europe under the Papacy was shattered and replaced by a fragmented system of sovereign monarchical states, which encouraged the estrangement of Europeans from one another based on territorial identity. Rule became increasingly territorialized. Warfare shifted from being about property to being about maintaining territorial sovereignty and the security of the state's inhabitants.

The specification of monarchy as the only legitimate form of the state encouraged the development of monarchical absolutism. Gradually, the monarch came to be seen as a source of all law, the owner of the realm who faced no restriction on his power. This represented a major break with medieval constitutionalism in which monarchs were constrained by the great council of the realm. Monarchs achieved their positions of absolute power by circumventing the great councils and ruling their territories directly through a staff of salaried administrative officials who were totally dependent upon them. The great council was 'put to sleep', that is, bypassed or suppressed and played little or no role in the governance of the realm. In some realms the great council disappeared completely. Local Rulers were brought under the control of the crown. Power was increasingly exercised without limitations, it was unbound or absolute.

Economic and social changes within monarchical absolutist states from the seventeenth to the nineteenth centuries produced a reaction to them, which brought forth a new form of the state. These changes created a powerful new class of subjects, mostly town dwellers who made their livings in commerce and industry, which believed that sovereignty was possessed by 'the people', not the absolute monarch, and was vested in institutions, constrained by the 'rule of law', that represented the people. The proponents of popular sovereignty were called 'liberals' because they sought to liberate (free) society and economy from absolutist rule and replace it with a form of the state that would allow individuals the freedom to live their lives the way they wanted, without guidance and direction from the state.

Liberals believed that the way to liberate individuals from the absolute state was to replace it with a 'constitutional state', that is, a state created by the people whose power was restricted by a constitution. Two forms of the constitutional state appeared as a consequence of the actions of liberals. One was based on the doctrine of the 'ancient' constitution, which maintained that there were certain legal principles that had been established over a long period of time, many centuries, which could be deduced from the history and customary law of the people. The most famous proponent of this view was the 'conservative' English thinker and politician Edmund Burke (1729–97), who famously argued that the British constitution was the manifestation of an ancient partnership between the dead, the living, and generations not yet born. He saw the British constitution as the embodiment of the collective wisdom, and the accretion of decision of the British people down through the ages. Ancient constitutionalism referred to medieval constitutionalism when monarchs were not absolute; their power and authority being limited by a complex web of vassalic duties and obligations and by the feudal rights and obligation of the great councils which compelled them to rule the realm jointly with it. Liberals who believed in the doctrine of ancient constitutionalism fought for a limited or constitutional monarchy.

The other form of the constitutional state was based on the doctrine of the 'written' constitution, drafted 'by the people'. This form of constitutionalism, unlike ancient constitutionalism, which relied on historical, mystical, or religious beliefs, was based on rational, moral, and philosophical arguments. Liberals of this persuasion believed that all human beings possessed the capacity to reason and could, therefore, perceive the unchanging moral order of the Universe, ordained by God, and manifested in Natural Law. 'Rational' human beings could contemplate Natural Law and discern for themselves that they possessed rights based on their common humanity exclusive of their particular social and political situation.

The most famous proponent of this form of constitutionalism was John Locke (1632–1704) who argued that the state should be limited to regulating the general conditions under which rights-bearing, independent individuals could exercise their power to make informed economic, social, and political choice with minimal restrictions. To create such conditions, the state had to be limited by a written constitution that divided its power among separate branches of government (legislative, executive, and judicial) and elevated the concept of individual rights above those of the state. Such a constitution was seen as a 'contract' between a pre-existing people living in 'a state of nature' and the state which can be broken if the state exceeds its authority and begins to violate individual rights. In this conception of constitutional state, no individual was obliged to obey the state unless he or she had consented personally to its authority.

During the eighteenth and nineteenth centuries liberal constitutionalists challenged absolutists for control of many European territorial states. Liberal constitutionalism flourished in Britain and its colonies in North America because Britain had the largest commercial class of all European monarchies thanks to the extensive industrialization and commercialization of its economy and urbanization of its population. On the European continent where commercialization, industrialization, and urbanization were less widespread, liberal constitutionalists were much less successful in changing the absolutist monarchies to liberal constitutional states. This resulted in prolonged and often bloody struggles between liberals and absolutists in these realms. In France, for example republicans, constitutional monarchists and absolutists struggled against one another for control of the state for nearly one hundred years after the French Revolution; that is, until the coming of the Third Republic in 1871 which abolished the monarchy forever and definitively established the French state as a liberal, constitutional republic.

Social and economic changes wrought by the Industrial Revolution of the late nineteenth and early twentieth centuries created major challenges to liberal constitutional states. Industrialization produced an abundance of material goods and abominable working conditions for the laboring class. Eventually, workers began to demand a living wage and better working conditions as well as a share of political power. Believing that the horrendous social dislocation, gross inequalities of wealth, and urban squalor produced by industrialization would eventually be dealt with by the 'trickle down' effect, which would spread wealth from the rich to the poor, liberal constitutionalists refused to go beyond judicially applied, minimally-intrusive reforms and the expansion of procedural democracy.

By the end of the nineteenth century, frustrated by the lack of significant progress of liberal reformism, workers began to support movements that sought to overthrow the liberal constitutional state and replace it with a different form of the state. Two variations of anti-liberal state appeared as a result of actions of these movements. One was based on the ideology of socialism as articulated by Karl Marx (1818–83), a German economist, journalist, and political organizer. Marx argued that the horrible conditions in which the working class found itself were the result not of individual short comings, as liberals argued, but on the capitalism's mode of production, which he saw as intimately connected to the liberal constitutional state. Marx argued that the form of the state was a reflection of the class holding power. Under **capitalism**, the bourgeoisie created a state that promoted its needs. Its police kept the working class in check, its economic agencies ministered to the capitalist economy; its wars opened overseas markets and secured its investments abroad. In a socialist state, the state itself would eventually 'wither away' because it would become unnecessary to maintain the capitalist mode of production and the suppression of the working class, or so Marx claimed.

Another variety of anti-liberal state was based on the thinking of the German idealist philosopher Georg Hegel (1770–1831), who, unlike liberals, saw the state as an active agent of change. Indeed, Hegel saw the state as it had emerged in Europe as the supreme manifestation of the rational nature of human beings. For Hegel, the state embodied the spirit of human history and the realization of a rational society. He argued that liberal-

ism's belief that individuals using their own initiative could produce a rational and just society was mistaken. The liberal constitutional state realized only a truncated version of human reason, one based on instrumental calculations of self-interest. Full realization of human reason required a state in which human beings gave self-conscious direction to organization of their shared ethical and social life. For Hegel, the realization of full human reason was manifested in struggles among sovereign states, which would lead, eventually, to the victory of the sovereign state, which in turn represented the most rational ethical life for its inhabitants, that is, true freedom.

Two prominent states in the twentieth century explicitly rejected liberal constitutionalism and embraced alternative forms of the state based on these philosophies. One was Russia, which after the socialist revolution in 1917, reorganized itself into a communist state (see **communism**) after attempts during the nineteenth century to transform its ruthless absolutist monarchy into a liberal constitutional one failed and the other was Germany which, in the wake of its defeat in World War One, attempted a liberal constitutional republic. The crisis of the Weimar Republic brought to power the National Socialist German Workers Party (NAZI) and the establishment of the anti-liberal and anti-socialist state (the Third Reich) ruled by a 'master race' of Aryans, united by love of the Fatherland, and dedicated to the protection of Germans from the evil machinations of so-called 'inferior races', especially Jews, and the so-called 'decadent' liberal constitutional democracies. The Weimar Republic was gradually replaced with a dictatorship, which claimed to represent the German 'Master Race'. Struggles for supremacy against neighboring states began with the invasion of the 'inferior'

Poles in 1939. This act of aggression started World War Two.

World War Two, which brought an end to the German Nazi state in 1945, and the subsequent **cold war** (1948–90) conditioned the states involved to become more centralized and to employ science and technology to rationalize territorial administration and intensify their control over economic and social life because without the total mobilization of all sectors of the society, modern, industrialized warfare could not be successfully waged. These tendencies, which were clearly evident in Nazi Germany and Soviet Russia, also appeared in liberal constitutional states such as the United States, Great Britain, and France. By the last decades of the twentieth century these tendencies brought forth a new form of the state.

This new form of the state, which can be called the managerial state, became dominant on the planet in the late twentieth century. While the managerial state continues to rely on liberal constitutionalism to create the appearance of a weak and limited state, it continuously monitors, organizes, controls, and regulates the social, economic, and political life within itself. The managerial state has diffused its power throughout these spheres and has assumed responsibility for the entire condition of contemporary society: the condition of its environment, its food supply, and the quality of its water; the relationships of its citizens; the habits they develop; their education; their health; and their ability to make a living. The managerial state, like earlier forms of the state, is based on an ideology, in this case, rational instrumentalism. In the managerial state, reason has come to be seen as the efficient application of means, or the invention of new ones, to achieve a given end. The managerial state is seen as the coordinator of all the complex subsystems that compose it and intervenes in them to make them function more efficiently.

The most famous theorist of the managerial state was the German historian, legal scholar and political sociologist, Max Weber (1864–1920), who argued that the rationalization of the state was historically inevitable because of the breakdown of the status-based social solidarity of feudalism and the emergence of industrialized urbanized states in the late nineteenth and early twentieth centuries. The most important aspect of this development for Weber was the advance of bureaucracy because of its technical superiority over other forms of administering wide territories and large populations.

The managerial state appears to represent progress toward greater individual freedom from domination because it retains the ideology of liberal constitutionalism and exercises control through familiar friendly institutions (e.g., schools, churches, charities) and routine practices (e.g., procedural democracy). The citizens of managerial states have come to accept and even welcome domination by the state and willingly comply with it to the degree that they perceive it as legal rational, democratic, and the font of their well being and prosperity.

As the managerial state has expanded in the late twentieth century, its citizens increasingly have come to be treated less as bearers of rights, as in liberal constitutional states, and more as efficient contributors to and consumers of state programs. In the managerial state, the political consciousness of the citizens becomes that of the rational consumer who looks to the state through the lens of utilitarian calculations of costs and benefits. Taxes, for example, come to be seen less as necessary contributions for the public good and more as the price of government programs and services.

Although information continues to circulate freely in managerial states, as it did in liberal constitutional ones, technology and the industrialization of the media industries and the concentration of the ownership of news and information. Increasingly, people in managerial states receive their information and interpretations of state policies as spectators outside the forums for political discussion and debates. In the managerial state, political information is produces and circulated like industrial products, such as soap and automobiles. To be financially successful, the corporations that produce the news must reach a wide audience; therefore, they tailor their information and news to the 'average' consumer. Increasingly in the managerial state, being a good citizen has come to mean 'keeping up with the news' not actively engaging in political activity and debate. Although the media are not owned by the public in the managerial state, the state does intervene to limit and at times direct the way in which information is presented, especially in times of war. In the managerial state, election campaigns take place primarily through the media and candidates adopt the same marketing strategies that business do when selling a product: they devise and strategically place advertisements for themselves and carefully control the timing and content of their public statements. They employ professional media and marketing consultants who help them shape the image they want to project.

The managerial state assumes responsibility for the prosperity of the economy. Under some circumstances the managerial state intervenes directly into the economy by nationalizing industries that fail as private enterprises but provide the public goods that the state needs, such as railroads and utilities; by subjecting private business and corporations to health, safety and environmental regulations; and by energizing the economy through government spending, providing subsidies to certain industries, by passing tariffs, and by manipulating the tax codes.

The managerial state also assumes responsibility for the welfare of its subject population. State programs such, as health insurance, social security, unemployment insurance, and aid to the poor, are important tools used by the state to manage prosperity and maintain public order. These programs channel money to consumers to ensure sufficient aggregate demand for the mass-produced goods of industrial corporations and to redirect labor to the new jobs the economy requires. They are also important components of the management of general social order by disciplining recipients of aid through program requirements and by ameliorating the worst dislocation of the industrial capitalist market place.

The managerial state manages political participation by the formalization and routinization of procedural democracy. The principal way that people participate in politics in the managerial state is through regular elections, which channel participation away from unpredictable, disruptive, and spontaneous forms of participation such as demonstrating, rioting, and throwing Molotov Cocktails. Elections domesticate and pacify participation and transform it into a routine, peaceful public activity. All managerial states regulate the way in which individual votes are translated into seats in a representative body and regulate the composition of the electorate.

The trend in managerial states has been toward fewer large parties that do not differ much from one another in terms of ideology or program. Such catchall parties seek to capture as many voters as possible by appealing to prudent administration, managerial ability, technical expertise, or personal characteristics of its candidates. Thus, elections in managerial states have become ritualistic confrontations between candidates and parties who claim to be best able to manage the state more effectively and efficiently than their opponents, rather than occasions for serious public debate and discussion about pressing issues. Increasingly, parties and candidates control their images by employing the marketing techniques of consumer manipulation used in commercial advertising in order to mobilize or demobilize voters. Public opinion polling is also used extensively. Governance becomes an exercise in maintaining popularity. These techniques have produced a significant level of disenchantment with politics among the voters and a general apathy toward public affairs, which is reflected in marked declines in the percentage of eligible voters who actually vote in managerial states.

The spread of the state beyond Europe

European feudalism was inherently aggressive and expansionist. Within Europe feudal politico-military practices were spread by military conquest and dynastic marriage from the core to the peripheries of the continent. Feudalism aggressively pushed outward the dominions of European centralizing monarchies to the east against Slavic peoples and to the south against the Muslims, who had occupied the Iberian Peninsula in 711. This expansionism homogenized Europe around the feudal institutions and practices whence the modern territorial state emerged.

European expansionism combined with religious fanaticism as well as the desire for booty and trade drove Europe's first attempt at external expansion, the Crusades. From the eleventh to the end of the thirteenth century European armies, at the instigation of various popes, repeatedly attacked the Muslim peoples of the eastern Mediterranean in order to establish and maintain hegemony over the holy sites of Christianity in Palestine. Four Christian feudal holdings, the County of Edessa, the Principality of Antioch, the Kingdom of Jerusalem, and the County of Tripoli, were carved out and maintained until 1290 when Muslim armies regained control over the area and expelled the Europeans.

Although Europeans were unable to maintain their presence in Palestine, European external expansionism continued elsewhere. The vehicle for this expansion was the increasingly centralized and territorialized states that were forming on the continent, each with its own economic base, centralized political institutions, and armed forces. The competitive relationship among the emergent territorial states within Europe began to spill over into oceanic sphere in the early fifteenth century producing a vast global quest for overseas colonies. The result was the permanent European domination of the globe. By 1650 Europeans had achieved military control over the Western Hemisphere, Siberia, coastal Africa, the Antipodes, and various archipelagos in the Pacific. By 1800 Europeans controlled 35 per cent of the globe's surface, by 1900 that total had been raised to 85 per cent. The global order beyond Europe at this point was one of rival colonial **empires**.

European domination of the globe was made possible by advances in maritime technology and the ability of the emerging territorial states of Europe to project military power beyond the continent. Europe's domination of the globe spread European politico-military norms and practices throughout the world and imposed them on non-European peoples.

In this way the idea that the territorial sovereign state, as it had emerged in Europe, was the only acceptable form of rule was spread throughout the world and became the global norm and laid the foundation for the present global system of sovereign territorial states.

European imperialism created states outside of Europe in two ways: first, states were created by the direct conquest and colonization of non-European peoples by European states. In this situation the idea of the state was directly imposed on tribal peoples whose governance was not oriented to formally demarcated, territorial space of European colonies. Direct conquest and colonization created new territorial political spaces that had not existed previously within which competition for control of that space, and its governing apparatus was engendered. Eventually, contending Europeanized indigenous elites vied with one another, often using ethnic appeals, for control of the colonial state.

Second, states were created by external inducement. In this situation, states emerged from indigenous forms of rule in areas of the globe not directly conquered by European states. Externally induced states were produced by the ability of certain non-European peoples, such as the Chinese, Japanese, and the Persians, to resist direct and complete European hegemony and survive into the present as independent entities by adopting the institutions and politics of the European state and molding them with indigenous traditions of rule.

State and nation

The force that transformed the world of European colonial empires into the current global order of sovereign states was **nationalism**, which began in Europe and spread to the rest of the world. During the eighteenth century in Europe the idea of a common national community to which all subjects of the state belonged; that is, a 'nation' bound together by a common language, religion, history, and culture, enabled the state to raise huge armies without creating a threat to the state itself. Thus, in Europe first, nations were created where none had existed previously in order to mobilize the human resources necessary to survival in a world of competitive, militarized states. Since then, the idea that the state should have a common national identity and be governed by individuals of that nation has become one of the most powerful forces in the current **international system**.

State boundaries have rarely conformed to a single linguistic, religious, or cultural community, however. Despite the efforts of states to create a uniform nation within their boundaries, many contain significant minority groups who do not share the official national culture. Many of these groups imagine themselves to be 'captured' nations and have formed political movements that claim the right of **self-determination** and have demanded autonomy within the state or an independent state of their own. Demands for autonomy and independence result from the belief of ethnic groups that:

1. the identity of the groups is being eroded by strong assimilationist policies of the majority or dominant ethnic group that controls the state;
2. their cultural identity can be maintained by breaking away from the state in which they find themselves and forming their own state; and
3. their nationalist aspiration can only be achieved with full sovereign statehood.

The demands of such groups are transforming the current global system of states by fragmenting existing ones. Essentially, the state boundaries imposed on the globe during the age of European expansionism are being redrawn by ethnic groups who were disregarded when these boundaries were laid down.

Challenges to the state

Ironically, as the number of sovereign states is increasing on the planet, the state as a form of governance is being challenged by economic and social forces that are rendering it more ineffective as an entity that can protect its citizens and assure their economic well being. In effect, while more states are coming into existence, their sovereignty is being diminished by changes in the nature of warfare, the **globalization** of economic life, and the tremendous increase in global nomadism.

During the medieval period, before the advent of the territorial state, war conducted by small contingents of highly trained aristocratic knights whose personal discipline, prowess, courage, and desire for honor were tested in brief, 'face to face' combat. The rise of the state made this form of combat anachronistic and transformed warfare. Warfare became an activity monopolized by the state and, increasingly, was waged by vast infantry based armies composed of quickly-trained individuals, each performing a small aspect of the war fighting enterprise. Initially, such vast armies fought each other in set-piece battles. A clean distinction between combatant and non-combatant was maintained and fighting was confined to designated battlefields so as to cause the least amount of damage to the civilian population.

The industrialization of warfare in the nineteenth century changed the nature of warfare. War fighting became a total effort of the state. Increasingly, states organized their entire industrial and social capacities to fight wars. The state came to be always 'at war' in some sense and the distinction maintained previously between combatants and non-combatants dissolved. In total war, civilians and soldiers were both combatants. The state began to manage weapons industries and commit vast resources to the development of new, more efficient weapons. War no longer involved close hand-to-hand combat where both combatants were simultaneously in harm's way. In total war, combat took place at vast distances, each side seeking to kill as many of the other side (including civilians) as possible with the minimum of casualties to one's side. The object of warfare was to forcefully penetrate the boundaries of the enemy state, utterly vanquish its people, and occupy its territory.

Industrialized total war challenged the ability of states, even the most powerful, to defend themselves effectively from attack and destruction by rival states. Advances in military technology in the twentieth century have made this even more difficult, if not impossible. The development of long-range strategic bombers during World War Two and the perfection of intercontinental ballistic missiles (ICBMs) during the cold war, made the territorial state vulnerable because there is no effective defense against these weapons. Such developments in the technology of warfare have created a severe challenge to the state's ability to use its military forces to defend its territory and population and has led many people to the conclusion that the continuation of the current global order based on the territorial state is not warranted by the realities of total war nor morally defensible in light of the ability of industrialized weapons, especially weapons of mass destruction, to kill indiscriminately vast numbers of people.

A second challenge to the state's ability to control its territory and population is globalization, which refers to that complex of economic structures and communications technologies that have emerged on a global scale that ignore the boundaries of sovereign territorial states. A world economy, dominated by **multinational corporations** (MNCs) made possible by improvements in transportation and telecommunications technologies have:

1. made good and services globally tradable as never before;
2. made it possible for MNCs to coordinate effectively and efficiently on a global scale their production, planning, and financial operations;
3. made information tradable; and
4. created a global market for currencies by facilitating the electronic flow of capital around the world.

Globalization has made it more difficult for states to maintain the value of their currencies, protect domestic markets with tariffs and regulations, and retain jobs. In short, globalization has challenged the ability of states to manage their economies and guarantee the economic well being of their populations.

A third challenge to the state, which is related to the first and second challenge, is global nomadism. As membership in a state no longer assures protection from military attack or security from poverty for many people who live within them, vast numbers of these people, especially from poor states, have become global nomads who move in and out of states seeking personal security and economic well being. For these people membership in a particular state is a matter of convenience, not patriotic loyalty. It is difficult for global nomads to develop a strong identity with the state in which

they happen to reside because their residency in it is temporary. In today's world economy many individuals take whatever nation-state offers them peace and **security**, even if it means they must abandon their original national identities. Some individuals move from state to state so frequently that they become de facto 'stateless' persons.

These challenges are seen by some observers as evidence that the nation-state is withering away and will be replaced eventually by a different form of **global governance**. Although the state has been weakened by these challenges, it remains the most powerful entity in the global order. Nevertheless, arguments about its decline and fall are plausible and discussions about what might and ought to replace it should be taken seriously. A number of alternative forms of global governance have been advanced.

One possibility would be a world government that would supersede the sovereignty of particular nation-states; another would be some form of global federalism among states in a particular region of the world; a third would be a deterritorialized, universal, ecclesiastical theocracy not unlike Christendom in Europe before the rise of the state; others see the collapse of the state leading to a condition not dissimilar to the heteronomy of the Middle Ages; finally some have argued that **liberal internationalism** in which a rational scientific orientation as a general creed of life and allegiances to principles of universal **human rights** and transnational solidarities are emerging against the parochial allegiances of nationality and religion mixed with the state, which many regard as being responsible for global prejudice, pestilence, and war. In this last alternative, the state would not disappear but would adopt governing structures based on rational principles. World peace would follow because states would share the same organizational format and would work out their differences not through war but through cooperative **multilateralism**.

Further reading

Andrew, V. (1987) *Theories of the State*, Oxford: Basil Blackwell.

Giddens, A. (1985) *The Nation-State and Violence*, Berkeley: California University Press.

Hall, J. A. and Ikenberry, G. J. (1989) *The State*, Minneapolis, MN: Minnesota University Press.

Opello, W. C. and Rosow, S. J. (1999) *The Nation-State and Global Order*, Boulder, CO: Lynne Rienner.

Paul, T. V., Ikenberry, G. J. and Hall, J. A. (eds) (2003) *The Nation-State in Question*, Princeton, NJ: Princeton University Press.

Poggi, G. (1978) *The Development of the Modern State*, Stanford: Stanford University Press.

Porter, B. (1994) *War and the Rise of the State*, New York: Free Press.

Spruyt, B. (1994) *The Sovereign State and its Competitors*, Princeton, NJ: Princeton University Press.

Strayer, J. R. (1970) *On the Medieval Origins of the Modern State*, Princeton: Princeton University Press.

Tilly, C. (1990) *Coercion, Capital, and European States, A.D. 990–1990*, Cambridge: Cambridge University Press.

See also: diaspora; multiculturalism; nationalism; self-determination; state formation

WALTER C. OPELLO, JR.

Neocolonialism

The term neocolonialism encapsulated the disappointment that many **Third World** citizens felt in the 1950s and 1960s as the euphoria accompanying independence wore off. Colonialism might be officially over but its consequences lived on, often embodied in local administrators who now occupied the same positions as their erstwhile rulers and pursued similar policies. As a consequence, neocolonialism assumed new applications. **Dependency** theorists used the term to describe strategies actively pursued by industrialized states to perpetuate their control over Third World economies. Third world elites employed the term to deflect domestic criticism from themselves to the machinations of first world nations. And first world leaders, despite rejecting colonialism and embracing universal **modernization**, began increasingly to revert to the stereotyping neocolonialism employed. Neocolonialism enjoyed a dynamic history.

In the mid-1960s when Ghanaian President Kwame Nkrumah coined the term, neocolonialism quite understandably described the state of many newly independent countries. Colonial authorities had rarely prepared their subjects for independence. If anything their actions disempowered subjects. Most Third World countries attained independence without the infrastructure and social transformation necessary to sustain vibrant and democratic economies, the hallmarks of postwar success for industrial nations. Consequently their peoples felt as if little had changed.

This history immediately set Third World countries apart from the rest of the world, certainly from the late industrializers of the nineteenth and early twentieth centuries who had never lost their autonomy. Recovering autonomy then became a central goal of most postcolonial societies, but always the spectre of neocolonialism lingered as a measure of the distance yet to travel. Academic debates in the 1970s reflected this also. Dependency theorists regarded neocolonialism as more than just the lingering consequences of colonialism. Neocolonialism represented a state of dependence actively perpetrated by industrial nations. The first world oversaw the maintenance of forms of unequal exchange, the creation of new forms of 'enclave' production, and the further disarticulation or fragmentation of Third World economies and their separate **integration** into the world economy. Their collusion with postcolonial regimes perpetuated the overdeveloped military and administrative nature of Third World states and assisted the regimes – like their colonial predecessors – to remain relatively autonomous of local classes.

Dependency researchers measured the consequences of neocolonialism in terms of continued helplessness. The societies neocolonialism imprisoned seemed incapable of following the path of first world states. They produced no similar class of strong and independent capitalists able to autonomously sustain growth and prosperity. Instead they possessed weak and state dependent capitalists (see **capitalism**) overshadowed by foreign capital and politicians determined to retain the privileges and **power** once exercised by colonial administrators. This outcome suited exiting colonial authorities keen to retain economic and political influence. They directed aid and military support directly to compliant leaders and conveniently overlooked **human rights** abuses, **corruption** and spending excesses.

Consequently neocolonialism also incorporated a sense of disillusionment that quickly become self-fulfilling prophecy whenever popular discontent at the uneven consequences of **development** threatened domestic stability. Because ruling classes were remote from the mass of their people, they tended to be conservative and to fear the consequences social reconstruction might have on their power bases. Often they sought to deflect popular discontent

externally by appealing to precolonial identities. They presented themselves as custodians of tradition protecting their people from Westernization, which they now projected as the real source of instability and the new colonial threat. Thus neocolonialists learned that the ideology of neocolonialism could be usefully employed to preserve their own status and power.

Nonetheless, such appeals had limited value. By employing tradition in this manner, rulers increased popular perceptions that the main divide in societies lay between tradition and modernity, a position that modernization strategists most often presented as the cause of backwardness. Ironically, it also served to deflect attention from the role modernization played in maintaining neocolonialism and frustrating popular expectations for change. Their strategies failed to develop a cohesive domestic economy. Instead they sought international advantage from national weakness by creating **free trade** or export zones to exploit the one resource Third World countries held in plenty – unregulated cheap labour.

During the 1970s many former European colonies also renegotiated the terms of trade for commodities such as sugar. Although these protectionist regimes provided farmers a small measure of price stability, they also perpetuated colonial commercial relationships, reinforced economic dependence on the markets of first world countries, and reduced institutional pressure for domestic reform and agricultural diversification. In short, by reducing further the possibility for developing linkages between agriculture and industry, town and country, as the basis for future growth, they demonstrated their neocolonial credentials, but at the cost of social harmony and **democratization**.

Varying degrees of authoritarianism invariably met the popular discontent social and economic segregation fuelled. As a consequence, the weak democratic institutions established belatedly on the eve of independence were weakened further. Political authorities connived with their militaries to transform political systems to better serve their own interests. After all, modernization planners prioritized stability and **order**, not social justice and equity. Like latter day colonists, they claimed that authoritarianism presented valid pathways to democracy and modernity.

Such pathways increasingly employed stereotypes to garner popular support. During the course of the late twentieth century appeals to exclusivity became a central hallmark of neocolonialism, just as it had been during the era of colonialism. Colonial authorities had justified their right to rule on the grounds that they were superior and different from the lesser peoples they ruled. Neocolonial successors did not challenge such ideas concerning exclusivity. They justified new segregations between peoples or reinforced old ones, thereby avoiding the need for democratization.

But neocolonial societies had to survive in an increasingly globalized world in which all forms of segregation not only disadvantaged communities but also contributed to global disharmony. The spate of **ethnic conflict**s and **genocide**s that shook the world in the late twentieth century were a direct consequence of neocolonialism, which reinforced difference rather than commonalities. Instead of dismissing the stereotypes and animosities that colonialism had exploited, neocolonialists exploited them anew, appealing to tradition, **nationalism**, religion, and patriotism.

The new first world ideology of immutable difference at the start of the twenty first century, the alleged **clash of civilizations**, similarly appealed to essentialisms. In doing so, it demonstrated the continued relevance of the term neocolonialism. It also demonstrated the validity of comparisons originally drawn by dependency theorists. But above all it demonstrated that without deeper democratization, the future development prospects of most former colonies will remain haunted by neocolonialism.

Further reading

Alavi, H. and Shanin, T. (eds) (1982) *Introduction to the Sociology of 'Developing Societies'*, London: Macmillan.

Fanon, F. (1968) *The Wretched of the Earth*, New York: Grove Press.

Nkrumah, K. (1965) *Neo-Colonialism: The Last Stage of Imperialism*, London: Nelson.

Said, E. W. (1993) *Culture and Imperialism*, London: Chatto & Windus.

See also: clash of civilizations; cold war; dependency; development; ethnic conflict; globalization; Marxism; modernization; postcolonialism; Third World

ROBBIE ROBERTSON

Neoliberalism

Neoliberalism is a recent concept and is open to conflicting interpretations. Its widespread adoption reflects the fashion for affixing prefixes such as 'neo' to well known political labels, ostensibly signifying that outdated ideological frameworks and/or historical paradigms were being reshaped for a late modern or postmodern world. In international relations, other examples include neoconservatism, neorealism and **neomedievalism**. In a world where the **levels of analysis** between international and domestic politics is being challenged and where debates on **globalization** are increasingly framing our understanding of world politics, neoliberalism has moved center stage.

Defining neoliberalism

Neoliberalism has taken on two distinct and partly contradictory definitions, reflecting its precursor, 'liberalism'. Liberalism is itself a complex mixture of meanings, reflecting the ambiguity of its central referents – the notion of liberty, the centrality of the individual, free-thinking and a critical bent of mind, as in Enlightenment philosophies – rather than a more holistic conception of society. It can also refer to support for civil freedoms and **human rights**. Furthermore, it can mean the necessity or desirability of free and/or liberal democratic political institutions, rooted in individual consent rather than collectivist ideologies. Freedom of religion and a critical attitude towards the social role of religion are also central for liberals, as in the separation of church and state. Finally, economic liberalism is associated with **capitalism**, implying an uneasy combination of *laissez faire* economics and pro-competitive economic regulation. Clearly there has been much room for conflict amongst these meanings. For example, rights to life, liberty and property can often conflict with each other in practice.

In continental Europe, the 'liberal' label has retained much of this fundamental *laissez faire* meaning as an ideology of the capitalist right – as distinct from more organic right wing ideologies such as fascism, elitism or certain forms of social Catholicism in the late nineteenth- and early twentieth centuries – applied mainly to small European parties of the center-right. In the United States, such liberalism is often referred to as 'nineteenth century liberalism' or 'classical liberalism', having much in common with 'conservatism'. In contrast, the term liberalism in the United States in the twentieth century became a label for the moderate center-left, based on the nineteenth century American Progressive tradition.

Historically, American-style liberalism has been closely linked to moderate social democratic views in continental Europe. Today, American conservatives and neoconservatives have demonized liberalism as the 'L-word' in an attempt to deny liberals the middle ground in American politics that used to be occupied by Presidents such as Franklin Delano Roosevelt and John F. Kennedy. In Australia, this center-left version of liberalism is referred to as 'social liberalism'. In the United Kingdom, liberalism, at least in the approach of the Liberal Democratic Party (formerly the Liberal Party) is seen as trying to take the best elements of both conservatism and social democracy while emphasizing individualism.

In international relations and **international political economy**, liberalism and neoliberalism can also be seen as having two analogous distinct meanings. The first of these derives from the tradition of **liberal internationalism** associated with the legacy of Woodrow Wilson and the **League of Nations**. Liberal internationalism involved the construction of international institutions composed of sovereign states (see **sovereignty**), the provision of **collective security** and the expansion of **international law** along relatively liberal lines. The **United Nations'** Universal Declaration of Human Rights is seen as a key document of this tradition along with United Nations' sponsorship of **development**, health, food and housing programs. However, the establishment of the **Bretton Woods** system of international economic institutions at the end of World War Two is also seen to represent international economic liberalism through the promotion and regulation of increasingly open international trade (through the General Agreement on Tariffs and Trade and now the **World Trade Organization**), an international monetary system (through the **International Monetary Fund**) and economic development (through the **World Bank**). The postwar system of **embedded liberalism** linked international economic liberalism with American-style domestic liberalism (or European-style social democracy) through Keynesian macroeconomic policies and the establishment of the welfare state.

In the study of international relations (IR), the term 'neoliberalism' or 'neoliberal institutionalism' refers to a school of thought that is distinct from 'neorealism'. According to neoliberals in IR, the development of the **international system** since World War Two has been characterized primarily by a broad but rather *ad hoc* proliferation of international **regimes**, whether of the broad kind such as the 'regime of embedded liberalism', or in the narrow sense of specific, quasi-autonomous problem solving institutions dealing with particular issue areas (the International Monetary Fund, the General Agreement on Tariffs and Trade, the International Labor Organization, specialized organizations for the **law of the sea**, shipping, intellectual property, etc.). This definition of neoliberalism was constructed in contradistinction to the huge influence (especially in the United States) of neorealists who argued that the autonomous state was the only genuine 'actor' in an 'anarchic' international system.

Neorealism in turn gave rise to **hegemonic stability theory**, which argued that in an anarchic system – where 'self-help', defection and free riding were the default positions and international cooperation a fragile reed – only an overwhelmingly well resourced great power (see **great powers**) could provide the **international public goods** of stability and **security** by paying the costs of those goods unilaterally and not depending on other actors to contribute key resources. In contrast, neoliberal institutionalists argued not only that international regimes had proliferated from the 1940s to the 1980s, but also that their widening scope of influence and control over increasingly significant and salient issue areas was giving them institutional autonomy and engendering habits of intergovernmental cooperation despite the alleged decline of US power in the system. Indeed, neoliberal institutionalism was taking over 'after hegemony'.

The second use of the term 'neoliberal' is quite distinct and is derived from the continental European, nineteenth century or 'classical' conceptions of liberalism. This usage – which focuses primarily on economic neoliberalism but has much wider implications – has become more widely accepted and has apparently supplanted 'neoliberal institutionalism' as the main way the word is used, not only in academic circles but also in policymaking and journalistic circles. Central to this form of neoliberalism is the assertion that the market is the core institution of modern – capitalist – societies and that both domestic and international politics are (and should be) increasingly concerned with making markets work well.

This overriding policy goal has several component parts. In the first place, it seeks to design and to establish institutions and practices that are market-based and market-led. Second, it is crucial to instil a culture of individualistic, market orientated behavior in people of all social classes, counteracting the '**dependency** culture' of the welfare state by 'ending welfare as we know it' (Bill Clinton) and deregulating the labor market. Third, governments and international institutions too should be internally imbued with market-friendly attitudes and practices. Fourth, barriers to international trade and capital flows should be progressively dismantled. The most efficient markets, in theory, are those with the largest numbers of buyers and sellers, so that an 'efficiency price' can be established that will 'clear the market'. (Clearing the market means that all the goods offered for sale will be purchased at a mutually acceptable price.) Therefore the most efficient markets ought in principle to be world markets.

This second type of neoliberalism developed out of the domestic programs of Margaret Thatcher and Ronald Reagan in the 1980s and from the return to fashion in academic economics of free market economists like Milton Friedman in the United States or more intellectual policymakers like Sir Keith Joseph in Britain. But the real springboard was the 1970s **crisis** of the post-Second World War economic **order**, both domestic and international. This crisis had several dimensions.

The first was the 'fiscal crisis of the state', in which the budgetary costs of social policies, public services, nationalized industries and bureaucracies were seen to grow faster than the tax base, leading neoliberals to propose the reduction of tax rates and government services with the aim of producing additional economic growth that would result in higher tax payments despite lower rates ('supply side economics'). The second involved the partial breakdown of 'social partnership' or 'neo-corporatist' arrangements – usually tripartite, state supported institutions or negotiating fora bringing together management, labor and bureaucrats – that had become increasingly important in

the 1960s for negotiating wages and working conditions. The 'stickiness' of wages, the slowdown in investment and organized labor in general were blamed for economic stagnation, leading to proposals to deregulate labor markets and abandon the postwar priority of full employment. A third dimension of the crisis concerned international and domestic economic conditions, from the reduction in the growth rate of world trade and an alarming rise in the 'new protectionism', mainly through the introduction of **non-tariff barrier**s, to increasing 'stagflation' (simultaneous stagnation and inflation). There was a fear of a return to the vicious circle of the sort of 'beggar-thy-neighbor' policies that were seen to have deepened the Great Depression of the 1930s. Finally, the Bretton Woods 'adjustable peg' system of managed exchange rates known as the 'dollar standard' or the 'Gold Exchange Standard' broke down; endemic exchange rate crises that had first led to the end of the dollar's link to gold (1971–3) were dramatically exacerbated by the Yom Kippur War of 1973–4 and the fourfold rise of oil prices that resulted. Further rises in inflation, interest rates and **Third World** debt regularly followed during the 1970s and early 1980s, entrenching the deepest recession since the 1930s.

The experience of the recession of the 1970s at first led to a wider crisis of the postwar consensus around domestic Keynesianism, 'indicative planning' and the welfare state. Once Keynesian macroeconomic fine tuning had failed to prevent stagflation, and neocorporatism came to be seen as a major source of rigidity preventing businesses from responding to these crises, key sections of the postwar coalitions in most developed capitalist countries began to defect. The ideological and cultural glue that the 'long boom' from the early 1950s to the early 1970s had reinforced, accepted even by most conservative parties in the 1950s, 1960s and early 1970s, dissolved.

Various middle class groups and, indeed, fractions of the working class began to vote for parties and leaders promoting the new brand of economically liberal 'conservatism', including the 42 per cent of trade unionists in Britain who voted Conservative in the key election of 1979 that brought Margaret Thatcher to **power**, while in the United States the 'Reagan Democrats' also became part of the new neoliberal consensus. The British Labor Party and the Democratic Party in the United States subsequently moved distinctly to the right, with labels like New Labor, the New Democrats and the **Third Way**. The failure of much of the 'socialist' program of French President François Mitterrand, elected in 1981, to pull France out of the slump led to his administration partly reversing course and then giving way to 'cohabitation' with rhetorically neoliberal conservatives, although much of French statism has remained. Germany and Japan are still in the midst of this transformation. The **European Union** has been seen as a driving force of neoliberalism too, especially in terms of competition policy and the development of the single market after 1985.

This process was not limited to the developed world. Much worse stagnation in the 1970s and 1980s in Soviet Bloc countries alienated many of the same groups – leading to the protests that brought down the Berlin Wall in 1989, the end of the **cold war**, and the establishment of a wide variety of neoliberal experiments in so-called 'transition countries'. Bureaucratic authoritarian governments in the developing world, especially those mired in the **debt trap** of the early 1980s, found their quasi-nationalist, quasi-socialist coalitions dis-

solving in hyperinflation and crony capitalism. The rapid industrialization taking place in many transitional and developing countries, fueled by **globalization**, created a demand for neoliberal policy innovations, broke up old sociopolitical coalitions and laid the groundwork for new coalitions to emerge seeking to mobilize both existing and potential new supporters.

Not all disillusioned groups bought the neoliberal package as a whole, but the politics of most countries seemed increasingly to revolve around the conflict between resisting neoliberal policies in order to preserve social values and/or entrenched positions, on the one hand, and attempting to capture the benefits of globalization by copying and internalizing neoliberal prescriptions, on the other. Severe social disruptions resulted, especially when particular socioeconomic groups became unemployed and impoverished, not only in developed countries but even more so in those developing countries that suffered most from overextended and/or collapsed states, deteriorating terms of trade (especially the 'commodity trap' whereby raw materials declined in relative value), and growing political divisions along communal or class lines. The rise in internal violence, **civil war**s, and even **terrorism** is widely imputed to the negative effects of neoliberal globalization. Endemic financial and economic crises from the Latin American debt crisis of 1982 to the Asian and Russian crises of 1997–8 and the Argentine crisis of 2001–2 demonstrate that adjustment to neoliberal policies and structural reforms can be a very painful and politically divisive experience.

At the same time, alternatives to neoliberalism have also been ineffectual and often incoherent. Mrs Thatcher famously said that 'there is no alternative' and that 'you can't buck the markets'. In the light of such increasingly influential and politically successful perspectives, key political and academic debates have revolved around whether globalization in its neoliberal manifestation is inevitable and whether there is a long-term process of 'convergence' taking place across the world. Indeed, embedded liberalism seems to have been succeeded by embedded neoliberalism.

At least four core dimensions of the embedded neoliberal consensus can be identified as component parts of a coherent package of 'necessary' reforms in the light of increasing **interdependence** and 'global realities'. The precise content of the package varies in different countries depending upon existing domestic institutions and practices, the stance of interest groups and their linkages across borders, and the changing global structure of markets and production. These dimensions of neoliberalism are a commitment to free trade, the reform of national financial management, reduced state intervention in the economy, and the restructuring of the relationship between the public sector and the private sector.

Free trade

The first dimension involves reducing barriers to trade and capital flows. Trade barriers were blamed for the decline in world trade that deepened the Great Depression of the 1930s, and the establishment of the General Agreement on Tariffs and Trade (GATT) in 1947 – an outgrowth of the Bretton Woods Agreement of 1944 – led to several rounds of tariff reductions and later attempts to tackle non-tariff barriers too, followed by the transformation of the GATT into the World Trade Organization and a range of regional and bilateral trade agreements. Free trade was in many ways the core building block of both embedded liberalism and later, neoliberalism. There has been a growing consensus that new trade barriers lead to a vicious circle of retaliation, leaving all participants worse off, whereas free trade, so long as it does not lead to serious short term structural disruption, is a long-term public good benefiting poor as well as rich countries by creating a virtuous circle of economic **development** and growth. Although free trade, or the uneven version of it that exists, especially in areas like agriculture, textiles, services and the like, has been criticized for 'going too far', even anti-globalization protestors today accept the need for lowering trade barriers on products where poorer countries have a comparative advantage.

Furthermore, since the collapse of the postwar adjustable peg exchange rate regime in 1971–3, several factors have led to a multiplication of cross-border capital flows. The combination of floating exchange rates, the globalization of financial markets and the failure of import substitution industrialization and international aid regimes to foster effective development has led to the widespread reduction of **capital controls**. Developed countries, led by both government deregulation and the increasing clout of internationally linked market actors in banks and securities markets, began seriously to reform their financial systems in the 1970s, while the International Monetary Fund, the Bank for International Settlements and other international regimes pushed for liberalization and established a range of standards and benchmarks for doing so, such as the Basel capital adequacy standards (1988). Meanwhile, formerly **Third World** countries, today called 'emerging markets', now look primarily to foreign sources – both **foreign direct investment** and international portfolio investment – for otherwise scarce capital. Despite frequent financial crises and the acceptance of some limited capital controls, the debate on international capital mobility today focuses chiefly on how to institute effective financial regulatory systems at national, regional (European, North American and Asian) and international levels in order to smooth adjustment to an open global capital markets regime.

The internationalization of production, linked to both trade and financial liberalization, has led to the increasing acceptance of a leading role for **multinational corporation**s. Although the project for a Multilateral Agreement on Investment that would have established international rules protecting MNCs from government intervention was dropped in the late 1990s in the face of widespread opposition, developed and developing states alike, along with the major international economic institutions, have come to see MNCs as desirable partners in the search for economic growth. All in all, freer trade, financial liberalization and the internationalization of production are increasingly taken for granted as core drivers of both domestic and international economies in the twenty first century and form the cornerstone of neoliberalism.

The reform of national financial management

The second key dimension of neoliberalism is the reform of national finances, especially the attempt to control inflation, seen as having in the 1970s undermined not only the long boom in the developed countries but also development in the Third World. This has involved a shift away from Keynesian macroeconomic demand management to a more structural approach to fiscal and monetary policy. With regard to fiscal policy, both personal taxation – especially at higher rates – and, increas-

ingly, corporate taxation rates have been widely lowered with the express intention of freeing up private capital for investment. Lower taxes have become a key part of the neoliberal consensus on both left and right and in some countries, especially the United States, and have been the centerpiece of vote winning strategies. Tax cuts legislated by the George W. Bush Administration have been criticized by Democrats as being a tax cut for the wealthiest, yet Democrats (like 'New Labour' in Britain) have also proposed tax cuts targeted on the middle class.

Balanced budgets are in theory another central tenet of embedded financial orthodoxy, although in the United States deep tax cuts under the Reagan Administration (1981–9) and the George W. Bush Administration (2001–present) have led to historically unprecedented budget deficits; indeed, the most rigorous budgetary discipline occurred under the Clinton Administration (1993–2001). The European Union's Growth and Stability Pact limits national budget deficits to 3 per cent of Gross Domestic Product, although this has been coming under strain recently. International Monetary Fund and World Bank aid has increasingly become subject to conditionality that requires recipient countries to run budget surpluses, and political leaderships of both left and right in many developing countries, for example Brazil, have adopted tight budgetary discipline. Another aspect of embedded financial orthodoxy has been the drive to reform state ministries and agencies in order to reduce waste and make them operate according to the same sort of efficiency standards used in successful businesses. Also management of the money supply has been increasingly carried out through open market operations and central banks have been made more independent of political control. Finally, macroeconomic management is generally carried out more through monetary policy (the manipulation of interest rates) than through fiscal policy (the manipulation of taxes).

Reducing state intervention

The third dimension of neoliberalism is a sea change in the character of state intervention in the domestic economy. Traditionally, both socialist and social democratic approaches to state intervention could be characterized as outcome orientated, and in the postwar period the key objectives of public policy were economic growth, the promotion of industrialization, full employment and a certain amount of redistribution of wealth and income through the tax system and the welfare state. With this package came a broad commitment to greater equality, especially with regard to social policy, even among center-right and right wing parties, in the wake of the Great Depression and World War Two.

The concept of 'regulation', widely used historically, was a general one that mixed together two distinct modes of intervention. The first involved direct or indirect public control of sectors of the economy and of social and public services in the name of the public interest. Regulators, whether in government departments or relatively independent agencies (the latter especially in the United States) often had considerable discretion to design and run services and set conditions – including some elements of planning – for the operation of various industries including energy, infrastructure and any sectors considered 'strategic' to the national economy. In France, for example, the state promoted 'national champion' firms meant to become major competitors in international and domestic markets. The second meaning of 'regulation', which devel-

oped primarily in the United States, is what has been called 'arm's length regulation'. The role of regulators by definition was not to intervene in order to produce particular outcomes, but rather to establish and enforce general rules for a particular sector, industry or service. The ostensible purposes of these rules were to prevent fraud, promote competition and restrict monopolitistic and oligopolistic practices, counteract 'market failures', enforce contracts and property rights, and generally provide a quasi-legal environment for actors (especially private market actors) to operate in efficient market fashion, although the effectiveness of such rules has been criticized in the light of recent scandals.

The latter of these two types of regulation is at the core of the neoliberal project, summed up in the aphorism that 'governments should steer but not row'. Ideally, governments ought not to run industries or provide services, but rather provide a working framework of rules for market actors to follow. Of course, some neoliberals and neoclassical economists argued that government should stop intervening in the economy entirely. Deregulation originally meant just what it said, repealing all rules that caused market participants to behave in any other way than in their own self-interest, ostensibly distorting markets and making them inefficient.

However, other neoliberals argued that it was the type of regulation that mattered and that arm's length 'prudential' regulations, the second type outlined above, were necessary in order to promote efficient market behavior. Deregulation was never really deregulation, but became the replacement of outcome orientated and discretionary interventionism with new market friendly regulations – a form of pro-market re-regulation. Indeed, in many cases the new regulations were more complex and onerous than the old type. A well-known example is that of insider trading regulation in financial markets, almost unknown (except in the United States) before the 1980s.

Despite the rhetoric of deregulation, neocorporatism in labor markets has been replaced not so much by the abolition of regulations – although employers' freedom to hire and fire has generally been increased – as by a wide range of new regulations and programs designed to 'enable', or actually compel, the poor and unemployed to enter the labor market through a combination of carrots (training, education, temporary employment subsidies) and sticks (reduced and time-limited welfare benefits), i.e. the 'workfare state'. Groups such as single mothers have been particularly targeted.

The core of the new regulatory approach is contractualization and 'ex post' regulation. Behavior is not constrained a priori but is subject to later litigation, including both judicial and quasi-judicial procedures, especially through independent regulatory agencies. Such rule-based systems, however, also require extensive monitoring and surveillance (rather than the exercise of discretionary 'ex ante' control) to determine whether agreed performance indicators or targets have been met. Ever more aspects of economic life are today subject to extensive regulation of this sort imposed by governments in both the developed and the developing world. Indeed, one of the main roles of the IMF, the WTO and the World Bank today is to proselytize the regulatory creed and spread 'best practices' throughout the world.

Public sector/private sector

The fourth core dimension of neoliberalism concerns the relationship of public and private sectors. Neoliberalism has always involved the privatization of many public and social services and greater experimentation with mixed public–private productive and distributive goods. However, the emphasis has shifted from the direct sale of government controlled industries, as in the United Kingdom under the Thatcher Government, to 'contracting out' services, public–private partnerships (PPPs) and the use of private sources of finance for public purposes, for example the UK's Private Finance Initiative (PFI) for the construction and operation of schools, hospitals, and prisons. Proponents argue that structural changes in the economy, especially the development of information and communications technology (ICT), have fundamentally transformed how firms work and shifted the boundaries between public and private sectors. Opponents argue that such services have a public character that is undermined by privatization. Another objection is that cost savings have not materialized and that governments have assumed private contractors' financial risks where cost overruns and quality deficiencies have occurred.

This dimension is linked with the shift to the regulatory approach discussed earlier. Contractualization, the use of financial performance indicators and ex post enforcement are at the heart of the system, along with hybrid forms of 'governance' such as special purpose bodies like development agencies at local, regional, national, transnational and international levels, as well as a focus on policy networks rather than formal processes. Neoliberalism involves the substitution, where deemed appropriate, of purpose built regimes for the organization of public life – regimes that straddle the public–private divide and involve market participants directly in the authoritative allocation of resources and values. Neoliberalism, like neomediev-alism, involves the fragmentation of government into crosscutting and over-lapping institutions and processes. The emerging embedded neoliberal con-sensus is not simply developing 'from below' as market forces and transna-tional interpenetration constrain govern-ments, international institutions and other political actors to behave in parti-cular ways. It is also a political con-struction, promoted and shaped in real time by 'political entrepreneurs' who must design projects, convince others, build coalitions and ultimately win some sort of political **legitimacy**.

The future of neoliberalism

Neoliberalism, like embedded liberalism before it, is 'overdetermined'. There are several interests, pressures and structural trends pushing in the same direction while scholars debate the relative sig-nificance and independence of these different variables. The first set of 'dri-vers' comprises state actors (politicians, bureaucrats and political parties) in for-mulating new public policies designed to overcome the legacy of the 'over-loaded state', 'stagflation' and the like – breaking up old and building new poli-tical coalitions at both elite and mass levels to win elections, or controlling and reshaping bureaucracies in order to promote marketization and global com-petitiveness. Other significant promoters of neoliberalism are **global governance** institutions such as the World Bank, the IMF, the WTO, the **Bank for Interna-tional Settlements**, and the **G8**. Neoli-beralism is fostered by political and economic power differentials among states too, especially between the United States and the rest of the world. Finally, the increasing dominance of the **dis-course** of neoliberalism gives actors who participate in the embedded neoliberal

consensus not only greater ability to proactively design neoliberal responses and solutions, but also entrenches, through socialization, reactions that internalize neoliberalism in the way people frame political and economic issues and choices.

Paradoxically, however, neoliberal public policies, whether at national, regional or international levels, do not merely constrain but also bring opportu-nities. Contemporary politics entails both a process of choosing between different versions of neoliberalism and innovating creatively within the new neoliberal playing field. Although the dimensions specified above constitute the bottom line of neoliberalism, their implications vary dramatically by policy issue area. Economic globalization and the new neoliberal politics have involved a 'reshuffling of the pack', as new groups, interests and political entrepreneurs have emerged; old interests and coalitions have either declined or adapted; and the pecking order of influence has been profoundly altered. But the need for sta-bilization and social integration has also forced such actors to innovate both in different issue areas and simultaneously across the complex, multiple levels and nodes of governance that characterize the present century.

These innovations at first glance seem quite disparate, but they all involve initial responses to the challenge of 'reinventing the social' in a neoliberal world. The promotion of competitive-ness is leading to new forms of micro-industrial policy which are especially significant for small and medium sized enterprises in an open world economy. Linking trade opening to environmental and labor standards gives additional leverage to a kind of extraterritorial social policy. Welfare spending has not significantly dropped and a range of welfare reforms have in some instances actually expanded welfare services. Demands for stricter and more accountable international rules and procedures for corporate governance, accounting standards, bond rating agencies, private mediation and arbitration procedures, antitrust regulation and the like are reshaping government–business relations. The World Bank's shift in the mid-1990s to prioritizing poverty reduction has changed the discourse of global governance towards more socially oriented goals, although whether it has changed the substance is hotly debated. Major international economic institutions, leading developed states and many **non-governmental organizations** (NGOs) increasingly emphasize **good governance** and **democratization** as key objectives necessary for stability and growth; indeed, some analysts would include these as a fifth dimension of the embedded neoliberal consensus. The World Social Forum and similar non-governmental organizations have shifted the focus of advocacy group debate from anti-globalization to alternative approaches to globalization. Political leaders such as Presidents Fernando Henrique Cardoso and Luiz Inácio Lula da Silva of Brazil have sought in both domestic and international forums to reinvent domestic social policies for a globalizing world. Kofi Annan's **Global Compact** seeks to develop a kind of transnational neocorporatism through collaboration with business to promote social goals. And, despite US withdrawal, the **Kyoto Protocol**, the **International Criminal Court**, the Ottawa Convention on Landmines and a range of other international agreements may prefigure a new kind of incremental public legal internationalism.

It can be argued that these innovations add up to a kind of alternative neoliberalism, competing politically with the more *laissez faire* type characteristic of Thatcherism and Reaganism over the shape of the a more open, globalizing world order. Thus we may be witnessing the emergence of a new 'social neoliberalism' that a few years ago would have seemed like a contradiction in terms.

Further reading

Baldwin, D. (ed.) (1993) *Neorealism and Neoliberalism: The Contemporary Debate*, New York: Columbia University Press.

Cardoso, F. H. (2001) *Charting a New Course: The Politics of Globalization and Social Transformation*, Lanham, MD: Rowman and Littlefield.

Evans, M. and Cerny, P. (2003) 'Globalisation and Social Policy', in N. Ellison and C. Pierson (eds) *Developments in British Social Policy*, Basingstoke: Palgrave, 19–40.

Moran, M. (2003) *The British Regulatory State: High Modernism and Hyper-Innovation*, Oxford: Oxford University Press.

Osborne, D. and Gaebler, T. (1992) *Reinventing Government*, Reading, MA: Addison-Wesley.

Williamson, J. (1990) 'What Washington Means by Policy Reform', in J. Williamson (ed.) *Latin American Adjustment: How Much Has Happened*, Washington, DC: Institute of International Economics, 5–20.

See also: capitalism; casino capitalism; embedded liberalism; foreign direct investment; free trade; liberal internationalism; structural adjustment program

PHILIP G. CERNY

Neomedievalism

An argument that the core structures of the emerging postmodern or post-Westphalian global political economy (see **Westphalia**) may bear a closer resemblance to medieval Europe than to the current international political system. Neomedievalism is a metaphor rather than a description of empirical reality; it is helpful in imagining modes of political and economic organization that may once again be networked rather than hierarchical and non-territorial.

The Peace of Westphalia (1648) is taken as the conventional point of demarcation marking the transition from medieval universalism to the modern state system. Late twentieth century **globalization** may mark another systemic transition, an evolution beyond the geographically rooted Westphalian political economy to an, as yet, undefined and unstructured postmodern **international** system.

The core of the Westphalian international system is territorial **sovereignty**: mutually exclusive geographic jurisdiction delimited by discrete and meaningful borders. In contrast to the complex, interwoven and overlapping system of political authority characteristic of medieval Europe with 'supranational centers' vested in an Emperor or Pope, the modern state system is based on territorial sovereignty and its corollaries of singular geographically based political authority and loyalty, unitary international political actors and state centrism.

Globalization, the emergence of an integrated world economy and electronically integrated global networks, renders the basic construct of territorial sovereignty and its assumption of singular, discrete political authority problematic. While states may still be the most important international actors, others institutions such as **non-government organizations**, **multinational corporations**, regional economic authorities and international organizations share **power**. Furthermore, both the deep **integration** of the world economy and the **information revolution** have rendered borders diffuse and permeable, blurred the sharp distinction between domestic and international affairs, and compromised the **authority** and power of states.

Neomedievalism argues that the modern era of mutually exclusive territoriality and geographically defined political authority may be an historical anomaly – a window about to slam shut: that territorial sovereignty is not historically privileged. The process of political evolution may not be linear and unidirectional and there are reasons to believe that the emergent post-Westphalian political system may take on some of the characteristics or attributes of the last pre-modern system of political organization, medieval Europe.

In the late 1970s, Hedley Bull (1995: 245) explored alternatives to the current state system and suggested that is conceivable 'that sovereign states might disappear and be replaced not by a world government but by a modern and secular equivalent of the kind of universal political organization that existed in Western Christendom in the Middle Ages'. He wondered whether a secular version of the system of overlapping or segmented authority that was characteristic of medieval political organization might replace the states system.

Neomedievalism is a metaphor rather than description of reality, it allows one to overcome the inertia imposed by immersion in the present and think about other possible modes of political and economic organization. Arguing by analogy facilitates thinking about non-geographic modes of organization by focusing on similarities between the immediate pre-modern period and emerging postmodern organizational structures.

There are a number of trends or aspects of the emerging global political economy that resemble medieval modes of political organization. The core construct of the modern mode of political and economic organization, mutually exclusive territoriality, has been rendered problematic by the internationalization of production, deep economic integration and the digital/ information revolution. Borders are increasingly permeable and diffuse and the sharp line separating domestic and international affairs has become much less distinct.

While states may still be the primary actors in the international system, they have lost power to a number of other actors such as **non-governmental organizations**, regional authorities, multinational firms and international organizations that have gained significant political authority. The emerging system is characterized by the re-emergence of multiple and overlapping political authorities, multiple, competing political institutions. Similarly, political loyalty has become fragmented, overlapping and more complex.

While global government is not a realistic possibility, **global governance** is a serious and problem-fraught issue. Once again there is concern about the need for some sort of authority or authorities at the center, international or supranational organizations with the resources and power necessary to contribute to some form of meaningful global governance.

Although a unifying force or ideology that is a secular equivalent of Western Christendom has not appeared on the horizon, technology and especially the information revolution, satellite communication and the internet have served to unify the peoples of the World, or at least to put them in closer contact with one another. Some have suggested that belief systems such as environmentalism might serve secular ideologies in the future.

The line between public and private property, and public and private authority, may be blurring as multinational firms and non-governmental organizations take on what were once public functions of the state. Last, private political violence appears to be remerging as

a problem, especially in the context of **failed state**s.

At the start of this century, we face a political system in transition that provides only a very dim and diffuse idea of its final shape and character. Three and a half centuries after Westphalia it is difficult to even imagine a political system organized on any other basis than geographic territory. Neomedievalism is useful to the extent it allows us to reason by analogy, to use an earlier form of political organization to break the hold territorial sovereignty has on our political imagination and begin to think about what a postmodern system will look like.

Further reading

Bull, H. (1995) *The Anarchical Society: A Study of Order in World Politics*, 2nd edn, New York: Columbia University Press.

Cerny, P. G. (1998) 'Neomedievalism, Civil War and the New Security Dilemma: Globalization as a Durable Disorder', *Civil Wars* 1(1), 36–64.

Cohen, B. J. (1998) *The Geography of Money*. Ithaca, NY: Cornell University Press.

Kobrin, S. J. (1998) 'Back to the Future: Neomedievalism and the Postmodern Digital World Economy', *Journal of International Affairs* 51(2), 361–86.

Winn, N. (ed.) (2004) *Neo-Medievalism and Civil Wars*, London: Routledge.

See also: failed state; global governance; globalization; multinational corporation; nation-state; non-governmental organization; sovereignty; Westphalia

STEPHEN J. KOBRIN

Newly industrializing country (NIC)

The term newly industrializing country, at its broadest level, is associated with particular states associated with specific patterns of economic growth and attendant material and infrastructural changes. Such states are different from older industrialized countries in that economic growth and related changes are a recent phenomenon deriving from the post-World War Two period. Typically, such countries are likely to have undergone a process of rapid industrialization, especially in the manufacturing or secondary sector. Additionally, economic growth is closely linked to the export of products in that sector. In the academic jargon, the term 'export led' growth is often used to describe this model of **development**. The geographical region of East Asia has traditionally had the greatest concentration of newly industrialized countries.

Specifically, South Korea, Taiwan, Hong Kong, and Singapore are often regarded as good examples of countries that have successfully appropriated this economic strategy of growth. The evolution of the model itself is often attributed to Japan. Countries that exemplify similar strategies of economic growth with a measure of success are referred to as newly industrializing countries. Many such countries like Malaysia and Thailand are physically located in Southeast Asia. More recent entrants into this category include larger and potentially more powerful countries like Brazil, China, and India. Newly industrializing countries collectively have great productive capacity. However, they have much lesser consumptive capacity. In this regard, newly industrializing countries are dependent on developed countries to absorb their exports.

Newly industrializing countries have tended to display a number of specific characteristics. The most pronounced of such characteristics involve a correlation between authoritarian regime types and rapid economic growth. Such regime types that involved a high level of central planning in the allocation of resources may be either of a bureaucratic or military nature. The emphasis of such regimes is on technocratic efficiency and the production process. Additionally, such countries have tended to depoliticize and suppress labor and other mass organizations that have the potential to challenge business led decision-making. The state may also engage in the creation of corporatist-type peak organizations to control labor unions and bring them in line with central policymaking. Finally, such countries have tended to function within the framework of a dominant or predominant party system as opposed to the liberal pluralistic model preferred by democratic theorists. Newly industrializing countries also tended to rely on performance based criteria for political **legitimacy**, a euphemism for the provision of high levels of economic growth and employment.

Newly industrialized countries have also from time to time been accused of maintaining a measure of protectionist tariffs to protect local infant industries, the agricultural sector or the higher value-added tertiary or service sector. Such protectionist measures have in the past attracted the ire of developed countries that argue for greater market access to newly industrialized countries as a reciprocal benefit for export-led growth that targets the developed and industrialized countries. Occasionally, developed countries, in order to protect their own interests and employment markets, impose quotas or tariffs on products originating from newly industrialized countries. Attempts by the United States to impose tariffs on steel products originating from China and South Korea are such an example. Governments of developed democratic countries are also subject to greater pressure from interest and lobby groups to protect home industries and jobs.

The original model, at least as envisaged by Japan, involved what came to be popularly referred to as the 'flying geese' strategy. This strategy assumed that Japan, as the originator of the model, would occupy the role of the lead 'goose' and determine both the productive capacity and technological development of the other newly industrializing countries. In other words, the Japanese model originally envisaged that other countries adopting this export-led model would facilitate Japan's further development and perform a subsidiary and supportive function. Such an arrangement has not been fully realized. Part of the reason for the plan being frustrated is the ability of newly industrializing countries to wean themselves away from Japan through transnational production and technology transfer arrangements with the United States and West European countries. Another reason for the failure of the model is that large developing countries like China have exhibited the ability to produce a parallel flock of geese through a gradated development of manufacturing within a single country.

The relative success of the export-led growth strategy up to the late 1990s in turn spawned a series of significant academic debates. The earliest of these pertained to the linkage between regime types and economic growth. Flushed with success, East Asian elites were convinced that authoritarian regime types that held democracy in check had the greatest potential to reap the benefits of robust economic growth. Contained within this argument was the repudiation of the Western model of development that correlated democratic governance with **capitalism**. In other words, East Asian elites argued that authoritarianism rather than democracy was suitable for rapid industrialization and economic growth. The linkage between regime types and economic performance continues to be a contentious subject among academics and policymakers, although it is generally acknowledged that economic development will eventually lead to a measure of democratic government as well.

Yet another argument deriving from this debate was that **Asian values**, broadly defined to include hard work, thrift, high savings, and a concern for collective communal welfare, contained within them the seeds for a model that was superior to the liberal political model advocated by Western countries. East Asian political elites seemed convinced that their model provided for both robust economic growth as well as political stability. Additionally, the correlation between Asian values and economic growth was meant to endorse authoritarian regime types where political obedience and respect for authority were cardinal features.

Both the debates on the correlation between regime types and economic development on the one hand, and the utility of Asian values on the other, have died a natural death since the Asian financial crisis of 1997. The crisis, which ravaged the economies of Indonesia, South Korea and Thailand, has led to a rethink on Asian values. The rethink is fueled, at least in part by the financial support provided by Western international agencies like the **World Bank** and the **International Monetary Fund**. Subsequent investigations into the causes of the crisis have also uncovered widespread financial mismanagement and **corruption** that has tainted the 'Asian model' of development.

The Neo-Marxist critique of newly industrializing countries was that the success of such countries was a function of dependent development. In other words, such countries functioned within and relied heavily on the global capitalist system in order to achieve growth and prosperity. Accordingly, the performance and growth strategy of these countries invariably upheld the Western capitalist system that is in turn dominated by the developed countries. Dependency theorists were also critical of newly industrialized countries that perpetuated an existing system that was responsible for unequal relationships and terms of trade that disadvantaged poorer less developed countries. Western industrialized countries, over time, came to acknowledge a certain responsibility in aiding the economic growth of less developed countries. The mooting of a New International Economic Order (NIEO) by less developed countries in 1972 is generally regarded as a response to the uneven terms of international trade and a call to attend to the discrepancy. However, the success of the newly industrialized countries helped, at least in part, to deflect the criticism that international trade could only weaken the economies of developing countries and subject them to greater levels of poverty.

Further reading

Gilpin, R. (1987) *The Political Economy of International Relations*, Princeton, NJ: Princeton University Press.

Jameson, K. and Wilber, C. (eds) (1996) *The Political Economy of Development and Underdevelopment*, 6th edn, New York: McGraw-Hill.

Krasner, S. D. (1985) *Structural Conflict: The Third World Against Global Liberalism*, Berkeley, CA: University of California Press.

Simon, D. (ed.) (1995) *Corporate Strategies in the Pacific Rim*, London: Routledge.

See also: development; post-fordism; world-system theory

NARAYANAN GANESAN

Non-governmental organization (NGO)

A non-governmental organization (NGO) is a private, voluntary, nonprofit association. Although an NGO may be domestic in character, operating within the confines of a single community, province, or state, in the field of International Relations (IR) NGO generally refers to a group whose membership and organizational activities cross national boundaries. To highlight this transnational dynamic, some scholars employ the term international non-governmental organization (INGO).

Largely a product of twentieth-century politics, NGOs have increased dramatically in number and influence since the 1970s and have flourished in an era of **globalization**. An accurate count of NGOs is hard to come by, due in part to their dynamic character and geographic diffusion, but the Union of International Associations (itself an NGO) puts the number at more than 40,000 worldwide. NGOs' varied goals and activities address a range of substantive global issues including **human rights**, human **security**, international trade, and **sustainable development**. Familiar examples of NGOs include Greenpeace, Oxfam, and Médecins San Frontières (Doctors Without Borders).

Although some NGOs work to preserve the status quo, most seek to effect changes in world politics. In the latter regard, conventional studies tend to portray NGOs as pressure groups seeking to influence state behavior on various international issues. These state referential studies acknowledge the significance of NGOs, but essentially consign them to the role of lobbying groups forced to work through mediators – states and international institutions – to realize their goals.

In the 1990s, the changing nature of international relations and alternative theoretical perspectives (such as **constructivism** and **feminism**) prompted scholars to consider NGOs in a different light; that is, as international actors in their own right. As such, NGOs perform important functions in global politics. Through their organizational activities, global networks, and interactions with other international actors, they influence domestic politics, participate in multilateral forums, promote interstate cooperation, and facilitate political participation. Since the end of the **cold war**, NGOs also have 'subcontracted' work for states and international institutions, for example by distributing food aid or assisting in **refugee** resettlement programs. In general, NGOs have become more visible and effective in each of these capacities since the mid 1990s.

Global campaigns, often conducted by networks of NGOs, garnered notable results in the late twentieth- and early twenty-first centuries. 'Anti-sweatshop' campaigns led to voluntary codes of conduct for **multinational corporation**s (MNCs) and renewed calls for international labor standards. A largely Internet-based campaign pooled the resources of widely divergent NGOs to halt talks on a Multilateral Agreement on Investment (MAI). And in a widely cited success story, a network of more than 1,200 NGOs from sixty countries known as the International Campaign to Ban Landmines (ICBL) helped forge an international treaty that prohibits the use, stockpiling, production and transfer of anti-personnel mines.

The landmine campaign initiated a lively debate that continues today about the changing roles and influence of NGOs in international relations. In this case, NGOs adopted novel networking and communication strategies that made particularly effective use of the Internet.

Working together with (mostly **middle power**) states, they also played an unprecedented role in the treaty's drafting and implementation – gaining a 'place at the table' (with state representatives) during the negotiating process and, following ratification, assuming specific (treaty mandated) responsibilities. The successful campaign prompted talk of a 'new **multilateralism**' among scholars and practitioners, and the ICBL received the 1997 Nobel Peace Prize in recognition of its work.

Thus, NGOs have firmly established themselves as influential actors that merit attention in the study of international relations. This is evident particularly in the context of globalization, as NGOs effect political change through 'transnational advocacy networks' (such as the ICBL) and, more broadly, contribute to the dynamics and processes of **global civil society**. In the former regard, NGOs not only advocate for legal and political change; they also serve as 'norm entrepreneurs' – creating and promoting common (global) values in areas such as **human rights**, poverty reduction, and environmental preservation. NGOs contribute to the development and maintenance of global civil society, as well, by helping to establish global civil society's constitutive network of social relations and creating channels of political opportunity for a variety of international actors.

Despite their positive contributions to international relations, NGOs have been criticized for institutional shortcomings and related failures. Although many NGOs call for transparency and accountability in international institutions, their own organizational structures can be hierarchical and undemocratic. Northern NGOs, with headquarters in the world's wealthier and more powerful countries, also tend to have more resources and enjoy greater visibility than NGOs in the global South. This imbalance and its attendant problems can create animosity among NGOs and lessen the effectiveness of (global) campaigns on certain issues. Since the late 1990s, both scholars and practitioners have increasingly become aware of these issues and begun to address them in theory and practice.

Over the past quarter century, nongovernmental organizations have become visible and influential international actors. In the coming years, in the face of continued globalization and change, NGOs likely will play an even greater role in world politics.

Further reading

Cusimano Love, M. (2003) 'Nongovernmental Organizations: Politics Beyond Sovereignty', in M. Cusimano Love (ed.) *Beyond Sovereignty: Issues for a Global Agenda*, 2nd edn, Belmont, CA: Wadsworth/Thomson Learning, 71–94.

Keck, M. E. and Sikkink, K. (1998) *Activists Beyond Borders: Advocacy Networks in International Politics*, Ithaca, NY: Cornell University Press.

Simmons, P. J. (1998) 'Learning to Live with NGOs' *Foreign Policy* 112, 82–96.

Warkentin, C. (2001) *Reshaping World Politics: NGOs, the Internet, and Global Civil Society*, Lanham, MD: Rowman & Littlefield Publishers.

See also: global civil society; globalization; transnational social movement

CRAIG WARKENTIN

Non-offensive defense

The principle that minimizing offensive military preparations and maximizing defensive ones reduces the risk of **war** and provides a viable basis for defending a society if war ever breaks out. Non-offensive defense is often used interchangeably with such terms as *non-provocative defense, defensive defense,* and *territorial defense*. A central assumption of these concepts is that manifestly defensive capabilities provide reassurance to others about one's intentions, thereby helping to escape or mitigate the **security dilemma** by reducing arms racing and the risk of pre-emptive war. Non-offensive defense does not distinguish between particular weapons as offensive or defensive; rather, it is the overall mix of weapons and policies that conveys defensive intent.

The main military (war-fighting) advantages of non-offensive defense are that fewer troops are generally required to defend territory than to take it; soldiers who are defending home territory are more likely to experience higher morale and therefore be better fighters compared to soldiers who are attacking; and the defending side has superior knowledge of local conditions. Against these strengths, non-offensive defense has two major disadvantages: its lack of operational mobility and its lack of counterattack capability. As for the first, defending troops must guard large tracts of territory, which renders them too dispersed to prevent an attacker from choosing an advantageous point of attack for a major offensive. The second disadvantage is that many non-offensive defense schemes seriously restrict the defending state's counter-offensive capability, especially at the strategic level. The problem here is that the defender must be able to retake occupied territory and, in some circumstances, attack and seize the aggressor's heartland, as in World War Two.

Historically, non-offensive defense has deep roots that can be traced, at least, to inter-war **arms control** negotiations (such as the Washington Naval Treaties of the 1920s and the Geneva Disarmament Conference of the 1930s) and to unilateral state practice (such as the French Maginot Line and the defense policies of small neutral states such as Sweden and Switzerland). In the 1950s and 1960s, defensive buffer zone and force disengagement proposals were advanced to help ease tensions along the Central European Front dividing East and West, most notably along the inner German border. However, such defensively oriented proposals were overshadowed by great power strategic doctrine (see **great powers**) that focused on nuclear weapons and the radical paradigm of punitive and offensive mutual **deterrence**.

By the 1980s, however, interest in non-offensive defense concepts emerged in two different, but related contexts. First, against a background of deteriorating East–West relations and **North Atlantic Treaty Organization** (NATO) plans to modernize its intermediate range nuclear forces (INF) and to implement conventional deep strike concepts designed for interdiction deep in Warsaw Pact territory, non-offensive defense advocates argued that NATO was, in fact, worsening the East–West security dilemma. Many advocated a more defensive **alliance** posture, combining minimum nuclear deterrence and non-offensive conventional measures. Such an approach, they claimed, would reduce arms racing, reduce the risk of war by pre-emption, win public support, and improve the international political climate.

Second, from the mid-1980s, non-offensive defense ideas were incorporated into the reformist platform, known as 'new thinking', adopted by Soviet leader Mikhail Gorbachev. Under new thinking, Gorbachev and his supporters embraced non-offensive defense – by then closely linked to the strategic security concept known as **common security** – promoting proposals for the

adoption of more defensive, and therefore reassuring, military postures for both NATO and the Warsaw Pact.

Under these proposals, the Soviet Union would withdraw key offensive military assets from Eastern Europe. Consequently, by 1989, Gorbachev and his supporters had made non-offensive defense a respectable topic in both East and West, illustrated by the mutual acceptance by both alliances of key defensive provisions in the 1990 Conventional Forces in Europe (CFE) Treaty.

Thus, while the end of the **cold war** in many ways vindicated important aspects of non-offensive defense theory, interest declined sharply in the 1990s. Under more fluid, post-cold war conditions involving the eruption of **civil wars**, serious doubts arose as to the relevance of non-offensive defense, which had been designed specifically to protect against external threats to states.

Moreover, non-offensive defense was largely overtaken by a surge in support for **humanitarian intervention**, an emerging norm that required offensive, not defensive, military capabilities. The main 1990s impetus for humanitarian intervention's revival was the 1990–1 Persian Gulf War. That war also revealed many ways in which comprehensive defensive schemes, tied to the special conditions of the static, bipolar cold war confrontation in Europe, did not translate easily in the 1990s security environment. The Gulf War's conduct demonstrated the apparent futility of small states adopting non-offensive defense against large, predatory neighbors and the need for an international counter-offensive to dislodge Iraqi forces from Kuwait. Moreover, the Gulf War gave rise to a new 'over the horizon' defense doctrine and a fresh **legitimacy** for professional armed forces (both of which were antithetical to non-offensive defense). However, post-Gulf War settlement arrangements (such as the **United Nations**' cease-fire resolution and the creation of a Demilitarized Zone along the Iraqi–Kuwaiti border) were clear expressions of the victors' wish for a constrained Iraq, reflecting the historical depth to which defensive norms for defeated states tacitly drive war termination processes.

Classical realists and strategic studies specialists tend to be skeptical of the offence/defense distinction when it is raised in the non-offensive defense context, even though the military depends on this distinction for planning purposes. Many realists also embrace the distinction in their support for **ballistic missile defense** (BMD), a system opposed by most non-offensive defense advocates as being provocative and not genuinely defensive. This realist skepticism notwithstanding, non-offensive defense – with its potential to mitigate the security dilemma – attracts theoretical interest from an eclectic range of perspectives, including **peace studies**, **constructivism**, and **critical security studies**.

Non-offensive defense should be seen as having three distinct, but complementary, meanings. The first of these is *normative policy advocacy*. This advocacy advances specific proposals for states and alliances, envisaging a progressively more secure world. There are many situations where non-offensive defense can contribute to conflict amelioration. For example, it remains relevant to the Korean peninsula (which mimics cold war conditions), and to the Russian–American, Sino–American, and Indian–Pakistani relationships. Indeed, a defensively armed, post-Hussein Iraq and a defensively configured, lightly armed Palestinian military could help resolve two thorny problems in the Middle East. The second meaning takes non-offensive defense to be a *general standard* for evaluating and judging defense policies and practices for all countries,

both large and small. Having such a standard provides a safeguard against the tendency of defense planners to apply offensive/defensive criteria to other states but not to their own. The third meaning equates non-offensive defense generally with *unnoticed defensive norms and practices* that underpin policymaking (as distinct from explicit schemes and proposals). Non-offensive defense norms and reassurances contributed to the successful diplomatic negotiations on German reunification and are central to regional debate about Japan's expanding security role. Theoretically, such contributions imply significant, unacknowledged levels of defensive thinking in international relations.

Further reading

Butfoy, A. (1997) *Common Security and Strategic Reform*, Basingstoke: Macmillan.

Gates, D. (1991) *Non-Offensive Defence: An Alternative Strategy for NATO?* Basingstoke: Macmillan.

Møller, B. (1991) *Resolving the Security Dilemma in Europe: The German Debate on Non-Offensive Defence*, London: Brassey's.

Møller, B. *et al.* (1998) *Non-Offensive Defence in the Middle East?* New York: United Nations Institute for Disarmament Research.

Wiseman, G. (2002) *Concepts of Non-Provocative Defence: Ideas and Practices in International Security*, Basingstoke: Palgrave.

See also: balance of threat; ballistic missile defense; strategic culture

GEOFFREY WISEMAN

Non-tariff barrier (NTB)

Until the 1980s, the main instrument for states to restrict imports from other states and to protect domestic industries was the tariff. A tariff is a tax imposed on goods imported from outside the country that is not imposed on similar goods from within the country. Import tariffs may be levied on an *ad valorem* basis, i.e., as a certain percentage of the estimated market value of the imported item. Alternatively, they may be levied on a specific basis, i.e., as a fixed amount per unit imported. Tariffs (sometimes called duties) may be imposed mainly to raise revenues because they are relatively cheap and easy taxes for a small or poorly organized government to collect. In developed industrial states they provide domestic producers of the good in question with an artificial competitive advantage over their foreign competitors, usually at the expense of domestic consumers of the product. Domestic producers enjoy higher prices, a bigger market share, and higher profits.

Since the 1980s, and in light of the substantial progress made in lowering tariffs through successive rounds of negotiations under the 1947 General Agreement on Tariffs and Trade (GATT), states have developed a host of NTBs to achieve the same goals as tariffs. Import tariffs levied on industrial products by the major industrial countries were reduced from a weighted average of about 50 per cent of product value in 1947 to around 5 per cent by the end of the twentieth century. Many NTBs are now regulated by the successor to GATT, the **World Trade Organization** (WTO). Whilst NTBs vary enormously across the **international system**, there are four main types.

First, trade may be restricted by the imposition or negotiation of various *quantitative* restrictions (QRs), such as quotas. These are usually regarded as more onerous than tariffs because of the more limited flexibility that they permit in trade and because they place greater limits on the extent to which foreign and

domestic sellers can compete. In 1962 several major textile trading countries established a temporary agreement regulating trade in cotton textiles in an attempt to protect their domestic industries. In 1973 the agreement was succeeded by the Multi-Fibres Agreement (MFA), enlarging its coverage to include wool and synthetic fibers. Another example of quantitative restrictions is the use of voluntary export restraints (VERs), which were predominantly imposed by the United States and the **European Union** against Japan and newly industrialized countries (see **newly industrialized country**) in order to protect certain domestic sectors, particularly textiles, cars and high technology industries. They essentially involve a bilateral agreement where the quantity and type of goods to be traded are fixed according to the requirements of the importing country.

Second, trade may be restricted by domestic *product regulations* demanded by governments. Some of these may not be explicitly targeted at international trade but they may affect the costs or feasibility of trade. Most obvious are the many regulations, standards, and other measures that restrict the form that a good may take or the manner in which it may be produced for sale in the domestic market. Such rules may be intended to protect the public safety or health, or they may only seek to insure compatibility of products that must be used in combination.

Third, governments may use *subsidies* to protect particular industries. Although the WTO bans subsidies provided directly for exports, it is far more difficult to regulate subsidies for overall production of a particular good or service. Subsidies that are not specific to particular firms or industries, subsidies for research and development, regional **development** and for adaptation to environmental regulation are not regulated at the international level.

Fourth, states may *dump* exports on overseas markets. Dumping is the export of a good for an unfairly low price, defined either as below the price on the exporter's home market or as below some definition of cost. The World Trade Organization permits anti-dumping import duties equal to the dumping margin – the difference between the actual and the 'fair' market price.

The use of NTBs has been the subject of much discussion in recent years. Two questions have dominated the debate. First, to what extent have NTBs replaced tariffs in restricting international trade? This is difficult to measure, since so many NTBs are hidden from view by their very nature. In many cases, even the identification of a non-tariff barrier is subjective; what is an NTB to one person is a legitimate activity to another. Second, are they necessarily to be condemned and brought under international regulation? Again, the literature is divided between those who see all NTBs as constraints on the evolution towards a **free trade system**, and others who believe that states have a legitimate reason to use them to protect their basic **national interests**. In any case, the debate is sure to remain high on the academic and diplomatic agenda, particularly at the highest levels of the World Trade Organization, whose mission has been complicated enormously by the new protectionism in international trade.

Further reading

Cottier T., Mavroidis, P. and Blatter, P. (eds) (2000) *Regulatory Barriers and the Principle of Non-Discrimination in World Trade Law: Past, Present, and Future*, Ann Arbor, MI: University of Michigan Press.

Grieco, J. (1990) *Cooperation Among Nations: Europe, America, and Non-Tariff Barriers to Trade*, Ithaca, NY: Cornell University Press.

Grynberg, R. and Turner, E. (2004) *Multilateral and Regional Trade Issues for Developing Countries*, London: Commonwealth Secretariat.

Wolf, C., Levaux, H. and Tong, D. (1999) *Economic Openness: Many Facets, Many Metrics*, Santa Monica, CA: Rand.

See also: managed trade; North American Free Trade Agreement; World Trade Organization

TERRY O'CALLAGHAN

North American Free Trade Agreement (NAFTA)

The world's first **free trade** agreement involving both developed and developing states, the 1994 North American Free Trade Agreement (NAFTA) is a trade liberalization agreement between Canada, Mexico, and the United States that created a market of almost 400 million people and has become established as one of the world's leading economic regions. During its negotiation NAFTA inspired deep controversy and its merits have continued to be debated throughout its first decade of existence.

In the second half of the 1980s the international trading system faced a number of challenges as the major economic powers struggled to agree in the Uruguay Round of GATT negotiations. A deadlock over agricultural trade reform between the United States and the **European Union** threatened the future of the global multilateral trade **regime**. With the future of the world's trading regime in the balance, a number of states looked to economic **regionalism** as a potential substitute for broader **multilateralism** in trade. The Europeans successfully negotiated the 1986 Single European Act creating a single market for goods, services and labor in the European Union by 1993. Also in 1986 negotiations began between the United States and Canada towards a Canada–US Free Trade Agreement (CUFTA), that was implemented in 1989 and would gradually eliminate the tariffs on many goods and liberalize investment between them by 1998.

As the CUFTA came into effect negotiations began toward a larger free trade agreement in North America, one that would include Mexico alongside Canada and the United States. The negotiations were spurred by a convergence in the economic ideological preferences of the three countries' heads of government: Prime Minister Brian Mulroney in Canada, President Carlos Salinas de Gortari in Mexico, and US President George H. Bush, all three of whom pursued liberal economic policies in their respective countries. Driven initially by President Salinas de Gortari's goal of modernizing the Mexican economy, the three states predicted substantial benefits from a free trade area in North America, both in the short and long term. The negotiation process extended from 1990 to 1992 when a preliminary agreement was signed.

The NAFTA negotiations were marked by heavy protests from social groups in the three countries. In Canada and the United States labor unions and small businesses argued that the agreement would result in a drain of economic activity south to Mexico, where wage levels were lower and employment and environmental regulations more lax. US Presidential candidate Ross Perot famously warned of 'a giant sucking sound' as American jobs and capital went south. In Mexico fears were expressed that Mexican **sovereignty** would be severely compromised by the deal and that Mexican business would be unable to compete against Canadian and US exporters. Some Mexicans also argued that an ecological nightmare would result as US industries moved their production to Mexico in order to be able to escape more stringent environmental restrictions north of the border.

A long and complex debate ensued in the US Congress and Canadian Parliament as opponents of the agreement lobbied legislators over NAFTA. Although public protest was also vigorous in Mexico, it had little impact on the legislative process due to the Mexican presidency's domination of the legislature in the early 1990s. Therefore it was primarily to address the concerns of opponents in Canada and the United States, and thus to secure legislative approval of the agreement, that in 1993 two side-deals with NAFTA were signed by the three states. The conclusion of these deals in the areas of environment and labor standards permitted the eventual ratification of NAFTA in November 1993. NAFTA came into force in January 1994 and in its first ten years it resulted in a far reaching liberalization of trade and investment between the three countries. The most immediate effects of NAFTA were to be found in the US–Mexico bilateral economic relationship, with tariffs removed on approximately half of all US goods entering the Mexican market in 1994 and a commitment to do the same for many other goods by the year 2009.

The NAFTA negotiations neatly encapsulated an important element in international relations, namely the links between domestic actors and foreign policy. Each of the states conducted their negotiations with each other whilst holding an ongoing dialogue with national actors from the economic sector in question. Thus in the case of the automobile sector negotiations, the auto industries from each country were consulted directly by their respective governments to gain their support for the final agreement. This greatly facilitated political backing for the NAFTA as industries lobbied legislators to support what they came to see as 'their' agreement. However it raised important questions about whose interests the NAFTA promoted and also about the democratic process.

One of the first challenges to NAFTA came in the form of the Mexican peso crisis of December 1994. As the Mexican economy fell into recession and the financial system was wracked by deep instability, the Mexican government applied for financial assistance from the **International Monetary Fund** (IMF). US President Clinton, facing criticism after his enthusiastic support for NAFTA, threw his political weight behind a financial aid package for Mexico that eventually totaled some US$50 billion. This support from the US presidency exemplified the growing levels of mutual dependence or **interdependence** between the NAFTA countries.

One of the key features of NAFTA has been the institutionalization of trade relations between the three economies. Disputes over interpretation of the rules of NAFTA and over breaches of those rules are resolved through a dispute settlement process provided for in the agreement. This has made trade relations more predictable than in the past but it has not eliminated commercial conflicts. Throughout the 1990s and early 2000s a number of high profile disputes continued between Canada and the United States involving softwood lumber, potatoes, salmon, and magazines. Likewise, Mexico and the United States found themselves in conflict over the issue of trucking and the trade of a number of agricultural goods. Furthermore, chapter eleven of NAFTA, dealing with the liberalization of capital flows in the region, has been cited in several lawsuits involving cross border investments totaling billions of dollars.

After ten years in existence NAFTA is generally accepted to have generated tangible benefits for each of the area's three national economies. However, although capital and jobs have been created in Mexico as a result of NAFTA, the distribution of those benefits has been far from even. Mexico is perhaps the best example of this, for whereas Mexican Gross Domestic Product (GDP) as a whole seems to have increased as a result of NAFTA, and investment and trade have benefited, that growth has been concentrated in a relatively small area of the country, mostly in the north near the US border, and in Mexico City. This is, in turn, creating political and social tensions between the regions of Mexico.

A key question for the future of NAFTA is the choice between deepening or widening of the existing agreement. Deepening NAFTA would involve the creation of new institutional arrangements that would bind the three existing members closer together, whereas widening would bring in new members from the rest of the Americas. In the mid-1990s the accession of Chile was discussed but resistance from the US Congress has meant that this option remains stalled.

Further reading

Cameron, M.A. and Tomlin, B.W. (2002) *The Making of NAFTA*, Ithaca, NY: Cornell University Press.

Gereffi, G., Spener, D. and Blair, J. (eds) (2002), *Free Trade and Uneven Development: The North American Apparel Industry after NAFTA*, Philadelphia PA, Temple University Press.

Pastor, R. A. (2001) *Toward a North American Community: Lessons from the Old World for the New*, Washington, DC: Institute for International Economics.

Thacker, S. C. (2000) *Big Business, the State, and Free Trade: Constructing Coalitions in Mexico,* Cambridge: Cambridge University Press.

See also: free trade; preferential trade agreement; regional trade bloc

DUNCAN WOOD

North Atlantic Treaty Organization (NATO)

A military **alliance** formed on 4 April 1949 by the United States, Canada, and ten Western European states (the United Kingdom, France, Belgium, the Netherlands, Luxembourg, Denmark, Italy, Norway, Portugal, and Iceland) to deter, and if necessary, to defend against potential Soviet-bloc aggression in Europe. While the original motivation for the alliance faded with the end of the **cold war**, NATO continues to play an important role in European **security** and world politics. There are currently twenty-six members of NATO. In addition to its role as a defensive military alliance, NATO has been active in building closer ties between its members and the former Soviet-bloc states and in **peacekeeping** and peacemaking missions.

The North Atlantic Treaty is a defensive alliance; obligations are invoked in the event of armed attack on one or more of the parties in Europe or North America (in other words, on their home territory or territorial waters). Article 5 states that 'The parties agree that an armed attack against one or more of them in Europe or North America shall be considered an attack against them all and consequently they agree that, if such an armed attack occurs, each of them … will assist the Party or Parties so attacked by taking … such action as it deems necessary, including the use of armed force, to restore and maintain the secur-

ity of the North Atlantic area.' The primary goal of the founders was to deter the Soviet Union or any other state from attacking a member by promising a joint military response. Should **deterrence** fail, the goal was to produce a combined military force that could defeat any attacker. No member state need rely on only national forces for ensuring security; states can depend on collective defense instead.

Shortly after NATO was formed, steps were taken to institutionalize military and political cooperation among the member states. By 1951, a headquarters and integrated command had been established, along with rules for procedure and equipment standardization and an active governing body with a permanent staff. A number of bilateral agreements were signed between member states to regulate military assistance and the stationing of forces on foreign territory. NATO also quickly expanded to include Greece and Turkey to the south (in 1952) and the newly recognized Federal Republic of Germany (in 1955). Alliance members created an integrated structure that fostered effective military collaboration and helped to make their promises of collective defense credible and dependable.

In the 1960s, conflicts emerged among the allies on issues of foreign policy and alliance management, leading France and Greece (on separate occasions) to withdraw from participation in the integrated command. No states, however, severed relations with NATO, and the alliance remained active throughout the cold war. When the cold war ended, the future of NATO seemed uncertain; its reason for being no longer existed. Yet, while the Warsaw Pact, its rival in the East, collapsed, NATO remained active. Members have found new ways to use the NATO structure to enhance security in Europe and North America.

One of the primary goals of the NATO members in the post cold war era is to encourage cooperative relationships with the states of the former Soviet-bloc. Parallel to the consultation and confidence building measures undertaken under the auspices of the **Organization for Security and Cooperation in Europe** (OSCE), NATO established the North Atlantic Cooperation Council (NACC) in 1991, followed by the Partnership for Peace (PfP) in 1994, and the Euro-Atlantic Partnership Council (EAPC) in 1997. These fora are intended to foster political consultation and discussion among all European and North American states, to encourage transparency in military planning and intentions, and to serve as a step toward integrating new states into NATO. In 1999, the Czech Republic, Poland, and Hungary became the seventeenth, eighteenth, and nineteenth members of NATO (Spain had joined in 1982), and protocols of accession were signed in 2003 for Estonia, Latvia, Lithuania, Bulgaria, Romania, Slovenia, and the Slovak Republic, allowing them to become full members upon ratification.

Russia voiced considerable opposition to the expansion of NATO eastward, and, in response, NATO members offered assurances that expansion would not be accompanied by significant increases in force levels or movement eastward of nuclear weapons. In 1997, NATO and Russia created a Permanent Joint Council for ongoing consultation. Russia also participates actively in the PfP and EAPC.

Since the end of the cold war, NATO has also found a new role as a **peacekeeping**, and occasionally a peacemaking, force. The crisis in the former Yugoslavia inspired NATO to adopt **crisis** management as one of its main goals. During the war in Bosnia-Herzegovina in the early 1990s, NATO forces worked to enforce **United Nations** sanctions and to protect UN peacekeepers. Following signature of the Dayton Accords in 1995, NATO formed a peacekeeping force to help implement the agreement. The goals were to demilitarize the area, to deter a resumption of fighting, and to ensure that the parties fulfilled their Dayton obligations. A crisis in the Kosovo province of Serbia in 1999 led to bolder action. NATO used air strikes against Serbian forces to end fighting between the Serbian government and ethnic Albanians. When Serb government forces withdrew from Kosovo, NATO forces assumed a peacekeeping role.

In 2001, Article 5 of the North Atlantic Treaty was invoked for the first time. NATO members declared that the terrorist attacks of 11 September 2001 on the United States were an attack against all NATO members. In 2003, NATO assumed command of the peacekeeping mission in Afghanistan, operating under a UN mandate.

While political consultation with nonmembers, confidence building, peacekeeping, and crisis management are not discussed in the North Atlantic Treaty and seem far removed from the founders' expectations, current NATO members find the organization useful for these purposes and have worked to adjust the structure to accommodate these goals. NATO's primary mission is to deter threats to the security of member states and to be prepared to defend states in the event of attack; it remains first and foremost a defensive military alliance. Yet the end of the cold war has opened the door to additional uses for this well integrated security organization.

Further reading

Haftendorn, H., Keohane, R. O. and Wallander, C. A. (eds) (1999) *Imperfect Unions:*

Security Institutions Over Time and Space,
New York: Oxford University Press.

Mattox, G. and Rachwald, A. (eds) (2001)
Enlarging NATO: The National Debates,
Boulder, CO: Lynne Rienner.

Sandler, T. and Hartley, K. (1999) *The Political Economy of NATO,* Cambridge:
Cambridge University Press.

Schmidt, G. (ed.) (2001) *A History of NATO –
The First Fifty Years,* Basingstoke: Palgrave.

See also: alliance; cold war; collective security; Organization for Security and Cooperation in Europe; security community

BRETT ASHLEY LEEDS

Nuclear proliferation

The proliferation of nuclear weapons has been a key issue in international **security** since these weapons were first developed and used in August 1945 by the United States against Japan. The **cold war** era was epitomized by fears of nuclear war between the **superpowers**, but there were also concerns that nuclear weapons might be acquired by an increasing number of states. The USSR had tested its first nuclear weapon (NW) in 1949, Britain tested in 1952, France in 1960, and China in 1964. These states came to be known as the five 'declared' nuclear weapon states (NWS). To prevent the further spread of NW, or what is known as horizontal proliferation, the Treaty on the Non-Proliferation of Nuclear Weapons (NPT) was concluded in 1968 and came into effect in 1970.

While preventing the non-nuclear weapons states (NNWS) – that is, those that had not tested a nuclear device by 1968 – from acquiring a nuclear weapons capability was the main aim of the NPT, the Treaty also included two other objectives: the transfer of nuclear technology for peaceful purposes to the non-

nuclear states, and an attempt to control vertical proliferation by encouraging the NWS to end the nuclear **arms race** and move to nuclear disarmament. These two provisions were part of the grand bargain between the NWS and NNWS; the latter group would forswear nuclear weapons in return for technology transfers and the promise of eventual disarmament on the part of the former.

The ending of the cold war eased fears of a nuclear exchange between hostile great powers but did not bring with it a halt to nuclear proliferation. The collapse of the USSR and resulting concern about the control of nuclear material and technology served to increase the dangers of proliferation. Various arms control treaties have reduced markedly the number of weapons held by the declared nuclear weapon states after the 1980s, representing a successful attempt to halt vertical proliferation. But the number of states that have acquired a nuclear weapons capability has increased. In addition to the original five NWS, there now exist a number of states which are self-declared nuclear weapon states (India and Pakistan, which both tested in 1998; India had previously conducted a 'peaceful' nuclear explosion in 1974) or non-declared nuclear weapon states (Israel, which has not tested but which is known to have a substantial arsenal) and others which are suspected of developing or coming close to developing a nuclear weapon (Iraq, North Korea). Finally, there have been instances of proliferation by states, both during the cold war and after, that have subsequently renounced their nuclear weapons capability: South Africa revealed in 1993 that it had developed six nuclear devices which were dismantled prior to its joining the NPT. Argentina, Brazil and Libya had also developed substantial programs that were subsequently jettisoned.

Nuclear weapon proliferation has been seen overwhelmingly as undesirable in world politics for a number of reasons, chief of which is the view that the greater the number of states that possess such weapons, the greater the risk of actual use of NW. Notwithstanding this, there are those who argue in favor of greater proliferation. The 'more is better' thesis is based on perceptions that nuclear weapons can be managed effectively, that deterrence has served to restrain their use and that such weapons provide strategic stability to relations between states. Underlying this view is a belief that the history of nuclear weapons during the cold war was a positive one, and that it was nuclear deterrence that kept the peace.

This pro-proliferation view has not enjoyed great support, either from analysts or policymakers. Critics draw attention to the pitfalls of deterrence theory, especially when practiced by weak states or those controlled by the military. The thesis is also roundly rejected by those arguing for the elimination of nuclear weapons, a process to which the NWS have committed themselves in the NPT. Similarly, the continuation of the NPT itself, despite its flaws, is testament to the international community's belief that proliferation is undesirable and must be contained.

The non-proliferation **regime** has thus been expanded and strengthened in recent years. The NPT was renewed indefinitely at the 1995 Review and Extension Conference and incorporated a set of principles and objectives for disarmament and non-proliferation, together with an expanded program for reviewing the treaty. Other key elements of the non-proliferation regime include the role played by the **International Atomic Energy Agency** (IAEA) in monitoring verification and compliance with the NPT, the completion of a Compre-

hensive Test Ban Treaty (CTBT) in 1996 (although it is yet to come into force), the establishment of a number of Nuclear Weapon Free Zones, the United States' Cooperative Threat Reduction program designed to control nuclear material and technology emanating from the former USSR, plans for a Fissile Material Cut-Off Treaty, the establishment of various groupings to address the supply side of nuclear proliferation, such as the Zangger Committee and the Nuclear Suppliers Group, and the Missile Technology Control Regime, designed to minimize development of delivery systems capable of carrying nuclear warheads.

These various measures can be seen as an ambitious and largely effective move on the part of the international community to halt proliferation. Fears that the number of nuclear states would rise to 30 or more by the end of the twentieth century have not been realized. Nevertheless, the non-proliferation regime has suffered a number of setbacks. In particular, the realization after the Gulf War in 1991 that Iraq had been developing a nuclear weapons program that was not detected by the IAEA and which was in contravention of Iraq's obligations under the NPT was something of a 'wake up' call to an international community which had become somewhat complacent in the 1980s. Similarly, the moves taken by North Korea in 1993–4 and again in 2003–4 to develop nuclear weapons revealed the limitations of the non-proliferation regime. When North Korea withdrew from the Agreed Framework negotiated in 1994, announced that it had developed a nuclear weapon and withdrew from the Treaty in 2004, there seemed little that collective action could do. As of 2004, negotiations continue between North Korea, the United States, China, Japan and South Korea in an effort to resolve this issue. Libya provided another example that non-proliferation norms and activities had not deterred that state from seeking nuclear weapons.

Further problems center on the unwillingness of the NWS to move to nuclear disarmament. Halting proliferation will require not just a strong non-proliferation regime, but also a genuine move to disarmament on the part of the existing nuclear weapon states.

Further reading

Sagan, S. and Waltz, K. (2002) *The Spread of Nuclear Weapons: a Debate*, New York: Norton.

Ungerer, C. and Hanson, M. (eds) (2001) *The Politics of Nuclear Non-Proliferation*, Sydney: Allen and Unwin.

See also: arms control; International Atomic Energy Agency; mutually assured destruction; weapons of mass destruction

MARIANNE HANSON

Nuclear utilization theory (NUT)

Central to the question of nuclear weapons are issues involving their possible use. Those issues involve much more than a philosophy of targeting. They involve questions of broad strategic doctrine. How is **deterrence** best sustained? How can the forces to sustain deterrence be minimized? How might we offset nuclear weapons states more attracted to doctrines of compellence? What do we do if deterrence fails? Such questions lie at the core of the principal targeting debates.

For US nuclear **war** planners, a key imperative has always been to maximize the range of options available to the president during a **crisis**. But publicity about such plans has often made Western publics more hesitant about nuclear weapons, and excited debates about the appropriate targeting focus of the arsenal. Should nuclear forces be shaped by counter-force or counter-value targeting polices? To what extent do war-fighting doctrines undermine deterrence doctrines? These concerns were a feature of the **cold war** years. Nor have they disappeared in the changing **security** environment. Indeed, several strategists point to a second nuclear age: an age when the nuclear armed players include not merely **superpower**s and **great power**s, but enduring rivals, **rogue state**s and possibly even non-state actors.

What are nuclear weapons good for? This question might seem trite, but it has been the central question of the world since 1945. How could weapons of massive destructive power be employed to make a positive contribution to international relations? Paradoxically, the primary use of such weapons had to lie in their non-use. Threats to use such weapons had to replace actual use, or the world would not survive. Threats to use nuclear weapons, coupled to doctrines of **containment**, served as the primary Western strategic policy during the cold war. It is important to remember that, at least in this sense, we 'used' nuclear weapons virtually every day of the cold war. It is entirely fallacious to argue, as some have done, that nuclear weapons were not 'used' during the cold war. On the contrary, they were used so effectively that Western policy-makers have been most reluctant to put them aside.

But even this 'non-using' form of 'use' derives its effectiveness from credible targeting strategies. Deterrence, which has been described as the science of things that do not occur, works because an actor credits an opponent with both a capability to punish any transgression, and the will to do so if pressed. Judgments about capability will intermesh with declaratory strategy: if a nuclear weapon state is threatening to apply a particular targeting strategy, say, targeting of silo-based missiles as part of a second strike capability, then it must demonstrate that it has the necessary combination of missile accuracy, warhead yield, and force protection to support that strategy. And it must also do what it can to demonstrate the will to resort to nuclear weapons use when pushed. Whatever deterrence country A's leaders may hope to bring to bear upon country B arises precisely from judgments made by country B's leaders about country A's ability and will to strike particular targets.

In this sense, strategies of deterrence are perhaps less clearly separable from strategies of war fighting than some critics of nuclear strategy might believe. And in this sense too, strategies of minimum deterrence raise particular difficulties, since small arsenals are generically incapable of supporting demanding targeting options. Indeed, they are of use only in targeting a small number of cities, and Western nuclear strategy has attempted overtly to avoid the indiscriminate targeting of civilians, not least because the strategy itself would be self-deterring to most policymakers called upon to enforce it. For this reason, Western policymakers have never been attracted to the idea of minimum deterrence.

Counter-value targeting is not exactly the same as the gross targeting of civilians: rather a counter-value strategy suggests that deterrence is maximized by the deliberate targeting of things that the adversary values. In the former Soviet Union, for example, the decades devoted by its leaders to the industrialization of the country would suggest to an observer that Soviet leaders placed a high value on industry. So a counter-value targeting strategy might threaten that industry. In practice, of course,

such a strategy might look little different from one of mere 'city busting', but it would be driven by different considerations.

Counter-force targeting suggests that the principal role for nuclear forces is to destroy opposing military forces (including nuclear weapons) that might be used during a conflict. In this sense, nuclear forces deter an opponent from beginning or continuing a particular aggression by destroying (or threatening to destroy) the military forces available to support such an aggression. Such strategies are often more attractive to policymakers, because they allow nuclear weapons to be brought to bear on the 'sharp end' of the military threat. But counter-force strategies are usually more demanding than counter-value strategies in terms of intelligence and the required attributes of force structure (such as accuracy). Some nuclear weapons states might not have a choice of a counter-targeting strategy, simply because their arsenal could not support the strategy.

So far, we have not seen the emergence of any nuclear weapon state that has propounded a doctrine of compellence – namely that it would resort to use of nuclear weapons *unless* another actor does something. Such attempts to compel behavior under duress of nuclear targeting would be highly strategically destabilizing, and could only be the strategic policy of an actor that itself had very little to lose.

For most of the **great powers**, and in particular for the United States, the need to deter opponents from possible aggression has entailed considerable conceptual complexity. In Western models of deterrence, we have seen the emergence of both 'pre-war' and 'intra-war' deterrence, suggesting that Western policymakers continue to see utility in the deterrence model beyond the firing of the first shell. These complexities were particularly marked during the cold war, when the diplomatic requirements of Western alliances required the United States to tell a coherent strategic story about extending nuclear deterrence to protect allies against even conventional threats of war.

Since the end of the cold war, and the possible emergence of a wider range of nuclear opponents, US nuclear strategy has turned to a different, and in some ways more difficult question: how to 'use' nuclear weapons to bear down upon contemporary threats, which are more likely to be regional and/or asymmetric in nature. Weapons and strategy seem likely to evolve to fit a changing strategic landscape, and we can already see signs of such evolution in recent debates amongst American scientists about the need to construct and test new species of nuclear weapons designed to destroy new kinds of targets.

Further reading

Ball, D. and Richelson, J. (eds) (1986) *Strategic Nuclear Targeting*, Ithaca, NY: Cornell University Press.

Baylis, J. and O'Neill, R. (eds) (2000) *Alternative Nuclear Futures: the Role of Nuclear Weapons on the Post-Cold War World*, Oxford: Oxford University Press.

Freedman, L. (2003) *The Evolution of Nuclear Strategy*, 3rd edn, Basingstoke: Palgrave.

Krepon, M. (2001) 'Moving away from MAD', *Survival* 43(2), 81–95.

Payne, K. B. (1996) *Deterrence in the Second Nuclear Age*, Lexington, KY: University Press of Kentucky.

See also: deterrence; mutually assured destruction; peace studies

ROD LYON

O

Offshore

A technique adopted by a growing number of states of dividing their territorial **sovereignty** into two realms: in one realm, normally the larger portion of their territorial sovereignty, they apply fully their regulations and taxation, while in the other realm, offshore, they relax or withdraw some of those regulations and taxation. Offshore denotes, therefore, not the geographical location of economic activity, but rather the juridical status of a vast and expanding array of specialized realms of activity.

There are three methods of setting up offshore economies: enclave zones, enclave sectors, and virtual offshore. The first are special economic zones typically separated by a perimeter fence and/or other physical barriers from the onshore economy. The second, which includes tax havens and flags of convenience, come about when states set up intentionally low or no taxation loopholes and/or little regulation in order to attract international finance, business or shipping into their territories. The third produces virtual or unregulated realms akin in legal status to the role the oceans or space is playing in **international law**. The third method produced the offshore financial markets or the Euromarket and is increasingly attracting e-commercial activity. In economic terms, the third method has had the deepest impact on the world economy, followed by the second and the first.

Virtual offshore

The Euromarket is a medium for lending and borrowing the world's most important convertible currencies. It is a wholesale or inter-bank market in which the commercial banks are its principal intermediates. Eurocurrency transactions are distinguished from conventional domestic or even international banking activities because these markets operate outside the jurisdiction of the national authority and are not subject to state regulations such as reserve requirements, reporting or, most importantly, taxation.

In 1957, the Euromarket emerged as the first financial market that was not directly regulated by any state. In contrast to the **Law of the Sea**, however, the legal status of the Euromarket has never been codified in any multilateral setting or documents which means, effectively, that the Euromarket persists due to the willingness of states to sustain it. In that sense, the Euromarket is only fictionally offshore, for it lives its life in the familiar financial centers of the world.

Whilst the offshore financial market is fully integrated, internally coherent and global, it is not located offshore in any literal sense. Rather, it is situated in and between different types of financial centers, all of which are located, physically and juridically in major onshore cities. The literature distinguishes among three types of offshore financial centers, or three different legal arrangements: the so-called 'spontaneous' offshore sites, such as London and Hong Kong; variations of International Banking Facilities (IBF) such as New York and Tokyo; and tax havens.

The offshore financial market is unregulated by states, but that does not mean that it is entirely unregulated. It is subjected to self-regulation by banks and other financial institutions as instructed by the Basle Concordant (Basle I and II). It is estimated that over 80 per cent of international financial transactions are taking place in this offshore market (Palan 2003).

Enclave sectors

The offshore financial market encouraged the emergence of offshore financial centers on tax havens. Tax havens can be defined as deliberate state policies aimed at attracting international trade by minimization of taxes and the reduction or elimination of other restrictions on business operations. Modern tax havens tend to offer the following:

- Minimal or no personal or corporate taxation;
- Effective bank secrecy law. Bank or state officials are often barred by law from disclosing the origins, character and name of holders of funds;
- Few, or preferably no restrictions on regulations concerning financial transactions, together with the maintenance of a code of anonymity and secrecy;
- The territory must possess political and economic stability – hence, preferred jurisdictions are dependencies of large, prosperous and stable states (e.g. the Channel islands and the Isle of Man which are both British dependencies);
- It should either be supported by a large international financial market or alternatively be equipped with sophisticated information exchange facilities and/or within easy reach of a major financial center. Gibraltar, for instance, has invested heavily in communication infrastructure.

The emergence of the modern tax havens has been a complex affair. Bank secrecy laws were enacted first in Switzerland in 1934, but corporate registration for tax purposes evolved in the UK prior to that period (Picciotto 1992). Today there are over seventy tax havens in the world and just about half of all international lending is routed through them (Palan 2003). Flags of convenience work on a similar principle. These are countries that offer easy registration, low or no taxes, and no restrictions on the nationality of crews. By transferring a ship from a genuine national register to a Flag of Convenience, an owner runs away from taxation, safety regulations and from trade union organization It is estimated that nearly 70 per cent of heavy shipping are located in flag of convenience states.

Enclave sectors

States set up special territorial zones, often called export processing zones or special economic zones in order to attract investment into their territories. Export processing zones (EPZ) are duty free zones dedicated to manufacturing for export. Most EPZs have few labor and environmental laws. Normally no customs duties are charged for importing raw materials, components, machinery, equipment, and supplies used to produce manufactured goods, provided these are then exported. EPZs tend to be relatively small, geographically spread areas within a country, the purpose of which is to attract export industries by offering them favorable investment and trade conditions as compared with the remainder of the host country. In particular, the EPZs provide for the importation of goods to be used in the production of exports on a duty free basis. These enclaves enjoy special economic concessions, including an extensive package of incentives and very often exemption from certain kinds of legislation that apply outside the zones. Among the most common of such exceptions is that EPZs generally allow the duty free entry of goods for re-export. Within these zones all the physical infrastructure and services necessary for manufacturing are provided: roads, power supplies, transport facilities, low cost rent buildings. In a number of cases restrictions on foreign ownership that apply in the country as a whole are waived for foreign firms locating in the zones. Export processing zones may be seen, therefore, as the manufacturing equivalent of tax havens. There are now over 850 export processing zones in the world employing over 27 million workers.

The offshore economy evolved from the beginning of the twentieth century, but began to flourish during the 1970s. Today, the offshore economy is fully integrated as some tax havens, such as Cayman Islands, Bermuda, the Channel Island and Bahamas evolved into large, if largely virtual, financial centers. The Euromarket also finances manufacturing relocation into the export processing zones, and growing capital mobility associated with **globalization** encourages flag of convenience and e-commercial activities. Indeed, offshore may be considered a cornerstone of globalization.

Further reading

Hampton, M. (1996) *The Offshore Interface: Tax Havens in the Global Economy*, Basingstoke: Palgrave.

Hampton, M. and Abbott, J. (eds) (1999) *Offshore Finance Centers and Tax Havens*, Basingstoke: Macmillan.

Palan, R. (2003) *The Offshore World: Sovereign Markets, Virtual Places, and Nomad Millionaires*, Ithaca, NY: Cornell University Press.

Picciotto, S. (1992) *International Business Taxation*, London: Weidenfeld and Nicolson.

See also: disintermediation; global financial center; multinational corporation

RONEN PALAN

Order

A sustained pattern of social arrangements, combining both a structural and a functional dimension. The structural dimension refers to how things are arranged, and the nature of the relationship among the constituent parts. This is what Saint Augustine (354–430 AD) meant when he referred to 'a good disposition of discrepant parts, each in its fittest place'. The functional dimension refers to the purpose of the arrangement. For example, a state may be structured for the purpose of enhancing individual or collective freedom, for centralizing or decentralizing decision making processes.

When the constituent parts are arranged in their proper place and achieve the intended purpose the whole is said to be well ordered. As a pattern repeated over time, orders produce structural regularities and functional goals that lend a certain amount of stability and perhaps even predictability to social interaction. In this respect, order is the opposite of chaos and disorder. At a minimum, well-ordered political societies are expected to enable cooperation and eliminate wanton violence.

Order in international relations is distinguishable from peace and stability. Peace is a particular order whereby the pattern of social arrangements excludes **war**. As we shall see, order and war are not mutually exclusive conditions, unlike peace and war. Order is also distinguishable from stability because stability and instability are properties of order. For example, there may be stable orders where patterns remain largely unchanged or evolve gradually over time, or unstable orders where patterns are subject to volatility or upheaval.

In the study of international relations, order has often been counterposed to justice, a particular pattern of social arrangements governed by principles of fairness. Order and justice then are not simply social arrangements, they are also values or ideals which political actors seek to institutionalize. A central question in much international relations theory has been the relationship between these two values. Should one be given priority over the other? Is it possible to strike a balance between them? Are they compatible social goods? Two powerful assumptions have guided thought about the relationship between order and justice. One is that order is a precondition of justice and various other social goals. The other is that the pursuit of justice in international relations can be radically disruptive of international order. This is illustrated by the Roman adage that justice should be done even though the world may perish.

However, the assumption that order and justice are mutually exclusive values or social arrangements has been challenged on the grounds that no order can expect to endure long without delivering some degree of justice. By rejecting the notion that order and justice are mutually exclusive, it becomes possible to pose normative as opposed to merely empirical questions about order. Who benefits from the particular order that prevails? Is the extant order compatible with the political community's espoused moral and political values? Does the prevailing order unjustly exclude the weak and vulnerable? We shall return to the question of who benefits below. For the moment, it is important to understand why order has long been perceived as a political virtue.

Why is order important?

Order has long been a chief preoccupation in the history of political thought. At least since the Ancient Greeks, ways of warding off chaos and disorder have been integral to political thought and practice. That so much attention is paid to the foundations of states and their constitutional arrangements is testament to the centrality of order in the history of political thought.

The great Florentine diplomat and writer Niccoló Machiavelli (1469–1527) devoted much of his most famous book *The Prince* (1532) to the establishment of firm foundations of princely rule. Foundations were equally significant in his *Discourses* (1531). For Machiavelli a well ordered political society was a republic wherein liberty is secured for itself and its citizens under the rule of law and through a mixed government combining ruler, aristocracy and people. In his eyes, Rome was the perfect republic because it allowed the three constituent parts of society (the ruler, the aristocracy and the people) to keep a check on each other. The republican mode of ordering the state was, for Machiavelli, a structural precondition of a free citizenry and achievement of the common good. It meant that conflict, while impossible to eliminate, could at least be managed and regulated in ways conducive to a dynamic social order. The constitutional arrangements Machiavelli envisaged for the republic were intended to stave off disorder by moderating conflict, reducing the frequency of violence and developing habits of civility in public life. These were crucial not just in ensuring that internal conflict would never destroy the state, but also in making the state secure against external attack.

Thomas Hobbes (1588–1679) was also prompted by a concern to stem disorder. In the face of civil wars and religious conflict, he believed that only the centralization of legal and political **authority** could neutralize conflict and secure domestic peace. The sovereign would be a supreme political authority with the right to lay down and enforce the law as a means of maintaining social order and providing security to individuals. Political and social order, therefore, were a product of the sovereign's ability to institute and maintain the law, that is, a system of rules. In the absence of the sovereign's enforcement capacity, Hobbes argued, it makes no sense to speak of law, or, by implication, order.

The arguments of Machiavelli and Hobbes were almost exclusively concerned with political order inside states. Little of their attention was directed at order among states. One of the first thinkers to systematically address the question of international order was the Dutch jurist Hugo Grotius (1583–1645). Like other early modern thinkers Grotius was disturbed by the way European rulers rushed to **war**, often on flimsy pretexts. This was, after all, a period in European history when civil and transnational religious wars were closely linked to **state formation**. He believed there was a lack of restraint on the exercise of violence, which made order within and between states precarious. To remedy the situation Grotius elaborated rules governing the external conduct of sovereign states, including rules relating to warfare.

Grotius's work lends itself to many different interpretations. In his texts, one can find arguments for restraint alongside numerous justifications for the use of force, particularly in connection with causes that furthered the commercial expansion of his native United Provinces in the East Indies. From the perspective of contemporary International Relations, what is important about Grotius is the manner in which his ideas were taken up and adapted by scholars known as the **English School**. The most important of these is the argument that order is a necessary condition for the realization of other human values. In its absence, the achievement of individual and community goals would be greatly limited.

To achieve a stable order, Grotius argued, violence has to be strictly regulated and restricted. This is as true for relations between states as it is for relations within them. It is important to note that adherents of the Grotian tradition are not opposed to war *per se*; in fact, they recognize that limited war can be an important instrument for defending or restoring international order. The pertinent point to recognize here is that despite appearances, war, like other social activities, is rule governed. War occurs in a rule governed context that establishes the grounds for its legitimate conduct (jus in bello) and purpose (jus ad bellum). This set of legal and moral rules is generally known as the **Just War** tradition and is the product of custom and established state practice.

For all three thinkers – Machiavelli, Hobbes and Grotius – order is a precondition of social existence. Without sustained patterns of social arrangements other social, political, economic or cultural needs and desires cannot be met. Order therefore is essential to securing the particular goods and values that societies seek to obtain for themselves, including, liberty, equality, and justice.

Rules and international order

Grotius' work provided the kernel of three important arguments about order that were taken up by later International Relations scholars, including Hedley Bull (1932–85), author of *The Anarchical Society* (1977) and a leading member of the English School. First, order, whether domestic or international, requires rules, though not perhaps a sovereign rule maker. By rejecting what he termed the 'domestic analogy', Bull prepared the ground for imagining, *contra* Hobbes, society without government and order without an orderer.

From this counter-intuitive notion it became possible to think of states forming a society among themselves. This is the second Grotian idea picked up by later international relations theorists. It led Bull and others to elaborate the common consciousness, rules and institutions that bind states loosely together, forming them into an **international society** and committing them to international order.

The third idea is that within this society of states, all sovereigns are the bearers of both rights and duties that ought to be respected. In the three hundred years that intervened between Grotius and the revival of his thinking in International Relations, the content of these rights and duties has changed but the basis of the argument has remained largely unchanged: namely, that all social orders, including primitive ones, rest on certain elementary or primary rules. These primary rules set limits on the conduct of individuals and states, specifying acceptable and unacceptable conduct; they are thought to include: restrictions on violence, respect for property, and honesty and trust.

At the level of international society, these primary rules correspond to the just war, respect for territorial sovereignty, and the principle of *pacta sunt servanda* (treaties must be observed). They are instrumental in providing a set of minimal conditions that allow states to live alongside one another, and make up what Bull calls the 'rules of coexistence'. To illustrate the nature and purpose of these rules, it is useful to invoke the analogy of an egg carton. Rules of coexistence function rather like an egg carton in that they separate and cushion sovereign states (or eggs), thereby enabling them to orient their actions toward mutual respect and toleration.

According to Bull and others, in international society order is a pattern of social relations that sustains the following functional goals. First, the preservation of the **international system** itself. Historically, the preservation of a system of sovereign states, each state having its own distinct cultural and political traditions, has often been beset by attempts to build universal **empire**s. From Alexander the Great and the Roman Emperors to Napoleon and Hitler, imperial ambitions have been held in check, often at a very high price in terms of the sacrifices made by troops fighting in counter-hegemonic wars. Through the **balance of power** and counter-hegemonic wars the system has resisted being transformed into a universal empire.

The second goal is the preservation of the **sovereignty** or constitutional independence of the members. All states have something to be gained from being part of a wider society. Their claim to exclusive jurisdiction over their territory and people is predicated on extending this right to other members. In this respect, ideas of mutual **recognition** and

reciprocity are built into the fabric of international society.

Security is the third goal of international society. As noted previously, this is not to be equated with peace, as states not only have a right to use force in self-defense, they may be required to participate in collective enforcement action against an aggressor (be this a state or a non-state actor). Aside from this narrowly circumscribed range of justifications, states must accept restrictions on the use of force and search for other means of resolving conflicts of interest. Since World War Two force is deemed legitimate only when it is used in self-defense or when authorized by the **United Nations** Security Council.

Bull's thinking on order is significant because of its normative content. Achieving these goals requires states to recognize a common set of rules and to believe their fates to be intertwined. It is the cooperative basis of international order that sets modern inter-state relations apart from previous systems in which the parts of the whole were connected in the absence of common rules and institutions. There is a further sense in which Bull's thinking on order is normative. The order established by states is only to be valued if it reflects global concerns about justice. The question of order, in the last instance, cannot be separated from the development of cosmopolitan ethical sensibilities (see **cosmopolitanism**) and the pursuit of a just world order.

How is order maintained?

Order, for Bull and the classical realists (see **realism**), is contrived. It is the daily responsibility of state leaders and diplomats to nurture and tend to its requirements. The international system is preserved and order maintained through **diplomacy** and the contrivance of the balance of power. The balance of power is a particularly important mechanism that operates through **alliance** formation, vigilant monitoring of threatening states, the delicate adjustments of **power** to power and the occasional resort to arms.

At about the same time that Bull published his study of order, Kenneth Waltz was writing a very different account of order in his classic work *Theory of International Politics* (1979). There is a logic of balancing in the international system, Waltz argues, whereby a growing preponderance of power in any one state will trigger the rise of countervailing powers or alliances, but the balance of power results from the spontaneous interactions of self-regarding units, not from contrivance. Waltz's belief in an automatic balancing mechanism is therefore at odds with a powerful strand of classical realist thought that emphasizes the deliberate construction of order out of **anarchy**. To examine the motives of any single actor, such as asking the question whether they behaved in such a way as to strengthen the balance of power, is to mistake the features of the system for the identity of the units. All we need to know, according to Waltz, is that states are **security** seekers, and in pursuit of this primordial goal, their behavior will generate patterns that correspond to different kinds of systemic order.

Many other realists believe, following Hobbes, that order depends on hierarchy and leadership; that is to say, an effective rule enforcer. This leads them to focus on hegemonic stability (see **hegemonic stability theory**) or the **concert of powers** as important mechanisms. For example, the international orders of *pax Britannica* or *pax Americana* are thought to be evidence that global rules, regimes, and institutions depend on the presence of a single dominant power willing to act as founder and custodian. Similarly, under certain historical circumstances, order can be the product of a central coalition of **great powers** managing international affairs, as in the Concert of Europe after the Napoleonic wars in the nineteenth century.

Hegemonic stability theory is an argument that contemporary realists have put forward to explain how order emerges in the international political economy. Rather than balancing against an external threat, as realism predicts that states will do in the security sphere, in the field of trade and finance it is in the interests of great powers to provide hegemonic leadership. Underlying this argument is a theory about the relationship between economic interests and the provision of **international public goods**. To establish the conditions of a trading system that maximizes the hegemonic state's power and influence, it must bear the burdens associated with it. This may include investing in weaker economies abroad and providing financial stability to the world trading system, both of which might be counter to the short-run interests of the state in question. It also requires a complex set of interstate bargains in order to persuade, cajole or force others to join in.

Liberal institutionalists agree with the claim that hegemonic states can bring stability to the system although they disagree with the explanation offered by neorealists for this outcome. Hegemonic states are not solely motivated by the prospect of their own gains so much as the optimal institutional order for all the players in the game. For an example of the working out of such a strategy in practice, we need look no further than the success of the liberal **hegemony** of the post-1945 era. In the aftermath of World War Two, the United States took the opportunity to 'embed' certain fundamental liberal principles into the regulatory rules and institutions of international society. Most importantly, and contrary to realist thinking, the United States chose to forsake short-term gains in return for a durable settlement that benefited all states. Central to this strategy was the creation of a range of important international institutions that constrained not only the actions of other states but also crucially that of the hegemon. The **Bretton Woods** systems of economic and financial accords, and the NATO security alliance (see **North Atlantic Treaty Organization**), are the best examples of the highly institutionalized character of American power in the post-1945 period. Advocates of this liberal hegemonic order note wryly that it was so successful that allies were more worried about abandonment than domination.

Therefore, for liberal institutionalists, order in the international political economy requires a cooperative arrangement that is codified by **regime**s and institutions. Such a position chimes with an English School account of order, outlined in broad terms above, although there are important differences. Liberal institutionalism is premised on a rational actor model of state behavior. On this logic, institutions provide incentives for states to cooperate as they increase transparency, pool information, and reduce transaction costs. Set against a cost-benefit interpretation of institutions, the English School, by contrast, argues that players in a game follow rules because it makes sense to them to do so. Rule compliance cannot be reduced to simple cost-benefit analyses. Compliance is certainly affected by cost-benefit analysis, but the factors included in such an analysis include several intangibles including reputation, recognition of the benefits issuing from international order, and an understanding that rules help constitute the very identity of states as sovereign entities.

Not only does the English School offer a more contextual account of how cooperation emerges, its view of institutions is much broader. While liberal institutionalists view institutions as a recent invention, the English School argues that practices such as diplomacy, **international law**, and great power coalitions have long been crucial to the management of international order. One of the drawbacks with this more historical approach is the lack of clarity in the relationship between order and society. Is the former a precondition for the latter or a consequence of it?

Despite the existence of ambiguities in the English School account of order, it is important to recognize that its view of institutions is not premised on a rational design approach. Institutions – of which **sovereignty** is perhaps the most important – are social facts external to all the actors but internalized by each. They are often reproduced 'blindly' without the actors' conscious awareness of the ongoing practice. One under-explored dimension of the constitutive nature of international order's institutions is the extent to which they are durable only in the presence of a common (or at least, converging) culture.

Another vitally important set of questions left unexamined by the English School pertains to the interaction between the international system and social forces. It should not be assumed that the visible pattern of order among states is the only or the most important pattern. Social and economic patterns also exist that shape international order. Robert Cox (1987), following a broadly Marxist approach (see **Marxism**), has argued that patterns of order at the global level cannot be properly understood without accounting for the changing modes of production and their impact on forms of state (whether mercantilist (see **mercantilism**), liberal, Keynesian, capitalist (see **capitalism**), and so on). The prevailing order among states is always a product of deeper social forces that have the capacity to reshape dominant modes of statehood. Cox is drawn to patterns not perceived by realism, liberalism or the English School, patterns of social and material production that affect the relationship between state and society and sustain prevailing forms of international economic order.

Thinking about order has also been shaped by more normative theoretical approaches that have critically analyzed the prevailing order's capacity to deliver security, **development**, democracy, peace or justice. Indeed, they have questioned the conventional meaning of these terms and for whom they are pursued. In the struggles to achieve a global order more reflective of these goals, identifying patterns of inclusion and exclusion has become central to the more radical approaches to the study of order. The writings of R. B. J. Walker (1988) and Andrew Linklater (1988), among others, have focused attention on the forms of exclusion that are built into the modern state, sustaining an international order that impedes progress toward a just world peace and cosmopolitan global order.

Threats to order

International orders, like all orders, are established against threats. They are intended to contain or hold at bay threats to sustained patterns of social arrangements and the social goods associated with them. Naturally, the character of threats changes according to time and place, and there are different intensities and sources of threat. However, there are some general propositions we can make about threats to order.

To begin with, we can say that international order is threatened when the functional goals sustaining international order come under attack. Tilts at universal empire, for example, constitute a threat to international order's first functional goal, the preservation of the international system. As already noted, throughout international history there have been several failed attempts to transform the system into a universal empire, but these have been defeated by counter-hegemonic alliances and balances of power.

A more historically familiar threat to international order takes the form of violent conduct against another sovereign state. Acts of aggression, invasion and occupation are an enduring feature of international relations, but they are also commonly seen as threats to international order because they attack the rights of sovereign states, undermining the functional goal of preserving the constitutional independence of international society's members. The rule of non-intervention, which prohibits coercive interference in the domestic affairs of states and is enshrined in the United Nations Charter under article 2.7, is the formal codification of the goal of maintaining states' independence. However, several instances in international history demonstrate that great powers are sometimes willing to sacrifice individual states for the perceived greater good of international order. Two prominent examples where the rights of sovereign states have been forfeited are the several partitions of Poland in the eighteenth century and Italy's 1935 invasion of Abyssinia. As these two examples would suggest, how the great powers interpret and maintain international order can precipitate resentment – and potentially revolt – among weaker or aggrieved states.

Order may also be threatened, therefore, by those dissatisfied with the status quo. Revolutionary France in the late eighteenth century, for example, chal-lenged the international order supported by Europe's *anciens régimes*. An alternative form of dissatisfaction with the status quo stems from those who feel exploited by the prevailing pattern of social arrangements or excluded from its social goods. Dissatisfied or aggrieved states may see the extant international order as unequal and serving the interests of the powerful at the expense of the weak.

The inequalities built into international society are in many respects the historical legacy of European practices of conquest and colonization from the fifteenth to the nineteenth century. During this period, two sets of rules and two orders existed simultaneously. Within the European society of states, a particular pattern of relations emerged around rules of coexistence and legal equality. The unique order produced inside Europe was not, however, replicated in Europe's dealings with outsiders. Different rules applied in Europe's relations with the extra-European world producing a more hierarchical or imperial order which served to legitimize the dispossession of indigenous peoples often under the aegis of the **standard of civilization**. Many of these entrenched inequalities remained in place until the middle of the twentieth century when **Third World** demands for justice in international relations surged. The demands made by decolonized Asian, African, and Latin American countries were based on a rejection of the dominant patterns of wealth and power distribution: in Bull's words, these calls for change amounted to a 'revolt against the West', or, more specifically, a revolt against Western dominance in international society. Among other demands, the Third World called for racial equality, economic fairness, national **self-determination** and cultural freedom.

The revolt against the West showed that the international order that had developed in the twentieth century, like any order, was by no means neutral. Rather, it produced global patterns of inequality and injustice. Uneven access to international public goods meant that hunger, malnutrition, and disease continued to grow in areas outside the **zones of peace**. The fact that international order could be sustained in the face of such widespread human suffering highlighted the tension between order and justice. Is it right to maintain an international order where a majority of the planet's population live in abject poverty? Is it more vital to maintain order among states than it is to deliver basic material needs and human security to the planet's population? These questions have generated further questions about the moral **legitimacy** of international order's privileging of state sovereignty and non-intervention, not least when states hide behind sovereignty to rationalize mass violence against their own citizens, or when state power and authority collapse, recreating a Hobbesian state of nature.

A further threat to international order derives from the existence of **failed state**s. When states lose the capacity to exercise power and authority over their territory, economic turmoil and political violence are the inevitable consequence. Whatever their causes may be, failed states represent a threat to international order because states are the principal building blocks of international order. When states break down various forms of disorder seem to flourish, from **ethnic cleansing** and **genocide** to 'warlordism' and **terrorism**.

A final threat to consider comes from non-state forms of violence. From piracy and privateering in early modern times to global terrorist networks in the twenty-first century, international order has long encountered 'private international violence'. Non-state violence poses a threat to international order because it challenges the state's monopoly over the legitimate instruments of violence. Moreover, it challenges international society's rules and institutions, especially those related to coexistence and the peaceful resolution of conflict. This is especially the case with the advent of global terrorist networks, where the violent interruption of everyday international life and the spreading of fear and mistrust places great strain on coexistence and cooperation.

Disorder, whether in the form of uncontrollable impersonal forces, like the crises of the world economy, or disaffected actors, like revolutionary states or terrorist groups, always looms as a threat to the prevailing order. The capacity of the institutions of international society to endure, in the face of new threats, in part depends on the degree of solidarity among the members and the strength of their commitment to the status quo. Where there is a disagreement over the prevailing framework of rules and institutions, the likely consequence will be disorder or the emergence of a new order. Conversely, external shocks will be absorbed when there is a consensus on the need to re-establish the enabling conditions of the previous order.

Conclusion

The search for order has, down the ages, been an elusive quest embarked upon by many leaders, advisors, and thinkers. As difficult as it might be to achieve order, it remains a constant desire in political life. David Hume (1711–76) appears to have been right in saying that the same love of order which urges humans to arrange books neatly in a library, drives the human search for well ordered political societies.

While a minority have believed there to be a natural quality to order, most have believed that it is contrived and something that needs to be managed. Admitting that order is constructed soon opens up into a broader issue about the normative value of a particular institutional arrangement. How are we to measure the success of one form of order over another? All orders produce winners and losers, or at least an unequal distribution of gains and losses. Does that mean that order is necessarily partial?

Our discussion of order has brought to the fore Hedley Bull's account in part because he believed that order was not only contrived but it was also a condition of social existence. Nevertheless, Bull was aware that no particular order guarantees justice, an equally vital political value. What made an order just was whether it provided for the possibility of reaching world order values such as **human rights**, **sustainable development** and a fairer world economy. Bull recognized, like many radical writers today, that international order often failed in these respects. Far from delivering the conditions for a just world order, the rules and institutions of contemporary international society often deny basic rights to billions of the world's inhabitants. International order, it may therefore be concluded, is always a sustained pattern of social exclusion. As Bull also recognized, such orders are likely to remain unstable as well as unjust.

Further reading

Bull, H. (1995) *The Anarchical Society: A Study of Order in World Politics*, 2nd edn, Basingstoke: Palgrave.

Bull, H. (1984) *Justice and International Relations, The Hagey Lectures*, Ontario: University of Waterloo.

Cox, R. W. (1987) *Power, Production and World Order: Social Forces in the Making of History*, New York: Columbia University Press.

Dunne, T. (1998) *Inventing International Society: A History of the English School*, Basingstoke: Macmillan.

Keene. E. (2002) *Beyond the Anarchical Society: Grotius, Colonialism and Order in World Politics*, Cambridge: Cambridge University Press.

Linklater, A. (1998) *The Transformation of Political Community: Ethical Foundations of the Post-Westphalian Era*, Cambridge: Polity Press.

Paul, T. V. and Hall, J. A. (eds) (1999) *International Order and the Future of World Politics*, Cambridge: Cambridge University Press

Suganami, H. (1989) *The Domestic Analogy and World Order Proposals*, Cambridge: Cambridge University Press.

Walker, R. B. J. (1988) *One World, Many Worlds: Struggles for a Just World Peace*, Boulder, CO: Lynne Rienner.

Waltz, K. (1979) *Theory of International Politics*, Reading, Mass: Addison Wesley.

See also: anarchy; authority; balance of power; concert of powers; English School; global governance; hegemonic stability theory; hegemony; international society; legitimacy; power; sovereignty; war

RICHARD DEVETAK and TIM DUNNE

Organization for Economic Cooperation and Development (OECD)

An international organization that exists to advance the economic interests and societal **development** of its member countries. The thirty member states represent the world's most industrialized countries. To advance the capitalist system (see **capitalism**) and to promote policy development that will facilitate macroeconomic growth, the OECD also engages in extensive outreach to non-member countries.

The Organization for European Economic Cooperation (OEEC) was the precursor to the OECD, established in 1948 to administer Marshall Plan funds for the reconstruction of Europe after World War Two. The core principles of the OEEC laid the seeds for the European Economic Community (EEC) and the **European Union** (EU). These principles included the development of intra-European trade through the reduction of tariffs, the creation of a European **free trade** area, and the efficient utilization of labor.

In September 1961, the OEEC was replaced by the OECD, consisting of the 18 European OEEC countries, plus the United States and Canada. By 1973, the number of member countries had grown to 24, with Japan, Australia and New Zealand broadening the OECD's geographic representation. Membership remained static until 1994, when Mexico became the first (and to date only) Latin American member state. A further five countries joined by 2000, four of which are European.

In common with other international organizations, each member pays an annual subscription, calculated on the basis of a formula related to the size of its economy. These are known as Part I contributions. The United States and Japan contribute nearly half of the Part I budget.

The OECD's mandate is managed through two intersecting processes. First, the OECD is involved in rule making. This includes legally binding agreements and non-binding guidelines or codes of practice. Existing across diverse fields, examples include Codes of fiscal liberalization, the Convention on Combating Bribery, and a 'Scheme' to apply international standards to trade in fruit and vegetables.

Second, the OECD member states seek solutions to common problems. This is enacted through 'peer learning' and 'peer influencing'. As an organization consisting of members at relatively similar stages of development, and often facing similar economic and social challenges, much work is devoted to peer learning in the form of international comparative studies. Two aims of this research and analytical work are to review divergent policy practice, and to suggest practical solutions that member countries can modify to their own national context. The OECD's comparative statistics and analytical reports are highly respected, and are frequently cited by government agencies, the private sector, and **non-governmental organization**s.

Peer influencing is crucial to the functionality of the organization. The OECD Convention asserts that all decisions must be reached by consensus, and therefore any single member may exert a veto. For this reason, peer influencing – negotiated outcomes – shapes much of the OECD's budget preparation and its program of work.

The OECD's work is organized by committee, with a permanent Secretariat (based in Paris) facilitating activities and managing much of the analytical work. With an annual budget in excess of US$200 million, the Organization's 200 committees cover topics ranging from trade policy to education, from science and technology to public governance.

The OECD is giving serious consideration to further enlargement. The OECD Convention places no limit on the number of member states, but the accession process is rigorous. Prospective members must demonstrate a commitment to an open market economy, democratic governance, and **human rights**. In general practice, prospective members act as observers to a range of committees, sometimes for years, prior to commencing the accession process.

In July 2004, the OECD embarked on an historic experiment. Breaking away from the consensus decision-making model, the OECD Council (its highest body) allowed the introduction of voting. For a decision to be passed, it requires the assent of 60 per cent of member countries, and cannot be opposed by three or more members that collectively contribute at least one quarter of the Part I budget.

There are two outcomes of this two-step voting system. First, the United States and Japan have been given virtual veto power. Each contributes nearly a quarter of the budget, and therefore each would only need the support of two further members to block any decision. Second, a European voting block could direct the Organization. Representing 76 per cent of the membership, European (and EU) preferences could become decisive.

For these reasons, any enlargement of the Organization has a sharpened geo-political edge. With the expansion of the EU from fifteen to twenty-five members in 2004, there are concerns that OECD enlargement does not further over-represent European members within the Organization. Therefore, in addition to the existing tests for membership, other factors that might be taken into consideration include the degree to which the country is influential at the global level, that the country has a like-minded approach to world affairs, and that the country will bring greater geographic diversity to the OECD.

While the OECD has no aspirations to become an Organization with universal membership (such as the **United Nations**), it is worth noting that in the mid-2000s there were only two member countries from Asia – Japan and South Korea. There were also no members from Africa, the Middle East, or South America. The OECD membership underlines the nature of wealth concentration, the status of democratic governance, and the relative stages of industrialization among the world's continents.

Further reading

Blair, D. (1993) *Trade Negotiations in the OECD*, London: Kegan Paul International.
Lawrence, R. (1996) *Single World, Divided Nations? International Trade and the OECD Labor Markets*, Washington, DC: Brookings.

See also: development; World Bank; World Trade Organization

DAVID COLEMAN

Organization for Security and Cooperation in Europe (OSCE)

The Organization for Security and Cooperation in Europe (OSCE) is a unique security organization. Although pan-European, it includes the North American states. Its focus is also very clearly on both the military and non-military aspects of security. It is arguably the key instrument in Europe for the early warning of conflicts, for conflict prevention and for post-conflict rebuilding. Its approach is both comprehensive (it addresses the broad aspects of security, including human security, politico-military security, and economic/environmental security) and cooperative (all states participate on an equal footing, with politically binding decisions in almost all cases taken by consensus). As an evolving organization, the OSCE is making an important contribution to the creation of a stable, democratic, and peaceful Europe.

The OSCE had its origins in the 1975 Helsinki Final Act, a document produced by the (then called) Conference on Security and Cooperation in Europe

(CSCE). The CSCE process itself had been in gestation since the 1950s, when the Soviet Union had started its calls for a pan-European security conference. On the clear understanding that they would not concede to the Soviet Union any legal recognition of the division of Europe, West European states, the United States and Canada eventually agreed to commence discussions with the Soviet bloc in 1972 in Helsinki. This meeting, which continued until August 1975, produced the Helsinki Final Act and launched the CSCE (or Helsinki) process.

Importantly, the provisions of the Final Act would come to have great relevance for European security in the post-**cold war** era. It contained agreements covering military and non-military dimensions of security, including ten principles designed to govern relations between participating states. These principles reaffirmed, *inter alia*, the peaceful resolution of disputes, the inviolability of state borders (but also specified that borders could be changed by peaceful means and with the consent of those involved, thus denying Moscow a formal recognition of the division of Europe) and respect for **human rights** and fundamental freedoms. This latter issue was pursued by the Western states and was to become central to the CSCE and the OSCE. The military dimensions of security included a series of **confidence and security building measures**, designed to ease the fear of unpredictable military threats. The Final Act also provided a framework for cooperation in economic, scientific, technical, and environmental affairs, and detailed specific human rights and humanitarian issues. It also provided for a Follow Up mechanism to ensure that compliance with provisions would be monitored and that the process would be an ongoing forum.

With the completion of the Final Act, the CSCE became a central reference point for an ongoing process of multilateral **diplomacy** providing a broad agenda and operational framework for East–West dialogue. Subsequent meetings were marked by acrimony but the advent of Mikhail Gorbachev to the leadership of the Soviet Union, and his clear commitment to the Helsinki process in the late 1980s, enabled the organization to reach agreement on a number of important issues, including human rights and negotiations for the reduction of conventional forces in Europe. The ending of the cold war was symbolized by the CSCE Charter of Paris for a New Europe, signed by all participant states in 1990.

With its broad membership, the organization was the logical forum for forging new relations between Atlantic, West European, East European, Central Asian states, and the new Russia. Many of the features associated with establishing European security in the post-cold war era – such as the articulation of norms and the promotion of **good governance** and human rights, together with practices of confidence building, regular dialogue and review, and the peaceful resolution of disputes – were already well established in the Helsinki process. The organization had been one of the very first expressly to link human rights and security and to establish processes of accountability and compliance with humanitarian norms, practices which eventually came to be emulated by other multilateral institutions. These elements were to be called on extensively as members sought to transform European political and security relations after the cold war.

The CSCE had been institutionalized in 1990 with a Secretariat in Prague, an Office for Democratic Institutions and Human Rights (ODIHR) in Warsaw, and the Conflict Prevention Center (CPC) in Vienna. A Follow Up meeting in Helsinki in 1992 further developed the organization's capacities for conflict prevention and the peaceful settlement of disputes, and established a High Commissioner for National Minorities, all seen as necessary in the evolving climate of inter-ethnic hostility and **civil war** in Yugoslavia facing Europe by this time. Various meetings continued to be held throughout the 1990s, including at Budapest in 1994, where the institution agreed to change its name to the OSCE, and at Istanbul in 1999 where a new Charter for European Security was adopted.

The OSCE conducts a number of interrelated practical activities designed to facilitate democratic political processes, to prevent or resolve conflicts, to promote civil society and to reinforce the rule of law in member states. These activities include early warning mechanisms (particularly with regard to ethnic conflict), protection of minorities through technical assistance with constitutional and other processes, monitoring and verification of elections, and the deployment of peacekeepers. Field operations have been undertaken in Southeast Europe, the Caucasus, Eastern Europe, and Central Asia; in 2003 some nineteen missions were underway. Additionally, the OSCE remains a primary instrument for conventional **arms control** and the expansion of confidence and security building mechanisms in Europe, all designed to provide strategic reassurance among member states.

The OSCE's primary decision-making body, located in Vienna, is the Permanent Council, comprising representatives from each of the member states (in 2003, the organization had fifty-five member states). A Chairman-in-Office (Foreign Minister of the state currently holding Chairmanship of the Permanent Council) assisted by past and future Chairs and the OSCE Secretary General from the Secretariat (also located in Vienna), has

responsibility for executive decisions. Annual Ministerial Councils are held, involving the Foreign Ministers of member states and/or Heads of Government. In addition to the Secretariat, the ODIHR and the CPC mentioned above, the OSCE also includes in its functional structure the Office of the High Commissioner on National Minorities (located in The Hague), the Office of the Representative on Freedom of the Media (located in Vienna), and the Court of Conciliation and Arbitration (located in Geneva). A separate body, the OSCE Parliamentary Assembly comprising over 300 representatives is based in Copenhagen.

The OSCE's role is an immensely broad one. What started as a conference designed to alleviate political and military tensions in a divided Europe during the cold war has evolved into a mechanism for creating a broad European **security** community. It has not been entirely successful; the failure of the organization to prevent or contain the conflicts in the former Yugoslavia and other regions of Europe reveals the ongoing difficulty of knitting together a diverse region whose history is marked by military and political conflict. Moreover, the organization, unlike NATO (see **North Atlantic Treaty Organization**), also concerned with European security, has no military capabilities of its own. Indeed the OSCE works closely with NATO, the **European Union**, the Council of Europe and the **United Nations** to pursue security in Europe. Without the possession of material incentives or the threat of military force, the OSCE has relied essentially on strengthening norms and fostering a climate of compliance with these norms through ongoing dialogue and intrusive monitoring measures. Its strength lies in its linking of both traditional and new security issues and its ability to establish, over time, a collective identity that leads to expectations of peaceful relations between member states. It has, over a period of almost three decades, helped to build a code of conduct for inter- and intra-state relations in Europe. Despite its failures therefore, it must be judged on its long-term contribution and the potential it carries for strengthening peaceful relations in Europe.

Further reading

Adler, E, (1998) 'Seeds of Peaceful Change: the OSCE's Security Community Building Model', in E. Adler and M. Barnett (eds) *Security Communities*, Cambridge: Cambridge University Press, 118–60.

Bothe, M., Ronzitti, N. and Rosas, A. (1997) *The OSCE in the Maintenance of Peace and Security*, London: Kluwer Law International.

Freire, M. R. (2003) *Conflict and Security in the Former Soviet Union: The Role of the OSCE*, Aldershot: Ashgate.

Sabahi, F. and Warner, D. (eds) (2004) *The OSCE and the Multiple Challenges of Transition*, Aldershot: Ashgate.

See also: collective security; European Union; peace-building

MARIANNE HANSON

Organization of Petroleum Exporting Countries (OPEC)

The Organization of Petroleum Exporting Countries (OPEC) is probably the best-known example of an international cartel, even though the diamond trade is more successfully controlled. A cartel is a national or international organization of producers who act in concert to fix prices, limit supply, divide markets, or set quotas. The cartel seeks maximum profits by driving out competition and by limiting production in times of over-supply. Cartels are usually criticized for eliminating the price benefits of competition. Their defenders argue that they distribute risks, stabilize markets, and protect weak members. Cartels often fail because member firms or states deviate from the rules of the cartel to serve their own interests.

OPEC was formed at a conference held in Baghdad in September 1960. There were five original members: Iran, Iraq, Kuwait, Saudi Arabia, and Venezuela. Between 1960 and 1975, the organization expanded to thirteen members with the addition of Qatar, Indonesia, Libya, United Arab Emirates, Algeria, Nigeria, Ecuador, and Gabon. Currently, OPEC consists of eleven member states (Ecuador dropped out in 1992 and Gabon withdrew in 1995), of which Saudi Arabia is the most powerful.

OPEC was set up to help unify and coordinate members' petroleum policies and to safeguard their interests. Among other activities, OPEC holds regular meetings of national oil ministers to discuss prices and, since the early 1980s, to set production quotas. OPEC also provides some financial assistance to developing countries through its OPEC Fund for International Development (founded in 1976), and conducts research on such topics as energy finance, technology, and relevant economic issues. The countries that make up OPEC produce about 40 per cent of the world's oil and hold more than 77 per cent of the world's proven oil reserves. OPEC also contains most of the world's excess oil production capacity.

It should be noted that OPEC did not establish the oil cartel. It simply took over an existing one. Before 1960, the 'seven sisters' (seven major oil companies including BP, Esso, Shell, Gulf and Mobil) controlled the price of oil. They worked together as an organized cartel controlling exploration, production, transportation, marketing and refining. During the 1960s, OPEC was unable to sustain the high oil prices of the 1950s. There were deep divisions between member states, and they often refused to respect quota resolutions. For example, Kuwait had a very low production rate so it demanded high quotas. On the other hand, Venezuela had a very high production rate that was being sold very cheaply, hence it demanded low quotas to increase the price of oil. By 1970 OPEC was merely a group of weak partners that depended heavily on income from oil, but could not create a cohesive policy.

In the early 1970s, however, the situation changed. In 1969 the American backed Libyan Government was overthrown by a military regime led by Colonel Gadaffi. He stopped the high production of Libyan oil. Moreover, Libya stopped trading with the major oil companies. Other countries followed the Libyan example. More importantly, the 1973 Arab–Israeli War finally led to an agreement among OPEC member states to reduce oil exports to countries that supported Israel. In 1973 exports were reduced by 50 per cent. In addition the price of oil rocketed, contributing to the widespread recession of the 1970s that also damaged the economies of non-oil exporting states in the **Third World**.

OPEC began to lose control of the price of oil in the late 1970s. For instance, responding to the oil shocks of the era, states began to conserve energy and use it more efficiently. Moreover they began to rely upon alternative energy sources. In Japan, the share of oil in total primary energy consumption fell by 23 per cent between 1973 and 1996, while the share of natural gas and nuclear energy increased by more than 10 and 14 per cent respectively. Recently, international environmental initiatives to cut carbon emissions and control **global warming** have accelerated this trend.

An expanding global oil supply has also reduced OPEC's **power**. During the 1970s, the OPEC countries took control of their oil industries and nationalized the foreign oil companies' operations on their soil. Deprived of the opportunity to invest in most of the OPEC countries, the major oil companies looked for opportunities in states such as Norway and the United Kingdom. As a result, OPEC's oil now accounts for only 26 per cent of the world's energy requirements outside the former Soviet Union and the United States, compared with 56 per cent twenty years ago. Oil ventures in the Central Asian states of the former Soviet Union will expand global sources of oil for the industrialized world.

Recent technological innovations have also played a role in increasing oil stocks. The expense and risk associated with finding and developing oil in difficult places has been reduced, as has the time it takes for oil to be brought onstream and produced. The revolution in oil technology has significantly expanded output among non-OPEC producers, most notably in the North Sea, the US side of the Gulf of Mexico, and off the shore of West Africa.

There is perhaps no better indicator of how much times have changed than the differing impacts of the two wars in the Persian Gulf. The Iranian crisis in 1979 and the Iran–Iraq War in 1980 created an oil shortage that proved to be a financial windfall for OPEC. But the aftershocks from the 1991 Gulf War have emerged as a mixed blessing. On the one hand, sanctions imposed on Iraq between 1991 and 2004 kept a major producer off the market. On the other hand, the **war** and its aftermath led to financial difficulties for both Kuwait and Saudi Arabia in spite of the latter's financial gain from the Iraqi embargo. Saudi oil replaced Iraq's oil market share by almost 80 per cent, in effect doubling its income. However, the extravagant spending and lavish subsidies bestowed on Kuwaiti and Saudi citizens, together with weapons purchases from the United States have helped to drain their coffers.

Nonetheless, the future is not bleak for OPEC. According to recent forecasts, global primary energy demand is expected to climb by 50 per cent by the year 2010, with fossil fuels still accounting for nearly 90 per cent of that consumption. Asian countries alone will account for 44 per cent of that increased demand, and present OPEC with a potential market opportunity, particularly if China continues to grow at an average rate of 8–9 per cent per year. Also, whilst many states have reduced their dependence on oil imports, the United States has increased its reliance on oil from the Middle East.

Further reading

Amuzegar, J. (2001) *Managing the Oil Wealth: OPEC's Windfalls and Pitfalls*, 2nd edn, London: I. B. Tauris.

Claes, D. (2000) *The Politics of Oil Producer Cooperation*, Boulder, CO: Westview.

See also: debt trap

MARTIN GRIFFITHS

Ozone depletion

A reduction in the concentration of atmospheric ozone, accelerated by anthropogenic emissions of Ozone Depleting Substances (ODS), most notably **chlorofluorocarbons (CFCs)**. Left unmarked, removal of the protective ozone layer would result in harmful increases in ultraviolet radiation at the Earth's surface. Recognition of this fact and increased understanding of the depletion mechanisms has resulted in the successful multilateral control of this potentially significant global environmental problem.

Ozone gas is a molecule with three oxygen atoms (O_3) and is the poisonous cousin of oxygen (O_2). It is concentrated approximately 19 to 30 kilometers above the Earth's surface, in the region of the atmosphere named the Stratosphere. The occurrence of ozone in this region is frequently referred to as the 'ozone layer', however concentrations are in fact extremely low (approximately one molecule in ten million) suggesting the 'ozone veil' may be a more appropriate term. Ozone is created in the stratosphere when highly energetic UV radiation splits oxygen molecules (O_2), which then join to form an ozone molecule (O_3) and a free oxygen atom. Solar radiation is greatest around the equator so most ozone is created in this region and then transferred to the poles by global wind patterns. Ozone creation is balanced by natural destruction, which occurs when ozone molecules react with various compounds containing nitrogen, hydrogen and chlorine. The reactions with these compounds are typically catalytic, which describes a set of reactions that result in the destruction of many ozone molecules while the molecule that started the reaction survives to continue the process. Therefore, for example, an individual chlorine atom can, on average, destroy nearly a thousand ozone molecules before it is converted into a form harmless to ozone. Natural concentrations of these reactive, or ozone destructive, compounds are usually very low in the stratosphere, maintaining the balance between creation and destruction. However, the balance was tipped when concentrations of man-made reactive compounds increased rapidly in the latter half of the last century, resulting in rapid ozone depletion.

We are now aware of the destructive nature of a range of man-made products, termed collectively, Ozone Depleting Substances (ODS). The most significant group of ODS are the CFCs which have caused up to 80 per cent of measured ozone depletion. The problem with CFCs is their chemical stability, the feature that makes them so attractive commercially. Released CFCs rise into the atmosphere where they may remain for decades up to a hundred years. CFCs are not 'washed' from the lower atmosphere by rain and are resistant to break down by other chemicals. As a consequence, CFCs remain stable for long enough periods to rise into the stratosphere. Here, CFC molecules are broken down by the action of solar ultraviolet (UV) radiation, releasing free chlorine, which then catalytically destroys ozone. Other ODSs include the halons (a group of compounds similar to CFC which contain bromine instead of chlorine, used primarily in fire extinguishers) and other less common compounds such as carbon tetrachloride (used in fire extinguishers, as an industrial solvent and agricultural fumigant, among other uses), methyl chloroform (an all purpose industrial solvent) and methyl bromide (a pesticide). The relative impact of an ODS is determined from the Ozone Depleting Potential (ODP) of the compound, where the ODP is the ratio of the impact on ozone of a chemical compared to the impact of a similar mass of CFC-11. Thus, the ODP of CFC-11 is defined to be 1.0. Other CFCs and HCFCs have ODPs that range from 0.01 to 1.0. The halons have ODPs ranging up to 10. In recognition of the strong scientific evidence of links between measured ozone depletion and the occurrence of these ODS, their production and use is now strictly controlled by the multilaterally negotiated Montreal Protocol (see **chlorofluorocarbons (CFCs)**).

The preservation of the 'ozone layer' is critical to the health of the planet as ozone provides a shield against potentially harmful ultraviolet (UV) radiation emitted by the sun. Ozone absorbs all UV with wavelengths shorter than about 290 nanometers (UV-C), most in the range 290 to 320 nanometers (UV-B) and little above 320 nanometers (UV-A). The shorter the wavelength the more damaging the radiation is to life. UV-C is relatively innocuous and UV-A is absorbed by oxygen gas, so increases in UV-B are directly linked to ozone depletion.

Since the 1970s, when ozone depletion was first detected, UV-B levels on the Earth's surface have increased significantly. Currently, levels in the northern hemisphere mid-latitudes are 4–7 per cent higher, with elevated levels in the spring and summer when solar radiation is greater. In the southern hemisphere mid-latitudes levels are about 6 per cent higher all year round. The most dramatic increases, however, have been recorded in the polar regions, particularly in the spring, with a 22 per cent increase in the Arctic and 130 per cent increase in the Antarctic.

Elevated levels in the polar regions are a result of enhanced local ozone depletion due to the presence of high level clouds that accelerate the depletion process, especially in late winter and early spring. Enhanced depletion is particularly marked in the Antarctic, the location of the famous 'ozone hole', which reached a record size of 25 million km^2, approximately two and a half times the size of Europe in September 1988. The size of this 'hole' is now monitored closely from space, by the Total Ozone Mapping Spectrometer (TOMS) and reductions in the extent of ozone depletion are used as a barometer for the success of the Montreal Protocol phase-out schedules for ODS.

If left unchecked, the impact of continued ozone depletion and associated increases in UV-B on population and environmental health would be significant. In humans elevated UV-B levels have been linked to the increased prevalence of acute conditions such as sunburn and snow blindness and chronic conditions including cataracts and skin cancer. As a result of contempory increases in UV-B, melanoma is now one of the most common forms of cancer among people with white skin. Indirect health effects have also been recorded, including immune system damage, which may result in increased susceptibility to cancer or infectious disease. The effects of increased surface radiation are predicted to be equally deleterious for other organisms, including livestock and crop species, posing the threat of reduced food availability and quality. Research suggests that in marine systems, even small increases in UV-B will substantially affect the growth of phytoplankton (the single celled plants at the base of the food chain), a matter of concern considering that 30 per cent of the world's protein is provided by the oceans.

Ozone depletion may also be linked to other problematic atmospheric processes including **global warming**. Cooling of the lower stratosphere, due to ozone destruction may have masked the warming effects of growing greenhouse gas emissions. Conversely, increases in greenhouse gases may reduce warming in the polar regions, resulting in more extreme winter conditions, increased stratospheric cloud formation and thus increased ozone loss. On a positive note, many of the ODS covered under the Montreal Protocol are strong greenhouse gases and their reduction under the schedules of the Protocol may potentially help to curtail the warming process.

The signing and adherence to the Montreal Protocol by developed and developing countries has resulted in the atmospheric concentrations of several of the most important ozone depleting gases peaking and now declining or projected to peak and then decline within the few years, thus reducing the threat to the ozone layer. Indeed, recent observational evidence suggests that ozone depletion in the upper stratosphere may have already peaked and will start to recover in the near future.

Without the Protocol, by 2050 ozone depletion would likely have been about ten times worse than the current levels. This level could potentially have doubled and in some areas quadrupled, the amount of ultraviolet-B radiation reaching the earth's surface. The consequences of increases of this magnitude on human health would have been significant, with estimates of 20 million more cases of skin cancer and 130 million more cases of eye cataracts relative to 1980. However, if the Protocol is fully implemented by all Parties, scientists predict that the ozone layer should return to pre-1970s conditions by around 2050.

Further reading

Jones, R. R. and Wigley, T. (eds) (1989) *Ozone Depletion: Health and Environmental Consequences*, Chichester: John Wiley & Sons.

Liftin, K. (1994) *Ozone Discourses: Science and Politics in Global Environmental Cooperation*, New York: Columbia University Press.

United Nations Environmental Program (UNEP) (2000) *Action on Ozone*, Nairobi: UNEP.

See also: biodiversity; chlorofluorocarbons; global warming

RAECHEL L. WATERS

P

Pacifism

There are several different sorts of pacifism, but they all include the idea that **war** and violence are unjustifiable, and that conflicts between states should be settled in a peaceful way. The word (but not the idea) is only a century old, and was first used in 1902 at the tenth International Peace Conference.

People are pacifists for a variety of reasons. One powerful motivating force is humanitarian outrage at the destruction caused by war. Economic motives have also played a part in pacifist arguments; pacifists condemn the economic waste of war, which they claim is avoidable. International cooperation and pacifism are closely connected, and pacifists usually advocate international agreements as a way to insure peace. Pacifism is also closely connected with movements for international disarmament. One of the strongest motivations in the promotion of peace has been religion, the objection to war being, in general, based on the belief that the willful taking of human life is wrong. The Eastern religions, especially Buddhism, decry war and advocate nonresistance. There has also been a strong pacifistic element in Judaism and Christianity. The Sermon on the Mount, in particular, contains a strong exhortation to peace. The Christian church generally voiced opposition to war as such (with the notable exception of the Crusades). Some later sects (especially the Anabaptists, Quakers, and Mennonites) elevated nonresistance to a doctrinal position.

As a social movement, modern pacifism began early in the nineteenth century. Peace societies were formed in New York (1815), Massachusetts (1815), and Great Britain (1816). Other countries followed, and similar societies were established in France and Switzerland. The first international peace congress met in London in 1843, marking the earliest attempt to organize pacifism on an international scale. Of course the peace societies were powerless to check the onset of World War One. Although the number of conscientious objectors (as pacifists were called at the time) was small, after the war the peace movement reappeared with greater vigor. Pacifism became widespread as a reaction to the scale of killing in World War One and the use of universal male conscription. In addition, the doctrine of non-violent resistance as applied in India by Mohandas K. Gandhi (1869–1948) gained attention and respect for the pacifist movement.

A concerted effort toward world peace was made not only in the peace congresses but also in such agitation as the pacifist resolution (1933) of the Students' Union at Oxford University. In 1828 William Ladd, one of the early American pacifists, welded the many local societies that had been established in the United States into the American Peace Society. The hopes placed in the **League of Nations**, however, failed to materialize, and some American pacifists placed their trust in **isolationism** and **appeasement** prior to World War Two. During the War the number of conscientious objectors in the United States and Great Britain was larger than in World War One.

After 1945 international contacts between pacifist organizations were restored; although a world pacifist conference projected for 1949 in India was postponed because of the assassination of Gandhi. At its meeting in 1948 the World Council of Churches was unable to reach agreement in regard to pacifism and the church. Although pacifists were not very active in the United States during the Korean War in the early 1950s, this was not the case during the Vietnam War in the 1960s and early 1970s, when pacifists and other antiwar groups joined together for several major protest marches in Washington, DC and other cities. More recent pacifist movements have tended to concentrate their efforts on urging unilateral or multilateral disarmament and the cessation of nuclear testing.

It is important to distinguish between different degrees of pacifism. *Absolute* pacifists believe that it is never right to take part in war, even in self-defense. They think that the value of human life is so high that nothing can justify killing a person deliberately. It is, however, hard to stick to this principle consistently, since it would prohibit the use of violence to rescue an innocent person who is being attacked and who may be killed. *Conditional* or selective pacifists are against war and violence in principle, but they accept that there may be circumstances when war will be less bad than the alternative, limiting their pacif-

ism to particular kinds of war, usually involving **weapons of mass destruction**, because of the uniquely devastating consequences of such weapons.

Many pacifists are heavily involved in political activity to promote peace. During a war many pacifists will refuse to fight or take part in *any* activity that might support the war, but some will take part in activities that seek to reduce the harm of war; e.g. by driving ambulances. Today, most democratic countries accept that people have the right of conscientious objection to military service, but they usually expect the objector to undertake some form of public service as an alternative.

As a national policy pacifism is unheard of, for the obvious reason that it will only work in a context of global disarmament. In any other circumstances adopting a pacifist stance may result in your country rapidly being conquered. However, the goal of pacifism, and of seeking non-violent solutions to disputes between states, plays a significant part in international politics, particularly through the work of the **United Nations**.

Those who oppose pacifism say that because the world is not perfect, war is not always wrong. Just as states have a duty to protect their citizens, citizens have a duty to carry out certain tasks in a **just war**. It does not matter that pacifists are motivated by respect for human life and a love of peace. Pacifists' refusal to participate in war does not make them noble idealists, but people who are failing to carry out an important moral obligation.

Further reading

Ackerman, P. and Duvall, J. (2001) *A Force More Powerful: A Century of Nonviolent Conflict*, Basingstoke: Palgrave.

Cahill, L. (1994) *Love Your Enemies: Discipleship, Pacifism and Just War Theory*, Minneapolis, MN: Augsburg Fortress.

Zunes, S., Kurtz, L. and Asher, S. (1999) *Nonviolent Social Movements: A Geographical Perspective*, Oxford: Blackwell.

See also: appeasement; just war; war

MARTIN GRIFFITHS

Pandemic

An outbreak of a disease over a widespread geographic area, usually covering multiple continents. Of all the present day pandemics (Influenza, Malaria, Tuberculosis, and Hepatitis C) HIV/AIDS (Human Immunodeficiency Virus/ Acquired Immune Deficiency Syndrome) has become a human, social and economic disaster on a scale never before experienced. Although we understand how the virus spreads and what factors fuel the pandemic, no reliable method exists to predict what the trajectory of the pandemic will be.

Not all pandemics are the same. While similarities have been drawn between HIV and the great plagues of the past and present pandemics, there are unique qualities associated with the HIV pandemic. This uniqueness is due not only to how the virus is spread but also to its timing. **Globalization** has a significant impact on how the virus spreads and on the way we think about and respond to the virus. While 95 per cent of HIV infections exist in developing countries, HIV/AIDS is arguably the most globalized pandemic ever experienced. HIV/AIDS is a product of globalization through **development**, global migration, the growing global economy and the internationalization of trade in sex and drugs. Global organizations, their policies and their funding drive the response to HIV/AIDS, through prevention programs and the supply of anti-retroviral therapy.

The HIV/AIDS pandemic is commonly understood both as a health issue and as a development issue. The **United Nations** Secretary-General Kofi Annan commented at the Special Session of the General Assembly on HIV/AIDS in February 2001 that AIDS is now 'the most formidable development challenge of our time'. More recently, HIV is seen as an example of a threat to national and global **security**, a link that still receives cursory attention by scholars of international relations.

More than 60 million people have been infected with the virus. Current estimates indicate somewhere between 34 and 42 million people are living with HIV. Now in its third decade, the number of people living with HIV continues to increase, with an estimated 4.8 million people newly infected with HIV in 2003. The pandemic continues to spread in most countries despite effective prevention strategies, such as safe sex education and the promotion of condom use.

Unlike most pandemics, HIV does not strike individuals at random, as is often the case with other communicable diseases. HIV is inextricably linked to issues of sex, sexuality, gender inequality, stigma and discrimination, **human rights** abuses, poverty and marginalization of specific behaviors. Governments are often reluctant to discuss activities that contribute to the spread of the virus, which ultimately hampers efforts to reduce the spread of the virus.

There is also a long time lapse between infection and the onset of clinically apparent diseases, which increases the chance for people who are positive to unknowingly pass the virus to others. In developing countries, it is common for people to discover that they are infected only when they become terminally ill, which may be years after infection. Such a long latent period reduces the urgency for authorities to act in the present, particularly when there are considered to be more immediate issues to deal with.

The HIV/AIDS pandemic is present in every continent. While it cuts across age, gender and social strata, the greatest impact falls on those who are vulnerable and upon those who are young. The largest share of a country's knowledge and skills are tied to those aged 20–40. This cohort also tends to be the most sexually active and therefore most at risk of HIV. Half of all new HIV infections are within the 15–24 year cohort.

HIV is also a threat to national and global security for a range of reasons. Because HIV/AIDS mainly affects the most productive members of society, there are considerable social, economic and political consequences for the future of many states. Sub-Saharan Africa has been most severely affected. Life expectancy has fallen to below 50 years. HIV has slowed economic progress, increased poverty and contributed to a reduction in food production. The ability of the governments of the worst affected countries of Africa to effectively respond to the pandemic has been weakened by the economic and social costs associated with the virus. Health budgets are often unable to cope with the growing demand for care and for treatment. In many cases the human capital is simply not available. Human security has been eroded, along with a reduction in productivity and the erosion of social cohesion. Decades of health, economic and social progress have been stripped away.

HIV has only recently begun to catch the attention of international relations scholars. This is partly due to the fact that Africa, which is where the effects of the pandemic have been felt the hardest, occupies a place of marginal importance in global economics and politics. While HIV/AIDS continues to decimate sub-Saharan Africa, the next quarter century will see a dramatic increase in level of infections throughout Asia and Eastern Europe, particularly in India, China and Russia. The UN estimates that without an effective response a total of 10 million Chinese could be infected with HIV and as many as 260,000 could be orphaned by the end of this decade. A geographic shift in focus may dramatically alter economic prospects and threaten the global military balance.

The first global health strategy was established by the **World Health Organization** (WHO) under the title of the Global Program on AIDS (GPA). While successful global strategies have been waged in the past against other pandemics, such as polio, never before has a global strategy incorporated so many organizations and attracted so much attention. Global networks have developed under GPA's guidance, such as the Global Network of People Living with AIDS Service Organizations (ICASO) and the International Community of Women Living with HIV/AIDS (ICW). These networks have enabled links to be formed with other **transnational social movement**s.

The United Nations Security Council began the twenty-first century by holding an unprecedented special session on AIDS and Africa, recognizing AIDS as an issue of human security and acknowledging its future impact on increased regional instability and issues of national security. AIDS was declared a global problem from which no country was safe. It was the first time that the Council had identified a health issue as a threat to peace and security. A year later, a United Nations General Assembly Special Session on HIV/AIDS (UNGASS) resolved to establish a fund with an annual expenditure on AIDS of between US$7 and US$10 billion by 2005. The fund (known as the Global Fund to fight AIDS, TB, and Malaria) has increased opportunities to rally international will and resources, the immediate aim being to increase the amount of money needed for prevention and treatment.

Further reading

Altman, D. (2003) 'AIDS and Security' *International Relations* 17(4), 217–27.

Eberstadt N. (2002) 'The Future of AIDS', *Foreign Affairs* 81(6), 22–35.

Joint United Nations Program on HIV/AIDS (UNAIDS) (2004) *2004 Report on the Global AIDS Epidemic*, Geneva, United Nations.

Kalipeni, E., Craddock, S., Oppong, J. and Ghosh, J. (eds) (2003) *HIV and AIDS in Africa*, Oxford: Blackwell.

Ostergard, R. (ed.) (2004) *HIV, AIDS and the Threat to National and International Security*, Basingstoke: Palgrave.

Price-Smith, A. (2001) *The Health of Nations*, Cambridge, MA: MIT Press.

See also: globalization; Third World; transnational social movement; World Health Organization

STEPHEN McNALLY

Partition

The division of the territory of a state, or other large area, into two (or more) separate, independent states. Partition has generally been performed or suggested as a solution to **ethnic conflict**; division of the territory between warring ethnic groups is seen as a potential means to resolve such conflicts. Partition is the ultimate aim of **secession** movements, which seek to separate a piece of territory from a **nation-state** and form a newly independent entity on it. Partition has also been employed or proposed by imperial powers as a means of dividing the territory prior to the granting of independence (e.g. India and Pakistan in 1947, or proposals for the partition of the Palestine Mandate in the 1930s and 1940s).

The benefits and costs of partition have been a topic of hot debate by scholars of ethnic conflict. Some have argued that once ethnic conflict reaches a certain level of violence, partition is the only possible solution to the conflict. This argument hinges on several points. First, the existence of ethnic violence, directed impersonally at members of another group simply because they belong to that group, is presumed to generate strong feelings of resentment and desires for revenge. Proponents of partition therefore argue that violence necessitates partition, because the emotional responses generated will prevent the two sides from living in peace in proximity to each other.

A related argument suggests that rational calculation, rather than emotion, would lead to the same conclusion. That is, with the onset of ethnic warfare, each side knows that the other is willing to use violence against itself. Any negotiated settlement in which the parties continue to inhabit the same land, therefore, allows for the possibility of future violence. Since neither side can rationally trust the other, such an arrangement is unacceptable, because it leaves the members of each group at the potential mercy of the other. Moreover, any attempt by one side to strengthen its ability to defend itself will be seen by the other as inherently threatening, creating an ethnic **security dilemma**. Partition into mutually defensible and separate enclaves, it is therefore argued, is the only solution.

Finally, supporters of partition as a solution to ethnic conflict point to the principle of **self-determination** as a normative argument in favor of granting ethnic groups their own nation-state. President Woodrow Wilson's argument following World War One, that no nation should be made to live subject to the rule of another, is seen as a normative rule that justifies partition on the grounds of granting ethnic or national groups their natural rights. Partition supporters point to the redrawn boundary between Greeks and Turks, following the fall of the Ottoman **empire**, as an example of a partitioned territory that eased ethnic tensions. They also blame the Western rejection of partition in Bosnia in the 1990s for exacerbating the problems there, by trying to force hostile ethnic groups to live together within the same state.

Other scholars, however, consider partition to be a questionable solution on ethical as well as practical grounds. Ethically, they argue that international support for partition will reward groups that engage in **ethnic cleansing**, and give incentive to groups living in ethnically mixed circumstances to drive their rivals out of the territory they want. Similarly, there are concerns that support for partition will encourage other ethnic groups to seek secession elsewhere, as it will become more legitimate and thus the chances of success will be greater. Ultimately, the normative concern is that support for partition will undermine the principle of the inviolability of borders, which is seen as an important anchor of stability for many regions of the world. Partition may also violate the rights of already displaced individuals who lost property or land in fleeing ethnic violence; this notion of a 'right of return' has been a stumbling block to the resolution of conflicts in Cyprus and Palestine.

Others oppose partition on practical grounds. It is argued that, when ethnic groups are closely intermixed, any partition plan will leave some members of each group on the 'wrong' side of the line. This leads to the need for 'resettlement', which, in addition to being normatively questionable, may create additional violence. Opponents of partition point to the 1947 division of the former British colony in South Asia into India and Pakistan, in which one million people died in crossing to the 'right' side of the India/Pakistan border, as an example of what can go wrong. In more recent cases like Bosnia, it has been argued that any attempted partition would displace tens or hundreds of thousands, or alternatively will leave groups in indefensible enclaves subject to oppression or retribution by the new authorities in that area.

Finally, some opponents of partition suggest that the act of dividing a state may not end the conflict, but simply shift it to a new setting. Eritreans fought for decades for their independence from Ethiopia, for example; yet within a few years of their successful secession in 1991, Ethiopia and the newly created state of Eritrea were at **war** with each other. Similarly, the separation of Greeks and Turks into different states may have kept their populations from being involved in direct local violence against each other, but it has not prevented several Greek–Turkish crises over the latter half of the twentieth century, some of which came dangerously close to war. Israelis fear that the creation of an independent state of Palestine, a partition solution first suggested by the British back in 1937, would simply give Palestinians who reject Israel's existence a sovereign base from which to operate in attacking Israel.

Since the end of the **cold war** and the collapse of the Soviet Union and related empires, the international community has tended to accept partitions that fall along previously established boundaries, like the internal borders of the Soviet states, or the republics within the former Yugoslavia. Additional efforts to create new partitions, however, have generally met with resistance from the international community, for fear that granting **legitimacy** to any one such claim would create a host of others. Hence, in the

1990s, Western powers and the **United Nations** resisted calls for the partition of Bosnia, as well as the separation of the Kosovo region from Serbia and the permanent division of Cyprus. In the early twenty-first century, the only partition movement with significant international support was the 'two-state solution' for Israel and Palestine, an anomalous case because of the unsettled legal standing of the territories occupied by Israel following the 1967 war. On the whole, therefore, partition remains a goal for many ethnic groups engaged in secession or **irredentism**, but it continues to be resisted by most of the world's major powers and international organizations.

Further reading

Byman, D. (1997) 'Divided They Stand: Lessons About Partition from Iraq and Lebanon', *Security Studies*, 7(1), 1–29.

Kaufman, C. (1996) 'Possible and Impossible Solutions to Ethnic Civil Wars' *International Security*, 20(4) 136–75.

Lake, D. and Rothchild, D. (1996) 'Containing Fear: The Origins and Management of Ethnic Conflict', *International Security* 21(2), 41–75.

Posen, B. (1993) 'The Security Dilemma and Ethnic Conflict' *Survival* 35, 27–47.

Zartman, I. W. (1995) 'Putting Things Back Together', in I. W. Zartman (ed.) *Collapsed States: The Disintegration and Restoration of Legitimate Authority*, Boulder, CO: Lynne Rienner, 267–73.

See also: ethnic cleansing; ethnic conflict; irredentism; nation-state; secession; self-determination

R. WILLIAM AYRES

Patriotism

Love of one's country, identification with it and with one's compatriots, and a special concern for its well-being and that of compatriots. A full account of patriotism would include the patriot's need to belong to a collectivity and be part of a wider narrative, to be related to a past and a future that transcend the narrow confines of the individual's life and its mundane concerns, as well as social and political conditions that affect the ebb and flow of patriotism, its political and cultural influence, and more. As a topic in philosophy and political theory, patriotism was rather neglected until the 1980s. Since then it has enjoyed considerable interest, due in particular to the resurgence of its cognate, **nationalism**, in many parts of the world. Philosophers discuss patriotism as a test case in the conflict of the requirements of universal morality with particular, local or personal attachments. Political theorists consider it in the context of the debate between liberals and communitarians (see **communitarianism**); some argue that a distinctively political version of patriotism should provide the ethos of the stable and well-functioning polity.

Patriotism is often confused with nationalism. Many writers use the two terms interchangeably. Others conflate country and nation and distinguish between patriotism and nationalism in terms of degree of the attachment. This approach need not, but as a matter of fact often does encourage the use of a double standard of the form 'us versus them' that has a foothold in common usage. When *we* love our country or nation and put it above others, that is patriotism, a natural, sensible, and unexceptional attitude; when *they* love theirs and act accordingly, that is nationalism, an overblown and dangerous passion. Yet the two can be readily distinguished in a way that helps clarify the issues and begs no moral questions, namely, in terms of their objects. A patriot loves her *patria*, her country, identifies with it, and shows special concern for its well-being and that of compatriots. A nationalist loves his *natio*, his nation (in the ethnic, rather than political sense of the term), identifies with it, and shows special concern for its well-being and that of conationals. Both attitudes, like any love, identification, and concern, admit of degrees. And in these matters the degree of a commitment is decisive for the assessment of its morality.

An influential tradition in philosophy, encompassing both Kantianism and some versions of utilitarianism, understands morality as essentially universal and impartial and seems to rule out all local, partial attachment. Its adherents argue that patriotism is a type of group egoism, a morally arbitrary partiality incompatible with the requirements of universal justice and common human solidarity. When one must choose between two persons, both in need of help, one of whom is a compatriot while the other is not, should one help the former, rather than the latter, because in doing so one will be helping a compatriot? If that is true when the two are equally in need, is it still true if the stranger is more in need of help than the compatriot? Another criticism is that patriotism makes for indifference to and indeed hostility towards other countries, encourages militarism, and leads to international tension and conflict.

The other main position in this debate considers patriotism a natural and morally appropriate expression of attachment to the land where one was born and raised and of gratitude one owes it for the benefits of life on its soil, among its people and under its laws. It is also seen as an important and indeed central constituent of the individual's identity. As some communitarians have argued, there is no morality as such; there are only moralities of particular communities. An individual can understand and adopt moral rules and values only in the particular version in which they are embodied in and endorsed by her community. She can become and remain a moral agent only when shaped and nurtured as such by her community. Patriotism and morality cannot be distinguished and contrasted; patriotism is rather a paramount moral virtue, if not the bedrock of morals.

Still other philosophers seek a middle ground. They distinguish between ordinary, unrestrained patriotism, which is vulnerable to criticism sketched above and must be rejected, and moderate patriotism, which is morally legitimate and indeed virtuous. The latter type of patriotism, defended most notably by Stephen Nathanson (1993), does not enjoin promoting one's country's interests by any means and in any circumstances, but rather acknowledges the constraints imposed by universal morality. It is not uncritical, but rather conditional on one's country living up to certain standards of value and deserving the patriot's devotion. Accordingly, it is not exclusive, but rather compatible with a decent degree of concern for all human beings. The contrast between extreme and moderate patriotism is captured in two sayings: the well known 'My country, right or wrong!' (originating with US naval officer Stephen Decatour, 1779–1820), and the less popular, 'My country, right or wrong! If right, to be kept right; and if wrong, to be set right' (ascribed to German-American politician Carl Schurz, 1829–1906).

While philosophers tend to debate patriotism as a moral issue, political theorists are interested primarily in its capacity to replace nationalism as the ethos of the well-ordered and stable state. A number of authors have advocated a distinctively political type of patriotism: one that puts aside, or deemphasizes, the pre-political ties among compatriots such as common ancestry, language, or culture, and enjoins love of, and loyalty to, one's polity, its laws and institutions, and the common liberty they make possible. Some are concerned with countries such as the United States or Switzerland, where a 'covenanted patriotism' is the only type of love of country readily available to an ethnically and culturally heterogeneous population. Others are motivated by the disastrous experience with nationalism, and propound 'constitutional patriotism' as an alternative, post-national basis of unity and stability of the liberal, democratic, and multicultural state, as well as an antidote to the temptation of 'chauvinism of affluence'. Still others remind us that patriotism was originally a political notion: that since ancient Rome, love of country was first and foremost love of the laws and institutions of one's polity and the rights and liberties they made possible. It was only in the nineteenth century that patriotic **discourse** and passion were conscripted into the service of the nation-state and became submerged in those of nationalism. These authors consider that a failure of citizenship, and call for reviving the original 'patriotism of liberty' (Viroli 1995).

The project of an emphatically political patriotism has been criticized on two counts. A merely political collective identity is no identity at all, and proponents of this type of patriotism in fact take for granted that certain cultural or ethnic identities are in place. Moreover, if it were possible to dispense with all pre-political identities and attachments and ground the polity solely on voluntary commitment of citizens to its laws and institutions, that would make their loyalty to it and to fellow citizens rescindable, defeasible, and much too insecure. If *that* is patriotism, then patriotism is not enough.

Further reading

Cohen, J. (ed.) (1996) *For Love of Country*, Boston, MA: Beacon Press.

Nathanson, S. (1993) *Patriotism, Morality, and Peace*, Lanham, MD: Rowman & Littlefield.

Primoratz, I. (ed.) (2002) *Patriotism*, Amherst, Humanity Books.

Primoratz, I. (2002) 'Patriotism: A Deflationary View', *The Philosophical Forum* 33(4), 443–58.

Viroli, M. (1995) *For Love of Country*, Oxford, Oxford University Press.

See also: communitarianism; cosmopolitanism; nationalism; nation-state

IGOR PRIMORATZ

Peace-building

Peace-building tries to create a culture of peace where attitudes and practices are based on non-violence, a respect for **human rights** and the promotion of intercultural tolerance. The concept of peace-building is complex because it has numerous layers of meaning and is intertwined with other aspects of peace. Broadly, it encompasses a wide range of political, developmental, humanitarian and human rights mechanisms that foster peace. Peace-building addresses immediate **security** and humanitarian needs and also the root causes of conflict. Formal peace-building activities include demilitarization, reintegrating former combatants into civilian society, monitoring past and existing human rights abuses, strengthening law accordingly and promoting non-violent conflict resolution and knowledge of democratic practices. Informal peace-building works toward social justice and equal rights with peace-builders utilizing transparent, open dialogue to build trust and develop positive relationships of tolerance and coexistence.

The **United Nations** distinguishes between peacemaking, **peacekeeping** and peace-building. Peacemaking includes mediation, conciliation, arbitration and negotiation necessary to bring hostile parties to agreement. Peacekeeping involves the use of multinational forces that keep parties from harming each other. Peace-building involves constructing the conditions in society through which peace is meaningful. Peace-builders may not be able to operate without peacekeeping support, and without peace-building work, peacekeepers cannot leave confidently. The UN understands peace-building as a means of preventing the outbreak, recurrence or continuation of violent conflict and thus accepts that it is wide ranging in scope. The UN situates peace-building as part of formal peace processes, along with early warning strategies, **preventive diplomacy**, **sanctions** and conflict prevention tactics. The activities that accompany these formal peace processes include conflict resolution, peace negotiations, reconstruction of infrastructure, the provision of humanitarian aid and reconciliation.

The United Nations Department of Political Affairs is the designated focal point for peace-building. It views peace-building strategies as small, temporary, catalytic and facilitating mechanisms. Political responsibilities cover crisis management including support for dialogue between conflicting parties, mediation, advocacy, the sensitization of national actors to human rights concerns and the protection of nascent democratic institutions, particularly through the political education of locally elected representatives, thereby strengthening the role of local leaders. In 2003, the UN had peace-building missions in Afghanistan, Bougainville, Burundi, Central African Republic, Côte d'Ivoire, Great Lakes Region, Guatemala, Guinea-Bissau, the Middle East, Somalia, Tajikistan, and West Africa. The UN admits to the overlap between peace-building and humanitarian activities. For example, in Tajikistan, slowing the flow of drugs into the country decelerates the flow of arms.

The UN Development Fund for Women (UNIFEM) defines women's peace-building to include women's activities that are directed toward replacing armed conflict and coercion with non-violent, justice-seeking behavior. Such activities create a new space for harmonious social relationships. However, many of UNIFEM's peace-building activities in places like Angola, Guatemala, Liberia, and Sierra Leone are classified as human rights or 'violence against women' initiatives. The UN and many international relations scholars place peace-building measures as part of post-conflict reconstruction. The former UN Secretary General Boutros Boutros-Ghali emphasized this view. Secretary General Kofi Annan links peace-building to structural reconstruction, and also to **sustainable development** and respect for human rights. Annan's view, like UNIFEM's view, expands the domain of peace-building. Many local **non-governmental organizations** (NGOs), community workers, grassroots human rights activists and local women's groups maintain that peace-building is important in the pre-conflict, conflict and post-conflict reconstruction stages. That is, peace-building includes all the processes that build peace. Agencies working with local grassroots peace groups understand peace-building broadly, to cover both formal activities covered by the UN and informal processes practiced within local communities.

Broad understandings of peace-building link peace with justice for two reasons. First, peace-building emerges in local settings and addresses immediate human

security needs. To sustain peace, the just fulfillment of material, social and spiritual needs must be maintained. Indeed, many community workers, local NGOs, church groups, labor activists, women, and social rights campaigners become peace-builders in everyday contexts of struggling to meet ordinary daily needs. Second, peace-building addresses root causes of conflict and is focused on social transformation. In many instances, political, social, economic and **gender** injustice, inequality and oppression are the root causes of conflict, manifest in sectarian and ethnic discrimination, apartheid or the dispossession of land. Conditions that free people from poverty, exclusion, oppression and injustice, also sustain human security. Thus, sustainable peace requires the formation of just institutions. The participation in inclusive democratic institutions by groups previously marginalized or discriminated against is integral to building peace with justice. Peace-builders strive toward improving equal citizenship in a non-violent context. Societal peace-building underpins the peacemaking at the representative, political level.

Democratic principles of participation, rights, social justice, and equality assist a democratic peace with justice. The common aspiration for a pluralist, open society characterized by inclusive, participative governance, encourages peace-builders to support initiatives that also encourage active citizenship. Accordingly, peace-building moves beyond a minimalist definition of negative peace as the absence of war to a vision of positive peace linked with justice. Thus it attends to both the immediate security needs and the core reasons for conflict. In peace-building, relationships, concrete situations and social and political institutions are transformed.

Hence peace-building is contextual, firmly grounded in a particular conflict with the specific historical, religious, economic, political, ethnic, and regional factors that contribute to hostilities and the need to build peace. Culturally specific and local approaches must be valued and promoted by external agencies. The local community defines what is important for their peace-building. A community development approach that respects principles of inclusion of gender, race, ethnicity, and religious and cultural difference is likely to create the conditions that allow conflicting parties to engage in dialogue about problems that have been perpetuated by conflict. Building alliances across **ethnic conflict** and political divides is imperative to building healthy relationships, despite the risks in exploring long held myths that have been sustained by hatred and bitterness. Even with fundamental differences within alliances, the realization of some shared goals, like the desire for peace or reintegrating combatants, begins to build mutual trust between previously conflicting groups. Women's coalitions in places like Burundi, Cyprus, Eritrea, Liberia, Northern Ireland, South Africa, Sudan, Uganda, and across the Middle East, the Balkans, and Southeast Asia have been particularly significant in bridging divides and building alliances.

Difficult challenges always remain for peace-builders, to deal with enormous matters of guilt, innocence, impunity, justice, punishment, forgiveness, and reconciliation. Many grassroots peace-builders concentrate on building positive relationships, healing emotional wounds, reconciling differences, restoring esteem, respecting rights, meeting basic needs, and enhancing equality. Much of this relationship building occurs through telling stories, sharing common experiences of suffering and victimhood, networking, and working together on common goals. Networks across class, racial, ethnic, and religious differences build reconciliatory relationships. Tangible signs of peace-building include the decrease in fear, the reduction of prejudice and the increase in trust, confidence, and optimism. Grassroots peace-builders maintain that ongoing peace-building practices are needed for sustainable peace and reconciliation. Peace-building involves all peace processes that create the conditions through which peace is meaningful.

Further reading

Darby, J. (ed.) (2002) *Contemporary Peace Making*, Basingstoke: Palgrave.

Jeong, H-W. (2002) *Approaches to Peace-Building*, Basingstoke: Palgrave.

Knox, C. and Quirk, P. (2000) *Peace-building in Northern Ireland, Israel and South Africa. Transition, Transformation and Reconciliation*, Basingstoke: Palgrave.

Porter, E. (2003) 'Women, Political Decision-Making and Peace-building,' *Global Change, Peace and Security* 15(3) 245–62.

Reychler, L. and Paffenholz, T. (eds) (2001) *Peace-building: A Field Guide*, Boulder, CO: Lynne Rienner.

See also: civil war; Organization for Security and Cooperation in Europe; peace enforcement; peacekeeping; United Nations

ELISABETH PORTER

Peace enforcement

Described by former **United Nations** (UN) Secretary General Boutros Boutros-Ghali – in *An Agenda for Peace* (1992) – as a military operation occupying the middle ground between **peacekeeping** and military enforcement (or **collective security**) against aggression, peace enforcement is an emerging doctrine representing the militarization of peacekeeping. Authorized by the Security Council, peace enforcement mandates have direct reference to Chapter VII of the UN Charter, authorizing the threat or use of force in self-defense and/or to ensure execution of operational mandates. The main function of peace enforcement is to maintain and/or restore peace and **order** in areas of armed conflict and instability. The idea of a new doctrine emerged as a response to the problems of post-**cold war** international insecurity: the proliferation of intrastate conflicts, and an upsurge of **nationalism** – with ethnic, religious, and cultural dimensions.

In the immediate post-cold war years, it became clear that the cold war type of traditional non-coercive peacekeeping operation, associated mostly with interstate conflict, was an inadequate response to intrastate conflict in failed or failing states. It is inadequate, particularly, where such conflicts are further complicated by a multitude of transnational elements – regional powers' interference, illicit arms transactions, and massive cross-border refugee movements. Consequently, post-cold war peacekeeping had evolved into complex multidimensional operations combining elements of traditional peacekeeping, **peace-building**, humanitarian relief, and where non-compliance with ceasefire agreements occurred, also elements of peace enforcement.

The notion of peace enforcement is first mooted in *An Agenda for Peace*, where a brief reference is made to the utilization of peace enforcers – better-armed and better-trained than peacekeepers – in clearly defined circumstances, and with terms of reference specified in advance. The idea is further expanded in *Supplement to An Agenda for Peace* (1995), referring to a distinct separation between the concepts of peacekeeping and peace enforcement in order to avoid undermining peacekeeping missions and endangering peacekeepers. This came about as a result of the failure of peacekeeping response to complex emergencies – particularly the UN's failed attempt to mix peacekeeping and peace enforcement in Somalia, and Bosnia-Herzegovina. Not unlike the UN's first attempt at the mixing of the two concepts in the Congo in 1961/2 – to end Katanga's attempt at **secession** from the Congo – the Somalia and Bosnia-Herzegovina experiences were also controversial and costly, and had severely undermined the credibility of UN peacekeeping.

Typical of intrastate conflict, in both Somalia and Bosnia-Herzegovina, consent of the parties was absent because state **authority** had collapsed, and the warring groups did not honor the various ceasefire agreements. Consequently, the Security Council 'beefed up' the existing peacekeeping operations with additional mandates authorizing the use of force. At the same time, however, the original peacekeeping mandates remained part of the operations, as did the peacekeeping principles of consent, impartiality and no enforcement, thus creating the dilemma of conflicting goals. In Bosnia-Herzegovina, while authorized to use force to protect civilians, the existing operation, the UN Protection Force (UNPROFOR (1992–5)), was geared to a non-coercive peacekeeping operation, and so the peacekeepers were unable to execute the enforcement mandate without endangering themselves. In Somalia, the second United Nations Operation in Somalia (UNOSOM-II (1993–5)), was mandated to 'use all necessary means' to disarm the warring factions and establish a secure environment for humanitarian relief. By becoming embroiled in the factional fighting, UNOSOM-II abandoned its impartiality. Conflicting goals, confusion and half-measures, and eventually failure in both Somalia and Bosnia-Herzegovina resulted in the death of peacekeepers and hundreds of civilians

in Somalia, and in the killing of thousands of Muslim men in Bosnia-Herzegovina. For the UN this meant a peacekeeping paralysis lasting several years.

The mixing of peacekeeping with peace enforcement, that is, using the same force to move from peacekeeping to peace enforcement and back again, poses political and military challenges to states contributing peacekeepers. Politically, while governments are prepared to commit troops to non-coercive operations, they are generally reluctant to involve their troops in situations where their own interests and **security** are not involved, and few, if any, governments are willing to commit their troops to an enforcement role in which they may suffer casualties.

Militarily, the quality and quantity of troops and equipment vastly differ between the two types of operation. Consequently, the concept of peace enforcement provokes much political and academic debate, concerning not only the details of the legal basis, authorization, principles, delegation and implementation of operations, but also how such operations be referred to. Since the Brahimi Report (2000), the UN, for instance, does not mention peace enforcement, but refers to two tier peacekeeping operations – UN led and commanded peacekeeping, and Security Council authorized, but non-UN led multinational force operations with robust mandates. The British, on the other hand, refer to 'peace support operations' in which peacekeeping and peace enforcement and part of a range of military operations.

However, most scholars agree on the general features that distinguish the concepts of peace enforcement, military enforcement and peacekeeping from each other: the Charter's provisions on the maintenance of international peace and security are the basis for all three types of operations. Both peacekeeping and peace enforcement operations, and most military enforcement actions, are authorized and mandated by the Security Council. UN peacekeeping operations have a multinational composition, and are mostly under UN command and control. On the other hand, since the Somalia and Bosnia-Herzegovina experience, peace enforcement operations are not under UN control, and like military enforcement actions, are led by a single country in coalition with other states. So for instance, in Bosnia-Herzegovina, UNPROFOR was a UN led and commanded peacekeeping operation with an enforcement element, while UNPROFOR's successors, the multinational military Implementation Force (IFOR (1995–6)), and the Stabilization Force (SFOR (1996 – still operational in 2003)) are authorized by the Security Council, but are led and commanded through NATO peace enforcement operations (see **North Atlantic Treaty Organization**). And the 1991 Operation Desert Storm to restore Kuwait's sovereignty by forcibly ending Iraq's occupation was a UN authorized, military enforcement action, undertaken by an American-led coalition. Furthermore, while all UN members share peacekeeping costs, peace enforcement and military enforcement operations are financed directly by the participating states. When combined with political and diplomatic efforts, both peacekeeping and peace enforcement offer the parties to the conflict a chance to restore peace.

However, the most important divergence of the three concepts concerns the principles of consent, impartiality, the use of force, and a ceasefire in place. First, while in peacekeeping state **sovereignty** is a key consideration, and therefore the consent of the parties to deployment of peacekeepers is an essential requirement, and in military enforcement consent is irrelevant, in peace enforcement consent is desirable but mostly unobtainable. Second, impartiality vis-à-vis the parties to the conflict, is also considered a key principle of peacekeeping, but military enforcement is always partial against a known aggressor, while in peace enforcement, impartiality (according to Brahimi's recommendations, and several national peace enforcement doctrines) is towards the execution of the mandate rather than the parties to the conflict. Third, the use of force in peacekeeping is limited to self-defense and defense of the mission, whereas the minimum of force may be used to implement a peace enforcement mandate, and all necessary force to win a **war** in military enforcement. Finally, a cease-fire in place is an essential prerequisite before peacekeepers are deployed, while in both military enforcement and peace enforcement operations, an existing ceasefire is not a consideration.

Although in some operations enforcement powers are extensive, underpinning a wide range of military and non-military tasks, the main purpose of peace enforcement is to restore and/or preserve peace, particularly, though not exclusively, in the anarchic and chaotic environment of intrastate conflict.

Further reading

Boulden, J. (2001) *Peace enforcement. The United Nations experience in Congo, Somalia, and Bosnia*, Westport, CO: Praeger.

Boutros-Ghali, B. (1992) *An Agenda for Peace*, United Nations, New York

Boutrous-Ghali, B. (1995) *Supplement to An Agenda for Peace*, New York: United Nations.

Findlay, T. (2003) *The Use of Force in Peace Operations*, Oxford: Oxford University Press.

Osman, M. A. (2002) *The United Nations and Peace Enforcement*, Aldershot: Ashgate.

Pugh, M. (ed.) (1997) *The UN, Peace and Force*, London: Frank Cass.

See also: collective security; humanitarian intervention; peace-building; peacekeeping; United Nations

ANN HUGHES

Peacekeeping

Peacekeeping is the help – in the form of a range of field operations – extended by the **United Nations** (UN) to member states, on the premise that a threat exists to international peace and **security**. UN peacekeeping may be offered either in response to a state's request or, unsolicited, to disputing parties. The purpose is to facilitate the implementation of political solutions to interstate or intrastate disputes, in order to stabilize and restore local and/or regional peace. Not mentioned in the UN Charter, the concept emerged during the **cold war** when the UN failed to implement the Charter's **collective security** enforcement arrangements.

The **authority** for the command and control of UN peacekeeping is derived from enabling Security Council resolutions. The implementation of the resolutions is delegated to the Secretary-General who is in charge of the executive functions involved in setting up and running peacekeeping (through the Department of Peacekeeping Operations – DPKO),. Since the UN does not have a standing army, operations are dependent on the willingness and ability of member states to contribute military and civilian personnel and equipment, while financing the operations is shared by all member states.

There are two distinct types of peacekeeping operations: the traditional, cold war-type, and the multidimensional, post-cold war-type. Traditional peacekeeping comprises:

1. observer missions – unarmed military observers, mandated to supervise truce and armistice agreements, etc. – the first of which, still in operation in 2003, was established in 1948 to supervise the Arab–Israeli cease-fire agreements;
2. military contingents – lightly-armed (for self-defense/defense of the mission) with tasks similar to those of observer missions, but also mandated to act as a buffer between hostile parties.

The idea of such a force came from Canada's Lester Pearson (for which he received the 1957 Nobel Peace Prize) while the development of the concept is due to former UN Secretary-General, Dag Hammarskjöld. Based on the Charter's doctrine of state **sovereignty**, Hammarskjöld established the guiding principles of traditional peacekeeping: consent of the parties, impartiality vis-à-vis the parties in the conflict, neutrality vis-à-vis the conflict, no enforcement, and the interposition of a UN presence between conflicting parties deployed after a ceasefire but before a settlement of the overall conflict.

Banned from influencing the military balance in a conflict, and thereby the political balance affecting diplomatic efforts to settle the conflict, contingents would not include the permanent members, or any state with interest in the conflict. The success of the first UN peacekeeping operation (as opposed to an observer mission), the 1956 first UN Emergency Force (UNEF-I) in facilitating a peaceful Anglo–French–Israeli withdrawal from Egypt, and its innovative approach in using military personnel in a non-enforcement role, set the standard for future peacekeeping.

With the exception of the Congo operation (1960–4), cold war peacekeeping – which comprised thirteen operations during 1945–88 – adhered to the Hammarskjöld doctrine. In the Congo, however, the UN became embroiled in civil war, and deviated from the principle of no enforcement. Although it was eventually successful, the operation made a number of states wary of peacekeeping for many years. The Congo notwithstanding, peacekeeping was considered a success (for which the UN peacekeeping forces, the 'blue helmets', received the 1988 Nobel Peace Prize), as a mechanism facilitating peaceful settlement of international conflicts, and a useful non-coercive device to pre-empt **superpower** involvement on behalf of their respective clients, thus reducing the risks of international destabilization.

The end of the cold war reduced the threat of conflict between the **great powers**, but also removed the constraints that inhibited certain conflicts, thus bringing about less control and **order**, characterized by the proliferation of intrastate and regional conflicts. This, together with the perceived success of cold war peacekeeping, resulted in an increased demand for and reliance on peacekeeping for the maintenance of international peace and security – hence forty-four operations were undertaken during 1988–2003. Consequently, peacekeeping evolved into multidimensional operations transcending the traditional role of peacekeeping, to encompass peace support operations (peacekeeping, peace-making, **peacebuilding**, and **peace enforcement**) comprising military contingents, observers, and civilians contributed by member states including the Permanent Five.

Rapid expansion brought about mixed results. Early operations were successful – Namibia (1989), Iran–Iraq (1988–91), and Afghanistan (1988–9). Others, however, failed, with enormous consequences, the killing of thousands of civilians, and the loss of credibility of UN peacekeeping in Rwanda (1994), and Bosnia-Herzegovina (1995).

The reasons for failure (not unique to the Rwanda and Bosnia-Herzegovina experiences) are complex. For instance, increase in demand for peacekeeping operations pushed the limits of UN resources, qualitatively and quantitatively (equipment, personnel, and finance) to breaking point, leading to the deployment of too few peacekeepers, too late, and at times with too weak a mandate. Relatively simple traditional peacekeeping operations were fairly cheap to set up and run. By contrast, multidimensional peacekeeping operations involve hundreds, if not thousands, of troops, various military and civilian specialists, and are consequently extremely costly. Organizing and setting up such operations are lengthy processes, while management in the field requires special skills. Moreover, increased demand coincided with military cutbacks in many Western states. Consequently, most UN peacekeeping contingents are drawn from developing countries, which at times may be ill-prepared in training, equipment and discipline for the complexity of the situations they find themselves in.

Most traditional peacekeeping took place within the context of interstate conflict, and peacekeepers acted as a non-coercive and impartial buffer between the parties. Most multidimensional peacekeeping operations, on the other hand, take place within the context of intrastate conflict, where, at times, there is no peace to keep, and some or all of the principles of traditional peacekeeping cannot be applied. While success can be partly attributed to the desire, on the part of the parties to the conflict, for peace, unambiguous Security Council mandates and conceptual clarity, backed by the political will and financial support of the international community are also essential.

Most of the above perquisites did not exist in the failed operations. There was no ceasefire in place, peacekeepers were confronted with anarchy and chaos, and consent of the parties could not be obtained or guaranteed. Moreover, in Bosnia-Herzegovina successive Security Council resolutions, mixing peacekeeping with peace enforcement resulted in conflicting goals contributing to operational and conceptual confusion. Consequently, in Bosnia-Herzegovina, peacekeeping stands accused of 'unthinking impartiality' in allowing Bosnian Serbs to overrun UN designated 'safe areas', and the eventual killing of thousands of Muslim men. Meanwhile in Rwanda, the combination of an overstretched DPKO, which ignored warnings of a looming disaster, and the lack of political will/interest of the international community, left an underresourced traditional-type peacekeeping force mandated to use force in self-defense only, to witness the genocide of Rwanda's Tutsi population.

The outcome was the loss of confidence in peacekeeping, and a crisis lasting from the middle to the end of the 1990s. Its efficacy and practicality in question, there followed a comprehensive reappraisal of the limits and potentials of peace operations – the Brahimi Report (2000). There are four significant recommendations:

1. the richer Western states to provide money and training for peacekeeping;
2. Robust and clearly defined mandates;
3. The redefinition of impartiality to be in relation to the mandate rather than the conflict;
4. Where armed resistance and noncompliance is encountered peacekeeping mandates should authorize the use of force.

While the report is not about the conceptual or actual division of labor between peacekeeping and **peace enforcement**, the post-Brahimi reality is a two tier system: UN led and directed 'blue helmet' operations, and UN authorized multinational peace enforcement operations, led and directed by a single state/group of states, mostly working alongside UN peacekeeping operations.

Further reading

Bierman, W. and Vadset, M. (1998) *UN Peacekeeping in Trouble: Lessons from the Former Yugoslavia*, Aldershot: Ashgate.

Goulding, M. (2002) *Peacemonger*, London: John Murray.

Warner, D. (ed.) (1995) *New Dimensions of Peacekeeping*, Geneva, Graduate Institute of International Studies.

See also: peace-building; peace enforcement; United Nations; war

ANN HUGHES

Peace studies

The interdisciplinary examination of the causes of social, cultural and political conflict and the possibility of peaceful solutions. The primary task of peace studies is not to directly analyze **war**, armed conflict or violence, but to focus on understanding obstacles to peace and to develop alternative ways to build sustainable civil and transnational peace. Peace studies examines the nature of conflict within and between societies and evaluates the conditions most likely to promote conflict resolution and peaceful, equitable, harmonious relationships of social coexistence. Interdisciplinary peace studies increasingly is important as governments, **non-governmental organizations** (NGOs) and international bodies struggle to find acceptable ways of resolving conflicts without recourse to violence.

Peace studies was first developed as an academic subject just after World War Two. Peace studies is sometimes called peace and conflict studies, conflict resolution, or peace and justice studies. Peace studies is now taught in more than one hundred universities worldwide. The Department of Peace Studies at the University of Bradford is the world's largest University Center for the study of peace and conflict. Peace studies is distinguished from other disciplines in four ways: its focus, selective interdisciplinarity, its specific values and its engagement with practical scenarios.

First, while its focus is explicitly on peace, non-violence and conflict transformation, attention also is given to war, violence and the nature of political conflict. Peace studies explicitly examines ways to build peaceful, just societies but there are other related areas of academic concentration. For example, conflict resolution, like peace studies, also emerged as a distinct field of academic study at the end of World War Two. It examines concepts and practices of social change, conflict resolution and mediation. This field provides diagnostic tools for analysis of conflicts and for the evaluation of alternative non-violent causes of action. **Development** studies emerged in the 1960s with a concern to promote positive changes in the economies, societies and politics of the poorer

countries of the world, where many conflicts and peace settlements occur. Peace studies also investigates international relations in order to understand how countries relate to each other, the changing relations between states and the **international political economy** of peace.

Second, courses taught in peace studies departments, centers, or faculties adopt a multidisciplinary approach, drawing on the traditional disciplines of anthropology, history, international relations, law, literature, sociology, philosophy, politics, psychology, and theology. Within peace studies and the related areas of conflict resolution, development studies, and security studies, there are many distinctive spheres of interdisciplinary study. For example, the role of international norms, institutions, and states in a peaceful world **order** is scrutinized in order to determine how governmental and intergovernmental institutions can become more effective and representative and strengthen their compliance with fundamental norms of **human rights** and peace.

Another interdisciplinary area is the impact of religion, philosophy, and cultural influences on peace. This area looks at the way the world religious traditions aggravate violence or encourage peace. It examines ethical debates on **just war** and posits theological and philosophical visions of global justice and peace through studying linguistic, literary, and historical dimensions of cultures of peace. Another broad interdisciplinary theme is concerned with the promotion of social, economic, and environmental justice. The focus in this theme is on social change with attention given to the role of NGOs, business enterprises, and states in fostering sustainable economic development, respect for rights, non-violent conflict transformation, **gender** equity and environmental protection. Other interdisciplinary topics examine the dynamics of inter-group religious or **ethnic conflict** and the conditions that give rise to violent clashes or conflict transformation, trying always to identify local and international responses that are able to encourage **peace-building**. There is an active collaboration and dialogue between disciplines and the general aims of peace studies. However, peace studies insists on integrating other academic fields within its distinctive values.

Third, these values explicitly regard conditions of war and certain kinds of violence as problematic. This does not mean that all students or researchers in peace studies believe in **pacifism** or condemn every call to arms, but the discipline does seek the diminishment of war and large-scale violence. It does not pretend to be neutral on the moral issues of peace and war. Additionally, the relationship between peace and justice is clear. Structures of social injustice and oppression are often causes of war and violent conflict. One cannot evaluate the ethical implications of violence without also considering the consequences they have for social and political structures. Further, any adequate understanding of the virtues of justice should include the conditions under which people ought to be free from violence and war. Peace studies adopts controversial normative stances. Peace studies promotes **human capabilities**, human security and well being.

Fourth, peace studies is engaged explicitly in concrete practices, case studies, and areas of the world where armed conflict and violence dominate. It is concerned with practical, ethical questions of how to realize peace and justice in the everyday world. Most peace studies departments or centers of peace and conflict studies facilitate dialogue between interested groups in the local community who are concerned with community relationships, interfaith concerns, and building positive cross-cultural interactions. They often seek students from war-torn regions. Weight is given to the particular problems facing students in their homeland. Attention is focused on the structural and human relational problems affecting countries in cases that students know best. Many students in peace studies undertake international study abroad programs. The emphasis is on facilitating cross-cultural understanding. The academic research area of peace studies produces practically useful scholarship on how to create a more just and peaceful world.

Graduates of peace studies work in a wide variety of careers, specializing in conflict management, conciliation, mediation, or negotiation. Some work in jobs where an understanding of the interconnectedness between the causes of violence is important. Graduates also work in positions where analytical skills are needed to identify adequate responses to humanitarian crises, aid, development, and justice concerns. Others advise their government or go into areas of **diplomacy** including the **United Nations** and its affiliates or defense planning. Others go into positions of leadership in religious, social, or political organizations. Some conduct research or formulate policy. Others go into community organizations for economic and **sustainable development**.

Further reading

Barash, D. (2002) *Peace and Conflict Studies*, London: Sage.

Darby. J. and MacGinty, R. (eds) (2000) *The Management of Peace Processes*, Basingstoke: Palgrave.

Galtung, J. and Jacobsen, C. G. (2000) *Searching for Peace. The Road to Transcend*, London: Pluto Press.

Jeong, H-W. (2000) *Peace and Conflict Studies*, Aldershot: Ashgate.

Nardin, T. (ed.) (1996) *The Ethics of War and Peace: Religious and Secular Perspectives*, Princeton NJ: Princeton University Press.

Samadda, R. (ed.) (2003) *Explorations in Themes of Conflict and Peace*, London: Sage.

See also: cold war; confidence and security building measures; structural violence

ELISABETH PORTER

Pluralism

A concept of **international society** in which **sovereign state**s are basic units, each with its own values and interests, which co-exist, and which relate not only on a basis of self-interest and expediency but also out of **recognition** of each other and regard for common norms and practices, especially **international law**, **diplomacy**, and political and commercial **reciprocity**. This conception of jurisdictional pluralism can be contrasted with **solidarism** and also with monism (law) and monotheism (theology): notions of a singular community or **authority** or law or deity above all others. Jurisdictional pluralism should also be distinguished from value pluralism (political theory) and sociological pluralism (social science). Value pluralism refers to the diverse civilizations and cultures of the world as expressions of freedom. Sociological pluralism refers to a society marked by overlapping membership affiliations and crosscutting social cleavages. This discussion will be confined to jurisdictional pluralism with a brief comment at the end on value pluralism.

The basic idea is of a society of states resting on universal principles of equal sovereignty, territorial integrity, and non-intervention: Article 2 of the **United Nations** Charter. These are among the primary jurisdictional markers of a pluralist international society. Pluralism is a conception of co-existing, territorial political systems each with its own government, ideology, interests, laws, and policies. States have their eye on each other. That is not only out of a Machiavellian concern for themselves: e.g. their own **security** or opportunity. It is also out of a 'constitutional' regard for norms and practices they have in common. That includes international legal norms that states observe in their relations, such as treaties they contract with each other. It also includes diplomatic practices and conventions they arrange among themselves. And, finally, it includes their reciprocal political interactions and commercial exchanges: such as the many institutions and activities involved with international organization, business, finance, trade, transport, travel, migration, etc. The fundamental units and agents of pluralism are therefore sovereign states: an assortment of contiguous but non-overlapping territories; a diversity of populations usually seen as distinctive peoples or nations; a plurality of independent governments.

In the pluralist conception of international society states are not exclusively engaged in struggle or even in rivalry or competition with each other. The pluralist image of international relations is not that of Machiavelli or Hobbes: a conception of conflicting national wills and clashing **national interest**s. Nor are states engaged in a common or joint enterprise that serves some overarching purpose. The pluralist image of international relations is not that of Dante or Kant. The society of states has no greater goal or final destination: it is not going anywhere; it is not geared to achieving perpetual peace; it has no **end of history**. Its very existence as a world that enshrines the values of local independence or freedom is what it is all about. It is a Grotian world between Machiavelli and Kant: what Hedley Bull (1995) labels 'the anarchical society'.

Here, then, is a conception of the population of the world not as humanity *tout court*, but as humanity compartmentalized into various territorially defined peoples, nations or citizenries. A pluralist international society caters for people around the world not by positing their cosmopolitan solidarity (see **cosmopolitanism**) but rather by accommodating the legitimate interests and concerns of the individual states of which they are citizens. (We could refer to these states as **nation-state**s.) According to pluralist theory, the people of the world belong to the world by being citizens of states. Following Hobbes, pluralism postulates that states exist for the security and benefit of their people. But pluralism goes far beyond Hobbes by extending that argument to the society of states as a whole: it, too, exists for the security and benefit of the populations of the numerous and various countries around the world. Citizenship or nationality is held to be more important in safeguarding and succoring human beings, indeed far more important, than any Kantian notion of human solidarity.

Pluralist international society is thus geared to humanity via the institution of statehood. States are posited as human organizations that recognize each other as members of the same exclusive club: the society of states. They show regard for the rights and legitimate interests of each other as fellow members of the club. They subscribe to the rules and practices of their association. When any member trespasses on those rules – and thereby fails their fellow members – they are seen to be placing themselves outside international society. Stepping outside in this way would be grounds for discipline in accordance with the rules

of the association, including (because it is an international association) the threat or use of armed force against them. *Force majeure* or **war** is the last resort for upholding pluralist international society and the rights and legitimate interests of its members.

That posited mutual recognition and regard of states, along with their affirmation and ratification of shared norms, is the metaphorical glue that helps to keep pluralist international society from deteriorating into a mere **international system** of competing and colliding states, each a law unto itself. That is not to say there will not be conflicts and collisions: wars, armed interventions, etc. It is only to suggest that the pluralist norms of international society exist to underscore and (as far as possible) to uphold the independence of states and their right to govern themselves in their own way providing they do not interfere with the right of other states to do the same. In other words, pluralism affirms the values of independence, **self-determination**, self-government, co-existence, non-intervention, and reciprocity.

Pluralist international society is, in that sense, a classical liberal doctrine applied not directly to people as members of the so-called community of humankind, or even to people as citizens of states, but rather to states as agents for the protection and well-being of their citizens. It is at this point that jurisdictional pluralism merges with value pluralism and becomes a prescription as well as a conception of international relations: it declares the freedom of cultures and civilizations to be themselves and to express themselves via the society of states. The state is seen as a vehicle of that freedom. It is not a freedom of one state or group of states to impose its culture or civilization on others. It is exactly the opposite. Here international pluralism is seen clearly as a doctrine of non-intervention. The only legitimate grounds for intervention is to discipline a state that has violated the rules of international society. Cultural **imperialism** and any other foreign imposition of religion or ideology or doctrine are contrary to pluralism. **Humanitarian intervention** is also contrary to it.

The main normative challenge to pluralism emerges at this point: how to deal with the obvious facts of the abuse of state **power** and **failed state**s. One conceivable solution is to make sovereignty conditional on the security and benefit of the citizens of states. But that could not be imposed on international society merely from one quarter or by one region: e.g. the West. Without the general consent of all states that solution would amount to an interventionist doctrine. Abusive governments or failed states may be a price pluralists have to pay for an international society that upholds local liberty across the world via the doctrine of non-intervention. However, according to the pluralist way of thinking, internally legitimate and effective states are not likely to be built by foreigners anyway, but only by the local people involved.

Further reading

Alderson, K and Hurrell, A. (2000) *Hedley Bull on International Society*, Basingstoke: Palgrave.

Berlin, I. (1992) *The Crooked Timber of Humanity*, New York: Vintage Books.

Bull, H. (1995) *The Anarchical Society: A Study of Order in World Politics*, 2nd edn, Basingstoke: Palgrave.

Jackson, R. (2000) *The Global Covenant: Human Conduct in a World of States*, Oxford: Oxford University Press.

Mayall, J. (2000) *World Politics: Progress and Its Limits*, Cambridge: Polity.

See also: English School; international society; law of peoples; solidarism

ROBERT JACKSON

Polarity

The distribution of military, economic, and other **war** making capabilities among members of the state system. According to neorealist theory, the structure of the system is defined by the way states are positioned or arranged, which is a function of how material capabilities are dispersed among them. When capabilities are concentrated in the hands of a single preponderant state, the system is said to have a *unipolar* structure. When two states hold significantly more capabilities than everyone else, the system possesses a *bipolar* structure. Finally, when capabilities are diffused among several roughly equal states, the system has a *multipolar* structure.

Neorealists maintain that system structure – how states are positioned relative to one another – shapes interaction patterns. Despite variations in culture, government, and other domestic characteristics, they expect different states to behave similarly when they hold similar positions within the system. Polarity is important because it defines how states are positioned, which, in turn, affects the decision latitude they possess. For example, states at the apex of unipolar structures have more latitude to use military force and intervene in the affairs of others than even the strongest states in multipolar systems, because there are no powerful rivals to obstruct their actions. In contrast, multipolar structures afford weaker states more foreign policy latitude than unipolarity provides. Rather than 'bandwagoning' with the hegemon (see **hegemony**) when facing pressure to conform with its wishes, they can maneuver among several **great powers**, forging ties with like-minded states to give themselves the opportunity to ward off potential threats. Thus a vulnerable state's position within the **international system** influences whether it copes with external pressure by accommodating the source of that pressure or balancing against it. In short, polarity configurations shape the calculus of foreign policy choice by affecting the decision latitude of both strong and weak states.

Whereas polarity pertains to the distribution of relative capability among states, the term polarization refers to the degree to which states cluster together in countervailing coalitions or blocs. The greater the discreteness between these groupings and the tighter the **alliance** bonds within them, the more polarized the state system. In other words, systems with low levels of polarization have distinct clusters of states, but the membership of these clusters tends to overlap. By way of contrast, systems with high levels of polarization contain two cohesive, mutually exclusive, adversarial blocs.

Several historical examples can be used to illustrate the distinction between polarity and polarization. The period from the Congress of Vienna in 1815 to the onset of World War One in 1914 was multipolar, with Austria–Hungary, France, Prussia/Germany, Great Britain, Russia, and Italy (from 1860) all holding the status of European great powers. Unlike the first half of this period, when the great powers engaged in multilateral cooperation (see **multilateralism**) under the auspices of the Concert of Europe, the latter half became increasingly polarized, with the Triple Entente of France, Great Britain, and Russia eventually facing the Triple Alliance of Austria–Hungary, Germany, and Italy. As this example shows, polarity and polar-

ization are independent phenomena. The members of a multipolar system can work in concert or they can split into rival blocs.

Bipolar systems can also vary in their degrees of polarization. Throughout the **cold war**, the Soviet Union and the United States were the dominant powers in the world. In the immediate aftermath of World War Two, both Moscow and Washington established military alliances to consolidate their paramount positions. Far from being flexible coalitions of fairly equal members, they were groups of secondary powers clustered around one of the two **superpower**s. However, these rigid, counterpoised blocs began to loosen over time. By the 1960s, the Sino–Soviet schism and the withdrawal of France from the integrated military structure of the **North Atlantic Treaty Organization** (NATO) revealed that the level of systemic polarization was declining, even though the structure of the state system remained bipolar.

Does the distribution of capabilities or the polarization of alliances affect the onset, magnitude, or severity of interstate war? One school of thought insists that a world polarized around two rival centers of power, each significantly stronger than the next tier of states, will be stable because the dangers of a dispute escalating to a catastrophic war encourages the bloc leaders to exercise caution when dealing with one another and restrain the actions of their subordinate allies. Conversely, a second school of thought maintains that a fluid, multipolar system will be stable because states that are adversaries on one issue may be allies on another, thus reducing the rigidity of conflicts. In rebuttal, the former submit that because of its ambiguous nature, multipolarity will promote war through miscalculation. The latter retort that bipolarity, lacking in flexibility and suppleness, will deteriorate into a struggle for supremacy.

Numerous studies have been undertaken to ascertain which argument can be sustained by empirical evidence. Is either polarity or polarization related to war? Given that periods of unipolarity are rare in modern history, most of the research has focused on whether bipolar or multipolar systems are more war prone. The findings from these studies have not always converged on the same conclusions, perhaps owing to the different ways that the researchers have tried to measure polarity and polarization. Nevertheless, two general patterns stand out. First, the distribution of material capabilities within the state system is not related to the onset of war; nevertheless it affects the amount of war should armed conflict occur. Wars occur in all types of polarity configurations, but multipolar systems tend to experience larger, more severe wars.

Second, although different polarity configurations do not raise or lower the probability of war, alliance polarization makes war more likely because the structural rigidity it fosters reduces the opportunities for a wide array of multifaceted interactions among states, therein decreasing the chances for cross-cutting cleavages to emerge. Cross-cutting reduces the odds of war, because opponents on one issue may be partners on another. They are not implacable enemies confined to an endless zero sum struggle. Alternatively, within an international environment of overlapping cleavages, adversaries have few interests in common, and thus become fixated on the things that divide them. Under these circumstances, minor disagreements are magnified into bigger tests of will where reputations are thought to be at stake.

In summary, different polarity configurations influence the latitude of a state's foreign policy choices, but they have not been found to increase or decrease the probability of war. Polarized systems are war prone, and if alliance polarization occurs within a multipolar structure, the resulting war will be large and severe. Peace is best preserved when there is a moderate amount of flexibility in the structure of alliances.

Further reading

Jervis, R. (1997) *System Effects: Complexity in Political and Social Life*, Princeton, NJ: Princeton University Press.

Geller, D. S. and Singer, J. D. (1998) *Nations At War: A Scientific Study of International Conflict*, Cambridge: Cambridge University Press.

Kegley, C. W. and Raymond, G. (1994) *A Multipolar Peace? Great-Power Politics in the Twenty-first Century*, New York: St. Martin's Press.

Sabrosky, A. N. (ed.) (1985) *Polarity and War: The Changing Structure of International Conflict*, Boulder: Westview.

Vasquez, J. A. (1993) *The War Puzzle*, Cambridge: Cambridge University Press.

Waltz, K. (1979) *Theory of International Politics*, Reading: Addison-Wesley.

See also: alliance; bipolarity; great powers; hegemonic stability theory; international system; power transition theory

GREGORY A. RAYMOND

Political risk analysis

Since the 1960s a rapidly growing proportion of firms procure their factor inputs through international outsourcing and offshore component production. By 2003, the number of **multinational corporation**s (MNCs) in the global economy had grown to 65,000, operating some 850,000 foreign subsidiaries and employing over 80 million people, with global sales in excess of US$10 trillion dollars.

The extent of overseas activity measured in terms of **foreign direct investment** (FDI) reflects a similar trend, with the total cumulative value of FDI standing at US$112 billion in 1967, growing to US$4.1 trillion in 1998 and expanding to US$7.1 trillion in 2002–3, despite interruptions associated with global economic slowdown (2000), terrorist attacks (2001) and the war on terror.

Emblematic of the growing importance of overseas commerce to global GDP has been the meteoric rise in the economic **power** enjoyed by MNCs. As primary agents of **globalization**, MNCs have witnessed annual increases in the volume of economic activity they generate, up from less than 5 per cent of global GDP in 1970 to 10 per cent in 2003, or one-fifth of total global private GDP. In terms of global trade, private commercial exchanges by MNCs now account for one-third of global exports, while the largest 100 MNCs are responsible for more than one quarter of all global FDI. Indeed, by the turn of the century fifty of the largest one hundred economic entities in the world were MNCs.

Not surprisingly, the revenues generated by some MNCs are far greater than the GDP of many **nation-state**s. The combined revenues of the largest ten MNCs in 2003, for example, exceeded the combined GDP of the worlds poorest one hundred nation-states, while the annualized revenues of one of the largest MNCs, Wal-Mart (US$260 billion), is bigger than the economy of Belgium (US$245 billion); Saudi Arabia (US$190 billion); Ireland (US$120 billion); Singapore (US$87 billion); as well as the GNP of 168 other nation-states. Ranked in terms of total trade sales, for example, Wal-Mart is China's eighth largest trade partner and is currently responsible for fully 10 per cent of the United States trade deficit with China.

Political risk in international relations

Globalization provides greater commercial opportunities as well as greater risk exposure in a world still prone to conflict and unlawfulness. However, risk exposure to multiple markets and disparate geographical locales has long been a feature of international investment and trade. Extortion and expropriation of the assets of foreign investors can be recorded as far back as ancient Greece and the Roman Empire. In the seventeenth and eighteenth centuries, high seas pirates posed ongoing risk for the British, Spanish, and French mariners importing exotic wares from the new world, while in the twentieth century invasion and armed aggression have been frequent occurrences threatening commercial and colonial holdings in Africa, Asia, and Latin America.

Risk, or more particularly political risk, is thus a feature with a long history in international relations. Yet for such an endemic characteristic of the international system it has received scant attention in the professional literature. In part, this is explained by the predominance of high politics in the twentieth century. Recurrent interstate **war** combined with the prospects of nuclear confrontation monopolized intellectual inquiry and theoretical efforts. Low politics, by contrast, tended to be marginalized. In addition, the primacy of the state and the **international system** have framed the dominant approaches to international relations. When non-state actors such as MNCs have been accorded a more central analytical role, theorists have tended to regard them through ideological blinkers. The spate of new left and **dependency** approaches of the 1960s and 1970s, for example, viewed MNCs as agents of powerful states (particularly the United States) or as instruments of

capitalism. In either case, MNCs were analyzed in terms of the impoverishment they brought to developing economies, for the wealth they transferred via profit repatriation to shareholders and corporate headquarters, how their activities destabilized developing countries, created a core-periphery relationship in the global economy, and promoted inequality in the global distribution of wealth and power.

Much of the literature in international relations has thus been ill disposed to view MNCs as anything other than either marginal or exploitive; predatory agents or subordinate to state actors. Little wonder that few theorists have chosen to view international relations through the eyes of MNC actors, and still fewer to devote much time to exploring political risk as a mediating relationship between states and non-state economic actors.

Locating risk

Political risk analysis strides numerous disciplines that address the relationship between state and non-state economic actors. While not the focus of their subject matter, to varying degrees scholars concerned with developmental politics and economics, political economists concerned with the issues of trade, investment and the activities of multinational enterprise, and students of international business exploring risk and risk exposure and its effects upon the overseas activities of firms, have all grappled with the problem of political risk. The ubiquity of political risk explains its empirical presence despite its conceptual absence in the study of international relations.

Political risk is normally understood as a function of international relations and as a product that grows out of cross-border activities. Indeed, political risk is intimately connected to the state system

and its organizing principle of **sovereignty**. Since 1648, sovereignty has been the guiding principle of the Westphalian system (see **Westphalia**), limiting the juridical scope of regulatory orders, property and individual rights, and exposing individuals, commercial actors and state agents to the vagaries of risk that arise from communitarian based social, political and economic orders.

Ironically, while globalization has witnessed the emergence of transnational regimes and the increasing standardization of international norms and rule governed behavior, the depth of these regimes has not been so great as to reverse the pernicious nature of sovereignty and the ubiquity of force, coercion, illegality and extortion, all of which remain the purview of intra-state jurisdiction. Even where such state excesses have been moderated with the global movement toward liberalization of financial markets, removal of **capital controls**, increasing recognition of international property rights and the rollback of protectionist measures, state discretion to transgress these rules has been recurrent, leaving political risk a continuing reality in the international environment.

The changing patterns of political risk

While the concept of risk through political action has been inherent in the international arena since the time of the ancient Greeks, its most recent intellectual pedigree emerged in the post-war period. In part, this has been a function of increasing capital flows from North America and Western Europe to developing economies. More particularly, of course, interest in political risk developed in response to the dangers posed to these investments. High profile incidents involving the nationalization of foreign interests in Cuba in 1959 and in Chile in 1972, as well as the expropriation of land holdings owned by the American United Fruit Company in Guatemala in 1951 and of petroleum extraction assets held by Texaco and Chevron in Nigeria in 1975, all provided demonstrable evidence of the perils faced by international investors.

These concerns tended to abate as the 1970s progressed, due partly to ideological shifts among ruling elites in emerging economies. The utility of private foreign investment capital to economic **development** and poverty reduction, as well as its centrality to successful **modernization** and industrialization, became the dominant mantra underscoring domestic political **legitimacy** and regime stability. Many ruling elites in emerging economies thus redirected their efforts to attracting FDI in order to accelerate development and secure regime legitimacy. This was particularly true throughout Asia, where the **newly industrializing countries** (NICs) of Singapore, Hong Kong, Thailand, and Malaysia, experienced high growth and massive inflows of FDI.

Nonetheless, foreign commercial interests continued to experience expropriation threats, most obviously with the tumultuous events at the close of the 1970s with the Iranian revolution and the prompt nationalization of its petroleum assets. Indeed, the 1980s produced as many expropriation claims against political risk insurers as the 1970s. Expropriation, however, has been only the most obvious form of political risk. The 1980s also witnessed new forms of political risk associated with a spate of sovereign defaults as a result of the **Third World** debt crisis that began in Mexico in 1982 and spread throughout Latin America and Africa.

More recently, interest in political risk has been boosted by a new wave of international concerns. The five-fold increase in private foreign capital flows from developed to developing countries between 1990 and 1997, for example, exposed private investors to the global vagaries of managed hedge funds and currency instabilities experienced with the Asian financial crisis. This was followed closely by rapid devaluation of foreign investments and currency exposures in Brazil and Argentina, the imposition of capital controls in Malaysia and ongoing trepidation over commercial transactions with China. Risk in the 1990s has thus centered on the problems of exposure to countries whose institutional capacity and prudential and regulatory structures prove both opaque and unstable. For investors engaged in more complex exposures to such markets, the paucity of internal governance structures and the absence of transparency create obstacles for market participants to gauge the risk environment in which they operate.

The changing forms of political risk are also apparent with the transition in governance structures currently being experienced among many emerging economies. Decentralization in Indonesia, for example, has complicated the legal and administrative corridors of responsibility, creating numerous avenues for misadventure, malfeasance, and nefarious activities by corrupt provincial officials. While in Indonesia this has articulated as a form of bureaucratic inertia creating administrative and legal bottlenecks for foreign investors, in Brazil it has witnessed renewed forms of expropriation by regional politicians.

Domestic political reorganization evident in many emerging economies, especially transition economies tentatively moving toward more inclusive forms of democratic representation, has generated new avenues to wrestle control of resources from foreign investors in ways best described as creeping expro-priation. The problem of governance, institutional capacity, and the adequacy of prudential regulation in emergent financial markets, thus poses a series of new, critical risk factors, all of which were particularly acute in the 1990s.

The most recent and obvious interest in political risk, however, stems from the events of 11 September 2001 and the turbulence associated with terrorist attacks in the Middle East, Bali, Jakarta, Kenya, Yemen, and Istanbul, the instability caused by geopolitical actions in Afghanistan and Iraq, and possible exposure to future terrorist attacks from fall-out due to the 'war on terror'. The events of 11 September 2001 exposed some of the world's leading companies to business continuity risk and the pro-spect of total loss; not just from the loss of data systems, communications and the destruction of operating infra-structure, but more importantly the loss of human capital and irreplaceable insti-tutional capacity.

Thankfully, such dramatic instances are infrequent. However, they illustrate the financial and commercial **inter-dependence** of the global risk environ-ment, the interconnection of financial markets and the ability of apparently isolated risk events such as the attacks in Washington and New York to be socially amplified through modern communi-cations media. For example, while the direct economic cost due to physical destruction of buildings and infra-structure amounted to something in the order of US$27 billion dollars, United States-wide losses as a result of the sub-sequent economic downturn ran to US$500 billion dollars, a figure undoubtedly dwarfed by the global eco-nomic slowdown.

Furthermore, the varied responses to the attacks, which range from increased military spending, additional force deployment, regime change in **rogue state**s, and the development of new pre-emptive military doctrines, represent new and perhaps more extensive deriva-tive risks than the attacks themselves posed; hazard exposure from force deployment, instability for the global **security**, political and economic order, and possible 'blowback' terrorist attacks in the future.

Political risk is thus prone to the dis-torting effects of amplification through global communications and interna-tional media. The amplification of poli-tical risk is an unavoidable byproduct of globalization, where the political, strate-gic, and commercial interdependence of national economies acts as a medium through which isolated risk events can be felt in disparate geographic localities but with global ramifications. It is this phenomenon that makes the emerging risk environment unique, and highlights antagonisms in the international order that will undoubtedly act as risk drivers well into the future.

Understanding political risk

The literature on political risk is diverse and remains at the 'pre-theory' stage of its evolution. Indeed, the vast bulk of political risk literature is readily identi-fied by its preoccupation with the iden-tification of key drivers and variables that comprise political risk and cause its var-iance.

These definitional explorations, how-ever, have been undertaken from dis-crete disciplinary corners, producing non-contiguous literatures. While the vast bulk of political risk literature is concerned with risk as it impacts on multinational enterprise, a not insignif-icant proportion of the literature approa-ches political risk from the perspective of conflict avoidance and the aversion of state failure, and has been developed by theorists concerned with peace and conflict studies and international relations (IR). These two approaches yield different definitional starting points and modes of analyses.

First generation approaches: the catalogue school

By far the dominant conception of political risk relates to its negative consequences for the cross-border investment activities of MNCs; where political risk is seen to arise from actions taken by host governments, government agencies, or political actors in host countries that adversely impact the operations, value or profitability of MNCs. On this understanding political risk is simply the amalgam of 'unwanted consequences of political activity', or, more specifically, the series of things that governments, their agencies or domestic political actors *do* that interferes with the business of multinational enterprise.

This conception of political risk analysis informs the work of what might be called the catalogue school, whose practitioners simply develop lists of the possible negative activities of governments in host countries that detract, or have the potential to detract, from business operations, value, and profitability. Political risk is conceived as government/political intrusion into otherwise sanguine, functioning and efficient markets. This approach dominated the initial wave of political risk literature that emerged in the early 1950s and, indeed, continues to exert significant influence today. It is a collective effort to disentangle the multifarious series of non-financial and non-market risks into discrete categories in order that they might be described, assessed, and their effects mitigated.

However, this first generation approach to political risk is conceptually flawed

and of limited methodological value. It assumes a rather simplistic view not just of political processes but also of markets. First, it assumes that markets are perfect or near perfect, prone to equilibrium, self-regulating and otherwise functional. Second, it assumes that markets are independent entities that are forced to interact with non-market actors and non-market signals, thus constructing a bifurcated image of the relationship between political systems and economic markets. The notion of imperfect markets, poor transparency, and activities like monopoly practices, organizational self-preservation, collusion, or any other anti-competitive activity, is excluded from the theoretical purview of such approaches, which imply that markets are not embedded in states or a broader societal polity, viewing the latter as intrusive to markets and alien to efficient market operation. This artificially disembeds markets and business relations from their socio-political contexts and sees all political activity as negative, market distorting, and detrimental to business and profitability. According to the catalogue school, political risks exist because of politics and governments, and can thus only be removed by limiting the power and regulatory reach of government.

First generation approaches to political risk thus tend to render analytically invisible the role of the state as an enabling agent of commercial practice. As economic historians have long recognized, nation-states and their regulatory arms are prescient to market operation and a necessary conduit to insure the transmission of market information and transparency. Rather than the presence of such actors, it is their *absence* that increases political risk. The great lesson of the 1997 Asian financial crises, for example, has been to affirm the centrality of functioning political systems and regulatory bodies for sound economic outcomes. Weak state capacity makes for poor economic outcomes, and weak state institutions create conditions prone to market failure or distortion. The recent and ongoing emphasis on **good governance** by leading international agencies like the **International Monetary Fund** (IMF) and **World Bank**, for example, stresses the importance of institutional capacity to support the operation of financial markets, market transparency and probity, and provide administrative and legal corridors for the transfer of assets, debt, and debt settlement. Without state and institutional capacity, markets very often implode or function inappropriately, and expose participants to risk.

The relatively crude conceptual apparatus offered by first generation political risk approaches thus leaves little room to develop methodological frameworks that treat seriously political processes and the manner in which they manifest and articulate with markets. Political risk is treated exogenously, as a set of market interventions with negative consequences. The fact that political risk can stem from the absence of effective, functioning political systems leaves this literature bereft of methodological tools to forecast political risk, analyze its likely future dimensions, and to manage its consequences.

Second generation approaches: the system–event school

Second generation political risk approaches implicitly recognize the limitations of the catalogue school. Delimiting political risk to the activities of governments forecloses consideration of state and system type, and of possible correlations between political systems and political risk. Moreover, intuitive and empirical observation suggests broad correlates exist between certain types of states and

the level and extensity of certain political risks. Particular state types, for example, display less stability, are more prone to nefarious political activity, crime, corruption, and regime change than are other state types. Different states thus have different political risk profiles, opening up the possibility of developing models that can link system characteristics with the likely development of specific political risk events. For political risk analysis, this holds out the prospect of developing prescriptive social science models able to alert investors, states and/ or stakeholders to future risk events and thereby avoid exposure to them.

Unlike first generation political risk approaches, second generation approaches understand the mutually constitutive nature of political systems and markets. On its own, economic growth is no indicator of low levels of political risk. Indeed, economic modernization can generate political risk in situations where the absence of political development, or the inability of the political system or political elites to accommodate the demands of emerging powerful constituencies, precipitates political crisis and radical political change.

Second generation approaches to political risk are informed by political modernization theory and the spate of studies surrounding the **decolonization** process and the emergence of numerous new, fragile states in the immediate aftermath of World War Two. While development economists attempted to distil the conditions necessary for economic growth, industrialization, and mass consumptive society, political scientists and sociologists were equally at work discerning the conditions necessary for political **modernization**, institutional development, and the emergence of mature, liberal democratic societies. What was it that caused societies to develop politically, for political cultures and political institutions to emerge and support complex economic systems and production networks?

The answers come predominantly from the identification of pattern variables endemic to cultural, social, and political modernization. Developed societies display certain social and political attributes; functional differentiation, specialization, individual autonomy, adaptation, and increasing complexity. They also display increasing socio-political differentiation facilitating wider freedoms from the binds of family, locality, and religion (individualism; separation of state and church; secularism, social atomization), but set amid integrative dynamics and technologies that otherwise reproduce social orders and create larger societal wide referents beyond familial/clan association (citizenship, **nationalism**). These evolutionary universals are associated with structural–functional attributes that, if identified, can be transplanted or diffused into emerging societies, helping quicken the pace of development and avert the social and political ills of political backwardness.

Structural–functional analysis generated a series of studies into the comparative strengths and weaknesses of specific state types, and the political, cultural, regulatory and social environment endemic to their composition, in the process producing comprehensive typologies. For political risk analysts it was only a short step to infer the probability of event scenarios like regime change, revolution, civil disturbance, or the degree of probity associated with specific types of emerging political systems. While not a predictive tool that could be correlated to specific future risk events, structural functional analysis could provide insights into the risks associated with specific stages in the political modernization cycle, and of possible trigger points that could pre-

empt political instability or derail further modernization.

Second generation approaches to political risk generally coalesce around what we might loosely term the system-event school. This school stresses the identification of events that impact on regime stability and detract from the incumbent regime's capacity to govern, or system characteristics which facilitate the emergence of political events and which detract from system stability, political maturation and legitimacy. Political risk is associated with events such as social or political unrest, expropriation, labor problems associated with strikes, problems associated with profit remittance such as currency controls, or events such as the imposition of import restrictions. These events derive from a specific system type, normally modernizing fragile states prone to be captured by domestic constituencies and otherwise not able to exert control and implement policy in the longer-term interests of the nation as a whole. Captured states, in other words, pursue policies that reflect the narrow sectional interests of ruling elites within emerging states, increasing the political risks for foreign investors and jeopardizing the longer-term economic benefits to the nation.

For second generation approaches, political risk exists along a spectrum that ranges from low to high and corresponds roughly to political systems that are undeveloped compared to those that are highly developed. The degree of political risk is therefore a reflection of the capacity of a state and its political system to manage political events, competing sectional interests, exercise legitimacy, and discharge the functions of statehood in a non-violent, stable, orderly, democratic manner.

Political risk and the possibility of political instability correlate inversely with the level of modernization and adaptability of a political system. More importantly, the level of political risk is positively correlated to stress caused by rapid economic modernization, where the political system can be overstretched to the point of crisis when confronted with complex demands occasioned by rapid development, social dislocation, and the emergence of issues for which it does not have the institutional capacity to absorb.

These insights suggest various investment strategies for avoiding political risk. First, identify the system type into which the country falls, then design investment strategies that reflect the political risk profile of the country. Thus, in the case of military dictatorships where legitimacy is low, the use of violence ubiquitous, and sudden regime change or popular uprising possible, avoid long term investments, use short term investment vehicles, minimize sunk costs, attempt to contain investments in liquid and easily withdrawn assets. Conversely, emerging societies promise the least political risk, inviting longer-term investment and able to support higher sunk costs with exposure to fixed infrastructure (mining, production) with relatively low political risk. Not unexpectedly, adaptive systems display the lowest levels of political risk and the highest levels of political stability, able to absorb long-term investments, high sunk costs, and multiple investment exposures.

While second generation approaches to political risk are a marked improvement over their predecessors in the catalogue school, their achievements have been modest. Part of the problem stems from the use of a circular logic. Low political risk and high political stability are manifest in systems that are developed, predominantly Western, liberal democratic, and capitalist. By definition any state that displays dissimilar characteristics represents a political risk and the possibility of instability. On this understanding, political risk is attributed to non-western states, thus betraying what critics allege to be ethnocentric values and neo-imperial attitudes.

Second generation approaches also display a capricious understanding of political stability and political risk. Why is political instability or regime change necessarily a risk to business? Political stability interrupted by sudden system change to replace despotic dictatorships, for example, generally signifies a reduction in political risk, greater political transparency, and can be the basis for less autocratic intervention into the economy. Moreover, sudden, dramatic political events such as regime change, apart from being infrequent, are not themselves always hazardous to business activity or the operations of MNCs. Regime change in Indonesia with the fall of President Suharto in 1998, for example, had no immediate consequences for the presence of foreign business interests. Indeed, many welcomed regime change and the possibility of greater economic freedom in the country.

Thus, the conflation of political instability and political risk, while intuitively appealing, is simplistic. While regime instability or sudden regime change can certainly 'spook' investors, there are few empirical grounds to infer a strong correlation between regime change, political risk and any impact upon the activities of foreign investors. Indeed, large risk events such as nationalization or expropriation normally occur under conditions of relative regime and political stability, and reflect state capacity, institutional depth and authority to undertake such activities. Put simply, second generation approaches to political risk only look at political events and system structure, but cannot establish direct correlations between these events and their impact upon firms.

In part, this problem arises from the system-events school's treatment of foreign investment as a ubiquitous category without allowing for variation in investment type. Different investment types interact with regulatory regimes, political systems, political coalitions, and political elites differently, and thus generate different forms of political risk. Attempting to build system wide correlations and universal theory ignores the fact that not all political events have the same risk implications for foreign investment. In Nigeria, for example, The Royal Dutch Shell company has successfully operated physical plant, equipment, and pipelines despite widespread civil unrest and continuing political instability; an environment that would be unthinkable for retail chains or manufacturers. The ability to analytically disentangle investment types and then demonstrate causality between political events, political systems and their impact upon various investments, thus escapes entirely the system-events approach.

A related problem is the limited comparative application of system-event stability theory. Can the attributes that contribute to political instability in one country be generalized? The development of such theory is elusive, since factors that produce instability in one state might not be relevant to other political systems or produce the same type of instability elsewhere. More fundamentally, what is meant by political instability? If it refers to regime change, can it be assumed that this will result in policy change? If not, then why focus on regime change when policy changes are likely to have the greater impact on economic actors? Conversely, should it be assumed that political stability promotes policy stability or continuity? Radical policy change often occurs in situations of political stability and reflects regime legitimacy and strong state and institu-

tional capacity to withstand domestic protest and lobby groups. In all, then, political instability might not be the most appropriate variable that needs measuring in order to assess political risk.

Finally, and with obvious hindsight, the system-events school has had few predictive successes. While this is a failure endemic to social science forecasting generally, it nonetheless highlights the analytical limitations of second generation approaches. One of the greatest political events of the twentieth century, for example, the fall of the Soviet Union, went without any prescience on the part of political scientists or international relations scholars. Likewise, the fall of Suharto, the popular revolution in the Philippines that disposed President Marcos, the fall of the Shah in Iran in 1979, the rollercoaster of political disruption in the wake of the Asian financial crises of 1997, or any number of similar sudden political events, have all escaped forecasting despite several decades of predictive model building. Unfortunately, the great hope of second generation approaches, especially in terms of better modeling, precision, and the ability to generate prescriptive outcomes, has not eventuated.

Third generation political risk approaches: method versus theory

Positivist political science enjoyed wide application in the 1950s through 1970s, underscored by a desire to replicate the prescriptive and predictive success of the hard sciences and a belief in the infallibility of rationalist–empirical epistemologies. Political risk analysis was no different, actively pursuing approaches aimed at greater predictive power. This desire stemmed from the nature of political events occurring in developing regions, and the political risks typically encountered by foreign investors. Expropriation and nationalization of foreign interests dominated political risk for the greater part of the post-war period. In 1975 alone, for example, there were eighty-three recorded cases of expropriation. Developing models or frameworks of analysis that might predict such events thus promised great rewards and was enthusiastically pursued.

By the 1980s, however, a sea change in host government attitudes toward external investment witnessed a marked shift in the types of political risks. From 1981 to 1992, for example, there were only eleven recorded expropriations. Increasingly, nation-states now compete for FDI and attempt to set in place policies that attract prospective investors. Large risk events like expropriations, ideologically motivated coups, mercantilist trade policies (see **mercantilism**), or tariff based protectionist policies (import substitution industrialization), have been a shrinking feature of the **international political economy**. These developments, combined with the spate of poor analytical outcomes associated with second generation approaches to political risk, have witnessed not just a reorientation in political risk analysis, but have also changed the expected outcomes from such endeavors. Political risk approaches are now more circumspect in their ambitions. They aim less toward grand theoretical correlations and more toward informed micro-analyses that emphasize the importance of context, and focus on project level analysis. These approaches fall into a number of discrete categories and offer very different insights, but all share a general rejection of the grand theoretic tradition of political science.

Third generation approaches to political risk abandon theory for method. Rather than attempt to develop explanatory schema with predictive capacity, they develop methods to evaluate the risk environment in relation to industry or project specific applications. This has thrown up a plethora of approaches, all with varying degrees of utility and none enjoying wide acceptance as the pre-eminent approach to political risk analysis. To add to the confusion, numerous consulting firms have also developed various 'systems' or risk assessment techniques that infuse the literature, creating a profusion of models all claiming to offer superior insights and greater maneuverability with regard to risk avoidance. However, the move toward particularistic micro-studies generally reliant on qualitative techniques and emblematic of third generation approaches has also proven unedifying. The main reason is that qualitative approaches remain reliant upon the agility and expertise of particular analysts, and the method of analysis is often deductive. They are difficult to test, a limitation especially acute for governmental and commercial organizations that need definitive analysis. The holy grail of political risk theorizing; constructing quantitative models that can provide testable propositions, or the construction of data sets that can relate accurate probability indices to specific risk events, policy changes, or country settings, thus remains a highly prized goal despite its difficulties.

Is there a way beyond this impasse? Can meaningful data sets be generated that successfully correlate risk with structural features in the political composition and political practices of nation-states, their institutions and the cultural/procedural norms that comprise their markets, social, political and juridical systems? This question sets a highly challenging task for political risk analysis. It involves the construction of data sets that allow analysts to examine the relationship between political and economic institutions, the interface between domestic norms, actors, institutions, and external influences and participants/ investors, and to understand the causal connections between all these spheres in terms of probabilities about their implications for country and political risk events in the present and immediate future.

New approaches

Perhaps as a result of information data profusion doubtlessly associated with advances in information technologies, numerous attempts are now being mounted to develop risk databases that attempt to correlate and or identify specific trigger points with particular risk events; events such as humanitarian crises, state failure and ethic conflict, for example. Not unnaturally, much of the most interesting of this work is being done in the foreign policy and international relations fields. Here, projects as diverse as PIOOM (Interdisciplinary Research on the Root Causes of **Human Rights** Violations); GIEWS (Global Information and Early Warning System) assessing food security and trigger points for hunger and famine; GEWS (Global Early Warning System); GEDS (Global Event Data System); FAST (Early Recognition for Tension and Fact Finding) and ICG (International Crisis Group) are all attempts at developing systematized methodologies for identifying trigger points prescient to various international risks associated with food security and famine, ethnic and religious tensions, **civil war**, interstate hostilities, energy crises and environmental sustainability.

Many of these organizations are involved in preliminary data collection, seeking to establish sufficient data in order to develop leading indicator models able to identify which sequence of events or triggers are precursors to regime instability, conflict, humanitarian crisis, or any series of other severe events. One of the more innovative, for example, the Country Indicators for Foreign Policy (CIFP), has grown out of a geopolitical database originally developed by the Canadian Department of National Defense in 1991.

The novelty of CIFP rests in its ambitions to move beyond risk analysis into a fully-fledged early warning system prescient to Canada's humanitarian approach to international affairs. Part of this has involved the development of a modeling technique for assessing country risk based on a cross-national 'index of severity', to better identify areas of stress that might be triggers for risk and crisis. The insights of the CIFP Index of Severity is its ability to develop indices measuring the *relative* performance of a state's capabilities rather than simply generating cross-national comparisons based on absolute performance indicators.

With this important innovation and caveat, the CIFP severity index develops a weighted index of nine composite risk indicators (armed conflict, governance and political stability, militarization, population heterogeneity, demographic stress, economic performance, human development, environmental stress, and international linkages). In addition, each of these composite indicators can be related to any combination or all of the other composite indicators (to a maximum of seventy-two potential linkages). The severity index thus assigns a weight to each indicator based on the number of linkages it is expected to have with others and thus its input into over-all severity.

Similar humanitarian early warning systems are also being evolved by organizations like the International Crisis Group (ICG) whose network of country and regional based representatives across five continents, maintain continual monitoring protocols based on field analysis and high-level advocacy to prevent and resolve deadly conflict. Peace researchers in the Netherlands and Scandinavia are likewise working toward early warning modeling based on collecting sufficient data and evolving trigger point identification techniques.

Such lead indicator modeling approaches and early warning systems harbor obvious utility for various aid agencies, **non-governmental organizations** (NGOs), international organizations, as well as governmental bodies. If perfected, they can provide vital and timely information helping avert humanitarian crises, **ethnic conflict** or inter-state hostilities. They thus have enormous practical utility in terms of pre-emptive decision making, humanitarian disaster preparedness and conflict avoidance. In contrast to second generation approaches that attempt to develop abstract typologies of political systems in terms of their risk characteristics vis-à-vis regime stability, social unrest or conflict propensity, new approaches are far more specific and actively seek to correlate particular institutions, trigger points, or event sequences and stresses to particular decision making practices, crises and outcomes. This represents a level of micro-institutional analysis that, if successful, will be able to correlate institutional type to the probability of risk events, or a sequence of events, stresses, strains and relative capability performances, to crisis episodes and conflict outcomes, a level of analytical precision that always escaped second generation approaches.

While still in their formative stages, the new approaches have spurned a renewed excitement about the potential of finally gaining greater analytical precision and of identifying which institutions matter, how they affect risk episodes and the societal risk environment. This obviously opens up the possibility of institutional engineering to help ameliorate all manner of economic and political ills; economic development and growth, enhancing institutional capacity and effective public policy delivery, increasing public sector resource efficiency, as well as contributing to better institutional probity and administrative transparency.

Further reading

Bernstein, P. (1998) *Against the Gods: The Remarkable Story of Risk*, 2nd edn, New York: John Wiley & Sons.

Conklin, D. (2002) 'Analyzing and Managing Country Risks', *Ivey Business Journal* 66(3), 37–41.

Dunning, J. H. (ed.) (1997) *Governments, Globalization and International Business* Oxford: Oxford University Press.

La Porta, R., Lopez-de-Silanes, F., Schleifer, A. and Vishny, R. (1999) 'The Quality of Government', *Journal of Law and Economic Organization* 15(1), 222–79.

Monti-Belkaoui, J. and Riahi-Belkaoui, A. (1998) *The Nature, Estimation, and Management of Political Risk*, Westport, CT: Quorum Books.

Pauly, L. W. and Reich, S. (1997) 'National Structures and Multinational Corporate Behaviour: Enduring Differences in the Age of Globalization', *International Organization* 51(1), 1–30.

See also: foreign direct investment; multinational corporation

DARRYL JARVIS

Population growth

At the beginning of 1992, the earth supported about 5.4 billion people, a dramatic rise since 1900, when it contained about 1.6 billion people. In 2000, the world population surpassed six billion people. Each day, the world's human population increases by about 250,000 people, or more than 80 million each year. This annual increase is approximately equal to the population of Mexico.

The rate at which the human population is growing can be illustrated by how little even catastrophic natural disasters slow it down. For example, in June 1990 an earthquake in Iran killed an estimated 40,000 people. Within six hours, new births worldwide replaced the number of people lost from this immense tragedy.

Population growth is not due simply to an increase in births but to the excess of births over deaths. Improvements in public health and medicine around the world propel population growth by enabling people to live longer. The growth feeds itself as greater numbers of young women survive to childbearing age and start to have children.

These advances are causing the world's population to double at a much faster rate than ever before. In the year 1000, the human population grew at a rate so slow that, had it continued, the world population would not have doubled for 575 years. By 1825, the doubling time had decreased to about 100 years. Today, the world's population doubles every 35 to 40 years.

But the growth rate varies greatly from country to country. In the richer, industrialized states such as the United States, Canada, Japan, and the countries of Western Europe, population growth averages 0.5 per cent per year. Germany and Hungary have rates that are sometimes less than zero, meaning that their populations are declining. The Russian population is expected to decline for the next twenty years, in part as a result of the AIDS pandemic in that country. In the developing nations, however, population growth is much higher. The highest growth rates occur in Africa and in Arab states on the Persian Gulf.

Although population growth rates expressed in percentages may seem insignificant, the difference between a worldwide 1 per cent rate of growth and a 3 per cent rate is the difference between adding 54 million people and adding 200 million people each year. A sustained worldwide growth rate of 3.7 per cent, for example, would cause the earth's population to double in only twenty years.

Many economists and social planners believe that economic **development** is the key to slowing population growth. In poor countries, where many people farm for a living, there is an economic advantage to having several children who can help with the work and provide for the parents in old age. When societies become economically and technologically advanced, however, modern agricultural techniques enable the production of the same amount of food using the labor of fewer people. In such societies, large families are unnecessary and may be costly. As a result, family size drops. This so-called demographic transition has helped to reduce the growth of populations in the wealthier, industrialized countries.

Unfortunately, a rapidly expanding population can by itself prevent a developing country from improving its economy. Its people can become poorer when its population growth outstrips its economic growth. Kenya, for instance, with a 1992 population of 24 million, will have 48 million people in 2012 if the current population growth rate continues. Few experts believe that Kenya's economic circumstances can improve sufficiently during that time to provide adequately for so many people. Kenya may be doomed to worsening poverty unless it can limit its population growth.

The human population is expanding in many regions simply because people lack awareness of birth control or the ability to limit the size of their families. In other cases, people in developing countries who want to limit the growth of their families lack access to contraception. Family planning methods are simply not available in large sections of the world. But attempts to slow population growth confront more than economic or educational problems. Human reproduction is a matter of great religious and cultural importance as well. The religious teachings of many people prohibit or discourage contraception. And some cultures traditionally value large families as a sign of prestige.

The problem of uncontrolled population growth prompted the government of China in 1955 to restrict families to only one child. China is one of the most densely populated countries in the world. It has the largest population, at one and a half billion people. China's 9.6 million square kilometers (3.7 million square miles) gives it a population density of about 119 people per square kilometer (309 people per square mile). But because the land is not all habitable, the density in inhabited places is much higher. By comparison, the United States, whose 280 million people live on a land area approximately equivalent to that of China, has a population density of only thirty people per square kilometer (seventy people per square mile).

China's population control program has not been a clear success. The government's rules are modified for special groups within the larger population. Also, families often desire male children, a wish that in practice may lead to the killing of female newborns or simply a disregard for governmental restrictions. Thus, there are more births than officially allowed in order to produce males. Over the last decade, despite many years' experience with the policy, the population of China was still increasing by about 1.4 per cent annually. At this rate, China's population will double in about fifty years.

It is difficult to estimate the consequences of the patterns of population growth. On the other hand, optimists would argue that the consequences will be benign, because continuing advances in food production and high-yield farming practices are likely to be more efficient. Technological advances have tripled the productivity of world cropland over the last century. In the 1990s alone they have helped expand the world grain harvest from less than 400 million tons in 1990 to nearly 1.9 million tons in 1998. Indeed, farmers have expanded grain production five times as much since 1900 as during the preceding 10,000 years since agriculture began. Pessimists, on the other hand, paint a more depressing picture of the future, pointing out that as many as 13 million people die every year from malnutrition and starvation, despite the fact that global food production continues to increase and total world food supplies are adequate. Of course, there are complex political and economic factors that lead to poverty and hunger in various regions. But some scientists fear that current demands for agricultural resources already exceed the earth's capacity to supply the population on a continuing basis. From 1950 until 1984, world agricultural production nearly tripled. In the mid-1980s, however, world agricultural production began to level off, and, in certain places, production declined.

Loss of farmland is a major cause of the decline in agricultural production. Usable farmland is lost for many reasons, but the major causes are erosion, **desertification** and salinization. Erosion and desertification occur when wind and water rob land of its nutrient-rich soil. Salinization is the accumulation of salts in the soil, a problem common in regions where irrigation is used. Finally, as cities grow, they take over land once available for agriculture. The result of all these factors is that less and less land must feed more and more people. Dwindling farmland is not the only problem, however. Across the entire globe, overpopulation continues to deplete croplands, fisheries, water resources, and energy supplies. Some scientists fear that uncontrolled population growth will thus produce dangerous conflicts among states and regions over access to the earth's natural resources.

Further reading

Kaplan, R. (2000) *The Coming Anarchy*, New York: Random House.

Leisinger, K. M., Schmitt, K. and Pandya-Lorch, R. (2002) *Six Billion and Counting: Population Growth and Food Security in the 21st Century*, Washington, DC: International Food Policy Research Institute.

McMichael, A. (2002) 'Population, Environment, Disease and Survival: Past Patterns, Uncertain Futures', *The Lancet* 359(9312), 1145–8.

See also: biodiversity; desertification; development

TERRY O'CALLAGHAN

Postcolonialism

A diverse and multifaceted approach to the study of north–south relations of domination and resistance, which aims to recover the position of marginalized peoples. Originating in the field of literary and cultural studies, postcolonial approaches to International Relations have become more prominent in recent years. These often proceed from a recognition of the Western character of mainstream International Relations, which has traditionally devoted little attention to **Third World** countries. Postcolonial approaches place the Third World and the subaltern at the center of analyses, and are concerned to uncover and change the complex **power**/knowledge relationships that maintain and reproduce the contemporary world **order**.

Situating postcolonialism

Postcolonialism is not a conventional theory or school of thought in the traditional academic sense, and some would even dispel its classifications as an 'ism'. Rather than a unified body of thought, postcolonialism is multiple, diverse, and eschews easy definitions or generalizations. Similarly, postcolonialism does not have a disciplinary 'home' and cannot be confined to any particular academic department. While originating as an approach to the study of **Commonwealth** literature in the late 1970s and early 1980s, its focus has since broadened to include other aspects of north–south relations and has made an impact in a wide variety of fields, including cultural studies, anthropology, history, geography, and politics.

In international politics, postcolonial analyses are relatively new and remain marginal. In large part, postcolonial approaches stem from a dissatisfaction with mainstream International Relations and its traditional focus on **superpower** politics, states, the **balance of power**, and so on. This focus is seen to result in a very narrow and statist analysis of world politics, excluding important aspects such as culture and **identity**. Moreover, international Relations is regarded as the **discourse** of the powerful. Born in Europe and currently dominated by the US academic community, the discipline continues to provide an account of the world as seen from the West, failing to capture and reflect the concerns of poorer countries and their peoples. Against this perceived universalism (and irrelevance) of conventional International Relations, postcolonial analyses of global politics place the Third World and marginalized peoples at the heart of their inquiries. Postcolonial writers are centrally concerned with culture and identity, and the colonial relationship (so often ignored by conventional international relations) is seen to be of continuing relevance to an understanding of both the (ex)colonizer and the (de)colonized. A key aim of postcolonial investigations is to expose the Eurocentrism of much mainstream scholarship, and to draw attention to the epistemological bases on Western power. This in turn has led to a focus on discourse and representations, which are regarded as forms of power that need to be challenged in order to effect political change.

It is clear from the above that postcolonialism has many intellectual affinities with the post-positivist turn in international relations (see **post-positivism**), and with **poststructuralism** and postmodernism more generally. However, to reduce or subsume postcolonialism within any of these approaches does not do justice to its originality, heterogeneity and multiple sources of inspirations. To be sure, thinkers commonly associated with poststructuralism such as Michel Foucault (1926–84), Jacques Derrida (1930–2004) and Jacques Lacan (1901–81) figure prominently in the pantheon of postcolonialism, but their ideas are frequently applied in novel and eclectic ways. Moreover, many of postcolonialism's proponents would argue that their explicit political commitment to the subaltern distinguishes their accounts from what are frequently regarded (rightly or wrongly) as the more relativistic analyses of postmodernism. In this respect, many postcolonial writers are in a close dialogue with the Marxist tradition of criticism (see **Marxism**), as evidenced for example by the use of the Gramscian term 'subaltern'. Again, a certain eclecticism characterizes the use of Marxist-inspired methodologies, combining its traditional materialism with detailed attention to the subjective effects of oppression. A third important source of inspiration for post-

colonialism comes from Third World intellectuals, like Franz Fanon (1925–61), Amilcar Cabral (1924–73), and Mahatma Gandhi (1869–1948), to mention a few. The approach also has important affinities with the Subaltern Studies group of Indian historiography, which has been motivated by a desire to retell history from the counter-hegemonic standpoints of the colonized.

Recognizing the diversity of postcolonialism's intellectual antecedents is important because critics have attempted to dismiss it as a predominantly Western discipline, associated with diasporic Third World intellectuals attempting to come to terms with their own conditions within the Western academe and reflecting the concerns of the rich and well educated rather than the poor and marginalized. While it is the case that many of its exponents, like Gayatri Spivak (1999) and Homi Bhabha (1994), are (or have been) based in Anglophone universities, the interpretation of postcolonialism as the West ignores the substantial influence of many Third World thinkers. Moreover, to pose the question of postcolonialism's geographical identity can be said to pursue the wrong line of inquiry, as a central aim of the approach is precisely to abandon such strict boundaries and classifications in favor of a focus on mutually constitutive relations. This can be illustrated through an investigation of the 'post' in postcolonialism.

The 'post' in postcolonialism

Much ink has been spilt on debating exactly what the postcolonial means and when it begins, and many of the criticisms of the approach arise from the fuzziness and ambiguities of the term and the vision of history that it employs. While the 'post' in postcolonialism signifies the end of colonialism as *direct* domination, it does not imply *after* **imperialism** as a global system of hegemonic power (see **hegemony**). Thus, many of the proponents of postcolonialism have no hesitation in maintaining that we live in a world that is simultaneously postcolonial and neocolonized, and stress the continuity of colonial power relationships. In other words, colonialism as conventionally defined in terms of formal settlement and control of other people's land and goods is in the main over, but many of its structures and relations of power are still in place. The 'post' in postcolonialism is not therefore to be understood as a dividing, temporal marker, but rather as an indication of continuity. The term attempts to transcend strict chronological and dichotomous thinking where history is clearly delineated and the social world neatly categorized into separate boxes, and seeks instead to capture the continuities and complexities of any historical period.

The colonial experience is nevertheless regarded as crucial to an understanding of contemporary politics. By the 1930s, colonies and ex-colonies covered 85 per cent of the land surface of the globe, and colonialism formed a key transformative encounter for both the colonizer and the colonized. Colonial power not only changed the ways of imposing and maintaining rule over the colonized, but also the terrain within which colonized people could respond to domination. The global reach of Western imperial power also brought new peoples and places into the world capitalist economy (see **capitalism**), and compelled them to remain, even after their formal independence, within this economic system. In this way, the colonial encounter is seen to mark a profound reordering of the world, and many postcolonial writers argue that the return to a pristine, unspoilt pre-colonial culture is impossible and have warned against such nostalgia for lost origins. Crucially however, this does not mean that the pre-colonial came to an abrupt end, but rather the present is regarded as a complex mix and continuation of different cultures and temporalities.

The connections between the past and the present, the colonial and the postcolonial, the north and the south thus emerge as a key focus of postcolonial investigations. Rather than pointing to fixed temporal and geographical periods and spaces, postcolonialism draws attention to continuities, fluidity and interconnectedness, economically, politically, and culturally between the North and the south. The constitutive relationship of the North and the South, the way in which the two produce and reinforce the identity of each other both in the colonial past and the postcolonial present, are key insights and concerns of postcolonial thinking. From this perspective, the meaning of common terms like 'Africa', the 'Third World' or the 'West' can only emerge from a recognition of their relationship to the 'other'. During colonialism, for example, the claims of 'civilization' came to rest on the deficiencies of 'barbarism', with the description of 'savages' reinforcing the 'civilized' character of Europeans and legitimizing the authoritarian nature of colonial rule. This constitutive relationship continues today, and postcolonial writers argue that postcolonial territories such as Africa continue to function as metaphors through which the West represents the origins of its own norms and develops its self image and identity.

Power/knowledge and the cultural production of postcolonial societies

Despite the diverse character of postcolonial studies, it is possible to identify certain common methodologies, themes and concerns that figure prominently in the writings of many key thinkers. Of central importance is postcolonialism's extensive engagement with the role of power in the formation of identity and subjectivity and the relationship between knowledge and political practices. While mainstream International Relations tend to conceive of power as a capacity located primarily in the state and as associated with economic and military might, postcolonial approaches employ a more complex understanding of power, drawing in particular on the thinking of Michel Foucault (1926–1984). In this formulation, power is no longer perceived as only repressive, nor is it understood in purely material or institutional terms. Instead, power is productive and creative of subjects. It is also intimately linked to knowledge, not in the purely instrumental sense that knowledge is always in the service of the powerful, but in terms of the production of truth and **rationality**. Truth, in the Foucauldian sense, is a thing of this world, produced through **discourse**s that establish dominant ways of understanding and representing social reality. Discourses, in other words, are practices that systematically form the objects of which they speak, that is, practices that have material effects. Analyses informed by such insights seek to establish how certain ways of understanding and representing the world became dominant, and to demystify and politicize their truths.

This power/knowledge nexus is central to postcolonial analyses of relationships of domination and resistance, and explains in large part their attention to discourses and representational practices. It is for example a key focus of Edward Said's *Orientalism* (1979), the book often credited with having spawned the field of postcolonial studies. Arguing that there is no such thing as a delivered presence, only representation, Said shows how in the case of the Orient knowledge and power went hand in hand and how there is no such thing as an innocent, objective academic standpoint. Said's central contention is that Orientalism was a systematic discipline through which European culture both managed and produced the Orient. For Said, the Orient was ultimately a political vision whose structure promoted a binary opposition between the familiar (the West/us) and the strange (the Orient/them). In this way, the Orient is revealed as central to European self-understanding and identity, while knowledge, representation and the ability to interpret social reality emerges as a form of power that influence identities and ways of life.

This perceived power of Western discourses to create so-called 'regimes of truth' that marginalize or silence other discourses and ways of being is not confined to the colonial period, but continues into the present. A contemporary illustration can be found in the discourse of **development**, which from a postcolonial perspective can be seen to continue many of the relationships of colonialism. The ability of the rich countries to set standards for what constitutes development and progress can be regarded as a form of power that conditions the choices available to Third World countries. Rather than focusing on the stated aims of development policies, a postcolonial approach seeks to uncover its effects and to question and destabilize the 'taken for granted' character of key concepts and categories. Thus, development and its opposite underdevelopment are not seen as self-evident or pre-ordained categories. Instead they are discursive constructs; particular ways of seeing and acting upon the world that reflect not only the conditions they describe but also the constellations of social, economic and political forces at the time of their emergence. With the problematization of 'underdevelopment', which is frequently dated to the US President Harry Truman's inaugural speech in 1949, social reality became ordered into new categories such as underdeveloped, malnourished, illiterate, etc. This ordering of the world not only shapes and influences the identities of Third World subjects, but also establishes Third World countries as objects of intervention, and normalizes the right of the north to intervene and control, adapt and reshape the structures, practices and ways of life of the south. Development discourse thus helps legitimize interventions in the Third World in order to remodel it according to Western norms of progress, growth and efficiency. Seen from this perspective, development is a form of power, and through its interventions the underdeveloped subject becomes known, categorized, incorporated into statistics, models and graphs, which in turn legitimate practices and facilitate the emergence of the developed, disciplined subject. Importantly, this interpretation does not entail a denial of the material condition of poverty or the disparities between rich and poor, but rather poses a challenge to their particular conceptualization and the political practices that they make possible.

Hybridity and identity

The understanding of power as not merely domination, but also as productive of subjectivities through various micro-technologies and relations is reflected in postcolonialism's concern with hybridity and identity. Identities and subjectivities were profoundly reshaped by the colonial experience, and accordingly colonialism finds continued expression through a multiplicity of practices, philosophies, and cultures imparted to and adopted by the colonized in more or less hybrid forms. The notion of hybridity marks both the continuities of colonialism, and its failure to fully dominate the colonized. Hybridity thus draws attention to the way in which the colonizer and the colonized are forged in relationship with each other, an observation that is central to Franz Fanon's analyses. According to Fanon, the white man's self-perception as moral, rational and civilized required the image of the Negro as barbaric and uncivilized. The notion of hybridity helps to break down this essentialized, binary opposition between the colonized and the colonizer, between black and white, self and other.

Whereas for many nationalists hybridity is experienced as a regrettable loss of traditional culture and identities, often leading to attempts to recover ancient cultural practices and symbols, for many postcolonial writers hybridity is not inherently bad, nor does it signify the total domination of the colonised. Instead, hybridity, especially in the formulation of Homi Bhabha, signifies the failure of colonial power to fully dominate its subjects, and shows their creativity and resilience. Where Said's *Orientalism* at times seems to exaggerate the ability of the West to produce the Orient and ignore the voice of the Oriental, Bhabha's treatment of hybridity shows that the colonized were not passive victims whose identities were narrated in a one-way process by colonial authority. On the contrary, the ambivalence of hybrid cultures and practices, the way in which they are 'almost the same, but not quite', is for Bhabha a sign of the agency and creativity of the colonized.

The clue to this interpretation of hybridity as a potential site of resistance and subversion is to be found in the manner in which it breaks down the symmetry of the self/other distinction. The exercise of colonial authority requires the production of differentiation between the white man as more civilized than the black, for example. Hybridity, however, disrupts this differentiation, as what is disavowed by colonial power is repeated back as something different. In this way, hybridity rules out recognition, as the differences that were relied upon to justify colonial power are no longer immediately observable. Mastery is constantly asserted, but always incomplete, always slipping. Herein lies the menace of hybridity and mimicry; it discloses the ambivalence at the heart of colonial discourse and has the potential to disrupt its authority. From the 'in between', hybrid identities can engender new forms of being that can unsettle and subvert colonial and postcolonial authority. More recently, the notion of hybridity has been invoked as a measure of local creativity and agency in the face of **globalization**. Hybridity is seen to signify the creative adaptation, interpretation and transformation of Western cultural symbols and practices, and shows that formerly colonized peoples are not simply passive recipients of an all-powerful Western culture. The notion of hybridity has also cast light on the importance of the postcolonial within industrialized countries, especially in terms of the politics of **diaspora**s.

At this point, it is important to note a certain unresolved tension within postcolonialism. On the one hand, it celebrates hybrid identities, while on the other, its explicit commitment to the subaltern frequently leads to a privileging of local cultures and identities and a concern for the cultural survival of marginalized peoples encountering powerful global cultures. National culture and its preservation was central to the thinking of both Fanon and Cabral. Such positions stand in a somewhat uneasy relationship to the emphasis on hybridity and the argument that there can be no pure or unsullied identity. In terms of political choices, the notion of hybridity serves to refute political and cultural positions that advocate a return to origin' or 'tradition'. The idea of pure cultures, in urgent need of being kept free from alien contamination is feared as the type of project that led to atrocities like **ethnic cleansing**, **genocide**, and apartheid.

This view in turn has informed critiques of movements like *negritude*, which is seen to reinforce imperial hierarchies between the colonized and the colonizer and to propose an essentialized identity or 'Africanness' that is not only impossible, but also politically potentially dangerous and damaging. Others, however, fear that to abandon the belief and pursuit of 'authenticity' is simultaneously to make resistance and opposition impossible. The anti-colonial struggles, for example, gained their force in large part from an appeal to a traditional, national identity different from that of Western modernity. In response to this dilemma, Spivak has argued for what she calls a strategic essentialism that allows for some form of essentialized identity in order to facilitate resistance, while at the same time recognizing that there can be no pure identities. The extent to which this move to strategic essentialism successfully resolves the tension within postcolonialism is, however, unclear. For many postcolonial societies, the challenge remains how to resist the modernity of the West in terms other than a return to a mythical, pre-modern past and how to avoid that the local voice, once heard, does not create its own forms of violence, silencing and suppressing new minorities and subalterns.

In this context, a focus on hybridity recognizes that local identities are not exhaustive and that appeals to fixed identities (even if national or local) can contain their own dangers and therefore seeks to advocate a more generous and pluralistic vision of the world, where the possibilities for oppressive identity claims are minimized.

Resistance

As discussed before, hybridity is intimately connected to resistance in that it signifies the creativity and adaptability of the subaltern in the face of power and demonstrates that the colonial encounter as well as contemporary North–South relations cannot be understood in terms of a one-way relationship of domination. Resistance is a recurring theme in postcolonial analyzes, and this focus is frequently invoked as one of its defining features. The commitment to the marginalized, or the subaltern, is also frequently said to differentiate it from the perceived relativism of postmodernism, and the stated aim of many postcolonial writers is to give voice and make visible those who are not normally heard or seen. In this regard, postcolonial approaches have much in common with the Subaltern Studies group of Indian historiography. This group of historians has argued that the conventional historical account of India's colonial experience and independence struggle is a history of the elite, systematically ignoring the agency and resistance of the subaltern. Seeking to rewrite history by retelling it from the point of view of the subaltern, these writers demonstrate not only that the colonial relationships of power were much more complex than commonly acknowledged, but also that the poor were not passive victims of imperial power.

Postcolonial approaches share much with this revisionist Indian project, and many writers seek to recover the subject positions of the marginalized or retell history from counter-hegemonic standpoints. This is not so much an attempt to speak on behalf of the subaltern, as an effort to mark the space of the silenced in conventional imperial history and contemporary accounts of world politics, history and culture. Nevertheless, the recovery of lost or previously silent voices is seen as a form of subversion or resistance, a way in which to break down the hegemony of dominant discourses. Again, Said's *Orientalism* can be seen as an important inspiration for this focus, as by drawing attention to the intimacy of power and knowledge, he made a first step towards challenging the hegemonic narratives of the West, a process which is sometimes referred to as 'the Empire writing back' in an attempt to destabilize discourses that constructed the colonial subject as the 'other'. This process of reinterpretation and 'giving voice' is regarded by postcolonial writers as central to overturning contemporary relations of domination between the north and the south. The fact that the Empire is now 'writing back', telling its own stories, becomes not only an act of resistance, but also a form of empowerment. From a postcolonial perspective then, resistance is also about refiguring the conceptual space in which we understand and act upon the world, and thereby create the possibility for alternatives ways of being and acting.

Postcolonialism's understanding of power as productive and ubiquitous has clear implications for the analysis of resistance. As seen in the interpretation of hybridity and ambivalence, resistance is often much more subtle than in mainstream political analyses in that it is not necessarily overt or in a direct relationship of opposition and polarity (colonized/colonizer, white/black). As such, postcolonialism illustrates the inadequacy of conventional binary oppositions between domination and resistance, and shows how resistance cannot be idealized as pure opposition to the order it opposed, but operates instead inside a structure of power that it both challenges and helps to sustain. Following Foucault's insight that power works through micro-processes and relations and should therefore be investigated from the 'ground up', postcolonial investigations of resistance tend to focus on everyday forms of behavior rather than the conventional preoccupation of political science with **revolution**s, armed struggles or large-scale political opposition. The subaltern, even in conditions of extreme domination, is found to have multiple ways of resisting and avoiding power, including mockery and ridicule. Dominance, in other words, is never total; the subaltern always has her own agency and subjectivity. Given postcolonialism's pervasive skepticism of metanarratives and universal truths, it should be noted that such local level micro-struggles against the dominant order take on a particular importance as they may give rise to alternatives ways of organizing life.

By drawing attention to the epistemic aspects of colonial and postcolonial power and violence, postcolonial writers have also problematized the target of resistance. The solution is no longer to be found simply in 'seizing' state power or the means of production. Instead, postcolonialism's project can be described as material, cultural, and epistemological, in that it entails a recognition that change of economic and political structures of domination and inequality requires a parallel and profound change in their epistemological and psychological underpinnings and effects. Hence, Ashis Nandy's (1983) argument that colonialism was first and foremost a matter of consciousness and accordingly needs to be defeated in the mind. That said, postcolonialism has been criticized for its overly discursive focus and for ignoring the structural inequalities of power and wealth between the north and the south. The focus on representations and discourses is seen by critics to be largely irrelevant to the everyday struggles of the poor and marginalized, and to reflect the concerns of the 'ivory tower' rather than the subaltern. What, critics ask, has postcolonialism got to say about the exploitation of the Third World by transnational **capitalism**, about the **debt trap**, or Western trade protectionism? The ability to mock power and the existence of hybridity, such critics maintain, may demonstrate the agency of the subaltern, but it does little to actually change the distribution of the resources domestically or globally. Hence, the poor continue to suffer, despite the counter-hegemonic narratives of postcolonial writers.

However, while it is the case that postcolonial critiques have frequently been concerned with representation and the past, this cannot be interpreted as a disregard for contemporary material or structural inequalities. Instead, the postcolonial project advocates a politics based on a recognition of the interconnectedness of the past and the present and of the intimate relationship between power, discourse and political institutions and practices. By making explicit the forms of rationality and the assumptions that underpin 'common sense' and various 'expert' knowledges and practices, postcolonialism not only helps expose the contingency of the current social and political order. It also provides crucial insights concerning the maintenance and reproduction of current relations and structures, and through such critiques postcolonial perspectives can help generate possibilities for transforming social and political conditions.

Further reading

Bhabha, H. (1994) *The Location of Culture*, London: Routledge.
Darby, P. (ed.) (1997) *At the Edge of International Relations. Postcolonialism, Gender and Dependency*, London: Pinter.
Fanon, F. (1986) *Black Skin, White Masks*, London: Pluto Press.
Loomba, A. (1996) *Colonialism/Postcolonialism*, London: Routledge.
Moore-Gilbert, B. (1997) *Postcolonial Theory: Contexts, Practices, Politics*, London: Verso.
Nandy, A. (1983) *The Intimate Enemy. Loss and Recovery of Self under Colonialism*, Delhi: Oxford University Press
Paolini, A. J. (1999) *Navigating Modernity: Postcolonialism, Identity and International Relations*, Boulder, CO: Lynne Rienner.
Said, E. (1979) *Orientalism*, Harmondsworth: Penguin.
Spivak, G. (1999) *A Critique of Postcolonial Reason: Toward a History of the Vanishing Present*, Cambridge, MA: Harvard University Press.
Young, R. (2001) *Postcolonialism. An Historical Introduction*, Oxford: Blackwell.

See also: decolonization; imperialism; neocolonialism; Third World

RITA ABRAHAMSEN

Post-Fordism

A generic term employed to describe a whole range of transformations in the organization of business and the state that have taken place since the early 1970s. The period between 1945 and 1970, often described as the Golden Age of Fordism, saw an unprecedented degree of sustained economic growth in the core capitalist economies of North America, Western Europe and Japan (see **capitalism**). Many believe that the principle cause for the rapid pace of economic growth sustained during that period was the high rate of productivity growth following the successful implementation and diffusion of techniques of mass production and distribution by **multinational corporation**s. These corporations developed and perfected high volume technologies of assembly line mass production and distribution of standardized products. They followed a model of business organization developed first by Henry Ford in the production of the Ford T car. The predominance of mass production techniques stimulated in turn, modern techniques of mass consumption. The combination of the business model with mass consumption techniques is captured by the term Fordism.

By the late 1960s, however, corporations increasingly experienced difficulties in sustaining such high rate of productivity growth. At the same time, the long period of sustained growth in the core capitalist economies produced a sufficiently large number of consumers in search of non-standardized, individualized products and services. The combination of these two trends contributed to a marked decline in corporate profit rates and a general crisis of Fordism. The crisis of the early 1970s, which manifests itself in, among other things, the collapse of the **Bretton Woods** agreement and the 1973 oil **crisis**, intensified the quest for an alternative, so-called Post-Fordist, model of production and distribution of goods.

No single model of business organization has prevailed during the period of post-Fordism. Hence, post-Fordism refers, at best, to a number of models, each of which has evolved since the 1970s. Indeed, considerable diversity and evolution of different business and organizational models renders the concept of post-Fordism less useful. Nonetheless, as a general category, post-Fordism is based on the dominance of a flexible and permanently innovative pattern of accumulation, characterized by the phenomenon of 'lean production'.

The concept of 'lean production' includes Just-in-Time (JIT) and Total Quality Control (TQM), extensively used by the Japanese auto industry beginning in the late 1960s. The industry shifted from mass-market production to market segmentation and niche marketing strategies, which requires highly skilled labor and emphasizes quality and services over quantity. Much earlier, IBM combined total quality management and lean manufacturing, just-in-time delivery, and price based costing. However, lean production was the term adopted to describe the general philosophy adopted by Japanese business of continually reducing waste in all areas and in all forms. Lean production consists of the techniques of Just in time (JIT) which refers to a production scheduling and inventory control technique that calls for any item needed at a production operation – whether raw material, finished item, or anything in between – to be produced and available precisely when needed. JIT was designed at Toyota specifically to cut waste in production. Lean production is also associated with Total Quality Control (TQM), which refers to activities involving managers and workers in a totally integrated effort toward improving performance at every level. Toyota aimed for the smallest possible batches replacing the American philosophy of optimal batch size. To achieve its aims, Toyota developed a new material controls method (the *kanban* system) and the aforementioned JIT technique. Consequently, the setup time for new product lines was reduced dramatically. By the early 1970s, Toyota could reset its press lines in three minutes compared to nearly four

hours for comparable manufacturers in the West. The production process became ever more sensitive to disturbances, and manufacturing quality aimed at zero defects. Small batch manufacturing led to the need for highly flexible workforce, with rapid and frequent relocation of personnel according to the production needs of the moment.

While Japanese lean production techniques were adopted in the automobile and electronic business, there was evidence that lean production was evolving in Europe and the United States in a direction known as 'flexible production', based on the rise of specialized industrial districts in Europe and the United States. In these districts, production took place for a small series of customer tailored products. New technologies were used to renew long-standing craft traditions and to improve product quality in a more participatory work environment.

Meanwhile in the telecommunication and computer sector a different type of industrial organization arose. The new competitive form is referred to as 'Wintelism' where the market dominance of companies like Intel (microprocessors) and Microsoft (Windows operating systems), exemplify the importance of knowledge to modern competitiveness and market success. The rising importance of standards and design is also connected with the restructuring of corporate as well as industrial forms of organization. Leading or 'brand-name' corporations are pursuing 'innovation intensive' activity while delinking from 'production intensive' activity. They outsource their productive capacity and concentrate resources to help pursue innovation at the product level, creating and enhancing the characteristics that define products and how they interact with other products. Thus, market-creating innovative capacity is increasingly hoarded 'in-house' by dominant corporations, and market-supplying capacity is allowed to migrate into the external economy.

The general pattern evolved increasingly towards what Richard Dunning calls alliance capitalism (1997). Dunning maintains that the traditional hierarchical corporation engaged in adversarial relationships with other corporations in the world is giving way to the sharing of information and the establishment of strategic alliances. Firms are increasingly engaged in collaborative arrangements in order to minimize uncertainty and transaction costs.

Like Fordism, the plethora of transformations in business organization extends well beyond process engineering, contributing to the rise of the 'competition state'. States are responding to accelerated capital mobility, the growing diversity in manufacturing operations, and organizational paradigms and business models by trying to supply the right mix of infrastructural support and macro- and micro-economic policies to encourage the location of high-value production chains in their territories (Palan and Abbott 1996).

Further reading

Amin, A. (ed.) (1994) *Post-Fordism: A Reader*, Oxford: Blackwell.

Dunning, J. H. (1997) *Alliance Capitalism and Global Business*, London: Routledge.

Lipietz A. (1987) *Mirages and Miracles: The Crisis of Global Fordism*, London: Verso.

Palan, R. and Abbott, J. (1996) *State Strategies in the Global Political Economy*, London: Pinter.

Palan, R (ed.) (2000) *Global Political Economy: Contemporary Theories*, London: Routledge.

See also: disintermediation; newly industrializing country; offshore

RONEN PALAN

Post-positivism

A term coined in the late 1980s to describe a group of theoretical approaches that reject positivism as an appropriate epistemology and methodology for the study of international relations. Post-positivist approaches include much work conducted under the labels of **constructivism**, **critical theory**, **feminism**, and **post-structuralism**. Normative approaches such as **communitarianism** and **cosmopolitanism** are also post-positivist.

Despite their differences, all these 'isms' can be seen as part of a post-positivist era in the study of international relations. All that this means is that positivism is no longer dominant in shaping the nature and limits of contemporary international relations theory, although the debate between supporters and opponents of positivism remains a controversial issue. Rather than explore all the manifestations of post-positivism, students should be clear what positivism is (or was!) in the field.

First, it is important to distinguish between epistemology and methodology. The term epistemology comes from the Greek word *epistêmê*, meaning knowledge. In simple terms, epistemology is the philosophy of knowledge or of how we come to know. Methodology is also concerned with how we come to know, but is much more practical in nature. Methodology is focused on the specific ways that we can use to try to understand our world. Epistemology and methodology are intimately related: the former involves the philosophy of how we come to know the world and the latter involves the practice.

Positivism is a philosophical movement characterized by an emphasis upon science and scientific method as the only sources of knowledge, a sharp distinction between the realms of fact and value, and a strong hostility toward religion and traditional philosophy. Positivists believe that there are only two sources of knowledge (as opposed to opinion): logical reasoning and empirical experience. A statement is meaningful if and only if it can be proved true or false, at least in principle, by means of the experience. This assertion is called the verifiability principle. The meaning of a statement is its method of verification; we know the meaning of a statement if we know the conditions under which the statement is true or false.

Thus in its broadest sense, positivism is a position that holds that the goal of knowledge is simply to describe the phenomena that we experience. The purpose of science is simply to stick to what we can observe and measure. Knowledge of anything beyond that, a positivist would hold, is impossible. Since we cannot directly observe emotions, thoughts, etc. (although we may be able to measure some of the physical and physiological accompaniments), these are not legitimate topics for scientific study.

In a positivist view of the world, science is seen as the way to get at truth, to understand the world well enough so that we might predict and control it. The world and the universe are deterministic. They operate by laws of cause and effect that we can discern if we apply the unique approach of the scientific method. Science is largely a mechanistic or mechanical affair. We use deductive reasoning to postulate theories that we can test. Based on the results of our studies, we may learn that our theory does not fit the facts well and so we need to revise our theory to better predict reality. The positivist believes in empiricism, the idea that observation and measurement is the core of science. The key approach of the scientific method is the experiment, the attempt to discern laws of behavior.

The only shared characteristic among those who call themselves 'post-positivist' in the study of international relations is a rejection of one or more aspects of positivism. Beyond that, post-positivism defies easy summary. It is perhaps best seen as a multi-dimensional attempt to broaden the epistemological and methodological horizons of the field. Although this attempt has led to claims by some scholars that the study of international relations has fallen into disarray, most scholars have welcomed the move toward post-positivism even if they remain suspicious of some of its manifestations in international relations theory.

Further reading

Brown, C. (1992) *International Relations Theory: New Normative Approaches*, New York: Columbia University Press.

Crawford, R. and Jarvis, D. (eds) (2001) *International Relations: Still An American Social Science?* New York: SUNY Press.

Lapid, Y. (1989) 'The Third Debate: On the Prospects of International Theory in a Post-positivist Era', *International Studies Quarterly*, 33(3), 235–54.

Smith, S., Booth, K. and Zalewski, M. (eds) (1996) *International Theory: Positivism and After*, Cambridge: Cambridge University Press.

Wendt, A. (1999) *Social Theory of International Relations*, Cambridge: Cambridge University Press.

See also: agent-structure debate; constructivism; cosmopolitanism; critical theory; foundationalism/anti-foundationalism; hermeneutics; inter-paradigm debate

TERRY O'CALLAGHAN

Poststructuralism

The name for a tradition within international relations scholarship that draws on deconstructive, interpretative, critical, psychoanalytic or genealogical (see **genealogy**) approaches to examine practices of global politics. It was previously called postmodernism, and is often aligned, by those who enjoy such categorizations, with post-foundationalist or post-positivist (see **post-positivism**) approaches. Both these labels, and indeed the description 'poststructuralism', are generally regarded as unhelpful by scholars who use such approaches. This is not just awkwardness on their part; to a certain extent the discomfort arises because notions of 'post' foundationalism and 'post' positivism imply the existence of that which they follow, namely foundations and positivism. This misunderstanding can lead, for example, to the complaint that poststructuralists are suggesting that we abandon foundations. However, they are not suggesting such a move. Rather, they argue that there are no such things as foundations or points of origin outside the **discourse**s that constitute them. In other words, to call any approach 'post-foundationalist' or 'post-positivist' assumes precisely the Archimedean point from which objective judgments can be made, an assumption that many of those labeled 'poststructuralist' find implausible.

Taken literally, the term 'poststructuralist' designates theoretical approaches that build upon and to a certain extent challenge structuralism. However, poststructuralism is not opposed to structuralism. It would challenge the notion of a centered structure and would ask whether a non-centered structure might be possible, but it would not want to throw out the idea of structure altogether. Additional confusion arises when the notion of poststructuralism is related to the so-called agent-structure problem in the study of international relations (see **agent-structure debate**). Poststructuralists are wrongly assumed to be on the side of agency, as opposed to structure. On the contrary, poststructuralist thinking considers what it might mean to regard both agent and structure as constituted by each other at the same moment.

The misunderstanding that the term 'poststructuralism' generates is one reason why scholars of international politics within this tradition dislike the label. Another reason is a dislike of the process of labeling altogether: such projects are regarded as homogenizing and totalizing. A third reason is that the label draws a series of disparate thinkers under one banner. What is called 'poststructuralism' in international relations scholarship tends to include work that draws on a range of writers whose differences are at least as important as their similarities.

Subjectivity

However, despite these differences, it is possible to trace certain ideas or concepts that are to a large extent shared by those labeled 'poststructuralist' and these concepts might thus be said to characterize this style of thinking. The first of these is the notion of a de-centered subject. This conception represents a move away from the fully self-present, though self-doubting, Cartesian subject, the subject who could say with certainty that 'I think therefore I am'.

The first move away from the Cartesian subject was toward what might be called the sociological subject. This is the subject who is formed by the social and economic environment. In other words the subject does not arrive in the world fully formed. Rather, the subject is developed by upbringing and socialization. It is in this context that the nature/nurture and freedom/determinism debate arises. How much of the self is a product of social upbringing and how much is a product of its inherent (genetic or spiritual) nature? The second move, to what would by some be called the 'poststructural' subject, involves the abandonment of any residual notion of pre-existing subjectivity. For this way of thinking, the 'subject' and the 'world' are not distinct entities. Rather, they are produced, as 'world' and as 'subject', through social, cultural and particularly political practices. This is often expressed by saying that both subject and social order are 'mutually constituted' or 'co-constituted'. Neither pre-exists the other. The subject is not in this sense born into a world. Instead, the subject produces the world of which it is a part as the same time as it is itself produced.

These types of statement are often misunderstood as implying some sort of denial of the existence of material reality; on the contrary, they are perhaps better taken as assertions that there is nothing outside the material, or that there is nothing outside the text. It is important to note the differences between concepts of the subject and subjectivity that retain the notion 'in the last instance' of a core or essential subjectivity and those that do not. Seeing the subject as fragmented, or as the potential holder of a diversity of identities or possible 'subject positions', which is often how poststructuralist thinking is characterized, is more a feature of thinking that retains an essential subject. Otherwise, how could there be fragmentation? What is there that could 'possess' a range of identities? Once the notion of an essential core is abandoned, however, identity can no longer be 'possessed' nor subjectivity 'fragmented'. It is important to note the distinction between this latter view of the subject and subjectivity and that taken by more constructivist approaches to international relations (see **constructivism**).

Several different strands of thinking contributed to the move from a Cartesian subject through a sociological subject to a postmodern subject. For example, in psychoanalysis the work of Sigmund Freud (1856–1939) proposed that people were not in control of their thoughts in quite the way that René Descartes (1596–1650) assumed. To account for certain symptoms that Freud observed in his patients, their dreams, slips of the tongue and jokes, it was helpful to propose that a large part of thinking takes place in a realm called the unconscious. In this realm, to which there is no conscious access, thinking processes are structured very differently; moreover, conscious thought is to be regarded as in many ways the lesser in importance. Ferdinand de Saussure (1857–1913) demonstrated that language was not a simple case of nomenclature or transparent communication of pre-existing ideas. The naming of objects in the world is arbitrary, and, moreover, the process of naming produces the object named as something that is separate from the continuum of 'things in the world'. Objects, in other words, are not presented as distinct, ready for naming. This can be seen by the way in which each language not only names objects differently, but has a distinct set of objects that it enables its speakers to 'see'. This means that people do not speak language. Rather, language 'speaks' people. What this means is that what is said – or indeed, thought – depends on what the specific language, and its way of seeing the world, makes it possible to say or think. This means that thinking, which for Descartes was intimately related to his individual existence (it was the one thing he could be sure of) is an inherently social activity that relies on language.

Language and discourse

An acknowledgment of the significance of language, discourse and interpretation is perhaps the second feature that approaches labeled as poststructuralist share. As well as pointing out the importance of language in constituting the world, Saussure noted that meaning in language depends not on positive value but on difference. Words mean what they do, not because of any link in sound with the object they represent, but because of the difference between one word and the next. What is said is meaningful because of the associations with what is not said. This notion is taken further in the study of discourse that takes place in Michel Foucault's (1926–1984) work. Whereas Saussure was interested in what *could* be said in any particular language, Foucault was interested in what *is* said in any specific epoch. He explored the connection between the various things that were said, and the other social practices in which these 'things said' were embedded in any particular era or *episteme*. He argued that different epistemes could be characterized by different ways of looking at the world, and in particular by distinct ideas of what might constitute an ordering principle, or a way of making sense of the world. Whereas a history of ideas approach would be concerned to trace the gradual evolution of a particular concept over time, Foucault's archaeology of knowledge, which he also designated a history of the present, aimed to demonstrate the discontinuity between different ways of ordering the world in different epochs.

A Foucauldian approach is also concerned to demonstrate the continuity between discursive practices and other social practices. Discourse is not confined to written forms or to language in the narrow sense, but extends to all symbolic systems and to any form of social practice that by definition involves such systems. One of Foucault's key contributions to contemporary thought and political analysis is his demonstration of the way in which knowledge is tied up with the forms of subjectivity to which it gives rise. He showed this in the case of the penal or prison system. He examined the way in which the prison as a form of punishment displaced earlier forms that had involved public executions and the demonstration of the sovereign's power over the subject's body by practices such as hanging, drawing, and quartering. The penal system, in contrast, involved a form of punishment that entailed disciplinary practices: confinement to an institution, continuous surveillance, the collection and storage of information about prisoners, their involvement in compulsory work programs, and so forth. The image of the panopticon is exemplary of this disciplinary practice: prisoners were held in cells structured in such a way that each prisoner could be seen by the prison guards at any time, but no prisoner could see either other prisoners or the source of surveillance. As a result, prisoners behaved as if they were continuously observed: they disciplined themselves. Foucault also crucially observed that although prisons always failed in their declared aim of rehabilitation (levels of re-offending by released prisoners were always high) they nevertheless continued as institutions. He argued that to understand this it is necessary to ask not 'Why did they fail?' but 'What was their function?' His response was that prisons delineate a class of person (the delinquent) as a distinct group that has no political voice.

Analogous forms of argument and analysis have since been applied to institutions of international politics. It has been proposed, for example, by Arturo Escobar (1994), that Third World **development** is a process that fails to produce its stated result (the economic development of 'underdeveloped' areas of the globe), but that continues nevertheless because it serves to delineate certain countries as in need of development and thus intervention. Aid practices in complex emergencies have been analyzed in the same way.

Power relations and biopolitics

Michel Foucault's work has also been of significance in relation to the third strand that is shared by so-called poststructuralist approaches to international politics: a different view of power. Traditionally power has tended to be thought of as something that can be possessed: states or individuals *have* power, and some have more than others. In this way of thinking it makes sense to talk of a **balance of power**, and of different forms of power (military, economic, or cultural, for example). Foucault suggests a new way of thinking of power. He argues that power should be seen not as something that a pre-existing entity can possess but rather as something produced in relationships, relationships that are to be seen as constitutive of those entities themselves. Thus Foucault does not speak of 'power' but of 'power relations'. Power is not held centrally but produced in a dispersed way, through a series of power relations that take place on a micro-level during social interactions. To understand how power works, which is fundamental to understanding global politics, it is necessary to examine the microphysics of power relations. This enables scholars to understand how relations of domination, when power is sedimented over long periods, arise, and how they might be challenged. It makes it possible to analyze resistance. In the Foucauldian view, power is not separate from resistance but rather implies it: were there no resistance, there would be nothing

that could properly be called a power relation.

Foucauldian thinking insists on the close relation between power and knowledge, or more accurately, on the inseparability of what he calls 'power/ knowledge'. He talks in terms of 'regimes of truth': systems of power relations that determine what mechanisms are used in any particular era to determine what counts as true. Each society has its own way of authorizing 'truth'. Intellectuals are closely implicated in these regimes. And each system of power relations produces particular subjects and at the same time generates knowledge about those subjects. For example, in the criminal justice system, records are kept of offenders. The sum of these records produces the delinquent as subject, as described above.

The detailed analysis of power relations leads to the identification of a series of different practices of power. Foucault argues that sovereign power, which he regards as entailing the power over death (the sovereign can put to death those it chooses) has more recently been supplemented by biopower; the power over life, or, more specifically, the power over populations. Biopower is expressed in disciplinary practices, such as are found in the prison, the barracks, the school or the hospital, and in forms of governmentality. The state increasingly operates through these practices, which are addressed to entire populations, rather than through the direct expression of sovereign power in relation to the individual subject. A somewhat different view of these types of power and politics is proposed by the political philosopher Giorgio Agamben (1998). He argues that from the start the Western form of the state has been biopolitical. It has relied on the separation, first made by the Greeks, between the home or domestic sphere and the *polis* or public realm. The former is seen as the realm of bare life, the latter that of politically qualified life. The political sphere is maintained only by the exclusion of particular forms of life, which Agamben calls *homo sacer*, or bare life. *Homo sacer* has no political voice; as a form of life it is included in the political realm only by its exclusion from it. The form of power that operates through the ban or the exclusion is sovereign power, according to Agamben; his work thus associates sovereign power and biopolitics. He argues that increasingly in the contemporary world all life has become bare life, life excluded from politics, and that sovereign power is to be seen no longer as the power over death, nor as the power over life, but the power *to make survive*.

Excess or lack

In addition to the shared interest in subjectivity, linguistic or discursive practices, and power relations, scholars working within what is called the poststructuralist tradition share a fourth concern, one that is perhaps more difficult to specify. This is an interest in what has been called variously the excess (or lack), the real, or the mystical. It is closely related to the question of the political in this thinking. What is alluded to here is an interest in that which falls out of language and discourse, that which has to be excluded in order for what we call social reality to constitute itself, or that which occurs at the moment of the founding of the state but is then forgotten.

This notion that is particularly apparent in the Lacanian tradition, where the subject itself is seen as constituted around a lack or a traumatic kernel. The lack or the excess can be explained by noting that once something has been named, that something both *never lives*

up to the name it is given and *is always more than* the name can encompass. For example, if a person is described as a 'political activist', then there are two possible responses. First, one might say, well, if that person is an activist, why do they not stand in elections, or go on demonstrations? Surely writing letters to one's representative or delivering election manifestos is not sufficient? Second, there is the opposite response. The person concerned is not just an activist: consider all the other things they do: they are a mother and an employee, for example, not just an activist. In Derridean thought, attention is drawn to the 'mystical foundation of authority', the way in which the 'origin' of a state or a system of laws is a 'non-founded founding moment': a moment that has nothing to rely on to justify or legitimate itself because it is the very point at which the source of law or legitimation will have been established.

It is interesting to note at this point the way in which this type of thinking leads to a questioning of the linearity of time. It is only when a legitimate source of law has been established that the processes that led to its establishment will be seen as legitimate. There is a certain non-linearity or retrospective character to the temporality involved here. A similar character can be noted in the case of subjectivity: if the subject becomes what it is in processes of interaction, then it only ever *will have been*. There is never a moment in the present at which it can be said that the subject 'is' anything in particular. By the time it has been acknowledged as something, it will already have become something slightly different, if only through its involvement in the process of recognition.

One of the features of poststructuralist thinking is the way it questions conceptions of politics and the political. In much of this work there is an attempt to distinguish *politics* (something that takes place in elections, political parties and government institutions and forms part of the realm distinguished from the economic or the social) from *the political*. The latter is more concerned with specifying what counts as 'politics' and establishing the institutional setting through which it can take place. Whereas politics operates within a settled agenda or framework that is taken for granted, the political takes place when that agenda itself is called into question. The political also refers to the processes that take place every day in order to reproduce that order, once established. The political moment is unsettled and unsettling, the moment of excess or of trauma. There have been a number of attempts within poststructuralism to rethink 'the political', but there are other scholars who would not want to define 'the political' at all but to focus on processes of re-politicization and de-politicization. James Ferguson, for example, in his book *The Anti-Politics Machine* (1994), looks at the way in which development practices in Lesthoto function to de-politicize a series of social practices and thus place them beyond political challenge.

The political moment is often seen as similar to what in Derridean thought is called the moment of decision. This is the moment of ethico-political responsibility. It is the point at which it is necessary to take an action that is not guaranteed, or indeed cannot be guaranteed, by rule or by law. Only such actions can be said to be responsible, not actions that follow rules, whether contained in legal or moral codes. The latter are not ethico-political acts but rule following technologies. Rules or laws are framed in general terms, and cannot be 'applied' directly to particular cases. They always have to be interpreted, or re-invented. Whether an ethico-politically

responsible action has taken place or not cannot be determined retrospectively, since afterwards it will often appear that the act has followed a rule, although it may have actually created or at least modified that rule. The moment of decision is an *aporia* or non-passage.

In this tradition, the political or political community has to engage with notions of hospitality or openness to the radical other, whether in the form of an 'other' such as the **refugee** or stranger, or in the form of the future as what is 'to come'. In both cases, there is an injunction not to close off possibility and futurity by any attempt to specify or limit what it is that hospitality is to be offered to, or what that hospitality might comprise. This radical openness refuses to set out a program or an agenda for a utopian future.

Research methods

What is called poststructuralism does not translate neatly into research methods, although it does give rise to certain ways of working and specific approaches. Despite the mythology surrounding these approaches, they are highly practical and many scholars in this tradition are engaged in detailed empirical analyses, involving for example, meticulous readings of texts, in depth participant observation, elite interviews, oral history, archive research and so on. Methods such as **deconstruction**, interpretative analysis, discourse analysis and **genealogy** are used to analyze the data that is gathered through empirical work. Often the focus of study will be the practices of other academics, as well as those of policymakers and workers in government or **non-governmental organizations**. It is important to note that poststructuralism is not just a method of textual analysis in the narrow sense of the study of written or spoken texts or discourses. It is an approach that treats social practices, objects and institutions as 'texts' in the broadest sense, in that they are capable of being interpreted in terms of their production of meaning, their discursive function and the power-relations and structures they produce and in which they are embedded. James Ferguson's work on development in Lesotho is again an excellent example here. He examines the way in which the development discourse produces a particular picture of Lesotho, and how interventions organized on this basis strengthen and expand bureaucratic state power while at the same time presenting a depoliticized view of the processes involved.

These types of analysis can lead directly to policy engagements. They do not lead to policy advice of the form 'if such and such a situation is found, do this': they lead to the recommendation to be suspicious of such suggestions, which can often be harmful and lead to counterproductive actions. In other words, they eschew prescriptive generalizations and encourage a focus on the specifics of particular situations. In ethical terms they advocate a focus on singularity: the singularity of the person or of the practice, the singularity of the situation in which policy decisions have to be made. In this way what is argued is not very different from the way in which many, perhaps most, people act in practice, but what is explicitly refused is the idea that there is a possibility of 'expert', objective, non-political knowledge that can provide impartial and universally applicable guidance for action. All knowledge is seen as situated in terms of power relations as well as in terms of the social and cultural background against which it is produced.

Poststructuralism in international relations

There are a large number of scholars in international relations who are using approaches that might be described as poststructuralist, even though many of them would prefer not to be subsumed under this label. This work examines the full diversity of topics that come under the rubric of international relations, for example, **security**, **war** and militarization, political economy, international ethics, **diplomacy**, international institutions, social movements, development, postcolonial politics, foreign policy, conflict resolution, migration, refugees, and citizenship, and includes scholars with expertise in a range of different parts of the world.

Poststructuralism and other traditions

Poststructuralist thinking within international relations is very closely related to other strands of work. Many writers within the feminist tradition count poststructuralist thinkers among those in their toolbox. Of course there are a number of different aspects of feminist and **gender** thinking in political theory and international politics. Some of these hold a more or less essentialist view of 'woman', though in most cases this is quite likely to be a strategic essentialism that can sit happily alongside poststructuralism. Other writers in the feminist tradition will be very critical of the way in which much poststructuralist thinking can often appear to be gender blind. Agamben's work, for example, makes no reference to the way in which women have always been regarded as outside the political realm nor does he acknowledge how feminist political theory has long since pointed this out.

There are similar issues concerning the relation of the poststructuralist tradition in general to questions of race and ethnocentrism. Foucault for example could be accused of ignoring the imperial setting in which the French thinking that he analyzes developed. However, there is a very rich literature in postcolonial studies that takes continental thinking very much to heart and uses it to analyze both colonial and postcolonial practices. This strand of thinking is increasingly being brought into international relations. It is invaluable in drawing into the discussion areas of the world that have been largely ignored by international relations scholars in the past, and practices of **imperialism** and colonialism whose analysis has been neglected despite their intimate relation to contemporary practices of intervention and **globalization**.

Much poststructuralist work draws strongly on certain elements of **Marxism**, and is closely related to 'post-Marxism'. Poststructuralist analyses of ideology in particular can be seen as close to Gramscian notions of commonsense, and the way in which discourses operate can be linked to Gramscian ideas of **hegemony**. On the whole, although poststructuralism might not want to make an abstract distinction between the material and the ideational (seeing such a distinction as socially constituted) poststructuralists would not want to refuse the importance of the economic, but rather to point out the extent to which it relies on, is implicated in and produced by discursive practices and relations of power.

Further reading

Agamben, G. (1998) *Homo Sacer: Sovereign Power and Bare Life,* Stanford, CA: Stanford University Press.

Campbell, D. and Shapiro, M. J. (1999) *Moral Spaces: Rethinking Ethics and World Politics,* Minneapolis, MN: University of Minnesota Press.

Der Derian, J. and Shapiro, M. J. (1989) *International/Intertextual Relations,* New York: Lexington Books.

Edkins, J. (1999) *Poststructuralism and International Relations,* Boulder, CO: Lynne Rienner.

Escobar, A. (1994) *Encountering Development: The Making and Unmaking of the Third World,* Princeton, NJ: Princeton University Press.

Ferguson, J. (1994) *The Anti-Politics Machine: 'Development', Depoliticisation, and Bureaucratic Power in Lesotho,* Minneapolis, MN: University of Minnesota Press.

Foucault, M. (2000) *Power: Essential Works of Foucault 1954–1984,* New York: The New Press.

Hindess, B. (1996) *Discourses of Power,* Oxford: Blackwell.

Shapiro, M. J. and Alker, H. R. (eds) (1996) *Challenging Boundaries: Global Flows, Territorial Identities,* Minneapolis, MN: University of Minnesota Press.

Walker, R. B. J. (1993) *Inside/Outside: International Relations as Political Theory,* Cambridge: Cambridge University Press.

See also: deconstruction; discourse; genealogy; identity/difference; power

JENNY EDKINS

Power

Power is a central concept in International Relations (IR). As so often in IR, the theoretical discussion takes its reference point from **realism**, since the role of power is central to this dominant worldview in the field. According to realists, the 'struggle for power' is the defining feature of international affairs and understanding power is the realist precondition for successful policy. More precisely, understanding power is essential to answer two key questions. Who can be expected to win in a conflict? Who governs international politics? Translated into the realm of theory, power becomes a central variable in a twofold causal link. For realists, power understood as resources or 'capabilities' is an indicator for the strength of actors, and consequently of their capacity to affect or control events. Likewise, a general capacity to control outcomes has been used as an indicator for determining how the **international system** is governed.

Power politics and the 'lump' concept of power in realist theories

At the broadest level, realism relies on the concept of the **balance of power** to generate hypotheses concerning international stability, and the likelihood of **war** among states. However, the balance of power only makes sense as a concept if there exists a common denominator for power in which all its dimensions can be coherently aggregated. At the level of the state, realist theory assumes that states are positional actors that are primarily motivated to maximize their relative power in comparison with other states. Again, this assumption requires that power be measurable, akin to the concept of money in economic theory. As John Mearsheimer (2001: 12) puts it, '[p]ower is the currency of great-power politics (see **great powers**), and states compete for it among themselves. What money is to economics, power is to international relations'. In this analogy, the striving for utility maximization expressed and measured in terms of money, parallels the **national interest** (i.e. **security**) expressed in terms of (relative) power.

This central assumption has been challenged, and many scholars argue

that the analogy between power and money is false. To aggregate power resources, one needs a common scale to measure their value, just as money provides a way of imputing value to disparate goods and services. Critics of realism claim that unlike money, power is not a *fungible* phenomenon. The term fungibility refers to the idea of a moveable good that can be freely substituted by another of the same class. Fungible goods are those universally applicable or convertible, in contrast to those goods that retain value only in a specific context. According to the critics, it is difficult to see how even apparently ultimate power resources like **weapons of mass destruction** might be of help in getting another state to change its monetary policies. Thus in international relations, power cannot play a corresponding role as a standard of value. It cannot be the 'currency' of great power politics. Actors are never sure about its real value in the variety of different (power) denominations. At best, power is segmented, usable within specific issue areas. The aggregation of power in a general 'balance' is inherently uncertain.

In response, realists have argued that diplomats have repeatedly been able to find an aggregate measure of power and hence the difference between money and power is one of degree, not of kind. Yet even if actors can agree on some approximations for establishing a rough ranking of power, these agreements are social conventions which by definition can be challenged and exist only to the extent that the agreements last. As David Baldwin argues, it 'is time to recognize that the notion of a single overall international power structure unrelated to any particular issue area is based on a concept of power that is virtually meaningless' (Baldwin 1989: 167).

Political pluralism: redefining the link between resources and outcomes

The rebirth of power analysis in IR/IPE over the last two decades has been inspired by what Baldwin (1989) calls the 'paradox of unrealised power'. For example, during the Vietnam War, the leading **superpower** had to accept a humiliating military and political defeat against the Vietcong. Some scholars tried to explain this paradox away by identifying the lack of 'will' on the side of the United States to use all its available resources, and to convert capability into power over outcomes. An explanation based on alleged conversion failures implies that the war did not show the relative weakness of the United States, but simply its unrealized strength. But such an explanation can re-arrange *ex post* any outcome to suit any power distribution. In other words, such an explanation has the scholarly implication that the significance of power cannot be empirically assessed, let alone employed as a predictor of outcomes.

A more 'pluralist' approach to power acknowledges that power is segmented into issue-areas. Consequently, control over resources, even issue specific ones, does not necessarily translate into control over outcomes. For example, in his discussion of **hegemonic stability theory**, Robert Keohane (1984) distinguishes between a crude systemic version that seeks to explain patterns of cooperation among states based solely on underlying shifts in the distribution of power, and a more sophisticated version in which the concept of leadership figures prominently. In Keohane's analysis, the latter version is preferable, undermining the utility of any simplistic explanation of national interests based solely on the distribution of power.

Another approach to the paradox of unrealized power has been proposed by David Baldwin (1989). His approach maintains a strong causal role for power by further specifying the relational and situational context that defines which policy instruments can count as actual power resources in specific issue areas. For Baldwin, there can be no useful assessment of power independent of situational factors unique to specific issue areas, and all generalizations about power are inherently contingent. He emphasizes that power is fundamentally a property of a relationship between two or more actors, and can only be understood in the context of that relationship. For example, if someone who is about to commit suicide is threatened at gunpoint to choose between his money and his life, he might not feel threatened at all. The gun as a power resource may therefore be powerless to achieve its intended outcome.

In other words, power comes not (only) from the utility attached to resources, but also from the value systems of human beings in their relations with each other. Value systems, in turn, cannot be simply assumed in any empirical analysis of power. Instead, the researcher has first to analyze the value systems of the interacting parties in order to establish what power resources exist in the first place. For this reason, Baldwin insists that one can only study power as a causal variable in circumscribed 'policy-contingency frameworks'. The framework specifies the scope and domain of power, as well as the norms and values within which interaction takes place. Once circumscribed, power can then be defined as a causal antecedent to an outcome. The price to be paid in this approach is that power analysis is a very poor predictive tool. The question should always be: power over whom, and with respect to what?

Structural power in the global political economy

In addition to thinking about power as a relationship between actors, one should also bear in mind an important distinction between *relative* power and *structural* power. The latter confers the power to decide how things shall be done, the power to shape frameworks within which states relate to each other, relate to people, or relate to corporate enterprises. The relative power of each party in a relationship is more, or less, if one party is also determining the surrounding structure of the relationship. Structural power defines the context within which interaction takes place, the resources considered important for assessing capabilities in the first place, and the outcomes that should be included in power analysis.

One version of structural power could be called *indirect institutional power*. This refers to the conscious manipulation of the institutional setting within which bargaining relations take place. Many important issues are decided before they reach the bargaining stage, indeed, often because they never reach it. Structural power has also been conceptualized as *non-intentional power*. The late Susan Strange (1988) suggested that we should think of power backwards from its effects, and not in terms of intended outcomes. As did Nye's later concept of 'soft power' (2004), her concept of structural power stresses both the diffusion of the origins of power (and the variety of power resources), and the diffusion of its effects. For Strange, power no longer lies mainly with states or with military capabilities, but with, for instance, the international control of **security**, production, credit and knowledge. Similarly, there is no reason to exclude from power analysis all those crucial effects that might not have been

intended by those who initiated them. For example, whether the interest rate policies of the German Bundesbank were intended to destabilize the European Monetary System in the late 1980s or not, is less significant than the fact that only a few players could have effected such an outcome. As the old Chinese saying has it, it makes little difference to the grass beneath whether the elephants above make love or war.

This analytical shift from intentions to effects focuses on systematic and structural frameworks, rather than the intentional features of power. Such an approach is still compatible with an individualist approach, yet one in which the role of unintended consequences is given a special place. Structural power can be understood in a third way as *systematic bias or impersonal power*. Based on the idea of 'non-decision-making', structural power includes not only a component of intentional agenda setting, but also an impersonal 'mobilization of bias' where social structures systematically favor certain agents over others.

Rule in world politics: the social construction of consensus and legitimacy

Poststructuralist and constructivist approaches (see **poststructuralism**; **constructivism**) have made an important contribution to our understanding of power by elaborating the intersubjective (ideational and/or discursive (see **discourse**)) origins of consensus and legitimacy, and exploring some of the ways in which social practices construct the very meaning of power and power politics. Steven Lukes' (1974) third dimension of power constitutes a good starting point for understanding these approaches. This dimension of power refers to those situations in which the behavior of an actor was influenced without any visible persuasion by, bargaining between, or overt conflict with another actor. Lukes' third dimension of power focuses on consent that results not from any obligation or threat, but from the internalization of values and ideas. Whereas in the law of anticipated reactions, consent follows an adaptation process, the third dimension of power is at work in situations where conflict is not even 'thinkable', where even a consciousness of divergent interests does not exist.

Poststructuralist and constructivist scholars conceive of this dimension of power as the reproduced outcome of rituals and discourses. Instead of seeing consensus as the consequence of open coercion or a more or less voluntary social contract, they look at how discourses and practices dispose agents in particular ways, and how 'taken for granted' or 'naturalized' habits become entrenched. Power shifts from being a potential or disposition at the level of the agent to a property of practices. Their analysis focuses more on the symbolic power inherent in the social construction of reality.

These approaches take the idea of 'double **hermeneutics**' very seriously. In the social sciences, observers interpret an already interpreted world, and how actors interpret the world – through the use of analogies, for example – has important implications for the way in which they behave. Certain 'naturalized' understandings evoke certain actions and empower certain agents. If an event is understood as analogous to 'Munich', for example, a collective memory is mobilized that authorizes some action and delegitimates others. 'Conventional wisdom' disposes us to understand the world in a certain way, to ask certain question and not others.

Paradoxically, the recent focus on the ubiquity of structural power has made it even more difficult to use the concept to develop a theory of power with any predictive capacity. For example, if power lies in the mobilization of a pre-existing bias in collective memory, we may be able to anticipate that certain analogies will be used by political actors, but we cannot predict which part of the collective memory – e.g. the Munich analogy or the Vietnam syndrome – will be more successfully mobilized. Moreover, the advantage of understanding customary practices and discourses as part of the reproduction of power has the analytical drawback of making power ubiquitous.

Conclusion: the politics of power analysis

Power analysis in IR/IPE has come to challenge the presumed twofold link in realist power analysis, that is, between control over resources and control over outcomes, and between control over outcomes and broader patterns of rule or governance. In conclusion, it is worth noting that power has a special status in the study of international relations. The term is used in practical contexts in which we are interested in what we can do to others and what others can do to us. Power becomes an indicator of politics as the 'art of the possible'. It is also important in moral/legal contexts where it functions as an indicator of effective responsibility: if actors could not have done an act (if they had not the capacity to do so), they cannot be found guilty for it. Put into a wider frame, power is about a counterfactual, that is, about things that could have been otherwise. Invoking power therefore asks for a justification for why things were done the way they were.

Consequently, narrow concepts of power (such as that employed by realists) diminish the realm where 'something can be done' and in which action needs to be justified. This is an important issue when discussing the non-intentional effects of power. By limiting the practical context to only those actions with which we intend to affect others, we rule out any moral judgments on unintended effects. Leaving out the 'collateral damage' of effects that were not intended mobilizes a status quo research bias and blinds us to the tacit power of the strong. The fundamental point is that invoking the presence of power *politicizes* issues.

Further reading

Baldwin, D. (1989) *Paradoxes of Power*, Oxford: Blackwell.

Caporaso, J. (1978) 'Dependence, Dependency and Power in the Global System: a Structural and Behavioral Analysis', *International Organization* 32(1), 13–43.

Connolly, W. (1974) *The Terms of Political Discourse*, Oxford: Martin Robertson.

Dowding, K. (1996) *Power*, Minneapolis, MS: University of Minnesota Press.

Guzzini, S. (1993) 'Structural Power: the Limits of Neorealist Power Analysis', *International Organization* 47(3), 443–78.

Keohane, R. (1984) *After Hegemony: Cooperation and Discord in the World Political Economy*, Princeton, NJ: Princeton University Press.

Lukes, S. (1974) *Power: A Radical View*, Basingstoke: Macmillan.

Nye, J. (2004) *Soft Power: The Means to Success in World Politics*, New York: PublicAffairs.

Mearsheimer, J. (2001) *The Tragedy of Great Power Politics*, New York: Norton.

Strange, S. (1988) *States and Markets: An Introduction to International Political Economy*, Oxford: Blackwell.

See also: authority; balance of threat; hegemony; poststructuralism; power transition theory; realism; relative gains/absolute gains

STEFANO GUZZINI

Power transition theory

Power transition theory is based on the assumption that the **international system** is a hierarchy of **power**, in which states are distinguished both by how powerful they are and by whether they are satisfied or dissatisfied with the international status quo. The theory hypothesizes that **war**s are fought among the strongest of states in the power hierarchy, and are fought to change or preserve the status quo. The theory is thus about **global governance**, great power war (see **great powers**), and the revisionist aims of some states.

The dominant power is the most important actor in power transition arguments. This state usually rises to its position of dominance by emerging victorious from an earlier great power war. Being the dominant power is advantageous because the dominant power establishes the international status quo. The status quo represents the formal and informal rules by which the international system is governed. The dominant power drafts these formal and informal rules on the basis of its own **national interest**s. Since World War Two the United States has been the international dominant power, and consistent with the theory, the United States consciously set about drafting new formal and informal rules to manage global relations in the mid 1940s. The United States was instrumental in constructing the **Bretton Woods** international economic order, the **United Nations**, and defensive alliance blocs such as the **North Atlantic Treaty Organization**.

In addition to the dominant power, power transition theory focuses on great power challengers. These are states rising in power such that they might rival the dominant power in capabilities. If they rise in power so much that there could be a power transition in which they would supplant the dominant power, war may ensue. Specifically, if the rising challenger is dissatisfied with the status quo constructed by the dominant power, it may use its capabilities to demand changes to the international status quo. If the dominant power resists these demands, the rising challenger may resort to war to enforce change.

The period of 'overtaking' is critical to power transition theory's expectations about when great power wars will occur, because when the rising challenger and the dominant power are roughly equal in power, i.e. when they are at parity, neither side is able reliably to predict who might win any war they might fight. If they are noticeably unequal in power, the stronger state will expect to win and the weaker will expect to lose. In such a power relationship the weaker side is expected to make concessions to the stronger to avoid fighting a losing battle. Thus, it is in the period of 'overtaking', and when the rising challenger is dissatisfied with the existing status quo, that great power war is most likely.

If the rising challenger is satisfied with the existing status quo, war is not expected. In such a situation neither the dominant power nor the rising challenger has any disagreement sufficiently significant to justify war. Consequently stability persists even with major fluctuations in power accompanying the power transition. Power transition theorists point to the overtaking of Britain (the previous dominant power) by the United States as an example of a satisfied and thus peaceful power transition. According to power transition theory, stability is also expected to prevail and war to be avoided when the dominant power is preponderant over all challengers. In such a situation even dissatisfied challengers do not make demands for revision of the international status quo,

because they lack the wherewithal to force the changes they desire.

Power transition theory has been empirically verified in a large number of quantitative analyses. It has also been adapted to account for war and peace within regional power hierarchies in addition to the traditional focus on the interactions of the great powers. Statistical analyses identify 'overtaking' among great powers, and among regionally powerful states, as especially bellicose, and also identify revisionist states (variously defined based on their armament acquisition behavior, their **alliance** portfolios, or territorial disagreements) as especially likely to provoke wars. In addition, power transition arguments have been used to explain why some **deterrence** relationships are stable while others are dangerous, why some **arms races** lead to war while others do not, and why some alliances are durable even when the threatening state that motivated the alliance's formation in the first place no longer poses a threat.

In addition, power transition theory offers an explanation for the empirical observation of a **democratic peace**, the finding that democracies are disproportionately less likely to be involved in any type of conflict with each other than are other regime types. According to power transition theory, states that are satisfied with the status quo have common interests in preserving the existing international **order** peacefully. Given that the dominant powers of the past two centuries (the period for which evidence exists to substantiate a democratic peace) have been democracies, it is no surprise that democracies have been disproportionately likely to be satisfied with the status quo. According to this reasoning, the observed empirical regularity of a separate peace among democracies is a subset of a more general peace among satisfied states.

Power transition theory is similar to, yet distinct from, many other theories of international relations. Like **hegemonic stability theory**, power transition theory sees the presence of a preponderantly powerful actor as conducive to peace and stability. Power transition theory differs from hegemonic stability theory, though, in that it does not require that the status quo be a collective good. Like long cycle theory, power transition theory sees structural elements of the international system (the distribution of power, and changes within it), as recurrently generating international conflicts that alter the system significantly. Unlike long cycle theory, however, power transition theory does not assign any specific periodicity to these events, and also draws attention to important non-structural characteristics of actors, such as their status quo evaluations.

Power transition theory was originally developed as an alternative to **balance of power** arguments identifying an equal distribution of power as a condition of peace. According to power transition theory, equality of power, or power parity, is dangerous. This is because at parity neither side can be sure of victory. More importantly neither side is confident that it will lose. This uncertainty about the likely outcome of any war that might occur thus emboldens both the dominant power and the rising challenger to be resolute in their demands and/or in their resistance to making concessions to change the status quo. In this way power transition theory is consistent with many formal models of international bargaining and war, which identify uncertainty about likely outcomes as well as about the intentions of states, as important causes of war.

Further reading

Kugler, J. and Lemke, D. (2000) 'The Power Transition Research Program', in M. Mid-

larsky (ed.) *Handbook of War Studies II*, Ann Arbor, MI: University of Michigan Press, 129–63.

Lemke, D. (2002) *Regions of War and Peace*, Cambridge: Cambridge University Press.

Organski, A. F. K. and Kugler, J. (1980) *The War Ledger*, Chicago, IL: University of Chicago Press.

Tammen, R. *et al.* (2000) *Power Transitions*, London: Chatham House.

See also: hegemonic stability theory; polarity; power; realism; war

DOUGLAS LEMKE

Pre-emptive use of force

The anticipatory use of force by one state against another state or non-state actor from which an attack is judged to be imminent. The pre-emptive use of force in international relations has a well-established lineage. During the **cold war**, the concept permeated thinking about nuclear weapons and the pre-emptive use of force was contemplated by both **superpower**s on several occasions. With the end of the cold war, the term faded from the strategic studies lexicon. However, the Bush administration's decision to formally embrace pre-emption as official US doctrine in the aftermath of the 11 September 2001 terrorist attacks (see **terrorism**) has meant that the term has acquired new currency in the academic and policy communities.

By its very nature, the concept of pre-emption assumes that the benefits of resorting to military force to forestall an armed attack outweigh the costs of defending against an attack that is regarded as inevitable. The pre-emptive use of force enshrines the superiority of the offensive in international relations. It assumes explicitly that the momentum for victory in any armed conflict lies with the state that retains the initiative in conducting offensive operations on the battlefield.

The operative words contained in the definition of pre-emption – anticipatory and imminent – presuppose that a state possesses two distinct capabilities. First, that it can verify, through the use of timely and reliable early warning intelligence assets, that there is an attack pending on its territory and/or its **national interest**s. And second, that the leadership of the state has both the military wherewithal and the political will to use decisive force to negate a threat before it is put into effect.

The ethics and legality of pre-emption continue to be subject to contention within the study of international relations. Those sympathetic to the concept argue that while it is proscribed under Article 51 of the **United Nations** Charter, pre-emptive use of force can be defended ethically because it accords closely with the *jus ad bellum* dimension of **just war** theory, which encompasses just cause and right intention. From this perspective, pre-emption can be justified because inaction in the face of an imminent military strike is morally unacceptable if it threatens the lives and well being of citizens within a given state. On the other hand, in addition to pointing to Article 51 of the UN Charter, critics of pre-emption maintain that it provides a cloak of **legitimacy** for those states that intend to use force for ulterior motives. They also argue that interpreting whether a threat is 'imminent' is far too subjective a process to have any agreed meaning in international relations.

While the pre-emptive use of force was rarely invoked during the cold war, two cases stood out. The most celebrated case was Israel's decision on 5 June 1967 to launch a pre-emptive strike against a coalition of Arab states follow-ing the rapid build up of Arab forces in the Sinai Peninsula. Facing the imminent onslaught of numerically superior Arab forces united by the goal of Israel's destruction, Israeli decision makers determined that they had no alternative but to strike first or suffer a massive defeat. The result was that on the first day of the 1967 War, Israel destroyed the large bulk of the Arab air forces while the planes were still lined up at air bases, thus ensuring Israeli air supremacy for the remainder of the conflict. This was decisive in allowing Israel to achieve a significant military victory in a mere six days.

The second case was the hair trigger nuclear alert postures of both **superpower**s. An important (though often overlooked) aspect of US and Soviet nuclear strategy was a shared assumption that in order to deter the other side from striking first, it was necessary to demonstrate a willingness, in force structure and disposition, to carry out a first strike at any time. Such a first strike would 'decapitate' the other side's ability to retaliate by effectively destroying its capabilities to do so. Although advocated most enthusiastically by a small minority who believed that victory was possible in a nuclear war, the option of pre-emption was generally regarded by American and Soviet policymakers as an effective (albeit risky) way of augmenting mutual **deterrence**.

In the wake of 9/11 on the American strategic mindset, the Bush administration gradually began to devote renewed emphasis to the option of pre-emption in its public statements. This culminated in the release of the US National Security Strategy in September 2002, which identified the threat of **rogue state**s transferring **weapons of mass destruction** (WMD) to terrorist groups as a justification for the pre-emptive use of force. According to the document, in dealing with the radically altered global **security** climate post-9/11, the 'reactive' posture of deterrence was no longer sufficient to safeguard national security: deterrence would need to be supplanted by the more 'pro-active' doctrine of pre-emption in neutralizing threats before they reached the North American mainland.

The fact that the United States had formally adopted pre-emption as part of its strategic doctrine coterminous with the build up of a massive Iraqi invasion task force led many observers to conclude that military action against Iraq represented the first step in implementing the doctrine in practice. But this ignored a critical distinction between pre-emptive use of force and preventive war. Even prior to the US-led invasion of Iraq it was obvious that the latter's WMD inventory did not pose an *imminent* threat against the United States and its allies. American led military action against Iraq was clearly a preventive war because it was aimed, *inter alia*, at preventing a future capability from emerging, rather than pre-emptively destroying an existing capability poised for use.

In embracing the doctrine of pre-emption, it is likely that the United States will face some short- to medium-term costs. One cost is already apparent: the Bush administration has been vulnerable to charges of inconsistency in not acting decisively to nullify North Korea's nuclear threat, a threat that is clear and present in contrast to Iraq's fragmented WMD capabilities. Indeed, by not confronting North Korea directly with military force following the promulgation of the pre-emption doctrine in September 2002, Washington has run the risk of diluting the credibility of US strategic doctrine more broadly.

In the longer term, the United States may be placed in the uncomfortable position of having to restrain allies (such as Israel or India) who seek to emulate America's pursuit of pre-emption against adversaries with whom Washington is seeking closer relations. Finally, by bestowing on itself the right to act pre-emptively, but not granting it to others, the United States risks further encouraging attempts by states concerned with Washington's drift toward **unilateralism** to 'bandwagon' against American global **power**.

Further reading

Freedman, L. (2003) *The Evolution of Nuclear Strategy*, 3rd edn, Basingstoke: Palgrave.

Gaddis, J. (2004) *Surprise, Security and the American Experience*, Cambridge, MA: Harvard University Press.

Lebow, N. R. (1987) *Nuclear Crisis Management: A Dangerous Illusion*, Ithaca, NY: Cornell University Press.

Litwak, R. (2002–3) 'The New Calculus of Pre-emption', *Survival*, 44(4), 53–80.

Wirtz, J. and Russell, J. (2003) 'US Policy on Preventive War and Pre-emption', *The Nonproliferation Review* 10, 1: 113–23

See also: al-Qaeda; deterrence; just war; revolution in military affairs

ANDREW O'NEIL

Preferential trade agreement (PTA)

Article XXIV in the 1947 General Agreement on Tariffs and Trade (GATT) allowed customs unions and **free trade** areas as exceptions to the **most favored-nation** (MFN) principle. This exception was designed to allow the countries of Western Europe to establish economic cooperation, which the twenty-three original contracting partners (including the United States) regarded as strategically important in the early stages of the **cold war**. Once included however, this exception could not be denied to other members.

For the next forty years, customs unions and free trade areas were mainly pursued by the Europeans, as they absorbed neighboring countries into economic union, or looser preferential trade arrangements in the case of Mediterranean and African countries. Some developing countries have also experimented with such **integration**, but with little success.

Since the **World Trade Organization** (WTO) was established, agreements under GATT Article XXIV have proliferated, with almost 300 PTAs proposed since 1995. This form of discrimination (extending preferences to selected countries) became popular after the US Congress approved the **North American Free Trade Agreement** (NAFTA) in 1993, and has continued following the 2002 Trade Promotion Authority (TPA) which granted the President of the United States authority to 'fast track' multilateral trade negotiations and to negotiate bilateral trade agreements. Preferential access to the largest and richest market in the world is attractive to other countries and it gives US negotiators the ability to pursue the interests of US business lobbies that are more difficult to protect in multilateral negotiations – for example, protection of intellectual property rights, increased market penetration for audiovisual products and other services, and liberalizing capital flows.

PTAs are not, however, a substitute for multilateral trade negotiations. They do not lead to universal **free trade** because they maintain trade barriers (including tariffs) against non-participating countries. While they do lower trade barriers between willing partners, as each PTA is established, global trade rules become more complicated. With so much intra-industry trade in components and services, it is difficult to define a country of origin for most products. Hence, which products passing between economies in a PTA should be eligible for 'preferences'? To define this intra-area trade, rules of origin are created that seek to measure the 'value-added' content of products passing between economies in a PTA.

Determining rules of origin has become one of the most contentious topics when finalizing PTAs. In many ways, rules of origin provide more protection from competition than tariffs because they regulate which goods (and services) are eligible for preferential treatment. It often takes several months longer to reach agreement on rules of origin than it does to sign the basic preferential trade agreement.

Once PTAs began to proliferate in the 1990s there was a strong incentive for other countries to join in, especially when access to large economies, such as those of Japan, the United States and the **European Union** (EU), were at stake. Many observers are concerned about the growth of PTAs in the global trading system. They worry that the large economies will form 'hubs' for a series of bilateral agreements ('spokes') with other countries. The bargaining power rests with the 'hubs', which can decide on the scope, rules and liberalization schedules for the 'spokes'. In other words, bilateral agreements give power to the major players.

Research shows that, historically, trade diversion has often outweighed trade creation in PTAs; that is, tariff discrimination displaces imports from low cost non-PTA sources with higher cost imports from partner countries within PTAs and that this cost outweighs gains from the more efficient distribution of production among PTA members. Hence, the global allocation of production may be less efficient than under multilateral forms of trade liberalization.

In contrast, administrative and other transaction costs can be lower in a PTA, which is particularly important for trade in services, the area where most economic growth is now occurring. With average tariffs on most manufactured goods and raw materials low, and few quantitative restrictions remaining, trade discrimination is becoming less important. However, the partiality of the major players to exclude agriculture and other sensitive sectors from their PTAs indicates that the proliferation of PTAs is less desirable than a comprehensive multilateral approach to trade liberalization.

One reason for the increased interest in PTAs – apart from the fear of being left out – is the interest in extending liberalization and market access beyond industrial tariffs to include services. Negotiations in the WTO incorporate all member states, they tend to proceed at the speed of the slowest participant, and are agreed on an MFN basis. This tends to slow liberalization in the fast growing, innovative service sectors.

More and more PTAs are being proposed. If uniform rules could be devised to apply to all PTAs, requiring for example, uniform rules of origin, schedules for complete liberalization and comprehensive commodity coverage (much of which is required by GATT Article XXIV) discrimination would be minimized. Such a harmonization of the rules may become possible if at some point the complex relations with 'spokes' becomes too cumbersome for the 'hubs'.

Further reading

Bagwell, K. and Staiger, R. (2003) *The Economics of the World Trading System*, Cambridge, MA: MIT Press.

Bhagwati, J., Krishna, P and Panagariya, A. (eds) (1999) *Trading Blocs: Alternative Approaches to Analyzing Preferential Trade Agreements*, Cambridge, MA: MIT Press.

Lawrence, R. (1996) *Regionalism, Multilateralism, and Deeper Integration*, Washington, DC: Brookings.

Schott, J. (2004) *Free Trade Agreements: US Strategies and Priorities*, Washington, DC: Institute for International Economics.

See also: free trade; managed trade; most-favored nation; North American Free Trade Agreement; regional trade bloc

MARTIN GRIFFITHS

Preventive diplomacy

Popular usage of the term preventive **diplomacy** can be traced to the activities of former **United Nations** Secretary General Dag Hammarskjöld (although its underlying logic has existed at least since the emergence of the modern state system; the Westphalian Treaty (see **Westphalia**) at its birth was an attempt to prevent the continuation of interstate warfare of the early seventeenth century; and indeed, its rationale is deeply imbedded in such fundamentals of statecraft as **deterrence**, reassurance and compellence). Hammarskjöld realized that early engagement by the global organization could act to forestall the destructiveness of conflict created by external military intervention and arms transfers. Preventive action stems from the more general reasoning that external interventions can be avoided or tempered if a region is made more autonomous in terms of **security**. Preventive action aims to fill the vacuum so that it will not provoke a hostile response from any of the major parties. When **crisis** threatens, traditional diplomacy continues, but more urgent preventive efforts are required – through unilateral and multilateral channels – to arbitrate, mediate, or lend 'good offices' to encourage dialogue between conflicting parties.

Preventive diplomacy has grown in importance due to the evolving nature of conflict. The shift from interstate to intrastate conflict is well documented. However, this change in itself has not been sufficient to generate a call for revised thinking on preventive action. It is the surrounding circumstances, the ability of complex conflicts to spread vertically and horizontally – in essence the potential of intrastate conflict to do harm to others, ordinary citizens, neighboring states, **refugee**s and minorities – that generates preventive diplomacy.

In the post-**cold war** era preventive diplomacy and conflict prevention became catch phrases for any activity, by any actor, to reduce the possibility of conflict, from **development** assistance to **human rights** activism, preventive **peacekeeping** activities, conflict resolution and post-conflict peacebuilding. The former UN Secretary General Boutros-Ghali (1992) offered a very general definition of conflict prevention. What he called preventive diplomacy is action to prevent disputes from arising between parties, to prevent existing disputes from escalating into conflicts and to limit the spread of the latter when they occur. He further suggested that the most desirable and efficient employment of diplomacy is to ease tensions before they result in conflict – or, if conflict breaks out, to act swiftly to contain it and resolve its underlying causes. Preventive diplomacy requires measures to create confidence; it needs early warning based on information gathering and informal or formal fact-finding; it may also involve preventive deployment and, in some situations, demilitarized zones. This is a very broad approach to preventive action, one that captures all perceivable stages of conflict, from prevention to resolution.

Michael Lund (1996) differentiates between 'peacetime diplomacy or politics' during eras of durable and stable peace, 'preventive diplomacy or conflict prevention' during areas of unstable peace, 'crisis diplomacy or crisis management' during a crisis situation, and 'peacemaking or conflict management' during war. Lund envisions 'peace enforcement or conflict mitigation' as the appropriate response to war situations, 'peacekeeping or conflict termination' as a means to defuse war and conflict, followed by 'post conflict peace building or conflict resolution'. Each of these stages requires different operational and institutional responses, while conflict prevention is only effective during a situation of unstable peace – when the signs for an emerging conflict become obvious to the informed outside observer. Bruce Jentleson (1999) echoes this more subtle interpretation of conflict prevention by distinguishing between 'normal diplomacy,' 'developmentalist diplomacy', 'preventive diplomacy' and 'war diplomacy'.

The UN Secretary-General's 2001 *Report on the Prevention of Armed Conflict* adopted the distinction made by the Carnegie Commission on Preventing Deadly Conflict (1997) between operational prevention, which refers to measures applicable in the face of immediate crisis, and structural prevention, which consists of measures to ensure that crises do not arise in the first place or, if they do, that they do not recur. Here the stress is on the need to address root causes of potential conflicts through long-term, structural prevention. In recognition of the potential catch-all character of the prevention agenda, however, there is a clear distinction between regular developmental and humanitarian assistance programs, on the one hand, and those implemented as a preventive response to problems that could lead to the outbreak or recurrence of violent conflict, on the other.

This distinction is affirmed by the International Commission on Intervention and State Sovereignty in its report *The Responsibility to Protect* (2001). The report stresses international, regional, national and local cooperation in both direct (operational) and root cause (structural) preventive efforts. Both reports emphasized the need for the UN and other inter-state, state and non-state actors to move from a culture of reaction to a culture of prevention. While both reports argued that the main responsibility for preventive efforts lies with national governments and civil society, intergovernmental organizations such as the UN and regional organizations play leading roles in strengthening the capacity of national and local actors to create conditions that foster peace. The UN and regional organizations' commitment and ability to promote and practice preventive strategies are key to sustained preventive efforts at national and local levels.

Kalypso Nicolaides (1996) provides a useful conceptual framework for determining how preventive diplomacy relates to conflict prevention. Preventive diplomacy is an operational response. It is premised on incentive structures provided by outside actors to change specific kinds of undesirable behavior. Preventive diplomacy is therefore, targeted and short-term and the preventive action taken relates directly to changes in conflict escalation and conflict dynamics. In this regard outside actors can seek to influence the course of events and try to alter or induce specific behavior through coercive and operational threats and deterrents or through less coercive strategies of persuasion and inducement.

Ultimately though, outside actors can work to influence the incentives of the relevant parties engaged in conflict but they cannot change the initial conditions that led to conflict in the first place. Thus, structural approaches emphasize capacity building to provide conflict prone societies with the means to address the root causes of conflict. In this sense, structural conflict prevention strategies, such as those focusing on human **security**, conflict transformation and development cast a much broader net. They tend to be long term and are generally applied across a range of countries, issues and actors. The goal is to transform conflictual behavior over time. This change in behavior can be dependent on institutional inducements – such as conditionality for membership in international institutions, **arms control** agreements and stability pacts or on the promotion of **sustainable development**, support for human security and regional confidence building mechanisms. The difference between operational and structural approaches is made clear through the analogy to the clinical and environmental approaches to health care. Clinical and environmental health care may both be preventively oriented. However, the former focuses on the treatment of sick individuals whereas the latter emphasizes a public health model that aims to prevent illness by focusing on its associated environmental factors.

Further reading

Boutros-Ghali, B. (1992) *An Agenda for Peace* New York: United Nations Press.

Carment, D. and Schnabel, A. (eds) (2003) *Conflict Prevention: Path to Peace or Grand Illusion?* Tokyo: United Nations University Press.

Carnegie Commission on Preventing Deadly Conflict (1997) *Final Report*, Washington, DC: Carnegie Foundation.

International Commission on Intervention and State Sovereignty (2001) *The Responsibility to Protect* (Ottawa: IDRC).

Jentleson, B. (ed.) (1999) *Opportunities Missed, Opportunities Seized: Preventive Diplomacy in the Post-Cold War World* Lanham, MD: Rowman & Littlefield.

Lund, M. (1996) *Preventing Violent Conflict*, Washington, DC: USIP Press.

Nicolaides, K. (1996) 'International Preventive Action: Developing a Strategic Framework' in Rotberg, R. (ed.) *Vigilance and Vengeance: NGOs Preventing Ethnic Conflict in Divided Societies*, Washington, DC: Brookings, 23–72.

United Nations General Assembly (2001) *Report of the Secretary-General on the Prevention of Armed Conflict*, A/55/985–S/2001/574, New York: United Nations.

See also: containment; crisis; diplomacy

DAVID CARMENT

Prisoner's dilemma

A model of social interaction falling within the broad category of **game theory** that illustrates how rational choices (see **rationality**) by individuals can lead to collectively inferior outcomes due to the structure of the situation. The prisoner's dilemma has been used extensively in international relations because it captures both the interdependent nature of international relations and the inability of parties to sign binding agreements given the anarchic structure of the **international system**. Scholars have employed the prisoner's dilemma to help analyze a wide variety of global issues, including **arms race**s, trade **wars**, environmental problems, cartel behavior, international **regime**s, and social mobilization.

Game theory is the mathematical modeling of interdependent decision-making. Game theory first emerged within economics in the 1920s *Theory of Games and Economic Behavior* in 1943. Although early theoretical and empirical work focused on zero sum games of pure conflict, research moved toward the broad category of non-zero sum games, which includes the prisoner's dilemma. As research on the prisoner's dilemma diffused across the social sciences, it became arguably the most explored game in international relations, political science, social psychology, and sociology.

The type of game known as Prisoner's Dilemma is a non-zero-sum game. The scenario involves two prisoners who are suspected of jointly committing a crime, but neither has yet confessed. They are held in separate cells, unable to communicate with each other. Each prisoner is told that:

1. if neither confesses both will go free;
2. if both confess they will both be imprisoned; and
3. if only one confesses, turning state's evidence against the other, that one will be positively rewarded while the other will serve a longer prison term.

Since each prisoner is better off confessing, given the action of the other (the reward is better than just going free, and the short prison term is better than the long one), the normal outcome in the *absence* of cooperation between the prisoners is for both to confess. Both could be better off than that equilibrium however, if they could somehow agree to cooperate and neither confess. Unfortunately for them, such cooperation is bound to be difficult since both have an incentive to break any agreement by confessing.

Variations of the prisoner's dilemma can be categorized on two dimensions: number of players (two versus *n*-person) and length of the game (single play versus iterated game). In general, the probability of cooperation decreases as the number of players grows large and increases as the game is lengthened. The two-actor game has been used to model state-to-state bargaining and oligopolies. In contrast, the *n*-person game has been applied to problems of social mobilization in comparative politics and **global warming** in international relations. When the number of players in the game increases, it becomes very difficult to monitor behavior and punish defectors.

In a single iteration game, it is never rational to cooperate with an opponent because they have no incentive to cooperate. However, repeated plays (or iteration) of the game increase the likelihood of cooperation because actors can reap a stream of benefits, employ complex strategies, and communicate tacitly. Although the benefit of mutual cooperation is small relative to the temptation payoff, the establishment of stable cooperation implies the sum of the reward payoffs across time will be larger than a single temptation payoff followed by a stream of mutual defections. As long as both players value the future to a sufficient degree, cooperation is rational in an iterated game.

In terms of strategies and communication, iteration allows the use of strategies that can communicate a message to the opponent. For example, in an iterated game an actor can play a *Tit-For-Tat* (TFT) strategy in which they cooperate on the first move and reciprocate on all subsequent moves. Experimental research and computer simulations have demonstrated the utility of TFT strategies in altering expectations and increasing cooperation. While TFT in no way guarantees cooperation, it does increase the probability of cooperation because the strategy is *nice* (i.e., initially cooperates), *simple* (i.e., easy for the other side to recognize what you are doing), *retaliatory* (i.e., punishes others for defecting), and *forgiving* (i.e., if the other side begins to cooperate again, you will reciprocate).

The prisoner's dilemma has been used extensively within international relations. Proponents of **realism** have used the single play game to illustrate how the structure of the situation can make cooperation difficult even between status quo states with similar preferences. Trade theorists have used the model to explain the propensity of states to adopt 'beggar-thy-neighbor' policies which can trigger tariff wars and the collapse of **free trade**. Advocates of **liberal internationalism** drew heavily on the iterated version of the prisoner's dilemma to illustrate how cooperation could emerge in **anarchy** among selfish states. Interestingly, the realist critique of the liberal argument did not attack the use of the iterated prisoner's dilemma to model state-to-state interaction. Rather, realists argue that the relative nature of power implies leaders will focus on relative payoffs rather than absolute payoffs. While the interpretation of payoffs has a significant impact on the probability of cooperation, both types of payoffs fit comfortably within the prisoner's dilemma model.

Further reading

Axelrod, R. (1984) *The Evolution of Cooperation*, New York: Basic Books.

Lake, D. A. and Powell, R. (eds) (1999) *Strategic Choice and International Relations*, Princeton, NJ: Princeton University Press.

Poundstone, W. (1992) *Prisoner's Dilemma*, New York: Anchor Books.

Stein, A. A. (1990) *Why Nations Cooperate: Circumstance and Choice in International Relations*, Ithaca, NY: Cornell University Press.

Von Neumann, J. and Morgenstern, O. (1943) *Theory of Games and Economic Behavior*, Princeton, NJ: Princeton University Press.

See also: anarchy; game theory; reciprocity; security dilemma

DAVID L. ROUSSEAU

R

Rationality

The ability of a unitary actor to maximize utility through decisions and actions. The decision maker analyzes costs and benefits in a situation, and chooses that option which will result in the most value, or smallest negative value in a 'no win' situation. In international relations, specifically through the lens of **realism**, this value is measured by its relation to the **national interest**. The rational actor model derived from this theory assumes that the entire universe of information is available to a given decision maker, and that the actor will be able to properly assess each option in full detail. This is, in turn, the underlying assumption behind rational actor theory, one of the prominent fields of research in international relations. From the assumption of rationality, the foundation of a large body of scholarship exists which (according to realists) captures the most important aspects of international relations.

The rational actor model is the backbone of rational actor theory. Unfortunately, this theory wrongly assumes that interests are the same from one actor to another, whether the actors are individuals or states. Individual differences are not taken into account. Instead, any divergence in behavior results from differing resources, geographical position, or other factors not within the realm of the decision maker's internal processing mechanisms. This divergence can be specified and modeled as a limit to the rational options available to the actor. From this assumption, mathematical models are derived, which are very general and abstract conceptions of how actors behave. One of the most well known types of mathematical models is **game theory**, which is derived from 'strategic rationality', where outcomes depend on the deliberate choices of other rational decision makers.

Rationality is also the basis of a model of decision-making – the rational decision making process – that contains a series of steps. The first step in this process is clarifying goals, followed by the rank ordering of these goals by importance, which allows for a solution if different goals conflict. The identification of alternatives to achieving these goals is then assessed, which is followed by an investigation into the consequences of these alternatives. Finally, a course of action is chosen from this process that will result in the maximal representation of utility. The development of formal models, specifically the rational actor model, is desirable since it allows for a clearer understanding of an argument or theory, through an objectively discernible equation, than that which may be attainable in more qualitative research. These models also allow for greater precision than other types of arguments, and are usually logically consistent.

There is a large body of literature devoted to the exploration of 'non-rational' sources of behavior, whether by individuals or by groups. Thus some studies have focused on the processes by which individual perception and cognition affect outcomes, as well as the influence of groups in decision making. In reality, decision makers are influenced by beliefs, values, and personality characteristics that differ from person to person. Further, it is usually impossible for an individual to process all information relating to a particular problem. Thus, selective processing comes into play, which constrains an individual's ability to act rationally. The use of groups may help to alleviate some aspects of rational decision making by diffusing responsibilities, but this comes with its own set of problems.

A significant critique of rational actor models comes from the field of political psychology, according to which it is unrealistic to assume that any decision making group would be able to possess the requirements of unlimited resources, time, and effort, along with the ability to understand all the dynamic aspects of the system that would render rationality possible. Further, rational actor theorists disregard group influences such as the establishment of entrenched departmental views, which constrain creativity and one's ability to deviate from standard procedures. Another problem associated with group decision making is **groupthink**, a social psychological concept of a group's susceptibility to making bad decisions due to the group environment, which often displays an 'irrational' adherence to the status quo.

'Limited rationality' is a broad term describing the subject of scholars who recognize the absurdity of pure rationality. This has led to several different methods of examining decision making in a more realistic fashion. Similarly, the term 'bounded rationality' is used by scholars who recognize the constraining effects of human and organizational factors in maximizing utility. What is sometimes called 'satisficing behavior' is linked to bounded rationality, and is demonstrated when an actor chooses the first available alternative that meets minimum acceptable standards.

Another major criticism of rationality comes from the substantivists, who maintain that the culture of a specific society differs from other societies, and that examining individual behavior 'thinly', only in terms of interests and beliefs, leaves out a vast amount of culturally specific information necessary to understanding individual reasoning. In other words, 'interests' and 'beliefs' are not transferable from one culture to another. For example, it is sometimes claimed that the cost/benefit aspect of rationality is based on economic behavior that is specific to free market cultures. Such behavior has no meaning in some premarket societies, and thus cannot be used to examine them.

Rationality can be examined at several different levels. State rationality is associated with which action best serves the interests of the state. Organizational or departmental rationality is associated with what will best suit a respective institution in terms of policy influence or resource acquisition. Rationality of individuals or groups is the examination of what interests suit their respective needs regarding the pursuit of influence and **power**. Differences between these forms of rationality exist, which reflect institutional, aggregate, or specific psychological influences. Levels of rationality also influence each other, however. For example, state rationality may filter out irrational decision-making resulting from an individual's flawed reasoning.

Conversely, individuals may be able to recognize a group's distorted outcome of a rational idea (perhaps as a result of the group problems mentioned earlier), and make changes accordingly.

Further reading

Schepsle, K. and Bonchek, M. (1997) *Analyzing Politics: Rationality, Behavior, and Institutions*, New York: Norton.

Simon, H. A. (1997) *Administrative Behavior: A Study of Decision-Making Processes in Administrative Organizations*, 4th edn, New York: The Free Press.

Walt, S. (1999) 'Rigor or Rigor Mortis? Rational Choice and Security Studies' *International Security* 23(4), 5–48.

See also: crisis; game theory; prisoner's dilemma

MARK SCHAFER and SAM ROBISON

Realism

Modern realist theories are regarded by their advocates as the current incarnations of an extended intellectual tradition. It is customary to trace realism back to antiquity, with claims that its arguments can be found in important works from Greece, Rome, India, and China. Smith (1986) and other surveyors, for example, suggest that Thucydides' *History of The Peloponnesian War* illustrates realism's skepticism for the restraining effects of morality. Realist arguments can also be found in Kautilya's *Arthashastra* from India. Jonathan Haslam (2002, 14) notes that 'Kautilya focuses on the position of the potential conqueror who always aims to enhance his power at the expense of the rest'. Realists also claim Niccolo Machiavelli (1469–1527) among their number (e.g. Carr 1939/1946, 63–4). Starting from a deeply pessimistic view of human nature, Machia-velli argues for strong and efficient rulers for whom **power** and **security** are the major concerns. Unlike individuals, such rulers are not bound by individual morality. '[A]ny action that can be regarded as important for the survival of the state carries with it a built-in justification' (Smith 1986, 12). Realists also identify with Thomas Hobbes (1588–1679) and his notion of a 'state of nature' where the absence of overriding authority allows human appetites to be pursued without restraint – individuals engage in constant conflict, with their lives being concomitantly 'solitary, poor, nasty, brutish and short'.

Political realism's prolonged existence gives it a distinct advantage over relatively youthful liberal alternatives (Morgenthau 1985: 4). It is important, therefore, to note that realist interpretations of antiquarian writings are often contested. Regardless of one's views on the longevity of realist thinking, however, there is more consensus that the millennia long record of inter-group conflict seems to support realism's pessimistic worldview. While realism's interpretation of particular episodes have been disputed, even its critics acknowledge that humankind has, in most times and in most places, lived down to realism's very low expectations.

Twentieth century realism

As the dominant tradition in the study of international relations, political realism has been implicated in virtually every major debate in the field in the last half of the twentieth century. In describing and appraising the tradition, it is customary to differentiate realism from other approaches, and to separate realist theories into distinct sub-groups. Accordingly, accounts of twentieth century realism typically distinguish political realist from liberal traditions, as well as describe succeeding iterations of realist theory.

Pessimistic and prudential, political realism suggests that state behavior is driven by leaders' flawed human nature, or by the preemptive unpleasantness mandated by an anarchic **international system**. Selfish human appetites for **power**, or the need to accumulate the wherewithal to be secure in a self-help world, explain the seemingly endless succession of **war** and conquest. Liberal understandings of international affairs suggest that states' foreign policies are driven by their domestic political arrangements, shared democratic norms, or commercial interests. Unlike realism, **liberal internationalism** holds out the promise of progress toward a more peaceful and enlightened world (though see Glaser 1997 for an unusually optimistic realist reading).

As the basis for prescriptive policy, the stakes in the competition between the realist and liberal worldviews were, and remain, high. The best realism has to offer the world is an armed and watchful peace anchored in mutual **deterrence**. The best that liberal internationalism has to offer is a community of like-minded states, at peace because war is unnecessary and costly. If political realism is correct, and states mistakenly pursue a foreign policy based on liberalism, they may fail to deter belligerence or to properly prepare for a war should aggression occur. If liberalism is correct, and states mistakenly pursue a foreign policy based on political realism, they may be missing the best opportunity to achieve international peace, and by their preparations for defense bring on the very conflict they are trying to avoid.

With respect to different iterations of realist theory, scholars typically distinguish between classical and neorealist variants. There are at least four different competing varieties of contemporary realism: neoclassical, rise and fall, offensive structural, and defensive structural realism. It should be noted that this descriptive strategy (which follows the sub-field's customary approach) is also implicated in recent appraisals that try to be more self-consciously rooted in relevant epistemology. For example, the realist tradition has recently been criticized for making self-serving adjustments to avoid contradiction by empirical anomalies. John Vasquez (1997) suggests that balance of power theory is empirically inaccurate, but that succeeding versions of the theory have become progressively looser to allow it to accommodate disconfirming evidence. A related critique was launched by Jeffrey Legro and Andrew Moravcsik (1999), who argue that recent realists subsume arguments that are more usually associated with competing liberal or constructivist (see **constructivism**) approaches. The result, they argue, is that realist theories have become less determinate, coherent, and distinctive. These critiques have sparked vigorous responses from realist scholars, who argue that the critics are mistaken in their descriptions of the tradition and in their application of metatheoretical criteria. The approach followed in this entry avoids a single definition of realism, opting instead to break the tradition down into several discrete research programs.

Classical Realism

Twentieth century classical realism is generally dated from 1939, and the publication of Edward Hallett Carr's *The Twenty Years' Crisis*. Classical realists are usually characterized as responding to then-dominant liberal approaches to international politics although scholars disagree on how widespread liberalism was during the interwar years. After

World War Two Hans Morgenthau's *Politics Among Nations: The Struggle for Power and Peace* became the undisputed standard bearer for political realism, going through six editions between 1948 and 1985.

According to classical realism, because the desire for more power is rooted in the flawed nature of humanity, states are continuously engaged in a struggle to increase their capabilities. The absence of the international equivalent of a government is a permissive condition that gives human appetites free reign. In short, classical realism explains conflictual behavior by human failings. Wars are explained, for example, by particular aggressive statesmen, or by domestic political systems that give greedy parochial groups the opportunity to pursue self-serving expansionist foreign policies. For classical realists international politics can be characterized as evil: bad things happen because the people making foreign policy are sometimes bad (Spirtas 1996, 387–400).

Although not employing the formal mathematical modeling found in contemporary rational choice theory, classical realism nevertheless posits that state behavior can be understood as having rational microfoundations. State strategies are understood as having been decided rationally, after taking costs and benefits of different possible courses of action into account.

The 1960s saw classical realism coming under increasing scrutiny. Scholars who disagreed with Morgenthau and other classical realists on substantive grounds closely parsed their work to find inconsistencies and contradictions. In addition, advocates of new behavioral and quantitative methodologies questioned the value of the traditional approach to inquiry. The 1970s saw the pendulum swing further against realism, with work focusing on **interdependence** and non-state actors finding new prominence and popularity.

Neorealism

The realist tradition was revived and revised with the publication of Kenneth Waltz's *Theory of International Politics* (1979), which replaced Morgenthau's *Politics Among Nations* as the standard bearer for realists. In his book, Waltz assumes that the international system is ordered anarchically and is characterized by low functional differentiation. The only variable in the theory is the distribution of capabilities.

One distinction between classical realism and neorealism is their different views on the source and content of state preferences. Contra classical realism, neorealism excludes the internal make-up of different states. Morgenthau's (1948) seminal statement of classical realism relied on the assumption that leaders of states are motivated by their lust for power. Waltz's 1979 theory, by contrast, omits leader's motivations and state characteristics as causal variables for international outcomes, except for the minimal assumption that states seek to survive.

In addition, whereas classical realism suggested that state strategies are selected rationally, Waltz is agnostic about which of several micro-foundations explain state behavior. States' behavior can be a product of the competition among them, either because they calculate how to act to their best advantage, or because those that choose unwisely are 'selected out' of the system. Alternatively, states' behavior can be a product of socialization. Since the theory provides such a minimal account of preferences and micro-foundations, it makes only indeterminate behavioral predictions, and Waltz is correspondingly reluctant to make foreign policy predictions. Waltz nevertheless suggests that systemic processes will produce convergent international outcomes.

Waltz notes that international politics is characterized by a disheartening consistency; the same depressingly familiar things happening again and again. This repetitiveness endures despite considerable differences in internal domestic political arrangements, both through time (contrast, for example, seventeenth- and nineteenth-century England) and space (contrast, for example, the United States and Germany in the 1930s). Waltz's purpose is to explain why similarly structured international systems all seem to be characterized by similar outcomes, even though their units (i.e. member states) have different domestic political arrangements and particular parochial histories. Waltz concludes that it must be something peculiar to, and pervasive in, international politics that accounts for these commonalities. He therefore excludes as *reductionist* all but the thinnest of assumptions about the units that make up the system – they must, at a minimum, seek their own survival.

By focusing only minor attention on unit-level variables, Waltz aims to separate out the persistent effects of the international system. Jervis (1997, 7) observes that '[w]e are dealing with a system when (a) a set of units or elements is interconnected so that changes in some elements or their relations produce changes in other parts of the system; and (b) the entire system exhibits properties and behaviors that are different from those parts'. Because systems are generative, the international political system is characterized by complex nonlinear relationships and unintended consequences. Outcomes are influenced by something more than simply the aggregation of individual state behavior, with a tendency toward unintended and ironic outcomes. As a result, there is a gap between what states want and what states get. Consequently, unlike classical realists, neorealists see international politics as tragic, rather than as being driven by the aggressive behavior of revisionist states (Spirtas 1996, 387–400). The international political outcomes that Waltz predicts include that multipolar systems will be less stable than bipolar systems; that interdependence will be lower in **bipolarity** than multipolarity; and that regardless of unit behavior, **hegemony** by any single state is unlikely or even impossible.

Partly because of its popularity, and partly because of its own 'take no prisoners' criticism of competing theories, Waltz's book almost immediately became a prominent target. As time went by, detractors chipped away at the book's dominance. Non-realist work, in particular liberal institutionalism and investigations of the **democratic peace**, became more popular. Realism's decline in the 1990s was amplified by international events. The closing years of the twentieth century seemed to provide strong support for alternative approaches. The Soviet Union's voluntary retrenchment and subsequent demise; the continuation of Western European **integration** in the absence of American-Soviet competition; the wave of **democratization** and economic liberalization throughout the former Soviet Union, Eastern Europe and the developing world; and the improbability of war between the **great powers** all made realism seem outdated. It appeared that liberal or constructivist theories could better appreciate and explain the changes taking place in the international arena. Not surprisingly, the post-9/11 arena seems much more challenging, and it comes as no revelation that political realism is regarded as being better suited to address threats to national security. It is, however, ironic that its renaissance is at least partly owed to transnational terrorist networks motivated by religious extremism, actors, and appetites that both lie well outside realism's traditional ambit.

Contemporary realism

There are at least four contemporary strands of political realism: rise and fall realism, neoclassical realism, defensive structural realism, and offensive structural realism. All four take the view that international relations are characterized by an endless and inescapable succession of wars and conquest. The four groupings can be differentiated by the fundamental constitutive and heuristic assumptions that their respective theories share. Briefly, the approaches differ on the sources of state preferences – the mix of human appetites for power and/or the need to accumulate the wherewithal to be secure in a self-help world – while agreeing that rational calculation is the microfoundation that translates those preferences into behavior.

'Rise and fall' realism

According to Robert Gilpin (1981) the rules and practices of the international system are determined by the wishes of the leading (i.e. most powerful) state. Since considerable benefit accrues to the leader, other great powers seek this pole position. 'Rise and fall' realism explains how states first rise to, and then fall from, this leading position, and the consequences of that trajectory for state foreign policies. In particular, the approach is concerned with the onset of great power wars that often mark the transition from one leader to the next. The microfoundation that explains this behavior is rational choice. Given a narrowing of the gap between the first and second ranked states, the leader will calculate

the need for preventive action. Failing that, the challenger will opt for a war to displace the current leader. The most prominent recent incarnation of 'rise and fall' realism is Dale Copeland's (2001) dynamic differential theory, which suggests that major wars are typically initiated by dominant military powers that fear significant decline. Copeland's theory also incorporates structural realist arguments, however, since he sees the main virtue of power as ensuring survival, rather than allowing the arrangement of international affairs to suit the dominant state's interests.

Neoclassical realism

Neoclassical realists suggest that what states do depends in large part on domestically derived preferences. For example, Schweller (1994, 92–9) insists that realism is best served by acknowledging and including different state motivations. As Rasler and Thompson (2001, 47) note, neoclassical realists stress a wider range of revisionist motives than classical realism's earlier reliance on human nature. 'Things happen in world politics because some actors – thanks to domestic structure and institutions, ideology, and ambitions – practice disruptive and predatory strategies'. The most prominent version of neoclassical realism is Randall Schweller's (1998) 'balance of interests' theory, which develops a typology based on whether states are primarily motivated by, and the extent of, their fear and greed. Thus, states rationally decide foreign policies depending on a combination of power and interests.

In addition to emphasizing the distinction between status quo and revisionist states, neoclassical realists also focus on the domestic 'transmission belt' connecting resource endowments and power. Neoclassical realists agree that material capabilities and the distribution of power are the starting points for an analysis of international outcomes. They insist, however, that state characteristics and leaders' views of how power should be used intervene between structural constraints and behavior. Accordingly, they also investigate domestic political features, such as the abilities of foreign policymakers to extract resources for the pursuit of foreign policy goals.

Defensive structural realism

This strand of realism developed, but is distinct from, neorealism. Like neorealism, defensive structural realism suggests that states seek security in an anarchic international system. The main threat to their well-being comes from other states. Whereas neorealism allows for multiple micro-foundations to explain state behavior, however, defensive structural realism relies solely on rational choice. This is a crucial difference, since it allows defensive structural realism to make determinate foreign policy predictions. The prime strategy for survival in defensive structural realism is balancing against states that increase their relative power. In one of its best known variants, **balance of threat** theory, state power is modified by proximity, the offense–defense balance, and intentions. While defensive structural realism also predicts that hegemony is improbable, unlike neorealism this outcome is produced by deliberate dyadic, and not automatic, balancing.

Defensive structural realism argues that, because states react quickly to defend against perceived threats to the status quo, power maximization is ultimately self-defeating. This hair-trigger reaction to threat also underpins their explanation for war in a world of status quo states. Defensive realists invoke the concept of the **security dilemma**, and

argue that defensive actions are often misinterpreted as aggressive behavior. Steps taken by states seeking to preserve the status quo are ambiguous, and are often indistinguishable from preparations for taking the offense. As a result, states threatened by those new, potentially offensive capabilities respond with military measures of their own, leaving the first state in as precarious a position, if not worse off, than before. This is international relations as tragedy, not evil: bad things happen because states are placed in difficult situations. In sum, defensive realists suggest that states should seek an 'appropriate' amount of power, not all that there is. If states do seek hegemony, it is due to domestically generated preferences; seeking superior power is not a rational response to external systemic pressures.

Offensive structural realism

Offensive structural realists disagree with the defensive structural realist prescription that states look for only an 'appropriate' amount of power. Its leading representative, John Mearsheimer (2001), argues that states face an uncertain international environment in which any state might use its power to harm another. Under such circumstances, relative capabilities are of overriding importance, and security requires acquiring as much power compared to other states as possible. The stopping power of water means that the most a state can hope for is to be a regional hegemon, and for there to be no other regional hegemons elsewhere in the world.

Offensive realists explicitly reject the defensive structural realist argument that states should avoid maximizing their power. This divergence is based, in part, on a different understanding of the security dilemma. Mearsheimer (2001) argues that increasing capabilities can improve a state's security without triggering a countervailing response. Careful timing by revisionists, buckpassing by potential targets, and information asymmetries all allow the would-be hegemon to succeed. Power maximization is not necessarily self-defeating, and hence states can rationally aim for regional hegemony.

Realism is a multifaceted and durable tradition of inquiry in international relations, with an extraordinary capacity for adaptation and modification. To be sure, its critics ask if the tradition still has any relevance in an allegedly shrinking and globalizing world where intra-state violence is more common than inter-state war. But those who are anticipating realism will become obsolete are likely to be in for a long wait to see their expectations fulfilled.

Further reading

Carr, E.H. (1939/1946) *The Twenty Years' Crisis*, New York: St. Martin's Press.

Copeland, D. (2001) *The Origins of Major War*, Ithaca, NY: Cornell University Press.

Donnelly, J. (2000) *Realism and International Relations*, Cambridge: Cambridge University Press.

Gilpin, R. (1981) *War and Change in World Politics*, Cambridge: Cambridge University Press.

Glaser, C. L. (1997) 'The Security Dilemma Revisited', *World Politics* 50, 171–210.

Haslam, J. (2002) *No Virtue Like Necessity*, New Haven, CT: Yale University Press.

Jervis, R. (1997) *Systems Effects: Complexity in Political and Social Life*, Princeton, NJ: Princeton University Press.

Legro, J. W. and Moravcsik, A. (1999) 'Is Anybody Still a Realist?' *International Security* 24(2), 5–55.

Mearsheimer, J. (2001) *The Tragedy of Great Power Politics*, New York: Norton.

Morgenthau, Hans. 1985. *Politics Among Nations: The Struggle for Power and Peace*, 6th edn, New York: McGraw-Hill.

Rasler K. and Thompson W. R. (2001) 'Malign Autocracies and Major Power Warfare: Evil, Tragedy, and International Relations Theory', *Security Studies* 10(3), 46–79.

Schweller, R. L. (1994) 'Bandwagoning for Profit: Bringing the Revisionist State Back In', *International Security* 19(2), 72–107.

Schweller, R. L. (1998) *Deadly Imbalances: Tripolarity and Hitler's Strategy of World Conquest*, New York: Columbia University Press.

Smith, M. J. (1986) *Realist Thought From Weber to Kissinger*, Baton Rouge: Louisiana State University Press.

Spirtas, M. (1996) 'A House Divided: Tragedy and Evil in Realist Theory', *Security Studies* 5(3), 385–423.

Vasquez, J. and Elman, C. (eds) (2003) *Realism and the Balancing of Power: A New Debate*, Upper Saddle River, NJ: Prentice Hall.

Vasquez, J. (1997) 'The Realist Paradigm and Degenerative versus Progressive Research Programs', *American Political Science Review* 91, 899–912.

Walt, S. M. (1987) *The Origins of Alliances*, Ithaca, NY: Cornell University Press.

Waltz, K.N. (1979) *Theory of International Politics*, Reading, MA: Addison-Wesley.

See also: agent-structure debate; anarchy; balance of power; critical theory; historical sociology; liberal internationalism; Marxism

COLIN ELMAN

Reciprocity

The provision of a benefit or the imposition of a cost in the form of a good or an action to another actor who has previously provided a benefit to or imposed a cost on oneself. The conditional exchange of tangible and intangible goods or actions is a widespread if not omnipresent practice in human society, one that ranges from ritualistic exchange of gifts or favors in traditional cultures to the practices of comity in **international law** and bargaining in international politics. Much research in political science has been devoted to analyzing the practice of reciprocity and its implications for cooperation, conflict, and strategic interaction in domestic and international politics.

The practice of reciprocity can be distinguished in terms of the degree of contingency and equivalence of exchange between two parties. Contingency refers to the sequence and timing of an action taken by one actor in response to an action taken by another. Actions taken by one actor immediately following and because of those taken by another are highly contingent, while those that are less motivated by or taken long after the actions of another are less contingent. Immediate payment for services rendered is a highly contingent exchange, while the offer of assistance to a friend or ally in need is generally a less contingent act.

The level of contingency in exchange is a function of at least three factors. These include the actors' expectations about future interaction (often referred to as the 'shadow of the future'), the degree to which each actor values future relative to current rewards from their exchanges with one another (often referred to as the 'discount rate'), and each actor's need for the other to respond quickly and its expectations that the other can respond in a timely manner. If both actors expect to interact with the other in the future, if they place a relatively high value on future interactions, or if they either do not need a quick response or they anticipate that the other may have difficulty in responding immediately, then the exchanges between them are likely to be less contingent than would otherwise be the case.

Equivalence refers to the perceived value of the goods or actions given and received. Precisely equivalent exchanges exist when the actors involved concur that the value and rate of exchanges

match mutually specified levels. Imprecise equivalence exists when the rate or value of exchange is either not specified or is inconsequential. It is important to note that the value of goods or actions exchanged is often interpreted subjectively by each actor, such that even the exchange of identical goods may not be seen as precisely equivalent if the goods received do not match the recipient's expectations. In negotiations over market access, for example, countries whose consumer markets differ in size may not consider an identical dollar value of exports to one another to represent equivalent access to each other's consumers. The level of precision in an exchange is a function of several factors including the compatibility of the actors' preferences, the relative **power** of each actor to alter the terms of exchange to its advantage, and the **legitimacy** of the process through which the exchange is conducted. The less actor preferences overlap, the more competitive their relationship, the less legitimate the exchange or the greater the probability of deceit, the more precisely the exchange is likely to be specified.

While the degrees of contingency and equivalence in a reciprocal exchange may vary, the interaction of two characteristics creates four ideal types: specific reciprocity, diffuse reciprocity, and two mixed patterns of reciprocity. Specific reciprocity refers to a highly contingent and precisely equivalent pattern of exchange. The strategy of 'tit for tat' – I will cooperate in kind if you do, but will not if you do not – represents this form of reciprocity. This strategy can lead to cooperation under a limited set of conditions, but it is fragile because expectations are narrowly defined and a single seemingly uncooperative action will likely spark a retaliatory defection, generating an exchange of mutual costs rather than mutual benefits. This makes transparency of actions, clarity in signaling, and verification extremely important. The exchange of political prisoners during the **cold war** between the East and West at Check-Point Charlie in Berlin is a good example of specific reciprocity. Whether it involved one person from each side or multiple prisoners from one side for one of high value from the other, each exchange involved very detailed agreements about who was getting what, for how much, and when.

Diffuse reciprocity refers to a noncontingent and imprecise pattern of exchange. Examples of diffuse reciprocity include the granting of normal trading status to all members of the **World Trade Organization** (WTO), compliance with customary international law, and the multifaceted exchange of information among allies. In each case, neither the timing nor the nature of the repayment is specified in advance. For example, members of the WTO are obliged to extend any trade concessions to all fellow members, regardless of whether the others have offered similar benefits. Whereas specific reciprocity is most likely to persist when transparency is high and the terms of exchange are clearly measurable, demands for transparency may undermine diffuse reciprocity by suggesting an inappropriate concern about score keeping or burden sharing. Also, in contrast to the practice of specific reciprocity, one or even several unexpected actions by the other are unlikely to undermine diffuse reciprocity. For example, repeated violations of an international rule do not necessarily indicate that the rule is not valid, nor does it change the expectation that states (including the violator) will comply with it under other circumstances.

Reciprocity may also exist when either the exchange is highly contingent but the value of that exchange is imprecise, or the degree of contingency is low and equivalence is precise. The first mixed ideal-type of reciprocity exists when actors demand an immediate action, but they leave the value of the action unspecified. For example, in March 1997, the US Congress threatened to impose sanctions against Mexico if it did not take immediate action to demonstrate its commitment to fighting drugs. On the eve of its deliberations, the Mexican government arrested a single corrupt drug chief. Even though this likely did little to address the drug problem, the US Congress accepted it as evidence that Mexico was a reliable partner in the fight on drugs.

The second ideal-type of mixed reciprocity is exists when the value of exchange is critical, but the timing is not significant. Negotiations involving the use of common pool resources, such as a shared water supply, represent this type of exchange. In such cases, it is critically important to specify the amount of water (or the good in question) to which each party is entitled. Once the allotments are determined, however, the timing or rate of consumption becomes less important. Like the others, these mixed patterns of reciprocity are likely to persist as long as each actor shares the same expectations in terms of the timing and value of the rewards and punishments it will receive from the other.

Further reading

Axelrod, R. (1984) *The Evolution of Cooperation*, New York: Basic Books.

Keohane, R. (1986) 'Reciprocity in International Relations', *International Organization* 40(1) 1–27.

Lepgold, J. and Shambaugh, G. (2002) 'Who Owes Whom, How Much, and When? Understanding Reciprocated Social Exchange in International Politics', *Review of International Studies* 28, 229–52.

See also: international law; prisoner's dilemma; recognition

GEORGE E. SHAMBAUGH

Recognition

Membership in the **international system** depends on the general recognition by other states of a government's **sovereignty** within its territory. Such recognition is extended formally through the establishment of diplomatic relations and by membership in the **United Nations** (UN). It does not necessarily imply that a government has popular support but only that it (usually) controls the state's territory and agrees to assume its obligations in the international system – to accept internationally recognized borders, to assume the international debts of the previous government, and to refrain from interfering in other states' internal affairs. In other words, the act of recognition establishes the status of a political entity in **international society**. That status provides the new state with formal equality in the context of **international law**, it is able to join international organizations, and its representatives are entitled to all the benefits of diplomatic immunity.

Since 1945 recognition has taken place primarily in the context of **decolonization**, although since the end of the **cold war** it has played an important role in the dissolution of states that have fragmented as **nationalism** has re-emerged as a potent force in international relations. The process has been surprisingly peaceful in some cases (for example, the former Czechoslovakia and the former Soviet Union) and extremely violent in others, particularly Yugoslavia.

There is no collective agreed practice, in law or politics, to guide state recognition. It is a unilateral decision rather than a collective one, and as yet there are no universal criteria for recognition. Some states are explicit in the criteria they use (for example, Britain) whilst others such as the United States prefer greater flexibility in determining whether to accord recognition. The British tend to rely on the effectiveness of control over a particular territory exercised by a fledgling state, but this preference is not shared by all states. For example, in 1967 five states (Gabon, Ivory Coast, Zambia, Haiti, and Tanzania) recognized Biafra's claim to independence from Nigeria. By 1970 Biafra acknowledged that it had not managed to establish such independence, leading to the withdrawal of recognition by the other African states. The advantage of the British position is that it signifies neither approval nor support of the new state. In contrast, the United States uses diplomatic recognition as an instrument of its foreign policy. Thus it recognized the State of Israel within a day of that country's unilateral declaration of independence in May 1948, but it refused to extend recognition to the People's Republic of China until 1979.

Since the late 1970s, although the United States has moved closer to the British position on recognition, there remains a lack of consensus in the international community over the conditions for recognizing new states or for withdrawing recognition from existing states. This became clear during the early 1990s in the context of the wars in Yugoslavia. In 1991 Germany argued that it would unilaterally recognize Slovenia and Croatia at the end of the year. Britain argued that such recognition was premature in light of the ongoing **war** with the nominal Federal Republic of Yugoslavia. There were powerful arguments on both sides of the issue. Germany argued that recognition would send a clear message to the Serbian government that its aggression could not continue without transforming a **civil war** into an inter-state conflict. On the other hand, in the absence of any commitment to assist Croatia militarily, it remained unclear why Serbia would heed the message. Ultimately, Germany succeeded in prevailing over dissenting voices in the **European Union**, but there is little evidence that recognition had any effect over the conflicts that continued throughout the first half of the 1990s.

The issue was again raised in 1999 during the conflict between Serbia and the Yugoslav Republic of Kosovo. This time the United States mobilized its NATO allies (see **North Atlantic Treaty Organization**) to bomb Serbia because of its repression of the Kosovars, but the United States refused to countenance Kosovo as an independent state. It argued that such recognition could lead to further fragmentation in the region, although it was difficult for many observers to see how Kosovo and Serbia could remain part of a single state after the war.

In short, the acts of recognition as well as the withdrawal of recognition remain political acts. They vary from state to state, and a particular state can use different criteria over time depending on its interpretation of the **national interest**. Whilst recognition provides a state with important privileges that come with membership of an exclusive club, it is not accompanied by any guarantees. The wars in Yugoslavia provide another good example of this lesson. When conflict broke out in Bosnia in 1992, the existing (Muslim) government was widely recognized by the international community. Such recognition was of little help in preventing the de facto partition of Bosnia three years later.

Further reading

Caplan, R. (2005) *Europe and the Recognition of New States in Yugoslavia*, Cambridge: Cambridge University Press.

Krasner, S. (1999) *Sovereignty: Organized Hypocrisy*, Princeton, NJ: Princeton University Press.

Peterson, M. (1997) *Recognition of Governments: Legal Doctrine and State Practice*, New York: St. Martin's Press.

See also: diplomacy; legitimacy; self-determination; Westphalia

MARTIN GRIFFITHS

Reflexivity

Reflexivity means referring to oneself, acting upon oneself or reflecting upon oneself. Reflexivity is used in virtually all fields of science. In the *Oxford English Dictionary* it is defined only with reference to its grammatical meaning, but mathematicians discuss the reflexivity of Abelian groups and of Banach Spaces, and reflexivity is central to discussions in topics as diverse as biology and organizational economic theory, the philosophy of science and anthropology. As this diversity of use indicates, the exact meaning and connotations of reflexivity are as varied and contested as the contexts of its usage. The focus here is on reflexivity as used in International Relations and International Political Economy (IR/IPE). As in the bulk of the social sciences, reflexivity in IR/IPE is mainly associated with the problematization of the observer in relation to the observed, that is, with the self-referential activities of researchers. This kind of reflexivity is increasingly central and positively valued. However, since there are diverse reasons for valuing reflexivity, the practical and theoretical meaning of reflexivity is not fixed.

There are three main reasons behind the increased importance of reflexivity in the study of international relations. First, the field has become far more open to diverse theoretical approaches over the past decade. In IR/IPE this is expressed by the epistemological or 'reflectivist' turn taken as **gender**, constructivist, and poststructuralist (see **constructivism; poststructuralism**) scholars entered the field. Common to all of these approaches is an explicit recognition of the complex relationship between theory and practice, or subject and object of analysis. Can the observer adequately understand and translate the meaning of observed activity to the context and language of the observer? Is translation between systems of meaning possible at all? How does the social embeddedness of the observer impact on what s/he can see, chooses to see and what is actually revealed by the observed? Is understanding a conceptual (semiotic) process or an aesthetic (mimetic) one?

A second reason for valuing reflexivity is its role in assessing how observation effects the observed. The meaning systems of observers may have real effects through their impact on policies and institutions structuring the social world. Finally, meaning systems produced by observers may impact on the observed by informing and reordering the latter's basic categories and meaning systems. It is highly contested whether the feedback effect of observation (in general or of specific observations) on the observed is, should be or can be emancipatory or will merely feed into evolving modes of social control and power/knowledge constellations (Sparti 2001). Either way reflexivity becomes essential for political and ethical reasons. Awareness of the importance of observation for the observed makes a strong case for reflexively assessing the impact of scientific activities on social reality.

A third explanation for the ascent of reflexivity is temporal and tied to the centrality of knowledge and observers in most influential accounts of the contemporary social world. Whether in 'knowledge society', 'risk society', 'network society', 'second/late modernity', or in 'post-modernity' we inhabit a world where 'experts' are increasingly pivotal.

The wide consensus about the significance of reflexivity is not matched by a consensus about what reflexivity means or how it should be practiced. Instead, the numerous differences among those who arrive at the conclusion that reflexivity is essential are reflected in the diversity of approaches to reflexivity. One way to simplify this diversity is to distinguish between three 'families' of reflexivity: cognitive, aesthetic and hermeneutic (Lash 1994) (see **hermeneutics**).

Cognitive reflexivity is an approach according to which meaning is important in the social world but its implications for science are minimized. This means that the social world can be described and understood by the observer in a realistic fashion through an analysis of prevailing **discourse**s, the spread of norms or the constitution of identity. This position is consistent with a universalist ethics, making it important to think about the emancipatory effects of research. On this account reflexivity does not necessarily have to be present and visible in all texts and research.

Aesthetic reflexivity is an approach that undermines all claims to scientific objectivity. Instead, the social embeddedness of the observer is fundamental to the assessment of claims and arguments. On this account meaning and knowledge are (increasingly) mimetic and intuitive rather than semiotic and conceptual. A correlate of this position is that there can be no universal ethics but only ethics of 'non-identity', of 'the other' or of 'difference'. This position results in a very different form of reflexivity. It becomes a key endeavor of non-scientific activity to embrace the radical uncertainty of all accounts of the world, to deconstruct (see **deconstruction**), undermine and reveal the power/knowledge nexus inherent not only in the categories of the observed world, but also in the text of the observer.

Hermeneutic reflexivity shares the esthetic understanding of meaning as fundamental not only for practice but also for theory, of knowledge as largely mimetic, and expressed in practices of power/knowledge. However, it rejects the relativism of esthetic reflexivity and instead tries to ground science. For this purpose, the narcissistic reflexivity of acknowledging the observer in the text is an inadequate remedy. It is not clear, for example, how travelogs, biographical fragments or imagined 'second voices' actually clarify the observer–observed relation. Instead, hermeneutic reflexivity strives to explicitly clarify the implications of our social embeddedness for theoretical inquiry. On this account, reflexivity is an integral part of all scientific work. It is essential to limit the impact of bias, and to recognize the (often unintended) impact of observers on the observed and more generally on the constitution of legitimate knowledge.

Further reading

Der Derian, J. (2001) *Virtuous War: Mapping the Military-Industrial-Media-Entertainment Network*, Boulder CO: Westview Press.

Harrison, E. (2004) *The International System: Strategies, Institutions and Reflexivity*, London: Routledge.

Lash, S. (1994) 'Reflexivity and Its Doubles: Structure, Aesthetics, Community', in Beck, U., Giddens, A. and Lash, S. (eds) *Reflexive Modernization*, Oxford: Polity Press, 110–73.

Lynch, M. (2000) 'Against Reflexivity as an Academic Virtue and Source of Privileged Knowledge', *Theory, Culture & Society* 17(3), 26–54.

Pels, D. (2000) 'Reflexivity', *Theory, Culture & Society* 17(3), 1–25.

Sparti, D. (2001) 'Making up People', *European Journal of Social Theory* 4(3), 331–49.

See also: hermeneutics; post-positivism

ANNA LEANDER

Refugee

An individual forced to leave his or her country for fear of persecution or threat to life. The term was first coined to apply to the several thousand Huguenots who were pushed out of catholic France with the revocation of the Edict of Nantes in 1685. Legislation relating specifically to refugees began to be introduced in the seventeenth century alongside the growing field of nationality laws. By the end of the nineteenth century displacement was starting to occur across Europe on a mass scale, as a result of political and social changes affecting the entire **international system**. Huge refugee flows were created by the inherent turmoil associated with events such as the breakdown of **empire**s into new states, World War One, wars in the Balkans and Russian pogroms. The League of Nations High Commissioner for Refugees (LNHCR) was established to deal with the growing problem, marking the beginning of intergovernmental action in the field. When LNHCR was dissolved in 1930, successive organizations took its place, leading to the foundation of the statute of the United Nations High Commissioner for Refugees (UNHCR) in 1950. This continuation of intergovernmental organization in the field has allowed the refugee as a concept to be viewed in state centric terms as the uprooted, mobile exception in contrast to the 'normal', sedentary citizen. Hence the refugee has been constructed since the outset as a 'problem' to be solved due to the way in which **international society** is organized amongst separate sovereign territorial states.

UNHCR remains the leading organization working in the field today, albeit restricted by the strategic preferences of donor and host states. But the fact that the system depends on the strategic preferences and self-interest of individual governments leaves it open to states' differing conceptions of the refugee. Indeed, the current persistence of the 'refugee problem' in international politics and successive unsuccessful attempts to respond to it is only partly attributable to politics or questions of resources. There are now so many different words used in everyday speech that any discussion of the issues is difficult. In different contexts refugees are referred to as economic migrants, illegal immigrants, asylum-seekers, displaced persons, political refugees, and stateless persons.

Attempts at definition go back to the early days of refugee regimentation when, in the inter-war period, various arrangements and legal instruments tried to categorize specific groups of refugees. These efforts culminated in the formulation of the Convention relating to the Status of Refugees in 1951, which describes a 'refugee' as any person who, 'owing to well-founded fear of being persecuted for reasons of race, religion, nationality, membership of a particular social group or political opinion, is outside the country of his nationality and is unable or, owing to such fear, unwilling to avail himself of the protection of that country'. Importantly the Convention grants an internationally recognized legal status and certain associated rights. Perhaps the most crucial of these is contained in Article 33 – the principle of *non-refoulement*, or the prohibition on returning an individual to a country where his or her life would be in danger. However, the definition itself is somewhat restrictive in insisting on individual persecution as the main criterion for refugee status. It was formulated in the climate of the **cold war** when such a criterion was practical within Europe. But since the 1960s mass displacements across Africa, for example, have affected whole communities rather than individuals. The 1967 Protocol removed the geographical limits of the Convention to beyond Europe, yet 'individual persecution' as the defining factor for refugee status remains inappropriate. Accordingly regional instruments have sought to expand the understanding of who constitutes a refugee. For example, The Organization of African Unity (OAU) Convention of 1969 includes the criterion of 'displacement due to external aggression, occupation, foreign domination or events seriously disturbing public order in part or all of the country'.

The 1951 Convention is also restrictive in requiring would-be refugees to cross an international border in order to be granted refugee status. The contemporary 'refugee problem' involves millions of individuals in qualitatively the same situation as a refugee but who remain within the borders of their state – so-called 'internally displaced persons' (IDPs). Crossing an international frontier is not always possible for displaced populations; many remain quite literally trapped within state borders, out of the reach of international aid and protection.

UNHCR has expanded its remit over the decades via its 'good offices' to work on behalf of those who do not fall within the Convention definition. They include individuals recognized as refugees under the OAU Convention and the Cartagena Declaration, those fleeing generalized violence or 'mandate refugees', internally displaced persons, those granted leave to remain in host countries on humanitarian grounds, and those granted temporary protection on a group basis. At the end of 2003 UNHCR classed 12.1 million people 'of concern' across the globe, including 9.7 million refugees, 4.3 million IDPs and almost one million asylum-seekers.

UNHCR advocates three durable solutions to the problem of refugees – repatriation, local (re)settlement and international resettlement. All these responses can be seen as attempts to 'reterritorialize' the refugee, to reinstate the individual in the 'normal' state–citizen relationship bounded by territory. Yet this attempt fails to appreciate that in the context of an international system based on sovereign territorial states, any solution can only be temporary until the next refugee movement occurs. Indeed, the refugee is an unavoidable if unanticipated consequence of erecting borders between separate sovereign territorial states, including states that fail to protect all individuals within their jurisdiction as citizens. Refugees have been forced outside the 'normal' state–citizen relationship into the gaps *between* states. It is a fundamental assumption of **international society** that states are good for their citizens, yet sovereign obligations are not always met. When a gap is created between the positive sovereignty of the individual state and the negative sovereignty of international society in which this state is situated, the discrepancy causes a failure both domestically and internationally, which leads to the creation of refugees. In other words refugees appear when the theory and practice of the international states system and the concept of sovereignty on which it relies fail to coincide.

A broader definition of the refugee than that contained in the 1951 Convention would seem to be called for, to take into account contemporary patterns of displacement. This should focus on the situation of individuals who have been forced out of the state–citizen relationship within the domestic political community, and who will be unable to return until the relationship is repaired, rather than the current focus on those who have been persecuted and have been able to cross an international boundary. International borders symbolize the boundaries of the domestic political community, but crossing one is not a necessary condition for becoming a refugee. 'Refugees' are created when norms of **good governance** within a state fail and individuals are forced to search for protection in another state. But the relationship between the state and the citizen may have broken down without a border crossing having taken place, hence the false dichotomy between 'refugee' and 'internally displaced person'.

Perhaps, however, the concept of the 'refugee' ultimately defies universal definition. We must ask whether one generalized term is appropriate for so many forced migrants with such diverse histories and experiences. What is clear is that the definitional issue in the case of the refugee is more than just a question of semantics. For many individuals the issue of who is and who is not included in the category is a matter of life and death.

Further reading

Feller, E., Türk, V. and Nicholson, F. (eds) (2003) *Refugee Protection in International Law*, Cambridge: Cambridge University Press.

Haddad, E. (2003) 'The Refugee: The Individual Between Sovereigns', *Global Society* 7(3), 297–322.

Hathaway, J. C. (1991) *The Law of Refugee Status*, Toronto: Butterworths.

Jacobsen, K. (2004) *Refugee Camps: A Problem of Our Time*, Basingstoke: Palgrave.

Shacknove, A. E. (1995) 'Who Is a Refugee?' *Ethics* 95, 274–84.

Soguk, N. (1999) *States and Strangers: Refugees and Displacements of Statecraft*, Minneapolis, MN: University of Minnesota Press.

See also: asylum; civil war; ethnic conflict; identity/difference; international society; international system; sovereignty

EMMA HADDAD

Regime

A set of principles, procedures, norms, or rules that govern particular issue areas in international relations. Regimes are important because they facilitate some form of **global governance** in an anarchical realm (see **anarchy**). They reflect the fact that states often have converging **national interest**s and are willing to cooperate to achieve certain outcomes. As a consequence, some scholars believe that regimes play a significant role in reducing the level of international conflict between states and facilitating cooperation at the international level.

Regimes can take the form of conventions, international agreements, treaties or international institutions. They can be found in a variety of issue areas, including economics, the environment, policing, transport, **security**, communications, **human rights**, **arms control**, even copyright and patents. Indeed, they exist in most issue areas where states have similar interests. The **World Trade Organization** (WTO), the **United Nations** Convention on the **Law of the Sea** (UNCLOS) and the **Chemical Weapons** Convention (CWC) are all examples of firmly established regimes.

A regime can be bilateral, multilateral, regional, or global in scope. It can also be formal and highly institutionalized or quite loose and informal. The WTO is a good example of a formal and institutionalized regime, while UNCLOS and the CWC have fewer institutional structures underpinning them. Yet they are similar in the sense that each requires compliance from states. States who have accepted the conditions set out by the regime are under an obligation to act according to its principles.

The notion of convergence is crucial to understanding the character of regimes. Regimes presuppose that states have similar interests across a range of issues and that these interests can best served by coordinated action. In other words, regimes provide a regulatory framework for states that facilitates a semblance of global governance. Imagine, for example, the difficulty in getting mail to someone on the other side of the world without a formal agreement governing the distribution of mail. Think for a moment about the chaos in the skies if there were no rules or procedures regulating airline traffic. Who would risk overseas flight under such circumstances?

Some scholars have argued that regimes function best when **power** is concentrated in the hands of a preponderant state. **Hegemonic stability theory** suggests that the presence of a hegemon makes it possible (and easier) to enforce rules and norms across an issue area. The role of the United States in putting in place an open trading system in the aftermath of World War Two is often cited as an example of the importance of power in determining the success of regimes.

Since the 1970s, theoretical inquiry into regimes has developed into a growth industry. Today, there are at least three main divisions within contemporary regime theory. Realist theories (see **realism**) stress the role of power in generating cooperation between states. Interest-based theories highlight the value of regimes in promoting the common interests of states, whilst knowledge-based theories focus primarily on the way that ideas and norms shape perceptions of international problems and the role of regimes in this process.

Despite the differences of emphasis in these approaches, all agree that regimes are an important source of stability in the international arena, particularly as states increasingly confront problems that do not respect territorial boundaries and which require international cooperation.

Further reading

Aggarwal, V. (1998) *Institutional Designs for a Complex World*, Ithaca, NY: Cornell University Press.

Cronin, B. (2003) *Institutions for the Common Good*, Cambridge: Cambridge University Press.

Spector, B. and Zartman, I. (eds) (2003) *Getting it Done: Postagreement Negotiation and International Regimes*, Washington, DC: United States Institute of Peace.

See also: relative gains/absolute gains; international public goods

TERRY O'CALLAGHAN

Regionalism

This term refers to intensifying political and/or economic processes of cooperation among states and other actors in particular geographic regions, although it is most often discussed in the context of trade flows. At least since the beginning of the 1980s, the world economy has become increasingly tripolar, with more than 85 per cent of world trade concentrated in three regions: East Asia, Western Europe, and North America. At the same time, these are also areas in which attempts to engage in some regional **integration** have taken place. The deepening and the expansion of the

European economic integration, increasing **interdependence** among three North American countries (United States, Canada, Mexico) as well as the transformation of the **Association of Southeast Asian Nations** (ASEAN) into a more economy-oriented association since the 1980s are examples of this trend. In contrast, other regions have been successively losing their share of the world market, and represent approximately one-tenth of the world trade volume.

Essentially, a region is a spatial concept. It is defined by a combination of geographical proximity, density of interactions, shared institutional frameworks, and common cultural identities. Regions can be identified empirically by relying on data on mutual interactions such as trade flows, similarities of actor attributes, and shared values and experiences. But one should also bear in mind that regions are dynamic entities. They are not so much measurable building blocs of the international **order** as spatially defined cultural, economic, and political constructions whose nature and functions are transformed over time.

The term 'regionalism' captures these dynamic aspects of regional cooperation defined as the growth of social and economic interaction and of regional identity and consciousness. Regionalism results from the increasing flow of goods, people, and ideas within a spatial entity that becomes more integrated and cohesive. Regionalism can develop 'from below' (i.e. from the decisions by companies to invest and by people to move within a region) or 'from above' (i.e. from political, state-based efforts to create cohesive regional units and common policies for them).

Practically everyone writing today on regionalism argues that it is growing strongly in almost every part of the world. This trend, sometimes depicted as the 'second coming' of regionalism (the first one took place in the 1960s), has been explained by several, often disparate factors. The alleged decline of US material hegemony, the end of the **cold war**, the rise of the Asia-Pacific region, and the export-led reorientation of **development** strategies in the **Third World** have all fostered a more decentralized **international system**. This has, in turn, enhanced the autonomy of regions and their dominant actors. The standard arguments on the rise of regionalism mention, at a minimum, the establishment of the **North American Free Trade Agreement** (NAFTA), the deepening integration in the **European Union**, and the growing economic interdependence in East Asia. Regional cooperation may also be promoted as a counterweight to the uneven **globalization** of the world economy. Finally, regionalism may be a reaction against dominant states that try to co-opt local actors by granting special privileges to them.

The main debate about regionalism is whether it is leading to a more polarized or a more cooperative world economy and world order. While the proliferation of regional **preferential trade agreement**s has raised concerns about their implications for the multilateral trading system, most observers argue that these two systems have not been contradictory. However, the relationship between regionalism and a multilateral system is a complex one, and it is becoming more complex as the number and the scope of regional initiatives increase. Ensuring that regionalism and **multilateralism** grow together (*open regionalism*) – and not apart (*closed regionalism*) – is perhaps the most urgent issue facing trade policymakers today.

Well-structured regional integration arrangements may be helpful to the strengthening of an open world economy, for three main reasons. First, regional arrangements can enhance the awareness of interdependence between trading partners, thereby enhancing the acceptance of international rules on the part of national governments and interest groups. Second, regional arrangements in general face similar challenges as those faced by the multilateral trading system. Therefore, the problems and solutions experienced during regional negotiations will be useful in overcoming similar difficulties that arise in the multilateral processes. Finally, increasing inter-regional cooperation mechanisms can serve as a building block for the strengthening of multilateralism. The stronger the cooperation among the three major traders of the world economy, Asia, Europe, and North America, the more likely it is for the world economy to be integrated globally, rather than be fragmented into several **regional trade bloc**s. Thus there can be a mutually supportive relationship between multilateralism and regionalism.

Further reading

Katz, B. (ed.) (2000) *Reflections on Regionalism*, Washington, DC: Brookings.

Mattli, W. (1999) *The Logic of Regional Integration*, Cambridge: Cambridge University Press.

Söderbaum, F. and Shaw, T. (eds) (2003) *Theories of New Regionalism*, Basingstoke: Palgrave.

See also: African Union; Arab League; Association of Southeast Asian Nations; European Union; globalization

TERRY O'CALLAGHAN

Regional trade bloc

An economic grouping of countries that are located close to each other and that seek to enhance trade and investments within a specific geographical area. Such blocs may be outward or inward looking. If they are outward looking, the primary aim of the grouping is to promote regional economic activities in a manner consistent with the encouragement of international trade along liberal lines and with minimum restrictions. In contrast, if the grouping is inward looking, then, the aim is to promote trade among members while disadvantaging non-members.

When regional trade blocs pursue a liberal model of **development**, their activities are likely to be consistent with international **regime**s committed to enhancing international trade and investment. At the broadest level, such regimes include the **World Trade Organization** (WTO) and the General Agreement on Tariffs and Trade (GATT). The United States and Western European countries have traditionally pushed for liberal international trading regimes. There are two major reasons for this decision. The first reason is the widespread conviction that liberal trading regimes generally enhance global production and consumption through the competitive deployment of relatively scarce resources. The second and perhaps more selfish reason is that liberal regimes allow industrialized countries greater access for their manufactured goods in the domestic markets of less developed countries.

Trading blocs that are convinced of the utility and persuasiveness of liberal economics invariably tend to be outward looking or open. However, contrarily, trading blocs whose members fear the loss of the domestic market and manufacturing sector to external competition tend to be inward looking or closed. Closed regional trading blocs prevent external intrusion into their markets by employing high tariffs, quotas, or a mixture of the two.

The transition from a closed to an open trading bloc is complicated by the fact that the 'high end' manufactured goods of industrialized countries have traditionally had a greater premium placed on them than the products of developing countries. Additionally, the value of agricultural goods is much lower than the value of manufactured goods. It was as a result of such considerations that many newly independent countries in Asia and Latin America adopted a policy of import substitution after the end of World War Two. There was also some concern that consistently negative trade balances would weaken these countries economically and leave them at the mercy of the industrialized countries. The popularity of nationalist, Marxist, and dependency theories (see **nationalism; Marxism; dependency theory**) in the 1950s and 1960s (all of which emphasized the unequal terms of international trade and unfavorable structural dependence on Western-inspired liberal trade) further worked against outward looking trade blocs. Additionally, newly independent and less developed countries were unprepared to surrender their **sovereignty** on economic policies to what were essentially developed countries. These sentiments culminated in the mooting of the New International Economic Order (NIEO) in 1972. Sentiments favoring **free trade** only coalesced after the success of the newly industrialized countries of East Asia (NICs) (see **newly industrialized country**) in achieving rapid economic growth through export-led development in the 1970s and 1980s.

Regional trade blocs may be found in different parts of the world among countries at different levels of development. For the most part, many of these blocs are open or outward looking. The oldest and perhaps most celebrated of such blocs was the European Economic

Community (EEC) which has now been subsumed under the broader rubric of the **European Union** (EU). Other significant and more recent blocs include the **North American Free Trade Area** (NAFTA) that combines Canada, Mexico, and the United States. In the Asia-Pacific region, the **Association of Southeast Asian Nations'** Free Trade Area (AFTA), the Asia-Pacific Economic Cooperation forum (APEC) and the Pacific Economic Cooperation Council (PECC) are also examples of regional trade blocs.

Regional trade blocs often have spillover effects on a number of sectors that may not be directly related to the enhancement of trade. Such spillovers may occur in sectors such as labor, technology, and capital flows. As a result of the supranational nature and thrust of regional trade blocs, such blocs have the potential for greater levels of functional regional integration. Subsequently, if there is sufficient political will and momentum on the part of member states, such blocs may eventually tend in the direction of regional integration, as is the case of the EU. Naturally, apart from positive political will, both the availability and willingness of trading blocs to bring enforcement mechanisms to bear on member states determine the progress and cohesion of such blocs.

Conversely, the two greatest threats to the institutionalization of liberally-inspired open trading blocs are state sovereignty and domestic interest and lobby groups. States, especially powerful ones that seek to retain a measure of sovereignty in economic and trade matters, have traditionally resisted integration that tends in the direction of supranationalism. Similarly, states that seek a measure of protection for infant industries or specific sectors have also resisted surrendering sovereignty in its entirety. So, for example, the agricultural lobby is extremely strong even in developed countries like France and Japan and such lobbies have in the past hindered the realization of broad-based open trading arrangements. More recently however, the WTO has availed itself for the resolution of trade disputes between states through legally binding arbitration. Consequently, it is likely that there will be a far greater drift towards liberal trading arrangements in the future. Nonetheless, it must be remembered that even the WTO is unable to enforce its decisions on individual countries.

Apart from questions pertaining to state sovereignty, another recent challenge to regional trade blocs and **multilateralism** in general is the increasing popularity of bilateral trading arrangements. Technically, such arrangements allow countries to cut deals 'on the side' and bypass regional trade blocs. In so far as such bilateral trading arrangements do not confer exclusive benefits at the bilateral level and are consistent with WTO and GATT rules, such infringements may be avoided.

Further reading

Gibb, R. and Michalak, W. (eds) (1994) *Continental Trading Blocs*, New York: John Wiley.

Mansfield, E. D. and Milner, H. D. (eds) (1997) *The Political Economy of Regionalism*, New York: Columbia University Press.

Ohmae, K. (1995) *The End of the Nation State: The Rise of Regional Economies*, New York: The Free Press.

See also: regionalism; World Trade Organization

NARAYANAN GANESAN

Relative/absolute gains

The payoffs from social interaction can be measured in several ways, including relative gains (i.e., how much do I gain relative to you?) and absolute gains (i.e., how much do I gain irrespective of your gain?) While proponents of **realism** tend to emphasize the importance of relative gains, advocates of **liberal internationalism** tend to focus on absolute gains. Virtually everyone agrees that focusing on relative gains decreases the probability of cooperation in any social interaction, including interstate bargaining.

Power is a relative concept. According to some realists, any gain in power by one state corresponds to a loss in the power of other states. For example, during the **cold war**, gains in power by the Soviet Union were considered power losses by the United States. The anarchic structure (see **anarchy**) of the **international system** means that shifts in power are dangerous because states can use their power to coerce other states. Thus, realists contend that foreign policy-makers must be acutely sensitive to the distribution of gains in any economic or military agreement. States will only approve of agreements that either preserve the existing **balance of power** or enhance the state's relative power. Given that realists believe that the competitive international environment will force all states to adopt similar preferences in the long run, the pursuit of relative gains should become universal. Only in rare cases (i.e., accords which perfectly preserve the balance of power) will international cooperation be possible, particularly among the **great powers**.

In the realm of **international political economy**, the relative/absolute gains debate can be traced to the liberal reaction to **mercantilism** in the eighteenth and nineteenth centuries. Mercantilists, who sought to increase wealth by maximizing exports and minimizing imports, viewed trade in zero sum terms. Any gain in trade by one country was a loss by another. Adam Smith (1723–90) and his followers countered that states could maximize national wealth by adopting a **free trade** strategy. By exploiting their comparative advantage, states could increase economic efficiency and thus the total size of 'the pie' to be distributed among the traders. Over the last two centuries, particularly since the end of World War Two, liberal trade policies have slowly supplanted mercantilist and autarchic strategies.

In the political sphere, realism with its emphasis on relative gains continued to be the dominant paradigm (with perhaps the brief exception of the interwar period). However, realism came under increasing attack from the liberal camp beginning in the 1980s and 1990s. Many liberals accepted some realist assumptions such as the importance of the international structure, the existence of selfish agents, and the irrelevance of domestic politics. Drawing on economic theory and employing game theoretic models, however, they argued that cooperation is possible even after adopting the pessimistic assumptions of their realist counterparts. Through repeated interaction and with the help of international **regimes**, states can encourage the emergence of cooperation by changing the expectations of other states.

Such arguments rely heavily on economic theory, which typically assumes actors are motivated by absolute gains. For example, while the theory of comparative advantage claims that all participants are better off after trade, it does not predict that the gains in trade will be evenly divided or will preserve the existing balance of power. However, realists contend that states cannot be motivated solely by the promise of absolute gains because it would threaten their very survival. Using an evolutionary argument, realists argue that states maximizing absolute gains are 'weeded out' in the long run because they find it difficult to survive in the rough and tumble world of international politics. While realists concede that a focus on absolute gains may maximize wealth, they contend that it cannot maximize **security**.

The debate between liberals and realists has important policy implications. For example, consider American policy toward the rise of China. Should the United States encourage or discourage China from joining economic institutions such as the **World Trade Organization** (WTO)? According to the realist argument, the United States should only encourage WTO membership if the United States gains more than China from China's membership. In contrast, liberals argue that membership is important because repeated cooperation within the economic sphere can change expectations about each side's willingness to cooperate on a range of issues. Although the United States eventually supported Chinese membership in the WTO and China joined the organization in 2001, the issues raised by liberals and realists were hotly debated in policy circles.

In the 1990s, **constructivism** entered the debate by linking shared identity to the salience of relative gains. Constructivists argue that interests are often a function of identity. Humans naturally define themselves by drawing lines between the 'in group' and the 'out group'. Members of the 'in group' are treated differently from members of the 'out group'. Constructivists claim that the promise of absolute gains may characterize motives with respect to social exchanges within the 'in group', and the prospect for relative gains may apply to relations with the 'out group'. This synthetic argument challenges the realist notion of exclusive interest in relative gains and provides liberals with a causal argument as to when absolute gains are likely to dominate.

The debate raises a number of important questions. First, is the salience of relative gains a constant or a variable? Both sides in the debate tend to treat it as a constant, which fails to explain the simultaneous existence of intense conflict in some dyads and cooperation in others. Future theoretical development needs to specify the conditions under which different motives drive behavior. Constructivism is one, but certainly not the only, way to explore the question of conditionality. Second, how does the inclusion of multiple actors alter the analysis? Most models within the liberal camp assume a two state world. However, some research has highlighted how the existence of multiple actors greatly complicates the analysis because state A's relative loss to state B may be a relative gain in relation to state C. Research needs to go beyond having identified the problem to modeling how individuals deal with gains in an *n*-person world. Third, how does the fungibility of power influence the salience of relative gains? Scholars employing formal models have claimed, for example, that if economic gains cannot be readily converted into military power or if the defense is dominant over the offense, then relative gains in the economic sphere are less problematic. Researchers need to empirically investigate these and similar claims from the formal literature. Finally, how do individuals calculate gains? We need more experimental and survey research to explore how individuals interpret payoffs and whether belief systems influence the calculation of gains.

Further reading

Baldwin, D.A. (ed.) (1993) *Neorealism and Neoliberalism: The Contemporary Debate*, New York: Columbia University Press.

Powell, R. (1991) 'Absolute and Relative Gains in International Relations Theory',

American Political Science Review 85(4), 1303–20.

Rousseau. D. L. (2002) 'Motivations for Choice: The Salience of Relative Gains in International Relations', *Journal of Conflict Resolution* 46(3), 394–426.

Snidal, D. (1991) 'Relative Gains and the Pattern of International Cooperation', *American Political Science Review* 85(3), 701–26.

Stein, A. A. (1990) *Why Nations Cooperate: Circumstance and Choice in International Relations*, Ithaca, NY: Cornell University Press.

See also: realism; liberal internationalism; prisoner's dilemma; regime

DAVID L. ROUSSEAU

Restorative justice

Restorative justice requires perpetrators of injustice to make redress to their victims for harms that they have caused. In international affairs, demands for restorative justice arise (for example) when states or nations seek the return of territory seized from them by acts of aggression; when states require reparations from a defeated enemy for losses incurred in fighting a **just war**; or when people seek compensation for injuries done to them by the officials or citizens of another state. Restorative justice, according to most accounts, requires rectification: that victims be restored to the situation they were in before the injustice took place or receive compensation equal to the value of what they have lost.

Restorative justice, so understood, should be contrasted with 'reconciliation' which deals with past injustices by aiming to create harmonious, or at least peaceful, relationships between perpetrators and their victims through acts of apology, acknowledgment of wrong, and forgiveness. However, the moral, practical, and theoretical difficulties that often accompany demands for rectification mean that those who seek a just way of dealing with the past wrongs will often be forced to adopt reconciliatory aims and processes.

Aristotle (384–322 BC) thought of restorative justice as a matter of righting the moral balance by ensuring that perpetrators of injustice could not profit from ill-gotten gains and that the victims would recoup what had been wrongly taken from them. This ideal of justice, though intuitively plausible, is often impossible to achieve and its pursuit may have undesirable effects – particularly in political cases.

Consider a relatively straightforward application of restorative justice to international affairs. At the end of the first Gulf War in 1991, Iraq, the aggressor, was forced to give back the territory it had taken from Kuwait and was required to pay reparations in the form of oil revenue for harm caused to Kuwaitis during the invasion. These payments provided some compensation for damage to property, but were not able to restore the moral balance. During the course of the Iraqi invasion inhabitants of Kuwait were killed, threatened, incarcerated, and insulted. Such harms, unlike property losses, are beyond compensation. Restorative justice as rectification has obvious limitations.

Since oil revenue is the main economic asset of Iraq, forcing Iraq to pay reparations from this income had the effect of making Iraqi citizens shoulder the burden for the harm done. Extraction of reparations becomes questionable from a moral point of view when this has the effect of harming those who are already suffering from economic disadvantage. Forcing Germany to pay reparations to the Allies after World War One has often been criticized because of the harm it did to German people. But extracting reparation payments from citizens becomes especially questionable in those cases where they had no way of controlling the unjust acts of their leaders – as was true in Iraq.

Demands for rectification become especially problematic when injustices are historical. Serbia claims Kosovo because the territory was part of a medieval kingdom ruled by ancestors of the Serbs until its conquest by the Ottoman Empire at the beginning of the fifteenth century. One of the problems with the Serbian claim is that the victim of injustice – the medieval kingdom – no longer exists. It is doubtful whether modern Serbia can demand restoration of territory simply because some of its people have ancestral, linguistic, or religious ties to former possessors. But the more serious difficulty is that other groups of people have for many centuries inhabited the territories that the Serbs claim. Whether Serbian, or similar claims, have any plausibility depends on the view that is taken about the origin and persistence of rights of possession.

The view about possession that seems most favorable to the Serbian claim insists that having a right to a possession depends on history, and not on existing needs. According to this view, if an individual or a group has legitimately acquired something and has not voluntarily surrendered it, then it belongs to them. So if it was taken from them unjustly they can demand its restoration. There are a number of problems with this account. One of them is that few, if any, states have obtained their territory without engaging in acts of conquest or other forms of injustice. But even if this problem is set aside, it is difficult to explain how a people's right to territory can persist hundreds of years after others have taken possession. Surely the more recent inhabitants have acquired a claim. More fundamentally, many theorists question

whether right of possession is so basic or absolute as to be proof against claims to resources based on present needs. Returning a group of people to the situation they were in before the injustice occurred may be unfair to those whose lives and fortunes have come to depend on the situation created by the injustice.

Not all demands for rectification are demands for the restoration of lost possessions. Some African leaders and organizations have demanded compensation for damages caused to their societies by the slave trade. Their claim is that Western states have been unjustly enriched by this trade and that Africans have been unjustly harmed, a situation that calls for restorative justice in the form of monetary compensation by Western societies to African states. The demand for compensation depends on a contrary to fact judgment: that African societies would be much better off now (and Western societies much worse off) if the slave trade had never existed. This claim is difficult to substantiate. Disadvantages presently suffered by African people are the result of a long and complex history and it is impossible to determine which of these harms, if any, can be attributed specifically to the injustice of the slave trade. The same can be said about the benefits enjoyed by people of Western states. But this means that there is no way of determining what compensation is owed, if any at all.

The difficulties of applying requirements of rectification to cases of historical wrongs have led some theorists to insist that restorative justice applies only to recent injustices (at best). Holding this position is compatible with the belief that wealth should be shared more equitably among the people of the world. However, ignoring historical injustices is not a satisfactory option. Injustices haunt the memories of members of political communities and blight their relationships with others. Moreover, recent and historical injustices are often inseparably related. Some groups have been subjected to a history of injustice, which involves a persistent failure of perpetrators to show respect for their existence and culture. Redress of some kind ought to be given for such wrongs, but there is no formula for determining what form it should take. Leaders have sometimes offered apologies for the past wrongs of their state. Prime Minister Blair apologized to the Irish for British indifference during the potato famine of the 1840s. Apology is not necessarily a substitute for compensation. Justice would be best served in many cases by aiming for a settlement between perpetrators and victims that all parties can regard as just, given present needs and conditions. This idea of justice incorporates the forward-looking orientation associated with reconciliation and, like reconciliation, it also requires acknowledgment of wrongs done.

Further reading

Barkan, E. (2000) *Guilt of Nations: Restitution and Negotiating Historic Injustice*, New York: Norton.

Brooks, R. L. (ed.) (1999) *When Sorry Isn't Enough: The Controversy over Apology and Reparation for Human Injustice*, New York: New York University Press.

Roberts, R. C. (ed.) (2002) *Injustice and Rectification*, New York: Peter Lang.

Thompson, J. (2002) *Taking Responsibility for the Past: Reparation and Historical Injustice*, Cambridge: Polity.

See also: law of peoples

JANNA THOMPSON

Revolution

There is an important divide in approaches to the study of revolution. On the one side interest focuses on the 'great revolutions' such as those of France (1789), Russia (1917) and China (1949), and views them in terms of fundamental transformations that impact on world history. On the other side revolutions are studied not for their greatness and therefore their rarity in history but for their similarity with other forms of political violence, such as riots, rebellions, and **civil war**s. The world historical approach concentrates on underlying material and structural conditions, and is concerned both with general causes and with explanation for outcomes. The violent action approach concentrates on the reasons for individual and collective behavior, for example frustrated expectations leading to aggression, and the role of organization in the process of revolution. It follows that there is neither one accepted definition of revolution nor agreement on the cases to which the term applies. It follows also that there are competing explanations for revolutions and debate over their international significance.

The role of revolutions in history was first highlighted by Karl Marx (1818–83) as the means by which one stage of history replaces another. So the French Revolution of 1789 signified the move from feudal to bourgeois society and a proletarian revolution was predicted to destroy **capitalism**. **Marxism** provided not only a scientific theory of revolution but also a justification for revolution and the organizational means for achieving it, the Communist Party. The first example of communist revolution occurred in Russia in 1917, the second in China in 1949 (see **communism**). Both revolutions drew attention to the significance of the role played by peasants as revolutionaries. The Chinese revolution also demonstrated not only the importance of the Chinese Communist Party but also of the communist guerrilla army. In 1959, the Cuban Revolution confirmed the importance of guerrilla tactics but, significantly, the Cuban guerrilla movement was independent of the Cuban Communist Party.

The dominant approach to revolutions, which concentrates on the great revolutions, is concerned with structural explanations induced from comparative historical analysis. This approach was pioneered by Barrington Moore (1966), whose work includes cases ranging from the English Civil War to the Chinese Revolution. Moore concentrates on differences in the commercialization of agriculture and the strength and weaknesses of social classes and class alignments to explain the bourgeois (liberal democratic), communist and fascist routes to the modern world. He argues that revolution plays a necessary role in the bourgeois and communist routes, and failure to have a revolution is crucial to the fascist route, which opts for 'revolution from above'. Communist revolutions, in Moore's analysis, are peasant revolutions, occurring in the twentieth century.

Comparing France (1789), a bourgeois revolution, with Russia (1917) and China (1911–49), both communist revolutions, Skocpol (1979) challenges Moore's social and economic explanation for revolution by highlighting the importance of state collapse. She argues that in all three cases the pre-revolutionary regimes were 'agrarian bureaucracies', which suffered state bankruptcy due to the costs of **war** and peasant rebellions. This highlighting of the importance of the state and of international as well as national factors continues through to her explanation for why, given that the causes were similar, the outcomes were different. Skocpol stresses the differences in the contexts of trade and the wars that broke out after the revolutionary overthrow. The need to mobilize for these wars and the bureaucratic cen-

tralization this required is given prominence in her view of post-revolutionary **state formation**.

Skocpol's focus on post-revolutionary state formation is reaffirmed in works explaining the outcomes of the revolutions in Iran and Nicaragua in 1979, where, in addition, emphasis is given to rival groups with conflicting ideologies struggling for state **power** in more complex international conditions. In both cases, class analysis has also reappeared, with particular emphasis given to the importance of the bourgeoisie in Nicaragua's liberal democratic outcome. In Iran the unique outcome of a Shi'a Islamic State has drawn attention to the failure of structural explanations to pay sufficient attention to the importance of ideas, including ideology and religion, and to specific actors and revolutionary organization.

Skocpol's own analysis of the Iranian Revolution introduced the 'rentier state', dependent on world market trade, as an underlying cause of the revolution and drew attention to the role of religious organizations in mobilizing revolution. The revolutions in Iran and Nicaragua have also furthered interest in revolutionary events in the **Third World** and moved theorizing in more recent comparative work to issues of **post-colonialism** and international markets. With neither case involved in foreign war before their revolutions but engaged in them afterwards, interest in the relationship between war and revolution has also broadened. Concentrating on the 'reign of terror' stage of revolution, O'Kane (1991) has challenged Skocpol's stress on foreign wars in state-building and argued for the primary importance of **civil war**s which need to be won before permanent state construction can begin. This argument has also rejected terror as an inevitable stage in revolution and has drawn attention to the differences between spontaneous revolutions and those involving guerrilla movements. The collapse of **communism** in Eastern Europe, 1989–91, has highlighted the impact of events which, while not themselves revolutions, have revolutionary consequences.

Interest in **Third World** revolutions and the effects of **modernization** on traditional societies through world trade and industrialization have an important source in Wolf's (1969) study of twentieth century revolutions. Wolf departed from Moore in arguing that not only were peasants important as revolutionaries in their own right but that differences between peasants were crucial. It was the 'free' peasants in their attempt to stay traditional in a modernizing society who were the most revolutionary. Concern with peasant revolutions was given impetus by events not only in China but also in Vietnam, which drew attention to the crucial role played by peasant guerrilla armies. Debate has also developed over the role of communist organization in raising consciousness. Scott (1976) argues that the traditional collective interests and history of rebellion against the state found in peasant villages is crucial to revolution in conjunction with communist party activity.

Study of peasant revolutions has also led to the application of rational choice theory, which focuses on the circumstances under which it is rational for an individual to join in revolutionary action. This may constitute joining a revolutionary organization or the revolution itself, once started. This approach highlights the importance of both private and community benefits in both winning support and building collective action. In concentrating on revolutionary action, rational choice approaches share interests with behavioral and psychological approaches rather than structural approaches to revolution. Importantly,

while not rejecting the value of a structural approach or challenging the relevance of international factors, rational choice theory draws attention to the necessity of retaining a focus on the actual revolutionary action taking place; to remember that revolutions are carried out by people and that it is necessary to understand why they take part.

Further reading

Davies, J. C. (ed.) (1997) *When Men Revolt and Why*, New Brunswick, NJ: Transaction Publishers.

Halliday, F. (1999) *Revolution and World Politics: The Rise and Fall of the Sixth Great Power*, Basingstoke: Palgrave.

Moore, B. Jr. (1966) *Social Origins of Dictatorship and Democracy:Lord and Peasant in the Making of the Modern World*, Boston, MA: Beacon Press.

O'Kane, R. H. T. (1991) *The Revolutionary Reign of Terror: The Role of Violence in Political Change*, Aldershot: Edward Elgar.

Scott, J. C. (1976) *The Moral Economy of the Peasant Rebellion and Subsistence in Southeast Asia*, New Haven, CT: Yale University Press.

Skocpol, T. (1979) *States and Social Revolutions: A Comparative Analysis of France, Russia and China*, Cambridge: Cambridge University Press.

Wolf, E. R. (1969) *Peasant Wars of the Twentieth Century*, New York: Harper and Row.

See also: agent-structure debate; state formation; Marxism

ROSEMARY H. T. O'KANE

Revolution in military affairs (RMA)

A revolution in military affairs (RMA) is a major change in the nature of warfare that renders obsolete a previous means of waging **war**. Technological advances are often the precursor to changes in warfare, but there can be no RMA until new technologies are combined with significant innovations in military doctrines and organizations. An RMA takes place when new military technologies lead to dramatic changes in military doctrine and organization that fundamentally alter the character and conduct of military operations.

This entry examines the Revolution in Military Affairs and some of its important trends and implications. After briefly placing the RMA in historical context, it gives an overview of the key technological, doctrinal and organizational elements that comprise the contemporary RMA. It then identifies those aspects of the RMA that have been most noticeably reinforced and validated by the Kosovo, Afghanistan, and Iraqi conflicts, and highlights some changes in direction post-9/11 that may influence the course and outcome of the RMA. It concludes with an examination of some of the implications of the RMA for the United States, its allies, and its enemies.

Historical context

There have been many RMAs over the course of history. Examples include the artillery revolution of the fifteenth century; the gunpowder revolution of the seventeenth century; the Napoleonic revolution; the land warfare revolution in the mid-nineteenth century that was propelled by the civilian technological advances of the railroad and telegraph; the interwar revolutions in mechanization and aviation; blitzkrieg, carrier aviation, amphibious warfare, and strategic aerial bombardment in World War Two; and the nuclear revolution in the **cold war** era.

Since the 1970s the **information revolution** in the civilian world has been driving a contemporary RMA. During the final decade of the cold war, advances in military technologies were accelerated by America's 'offset' strategy of using the West's technological superiority to compensate for the Soviet Union's quantitative advantage in military forces and equipment. The changing nature of the threat in the first post-cold war decade, combined with budget reductions and the political imperative of reducing friendly casualties and civilian collateral damage, served to further press advances in military technologies. These in turn facilitated some initial accompanying doctrinal and organizational changes in the way that militaries operate. The terrorist attacks of 11 September 2001 marked a new stage in world affairs and have inevitably impacted on the course and speed of these developments.

Elements of the RMA

Today's RMA centers on several key technologies, doctrines and accompanying organizational changes. Probably the best-known technological advance in modern warfare is the development of precision-guided munitions. Such munitions were first developed in the latter stages of the Vietnam War but have increased dramatically in terms of accuracy since about the mid-1980s, and even more so since the Gulf War. At a time when there is growing public intolerance for casualties, precision-guided munitions also offer the possibility of destroying military targets without substantial civilian damage. Advances are also being made in low-observable technologies or what is commonly referred to as stealth. Stealthy platforms have an advantage over their non-stealthy counterparts because of their ability to go undetected into high-threat areas and deliver precision-guided munitions.

More than the contribution of any particular military platform, it is the potential of new military technologies to reduce the 'fog of war' that could change the way wars are fought. Sensors in satellites, manned aircraft or unmanned aerial vehicles can now monitor virtually everything that is going on in a particular battle area, dramatically improving intelligence gathering, surveillance and reconnaissance capabilities. The net result of all the space-based, manned and unmanned platforms is the potential for commanders to have complete, real-time knowledge of where all enemy and friendly forces are in a battle area.

Enhancing surveillance is only part of the story; equally important for cutting through the fog of war is having the command and control systems to act on information. Advanced command, control, communications, computers, and intelligence processing are being designed to make sense of the vast amount of data that is gathered, display it in a useful fashion on screen, and assign targets to weapons and platforms. Advanced command and control arrangements are meant to enable commanders to be in constant and instant contact with their forces at all levels, giving them the ability to control a battle from one moment to the next.

Precision weapons, stealth, and advanced technology for seeing the battlespace more clearly and communicating with military forces more quickly are the key military technologies that are associated with the contemporary RMA. But new technologies alone do not make a revolution; there must also be changes in military doctrine as a result of this new technology. Today's RMA involves a number of new military doctrines, one of which is joint doctrine. The RMA is bringing about an increasingly integrated battlefield, with the Army, Navy, and Air Force working ever more closely together. Operations are characterized by Air Force precision force preparing the battlefield for ground forces, and airlift

assets transporting troops to the theater of operations. Manned and unmanned surveillance aircraft and satellites operate throughout the campaign supporting all three services. Naval forces provide off shore logistical support, sealift and precision force against ground targets. The trend toward joint operations is placing a premium on interoperability among forces.

Beyond joint doctrine, there are changes in naval doctrine. A key shift here is toward littoral warfare. In contrast to the cold war scenario of battling against a large, opposing surface force at sea, navies are now preparing to project force from the sea directly ashore, whether in the context of a regional war or a **peacekeeping** operation. The littoral region is a perfect battleground for joint warfare because effective operations in this environment require that the Navy work closely with the Army. The US Navy is also shifting from platform-centric to network-centric warfare. This concept places the emphasis on the sensor and surveillance systems of a group of warships, submarines or aircraft, rather than on the particular attributes of the platform itself.

Land warfare specialists argue that regardless of the high tech changes taking place, it still takes ground forces to achieve US military objectives. Most of the military missions that the United States has faced since the end of the cold war have depended on ground forces backed by air and sea power. This was the case in Bosnia, Kosovo, Afghanistan and Iraq. Even during the first Gulf War Iraqis endured long-range precision strikes but did not surrender until coalition ground forces were on the battlefield.

Although ground forces continue to be necessary, their characteristics are changing. The unpredictable nature of threats in today's international **security** environment necessitates that military forces have the ability to respond quickly to almost any situation. This, in turn, demands smaller, more mobile and flexible ground forces that are still highly lethal. The idea is to change from a forward-deployed Industrial Age army trained and equipped to stop a Soviet advance in Europe, to an Information Age power projection army that can operate anywhere in the world.

Meanwhile, air-power proponents argue that the ability of modern air power to affect land warfare has crossed a threshold over which its effects are fundamentally greater than before. They argue that advances in precision munitions have made air power the decisive force in war and that this has allowed for a doctrine of disengaged combat. Using long-range precision weapons, a substantial amount of force can be applied from a safe distance away. Ground commanders do not have to directly face the enemy until the costs of such contact have been significantly reduced. Air power proponents argue that the principal role of land power in war is now to secure a win at the end, rather than achieve it.

Unmanned combat is also a new military doctrine. Many military experts predict a long-term move away from manned fighters and toward unmanned combat. Armed unmanned aerial vehicles were used extensively in Afghanistan and Iraq and the United States has an unmanned combat aerial vehicle under development. Unmanned combat aircraft have a number of advantages over their manned counterparts. They are less expensive, they remove the risk of aircrew casualties and, in some cases they may even be able to outperform manned aircraft. Without a pilot to consider, unmanned tactical aircraft may be able to travel substantially faster, higher, and longer than manned fighters and could also be made smaller and steal-

thier. In the future, it is conceivable that manned fighters may be used for only a limited number of roles, such as shooting down the most advanced enemy aircraft. The bulk of an air force may be made up of unmanned aircraft.

It is not only the tools and doctrines of warfare but also the organizations that use them that make for revolutionary change in war. The invention of the tank did not bring about an armored warfare revolution until such time as Germany placed it in the context of a Panzer division – a combined arms organization built around the tank and including artillery, engineers and infantry. Today's organizational transformation requires that with the shift from mass destruction to precision warfare come a parallel shift from mass armies to smaller, more rapidly mobile forces and units.

Meanwhile, the emphasis on high quality weaponry has reduced the relative importance of numbers and placed a premium on high-quality troops. Militaries of the future will rest primarily on professional forces, as opposed to conscript forces. The balance between quantity and quality has shifted in favor of quality. At the same time, the centralized decision making of the bureaucratic organization, which dominated the Industrial Age, must change to reflect the decentralization of the Information Age. Advanced military technologies will, in theory, allow soldiers to know as much about a battlefield as generals. It follows that military organizations must become 'de-layered', with soldiers accorded more leeway in taking initiatives. Such a change must be accompanied by new command protocols so as to avoid chaos on the battlefield.

As the organizations change, so too must the people, with new career possibilities, educational requirements, and promotion paths becoming essential. Increased responsibility at lower echelons must be coupled with enhanced skill levels. The changing nature of warfare will also call for new types of skills altogether. Finally, new military organizations must have the flexibility to switch rapidly from one type of contingency to another. This is best achieved through 'flexible force packaging', a concept which demands that units from one organization be interoperable with those of another. Units must be modular in the sense that they can be brought together with other units to produce a force package that is tailored to a specific task at hand.

RMA Trends: Kosovo, Afghanistan and Iraq

Those, in brief, are some of the key technologies, doctrines, and organizational changes associated with the RMA. Military operations in Kosovo, Afghanistan, and Iraq reinforced and validated a number of these elements, but also raised some caveats that give preliminary indication of possible changes in the ultimate course of the RMA.

All three operations confirmed the utility of advanced precision munitions and their associated doctrines in modern warfare. In Kosovo, precision air power helped bring about an end to hostilities. In Afghanistan it allowed the United States to do much of the work of combating international **terrorism** from safe standoff distances. And in Iraq, precision firepower from a variety of American and British platforms targeted and destroyed numerous very specific regime-oriented objectives, including command-and-control sites, communications lines, and air defense installations.

Since the end of the cold war there has been a trend toward the increased used of precision munitions in military campaigns. Some 68 per cent of the bombs dropped on Iraq in 2003 were precision-guided, as compared to about 9 per cent in the first Gulf War, 35 per cent during the Kosovo air campaign, and 60 per cent in Afghanistan. A growing proportion of these precision bombs are, in turn, satellite-guided. They include Joint Direct Attack Munitions attached to bombs launched by bombers or fighter aircraft, and Tomahawk cruise missiles launched from ships and submarines. Satellite-guided weapons have an advantage over their laser-guided counterparts in that they are not limited by weather conditions, such as clouds, rain or sandstorms.

The second Gulf War (2003) stands in contrast to the first Gulf War, Kosovo, and Afghanistan in that coalition forces did not spend weeks softening up enemy air defenses with air strikes before committing ground forces, as a doctrine of disengaged combat would call for. But this observation must be placed in context. The two Gulf Wars are best seen as part of a single picture that includes the first Gulf War's air strikes, twelve years of **sanctions** that hindered the Iraqi regime's ability to rebuild high value targets, and a similar period of no-fly zone enforcement which eliminated many remaining precision force targets. In essence, the battlefield for the second Gulf War had been prepared long before the war began.

Each succeeding war in the post-cold war era has reinforced the centrality of advanced intelligence gathering, surveillance and intelligence capabilities to twenty-first century warfare and especially the value of unmanned aerial vehicles (UAVs) in providing this information. American and Israeli short range tactical UAVs were used extensively in the first Gulf War. Longer range Predator UAVs made their debut in Bosnia and were deployed in greater numbers in Kosovo. Both the Predator and the strategic Global Hawk UAV figured prominently in the war on terrorism in

Afghanistan. Geared toward monitoring troop movements, the Predator adapted easily to the task of tracking terrorists. The high-altitude Global Hawk, with its cloud-penetrating sensors, conducted extensive strategic surveillance and reconnaissance. In Iraq, Predator UAVs flew over coalition forces headed to Baghdad, giving ground commanders up-to-the-second information on what lay ahead, while Global Hawk UAVs provided continuous sensor coverage of large sections of Iraqi territory.

With the help of UAVs the campaign in Afghanistan saw the realization for the first time of what the Pentagon is calling 'persistent' intelligence, surveillance, and reconnaissance (ISR). This refers to the ability to provide a real time, continuous flow of information to whatever ground, air, or naval platform is needed to provide an appropriate response. Persistent ISR has important ramifications for command and control and the revolutionary objective of giving force commanders the ability to control a battle from one moment to the next. During the first Gulf War it took hours to get a Pioneer UAV over a particular area, and sometimes days to get the information to a commander. Lag times had diminished significantly by the time of the Kosovo campaign with the use of Predator and Hunter UAVs, but the information was still not flowing quickly enough to those who needed it. In Afghanistan sensor information from Predator UAVs was fed in real time into the cockpits of American gunships and strike aircraft, allowing them to respond within minutes against Taliban targets. Similarly, in the second Gulf War Predator UAVs sent live video transmissions to American gunships.

The RMA's prediction that sea, land, and air forces will work ever more closely together was borne out in the Afghanistan and Iraq campaigns. The war on terrorism in Afghanistan campaign saw extraordinary synchronization between land and air power, including naval air power. Special operations forces on horseback provided target information back to the ships, bombers, and fighter aircraft firing precision weapons, dramatically enhancing their accuracy and effectiveness. In Iraq, Army Black Hawk helicopters called in close air strikes from Royal Navy Harrier fighter jets, US Air Force A-10 Warthog tank busters, and US Navy F-18s. Strategic bombers provided close air support to ground forces, while heavy armor supported special operations forces. Special forces also called in air strikes against critical regime targets. While the concept of air-land coordination in battle has been around for almost as long as the airplane, the Iraqi conflict demonstrated an unprecedented partnership between air power and ground maneuver. General Richard Myers, Chairman of the Joint Chiefs of Staff, attributed the efficient progress of the war to a vastly improved picture of the battlefield, and a new willingness on the part of commanders to use the most appropriate capabilities available, regardless of which service was providing them.

It follows that all recent military campaigns have reinforced the naval trend toward littoral warfare. During the Kosovo air campaign a significant portion of the land attack precision strikes were carried out by Tomahawk cruise missiles launched from US and British ships in the Adriatic littorals. In Afghanistan US and Royal Navy surface ships and submarines launched Tomahawk cruise missiles against Afghan targets, while carrier-based fighter aircraft dropped precision-guided bombs. This was similarly the case in the second Gulf War, during which US and British ships and submarines launched more than 750 cruise missiles.

The Iraqi conflict may be remembered as the one where advanced intelligence, surveillance, reconnaissance, and command and control technologies first most clearly meshed with increased jointness to produce a force multiplier effect. The combination of rapid targeting information and tightly integrated air and ground attacks produced an unbroken string of tactical victories. A greater ability to link disparate weapons systems, aircraft, and ground troops into a common information net enabled the United States to coordinate operations better than ever, making its military punch more powerful than the sum of its parts. In Iraq the era of network centric warfare seemed to have truly arrived.

A notable development has been the large and growing role of special operations forces. American and allied Special Forces played the central land force role in Afghanistan. This is perhaps not surprising since these forces currently most closely resemble what the RMA foresees as the type of ground forces necessary for the future – rapidly deployable and highly mobile forces that can move swiftly over the battlefield in widely dispersed locations, while remaining highly lethal (in this case by calling in air power). These trends are facilitated by technology but driven by the character of the international security environment. The global nature of the war, the nature of the enemy, and the need for fast, efficient operations in combating terrorist networks have all contributed to the need for an expanded role for Special Operations forces. Some 6,000 special operations forces were deployed to Afghanistan but even this large (by historical standards) figure was surpassed in Iraq where 10,000 Special Forces were deployed in the war's first week. Indeed, Iraq was one of the biggest special operations missions ever, with the Army's Delta Force and Rangers

in the west and Special Forces in the north and south. Although the details have not fully emerged, it is likely that special operations forces played an even greater role in Iraq than in Afghanistan, seizing control of air bases, securing oil fields from sabotage, calling in air strikes, eliminating the scud missile threat to Israel, and forming a northern front.

Beyond the growing role of special operations forces the Iraqi conflict gave mixed signals on the sorts of land forces required for the future. The specter of Abrams and Challenger main battle tanks, and Bradley and Warrior armored fighting vehicles moving over the desert demonstrated, in effect, that the heavy ground forces consigned to the dust bin by the RMA are still relevant to the conduct of post-cold war conflicts. After sitting out the Kosovo conflict and contributing only special operations forces to the war in Afghanistan the Army entered Iraq before the major air campaign got underway and remained at the center of the battle throughout. These developments gave pause to the air power notion that the principal role of land power may now be to secure a win, rather than achieve it.

That said, the second Gulf War demonstrated some consistencies with the land force predictions of the RMA. The number of American and British forces deployed in and around Iraq – about 300,000 soldiers – was less than half the size of the coalition force deployed to carry out the first Gulf War's objectives. Even this force took some time to put in place and some Pentagon officials believe that the value of the Abrams tank, for example, was undercut by the difficulty of transporting them to theater. A future conflict may not allow so lengthy a period of time to deploy forces to a regional conflict.

More than anything the conflict in Iraq in 2003 highlighted the value of speed in conducting twenty-first century ground operations. Speed of action is at the center of the post-9/11 US military doctrine of rapid decisive operations that calls for integrating air power, special forces and mobile ground formations to enable the American military to be more effective with less mass. The idea here is not to overcome the enemy with overwhelming force but to apply decisive firepower at the right enemy forces at the right time. Thus while the army has been given a boost by the Iraqi conflict, the focus is likely to continue to be on efforts to make ground forces more mobile and rapidly deployable than in the past. This involves restructuring forces into smaller units and fielding lighter equipment, as foreseen by the RMA. The requirement for tanks, or for a platform with the tank's capabilities, has not disappeared in the post-9/11 security environment; rather these platforms need to be made more mobile and deployable. This is similarly the case with respect to artillery. Both Iraq and Afghanistan illustrated the necessity of precision strike weapons at the tactical level in the form of precision artillery and mortars. The lack of such a capability in Afghanistan forced ground forces to rely on precision firepower from above. This was effective but it made some military maneuvers much more difficult than would have otherwise been the case.

Post-war stabilization efforts in the Balkans, Afghanistan, and Iraq also hold lessons for ground forces of the future. The RMA calls for army component units to be smaller and more mobile. But smaller units no longer mean a smaller overall size of army – this idea was relevant only in the immediate post-cold war era and especially in the context of the necessary transition from conscript to professional forces in many European countries. In the future security environment ground forces will be playing central roles in both war fighting and **peacebuilding** and it will be critical that Western armies are large enough both to win the war and to consolidate the peace.

The twenty-first century has witnessed the debut of the revolutionary air doctrine of unmanned combat using unmanned combat aerial vehicles. In the war on terrorism in Afghanistan Predator UAVs, which are designed and built for surveillance missions, were modified so that they could conduct combat operations. Drones armed with precision-guided Hellfire missiles carried out dozens of strikes in Afghanistan with a reportedly impressive rate of accuracy. In 2002 a CIA-operated Predator UAV armed with Hellfire missiles targeted *al-Qaeda* members in Yemen. And in the 2003 war in Iraq armed Predator UAVs fired more than a dozen Hellfire missiles.

In future conflicts we can expect to see unmanned aerial vehicles that have been designed from the outset as a combat platform to carry out operations. Indeed, Congress has already mandated that one-third of America's tactical-strike aircraft is to be unmanned by 2015. But although armed Predator UAVs have proven themselves in recent conflicts, these developments must be treated with some skepticism. Battlefield successes have been chalked up against adversaries with little or no air-to-air strike capability. The Taliban had no air force and Saddam Hussein chose not to use whatever planes he had left over from the first Gulf War. It remains to be seen how an unmanned combat aerial vehicle would fare against an enemy air superiority aircraft.

Conflicts in post-cold war and post-9/11 eras have reinforced the doctrinal trend away from short-range land-based tactical aircraft. Such aircraft were originally designed for a confrontation in Europe and are inevitably reliant on the existence of allied bases close to the scene of the trouble. But in the new international security environment such bases are unlikely to be available. In Afghanistan, for example, US Air Force fighter aircraft were all but shut out of the war on terrorism because of the lack of US basing rights in Central Asia. Although the Joint Strike Fighter contract was awarded in 2002, it is conceivable that buys of the land-based variant could be reduced. The shortfall is likely to be made up not only with unmanned combat aerial vehicles, but also long-range strategic bombers, which delivered a significant proportion of the precision munitions in the Kosovo, Afghanistan, and Iraq campaigns. The Pentagon's decision to proceed with a new fleet of aircraft carriers is also testament to the continuing emphasis on carrier-based aircraft for precision strike missions ashore.

Implications of the RMA

The RMA raises some important implications for the United States, its enemies, and its allies. In its pursuit of the RMA, the United States could find itself focusing too much on technology for conducting effective military operations to the detriment of other important factors. The RMA places significant emphasis on the merits of using advanced technologies to see all enemy and friendly forces and platforms in the theater of war. But increased information, or data, does not equate to increased knowledge and understanding; it could just as likely lead to 'sensory overload'. Similarly, the RMA vision includes the ability of commanders to receive and transmit information and decisions in real time. Yet increasing the speed of data transmission does not appreciably quicken political and strategic decision-making, nor improve its quality. In short, advanced technology can go a long way toward decreasing the

fog and friction of war, but it cannot eliminate them altogether. An excessive focus on advanced technologies could cause military leaders to ignore or place less emphasis on other key requirements for war winning, including readiness, force structure and, perhaps most importantly, training.

The RMA has also contributed to the search for asymmetric counters to US power on the part of America's enemies. The 1991 Gulf War, as well as several conflicts since then, have provided dramatic demonstration of America's superior conventional capabilities, making it unlikely that future adversaries would confront the United States on the modern battlefield. The United States' military superiority on the conventional battlefield, in turn, has provided incentives for its adversaries to seek unconventional alternatives. Well before 11 September 2001 it was recognized that potential enemies were likely to develop asymmetric counters to US technological superiority – including terrorism, information warfare, ballistic missiles, and/or the use of **weapons of mass destruction** – to exploit US weaknesses and vulnerabilities. Asymmetrical assault is the only strategy that makes sense for potential US adversaries, since they cannot compete under the traditional rules. The rise of asymmetric warfare is compounded by the fact that the RMA creates increased vulnerabilities on the part of US forces, and therefore increased opportunities to carry out asymmetrical assault. For example, outgunned forces could use jamming gear to attack the electronic eyes and ears that have become ever more crucial to US war fighting efforts.

Finally, the RMA has accelerated the growing technology and capability gap between the United States and its allies. America is proceeding much further and faster with respect to the RMA than other

NATO allies (see **North Atlantic Treaty Organization**) and this is having a real impact on the Alliance's ability to take part in US-led coalition operations. During the Gulf War, US superiority in information systems and electronics meant that its military communications were speedier and more sophisticated than those of its allies. The Kosovo operation highlighted problems in weapons compatibility and indicated that European air forces would be unable to operate alongside US fighters in future conflicts until such time as they upgrade their communications systems. The technology and capability gap between America and its allies is likely one of the reasons why the United States did not request that NATO take part in the war on terrorism in Afghanistan. Although problems of compatibility have been an issue for the Alliance since its inception, the difference today is that US advancements in communications, data processing and precision-guided weapons are in the process of completely eclipsing those of its allies and casting into question their ability to function together.

Despite NATO's efforts to close the technology and capability gap, including the Defence Capabilities Initiative of 1999–2002 and the Prague Capabilities Commitment launched at the 2002 NATO summit, the gap persists and continues to widen. This gap has implications well beyond the creation of compatible forces among allies. At a time when the nature of the international security environment demands they work ever more closely together in addressing the sources of terrorism, America and its allies are increasingly unable to do so. This inability may be feeding a vicious circle that could have potentially destabilizing global effects. On the one hand, allies resist efforts to increase their military capabilities out of a perception that even if they took con-

crete steps to close the gap, the United States would not hear their voice and would act unilaterally. On the other hand the United States, with only a few allies that can make a meaningful military contribution to combating international terrorism, feels increasingly compelled to act unilaterally in the world.

Further reading

Cohen, E. (1996) 'A Revolution in Warfare', *Foreign Affairs*, 75(2), 37–54.

Gongora, T. and von Reikhoff, H. (eds) (2000) *Toward a Revolution in Military Affairs* Westport, CT: Praeger.

Matthews, R. and Treddenick, J. (eds) (2001) *Managing the Revolution in Military Affairs*, Basingstoke: Palgrave.

Sloan, E. C. (2002) *The Revolution in Military Affairs*, Montreal: McGill-Queen's University Press.

Yost, D. (2000–01) 'The NATO Capabilities Gap and the European Union', *Survival* 42(4), 97–125.

See also: ballistic missile defense; pre-emptive use of force; war

ELINOR C. SLOAN

Rogue state

The term 'rogue state' is often used interchangeably with the terms 'outlaw state' and 'pariah state'. In the 1990s the term was increasingly used by US policymakers to describe countries that possessed **weapons of mass destruction** (WMD) (e.g. North Korea, Iran, Iraq, and to a lesser extent Libya and Syria), had engaged in aggressive behavior toward other states, and which had direct or indirect links with **terrorism** (for example: Iran (suspected of bankrolling and arming Hezbollah in Lebanon); Iraq (unsubstantiated claims of Saddam Hussein's links with **al-Qaeda**); Libya (substantiated bombings of civilian airliners, including Pan Am flight 103 in December 1988 over Lockerbie); North Korea (various incidents mostly against South Korea); Sudan (hosting of Muslim terrorist groups since 1989); and Syria (support for Palestinian groups, including Hamas and Jihad)).

The origin and widespread use of the term within US policymaking circles explains the contested nature of the concept 'rogue state', which is applied to a wide variety of countries, not all of which exhibit similar patterns of behavior. This wide usage renders the term both controversial and elastic. Like 'beauty', a 'rogue state' seems to be 'in the eyes of the beholder'.

Specifically, a 'rogue state', as conceived of by its inventors, sums up a number of criticisms leveled against countries (such as Afghanistan under the Taliban, Iran, Iraq under Saddam Hussein, Libya until it agreed to abandon weapons of mass destruction and cut its links with terrorism in 2004, North Korea, Somalia, Sudan, Syria) which happen to share a number of features that are usually not mentioned by those who use the term. In addition to their questionable behavior, rogue states are usually non-western, poor, authoritarian, non-Christian, formerly client states of the Soviet Union until its dissolution in 1991 (Iraq, Libya, Somalia, Syria, North Korea, Afghanistan, and Cuba). Moreover, the usual list of rogue states contains countries that aspire to dominate their respective regions (Iran, Iraq, Libya, Syria), and perhaps most obviously, have weak or no diplomatic links with the United States.

As a construct, the term 'rogue state' stresses contrast, thus identifying a form of 'otherness'. Critics argue that the use of the term tells us more about its inventors' **discourse** than the countries it designates and condemns. If the term 'rogue state' refers to states that are non-Western, non-Christian, poor, authoritarian, and belligerent, then its opposite meaning would read 'Western', 'Christian', 'rich', 'democratic', 'civilized', and 'peaceful'. Of course, this representation serves to highlight the dichotomous nature of the discourse surrounding the notion of the rogue state. Critics argue that the term is used for self-validation and the invalidation of political and ideological 'otherness'. But the term does not only signify a mode of discourse about 'otherness'. It also describes flaws, such as autocracy and illegal behavior that may be empirically demonstrable in many states, Western and non-Western.

In the 1990s the term 'rogue state' assumed a high profile in the parlance of US policymakers following several foreign policy setbacks (particularly in Somalia in 1992). It should also be noted that the term came into use soon after the collapse of the Soviet Union in 1991. Confronted with expectations of a 'peace dividend' in the wake of the **cold war**, the term was invoked both to remind Americans that the United States still confronted important enemies abroad, and to provide a justification for the development of a **ballistic missile defense** system against countries whose potential possession of nuclear weapons posed a great danger to US **security**.

In the 1990s, US foreign policymakers sought to translate their anti-rogue state rhetoric into practical policy, ranging from the imposition of **sanctions** (particularly against Saddam Hussein's Iraq) to the use of force, the most dramatic example of which was the March 2003 Anglo-American invasion of Iraq.

US frustration with rogue states is not particularly novel. For example, the US bombing of Libya (1986) and Clinton's cruise missile attacks against Afghanistan and the Sudan (1998, following the terrorist attacks against US embassies in

Tanzania and Kenya) reflect a long pattern of enmity and the desire to use force to change rogue state behavior. But such responses also inspire critics to claim that the only remaining **superpower** is itself a rogue state. They point to a litany of unilateral actions by the United States, some of which meet the very criteria invoked by American policymakers to categorize rogue states. They point to the United States' track record of international double standards. Many critics fault the United States for its own possession of the deadliest arsenal of WMD, a dismal record of support for authoritarian regimes, and for its support of Israel. Others condemn the United States' illegal use of force against Iraq in 2003 as well as its outright disdain for **multilateralism**, particularly under the Bush Administration.

There is evidence to suggest that the use of the term by US policymakers was in decline prior to 11 September 2001. Since then, of course, it has been reinvigorated by the Bush Administration as part of its rhetorical arsenal in the war on terror. However, there are good reasons to suspect that its employment is increasingly counter-productive. Countries labeled as rogue states are more likely to become entrenched in their animosity toward the United States and its allies, whilst the term makes it difficult for the United States to pursue anything but a belligerent foreign policy toward states that it identifies as rogues.

Further reading

Blum, W. (2002) *Rogue State: A Guide to the World's only Superpower*, London: Zed Books.

Henriksen, T. (1999) *Using Power and Diplomacy to Deal With Rogue States*, Washington, DC: Hoover Institution Press.

Hoyt, P. (2000) 'The "Rogue State" Image in American Foreign Policy', *Global Society*, 14, 297–310.

Lennon, A. and Eiss, C. (eds) (2004) *Reshaping Rogue States*, Cambridge, MA: MIT Press.

Niblock, T. (2001) *Pariah States and Sanctions in the Middle East*, Boulder, CO: Lynne Rienner.

Prestowitz, C. (2003) *Rogue Nation: American Unilateralism and the Failure of Good Intentions*, New York: Basic Books.

Tanter, R. (2003) *Classifying Evil: Bush Administration Rhetoric and Policy towards Rogue Regimes*, Washington, DC: Washington Institute for Near East Policy.

See also: al-Qaeda; anti-Americanism; terrorism; weapons of mass destruction

LARBI SADIKI

S

Sanctions

Sanctions are punitive measures used as an instrument of **power**. They can be and are imposed on any actor in world politics: states, governments, governing elites, corporations, or entire nations or peoples. Likewise, sanctions can be and are imposed *by* any actor in global politics – from intergovernmental organizations like the **United Nations** to ordinary groups of consumers who decide to boycott the products of a particular company.

Punitive measures include any measure that interrupts normal intercourse or exchange in global politics. In the last century, however, the commonest have been economic sanctions, including *boycotts* and *embargoes*, either general or specifically targeted at particular goods, industries, or sectors of the economy. In addition to interrupting the flow of goods, the freezing or seizure of assets, including financial assets, is another common sanction. Sanctions can also extend to disrupting normal relations, communications or exchanges, or sporting activities.

The purpose of interrupting 'normal' business by imposing economic sanctions involves a simple calculation by those who invoke sanctions (or the 'sender'): the sender believes that what the 'target' is doing, or has done, is wrong, and believes that the imposition of sanc-

tions on the target will also impose sufficient costs that the target will abandon its wrong-doing. Thus, for many, sanctions are merely one of the coercive tools of power.

However, sanctions also have a punitive purpose. Some actors impose sanctions for no other reason than wanting to impose harm on a wrong-doer for the sake of punishment, for the same reason we punish criminals: to exact retribution for a wrong done to us; to entrench a particular norm; or to 'correct' or rehabilitate the wrong-doer.

Economic sanctions were a crucial part of the system of **collective security** established by the **League of Nations** after World War One. Many believed that if all members of the League could agree to impose economic sanctions against any state that used force as a tool of foreign policy, **war** could successfully be avoided. The belief was that no government could survive the crushing economic harms that universal economic sanctions would bring.

But economic sanctions did not prove to be an effective tool of statecraft. In the interwar period (1919–39), many governments simply refused to impose sanctions against states that used force. In the **cold war** period, economic sanctions were often used, but most analysts agree that they rarely managed to cause a target to change its behavior. At best, sanctions were one of a range of instruments of power that contributed to changing a target's behavior. This certainly was the case with *apartheid* in South Africa: sanctions – including sanctions on sports – turned South Africa into a **rogue state**, but sanctions were but one part of a broad dynamic that prompted the *apartheid* regime to negotiate itself out of office. Likewise, some have argued that the efforts by the United States to keep the Soviet Union economically marginalized and cut off from intercourse with the global capitalist economy was one of the factors that led to the collapse of the Soviet Union in the late 1980s.

In short, by the early 1990s, it was clear that economic sanctions in global politics did not 'work' in precisely the way claimed by those who were invoking them. On the other hand, however, it was increasingly recognized that economic sanctions did have powerful effects on those against whom they were imposed. Sanctions might not work if their purpose is to get governments to change their behavior. But sanctions surely work in producing negative effects on ordinary people. Because sanctions interrupt the flow of normal business, they have highly negative effects on ordinary people. Moreover, because they make certain goods and services scarce, sanctions invariably criminalize the economy that they target, since criminals are expert in ensuring that goods targeted by the state get to customers. Finally, sanctions may have profoundly negative effects on ordinary people, but they have little impact on those who rule over them, since elites are always able to find ways around shortages.

The increasing awareness of this paradox of sanctions – sanctions don't work, while they work all too well – gave rise in the late 1990s and early 2000s to what are known as 'smart sanctions': punitive economic instruments that are designed to avoid hurting 'ordinary' people, but to target only those who are responsible for some wrong-doing – usually leadership elites and their families and supporters.

Further reading

Cortright, D. and Lopez, G. A. (2002) *Smart Sanctions: Targeting Economic Statecraft*, Lanham, MD: Rowman and Littlefield.

Doxey, M. (1996) *International Sanctions in Contemporary Perspective*, 2nd edn Basingstoke: Palgrave.

Nossal, K. R. (1989) 'International sanctions as international punishment', *International Organization* 43, 301–22.

Pape, R. (1997) 'Why Economic Sanctions do not Work', *International Security* 22 90–136.

Weiss, T. G., Cortright, D., Lopez, G. A. and Minear, L. (eds) (1997) *Political Gain and Civilian Pain: The Humanitarian Impacts of Economic Sanctions*, Lanham, MD: Rowman and Littlefield.

See also: diplomacy; League of Nations; power

KIM RICHARD NOSSAL

Secession

An attempt by an ethnic or national group to remove control of its population and territory from the state in which it resides, and establish self-rule. Secession is engaged in by groups which do not have their own **nation-state**, but which live under the **authority** of a government controlled by other groups. The ultimate goal of secession is the creation of a new, independent nation-state for the group and on the territory that the group considers its 'homeland'. However, secessionist movements may also aim at varying degrees of autonomy or self-governance within the framework of existing boundaries. Secession is related to **irredentism**; while the latter seeks to remove a people and its territory from the control of one state and attach it to a different one, the former seeks to simply withdraw from the state in order to have its own independent existence. Secession can therefore be seen as a prelude to irredentism; in India, for example, the successful secession of Kashmir from India could be a step toward irredentist unification with Pakistan.

Secession has its roots in the promulgation of the principle of **self-determination** by US President Woodrow Wilson following World War One. Wilson's argument was that peoples should have the right to govern their own affairs – the right to determine for themselves how their society should be run. This idea was in response to the historically unstable Balkan region in Europe, in which various peoples (Serbs, Croats, Bosnians, Macedonians, Albanians, Romanians, etc.) had been subject to the rule of foreign powers (Ottoman Turks or Austrian and Hungarian Catholics). This generated resentment, instability, and a series of wars in the region, ultimately leading to the **crisis** that touched off World War One. The right of national self-determination was supposed to keep this from happening again, by insuring that the boundaries of nation-states coincided with the populations living within them.

The principle of self-determination, applied to the problem of national or ethnic groups subject to the rule (and, often, oppression) of others, leads directly to the desire for secession. If self-determination is a national right, then peoples who do not have their own nation-state, but desire to do so, ought to be able to form their own, separate from the authority of the 'foreign' government they live under. In the middle of the twentieth century, this reasoning fueled a vast wave of anti-colonial movements,

as peoples in Africa and Asia sought self-rule in place of government by a distant colonial power.

The new states created by these movements, however, tended to be set up within boundaries that had been drawn by the colonial powers, without respect to the distribution of local ethnic groups and populations. This left a great many states in Africa, the Middle East, South and Southeast Asia with numerous ethnic and national groups within their borders. All of these groups became potential secessionist movements; while some groups were successful in capturing control of the newly-created states (like the Hindus in India, or the Urdu-speaking Muslims in Pakistan), others were denied access to political, economic, or social **power**. In 1991, the collapse of the Soviet Union triggered a new round of **state formation**, leaving some ethnic minorities within new boundaries and subject to new governments in Eastern Europe, the Caucasus and Central Asia. Like the Balkan region in Europe in the early twentieth century, therefore, much of the world retains the conditions that can create secessionist movements.

Because of this historical legacy, secession has become a nearly global phenomenon. Secessionist movements have occurred in Africa (e.g. Ethiopia, Nigeria, Niger, Morocco, and Congo), the Middle East (Iraq, Iran, and Turkey), South Asia (Pakistan, India, and Sri Lanka), and East and Southeast Asia (China, Burma, Indonesia, and the Phillipines). Secessionist movements are still unresolved in parts of Eastern Europe (Serbia, Bosnia, Croatia, and Macedonia), in the Caucasus (Armenia, Azerbaijan, and the Chechen region of Russia), and even in Western Europe (the Basques in Spain, Corsicans in France, and Northern Ireland in the United Kingdom). Only in the Western Hemisphere is the phenomenon relatively rare, with few cases of secessionism in either North or South America (exceptions being the Quebecois in Canada and the Miskitu in Nicaragua). Overall, however, secessionist movements remain a significant challenge; in the latter half of the twentieth century, some eighty violent conflicts had been spawned around the world by secessionist demands.

Despite its prevalence since the end of World War Two, secession rarely succeeds in establishing an independent state. Some scholars have argued that success hinges on the support of an outside power assisting the secessionist movement. This view points to the successful secession of Bangladesh from Pakistan, largely accomplished by Indian intervention, as an example. Others point to different cases – like the Eritrean secession from Ethiopia in 1991 – in which there was no significant outside intervention. In general, secessionist movements are at a disadvantage, because they confront the government of the state from which they are trying to secede. In general, governments tend to have access to resources – the military, tax revenues, state-run media, and the like – that are not available to would-be secessionists, putting the latter at a disadvantage. Even battlefield success may not be enough to win permanent secession over the objections of the central government; in 1996, Chechen secessionists defeated the Russian military decisively, only to have Chechnya invaded by Russia again three years later.

Although outside intervention to aid the secession movement is an important factor in determining success, most international intervention tends to discourage rather than encourage secession. This is mainly because of the fear of 'contagion' – the concern that successful secession in one place will encourage more secessionist demands among other

groups nearby, or even in other parts of the globe. This argument was used by the US government during its intervention into the Balkan civil war against the **partition** of that country; it has also been used consistently by the government of India in defense of its determination to thwart the secession of Kashmir. While scholars disagree over whether secessionism is genuinely 'contagious', or whether it responds primarily to internal causes, most international policymakers are clearly concerned with the possibility, and thus tend to discourage secession, particularly by violent means.

The relatively low rate of success on the part of secessionist movements, however, does not seem to discourage groups from trying it, often leading to serious **ethnic conflict**. So long as the boundaries of states do not coincide with the distribution of ethnic groups, and so long as some ethnic groups are discriminated against by those who control governments, secession will remain a significant issue on the international stage.

Further reading

Ayres, R. (2000) 'A World Flying Apart? Violent Nationalist Conflict and the End of the Cold War', *Journal of Peace Research* 37(1), 105–17.

Carment, D. and James, P. (1997) 'Secession and Irredenta in World Politics: The Neglected Interstate Dimension', in D. Carment and P. James (eds) *Wars in the Midst of Peace: The International Politics of Ethnic Conflict*, Pittsburgh, PA: University of Pittsburgh Press, 194–231.

Gurr, T. (1993) *Minorities at Risk: A Global View of Ethnopolitical Conflicts.* Washington, DC: United States Institute of Peace.

Gurr, T. (2000) *Peoples Versus States: Ethnopolitical Conflict and Accommodation at the End of the 20th Century*, Washington, DC: United States Institute of Peace.

Heraclides, A. (1997) 'The Ending of Unending Conflicts: Separatist Wars', *Millennium: Journal of International Studies*, 26(3), 679–707.

See also: ethnic conflict; ethnic cleansing; irredentism; nation-state; partition; self-determination

R. WILLIAM AYRES

Security

One of the most persistent challenges confronting scholars since World War Two has been the study of 'security' as a key concept in the International Relations literature. Part of the problem in analyzing the concept has been the understandable inability of writers in the field to agree on a single, all-encompassing, definition of the term. But even if a suitable definition is within reach (say, protection from harm), there is still the issue of what constitutes the most appropriate level of analysis (see **levels of analysis**) for security studies? What is the prime object of security? Should it be the state or the individual? What types of threats to security should be accorded priority? Threats involving the use of force? Or threats that challenge the **sovereignty** of the state? Should the focus be on short term or longer term threats?

That these questions remain the subject of often vigorous contention in the academic world explain partly why the sub-field of security studies has struggled to find direction since the end of the **cold war**. There are a multitude of competing agendas and research paradigms that make security studies an especially pluralistic area within the broader International Relations discipline. Whether this diversity is cause for celebration or condemnation remains an open question. But what is clear is that the sub-field of security studies today looks very different from the cold war period, when the study of international security was essentially about the study of **super-power** strategy.

The origins of the sub-field owe much to the shared belief among many, mainly realist (see **realism**), scholars after World War Two that the pervasive influence of idealism in Anglo-American intellectual thought during the inter-war period was largely responsible for the failure of the Western powers to take a firm stand against Nazi aggression in Europe during the 1930s. Apart from their lack of will, Western powers had been seriously negligent in allowing their military capabilities to decline appreciably with elites in these countries following the misguided counsel of idealists by placing excessive faith in the capacity of international institutions (particularly the **League of Nations**) to safeguard national security.

Early postwar security analysts sought to inject the International Relations discipline with a more concerted focus on the role of strategy. Examining the reasons why states use force as an instrument of policy was regarded as crucial in fostering strategic stability between the two superpowers. More broadly, the sub-field of security studies was dominated by classical realist assumptions about the degree of evil, lust for **power**, and tragedy inherent in the human condition; this was the philosophical prism for looking at international relations in general and the issues of security and strategy in particular. A fundamental corollary of embracing realist assumptions was an acceptance of **war** as a *recurring* scourge on humanity. From the perspective of the emerging field of security studies, rather than wishing war away through pious platitudes, the phenomenon needed to be studied in a spirit of detailed and dispassionate scholarship.

Throughout the 1950s and 1960s, in a period often characterized as the 'Golden Age' of security studies, the academic community was preoccupied with analyzing, interpreting, and explaining the strategic dimension of US–Soviet confrontation. By and large, the overriding focus was the impact of the nuclear revolution on the dynamics of the superpower relationship. Two consequences flowed from this: nuclear **deterrence** emerged as the single most important strategic concept in the security studies lexicon (which remained the case until the end of the cold war); and US–Soviet relations became the orthodox academic template for analyzing international security.

In the early to mid-1970s, a shift in the security studies literature began to occur. Looming defeat for the United States in Indo-China and the flowering of détente between Washington and Moscow led some to question the wisdom of the traditional issue area focus of security studies. Rising disenchantment with the excessively 'strategic' purview of the sub-field led to increasing interest in 'transnational' security issues, including international **terrorism** and organized crime. This shift was largely a consequence of the rise of '**interdependence**' as a concept in the International Relations literature and the concomitant view that the dynamic impulses of international security went well beyond the bilateral US–Soviet relationship.

While the core focus of security studies throughout the 1970s remained East–West confrontation – with particular attention being devoted to supplementing earlier ideas about rational deterrence theory – an increasing number of scholars were exhibiting strong interest in developing 'non-military alternatives' to security in the emerging area of **peace studies**. With the advent of the 'second cold war' in the late 1970s, the focus of security studies turned more resolutely towards 'hard' East–West strategic issues such as nuclear weapons employment policy, the conventional force balance in Europe, and maritime strategy. Indeed, with the notable exception of the rise of peace research in Western European academic institutions, security studies reverted to a more traditional strategic focus during the 1980s.

Not surprisingly given its intellectual roots, the security studies community was thrown into conceptual disarray following the demise of the cold war: What (if anything) would supplant the international security template of East–West confrontation? The end of **bipolarity** provided an opportunity for those who had been arguing vocally in favor of a 'new' agenda for security studies, an agenda concerned less with issues pertaining to the use of force (i.e. strategy) and more concerned with issues such as the natural environment, population levels, and global poverty. Concern with these 'new' security issues has reflected a broader endeavor on the part of some scholars to eschew the state as the referent point for discussing security in international relations in favor of 'societal' and 'human' security. From this perspective, safeguarding human welfare should become the priority for scholarly analysis instead of safeguarding the territorial **sovereignty** of the state. This, in turn, has provoked something of a backlash from a number of observers who argue that the pendulum has swung too far away from strategic issues toward intellectual 'fads'.

Despite almost one-and-a-half decades having passed since the end of East–West confrontation, the shape of security studies remains fluid and uncertain, with most of the key research debates unresolved. The crucial question facing those who study security remains:

What priorities should determine how the concept is examined? All observers may converge on this key research question, but agreement on an answer still seems a long way off.

Further reading

Alagappa, M. (1998) 'Rethinking Security: A Critical Review and Appraisal', in M. Alagappa (ed.), *Asian Security Practice: Material and Ideational Influences*, Stanford, CA: Stanford University Press, 27–64.

Baldwin, D. (1995) 'Security Studies and the End of the Cold War', *World Politics* 48(1), 117–41.

Buzan, B. (1991) *People, States and Fear: An Agenda for International Security Studies in the Post-Cold War Era*, 2nd edn, Brighton: Harvester Wheatsheaf.

Cha, V. (2000) 'Globalisation and the Study of International Security', *Journal of Peace Research* 37(3), 391–403.

Hough, P. (2004) *Understanding Global Security*, London: Routledge.

Kolodziej, E. (2005) *Understanding Security*, Cambridge: Cambridge University Press.

Miller, S. (2001) 'International Security at Twenty-Five: From One World to Another', *International Security* 26(1), 5–39.

See also: collective security; common security; critical security studies; security community; security dilemma

ANDREW O'NEIL

Security community

A concept that was originally developed by Karl Deutsch and his associates in the 1950s. He defined a security community as 'a group has become integrated, where **integration** is defined as the attainment of a sense of community, accompanied by formal or informal institutions or practices, sufficiently strong and widespread to assure peaceful change among members of a group with "reasonable" certainty over a "long" period of time' (Deutsch 1957: 5). Security communities may either be *amalgamated*, involving a formal merger of previously autonomous political units, or *pluralistic*, in which case actors retain their independence and **sovereignty**, but share common subjective feelings about 'we-ness' and the improbability of **war** among themselves.

The main characteristics of security communities include mutual **interdependence**, mutual responsiveness, and the pacification or the abandonment of the use of force. Security communities are formed when a group of political units develop common political values, are able to respond to one another's messages, needs, and actions quickly, adequately, and without resort to violence; and enjoy mutually predictable political, economic, and social behavior. More recent scholarship on security communities has identified four key features: a fundamental, unambiguous and long-term agreement among actors about the avoidance of war, the absence of any **arms race**; the existence of formal or informal institutions and practices for reducing, preventing, managing and resolving conflicts, and a high degree of political and economic integration.

Deutsch's work challenged **realism**'s belief in the necessity and inevitability of war. The sources of change in world politics are not to be found in violent shifts in the distribution of **power**, but in fundamentally peaceful and social processes involving the perceptions and identifications of people. While measuring material transactions as indicators of integrative processes that result in security communities, Deutsch also viewed their development as an exercise in identity-building (see **identity/difference**).

After being neglected by a realist-dominated field for much of the **cold**

war, the concept of a security community has been resurrected in post-cold war constructivist scholarship (see **constructivism**). The concept has been further developed in four main ways. First, compared to Deutsch's transactionalism, recent constructivist writings on security communities have adopted a more qualitative and sociological approach. There is a much greater emphasis on the role of norms and actor socialization in the development of security communities.

A second advance has been the exploration of the process of community building, including the identification of factors that generate security communities, account for the various stages of their development and explain regional variation in the end product. In an important recent contribution to the literature on security communities, Adler and Barnett (1998) have sketched a social constructivist and path-dependent approach to the origin and evolution of such communities. They identify three stages in the development of security communities, each of which is marked by a number of characteristics. The *nascent phase* contains a number of 'triggering mechanisms' including threat perceptions, expected trade benefits, shared identity, and organizational emulation (learning from the experience of other multilateral organizations). The *ascendant phase* is marked by tighter military coordination, reduced fears on the part of one actor that others within the group represent a threat, and the beginnings of cognitive transition toward intersubjective processes and collective identities that begin to encourage dependable expectations of peaceful change. The main characteristics of the *mature phase* are greater institutionalization, supranationalism, a high degree of trust, and low or no probability of military conflicts. A mature stage may be 'loosely coupled' (a minimalist version)

or 'tightly coupled' depending on the degree of trust and institutionalization of the community. Loosely coupled security communities are minimalist in nature. Tightly coupled security communities have more stringent standards, including a 'mutual aid society' providing for collective and cooperative efforts to help each other and offer joint solutions to common problems. They should also have some characteristics of supranationalism, which might include common national institutions as well as supranational and transnational institutions, and some form of **collective security** agreement.

Third, there has been an attempt to apply the concept to non-Western regional settings. Deutsch's original work was concerned mainly with Europe and the Atlantic. He cited two examples of pluralistic security communities: Sweden and Norway after 1905, and the United States and Canada after 1815. Since then, such communities have been identified in the **European Union**, North America, and between the United States and Japan. The absence of reference to such communities in the **Third World** is hardly surprising given the much higher incidence of inter-state conflict in the Third World, particularly in sub-Saharan Africa. Another factor impeding the development of security communities in the Third World is the relative absence of significant economic interdependence and political pluralism. In much of the literature on security communities, it is assumed that a true security community must also be a democratic security community.

Some of the recent literature uses security community building as an analytic framework to investigate the progress of **regionalism** in Southeast Asia and the Southern Cone of Latin America. It highlights the fact that the original members of the **Association of Southeast**

Asian Nations (ASEAN) have not fought a war among themselves since their inception in 1967. A stable peace also exists among the Southern Cone nations. Both ASEAN and the Southern Cone nations have developed a significant and long-term habit of regional interaction, which makes intra-regional relations relatively more peaceful and predictable than many other parts of the Third World.

Finally, the contemporary understanding of security communities has moved away from the original tendency to view community building as a linear process. The current emphasis is on the process, rather than the end product *per se*. Security communities may rise and decline. They may unravel in response to a variety of internal and external circumstances. Recent work on security communities argues that the sources of decline of security communities need not be external to the socialization process. Rather they can result from such intra-mural developments as the widening of membership and deepening of cooperation, and the reluctance of member of such communities to adapt to changing norms and ideas about cooperation such as those concerning sovereignty and the doctrine of non-interference in the internal affairs of states.

Further reading

Acharya, A. (2001) *Constructing a Security Community in Southeast Asia: ASEAN and the Problem of Regional Order*, London: Routledge.

Adler, E. and Barnett, M. (eds) (1998) *Security Communities*, Cambridge: Cambridge University Press, 198–227.

Deutsch, K.W., Burrell, S. A., Kann, R. A., Lee, M., Lichterman, T. M., Lindgren, R. E., Loewenheim, F. L. and van Wagenen, R. W. (1957) *Political Community in the North Atlantic Area*, New York, Greenwood Press.

See also: collective security; common security; security

AMITAV ACHARYA

Security dilemma

States residing in the anarchic **international system** face a dilemma between arming and not arming: while not arming may place the country's **security** at risk in the short run, increasing defense spending can trigger arming by neighboring states which can result in a net loss of security for all states in the long run. The dilemma even exists among status quo states because any arming, even for defensive purposes, can appear threatening to other states. The security dilemma is an example of a collective action problem in which strategies that are rational from an individual perspective result in a collectively inferior outcome. Thus, the security dilemma is often modeled as a **prisoner's dilemma** game.

The anarchic structure of the international system permits states to use military force to pursue political objectives. Given the absence of an international body with coercive power sufficient to control the behavior of states, each state must ultimately rely on itself for security. Traditionally, states have enhanced their security through either increasing domestic defense spending or forming **alliance**s. Unfortunately, these policies can appear threatening to other states. While the security dilemma is often viewed as a constant in international relations, several authors emphasize that it is a variable that can be influenced by a variety of factors at the systemic, interstate, domestic, or individual level. In general, while realists (see **realism**) view the security dilemma as largely fixed due to the anarchic structure of the international system, liberal internationalists contend that a variety of factors can influence the dilemma (see **liberal internationalism**).

At the systemic level, liberals and realists agree that the technological balance between offense and defense can influence the severity of the security dilemma and the harshness of **anarchy**. When offense dominates defense (i.e., when taking territory is easier than defending it), the security dilemma is heightened because states are vulnerable to surprise attacks and slight shifts in the **balance of power**. At the interstate level, liberals contend that international **regime**s can reduce the security dilemma by reducing transaction costs, monitoring behavior, and providing rewards and penalties. At the state level, domestic structures and norms can also influence a state's interpretation of the behavior of others. For example, proponents of the **democratic peace** argue that shared institutional structures and beliefs reduce the likelihood that defensive actions take by one democracy will be viewed suspiciously by other democracies. Similarly, Lenin's contention that capitalist states are inherently prone to **imperialism** implies that the proliferation of capitalist states should increase the severity of the security dilemma. Finally, at the individual level, liberals and more recently proponents of **constructivism** argue that the line drawn between the 'in-group' and the 'out-group' may influence threat perception. The arming of a member of the in-group is likely to be viewed as far less threatening than the arming of a member of the out-group. Recent experimental evidence supports the claims that individuals are much more likely to cooperate with the in-group and that individuals view gains by the out-group as threatening.

Conceiving of the security dilemma as a variable implies that states can consciously influence the harshness of the security dilemma through multilateral, bilateral, and unilateral policies. At the multilateral level, treaties such as the Chemical Weapons Convention can reduce the security dilemma by monitoring the behavior of members and providing support to victims of **chemical weapons** attacks. At the bilateral level, **arms control** agreements can decrease the security dilemma. Finally, states can unilaterally reduce the security dilemma for their neighbors by limiting the offensive orientation of their tactics and the offensive capabilities of their weapons. For example, the Swedish government's decision to forgo a flight refueling capability for its air force during the **cold war** was an explicit attempt to reduce the security dilemma with the Soviet Union by limiting aircraft to short-range defensive missions.

Unfortunately, the ability of states to moderate the security dilemma is limited because offensive and defensive weapons are often indistinguishable (e.g., a tank can be used for both offensive and defensive purposes). Moreover, even weapons and strategies that are viewed as purely defensive, such as digging moats or building fixed fortifications, can be used for offensive purposes in conjunction with other weapons systems. For example, fixed fortifications can allow states to concentrate forces in other areas of the battlefield in the hope of breaking through the opponent's lines. In the current era, the development of **ballistic missile defense** (BMD) systems have been highly controversial for precisely these reasons. While BMD systems are purely defensive by themselves, they can be viewed as offensive systems if they are used in conjunction with offensive ballistic missiles. For example, a robust BMD system would in theory allow its possessor to conduct nuclear attacks with impunity because other nuclear powers no longer possess a secure second strike capability. The security dilemma nicely captures the concerns of all parties with respect to the proposed deployment of the BMD system by the United States. While many Americans may sincerely believe that their weapons are only for defensive purposes, the fact that the weapons could be used to coerce others implies a possible decrease in security for others. If other states respond by increasing their spending on **weapons of mass destruction** or conventional weapons, all states (including the United States) could find themselves worse off in the long run.

It is important to note that the security dilemma is the product of **anarchy** at the systemic level. While it can be reduced by state policies, it will not be eliminated until the anarchic structure is replaced by a hierarchical structure. While this may occur within certain regions (such as Western Europe), the emergence of hierarchy at the international level appears remote at the current time.

Further reading

Glaser, C. (1997) 'The Security Dilemma Revisited', *World Politics* 50(1), 177–201.

Hertz, J. (1950) 'Idealist Internationalism and the Security Dilemma', *World Politics* 2(2), 157–80.

Jervis, R. (1978) 'Cooperation Under the Security Dilemma', *World Politics* 30(2), 167–214.

See also: anarchy; arms race; ballistic missile defense; non-offensive defense; prisoner's dilemma; regime

DAVID L. ROUSSEAU

Self-determination

The right or claim by a group to have a separate and distinct political identity, and to govern itself. Self-determination is one of the most contested claims or collective rights in contemporary international relations. There are two key moments in the history of **international society** that provide the historical context for understanding the main obstacles to reconciling self-determination with **international law** and **order**. The first symbolic moment is the Westphalian settlement (1648) (see **Westphalia**) that inaugurated the modern states system based on the principle of **sovereignty**. The second is the French Revolution (1789) when the concept of *national* self-determination was promoted as a democratic ideal of representative government, theoretically applicable to all humankind. In the political thought of the Enlightenment, governments should be based on the will of the people, not the monarch. People not content with their government should be able to secede and organize themselves as they wish. This strain of political thought meant that people were no longer mere subjects of the monarch, they were now citizens of the **nation-state**. From its inception, the concept of national self-determination was a threat to the legitimacy of the established order, and remains so today. However they are defined, there are simply many more nations than there are states, and there are no juridical processes available to redistribute humanity according to the principle of national self-determination without a severe disruption to the territorial integrity and rights of existing states. In short, there is a fundamental tension between national self-determination and contemporary international society.

The historical context

Contemporary international society is an evolution of the European society of states, which, in turn, grew out of what was regarded as the universal Christian society of medieval Europe. This pre-modern idea of international society was conceived by the natural law thinkers of the period as a universal society of humankind bound in their relations with each other by moral laws derived, in part, from the natural law tradition, but also from the traditions and customs of Empire and Church in Christian Europe. The transformation of Christian international society into European international society was an outcome of the changing structures of political **power** in Europe and the intellectual challenges of the period.

The Reformation weakened the political and moral **legitimacy** of the Universal Church and the Holy Roman Empire, and challenged also the idea of a single moral **authority** in the political community. At the same time, the notion of political sovereignty and a conception of the state exercising exclusive jurisdiction over a territory and its inhabitants were becoming clarified. Despite the conflicts between European state-makers to establish territorial boundaries, they shared a common culture and a common interest: a desire to establish territorial control, the institutions of the state, and a monopoly of violence over the populations they ruled. The establishment of separate governing authorities over distinct territorial areas, claiming independence from both **empire** and Church externally, and superiority over all other actors internally, marked the beginning of international society in its modern form. The idea of international society is derived from two others. The first of these is the very ancient idea of a universal society of mankind: a great community more inclusive than the particular communities into which humanity is divided and governed by a law of nature superior to the particular laws of these more restricted communities. The second is the idea of a system of states, understood as a multiplicity of independent political communities coexisting within a certain geographical area.

As the inter-woven authorities of medieval Europe were dissolving and recombining into sovereign states, the doctrine of sovereignty served as justification for territorial rulers to free themselves from traditional sources of authority. Yet while the absolutist monarch claimed to be the ultimate source of earthly law, it was an authority that was itself held to derive from God. For Jean Bodin (1530–96) – who is rightly considered the father of the modern theory of sovereignty – the term 'absolute' referred to the lack of a higher *earthly* authority. What was once a source of unity, however, gradually emerged as a source of disunity as the Reformation pitted Catholic and Protestant rulers against each other. According to the conventional interpretation of international society, the Westphalian Peace Treaties constituted for the first time an international society in which the relations between diverse feudal entities and the hierarchical claims of **empire** and Papacy were, at least in Europe, superseded by formal relations between modern sovereign states. The consolidation of exclusive sovereignty resting on the internal monopolization of the means of violence translated into exclusive control by central rulers of the instruments of foreign policy, namely control of the army, **diplomacy** and treaty making. International relations came to be institutionalized in permanent embassies, coordinating international affairs through regular diplomatic intercourse governed by codified and binding diplomatic protocols.

By the mid-seventeenth century, only central rulers in charge of these prerogatives became subject to and makers of **international law**, based on mutual

recognition to the exclusion of rivaling domestic centers of power. Sovereignty had repressed the independence of the nobility to act legitimately as autonomous warlords, blurring any clear distinction between domestic and international spheres. With the consolidation of the means of violence by multiple sovereigns and the establishment of bounded territoriality, the field of politics was formally differentiated into separate domestic and international spheres, based on internal political hierarchy and external **anarchy**. After the Westphalian settlement, non-sovereign lords and other corporate actors 'dropped out' of international relations in Europe. At the same time, political sovereignty and the **discourse** of *raison d'etat* secularized international relations by undermining the power of religion as the dominant mode of legitimacy, curtailing the universal ambitions of the Roman Catholic Church. The separation between international politics and religion entailed the recognition of the peaceful coexistence between legally equal members of international society, embodied in a code of international law that acknowledged mutual recognition, non-interference, and religious toleration between states if not within them. Henceforth, universal conceptions of empire or *res publica christiana* gave way to the workings of the **balance of power** as the natural regulator of competitive international relations in a multipolar anarchical environment.

The vestiges of the original connection between sovereignty and the sovereign or monarch remain in modern usage with the tendency to treat sovereign states as individuals. However, the authority of the state has gradually been seen to derive from the people or commonwealth, and not with an individual sovereign. The people's acknowledgment of a central governing authority within a specified geographical territory, and its reciprocal recognition from other states, confers on the state its sovereignty. However, the recognition of a central authority does not imply approval of the form it takes. An unpopular and oppressive totalitarian regime is no less sovereign in international law than a popularly elected, democratic republic. Sovereign states are, by international law, equal, and sovereign equality is the basis upon which the **United Nations** operates, at least in the General Assembly if not the Security Council. This principle of sovereign equality guarantees equal participation by all states in international relations. This sovereign equality has as its content the following elements: states are legally equal and every state enjoys the rights inherent in full sovereignty. Every state is obligated to respect the fact of the legal entity of other states. The territorial integrity and political independence of a state are inviolable. Each state has the right to freely choose and develop its own political, social, economic, and cultural systems. Finally, each state is obligated to carry out its international obligations fully and conscientiously and to live in peace with other states.

One point to notice here is that sovereignty is not absolute. States can have international obligations that they accrue when they enter into international treaties and agreements. Of course, states are free not to enter into these agreements to begin with, but once they have done so, they have given up a certain measure of sovereignty to the international community.

The framework of international law that emerged from the practices and agreements of emergent European states in the sixteenth and seventeenth centuries always exhibited critical tensions. Its chief contradiction lay in justifications of rules and practices rooted, on the one hand, in the prescriptive sovereignty of states and, on the other, in Christian obligations to other human beings. Christian theology was conducive, however, to a rather sharp separation of the temporal and the spiritual, which in practice devolved almost unlimited domestic license to temporal rulers, epitomized in the edict from the Gospels to 'render unto Caesar what is Caesar's'. Nonetheless, within the constraints of the jealously guarded rights of states, important rules, especially relating to the conduct of **war**, codified a mutual interest in limiting the destructive side effects of war. Such rules were often justified with reference to the Christian principle of protecting the innocent, which promoted rules designed to limit the destructive impact of war on civilians and their property, and to enjoin compassionate treatment of prisoners of war.

The second crucial 'moment' in the evolution of international society exposed this contradiction in ways that have yet to be adequately dealt with at the international level, and which arguably cannot be dealt with within the existing architecture of international law. Following the French revolution, dynastic sovereignty – the divine right of monarchs – has given way to justifications of territorial exclusivity based on the idea of the nation-state, the self-determination of 'peoples', and popular sovereignty. Meanwhile, Christian compassion has given way to the more secular language of **human rights**. The modern nation-state is now justified on the grounds of its expression of the unity and will of the nation that it represents. What was a prudential response by European princes to the carnage of the Thirty Years War (1618–48), namely the prohibition against intervening in the internal affairs of other states, has become entrenched in international law as a normative principle of paramount

importance. Justification for the principle of non-intervention can thus be given not only with reference to pragmatic considerations of order and territorial integrity, but also with reference to the idea that political communities should be free to determine their domestic affairs according to their own particular values and beliefs.

Nonetheless, the new principle of territorial differentiation did not entirely replace its dynastic predecessor. Instead, it has been grafted onto it in fits and starts. After the Napoleonic Wars, Poles, Italians, Magyars, and Germans, as well as the ethnic minorities living among them, all advanced claims to self-determination. The Congress of Vienna in 1815 did not accept self-determination as a basis for reshaping the map of Europe, but similar demands from the oppressed peoples of the Austro-Hungarian and Russian empires later received more favorable treatment. After the revolutions of 1848, national movements led to the formation of two new unified states, Germany and Italy.

Only after World War One, when the former European system began to disintegrate, did the principle of self-determination acquire principled advocacy through international figures as ideologically diverse as Vladimir Lenin and President Woodrow Wilson. Despite Wilson's goal of enshrining the principle of self-determination within the **League of Nations**' Covenant, the practical difficulties of realizing the principle prevented its inclusion in the document's final text. Self-determination was only indirectly recognized as applicable to those territories placed under the League's mandate and to those colonies that became independent states after World War One. In fact, the League's Covenant essentially established the inequality of peoples. Under Article 22, lands that received the status of mandated territories were to be guided by the 'advanced nations'. This arrangement essentially legitimized the colonial system.

World War Two once again changed the political landscape, but the principle of self-determination affected these changes in the immediate postwar era only to a slight degree. During work on the United Nations Charter, differences of opinion over the use of the words 'people', 'nation,' and 'state'. The right to self-determination in the Charter is associated only with 'peoples', and the notion of 'non-self-determined peoples' corresponds to what was traditionally described as a colony.

Determining exactly who (or what) the right of self-determination applies to remains its most disputed aspect. President Wilson and Lenin considered 'peoples' and 'nations' to possess this right, but they did not specify the meaning of these terms. In the post-World War Two era, it has been more or less commonly accepted that the right to self-determination applies only to colonies, which filled the ranks of the United Nations as sovereign states during the wave of **decolonization** in the 1950s and 1960s.

The injustice of the colonial system led the UN General Assembly on 14 December 1960, to adopt the Declaration on the Granting of Independence to Colonial Countries and Peoples, whose preamble emphasizes that the refusal or obstruction of collective freedom brings about the intensification of conflicts. Article 2 states that '[a]ll peoples have the right to self-determination; by virtue of that right they freely determine their political status and freely pursue their economic, social, and cultural development'. Furthermore, Article 3 states that '[i]nadequacy of political, economic, social, or educational preparedness should never serve as a pretext for delaying independence'.

Despite these developments, the debate over self-determination was by no means concluded. There were as many opinions informing the Declaration on Decolonization as there were new countries it applied to. The UN Commission on Human Rights has still declined to define the word 'people' and the term acquires little more precision in the UN charter itself. In practice the right of self-determination has been attributed to all colonies, but the principle of *uti possidetis* has been applied, the effect of which has been to ensure that self-determination takes place within the boundaries determined by the colonial powers, or within pre-existing boundaries of federal systems in the case of the breakup of composite states such as the old Soviet Union.

War, peace and the nation-state

Before examining the problem of national self-determination as a legitimation of territorial exclusivity in contemporary international society, it is worth noting that there has been a general decline in the incidence of war among the great powers over the last four hundred years. Since World War Two **civil war** has become more common in the world than international war. For the post-cold war decade, the discrepancy is clear: ninety-two violent civil conflicts in the decade 1989–98, nine civil conflicts with foreign intervention, and only seven pure interstate violent conflicts. In 1995, all of the thirty major armed conflicts fought in the world were civil wars. The pattern is particularly noteworthy in light of the growing number of states in international society. From 1840 to 1914, the number of states in the system was highly stable, varying roughly between thirty-five and forty-three. By the eve of World War Two, however, that number was over sixty; by the 1960s, it had doubled to 120; and in 2004 there were 191 states represented in the UN General Assembly. War was becoming less common for everyone, not just the great powers. The combination of the two trends marks a significant change in international relations. Civil wars and international wars were roughly comparable in frequency for nearly two centuries between 1816 and 1980. Today, civil war is far more common than war between states.

The international system has been shaped fundamentally by the principles of sovereignty and national self-determination. Indeed, nation-states and the **international system** mutually constitute each other according to these principles. International war has declined, in part, because the principle of national self-determination and the norm of mutual recognition of sovereignty have produced a highly successful system of managing interstate conflict by increasingly delegitimizing military conquest. In the nineteenth century, international norms limited legitimate conquest only to certain areas. Since World War Two, conquest has become so illegitimate that it is rarely attempted and even less often successful. There is an irony here: against those who condemn **nationalism** as the evil doctrine that spawned the Napoleonic and World Wars, one could well argue that nationalism has increasingly promoted international peace in the last two centuries.

Within states, however, the principles of state sovereignty and national self-determination may oppose each other, sometimes leading to civil war. Inside multinational states, competition for power can become a competition for sovereignty over ethnic rivals, leading groups to see threats to their existence. This suggests that, ironically, the fact of international anarchy ameliorates many international conflicts and makes their

management easier, by offering sovereign equality as a solution, while competition for sovereignty exacerbates domestic conflict and makes severe violence more likely. This insight implies that the standard argument that world peace would require a world sovereign is wrong, because creating one would raise the stakes in international politics into the question of 'who rules'. Instead, strengthening identities, norms, and non-sovereign institutions to underpin the relatively peaceful world order is the proper path to improved world **security**.

The end of the **cold war** and collapse of the Soviet Union can be explained in part as a result of pressures for national self-determination. When Mikhail Gorbachev began to respect the principle of national self-determination in Eastern Europe, the result was a nationalist assertiveness of unexpected power in the East European satellite states, resulting in the fall of the Iron Curtain and the Berlin Wall. The same sort of nationalist assertiveness then spread to the Soviet Union itself, ultimately leading to its disintegration into its fifteen component and nationally defined parts. The end of the cold war further entrenched the national principle as the foundation of the international order, and the end of the Soviet empire delegitimized the institution of satellite states. Thus a stronger norm of respect for state sovereignty has solidified the international consensus against international aggression, as Iraq discovered to its cost in 1991.

The principle of a people's right to self-determination originally promoted peaceful coexistence between states. But in the modern world this principle has become problematic as demands for self-determination have sparked many conflicts that blur the line between civil war and inter-state war. We can identify four ways in which the principle of self-determination presents a problem.

First, as already mentioned, there are no clear criteria for what constitutes a people, and so what groups possess the right to self-determination. Second, groups often assert a right to self-determination without considering other competing rights and principles, such as the principle of the territorial integrity of states. Third, the principle of self-determination is often asserted in a dogmatic way, without regard to its costs or consequences. Fourth, the indiscriminate assertion of the right to form one's own nation-state actually threatens to undermine the security and stability of the whole international system – a system which is based, ironically, on respect for the nation-state. Since the early nineteenth century, it cannot be said that the society of states has managed these difficulties with great success. The **great powers** have not been able to determine consistently the priority that should be accorded to the competing principles of territorial sovereignty and national self-determination.

Beyond the impasse

In the twenty-first century, the principle of self-determination is in dire need of creative analysis and far greater flexibility in the manner of its expression than it has received thus far. Prior to the end of the cold war, self-determination was limited to its close identification with the process of decolonization. Since that process is now complete, at least in a formal sense, both the meaning of 'the self', and how that self determines how it should be governed, are ripe for imaginative reinterpretation. Unfortunately, although the principle has been the focus of renewed scholarly attention in recent years, that has yet to be translated into effective global policy. As a result, which groups get to enjoy self-determination and which do not is in

large part a function of violence and the visibility of particular political struggles.

Today, the principle of self-determination is proclaimed by, and on behalf of, non-state populations as diverse as the Kurds, the Quebecois, the Basques and the Palestinians. Although the international community bestows a measure of legitimacy to some of these struggles, it does so in a haphazard manner. In part this is because self-determination struggles have appealed to opposing values of community and individuality that coexist uneasily. Self-determination involves a conflict between two competing selves. As an expression of democracy, the principle is apparently a simple one. Let the people rule! As has often been said, however, the people cannot rule until it is decided who are the people. And that decision, once taken, bestows upon the representatives of the people a great deal of leeway in limiting popular participation in the political process. It should also be noted that self-determination has adopted expansionist as well as disintegrative forms throughout history. It has been used as an imperial doctrine to justify the expansion of the United States through *manifest destiny*, the conquests of Napoleonic France and, most notoriously, Hitler's quest for a greater Germany. Since the end of the cold war it has taken on disintegrative forms in the former Soviet Union and of course, Yugoslavia.

In the United Nations, the promotion of the principle of self-determination is sometimes celebrated as one of the organization's main purposes. The Charter of the United Nations (1945) begins by affirming a 'respect for the principle of equal rights and self-determination of peoples'. At the same time, however, the liberal and democratic values that underpin the appeal of self-determination were mooted as the principle was implemented solely as an instrument of decolonization. It is a measure of how insignificant self-determination was thought to be by the drafters of the Charter that it appears only twice in the whole document. Certainly no right to self-determination flowed directly from the Charter. Prior to 1945, international law knew of no specific right to self-determination, and within the Charter the principle is clearly subordinate to the prohibition on the use of force, to the right to territorial integrity (Article 2), and to the general commitment to ensuring peace and security (Ch. VII).

The two decades following the drafting of the Charter and the 1948 Universal Declaration on Human Rights were marked by the end of **imperialism**. Most of the colonial powers became increasingly committed to divesting their colonial territories, and an Afro-Asian bloc began to find its voice in the United Nations. In 1960 and again in 1970, the General Assembly passed two Resolutions that provided the principle of self-determination with some international legal status even as they limited the scope of its application. Both the Declaration on the Granting of Independence to Colonial Countries and Peoples (1960), and the Declaration on Friendly Relations (1970), explicitly link self-determination to decolonization. They did not recognize any right to what might be called *internal* self-determination (i.e., the right to representative government), nor did they recognize any need to alter territorial frontiers between ex-colonies that had been determined by Europeans with little or no consideration of the wishes of their subjects.

Since the end of decolonization, it has become clear that the diplomatic compromises that facilitated the transfer of political authority during that era are now obsolete. Today, the principle of self-determination lacks both definition and applicability. Saving it from a complete descent into incoherence will require a renewal of the links between autonomy, democracy, **human rights** and the right to self-determination. Central to cultivating this renewal should be the adoption of a more liberal and expansive interpretation of the meaning of self-determination. Self-determination does not have to mean **irredentism**, **secession** and the violent renegotiation of territorial frontiers. The promotion of minority rights, devolution, federalism and greater acknowledgment of the legitimacy of cultural self-expression are all expressions of self-determination. It should be noted that such modes of achieving self-determination cannot be legislated in advance of particular contexts. Secession, border revision, federation, regional or functional autonomy, cultural pluralism; there are many possibilities and no reason to think that the choice of one of these in this or that case makes a similar choice necessary in all the other cases. The recognition of group rights at the expense of individual ones, however, is not consistent with the ethical attraction of this much-abused concept. When applied without criteria and limitations, it ends up producing devastating results. We must continue to respect the principle of self-determination, but as a relative, not absolute, value. While the international community is not equipped to rule on whether any group is actually a 'people', it can evaluate and set limits on the means by which putative peoples pursue their claimed rights to self-determination. Similarly, the principle of state sovereignty is important, but it cannot be taken as absolute. State sovereignty must be limited by the rules necessary to maintain coexistence. Acceptance of limited sovereignty is the only way to make the state compatible with the existence of international **interdependence**, of an international order, and with internal levels of authority at the regional and local levels.

Further reading

Clarke, D. and Jones, C. (eds) (1999) *The Rights of Nations*, Basingstoke: Palgrave.

Danspeckgruber, W. (ed.) (2001) *The Self-Determination of Peoples: Community, Nation and State in an Interdependent World*, Boulder, CO: Lynne Rienner.

Hannum, H. (1996) *Autonomy, Sovereignty, and Self-Determination: The Accommodation of Conflicting Rights*, Philadelphia, PA: University of Pennsylvania Press.

Musgrave, T. (2000) *Self-Determination and National Minorities*, Oxford: Oxford University Press.

Raic, D. (2003) *Statehood and the Law of Self-Determination*, New York: Kluwer Academic.

Sellers, M. N. S. (ed.) (1996) *The New World Order: Sovereignty, Human Rights and the Self-Determination of Peoples*, New York: Berg.

Shapiro, I. and Kymlicka, W. (eds) (2000) *Ethnicity and Group Rights*, New York: New York University Press.

See also: ethnicity; irredentism; nationalism; nation-state; recognition; secession; sovereignty; Westphalia

MARTIN GRIFFITHS

Socialism

For the greatest part of the twentieth century, socialism has meant the abolition of private enterprise and of private ownership of the means of production, and the creation of a system of planned economy in which the enterpreneur working for profit is replaced by a central planning body. Today, very few people who call themselves socialist seem prepared to advocate this kind of socialism. In fact those ideas seem in danger of extinction, surviving only in Vietnam and Cuba.

The original, and unifying, political platform of socialists after World War Two (particularly in Europe) included nationalization, central planning, high and rapidly rising levels of public spending and taxation, highly progressive if not confiscatory income tax rates, exchange controls, and wage and price controls. By the end of the 1960s, many of these policy prescriptions had been abandoned, and a second kind of socialism became prevalent. Its political program was exemplified by the British Labour party. It consisted of a combination of Keynesianism, deficit spending, wage and price controls (or incomes policy, as it was called in Britain), and the Phillips curve (the idea that you could reduce unemployment by increasing inflation).

In a Keynesian world, price stability was not necessarily desirable. Most Keynesians were convinced that inflation was the unavoidable price of economic growth, that there was a stable trade-off between inflation and unemployment, that it was possible to reduce interest rates through monetary expansion, and that the time horizon for monetary policy decisions had to be dictated by the needs of short-term stabilization policies. All of these views have come under sustained criticism over the last thirty years.

For example, there is no evidence that economic growth inevitably involves price inflation. On the contrary, there are good reasons to believe that monetary instability hinders long-term projects and makes economic growth more difficult, as illustrated by the experience of a number of Latin American countries. In addition, the idea of a stable trade-off between inflation and unemployment is thoroughly discredited: an unexpected acceleration of inflation may temporarily reduce unemployment but this effect is usually short-lived. As for stabilization policies, it is now largely (though certainly not unanimously) agreed that our insufficient knowledge, unreliable short run macroeconomic forecasts, and variable time lags in the impact of monetary policy decisions, make it likely that attempts at 'fine-tuning' the economy often result in additional, avoidable instability. Finally, budget deficits were regarded as the ultimate propellant of economic growth when most economists believed that high employment and stability could be achieved through appropriate manipulations of the budget. In recent times, however, we have witnessed a reversal in the conventional wisdom. Deficits are now blamed for many different economic problems: inflation, unemployment, slow growth, the stock market crash, high interest rates, balance of payments difficulties, instability of exchange rates and a variety of other troubles.

While some of these criticisms are of dubious validity, it is increasingly recognized that, whereas deficit financed increases in public spending change the structure of total spending (by transferring funds from the private to the public sector), their long run impact on the level of aggregate demand may very well be negligible in most cases. It is harder to increase the size of government when spending must be financed with an increase in explicit taxation.

The birth of today's socialism can be traced to the failure of Keynesianism. One of the main factors in the historical changes that have marked the 1980s and the 1990s has been the liberalization of the international movement of goods, services, and capital. As a result governments that 'mismanage' their countries are penalized by the outflow of capital. The importance of capital movements in forcing governments to adopt certain policies cannot be overemphasized. High inflation countries, high deficit countries, countries with unreliable legal frameworks, or excessively punitive to private productive investments are forced by capital movements to 'mend their ways'. **Globalization** has promoted pro-market, neoliberal policies (see **neoliberalism**) and, by so doing, it has undermined the basis of post-war socialism. At the beginning of the 1990s, many people thought that we had come to a radical change of the political paradigm, so that the principles of a 'free society' were going to rule unchallenged everywhere, and socialism had come to an end. The events of the 1980s had convinced many observers that the struggle was over: capitalism had won.

However, over the past decade there has been a revival of socialism, especially in parts of Western Europe. The renewed popularity of socialist parties in recent years owes much to the crisis in financial markets, which many people have blamed on excessive market freedom. While defining contemporary socialism is nearly impossible, there are certain policy prescriptions that are common to many if not most socialist parties. Their common denominator is given by the fact that contemporary socialists have come to tolerate the market system because of its superior efficiency, but they do not accept the implications of an order based on individual liberty. Their position, in other words, is based on hostility toward a society arranged as much as possible on the principle of individual choice.

Unlike the socialists of the early post-war era, contemporary socialism is characterized by a heavy reliance on the regulation of **capitalism**. State regulation is for today's socialists what public ownership of the means of production and central planning were for socialists half a century ago. In this, as in other areas (like taxation, environmental protection, public spending, etc.), the difference between socialists and liberals is quantitative rather than philosophical. A good example is given by labor market regulation, especially in Europe, and attempts to harmonize taxes to limit capital movements across territorial borders. Another area where contemporary socialists and liberals differ is environmentalism. They both agree that some amount of environmental protection is necessary. The difference between the two is in the amount of environmental protection deemed desirable and in the ways to achieve it – socialists tend to rely on governmental regulation, liberals on market mechanisms.

We no longer live in an era of great ideological confrontation between liberalism and socialism; there are fewer differences between liberals and socialists today than in the past. This is because 'socialism' is arguably an empty shell – the label continues to be used, but its content has been lost, possibly forever. However, while socialism may be dead, statism is not. The focus of political debate has shifted from the general architecture of society to the desirability of specific policy proposals. The twentieth century has produced the largest increase in the size of government in the history of humankind. In 1900 the ratio of government spending to GDP in most advanced industrialized economies was 10 per cent, in the 1950s it was 30 per cent, and it is now roughly 60 per cent. As long as government spending remains at these levels within most advanced industrialized countries, the egalitarian ideals that lie at the heart of socialism will continue to inspire proposals for the regulation of capitalism by the state.

Further reading

Callaghan, J. (2000) *The Retreat of Social Democracy*, Manchester: Manchester University Press.

Geoghegan, V. (1998) 'Socialism' in R. Eccleshall, V. Geoghegan, M. Lloyd, I. Mackenzie, R. Wilford, M. Kenny and A. Findlayson (1998) *Political Ideologies*, 2nd edn, London: Routledge, 91–117.

Muravchik, J. (2002) *Heaven on Earth: The Rise and Fall of Socialism*, San Francisco, CA: Encounter Books.

Stiglitz, J. (1997) *Whither Socialism?* Cambridge, MA: MIT Press.

See also: capitalism; communism; Marxism; third way

MARTIN GRIFFITHS

Solidarism

A concept of **international society** in which sovereign states are united in pursuit of common purposes which serve as their ultimate *raison d'être*, and in which world politics is a collective process of coordinated and cooperative activities leading to joint destinations. Solidarism is closely related to the concepts of monism (law) and monotheism (theology). It can be contrasted with **pluralism**. International society is not about coexistence: it is more than a framework for ordering and civilizing the relations of states. It expresses common purposes and is geared to pursuing them by collective means. International history is progressive and not merely repetitive, in the sense of recurrent **war**. Among such purposes are **collective security**, **human rights**, human security, democracy, world prosperity, and global environmental protection. Processes of world politics – such as **democratization** and **globalization** – serve such purposes. Perhaps the final destination is human emancipation via worldwide democracy. That is sometimes referred to as the **end of history**. The ultimate purpose of international solidarism, therefore, may be to bring into existence a peaceful and prosperous world based on justice for people everywhere.

Solidarism is a conception of international society in which the common interests and shared concerns of people across the world are more fundamental than the borders that divide them into separate **nation-state**s with distinctive and potentially conflicting **national interest**s. States exist but they are agents of the international community and not only their people. People are not only citizens of a state but they are also citizens of the world. Solidarism posits international cohesion, camaraderie, cooperation and concord. Unity is the desirable condition of world affairs; disunity is undesirable and perhaps even unnatural. Solidarism is evident in global environmental protection, global prosperity, global civil society and global governance. Solidarism presupposes a world community of some sort and prefigures a world authority and even, in some versions, a world government.

The archetype of solidarism is the Kantian idea of a cosmopolitan (see **cosmopolitanism**) world community that extends far beyond the boundaries of states and embraces the entire human population of the earth on a basis of right or law: what Kant (1724–1804) refers to as cosmopolitan right or *jus cosmopoliticum*. Kant thereby emphasizes the wholeness and 'interconnectedness' of international society. He speaks of a world 'community of reciprocal action' and he envisages nation-states 'uniting for the purpose' of regulating such commercial intercourse open to all. Kantian solidarism may also be evident in efforts to establish human security as a purpose of international relations and to justify **humanitarian intervention** as necessary to provide security to populations of abusive states or **failed state**s. Governments are seen to have not only a duty to safeguard their own citizens but also

an obligation to protect people everywhere regardless of their citizenship. People across the world share that same obligation.

Cosmopolitan solidarism views war as a fundamental problem facing humankind and holds up as the highest goal of world politics the elimination of war on a permanent basis and thus the establishment of perpetual peace. Here war is no longer an inherent right of independent states or even an institution of the society of states but, rather, war is a collective right of international society as a whole. The overriding and fundamentally justifying purpose of the threat and use of armed force is to establish collective security on a worldwide basis. Armed forces exist to uphold the 'universal right of mankind' and to provide human security, which is the basis of collective security and the foundation of civil society. Kant speaks of the effort to establish universal and lasting peace as the 'entire ultimate purpose' of world affairs. Everything else is secondary. Peace is for people and not just for rulers or governments. Once final peace has been achieved the principle problem of international relations will have been solved.

Closely related to cosmopolitan solidarism and indeed growing out of it is political solidarity registered in the process of worldwide democratization. Kant conceives of perpetual peace as resting on a foundation of republican government (the *Rechtsstaat* or rule of law). Today we think of that in terms of democracy. Democratic peoples (unlike autocratic rulers) are portrayed as peace loving, and it follows that democracies do not fight each other. That supposed non-belligerent nature of democracy is a justification for condemning and wherever possible eliminating all other forms of government and installing democracy on a worldwide basis. That is not only expected to bring about a peaceful world but is also held to be the only form of government that fully respects the dignity of human beings and lays the foundation of human emancipation. Here solidarism is conceived as a collective endeavor to reach the ultimate destination of world politics: the final stage of historical development: the end of history.

A different conception of solidarism is evident in the utilitarian notion of globalization. That is a global economic process that is based on a worldwide division of labor and is conducive to higher standards of living across the world: world prosperity. Here, too, the referential framework is not merely the prosperity of countries individually or even international prosperity resting on reciprocal **most-favored nation** rules. Rather, it is economic progress and prosperity of the world as a whole, the entire world community. It is based on the welfare of all people across the world and no longer only on the welfare of nation-states. In that sense, one would speak not only of the Gross National Product (GNP) but also and even more the Gross World Product. That would be the basic economic indicator. It would determine investment and the allocation of scarce resources worldwide without the intervening or foreclosing consideration of GNP. Economic welfare would finally be a global and not merely a national issue. National economic development would be not an end in itself but a means of world prosperity, that is the prosperity of all the world's people, which would be the ultimate purpose.

Much of the foregoing discussion is about prospects and possibilities rather than actualities, the future more than the 'here and now'. That is owing to the fact that international solidarism confronts realities of the nation-state and the national interest. It also confronts realities of the division of the world population by culture, history, language, religion, civilization, etc. And it confronts difficulties of providing **international public goods** beyond the nation-state or the pluralist society of states. The twentieth century solidarist vision of collective security ran up against these limits. Governments showed themselves to be far more ready to provide security for their own people and their allies than the people of the world. They were unwilling to make armed force the collective instrument of international society as a whole. Citizens, too, were far more willing to identify with, pay taxes to, and fight for their own country and its allies than humankind in general. If asked to fight for humanity they might be left wondering what to do. Moreover, there was always a threatening 'other' out there. Wars against terrorists have not significantly altered that perception and inclination. National security and international security is the fundamental responsibility of nation-states and the society of states. Their sense of responsibility for human security is far more discretionary, if in reality it exists at all, and in most abusive states or failed states people are still left largely to fend for themselves.

Much the same can be said of economic prosperity and welfare: the nation-state is still the basic solidarist unit. **Free trade** and related international economic activities are supported and sustained only as long as they serve the interests of nation-states and their citizens. The world economy, considered as a collectivity, is a vague and poorly understood idea as compared to the national economy. Its emotional significance and impact is even less. The welfare of people around the world regardless of national citizenship is an almost invisible consideration and concern as compared to the welfare of Americans, Japanese, Germans, etc.

Recalcitrant facts such as these are major obstacles to the construction and operation of international society on solidarist principles.

Further reading

Booth, K. (1991) 'Security and Emancipation', *Review of International Studies* 17(4), 313–26.

Bull, H. (1995) *The Anarchical Society: A Study of Order in World Politics*, 2nd edn, Basingstoke: Palgrave.

Evans, G. and Sahnoun, M. (2001) *The Responsibility to Protect: Report of the International Commission on Intervention and State Sovereignty*, Ottawa: International Development Research Center.

Mayall, J. (2000) *World Politics: Progress and Its Limits*, Cambridge: Polity.

Wheeler, N. and Dunne, T. (1996) 'Hedley Bull's Pluralism of the Intellect and Solidarism of the Will', *International Affairs* 72(1), 91–107.

See also: cosmopolitanism; English School; international society; pluralism

ROBERT JACKSON

Sovereignty

From the perspective of some of the key theoretical positions in the study of international relations (IR), sovereignty is the most important constitutive principle that shapes contemporary international relations. Sovereignty is characterized as a constitutive principle because it is the defining attribute of the modern state and without states, of course, there would be no international relations. It is possible to trace **state formation** and international relations back in time for more than five millennia, and from this world historical perspective the emergence of sovereignty, at the end of the medieval era, is considered to be a recent and quintessentially modern phenomenon. The acquisition of sovereignty, moreover, not only transformed the nature of the state, but it also transformed the nature of international relations. Although it took several centuries for the modern sovereign state to consolidate, by the time of the Westphalian settlement (1648) (see **Westphalia**), it is usually accepted that we can start to define European states as sovereign entities. By that juncture, many of the features from the preceding medieval era that were fundamentally at odds with the establishment of the sovereign state had been swept to one side, while, at the same time, the conditions necessary for the formation of the modern sovereign state were starting to be put in place. In particular, the conception of sovereignty had been formally articulated and so it became possible to conceive of the state as a sovereign entity.

Sovereignty presupposes that the state is a territorially bounded unit with an inside and an outside. As a consequence, it is necessary to explore state sovereignty from both an internal and an external perspective. This may appear to be a patently obvious point, but Europeans had not previously thought about crucial concepts related to sovereignty, such as, **authority**, **power** and politics from these two different perspectives. Indeed, during the medieval era, and even as late as 1648, there was still no conception of a geographical area defined as Europe embracing a distinctive set of states. Instead, there were references to *respublica christiana* or christendom. The idea of Europe and the sovereign state were both features, therefore, of the modern era.

From an internal perspective, the sovereign state is conceived to be an entity that can exercise supreme authority within its own territorial boundary. That is to say, a state is sovereign because it is acknowledged that there is no external organization that can exercise authority within the territorial boundaries of that state. For the early theorists of sovereignty, such as Jean Bodin (1530–96) and Thomas Hobbes (1588–1679), the idea of supreme authority operating within the state represented the essence of sovereignty and it was this factor that primarily distinguished the modern era from the medieval era. But in the contemporary world, the external dimension of sovereignty is considered to be equally important. To acquire external sovereignty, a state must be recognized by the other sovereign states and identified as an equal member of the **international society**. When these two dimensions of sovereignty are put together, then it is seen to follow that sovereign states have an international obligation or duty to abide by the norm of non-intervention. In other words, sovereignty requires all states to acknowledge that they have no right to intervene in each other's domestic affairs.

Although sovereignty was regularly depicted as a key component of international relations throughout the twentieth century, there were always political philosophers who questioned whether the concept had either a useful or a meaningful role to play in the analysis of the state. There were also political scientists who wished to dispense with the idea of the state altogether and replace it with the concept of a political system. But in IR it was generally taken for granted that it was both necessary to draw on the idea of the state and appropriate to describe it as a sovereign unit. From the 1960s, onwards, however, the potential for states to maintain their sovereign status was called into question with increasing frequency. This trend accelerated in the 1990s with the growing belief that the forces of **globalization** had the capacity to erode sovereignty. And as

the impact of the **cold war** began to wane, **cosmopolitanism** gained ground and there were persistent demands by liberal cosmopolitans on governments in the developed world to promote **democratization** and to engage in **humanitarian intervention** at the expense of the sovereignty of states that operated in the **Third World**. Equally striking, at this time, was the simultaneous widening and deepening of the **European Union**, thereby threatening to undermine the sovereign state at its point of origin. For many analysts, therefore, the coming together of all these developments appeared to lead to the inexorable conclusion that the sovereign state is in the process of terminal decline.

Paradoxically, and partially in response to this assessment, there has been a resurgence of interest in sovereignty in IR over the last twenty years and a sophisticated literature on the concept is emerging. A common feature of this literature is the presumption that despite the centrality of sovereignty in our understanding of international relations, the idea has been inadequately conceptualized. As a consequence, it has been argued that it is not possible to evaluate claims about the demise of the sovereign state without developing a more effective framework for thinking about the nature of sovereignty. In the attempts to develop a more sophisticated understanding of sovereignty, three main lines of analysis have been advanced. Although they all support the general conclusion that the role being played by sovereignty in international relations is much more complex than has been generally recognized, they also diverge in some significant ways. Moreover, each line of analysis can be associated with one of the major contemporary IR Schools of thought: **realism, constructivism** and the **English School**. By examining the approach to sovereignty developed within the context of each of these Schools, the reason why the concept needs to be treated as both complex and contested becomes more apparent.

Realism

At first sight, it might seem surprising that realists should be paying close attention to the idea of sovereignty. Traditionally, realists have insisted that states should be regarded as autonomous actors and they have even acknowledged that states can be identified as sovereign units. But it has always been assumed that the long-term survival of states can be accounted for, most effectively, by the existence of a **balance of power**, rather than by the presence of a set of norms or constitutive principles operating within an international society. Realists, however, have begun to reassess the nature of the state, in general, and sovereignty, in particular, as a response, on the one hand, to the significance now frequently being attached to international **regime**s, norms and constitutive principles and, on the other hand, to the frequent claims that because state sovereignty is being systematically challenged in the contemporary world it has to be acknowledged that the state is in retreat. Realists are skeptical about both of these claims and they are now fighting a vigorous rearguard action to demonstrate that the international norms associated with sovereignty have persistently been violated ever since the time of the Westphalian settlement, and so, as a consequence, because these violations have been such a habitual feature of international politics in the past, there is little reason to suppose that current violations are going to eliminate the sovereign state in the future.

Potentially the most damaging aspect of the realist critique of the constitutive approach to sovereignty is the claim that the independence of reputedly sovereign states has been effectively and persistently compromised ever since the Westphalian settlement. In making this claim, realists also acknowledge that it is necessary to move beyond the undifferentiated conception of the sovereign state as an autonomous unit that they have traditionally relied on. So in addition to the distinctions already drawn between internal and external sovereignty and the rules associated with non-intervention (Westphalian sovereignty), realists have also drawn attention to **interdependence** sovereignty, which focuses on state control of transborder activities. Once it is accepted that there are different sets of norms and rules associated with these different aspects of sovereignty, then it follows that it can no longer be considered as an 'all or nothing' concept. The differentiation of sovereignty is sometimes referred to as the 'basket approach', with each state's basket containing a distinctive set of sovereign rights. It follows that in contrast to pregnancy, there are dimensions of sovereignty. And it could well be that there are relatively few states that can be considered fully sovereign.

Throughout the history of modern states sovereignty has been compromised regularly on both a voluntary and an involuntary basis. States are shown to have signed up, voluntarily, to both general conventions and specific contracts that have imposed limitations on their sovereignty. International conventions are, primarily, a feature that began to develop in the twentieth century when states regularly became signatories of international treaties that established, for example, a wide variety of universal rights for the individual. By signing these treaties, it can be argued that the states voluntarily imposed limitations or constraints on their own domestic authority. But voluntary constraints of this kind are not just a feature of the twentieth century. Ever since the Westphalian settlement, states have been willing to sign specific contracts with other states that have also conceded domestic autonomy on a voluntary basis. For example, states have signed contracts that oblige them to defend the rights of religious and ethnic minorities within their own boundaries.

Compromising sovereignty, however, is even more significant when it takes place on an involuntary basis. Yet, again, realists have brought into focus how frequently states have found their sovereign rights being disregarded by other states. During the cold war, for example, both the United States and the Soviet Union insisted that they had a right to intervene within their own spheres of influence, with the result that forcible interventions became a characteristic feature of cold war politics.

Once it is acknowledged that many, if not most states are less than fully sovereign, the idea that there is a constitutive principle of sovereignty that underpins an international society of states becomes difficult to sustain. Traditionally, realists have accepted that states have maintained their independence only if they possess the power to resist attacks on their sovereignty or if their independence is deemed necessary for the maintenance of the balance of power, in which case other states will ensure that their sovereignty is preserved. From this perspective, sovereignty is an epiphenomenal feature of international relations. But other realists have questioned this assessment and think that it is necessary to extend the discussion of sovereignty. They are particularly interested in the fact that although the whole raft of norms associated with the various dimensions of sovereignty have always been systematically compromised, nevertheless, states have consistently maintained that they possess an unequivocal right to full sovereignty. So despite the fact that sovereignty is not an embedded or institutionalized feature of international relations and norms are not consequential, in the sense of constraining the behavior of states, these norms have nevertheless still proved to be extremely durable. Realists have attributed the resilience of sovereignty to what is termed 'organized hypocrisy' (Krasner 1999).

This term draws attention to the fact that rulers take the idea of sovereignty very seriously, but if it is seen to be in their interests either to compromise the sovereignty of their own state, or to violate the sovereignty of another state, then they will not hesitate to do so. The durability of sovereignty demonstrates that it is an important and organized feature of international relations, but the ease with which rulers violate sovereignty indicates that there is a significant element of hypocrisy about their verbal adherence to the norms associated with the concept. Rather than seeing sovereignty as an institution, therefore, it is treated as a 'cognitive script' that tells rulers how to behave in a given setting. Under normal circumstances, rulers will automatically follow the script. It can be equated, as a consequence, with a standard operating procedure or the default procedure on a computer. But, as with a computer, there may be reasons to change the default setting. In this event, the rules associated with sovereignty will be set to one side and another set of rules brought into play and the rulers will start to operate on the basis of a different cognitive script.

Constructivism

From the realist perspective, the institutionalized character of sovereignty has been so firmly entrenched in IR that it has blinded the discipline to how habitual the violations of sovereignty have always been in international relations. It follows that while the significance attached to contemporary violations of sovereignty is seen to be exaggerated, by the same token, so too is the potential for sovereignty to be viewed as a constitutive principle of international relations. Constructivists agree with the first of these propositions, although for different reasons to realists, while sharply contesting the second. But their overarching problem with the realist perspective is that it fails to comprehend the nature of constitutive rules and constructivists insist that sovereignty needs to be defined in terms of these rules. As a consequence, from their perspective, sovereignty cannot be treated as a 'cognitive script' or in terms of a default position, because these metaphors associate sovereignty with regulative rules rather than constitutive rules. For the constructivist, the difference between these two types of rules is of fundamental importance. A change of regulative rules moves us from one strategy to another within a given game whereas a change in constitutive rules transforms the kind of the game that we are playing. So in terms of international relations, it follows that different regulative rules can operate within a particular historical era, whereas a change in constitutive rules moves us from one historical era into another. From the constructivist perspective, therefore, it was the emergence of the new sovereignty rules that precipitated the transformation from the medieval era to the modern era.

This transformation reflected an exceptionally complex process and there are major debates amongst historians about how and why it took place. But what is not in dispute is that the rules of the game before and after the transformation took on radically different forms. In the earlier period, Christianity provided a source of unity across medieval Europe, but power and authority within this area was extremely fragmented and decentralized. Control of any given territorial area was never in the hands of one person and so political allegiance could not be territorially determined. There was no clear hierarchy of power because so often authority relations overlapped with each other. For example, Henry II, king of England, was also the duke of Normandy. As a duke, he was obliged to pay homage to Louis VII, king of France, which he duly did. In Normandy, although obviously not in England, Henry was, effectively, Louis's steward and he had rights and duties with respect to him as well as to the inhabitants of Normandy. So this stewardship had to be conducted in accordance with natural law and right reason. And the actions of Louis were subject to the same constraints. But by the end of the medieval era, very different ideas began to exert an influence. In particular, attention was focused on the Roman law of *dominium* (property). For the Romans, landowners had absolute power over their own property and this provided a useful model for the rulers of the nascent states that began to emerge at the end of the medieval era. The complex and crosscutting political ties that existed in the medieval world initially confronted the rulers of the emerging sovereign states with both internal and external threats to their authority. But with the passage of time, these threats were largely overcome and as kings consolidated their power, so sovereignty achieved the status of a constitutive rule.

A crucial implication of depicting sovereignty in constitutive terms is that the concept is then imbued with an inter-subjective status. In other words, rulers acknowledge that their own claim to sovereignty requires them to accept the claim to sovereignty made by all other sovereign members of the international society. By implementing the complex body of rules associated with sovereignty, states then constantly reproduce the international society that is constituted by sovereignty. But if this account of sovereignty is accepted, then the systematic violations of sovereignty identified by the realists become deeply problematic. If sovereignty is no more than a cognitive script that can readily be replaced by an alternative cognitive script, then sovereignty must be an extremely precarious phenomenon. This is not the case, argue constructivists, because the violations are never considered to threaten the constitutive nature of sovereignty. When sovereignty is violated, the perpetrator will almost invariably endeavour to demonstrate that the violation can be justified and so it does not threaten the sovereign constitution of international society. This is not a case of hypocrisy; on the contrary, the violation helps to substantiate the claim that sovereignty is indeed a constitutive element of international society.

Constructivists, however, have taken the argument further. Starting from the position that sovereignty simultaneously determines or certainly reflects both the character of the international society and the identity of states, constructivists have gone on to demonstrate that during the modern era, the identity of the sovereign state has undergone some dramatic transformations, thereby challenging the traditional view that sovereignty is a fixed and unchanging principle. There has been a tendency to project our contemporary understanding of sovereignty back to the origins of concept and, by doing so, there is a failure to recognize what a very different conception of sovereignty existed at the time of the Westphalian settlement. It is taken for granted in the contemporary world that sovereign equality prevails, that states

have a monopoly on the legitimate use of force, and that there is a sovereign right to **self-determination**. But in 1648, none of these features of sovereignty existed. At that time, sovereign authority was vested with the king and individuals were regarded as subjects rather than citizens. There was certainly no conception of self-determination. And as God's lieutenants on earth, kings had the responsibility to maintain a divinely ordained, hierarchical social order, with their own position in the hierarchy determined by their reputed proximity to God. So states were not sovereign equals but operated within a God-given hierarchy. At that time, states did not attempt to establish a monopoly on the legitimate use of force. Non-state actors, such as mercenaries and pirates, authorized by the state, were responsible for much of the international violence that took place. Constructivists have not only demonstrated that a very different conception of sovereignty prevailed at the time of the Westphalian settlement, but also that the current conception of sovereignty is a very recent development. What we now take to be the essential characteristics of a sovereign state are seen to be very largely a product of the nineteenth and twentieth centuries.

The English School

Assessments of sovereignty almost invariably take place in the context of Europe, where the concept originated. But sovereignty is now a universal phenomenon and the English School has taken a particular interest in the global expansion of sovereignty. Initially, the English School focused on the idea of a **standard of civilization** that had to be met before a new state could be accorded sovereign status. On this basis, the English School revealed how the European international society of sovereign states steadily expanded until the present day when it is effectively worldwide. The founding fathers of the English School insisted that their analysis was not Eurocentric, but only an acknowledgment that sovereignty was a European invention. Despite this defence, their analysis continued to be subjected to criticism on the grounds that it produces a sanitized version of how international society evolved, effectively erasing the brutality and racism that accompanied European **imperialism**. But the analysis has now also been challenged from within the English School on the grounds that it fails to accommodate the fact that after the formation of the modern sovereign state, the Europeans began to establish two very different kinds of international **order**.

From this alternative perspective, the English school, indeed, IR in general, is seen to make the mistake of focusing exclusively on the international order that formed in Europe. The alternative account, by contrast, demonstrates that in addition to Europe's international society, the Europeans also established an extra-European order that operated on the basis of very different principles to those that governed the international order established in Europe. What is most striking about this assessment, distinguishing it from the orthodox English School account, is the assertion that the contemporary international order, far from being a universalized version of the European order, is, on the contrary, an extremely unstable combination of both the European and the extra-European international orders.

The divide between these two modes of international order was clearly in evidence by the nineteenth century. From the conservative perspective of European diplomats and historians, the main virtue of an order built on sovereignty was that

it tolerated the existence of divergent but equally civilized communities. But these conservative thinkers found it necessary to draw a sharp distinction between a longstanding European civilization and conditions in other parts of the world where it was considered that civilization had not yet developed. European conservatives accepted, however, that it was morally desirable for civilized people to promote civilization within the uncivilized world. This impetus, however, led to the formation of a second very distinctive international order. Relations amongst European states were constrained by **international law** but it only applied to fully sovereign states. But it was presupposed that the inhabitants of extra-European territory lacked the level of civilization to exercise full sovereignty. So when the European states operated outside of their own international society, they were only constrained by their own constitutional law.

Two crucial factors regulated Europe's relations with the extra-European world. One encouraged colonization on the basis of a right to appropriate territory – the principle of *occupatio* – provided that the appropriators made improvements to the land over which they established ownership. This principle was applied extensively in Africa and the Americas. However, when the Europeans confronted established states in other parts of the world, they avoided direct rule. Instead, they drew on the idea of divided sovereignty. The Europeans took control of certain essential functions, such as the regulation of foreign policy, leaving the indigenous state to control other essential functions. Divided sovereignty is often treated as either an oxymoron or a throwback to the medieval era. In fact, the idea was never absent from European legal thinking. The division of sovereignty, however, combined with the injunction to promote civilization, provided the Europeans with an automatic right to intervene across the extra-European world.

According to the orthodox English School assessment, during the course of the twentieth century, sovereign rights were then extended across the globe. But the alternative English School account considers that this assessment provides less than half the story. First, it ignores the fact that the significance attached to the importance of civilization was not eliminated by the extension of sovereign rights. On the contrary, the Europeans, confronted by the events of the two world wars, were forced to reflect on their own deficiencies with respect to the standard of civilization. There are no states in the world that fully live up to established **human rights** legislation. Second, the orthodox account fails to acknowledge that many newly established states in the contemporary international order lack many of the key attributes of statehood that were required before sovereignty would be extended to states in the European international order. States have been granted external sovereignty before internal sovereignty has been established. These states have been designated as 'quasi-states'. Indeed, it has been argued that in some parts of the globe, the situation has deteriorated even further and 'quasi-states' have now become **failed state**s and that these territories simply cannot be strait-jacketed into the Westphalian order that builds on the assumption of sovereign states. These assessments represent a serious challenge to the orthodox English School account that depicts the European international order being extended across the globe in an uncontroversial fashion. On the contrary, it has to be accepted that the European and extra-European international orders that were consolidated in the nineteenth century have fused in a complex and unstable fashion.

The future of sovereignty

It has been suggested by some political philosophers that the sovereign state has such a firm grip on the way that politics is conceived that it proves extraordinarily difficult to open up space for conceptualizing what politics could look like in the absence of the sovereign state. Poststructuralists in IR (see **poststructuralism**) have also stressed that because we are no longer living in a Westphalian era, politics, sovereignty and subjectivity all need to be redefined to take account of the fact that it no longer makes any sense to try to delineate the world in terms of distinct realms that operate inside and outside the sovereign state. Neither of these positions, however, takes sufficient account of how extensively the idea of sovereignty has been rethought within IR over the last two decades or so. For rather different reasons, realists, constructivists, and the English School have all come to the conclusion that the idea of a Westphalian era governed by an unchanging principle of sovereignty is simply untenable. Inevitably, these reassessments have affected how these divergent schools of thought have assessed the future of sovereignty.

Because realists acknowledge that sovereignty has never been a sacrosanct principle in the past, they have little reason to suppose that it will dictate the shape of international relations in the future. So from the realist perspective, states will constantly find that there are problems with trying to adhere to the idea of sovereign independence and they will search for and find pragmatic solutions that either violate or compromise sovereignty while still continuing to espouse the virtues of sovereignty. Indeed, international lawyers frequently push this argument further and insist that when states establish treaties that compromise their own sovereignty, they are, in fact, confirming and consolidating sovereignty.

Constructivists have looked closely at the theoretical and empirical implications of this position and demonstrated how the state practices that define and constitute sovereignty have changed radically across the centuries. From their perspective there is also no reason to suppose this process will come to a halt in the future and so it can be anticipated that the nature of sovereignty will continue to be reconstituted. The area that is most susceptible to redefinition at the moment, according to English school theorists, relates to humanitarian intervention. The International Commission on Intervention and Sovereignty has stressed, however, that intervention and sovereignty do not have to be regarded as mutually exclusive concepts and that there is a desperate need for the international community of states to accept that they have a responsibility to intervene, albeit under clearly specified circumstances, in order to protect human life. These circumstances, of course, are unlikely to be uncontested. Nevertheless, all three theoretical perspectives presuppose that sovereignty will continue to be a defining feature of international relations.

Further reading

Biersteker, T. J. and Weber, C. (eds) (1996) *State Sovereignty as Social Construct*, Cambridge: Cambridge University Press.

Gelber, H. G. (1997) *Sovereignty Through Interdependence*, London: Kluwer Law International.

Hinsley, F. H.(1986) *Sovereignty*, 2nd edn, Cambridge: Cambridge University Press.

Jackson, R. H. (1990) *Quasi-states, Sovereignty, International Relations and the Third World*, Cambridge: Cambridge University Press.

James, A. (1986) *Sovereign Statehood: The Basis of International Society*, London: Allen & Unwin.

Krasner, S. D. (1999) *Sovereignty: Organized Hypocrisy*, Princeton, NJ: Princeton University Press.

Krasner, S. D. (ed.) (2001*) Problematic Sovereignty: Contested Rules and Political Possibilities*, New York: Columbia University Press.

Lyons, G. and Mastanduno, M. (eds) (1995) *Beyond Westphalia?: State Sovereignty and International Intervention*, Baltimore, MD: Johns Hopkins University Press.

Philpott, D. (2001) *Revolutions in Sovereignty: How Ideas Shaped Modern International Relations*, Princeton, NJ: Princeton University Press.

Reus-Smit, C. (1999) *The Moral Purpose of the State*, Princeton, NJ: Princeton University Press.

Spruyt, H. (1997) *The Sovereign State and Its Competitors: An Analysis of Systems Change*, Princeton, NJ: Princeton University Press.

Thomson, J. E. (1994) *Mercenaries, Pirates and Sovereigns*, Princeton, NJ: Princeton University Press.

See also: constructivism; empire; humanitarian intervention; international society; realism; self-determination; state formation; standard of civilization; Westphalia

RICHARD LITTLE

Standard of civilization

A means historically used in **international law** to distinguish between civilized and uncivilized nations or peoples in order to determine membership in the **international society** of states. The concept entered international legal texts and practice in the eighteenth and nineteenth centuries under the influence of anthropologists and ethnologists who drew distinctions between civilized, barbarian, and savage peoples based on their respective capacities for social cooperation and organization. Operating primarily during the European colonial period, and sometimes referred to as the classical standard of civilization, it was a legal mechanism designed to set the benchmark for the ascent of non-European nations to the ranks of the civilized society of states. Membership in international society conferred full **sovereignty** upon a state entitling it to full **recognition** and protection under international law.

The general test of whether a nation was deemed civilized revolved around its degree of socio-political organization and capacity for self-government in accordance with accepted European standards. A civilized state required:

(a) basic institutions of government and public bureaucracy;
(b) organizational capacity for self-defense;
(c) published legal code and adherence to the rule of law; and
(d) recognition of international law and norms, including those on the conduct of **war** and diplomatic exchange.

If a nation could meet these requirements it was generally deemed to be a legitimate sovereign state entitled to full recognition as an international personality. In essence, a government had to be sufficiently stable to allow it to enter into binding commitments under international law, and possess the will and capacity to guarantee the life, liberty and property of members of foreign civilized states living and operating within its borders.

The inability of many non-European societies to meet these European criteria and the concomitant legal distinction that separated them from civilized societies led to the unequal treaty system of capitulations. The right of **extraterritoriality**, as it was also known, regulated relations between sovereign civilized states and quasi-sovereign uncivilized states in regard to their respective rights over, and obligations to, the citizens of civilized states living and operating in countries where capitulations were in force.

The formal standard of civilization was effectively rendered redundant at the close of World War Two. The abrogation of the laws of war as seen in the nature of the totalitarian aggression perpetrated by members of the 'civilized' world highlighted the anachronism of maintaining a legal distinction between civilized and uncivilized states. The use of nuclear weapons and the subsequent evolution of the concept of **mutually assured destruction** further undermined the **legitimacy** of distinguishing between degrees of civility. The war also prompted a growing number of sovereign states to recognize that the claims of anti-colonial movements in much of the **Third World** to their right of sovereign, independent self-government was increasingly justified and legitimate.

While it might be accurate to mark the post-war demise of the formal standard of civilization, that is not to say that something similar did not continue to serve much the same purpose in practice, at least in the conduct of international politics if not in international law. During the **cold war** era, the Westphalian states system was effectively a two-tiered system divided along much the same lines as in the colonial era. It was a system whereby the **superpower**s and their allies abided by an understanding that peace in Europe should be maintained at any cost, while at the same time the contest for influence in the Third World was keenly pursued, often by means of violent proxy wars.

Today the world continues to be divided according to states' capacities for socio-political organization or systems of government, and still in accordance with Western standards. Rarely are states still explicitly termed civilized or uncivilized, rather, distinctions are now drawn between states that are increasingly referred to as either well ordered or not well ordered; civic or predatory; postmodern, modern, or pre-modern; legitimate or rogue (see **rogue state**); and in the extreme, good or evil. This development, along with the post-cold war promulgation of ideas such as the **end of history** thesis, have made possible both implicit and explicit calls for the reintroduction of a standard of civilization for the twenty-first century. The post-cold war order is generally more receptive to suggestions that liberal democracy and the values associated with it, such as **human rights** and free markets, are universal aspirations. Hence comes the argument that human rights and democratic governance serve as the appropriate standard of civilization for the twenty-first century, and there is evidence that such a standard is at times applied in practice, albeit selectively. Some go further to suggest that human rights and democracy combined with policies that promote neoliberal (see **neoliberalism**) economic **globalization** are a more appropriate standard for the interdependent world of the twenty-first century.

As with the classical standard of civilization, the current measure of civilization revolves around non-Western states' capacity to govern themselves in such a manner that they can engage with the West in their adherence to international law. For some, the identification of different zones of civilization is nothing more than a description of existing or emergent political realities, but on another level its normative advocates see the West as the vanguard of global **order**. While there is a need to distinguish between different types of states on the basis of their **legitimacy**, there are

detrimental consequences to the enforcement of any standard of civilization. For the theory of different shades of civilization necessarily requires differential treatment – that is, double standards – where the boundaries of those zones intersect; on the one hand privileging members of the international society of civilized sovereign states, and on the other setting high barriers to entry for those who are excluded.

Further reading

Fidler, D. P. (2000) 'A Kinder, Gentler System of Capitulations? International Law, Structural Adjustment Policies, and the Standard of Liberal, Globalized Civilization', *Texas International Law Journal* 35(3), 387–413.

Gong, G. W. (1984) *The Standard of 'Civilization' in International Society*, Oxford: Oxford University Press.

Koskenniemi, M. (2001) *The Gentle Civilizer of Nations: the Rise and Fall of International Law, 1870–1960*, Cambridge: Cambridge University Press.

See also: clash of civilizations; decolonization; extraterritoriality; good governance; imperialism; international society; law of peoples; nation-state; neocolonialism; sovereignty

BRETT BOWDEN

State formation

Despite arguments that the effects of **globalization** may be undermining the **authority** of the **nation-state**, states remain crucially important actors in contemporary global politics and if scholars of international relations are to fully understand them and the sort of changes they may be going through, we also need to understand how this institutional form, which came to dominate the globe, developed. States have formed in different geographical areas, in different historical periods and under very different conditions. The early development of the modern state occurred in Western Europe, and this was followed by later episodes of state formation in the nineteenth century culminating in a number of new states gaining recognition after World War One; during the period of **decolonization** following World War Two; and, more recently, following the end of the **cold war**. Thus, while an understanding of the general processes involved in state formation is important we should also be attentive to the particularities of different epochs and, within these, the differences as well as similarities between states. Having said that, most work on state formation with which international relations scholars are familiar focuses on early modern state building in Western Europe and the discipline would benefit from a wider focus. Nonetheless, this is where this account begins. This is followed by a brief account of the successive phases of state formation and an overview of contending approaches.

The development of the modern state was a gradual process in which rulers in core areas of Western Europe, slowly gained centralized control over the means of violence and the means of revenue collection, resulting in the formation of the early 'core' states of Spain, England, and France. The first of these two interconnected processes began with monarchs wresting secular authority from the Catholic Church and the Holy Roman Empire, and disarming the nobility. In time, this consolidation of control of the means of violence would lead to the development of standing national armies, rather than the earlier reliance on mercenaries. As monarchs extended their rule, they were able to better organize the second aspect of control, the routine extraction of funds from their populations. This was something that they needed to do in order to fund the **war**s in which they were often engaged and it also played an important role in the economic **development** of states as feudalism gave way to **capitalism**.

Thus when we refer to the modern state we are referring to a centralized political **authority** which has legitimate control over the means of violence within a clearly demarcated physical territory and over a defined population, though exactly how this population has been defined has differed over time. While the territorial sovereign state has undergone many changes and challenges, the claim that it is the state, and the state alone, that legitimately controls and uses the means of violence remains a central aspect of the **legitimacy** claims made by states today. Implicit within this is the claim that when non-state actors use violent means, this is illegitimate in the absence of state sanction.

Phases of state formation

In the fourteenth century Europe was wracked by conflict. This crisis was exacerbated (or precipitated depending on your point of view) by economic recession, plague, widespread crop failures and **famine**. In a short period the population was decimated with the result that labor was scarce and those who sought to sell their labor began to move more freely and feudal authority structures lost much of their legitimacy. In short, this was a time of social and political fragmentation and conflict. Nonetheless, arising out of this devastation a number of monarchs managed to consolidate their authority in a surprisingly short time with Spain, England, and France emerging as the frontrunners.

Importantly, these rulers would not have seen themselves as 'state-builders' but they were intent on restoring order in their realms and expanding the reach of their authority. To do this they embarked on programs of centralizing authority and pacification within their proto-states and of war externally in order to either extend their imperial reach or to protect their realms from the imperial ambitions of others. In so doing they created the foundations of the territorial sovereign state and, at the same time, sharply defined the hitherto amorphous boundary between the domestic and the international realms. In so doing they were initiators of the transition to a new institutional form, which was imitated as it proved its viability over time. By the end of the twentieth century this institutional form would be the first form of political authority in history to be genuinely global in its reach.

The early states were also colonial powers that did not entertain any conception of the rights of colonial peoples to independence. However, by the nineteenth century and into the early twentieth century national sentiment was stirring within many colonial possessions but these claims would not come to fruition until after World War Two. In the nineteenth century both Italy and Germany became unified national states and in central and Eastern Europe nationalist sentiment, and the aspiration to independent statehood, was on the rise within the Habsburg, Russian, and Ottoman Empires. Greece gained independence from the latter in the 1820s and Serbia, Romania and Bulgaria followed suit later in the century. World War One dealt the final blow to these **empire**s and as the war drew to a close a number of groups claimed independent statehood, including Czechoslovakia, Yugoslavia, and Poland, while others such as Hungary and Turkey that had been at the core of empires, were also recognized as sovereign states, within newly demarcated boundaries. The tasks faced by state builders varied, but all of them faced the problem of building a cohesive, legitimate, central authority and a unitary national identity. This was not as easy as nationalists might have hoped (see **nationalism**). Despite shared ethno-linguistic characteristics, in many cases there were very different histories to be overcome by those that came together in the new states. For example, in Yugoslavia, Croatia, and Slovenia had been part of the Hapsburg Empire while Serbia, Montenegro, and Bosnia had been part of the Ottoman Empire.

Despite these often very different histories the right to national **self-determination** that was acknowledged in the post-World War One period was based on a racial and ethnic conception of national identity. However, as the populations were extremely heterogeneous, no matter how the boundaries were drawn it was inevitable that a number of minorities would find themselves within each new state. This did not 'fit' with nationalist ideology, particularly as minorities were likely to have loyalties to neighboring states. Many Germans, Austrians, Russians, and Hungarians found themselves outside their 'home' states, giving rise to the fear of **irredentism**. At the international level there was much concern that minorities would be vulnerable to discrimination and ill-treatment and for the first time this was seen as an issue for which the international community should take responsibility. The **League of Nations** Minorities Treaties were an attempt to set standards for the appropriate treatment of such minorities. However the new states, which came under the provision of the treaties system, saw the treaties as discriminatory. They were the object of much resentment and proved to be ineffective in protecting minority rights. Furthermore, Germany did not come under the treaties' system yet it was here that the Holocaust took the lives of an estimated six million

Jews during World War Two, as well as those of other minority groups. Thus when colonial possessions gained independence in the post-World War Two period the international community shied away from racial or ethnic definitions of the national communities that were to gain independent statehood, referring instead to the existing colonial boundaries as the boundaries of the new states.

Just as World War One brought the European and Ottoman Empires to an end, so too World War Two contributed to the collapse of colonial empires in Asia and Africa. Claims by non-Western peoples to the right to self-determination were rejected after World War One but after 1945 they pressed their claims even more vigorously. Although some colonial powers (for example the Dutch in what was to become Indonesia) resisted these claims, the legitimacy of this form of rule no longer held. Since 1945, when the **United Nations** (UN) had fifty member states at its inception, more than eighty post-colonial states have joined the organization. So what then was the process of state building that took place in post-colonial states? Under the Declaration of the Granting of Independence to Colonial Countries and Peoples (UN General Assembly 1960), it was asserted that all people have the right to independence and that this should take effect immediately without reference to whether or not a country was 'ready' in social, political or economic terms. Cast as a **human rights** claim, the declaration emphasized the injustices suffered under colonial rule and this legitimated immediate independence.

While it is hard to generalize about such a large number of states, these state builders faced a number of tasks under conditions very different to those faced by early state builders. They inherited domestic institutions that were often inappropriate and were faced with having to govern states that existed territorially and legally but which, once the first euphoria of independence had passed, faced problems of maintaining a legitimate central authority and, often, a lack of state capacity. They were also faced with the task of creating national identities out of great diversity, as the new boundaries enclosed many different ethnic groups (or in some cases cut across communities). The simultaneous tasks of state and nation building have been undertaken in different ways but the potential for the ill-treatment of minorities was not allayed by the rejection of race or ethnic identity as the basis of the international **recognition** of the right to self-determination. Many states soon suffered instability, elite **corruption** and the emergence of authoritarian regimes, some of which received arms from their respective **superpower** patrons during the cold war. Access to modern weaponry served to make such regimes resistant to domestic challenges to their authority.

As Charles Tilly (1985, 1990) points out, Western European states formed over a number of centuries and, over time, rulers conceded authority to their subjects and refrained from overt coercion to maintain their legitimacy. States that came into existence in the twentieth century, in contrast, arrived in a very different environment where external military support could mitigate against claims for democratic government. As the current process of **democratization** demonstrates, institutional development takes time and there is no guarantee that democratic, representative institutions will be a universal outcome.

In the post-cold war era the world witnessed yet another phase of state formation as the Soviet Union collapsed, followed by the violent disintegration of the former Yugoslavia and the peaceful 'velvet divorce' between the Czech

Republic and Slovakia. War in the former Yugoslavia witnessed the return of the 'ethnic principle' of state formation in the claims made by nationalists who embarked on programs of **ethnic cleansing** in attempts to create homogeneous national states. The international community did not accept this as legitimate, yet in practice conflicting signals were given to the contending parties. Regional concern with order and stability often took precedence over demands for the respect of **human rights**. There have also been conflicts in parts of the former Soviet Union, as struggles over what form the state should take are still being played out in the Central Asia and the Caucasus.

From this brief overview it is clear that later phases of state formation have taken place under very different conditions to earlier ones. The early statemakers not only 'made' their states, but as they jostled for position against one another they created the **international society** into which later states were admitted at independence. Thus new states arrived into an increasingly institutionalized international environment and were constituted according to dominant norms within this system. Such norms can of course be challenged or revised, as the story of the changing content of self-determination in the wake of the two World Wars and the delegitimation of colonialism demonstrates. What this should alert us to, as both Tilly and Georg Sørensen (1997) point out, is that while we may identify many similarities between states at the international level we should also be sensitive to the different conditions under which they were constituted and what this means for their governance, both domestic and international. This is not an evolutionary argument according to which there is a single path that all states must follow. On the contrary, we must recognize that

legal recognition as a state (or juridical sovereignty) is an important part of the story but states have different histories and varying capacities for empirical sovereignty, that is, the capacity to function effectively at the domestic as well as the international level. The issue that highlights many of these problems is contemporary state failure (see **failed state**) and the emergence of various forms of **humanitarian intervention**, which are beyond the purview of this entry. However, there are important questions to be asked about the extent to which the contemporary international community can intervene and assist the rebuilding of states. We now turn to a brief overview of different approaches to state formation.

Contending approaches to state formation

Mainstream theories of international relations explicitly bracket off processes of state formation. For example, realist scholars (see **realism**) such as Kenneth Waltz (1979) focus on the anarchic structure (see **anarchy**) of the **international system** and how it forces states to undertake 'self-help' in the absence of any overarching authority. Thus, what happens inside states or how states came to exist in the first place is not relevant to this model. As long as the basic functions of statehood are performed by a central government that has control over the means of violence, over a defined population and over a defined territory, we do not need to inquire further into the nature of the state in order to study international relations. Other mainstream theories, such as liberal institutionalism, argue that states do not only operate in terms of self-help but can cooperate for mutual gain. Despite this difference, they share realism's basic assumption that the state can be assumed to be a rational, unitary actor. This view was challenged in the 1980s by critical theorists (see **critical theory**) who argued that rather than regarding states as presocial 'facts', scholars of international relations should investigate the way in which states, and the states system of which they are part, are constituted through social, political and cultural practices. Thus Robert Cox (1982) argued that understanding international relations requires investigation of the different forms of state/society entities in history. He focused on the role of production in state formation and its impact on international relations, as social forces within states overflow state boundaries, and the international system in turn acts back on states and their constituent societies. Critical theorists argued that there is nothing inevitable about the dominance of the modern state as an institutional form and it should not be taken for granted. Understanding how it had become dominant would allow insight into possible changes and challenges to this institutional form of rule in the international system. Nonetheless, most critical theorists were not working specifically on state formation so much as challenging the reification of dominant ideas such as sovereignty and territoriality as well as critiquing the epistemological bases of mainstream theories.

In general, until the advent of critical approaches, international relations scholars had overlooked accounts of state formation. However, scholars in other fields have not done so and international relations scholars have been able to draw on the work of historical sociologists (see **historical sociology**) and institutional economists. It is to a brief overview of their accounts that we now turn.

Materialist accounts, such as that of Immanuel Wallerstein (1974) explain the development of states and the states system as a function of the world economy,

stressing the economic interests of state-builders. While Wallerstein characterizes the disorder of the fourteenth century as the outcome of economic pressures, the fifteenth century construction of what was to become a new order – involving neither the total collapse of the world-economy nor its transformation into a world-empire – was understood as a prerequisite of economic resurgence. Thus he argues that the capitalist world-economy needed and assisted the centralization of authority within a number of core states such as Spain, France, England, and later, the Netherlands. In this view 'strong states' were necessary for economic **development**. Statism, the claim that states should legitimately be the holders of centralized power, was the prevailing ideology of the world-economy. In this account economic factors are clearly seen to determine political outcomes. States were formed in response to the needs of the world economy and they, in turn were structured differently according to the needs of the world economy. This view has been criticized for being economically reductionist and for failing to account for the more complex relationship between the political, economic and indeed the cultural aspects of state formation. Thus, critics argue that it is not adequate to see states and the states system as merely the political superstructure of the capitalist world economy.

Institutional accounts also take the economic motivation of actors as a given, though from a position of methodological individualism rather than being driven by the logic of the capitalist system as such. This means that events can be explained as outcomes of the rational choices made by important individual actors. Thus state building in early modern Europe is understood as the expression of forms of institutional rationality that were dominant at the time. As noted above, even within the same epochs of state formation there were differences between states, and institutional accounts have much to tell us about the choices that state-builders made with regards to property rights and sort of states that resulted from their choices. Like Wallerstein, institutionalists take the interests of state builders for granted, assuming that they were motivated entirely by the desire for economic gain. Douglass North and Robert Thomas (1973) argue that the modern state became the most viable form of political and economic organization because it was the most efficient provider of private property rights. Granted, in the earliest phases of state formation coercion was the most salient means of consolidating power. However, as rulers engaged in internal pacification and external expansion via war and dynastic marriage, they needed increased revenue in order to maintain themselves and they chose different options to generate revenue. According to this view, the key to the different paths of development in early modern Europe are the deals rulers struck in order to raise revenue: the concessions they made, who they made them to and how they made them. Thus the institution of private property rights developed out of the trading of privileges for revenue that occurred between rulers and their subjects, particularly the nobility and the rising merchant class. Those rulers who instituted and enforced private property rights allowed economic efficiency and growth and provided a model of success, while those who continued to support monopoly rights, as in Spain, blocked innovation, efficiency and longer term growth. Thus England and the United Provinces (the Netherlands) became successful capitalist states while Spain, an earlier front-runner, declined.

Despite the emphasis here on institutional choices, the institutional approach could, nonetheless, lead us to assume that the dominance of the *form* of the modern state was inevitable. In his account of state formation Hendrick Spruyt (1994) argues that the success of this institutional form against competitors that developed in late medieval and early modern Europe, namely city states and city leagues, needs to be explained rather than taken for granted. What then made the sovereign state so successful as a form of rule? According to Spruyt, what became the nation-state outlasted its competitors because it could meet both the internal needs of centralized authority and administration, and the external need to be recognized as a legitimate actor that could make and keep agreements in the long term. At the center of these capacities is the concept of territorial sovereignty. The territorial demarcation of the fixed boundaries of the political authority meant that the reciprocal recognition of states as legitimate political actors was possible. Because states were compatible in this way, they could make and keep long-term agreements and the success of this institutional form meant that others either copied it or defected to it.

Spruyt accepts the important role of warfare in state making but asks why the state was better than its competitors at waging war. Size and military capacity alone cannot explain its superiority, as at times city states and city leagues outstripped states on these criteria. What was crucial, Spruyt argues, was institutional efficiency, and the key to effective institutional organization was the presence of 'clear sovereign authority'. It is the presence or absence of such authority that accounts for variation between units. If we look at the competitors to the sovereign state, we see a great many differences. City leagues had no internal borders, no hierarchy, no agreements on weights or currency, and diverse legal codes. Sovereign actors benefited from the Leagues' lack of unity. Importantly, the lack of a clearly defined sovereign authority made it hard for the leagues to *credibly* commit to international agreements. Like city leagues, city states had no internal hierarchy, lacked internal unity, and made no moves toward the rationalization of economic practices or the unification of legal codes. However, they did survive for quite some time. Spruyt argues that this was possible because the city states were represented by dominant cities and were thus able to behave like sovereign states (i.e. as unitary actors, despite their internal differences) in their external actions, and were thus considered legitimate actors in the international system.

While institutional accounts give important insights into the variation in institutional forms and patterns of bargaining within states between rulers and subject, they can be criticized on the same grounds as Wallerstein, that is, not all decisions made by state-builders can necessarily be explained in terms of the desire for economic gain. Thus we now turn to power based explanations.

There are a number of power-based explanations of state building, which in different ways emphasize the role of violence in the development of sovereign states. Such explanations trace the process by which monarchs gained control over the means of violence and taxation, both of which were necessary to further war making. An important part of this process was the 'taming' of the nobility, which occurred over a long period. The means by which absolutist rulers gained ascendancy, by manipulating the **balance of power** between the nobility and the bourgeois, is exemplified by Louis XIV's France. Louis successfully maintained his own position by

controlling and manipulating tensions between these competing groups.

Power-based explanations of state formation identify two key factors that drove the development of the state: changes in military technology, and the pressure of the states system as a primary 'source' and 'condition' of state formation. Priority is given to the international system as the structure that shapes states as agents. However, Charles Tilly offers a nuanced power-based explanation of state formation that takes into account institutional developments and economic factors. Like the institutionalists, Tilly argues that although war and coercion were the driving force behind the formation and early development of states, as states stabilized and grew they became less coercive as institutions developed, and capital and rulers struck bargains with one another. Unlike institutionalists, however, Tilly rejects the idea that processes of state building were the outcome of rational choices. Nor does he reduce state formation to a by-product of the development of the capitalist world-economy. In his view states emerged as the contingent outcome of the struggle for power which pushed rulers to consolidate their realms in order to fight wars.

Tilly identifies how the process of internal consolidation was concomitant with the differentiation of the internal and external aspects of the state. In the early modern period, states had to deal externally with the impact of other states and the pressure from the system of states as it began to take shape. These processes were inextricably bound up with the struggles over centralization, pacification, and the construction of single, sovereign identities, all of which were internal to states. As they armed against external threats, states gained an internal monopoly over the means of violence and the boundary between the internal and the external aspects of states sharpened. Thus, Tilly argues, states made war and war made states. Tilly asks important questions about state formation with equally significant implications. Early modern states might have begun as 'protection rackets' whereby state rulers offered protection to their subjects from threats that they themselves created but, as institutionalists argue, as Western European states stabilized over time they became less coercive. Institutions developed to mediate relations between national governments and citizens.

While materialist, institutionalist and power-based accounts discuss 'internal pacification' or the 'homogenization' of populations within states, their primary focus is not on the construction of collective identities within states as an integral part of state formation. In contrast, constructivist accounts (see **constructivism**) of state formation focus on the construction of interests and identities both within the state and internationally. Underlying this approach is the argument that the shift to the territorial sovereign state was a shift to a new form of collective political identity. An important early contribution to this is John Gerard Ruggie's (1993) argument that the changes that brought about the modern states system represent an epochal shift to a new spatial configuration of political authority – the territorially bounded sovereign state – and to a new social *episteme* in which the way the world is conceived also radically changed. Ruggie's interest in the development of both modernity and the early modern state arises from a desire to understand contemporary conditions in their historical context. He is interested in exploring whether we are once again seeing an epochal shift toward a new form of post-sovereign authority, particularly in Europe. Other constructivist

accounts examine the targeting of minorities in the construction of collective state identities in both the pre-nationalist and nationalist phases of state formation in Europe (Rae 2002) and the institutional shifts that have occurred as territorial-state sovereign actors were nationalized in the nineteenth and twentieth centuries (Hall 1999).

Thus there are a number of different accounts of state formation, which emphasize material, institutional, or power-based factors, with more recent constructivist accounts investigating the social construction of collective identities. While a number of scholars have investigated early state formation in order to better understand contemporary states, international relations scholarship would benefit from more sustained attention to the conditions under which states have formed in the twentieth century and the ramifications of these processes for the contemporary system of states.

Further reading

Ayoob, M. (1995) *The Third World Security Predicament: State Making, Regional Conflict, and the International System*, Boulder, CO: Lynne Rienner.

Cox, R. (1982) 'Social Forces, States and World Orders: Beyond International Relations Theory', *Millennium: Journal of International Studies* 10(2), 126–55.

Hall, R. B. (1999) *National Collective Identity: Social Constructs and International Systems*, New York: Columbia University Press.

North, D. C. and Thomas, R. P. (1973) *The Rise of the Western World: A New Economic History*, Cambridge: Cambridge University Press.

Rae, H. (2002) *State Identities and the Homogenisation of Peoples*, Cambridge: Cambridge University Press.

Ruggie, J. G. (1993) 'Territoriality and Beyond: Problematizing Modernity in

International Relations', *International Organization*, 47(1), 139–74.

Sørensen, G. (1997) 'An Analysis of Contemporary Statehood: Consequences for Conflict and Cooperation', *Review of International Studies* 23(3), 253–69.

Spruyt, H. (1994) *The Sovereign State and Its Competitors*, Princeton, NJ: Princeton University Press.

Tilly, C. (1985), 'War Making and State-Making as Organized Crime', in Peter B. Evans, Dietrich Reuschemeyer and Theda Skocpol (eds) *Bringing the State Back In*, Cambridge: Cambridge University Press, 169–96.

Tilly, C. (1990) *Coercion, Capital and European States, AD 990–1990*, Oxford: Blackwell.

Wallerstein, I. (1974) *The Modern World-System*, Vol. 1, San Diego, CA: Academic Press.

Waltz, K. (1979) *Theory of International Politics*, Reading, MA: Addison Wesley.

See also: historical sociology; nation-state; nationalism; self-determination; sovereignty

HEATHER RAE

Strategic culture

The manner in which established cultural beliefs and customs within a state shapes its approach to the use of force. The term was first coined by Jack Snyder (1977) to elucidate what he portrayed as the contrasting national belief systems shaping American and Soviet thinking about military doctrine in general and nuclear strategy in particular. According to Snyder, strategic culture was the sum total of ideas, conditioned emotional responses, and patterns of habitual behavior that members of a national strategic community have acquired through instruction or imitation and share with one another. Others have sought to broaden the concept by according increased emphasis to outcomes, rather than process. For instance, some scholars have suggested that the United States' uniquely determined pursuit of **ballistic missile defense** since 1945 reflects an intense fear of pre-emptive attack, ingrained deeply within the US strategic psyche traceable to the strikes on Pearl Harbor in 1941.

A useful way of illustrating the term further is to compare and contrast ideas about Western strategic culture of the type said to be found in North America and Europe, and Eastern strategic culture supposedly typified by states in the Asian region, especially China. A comparison is often drawn between the thinking of the nineteenth century Prussian military theorist, Karl von Clausewitz (1780–1831) and the fourth century BC Chinese theorist Sun Tzu. In his writings on strategy, Clausewitz attached priority to the idea of offensive **war** aimed at the total destruction of enemy forces, which he identified as the main criterion for achieving success. Although emphasizing the importance of victory in war, Sun Tzu argued that it could be attained with a minimum of fighting – by knowing the enemy 'inside out', deceiving the enemy prior to and during any conflict, and by exploiting the enemy's psychological weaknesses (referred to as the 'indirect approach' to warfare). In contrast to Clausewitz, Sun Tzu maintained that the supreme art of war is to subdue the enemy without fighting. The Vietnam War can be seen as a classic clash of these two strategic cultures, with the United States measuring its success primarily by reference to the enemy 'body count' in direct combat engagements, while the North Vietnamese devoted primacy to undermining the will of the United States to prosecute the conflict as a whole.

However, we need to avoid excessive generalization when talking about strategic culture. The fact that the strategic cultures of individual countries in specific regions may share certain themes does not mean that they are synonymous. It may be tempting to accept the notion that there exists a homogeneous European strategic culture or a uniform Asian strategic culture, but it overlooks the very real fissures separating countries in these regions on the issue of strategy. In the case of Europe, Germany's geography and its historical experience mean that its strategic policymakers have views about the use of force that are inconsistent with those of their counterparts in Britain whose history and geographical circumstances distinguish it from other countries on the continent. In Asia, which is even more diverse in terms of historical experience, regime type, and geography, there is much less scope for convergence among states.

While falling out of favor in the immediate post-cold war era, the concept of strategic culture has experienced something of a renaissance in recent years. A number of scholars have argued that strategic culture provides a critical variable that can supplement, and in some cases overshadow, the role of material capabilities in explaining state behavior with respect to the use of force in international relations. Increasingly, the term has been associated with the constructivist paradigm in international relations theory (see **constructivism**). Nevertheless, the value of the concept itself as an explanatory tool has been the subject of a spirited debate within the literature.

Proponents of the concept maintain that it provides a useful window into understanding the reasons why individual states embrace certain doctrines and policies as part of their national strategy. They argue that it is more than just an academic exercise in abstract theorizing. According to this perspective, recognizing the significance of strategic culture serves four inter-related purposes. First, and most importantly, it erodes the impact of ethnocentrism in strategic analysis. That is, it helps to overcome, or at least mitigate, the effects of 'mirror imaging' in dealing with other states. Second, it improves the capacity to 'know thine enemy' by sharpening insights into the intentions of other decision makers which can contribute to more complete and thus more accurate intelligence assessments. Third, it sensitizes the analyst to the role and impact of history and political culture in determining an individual state's military posture, which can help to circumvent the ever-present trap of misperception. And fourth, understanding a state's strategic culture can help to explain what superficially appears to be 'irrational' behavior.

In contrast, those critical of the concept's utility argue that culture is essentially peripheral in determining how and why states choose particular strategic postures. Culture may have some effect at the margins, but there are other, more significant variables at play. From this perspective, the nature of the external **security** environment, the structural dimensions of **balance of power** politics, geographical circumstances, and material political, economic, and military capabilities are the decisive variables shaping states' strategic doctrines and policies. Furthermore, advocates of this viewpoint maintain that reifying the concept of strategic culture runs the risk of exaggerating supposedly 'intrinsic' differences between states. If one looks hard enough for cultural distinctiveness, one will find it.

While it is important to be aware of the debate between these contrasting schools of thought, we can appreciate the role of strategic culture without necessarily endorsing the view that it is the dominant variable determining individual countries' strategic postures. One avenue of scholarship that needs to be developed further in order to determine the extent to which strategic culture can contribute toward explaining state behavior are country case studies. Only with a better understanding of the approach of individual states to the formulation and execution of strategy can we gain a greater insight into the value of strategic culture as an explanatory variable in international relations.

Further reading

Booth, K. (1979) *Strategy and Ethnocentrism*, London: Croom Helm.

Booth, K. and Trood, R. (eds) (1999) *Strategic Culture in the Asia-Pacific Region*, Basingstoke: Palgrave.

Gray, C. (1999). 'Strategic Culture as Context: The First Generation of Theory Strikes Back', *Review of International Studies* 25(1), 49–69.

Johnston, A. (1995) 'Thinking About Strategic Culture', *International Security* 19(4), 32–64.

Lantis, J. (2002) 'Strategic Culture and National Security Policy', *International Studies Review* 4(3), 87–114.

Snyder, J. (1977) *The Soviet Strategic Culture: Implications for Limited Nuclear Operations*, Santa Monica, CA: Rand Corporation.

See also: non-offensive defense; security; security community

ANDREW O'NEIL

Structural adjustment program (SAP)

Structural adjustment programs involve large scale, long-term, concessional lending by multilateral organizations to low income countries under the condition that the borrowing countries will shift the structure of their economy in the direction of a market oriented system. Adjustment programs may vary considerably from country to country, but they usually require states to sell state owned enterprises to private citizens, limit the growth of state financed domestic credit by raising interest rates, reduce inefficient subsidies and social programs, relax import tariffs and quota restrictions to increase competitive economic activity, and dismantle ineffective controls on the movement of financial capital. The central aims of the program are to restore the role of market prices as an information signaling mechanism and to eliminate policies that distort market-based incentives. The policies are guided by a belief that economic liberalization can significantly strengthen aggregate supply, which is viewed as an essential component in restoring a country's external creditworthiness and ensuring long-term economic viability. Conditions can be enforced either as a precondition for 'stand-by' loans and extended financial assistance, or through a combination of economic surveillance and the ability to withhold the release of loan installments (tranches) for failure to meet agreed performance criteria. Structural adjustment programs usually have a time horizon that exceeds three years.

Structural adjustment is not the same thing as economic stabilization. Stabilization involves policies to overcome short-term deficits in the balance of payments and to control inflation. Fiscal spending restrictions and monetary measures (including currency devaluation) are used to reduce aggregate demand and encourage increased exports. Stabilization programs usually have a time horizon of one to two years. The failure of stabilization policies to restore economic growth in developing economies as well as a decline in access to international finance resulted in a greater emphasis on supplementing macroeconomic stabilization policies with long-term structural adjustment by the mid-1980s.

Critics commonly contend that SAPs were imposed on developing countries under crisis conditions, without suffi-cient institutional authority, and that they included inappropriate and coun-terproductive policy components. It is correct that immediately following the 1982 Latin American debt crisis, debtor countries were strongly encouraged to undertake **International Monetary Fund** (IMF) supervised stabilization and struc-tural adjustment programs in exchange for country-specific debt rescheduling and refinancing negotiations with public and private creditors. As default by a cartel of debtor countries would have threatened the stability of the interna-tional financial system, and conse-quently further decreased the needed access to credit in low-income countries for **development** and debt servicing, the preference for negotiated settlements over default was appropriate. However, the IMF does deserve blame for not suf-ficiently emphasizing substantial debt forgiveness as a necessary component of the negotiation process with private and public creditors.

In terms of institutional authority, the IMF has a mandate from its member countries to develop countermeasures to trends that threaten an increasingly inte-grated international financial system. Thus, the IMF is authorized to handle complex negotiations between banking syndicates and sovereign borrowers. Although the leading role in administer-ing SAPs has shifted back and forth between the **World Bank** and the IMF over the years, this is not evidence of a lack of institutional authority. Although the World Bank developed its first struc-tural adjustment program in 1979, the World Bank allowed the IMF to take the lead in managing the fallout from the debt crisis in the early 1980s. In the immediate aftermath of the debt crisis, the World Bank continued to focus on long-term development issues. The World Bank became more involved after

the 1985 annual Fund/Bank joint meet-ing in which US Treasury Secretary, James A. Baker, requested additional financial support from the World Bank group and the Inter-American Develop-ment Bank (IADB). After an episode in which the World Bank offered four loans to Argentina while the IMF continued to insist on more substantial fiscal reforms, the multilateral organizations began developing better policy coordination.

The most penetrating criticisms have argued that the design of SAPs is detri-mental to the economic viability of low-income countries. However, as the IMF and World Bank believe that such coun-tries cannot achieve long-term economic growth without structural adjustment, it could be argued that the multilateral institutions are acting in the interests of the debtor countries. They provide assis-tance to debtor countries in designing adjustment programs and support those programs through their own financial facilities and by cajoling commercial banks to continue lending. Moreover, it is necessary to note that countries seek-ing multilateral assistance are already experiencing serious economic difficul-ties. Measuring the success or failure of SAPs is difficult since it is not possible to know *ex post facto* how a country would have fared with a different program design and implementation, or indeed without any adjustment program.

Nevertheless, critics contend that adjustment programs often hinder the critical role of developmental states in promoting economic growth. The need for strong states to overcome market risks, catalyze entrepreneurial activities, enforce legal codes, and supply public goods in late industrializing societies has been well documented in the 'develop-mental state' literature. Hence, policies designed to expand market forces *at the expense of* state capacity in developing countries are counterproductive. SAPs that promote financial liberalization also may contribute to the destabilization of the domestic monetary system in countries with weak currencies and insufficient financial regulatory agencies, as demonstrated during the East Asian financial crisis in the late 1990s. Finally, critics have linked SAPs to increased income inequality and severe hardship from the termination of food and social subsidies.

Although the criticisms are valid, they often fail to examine the bargaining that occurs between a multilateral institution and its member countries as well as the level of institutional learning that happens over time. As the debt crisis receded in the late 1980s, the IMF and World Bank became increasingly flexible in their policy recommendations and even endorsed certain heterodox approaches to structural adjustment. In response to external critics and internal debate, the IMF began working with the World Bank, UNICEF, and the **International Labor Organization** (ILO) in the mid-1980s to redesign adjustment programs to mitigate their negative effects on the poor through targeted subsidies, direct wage support, and the protection of education and health expenditures. These policies, embodied in the slogan 'structural adjustment with a human face' have shifted the main goals of adjustment policies to include poverty reduction, human development, and debt-service relief.

Finally, it should be noted that many criticisms of SAPs are often predicated on the assumption that technocrats and other policymaking elites in the developing world were opposed to the end goal of structural adjustment. However, elites in low-income countries often silently endorsed the end goal while vociferously decrying the IMF and World Bank for the 'imposition' of austerity measures. Nevertheless, through inter- and intra-institutional debate and

learning, the character of structural adjustment has gradually been transformed to incorporate the goal of poverty alleviation.

Further reading

Boughton, J. (2001) *Silent Revolution: The International Monetary Fund 1979–1989*, Washington, DC: International Monetary Fund.

Haggard, S. and Kaufman, R. (eds) (1992) *The Politics of Economic Adjustment: International Constraints, Distributive Conflicts, and the State*, Princeton, NJ: Princeton University Press.

Nelson, J. M. (ed.) (1990) *Economic Crisis and Policy Choice: The Politics of Adjustment in the Third World*, Princeton, NJ: Princeton University Press.

See also: conditionality; good governance; International Monetary Fund; neoliberalism; World Bank

VIKASH YADAV

Structural violence

This is a key concept in the field of **peace studies** and was first coined by one of the pioneers in the field, Johan Galtung (1985). Most of us think of peace intuitively in negative terms, as the absence of war or armed conflict. Peace is the opposite to what is observable, measurable and very real in its direct effects – **war**. Thus throughout the years of the **cold war** between the former Soviet Union and the United States, many of those observers who supported nuclear **deterrence** and the condition of **mutually assured destruction** (MAD) claimed that whatever its costs, it helped to maintain a 'long peace' between the two main antagonists. However, the idea of structural violence (and its associated term 'positive peace') refers not merely to the observable use of force between states, but anything avoidable that prevents or impedes human fulfilment or self-realization. In turn, the latter is usually conceived by peace researchers in terms of the satisfaction of fundamental human needs, which can be physiological, ecological, economic and spiritual. The concept of structural violence, therefore, is much broader than the conventional focus of students in the Anglo-American study of international relations on war and the use of direct, physical armed force between states.

More specifically, the term alludes to the structures that maintain the dominance of one group at the center of **power** over another group, usually the majority, at the periphery. For the latter, structural violence can manifest itself as low wages, illiteracy, and poor health, few legal or political rights, and very limited control over their lives. If they resist or try to change their condition of misery by direct action, they may be met with direct violence.

The concept of structural violence was first used in the context of colonial situations. Galtung himself drew upon his fieldwork in Rhodesia under British colonial rule. Today, the concept is used more widely to encompass the enduring and often insidious ways in which harm is inflicted upon individuals by repressive political, economic, and cultural structures. In comparison with direct violence, structural violence works slowly but some would argue that it kills many more people in the long term. One way of measuring structural violence is to subtract average life expectancy for the world from the highest national life expectancy, year by year, and divide by the highest life expectancy to provide a rough indicator of preventable, premature deaths. This translates into at least 17 million people per year; usually children in the **Third World**, who die from hunger or preventable disease.

Of course, death is not the only effect of structural violence on its victims. There are four types of violence in global politics. First, there is the *classical violence* of the conventional literature, which refers to the deliberate infliction of pain, such as in war, torture, or inhuman and degrading punishment. Second, there is the *deprivation* of our fundamental material needs for shelter, clothing, food, and water. Third, *repression* refers to the loss of human freedoms to choose our beliefs and speak out on their behalf. Finally, *alienation* is a form of structural violence against our identity and our non-material needs for community and relations with others. Structural violence refers to the second, third, and fourth types of violence. It does not need to be observed taking place between a perpetrator and a victim. Rather, it may be built into a social order or political and economic structure.

Just as the absence of war (or negative peace) is the preferred alternative to direct violence, positive peace is preferred to structural violence. In essence, positive peace involves the presence of structures that provide increasing degrees of political liberty and social justice. The concept of structural violence has little explanatory use, however. It is simply a way of describing what, in the Third World in particular, is a familiar, if depressing, reality. There is no obvious link between structural and direct violence – poverty and oppression does not necessarily lead to revolt. The concept of structural violence was an interesting concept in helping to define the scope of peace studies and it remains a useful rhetorical device for activists who seek to justify struggles against economic oppression. One might argue, however, that the concept is far too broad. Not only are there perfectly good terms to describe what often is called structural violence (e.g. injustice, alienation, oppression, etc.), but there is also something distasteful in conflating such phenomena with Nazi **genocide**. Nevertheless, for revolutionaries, structural violence provides a good reason for armed struggle. By blurring the distinction between direct violence and other forms of 'violence', use of the former to end the latter is thereby justified.

Further reading

Galtung, J. (1985) 'Twenty-five Years of Peace Research: Ten Challenges and Some Responses', *Journal of Peace Research* 22, 141–58.

Lawler, P. (1995) *A Question of Values: Johan Galtung's Peace Research*, Boulder, CO: Lynne Rienner.

See also: failed state; peace studies; power

MARTIN GRIFFITHS

Suicide terrorism

Over the past decade, several countries all over the world have been forced to contend with the phenomenon of suicide attacks. Radical activists from such diverse countries as Iraq, Turkey, Sri Lanka, Lebanon, as well as Palestinians have elected to use suicide as a weapon in terrorist attacks aimed at various targets – both civilian and military – where large crowds tend to gather.

Suicide attacks constitute an additional stage in the escalation of **terrorism**, with the clear intention of causing the maximum number of casualties and damage, and to strike a blow to public morale. A suicide attack is an operational method in which the very act of the attack is dependent upon the death of the perpetrator. The terrorist is fully aware that if he or she does not die, the planned attack will not be implemented. The attack is usually carried out by acti-

vating explosives worn or carried by the terrorist in the form of a portable explosive charge, or planted in a vehicle.

It is important to correctly define a suicide attack, for there are different types of attacks that may be mistakenly considered as belonging to this special category. On many occasions, the perpetrator of an attack sets out with the knowledge that there is a good chance of being killed in the course of an attack (for example in trying to force a bus over a cliff). In spite of the imminent danger to the terrorist's life, as long as there is a possibility of the attack being carried out without the terrorist being forced to kill himself or herself during the course of the attack, this is not a suicide attack. Sometimes the terrorist makes concrete preparations for the possibility of death as a result of the attack (preparing a will, carrying out purification ceremonies, etc.). However, these preparations in themselves do not turn the attack into a suicide attack. In some attacks, the terrorists are equipped with arms or explosives for blowing themselves up should the attack go wrong, (for example if the attack fails, or if **security** forces break into a building where terrorists are holding hostages). The existence of such arms or explosives – and even the decision to use them – does not constitute adequate grounds for the attack to be defined as a suicide attack. In a true suicide attack, terrorists know that the attack will not be executed if they are not killed in the process.

Suicide attacks are attractive to terrorist organizations, as they offer them a variety of advantages. First, they usually result in many casualties and cause extensive damage. Second, suicide attacks attract wide media coverage. A suicide attack is a newsworthy event for the media as it indicates a display of great determination and inclination for self-sacrifice on the part of the terrorists.

Third, although a suicide attack is a very primitive and simple attack, the use of suicide tactics guarantees that the attack will be carried out at the most appropriate time and place with regard to the circumstances at the target location. This guarantees the maximum number of casualties (in contrast to the use of technical means such as a time bomb or even a remote controlled explosive charge). In this regard the suicide bomber is no more than a sophisticated bomb – a carrier that brings the explosive device to the right location and detonates it at the right time.

In a suicide attack, as soon as the terrorist has set off on the mission success is virtually guaranteed. It is extremely difficult to counter suicide attacks once the terrorist is on their way to the target; even if the security forces do succeed in stopping the terrorist before the intended target is reached, the terrorist can still activate the charge and cause damage. Thus the need for accurate intelligence concerning the plans of the terrorist organizations is crucial. Fourth, planning and executing the escape route after a terror attack has occurred is usually one of the most complicated and problematic stages of any terrorist attack. Suicide attacks require no escape plan. Finally, since the perpetrator is killed during the course of the suicide attack, there is no fear of the terrorist being caught afterwards, interrogated by the security forces and passing on information liable to endanger other activists.

Suicide attacks are considered attractive by groups of religious and nationalistic fanatics who regard them as a kind of Holy War and a divine command. The phenomenon has seen a growing popularity especially among Islamist fundamentalist terror groups. For Hamas, for example, the perpetrator of the suicide attack is not considered to have committed suicide. Rather, the perpetrator

perceived to be a *shahid* – a martyr who fell in the process of fulfilling a religious command, the *Jihad* or 'Holy War'.

Suicide attacks may provide the *shahid* and his families with substantial rewards. The majority of the *shahids* come from a low social status background. They improve their social status after their death as well as that of their families. In some cases, the family of the *shahid* is showered with honor and praise, and receives financial rewards for the attack.

There are a number of common characteristics of the *shahid* which serve as a basic profile of the suicide bomber. They are usually young (between 18 and 30 years of age), single, unemployed and from a poor family. The reason for committing a suicide attack for most of the *shahids* is therefore first and foremost religious fanaticism combined with nationalist extremism, and a wish for revenge, but not personal despair.

Suicide terrorists rarely volunteer for these missions. Instead, they are usually selected by terrorist organizations after a close examination and over a long time of acquaintance. After potential suicide terrorists are selected, they usually participate in long training sessions in order to test their attitudes and performance under pressure and in life-threatening situations. Only the trainees who are both willing and cool-headed are permitted to move onto the next stage. Subsequently they usually disappear from their homes without farewell, while they begin several days of intensive training in order to understand all operational aspects of the mission and learn how to deal with the explosive device. At this time they also undergo a process of physical and mental 'purification'.

Any country faced with a struggle against this type of terrorism must do its utmost to protect the population, and to provide them with a feeling that things can and will be done against suicide attacks in order to decrease the damage to the public morale. A state faced with suicide attacks must thwart these attacks through intelligence, operational (counter-terrorist) measures, and protective (anti-terrorist) measures. To these steps must be added psychological measures. Intelligence is the first link in the chain of thwarting any terror attack, and is of the utmost importance in thwarting suicide attacks before they are put into practice.

Intelligence and operational measures alone are not sufficient. Of foremost importance is the task of supporting and strengthening the civilian population in dealing with suicide terrorism. It should be borne in mind that the main victims of terrorism in general and suicide attacks in particular are civilians, and it is they who are on the front line in the fight against terrorism. In contending with the phenomenon of suicide terrorism we should bear in mind that the suicide attack is not an act of a lone lunatic or desperate terrorist who decides to attack as an act of revenge. Rather it is a well-planned terror attack, which demands extensive preparations and the involvement of a number of activists and leaders. Therefore, countering this wave of terrorism requires a combination of effective intelligence, operational activity, security and psychological measures combined with international cooperation in the fight against the organizations responsible for such attacks.

Further reading

Hoffman, B. (1999) *Inside Terrorism*, New York: Columbia University Press.

Reuter, C. (2004) *My Life Is a Weapon: A Modern History of Suicide Bombing*, Princeton, NJ: Princeton University Press.

Stern, J. (2003) *Terror in the Mind of God*, New York: HarperCollins.

See also: al-Qaeda; terrorism

MARTIN GRIFFITHS

Superpower

This term was used during the **cold war** era (1945–91) to describe the superordinate **power** of two states, the United States and the Soviet Union. Prior to the Second World War, the world's states tended to be divided into two simple categories: **great powers** and all others. The cold war made the dichotomy obsolete. In 1941, both the USSR and the United States were drawn into the broader global conflict – the USSR after Nazi Germany invaded it in June, and the United States after the Japanese attack on Pearl Harbor in December. The war-making capabilities of these two states were so dramatically vaster than the other great powers fighting World War Two – Britain, France, Germany, Japan – that the term great power no longer seemed appropriate to describe two states as unequal in capability as the USSR and the United States.

The term was made popular by William T. R. Fox, who in 1944 published a book about the likely shape of global politics after the **war**. *The Super-Powers* was an exploration of the changes wrought by conflict and the mobilization of the huge industrial power of the United States and the Soviet Union against Germany and Japan. Henceforth, Fox argued, there would be 'world powers' (or superpowers) and 'regional powers'. In Fox's view, there were only three such world powers: the United States, Britain, and the Soviet Union.

Fox's new terminology caught on, particularly for the two states which enjoyed a superordinate position in the post-1945 global system, the United States and the USSR. But the term was defined inductively: the USSR and the United States were superpowers by virtue of their attributes and their 'distance' in power capability from all other countries in the international community. But what were these attributes? While there is no clear and uncontested definition of superpower, generally this term was derived inductively from the following five attributes of both the United States and the Soviet Union.

First, and in keeping with Fox's original observation, both superpowers were indeed world powers: their interests were truly global, as was the scope of their attempts at power projection. Indeed, the forty-five years of rivalry between the United States and the USSR was marked by a constant attempt by the United States government to keep Soviet global power as confined as possible, and an equally constant attempt by the government in Moscow to expand Soviet power and influence. This rivalry was truly global, conducted in all regions of the world.

Second, each superpower had a sizable population, relative at least to other major powers. A large population was crucial for the projection of military power globally and the prosecution of total war. It was also necessary for a superordinate economic capacity.

Third, each superpower had a superordinate economic capacity (again, relative to other states), including ample indigenous supplies of food and natural resources necessary for industrial production. And both the United States and the USSR enjoyed a high degree of autonomy, not having to depend on international intercourse for their economic wealth.

Fourth, both superpowers occupied a continent-sized landmass. The geographical size of superpowers was critical for their superordinate power. Most importantly, a continent-sized power was highly resistant to invasion. As the Germans had discovered after 1941, the vast size of the USSR allowed the Soviet defenders to withdraw in the face of invasion, stretching the supply lines of invaders. The United States was even more immune to invasion, not only because of its vast size but also because of the protection afforded by three oceans.

Finally, and perhaps most importantly, both superpowers worked on acquiring a well-developed capacity to wage nuclear war. To be sure, this capacity only developed slowly: in the 1950s the primary means of delivering nuclear and thermonuclear devices was via manned bombers. But over the quarter century after the first atomic bombs dropped by the United States on Japan, both superpowers acquired more and more capacity – eventually gaining what was known as 'second-strike capability' (in other words, each side was capable of surviving an initial attack, or first strike, by the other side – with enough nuclear weapons to deliver a devastating counter-attack).

Eventually, second-strike capability would become the defining characteristic of superpower. Thus, while China occupied a continent-sized landmass, had the world's largest population, and a growing economy, its nuclear capacity was exceedingly limited. Certainly China could not have withstood a pre-emptive strike by either the USSR or the United States against its limited nuclear arsenal with enough residual capacity to launch a counter-strike. Thus, while some argued that China was a superpower, it was not a widely accepted claim.

The term superpower continued to be used in the early post-cold war period (1991–2001) to apply to the United States – which was usually described as the sole remaining superpower.

However, its use has been slowly fading as its applicability has diminished. The term no longer adequately captures the huge gap in power between the United States and all other countries that has grown since the formal end of the cold war in 1991 and the collapse of the other superpower, the Soviet Union.

The distance that had existed between the United States and all other major powers during the cold war also expanded in the decade after the end of the cold war. The countries of the **European Union** (EU) had a population and industrial/economic capacity equal to that of the United States, but the EU was no more organized to conduct the statecraft of a great power, much less a superpower. Despite its developed industrial and economic base, Japan's overall power capabilities relative to those of the United States declined after the end of the cold war. China's economy grew dramatically; its population, the world's largest, continues to grow; it had more military capability than in 1989. But the growth of its power resources over the post-cold war period has been more than matched by growth in American power. Finally, India also experienced considerable growth: it has a sizable middle class, and it has successfully demonstrated its nuclear capability. But like the other major powers, Indian capacities cannot come close to those of the United States.

For these reasons, a new term – hyperpower – has become more popular to describe and analyze American power in the post-9/11 era, suggesting that in time 'superpower' will be used exclusively to describe the United States and the USSR during the cold war.

Further reading

Fox, W. T. R. (1944) *The Super-Powers: The United States, Britain, and the Soviet Union – Their Responsibility for Peace*, New York: Harcourt, Brace.

Huntington, S. P. (1999) 'The Lonely Superpower', *Foreign Affairs* 78,: 35–49.

Nye, J. S. (1990) *Bound to Lead: The Changing Nature of American Power*, New York: Basic Books.

See also: great powers; hegemony; hegemonic stability theory; middle power; power

KIM RICHARD NOSSAL

Sustainable development

Despite the fact that this concept has become common currency in the early twenty-first century, it is a confused and sometimes contradictory idea and there is no widespread agreement as to how it should work in practice. According to advocates of sustainable development, three priorities should be incorporated into all development programs; the maintenance of ecological processes, the sustainable use of resources, and the maintenance of **biodiversity**.

Sustainable development gained credence thanks to the World Commission on Environment and Development (WCED; also known as the Bruntland Commission after its chair, Gro Harlem Gruntland of Norway), which was formed by the **United Nations** (UN) in 1983 and reported four years later. The Commission emphasized that the integration of economic and ecological systems is crucial if sustainable development is to be achieved, and the Commission defined sustainable development as that which meets the needs of the present without compromising the ability of future generations to meet their own needs. Although this definition is fairly concise, it is nonetheless open to varying interpretations. What exactly is a *need*, for example, and how can it be defined? Something that is considered a need by one person or cultural group may not necessarily be thought of as such by another person or cultural group. Needs may also vary through time, as does the ability of people to meet their needs. Likewise, the meaning of **development** can be interpreted in many different ways.

Despite the difficulties in pinning down sustainable development and understanding how it should be applied, calls for its adoption have been made by various international lobby groups, notably at the UN Conference on Environment and Development (UNCED), otherwise known as the Earth Summit, in Rio de Janeiro in 1992. But although use of the term sustainable development has become increasingly widespread, the fact remains that it is still an ambiguous concept. Perhaps this should not be surprising, since the word 'sustainable' itself is used with different connotations. When we sustain something, we might be supporting a desired state of some kind, or, conversely, we might be enduring an undesired state. These different meanings have allowed the concept to be used in varying, often contradictory ways.

Further confusion over the meaning of the term *sustainable* stems from its use in a number of different contexts, such as ecological sustainability and economic sustainability. A central tenet of ecological sustainability is that human interaction with the natural world should not impair the functioning of natural biological processes. Hence concepts such as 'maximum sustainable yield' have been developed to indicate the quantity of a renewable resource that can be extracted from nature without impairing nature's ability to produce a similar yield at a later date. Economic sustainability, however, tends to give a lower priority to ecosystem functions and resource depletion.

One strength of the sustainability idea is that it draws together environmental, economic and social concerns. In practice, most would agree on a number of common guiding principles for sustainable development, including the continued support of human life, the maintenance of environmental quality and the long-term stock of biological resources, and the right of future generations to resources that are of equal worth to those used today.

Much research and thinking about sustainable development has focused on modifying economics to better integrate its operation with the workings and capacity of the environment, to use natural resources more efficiently, and to reduce flows of waste and pollution. The full cost of a product, from raw material extraction to eventual disposal as waste, should be reflected in its market price, although in practice such a 'cradle to grave' approach may prove troublesome for materials such as minerals.

A key issue in the sustainable development debate is the relative roles of economic growth (the quantitative expansion of economies) and development (the qualitative improvement of society). In its first report, the WCED suggested that sustainability could only be achieved with a five-fold to ten-fold increase in world economic activity in fifty years. This growth would be necessary to meet the basic needs and aspirations of a larger future global population. Subsequently, however, the WCED has played down the importance of growth. This makes some sense, because many believe that it has been the pursuit of economic growth, and neglect of its economic consequences, that has created most of the environmental problems in the first place.

The change of thinking on economic growth has been reflected in the two types of reaction to calls for sustainability that have been made to date: on the one hand, to concentrate on growth as usual, although at a slower rate; and on the other hand, to define sustainable development as development without growth in 'throughput beyond environmental capacity'. The idea of controlling 'throughput' refers to the flow of environmental matter and energy through the socio-economic system. This does not necessarily mean that further economic growth is impossible, but it does mean that growth should be achieved by better use of resources and improved environmental management rather than by the traditional method of measuring economic 'throughput'.

One indication of the degree of change necessary to make this possible is in the ways we measure progress and living standards at the national level. For example, the gross national product (GNP) is essentially a measure of economic throughput and it has severe limitations with respect to considerations of environmental and natural resources. The calculation of GNP does not take into account any depletion of natural resources or adverse effects of economic activity on the environment, which feedback costs on such things as health and welfare. Indeed, conventional calculations of GNP frequently regard the degradation of resources as contributing to wealth, so that the destruction of an area of forest, for example, could be recorded as an increase in GNP. The need to introduce environmental parameters is now widely recognized, and some scholars believe that suitably adjusted measures of 'green GNP' could provide a good measure of national sustainability.

Further reading

Brown, L. (2003) *Plan B: Rescuing a Planet under Stress and a Civilization in Trouble*, New York: Norton.

Daly, H. (1996) *Beyond Growth: The Economics of Sustainable Development*, Boston, MA: Beacon Press.

Kenny, M. and Meadowcroft, J. (eds) (1999) *Planning Sustainability*, London: Routledge.

See also: capitalism; development; global warming

TERRY O'CALLAGHAN

T

Terrorism

The threat or the act of politically motivated violence directed primarily against civilians. As a method of employing violence, terrorism denotes a peculiar model of political behavior. In the spectrum of political violence, terrorism is unique. Terrorists seek to influence a wide audience by generating fear. Other forms of political violence include attacks against infrastructure (sabotage), assassination of political leaders, guerrilla warfare, and **ethnic cleansing**. While attacks against civilians (soft targets) are the commonest in the initial wave of terrorist operations, terrorist groups often develop the capability to attack **security forces** (hard targets). Today, about half of all attacks staged by terrorist groups are against security forces. The tactical repertoire of contemporary terrorist groups includes forms of political violence other than terrorism. For instance the Free Aceh Movement (GAM) conducts guerrilla warfare against Indonesian security forces, the National Liberation Army (ELN) has sabotaged gas and oil pipelines in Colombia, and Basque Fatherland and Liberty (ETA) has assassinated moderate politicians in Spain.

Terrorism differs from common crime. While terrorism is driven by political motives, crime is usually driven by economic motives. With the decline of state sponsorship, however, terrorist groups increasingly resort to crime to build their capacities and capabilities. For instance, the Revolutionary Armed Forces of Colombia (FARC) extorts money from foreign companies in Colombia, the Islamic Movement of Uzbekistan traffic narcotics, the Revolutionary United Force of Sierra Leone (RUF) smuggle diamonds, and **Al-Qaeda** engages in credit card fraud. Thus contemporary terrorist groups traverse along the political violence–criminality nexus.

During the **cold war** it was common to distinguish between two forms of terrorism. Domestic terrorism – also referred to as national terrorism – refers to acts of terrorism committed within the territorial borders of a country involving citizens and interests only of that country. International terrorism refers to acts of terrorism involving citizens or the territory of more than one country. However, almost all the major terrorist groups have developed an external presence in recent years. By building robust external support networks, even domestic terrorist groups have developed an international dimension. Therefore, the distinction made during the cold war between domestic and international terrorism is of declining relevance today.

Terrorist organization and infrastructure

Terrorist organization consists of the terrorist group and its support base. The terrorist group includes the leadership, the middle level cadres and the recruits who are constantly trained and assigned political and military activities. The life-blood of a terrorist group is dependent on the support it generates from its like-minded ethnic or religious brethren. The terrorist support base consists of colla-borators, supporters and sympathizers who provide political, financial and military support. Not all support is voluntary. Coercion, intimidation, rob-bery and organized crime are the norm in terrorist methods of generating finan-ces. The strength and the size of the group depend on the support base. The ability of the group to sustain its oper-ations depends on the capacity of the support base to replenish the group's human and financial losses.

Terrorist groups usually have two operational wings – an overt/semi-covert political wing and a clandestine military wing. While the political wing engages mostly in support functions, the military wing engages in operational functions. The political wing operates through front organizations. These terrorist affiliated infrastructures, some of which are legally registered as charities and non-profit organizations, build political and financial support for the military wing. Terrorists will use these affiliated infrastructures to disseminate propaganda; generate recruits, supporters, and sympathizers; raise and launder funds; secure forged, adapted and genuine identifies; hire, rent or buy safe houses and vehicles; gather intelli-gence; procure weapons, dual technolo-gies and other supplies; and transport supplies to the theatre of conflict.

The military wing is responsible for mounting final reconnaissance or sur-veillance of the intended target and executing the operation. To ensure operational security, terrorists assigned to conduct intelligence and military operations are usually organized in the form of compartmentalized cells. Although the bulk of the active terrorist groups are from the global south, they have estab-lished significant support networks in North America, Europe, and Southeast Asia. Liberal democracies are conducive for terrorist groups to establish state-of-the-art propaganda, fund raising, pro-curement and shipping infrastructures. Some of the support networks mutate into operational networks that conduct assassinations, bombings, ambushes, and direct attacks.

Terrorist belief systems

To advance their aims and objectives, terrorist groups develop ideologies or belief systems to politicize, radicalize, and mobilize actual and potential fol-lowers. By conducting a terrorist cam-paign within an ideological framework, a terrorist group seeks to advance its aims and objectives. Three principal ideological strands have generated the fuel required to spawn and sustain ter-rorist campaigns around the world.

Ideological terrorism is driven by left wing and right wing ideologies. **Marx-ism**, Leninism, and Maoism provide the ideological fuel to left wing terrorist groups to advance their aims and objec-tives. They seek to overthrow existing regimes and to establish communist states (see **communism**). Most of the groups driven by left wing ideologies – Communist Combatant Cells (CCC) of Belgium, Red Army Faction (RAF) of Germany, Red Brigades (RB) of Italy, Action Direct (AD) of France – disin-tegrated with the end of the cold war. Although the ideological justification for these groups to continue ended with the death of the Soviet **empire**, a few groups driven by left wing ideologies survived in the poorer regions of the world. They include FARC in Colombia, Tupac Amaru Revolutionary Movement

(MRTA), Sendero Luminoso (Shining Path), New People's Army (NPA) in the Philippines, People's War Group (PWG) in Andhara Pradesh in India. Of these groups, FARC, Nepal Maoists and NPA poses a severe national security threat to Colombia, Nepal and the Philippines. Among the left wing groups still active in Europe are the Revolutionary Organization 17 November and Revolutionary Nuclei, both of Greece, and the Revolutionary People's Liberation Party (DHKP-C) in Turkey.

Groups driven by right wing ideologies include the Ku Klux Klan, Aryan Nations (Church of Christian Aryan Nations, Church of Jesus Christ Christian), Aryan Liberation Front, Aryan Brotherhood, Arizona Patriots, the American Nazi Party (National Socialist Party, United Racist Front), and the (United Self-Defense Forces of Colombia: AUC). A group driven by a right wing group conducted the bombing of the Alfred P. Murrah Federal Building in Oklahoma City on 19 April 1995. Overall, groups driven by right wing ideologies pose a low threat compared to other categories of terrorism. In contrast to the left wing groups, the bulk of the right wing groups are located in North America and in Western Europe. Most right wing groups are neo-Nazi, neo-fascist, anti-Semitic, and racist groups. These groups attack immigrants and refugees, mostly of Asian and Middle Eastern origin.

The first wave of *ethno-nationalist terrorism* was by national liberation movements directed against the Colonial rulers. They included the Irgun and Lehi opposing the British rule in Palestine in the 1940s and French rule in Algeria in the 1950s. Contemporary groups driven by ethno-nationalism can be divided into three sub-categories. They are groups fighting for autonomy, unification, or reunification (**irredentism**). For instance, Al Aqsa Martyrs Brigade, Jammu and Kashmiri Liberation Front (JKLF), and the Liberation Tigers of Tamil Eelam are fighting for independence from Israel, India, and Sri Lanka respectively. The members of these groups are motivated by Palestinian, Kashmiri and Tamil **nationalism**. Similarly, Continuity and Real IRA are fighting for unification or reunification with the Republic of Ireland. Likewise, the PKK is fighting for linguistic and cultural autonomy for the Kurds in Southeastern Turkey. In comparison to the other categories, ethno-nationalist conflict produces the largest number of fatalities and casualties; internally displaced persons and **refugee** flows; and the biggest **human rights** violations. Groups that have adopted virulent ethno-nationalist ideologies pose a significant threat to their opposing ethnic communities and governments.

Politico-religious terrorist groups driven by religiosity include those from the Christian, Jewish, Sikh, Hindu, Buddhist, and Islamic faiths. They include Army of God in the United States, Kach and Kahne Chai of Israel, Babbar Khalsa International of Punjab, India, Aum Shinrikyo (recently renamed Aleph) of Japan, Islamic Resistance Movement (Hamas), Palestinian Islamic Jihad (PIJ), and Armed Islamic Group of Algeria. Aum, an apocalyptic group, aimed to take over Japan and then the world. In contrast to other Islamist groups campaigning within their territories, Al-Qaeda and Lebanese Hezbollah (to a lesser extent) have a global or a universalistic Islamic agenda. To justify violence, politically motivated religious leaders propagate corrupt versions of religious texts often misinterpreting and misrepresenting the great religions such as **Islam**.

Of the religious category of groups, Islamists or groups motivated by radical Islamic ideology are the most violent. Two pivotal events in 1979 – the Islamic

Revolution in Iran and the Soviet intervention in Afghanistan – led to the increase in number of groups driven by Islamism. After successfully defeating one **superpower**, the Islamists turned their energies toward building a capability to defeat the remaining superpower, the United States and its allies in the Muslim world. With martyrdom becoming widespread and popular among Islamist groups throughout the 1980s and 1990s, the scale of violence unleashed by Islamist groups has escalated dramatically. For instance, the Palestinian Liberation Organization, the Popular Front for the Liberation of Palestine, and the Abu Nidal Organization killed far fewer people than their contemporary Islamist counterparts – Hamas and PIJ.

In addition to the categories already mentioned, terrorist campaigns are also driven by ideologies that lack mass appeal and therefore are not very common. They are state sponsored, anarchist, and single-issue terrorism. As terrorism is a low cost/high impact form of violence, states wishing to advance their foreign policy goals have supported terrorist groups. As a result of **sanctions** imposed by the international community against states that sponsor terrorist groups, this clandestine surrogate form of warfare has declined dramatically since the end of the cold war. Although the US government accuses a range of countries for supporting terrorism, there is no evidence that North Korea, Sudan or Cuba is sponsoring terrorism today. Throughout the 1990s, however, Sudan and Libya were active sponsors of terrorism. Although the scale of sponsorship has declined, Iran, Syria, and Lebanon continue to support terrorism. The US list does not include another dozen countries that clandestinely support foreign terrorist groups. Single-issue terrorist groups include violent animal rights and anti-abortion groups that seek to change a specific policy or practice rather than the political system.

Motivation: why people join or support terrorist groups

By the cunning use of propaganda, terrorist groups have a high capacity to indoctrinate and motivate their ethnic and religious brethren to join them as full time and part time members, collaborators, supporters and sympathizers. Protracted socio-economic and political conflicts create the conditions for the spawning and sustenance of virulent ideologies. Those indoctrinated join, collaborate, support or sympathize with terrorist goals, aims, and objectives. Conditions of poverty, lack of education and unemployment often produce terrorist recruits and supporters. However, Osama bin Laden comes from the richest non-royal Saudi family and his principal strategist Dr Ayman Al Zawahiri is from one of the most educated families in Egypt. Although those who live in poverty, the unemployed, or the underemployed are most vulnerable to ideological indoctrination, it is not deprivation or relative deprivation but ideological indoctrination that generates recruits and supporters for terrorism. As the socio-economic and political conditions in the Global South – including much of Asia, Africa, the Middle East, Latin America, and the former USSR – are conducive for the inculcation of terrorist ideologies, the bulk of the terrorist groups are located in the poorer regions of the world. Both territorial and migrant communities harboring actual and perceived grievances and aspirations provide significant political, economic and military support for terrorist groups.

Some of the most committed members of terrorist groups are those who have been directly affected by political violence, often by a state or a state-sponsored group. The victims perceive joining or supporting a terrorist group as a vehicle to seek revenge or to bring about an alternative form of government. By its own political and military actions, it is hard for a terrorist group to grow in strength and size. To generate widespread public support, terrorist groups provoke **security** forces to over-react. A restrained law enforcement response is therefore critical to prevent terrorist groups from expanding their support bases. Other recruits join terrorist groups because they have failed to achieve their political goals by non-violent means. In their minds, terrorism is justified because there is no other path available.

Although conscription is not widespread and is often highlighted by governments for propaganda purposes, terrorist groups also coerce some recruits to join or support them. In an atmosphere of fear and uncertainty, a potential recruit can be threatened by a terrorist group to join or support a group. Such recruits harbor the belief that joining or supporting a terrorist group may facilitate the protection of his or her family. Finally, some are attracted to terrorist and guerrilla groups by the prospect of becoming members of a secret organization. They may feel a sense of excitement in being different from the rest of society. As opposed to the ordinary public, a terrorist can command **power** and strength. As contemporary terrorist groups engage in organized crime – from trading in diamonds to trafficking in narcotics and human smuggling and credit card fraud – joining a terrorist group is perceived lucrative by a few. Often in conflict zones, the opportunities for livelihood are limited.

Research demonstrates that a terrorist group by its own action cannot be successful. Often government over-reaction or under-reaction generates overwhelming support and recruits for terrorism. It is inappropriate government actions that drive individuals to become terrorists or to support terrorism. Mass arrests by the security forces – including arrests on mistaken identity or on false information provided by a personal enemy – can humiliate and turn a non-terrorist sympathizer into a terrorist sympathizer. Similarly, collateral damage by the security forces where death of one's mother, father, brother or sister can motivate one to join a terrorist group. Therefore, intelligence is paramount to accurately identify and pin-pointedly target the terrorist and the terrorist infrastructure. For every terrorist killed or captured, if the terrorist group can recruit five more, the battle is lost. The policy of collective punishment meted out in Israel and in some other theaters of conflict has proved to be counter productive. Often when a colleague is killed, the security forces tend to enforce collective punishment.

Terrorist training and weaponry

Terrorist groups pose a significant threat to domestic, regional and international **security** because of the access they have to professional training and weaponry. The quality of training and weaponry available to terrorist groups has dramatically changed over the years. During the cold war, each of the **superpower**s provided training to a number of terrorist groups. They controlled the level of training, weapons and targeting to ensure that the conflicts did not escalate.

Over the last three decades, terrorist training infrastructure has moved from the Middle East to Asia. In the 1970s and 1980s, the Syrian controlled Bekka valley in Lebanon was the main center for training for over forty foreign terrorist groups. In the 1990s, the center of gravity in international terrorism shifted from the Middle East to Central Asia. Afghanistan became the major center for training at least two dozen groups until US military intervention in October 2001.

Today, many terrorist groups have access to the same level of training available to security forces personnel. Four factors have facilitated terrorist access to professional training. First, the US sponsorship of anti-Soviet *mujahidin* groups throughout the 1980s included provision of field manuals reserved for the US military, including the US special forces. Second, several former security forces personnel from Egypt to Algeria and the United States participated both in the anti-Soviet and the subsequent global *jihad* campaigns that followed. For instance, Captain Ali Mohommad, an Egyptian who later joined the US Special Forces, was Al-Qaeda's principal military instructor in Afghanistan, Sudan, Somalia and Bosnia and also trained Osama bin Laden's bodyguard contingent. Third, there has been a proliferation of security companies and former security forces personnel willing to serve as both trainers and mercenaries (see **mercenary**), especially since the end of the cold war. Finally, certain intelligence agencies of governments continue to provide training to foreign terrorist groups as a means of advancing their foreign policy aims and objectives against inimical states. For instance, the Revolutionary Guards of Iran continues to train Hezbollah. As such, a well-connected or a well-endowed terrorist group can gain access to high quality training hitherto reserved for professional militaries.

What is apparent is that there is a generation of terrorists with knowledge comparable to regular soldiers in service of governments. Well-funded groups have hired some of the best available Special Forces trainers in the world. Therefore, to fight contemporary terrorism, it is essential to provide highly specialized counter-terrorism training to troops assigned for counter-terrorism functions. As most terrorists are better trained, better armed and better motivated, regular troops and policemen are likely to be unsuccessful without specialized training. The response of the German police to the massacre of Israeli athletes in the Olympic village in Munich in 1972 provides an insight to the difficulty of fighting terrorism without creating elite forces. Training and equipping highly specialized counter-terrorist forces remain at the heart of sound planning and preparing to fight contemporary terrorism.

Information on how to manufacture explosives or an explosive device is available in the public domain via the Internet, textbooks, pamphlets, etc. However, manufacturing and transporting explosives and explosive devices require specialized training and extraordinary skill. More importantly, with the end of the cold war, the international **arms trade** has grown rapidly. The widespread availability of firearms (notably small arms and light weapons) has increased the threshold for terrorist attacks. For example, there are nearly fifty million copies and variations of the A. Kalashnikov (AK/AKM) rifle, the most used weapon in the world. Easy to procure, conceal, transport, train, and use, small arms and light weapons will remain the weapons of choice of terrorists in the foreseeable future.

The widespread availability of weapons has provided terrorist groups access to small arms, medium size, and heavy infantry weapons. With easy access to the saturated weapons market, many terrorist groups have replaced their improvised weapons with commercially manufactured weapons. Many countries in Southeast Asia, sub-Saharan Africa, and the Balkans (mostly Croatia) are known to sell weapons without proper verification. In these regions terrorist groups have gained access to sophisticated weapons, dual technologies, and professional trainers. Saturated arms markets in Eastern Europe and the southern belt of the former Soviet Union and in other regions where cold war conflicts have ended feed the international arms pipelines of several terrorist groups.

Mass casualty weapons

Chemical, biological (see **chemical weapons**; **biological weapons**), radiological, and nuclear (CBRN) weapons are not synonymous with mass casualty weapons. Similarly, CBRN attacks are not synonymous with mass casualty attacks. 9/11 demonstrated that a terrorist group can kill several thousand people without resorting to CBRN weapons. Although classified as **weapons of mass destruction** (WMD), not all CBRN terrorist attacks have resulted in mass casualties. With the exception of the nerve gas attack by Aum Shinrikyo of Japan that killed twelve people, none of the other chemical, biological and radiological attacks have resulted in significant casualties. Most terrorists have not used CBRN material due to problems of access. Even terrorist groups with access to chemical, biological, and radiological materials may be reluctant to use them as weapons due to problems of delivery, lack of control, fear of overwhelming retaliation, and in some cases, loss of public support. The trend is for terrorists to conduct mass casualty attacks using conventional means such as hijacked fully fuel laden passenger aircraft used as guided missiles or coordinated simultaneous bombings of high rise buildings and population centers. Nonetheless, a handful of terrorist groups such as Aum Shinrikyo and Al-Qaeda have expressed a sustained long-term interest to acquire, develop and use CBRN weapons.

Construction of a nuclear device is not yet within the reach of a terrorist group. However, the US government has expressed concern over a state sponsor providing a nuclear device or radiological material to a terrorist group. In the past ten years, the **International Atomic Energy Agency** estimated 175 cases of trafficking in sensitive nuclear material. A radiological dispersal device or a 'dirty bomb' could be constructed using nuclear material such as uranium or plutonium from dismantled warheads or from a nuclear power plant. Such a device is unlikely to kill large numbers of people but will render a large area uninhabitable and generate mass panic.

Terrorist tactics and targets

Hijackings, kidnapping, and hostage taking belong to one sub-category of tactics. As terrorists are copycats, hijackings, hostage taking and kidnappings become fashionable during certain periods. In addition to these tactics, terrorist groups also use threats to advance their aims and objectives. The threat of a violent action to cause fear or coerce an action or inaction is also an act of terrorism. Terrorist targets include people and infrastructure on land, in the air and at sea. While human targets include political leaders, administrators, military personnel, business leaders and population centers, infrastructure targets include aviation, maritime, symbolic, and other national critical infrastructure. Symbolic and high prestige targets are a high priority for terrorists. By attacking a symbolic or high prestige target, the terrorist group's power and influence is magnified, prompting the government to engage in massive retaliation and thereby increasing the terrorist influence.

Some terrorist groups such as Hezbollah, FARC, ELN, AUC, and Al Ansar Mujahidin are notorious for hostage taking and hostage holding. Although most hostages are eventually freed a few groups – whether their demands are met or not – kill their hostages. Hostage-taking for large cash ransoms is the fastest growing form of terrorist activity in Colombia, Chechnya, Mexico, Yemen and the Philippines. Even **United Nations** peacekeepers, officials and aid workers have been taken hostage in Bosnia, East Timor, and Sierra Leone. Many of these countries lack either the resources to control the security environment or the elite units to respond to a hostage taking.

Hijacking

A hijacking occurs when a vehicle or transportation system is forcibly taken over by a terrorist or a group of terrorists. The vehicle or transportation system can be public or a private conveyance (car jacking) and it can be for the purpose of inciting fear and/or murder. In contrast to other tactics, hijackings give terrorists mobility, an opportunity to highlight their grievances and media attention. The hijacking of aircraft beginning in the late 1960s has been the single biggest threat throughout history. By the early 1970s, Israeli eliminated the threat of hijackings by introducing sky marshals and a range of other initiatives. The countermeasures displaced the threat, forcing Palestinian hijackers to consider other options.

Kidnapping

A kidnapping occurs when an individual or a group of persons are abducted by force to be used for ransom or coercion. To increase the ransom payment or coercive power, some terrorist groups

refrain from immediately publicizing that they have abducted a person. Often the person targeted is a prominent political or military figure, a wealthy person or a businessman, and an opponent. As it is a lucrative industry in some countries, terrorist groups such as FARC subcontract kidnappings to other organizations. In addition to demanding funds, terrorist kidnappings are motivated by publicity, to gain political concessions, to release terrorist detainees and prisoners, and for revenge and retaliation.

Although governments prohibit families and businesses from negotiating the release of kidnapped victims by payment of ransom, experience shows that this is virtually unenforceable. Permitting families and companies to pay a ransom for the release of a family member or employee provides the law enforcement authorities with the best possibility to capture the kidnappers. A highly trained professional police force can monitor the contacts between the captors and the negotiators. For example, the success of the police has led to remarkably low incidents of kidnapping in the United States.

The most publicized kidnapping of an individual by a terrorist group was the kidnapping of Aldo Moro, a former Prime Minister of Italy, by the Red Brigades on 16 March 1978. Moro's death resulted in a political crisis, prompting the Italian government to strengthen the legal framework for fighting terrorism. Within four years of the kidnap and murder of Moro, Red Brigades kidnapped US General James Dozier but he was subsequently released.

Suicide terrorism

Suicide terrorism is one of the most difficult forms of terrorist threats to manage. Although a suicide terrorist attack is nearly impossible to thwart once the bomber has been launched into battle, by investing in developing high grade intelligence a suicide attack can be detected and disrupted in the planning and preparation stages. In a suicide bomb attack, the bomber intends to kill himself or herself and to destroy his or her targets by using an improvised explosive or non-explosive device. In constrast to a non-suicide terrorist who seeks to survive to fight another day, a suicide terrorist is indoctrinated to kill and die with the completion of the mission. As the suicide terrorist concentrates maximum attention and effort to destroy the target and not to protect himself or herself, it becomes difficult to stop a suicide attack once the bomber has been launched. Traditional law enforcement is based on the principle of **deterrence** by punishing the perpetrator. While destroying his or her target, the suicide terrorist defies punishment by actively seeking his or her death. Suicide terrorists have inflicted severe damage to targets such as US diplomatic targets in East Africa, the World Trade Center and the Pentagon. By willing to die, a terrorist retains a high potential to destroy asymmetric targets that cannot be successfully attacked using non-suicide terrorist operations. Furthermore, by integrating suicide terrorism to the CBRN realm, the potential for destruction will be unprecedented.

Aviation terrorism

In addition to the terrorists trained in flying schools in Western Europe and in North America prior to the attacks of 11 September 2001, terrorists have also been trained in flying schools from Australia to Pakistan and Sudan during the last decade. Since learning to fly was not a criminal offence, throughout the 1990s Britain, France, Australia, and other countries turned a blind eye to terrorists and their known local supporters learning to fly. In addition to the suicidal hijacking threat, there are other forms of terrorist threat that persist today. A number of terrorist groups, including Al-Qaeda, have attempted to infiltrate airports with the intention of planting bombs in airline cargo. For instance, an Al-Qaeda cell in northern Germany penetrated airport security in Amsterdam during the planning stage of 9/11 with the intention of planting bombs in American passenger planes.

However, since 9/11, improvements to aircraft security have prompted terrorist groups to invest in acquiring the ability to shoot down aeroplanes using missiles. Although the *military* aviation industry has suffered as a result of the proliferation of Surface to Air Missiles (SAMs), this threat is gradually extending to the commercial aviation realm. Terrorist groups that have gained access to SAMs could target flying targets with great force. The most popular of the aerial weapons are the SA-7s (also known as Grail) using an optical sight and a tracking device with an infrared seeking mechanism. The SA-7 has an effective range of 6,125 meters and an altitude of 4,300 meters. Its US version Stinger (also known as FIM92A) is an infrared-guided shoulder launched SAM with a maximum range of 5,500 meters and an altitude of 5,250 meters. That means most aircraft could be targeted only when flying at low levels, during take-off or when landing. Although the US Congress in 1985 approved the transfer of SAMs to the Afghan *mujahidin* and to UNITA in Angola, the CIA expressed reservations. In the 1990s, the CIA unsuccessfully attempted to buy back Stinger missiles that survived the anti-Soviet Afghan campaign (1979–89). During the same period, many terrorist groups purchased SA-14s, an advanced version of the SA-7. In December 2001, a Sudanese member of Al-Qaeda fired a Stinger missile at a US warplane near the Prince Sultan airbase in Saudi Arabia. By enhancing perimeter security and by using antimissile flares, military aircraft have minimized the threat but commercial aircrafts remain vulnerable to terrorist attack. With the decline in the threat of hijacking, including suicide hijacking, due to increased security, the threat of SAMs to the aviation industry is likely to increase.

The future of terrorism

Al-Qaeda's coordinated suicide airborne attacks aimed at destroying America's outstanding landmark targets – the World Trade Center, the Pentagon and the White House – on 11 September 2001, demonstrated the escalating terrorist threat posed to civilian and military infrastructure. Before the attacks, the total number of US fatalities from three decades of international and domestic terrorism was less than 3,000. On 11 September 2001 the attacks conducted by nineteen suicide hijackers killed 3,100 citizens from seventy-eight countries. In our own lifetime, the face of terrorism is rapidly changing. Terrorism has emerged as the single biggest security threat to both governments and societies. Hitherto perceived as a law and order problem, terrorism today is regarded as a threat to national security.

Further reading

Buckley, M. and Fawn, R. (eds) (2003) *Global Responses to Terrorism*, London: Routledge.

Freedman, L. (ed.) (2002) *Superterrorism: Policy Responses*, Oxford: Blackwell.

Gunaratna, R. (2003) *Inside Al-Qaeda; Global Network of Terror*, New York: Columbia University Press.

Howard, R. D. and Sawyer, R. L. (2003) *Terrorism and Counter Terrorism: Under-standing The New Security Environment*, New York: McGraw-Hill.

Shanty, F. and Picquet, R. (eds) (2003) *Encyclopedia of World Terrorism*, New York: M. E. Sharpe.

Wilkinson, P. (2001) *Terrorism Versus Democracy, The Liberal State Response*, London: Frank Cass.

See also: al-Qaeda; biological weapons; chemical weapons; rogue state; suicide terrorism; weapons of mass destruction

ROHAN GUNERATNA

Third way

The ideas of the third way and 'new' social democracy enjoy a wide if fragile influence on the theory and practice of Western democratic politics. Political victories of self-consciously 'third way' governments through the 1990s – best represented by the Clinton Administration in the United States, the Blair 'New Labour' Government in the UK and the Schroder Government in Germany – have been no small achievement given the ubiquity of **neoliberalism** in Western democracies. However, there has always been doubt about the distance of the third way from neoliberalism. The longer third way governments have been in office, the more this doubt has grown.

The political and academic literature on the third way is now extensive covering both analysis of social change and advocacy and argument about political and policy responses to those changes. Anthony Giddens is perhaps the intellectual most closely associated with the articulation and defense of the third way but others (including Will Hutton, Geoff Mulgan, and Stuart White in the UK, and Robert Reich, Amitai Etzioni, Robert Putnam, and William Galston in the United States) have contributed to the articulation of a broadly third way analysis and policy agenda. The Democratic Leadership Council in the United States and the Demos think tank in the UK have both been important in taking third way ideas into the wider public domain.

For third way thinkers, we live in an era of dramatic social and economic change that challenges the basis of social **order** and the **legitimacy** of democratic governance in modern societies. Economically, the falling away of the manufacturing economy and the growth of the new service and high technology/information economies has created a new dynamic of inclusion and exclusion in modern societies and a growing gap between winners and losers. It is common to read of the '30-40-30' society to describe the changes taking place – 30 per cent winners, 40 per cent declining middle, and 30 per cent new poor/underclass. Of particular significance are the growing social and political gulfs that come with this new division. Like many others, 'third wayers' see the new economy as increasingly driven by global forces. For them, **globalization** is eroding the **power** and role of national governments. The new economic dynamic at work in the world is increasingly between regional and global levels – a latter day expression of the 1970s injunction 'act local, think global'.

Socially, third way thinkers see new relationships emerging between individuals and their community. Giddens argues that our understanding of individualism is moving from one dominated by narrow self-interest and 'me generation libertarianism', to one that stresses the virtues of cultural pluralism and lifestyle choice. For him, modern individuals are becoming more 'socially reflexive' – conscious of both their individuality and their social and cultural identities and the sense of citizenship that goes with those identities. Etzioni's more critical communitarian (see **communitarianism**) view is that modern individualism of all kinds is eroding reservoirs of community and social capital (the trust and social cohesion engendered by social institutions like the family and the local civic realm) necessary for social cohesion.

Third way thinkers argue that these changes are shifting the grounds of political agency in modern societies. Citizens are increasingly disengaged and cynical about conventional political insititutions. Mainstream democratic political processes lack legitimacy. People are less confident that 'politics-as-usual' is capable of delivering positive benefits. An ugly populist 'anti-political' mood is growing. Some, like Giddens, see the growth of an arena of 'sub-politics' (including social movements and **global civil society**) outflanking conventional political institutions, and laying the grounds for the practice of a new kind of politics.

The last major theme of third way analysis focuses on an argument about risk and the risk society. Giddens suggests that the increasing human influence on the world (there is less and less that conscious human action does not affect in some way) drives a new imperative to manage the risks associated with that impact in more active and creative ways. This has consequences for how social democratic governing is conceived and practiced. In the international arena, this outlook informs the third way defense of **humanitarian intervention**.

On the basis of this broad analysis, third way thinkers set out a political and policy agenda with many dimensions. The starting point is that, in order to both respond to the new issues confronting modern society and to restore the relevance of progressive politics, most of the social democratic tradition should be ignored and dismissed. In particular, the traditional social democratic ambition to build a socialized economy and public sector alongside private markets – decommodifying areas of life deemed central to human needs, and establishing public institutions charged with ensuring a robust reconciliation of equality and freedom – is attacked by third way thinkers as tainted by association with **communism** and state **socialism** as they were practiced in the twentieth century. For third way thinkers, we should not return to what they see as the dark days of authoritarian big government with its lack of democratic accountability.

Nevertheless, the third way reflects a semblance of social democratic commitment both in the values it defends and in the new alliances it sees between government and civic institutions in building the capacities of people to live decent lives, albeit within a society primarily shaped by private markets and capitalist processes. Some have coined various acronyms to characterize the balances at work in third way agendas – CORA (community, opportunity, responsibility, accountability), RIO (responsibility, inclusion, opportunity) and PAP (pragmatism and populism).

Giddens' articulation of a third way political agenda is perhaps the best distillation. He invokes a number of principles – the promotion of economic globalization against protectionism; equality and freedom maximizing individual autonomy; 'no rights without responsibilities' particularly in access to state welfare; 'no authority without democracy' in the exercise of government; and the reconciliation of modernizing, cosmopolitan, democratic and conservative ideals which allow change to be embraced but in a 'precautionary' manner. On the basis of these principles, Giddens outlines an integrated political program addressing the need for change and reform across the major sectors of society – state, civil society, economy and nation.

At the level of the state, the issue is not neoliberal shrinkage or social democratic expansion of government but its reconstruction to make it more democratic. The legitimate authority of government needs renewal on an active basis. This will entail a number of things including 'downward' and 'upward' devolution of power from the national level of government to ensure adequate responses to globalization, constitutional reform to ensure greater transparency and openness in government, and greater administrative efficiency in bureaucracy. While greater devolution of power might splinter the capacity to respond to social and economic problems within regions, Giddens argues that more deliberative democracy requires more experimentation at the local level, and that reinventing government on democratic principles should also mean reasserting the effectiveness of government in the face of markets.

Giddens' agenda for civil society connects with recent American communitarian, civic renewal, and social capital debates. The common issues here are the problems of the decline in trust and confidence, particularly in politicians and government, and the erosion of connectedness to and belonging in society. While recent American answers to these problems stress the virtues of self-reliant local community initiative as the best way forward, Giddens emphasizes the importance of local community action in partnership with government. Civil society is not a source of spontaneous order and harmony. For him, only government can adjudicate inevitable conflicts within and between local communities.

It is probably third way ideas about the mixed economy, the welfare state and the pursuit of equality that best expresses its critique of and distance from the social democratic tradition. For example, against the view that the mixed economy involves separate roles for the public and private sectors with a large part of industry in public hands, Giddens defends the idea of the 'new mixed economy', which looks for a synergy between public and private sectors, utilizing the dynamism of markets but with the public interest in mind. The private, market sector of the economy should become more important with government pursuing public objectives through regulation.

Third way thinkers also argue that welfare and equality should be pursued in quite different ways from the past. The traditional welfare response to inequality stressed the protection and **security** of people against material and related deprivation. This approach is overwhelmingly negative for many third way thinkers. The traditional welfare state is seen as undemocratic and paternalistic. In line with his argument about the changing role of security and risk in society, Giddens argues that the purpose of the welfare state should move from a protective and negative role toward ideas of 'positive welfare' that seek to develop a society of 'responsible risk takers'. Welfare should increasingly center on the provision of the necessary resources and skills (education in particular) for full participation in mainstream economic and social life. The cultivation of human potential should as far as possible replace 'after the event' redistribution even though redistribution will continue to be important.

Third way thinkers see equality less in terms of the distribution of material goods and income and more in terms of issues of diversity, inclusion and exclusion in society. Welfare policy should increasingly attend to those issues that reproduce social exclusion like access to work and education. A social investment welfare state should be created to pursue a positive welfare agenda based upon investment in human capital wherever possible, rather than the direct provision of economic maintenance. In line with the emphasis on civil society, welfare benefits – to the extent that they remain – should be localized and integrated with programs for the active development of civil society.

Many of the third way ideas about welfare and equality center on ideas of stakeholding and 'asset-based' egalitarianism – providing citizens with the skills, capacities and assets that increase their stake in the wider society, and their opportunity to participate in it, particularly in the spheres of employment and self-provision of goods like housing.

Lastly, and consistent with proposals associated with the notion of **cosmopolitan democracy**, third way thinkers defend cosmopolitan views about the nation, democracy and culture, and promote the idea of **global governance** to respond to the forces now shaping the internal structure of states and the global issues that will require attention in the future.

The debate about the third way

As a center-left strategy, third way thinking has been extensively criticized for analytical imprecision, and for the vagueness and timidity of its reform agenda. Perhaps the most significant imprecision is the way in which third way thinkers treat state socialism and old style liberal social democracy as one and the same. For third way thinkers, both suffer from a shared belief in the virtues of economic planning and state action, and a too ready opposition to private markets. There is no acknowledgment of the radically different politics and purposes of both enterprises. The damning of 'mixed economy' liberal social democracy by association with illiberal state socialism is seen by many as a ploy to buttress the third way claim that there is no alternative to accommodating liberal market capitalism on the latter's terms. Third way thinking rules out the mainstream social democratic attempt to build robust public institutions and a public economy at arm's length from private capitalist markets.

There is a strong relation between the timidity of the third way idea and the vagueness of the more specific policy ideas that go with it. For example, on the role of government there is some inconsistency. In his introduction to *The Global Third Way Debate* (2001), Giddens argues that 'we must avoid the traditional leftist strategy of putting more and more tasks into the hands of the state'. Nevertheless, he claims that we must also rediscover 'an activist role for government, restoring and refurbishing public institutions', and understand that 'the role of markets must be kept confined' through government intervention and regulation. Just how the latter can be pursued without giving the state and the public realm more capacity is not answered. On equality and the means of tackling it, there is also some scope for confusion. On the one hand, third way advocates argue that the creation of an egalitarian society remains an important objective. On the other hand, they are often opposed to increasing tax rates for the rich.

Beyond the imprecision, there has been extensive debate about the third way arguments and their political and policy expressions, particularly in the United Kingdom. Much of this debate has taken place on the radical and center-left. The critical arguments of Alex Callinicos (2001), Stuart Hall (2003) and David Marquand (2004) are representative.

Callinicos' critique of the third way is developed within the framework of a broadly Marxist (see **Marxism**) critique of the new global capitalism and the politics which accompanies it. His argument runs as follows. The role of government and democratic politics in the new global era is constrained by the need to appease the demands of capital. In contrast to those who are optimistic about economic growth in the context of the **information revolution** and the 'network' society, Callinicos sees a familiar crisis-prone economic cycle. On equality, the third way strategy is too glib. Drawing mainly on British experience, Callinicos argues that the third way employment policy leaves unaddressed the nature and pay of the jobs on offer. Underlying **power** and class divisions shaping the education system are not tackled by third way education policies. In general, inequality has worsened during the Blair era and the response has been timid. Callinicos believes that the third way emphasis on 'community' and the balancing of rights with responsibilities is authoritarian. Individual rights are central to a robust conception on equality and should accompany a more ambitious collectivist political agenda. Finally, the third way's international agenda based upon the idea of humanitarian intervention raises difficult problems of **sovereignty** and inequalities of power that it cannot solve.

Callinicos' alternative consists of a number of 'anti-capitalist theses', among which the following are central to his overall argument. First, regulation and reform of global capitalism is limited by the power of **multinational corporations** whose interests are reflected in national and international political institutions. Nevertheless, capitalist accumulation continues to depend upon wage labor.

Despite the fragmentation and individualization of work; there is a potentially strong allegiance between the labor movement and new transnational social movements. Alternative models of society beyond neoliberalism and the third way will emerge, and those that pursue the revolutionary transformation of capitalist society will be better than reformist models on the grounds that the former gives greater priority to human needs and subjects the allocation of resources to democratic control.

Stuart Hall's critique focuses on the political and policy directions of Blair's New Labour Government, the main example of third way thinking in practice. Much of the concern of the British left about New Labour has focused on how the Blair Government can be characterized in the broad sweep of British reform politics and, in particular, how much distance the New Labour Government has moved from Thatcherite neoliberalism.

Hall argues that even though globalization, neoliberalism and the economic and social changes associated with them constitute the terrain shaping modern democratic politics, left reformers still have a choice. They can either articulate and pursue progressive alternatives to neoliberalism or accommodate themselves to the neoliberal mainstream. He argues that the Blair Government has adopted the latter stance since its election in 1997, dressing up its adaptation in third way rhetoric.

For Hall, the New Labour Government represents 'a double or hybrid regime' composed of a dominant neoliberal strand and a subordinate social democratic strand. The resulting balancing act involves a complicated and difficult reconciliation of opposites. There has been attention to the needs and interests of losers from neoliberal reform through some measure of redistribution, and the setting of a minimum wage and family tax credits. But the policy mainstream reflects an increasingly centralist managerialism in which private and individual interests are favored over collective and public ones. The ever more careful management of the political process through public relations and 'spin' is required to reconcile the tensions between what have traditionally been opposing interests and viewpoints. As a left strategy, particularly a strategy wishing to distinguish itself from the neoliberal and capitalist mainstream, the New Labour/third way political and policy framework is very limited.

From a different, more centrist and liberal political viewpoint, David Marquand highlights many of the same tensions and difficulties in the New Labour and third way project. For him, there is a substantial continuity between Thatcherite neoliberalism and New Labour/third way reflected in the continued undermining of ideas and practices associated with 'the public realm' and political and social citizenship in contemporary British politics and public life. Through an historical analysis of British democracy over the past century, Marquand argues that the current period reflects a 'hollowing-out' of the public institutions and interests – particularly professional interests – which are, for him, essential to the proper functioning of a democracy. New Labour and the third way offer no real support to the values and practices associated with the public realm.

Marquand argues that the basic reason for this lack of support is that Blair's New Labour Government has internalized the axioms of the capitalist renaissance of our time: privatization, de-regulation, **free trade**, low taxation, and budgetary orthodoxy. While he acknowledges, like Hall, that there has been some policy innovation to address the needs and interests of the losers from economic change, the New Labour experience suggests that the neoliberal revolution continues unabated.

In many ways, much of the critique of the third way is reflected in a broadly left liberalism. For left liberals, free market capitalism is winning out over the mixed economy. The new economy is dynamic but it is producing a more divided, unequal society. Structural economic change and the unemployment and less secure employment that go with it are one of the main causes of the new inequality. Rather than higher levels of risk being a cause for celebration, the new economy and society are producing unnecessary exposure to life's vagaries and worsening levels of hardship. The 'social accord' or 'social compact' between all groups in society and upon which any civilized democratic society depends is breaking down. Unless there is a broad fairness and justice at play, a society's coherence is lost.

National government and programs of social democratic reform in welfare, education, health, law, and social insurance in the Western democracies in the second half of the twentieth century have been very important in establishing that coherence and, in the process, creating decent societies. For left liberals, if we are to recreate more stable and equal societies in the future, we need to reimagine the national role, not abandon it. Civilized capitalism entails public and political management to create a genuinely mixed economy which shares economic and political power across classes and social groups, and in the process achieve egalitarian outcomes. The pursuit of full employment should be a central aim in managing the mix.

The strategic principles involved in this 'reimagining' are opposite to those stressed by third way thinkers. Rather than celebrate fragmentation, risk, flexibility, and the virtues of the local community, the left liberal vision centers on macro and holistic conceptions and responses to problems. It stresses full employment and economic and social stability as the overall aims, and defends an integrated mixed economy with separate public and private sectors as the best means of achieving them. The strategic question is which goods and economic sectors should be commodified and which should be decommodified. An underlying assumption of the left liberal stance is that social **order** is organized and shaped from the top down as much as it is from the bottom up, especially if egalitarian economic and social outcomes are to be achieved.

The left liberal moral outlook is also pluralist but with liberal humanist roots. Against the postmodernism of the third way, some left liberals defend views about our common humanity as a more robust foundation for social democracy. They defend an essentialist view of human nature, a more or less coherent and settled account of what it is to be human grounded in views about human beings as needy, vulnerable and sociable. Free choice does not entail heroic individualism in free markets. Rather it is often characterized by tragic choice between ultimately incommensurable ends. Such choice entails a good deal of inner conflict, which in turn is reflected in social and political conflict.

The moral problem for communities is how to manage and resolve that conflict. Rather than assume the virtues of cooperation, community and mutual obligation, and pitch for devolved authority and institutions as the best arena to achieve them, left liberals take a different tack. They are more comfortable with the fact of conflict in society, indeed they see the scope for such conflict – within reason – as a touchstone of any healthy democracy. For them, we might want to aim for a more cooperative society but that must be based in much broader notions of community ultimately grounded in ideals of political, social and economic citizenship and the general public interest. For left liberals, the main institutional expressions of this ideal of community are public institutions through which impartiality and the public interest are encouraged to flourish.

The new progressivism

By the early 2000s, after a period of fairly intense criticism, the third way notion seemed increasingly exhausted. Political leaders and intellectuals associated with the third way began to use the more open term the new progressivism to describe the reformist task facing the center-left. New progressives have put forward revised views about the role of markets and the state in shaping modern society, the challenges of citizenship and welfare provision in a changing context, and the political and policy dilemmas at the global and international level involving ongoing economic change, immigration, **terrorism**, and technological and environmental change.

Giddens remains at the center of the new thinking. For him, the 'first wave' of third way policies in the 1990s is no longer relevant or useful. Giddens' understanding of neoprogressivism is some way to the left of the third way in its defense of the public sphere, public interests and public goods – or what he somewhat clumsily refers to as the need for 'publicization' in contrast to privatization. Ideas of the 'embedded market', the 'civil economy' and the 'ensuring state' are deployed to define a strategy which is not simply concerned with 'what works' – a favored third way position in the 1990s. Rather, ongoing problems in the new capitalism require a

stronger, more principled stance to the guidance and regulation of business by both civic institutions and the state. And rather than the third way notion of an 'enabling state' that provides resources to facilitate and empower citizens without much concern for the outcomes, the idea of the 'ensuring state' recognizes that the state also has obligations of care and protection for its citizens, and that some of these obligations should be provided as guarantees. Nevertheless, the emphasis on the role of choice and pluralism in the structure and practice of government should remain.

On welfare policy, new progressives are critical of the excessive emphasis on education in earlier third way thinking. Some scholars of the welfare state defend a welfare policy framework addressing the needs of working women and pre-school children through the provision of universal day care and greater work flexibility.

On global issues, the character of the neo-progressive argument is perhaps best seen as expressing a 'principled toughness'. On immigration, terrorism, and globalization more generally, Giddens argues that the emphasis should be on building multilateral responses but in ways which do not retreat from the need to take strong stances – for example, on the use of force to advance cosmopolitan, liberal ideals, and on the need to build a cultural bargain beyond **multiculturalism** as the foundation of immigration policy.

Further reading

Callinicos, A. (2001) *Against the Third Way: An Anti-Capitalist Critique*, Cambridge: Polity Press.

Gamble, A. and Wright, T. (eds) (1999), *The New Social Democracy*, Oxford: Blackwell.

Giddens, A. (1998) *The Third Way: The Renewal of Social Democracy*, Cambridge: Polity Press.

Giddens, A. (ed.) (2001) *The Global Third Way Debate*, Cambridge: Polity Press.

Giddens, A. (ed.) (2003) *The Progressive Manifesto: New Ideas for the Centre-Left*, Cambridge: Polity Press.

Hall, S. (2003) 'New Labour's Double-Shuffle', *Soundings* 24, 10–24.

Marquand, D. (2004) *Decline of the Public: The Hollowing-out of Citizenship*, Cambridge: Polity Press.

Martell, L. (ed.) (2001) *Social Democracy: Global and National Perspectives*, Basingstoke: Palgrave.

Mulgan, G. (ed.) (1997) *Life after Politics: New Thinking for the Twenty-First Century*, London, Fontana Press.

See also: capitalism; casino capitalism; democratic deficit; globalization; neoliberalism; socialism

LIONEL ORCHARD

Third World

This term is used (loosely) to refer to the economically underdeveloped countries of Asia, Africa, Oceania, and Latin America, considered as an entity with common characteristics, such as poverty, high birth rates, and economic dependence on the 'advanced' countries. The *First World* is the developed world – the United States, Canada, Western Europe, Japan, and the newly industrializing countries (Hong Kong, Singapore, South Korea, and Taiwan) (see **newly industrializing country**), Australia and New Zealand. The *Second World* is the ex-communist world led by the former Soviet Union (USSR). With the demise of the USSR and the communist bloc (see **communism**), there is of course no longer a Second World. The Third World is the underdeveloped world – agrarian, rural and poor. Many Third World countries have one or two developed cities, but the rest of the country is poor. Many parts of Central and Eastern Europe should probably be considered part of the Third World. Today, Russia could also be considered a Third World country with nuclear weapons. In general, Latin America, Africa, and large parts of Asia are still considered parts of the Third World.

The term 'Third World' is not universally accepted. Some prefer other terms such as 'the South', 'non-industrialized countries', 'less-developed countries', or 'emerging nations'. Nonetheless, the term 'Third World' is probably the one most widely used in the media today. Of course, no term adequately describes all non-First World, non-industrialized, non-Western countries accurately.

Insofar as one can make useful generalizations, the underdevelopment of the Third World is marked by a number of common traits; distorted and highly dependent economies devoted to producing primary products for the developed world and to provide markets for their finished goods; traditional, rural social structures; high rates of **population growth**; and widespread poverty. Nevertheless, the Third World is sharply differentiated, for it includes countries at various levels of economic **development**. And despite the poverty of the countryside and the urban shantytowns, the ruling elites of most Third World countries are wealthy.

This combination of conditions in Asia, Africa, Oceania and Latin America is linked to the absorption of the Third World into the international capitalist economy, by way of conquest or indirect domination. The main economic consequence of Western domination was the creation, for the first time in history, of a world market. By setting up throughout the Third World sub-economies linked to the West, and by introducing other modern institutions, industrial **capitalism** disrupted traditional economies and, indeed, whole societies.

Because the economies of under-developed countries have been geared to the needs of industrialized countries, they often comprise only a few modern economic activities, such as mining or the cultivation of plantation crops. Control over these activities has often remained in the hands of large foreign firms. The prices of Third World products are usually determined by large buyers in the economically dominant countries of the West, and trade with the West provides almost all the Third World's income. Throughout the colonial period, outright occupation severely limited the accumulation of capital within the foreign-dominated countries. Even after **decolonization** (in the 1950s, 1960s, and 1970s), the economies of the Third World developed slowly, or not at all, owing largely to the deterioration of their terms of trade – the relation between the cost of the goods a state must import from abroad and its income from the exports it sends to foreign states. Terms of trade are said to deteriorate when the cost of imports rises faster than income from exports. Since buyers in the industrialized countries determined the prices of most products involved in international trade, the worsening position of the Third World was scarcely surprising. After 1973, only the oil-producing countries succeeded in escaping the effects of the Western domination of the world economy.

No study of the Third World could hope to assess its future prospects without taking into account population growth. In 2000, the earth's population was more than six billion people, 80 per cent of whom live in the Third World. This population growth will surely prevent any substantial improvements in living standards there as well as threaten people in stagnant economies with worsening poverty.

The Bandung Conference, in 1955, was the beginning of the political emer-gence of the Third World. China and India, two states whose social and economic systems were sharply opposed, played a major role in promoting that conference and in changing the relationship between the Third World and the industrial countries, capitalist and communist. As a result of decolonization, the **United Nations**, at first numerically dominated by European countries and countries of European origin, was gradually transformed into something of a Third World forum. With increasing urgency, the problem of under-development then became the focus of a permanent, although essentially academic, debate. Despite that debate, the unity of the Third World remains hypothetical, expressed mainly from the platforms of international conferences.

Foreign aid, and indeed all the efforts of existing institutions and structures, have failed to solve the problem of underdevelopment. The United Nations Conference on Trade and Development (UNCTAD), held in New Delhi in 1971, suggested that 1 per cent of the national income of industrialized countries should be devoted to aiding the Third World. That figure has never been reached, or even approximated. In 1972 the Santiago (Chile) UNCTAD set a goal of a 6 per cent economic growth rate in the 1970s for the underdeveloped countries. But this, too, was not achieved. The living conditions endured by the overwhelming majority of the people who inhabit the poor countries have either not noticeably changed since 1972 or have actually deteriorated.

Whatever economic development has occurred in the Third World has not been distributed equally between countries or among population groups within them. Most of the countries that have managed to achieve substantial economic growth are those that produce oil: Algeria, Gabon, Iran, Kuwait, Libya, Nigeria, Oman,

Saudi Arabia, the United Arab Emirates, and Venezuela. They had the money to do so because after 1973 the **Organization of Petroleum-Exporting Countries** (OPEC), a cartel, succeeded in raising the price of oil drastically. Other important raw materials are also produced by underdeveloped countries that have tried to form cartels similar in form to OPEC. For example, Australia, Guinea, Guyana, Jamaica, Sierra Leone, Suriname, and Yugoslavia formed the Bauxite International Association (BIA) in 1974; and Chile, Peru, Zaire, and Zambia formed a cartel of copper producing countries in 1967. But even strategic raw materials like copper and bauxite are not as essential to the industrialized countries as oil, and these cartels therefore lack OPEC's strength; while the countries that produce cocoa and coffee (and other foods) are even less able to impose their will.

All international agencies agree that drastic action is required to improve conditions in Third World countries, including investment in urban and rural public work projects to attack joblessness and underemployment, institutional reforms essential for the redistribution of economic power, agrarian reform, tax reform, and the reform of public funding. But, in reality, political and social obstacles to reform are a part of the very nature of the international **order** and of most Third World governments.

Further reading

Handelman, H. (2002) *The Challenge of Third World Development*, 3rd edn, Upper Saddle River, NJ: Prentice Hall.

Harrison, P. (1990) *Inside the Third World: The Anatomy of Poverty*, 3rd edn, Harmondsworth: Penguin.

Thomas, C. and Wilkin, P. (2004) 'Still Waiting After All These Years: The Third World on the Periphery of International Relations', *British Journal of Politics and International Relations* 6, 241–58.

Weber, H. (2004) 'Reconstituting the Third World? Poverty Reduction and Territoriality in the Global Politics of Development' *Third World Quarterly* 25(1), 187–206.

See also: decolonization; development; neocolonialism; postcolonialism; world-system theory

TERRY O'CALLAGHAN

Transnational crime

Crimes that take place across territorial borders, and which are therefore outside the **sovereignty** or jurisdiction of a single state. While criminal networks have historically utilized dispersed migrant communities, fluid borders and cross-jurisdictional safe havens, the growth of transnational crime reflects changes in the **international system** and the rapidly increasing movement of people and goods. Since 1989 there has been a dramatic growth in international criminal activities. This growth potentially distorts domestic and international finance, and threatens the stability and sovereignty of **nation-state**s.

Figures on the annual profits from transnational crime are impossible to verify, but most estimates claim that annual revenues from the drug trade exceed US$500 billion, and combined organized crime is worth at least one trillion US dollars, or 3 per cent of world gross domestic product. The expansion of trade, ease of transport, communications and global **population growth** has increased transnational criminal activities. In addition, the deregulation of the international financial system and the increase in technological transfers has facilitated the movement of illegal profits and funds used to support and expand these activities.

Transnational criminal activities include drug production and smuggling, arms trafficking, trade in illicit commodities or stolen goods, human smuggling, trade in art and antiquities, the wildlife trade and financial crimes such as **money laundering**, fraud, and embezzlement. Other commodities that have entered the criminal market include the trade in nuclear materials, chemicals, precious metals, and corporate espionage for business advantage. Activities such as piracy also constitute transnational crime, as is any illegal activity, conspiracy or illegal commodity that crosses sovereign borders. Many illicit criminal networks feed each other, by permitting the growth of parallel industries that are needed to invest proceeds or raise funds for transnational crimes. For example, the international trade in 'people smuggling' for illegal migration follows similar networks already established for the illegal sex industry and bonded labor. Similarly, the international drug trade is linked with allied criminal industries such as auto theft and smuggling across borders.

Major transnational criminal networks include the Italian *mafia*, the Japanese *yakuza*, Chinese *triads* and Russian *mafiya*. Many of these groups have been transnational in character for decades, utilizing migrant communities in a host of countries through family connections, secret societies, and business activities. They often blend into existing ethnic communities, using the barriers of language and community solidarity to thwart legal detection. More recent groups include Colombian, Mexican, Nigerian, and Albanian cartels. These ethnic groups utilize dispersed migrant communities in several countries, in which criminals can operate and detection by law enforcement officials is difficult. Non-ethnic based groups in a host of states such as motorcycle gangs

cooperate in the production and transit of amphetamines.

The extent of cooperation between such transnational criminal networks (TCNs) is often overestimated, but cooperation between ethnic organized crime networks is a reflection of their increased sophistication. They operate in a similar manner to legitimate firms, instituting joint ventures for certain schemes and using the comparative advantage of one venture to facilitate other businesses. Not all groups are rigidly hierarchical, they are often dynamic networks that adapt swiftly to changing conditions or market shifts. This fluidity reflects the changing nature of global trade and also how difficult detection can be. Conversely, competition between groups has increased the level of violence in urban areas as many groups fight for the control of domestic and regional markets.

The increased cooperation between transnational criminal networks and other non-state actors has added further complexity for states in their attempts to manage the rise in transnational crime. Mergers have taken place between groups motivated by profit and politically motivated groups, such as terrorists and insurgents. Most illegal political movements pursue criminal enterprise to gain funds for their cause, utilizing their advantage in organized violence and extraterritorial control. The involvement of groups such as the Sri Lankan Tamil Tigers, the Kurdistan Workers Party (PKK), Colombian FARC guerillas, and Middle Eastern terrorists in such ventures as drug smuggling, credit fraud, and money laundering has added a further layer to transnational crime.

The threat to the **nation-state** posed by TCNs is dependent on the strength of state institutions. Stable democracies with effective law and order institutions have primarily identified transnational crime as a legal issue and act primarily on domestic breaches of the law. On the other hand, small and unstable states are vulnerable to penetration and even capture by criminal networks through the **corruption** of state officials and the electoral process, and the distortion of illicit profits in the legal economy. Small Caribbean states are the best examples of this capture, although larger territories such as Macau and Cambodia have become havens for major TCN bosses. Some jurisdictions even sell citizenship papers and passports to TCN members to grant them immunity from extradition. The effects of transnational crime are not simply a legal issue. The extent of infiltration of criminal networks weakens state institutions through greater corruption, has a deleterious effect on **human rights** and freedom of expression, and diverts state resources from more productive pursuits.

Large states experiencing economic transition are particularly vulnerable to transnational crime. In Russia after the end of the **cold war**, scores of criminal syndicates forged networks with business and political elites in a complex of corruption and illegal enterprise. Although long a part of Russian society, the post-Soviet era witnessed an explosion in the number of crime gangs, estimated to be between three to four thousand organizations with over 100,000 full time members. From this domestic base, Russian organized crime has spread to Europe, North America, and East Asia. Its activities range from smuggling, trafficking in illegal goods and people, to sophisticated computer fraud and money laundering. The spread of criminal involvement in the Russian transitional economy has caused serious distortions to state and international efforts to change to a market system.

International society has been slow to respond to the threat of transnational crime. Although the **United Nations** began seeking greater cooperation and international treaty agreements in the 1970s, and multilateral bodies such as Interpol have long cooperated in intelligence and joint investigations, transnational crime is not just a law enforcement issue. Hence cooperation among states is increasingly focusing on broader political and economic developments. Recognizing the need for greater international cooperation, 125 states signed the UN Convention against Transnational Organized Crime in Palermo in 2000. This treaty created the framework for greater cooperation between the legal, financial, and intelligence arms of states to cooperate in more effective ways, calling on all signatories to outlaw membership in a criminal organization, money laundering, corruption, and the obstruction of justice. The Convention does little in forcing states to enact a generalized set of laws, but it does establish a set of norms that states should work toward implementing. Further multilateral efforts through the United Nations Office of Drugs and Crime (UNODC) seeks to coordinate information and programs with member states to monitor criminal activities such as kidnapping, trafficking in persons, corruption, money laundering and drug production. Training in police methodology and detection methods also assists weak states in facing the challenge of criminal penetration. However, while there is a concerted international will to curtail the activities of criminal networks, countervailing methods are thwarted by the ability of criminals to respond to updated legal measures. Being able to access multiple jurisdictions and employing violence and corruption, transnational criminals are increasingly capable of evading detection.

Further reading

Berdal, M. and Serrano, M (eds) (2002) *Transnational Organized Crime and International*

Security: Business as Usual? Boulder, CO: Lynne Rienner.

Friman, H. R. and Andreas, P. (1999) *The Illicit Global Economy and State Power*, Lanham, MD: Rowman & Littlefield.

Shelley, L. I. (1995) 'Transnational Organized Crime: An Imminent Threat to the Nation State?' *Journal of International Affairs* 48(2), 463–89.

Williams, P. and Vlassis, D. (2001) *Combating Transnational Crime: Concepts, Activities and Responses*, London: Frank Cass.

See also: arms trade; money laundering; nation-state; offshore; terrorism; United Nations

DAVID SCOTT MATHIESON

Transnational social movement (TSM)

A group whose members share common social understandings and work across national boundaries to bring about transformative political change. Toward this end, a TSM coordinates its activities and engages in sustained interactions with political opponents to challenge the status quo on a targeted issue or set of issues. The nature and effectiveness of a transnational social movement are largely determined by the interplay of two dynamic processes, contentious politics and collective action, which also serve as key reference points in the study of TSMs. The notion of 'contentious politics' characterizes the nature of the interactions between a transnational social movement and its opponents, as well as the context within which these occur. 'Collective action', broadly construed, refers to a TSM's organizational capabilities and the manner in which these are employed.

The notion of transnational social movements is heavily indebted to that of national social movements, the study of which has taken various forms since the 1960s. The first approach, dominant in the late 1950s and early 1960s, was based on 'collective behavior theory' and focused on the grievances that give rise to social movements. This approach marked a productive start to the study of contemporary social movements, in that it sought to explain why they happen; but it viewed social movements as falling outside the social mainstream, considered them motivated by anomie or deprivation, and paid little attention to how collective action occurs. A second approach, grounded in 'resource mobilization theory', arose in the late 1960s and early 1970s. This approach examined the organizational dynamics of social movements, focusing on the means available to collective actors, in an effort to explain how movements occur. Thus, for example, personal resources, professionalization, and financial support came to be regarded as necessary components of a viable social movement.

Since the late 1980s, scholars have focused on the role of culture and ideas in creating and sustaining social movements, arguing that sufficient resources are not enough to insure a movement's success. According to this approach, for a social movement to sustain itself over time, it must connect its language and activities to the ideational constructs of members and potential supporters. This is accomplished through a process of 'framing' organizational goals and activities in ways that make sense (or ring true) to people on a personal level. Because conditions and attitudes change over time, effectively maintaining 'frame alignment' is an important and ongoing process for a successful social movement. Within this context, a social movement also develops a 'repertoire of contention', that is, a set of organizational strategies and practices that are employed over time in campaigns for change.

Well into the 1980s, sociologists dominated the study of social movements.

Consequently, analytical frameworks made few connections between social movements and politics. Political scientists and political sociologists began articulating such connections in the late 1970s, leading to the development of a 'political process model' in the early 1980s. This model adds an important dimension to the study of social movements, by calling attention to the opportunities and constraints created by political institutions and processes, how these vary over time and place, and the ways in which they facilitate or hinder a social movement's success.

By the 1990s, the advent of **globalization** was prompting scholars to extrapolate their conceptual schema for studying national social movements to the international level, facilitating a focus on transnational social movements. This broader focus has created some analytical confusion, in that TSMs are sometimes conflated with networks of **non-governmental organizations** (NGOs). Although similar in many respects, the two can be distinguished primarily by the nature of their constitutive connections. A transnational social movement is connected by members' shared social understandings, and thus is rooted simultaneously in the domestic social networks of several societies. An NGO network, on the other hand, generally is connected by shared positions on particular issues, often in the face of variant social understandings, and is not substantively integrated into domestic social networks. Definitions of transnational social movements nevertheless vary, with some more restrictive than others. By way of illustration, Greenpeace is often cited as a representative TSM. In essence, Greenpeace is a non-governmental organization. Yet its constitutive social connections are rooted in the domestic societies of several countries; it has developed and employed a (widely

recognized) repertoire of contention over the past three decades; and it has mounted effective and sustained campaigns for change under the mantle of a single organizational structure.

In the contemporary era, TSMs have increased their effectiveness by taking advantage of technology, liberalization, and the ebbing of state control that are characteristic attributes of contemporary globalization. This suggests that transnational social movements will continue to have a significant impact on the dynamics and processes of international relations.

Further reading

Khagram, S., Riker, J. V. and Sikkink, K. (eds) (2002) *Restructuring World Politics: Transnational Social Movements, Networks, and Norms*, Minneapolis, MN: University of Minnesota Press.

Melucci, A. (1996) *Challenging Codes: Collective Action in the Information Age*, Cambridge: Cambridge University Press.

O'Brien, R., Goetz, A. M., Scholte, J. A. and Williams, M. (2000) *Contesting Global Governance: Multilateral Economic Institutions and Global Social Movements*, Cambridge: Cambridge University Press.

Smith, J., Chatfield, C. and Pagnucco, R. (eds) (1997) *Transnational Social Movements and Global Politics: Solidarity Beyond the State*, Syracuse, NY: Syracuse University Press.

Tarrow, S. (1998) *Power in Movement: Social Movements and Contentious Politics*, 2nd edn, Cambridge: Cambridge University Press.

See also: critical theory; global civil society; globalization; non-governmental organization

CRAIG WARKENTIN

Trusteeship

The idea of trusteeship in **international society** presupposes a relationship in which a legal person (a state or international organization) is responsible for the general well being of a group of people who are deemed to be incapable of directing their own affairs. Fundamental to the procedural assumptions of trusteeship is the non-consensual and coercive character it discloses. Trusteeship assumes that the virtuous shall rule on behalf of the less so; that ruler and subject are joined in a relation of inequality; and that the powers of government should be exercised so as to secure the happiness of those who are incapable of directing their own affairs.

Crucially, then, trusteeship implies a mode of relations that is alien to that implied by sovereign statehood, especially the prevailing notion of popular **sovereignty**. The consent of the governed has no place in an arrangement of trusteeship: command and obedience **order** relations between trustee and ward. Trusteeship invokes a paternal relationship whereby dependent peoples are coerced, in much the same way that a parent coerces a child, for the sake of their own happiness. In this context trusteeship may be thought of as an arrangement suitable for peoples thought to be incapable of undertaking the civil and moral responsibilities that come with political independence.

The international history of trusteeship is intelligible mainly in the context of Anglo-American experience. Out of late-eighteenth-century debates concerning misrule in British India emerged the principle, enunciated most famously by Edmund Burke (1729–97), which would come to define the idea of trusteeship in the British Empire as well as in international society: all political **power** must be exercised ultimately for the benefit of peoples subject to it. The architects of **empire** embraced this principle, at least as a matter of declared policy, in justifying alien rule. Empire, they claimed, and

the preponderant power that sustained it, could be made to serve the cause of the world's most disadvantaged peoples.

The argument for a benevolent trusteeship underwritten by imperial power proved to be most influential in nineteenth-century Africa, a continent the European mind imagined as having been left destitute by endemic **war**, barbarous customs, and most devastating of all, 'illegitimate commerce' – the trade in human beings. In the Berlin Act (1885) members of European international society agreed to establish a system of **free trade**, abolish slavery and the slave trade, and take steps to spare the peoples of Africa the ravages of European war, all of which were meant to secure the 'native African' in a state of moral and material well-being. These obligations were not, however, premised on a disinterested humanitarian concern for the plight of the native African; they were premised on the conviction that the exploitation of Africa's natural bounties should reciprocally benefit Europeans and Africans alike.

That the promises undertaken in the Berlin Act were often observed in the breach – the Congo Free State being the most egregious offender – did not discredit the idea of trusteeship. Rather the framers of the **League of Nations** mandates system set out to remedy the defects of the Berlin Act, its wholly inadequate provisions of accountability in particular, by subjecting the tutelage of dependent peoples (detached from the German and Ottoman empires after World War One) to the scrutiny of international supervision. All three classes of mandate, A, B, and C, while different in respect of particular tutelary responsibilities, were administered under the supervision of the Permanent Mandates Commission, one of the principal organs of the League of Nations. The great innovation of the mandates system was that it combined the idea of a 'sacred trust', that preponderant power should be exercised on behalf of the world's 'backward' peoples, with internationally recognized and supervised securities against the abuse of that trust.

The **United Nations** trusteeship system to which the mandates were assimilated at the end of World War Two (save for South West Africa) differed only slightly in purpose from the mandates system. It is possible to discern in the United Nations Charter two distinct and contending notions of trusteeship. Chapter XI, the declaration on non-self-governing territories, reflects the British tradition of imperial trusteeship and Chapters XII and XIII, which establish the trusteeship system, reflects the American tradition of international trusteeship. Whereas the former contemplates the end of trusteeship as consisting in self-government within empire, the latter contemplates full and complete independence, in addition to self-government, as the end of trusteeship.

The **legitimacy** that trusteeship enjoyed for nearly two centuries collapsed rather suddenly in the onslaught of **decolonization**. Inability attributed to political, economic, and social backwardness was no longer a morally justifiable reason for withholding political independence. For the claims of fundamental human equality and the **self-determination** of peoples disallowed all appeals to ability or experience: political independence became a categorical right and political dependence a categorical wrong. But far too many of the states that emerged out of **decolonization** provided little in the way of social good and posed a great threat to the personal **security** of their citizens.

It is the appalling conditions of life for which these places are conspicuous that has resurrected interest in trusteeship. Trusteeship is increasingly seen as a way

of responding to the disorder and injustice that is often associated with so-called failed (see **failed state**), collapsed, outlaw, rogue (see **rogue state**), unjust, and 'quasi' states. International involvement in conducting the day-to-day affairs of government in Bosnia and Herzegovina, and in East Timor until it achieved independence, points to an increasing willingness of international organizations and individual states to assume responsibility for places ravaged by **civil war**.

However, international involvement in Kosovo since the late 1990s most closely resembles the classical idea of trusteeship that flourished in the age of empire. The *de facto* United Nations supervised trusteeship in Kosovo was established, just as protectorates were established in nineteenth-century Africa to put down slavery and the slave trade, through the use of force in order to redress an urgent humanitarian crisis. And just as colonial administrators were responsible for instructing native Africans in respect for human personality, **good governance**, and legitimate commerce, so too are international authorities, who enjoy supreme civil authority as stipulated in Security Council resolution 1244, responsible for supervising the reconstruction of Kosovo in accordance with the prevailing international legitimacy: **human rights**, democracy, and the free market economy.

But the resurrection of trusteeship generally runs up against very deeply rooted injunctions against all forms of political dependence. Post-colonial international society is still based on the conviction that accession to sovereign statehood entails passage through a one-way door. In this context, experience in Kosovo is an anomaly, suggestive of the nineteenth century practice of extinguishing the independence of people, and subjecting them to the will of an alien **authority** because they are unable to make good use of their liberty. They will be governed for their own good and for their own happiness until they are once again able to take their place as full and equal members of the international community.

Further reading

Bain, W. (2003) *Between Anarchy and Society: Trusteeship and the Obligations of Power,* Oxford: Oxford University Press.

Caplan, R. (2005) *International Governance of War-torn Territories: Rule and Reconstruction,* Oxford: Oxford University Press.

Hall, H. D. (1948) *Mandates, Dependencies, and Trusteeship,* London: Stevens & Sons.

Lugard, F. D. (1929) *The Dual Mandate of Africa,* London: William Blackwood & Sons.

Robinson, K. (1965) *The Dilemmas of Trusteeship: Aspects of British Colonial Policy Between the Wars,* Oxford: Oxford University Press.

See also: democratization, failed state; humanitarian intervention, imperialism, neocolonialism; sovereignty

WILLIAM BAIN

U

United Nations (UN)

The United Nations (UN) is currently the only universal multilateral organization in the world, with a membership of 191 countries from all geographical regions of the world. It is sometimes referred to as an institution or a set of **regime**s. The primary responsibility of the UN is to maintain international peace and **security**. Its other goals, which are no less important, include **sustainable development** and poverty alleviation, the promotion of science and technology for **development**, the setting of appropriate standards for environmental management and human habitation, and the generation and consolidation of norms of **global governance**, including **democratization**, social justice and **human rights**.

The UN business is conducted in six different languages: Arabic, Chinese, English, French, Russian, and Spanish. Most of its functions take place through five major organs: the General Assembly; the Security Council; the Economic and Social Council; the International Court of Justice; and the Secretariat. Its sixth organ, the Trusteeship Council, has no function because there are no colonies or trust territories for it to report on, and because Article 78 of the Charter prohibits the establishment of **trusteeships** over member states, even if they are **failed state**s. The UN Secretary-General Kofi Annan's Millennium Report to the General Assembly encapsulates the responsibilities, goals and aspirations of the UN at the beginning of the twenty-first century. The report identifies the UN's role in **globalization** and global governance, its efforts to promote freedom from want and freedom from fear, its environmental agenda, and the possibility for UN reform.

At a conference at the United Nations University in Tokyo in January 2000, the Deputy Secretary-General Louise Fréchette emphasized three broad imperatives for the UN: **legitimacy**, instruments, and institutions; and effectiveness. These are important factors, but they came under considerable public scrutiny when the US government announced in 2002 that it sought to invade Iraq and wanted UN authorization to do so. Some commentators and policymakers argued that the UN would lose its legitimacy, relevance and effectiveness if it failed to authorize the invasion of Iraq requested by the world's only **superpower**. Others claimed that the UN would lose its independence, legitimacy, and moral standing if it authorized an unwarranted war simply because one of its permanent members wanted it. These claims and counter-claims, which attempted to define the legitimacy and relevance of the UN in terms of its role in the

American-led invasion of Iraq, raised important questions about the organization's relationship with two issues: **war** and global governance. Why should the UN be required to authorize war when it was established primarily to put an end to interstate war? Why should the UN, which is based on **solidarism**, be assumed to lose legitimacy and relevance when it refuses to serve as an instrument of one country's selfish national interests? How does the world view the role of the UN in global governance in the twenty-first century? This essay seeks to address these questions by examining the continuing role of the UN in war and conflict prevention, and in global governance.

According to Hedley Bull (1995), war is one of the five major institutions of **international society**. The other major institutions (used here to refer to a stable set of rules, principles and norms) are the **balance of power**, great power management (see **great powers**), **international law** and **diplomacy**. Bull claimed that these institutions were the bedrock of international **order**.

To provide a broad perspective of the UN, this article uses insights derived from **constructivism**, the **English school**, **idealism** and **realism**. The choice of these perspectives has no significance beyond the assumption that they are among the most widely used theoretical frameworks in the discipline of International Relations. The first hypothesis is that the UN's identity and interests in global politics are, in large part, shaped by war and the fear of war. The second hypothesis is that the UN's survival and continued relevance in global politics are largely determined by how effective its role in global governance is. The next section looks at the structure of the UN, followed by a discussion of the UN's relationship with war and its role in global governance.

Structure

The structure of the UN refers to its four main component organs, which are the General Assembly, the Security Council, the Economic and Social Council, and the Secretariat. All these organs are on a par, which means that none of them has **power** of the other. For example, the Secretary-General may make a recommendation to the Security Council on matters relating to peace and security, but the Security Council can ignore his/her advice if it chooses. The Security Council may take action, which may appear to contravene international law, but the International Court of Justice does not have the mandate to sit in judgment over the efficacy of the decisions of the Security Council. Indeed, only the Security Council or the General Assembly may review its own earlier decisions and, if need be, revise them.

The General Assembly comprises all the members of the UN, which are considered to possess sovereign equality. For example, the newest member, East Timor, with a tiny population and a military force that is too small to defend its borders, is equal to China, with a population of more than one billion and a huge military force. Some analysts view the General Assembly as the most democratic element in the UN system because all members cast equal votes on any issue. However, the influence that small states exercise in the General Assembly is determined by the structure of the **international system**. For example, during the **cold war**, when the international system was bipolar, developing countries exercised leverage because they could play the Soviet Union against the United States or vice versa. With the end of the cold war, followed by the collapse of the Soviet Union and the emergence of the United States as the sole superpower, developing countries lost the freedom of action that they enjoyed between the 1950s and the 1980s.

The General Assembly has the mandate to deal with any question or any matter that falls within the UN Charter. These include economic, educational, health, environmental, and security issues. In its deliberations, the General Assembly may make recommendations to any other organ of the UN or to member states. For example, acting under Article 96 of the Charter, the General Assembly requested the International Court of Justice in late 2003 to provide an advisory opinion on the legality of Israel's 'security fence' around the West Bank. The resolutions of the General Assembly are not binding on member states to the same extent as Security Council resolutions are. This has created the wrong impression that the General Assembly resolutions are of no consequence or that they lack legal effect. Its resolutions have a normative function, and also serve as a source or potential source of **international law** because the International Court of Justice takes some of them into account in its rulings.

The Charter restricts the General Assembly's role in international peace and security. Indeed, according to Article 12 of the Charter, the General Assembly cannot make recommendations on a security problem that is still under consideration by the Security Council. The most visible part of the General Assembly at work is the plenary, which lasts from September to December every year, when heads of state or government or their representatives present speeches. This is also the time when the Secretary-General presents his agenda for the coming year. However, much of the General Assembly's work takes place through its seven committees away from the public limelight. The committees of the General Assembly include: the General Committee, Credential Committee, Disarmament and International Security Committee, the Special Political and Decolonization Committee, the Economic and Financial Committee, the Administrative and Budgetary Committee, and the Legal Committee. Some of the General Assembly's responsibilities overlap with those of the Security Council.

The primary responsibility of the Security Council is to maintain international peace and security, although what constitutes security has been changing over the years. In the initial period, threats to peace and security were defined in terms of the aggression of one state against another state. However, since the 1990s, humanitarian disasters have been described as threats to international peace and security. The Security Council comprises fifteen members, five of which – China, France, Russia, Britain, and the United States – are permanent members. The other ten members hold seats for two calendar years and are prohibited from serving two consecutive terms. The non-permanent members are expected to be elected from those countries that have performed significant roles in international peace and security, and they represent the five geographical groupings within the UN: Africa (3 members), Americas (2), Asia (2), West European and other states (2), and Eastern Europe (1).

The presidency of the Security Council is held for one month at a time, and rotates according to the alphabetical order of the members' names in their English version. Ultimate power in the Security Council is wielded by the permanent members, which are the World War Two victors. Article 27 of the Charter says that decisions of the Security Council on procedural issues require only nine votes, but on any other matter they need nine votes, plus the concurrence of the five permanent members. Thus, any one of the five permanent members can cast a veto on anything other than procedural matters. It is the permanent members that constitute the great power concert in the modern world (see **great powers**). If the permanent members reached a consensus that protecting human rights was more important than respecting sovereignty in some circumstances, nothing would prevent them from enforcing such an understanding. Much of the time, the decisions of the Security Council reflect the narrow interests of the permanent members, not necessarily the will of international society. Indeed, as the crisis over Iraq from 1991 to 2003 indicated, the Security Council can become a highly politicized body.

It is generally acknowledged that the Security Council is unrepresentative of the general membership in several ways. First, in terms of numbers, when the UN was established in 1945, five permanent members represented fifty-one member states. By 2004, the same five permanent members represented 191 member states. In racial terms, Caucasians are over-represented, with only one Asian, and no African, permanent member. From the perspective of geographical regions, Africa and Latin America have no permanent members on the Security Council. It is partly for these reasons that many critics have criticized the Security Council for being out of touch with the current international political and economic realities. Since the early 1990s, there have been numerous proposals for reform of the Security Council, but effective reform will come about only if the permanent members agree to dilute their powers.

Unlike the Security Council, the Economic and Social Council (ECOSOC) has been more flexible in accommodat-

ing the interests of the developing countries. ECOSOC is the most diverse of all UN bodies. It coordinates the work of fourteen UN specialized agencies, ten functional commissions and five regional commissions. According to the Charter, ECOSOC deals with international economic, social, cultural, educational, scientific, health and related matters. It facilitates international cultural and educational cooperation while also encouraging universal respect for human rights. It comprises fifty-four member states, eighteen of which are elected every year, and retiring members are eligible for re-election. Its seats are based on a geographical formula: Africa (14), Western Europe (13), Asia (11), Latin America and the Caribbean (10), and Eastern Europe (6). ECOSOC's regional commissions are the Economic Commission for Africa (ECA), the Economic Commission for Europe, the Economic Commission for Latin America and the Caribbean, the Economic and Social Commission for Asia and the Pacific, and the Economic and Social Commission for Western Asia. The main functions of these regional commissions are to work closely with member states in their regions to try to overcome obstacles to economic growth, trade, and **development**. For example, the ECA's role is to support the economic and social development of the fifty-three African states, foster regional **integration**, promote international cooperation for Africa's development and enhance the UN's role in Africa.

The UN's specialized agencies, such as the UN Children's Fund (UNICEF), the **World Health Organization** (WHO), the **United Nations Development Program** (UNDP), the Food and Agriculture Organization (FAO), the UN Environment Program (UNEP), the UN Commission on Human Rights, the UN High Commissioner for **Refugee**s (UNHCR), the UN Conference on Trade and

Development (UNCTAD), the UN Development Fund for Women, and the World Food Program (WFP), are also affiliated with ECOSOC. These agencies, which are technically subsidiary agencies of the General Assembly, play important roles in **peace-building** and have participated with **peacekeeping** operations in the reconstruction of so-called failed states. It is these agencies that are in the forefront of the programs that promote freedom from want. It is also these agencies that map out strategies for sustaining our future. Some of them are concerned with capacity building, poverty alleviation, the preservation of forests, fisheries and **biodiversity**, and the spread of scientific know-how, especially in developing countries. These agencies play important roles in setting the global agenda. For example, it is the UNDP that popularized the concept of human security, which was subsequently taken up by the UN Secretariat and the rest of the world.

The Secretariat, headed by the Secretary-General, comprises an international civil service that serves other principal organs of the UN. Its members answer to the UN alone for their activities and take oaths not to receive or seek instructions from any other authority. The Secretariat is based in New York, but it has offices in Addis Ababa, Bangkok, Beirut, Geneva, Nairobi, Santiago, and Vienna. The responsibilities of the Secretariat are varied, ranging from administering peacekeeping operations to monitoring human rights violations and preparing studies on **sustainable development**. The Secretary-General is appointed by the General Assembly on the recommendation of the Security Council. This means a permanent member of the Security Council can use its veto power to deny this office to a person it does not like, as the United States did in 1996 when Boutros Boutros-Ghali was seeking a second term.

The Secretary-General's length of term is not specified in the Charter, but they have conventionally served five-year terms. The number of terms each person may serve is also not specified in the Charter, but in practice most of them have served a second five-year term.

The Secretary-General and the Secretariat can take important decisions on international disputes. According to Article 99 of the Charter, the Secretary-General may bring to the attention of the Security Council any matter, which, in his/her opinion, may threaten the maintenance of international peace and security. As the CEO of the UN, the Secretary-General attends the meetings of the General Assembly, the Security Council and the Economic and Social Council, and presents reports to them. He/she is required to make an annual report to the General Assembly highlighting the work of the UN. Some of the Secretary-General's functions on conflict prevention take place through 'Good Offices'. Through them different Secretaries-General have brokered peace and averted **war** in many parts of the world.

The UN and war

The UN has a complex relationship with war, which can be explained in at least three ways. The first is that it was World War Two that led to the creation of the UN in 1945. The second is that the UN was established to eliminate conditions that lead to interstate wars. The third is that the UN has occasionally authorized war in order to rescue people from **famine** and starvation or to maintain international peace and security. This section discusses each of these relationships in turn.

The first issue to note is that it was due to the violence and brutality associated with World War Two that the UN was established. The war broke out in 1939 largely as a result of the global ambitions of Nazi Germany. However, the war was also partly blamed on weaknesses in the structure and functioning of the twenty-year-old **League of Nations**. For this reason, the victorious countries were determined to establish the UN and other international regimes that would ensure peace and prosperity. In this sense, the UN is essentially a product of war. This vindicates Bull's claim that war is a pivotal institution of international society. Bull considered war to be a central feature of international society and claimed that it was war, and the threat of war, that determined the shape and rules of international society. He argued that war was not the only determinant of the nature of international society, but that it was so basic that even terms like great powers, **alliance**s, spheres of influence, balances of power (see **balance of power**) and **hegemony** were scarcely intelligible except in relation to war and the threat of war. This **English School** perspective provides a rationale for viewing the UN and other international regimes after 1945 as products of war.

The second issue is that the UN's primary function is to put an end to inter-state war and foster international peace and security. The preamble of the Charter claims that the UN was established to save succeeding generations from the scourge of war. Moreover, Article 1(2) of the Charter says the principal purpose of the UN is to maintain international peace and security. Kofi Annan's *Millennium Report* talks of freedom from fear. To achieve this goal, the UN uses various strategies that are likely to eliminate the main causes of war. At the military and armaments level, the UN seeks to halt the **arms race** by proposing various **arms control** measures. It also seeks to curb the **arms trade** with a view to reducing the dangers posed by small arms, nuclear weapons, the proliferation of missile technology and weapons of mass destruction. The UN also uses **sanctions** as a non-military way of compelling countries to abide by **international law** and norms.

The UN also pursues other programs, such as peace-building, peace-making and conflict prevention in efforts to discourage war. Another major war-averting instrument that the UN frequently resorts to is peacekeeping. Through peacekeeping operations, the UN has intervened in numerous conflicts without compromising the sovereignty of the states in question. In pursuit of conflict prevention, the UN has been involved in poverty alleviation programs, the promotion of healthy and balanced economic development, the preservation of the environment, and the protection of human rights. Thus, in efforts to reduce the likelihood of war, the UN, through its specialized agencies, such as WHO, UNDP, and FAO, has undertaken extensive social and economic measures, especially in developing countries.

The third element in the relationship between the UN and war is that the UN has occasionally authorized war in order to end human suffering on a grand scale or to maintain international peace and security. UN-authorized war generally takes the form of **peace-enforcement** operations, which were authorized for several contingencies, including Korea in 1950, Iraq in 1990, Somalia in 1992–3, Haiti in 1994, and East Timor in 1999. The UN does not have its own military forces, so most of its peace-enforcement operations have been subcontracted to interested parties. The only peace-enforcement operation that was commanded and controlled by the UN Secretariat was the second UN Operation in Somalia in 1993–5. Prior to this, and after it, all peace enforcement operations were subcontracted to states. There have been other occasions when the Security Council has refused to endorse war efforts by interested parties. For example, it refused to approve the NATO (North Atlantic Treaty Organization) intervention in Kosovo in 1999, and declined to authorize the American-led invasion of Iraq in 2003.

Whether the UN authorizes war or not depends on how such a war advances the UN's aims. In the case of the intervention in Kosovo, some members of the Security Council believed that it would violate Yugoslavia's sovereignty and set a precedent that would lead to more global instability. However, the UN Secretary-General did not condemn it outright. Instead, he argued that the Security Council and the UN as a whole would in future have to weigh the balance between respect for sovereignty and respect for human rights. In the case of Iraq in 2003, the majority of Security Council members believed that there was no convincing evidence that Iraq was a threat to international peace and security. They also believed that the principle of pre-emptive war, which the US advocated, would undermine peremptory norms of international law and possibly lead to greater instability in the world.

The UN and global governance

Explaining the role of the UN in global governance is complicated by several factors. The first is that there is no clinical definition of global governance. For purposes of this entry, global governance refers to the structure of rules, norms and institutions that global actors have established to provide order and certainty. The second complicating factor is that the UN is not just a product of global governance, but also a leading generator of the ideas, norms, rules and principles that constitute global governance. When the World War Two victors created the UN, they were participating in global governance. And when the UN engages in peacekeeping, development activities and the promotion of human rights, it enhances global governance. It is the UN's practice of generating norms, ideas and principles that, in turn, shapes its identity. In this sense, the UN and global governance are inseparable. The third complicating factor is that the UN represents different things to various groups, including analysts from rival perspectives. The remaining part of this section will explain how realists, idealists and constructivists view the role of the UN in global governance.

Realists care about the legitimacy of the UN, but for them this legitimacy is derived from the UN serving as an instrument of state interests. A UN without the potential to serve as a device through which states use their power to pursue **national interest**s has little legitimacy for realists. There is little doubt that an organ like the Security Council provides a platform for power politics. What concerns developing states is that most of the power within the UN is held by Western countries, which dominate the international system politically, economically, technologically, and militarily. Western countries also have the means to promote their values and norms more effectively than the non-Western states. That is why some analysts argue that the West uses international institutions, military power, and economic resources to run the world in ways that will maintain Western predominance, protect Western interests and promote Western political and economic values. If the UN is to remain acceptable to the majority of people around the world, it has to erase the perception that it serves as a mechanism through which the values of powerful states are imposed on the weaker ones.

If realists have been mainly interested in the pursuit of national interests, idealists have been interested in the UN's universal and progressive character. Idealists believe that the UN has put power politics under check and facilitated the collective management of **international public goods**. From some idealist perspectives, the UN derives legitimacy from its inclusiveness and its potential to bring about human progress. They argue that the greatest strength of the UN is that it is the only universal forum for international cooperation and management. On the issues of democratization and participation, some idealists argue that the UN has neglected non-state actors for too long. Hence the increasing calls for the UN to involve the so-called **global civil society** more deeply in global governance. There is no doubt that a good number of NGOs have achieved phenomenal success in specific issue areas. However, the search for a mechanism for their participation with the UN in global governance has raised difficult questions. Some critics argue that NGOs have the capacity to do a great deal, but they have no obligation to do anything. Voluntary organizations are not accountable, even in theory, to those whom they serve. They suggest that the UN requires great ingenuity to pursue democratization without compromising the effectiveness and universal acceptability of its action.

For constructivists, the legitimacy of the UN is derived largely from its constitutive and transformative character. The UN is both a product, and a producer, of ideas, norms and state interests and identities. It has been an agent of transformation. It has generated numerous ideas on such issues as development, the environment, human rights, women's rights and peacekeeping. In this respect, the UN has become an important norm-setting organization. As the interests, preferences and identities of member states are neither fixed nor exogenously given, the UN has participated, however marginally, in influencing the way they are defined and redefined.

However, there is a perception in the developing world that the UN's transformative power has been harnessed by the West and works to the detriment of non-Western interests. Some of these criticisms were made at the 1993 UN conference on human rights in Vienna, where China and developing countries described the universalization of human rights as a conspiracy by Western governments to pressure non-Western states to change their identities and political and economic systems. However, the Vienna Declaration and Program of Action stated that human rights were universal, indivisible and interdependent, and interrelated, while also recognizing the significance of national and regional particularities and various historical, cultural and religious backgrounds. The Vienna Declaration underscored the clash of two principles – universalism and relativism. Western countries and NGOs from both the North and the South supported the universalist perspective, while non-Western states took the relativist line. The conference also underlined the imperative for the UN to devise a formula through which its ideas and norms in the future would reflect the diversity of the global village.

Critics argue that the exigencies of global governance require the UN to rethink its norms, structures, procedures, and practices. If the UN were to make a major difference to global governance, it would need to address more seriously the imperative for democratization in its agencies, taking account of growing demands for transparency and popular participation. Greater openness would not be achieved without creative efforts to recast sovereignty. For example, in discharging their responsibilities in the human rights area, UN Secretaries-General have often been constrained by the UN Charter, especially Article 2(7) that prohibits intervention in matters that are essentially within the domestic jurisdiction of any state. This part of the Charter has previously been interpreted in a manner in which it has indirectly shielded dictators from the international scrutiny of their human rights records. However, in his address to the General Assembly in September 1999, the Secretary-General said there was nothing in the Charter that precluded recognition that there were rights beyond borders. Some critics argue that this line of re-thinking should be stretched further. With the rapid changes brought about by globalization, what was essentially within the domestic jurisdiction of states in 1945 may not remain so in this millennium. Analysts argue that it is incumbent upon the UN administrators to reinterpret the Charter consistently to reflect the new global realities.

The UN Secretary-General's 1999 speech reflected the extent to which international law and diplomacy have changed in response to shifts in global values. Some of the most important changes in international law and diplomacy stem from the growth in international humanitarian law and the proliferation of international human rights instruments since the end of World War Two. The 1948 Universal Declaration of Human Rights was the most significant step in efforts to universalize rights. The impetus for it was the brutality of World War Two, and especially the extermination of Jews. The international society's response to the Jewish holocaust was to establish the Nuremberg tribunal. This was a normative development in at least three respects. First, Nuremberg placed human rights in the domain of global politics. Second, it helped redefine aspects of morality at the global level. Third, for the first time in history it gave coherence to the idea of **crimes against humanity**, in which individuals, rather than governments, were held responsible for war atrocities. The idea of crimes against humanity stems from the assumption that each human being has a duty to other human beings. These developments have had an impact on international law and diplomacy, which, in turn, have affected the practice of sovereignty. This development is one of the UN's major contributions to global governance.

Further reading

Bull, H. (1995) *The Anarchical Society: A Study of Order in World Politics*, 2nd edn, Basingstoke: Palgrave.

Falk, R. A., Kim, S. S. and Mendlovitz, S. H. (eds) (1991) *The United Nations and a Just World Order*, Boulder, CO: Westview.

Makinda, S. M. (1998) 'The United Nations and State Sovereignty: Mechanism for Managing International Security', *Australian Journal of Political Science* 33(1), 101–15.

Roberts, A. and Kingsbury, B. (eds) (1993) *United Nations, Divided World*, Oxford: Clarendon.

Price, R. and Zacher, M. (eds) (2004) *United Nations and Global Security*, Basingstoke: Palgrave.

Simma, B (ed.) (1994) *The Charter of the United Nations*, Oxford: Oxford University Press.

Sloan, B. (1991) *United Nations General Assembly Resolutions in Our Changing World*, New York: Transaction Publishers.

Thakur, R. and Newman, E. (eds) (2000) *New Millennium, New Perspectives: The United Nations, Security and Governance*, Tokyo: United Nations University Press.

United Nations (2000) *We the Peoples*, New York: United Nations.

Weiss, T. G., Forsythe, D. P. and Coate, R. A. (2001) *The United Nations and Changing World Politics*, 3rd edn, Boulder, CO: Westview,

See also: global compact; collective security; global governance; League of Nations; multilateralism; United Nations Development Program

SAMUEL M. MAKINDA

United Nations Development Program (UNDP)

A specialized agency within the **United Nations** system, with particular oversight of technical assistance. Like the majority of the UN's agencies, UNDP reports formally to the Economic and Social Council. The UNDP is perhaps best known for its *Human Development Report*, an annual publication in which a country's 'wealth' is calculated by the well being of its citizens. The statistics collected broaden the measurement of fiscal health from the traditional econometric rankings of Gross Domestic Product and the balance of trade to include a wider catchment of social, political and economic indicators. It takes into account Human Development Indicators such as access to education and health care, life expectancy, indicators of gender equity, the distribution of wealth and many other socio-economic variables to produce a global league table of relative disadvantage.

Established in 1966, UNDP's organizational antecedents stretch back to the 1940s. At that time technical assistance – a theme that embodies economic and social concerns – was in most cases a component of major infrastructural and public works projects. With the establishment of the United States' 1948 Marshall Plan for European reconstruction, UN-led technical assistance projects were directed primarily to developing countries. In 1949, this division of labor between the United Nations and the United States was for-

malized through the creation of the Expanded Program of Technical Assistance for Economic Development of Under-Developed Countries (EPTA).

In 1958, the UN Special Fund was established. Like EPTA, the Special Fund followed a technical assistance mandate. With project timelines of up to five years, it provided an adjunct to EPTA's short-term interventions. In an era of 'manpower' forecasting, infrastructure expansion, and massive capital works in the decolonizing world, the complementarity between the two agencies became evident. In January 1966, they merged to form UNDP.

The 1970 'Consensus' of the UNDP Governing Council led to the creation of 'development co-operation cycles'. The term refers to five-year multi-sectoral plans geared toward holistic country-based **development**. As a result of these moves, the UN General Assembly created the category of 'Least Developed Country' (LDC).

A major facet of UNDP operations is its country office network. With a limited presence in industrialized countries, the country offices are headed by Resident Representatives/Coordinators acting as 'on the ground' liaisons between the national government and UN agencies. Nineteen EPTA offices existed in 1952, with projects financed in a total of ninety-seven countries and territories. By the mid-1990s, UNDP had operations in 175 countries and territories, with liaison offices in 136 countries. Numbers remained relatively constant in subsequent years, with 166 country offices in the mid-2000s. While this decentralized approach has certain operational advantages, it can come at the cost of organizational consistency. For example, as part of the 2001 'change process', a global survey of UNDP staff revealed that most of them did not have a clear understanding of the organization's goals. The survey revealed a significant disjunction between the targets set in the New York headquarters and the operations of country-based officers.

UNDP typically partners other agencies in aid projects. Working across a multiplicity of sectors (including rural development, urban renewal, education, health, energy production, and telecommunications), UNDP's habitual focus is on vocational development and technical assistance projects with direct economic impact. UNDP has consistently held that economic growth and fiscal efficiency is imperative to socio-political stability. As every country is at least a token donor, UNDP has traditionally argued that this is a testament to its political and ideological neutrality as an aid agency. In January 1994 the forty-eight member Governing Council was replaced by a thirty-six member Executive Board. UNDP is headed by an Administrator, and since its inception all but one UNDP Administrator (Mark Malloch Brown, appointed July 1999) has been an American citizen.

The UNDP's funding base has progressively grown. In 1972, at the commencement of UNDP's first planning cycle, voluntary contributions were close to US$250 million. Reflecting the oil shocks of the early 1970s, and the associated drop in Official Development Assistance (ODA), government contributions to UNDP stagnated. In 1975, UNDP faced financial austerity. Thus commenced (first under the leadership of Administrator Rudolph Peterson and consolidated under the long-serving Administrator Bradford Morse) an extended process of diversifying UNDP's fundraising activities. Although this process was financially successful, resulting in a four-fold increase in technical assistance funding by 1984, it had long-term organizational consequences. The subdivision of financing, for example, into 'core' and 'non-core' budgets has allowed bilateral donors to tie an increasing proportion of their aid to specific projects (non-core), while minimizing their donations to UNDP's discretionary core coffers. In 1980, core contributions represented 90 per cent of UNDP resources but by 1994, roughly half of the voluntary contributions by member countries flowed to UNDP's core budget (US$928 million) and half to non-core funds (US$912 million). By 2000, core contributions had dropped below 30 per cent of assets (US$634 million) compared to US$1.56 billion pledged to specific non-core, non-discretionary programs or country-based projects. Although the overall UNDP budget expanded to US$3.2 billion in 2003, the decline in the proportion of funds directed to the core budget continued, falling to 24 per cent of UNDP assets.

In 1994, UNDP Administrator James Gustave Speth instigated the 'Initiatives for Change' process, which placed the concept of Sustainable Human Development at the centre of UNDP operations. Focusing on poverty elimination, job creation, environmental regeneration and the advancement of women, UNDP sought greater international cooperation, support for country-driven **development**, and the modest inclusion of civil society in development planning. Under Administrator Mark Malloch Brown this general emphasis continued, with UNDP resources directed toward public sector reform, democratic governance, poverty reduction and upstream policy advice.

The UN Millennium Development Goals have realigned UNDP operations. Derived from the Millennium Declaration, and adopted unanimously by UN member countries in September 2000, the Millennium Development Goals are time-based development targets. UNDP was subsequently tasked by the UN

Secretary-General, Kofi Annan, to act as the coordinator of the Millennium Development Goals within the UN system. Like many UN agencies, UNDP has been obliged to undertake almost continuous reform. In 1999, UNDP introduced its 'Results Oriented' Annual Report (ROAR). Tellingly, the 2004 Annual Report proclaimed the arrival of a 'New UNDP'. In that year, Malloch Brown commenced a second four-year term as Administrator.

Further reading

Jones, P. W. and Coleman, D. (2004) *The United Nations and Education: Multilateralism, Development and Globalization*, London: Falmer.

UNDP (various editions) *Human Development Report*, New York: United Nations Development Program.

UNDP (1999) *UNDP in the 1990s: The Story of a Transformation*, New York: United Nations Development Program.

See also: development; foreign aid; United Nations

DAVID COLEMAN

Uti possidetis

The legal principle of *uti possidetis* protects existing borders during the process of creating new states. Both the norms of territorial integrity and *uti possidetis* constitute limitations on the right to **self-determination**. As a customary rule of **international law**, *uti possidetis* delimits the international borders of a new state upon its emergence as a subject of international law. The new state retains its pre-existing boundaries at the precise moment of its birth, which are elevated to the status of its international frontiers unless all concerned states agree otherwise. These pre-existing boundaries could be the former state's international frontiers with other independent internationally recognized entities; the internal administrative divisions of the predecessor state in case of a successful dissolution or **secession**; or in the case of **decolonization**, the former administrative delimitations within a colony. A new state is therefore stuck with its colonial heritage as the principle of *uti possidetis* freezes the territorial situation as it exists at the precise moment of independence.

Uti possidetis originated as a rule of Roman law, found acceptance as part of international Law and eventually constitutional law in South and Central America during decolonization in the early nineteenth century, and re-emerged in Africa in the middle of the twentieth century again in the context of decolonization. It has also been applied to the dissolutions of Yugoslavia and the USSR in the post-colonial context.

In Spanish America, *uti possidetis* transformed borders *between* various Spanish colonies into the international borders of new states. Although the application of the principle did not lead to arbitrary divisions of ethnic communities in Spanish America, African colonial boundaries were significantly different. The colonial penchant for geometric lines has left Africa with a high concentration of states whose frontiers are drawn with little or no consideration for factors of geography, **ethnicity**, economic convenience or reasonable means of communication that have played a part in boundary determinations elsewhere. However, *uti possidetis* prevailed over rival suggestions for redrawing borders during the decolonization of Africa, and the new African states pledged to respect the principle. It also suited the colonial powers because immediate decolonization had become a political imperative for them and a redrawing of borders would have meant an undesirable, prolonged and messy involvement with former colonies. While the application of *uti possidetis* in Africa during decolonization can be viewed from the pragmatic perspective of having been the only possible solution that resolved many if not all border disputes, it can also be blamed for the numerous bloody and prolonged ethnic conflicts that Africa has endured and continues to endure.

Uti possidetis is often defended as a political and legal rule that is imperative for the successful emergence of a new state in international law. It determines the exclusive territorial jurisdiction of a new state, which is a pre-condition for the exercise of **sovereignty** and statehood. *Uti possidetis* functions as an aid to the exercise of self-determination by making it orderly and therefore more acceptable. It offers a practical solution involving minimum disruption in a potentially difficult situation, provides the stability, peace and **security** required for nation building after independence, and reduces the potential for conflicts by providing instant borders. As all borders are ultimately 'unnatural', a national identity can be built up and the goals of internal self-determination realized within any borders. It has been argued that in the absence of an inherited borders rule like *uti possidetis*, the borders of new states can only be determined by application of the doctrine of 'effective control' or by the use of brute force. Existing states, which happen to share a border with the new state, are also guaranteed acceptance of this international border by the emerging state thus removing the threat to the territorial integrity of other states.

In the context of modern day breakups of states, *uti possidetis* comes into conflict with the now well-established right of self-determination of peoples.

Though *uti possidetis* is of practical use in the process of emergence of a new subject of international law in that it provides the new state with a territorial legitimation, it also establishes a limitation on the right of peoples to self-determination. By pre-determining the territorial outcome of the process of emergence of a new state, *uti possidetis* restricts the availability of the right of self-determination to peoples who happen to inhabit a territorial unit. A people who might otherwise satisfy even the most conservative requirements of objective similarity and subjective group consciousness and thereby fully qualify as a distinct ethnic group, would by the application of *uti possidetis*, be denied a collective exercise of the right to self-determination if they happen to reside on both sides of an internal administrative division in a contiguous colonial unit or a state which is in the process of dissolution. *Uti possidetis* therefore undermines self-determination where pre-existing territorial divisions do not coincide with demands by a people for independent statehood. The basic problem with *uti possidetis* is that it forces peoples to live in political groups they may not want to be a part of.

A blind application of the rule of *uti possidetis* which limits 'territorially' the availability of an otherwise legitimate right of self-determination cannot have any inherent value apart from being a pragmatic rule in the absence of alternatives. While *uti possidetis* might postpone border disputes, its failure to prevent their re-emergence and its failure to eradicate the roots of future **ethnic** conflict and the persecution of minorities points to the need for an alternative framework which might better address concerns of lasting peace, stability, **human rights** and a just world **order**.

Further reading

Casesse, A. (1995) *Self-Determination of Peoples: A Legal Reappraisal*, Cambridge: Cambridge University Press.

Crawford, J. (1979) *The Creation of States in international law*, Oxford: Clarendon Press.

Musgrave, T. D. (1997) *Self-Determination and National Minorities*, Oxford: Clarendon Press.

Ratner, S. (1996) 'Drawing a Better Line: *Uti Possidetis* and the Borders of New States' *American Journal of International Law* 90, 590–624.

Shaw, M. N. (1997) 'Peoples, Territorialism and Boundaries', *European Journal of International Law* 3, 477–506.

See also: decolonization; international law; self-determination; Westphalia

MARTIN GRIFFITHS

W

War

In the contemporary popular imagination war is commonly viewed as a particular sort of state activity carried out by organized and identifiable military forces, employing lethal weapons, directed against the armed forces of one or more adversaries. But recently, many other types of activities have also been characterized as 'wars'. There is the 'war on drugs', the 'war against terrorism', 'gang wars', and even the 'war against cancer'. We employ terms such as **ethnic conflict**, insurgency, irregular war and **terrorism** to suggest less conventional methods of using armed force. We would become involved in an endless debate as to what exactly counts as a war were we to include virtually any activity that involves the use of violence.

The classical definition of war offered by Karl von Clausewitz (1780–1831) in the early nineteenth century asserts that the essential characteristics of war include a public agent (often but not exclusively states), a political purpose, and organized force. This definition excludes spontaneous riots, organized criminal activity, some terrorist activity, and research into diseases.

Contemporary research into war distinguishes between interstate wars, **civil wars**, and wars by states against non-state targets, as in wars of colonial conquest (extra-state wars). Interstate wars can include armed interventions and wars waged by coalitions and **alliance**s. Intrastate wars can include civil wars (attempts to gain control of the political apparatus), wars of **secession**, and wars between distinct social groups and the government. Armed conflicts that have fewer than 1,000 casualties may include border raids, various types of 'incidents', retaliations, and the like, but these are not included as wars. It does not matter whether force is used by conventional armies arrayed against each other on battlefields, or by local groups of guerrillas that emphasize stealth and secrecy. These are questions of strategy and tactics, developed according to the agents' peculiar strengths and weaknesses. Thus terms such as 'irregular war', 'guerrilla war', 'unconventional war', and 'revolutionary war' tell us only that particular styles of fighting are involved, not that the war is of a fundamentally different kind.

The incidence of war

War has been one of the hallmarks of relations between distinct polities, whether they are city-states, **empire**s, tribes, kingdoms, or modern states. Evidence of organized warfare goes back at least 8,000 years to the ancient civilizations of the Middle East (Sumeria, Egypt, for example) and to the Chou civilization (twelfth century BC). In the latter, the use of organized force was particularly frequent during the 'Period of the Warring States' (403–221 BC), during which the number of states dwindled from approximately 170 to about one dozen. Those that disappeared were the subjects of conquest, dismemberment, and annexation. Relations between independent polities were similar in ancient Greece, during the Roman period, the entire Mediterranean basin for many centuries, the Italian city-states during the Renaissance, and the great armed confrontations and conquests by the Europeans and Americans over African, Latin and North American, and Asian indigenous societies.

However, the raw incidence of interstate war is not an adequate measure of the safety of the international community. If wars between states were a constant risk we would expect them to increase with the expansion of the **international system**. As the international system has grown from an average membership of about twenty states in the nineteenth century to almost 200 today, the risks of war for the average state have declined dramatically. In this sense, the world has become substantially safer.

Several other facts about the incidence of interstate war need emphasis. In the last five centuries, and particularly since the early eighteenth century, war has been primarily though not exclusively a great power activity (see **great powers**). Since 1945, the United States has become involved in or launched more wars and armed interventions than all the other great powers combined. Colonial wars of conquest and subjugation (extra-state war), a common type of war in the nineteenth century, have become obsolete. The incidence of intrastate wars has been moving steadily upward, with a particularly significant increase since 1960. This has been the legacy of colonialism and the birth of dozens of 'weak' states that, while possessing formal **sovereignty**, lack many of the attributes of sustainable statehood. The problem of civil wars, state collapse, and armed secessions, most leading to various types of humanitarian catastrophes, will remain the main problem on the international agenda. The general pattern of contemporary war, then, is one of diminishing interstate armed conflicts and expanding domestic conflicts.

Why war? Issues, interests, and values that generate armed conflict

Analysts have attempted to explain why interstate wars recur throughout history. Some have emphasized human nature or biological drives. This line of reasoning leads nowhere since it fails to explain immense variations in the locales and agents of war. Sweden has not been at war since 1721; Israel has fought four wars and two *intifadas* in its brief history; and the United States has used military force in the last half century more often than all other states combined. To claim that human nature accounts for war is analogous to an explanation of automobile accidents because we have automobiles. Yet others have emphasized the characteristics of the public agents – in this case, states – as the best explanations. Great Powers have been involved in wars more often than smaller powers, but other state characteristics such as level of **development** or size do not explain most of the variance in war incidence. However, type of polity does make a difference: democracies do not go to war against each other. Finally, there is a body of research that seeks to find correlations between characteristics of the international system and war. The most famous is **balance of power** theory. It hypothesizes that in the face of imminent **hegemony**, other states will form coalitions to balance the threat.

Other avenues of research have examined the relationship between power distributions – for example, bipolar, tripolar, and multipolar – and war, but the results have not been robust. Wars have recurred in systems with all types of power distributions, including those that were both balanced and unbalanced.

Political agents have a variety of purposes including economic welfare, **security** in the broadest sense, gaining international reputation and stature, and in a few cases, remaking the world in their own image through some great ideological crusade. They occasionally go to war to defend or achieve these purposes. Take two extreme cases, at each end of a continuum of purposes and interests. Bhutan, a mountain kingdom situated between India and Tibet, has sought primarily to raise the welfare of its peasant population, and otherwise to be left alone. At the other extreme, Adolph Hitler had a dream of creating a 'Thousand Year Reich' within a 'New Order' that would require transforming the relations between sovereign states into relations between a hierarchy of races, with Aryans commanding a descending order of Latins, Slavs, and Africans, and with the physical liquidation of Jews and Gypsies. Hitler pursued this grand vision of a new world **order** through armed conquest. Conquered peoples were to be used as slave labor for the master race. Between these two extremes of Bhutan and Nazi Germany, most states most of the time seek to stimulate economic growth, promote the national culture, and join with other states to help achieve common purposes in the domains of science, technology, health, culture, education, and the like.

To understand war, then, we need to examine the kinds of issues – values, purposes, and interests – that generate conflict. Wars result primarily from situations where two or more political

agents are not able to achieve or defend their multiple purposes through negotiations, collaboration, and other peaceful means. What have been the major issues that lead to armed conflict? In primitive warfare, the main purpose was loot, treasure, and slaves. Later, dreams of empire, conquest of land and peoples, motivated vast military expeditions. In seventeenth century Europe, the contest between Catholic and Protestant princes was a foundation for the Thirty Years' War (1618–48) that devastated most of central Europe. For the remainder of the seventeenth century, states went to war primarily over issues of trade and fisheries (over which there were three wars between Holland and England in less than thirty years), colonial monopolies, and territory. Issues of dynastic succession were also prominent sources of war. In the eighteenth century, contests over territory continued to generate wars, followed by trade and succession problems. In the nineteenth century, wars to create states were the most prominent type. The United Provinces (Holland) launched the first modern 'war of national liberation' in the mid-seventeenth century. The Americans fought to free themselves from the British Crown in 1776. Armed revolts followed in the Spanish empire in Latin America in the 1820s. Greece fought a war of independence in the late 1820s and early 1830s, Hungarians and Poles rebelled for independence in mid-century, and wars that led to the unification of Germany and Italy took place in the second half of the nineteenth century. Wars to create the new states of Central and East Europe attended the collapse of the Russian, Ottoman, and Austro-Hungarian empires at the end of World War One. Nineteen wars of 'national liberation' against the colonial powers began in earnest after World War Two. Three wars for independence were the consequence of the collapse of Yugoslavia after 1991. Secessionist wars, all fought to establish independent states – in Kashmir, Sudan, Palestine, and elsewhere – continue. The value of national **self-determination**, defined as independent statehood, has been the source of more wars than any other issue in the last two hundred years. In addition to this major source of conflict, armed interventions, often for ideological reasons, have been used to install 'friendly' regimes or to oust governments that are deemed ideologically incorrect or tyrannical. In the last century, territory has declined significantly as a source of conflict, and commercial issues are no longer resolved through military force.

The most devastating and widespread wars of the last one-half millennium have been the consequence of dreams or long-range goals of reorganizing the international system or establishing paramountcy in Europe. The fear of Hapsburg/Catholic hegemony in Europe in the seventeenth century was a major source of the Thirty Years War. Although Louis XIV went to war at least twice late in the seventeenth century largely for reasons of glory and personal prestige, many of the kings and princes of the era genuinely feared that the 'Sun King' was attempting to establish what would amount to a French-based continental empire. A century later, Napoleon not only dreamed of creating a new European order based on his family's predominance but also engaged in serial warfare to establish it. Whatever its intentions in 1914, by the later stages of the Great War, German aspirations had grown to include an expanded overseas empire, overlordship over vast swaths of Russia and central Europe, and hegemony over the low countries and France. Hitler's dreams were, as noted, even more spectacular. In each of these cases, those who did not share the dreams and visions went to war to protect their

independence. National independence and territorial integrity thus remain the fundamental values of the international community – they are specified as such in the Charter of the **United Nations** – and those that threaten them are likely to cause wars.

The changing character of war

The technology of warfare did not change significantly between the pre-Christian era and the fifteenth century, approximately. There were essentially two environments on which battles took place: on land and on the sea. Military technology was geared to the actions of massed men on foot or on horseback, or on naval vessels whose range was inherently limited by seasonal factors and lack of maps and knowledge of far away seas. The application of gunpowder and the development of cannons in the fifteenth century significantly changed defensive arrangements, rendering walled towns and castles increasingly vulnerable. By World War One, two entirely new environments were opened up to military action: the skies and undersea. Along with long-range (e.g., more than 30 kilometers) cannons, cities and towns were now capable of being destroyed in a matter of days, and shipping was vulnerable to relatively hidden submarines. World War Two demonstrated how war had changed from a duel between professional armies in the eighteenth century to a struggle between nations. Massive firebomb raids by the Allies in 1945 against Tokyo, Hamburg, and Dresden and the atomic bombs on Hiroshima and Nagasaki killed more civilians (about 350,000) in several days than all the battle casualties of the eighteenth century. With the development of hydrogen warheads and intercontinental ballistic missile to carry them, those who possess them are now capable of destroying large cities and populations of over ten million in a matter of minutes. Most contemporary strategists emphasize that such weapons cannot be used in the classical sense of employing armed force to defend or achieve known political objectives. To use such weapons and face the certainty of retaliation through **mutual assured destruction** (MAD) deployments, would mean mutual national suicide; hence, the purpose of these weapons is primarily to deter, that is, to prevent rather than to prosecute war.

Recent technological developments – sometimes referred to as the **revolution** in military affairs – re-establish the classical idea of using force to diminish or destroy the adversary's capacity to resist. With precision-guided weapons, laser technology, and various devices that reduce the 'fog' of war, recent interstate wars, particularly those led by the United States, have demonstrated that operations directed primarily at military and command and control targets can be more effective in defeating an adversary than massive bombing raids such as those conducted in World War Two.

Ideas about war, along with technology, have been no less important in changing its characteristics. The Thirty Years War involved large, undisciplined mercenary armies that were under only limited political control, forced to survive through plunder and indiscriminate killing of those who resisted. Many of the original issues that had led to armed conflict were lost in the carnage, and killing appeared to become purposeless and systemic.

At a time when the nascent dynastic states of Europe were already weak from internal rebellions and numerous challenges to the sovereignty of the princes, the Thirty Years War was a powerful learning experience. The princes, led by dynasts such as Louis XIV of France,

learned that if they wished to consolidate their hold on **power** and establish strong states, they would have to develop professional armed forces under central state **authority**. The eighteenth century was an era of military institutionalization in Europe. The leading dynasts created military academies, increasingly selected their leading officers on the basis of merit rather than family lineage, and fostered the development of the 'science' of military strategy. Karl von Clausewitz, an officer in the service of the Prussian king during the Napoleonic Wars, wrote his classic *On War* to summarize both the advantages and shortcomings of military thinking during the era of the Enlightenment. He popularized the view that force is an instrument of statecraft. It is to be used primarily in conjunction with **diplomacy** as a last resort when other means of persuasion have failed. In this sense, war is a continuation of diplomacy by violent means. It is not a substitute for diplomacy, or divorced from it. Much of the modem philosophizing about war has taken as its starting point the Clausewitzian notion of armed conflict as part of a process of persuasion and bargaining between states.

In the twentieth century, other ideas about war become popular in some quarters. Certain writers during the early years of the Bolshevik regime in Soviet Russia praised war as an instrument of revolution. The war experience was one that could help mobilize people, and particularly the working class, to overthrow their bourgeois regimes. Important doctrinal innovations by Mao Tse-tung, Lin Piao, and Vo Nguyen Giap in the 1960s and 1970s emphasized the importance of mobilizing the people for war against imperialism. Trained armies were important, but victory could be gained only through effective work with, and through, the 'people'. 'People's

War' was a popular moniker for this type of armed struggle, and was designed to distinguish it from the Clausewitzian, classical European idea of war as an armed contest between professional armies, in an environment where soldiers and civilians were to be kept distinct from each other.

Nationalism, including the idea that each citizen has a moral obligation to offer his or her welfare and even life to the greater purposes of the nation and its embodiment in the state, has also helped transform interstate war. Where armies numbered in the tens of thousands in the eighteenth century, by World War Two they ran, as in the case of the Soviet Union, to more than ten million. War had become an undertaking requiring the mobilization of the entire population and the transformation of the economy from producing goods for public consumption into production of war materiel. The purposes of war also changed, from pursuing or defending discreet interests such as a piece of territory or a colony, to unconditional surrender and the punishment of an entire vanquished population. In 1919 the victors imposed a draconian peace treaty on the defeated Germans, stripping them of their navy and colonies, taking some of their territories, imposing socially ruinous economic reparations, and in general isolating Germany from any activity in international diplomacy. In 1945, the victors vanquished Nazi Germany and Japan under a doctrine of 'unconditional surrender' and did not restore them to sovereign status for several years.

Limitations on the use of force

One can observe throughout recorded history the inclination of polities within a common culture to adopt norms and even laws that limit both when force can be used legitimately (*jus ad bello*) and how that force should be used (*jus in bello*). The Chinese rulers of the 'Warring States' period (403–221 BC) and the Greek city states, for example, developed numerous rules of etiquette and propriety relating to the conduct of war, although they seldom bothered to enunciate doctrines of **just war**. The Chinese had regulations dealing with the treatment of prisoners; The Greeks had their famous truces that were to take place during the Olympic games. But wars between polities from different civilizations were seldom constrained by rules of any kind. The Mongols, who in the twelfth through fourteenth centuries swept through much of present-day Middle East, Russia, and East Europe, offered no mercy to those who resisted: the defeated were slaughtered and those that survived were quickly enslaved. Similarly, the Spanish conquistadors, the Germans who 'pacified' the natives in their African colonies, and the Americans in their conquest of the continent, offered no quarter to indigenous peoples who resisted. Men, women, and children were destroyed indiscriminately.

Notions of just war began to develop in medieval Europe. The Pope and other church authorities judged which parties to a conflict fought for a just cause. Those who did not meet certain criteria faced the possibility of excommunication. In the seventeenth century, international lawyers and legal philosophers wrestled with the problem of defining the criteria under which armed force could be used legitimately, but they faced strong opposition from the nascent monarchs who insisted that the right to go to war was an inherent attribute of sovereignty that cannot be limited. Throughout the century, the monarchs went to war, often on flimsy or trumped up grounds, conquered their neighbors' territories and colonies, annexed them to their own domains, and sold off or partitioned other conquests. The first significant limitation on the right to use armed force appeared at the Congress of Vienna (1815), when the great powers agreed that they would use armed force only with the consent of their colleagues, and that conquests had to be approved by them as well. Policy did not always follow doctrine throughout the nineteenth century, but by the end of that era publics and political parties had sought to limit the right to use force through major conferences and treaties.

World War One was the final catalyst. In the eighteenth century, war had been popularly constructed as an event that carried with it the possibility of glory, reputation, and dynastic brilliance. By 1919, broad publics, reacting to the eight million casualties of the Great War, portrayed war as a national disaster, a disease, and a curse against the upward movement of societies to ever-higher levels of civilization. The Covenant of the **League of Nations** symbolized a dramatic change in perceptions of war. War was now to be legitimate only in self-defense, and if ordered by the organs of the League against an aggressor (the idea of **collective security**). The 1928 Pact of Paris declared that aggressive war constituted a crime against humanity. Both Nazi and Japanese war leaders were indicted in 1945 under this criterion. Under the Charter of the United Nations states can legitimately use military force only for individual or collective self-defense, or in response to a determination by the Security Council that a particular situation is a threat to the peace, a breach of the peace, or an act of aggression. Under other contemporary doctrines and norms, the old right of conquest has been abrogated: states will not accept as legitimate any act of conquest or assaults against the territorial integrity or independence of states. Any regime of occupation is con-

sidered temporary and the occupier must observe numerous constraints under international law. The near-universal criticism against the United States attack on Iraq in 2003 without **United Nations** approval demonstrates the extent to which the use of force today requires community endorsement in order to attain **legitimacy**.

The Laws of War (*jus in bello*) have proliferated as war has become increasingly destructive. The list of regulations includes, among others, the 1863 United States General Order No. 100 (the Lieber Code), the 1864 Geneva Convention for the protection of the sick and wounded, the 1868 St Petersburg Convention prohibiting the use of certain kinds of missiles (and also reiterating the Clausewitzian notion that the only legitimate object which States should endeavor to accomplish during war is to weaken the military forces of the enemy), the 1899 and 1907 Hague Conventions, the 1922 Hague Aerial Bombardment Rules, and the 1949 and 1977 Geneva Protocols. All of these instruments contain rules that seek to minimize human suffering and to protect non-combatants from military assaults, abuses of **human rights**, pillage, and **war rape**.

There has been an almost perfect inverse correlation between the number of codified laws limiting the use of force and actual combat activity. Statistics of civilian casualties tell the tale. In World War One, approximately 5 per cent of the casualties were civilians. In World War Two, about half of the 50 million people who perished from military operations and deliberate massacres were civilians. The Nazi regime not only targeted civilians in massive terror air raids, but also built a large bureaucratic machinery to liquidate designated populations, including Jews, Gypsies, Soviet prisoners of war, and others. In the numerous wars since 1945, most of which have been of the civil or secessionist type, about 90 per cent of the victims have been civilians. Indeed, the overwhelming fact of most recent intra-state wars has been the deliberate targeting of civilians, including women and children, in military operations. The codification of restraints on the use of military force thus has not been effective in protecting the innocent. The 'revolution in military affairs' and its emphasis on targeting only military assets may help reverse this situation, but only the United States and a few other governments possess the technology to conduct war in a restrained manner.

The de-institutionalization of war

Starting in late seventeenth century Europe, war became institutionalized. The governments of the day developed scientific rules of strategy, transformed their rag-tag mercenary forces into a career, provided professional instruction through military academies, and most important, developed norms, rules and etiquette that helped establish and maintain clear distinctions between combatants and civilians, between combatants and neutrals, and between the armed forces and the political authorities under whose command they operated. There were common repertoires of strategy, tactics, logistics, and armaments, as the dynasts copied each other's innovations in each domain.

Contrast a typical contemporary intrastate war with an interstate war in the eighteenth century. In the latter era, governments typically issued a formal declaration of war before hostilities began. In the course of the war, they did not attack unarmed citizens, except in some instances when a town or city refused to surrender after siege. The purpose of armed combat was to maneuver

adversaries into untenable tactical positions, and to induce them to surrender. Surrenders were formalized through ceremonies in which defeated forces were disarmed, and then turned loose to return to their homes. Peace negotiations ended hostilities, after which the normal rules of international diplomacy were restored. Wars had distinct beginnings and endings, and rarely lasted more than three years.

Many wars of the past one-half century have displayed dramatically different characteristics. Atrocities, usually committed against innocent civilians, usually announce the beginning of an armed conflict within states. While some wars have had as their main purpose the goal of national self-determination or secession from an already established state, many others have had little purpose other than looting, grabbing control over natural resources, engaging in illegal trade activities, procuring women and slave labor, and extorting revenues from peasants. Operations typically target civilians, and lacking trained armies, the parties resort to impressing children (about 300,000 in the early twenty-first century) or hiring mercenaries (see **mercenary**). Terror is a standard practice in the military campaigns, and many combatants, often termed 'militias', are under no effective political control. They establish their own 'state within a state', sustain themselves primarily through criminal activities and terror, and generally have little interest in resolving the conflict because to do so they would have to forgo economic opportunities. The parties enter into peace negotiations primarily to gain time and even more loot; most cease-fires and truces are violated within a short period from the time of signing. The average post-1945 war has lasted about a quarter of a century and some continue considerably longer. Lacking clear political purposes, encouraging systematic violations of the Laws of War and humanitarian law, having no underlying ideas or theories of military strategy, and few of the characteristics of a military profession, these wars populate that unclear dividing line between war and criminality. Such wars have become de-institutionalized. Their victims are to be found in Burma (Myanmar), Sri Lanka, Palestine, Sudan, Rwanda, Burundi, Nigeria, Liberia, Sierra Leone, Bosnia, Kosovo, Tajikistan, Kashmir, the Congo, and many other places. Many wars have taken place within former colonies, where states are weak in **legitimacy**, **security** is scarce, societies are split between religious, ethnic, and language divisions, resources are available for plunder, and economic conditions are in a downward spiral. To the extent that these conditions continue to prevail in some areas of the world, intrastate wars will continue to be a prominent feature of contemporary life. At the same time, if present trends continue, interstate wars will become increasingly rare. Most states most of the time no longer face serious threats from their neighbors. The growing sense of international peace and security, defined as a declining fear of facing external aggression, is indicated by the reconfiguration of armed forces in many countries. Increasingly, they define their missions to include participation in multilateral **peacekeeping** and **peace enforcement** actions and dealing with domestic problems such as drug running and natural disasters.

Further reading

Ballentine, K. and Sherman, J. (2003) *The Political Economy of Armed Conflict: Beyond Greed and Grievance*, Boulder, CO: Lynne Rienner.

Best, G. (1994) *War and Law since 1945*, Oxford: Oxford University Press.

Holsti, K. J. (1991) *Peace and War: Armed Conflicts and International Order 1648–1989*, Cambridge: Cambridge University Press.

Holsti, K. J. (1995) *The State, War, and the State of War*, Cambridge: Cambridge University Press.

Howard, M. (1976) *War in European History*, Oxford: Oxford University Press.

Ignatieff, M. (1998) *The Warrior's Honour: Ethnic War and the Modern Conscience*, Toronto: Viking Press.

Keegan, J. (1993) *A History of Warfare*, New York: Alfred A. Knopf

Sarkees, M. R, Whelan, F. W. and Singer, J. D. (2003) 'Inter-State, Intra-State, and Extra-State Wars: A Comprehensive Look at their Distribution over Time, 1816–1997', *International Studies Quarterly* 47(1), 49–70.

Smith, M. (2003) 'Deconstructing Low Intensity Warfare', *Review of International Studies* 29(1), 19–38.

Van Creveld, M. (1991) *The Transformation of War*, New York: The Free Press.

See also: civil war; failed state; just war; mercenary; patriotism; revolution in military affairs; state formation; terrorism; United Nations; war crime; weapons of mass destruction

KALEVI J. HOLSTI

War crime

The violation of the laws of warfare or customs of **war** committed by any persons, military or civilian. Not all breaches of the laws and customs of war are war crimes. War crimes are offences against the laws of war for which an individual may be held criminally liable. They are distinguished from traditional criminal laws by reason of the fact that they are committed in association or connection with an armed conflict. They are generally more heinous and brutal than traditional crimes and demonstrate a ruthless disregard for the sanctity of human life with a wanton interference with rights of property unrelated to military necessity.

National war crimes codes regulating the conduct of armies have existed for centuries. The first significant national modern war crimes code that went beyond matters of strict military discipline was drafted by Dr Francis Lieber. In 1863 President Lincoln instructed the War Department to settle a series of instructions for the United States Army to use in the Field of battle during the course of the Civil War. These instructions were prepared by Lieber, a Professor of Law and Political Science at Columbia University. The instructions comprised some 159 Articles covering such matters as 'military necessity', punishment of crimes against the inhabitants of hostile countries, and the treatment of prisoners of war and spies.

At around the same time, in Europe, Czar Alexander II of Russia sponsored an international conference to ban the use of lightweight bullets that exploded upon contact with human flesh. As a consequence, the 1868 Declaration of St Petersburg prohibited the use of these bullets. This was the first international convention in modern times to prohibit the use of a particular weapon of war. The Declaration also provided that the 'only legitimate objective of war is to weaken the military forces of the enemy and that the unnecessary use of weapons which uselessly aggravate suffering were contrary to the laws of humanity'.

In 1899 Czar Nicholas II of Russia proposed the holding of another Conference, this time in The Hague, the Netherlands. The purpose of the conference was to consider banning the dropping of bombs from balloons, the use of poisonous gases and expanding bullets, known as 'dumdum' bullets, during war. The 1899 Hague Convention, which was the result of this Conference,

adopted these prohibitions but significantly also introduced the first laws and customs of war on land. The Laws and Customs of War (further modified in 1907) provided for the care of prisoners of war, flags of truce, treatment of the inhabitants and property of occupied territories, and prohibited rape and pillage.

Other Conventions settled upon at The Hague in 1907 included Conventions dealing with Enemy Merchant Ships at the outbreak of Hostilities; The Conversion of Merchant Ships into War Ships; The Laying of Automatic Submarine Contact mines; Bombardment by Naval Forces; and laws of Neutrality.

This attempt to contain the use of excessively destructive weapons of war spurned a proliferation of similar Conventions and Declarations throughout the course of the twentieth century including the Geneva Gas Protocol 1925 which banned the used of poisonous gases as a weapon of war. The protocol was eventually replaced by the Biological Weapons Convention (1972). Other **arms control** conventions included The Conventional Weapons Convention 1980 and the additional protocols of 1995 and 1996; The Chemical Warfare Convention 1993; and the 1997 Ottawa Treaty banning the use of anti personnel land mines.

The Laws of War prohibiting the use of excessively destructive weapons during armed conflict, (gas, bombs, bullets) and the conduct of soldiers, (rape, murder, and pillage), were not originally intended to apply to individuals, but only to the responsible state as a basis of claiming compensation or reparation. Thus although the conduct was prohibited the laws did not give rise to individual criminal responsibility at the international level. This situation was to change after World War One when individuals were held individually liable for the commission of certain war crimes.

The laws and customs of war discussed above are generally referred to as the Hague Laws, which are to be distinguished from the Geneva Laws which are known as international humanitarian laws. However the serious breach of an international humanitarian law can still be a war crime for which a person can be individually responsible.

The Geneva Laws had their origins in the middle of the nineteenth century, when Henry Dunant, a Swiss banker, observed the cruelty of war at Solferino in northern Italy. Dunant was struck by the total lack of regulation concerning the removal of the dead and wounded after battle. In 1862 he wrote *Memory of Solferino*. The book suggested that neutral 'relief societies' should be formed to care for the sick and wounded in times of war. He further suggested an international conference to consider and adopt an international agreement on how to care for the soldiers wounded in battle.

In 1864 such a conference was held in Geneva, Switzerland. It concluded by agreeing upon a short Convention that focused on providing a means by which medical attention could be provided to soldiers wounded in battle. It also saw the creation of the Red Cross Society, with its distinctive Red Cross emblem that enshrined the four Red Cross principles of neutrality, humanity, impartiality, and respect for the individual.

The Geneva Conventions first proposed by Henry Dunant were modified and updated throughout the course of the twentieth century. The Geneva Conventions of 1906 made greater provision for the care of wounded and sick soldiers, and were updated in 1929. Following World War Two the Geneva Conventions were again extensively overhauled at a Conference in 1949. As a result of this Conference, four new Geneva Conventions were adopted, each dealing with a specific subject area.

These included the treatment of wounded and sick members of the armed forces, wounded and sick civilians, and the treatment of prisoners of war. The 1949 Geneva Conventions were primarily directed at the regulation of conduct in the course of an international armed conflict. If the conflict is 'international' in character and if 'grave breaches' of the 1949 Geneva Conventions have been committed, then states have an international obligation to ensure that the offenders are brought to justice.

This limitation on the application of the 1949 Geneva Conventions to international armed conflicts was modified in 1977 to cater for the greater protection of civilians in both internal and international armed conflict. Thus the 1977 Additional Protocols when coupled with the 1949 Convention, now constitute the most important source of Geneva law.

Further reading

Dörmann, K. (2003) *Elements of War Crimes*, Cambridge: Cambridge University Press.

Jokic, A. (ed.) (2001) *War Crimes and Collective Wrongdoing*, Oxford: Blackwell.

Kittichaisaree, K. (2001) *International Criminal Law*, Oxford: Oxford University Press.

Maogoto, J. N. (2004) *War Crimes and Realpolitik: International Justice from World War One to the 21st Century*, Boulder, CO: Lynne Rienner.

Roberts, A. and Guelff, R. (1989) *Documents on the Laws of War*, Oxford: Oxford University Press.

See also: crimes against humanity; genocide; just war; war

GRANT NIEMANN

War rape

The rape of women and girls has been a ubiquitous feature of warfare from primitive times. Females are often viewed as 'spoils of **war**' to be sexually assaulted at will, often as a prelude to their enslavement or murder. Rape reflects broader patterns of misogyny (hatred of women) that have pervaded male-dominant societies throughout history, and are especially pronounced in the hypermasculine context of war (Price 2001).

Particularly in the contemporary era, rape of women and girls has been used as a form of **terrorism** to coerce broader communities or populations into surrendering or fleeing. It has been adopted as a means of humiliating community males by emphasizing their inability to protect 'their' women from sexual attack. It has also been used as a form of torture by **security** forces around the world – a practice that reached a zenith during the era of 'national security states' in Latin America and elsewhere during the 1970s and 1980s.

A number of twentieth-century cases have become paradigmatic of war rape. First was the 'Rape of Nanking' in 1937–8, in which tens of thousands of Chinese women and girls were raped by occupying Japanese troops, with the attacks often followed by savage mutilation and murder (Chang 1997). Gendercidal massacres of some 200,000 Chinese men took place during this period (see **gendercide**); an unknown number of men were also raped. In Berlin in 1945, victorious Soviet forces staged a weeks-long rampage of mass rape against German women and girls. When the Pakistani army staged its genocidal crackdown on ethnic Bengalis in East Pakistan (present-day Bangladesh) in 1971 (see **genocide**), gendercidal massacres of Bengali men and boys were accompanied by the rape of some 200,000-400,000 Bengali women. Many of these women were forcibly impregnated and experienced severe social isolation after giving birth. According to Brownmiller, the Bangladeshi atrocities marked the first time that

serious international attention was devoted to wartime rapes of women. This came about in part because of efforts by the independent Bangladeshi government to publicize women's suffering, and in part because of 'a new feminist consciousness that encompassed rape as a political issue' (Brownmiller 1975: 84) (see **feminism**).

This developing feminist consciousness was poised to confront war rape in a far more concerted fashion during the war that consumed former Yugoslavia in the first half of the 1990s. Rape has long been illegal under **international law**. But until recently, it has tended to be 'characterized as an outrage upon personal dignity, or as a crime against honor', separate from 'crimes of violence, including murder, mutilation, cruel treatment, and torture' (Copelon 1998: 65). This changed in the wake of the concerted attention that western media and feminist activists paid to the systematic rape of females as a strategy of war and **ethnic cleansing** in Bosnia-Herzegovina. The International Criminal Tribunal for the Former Yugoslavia (ICTY) was the first to define rape as a **crime against humanity**, and conduct its prosecutions accordingly. The even greater prevalence of rape as an atrocity during the Rwanda genocide of 1994 led to the 1998 conviction of Jean-Paul Akayesu, a former mayor, by the International Criminal Tribunal for Rwanda (ICTR). This marked the first time that a sentence was handed down for rape in a context of **civil war**. Rape was also declared to fall within the mandate of the new **International Criminal Court**. Despite these advances, however, news accounts and **human rights** reports from around the world attest to the continued prominence of rape in contemporary warfare.

Rape of women and girls in war should be set alongside related phenomena such as sexual torture, forced prostitution, and sexual slavery. All these crimes feature rape as an essential tool of violence and subjugation. Perhaps the most dramatic symbols of the wartime sexual victimization and exploitation of women are the so-called 'comfort women', victims of the regimen of forced prostitution instituted by Japanese occupiers in East and Southeast Asia during World War Two. At least 100,000 women, mostly Korean, Indonesian, and Filipina, were tricked and/or coerced into providing sexual services for Japanese troops. To the extent that this was deceptive and/or coercive, it can be considered under the rubric of war rape. In recent years, surviving 'comfort women' have mobilized to seek an apology and compensation from the Japanese government.

Considerable debate has taken place over the concept of genocidal rape, prompted in large part by the war in the Balkans and the genocide in Rwanda during the 1990s. The concept was deployed by Beverly Allen (1996) to designate a military policy of rape for the purpose of genocide. Allen isolated three main forms of genocidal rape: those inflicted in the presence of family and community members to terrorize the targeted community into fleeing; random rapes in detention centres and concentration camps, often as part of torture; and rape in specially-designated rape camps, in which women are often killed following the assault, or forcibly impregnated in the hope that the victim will bear the rapist's child.

Some scholars have criticized the conflation of rape with genocide. Rhonda Copelon (1998: 64) contends that 'rape and genocide are separate atrocities'. Many such critiques, however, place excessive emphasis on death and physical destruction as features of genocide. Under international law, genocidal strategies can also include the infliction of physical and psychological damage on members of a targeted group, as well as the prevention of births within a group. These commonly result (the latter through forced impregnation) from systematic campaigns of rape in war, genocide, and **ethnic cleansing**. The validity of the concept of genocidal rape was further bolstered by events in Rwanda between April and July 1994. Not only was rape a standard component of the assault against Tutsi communities, but the high rates of HIV infection among Hutu troops and militias meant that their victims confronted the fear and possible reality of death by AIDS as a consequence of the attack(s). It is notable that the conviction of Jean-Paul Akayesu by the ICTR included a judgment that rape had been used as a form and strategy of genocide.

In both domestic and international contexts, rape has overwhelmingly been viewed as a crime inflicted upon women by men, although male family and community members are often part of the designated audience of the assault. Only very recently has attention begun to be paid to the rape of males, both in conflict situations and in domestic society. According to Joshua Goldstein (2001), the rape of male soldiers and non-combatants is intimately bound up with other gender-specific atrocities by victorious against defeated males, including castration and large scale gendercidal killing. The intent is not only to inflict physical suffering, but to 'feminize' enemy males by exposing them to violations typically directed against females.

Further reading

Allen, B. (1996) *Rape Warfare: The Hidden Genocide in Bosnia-Herzegovina and Croatia*, Minneapolis, MN: University of Minnesota Press.

Brownmiller, S. (1975) *Against Our Will: Men, Women and Rape*, New York: Bantam Books.

Chang, I. (1997) *The Rape of Nanking*, New York: Basic Books.

Copelon, R. (1998) 'Surfacing gender: Reconceptualizing crimes against women in time of war', in L.A. Lorentzen and J. Turpin (eds) *The Women & War Reader*, New York: New York University Press, 63–79.

Goldstein, J. (ed.) (2001) *War and Gender*, Cambridge: Cambridge University Press.

Hicks, G. (1994) *The Comfort Women*, New York: Norton.

Moser, C. and Clark, F. (eds) (2001) *Victims, Perpetrators or Actors? Gender, Armed Conflict and Political Violence*, London: Zed Books.

Price, L. S. (2001) 'Finding the Man in the Soldier-Rapist: Some Reflections on Comprehension and Accountability', *Women's Studies International Forum* 2(2), 211–27.

Stiglmayer, A. (ed.) (1994) *Mass Rape: The War against Women in Bosnia-Herzegovina*, Lincoln: University of Nebraska Press.

See also: gender; gendercide; war; war crime

ADAM JONES

Weapons of mass destruction (WMD)

Weapons that kill and injure large numbers of people, destroy cities and critical infrastructure, and potentially render the natural environment uninhabitable. The term is generally used to refer collectively to nuclear, **chemical**, and **biological weapons** systems. These weapons are also known by the acronyms ABC (atomic, biological, chemical) and NBC (nuclear, biological, chemical).

Nuclear weapons are the most destructive of the three. Indeed, some scholars argue that they are the only true weapons of mass destruction (WMD). They employ nuclear fission or nuclear fusion to create an explosive force equivalent to many thousands of kilograms of TNT. Depending on the yield of these weapons, they have the potential to destroy everything within a ten to twenty kilometer radius from 'ground zero'.

While not destructive to cities and critical infrastructure, chemical weapons use the toxic properties of man-made chemicals such as Sarin, VX, and Tabun to kill and incapacitate people. Similarly, biological weapons kill by spreading weaponized micro-organisms (and viruses) such as smallpox, anthrax, and tularaemia through the air. Once inhaled, they replicate themselves in the human body causing infection and death. Radiological weapons are sometimes referred to as WMD. These so-called 'dirty bombs' use a standard explosive such as TNT or dynamite in conjunction with radioactive material. Once exploded, these devices spread the material around the blast site, contaminating the environment and anyone who comes in contact with it. Their destructive potential lies both in the explosive force of the weapon and the ability of the radioactive material to cause cancer and other long-term illnesses in humans. Whether 'dirty bombs' should be classified as WMD is an open question. The amount of radioactive material required to kill thousands of people would be substantial and very difficult to handle given the levels of radiation involved. Consequently, these weapons are at the lower end of the scale of lethality and more appropriately regarded as a conventional weapon.

Another candidate for inclusion in the list of WMD is fuel-air devices and cluster bombs. There is no doubt that these weapons are highly destructive to life and property, but there are two reasons why this interpretation should be resisted. The first is that regardless of the destructive power of sophisticated conventional weapons, they pale into insignificance when one considers the consequences of a nuclear detonation. For example, the nuclear weapons detonated over Hiroshima and Nagasaki at the end of World War Two killed over 100,000 people in the first two days, and many more died in the coming months and years from radiation related diseases. Moreover, the Hiroshima bomb destroyed almost 90 per cent of one of Japan's largest cities.

The consequences of a biological weapons attack are equally shocking. According to some estimates, one hundred kilograms of anthrax spores spread over a 300 square kilometer area could kill somewhere between one and three million people. However, the **World Health Organization** (WHO) estimates that a similar amount of anthrax could kill 200,000 and incapacitate 250,000. Regardless of the differences in existing estimates, it is clear that the collateral damage from weapons of mass destruction is of a different order of magnitude to conventional weapons.

The second point is that weapons of mass destruction are portable and relatively easy to conceal. A nuclear device capable of destroying a medium size city can be carried in a small suitcase. The Sarin gas attack that killed twelve and injured 5,500 people in a Tokyo subway consisted of two small pouches of a chemical agent. In contrast, large conventional weapons are often 500 to 1,000 kilograms in weight and require sophisticated high altitude bombers to facilitate delivery to their target.

While nuclear weapons are an invention of the twentieth century, the military use of chemical and biological agents is almost as old as **war** itself. The contamination of wells and the use of poison-tipped arrows was a common practice in ancient times. In the fourteenth century, the Tartars catapulted the corpses of plague victims into the besieged city of Kaffa in the Ukraine. In the seventeenth century, the British army is reported to have given blankets infected with smallpox to native American Indians in the hope of reducing their ability to fight. More recently, the Japanese developed a sophisticated chemical and biological weapons program (Unit 731) in Manchuria that lasted from 1932 until the end of the Second World War. Many thousands of people died as a consequence of this program, including 1,700 Japanese troops.

Chemical weapons played a major role in World War One. Phosgene, mustard, and chlorine gas killed almost 100,000 soldiers and injured more than one million. In all, some 129,000 tons of gas were used during the conflict, with the Germans by far the biggest users (68,000 tons). So concerned were leaders about the horrifying effects of these agents that in 1925 the **League of Nations** sought to ban the manufacture, use and stockpiling of these weapons.

The threat of a nuclear exchange between Russia and the United States of America has receded since the end of the **cold war**. However, this has not eliminated the threat posed by these weapons. There are two sources of concern. The first is that these weapons may be developed or acquired by sub-state actors such as criminal organizations or terrorist groups. Documents captured by British soldiers in Afghanistan suggest that **al-Qaeda** had successfully built a small radiological device. According to other sources, the organization has actively sought to acquire the material necessary to construct a nuclear device and has experimented with chemical agents.

The second area of concern is **rogue state**s such as Iran and North Korea. Both countries are actively pursuing a nuclear capability, with North Korea the more advanced of the two. Also, both countries have large stockpiles of chemical weapons and active biological weapons programs. While **deterrence** may help to reduce the danger posed by such states, the problems associated with horizontal proliferation are more challenging. Chemical and biological weapons are relatively cheap to develop and, as the Tokyo subway attack demonstrates, they are difficult to detect.

The world has lived with WMD for more than a century and will continue to do so in the future. Some scholars predict the development of weapons that can alter human DNA (genetic weapons) or destroy electronic and communications systems (E weapons). Others have gone as far as to suggest that WMD could be developed using artificial intelligence and robotics. Such 'Terminator' technology may seem far-fetched at present, but at the end of the nineteenth century, the idea that an entire city could be destroyed with a single blast would have also seemed fanciful. The good news is that most experts rate the prospect of a nuclear, biological, or chemical weapons attack on a civilian population as low. The challenge for policymakers is to ensure that it remains this way.

Further reading

Betts, R. (1998) 'The New Threat Of Mass Destruction', *Foreign Affairs* 77(1), 26–41.

Butfoy, A. (2001) 'Controlling the Spread of Weapons of Mass Destruction', in M. Hanson and W. Tow (eds) *International Relations in the New Century*, Oxford: Oxford University Press, 38–54.

Hutchinson, R. (2003) *Weapons of Mass Destruction: The No-Nonsense Guide to Nuclear, Chemical and Biological Weapons Today*, New York: Weidenfeld & Nicholson.

Mathiason, J. and Andemicael, B. (2004) *Eliminating Weapons of Mass Destruction*, Basingstoke: Palgrave.

Panofsky, W. (1998) 'Dismantling the Concept of Weapons of Mass Destruction', *Arms Control* 28(3), 3–8.

See also: arms control; biological weapons; chemical weapons; nuclear proliferation; terrorism

TERRY O'CALLAGHAN

Westphalia

The Peace of Westphalia ended the Thirty Years' War, a complex struggle that began in 1618 as a religious conflict within the Holy Roman Empire between the ruling Catholic Hapsburg dynasty and their Protestant subjects in Bohemia. Over the next three decades, the **war** evolved through a series of phases into a wider political conflict, pitting the Austrian and Spanish branches of the Hapsburgs together with their allies among the Catholic German princes against Denmark, Sweden, France, and their allies among the Protestant German princes. By the time the exhausted belligerents reached a preliminary agreement in 1641 to negotiate a comprehensive peace settlement, much of central Europe was devastated. At least half a million troops had died in combat and civilian casualties were far greater, especially in Germany where most of the fighting occurred. Some commentators put the loss of life at about one quarter of Germany's population; others estimate that it may have declined by as much as two-thirds.

Under the terms of the 1641 Treaty of Hamburg, two peace conferences were convened simultaneously in neighboring Westphalian cities, with the envoys of the Catholic princes and states assembled in Münster and the envoys of the

Protestant princes and states meeting in Osnabrück. The two conferences were considered part of a single international congress, whose final peace treaties were signed on 24 October 1648, and ratified the following February. The details of their execution were worked out at a conference held in Nurnberg between April 1649 and June 1651.

The delegates at Münster and Osnabrück faced two types of decisions, the first pragmatic and the second philosophical. The former dealt with questions of reallocating territory, resources, and titles in a way that would settle the material issues underlying the Thirty Years' War. The latter dealt with the rules of statecraft that would govern postwar diplomacy. The delegates' tasks were complicated by the absence of a preexisting body of procedures from which they could draw. Thorny questions of protocol arose at every step in the negotiations, forcing the delegates to cobble together rules of **order** as they went. Their efforts produced a monumental legacy, however. Through this painstaking process of trial and error, they developed the modern system of conference **diplomacy**.

The pragmatic decisions made by the delegates on material issues were designed to redraw the map of Europe so that a new **balance of power** could be established. Under the terms of the peace agreements, the **power** of the Hapsburgs was weakened, with the Holy Roman Empire limited in its sphere of influence to Austria and parts of Germany. France became the dominant power on the continent, and was now bordered by weak, fragmented states that posed no real threat to its **security**. Sweden received control of the north German coast, and the United Provinces of the Netherlands became independent from Spain. Although the government in

Madrid made peace with the Dutch, it continued hostilities against France until the 1659 Treaty of the Pyrenees.

The philosophical decisions made on rules of statecraft were designed to create a normative order that would support the new balance of power. The Westphalian normative order was important for numerous reasons. First, it secularized international politics by divorcing it from any particular religious footing, anchoring it instead on the tenets of **national interest** and reason of state. Second, Westphalia promoted **sovereignty**, the legal doctrine that no higher **authority** stands above the state, except that which the state voluntarily confers on any organization it may join. Third, Westphalia accepted a conception of **international society** based on the legal equality of states. All sovereign states possessed the same rights and duties. They had the right to handle matters within their boundaries without outside interference, as well as the duty to abstain from intervening in the domestic affairs of other states.

In short, the Peace of Westphalia not only brought the Thirty Years' War to a close; it ushered in a new diplomatic era whose influence still colors contemporary world politics. The Treaties of Münster and Osnabrück consolidated a normative order whose sundry rules of behavior had been gradually accumulating since the onset of the Protestant Reformation. They overturned the medieval system of centralized religious authority and replaced it with a decentralized system of sovereign, territorial states. For some scholars, the Westphalian treaties mark the birth of the **nation-state**, the primary subject of modern **international law**.

Following the implementation of the Treaties of Münster and Osnabrück, a ceasefire was declared, prisoners were released, and troops returned home.

Still, some fighting continued. France and Sweden clashed with neighboring states for the next half century, and the rulers of the new Germanic states created in the peace settlement began quarreling over border issues. While the delegates at Münster and Osnabrück briefly considered the idea of **collective security**, they eventually embraced balance of power politics as the means for maintaining security. Yet the Westphalian world of international **anarchy** and national self-help did not dampen the incidence of **war**. In retrospect, it failed as a formula for lasting peace because peace was never the primary objective of the balance of power. Survival of the members of the state system was the goal, and to survive it was assumed that wars would have to be fought, especially to block states with hegemonic ambitions.

Over the past three and a half centuries, the principles and practices embodied in the Treaties of Münster and Osnabrück gradually spread from Europe to the rest of the world. Increasingly, however, scholars and policymakers are asking whether they continue to be applicable in the twenty-first century. Contemporary world politics is shaped by centripetal and centrifugal forces. At the same time that **globalization** is pulling many of the planet's inhabitants together, fragmenting processes are pushing people apart. The world is simultaneously becoming more **cosmopolitan** and more parochial. Powerful non-state actors now vie with sovereign states. Intricate webs of transnational exchange compete with the emotional ties of national identity. Nation-states are becoming enmeshed within intricate networks of transnational governance that include corporations, banks, and intergovernmental and **non-governmental organizations**. In sum, the world today is being shaped by forces that challenge the Westphalian state-centric view of world politics.

Further reading

Doran, C. F. (1971) *The Politics of Assimilation: Hegemony and Its Aftermath*, Baltimore: Johns Hopkins.

Falk, R. A. (1998) *Law in an Emerging Global Village: A Post-Westphalian Perspective*, Ardsley: Transnational.

Kegley, C, W., Jr. and Raymond, G. (2002) *Exorcising the Ghost of Westphalia: Building World Order in the New Millennium*, Upper Saddle River: Prentice-Hall.

Parker, G. (1984) *The Thirty Years' War*, London: Routledge.

Wedgwood, C. V. (1944) *The Thirty Years' War*, London: Jonathan Cape.

See also: anarchy; balance of power; international law; international society; national interest; nation-state; order; sovereignty

GREGORY A. RAYMOND

Women and development

A broad concept used analytically to understand women's role in international **development** and normatively to promote their effective participation in politics and society. More narrowly the term refers to a particular model of development, grounded in neo-Marxist **feminism**, that emerged in the late 1970s. The notion of women and development has been variously interpreted and applied since becoming part of development **discourse** in the 1970s, but it has retained its primary focus on the particular experiences and perceived needs of women in developing countries. There is now broad agreement that women should (and do) play an important role in development, although scholars and policymakers continue to debate the nature, purpose, and effects of women's participation.

Pre-colonial societies in much of the non-Western world accorded women a relatively high status. Thus, for example, women could often own property or hold political office. The advent of European **imperialism**, and the institutionalization of Western values in colonized territories, diminished this status. Because colonizers regarded the public sphere (politics and the formal economy) as men's domain and the (home-based) private sphere as women's 'proper place', women lost much of their socioeconomic **power** and were (further) marginalized as political actors.

The end of the colonial era and the onset of the **cold war** brought increased attention to political, economic, and social conditions in former colonies. As a result, development programs were implemented (with mixed success), but few of these paid specific attention to women. This began to change in 1970, when a seminal study by Danish economist Ester Boserup helped place 'women and development' on the international agenda. Documenting her analysis with data from various countries, Boserup argued that – contrary to prevailing wisdom – development programs intended to facilitate **modernization** generally were not benefiting women and, in many cases, were proving detrimental to them. Subsequent studies have both supported and contradicted Boserup's conclusions. This has led to continued debate and the development of contending approaches to issues of women and development. These approaches have been variously categorized, based on their theoretical orientations and/or the nature of their policy prescriptions.

One classification scheme identifies three approaches – 'women in development' (WID), 'women and development (WAD), and **'gender** and development' (GAD) – that are distinguished primarily by their theoretical perspectives. The first of these, WID, developed in the early 1970s in the wake of Boserup's study. Solidly grounded in liberal feminism and modernization theory, this approach seeks to better integrate women into development programs and economic systems without challenging existing social structures. Policy prescriptions thus focus on insuring equality of opportunity, and increasing women's participation in areas such as education and employment. Despite some conceptual shortcomings, WID has legitimated the separate study of women's experiences and perceptions with regard to development. WAD, a second approach that emerged in the late 1970s, is critical of modernization theory and the WID approach. Adopting a neo-Marxist feminist perspective, WAD focuses attention on women's role in society as determined by inequitable social structures. Thus, rather than supporting the integration of women into existing programs, the WAD approach calls for carefully designed strategies and targeted development policies that can alleviate broader social inequities. WAD arguably represents an improvement over WID. Nevertheless, like the WID approach, it remains preoccupied with women's income-generating ('productive') activities and fails to address their unpaid ('reproductive') household labor. A third approach, GAD, took shape in the 1980s. Based on socialist (see **socialism**) and postmodernist feminisms, and significantly broader in scope than WID or WAD, GAD takes a holistic approach to women and development issues by focusing on socially constructed gender roles and their implications. Policies consistent with the GAD approach reject the public/private dichotomy, challenge patriarchal social structures, and seek to facilitate women's empowerment. GAD's critical and transformative orientation makes it a relatively less popular, yet potentially more effective, approach than either WID or WAD.

Another typology distinguishes approaches to women and development by a combination of their theoretical orientation and policy prescriptions. Theoretically, a key distinction is made between liberalism and structuralism. Liberal approaches advocate capitalist strategies (see **capitalism**) or emphasize modernization processes, while structuralist approaches support socialist strategies or focus on **dependency** relationships. Policy prescriptions are distinguished by their emphasis on 'practical gender needs' or 'strategic gender needs'. Those that address practical gender needs are defined in terms of women's gendered social position and do not threaten patriarchal structures. Examples include teaching women dressmaking or providing childcare facilities at a mother's workplace. Policies that address strategic gender needs, on the other hand, challenge the status quo and seek to erode patriarchal social structures. Examples include teaching women masonry or providing childcare facilities in a father's workplace. Those who employ this typology regard approaches to women and development as an ongoing process, by which institutions and policymakers have adopted various theory/policy combinations since the 1970s based on political ideology and lessons learned. Most recently, the 'empowerment' approach has gained currency. Similar to GAD, this approach combines a mix of liberalism and socialism with an emphasis on addressing women's strategic gender needs.

Since the 1990s, as suggested by the development of GAD and empowerment approaches, conceptions of women and development have become increasingly holistic in orientation and more fully integrated into development thinking. For example, the Gender Related Development Index (GDI) and Gender Empowerment Measure (GEM) – indicators created by the **United Nations Development Program** (UNDP) to measure gender inequalities – are increasingly used to help determine the effectiveness of development programs. The GDI focuses broadly on women's quality of life, as measured by their life expectancy, education, and income relative to men. The GEM measures women's formal participation in politics and the economy, their relative decision-making power in society, and their control over economic resources.

Since the 1970s, a focus on the particular needs and experiences of women has done much to improve the effectiveness of international development programs. Particularly since the 1990s, the concept of 'women and development' has productively expanded to include gender (the socially constructed roles of both men and women) and its implications for development.

Further reading

Beneria, L. (2003) *Gender, Development and Globalisation: Economics as if All People Mattered*, London: Routledge.

Boserup, E. (1970) *Women's Role in Economic Development*, London: Allen and Unwin.

Rathgeber, E. M. (1990) 'WID, WAD, GAD: Trends in Research and Practice', *Journal of Developing Areas* 24(4) 489–502.

Parpart, J. L., Connelly, M. P. and Barriteau, V. E. (eds) (2000) *Theoretical Perspectives on Gender and Development*, Ottawa, Canada: International Development Research Centre.

Tinker, I. (ed.) (1990) *Persistent Inequalities: Women and World Development*, Oxford: Oxford University Press.

See also: development; feminism; gender; modernization; sustainable development

CRAIG WARKENTIN

World Bank

One of the **United Nations'** (UN) specialized agencies whose stated objectives are the promotion of **sustainable development** and poverty reduction, together with all the other Millennium Development Goals agreed to by UN members in September 2000. The World Bank pursues these objectives through lending, the production of research and economic analysis and the provision of policy advice and technical assistance. It is a large organization employing some 10,000 **development** professionals (including economists, educators, environmental scientists, financial analysts, anthropologists, engineers, and many others) from over 140 countries. Three-quarters of its employees work in its headquarters in Washington DC and the rest work in the Bank's 109 'country offices'.

Structure of the Bank Group

The World Bank Group consists of five closely associated institutions. The term 'World Bank Group' encompasses all five institutions. The term 'World Bank' refers specifically to two of the five, namely, the International Bank for Reconstruction and Development (IBRD) and the International Development Agency (IDA).

IBRD was established in 1945. It provides lending services to members in need of development assistance – IBRD's main activity – as well as non-lending services (including analytical and advisory services). As of 2003 it has 184 members, whose capital contributions amount to only a small fraction of the Bank's total lending. To fund its activities, IBRD raises almost all its money by issuing bonds on the world's financial markets. As a result of government members' guarantees on all Bank lending, IBRD enjoys an AAA credit rating that allows it to borrow at the lowest market rates available. IBRD then lends these borrowed funds at a small mark-up. The IBRD does not aim to maximize profits but has earned a net income each year since 1948. Loans are to middle-income developing countries and to some low-income countries that are regarded as creditworthy. These countries would be able to borrow from commercial sources but only at much higher interest rates; moreover conditions for repayment of IBRD loans are also more favorable than the private sector, as loans are normally of a fifteen- to twenty-year duration with a three to five year grace period. In the fiscal year 2003, IBRD provided loans totaling US$11.2 billion, in support of ninety-nine projects in thirthy-seven countries. Approximately half of these loans were to Latin American and Caribbean countries and one-fifth were to states in Europe and Central Asia.

IDA was established in 1960 to provide lending to poorer countries on highly concessional terms, as these countries have little or no capacity to borrow on market terms. IDA is the world's largest source of concessional finance for the poorest countries. In the fiscal year 2003, IDA provided US$7.3 billion in financing for 141 projects in fifty-five low-income countries. About half of this credit was to sub-Saharan African countries and one-third to South Asian countries. Eligibility for access to IDA resources is governed by two basic criteria: a country's relative poverty (as measured by per capita income) and its lack of creditworthiness for IBRD resources. IDA lending is financed from the profits of the entire World Bank group and by grants from the governments of rich member countries, which every four years replenish the IDA fund. The fund was replenished most recently in 2002, with nearly US$9 billion from thirty-eight donors and another US$6.6 billion from the Bank's resources. IDA finances basic economic and human **development** projects. Its credits are very long-term (thiry-five to forty years, including a ten year grace period). IDA staff are integrated with those of the IBRD, so that the same staff are involved in both aid and non-aid work.

The International Finance Corporation (IFC) was founded in 1956 to encourage the growth of productive private enterprises in developing countries by providing long-term loans, guarantees, and risk management and advisory services to its clients. Unlike the Bank, IFC lends to private sector institutions without guarantee of repayment by the member government concerned. It also takes equity shares in private sector enterprises. IFC invests in projects in markets that commercial investors deem as too risky in the absence of IFC participation. One of its major activities is the development of financial markets in developing countries.

The Multinational Investment Guarantee Agency (MIGA) was created in 1988 to stimulate foreign direct investment into developing countries by providing guarantees to foreign investors against losses caused by non-commercial risks, such as expropriation, currency inconvertibility and transfer restrictions, armed conflict, and civil unrest. The creation of MIGA can be seen as a response to the debt crisis of the 1980s, when sovereign risk caused high interest rates on developing countries borrowing or precluded these countries' access to new loans even at high rates. MIGA also provides technical assistance to help countries disseminate information on investment opportunities.

The International Center for Settlement of Investment Disputes (ICSID) was established in 1966 to promote private foreign investment by providing international facilities for conciliation and arbitration of investment disputes, in this way helping to foster an atmosphere of mutual confidence between states and foreign investors. ICSID plays a purely juridical function. It also has research and publishing activities in the areas of arbitration law and foreign investment law.

History

The IBRD was created at the **Bretton Woods** talks in 1944. Its intended purpose was to finance the reconstruction in Western Europe after World War Two and promote economic development in other parts of the world by helping productive capital investments. In practice, however, the IBRD did not take part in the reconstruction, which was financed by the Marshall Plan.

With reconstruction in Europe completed by the late 1950s, development financing became IBRD's main role, which was justified by the existence of capital market imperfections hindering the flow of capital to developing countries. These countries needed investments with a longer horizon and lower interest rates than the private capital markets were ready to finance.

IBRD lending, however, was at near-market interest rates, which were higher than the rates of return that projects in many poor developing countries could yield. With the creation of IDA for the purpose of lending at preferential rates, the World Bank was transformed into a development agency. Bank lending came to be justified not only because of capital market imperfections, but because of the nature of the development process.

Poverty alleviation was not part of the original mandate of the Bank and, at the time, the Bank's intervention was not aimed at poverty reduction directly.

Rather, since it was believed that growth and development would 'trickle down' and reduce poverty, the Bank chose to concentrate on projects for economic infrastructure, seen as the primary means of generating growth. Moreover, since the prevailing economic theories suggested the existence of a trade-off between growth and income distribution, expenditure on welfare was regarded as counter-productive and the Bank avoided lending for social services or redistribution purposes.

In the 1960s, the World Bank grew rapidly. Its membership more than doubled, its staff trebled, and both the volume of lending and its geographical distribution – which up to the early 1950s were restricted to fewer than twenty loans a year, mostly in Europe and Latin America – expanded significantly. But it was under McNamara's presidency (1968–81) that the intensification of lending was greatest, with commitments reaching US$80 billion, equivalent to 86 per cent of total Bank lending until then. Even career prospects within the Bank were directly linked to the size of the project portfolio. McNamara's presidency also saw a major growth in development research within the Bank.

In an international environment characterized by grossly insufficient official lending and persistent protectionism in developed countries, the Bank saw its role to provide as much credit as possible to support the developing countries in their growth effort. There were concerns, however, that growth would exacerbate inequality in income distribution and even reduce the standards of living of the poorest groups, which could lead to the spread of **communism**. The 'trickle-down' approach to poverty reduction was replaced by a new development strategy primarily directed to the alleviation of poverty, mainly through

the funding of a 'new style' of projects for rural development, urban infrastructure, education and health. Agriculture, in particular, saw its share in Bank lending increase from 18.5 per cent in 1968 to 31 per cent in 1981. To influence governments' distributive policies the Bank started to propose agrarian reforms to distribute land to the poor farmers and limit the size of landholding. It was also in favor of the adoption of more labor-intensive methods of production and supported public works projects, the introduction of food subsidies, highly progressive taxes, and government expenditure on welfare.

The dramatic increase in indebtedness in developing countries did not constitute a major reason for concern. For example, after the first hike in the price of oil and raw materials in 1973, the Bank maintained a sanguine view of the trend in developing countries' export prices and continued to regard debt accumulation as the main means through which developing countries could develop their infrastructure – particularly electricity production – and increase production for export. Moreover, the obligation of debt repayment would be a strong incentive to reinvest part of the export receipts for the modernization of agriculture and the improvement of the export industry. Optimistically, this would have a cumulative effect, speeding up the process of development and fueling world growth.

With the second oil price hike in 1979, the Bank started to shift from project-based lending to policy-based lending. One reason for this change was that project lending was not seen as an appropriate vehicle for aid funds under the circumstances at the time, because the disbursement of project funds was too slow. By contrast, indebted developing countries were in need of balance of payments assistance, which required speedy disbursements of funds. A second reason was the realization that many developing countries were not in need of more projects. In fact, many countries had already started more projects than they could sustain and, particularly in an economically depressed environment, it had become almost impossible to identify potentially profitable projects, even at subsidized interest rates. A related reason was that, since project success was crucially dependent on the general economic situation, the Bank could no longer encourage economic growth without due regard to macroeconomic stability.

With the debt crisis that started in 1982 private sector capital flows to developing countries disappeared. The **International Monetary Fund** (IMF) and the World Bank had to intervene to sustain the payments positions of the indebted countries and prevent their outright default, which with over-exposed creditors could have caused an international banking crisis. Their intervention involved a debt rescheduling in conjunction with new loans, which were used to pay the interest on the existing debt. The 1980s became known as the 'adjustment decade' and the World Bank's structural adjustment lending – through Structural Adjustment Loans (SALs) and Sectoral Adjustment Loans (SECALs) – assumed major importance from 1983 onwards.

Indebted countries were required to stabilize their economies – reduce inflation, rationalize and stabilize the exchange rate, increase interest rates, reduce public expenditure, increase taxation, and eliminate subsidies – and undertake supply-side structural reforms – trade liberalization, privatization of state-owned enterprises, liberalization of the foreign direct investment regime, and market deregulation. Taken together, this set of policies formed what came to be

labeled as the 'Washington Consensus', which was to dominate Bank (and IMF) thinking for many years.

In this neoliberal agenda (see **neoliberalism**), macroeconomic stabilization receives priority over growth because it is the necessary foundation for sustainable growth. The latter would be triggered by the removal of distortions by means of **structural adjustment programs** that would in turn lead to the reduction of poverty. In this new version of the 'trickle-down' argument, openness and liberalization are the causal factors of growth, rather than state-led initiatives as in the earlier version.

Various factors contributed to this radical shift in Bank philosophy. One was the nature of external shocks, which required adjustment and macroeconomic stabilization above economic growth. Another factor was the appointment of the conservative Clausen (1981–6) to the presidency of the Bank, at a time when neoliberal governments were in power in the United States and Western Europe and neoliberalism was the new orthodoxy. Forces internal to the Bank were also important contributing factors. The Bank's own assessment of the effectiveness of poverty-oriented lending had in fact highlighted rather disappointing results. In particular, the Bank recognized that it lacked any real influence on borrowing governments' distributive policies and that poverty projects – which were concentrated in just a small number of areas, such as rural development, urban housing for the poor, and water supply projects – had on the whole a rather limited impact on poverty. As a result of this internal evaluation, the Bank had already begun to move away from intervention aimed at direct poverty reduction.

The Bank changed its emphasis again under Barber Conable's presidency (1986–91). On the one hand, the push for generalized policy reform and market liberalization remained strong and the idea that these reforms would help growth and hence reduce poverty was maintained. On the other hand, poverty alleviation and the mitigation of the social costs of structural adjustment through social expenditures programs (including the establishment of social safety nets) were given greater prominence.

However, it was not until 1996 – under a new president (James Wolfensohn, who was appointed in 1995 by the Democratic US administration to succeed the previous Republican appointee and who was reappointed in 1999 until 2005) and under pressure particularly from other international organizations and **non-governmental organization**s (NGOs) – that the Bank acknowledged that external debt could be a deadweight for the development of poor countries. The Bank launched the Heavily Indebted Poor Countries (HIPC) Initiative to reduce overall indebtedness. This initiative, which linked debt relief to the implementation of structural adjustment programs, was not successful, however. Three years after it was put into practice, only two countries had begun to receive significant debt relief.

While the Bank has maintained a clear orientation toward the private sector and 'orthodox' economic policies, Wolfensohn's presidency has marked a notable change in this institution by establishing the fight against poverty as the Bank's main mission. In 1999, the Bank launched three strategies that represented a significant development in Bank thinking and underpin much of its current activity, namely, the Comprehensive Development Framework (CDF), the Enhanced-HIPC Initiative and the Poverty Reduction Strategy Papers (PRSP). The CDF forms the basis for the Bank's work in all countries. It is an approach to develop-

ment assistance that proposes a comprehensive view of development, in the sense that it pays attention to economic and structural as well as social reforms and considers the problem of ensuring coherence between them. The CDF is a framework for all 'development stakeholders' – government, civil society, multilateral donors, and NGOs – to define a long-term, poverty-focused development program in partnership. The CDF aims, therefore, to enhance local ownership of the development process.

The enhanced-HIPC initiative aimed to raise the number of countries eligible for debt relief and increase the quantity and speed of relief. It also intends to reinforce the link between debt relief and poverty reduction, since for a country to obtain debt cancellation through the HIPC initiative, it is necessary to produce a plan (a PRSP) giving details of its poverty reduction strategy.

The PRSP is based on the CDF approach and is thus expected to be prepared by the countries themselves with the participation of civil society. In this document, countries are expected to provide an analysis of poverty and its determinants in the specific country context, and to define a specific strategy for poverty reduction, paying attention to maintaining coherence between macroeconomic, structural, and social reforms.

From the Bank's perspective, the PRSP approach is an aid mechanism that takes forward the CDF principles and implements them. As the CDF has no financial arrangements attached to it, there are no incentives for countries to adopt a CDF approach. By contrast, preparation of a PRSP is a requirement not only for obtaining debt relief under the HIPC initiative but also for access to concessional lending from the World Bank (IDA) and the IMF.

However, the PRSP is only a requirement for the poorest countries whilst the

CDF will also apply to middle income countries. The PRSP is envisaged as a three-year strategy (although in practice it is likely to be an on-going strategy with consecutive three-year plans), fitting into typical Bank and Fund program cycles, whereas the CDF process should yield a longer-term strategy.

The CDF and PRSP represent a new aspect of the Bank's philosophy that reflects not only the replacement of the trickle-down doctrine with the view that certain forms of poverty reduction are necessary conditions for sustained growth, but also a broader reconsideration of the nature of development and of development strategies. At least in rhetoric, it has been recognized that rapid market liberalization may result in increasing inequality, poverty, and macroeconomic volatility. It has also been accepted that greater participation in the decision-making process by recipient countries' governments and local groups is essential for the implementation of successful and sustained policy reforms. In turn, this requires the development of capacities within countries to plan and implement their own development strategies and that there must be institutions free of corruption that can strengthen the rule of law. As part of its **good governance** agenda, the Bank has emphasized institutional reforms for the modernization of the state.

Despite the rhetoric about the above three strategies, however, there are concerns about the translation of these views into practice. Notwithstanding an accelerated pace of implementation, progress under the enhanced-HIPC has been slow: the amount of debt canceled remains small and, as of September 2003, only six countries have completed the HIPC process.

As to the focus of the Bank on poverty alleviation, it appears to have resulted in the addition of modest social safety nets and targeted social spending programs to otherwise traditional stabilization and structural adjustment policies. The latter continue to stress the need for liberalization of trade, financial, and agricultural sectors and the centrality of the market even in key areas of anti-poverty policy, such as education and health. Countries have had greater autonomy in designing safety nets and social spending programs than in formulating their own stabilization policies or planning alternative paths to poverty reduction. The formulation of PRSPs has often resided with small technical teams from the ministries of the economy, without much consultation or participation or a proper analysis of the consistency between the program policies and the objective of poverty reduction. Even where some forms of consultation have taken place, there have been concerns that these have often involved specific civil society groups that are financially dependent on donors, and that the role of parliament has generally been limited.

Moreover, the use of **conditionality** still gives the IMF and World Bank a major influence on policy design. While there has been a decline in the average number of World Bank conditions, the biggest reduction has occurred in non-binding conditions, with a smaller proportionate reduction in the more serious, legally binding conditions. This has led to the call for a drastic streamlining of conditionality.

The 'Knowledge Bank'

The World Bank is not only a provider of financial assistance but also a provider of knowledge. As a 'Knowledge Bank', as it has been referred to, it has gradually assumed the role – not originally anticipated – of defining and disseminating a model of 'best development practice'. Research within the Bank is strongly policy oriented and has a definite cross-country dimension. To ensure that the results of research are integrated into the Bank's operational work and policy advice, researchers spend about one third of their time working directly with operational units.

Research is mostly undertaken within the Bank's research department in units that are under the direction of the Chief Economist, who has overall responsibility for the Bank's research program. In addition, most departments throughout the institution perform some research. Operational departments carry out Economic and Sector Work (ESW) on all developing country members in support of their lending operations. This work usually involves a Country Economic Memorandum (a comprehensive analysis of a country's economic performance and prospects) or more topic-focused reports, such as Poverty Assessments, Public Expenditure Reviews and Labor Market Studies. This type of work underpins the Bank's policy advice. Work on a country could also include a wide range of sectoral studies, such as Reviews of the Transport Sector or Health and Education Sector Reports, which provide the foundation for lending operations in those sectors. The amount of resources allocated to research and ESW makes the World Bank the largest development research institution in the world.

As an integrated institution undertaking both research and lending operations, the World Bank can draw on unparalleled cross-country evidence and experience on the merits of policy experiments and project interventions. The dissemination of such knowledge, which no developing country would have the capacity to assemble, is invaluable for any country considering similar policy actions.

The World Bank also collects large quantities of detailed data from international organizations, private institutions, and statistical offices of almost all countries. In addition, the Bank directly collects data from living standards surveys and external debt reports, as well as country economic reports, sector and project work and research papers. The Bank places these data in the public domain.

Governance system and political influence

The World Bank is run like a cooperative, with its member countries as shareholders represented by a Board of Governors. The Governors, who normally are the Ministers of Finance or Central Bank Governors from each country, are formally the ultimate policymakers in the World Bank. As the Board of Governors only meets once a year, decisions on the management of the bank are delegated to the Executive Board, which sits in almost continuous session. Every member government of the World Bank is represented by an Executive Director. However, representation on the twenty-four member Executive Board is not equal. Only the largest shareholders – the United States, Japan, Germany, France, and the United Kingdom – along with China, Saudi Arabia, and the Russian Federation, have their own Executive Director on the Board. Each of the other sixteen Executive Directors are elected to represent groups of countries, known as 'constituencies'. For example, twenty-two African countries are represented by one Executive Director.

Governance within the Bank is based on a weighted voting system. For example, on the Executive Board of the IBRD, the United States has 16.41 per cent of the votes, which is the largest share of any country. The other largest percentage shares for individual countries are: Japan (7.87); Germany (4.49); France

(4.31); United Kingdom (4.31); China (2.79); Saudi Arabia (2.79); Russian Federation (2.79). The United States is therefore in a very powerful position relative to the other countries. European countries do not vote collectively as members of the **European Union** (EU), and so they cannot in practice counterbalance the US vote. Even if the United Kingdom, France, and Germany vote together their collective vote is still less than the United States. All other EU countries are represented in groupings with other countries. For example, the group that comprises Albania, Greece, Italy, Malta, Portugal, and San Marino has 3.51 per cent of the votes; the group with Austria, Belarus, Belgium, the Czech Republic, Hungary, Kazakhstan, Luxembourg, the Slovak Republic, Slovenia, and Turkey has 4.80 per cent.

The weight assigned to each country's vote is roughly based on the relative size of its economy. Nevertheless, it has been shown that the allocation of votes does not reflect strictly technical criteria. Historical accounts demonstrate that the initial distribution of vote shares was rather determined by US political preferences. Subsequent periodical adjustments to the shares have also been influenced by political considerations. The voting share of the United States is not only the largest of any country but also confers the United States veto power over all decisions that require a special majority of 85 per cent, such as those relative to the approval of amendments to the IBRD's articles. The United States is the only country to enjoy such a veto on all major decisions. Other countries have rarely grouped together to veto decisions.

In practice, the Executive Board works by consensus and formal votes are virtually never taken. This does not mean that the share allocation of votes is irrelevant, however. To the contrary, work within the Bank reflects an awareness of the extent of consensus determined by the relative voting strength. For example, if it is known that the United States does not approve of a loan or a policy, it is unlikely even to come before the Board. Consequently, US influence, while often exercised informally, is probably felt throughout the Bank.

Nevertheless, the United States may not enjoy full control over the Bank's activities, since the belief by member states that the Bank has a certain degree of independence is necessary for the Bank's **legitimacy**. Executive Directors are not only representatives of their countries but also officers of the Bank and, as such, do not take decisions only on the basis of narrow **national interest**s.

The financial structure of IBRD confers it a high degree of autonomy from member countries' interference, since the Bank does not rely on their contributions to fund its activities. However, political pressures might influence decisions over the use of the Bank's surplus funds. Unlike IBRD, IDA does not enjoy financial independence, since it relies on periodic replenishments by member governments, and is open to their pressures. For example, the United States is the provider of one-fifth of IDA funds and this gives the United States great influence within IDA. Japan is also a major donor.

US leverage extends, however, beyond IDA, as the United States has sometimes threatened to reduce or even withhold its funding share in replenishments of the IDA fund in order to influence policy in the World Bank as a whole. The seriousness of such a threat does not derive simply from the potential reduction in the US contribution but from the fact that the contributions of the other IDA members are often in proportion to that of the United States. Hence, if the United States diminishes its contribution, the effect becomes magnified through the reduction in everyone else's contributions.

In theory the Bank's lending activities are insulated from political interference, since the Bank's Articles of Agreement prohibit the Board from taking politics into account in its lending decisions. In practice, however, historical accounts and more formal empirical studies present evidence that political considerations have been highly influential in determining who borrows from the Bank. For example, the political pressures of the **cold war** heavily influenced World Bank lending throughout the period 1948–90. Even in the aftermath of the cold war, there is evidence that some of the Bank's lending decisions have been influenced by US strategic considerations and interests. Thus political influence on lending activities is likely to be reflected in the decision to approve a loan or the nature of conditionality rather in the inclusion of specific elements in the policy content of the loan.

Political influence can also affect the Bank's research work and policy advice. For example, it has been argued that the Bank's push for the 'Washington Consensus' in the 1980s probably reflected US pressure and policy preferences, since even among the Bank's staff there were many critics of the neoliberalism. The Bank's president – who chairs the meetings of the Board of Directors and is responsible for the overall management of the Bank – exerts such a strong influence on the institution that it has been said that the Bank tends to reflect the personality of its head. The president is, by tradition, a US national and is elected for a five-year renewable term.

Further reading

Buira, A. (ed.) (2003) *Challenges to the World Bank and IMF: Developing Country Perspectives*, London: Anthem Press.

Gilbert, C. L. and Vines, D. (eds) (2000) *The World Bank: Structure and Policies*, Cambridge: Cambridge University Press.

Kapur, D., Lewis, J. P. and Webb, R. (1997) *The World Bank: Its First Half Century, Vol. 1: History; Vol. 2: Perspectives*, Washington, DC: Brookings.

Miller-Adams, M. (1999) *The World Bank: New Agendas in a Changing World*, London: Routledge.

Mosley, P., Harrigan, J. and Toye, J. (1991) *Aid and Power: The World Bank and Policy-based Lending, Vol. 1: Analysis and Policy Proposals; Vol. 2: Case Studies*, London: Routledge.

Pincus, J. and Winters, J. (2002) *Reinventing the World Bank*, Ithaca, NY: Cornell University Press.

Tarp, F. and Hjertholm, P. (eds) (2000) *Foreign Aid and Development: Lessons Learned and Directions for the Future*, London: Routledge.

World Bank (2003) *A Guide to the World Bank*, Washington, DC: World Bank.

See also: Bank for International Settlements; debt trap; development; foreign aid; structural adjustment program

ALBERTO PALONI

World Health Organization (WHO)

A specialized agency of the **United Nations** established in 1948 to encourage international cooperation to improve global health. WHO defined health in a non-medical and positive way as a state of complete physical, mental, and social wellbeing and not merely the absence of disease or infirmity. WHO has been seen as having a special responsibility for the health of the world's poor. At times in its history it has been seen to pursue this mandate well. At others, and increasingly in the past two decades, its performance has been criticized for being insufficiently focused on health inequities between and within rich and poor countries, and too concerned with economic efficiency, in accordance with the neoliberal (see **neoliberalism**) agendas of bodies such as the **World Bank** and private corporations. WHO has its administrative headquarters in Geneva. It has six regional offices throughout the world that vary in the quality of their performance. The World Health Assembly attended by all member states meets annually and is the supreme policymaking body. It is represented between Assembly meetings by the Executive Board. The organization is financed primarily from annual contributions made by member governments on the basis of their relative ability to pay.

WHO has five main functions. First, it conducts research and assists with the transfer of research from researchers to public health practitioners. The research relates to a range of communicable and non-communicable diseases. Second, it provides global leadership in responding to **pandemic**s, epidemics and endemic diseases. This is done through improvement of laboratory services, preparing health systems to undertake early diagnosis and health promotion and encouraging mass campaigns for vaccination. Its most significant achievement in this area has been in leading the eradication of smallpox. Third, it encourages the strengthening of national health systems and establishment of strong and effective district health systems. Fourth, WHO has a global advocacy role for health. There is much discussion about how effectively WHO fulfills this role, given the actions of powerful interests that attempt to influence the WHO agenda. Finally, WHO provides global leadership for new ideas in the provision of health services and in ways of promoting health. This function was evident through the 1978 Alma Ata Declaration of Health for All by the Year 2000 and the 1986 Ottawa Charter of Health Promotion. Both of these documents have been used throughout the world to inspire health workers and to re-orientate health systems toward community oriented health systems that place emphasis on disease prevention and health promotion rather than just cure.

The Alma Ata Declaration has inspired many who took up its vision of comprehensive primary health care (PHC) and used it to argue for community driven health services based on an understanding of the social and economic determinants of health. In contrast to this view, others have argued for a more selective interpretation of PHC. This strand of thinking has given rise to a series of global initiatives that have been designed to tackle specific diseases. In recent years the WHO has put much emphasis on partnerships with private sector organizations. Examples are the Roll Back Malaria Partnership, Stop TB and the Global Alliance for the Elimination of Leprosy. These private partnerships have attracted criticism from those who argue that they may compromise WHO's independence.

An ongoing debate has occurred about whether the role of WHO is to act in a selective manner by emphasizing technical intervention (e.g. vaccination campaigns to eradicate certain diseases) that are primarily donor-driven and promote vertical programs at the expense of developing robust, integrated, and comprehensive health systems that respond to local community concerns and are driven by community identification of need. Critiques of technical interventions argue that they are often not tailored to local circumstances and are therefore unsustainable. Furthermore, they often do not take account of existing programs, fail to involve communities in any meaningful way and largely ignore the social and economic determinants of health.

In the past decade WHO has struggled to maintain its position of global leadership in health matters. While once it was seen as the conscience of global health, it has appeared to lose its focus more recently. To some extent the mantle of WHO was taken over by the **World Bank**, which became the biggest funder of public health programs in the 1990s. The Bank's work has been criticized on the grounds that it sees health almost solely in terms of its contribution to economic **development** and that it proposes only selective, technical responses to diseases. WHO has not substantially challenged the World Bank view and, in fact, has reinforced its position with its Commission on Macroeconomics and Health, which again saw health in terms of its role in economic advancement rather than as a fundamental human value.

Two recent events have helped to restore WHO's leadership position. First the SARS epidemic in 2003 suggested that WHO is still the recognized leader in response to global epidemics. Its central role in investigating the outbreak and working with national governments through the provision of technical expertise was evident during this crisis. Second, WHO showed leadership in establishing the framework convention on tobacco control. This has been achieved despite considerable pressure and lobbying from the tobacco industry. WHO commonly faces lobbying from interests that oppose its public interest stance. For instance the food industry lobbies against dietary guidelines that recommend less sugar in diets and the Pharmaceutical industry lobbies intensively against WHO's essential drug list which is intended to ensure a better supply of drugs to the world's poor – an issue heightened by the Acquired Immunity Deficiency Syndrome (AIDS) epidemic.

WHO has also been criticized by civil society groups who maintain that it has lost touch with its original aim of promoting the health of the world's poor. Discontent reached such a point in 2000 that a coalition of civil society groups organized a People's Health Assembly as an alternative to the World Health Assembly on the ground that the latter body no longer represented the interest of ordinary people. A test for the new Director General, Dr Lee Jong-Wook, will be whether he can counter these critical voices from civil society and demonstrate a strong commitment to global and local health equity and to the strengthening of health systems that are responsive, sustainable and can deliver services to the poor.

WHO has the opportunity to reestablish its position as a global leader and advocate for the health of the poor against the negative effects of economic **globalization** (including the increasing concentration of wealth, the growing power of private corporations and unfair trading relationships). In this vision WHO would form partnerships with civil society organizations and the governments of poor countries to advocate for such structural reforms as fairer trade, against patents that appropriate indigenous knowledge and make drugs unaffordable, and argue in favor of redistributive taxes and effective public health sectors that are based on strong PHC services, accessible to all people.

Further reading

Beigbeder, Y. (2004) *International Public Health*, Aldershot: Ashgate.

Garrett, L (2000) *Betrayal of Trust: The Collapse of Global Public Health*, New York: Hyperion.

McKee, M., Garner, P. and Stott, R. (eds) (2001) *International Cooperation and Health*, Oxford: Oxford University Press.

Waitzkin, H. (2003) 'Report of the WHO Commission on Macroeconomics and Health: a summary and critique' *The Lancet* 361, 523–6.

See also: pandemic; United Nations

FRAN BAUM

World-system theory

World-system theory emerged in the 1970s as a reformulation of historic forms of global rule. Its progenitor, Immanuel Wallerstein, argued that inter-societal rule is a significant feature of human history. In particular, he distinguished between world-economies and world-empires, offering a historical theory regarding their distinctive political-economic dynamics. He argued that a world-empire's trajectory is governed by the eventual atrophy of its **power** to sustain a far-reaching **empire** from a single political center, whereas a world-economy's trajectory is more dynamic since it is governed by the competitive relations among a multiplicity of states. These relations are structured by a coaxial division of world labor, whose stratified socio-technical divisions correspond to an interstate political hierarchy.

Wallerstein deployed the concept of the modern world-system to intervene in the debate about the rise of **capitalism**. This debate addressed the transformation of feudal relations of fealty and bonded labor into capitalist relations governed by the cash nexus, where access to material livelihood depends upon labor and commodity markets. Interpretations of the transformation are divided between those that emphasize market expansion via a consequential merchant capitalist class, and those that account for the transformation of labor relations through peasant resistance to super-exploitation by financially pressed feudal lords, and the substitution of hired labor in increasingly commercial landed relations.

World-system analysis sought to transcend this debate by arguing that capitalism originated in the formation of a world-economy in the sixteenth century. That is, the historic dynamic lay neither in labor nor market relations, but in the political relations attending an emerging division of world labor. Expanding markets were structured by global relations of production, related to a hierarchical division of labor comprising wage labor in the European 'core', sharecropping in the Eastern European 'semi-periphery', and slave and bonded labor in the American 'periphery'.

Contra Karl Marx, who viewed wage labor as capitalism's *differentia specifica*, Wallerstein argues that the secret of capitalism lies in the inability of any one state to monopolize trading profits deriving from the world division of labor. The dynamics of the interstate system produce cycles of rivalry and **hegemony** as the political expression of an interstate system in which states and their firms create, and compete for, markets (but not always in synchrony). The rising hegemon's task is to deploy its industry, through military and commercial **power**, to establish world market dominance. Once achieved, the hegemonic state elaborates a policy of world-economic liberalism to maximize its commercial reach and financial returns. Hegemonic succession depends on a successful military and commercial challenge and the restoration of single power dominance.

Thus, in the twentieth century, as the sun set on the British empire, the United States emerged as its successor after two World Wars, a period of industrialization following unification via the American **civil war**, the devastation of rival states (Germany and Japan), and the **containment** of the Soviet empire. In the twenty-first century, as Giovanni Arrighi (1994) has noted, the elements of hegemony are now dispersed: the United States has the guns, Japan has the money, and China has the labor. Whether a world-empire will replace the world-economy is a question that can only be settled in the long run.

World-system analysis serves two principal functions. Methodologically, it offers the possibility of historicizing the social categories of the modern world. States, as institutions of the world-economy, can be understood as territorial political organizations whose domestic relations are simultaneously international relations. Modern states' internal configurations are conditioned by their strategic position in the world division of labor and the associated political, interstate, relations. In turn, interstate relations structure the division of world labor, and determine whether world history is in a period of state hegemony or inter-state rivalry. Thus nineteenth century Britain refashioned this division through its pursuit of the informal 'workshop of the world' empire, whereby the concentration of manufacturing in England depended on an expansion of agricultural production in both tropical (colonial) and temperate (settler) zones. The late nineteenth century response of Britain's rival states (Germany, the United States, Japan, and France) was to embrace economic protectionism and imperialism, and partly imitate the workshop model. Today, we are witnessing political struggles over **World Trade Organization** (WTO) rules as mechanisms for an uneasy juxtaposition of Northern protectionism and Southern economic liberalization. This expresses an elemental tension between the territorial logic of (possibly declining) core states, under electoral pressure to protect employment and social entitlements, and the capitalist logic of corporate and financial interests, under competitive pressure to access labor and currency markets globally through liberalization. It also reveals the contentious politics involved in re-divisions of world labor. The methodological contribution of world-system analysis, therefore, is to assert the historical perspective of the long-term, allowing us to hypothesize about such relational trajectories among states and between states and firms, and how these in turn restructure the capitalist world-economy.

The second function of world-system analysis is epistemological, in the sense that Wallerstein perceives it as a critique of social science, rather than a theory or a 'sociology of the world'. Central to this intervention is a powerful critique of the development 'paradigm'. Wallerstein views 'developmentalism' as an organizing myth privileging a Eurocentric world vision and a European-centered **geopolitics**. In this view, the European social science canon has bequeathed to us a set of categories centered on the state-society nexus, projected as a universal in the contemporary world. Political science, economics, sociology, anthropology and even history have all been harnessed to the endeavor of accounting for an apparent evolutionary differentiation among societies, where core states represent the future path (**'development'** or modernity) for successor semi-peripheral and peripheral states.

Development is regarded, through the world-system lens, as a misconstrued and misleading *national* strategy in a *hierarchical world* where only some states 'succeed', and then justify their superior power in developmentalist terms. World-system analysis explains the superiority of core states as the result of power relations stemming from their strategic position in the world division of labor. This power includes the ability to exploit weaker, peripheral states, sometimes via semi-peripheral states as regional powers, whose geopolitical status and middle-income profile is presented as the next step in the evolutionary path of development. This tripartite relation is a permanent feature of the capitalist world-economy, even though membership of these geo-political subdivisions may change over time. Thus China's current trajectory portends a massive shift in the political balance and world division of labor during the twenty-first century, and perhaps a significant erosion of what has been until now understood as 'development' in the core states. The lesson of world-system analysis is that development is not a linear path traversed individually by states arrayed along a continuum. Transformations within states are not independent of global economic transformations, and vice versa.

Further reading

Abu-Lughod, J. (1989) *Before European Hegemony: The World System A.D. 1250–1350*, New York: Oxford University Press.

Arrighi, G. (1994) *The Long Twentieth Century: Money, Power and the Origins of Our Time*, London: Verso.

Arrighi, G., and Silver, B. (1999) *Chaos and Governance in the Modern World System*, Minneapolis: University of Minnesota Press.

Chase-Dunn, C. (1998) *Global Formation: Structures of the World-Economy*, 2nd edn, Boulder, CO: Rowman and Littlefield.

Frank, A. G. and Gills, B. K., (eds) (1993) *The World System: Five Hundred Years or Five Thousand Years?* London: Routledge.

So, A. (1990) *Social Change and Development: Modernization, Dependency, and World-System Theory*, Newbury Park, CA: Sage.

Wallerstein, I. (1974) *The Modern World System I: Capitalist Agriculture and the Origins of the European World-Economy in the Sixteenth Century*, New York: Academic Press.

Wallerstein, I. (1980) *The Modern World-System II: Mercantilism and the Consolidation of the European World-Economy, 1600–1750*, New York: Academic Press.

Wallerstein, I. (1989) *The Modern World-System III: The Second Era of Great Expansion of the Capitalist World Economy, 1730–1840s*, New York: Academic Press.

Wallerstein, I. (1999) *The End of the World As We Know It. Social Science for the Twenty-First Century*, Minneapolis, MN: University of Minnesota Press.

See also: dependency; development; historical sociology; modernization

PHILIP McMICHAEL

World Trade Organization (WTO)

An international organization responsible for overseeing the rules governing trade between states. The WTO itself does not set the rules. Rather, they are the result of agreements negotiated among the member governments, and are intended to prevent discrimination in trade. Some 150 countries are currently members of the WTO, and most other countries are negotiating membership. Russia is the largest country that is not yet a member. Essentially, the WTO facilitates multilateral trade negotiations, is entrusted to monitor implementation and enforce compliance with the agreements reached, and also provides technical assistance to developing countries in implementing the agreements.

A brief history

The WTO was established in 1995 as a successor to the General Agreement on Tariffs and Trade (GATT). In an organizational sense this was a change of name, as the WTO Secretariat replaced the GATT Secretariat as the body responsible for overseeing multi-lateral trade negotiations and imple-menting GATT Agreements. However, the actual change is greater than a change in nomenclature, as an institu-tion the WTO has an enhanced role and broader remit than the GATT Secretariat. Specifically, the WTO has legal status as an international organization responsible for trade between states. The GATT, in contrast, lacked a proper legal founda-tion and was not treated as an organiza-tion in **international law**. To appreciate the role of the WTO as an international organization, it is useful to review briefly the history of the GATT.

Twenty-three countries were signa-tories to establishing the GATT on 30 October 1947. The signatories, known as contracting parties, engaged in 'rounds' of multilateral trade negotiations where they offered tariff concessions to each other on a product-by-product basis. The number of countries (contracting parties) that exchanged tariff concessions varied from thirteen to thirty-eight during the first four rounds, up to the late 1950s, but mostly comprised industrialized states and large developing countries. In the Dillon Round (1960–1), the then members of what was to become the European Economic Community (EEC) negotiated as a group for the first time. The first major change in the approach of the GATT was during the Kennedy Round (1964–7) when the product-by-product approach was replaced by a lin-ear or across-the-board method of tariff cuts. The aim of a 50 per cent tariff cut was achieved for many manufactured products and the number of contracting parties increased to sixty-two as many newly independent developing countries joined GATT. Agreements on measures to provide preferential treatment for

developing and least developed coun-tries were also reached in the 1960s.

The Tokyo Round (1973–9) saw the next major evolution of the GATT as specific agreements were reached in a number of areas other than tariff cuts. Throughout its history the GATT had been devising a set of rules to 'bind' countries to their commitments and to prevent countries from adopting non-tariff trade measures that would under-mine agreed tariff reductions. Specific agreements were reached covering anti-dumping, subsidies and countervailing measures, customs valuation and import licensing, and technical barriers to trade. Although the negotiations on tariff reductions had been limited to manu-factured products, and the Tokyo Round resulted in the weighted average tariff on manufactures for the nine major indus-trial countries being reduced from 7.0 per cent to 4.7 per cent, there were spe-cial agreements on dairy products and bovine meat. The scope of trade issues covered by the GATT increased sig-nificantly during the 1970s, and over 100 countries participated in the Tokyo Round.

The Uruguay Round (1986–94) saw the final major and significant broad-ening and updating of GATT rules to encompass trade in agriculture, textiles and clothing, and trade in services (under a separate agreement). There were agreements on a number of major trade-related issues and relatively tech-nical issues (discussed below). The Uru-guay Round Agreement (URA) was signed in Marrakech in December 1994 by 123 contracting parties, and estab-lished the WTO. A particular feature of the URA was that the contracting parties signed up for the Agreement in its entirety (the 'single undertaking' approach) and then became members of the WTO. Once established, the WTO was responsible for overseeing the implementation of the URA as a body of agreed trade rules to which all members were committed, and for continuing the process of multilateral negotiation of trade rules.

The functions of the WTO

The WTO has two broad types of functions, those associated with facilitating trade negotiations (setting the rules) and those associated with administering trade agreements (compliance with the rules). The structure of the WTO overlaps with these functions. At the pinnacle of WTO decision-making is the Ministerial Conference, where trade representatives from the member states get together at least every two years to negotiate on trade issues. The level below this is the General Council, comprising countries' trade representatives in Geneva, which meets several times a year in Geneva to continue discussions. Reporting to the General Council are a number of specific councils, committees, working groups and working parties that address particular issues and meet regularly in Geneva. Thus, discussions and negotiations on trade are ongoing, although agreed decisions are only reached at the Ministerial Conferences. The WTO Secretariat provides technical and administrative support to all of these decision-making and discussion bodies. These comprise the facilitation functions of the WTO.

The functions of the WTO that support the administration of trade agreements fall into three categories. First, the WTO *monitors compliance* by reviewing, on a regular basis, the trade policies of member states through the Trade Policy Review Mechanism. The WTO Secretariat undertakes and publishes Trade Policy Reviews of member countries, every few years for major economies such as the **European Union** (EU) and the United

States, and about every five years for smaller countries. These reviews are comprehensive and amount to a progress report on the countries. The General Council meets as the Trade Policy Review Body to discuss and evaluate the country reviews, and the country being reviewed faces questions from other members regarding its trade policies.

Second, the WTO has an *enforcement role* that is exercised through the Dispute Settlement Understanding (DSU). This is a very important function, as it is in this way that the WTO acts as a third party enforcer of agreements. If a member feels that another member is failing to comply with its obligations it can bring the dispute to the WTO. An independent panel of experts is appointed to hear the case and deliver a ruling. Under the GATT, all parties to a dispute had to agree to *accept* the panel's ruling, which meant that the offender could prevent acceptance of the ruling. The DSU has more force, as under the WTO all parties must agree to *reject* the ruling. The DSU provides for the appellant to seek remedy, although countries are encouraged to settle their differences through consultation. The DSU has proved quite effective, and in the first eight years of its existence the WTO heard as many disputes as the GATT under its entire existence (1947–94). Furthermore, the DSU has made it easier for smaller countries to take their disputes to the WTO and win them against major trading countries.

Third, the WTO provides *technical assistance* to developing countries to enable them to comply with agreements. Trade Agreements are a body of law, and it can be very costly in terms of technical and legal expertise to implement the many elements of an agreement. For example, meeting customs valuation requirements or technical and public health standards requires training of officials in every country, the provision of testing equipment and can even require a country to rewrite parts of its legislation. Developing countries, especially the poorest, require technical and financial assistance to comply with the agreements. The WTO, supported by donors, provides such assistance.

It is important to distinguish these two types of roles of the WTO, as a facilitator and as a monitor, because many of the criticisms of the WTO as an institution (especially those often heard from anti-**globalization** protestors, are based on misperception). It is often implied, for example, that the WTO is the 'rule-maker' and governs world trade. The WTO itself does not make or negotiate trade agreements. It is the member governments who negotiate agreements by multilateral consensus. All members of the WTO are parties to the negotiations and any one member can prevent agreement being reached. This is the main reason why negotiating rounds are slow processes, and many Ministerial Conferences are concluded without reaching a significant agreement. In a sense, the WTO is a court that monitors and adjudicates compliance with the body of international trade law.

The next two sections discuss, respectively, the principles underlying trade rules in the WTO and the remit (the range of trade and trade-related issues) for which the WTO has some responsibility. The penultimate section discusses the process and progress of negotiations of trade rules and agreements under the WTO.

The principles of trade rules

The WTO oversees a rule-based system for trade between states. In this sense, the WTO can be seen as an independent third party that monitors and enforces compliance with the trade rules agreed to by members. The rules cover a wide range of issues, but essentially are concerned to apply the principle of non-discrimination to market access and the treatment of imports and exports. The objective is that all countries that are parties to the agreement (members of the WTO) are treated in a non-discriminatory manner by all other countries (the general exception is that there can be discrimination in favor of poorer countries). In the early days of the GATT, the agreements related primarily to tariffs (import taxes) on trade in manufactures between industrialized countries. Over time, as more countries became signatories to the GATT, the rules extended to non-tariff barriers, export subsidies, treatment of developing countries and, in the URA, to all trade (not just manufactures) and a range of trade-related issues. Despite the increase in scope, the rules for trade were based on two fundamental principles of non-discrimination.

The first principle is **most favored nation** (MFN), which stipulates that each country should be treated by each other country at least as well as the country 'most favored' by the other. In effect, MFN established how developed countries would be treated, and no members could be less favorably treated. Countries declare their MFN tariff rates, and no country that is party to the agreement can face tariffs above the MFN rate. In a sense this is a misnomer, as certain countries can be granted preferences, such as tariffs lower than the MFN rate, and can be treated more favorably than the (so-called) most favored nation. However, the principle is that MFN establishes the baseline and no country can be treated worse than this. Countries can only be treated 'better' than MFN by special agreement. For example, it has long been recognized that the least developed countries should be granted preferential treatment, more favorable than MFN. This is known as Special and Differential (S&D) treatment, and is on terms negotiated in trade agreements. Similarly, developing countries have often been granted preferences that are more favorable than MFN, but less favorable than S&D. An example is the Generalized Scheme of Preferences (GSP), whereby GSP tariffs are lower than MFN tariffs. Countries that form a regional trade arrangement (RTA) can also treat members of the RTA more favorably than MFN.

The second fundamental principle is national treatment (NT), which stipulates that products from other countries should be treated in the same way as products produced domestically. Whereas MFN relates to the treatment of goods from other countries at the border (the process of importation), NT relates to the treatment of imports once they have entered the country. Although the complete logical extension of NT is that domestic and foreign products should be treated identically, the qualification 'once they have entered the market' permits levying tariffs on imports. Thus, the structure of tariffs (more strictly, the structure of border restrictions) should accord with the MFN principle and the subsequent treatment of imports should accord with the NT principle.

The NT principle underlies the extension of trade rules, especially in the Uruguay Round, to a variety of non-tariff and trade-related issues. At issue is whether there are government policies and regulations that have the effect of discriminating against foreign producers and/or distort patterns of trade. For example, a country may require that products meet certain public health standards, known in the WTO as Sanitary and Phyto-Sanitary (SPS) standards. The requirement is that the same SPS and technical standards are applied to foreign products as to domestic products.

Another example arises if governments impose specific 'performance requirements' on foreign-owned firms producing in the country, such as that a minimum share of their inputs must be procured from local suppliers. These requirements are discriminatory if they do not also apply to domestic firms, and can distort trade (e.g. the firm may be prevented from importing because it has to purchase locally).

So far we have only discussed the rules from the perspective of imports. What are imports for one country are exports for another country. The WTO rules actually say much less about exports than about imports, the major agreement being the rules that prohibit subsidies on exports. The basic reason is that provided exports are sold at their market price, trade rules can be limited to the treatment of imports. Thus export subsidies are generally prohibited. In cases where government policies have the effect of subsidizing exports, or the products are being sold at below market prices (dumping), importing countries are allowed to take action (countervailing or anti-dumping measures) against the subsidized imports.

The scope of trade and trade-related issues

The Final Act of the URA (the full legal text) is a vast document, detailing all elements of the Agreement and including the binding commitments on tariffs and non-tariff barriers of each member country. At the core of the URA are the *Agreement Establishing the WTO*, including that the URA is a single undertaking, the *GATT 1994*, updating interpretations of GATT Articles, and the *Uruguay Round Protocol*, listing the market access commitment of all countries. There are then a series of further agreements relating to agriculture, services, textiles and clothing, trade related investment measures, trade related aspects of intellectual property rights, antidumping, subsidies and countervailing measures, and safeguards. A number of agreements relate to 'technical' issues, including SPS, technical barriers to trade, customs valuation, pre-shipment inspection, rules of origin, import licensing, and government procurement. Finally, a number of 'decisions' or 'understandings' relate to the operation of the WTO. These include the Trade Policy Review Mechanism, the Dispute Settlement Understanding, measures to assist least developed and net food importing countries, and proposals for coherence in global economic policymaking.

We limit coverage here to some of the most important elements of the URA that are core elements of the WTO agenda of trade negotiations. In particular, we focus on those issues of greatest concern to developing countries, as the increased voice of the developing countries represents a major difference between the WTO and the previous GATT system (this is discussed in the final section below). The five issues summarized here have been the principal sources of disputes and delays in trade negotiations under the WTO.

Agreement on agriculture (AoA)

Liberalizing agricultural trade was a new issue in the Uruguay Round and disagreements between the **European Union** (EU) and the United States on this issue were the major reason for delays in reaching a final agreement. The principal issues covered in the AoA relate to developing countries being given greater market access for their exports, and developed countries implementing significant reductions in export subsidies and domestic supports offered to their domestic sector. Most developed countries provide significant subsidies to their farmers, especially the EU, the United States, and Japan. These subsidies distort world trade by reducing the level of imports into protected countries, while associated export subsidies reduce the world price of affected commodities (especially grains and dairy products). The elimination of subsidies would benefit other food exporters, and during the Uruguay Round these countries formed a lobby to promote liberalization, known as the Cairns Group (including countries such as Australia, Canada, Brazil, Argentina, and Thailand). On the other hand, the removal of export subsidies could increase world prices of temperate foods, with an adverse impact on net food importing countries. Some of the latter (Egypt, Mexico, Jamaica, Peru, and Morocco) formed the Food Importers Group, whose concerns were reflected in the Decision on measures to assist adversely affected food importers.

The AoA has resulted in a switch from subsidies that distort production towards subsidies based on environmental or non-production criteria. Developing countries would like greater latitude to apply subsidies for **development** purposes. This is an issue being addressed in ongoing negotiations in the context of the 'Development Box'. The issue of a 'food security box' is of increasing importance in the context of promoting small food producers in developing countries. For agricultural exporters the main achievement was bringing agriculture under GATT disciplines and the promise in the agreement of future progressive liberalization of trade in the sector. This promise has still to be delivered; dissatisfaction with the progress of certain developed countries in reducing their support to farmers and eliminating export subsidies has been a major source of disputes in WTO Ministerial Conferences.

The Agreement on Textiles and Clothing (ATC)

The Multifibre Arrangement (MFA) governed trade in textiles and clothing from 1974 until it was replaced by the ATC in 1995. The MFA was a framework of bilateral and unilateral restrictions and quotas that severely distorted trade in textiles and clothing. The ATC stipulated that quotas would be eliminated and integrated gradually (in four phases) into normal GATT rules by 2005 (i.e., the quotas will be replaced by tariffs). The ATC specified the percentage of products to be brought under GATT rules in each phase, and that the quota restrictions would be phased out by allowing quota levels to grow annually, and at an accelerating rate. From 2005, once the quotas have been eliminated and the ATC implemented, negotiations will proceed on liberalizing tariffs on trade in textiles and clothing. The basic objective is to replace the quotas under the MFA with tariffs, which are more transparent and less distortionary. Two areas of particular concern have arisen in implementing the ATC and are the subject of ongoing discussions. The first is where countries make recourse to antidumping actions against cheap imports of textiles and clothing, which should be covered in the Agreement on Antidumping. The second relates to the Rules of Origin applied in the sector, which many developing countries argue are too restrictive and complicated.

General Agreement on Trade in Services (GATS)

The GATS is a framework agreement with general provisions for all service sectors, and some sector-specific annexes, in which the principles of non-discrimination are applied less strongly than in the GATT. Specific agreements have been signed for information technology (1997), telecommunications (1998), and financial services (1999), including banking, insurance and securities. Other discussions to date have related to distribution and transport services, environmental management (that includes certain water utilities) and tourism. Countries offer commitments (concessions) and make requests in the GATS; exceptions to MFN can be specified and NT has to be negotiated. The GATS adopts what could be described as a menu approach rather than a single undertaking.

Countries make scheduled commitments, on market access, MFN and NT, under four separate modes of supply. Mode 1 relates to cross-border supply, where residents can purchase services from a foreign provider (based in a foreign country). Mode 2 covers consumption abroad, allowing the purchase of services when the consumer is in a foreign country. Mode 3 relates to commercial presence, and thus covers foreign direct investment by service providers. This is the most important mode in terms of the proportion of trade in services covered, and is related to the treatment of investment in the WTO (see below). Mode 4 relates to movement of natural persons, where the supplier is allowed to bring personnel overseas. This is potentially quite important to developing countries that could provide labor-intensive services. There is a specific Services Council that reports to the General Council of the WTO on progress in GATS negotiations.

Agreement on Trade Related Investment Measures (TRIMs)

These rules limit the performance requirements that governments can impose on foreign firms operating in the country. They are termed investment measures because they relate to **multi-national corporation**s that have engaged in **foreign direct investment** (FDI) and are undertaking production activities in the host country. They are trade related because the requirements impact on trade flows, in one or more of three essential ways. The firm may be potentially able to export, and the TRIM may relate to export requirements (e.g. stipulating a share or value of output to be exported). Alternatively, the firm may be producing import-competing goods, and the TRIM may restrict such competition (e.g. limiting the share or value of output that can compete with imports). Finally, the firm may import inputs that are available locally, and the TRIM may require some minimum amount of inputs be sourced from local producers (such as local content requirements). It follows that the removal of TRIMs should remove distortions to trade flows, and such removal is the intention of the TRIMs Agreement. The principle criticism of the TRIMs Agreement is that it restricts the actions of one party (the government) but imposes no reciprocal restraints or obligations on the other party (the multinational firm).

Under the WTO, discussions on TRIMs have been encompassed by broader discussions on the treatment of investment. With the increasing **globalization** of markets and growth in cross-border transactions the question arises if cross-country differences in investment and competition standards are becoming important non-tariff barriers to trade. The Singapore Ministerial meeting of December 1998 established a Working Group on Trade and Competition Policy, including anti-competitive practices, within the WTO. The issue was not whether the WTO should negotiate rules and implement an action agenda in this area, but whether there should be an exploratory work program to identify

areas requiring further attention. Whether there is a case for binding multilateral rules on investment and competition policy within the WTO framework has been rather controversial. The EU and the United States have been strong proponents of introducing such an agenda, these being two of the so-called Singapore Issues introduced at the Doha Ministerial (the others are government procurement and trade facilitation), but developing countries are strong opponents.

Agreement on Trade-Related Aspects of Intellectual Property Rights (TRIPs)

The aim of the TRIPs Agreement was to develop rules for minimum standards of intellectual property protection, and developing countries were given five years to implement the proposals (i.e. until 2000) while the least developed had eleven years, and longer if required. Articles in TRIPs increased the protection for well-known trademarks, including wording to discourage 'confusing' trademarks, and endorse 'geographical indications' such as for wines and foods. Article 27 requires that 'patents shall be available for any inventions, whether products or processes, in all fields of technology'. Included are plants, animals and biotechnological processes, although there is recognition of the need to protect plant varieties and breeder's rights. It also covers pharmaceuticals. These are the areas of greatest dispute between developed and developing countries, especially regarding access to medicines for HIV/AIDS and other diseases. The TRIPs Agreement prohibits producers of generic drugs from exporting, and therefore prevents poor countries from importing cheap generics rather than expensive patent-protected drugs. However, a public health clause allows countries to produce generics under license. There have been extensive negotiations on how to provide cheap medicines to poor countries within the confines of the TRIPs Agreement. To date, the United States, representing the interests of large pharmaceutical companies, has been the major obstacle to reaching an agreement.

Multilateral trade negotiations

The practice of the GATT, as carried over to the WTO, is that agreements are an outcome of negotiating Rounds, launched, continued and culminating at Ministerial Conferences. For example, the Doha Ministerial in November 2001 launched the Doha Round of negotiations which, given specific emphasis on meeting the needs of developing countries, has been referred to as the Doha Development Agenda (DDA). The failed Cancun Ministerial in September 2003 was a failure to agree on how to proceed with the DDA. The failure to reach an agreement at Cancun does not mean that the Round is over. Rather, what has happened is that member countries have not agreed priorities for which issues to include in the DDA negotiations.

An important feature of the WTO as a negotiating process, in contrast to the GATT process, is that developing countries have an increased voice. This is due to three main changes. First, whereas the GATT was between contracting parties, who could choose what to sign up to, the URA and subsequent WTO agreements are single undertakings based on unanimity. Member countries must accept all aspects of the agreement, and all member countries must reach agreement. Second, a somewhat subtle change is that all signatories to the URA became members of the WTO at its establishment. Consequently, developing countries can view themselves as

founding members of the WTO on an equal negotiating basis as any other member. This may have encouraged developing countries to be more active and engaged participants in the WTO than they were under the GATT. Third, the developing countries have cooperated to form negotiating groups. The most important of these is the so-called Group of 21 (G21) formed at the Cancun Ministerial, where large and economically important developing countries (Brazil, China, India, and South Africa) lead a group of mostly Latin American countries. Also, since the Doha Ministerial, African countries have acted as a group, while regional groups such as CARICOM or MERCOSUR have often acted as a group.

Acting together not only increases the voice of small countries, but also facilitates their participation. Given the vast array of issues in the URA and thus in subsequent WTO negotiations, small countries (unlike the EU and the United States) simply do not have enough officials and representatives to participate in all aspects of negotiations. By acting together, developing countries can ensure that they have representatives at all negotiations. The difficulty for developing countries acting as a group, however, is that their negotiating interests often diverge. In particular, the interests of the large developing countries (as represented by the G21) are quite different to those of the smaller and poorer countries (such as the African Group). This is most evident in respect of agriculture. The differences between food exporters and importers have been mentioned above. Similarly, many of the poorest countries benefit from S&D preferential market access, to the EU in particular, for the tropical commodities they export; bananas, and sugar are two examples that have given rise to disputes in the WTO. For example, full liberalization of the EU

Sugar **regime** would be costly to some developing countries (e.g. Mauritius, Cote d'Ivoire), with the benefits going to richer countries such as Brazil and even Australia.

The failure of WTO members to reach an agreement at the Cancun Ministerial has resulted in some questioning of the structure of trade negotiations in the WTO. Some commentators have argued that too many countries are involved and the principle of unanimity makes it too difficult to reach agreement. Indeed, both the EU and the United States expressed their willingness, if not determination, to pursue alternatives to multilateral negotiation, i.e. to negotiate bilateral agreements. This would run counter to the fundamental basis of the WTO: the full benefits of trade liberalization are only realized if all countries act together. There have been proposals to introduce majority voting in the WTO, as unanimity implies that any one country can exercise a veto. This is unlikely to resolve the problems, as it seems unlikely that any rule other than 'one member one vote' would be acceptable to the majority of members. As the majority of members are developing countries that have demonstrated their ability to work together, majority voting would probably not have altered the outcome at Cancun (unless to approve an agreement that the EU and the United States objected to).

An alternative view is to lay the blame for failure at Cancun against the breadth of issues rather than the number of countries. WTO members could have reached agreement on many important issues, and this would have ensured progress. There were two areas on which agreement was highly unlikely. The first was agriculture, as both the EU and the United States, in particular, were perceived by almost all other members as moving too slowly on implementing the AoA. The second was whether to include

investment and competition policy on the agenda, as developing countries were united in opposing their inclusion. The 'single undertaking' approach makes it difficult to reach an agreement when the scope of issues is very broad and some trade-related issues are highly contentious. If Ministerial Conferences concentrate on a narrow range of issues, agreement is more likely.

As negotiations are continuing in Geneva, the failure to reach an agreement at Cancun is not a failure of the WTO. In fact, in an important sense it shows that the WTO works – multilateral negotiations must accommodate all countries, and Cancun showed that developing countries can exercise their voice in the WTO. The most important lesson from Cancun is that the process can work, but the interests of all countries should be respected. This is most likely to be achieved if the scope of negotiation issues is limited. It will not be achieved if the number or the voice of negotiating countries is restricted. The inclusion of all countries in multilateral negotiations is the hallmark of the WTO.

Problems with the WTO

In conclusion, it is appropriate to comment on two major problems with the WTO. The first is how to reflect fairly the interests of all countries; the second is the fact that the rules only apply to governments, whereas most world trade is actually between companies. Aspects of the former have already been considered in respect of the difficulty of reaching agreement when there are so many negotiating parties. Although in principle unanimity gives each member equal **power**, in practice big economies are more powerful than small economies. This imbalance of economic power is manifested behind the scenes when, for example, a small country is promised

foreign aid or preferences in return for accepting the terms of agreement favored by the large country. It is argued that this represented the reality of many GATT rounds. This strategy has lost its efficacy under the WTO, as developing countries see the benefits of acting together and large developing countries are able to resist bribery. This underlying reality of international relations is one reason to argue against bilateral negotiations or any form of majority voting. The poorest countries deserve special and preferential treatment precisely because they are disadvantaged in world trade.

Finally, it should be noted that although the WTO negotiates trade as being between countries, most trade is actually within and between multinational companies. While this is a reason why trade issues cannot be properly addressed in isolation from investment and competition issues, the WTO is not currently equipped to address these concerns because it has no jurisdiction over private companies. WTO agreements limit the ability of governments to use restrictive trade measures, but do not impose any limits on the ability of companies (multinational or national) to engage in restrictive business practices. The latter practices are appropriately addressed in competition policy, and will in practice be related to issues of investment policy. Actually, aspects of competition policy are already present in the URA (in GATS and TRIPS in particular), while aspects of investment policy are present in GATS and TRIMs. As the scope of trade and trade-related issues covered by the WTO expands, the need to address the behavior of compa-

nies will be greater. Unfortunately the WTO is not, as constituted, an appropriate multilateral forum to address these issues.

Further reading

Brown, A. (2003) *Reluctant Partners: A History of Multilateral Trade Cooperation 1850–2000*, Ann Arbor, MI: University of Michigan Press.

Das, D. (2003) WTO: *The Doha Agenda, The New Negotiations on World Trade*, London: Zed Books.

Das, D. (2001) *Global Trading System at the Crossroads*, London: Routledge.

Drabek, Z. (ed.) (2001) *Globalization Under Threat: The Stability of Trade Policy and Multilateral Agreements*, Cheltenham: Edward Elgar.

Laird, S. (2002) 'A Round by Any Other Name: The WTO Agenda After Doha', *Development Policy Review*, 20(1), 41–62.

Matthews, A. (2002), 'Developing Countries Position in WTO Agricultural Trade Negotiations', *Development Policy Review*, 20(1), 75–90.

Morrissey, O. (2002) 'Investment and Competition Policy in the WTO: Issues for Developing Countries', *Development Policy Review*, 20(1), 63–73.

Narlikar, A. (2003), *International Trade and Developing Countries: Bargaining Coalitions in the GATT and WTO*, London: Routledge.

World Trade Organization (2003) *Understanding the WTO*, 3rd edn, Geneva: WTO.

See also: free trade; International Monetary Fund; international political economy; most-favored nation; multilateralism; non-tariff barrier

OLIVER MORRISSEY

Z

Zone of peace

Terms such as the 'long peace' and 'zone of peace' have been usually associated with the absence of **war** in Europe during the **cold war** (1945–89), and with the separate peace among democracies progressively developed throughout the last two hundred years (the so-called **democratic peace**). There are three alternative, and sometimes overlapping definitions of a zone of peace. First, the term refers to a legally recognized 'zone' such as a Nuclear Weapon-Free Zone. Second, it refers to a political 'zone' involving exclusively liberal/democratic countries. Third, the term refers to a spatial 'zone' of international peace that might extend into several regions of the **Third World**.

In terms of international **security** and **international law**, the idea of a 'zone of peace' overlaps with that of a Nuclear Weapon-Free Zone. One of the most innovative developments in the post-World War Two period in managing international problems has been the creation of a series of territorial **regime**s designed to meet the challenge of militarization, modern weapons technology, and intervention that stop short of outright aggression. Progressive application of the principles of demilitarization, denuclearization, and the exclusion of military competition has led to the creation of regions free of nuclear competition and deployment. These include, among others, Antarctica (1959); the Latin American region (Treaty of Tlatelolco, 1967); the South Pacific (Treaty of Raratonga, 1985); the South Atlantic (**United Nations** declaration of October 1986); the Indian Ocean (Declaration of 1971); a Zone of Peace, Freedom, and Neutrality by the **Association of Southeast Asian Nations** (ASEAN) in 1971; and the declaration of Mercosur (Argentina, Brazil, Paraguay, Uruguay, Bolivia, and Chile) as a Zone of Peace in 1998. Other legal declarations have been extended to cover the Central American countries (after 1987), and parts of the African continent (in the 1990s). This legal idea (and ideal) overlaps with a broader concept of a zone of peace to include the dismantling of military systems, the prohibition of the deployment of nuclear weapons in a specific geographic area, and a firm commitment to social justice and **human rights** as the basis for a more radical social transformation on a global scale.

A second, political definition of a zone of peace focuses exclusively upon the liberal zone of peace among democracies. This zone of peace includes only Western Europe, the United States, Canada, Japan, and the Antipodes, which together contain about 15 per cent of the world's population. This zone of peace and democracy is not a club that governments establish and into which they can invite any other country to join. Instead, it is a structural and normative result of the democratic character of the countries comprising the democratic peace. The countries in this zone of peace are modern and wealthy democracies that not only will refrain from fighting each other, but also form a pluralistic **security** community based upon common values and a shared identity. This is a very restrictive definition of a zone of peace, which reflects simultaneously the existence of both international peace among the members of the zone, and domestic peace within their borders.

Finally, a third definition of a zone of peace can be expanded into other historical periods in the European continent and to contemporary regions of the Third World. In this sense, a zone of peace can be defined as a discrete geographical region of the world in which a group of states have maintained peaceful relations among themselves for a period of at least thirty years – a generation span – although **civil war**s, domestic unrest, and violence might still occur within their borders. This definition refers strictly to the international relations domain. Moreover, no particular type of political regime is a prerequisite for membership in a given zone of peace. This is a very minimalist definition of a zone of peace, which should be clearly distinguished from the two previous ones. Accordingly, the following zones of peace can be identified since 1815:

1. Europe, 1815–48;
2. Europe, 1871–1914;
3. Western Europe, since 1945 (including Scandinavia);
4. Eastern Europe, 1945–89;
5. North America, 1917 to the present;
6. South America, 1883 to the present;
7. West Africa, 1957 to 1999;
8. East Asia, since 1953;
9. Australasia, since 1945; and
10. the ASEAN countries of Southeast Asia, since 1967.

According to this third definition, zones of peace in the **international system** develop when states are conservative in their territorial claims – in other words, when they are usually satisfied with the territorial status quo of their international borders, and of their region in general. Within these zones of peace we should expect no international wars among the state-members of the given region, although domestic and international conflict might still persist. Within this broad and loose definition it is possible to make a distinction between three gradations or categories of zones of peace in an ascending order of quality and endurance:

1. a zone of negative or precarious peace (mere absence of war), in which peace is maintained on an unstable basis by threats, **deterrence**, or a lack of will or capabilities to engage in violent conflict at a certain time;
2. a zone of stable peace (no expectations of violence), in which peace is maintained on a reciprocal and consensual basis. The zone is a community or society of **nation-state**s satisfied with the status quo. Domestic and international conflict might occur, but it is kept within non-violent limits;
3. a pluralistic security community of nation-states, with stable expectations of peaceful change, in which the member states share common norms, values, and political institutions, sustain an identifiable common identity, and are deeply **interdependent**.

The concept of a pluralistic security community is directly linked to the notion of **integration**.

The genesis of a zone of peace can often be attributed to the last war and its aftermath in the region. Conversely, its decay and potential disruption can be the product of a growing dissatisfaction with the status quo, the rise of **nationalism** in the zone involving secessionist or irredentist claims (see **secession**; **irredentism**), and/or changes in the distribution of **power**, or changes in the perception of that distribution.

Although there is a serious problem of aggregating the relationships of a number of peaceful dyads within a specific geographical region into one single characterization of that zone of peace as negative or stable, a regional pattern can be nevertheless traced that encompasses more than the sum of the dyads in a given region. Moreover, the geographic characterization of a zone of peace does not rule out the possibility that a member-state in a given zone might participate in an extra-regional war beyond its immediate borders (i.e., the United States in Vietnam in 1965–75 and in Iraq in 1991 and 2003; the United Kingdom in the Falklands/Malvinas War of 1982 and in Iraq in 2003). Thus, membership of a state in a zone of peace does not necessarily imply that it has a peaceful attitude toward international relations in general.

Further reading

Kacowicz, A. M. (1998) *Zones of Peace in the Third World: South America and West Africa in Comparative Perspective,* Albany, NY: SUNY Press.

Singer, M. and Wildavsky, A. (1993) *The Real World Order: Zones of Peace/Zones of Turmoil,* Chatham, NJ: Chatham House.

Subedi, S. P. (1996) *Land and Maritime Zones of Peace in International Law,* Oxford: Clarendon.

See also: democratic peace; liberal internationalism; security community; war

ARIE M. KACOWICZ

Index